# CATIA V5
# FEA Tutorials

**Release 17**

**Nader G. Zamani**
University of Windsor

**ISBN: 978-1-58503-432-1**

SDC
PUBLICATIONS
Schroff Development Corporation

www.schroff.com
www.schroff-europe.com

## Examination Copies:

Books received as examination copies are for review purposes only and may not be made available for student use. Resale of examination copies is prohibited.

## Electronic Files:

Any electronic files associated with this book are licensed to the original user only. These files may not be transferred to any other party.

# Preface

The objective of this tutorial book is to expose the reader to the basic FEA capabilities in CATIA V5. The chapters are designed to be independent of each other allowing the user to pick specific topics without the need to go through the previous chapters. However, the best strategy to learn is to sequentially cover the chapters.
In order to achieve this independence, there was a need to repeat many topics throughout the workbook. Therefore, we are fully aware of the redundancy introduced in the chapters.

In this workbook, the parts created in CATIA are simple enough that can be modeled with minimal knowledge of this powerful software. The reason behind the simplicity is not to burden the reader with the CAD aspects of package. However, it is assumed that the user is familiar with CATIA V5 interface and basic utilities such as pan, zoom, and rotation.

Although the tutorials are based on release 17, they can be used for earlier releases with minor changes. The workbook was developed using CATIA in a windows XP environment. Nevertheless, it can be used for NT and UNIX platforms with minor differences.

# Acknowledgments

I would like to thank Mrs. Mojdeh Ramezani-Zamani for her valuable assistance in the preparation of this document and to Ali and Ahmad for encouragement and support in this project. Special thanks to Dr. Jonathan Weaver from the University of Detroit Mercy, who introduced me to the "Knowledge" and the "Digital Mock Up" workbenches in CATIA.
Finally, I would like to thank the Schroff Development Corporation for providing me with the opportunity to publish this tutorial.

# NOTES:

# Table of Contents

# NOTES:

# Chapter 1

# Introduction

The finite element analysis is a powerful tool which can be used to approximately solve the field equations in engineering. These field equations can originate from different subjects such as, solid mechanics, heat transfer, fluid mechanics, and electromagnetism. The mathematical nature of such field equations can be either linear or nonlinear depending on the degree of the approximation.

This tutorial workbook deals primarily with the subject of linear stress analysis as available in CATIA V5. There are third party packages that can be licensed as add-on modules which can extend the limited capabilities to nonlinearities and transient dynamics.

It is important for the users of this document to be fully aware of the limitations of the FEA analysis in CATIA. The following is a summary of the points to remember.

**a) Material Linearity**

In CATIA, it is assumed that the stress and stress are linearly related through Hook's law. One should not try to model rubber-like materials, where although elasticity is maintained, linearity is non existent. In the case of metals, one should avoid loading the material into the plastic region.

**b) Small Strains**

The strains used in CATIA are the infinitesimal engineering strains which are consistent with the limitation in (a). As an example, problems such as crushing of tubes cannot be handled by software.

**c) Limited Contact Capabilities**

Although CATIA is capable of solving certain contact problems, they are within the limitations established in (a) and (b). Furthermore, no frictional effects can be modeled by the software.

**d) Limited Dynamics**

The transient structural response in CATIA V5 is based on modal superposition. Therefore sufficient number of modes have to be extracted in order to get good results. The direct integration of the equations of motion is not available at this point.

**e) Beam and Shell Formulation**

In these elements, the shear effects are neglected. Therefore, the results for thick beams and shells may not be very accurate.

Although the limitations (a) through (e) may seem to be severe, the basic machine design problems in industry can be carried out with the aide of CATIA's FEA module. Checking machine design handbooks quickly reveals that such problems are governed by linear elastic analysis in the first place.
A common question by the novice, regardless of the package used, is whether the mesh is fine enough. The answer is that one does not know unless several other runs are made where the mesh is progressively made smaller. This process is referred to as mesh refinement.

The user should then compare the results. If the differences are insignificant to his/her satisfaction, the mesh is satisfactory. It is clear that a single run, in the absence of an error indicator, does not provide enough information on the validity of the mesh. CATIA V5 has adaptive meshing capabilities which can be used to asses the accuracy of the results.

Another common question is, "Will the part break?". Generally speaking, FEA packages do not provide a direct answer to this question. The modes of failure and the stress level are the responsibility of the user. Although CATIA's material database provides the yield strength of the metals, it does not use it for calculation purposes.

The final frequently asked question is "Do I have the right restraints and loads?". Unfortunately, there is no direct answer to this question either. Boundary conditions that can be imposed in packages are mathematical idealizations to the actual conditions which are never known. The same is true with loads. Therefore, to a great extent, engineering judgments dictates how the restrains and loads in an FEA package should be used.

Do not let the color contours fool you. Check the stress levels to see whether they are in the elastic range. Finally, keep in mind the deformed shapes are scaled considerably otherwise one cannot distinguish between the deformed and undeformed configurations.

It is always a good idea to start with a coarse mesh in your preliminary runs. This allows you to identify any errors in the boundary conditions quickly. Animating the deformation can be quite helpful for this purpose. Once satisfied with the coarse mesh run, try refining the mesh. You also have to know the limitations of you hardware; a sufficiently fine mesh can bring the biggest computer in world to its knees.

Keep in mind that the stress contours in CATIA are color coded with the dark blue representing the smallest variable magnitude. Since this tutorial book is printed in black and white, to avoid the contour plots being mostly black, the color map has been changed for the majority of these plots.

# NOTES:

# Chapter 2

# Analysis of a Bent Rod with Solid Elements

## Introduction

In this tutorial, a solid FEA model of a bent rod experiencing a combined load is created. No planes of symmetry exist and therefore model simplifications cannot be made. Finally, the significance of the von Mises stress in design equation is discussed.

## 1 Problem Statement

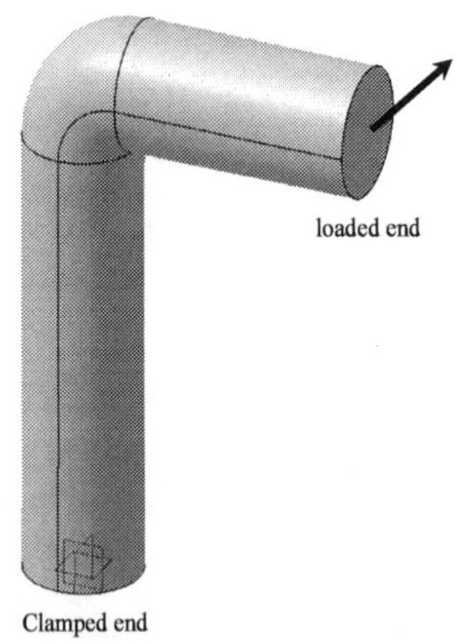


The bent rod, shown to the right, is clamped at one end and subjected to a load of 2000 lb as displayed. The steel rod has a Young's modulus of 30E+6 psi and Poisson ratio 0.3.
The nominal dimensions of the rod are also displayed below.
Although this problem is more efficiently handled with beam elements, we propose to use solid elements.
There are two main types of solid elements available in CATIA V5, linear and parabolic. Both are referred to as tetrahedron elements and shown below.

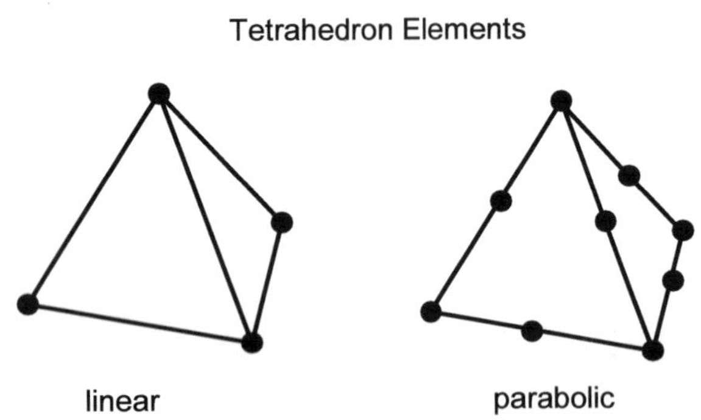


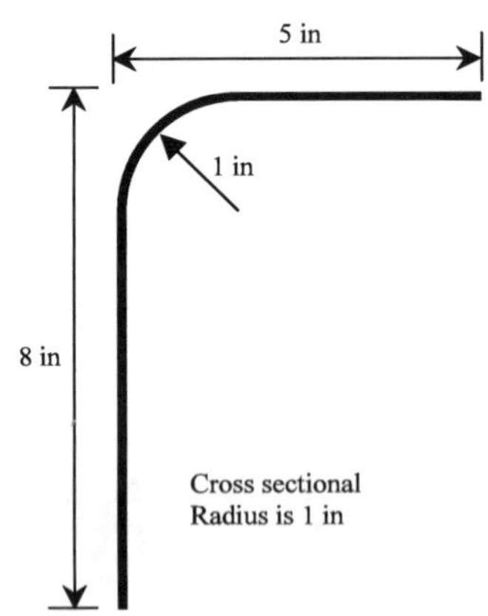


The linear tetrahedron elements are faster computationally but less accurate. On the other hand, the parabolic elements require more computational resources but lead to more accurate results. Another important feature of parabolic elements is that they can fit curved surfaces better. In general, the analysis of bulky objects requires the use of solid elements. Hexahedral elements are also available on a limited basis in recent releases of CATIA. These elements will be discussed in a later chapter.

## 2 Creation of the Part in Mechanical Design Solutions

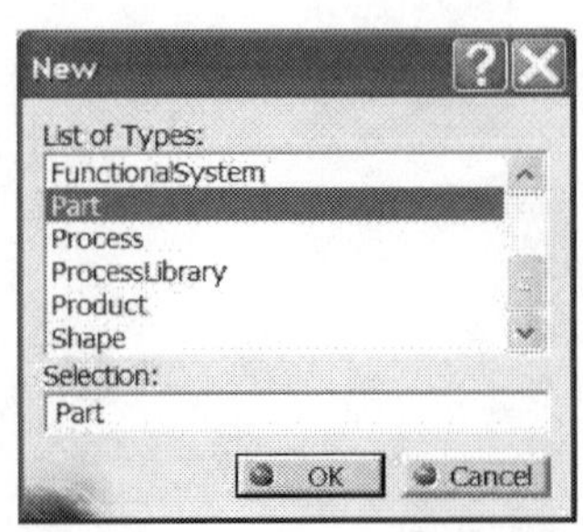


Enter the **Part Design** workbench  which can be achieved by different means depending on your CATIA customization. For example, from the standard Windows toolbar, select **File > New** 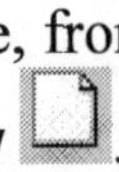. From the box shown on the right, select **Part**. This moves you to the **Part Design** workbench and creates a part with the default name **Part.1**. See Note#1 in Appendix I.

In order to change the default name, move the cursor to **Part.1** in the tree, right-click and select **Properties** from the menu list.

From the **Properties** box, select the **Product** tab and in **Part Number** type **wrench**. This will be the new part name throughout the chapter. The tree on the top left corner of the screen should look as displayed below.

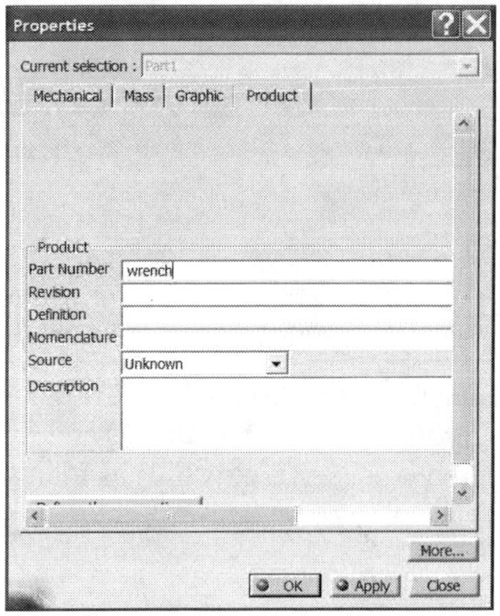


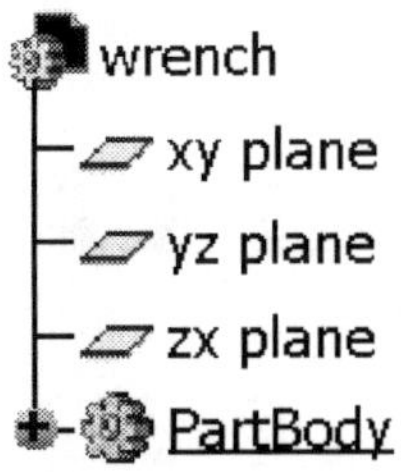


From the tree, select the **xy** plane and enter the **Sketcher**. In the **Sketcher**, draw a circle, and dimension it. In order to change the dimension, double-click on the dimension on the screen and in the resulting box enter radius 1. Your simple sketch and the **Constraint Definition** box used to enter the correct radius are shown below.

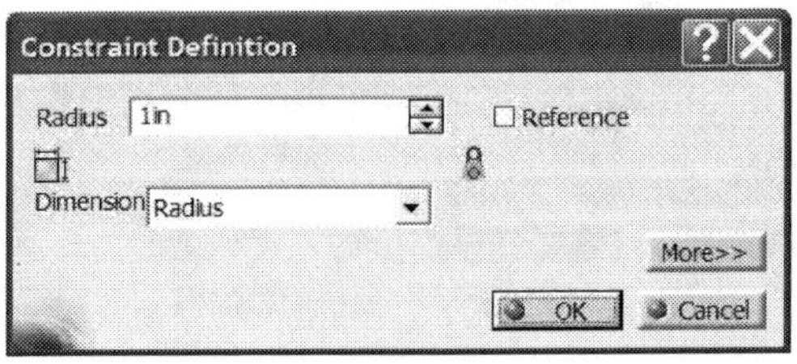


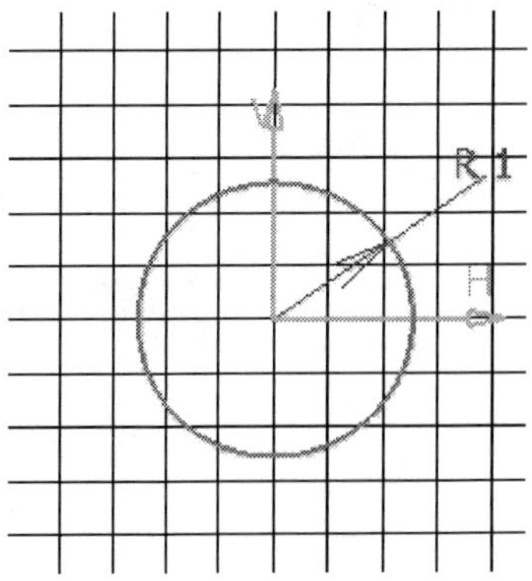


Leave the **Sketcher**.

From the tree, select the **yz** plane and enter the **Sketcher**. Draw the spine of the bent rod by using **Profile** and dimension it to meet the geometric specs. In the **Sketcher**, the spine should match the figure shown next. Upon leaving the **Sketcher**, the screen and the tree should resemble the following figures.

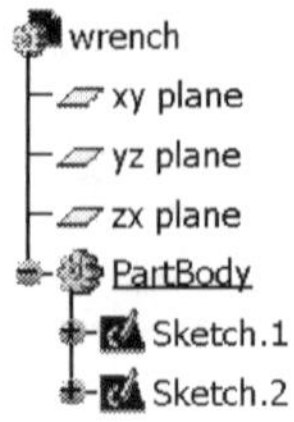


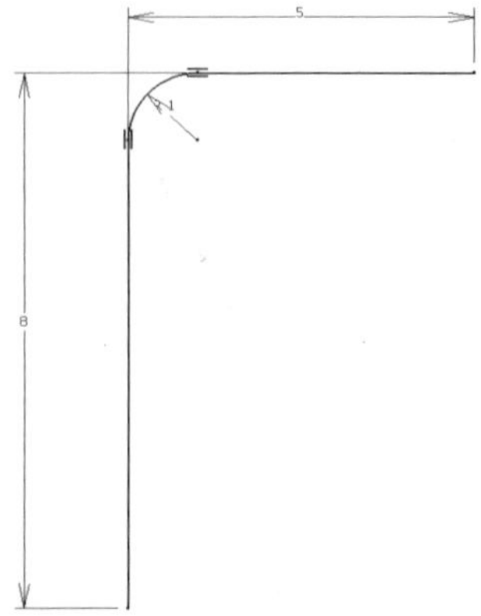

You will now use the ribbing operation to extrude the circle along the spine (path). Upon selecting the rib icon , the **Rib Definition** box opens. For **Profile** select the circle (**Sketch.1**) and for the **Center Curve** select (**Sketch.2**) as indicated. The result is the final part shown below.

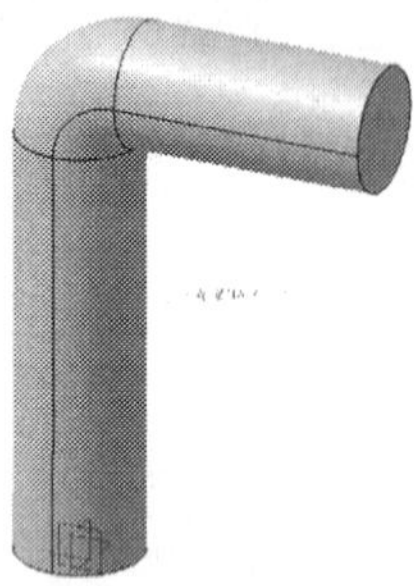

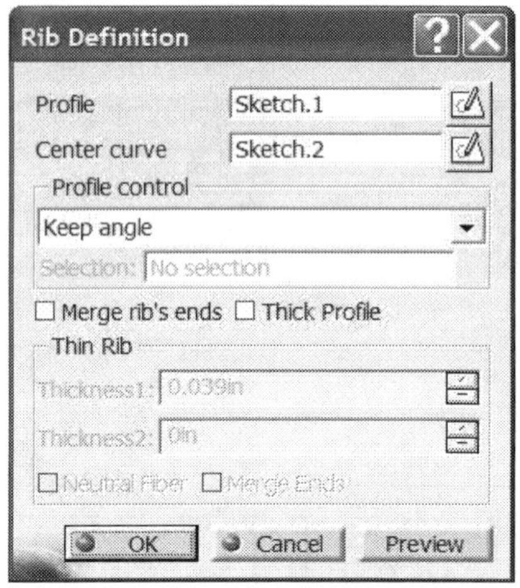


The next step is to apply material properties on the part created.

Use the **Apply Material** icon  from the bottom row of toolbars. The use of this icon opens the material database box shown next.

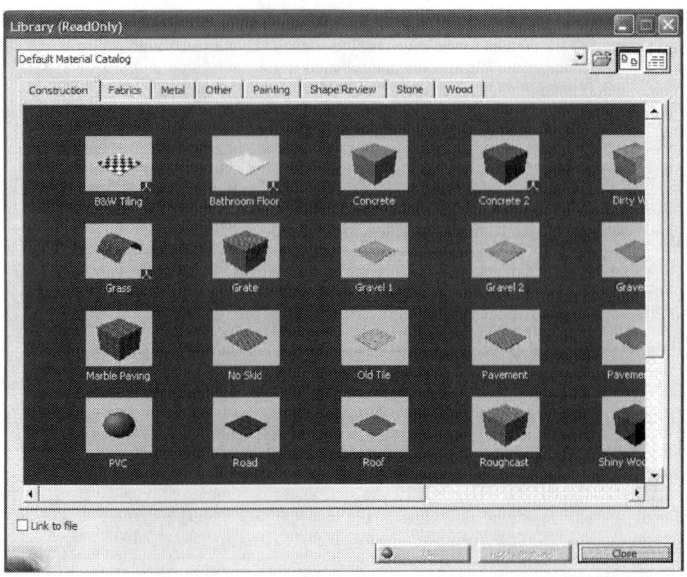

Choose the **Metal** tab on the top; select **Steel**. Use your cursor to pick the part on the screen at which time the **OK** and **Apply Material** buttons can be selected.
Close the box.
The material property is now reflected in the tree.

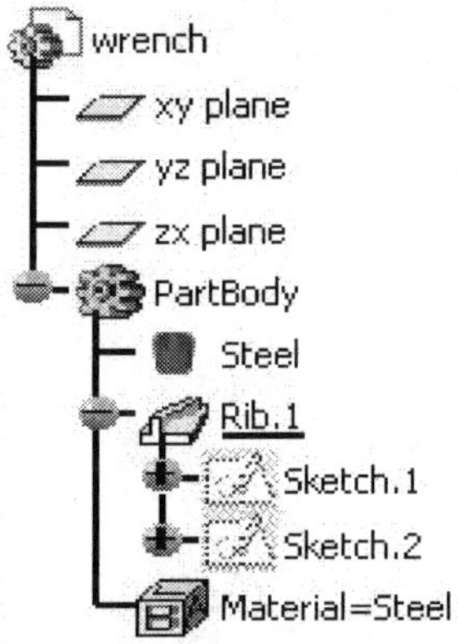


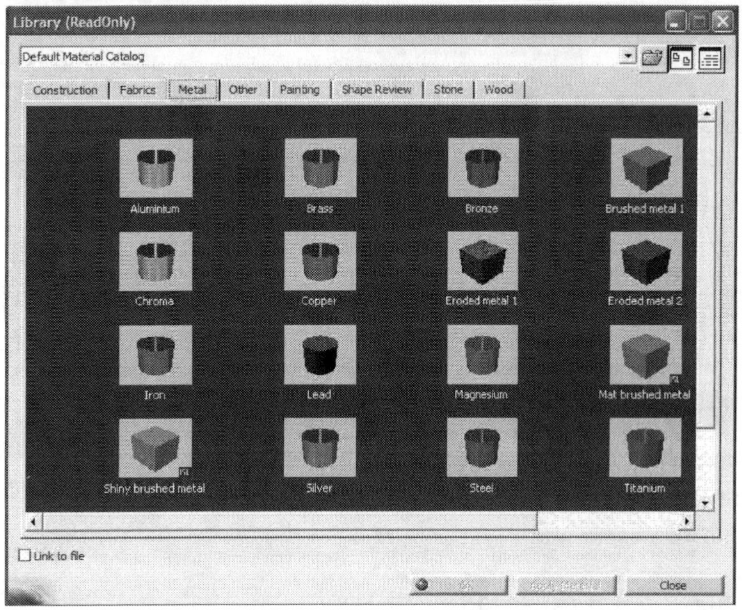


In order to inspect the values of the material properties assigned, double-click on **Steel** in the tree. It may take a minute before the database is searched. You will notice that the **Properties** box shown below opens. Choose the **Analysis** tab from this box, and the values will be displayed. Note that these values can be edited.
Since your Young's modulus and Poisson ratio are different from what is shown, in appropriate boxes, type Young's modulus = **3E+7** and Poisson ratio =**.3**. Press **OK**.

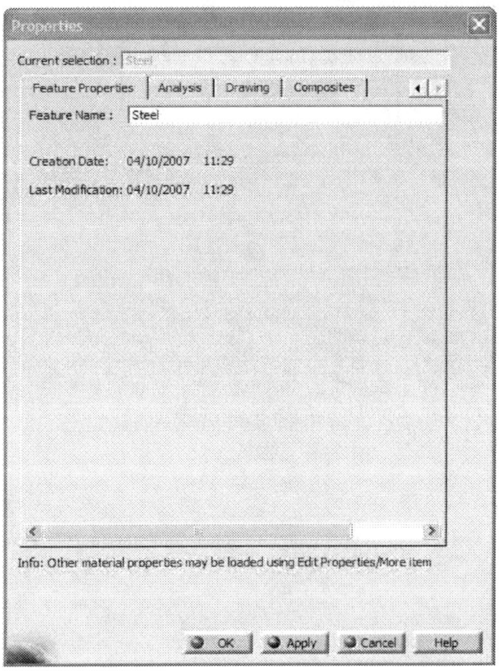


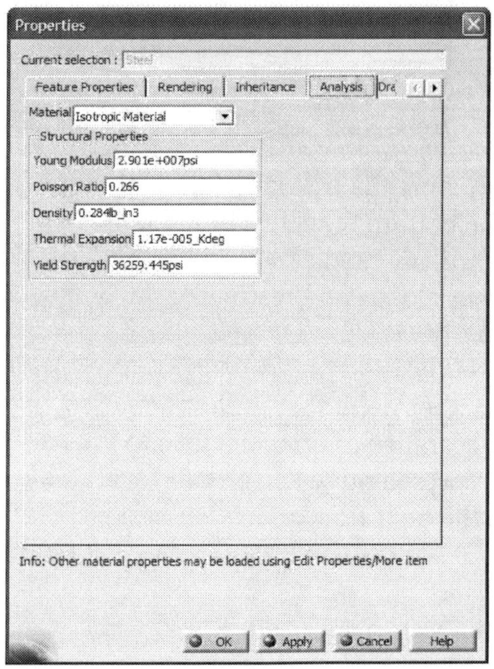

If the part is still "gray", one can change the rendering style. From the **View** toolbar

, select the **View mode** toolbar

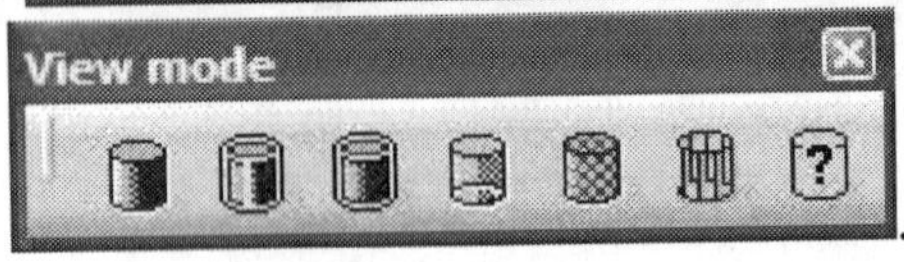


.

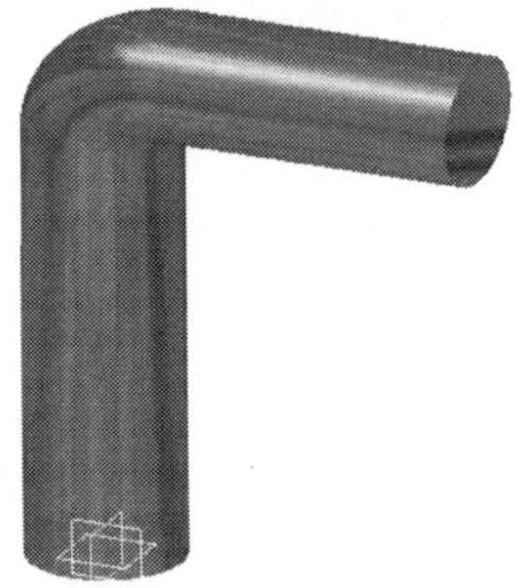

Next choose the **Shading with Material**
The part now appears shaded as shown on the right.

## 3 Entering the Analysis Solutions

From the standard Windows toolbar, select

**Start > Analysis & Simulation > Generative Structural Analysis**
There is a second workbench known as the **Advanced Meshing Tools** which will be discussed later.

The **New Analysis Case** box pops up. The default choice is **Static Analysis** which is precisely what we intend to use. Therefore, close the box by clicking on **OK**.

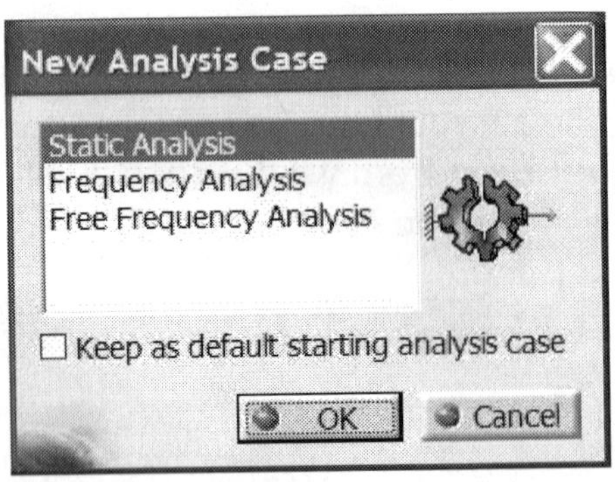


Note that the tree structure gets considerably longer. The bottom branches of the tree are presently "unfilled", and as we proceed in this workbench, assign loads and restraints, the branches gradually get "filled".

Another point that cannot be missed is the appearance of an icon close to the part that reflects a representative "size" and "sag". This is displayed in the next figure.

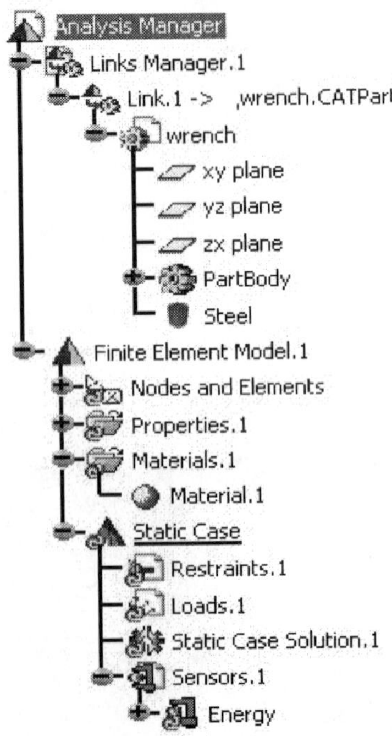

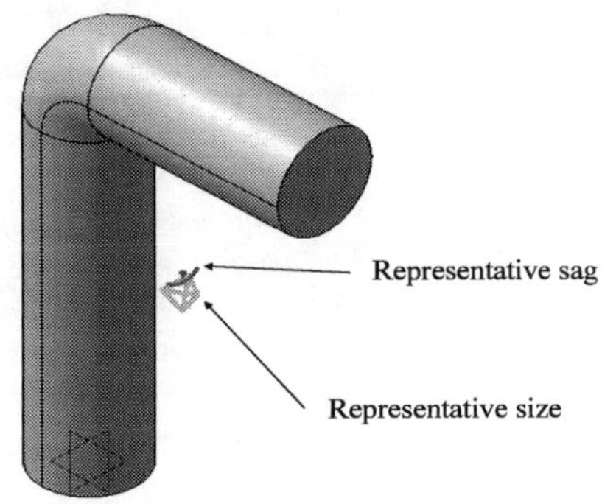


The concept of element size is self-explanatory. A smaller element size leads to more accurate results at the expense of a larger computation time. The "sag" terminology is unique to CATIA. In FEA, the geometry of a part is approximated with the elements. The surface of the part and the FEA approximation of a part do not coincide. The "sag" parameter controls the deviation between the two. Therefore, a smaller "sag" value could lead to better results. There is a relationship between these parameters that one does not have to be concerned with at this point.

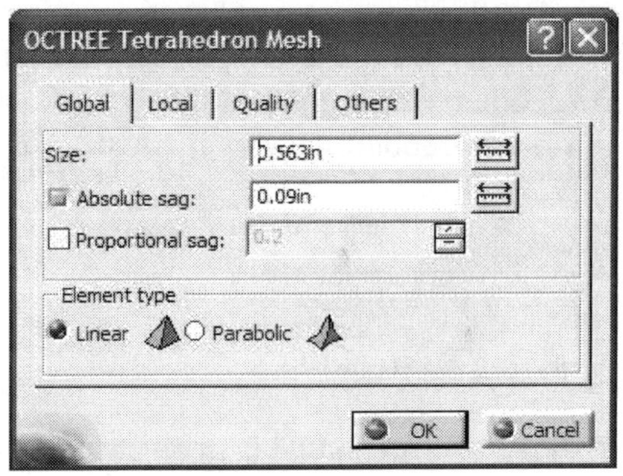


The physical sizes of the representative "size" and "sag" on the screen, which also limit the coarseness of the mesh can be changed by the user. There are two ways to change these parameters:
The first method is to double-click on the representative icons on the screen which forces the **OCTREE Tetrahedron Mesh** box to open as shown to the right. Change the default values to match the numbers in the box.
Notice that the type of the elements used (linear/parabolic) is also set in this box. Close the box by selecting **OK**.
The second method of reaching this box is through the tree.
By double-clicking on the branch labeled **OCTREE Tetrahedron Mesh** shown below, the same box opens allowing the user to modify the values.

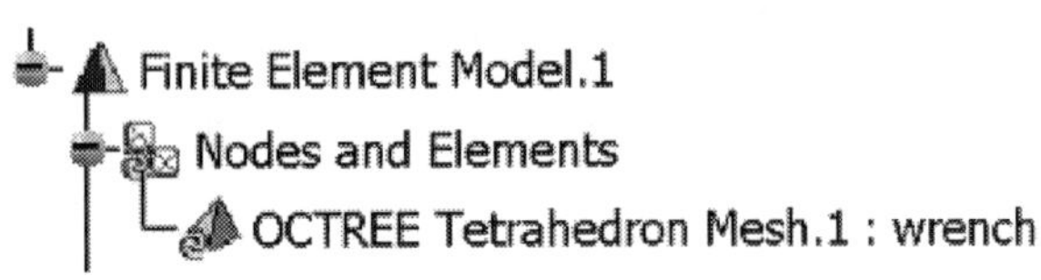


In order to view the generated mesh, you can point the cursor to the branch **Nodes and Elements**, right-click and select **Mesh Visualization**. This step may be slightly different in some UNIX machines. Upon performing this operation a **Warning** box appears which can be ignored by selecting **OK**. For the mesh parameters used, the following mesh is displayed on the screen. See Note #2 in Appendix I.

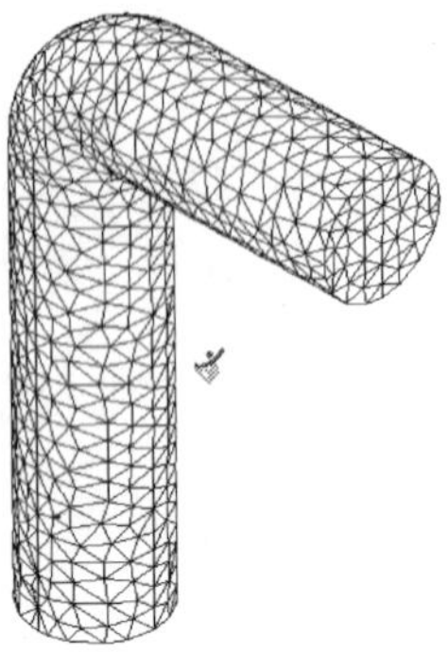

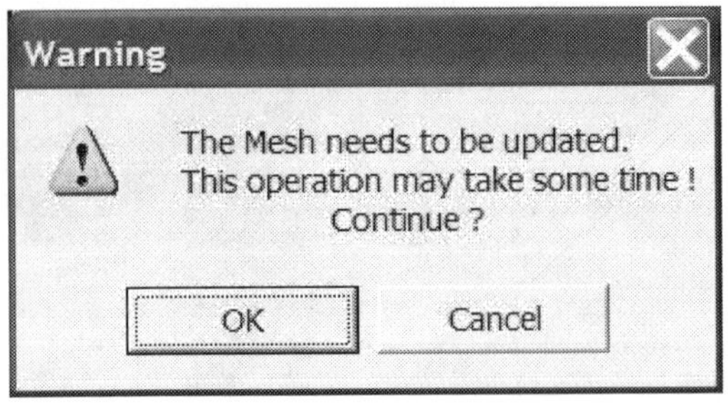


The representative "size" and "sag" icons can be removed from the display by simply pointing to them right-click and select **Hide**. This is the standard process for hiding any entity in CATIA V5.

Before proceeding with the rest of the model, a few more points regarding the mesh size are discussed. As indicated earlier, a smaller mesh could result in a more accurate solution; however, this cannot be done indiscriminately. The elements must be small in the regions of high stress gradient such as stress concentrations. These are areas where the geometry changes rapidly such as bends, fillets, and keyways.
Uniformly reducing the element size for the whole part is a poor strategy.

CONGRATULATIONS! You now have a mesh with the correct material properties. Regularly save your work.

**Applying Restraints:**

CATIA's FEA module is geometrically based. This means that the boundary conditions cannot be applied to nodes and elements. The boundary conditions can only be applied at the part level. As soon as you enter the **Generative Structural Analysis** workbench, the part is automatically hidden. Therefore, before boundary conditions are applied, the part must be brought to the unhide mode. This can be carried out by pointing the cursor to the top of the tree, the **Links Manager.1** branch, right-click, select **Show**. At this point, the part and the mesh are superimposed as shown to the right and you have access to the part.

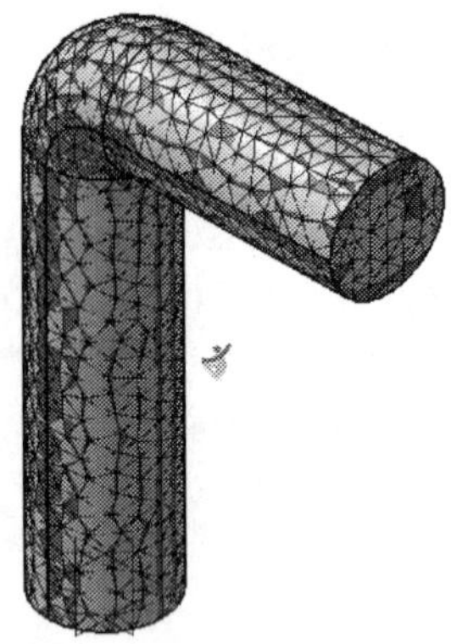

If, the presence of the mesh is annoying, you can always hide it. Point the cursor to **Nodes and Elements**, right-click, **Hide**.

Instead of hiding the mesh as indicated above, one can point the cursor to the **Mesh.1** item in the tree, right-click, and select **Activate/Deactivate**. The result is that the mesh is hidden and the part is displayed. The steps are graphically in the next figure.

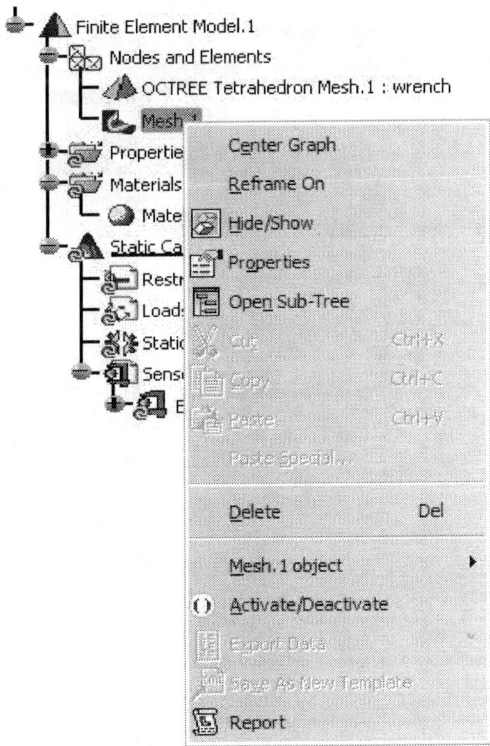


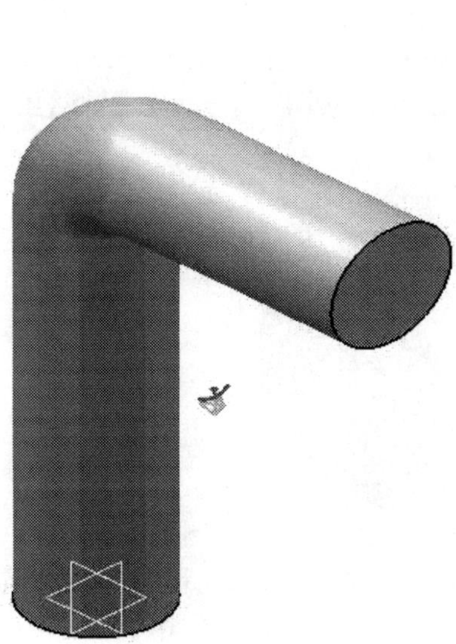

In FEA, restraints refer to applying displacement boundary conditions which is achieved through the **Restraint** toolbar 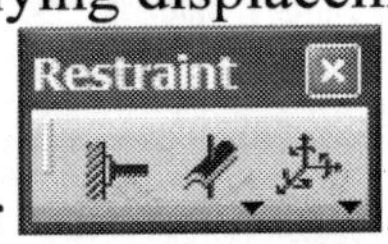

. In the present problem, you can assume that the base of the longer section is clamped. The **Clamp** condition means that the displacements in all three directions are zero. Select the **Clamp** icon  and pick the bottom face of the rod. Be careful not to pick the circumference (edge) of the circle instead of the face. In that case, only two restraint symbols will be shown attached to the circumference.

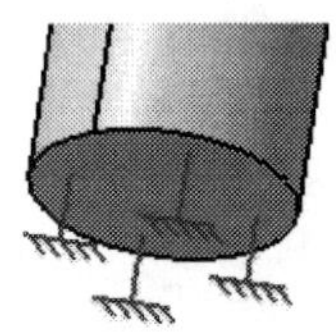

**Applying Loads:**

In FEA, loads refer to forces. The **Loads** toolbar 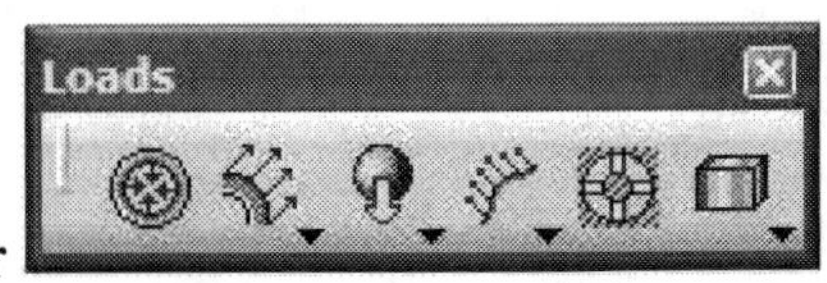

is used for this purpose. Select the **Distributed Force** icon , and with the cursor pick the other face of the rod which is loaded. The **Distributed Force** box shown below opens. A visual inspection of the global axis on your screen indicates that the force of magnitude 2000 lb should be applied in the negative x-direction.

Although in our problem the 2000 lb force is applied in the global direction x, it is possible to apply forces in the local direction specified by the user. Upon selection of the appropriate face, the force symbols will appear as shown below.

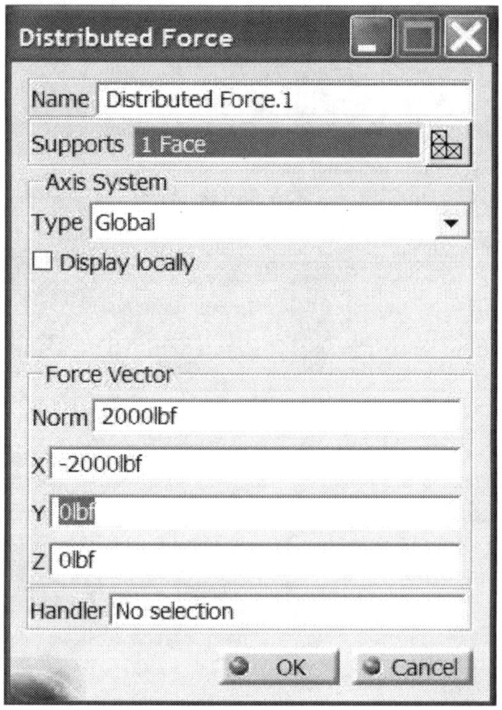


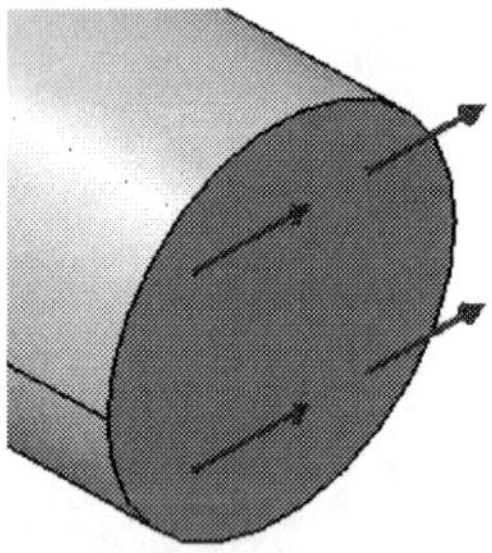

If the circumference of the circle is accidentally picked, only two arrows attached to the circle will appear. Although in our present problem there may be small differences in the results, one should apply the loads and restraints as intended.

The portion of the tree which reports the restraints and loads is shown below.

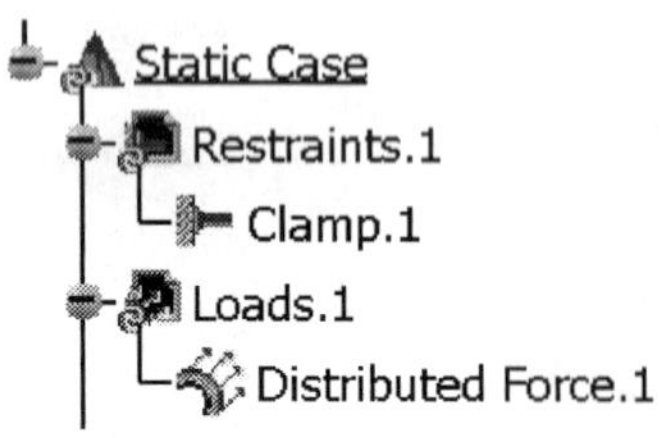


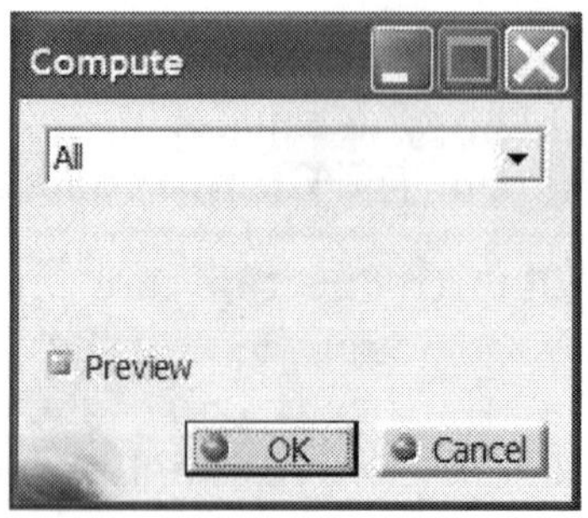


**Launching the Solver:**

To run the analysis, you need to use the **Compute** toolbar  by selecting the **Compute** icon . This leads to the **Compute** box shown above. Leave the defaults as **All** which means everything is computed.
Upon closing this box, after a brief pause, the second box shown below appears. This box provides information on the resources needed to complete the analysis.
If the estimates are zero in the listing, then there is a problem in the previous step and should be looked into. If all the numbers are zero in the box, the program may run but would not produce any useful results.

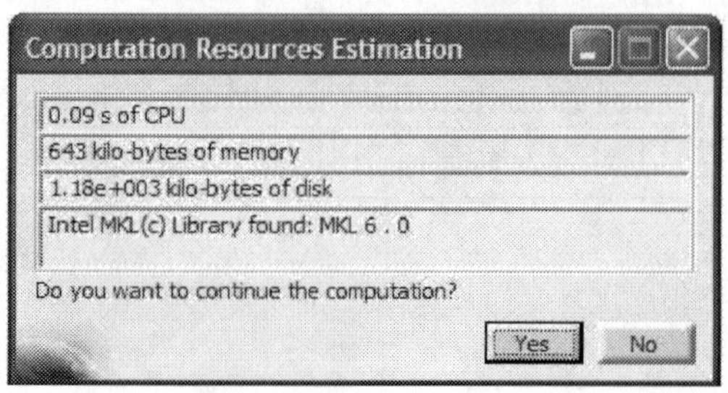

The tree has been changed to reflect the location of the Results and Computations as shown below.

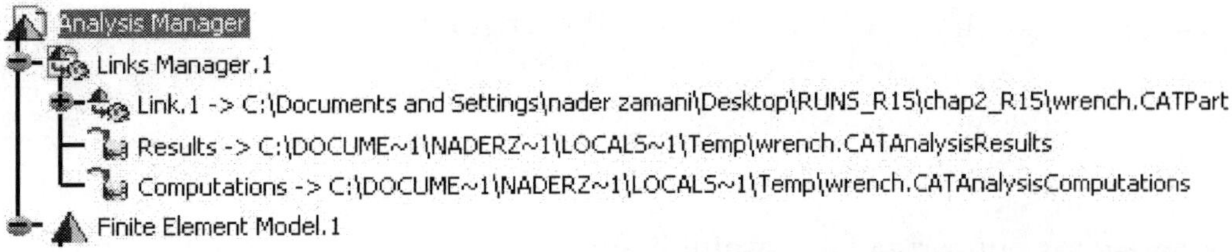


The user can change these locations by double-clicking on the branch. The box, shown on the right, will open and can be modified.

**Postprocessing:**

The main postprocessing toolbar is called **Image** 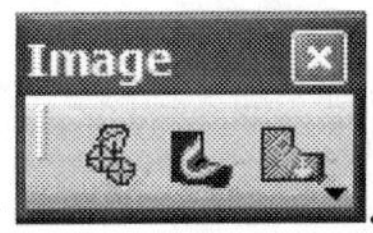 . To view the deformed shape you have to use the **Deformation** icon. The resulting deformed shape is displayed below.



The deformation image can be very deceiving because one could have the impression that the wrench actually displaces to that extent. Keep in mind that the displacements are scaled considerably so that one can observe the deformed shape. Although the scale factor is set automatically, one can change this value with the **Deformation Scale Factor** icon in the **Analysis Tools** toolbar  .



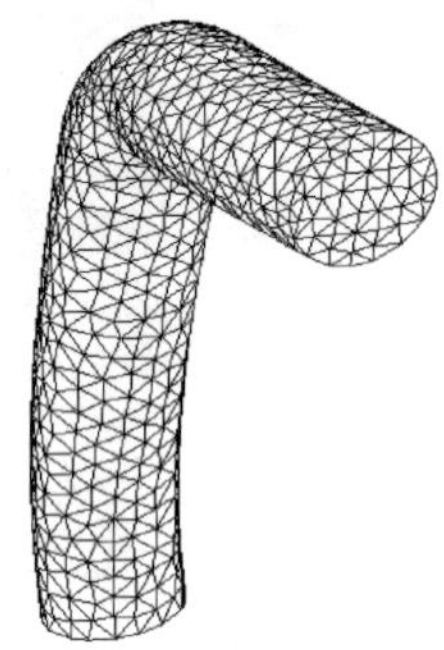

Clicking on the above icon leads to the box shown on the right where the desired scale factor can be typed. The deformed shape displayed corresponds to a scale factor of 46.017. The displayed value on the screen is 46.017 times the actual maximum displacement.

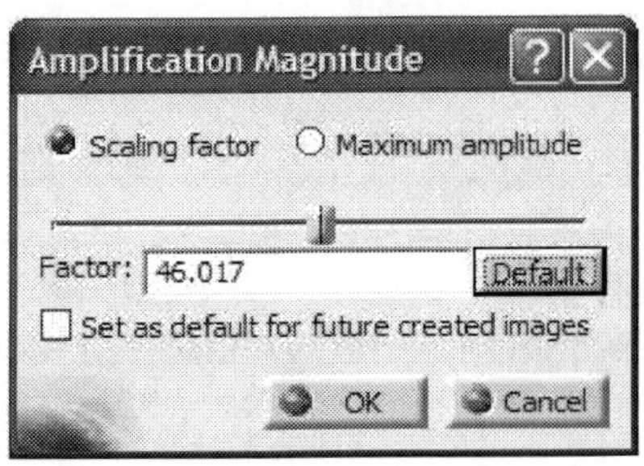

In order to see the displacement field, the **Displacement** icon in the **Image** toolbar should be used. The default display is in terms of displacement arrows as shown on the right. The color and the length of arrows represent the size of the displacement. The contour legend indicates a maximum displacement of .0353 in.

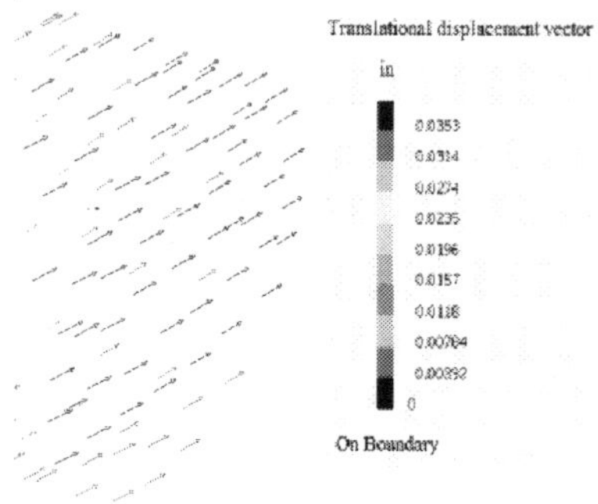


The arrow plot is not particularly useful. In order to view the contour plot of the displacement field, position the cursor on the arrow field and double-click. The **Image Edition** box shown below opens.

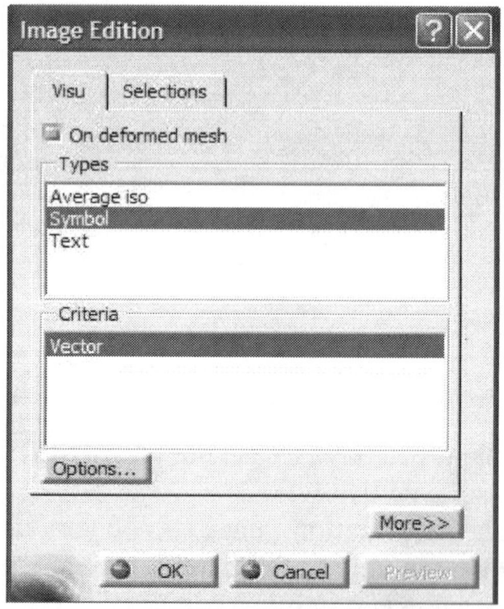


Note that the default is to draw the contour on the deformed shape. If this is not desired, uncheck the box **On deformed mesh**. Next, select **AVERAGE-ISO** and press **OK**.
The contour of the displacement field as shown is plotted.

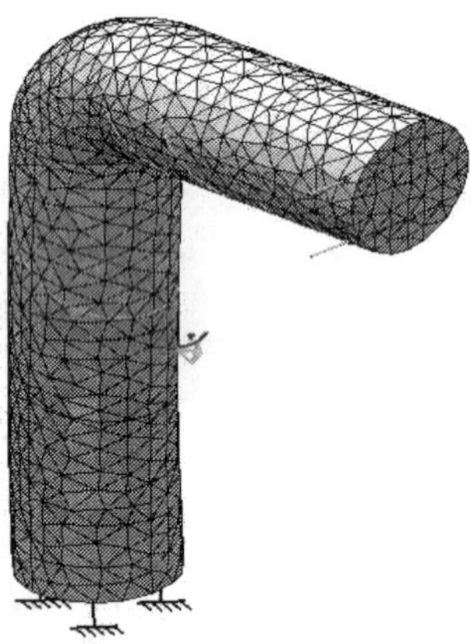

It is difficult to read the contour lines from the above figure. You can change the render style by using

**Shading with Material** icon in the **View Mode** toolbar

Note that the elements are not showing in this plot. If you prefer that the elements are displayed at the same time, you need to go through the following step.

Select the **Custom View Mode** icon from the above toolbar. In the resulting pop up box, make sure that **Edges and points** is checked.

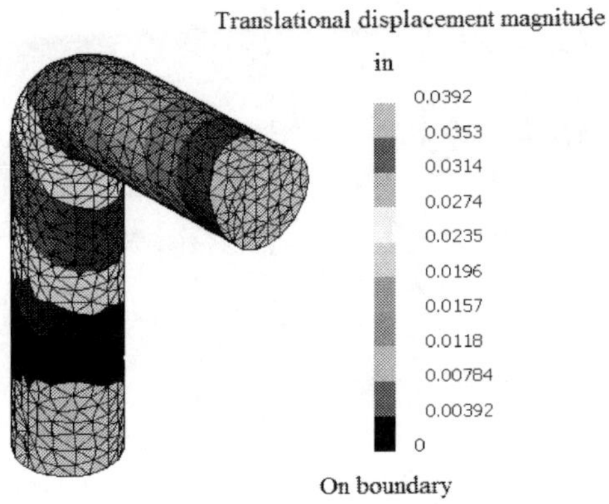


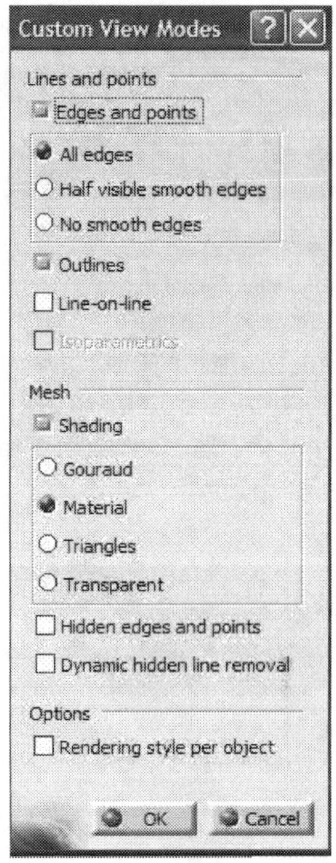


Ignoring the fillet radius of the bend, the beam bending solution of this problem can be obtained using Castigliano's theorem. This approximate value is .044 in which is in the same ball park as the FEA solution of .0392 in. The discrepancy is primarily due to the large bend radius.

Clearly, the maximum displacement is at the point of the application of the load, in the negative x-direction. (Note: The color map has been changed; otherwise everything looks black in the figure.)

The next step in the postprocessing is to plot the contours of the von Mises stress using the **von Mises Stress** icon  in the **Image** toolbar.
The von Mises stress is displayed to the right.

The maximum stress is at the support with a value of 2.06E+4 psi which is below the yield strength of most steels.

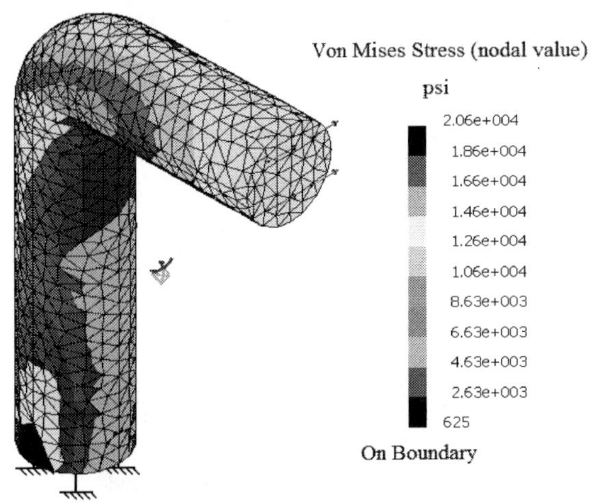

Double-clicking on the contour legend leads to the **Color Map** box displayed on the right.

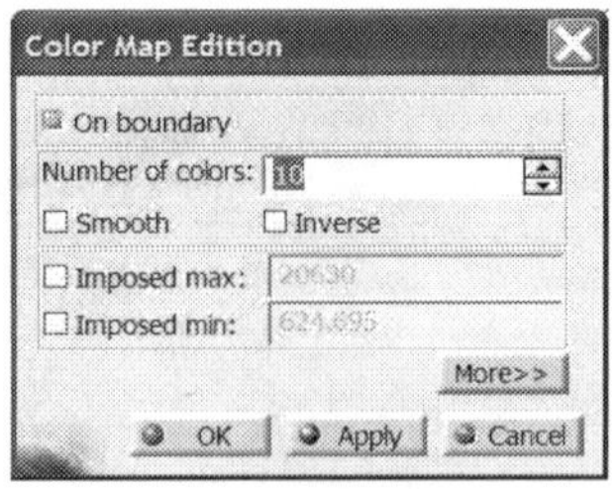


The contour can be plotted as **Smooth** or **Stepped**. The number of color bands is also specified in this box. Finally, the user can describe the range of stresses to be plotted.

Occasionally, you may be interested in plotting the von Mises stress contour in either the load area or the support section. In order to achieve this, double-click on the contour levels on the screen to open the image edition box. Next use the **Selections** tab as shown below. Here, you have the choice of selecting different areas.

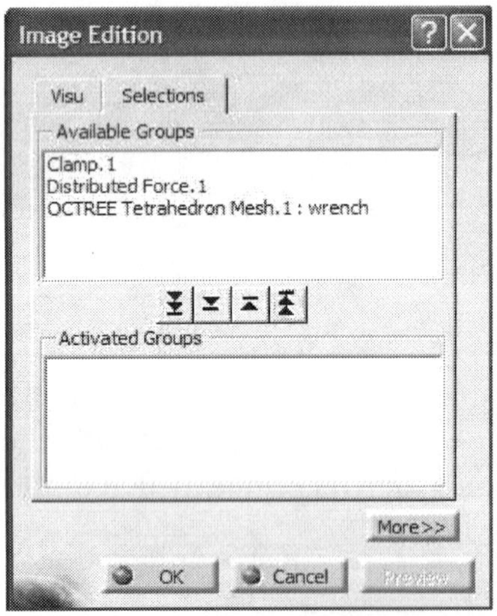


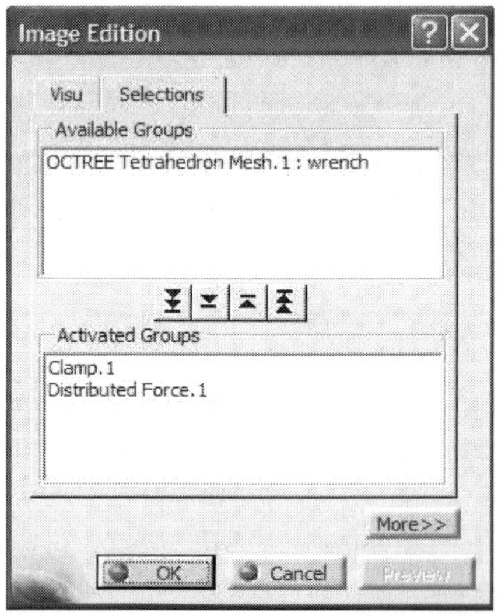


The contours on the right display the von Mises stress at **Distributed Force.1** and **Clamp.1** sections.

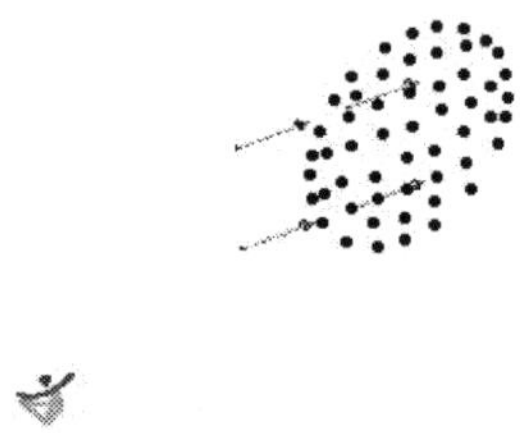

Unfortunately in the current release of CATIA this contour is rather useless. In a later chapter, you will be shown how to use the **Group** concept to generate a better contour plot as indicated below.

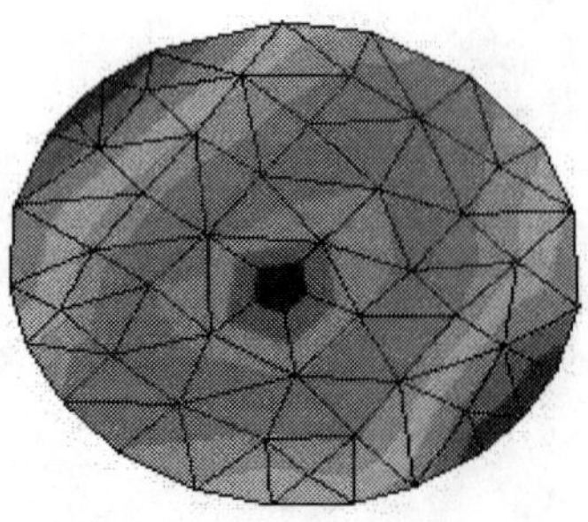

As the postprocessing proceeds and we generate different plots, they are recorded in the tree as shown. Each plot generated deactivates the previous one on the screen. By pointing to a desired plot in the tree and right-clicking, you can activate the plot. Clearly any plot can be deleted from the tree in the usual way (right-click, **Delete**).

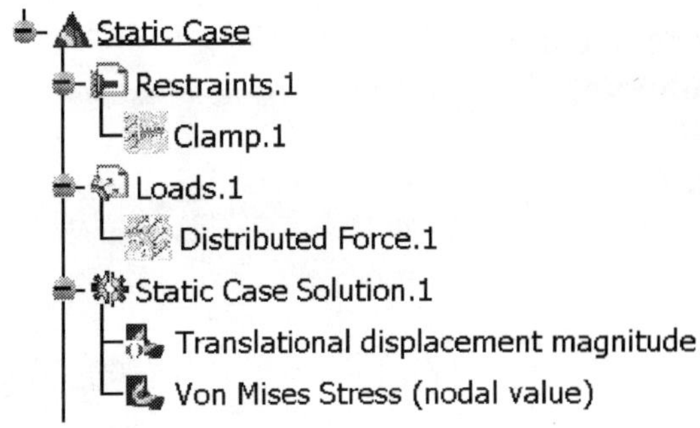


The location and magnitude of the extremum values of a contour (e.g. von Mises stress) can be identified in a plot. This is achieved by using the **Image Extrema** icon in the **Image Analysis** toolbar

.

Before the plot is generated, the **Extrema Creation** box pops up as shown to the right. If the default values are maintained, the global maximum and minimum are found and their location pin-pointed in a contour plot as displayed below.

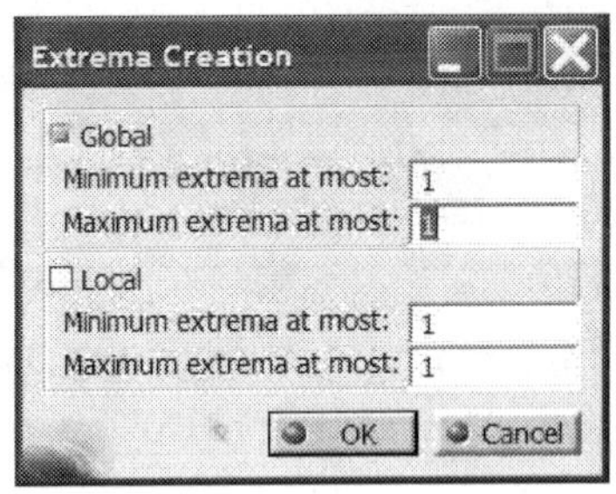

At this point we have generated two plots. The displacement and the von Mises stress contours which can be displayed individually. However, CATIA also allows you to show both plots side by side.

First make sure that both images to be plotted are active in the tree. If not, point to the graph in the tree, right-click, select **Active**.

Click the **Image Layout** icon from the **Image Analysis** toolbar. The **Images** box, shown to the right, asks you to specify the direction along which the two plots are expected to be aligned.

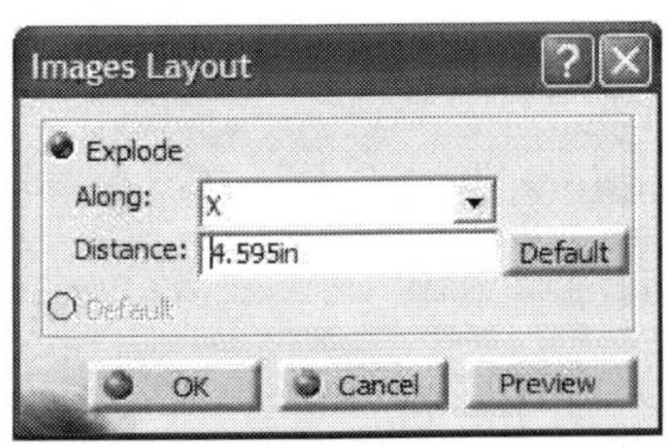

The outcome is side-by-side plots shown below. (Note: The color map has been changed otherwise everything looks black.)

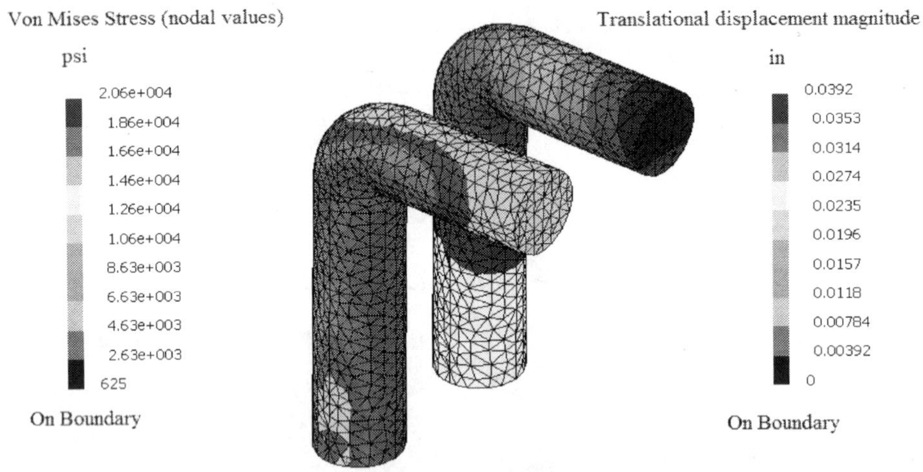


Before describing how the principal stresses are plotted, we like to elaborate on the significance of the von Mises stress plot.

The state of stress is described by the six Cauchy stresses $\{\sigma_x, \sigma_y, \sigma_z, \tau_{xy}, \tau_{xz}, \tau_{yz}\}$ which vary from point to point. The von Mises stress is a combination of these according to the following expression:

$$\sigma_{VM} = \sqrt{\frac{1}{2}\left[(\sigma_x - \sigma_y)^2 + (\sigma_x - \sigma_z)^2 + (\sigma_y - \sigma_z)^2 + 6(\tau_{xy}^2 + \tau_{xz}^2 + \tau_{yz}^2)\right]}$$

For an obvious reason, this is also known as the effective stress. Note that by definition, the von Mises is always a positive number. In terms of principal stresses, $\sigma_{VM}$ can also be written as

$$\sigma_{VM} = \sqrt{\frac{1}{2}\left[(\sigma_1 - \sigma_2)^2 + (\sigma_1 - \sigma_3)^2 + (\sigma_2 - \sigma_3)^2\right]}$$

For many ductile materials, the onset of yielding (permanent plastic deformation) takes place when $\sigma_{VM} = \sigma_Y$ where $\sigma_Y$ is the yield strength of the material. For design purposes, a factor of safety "N" is introduced leading to the condition $\sigma_{VM} = \frac{\sigma_Y}{N}$.

Therefore, a safe design is considered to be one where $\sigma_{VM} < \frac{\sigma_Y}{N}$. The von Mises stress contour plot allows you to check the above condition.

The **Cutting Plane** icon  from the **Analysis tools** toolbar 

can be used to make a cut through the part at a desired location and inspect the stresses inside of the part. The **Cut Plane** box allows you to keep the plane or to remove it for display purposes. A typical cutting plane is shown below.

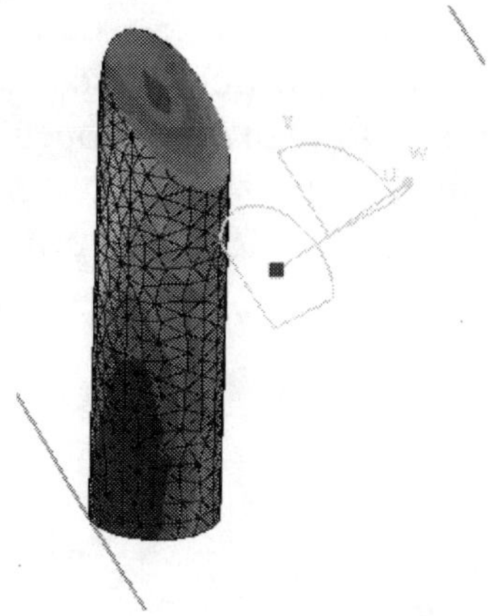

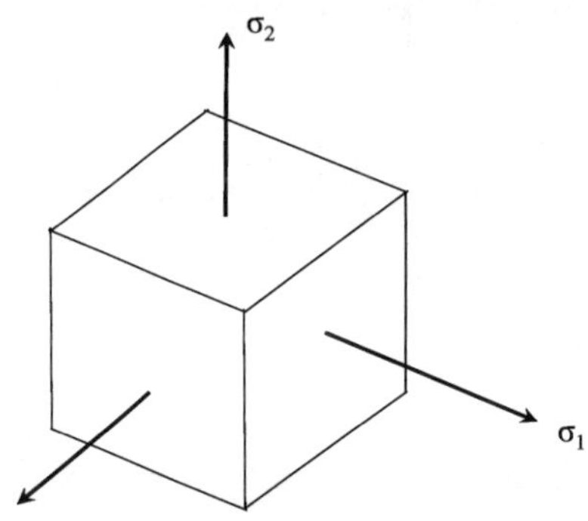


The principal stresses are postprocessed next. The principal directions are three mutually perpendicular directions along which only normal stresses act. These normal stresses are known as the principal stresses. The figure to the right displays the principal directions $x_1$, $x_2$, and $x_3$, together with the principal directions $\sigma_1$ , $\sigma_2$, and $\sigma_3$. The standard convention in stress analysis is to label the stresses according to $\sigma_1 \geq \sigma_2 \geq \sigma_3$. The principal stresses are important for both theoretical reasons and practical ones. In experimental stress analysis, the positioning of strain gauges relies on the principal directions on the surface of a part.

From the **Image** toolbar ,


select the **Principal Stress** icon 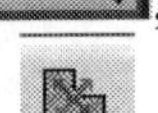. The result is the principal stress directions in the vector form as displayed to the right. Due to the large number of arrows, the interpretation of this plot is difficult. A zoomed view of the tip is also shown below.

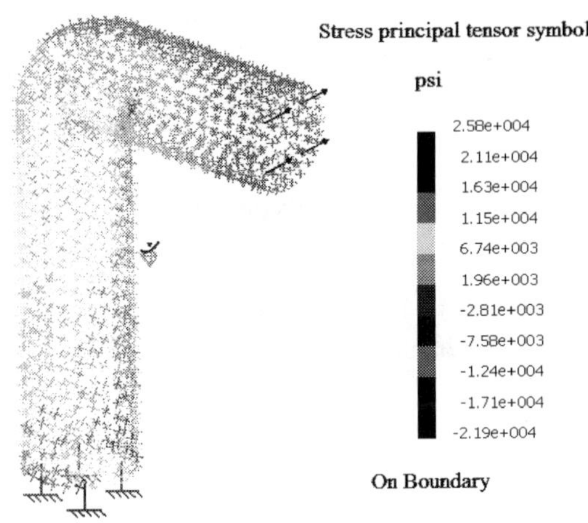


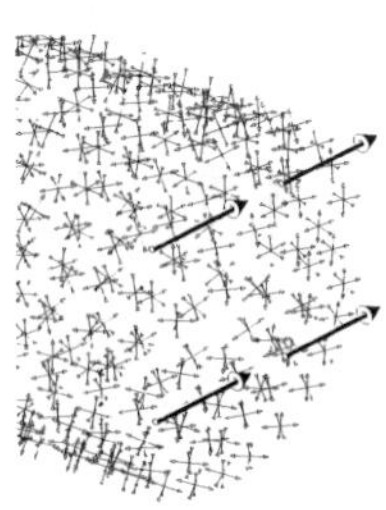

You can improve on the display of principal stresses by selecting a specific stress component to be plotted. To do so, double-click on the arrows on the screen which causes the **Image Edition**, shown to the right to open. Click on the **More** button to expand the window as shown below. Choose the **Component C11**. In CATIA, C11 represents $\sigma_1$, the largest principal stress.

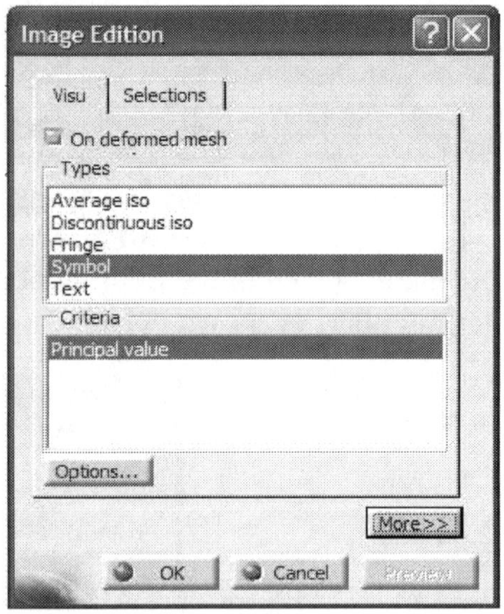


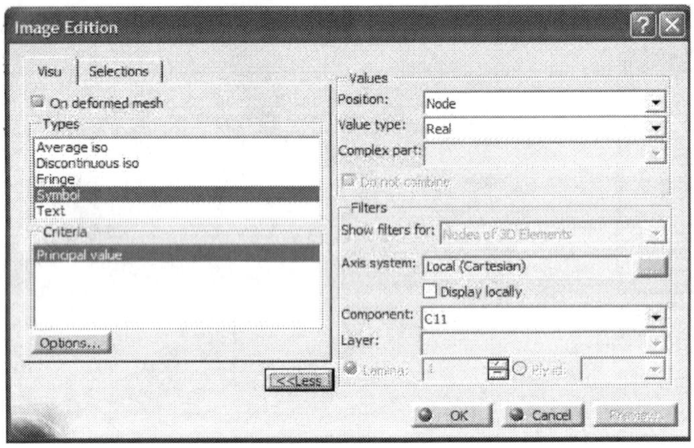


At this point the vector plot displays only the directions associated with $\sigma_1$ as shown in the plot below.

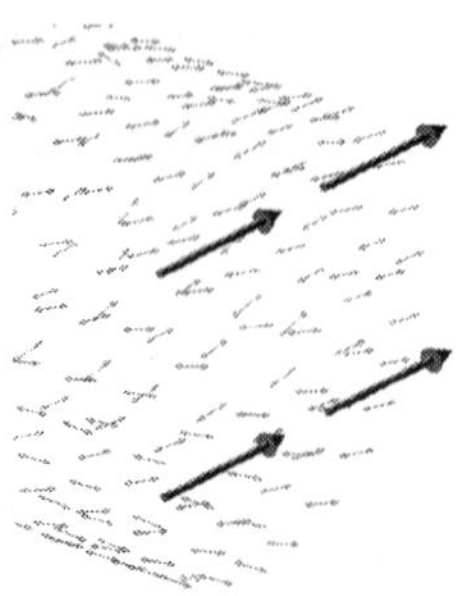

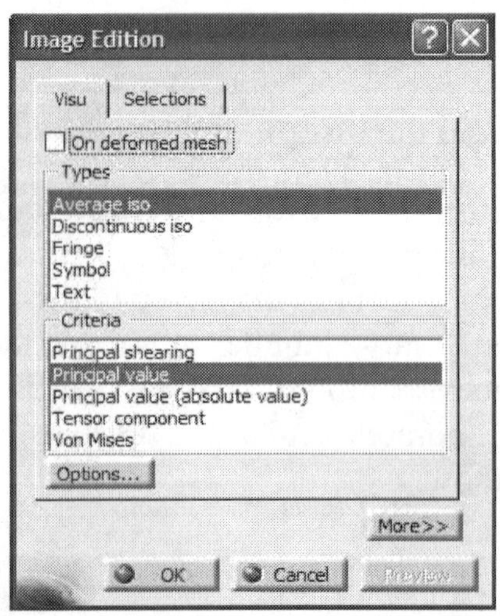


An alternative to the vector plot of the principal stress is the contour plot of $\sigma_1$. This can be achieved through the **Image Edition** box, under the **Visu** tab. You should select **AVERAGE-ISO** instead of **Symbol**. The resulting contour plot is shown below.

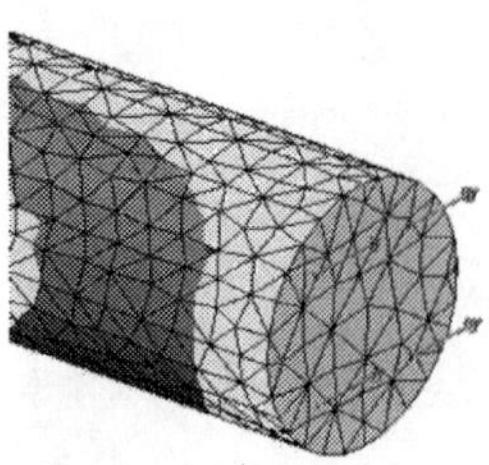

Using the icon **Generate Report**  in the **Analysis Results** toolbar 

an HTML based report can be generated which summarizes the features and results of the FEA model. The first page of this report is displayed below.

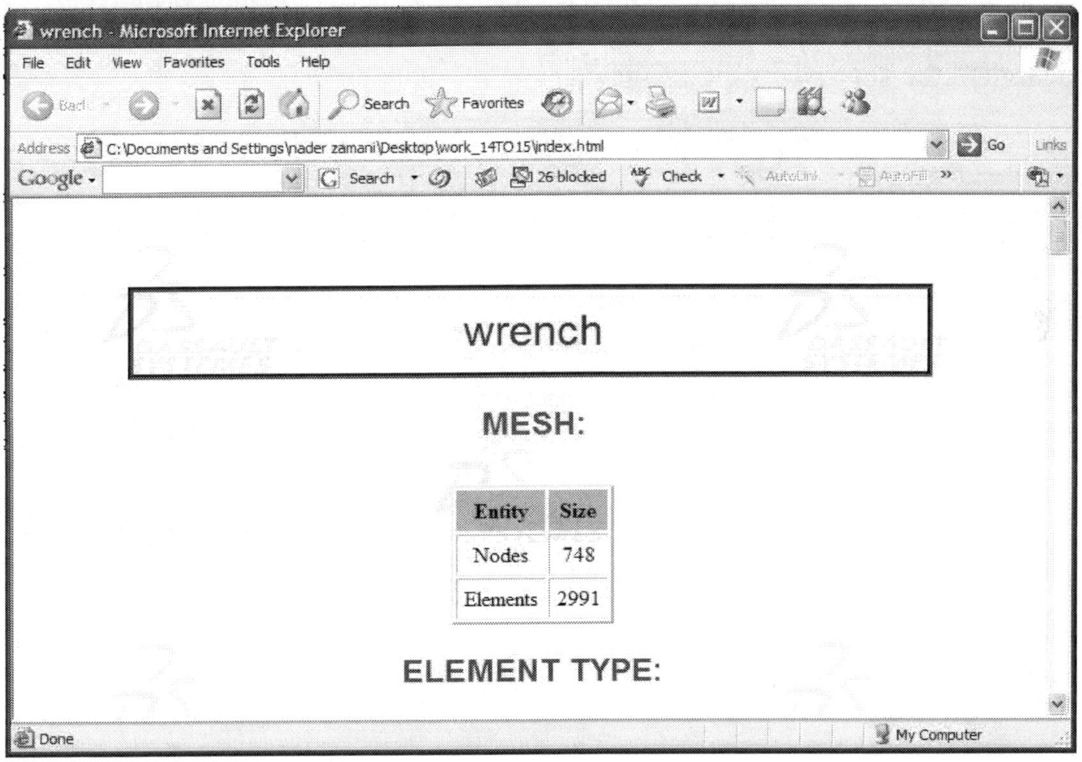


Finally, animation of the model can be achieved through the **Animate** icon  in the **Analysis Tools** toolbar 

and AVI files can easily be generated.

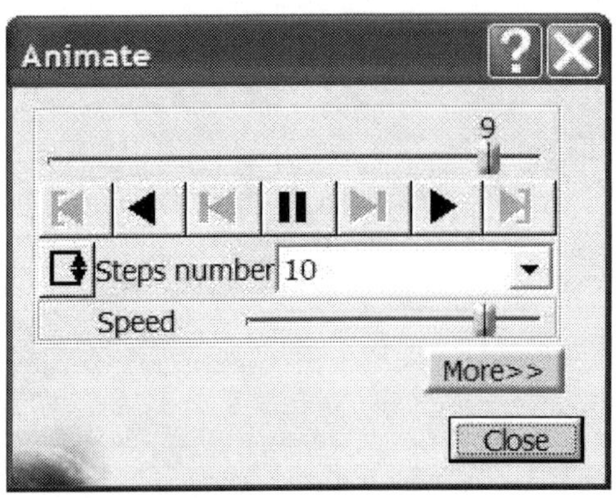

# Exercises for Chapter 2

## Problem 1: Analysis of a Foot Pedal

The foot pedal shown below is made of steel with Young's modulus 30E+6 psi and Poisson ratio 0.3. The pedal is loaded with a normal force of 100 lb along the edge shown. The other end of the pedal is clamped. The geometrical dimensions are provided at the bottom of the page where all the dimensions are in inches.

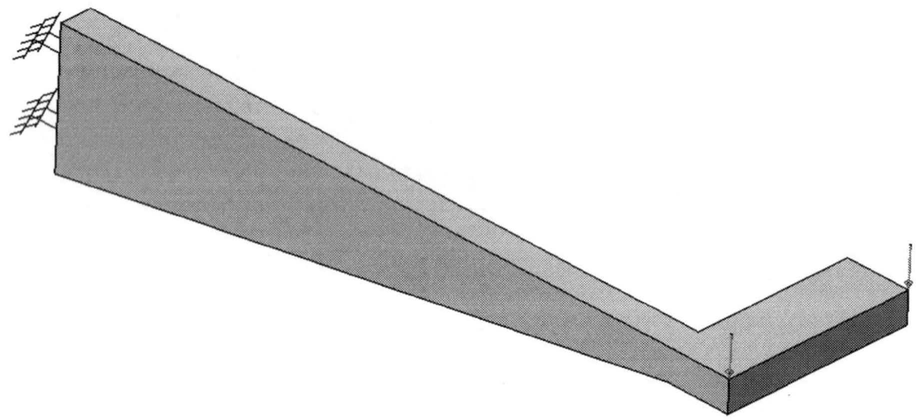

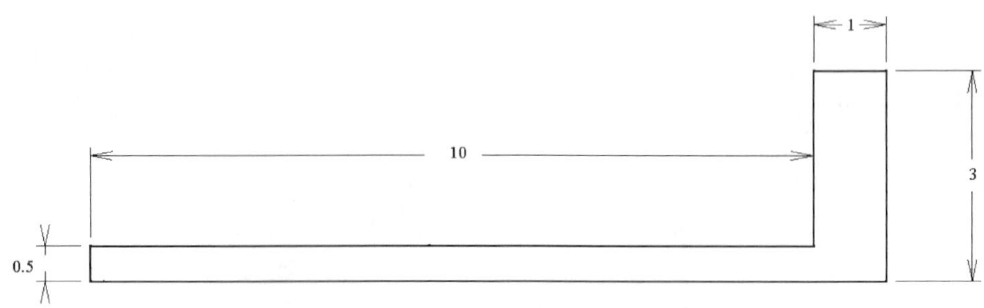


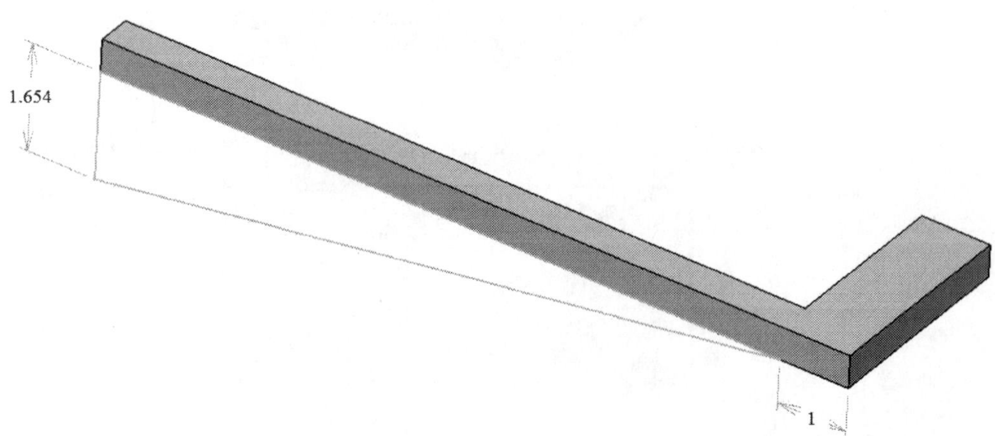

Try running the model with the two different element "size" and "sag" with both the linear and parabolic type of elements. Record the results in terms of the maximum displacement and the maximum von Mises stress in a table and comment on the results. The run time of the parabolic elements with element size of 0.1 could be substantial depending on the type of processor used.

Partial Answer:

| **Size = .3, sag = .05** | | |
|---|---|---|
| Element Type | Linear | Parabolic |
| Maximum Displacement | .0158 in. | .0227 in. |
| Maximum von Mises Srtess | 5.32E+3 psi | 1.1E+4 psi |

| **Size = .1, sag = .05** | | |
|---|---|---|
| Element Type | Linear | Parabolic |
| Maximum Displacement | .021 in. | .0229 in. |
| Maximum von Mises Stress | 9.43E+4 psi | 1.6E+4 psi |

The above tables reveal an extremely important fact about finite element analysis. Making a single run and accepting the results at face value is a serious mistake. Note that for linear elements as the mesh is refined, there is a significant change in both displacement and von Mises stress. The user should not accept either value as being correct and must refine the mesh further. The refinement should reach a point at which the difference with the previous mesh is not deemed to be significant to user. This process is referred to as a mesh convergence study.

Keep in mind that the refinement need not be uniform throughout the part. One should perform the refinement in the critical areas only. It is clear that parabolic elements are superior in accuracy to linear element. Furthermore, note that although the displacement seems to have stabilized, the von Mises is still unreliable. It is well known that the displacements in FEA are more accurate than stresses. The reason is that the stresses are obtained by differentiating the displacement, a process which magnifies the error.

## Problem 2: Analysis of a Cylindrical Bar under Torsion

The cylindrical bar shown below has a clamped end. The other end is subjected to a couple caused by opposite forces on magnitude 1000 lb separated by 1.5 in. This is equivalent to a torque of 1500 lb.in applied to the cylinder. The material is steel with Young's modulus 30E+6 and Poisson ratio of 0.3.
The diameter of the cylinder is 1 in. and the dimensions of the loaded end are shown below. Although not showing, the length of the padded cylinder is 5 in. and the length of the padded rectangle is 0.5 in. All sharp corners at the loaded end have surface fillet of radius 0.1 in.

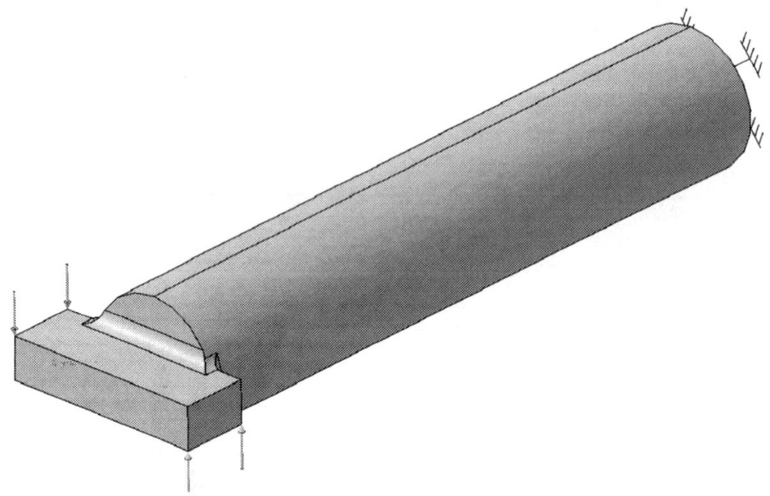

draw the rectangle on the circular face, then pad it away .5 in

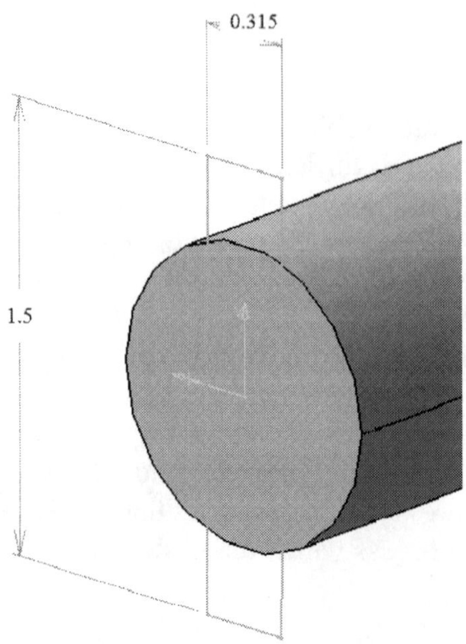


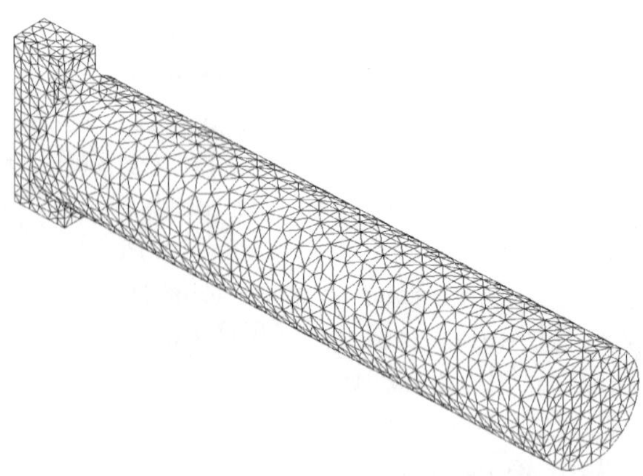

Model the part with linear solid elements with size = 0.1 and sag = 0.025 which results in the mesh shown in the previous page. Compare the hoop stress (The hoop stress is the largest principal stress "C11") with the theoretical solution from strength of materials.

Partial Answer:

The strength of materials solution is based on $\tau = \frac{Tr}{J}$ where T is the applied torque, r is the radius of the cylinder and J is the polar moment of inertia. In terms of the diameter, $r = \frac{D}{2}$, and $J = \frac{\pi D^4}{32}$. The hoop stress "C1" which numerically equals $\tau$ is calculated from $\frac{16T}{\pi D^3}$. For the present problem, $T = 1500$ lb.in and $D = 1$ in. Based on these parameters, a value of 7643 psi for the hoop stress is predicted.
The FEA results can be assessed by plotting the contour of "C1" at the clamped section. The resulting plot shown below agrees quite well with 7643 psi obtained earlier. The circular fringe patterns are another qualitative check on the validity of the FEA results.

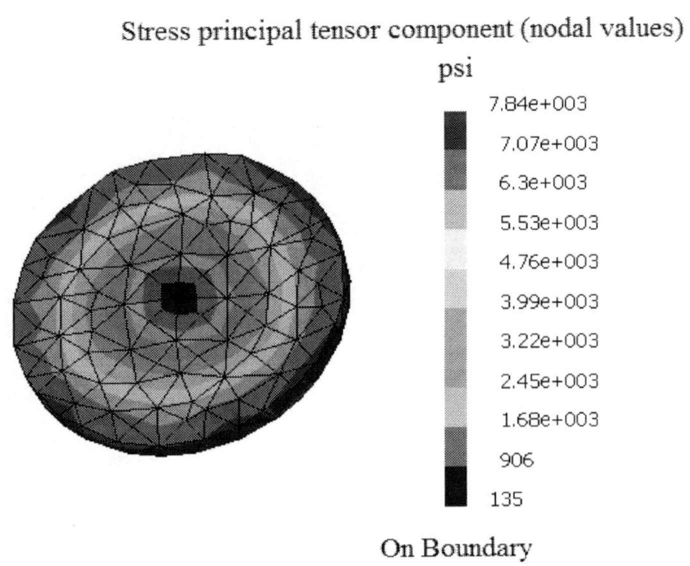

# NOTES:

# Chapter 3

# Axially Loaded Block with Stress Concentration

## Introduction

In this tutorial you will create a solid model of a notched block which is axially pulled. Symmetry is used to reduce the size of the model. The FEA results are compared with the existing analytical solution.

## 1 Problem Statement

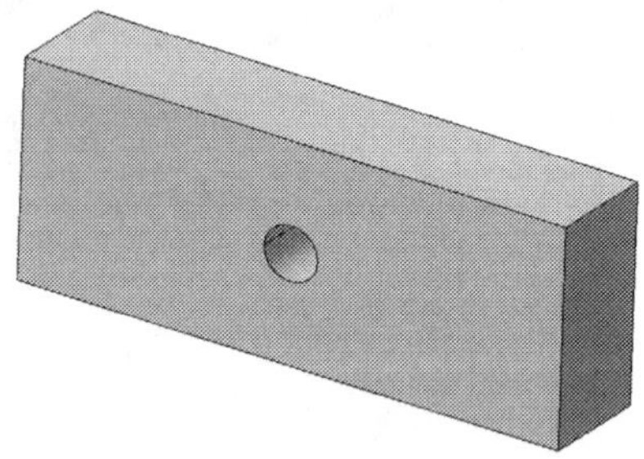

A block of dimensions 2x4x10 in. has a central hole with radius 1 in. as shown to the right. The block is made of aluminum with Young's modulus 10.15E+6 psi and Poisson ratio of 0.346. A tensile load of 2000 lb in the axial direction is applied to the ends of the block, causing it to elongate. The presence of the hole causes a stress concentration at the top and the bottom of the hole. In this chapter, you will use the solid tetrahedron elements described earlier to model the block.
This particular problem is very popular (and important) in the FEA area because it has an analytical solution that one can use to asses the computational results. To be more specific, provided that the block is sufficiently long and $\frac{d}{W} \leq .65$, the ratio of the maximum stress to the nominal stress can be approximated with the following formula

$$K_t(\tfrac{d}{W}) = 3.0039 - 3.753(\tfrac{d}{W}) + 7.9735(\tfrac{d}{W})^2 - 9.2659(\tfrac{d}{W})^3 + 1.8145(\tfrac{d}{W})^4 + 2.9684(\tfrac{d}{W})^5$$

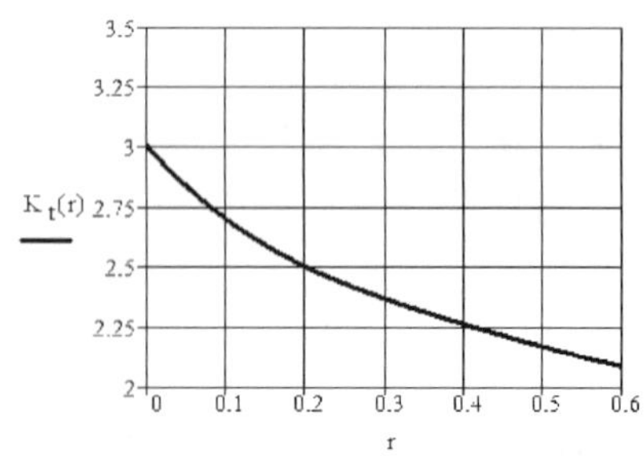


In the above expansion, W is the width of the block and d is the diameter of the hole. For the given dimensions, W = 4 in. and d = 1 in., therefore, the $K_t$ formula can be used. The graph of the stress concentration factor as a function of $r = \frac{d}{W}$ is given to the right. The nominal stress in the calculation of $K_t$ is based on the net section, i.e. $\sigma_{nom} = \dfrac{F}{(W-d)h}$ where $h = 2$ in. is the thickness of the block.

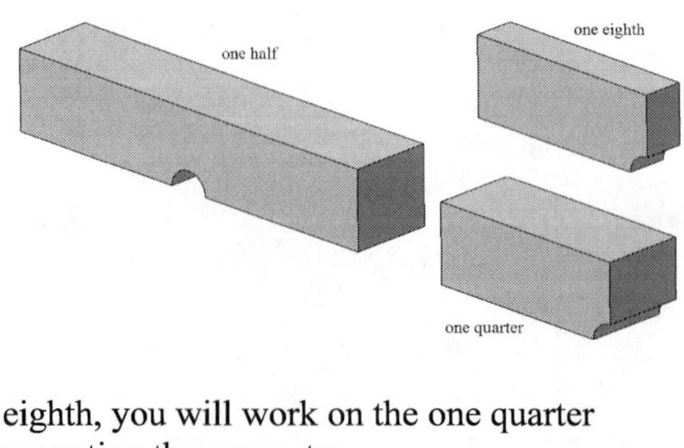


An important feature of this problem is the presence of three planes of symmetry. Therefore, there is no need to model the full block. Instead, one can concentrate on a half, quarter, or eighth of the geometry as displayed on the right.
Although the best strategy is to model one eighth, you will work on the one quarter model. In the next two pages, you will be generating the geometry.

## 2 Creation of the Part in Mechanical Design Solutions

Enter the **Part Design** workbench which can be achieved by different means depending on your CATIA customization. For example, from the standard Windows toolbar, select **File > New**. From the box shown on the right, select **Part**. This moves you to the **Part Design** workbench and creates a part with the default name **Part.1**. See Note #1 in Appendix I.
In order to change the default name, move the cursor to **Part.1** in the tree, right-click and select **Properties** from the menu list.

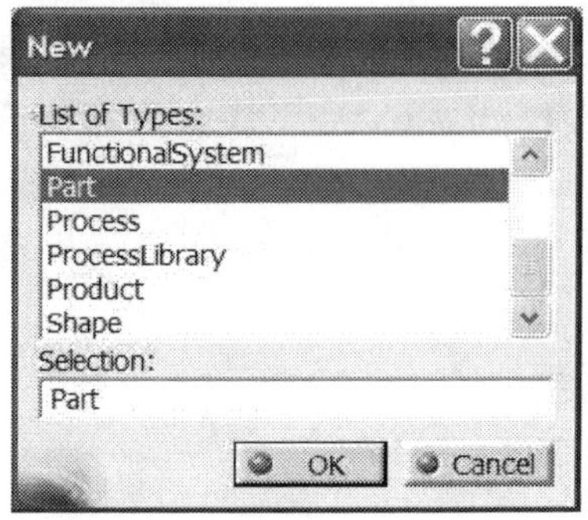


From the **Properties** box, select the **Product** tab and in **Part Number** type **block_with_hole**. This will be the new part name throughout the chapter. The tree on the top left corner of the screen should look as displayed below.

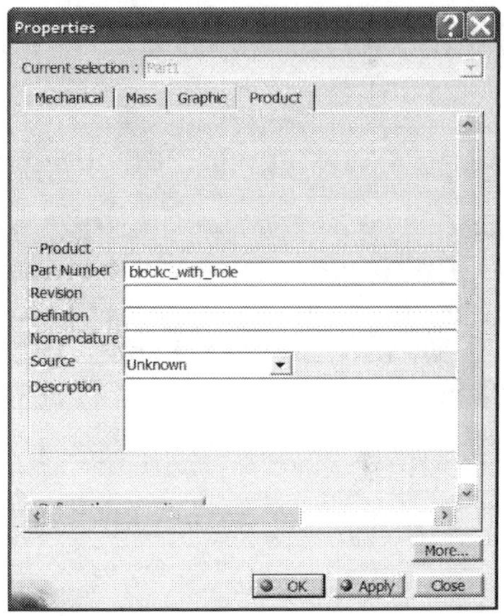


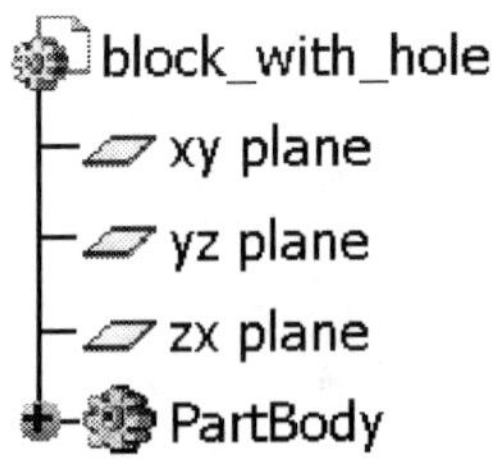


From the tree, select the **yz** plane and enter the **Sketcher**. In the **Sketcher**, draw a circle centered at the origin, and dimension it. Make sure that the center of the circle is at the origin of the sketch plane; otherwise, several extra steps are required in the construction of the model. The circle drawn may not have the correct radius. In order to change the dimension, double-click on the dimension on the screen and in the resulting box enter radius 0.5. Your simple sketch and the **Constraint Definition** box used to enter the correct radius are shown below.

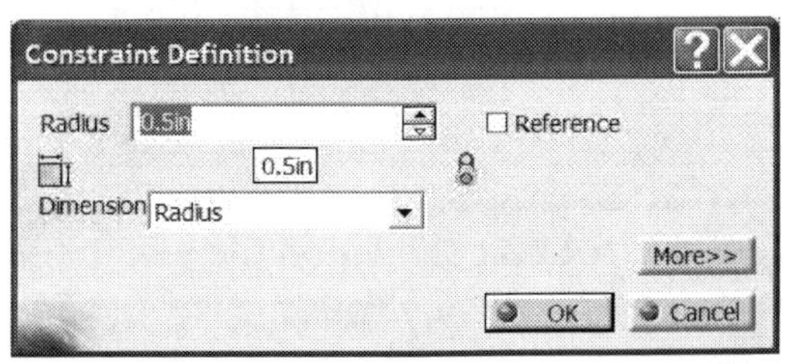


Use the **Profile** toolbar

and the icon **Centered Rectangle**, to construct a rectangle as shown in the image below and dimension to be 10x4 in. Make sure that the center of the rectangle is at (0,0).

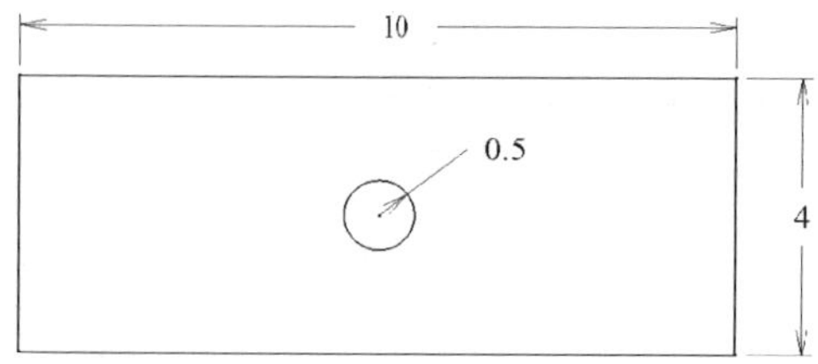


Upon leaving the **Sketcher**, the screen and the tree should be as shown below.

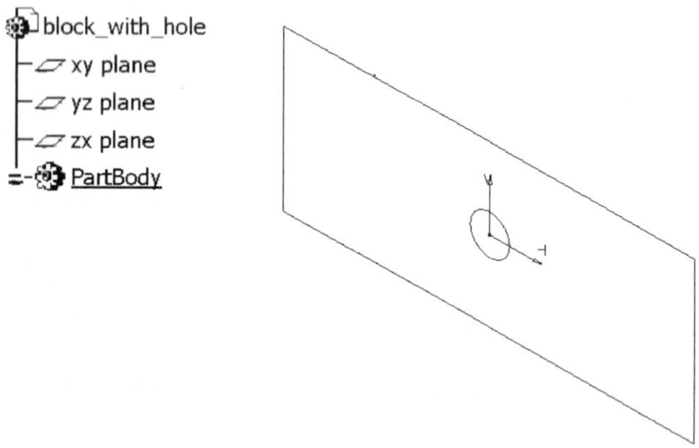


You will now use the **Pad** operation to extrude the sketch. Upon selecting the **Pad** icon, the **Pad Definition** box shown to the right opens.
In the **Length** box, type 1 and make sure to check the **Mirrored extent** button. This extrudes the sketch in both directions for a distance of 2 in., which is the thickness of the block.

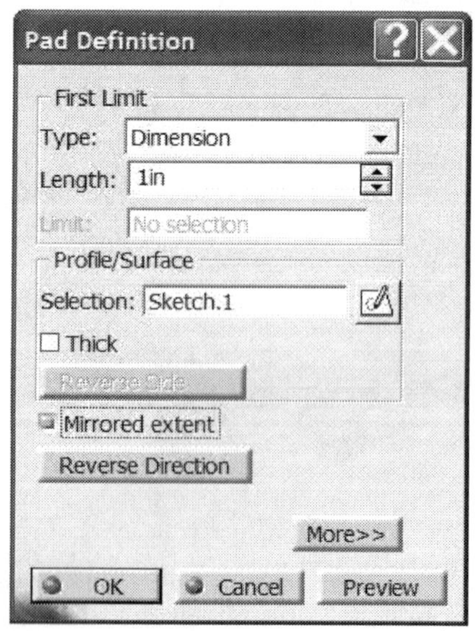


The result is our full block with a hole shown below.

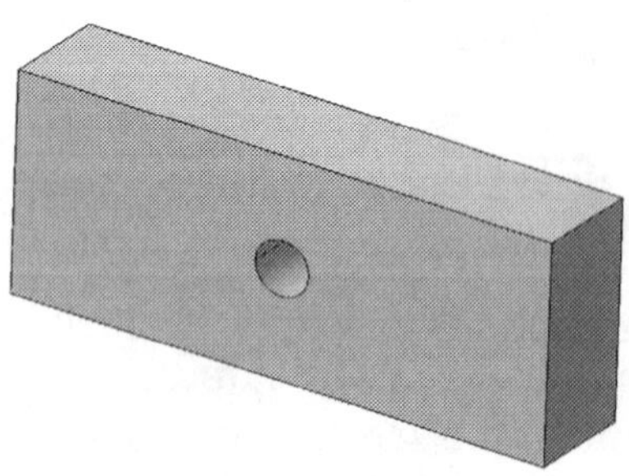

At this point, you will cut the block with the existing planes **xy** and **zx**. From the **Surfaced-Based Feature** toolbar, select the **Split** icon. The **Split Definition** box shown on the next page opens. The arrow displayed on the part indicates which half is to be kept. In case, the arrows points in the wrong direction, simply click on it, and it reverses. The tree, immediately after the **Split** operation, is also shown below.

The main reason behind the centering of the circle and the rectangle at the origin, and using the **Mirror Extent** feature in padding, was to be able to use the standard **xy, zx** and **zy** planes for reducing the model as described.

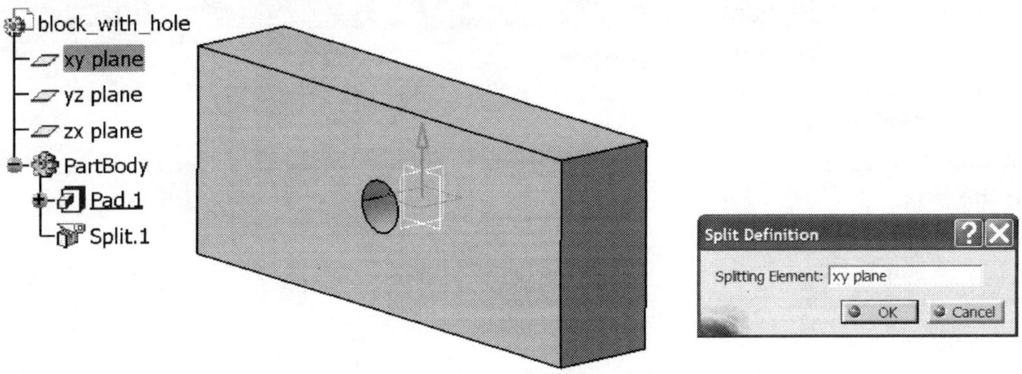


**Save your work regularly.**

Once again select the **Split** icon , this time choose the **zx** plane to reduce the model.

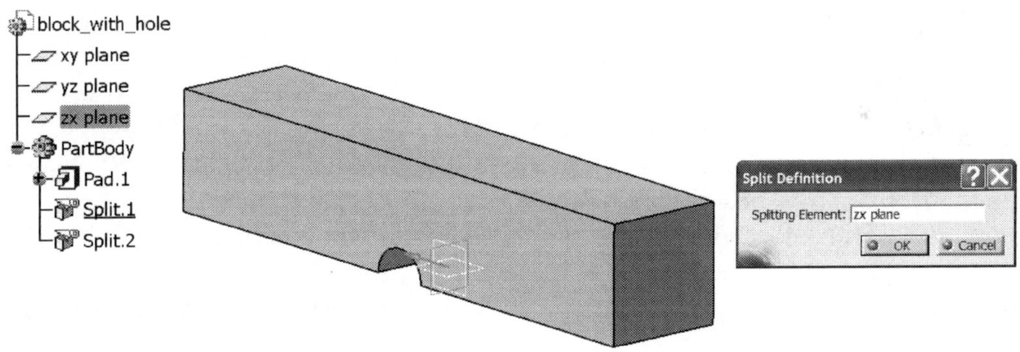


The outcome of splitting the block twice is displayed below.

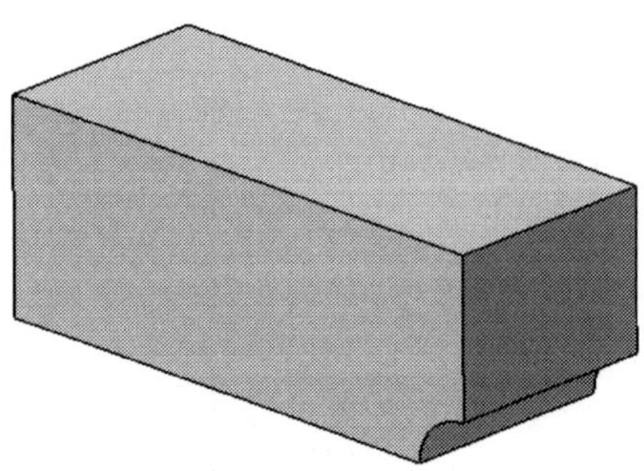

At this point we apply the default aluminum material properties to the part. Select the **Apply Material** icon . The use of this icon opens the material database box below.

Use the **Metal** tab on the top, select aluminum. Use your cursor to pick the part on the screen at which time the **OK** and **Apply Material** buttons can be selected.
Close the box.
The material property is now reflected in the tree.

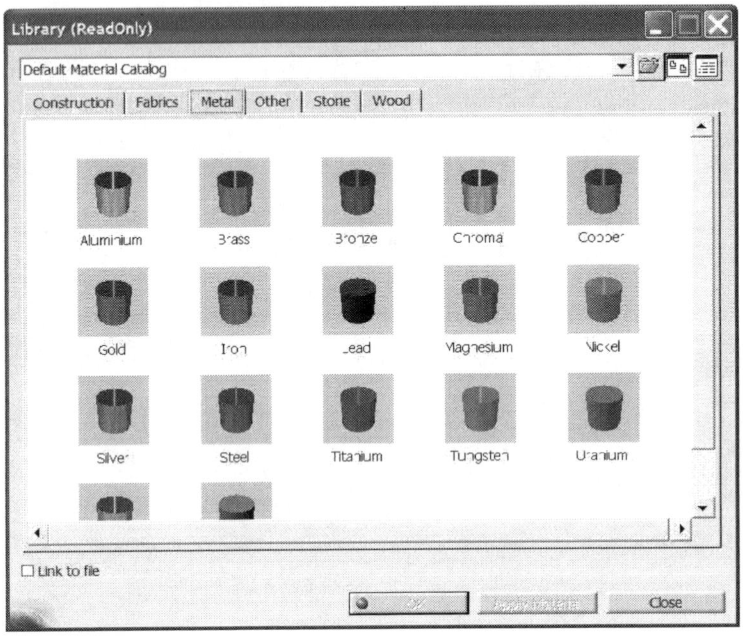


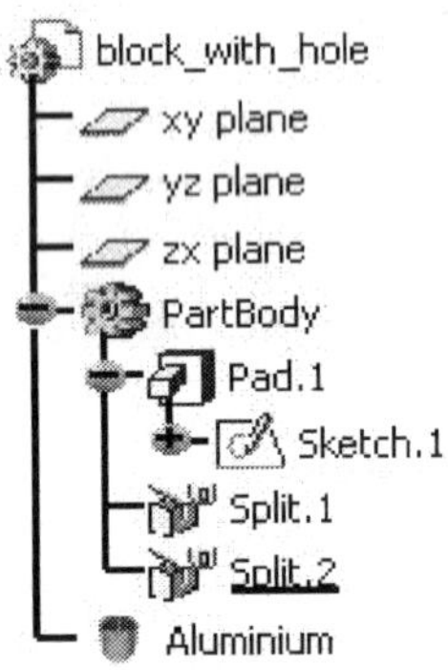


In order to inspect the values of the material properties assigned, double-click on **Aluminum** in the tree. It may take a minute before the database is searched. Next you will see the **Properties** box shown below opens. Chose the **Analysis** tab from this box and the values will be displayed. Note that these values can be edited.

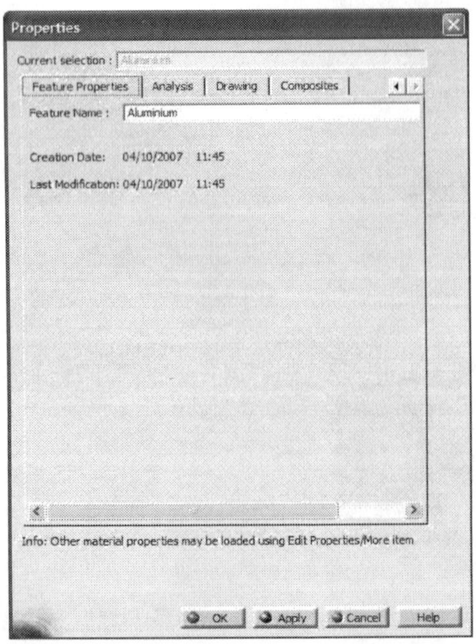


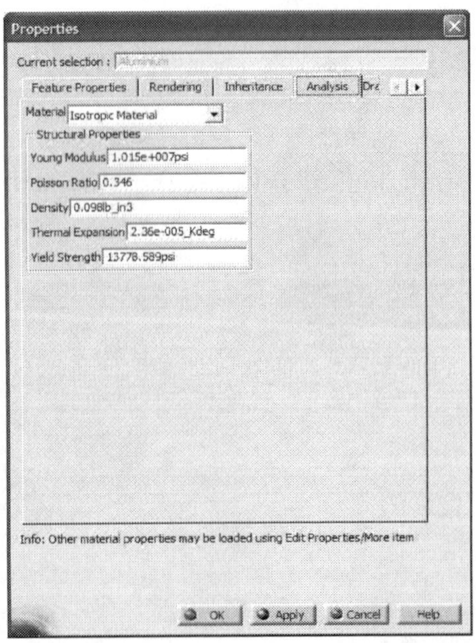

If the part is still "gray", one can change the rendering style. From the **View** toolbar

, select the **View Mode** toolbar

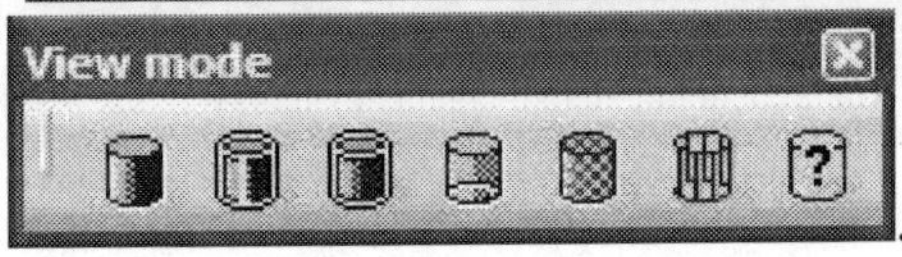


.

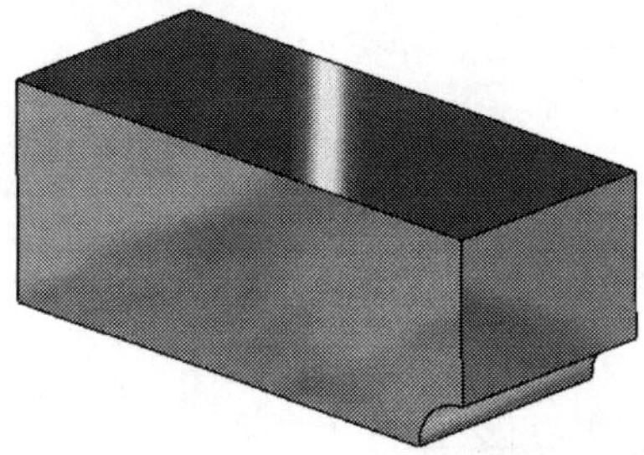

Next choose the **Shading with Material**  icon. The part now appears shaded as shown on the right.

## 3 Entering the Analysis Solutions

From the standard Windows toolbar, select

**Start > Analysis & Simulation > Generative Structural Analysis** 
There is a second workbench known as the **Advanced Meshing Tools** which will be discussed later.

Upon changing workbenches, the box **New Analysis Case** becomes visible. The default choice is **Static Analysis** which is precisely what we intend to use. Therefore, close the box by clicking on **OK**.

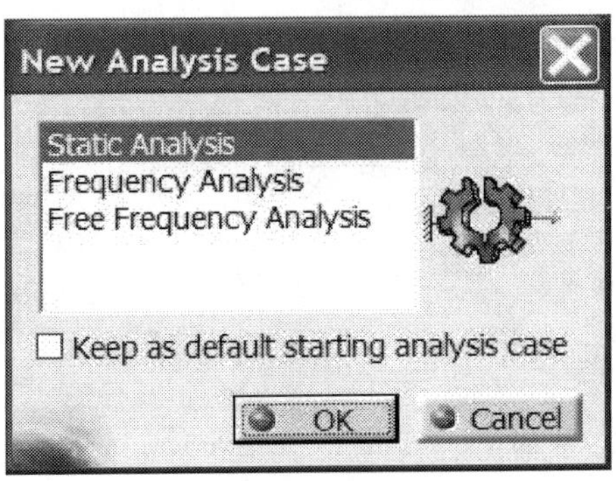


It happens frequently that one forgets to apply the material properties prior to entering the **Analysis & Simulation** workbench. In that case one gets a **Warning** message. There are two options, one is to select the **Cancel** button, and returning to the **Part Design**. After applying material properties, return to the **Analysis & Simulation** workbench.

The alternative is to use the **3D Property** icon  from the **Model Manager** toolbar

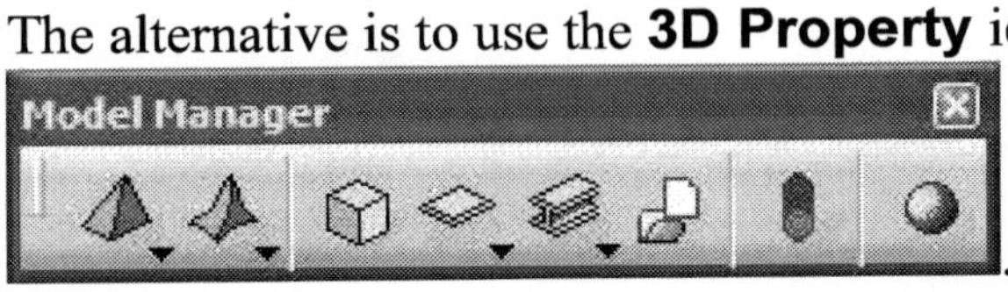


. This will be discussed further later.

On the screen you obverse a longer tree structure together with a representative element "size" and "sag" as shown. The bottom branches of the tree are all "unfilled", however, as we proceed further in modeling, they get "filled".

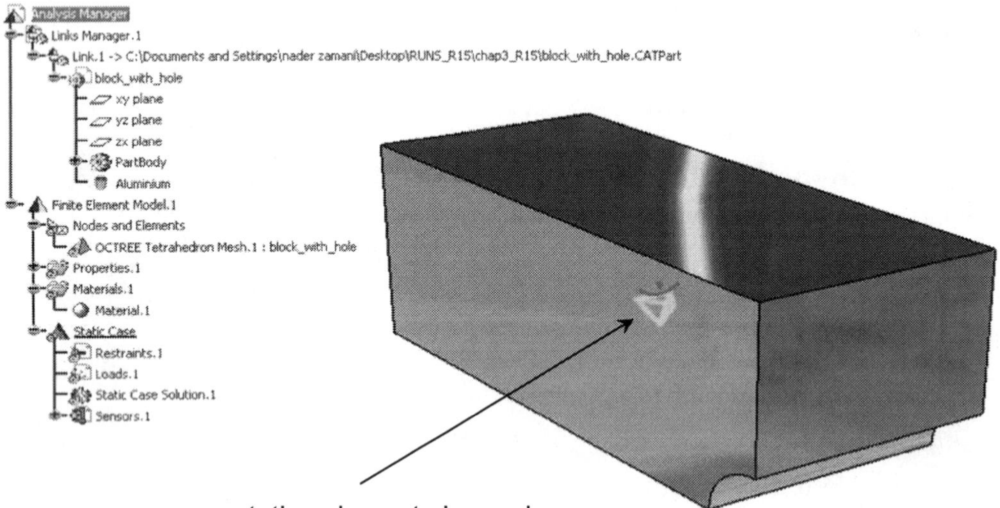


representative element size and sag

As indicated in the previous chapter, the element "size" and "sag" have a direct bearing on the accuracy of the FEA results. If you are not happy with the default values, there are two ways to change these values.

The first method is to double-click on the representative icons on the screen which forces the **OCTREE Tetrahedron Mesh** box to open as shown to the right. Change the default values to match the numbers in the box.

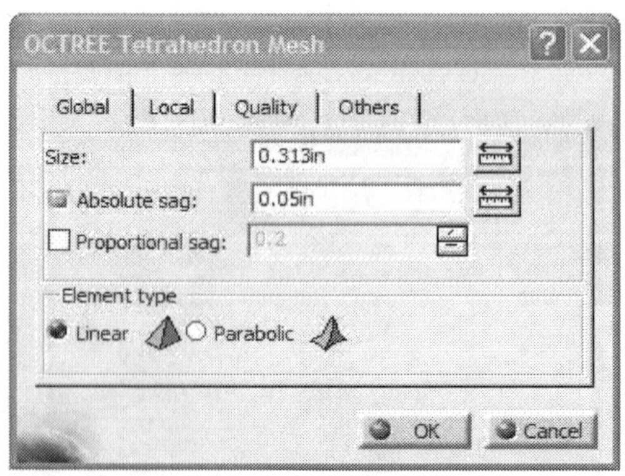


Notice that the type of the elements used (linear/parabolic) is also set in this box. Close the box by selecting **OK**.
The second method of reaching this box is through the tree.

By double-clicking on the branch labeled **OCTREE Tetrahedron Mesh** shown below, the same box opens allowing the user to modify the values.

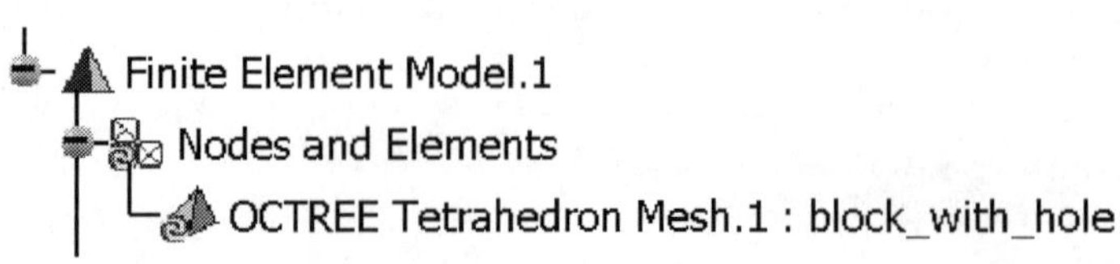

In order to view the generated mesh, you can point the cursor to the branch **Nodes and Elements**, right-click and select **Mesh Visualization**. This step may be slightly different in some UNIX machines. Upon performing this operation a **Warning** box appears which can be ignored (select **OK**). For the mesh parameters used, the following mesh is displayed on the screen. See Note #2 in Appendix I.

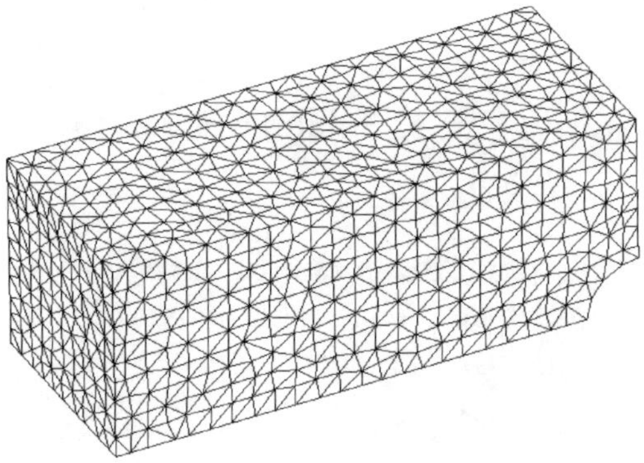

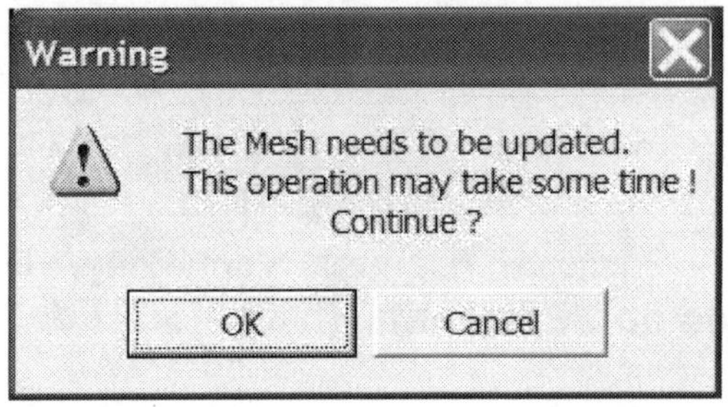


The representative "size" and "sag" icons can be removed from the display by simply pointing to them right-click and select **Hide**. This is the standard process for hiding any entity in CATIA V5.

CONGRATULATIONS! You now have a mesh with the correct material properties. Regularly save your work.

Once again, the reader is reminded that the accuracy of the results depends on the element size. However, one needs to create small elements only in regions of high stress gradient, such as stress concentration regions. In the present problem, these are regions immediately above and below the circular hole. The present strategy of uniformly reducing the size of the elements is unnecessary.

**Assigning Material Properties:**

This step is already completed and was accomplished using the icon  while designing the part.

**Applying Restraints:**

CATIA's FEA module is geometrically based. This means that the boundary conditions cannot be applied to nodes and elements. The boundary conditions can only be applied at the part level. As soon as you enter the **Generative Structural Analysis** workbench, the part is automatically hidden. Therefore, before boundary conditions are applied, the part must be brought to the unhide mode. This can be carried out by pointing the cursor to the top of the tree, the **Links Manager.1** branch, right-click, select **Show**.

At this point, the part and the mesh are superimposed as shown and you have access to the part.

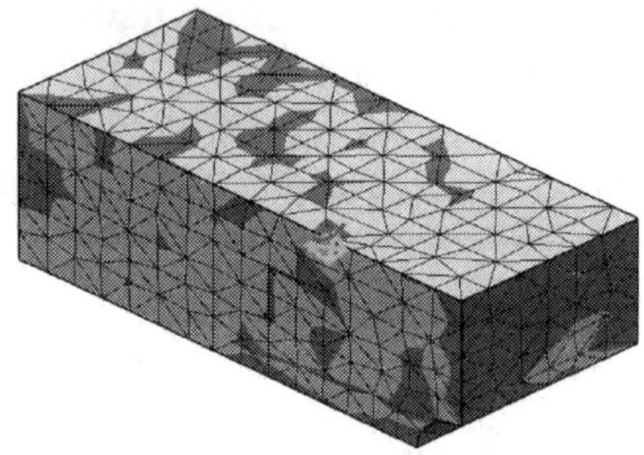

If, the presence of the mesh is annoying, you can always hide it. Point the cursor to **Nodes and Elements**, right-click, **Hide**.

Instead of hiding the mesh as indicated above, one can point the cursor to the **Mesh.1** item in the tree, right-click, and select **Activate/Deactivate**. The result is that the mesh is hidden and the part is displayed. The steps are graphically in the next figure.

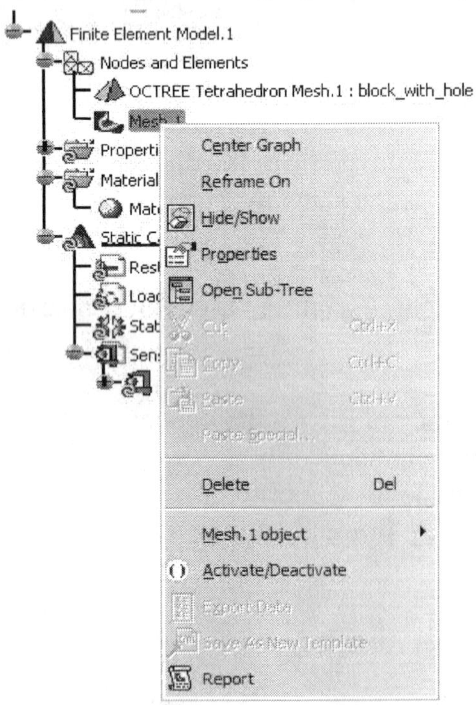


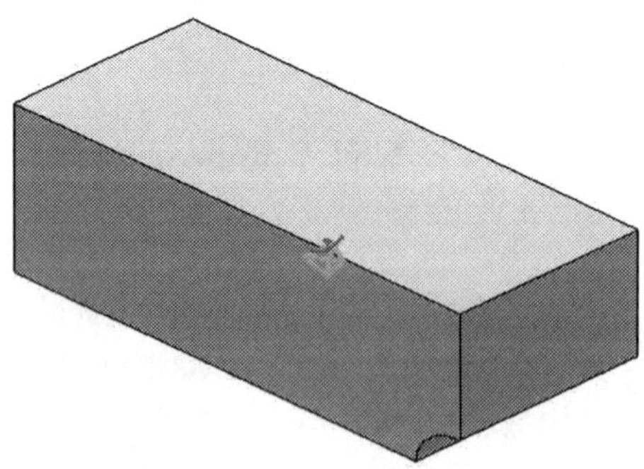

The planes shown in the figure to the right are called planes of symmetry. Points located on such planes do not move normal to these planes. Very frequently such points are said to have a "roller" boundary conditions.

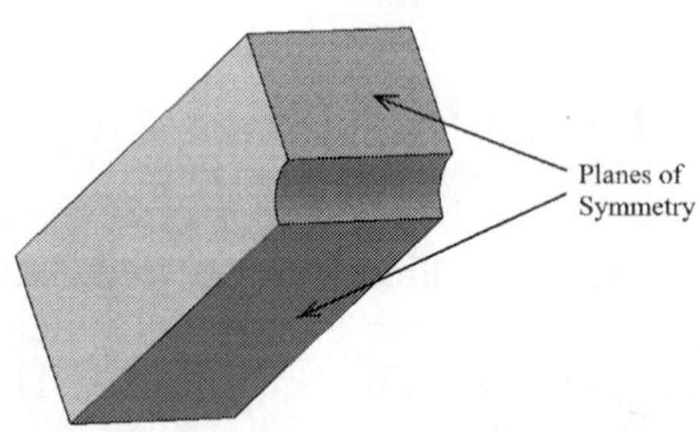

In CATIA V5 planes of symmetry are easily modeled by the **Surface Slider** icon (the part <u>must</u> be in the show mode in order to apply boundary conditions).

From the **Restraint** toolbar 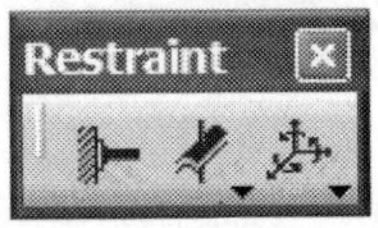

select the **Surface Slider** icon . The corresponding box shown below opens and you can select the two symmetry planes (faces). The resulting roller (slider) icons are also presented below to the left.

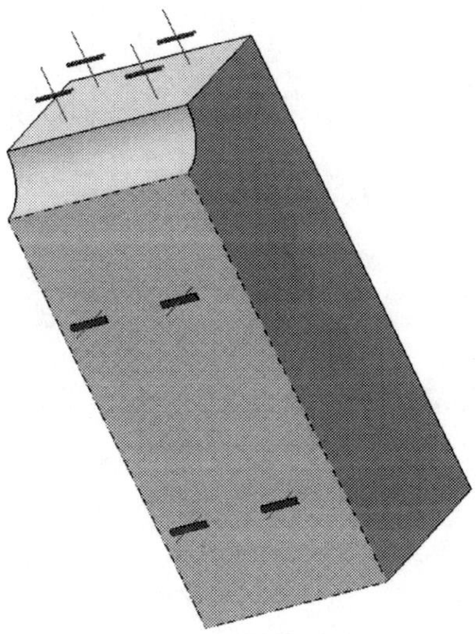

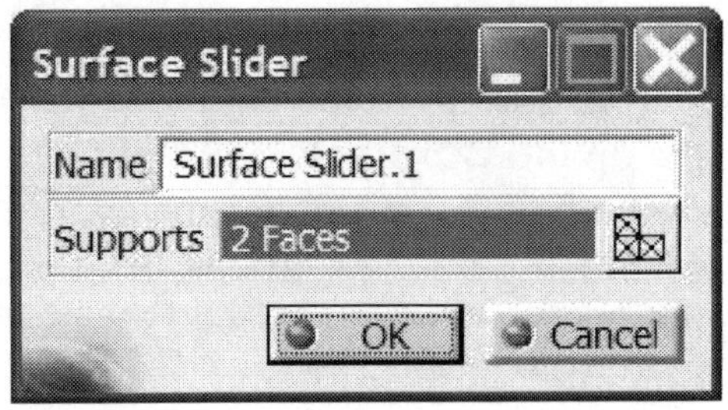


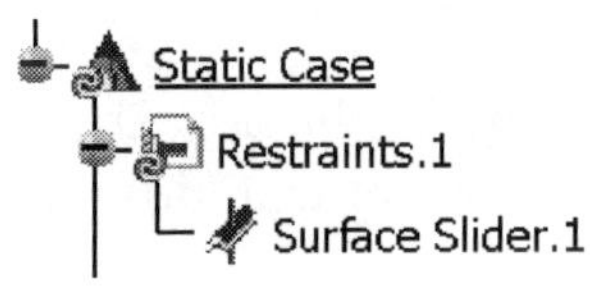


**Applying Loads:**

In FEA, loads refer to forces. The **Load** toolbar 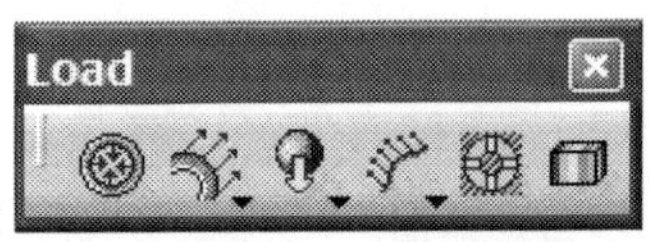

is used for this purpose. To begin with, we apply the end load as pressure. The force of 2000 lb over the end area is equivalent to a pressure of 250 psi. Clicking on the **Pressure** icon 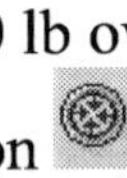 opens the **Pressure** box shown. For the **Support**, select the face where pressure is applied and as value type -250. All FEA packages have adopted the convention that a positive pressure is compressive while a negative pressure is tensile.

The **Pressure** icon will be displayed on the loaded surface of the part as shown.

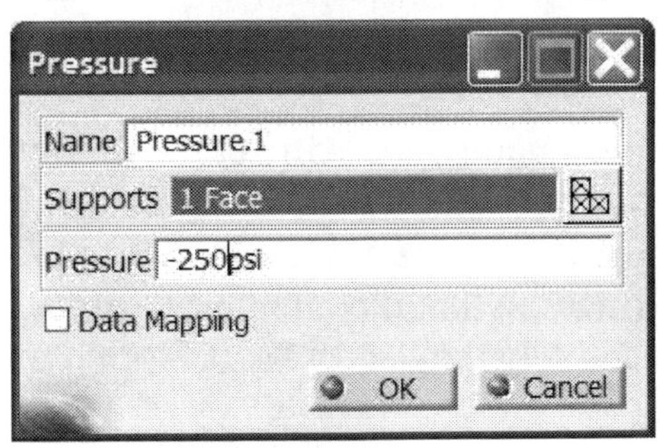


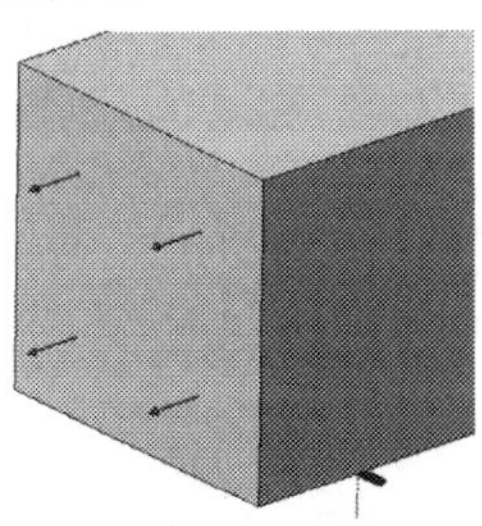

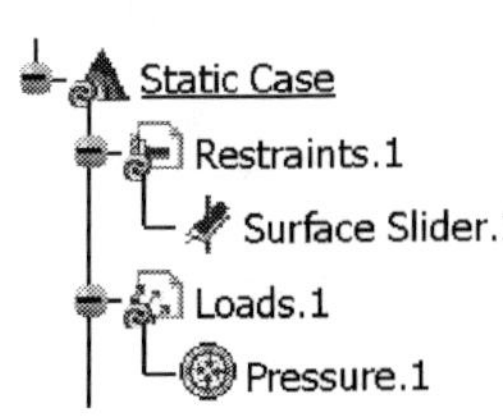

The branch of the tree pertaining to **Loads.1** is also displayed above.
It seems that all the restraints, and loads are applied and we are prepared to run the analysis.

**Launching the Solver:**

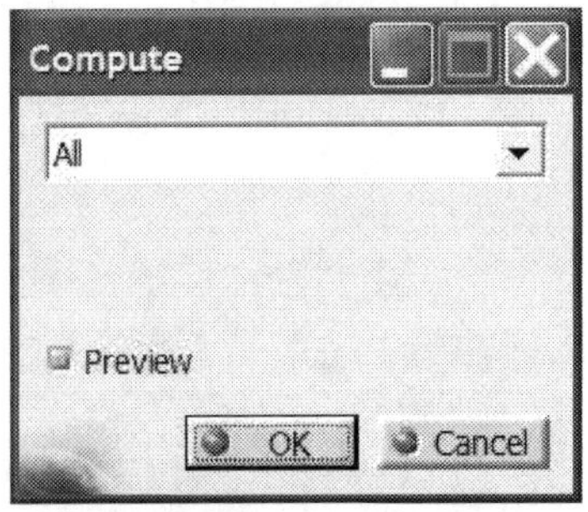


To run the analysis, you need to use the **Compute** toolbar  by selecting the **Compute** icon . This opens up the **Compute** box shown to the right. Leave the default as **All** which means everything is computed. Upon closing this box, after a brief pause, the second box shown below appears. This box provides information on the resources needed to complete the analysis.
If the estimates are zero in the listing, then there is a problem in the previous step and should be looked into. If all the numbers are zero in the box, the program may run but would not produce any useful results.

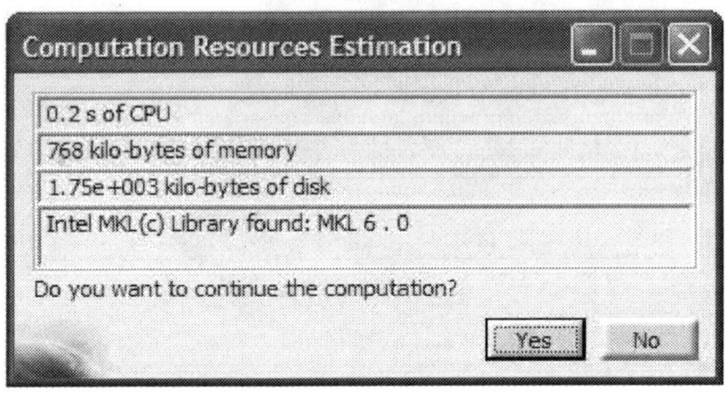


The tree has been changed to reflect the location of the **Results** and **Computations** as shown below.

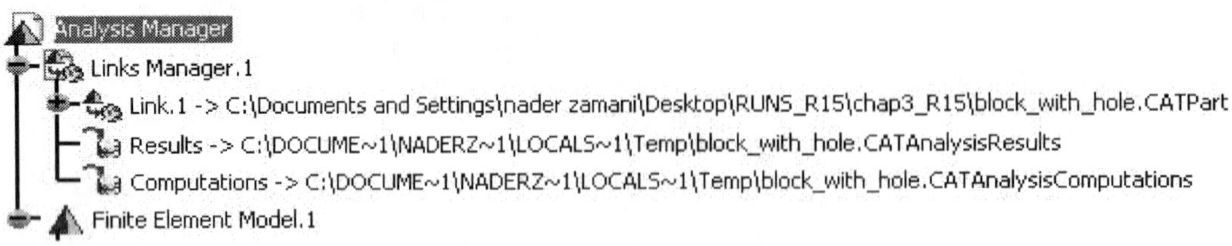


Unfortunately you will get the following **Error** box. Usually this box implies that the part is not fully restrained. In our model, the block is free to move in the x-direction as a rigid body. Some commercial packages rectify the situation by adding a small artificial stiffness in that direction, preventing the rigid body motion. In those packages, effectively they add a “soft” spring in the appropriate direction, resulting in a stiffness.

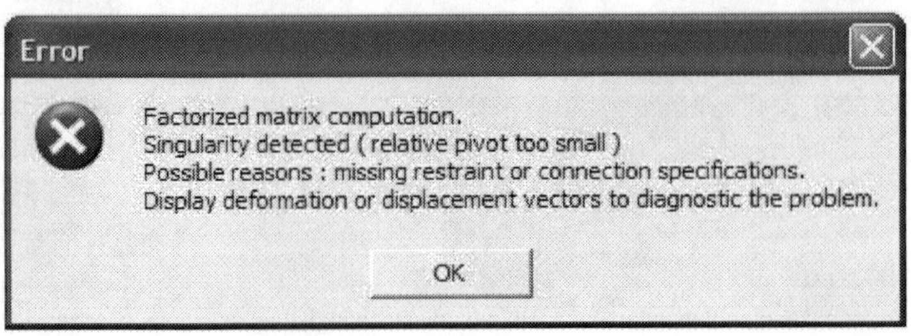

You achieve the same effect by selecting an arbitrary point and prevent it from moving in the x-direction. Use the **Restraint** toolbar 

and select the **User-defined Restraint** icon 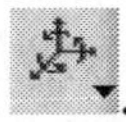.

The above action opens up the **User-defined Restraint** box shown to the right. Pick any arbitrary vertex and check the **Restrain Translation 1** box. The directions 1, 2, and 3 correspond to the global x, y, and z directions.
The single red arrow will show on the vertex.

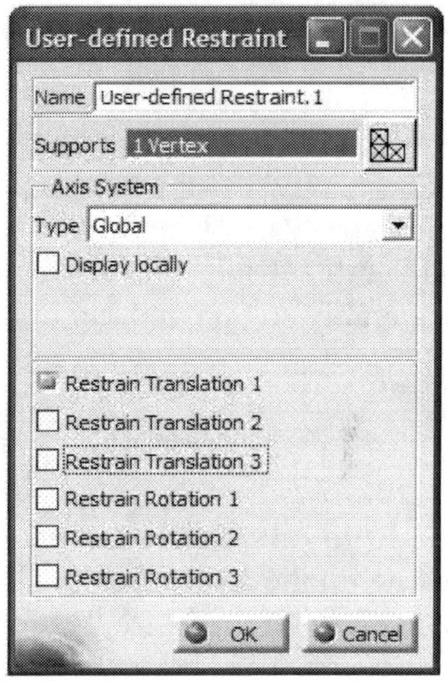


vertex picked to prevent rigid body motion

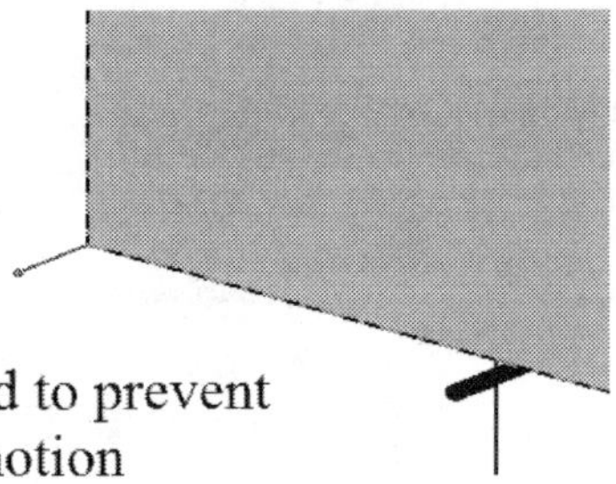

You are reminded that ordinarily the solid tetrahedron elements do not have rotational degrees of freedom; therefore, one cannot directly impose rotation or moment on them. Whether the **Restrain Rotation** boxes are left checked or not, there will be no impact on the results. The concept of "virtual parts" to be discussed in another chapter can be used to apply rotation and moment on solids if needed.

Now press on  to run the problem. This time, the run completes without an error. The tree has been changed to reflect the location of the Results and Computations as shown below.

The user can change these locations by double-clicking on the branch. The box, shown on the right, will open and can be modified.

## Postprocessing:

The main postprocessing toolbar is called **Image** 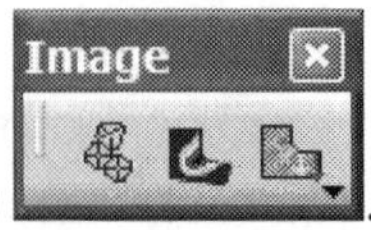

. To view the deformed shape you have to use the **Deformation** icon . The resulting deformed shape is displayed below.

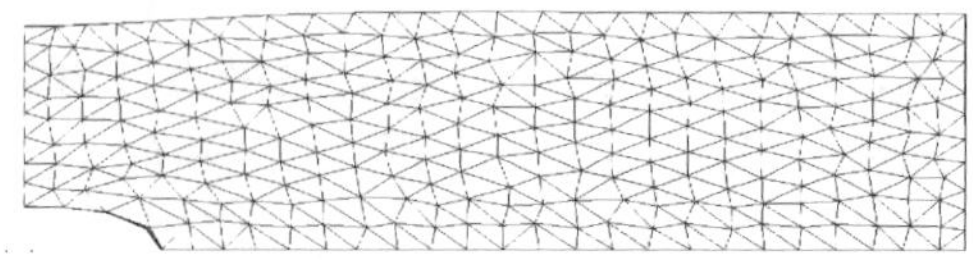

The deformation image can be very deceiving since one could get the impression that the block actually displaces to that extent. Keep in mind that the displacements are scaled considerably so that one can observe the deformed shape. Although the scale factor is set automatically, one can change this value with the **Deformation Scale Factor** icon  in the **Analysis Tools** toolbar 

.

Clicking on the above icon leads to the box shown on the right where the desired scale factor can be typed. The above deformed shape corresponds to a scale factor of 9698.9.

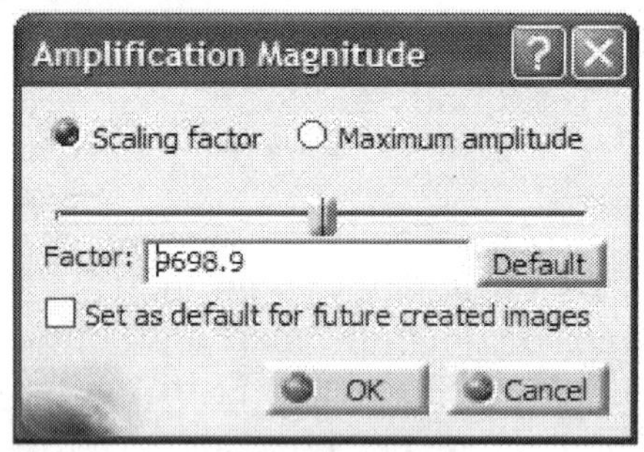


In order to see the displacement field, the **Displacement** icon  in the **Image** toolbar should be used. The default display is in terms of displacement arrows as shown on the right. The color and the length of arrows represent the size of the displacement. The contour legend indicates a maximum displacement of 0.000132 in.

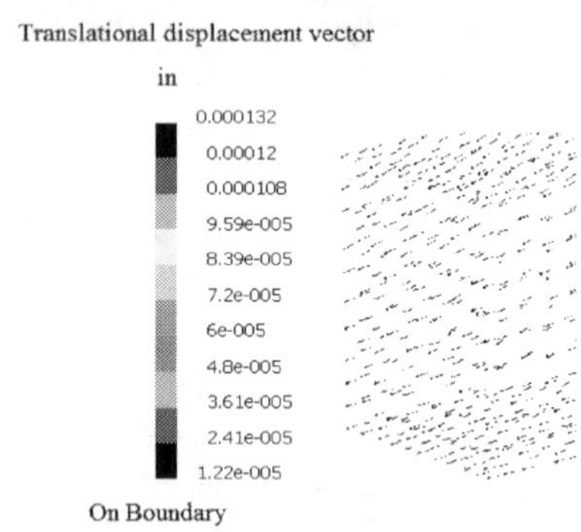


The arrow plot is not particularly useful. In order to view the contour plot of the displacement field, position the cursor on the arrow field and double-click. The **Image Edition** box shown in the next page opens.

Note that the default is to draw the contour on the deformed shape. If this is not desired, uncheck the box **On deformed mesh**. Next, select **AVERAGE-ISO** and press **OK**. The contour of the displacement field as shown in the next page is plotted.

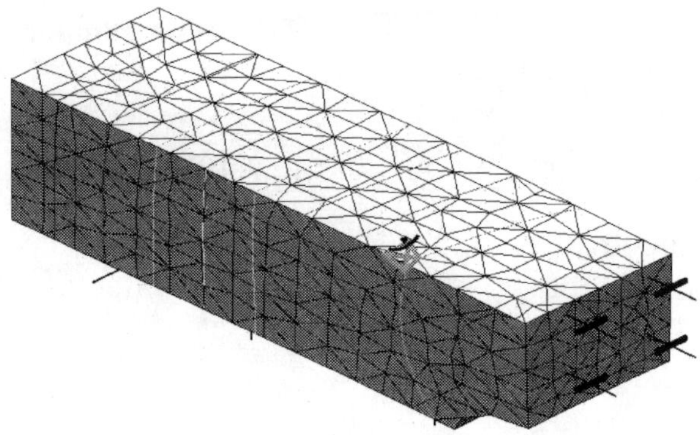

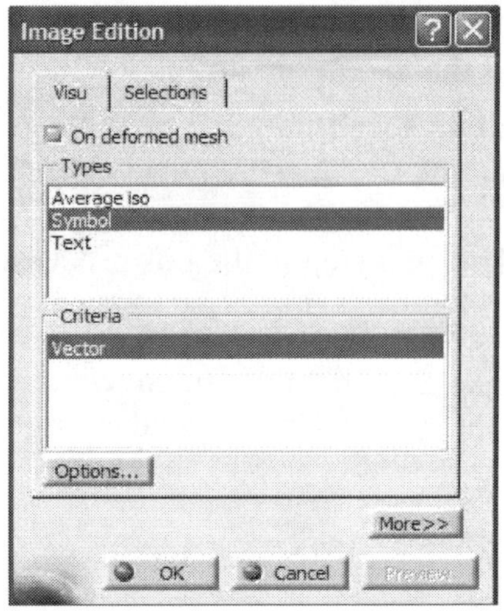


It is difficult to read the contour lines from the above figure. You can change the render style by using **Shading with Material**  icon in the **View mode** toolbar 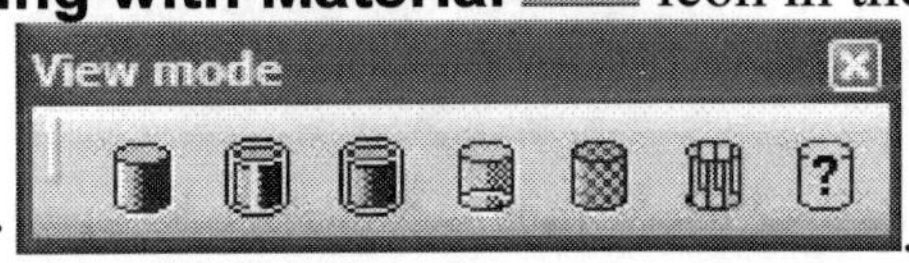.



Note that the elements are not showing in this plot. If you prefer that the elements are displayed at the same time, you need to go through the following step.

Select the **Custom View Mode** icon  from the above toolbar. In the resulting pop up box, make sure that **Edges and points** is checked.

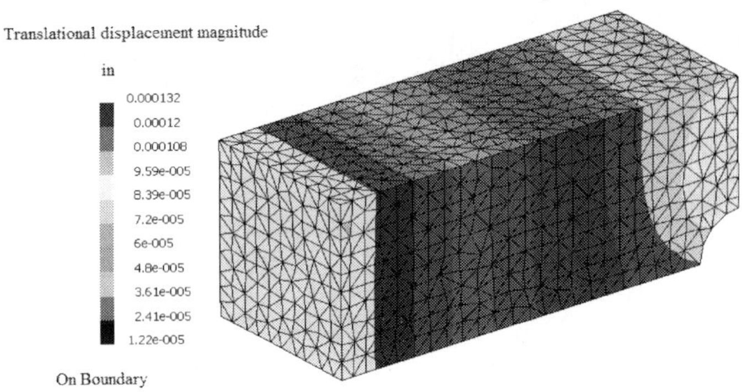


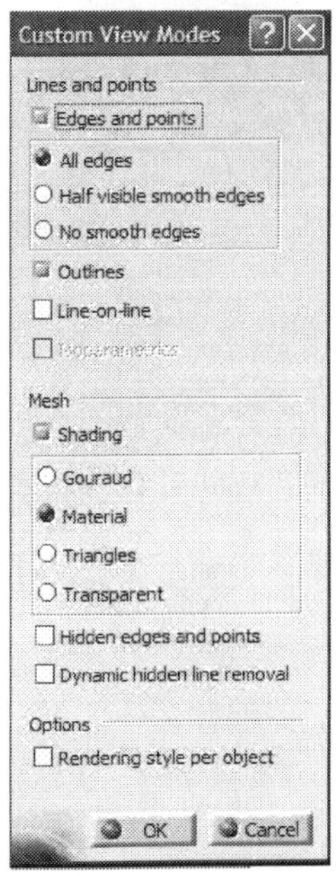


(Note: The color map has been changed; otherwise everything looks black.)

If you ignore the effect of the hole, elementary strength of materials provides an estimate of the maximum deflection through the formula $\delta = \frac{FL}{AE}$.
Upon substituting, $F = 2000$, $A = 16$, $L = 10$, and $E = 10.15E + 6$, one can get $\delta = .0001232$ which is in agreement with the FEA result.

The next step in the postprocessing is to plot the contours of the von Mises stress using the **von Mises Stress** icon  in the **Image** toolbar. The von Mises stress is displayed below. The maximum stress is at the top of the circle with a value of 603 psi which is below the yield strength of all steels.

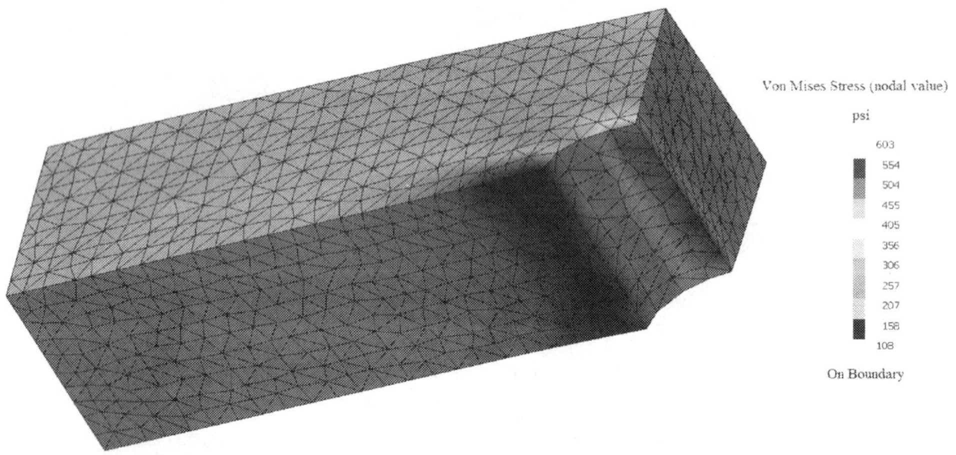


Double-clicking on the contour legend leads to the **Color Map** box displayed below. The contour can be plotted as **Smooth**, or **Stepped**. The number of color bands is also specified in this box. Finally, the user can describe the range of stresses to be plotted.
The first contour plot in this page uses the **non-smooth** format whereas the one immediate above uses the **Smooth** format.

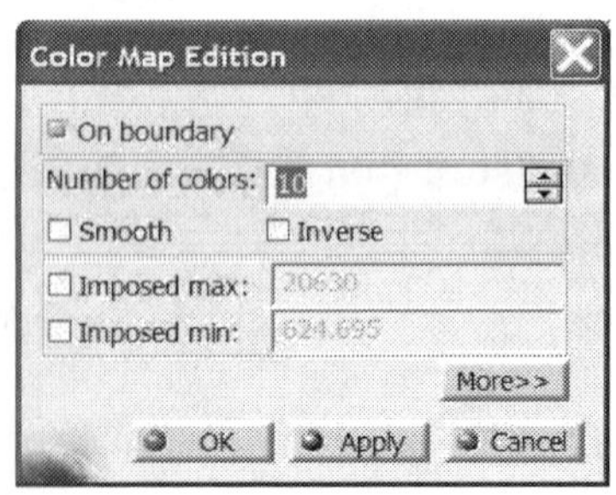

Occasionally, you may be interested in plotting the von Mises stress contour in either the load area or the support section. In order to achieve this, double-click on the contour levels on the screen to open the **Image Edition** box. Next use the **Selections** tab as shown on the right. Here, you have the choice of selecting different areas. Select **Pressure.1**, and use the button . The contour below displays the von Mises stress at **Pressure.1** section.

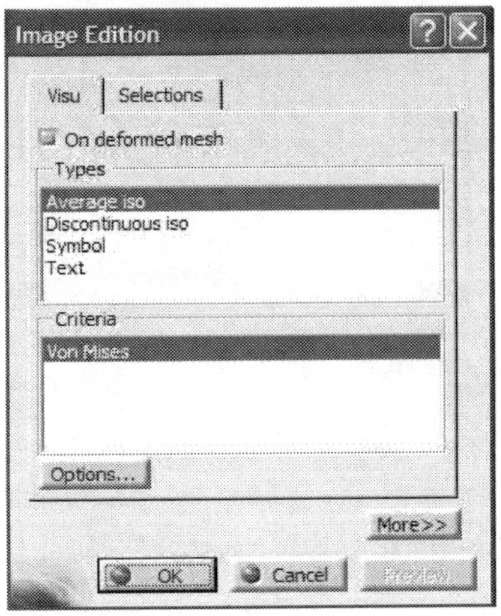


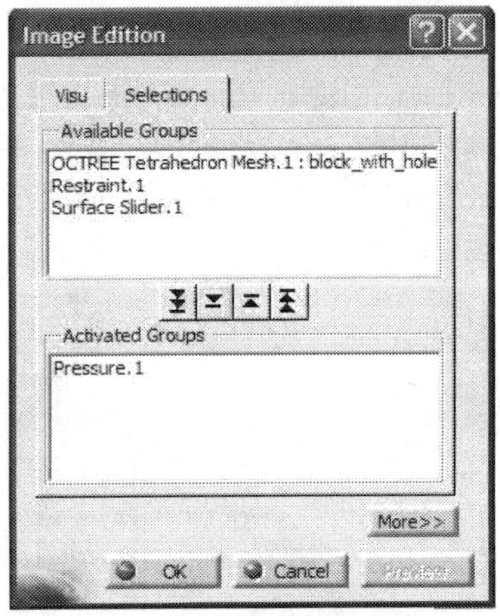


The different colors can be deceiving in this plot. However, a quick glance at the contour legend reveals that the stress is the pressure of 250 psi which was applied.

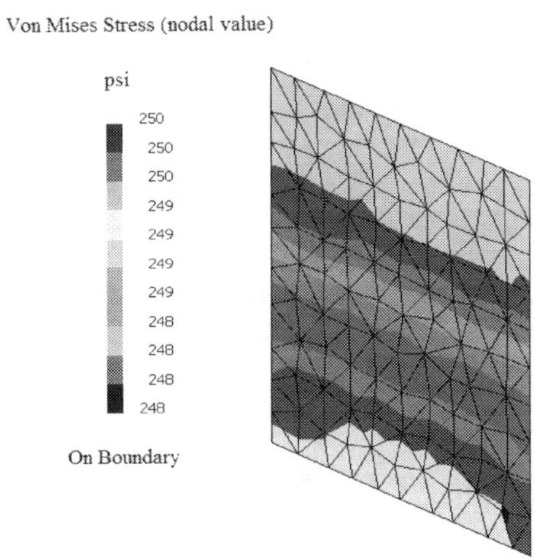


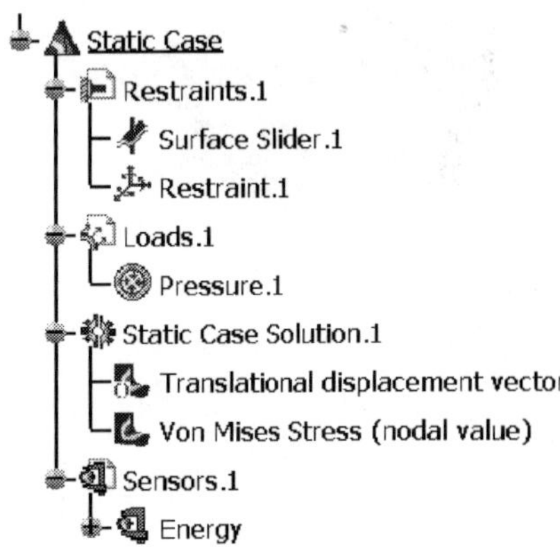


As the postprocessing proceeds and we generate different plots, they get recorded in the tree displayed above. Each plot generated, deactivates the previous one on the screen. By pointing to a desired plot in the tree and right-clicking, you can activate the plot. Clearly, any plot can be deleted from the tree in the usual way (right-click, **Delete**).

The location and magnitude of the extremum values of a contour (e.g. von Mises stress) can be identified in a plot. This is achieved by using the **Image Extrema** icon in the **Image Analysis** toolbar

.

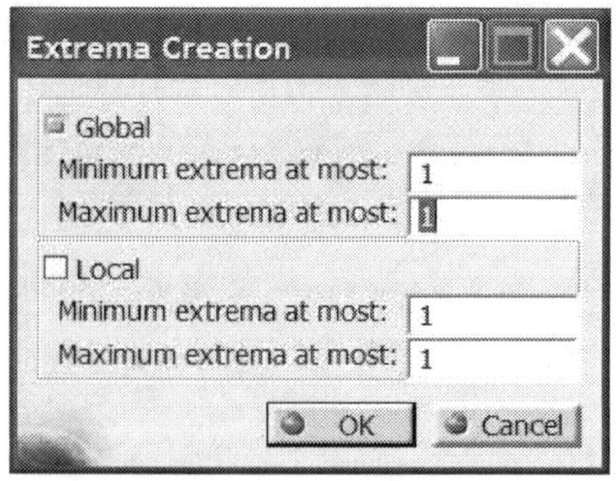


Before the plot is generated, the **Extrema Creation** box pops up as shown to the right. If the default values are maintained, the global maximum and minimum are found and their location pin-pointed in a contour plot as shown next.

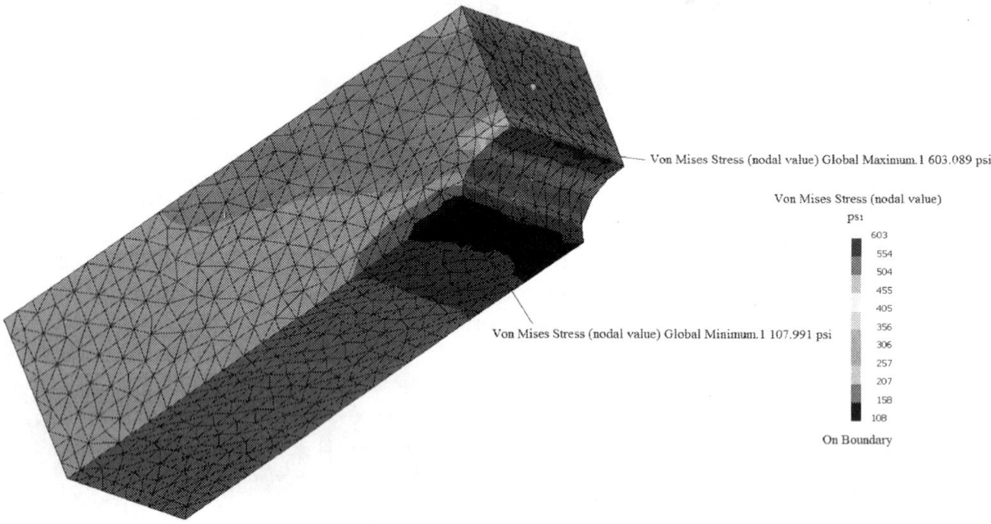


At this point, we have generated two plots. The displacement and the von Mises stress contours which can be displayed individually. However, CATIA also allows you to show both plots side by side.
First make sure that both images to be plotted are active in the tree, if not, point to the graph in the tree, right-click, select **Active**.

Click the **Image Layout** icon from the **Image Analysis** toolbar. The **Images** box, shown to the right, asks you to specify the direction along which the two plots are expected to be aligned. The outcome is side-by-side plots shown below. (The color map has been changed; otherwise everything looks black.)

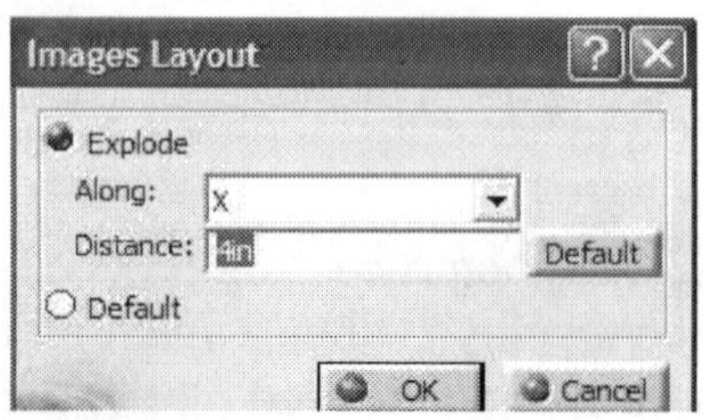

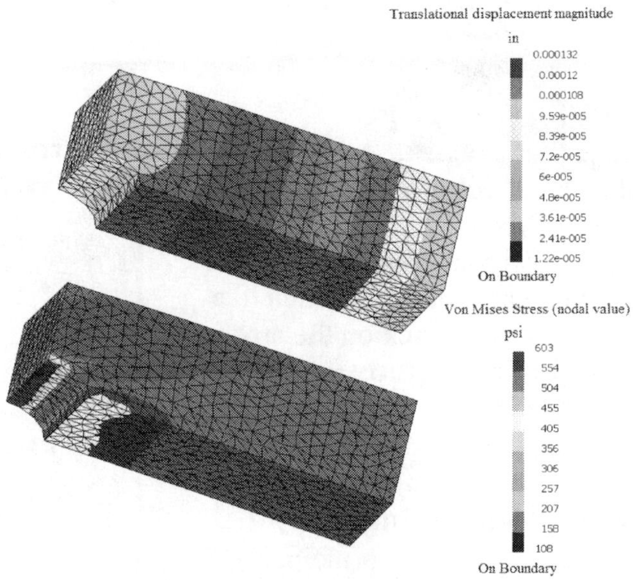


The **Cutting Plane** icon  from the **Analysis Tools** toolbar can be used to make a cut through the part at a desired location and inspect the stresses inside of the part. The **Cut Plane** box allows you to keep the plane or remove it for display purposes. A typical cutting plane is shown below.

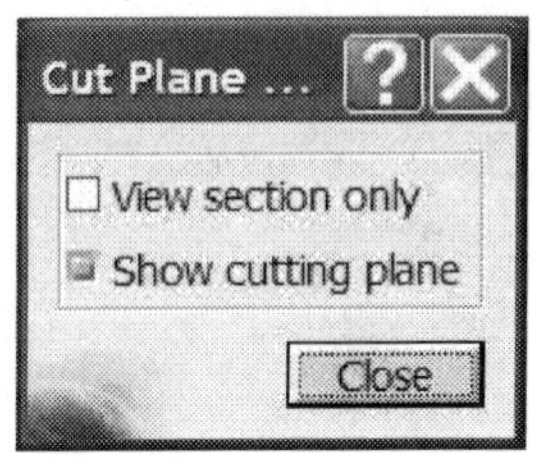


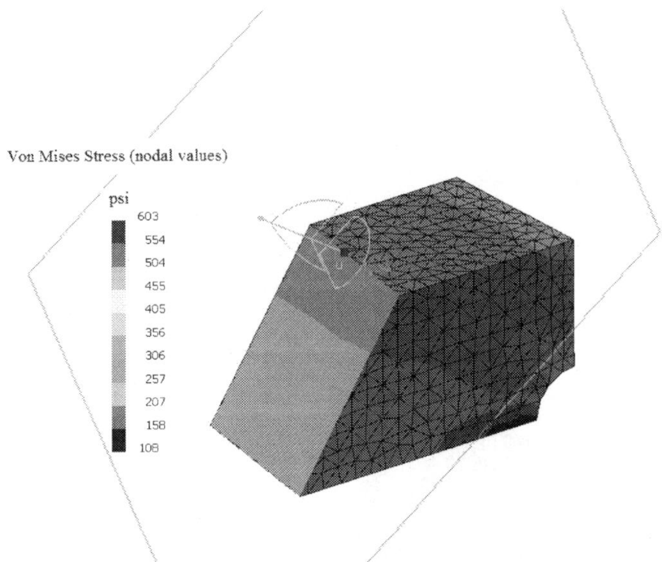

The principal stresses are postprocessed next.

From the **Image** toolbar , select the **Principal Stress** icon 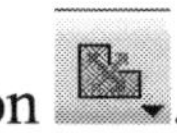. The result is the principal stress directions in the vector form as displayed on your screen.

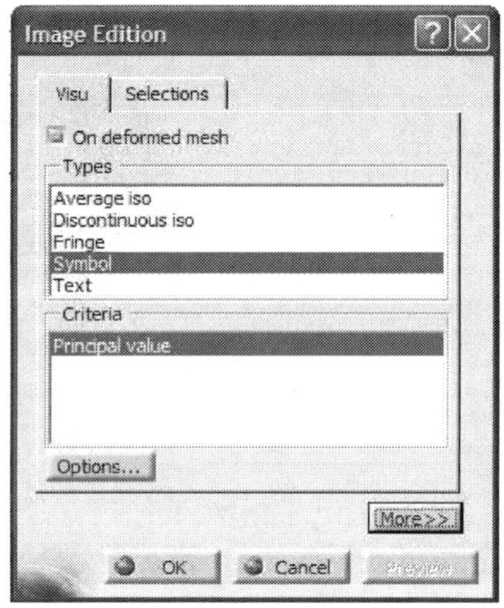


Due to the large number of arrows, the interpretation of this plot is difficult. You can therefore switch to a different style of plotting. Double-click on the arrows on the screen to open the **Image Edition** box on the right and select **AVERAGE-ISO**.

Click on the **More** button to expand the window as shown below. Choose the **Component C11**. In CATIA, C11 represents $\sigma_1$, the largest principal stress.

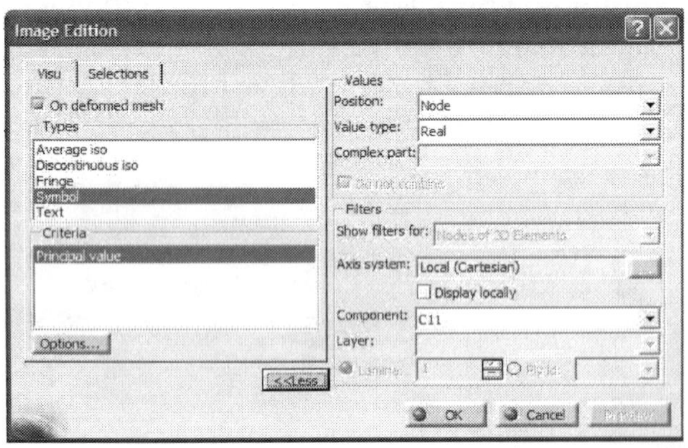


Keep in mind that CATIA uses C11, C22, and C33 to represent the largest, intermediate, and smallest principal stresses.

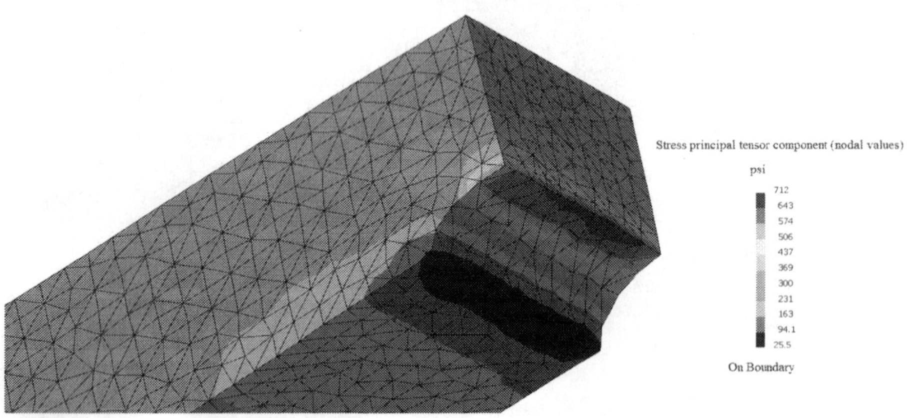

At this point, you can calculate the stress concentration factor from the FEA results. The maximum tensile stress which is retrieved from the above contour is 712 psi. With the nominal stress (calculated based on the net section) being 333psi, a stress concentration factor of 2.136 is obtained. The theoretical value from the formula provided on the first page of this chapter is 2.429.

Using the icon **Generate Report**  in the **Analysis Results** toolbar , an HTML based report can be generated which summarizes the features and results of the FEA model. The first page of this report is displayed below.

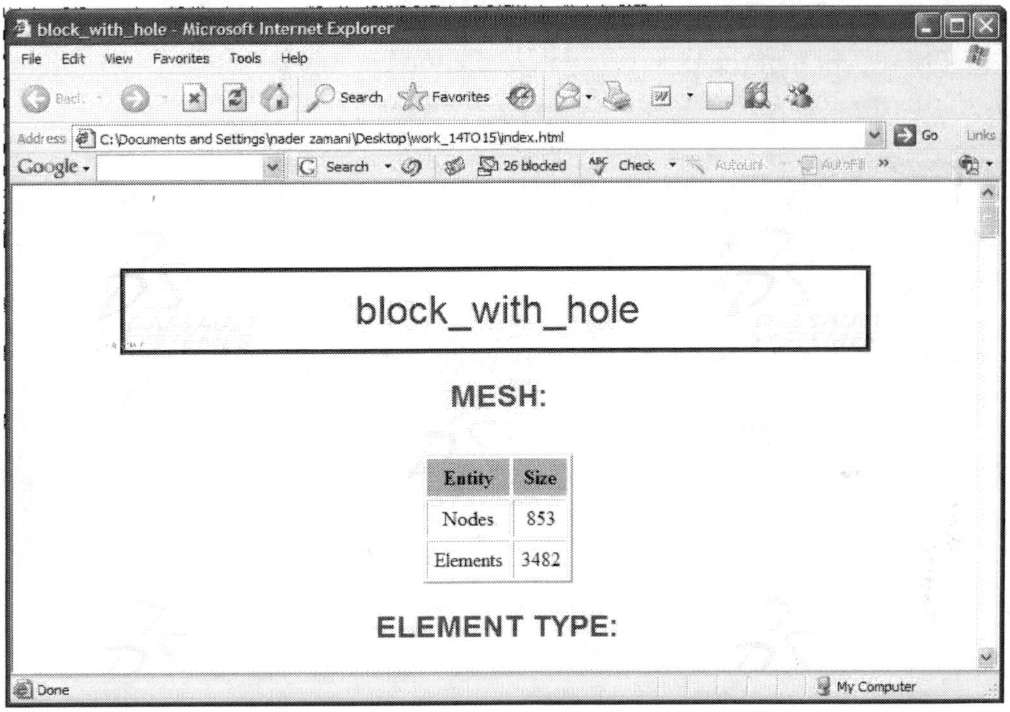


Finally, animation of the model can be achieved through the **Animate** icon  in the **Analysis Tools** toolbar  and an AVI file can easily be created.

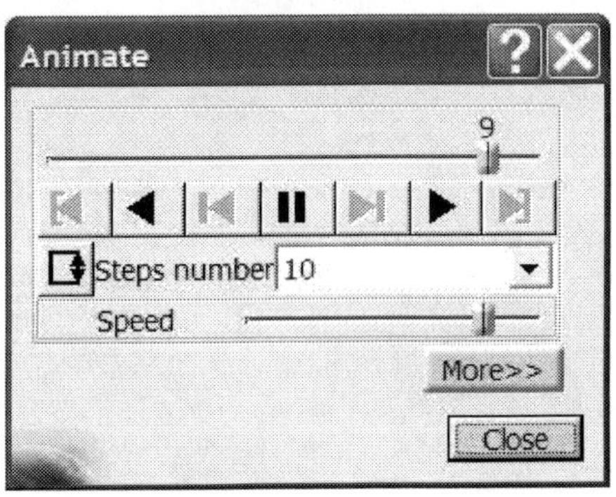

# Exercises for Chapter 2

## Problem 1: Analysis of a Pressurized Thick-walled Cylinder

A long thick pipe made of steel is pressurized at 1000 psi. The inside and outside radii of the pipe are 2 in. and 3 in. respectively. Use solid elements together with symmetry reduction to solve the problem in CATIA.

Partial Answer:

The statement that the pipe is long implies that it is in a state of plane strain. This in turn means that if a section of the pipe is isolated, the top and the bottom sections do not move axially. Furthermore, one needs to take only a quarter of the isolated pipe for modeling purposes.

The geometry to be modeled is shown below. For the height of the section, use 5 in. However, the results are independent of this value.

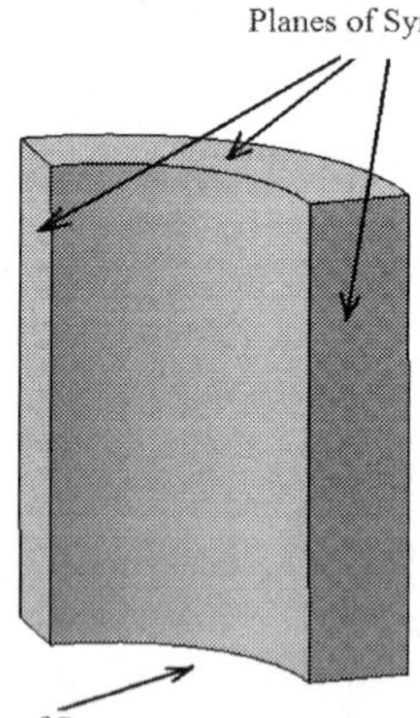


The hoop stress is the maximum principal stress and it is largest at the inside radius of the tube. The other two principal stresses are the radial and axial stresses.

The analytical expression for these stresses can be obtained from elementary strength of materials and are provided below.

$$\sigma_{hoop} = \frac{P}{R_o^2 - R_i^2}\left[R_i^2 + \frac{R_i^2 R_o^2}{r^2}\right]$$

$$\sigma_{radial} = \frac{P}{R_o^2 - R_i^2}\left[R_i^2 - \frac{R_i^2 R_o^2}{r^2}\right]$$

$$\sigma_{axial} = \frac{P R_i^2}{R_o^2 - R_i^2}$$

Here, $R_i$ and $R_o$ are the inside and outside radii and P is the internal pressure. The location along the wall is designated by r.

## Problem 2: the Difference between Pressure and Force Loading

Reconsider the problem solved in this chapter. Instead of applying a pressure of 250 psi to the end face, apply distributed force of 1000 lb and observe the difference.

Partial Answer:

Plotting the deformation and von Mises stress, you will obtain the following figures.

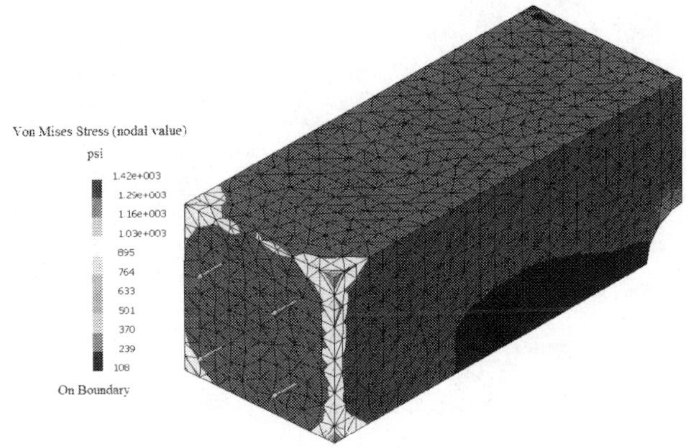

In dealing with solid elements, it is recommended to avoid using concentrated or line forces. Theoretically, the stress below a concentrated force is infinite and this is why the nonphysical stresses have developed in the above contour. The deformation pattern is also not reasonable.

In mechanics, the St. Venant principal states that the local effects die down as you get further from the source of disturbance. This statement translates into the fact that the stresses close to the notch are not significantly different from the case of pressure loading.

# NOTES:

# Chapter 4

# Stress Analysis of a Rotating Disk

## Introduction

In this tutorial you will be using the concept of symmetry to reduce the size of a solid model. The loading used is centrifugal and implemented by specifying a constant angular velocity. The calculations are performed with solid elements.

## 1 Problem Statement

A disk with inside radius of $R_i = 1$ in., outside radius of $R_o = 6$ in., and height of $h = 1$ in. is rotating about its axis at an angular velocity of 113 rad/s. The disk is made of steel with Young's modulus of 30E+6 psi and Poisson ratio of 0.3. The density of steel is assumed to be $\rho = 7.2E\text{-}4\ lb.s^2/in^4$.
In this chapter, you will be using CATIA and solid tetrahedron elements to predict the stresses developed in the disk due to centrifugal forces.
Although the mid-plane of the disk is a plane of symmetry you will not use this feature, however, you will take an arbitrary sector of the disk for modeling purposes. The original disk, together with a $30^\circ$ sector are shown below.

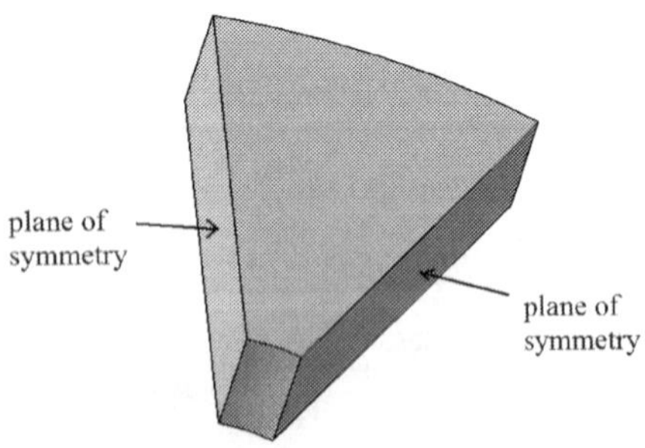


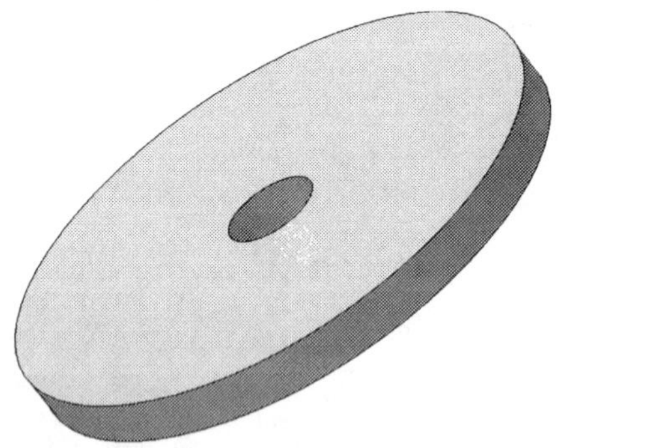

The spinning disk problem is a good benchmark because it has an analytical solution which can be used for comparison purposes. One can show that the three principal stresses are, hoop, radial and axial stresses described by the following relationships.

$$\sigma_{hoop} = \frac{3+\nu}{8}\left[\left(R_i^2 + R_o^2\right) - \frac{1+3\nu}{3+\nu} r^2 + \frac{R_i^2 R_o^2}{r^2}\right]\rho\omega^2$$

$$\sigma_{radial} = \frac{3+\nu}{8}\left[\left(R_i^2 + R_o^2\right) - r^2 - \frac{R_i^2 R_o^2}{r^2}\right]\rho\omega^2$$

$$\sigma_{axial} = 0$$

In these formulas, $\rho$, $\omega$, and $\nu$ are the density, angular velocity, and Poisson ratio respectively. For the parameters supplied in this problem, the distribution of the hoop and radial stresses as a function of "r" are also displayed on the right.

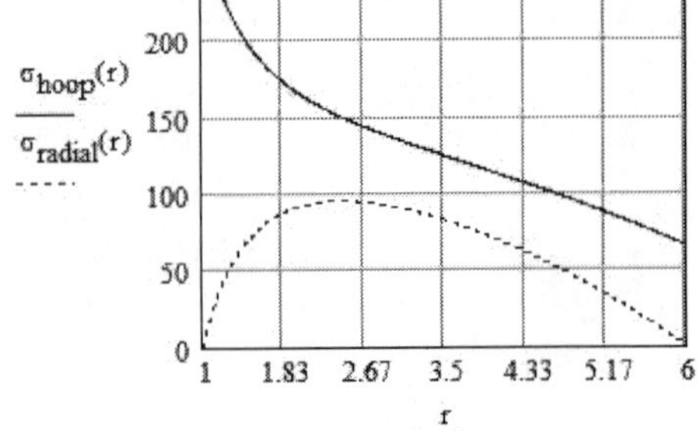

## 2 Creation of the Part in Mechanical Design Solutions

Enter the **Part Design** workbench which can be achieved by different means depending on your CATIA customization. For example, from the standard Windows toolbar, select **File > New**. From the box shown on the right, select **Part**. This moves you to the **Part Design** workbench and creates a part with the default name **Part.1**. See Note #1 in Appendix I.
In order to change the default name, move the cursor to **Part.1** in the tree, right-click and select **Properties** from the menu list.

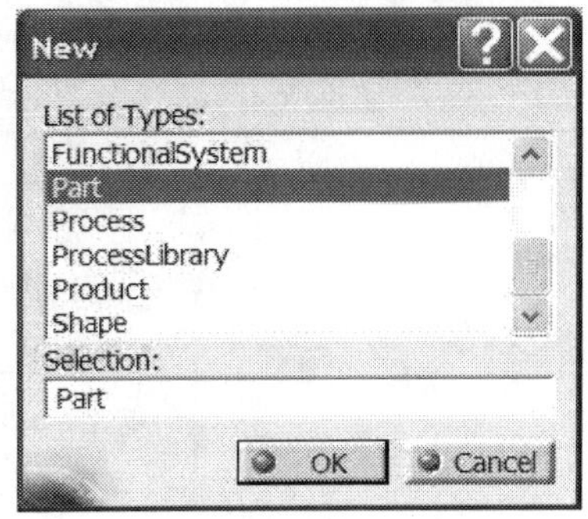


From the **Properties** box, select the **Product** tab and in **Part Number** type **rotating_disk**. This will be the new part name throughout the chapter. The tree on the top left corner of the screen should look as displayed below.

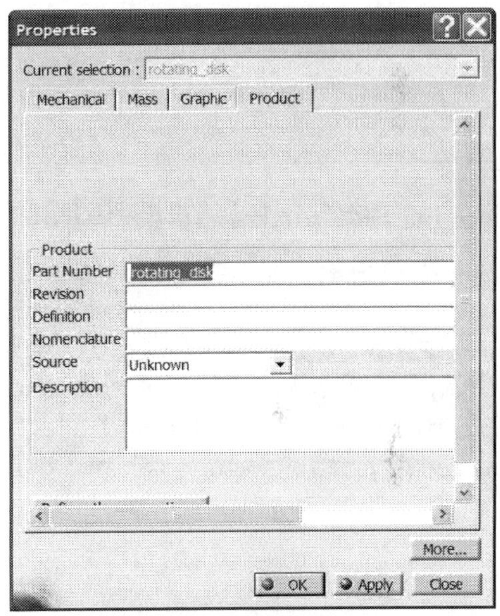


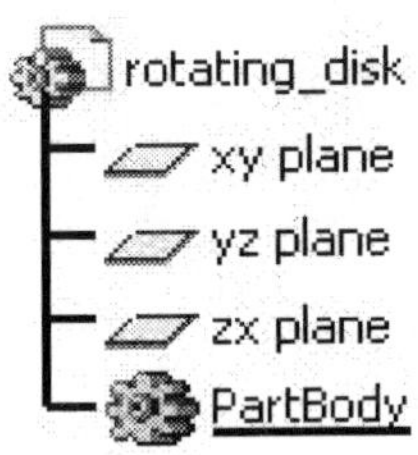


From the tree, select the **yz** plane and enter the **Sketcher**. In the **Sketcher**, use the **Profile** toolbar to draw a rectangle and dimension it. In order to change the dimension, double-click on the dimension on the screen and in the resulting box enter the correct value. Your simple sketch and a typical **Constraint Definition** box used to enter correct dimensions are shown below.

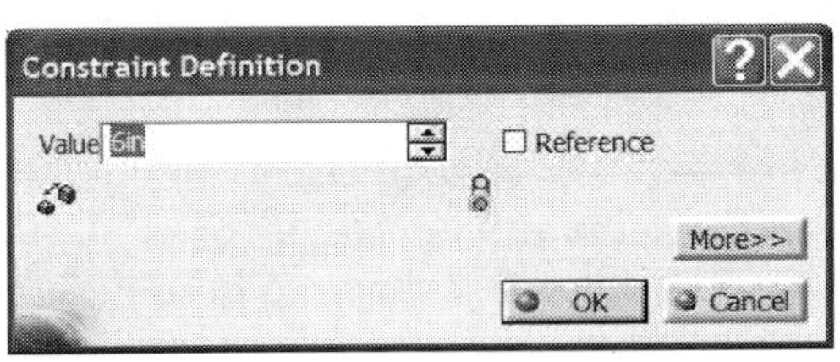


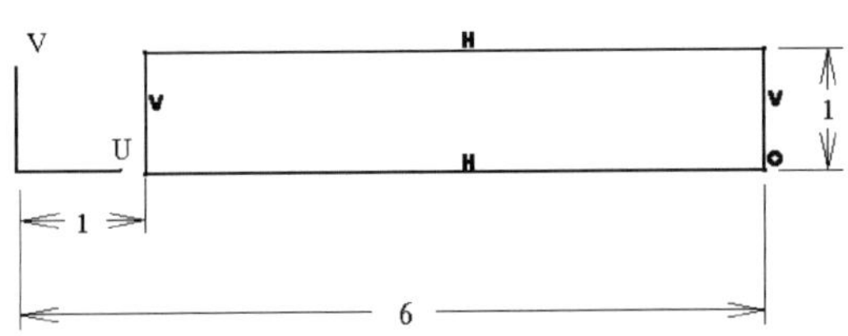

It is important that the left edge of the sketched rectangle be 1 inch away from the **v-axis** in the sketch plane. Leave the **Sketcher**.

Upon leaving the **Sketcher**, the screen and the tree should look as shown below.

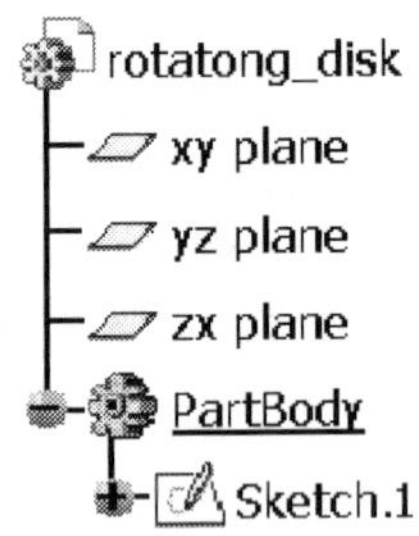


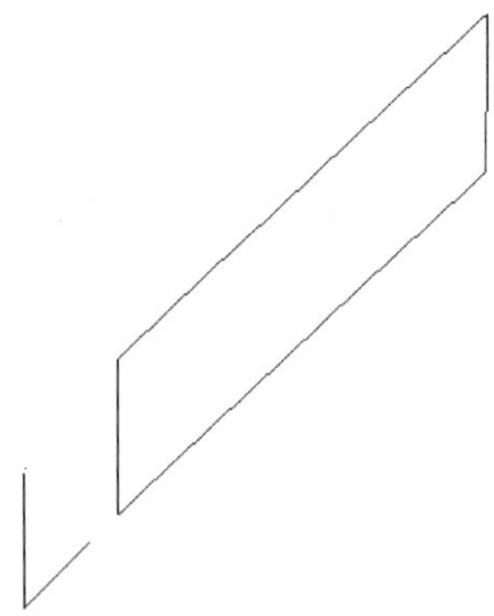

From the **Sketch-Based Features** toolbar 

, select the **Shaft** icon, which causes the **Shaft Definition** box shown below to open.

In the **First angle** box, type **30**. For the **Selection** box, pick **Sketch.1** from the tree. Finally, for the **Axis Selection** box, right-click and select the **Z Axis**. The result is a 30° sector as shown below.

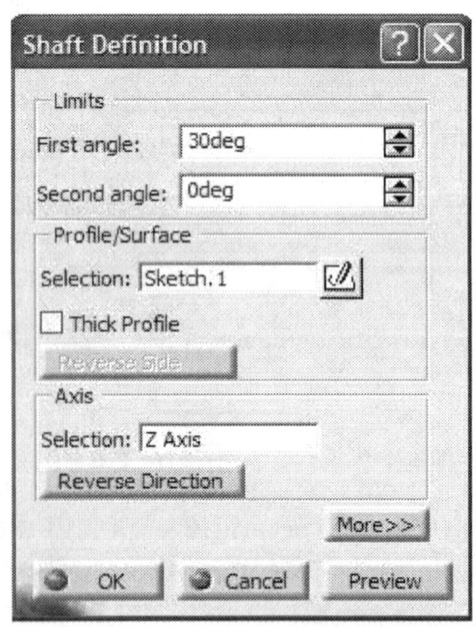


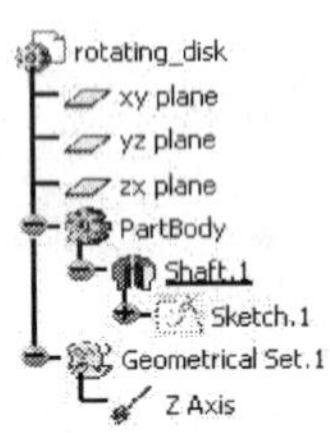


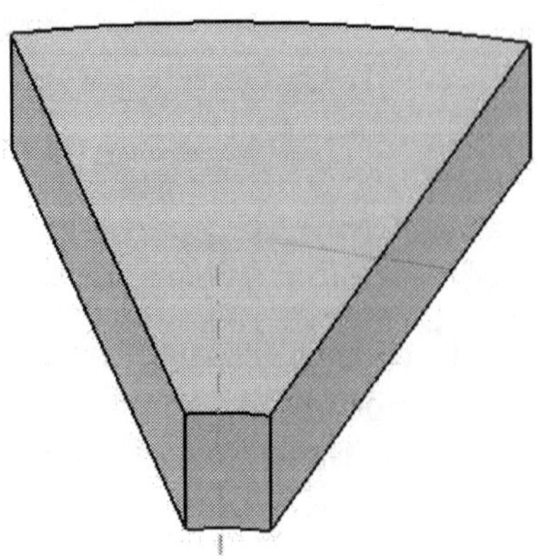

In anticipation of performing FEA calculation for our part, we will construct two local coordinate systems. One will be used to specify the direction and center of rotation, the second local system will be used to specify the roller boundary condition on the inclined plane.

A simpler approach to the latter objective is to employ the **Surface Slider** icon. We choose to do it differently to demonstrate other options available in CATIA.

Use the **Reference Element** toolbar 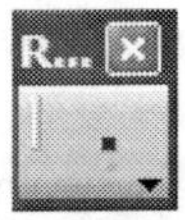 to select the **Point** icon 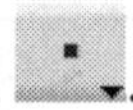. The **Point Definition** box shown below opens. Using the default information, a point at (0,0,0) will be created. Although it may be difficult to see, an "x" mark on the computer screen represents the point constructed.

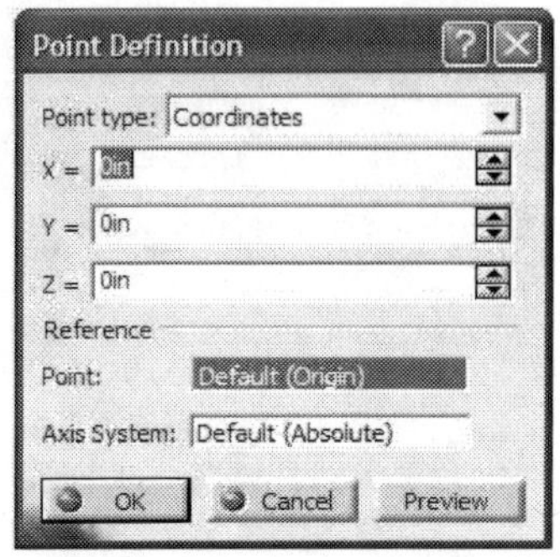


The next step is to create a local coordinate system at this location.

From the **Tools** toolbar , select the **Axis System** icon 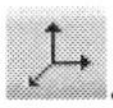. At this point, the **Axis System Definition** box shown on the right opens. Use the cursor to pick the point constructed immediately above. You will see that an axis system is displayed on the screen, and the tree is modified as shown to reflect the last two steps.

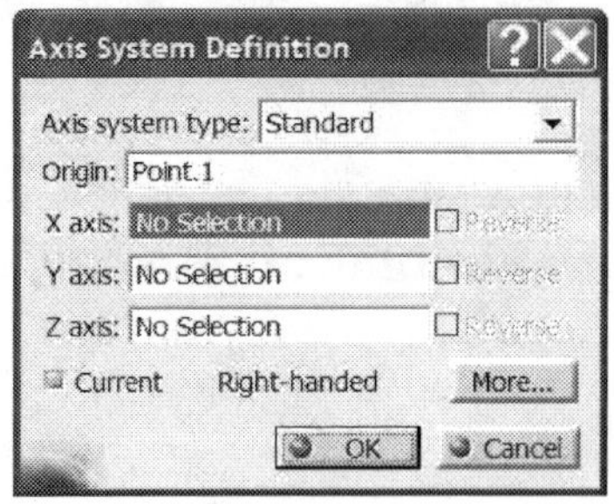


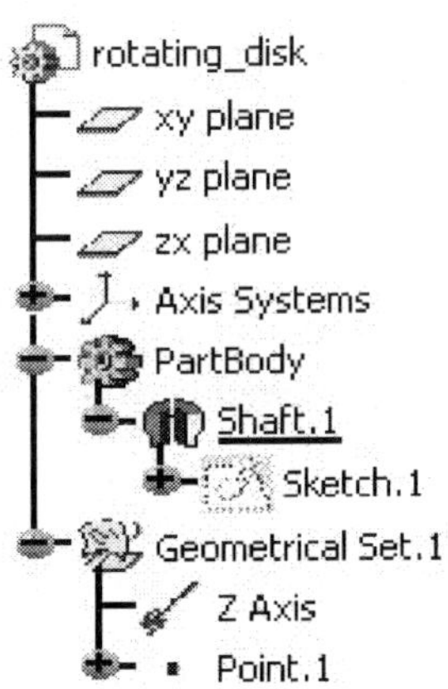

You now construct the second local coordinate system. Select the **Axis System** icon 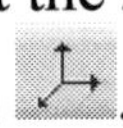.

As the origin, select the vertex of the sector as shown on the right. Finally, select the edges displayed to define the local x and y orientations.

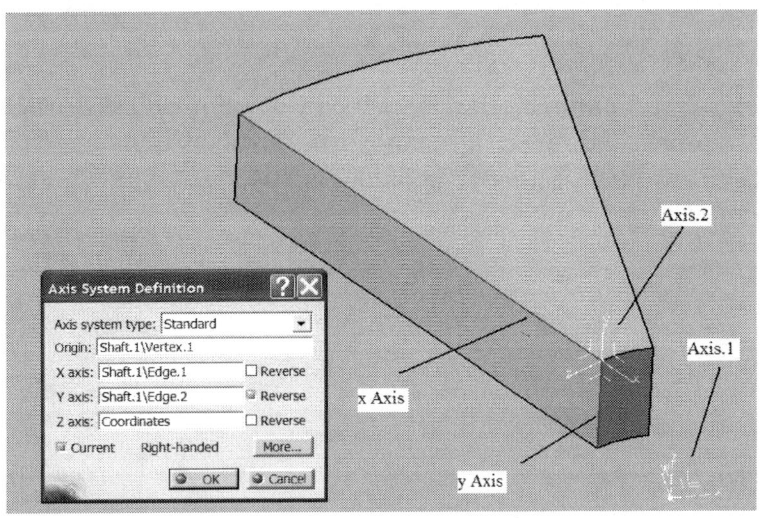

The two local coordinate systems and the associated tree status are displayed.

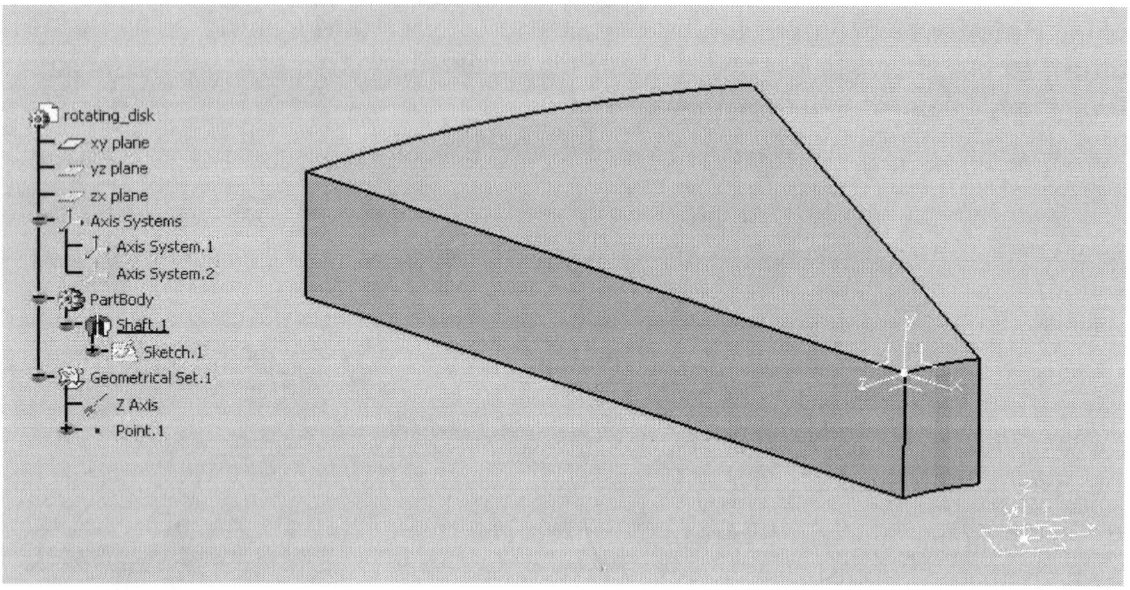


Although the material property can be assigned at this point, you will defer it until after the **Simulation & Analysis** workbench is entered.
**Regularly save your work.**

## 3 Entering the Analysis Solutions

From the standard Windows toolbar, select

**Start > Analysis & Simulation > Generative Structural Analysis**
There is a second workbench known as the **Advanced Meshing Tools** which will be discussed later.

The first thing one can note is the presence of a **Warnings** box indicating that material is not properly defined on rotating_disk. This is not surprising since material has not yet been assigned. This will be done shortly and therefore you can close this box by pressing **OK**.

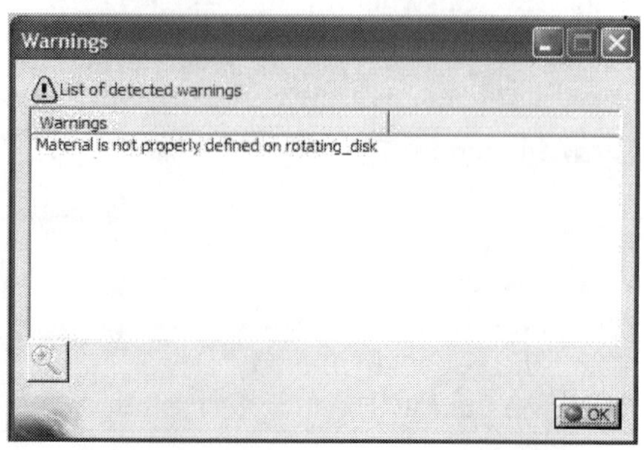

A second box shown below, **New Analysis Case** is also visible. The default choice is **Static Analysis** which is precisely what we intend to use. Therefore, close the box by clicking on **OK**.

Finally, note that the tree structure gets considerably longer. The bottom branches of the tree are presently "unfilled", and as we proceed in this workbench, assigning loads and restraints, the branches gradually get "filled".

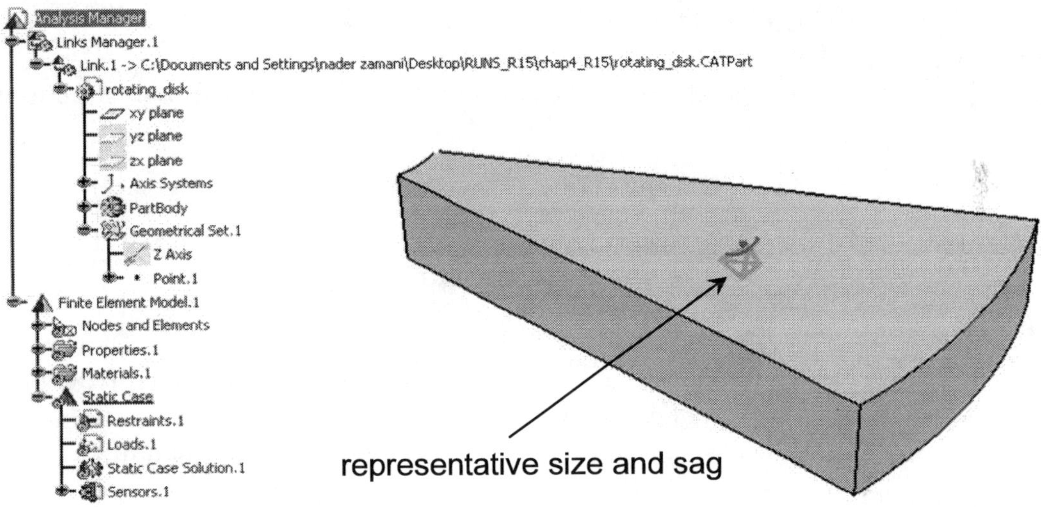


Another point that cannot be missed is the appearance of an icon close to the part that reflects a representative "size" and "sag". This is displayed above.

The concept of element size is self-explanatory. A smaller element size leads to more accurate results at the expense of a larger computation time. The "sag" terminology is unique to CATIA. In FEA, the geometry of a part is approximated with the elements. The surface of the part and the FEA approximation of a part do not coincide. The "sag" parameter controls the deviation between the two. Therefore a smaller "sag" value could lead to better results. There is a relationship between these parameters that one does not have to be concerned with at this point.

The physical sizes of the representative "size" and "sag" on the screen, which also limit the coarseness of the mesh can be changed by the user.

There are two ways to change these parameters:
The first method is to double-click on the representative icons on the screen which forces the **OCTREE Tetrahedron Mesh** box to open as shown to the right. Change the default values to match the numbers in the box.
Notice that the type of the elements used (linear/parabolic) is also set in this box. Select **OK**.
The second method of reaching this box is through the tree. By double-clicking on the branch labeled **OCTREE Tetrahedron Mesh** shown below, the same box opens allowing the user to modify the values.

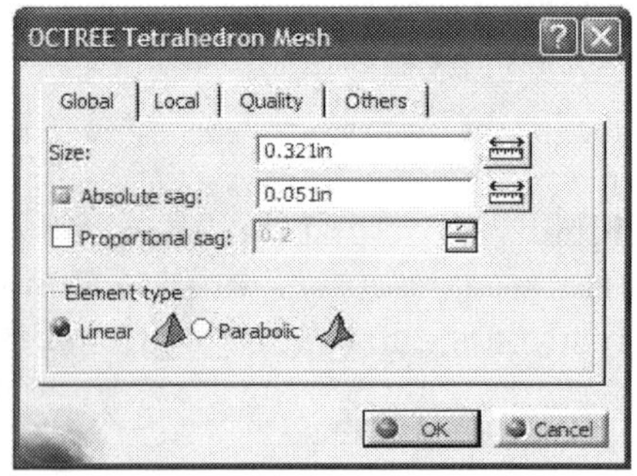


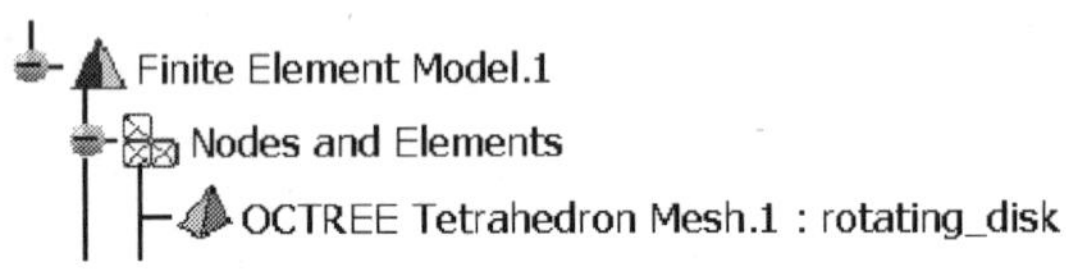


In order to view the generated mesh, you can point the cursor to the branch **Nodes and Elements**, right-click and select **Mesh Visualization**. This step may be slightly different in some UNIX machines. Upon performing this operation a **Warning** box appears which can be ignored (select **OK**). For the mesh parameters used, the following mesh is displayed on the screen. See Note #2 in Appendix I.

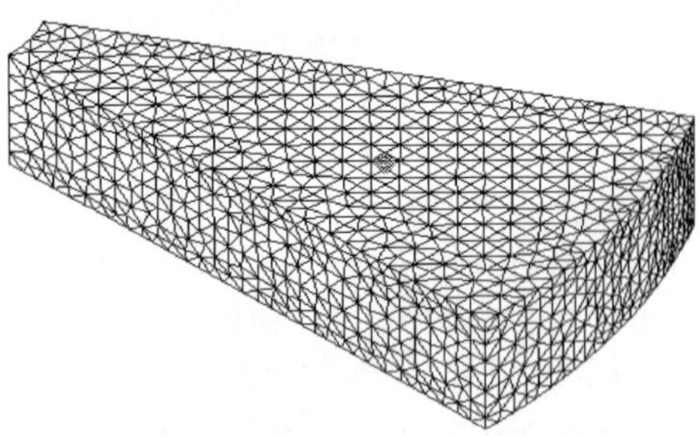

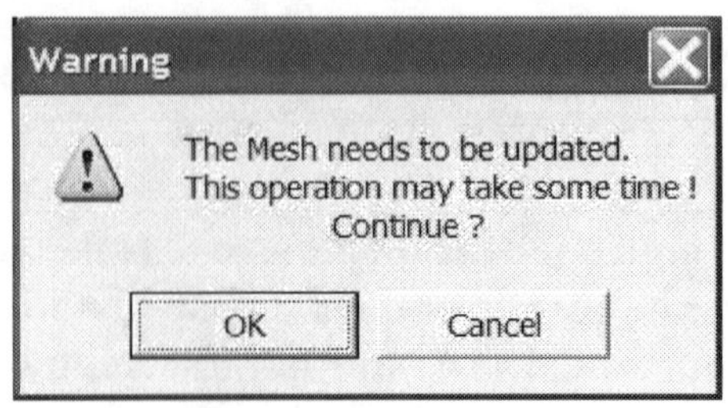


The representative "size" and "sag" icons can be removed from the display by simply pointing to them, right-click and select **Hide**. This is the standard process for hiding any entity in CATIA V5.

Before proceeding with the rest of the model, a few more points regarding the mesh size are discussed. As indicated earlier, a smaller mesh could result in a more accurate solution, however, this cannot be done indiscriminately. The elements must be small in the regions of high stress gradient such as stress concentrations. These are areas where the geometry changes rapidly such as bends, fillets, and keyways.
Uniformly reducing the element size for the whole part is a poor strategy.

## Assigning Material Properties:

A simple check of the lower branches of the tree reveals that the **Update** icon  is present. This occurs because a mesh has been created, but no material properties have been assigned. Although material could have been assigned at the part level with the **Apply Material** icon , we choose to do it differently.

Using the **Model Manager** toolbar 

select the **User Material** icon 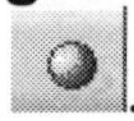. This action opens the material database box.

Choose the **Metal** tab on the top; select **Steel**. Use your cursor to pick the part on the screen at which time the **OK** and **Apply Material** buttons can be selected.
Close the box.
The material property is now reflected in the tree.

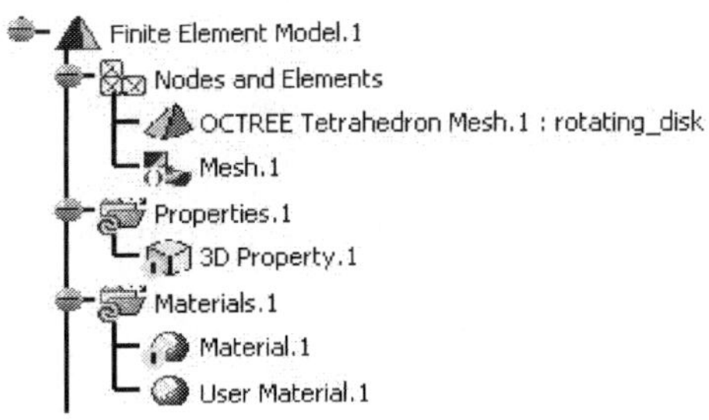


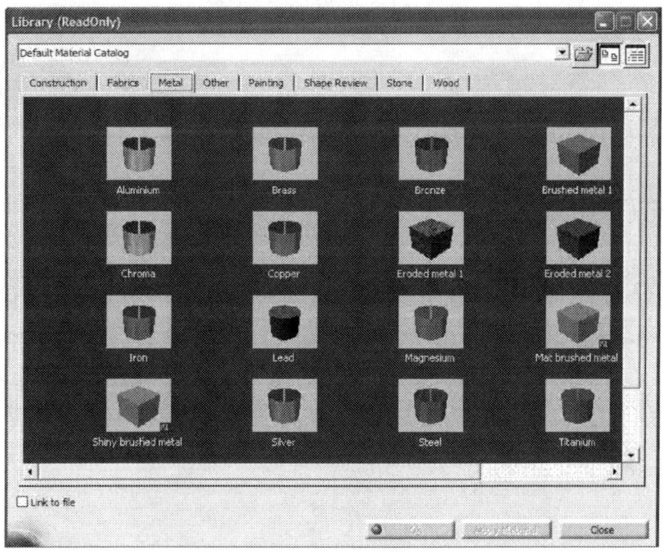


In order to inspect the values of the material properties assigned, double-click on **Steel** in the tree. It may take a minute before the database is searched. You will notice that the **Properties** box shown in the next page opens. Choose the **Analysis** tab from this box, and the values will be displayed. Note that these values can be edited.
Since your Young's modulus and Poisson ratio are different from what is shown, in appropriate boxes, type Young's modulus = **3E+7**, Poisson ratio =**.3** and Density = **7.2E-4**. Press **OK**.
Note that the value 0.284 is obtained by multiplying the given density of 7.2E-4 lb.s$^2$/in$^4$ by 384 due to unit conversion.

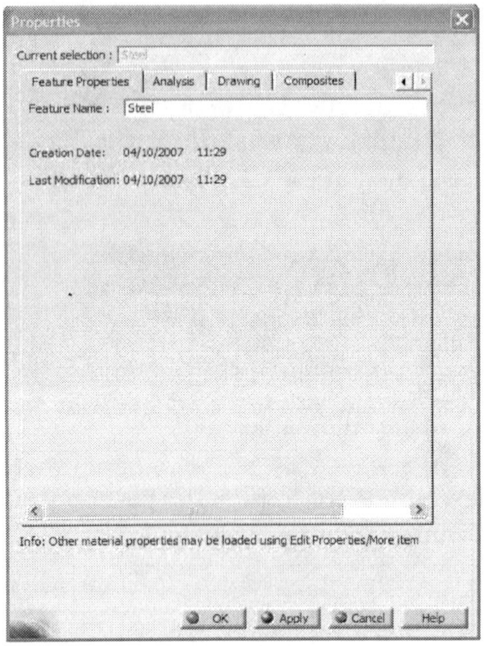


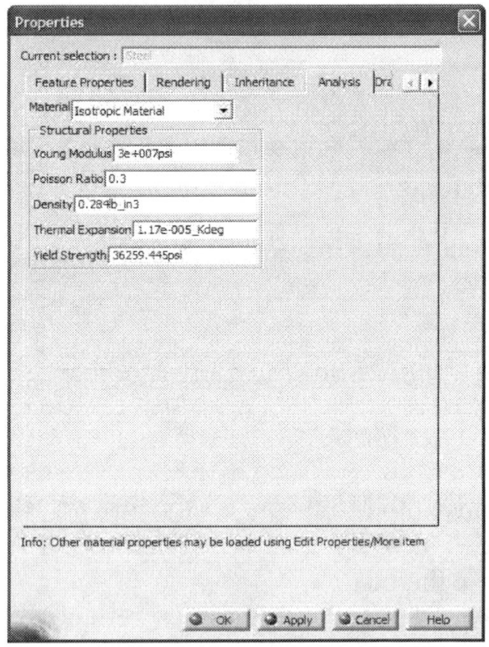


The mere fact that material properties are now specified does not mean that the elements are using it. This can be verified by selecting the **model checker** 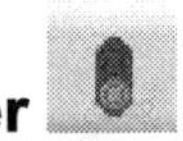 icon from the **Model Manager** toolbar 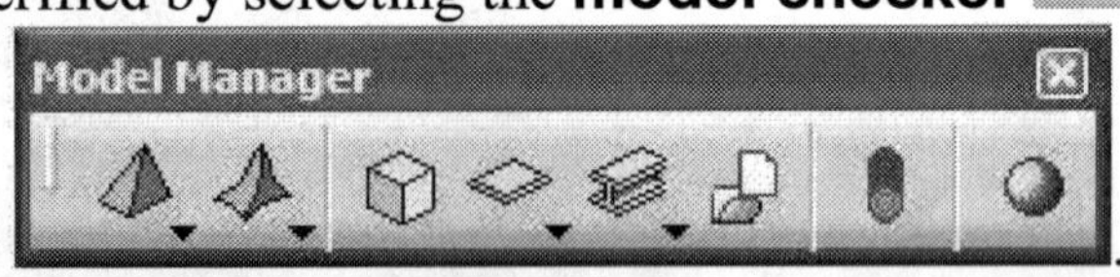

.

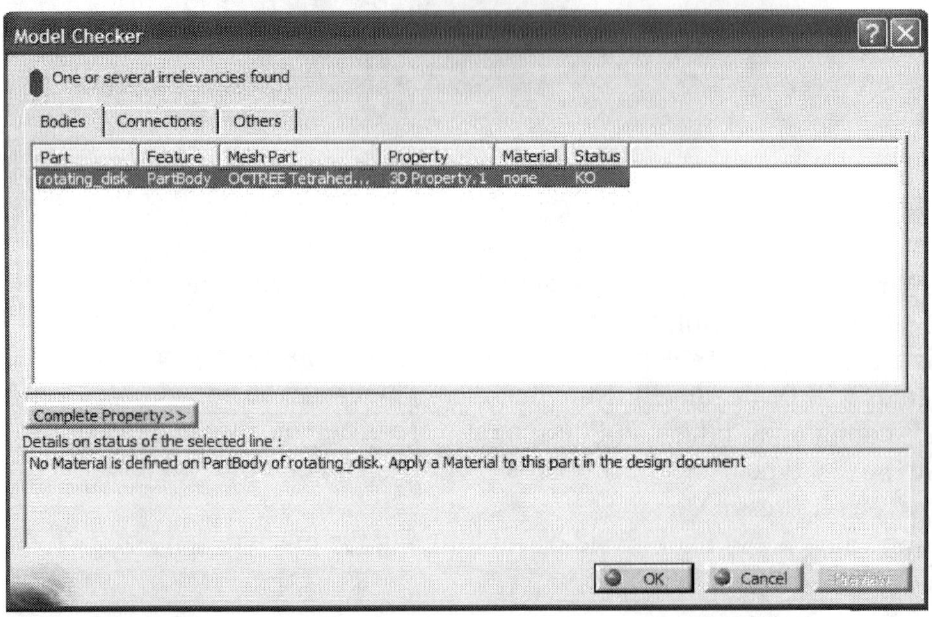


There is a clear indication that material is not detected by the FEA module.

We have to go through an additional step to accomplish this.
On the branch of the tree labeled **3D Property.1**, double-click. This action opens the box shown to the right, select the button **User-defined Material** and move the cursor to the **Material** line. You are now in a position to select the branch of tree labeled **User Material.1**.
This is the material that you created in the previous step. Note that before selecting this item from the tree, the **Material** data line in the box is plain blue (blank). It is only after the tree selection, that you see the box exactly shown on the right.

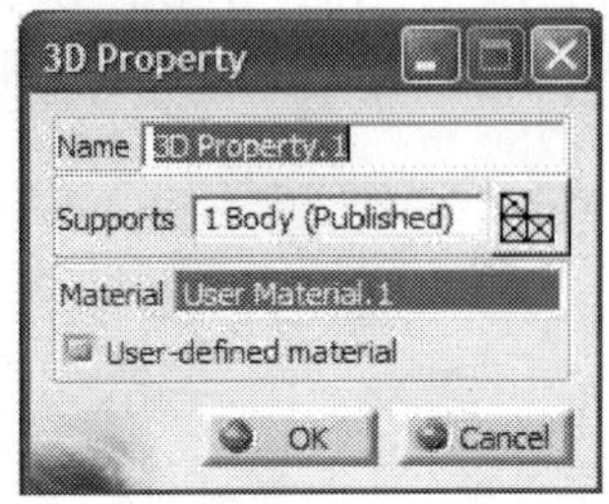


The tree status for the above selection is shown below.
The final step is pointing the cursor to **Nodes and Elements** in the tree, right-click, and select **Mesh Visualization**. See Note #2 in Appendix I.

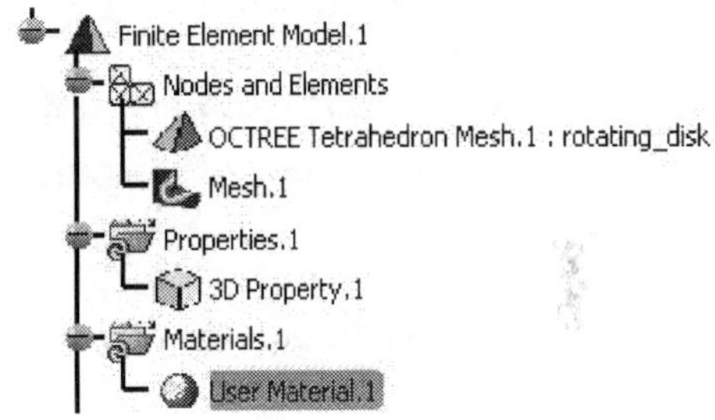


CONGRATULATIONS! You now have a mesh with the correct material properties.
Regularly save your work.

**Applying Restraints:**

It was indicated earlier that the easiest way to apply the boundary conditions on the symmetry planes is using **Surface Slider** icon . However, you will do this only for the side that lies in the global **zy** plane. For the inclined side, you will use the **User-defined Restraint** icon 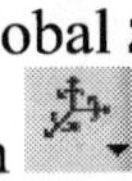 applied to the **Axis System.2**.

From the **Restraint** toolbar 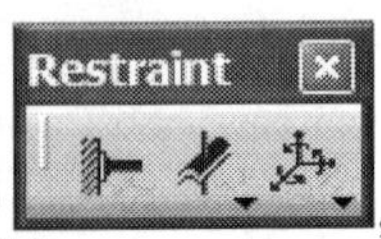

, select the **Surface Slider** icon . Once the box shown on the right opens, using the cursor, pick the face of the part lying in the **zy** plane as indicated below.

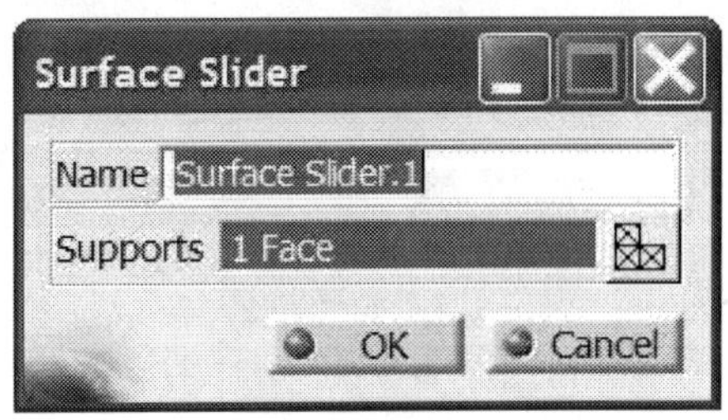


Keep in mind that the restraints are applied to the part, and therefore, the part must be in the **Show** mode. If the part is not showing, point the cursor to **Links Manager.1** in the tree, right-click, and select **Show**.

The red cylindrical icons on the face, are indications of the symmetry plane condition prevailing.

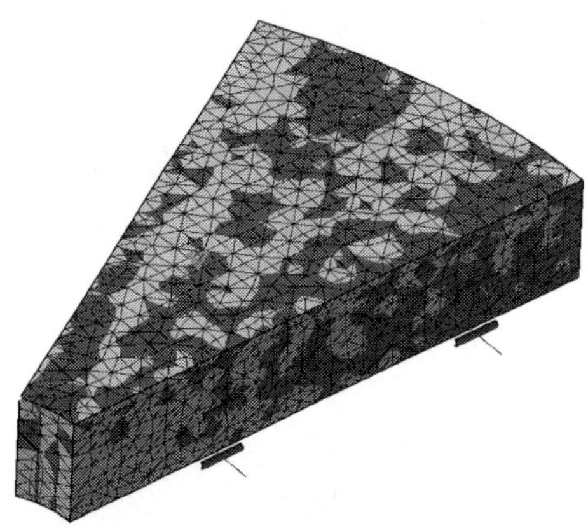

To apply the restraint on the inclined face, select the **User-defined Restraint** icon .
The box to the right opens. Note that the default Axis System is **Global**. You have to change that to **User**. With the cursor, pick the **Axis System.2** icon on the screen. This coordinate system is recorded in the box.

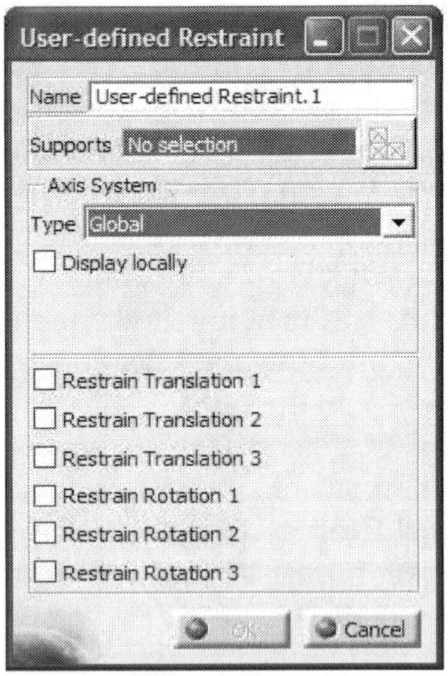


For the **Supports**, pick the inclined face, and keep only **Restrain Translation 3** checked. Remember, ordinarily **Restrain Rotation** has no role in solid elements. Furthermore, **Restrain Translation 3** indicates that there is no "z" displacement in the local coordinate system 2.

The final **User-defined Restraint** box and the part on the screen are shown below.

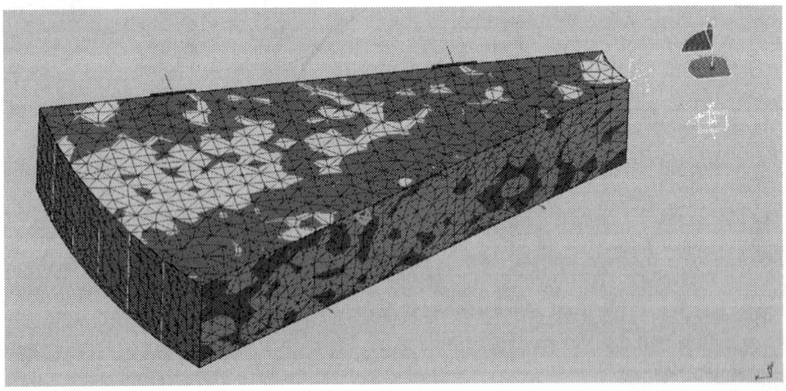

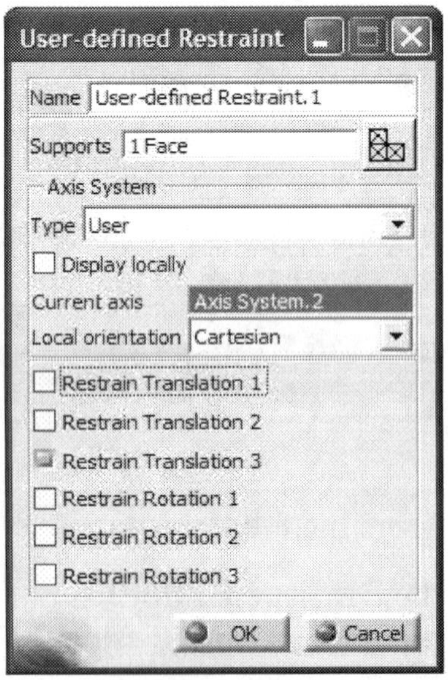

## Applying Loads:

From the **Loads** toolbar 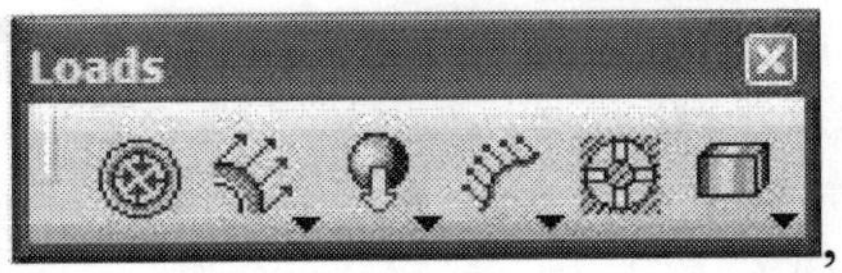

, select the **Rotation Force** icon . The associated definition box is shown below. This icon belongs to the **Body** toolbar 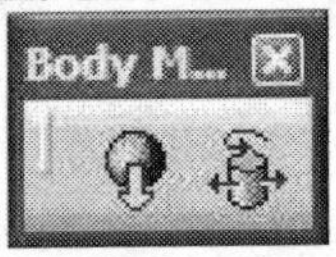

.

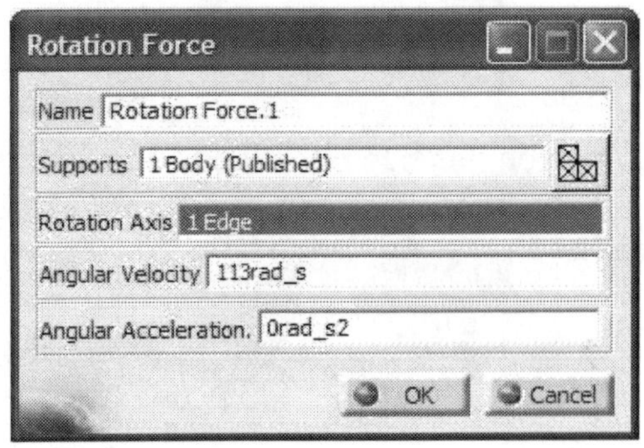


For the **Supports**, pick the part on the screen. For the rotation axis, pick the z-axis of the coordinate system 1, **Axis System.1**, with the angular velocity being 113 rad/s.

The **Rotation Force** icon on the screen is displayed about the "z" axis as shown in the following figure.

The tree after imposing this load is also shown below.

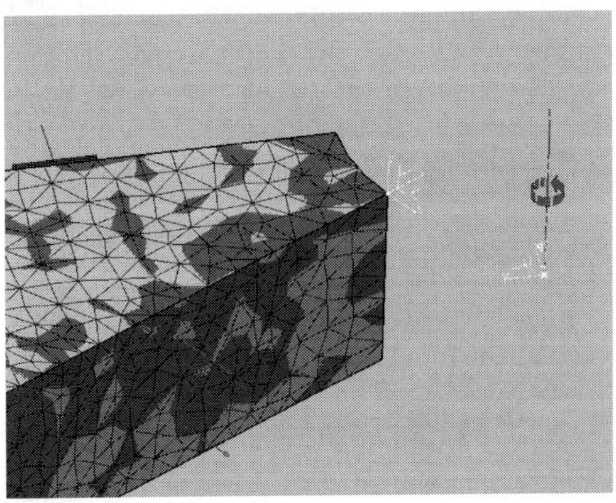

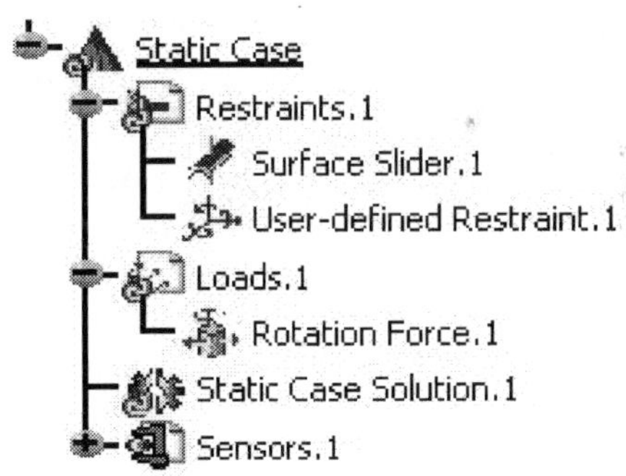


It seems that all the restraints, and loads are applied and we are prepared to run the analysis.

## Launching the Solver:

To run the analysis, you need to use the **Compute** toolbar 

by selecting the **Compute** icon . This opens up the **Compute** box shown to the right. Leave the defaults as **All** which means everything is computed.

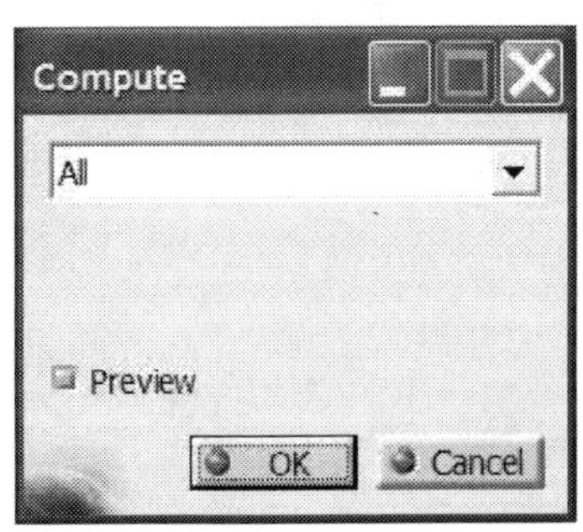

Upon closing this box, after a brief pause, the second box shown below appears. This box provides information on the resources needed to complete the analysis. If the estimates are zero in the listing, then there is a problem in the previous step and should be corrected. If all the numbers are zero in the box, the program may run, but would not produce any useful results.

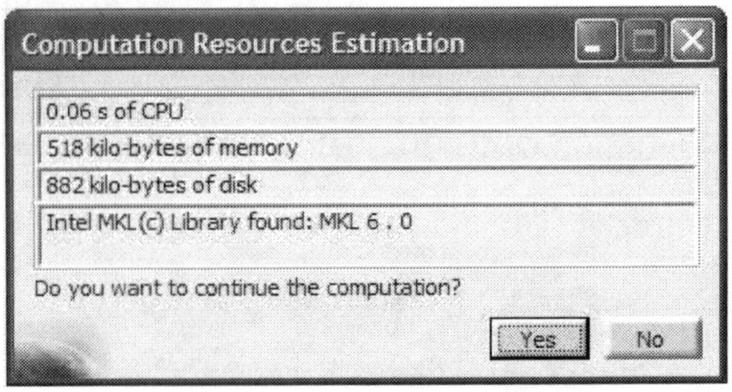


The tree has been changed to reflect the location of the **Results** and **Computations** as shown below.

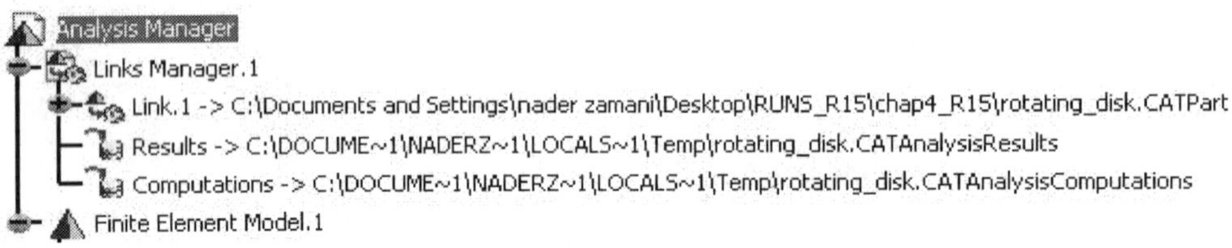


Unfortunately you will get the following **Error** box. Usually this box implies that the part is not fully restrained. In our model, the block is free to move in the x-direction as a rigid body. Some commercial packages rectify the situation by adding a small artificial stiffness in that direction, preventing the rigid body motion. In those packages, effectively they add a "soft" spring in the appropriate direction, resulting in a stiffness.

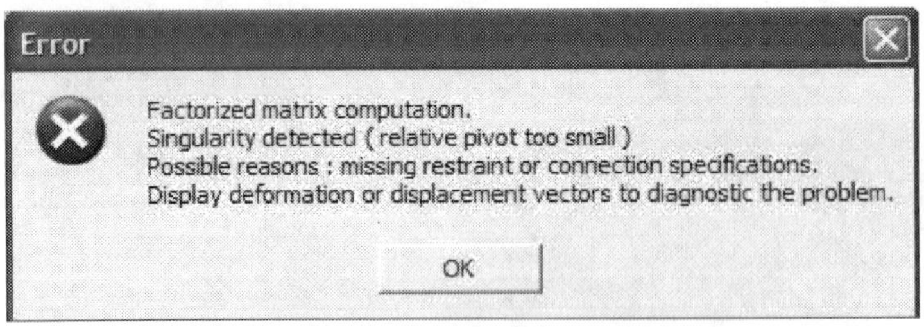


You achieve the same effect by selecting an arbitrary point and prevent it from moving in the z-direction. Use the **Restraint** toolbar 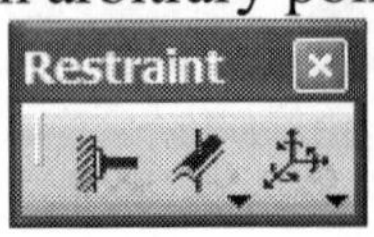

and select the **User-defined Restraint** icon 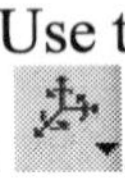.

The above action opens up the **User-defined Restraint** box shown on the next page. Pick any arbitrary vertex and check the "**Restrain Translation 3**" box. The directions 1, 2, and 3 correspond to the global x, y, and z directions. Make sure that the **Axis System Type** is set to **Global**.

The single red arrow will show on the vertex.

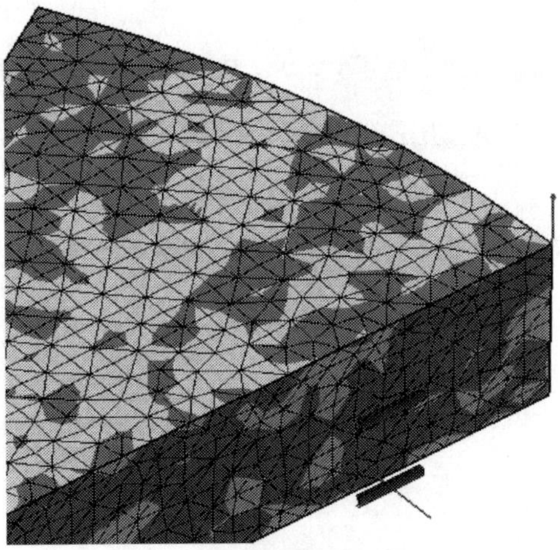

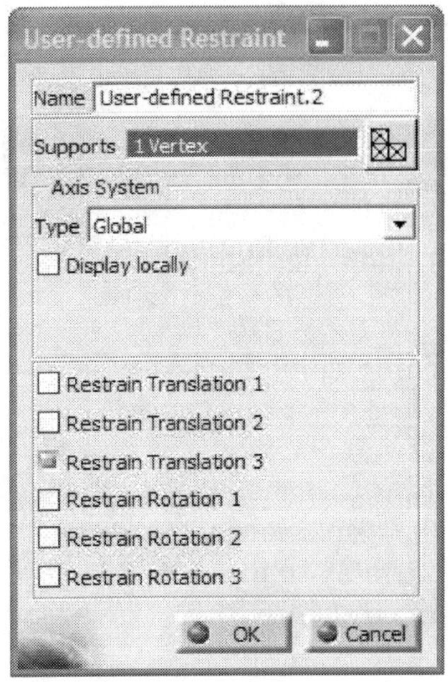


You are reminded that ordinarily the solid tetrahedron elements do not have rotational degrees of freedom; therefore, one cannot directly impose rotation or moment on them. Whether the **Restrain Rotation** boxes are left checked or not, there will be no impact on the results. The concept of "virtual parts" to be discussed in another chapter can be used to apply rotation and moment to solids if needed.

Now press on  to run the problem. This time, the run completes without an error. The tree has been changed to reflect the location of the Results and Computations as shown below.

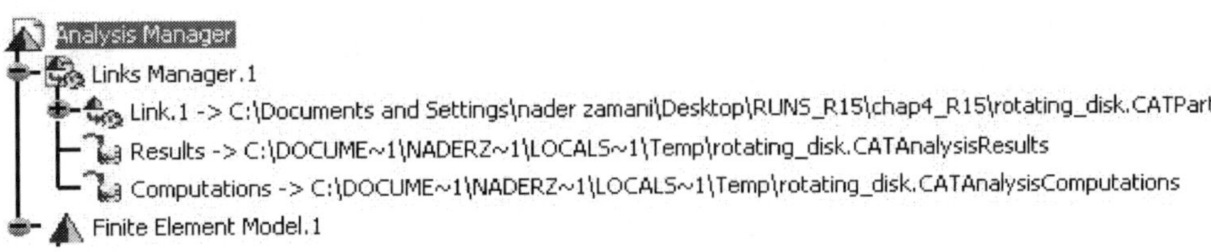


The user can change these locations by double-clicking on the branch. The box, shown below, opens and can be modified.

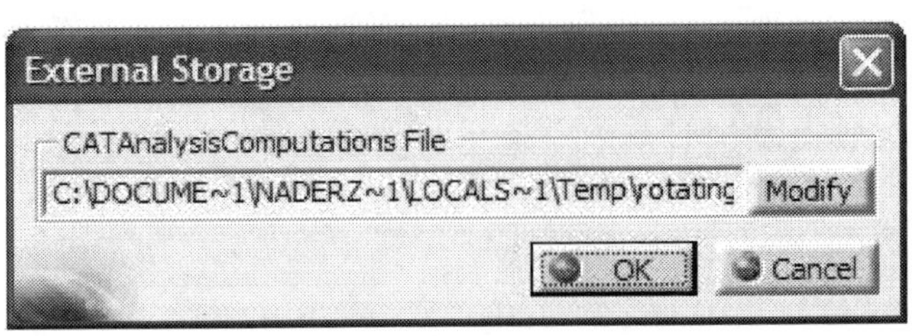

**Postprocessing:**

The main postprocessing toolbar is called **Image** 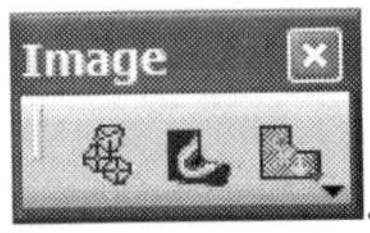

. To view the deformed shape you have to use the **Deformation** icon . The resulting deformed shape is displayed below.

The deformation image can be very deceiving since one could get the impression that the block actually displaces to that extent. Keep in mind that the displacements are scaled considerably so that one can observe the deformed shape.

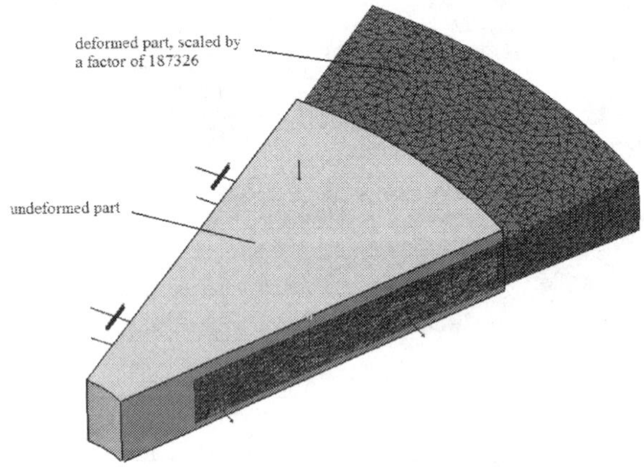


Although the scale factor is set automatically, one can change this value with the **Deformation Scale Factor** icon  in the **Analysis Tools** toolbar

.

Clicking on the above icon leads to the box shown on the right where the desired scale factor can be typed. The above deformed shape corresponds to a scale factor of 81775.

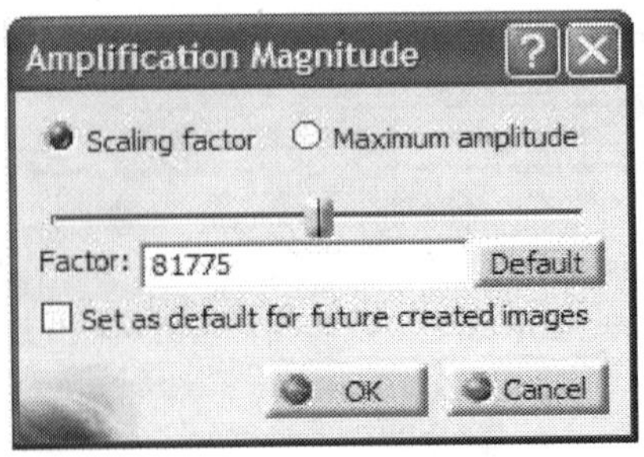


In order to see the displacement field, the **Displacement** icon  in the **Image** toolbar should be used. The default display is in terms of displacement arrows as shown on the next. The color and the length of arrows represent the size of the displacement. The contour legend indicates a maximum displacement of 9.65E-6 in.

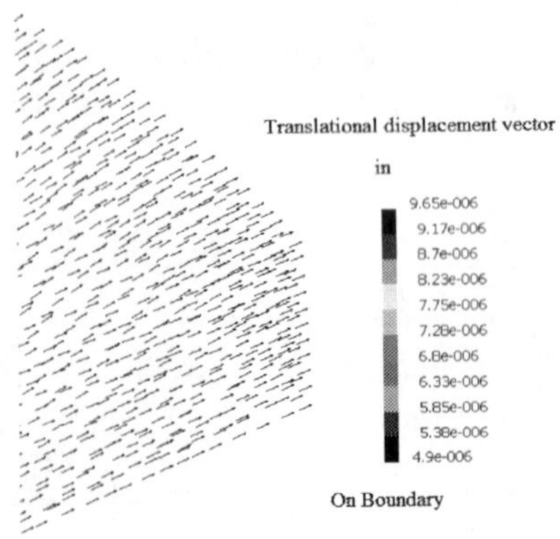


The arrow plot is not particularly useful. In order to view the contour plot of the displacement field, position the cursor on the arrow field and double-click. The **Image Edition** box shown below opens.

Note that the default is to draw the contour on the deformed shape. If this is not desired, uncheck the box **On deformed mesh**. Next, select **AVERAGE-ISO** and press **OK.**

The contour of the displacement field is plotted below. (Note: For visibility purposes, the color map has been changed.)

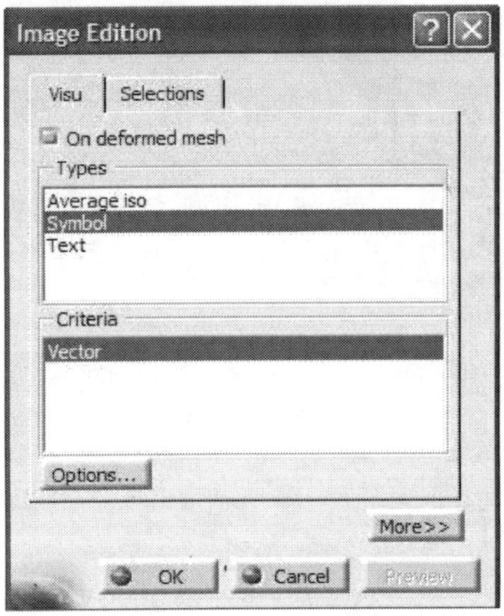


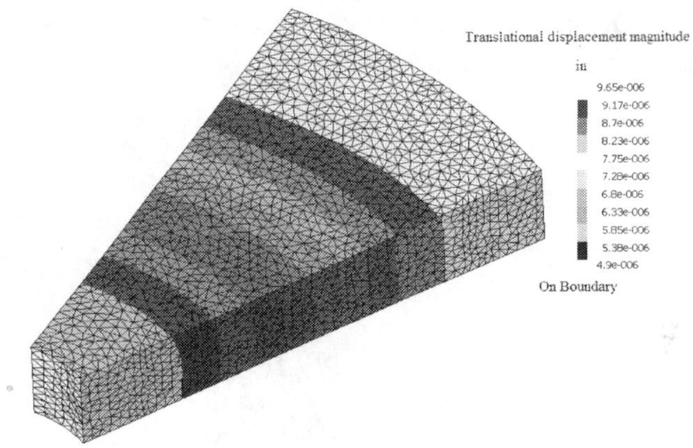


Note that the displacements of all the points equidistant from the center are the same. This is why contour is perfectly circular in pattern. This statement also applies to the contours of all stresses.

The next step in the postprocessing is to plot the contours of the von Mises stress using the **von Mises Stress** icon  in the **Image** toolbar. The von Mises stress is displayed to the right. The maximum stress is at inside surface of the hole, in agreement with the analytical solution provided in the beginning of the chapter.

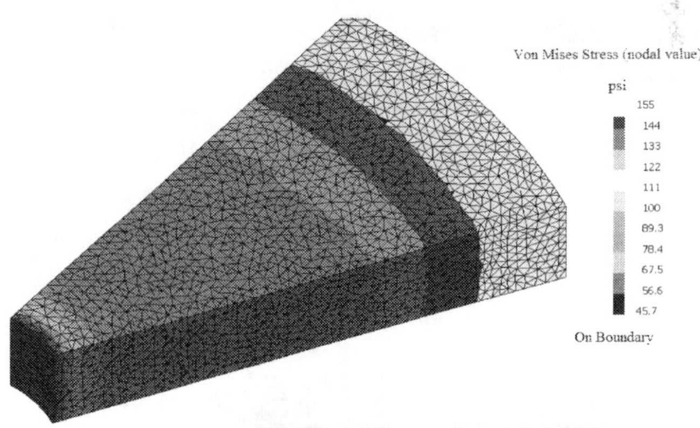


Double-clicking on the contour legend leads to the **Color Map** box displayed below. The contour can be plotted as **Smooth**, or **Stepped**. The number of color bands is also specified in this box. Finally, the user can describe the range of stresses to be plotted.

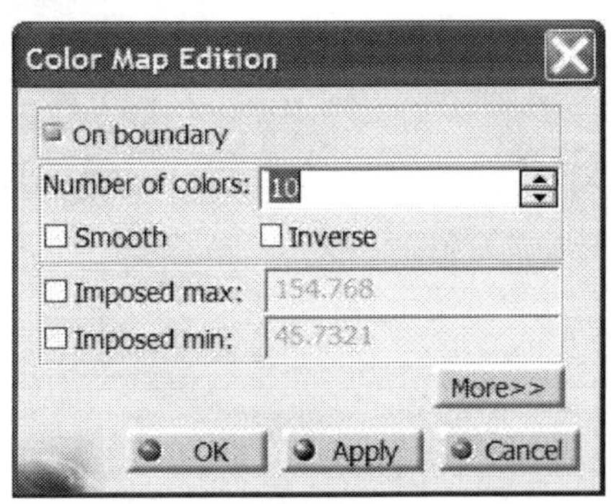

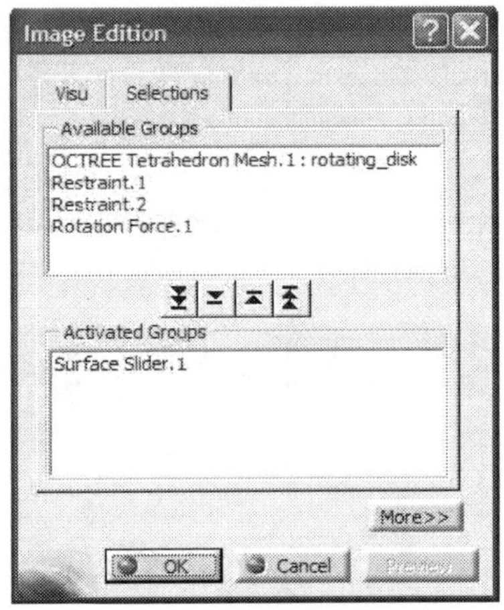


Occasionally, you may be interested in plotting the von Mises stress contour in either the load area or the support section. In order to achieve this, double-click on the contour levels on the screen to open the **Image Edition** box. Next use the **Selections** tab as shown on the right. Here you have the choice of selecting different areas. Select **Surface Slider.1**, and use the button . The contour below display the von Mises stress at **Surface Slider.1** section.

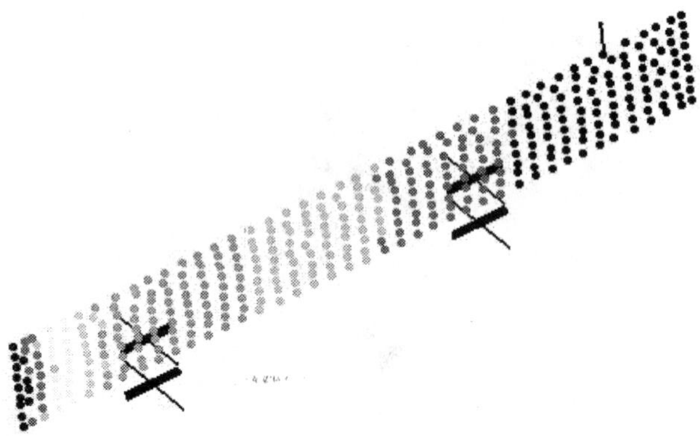

As the postprocessing proceeds and we generate different plots, they get recorded in the tree as displayed below. Each plot generated, deactivates the previous one on the screen. By pointing to a desired plot in the tree and right-clicking, you can activate the plot. Clearly any plot can be deleted from the tree in the usual way (right-click, **Delete**).

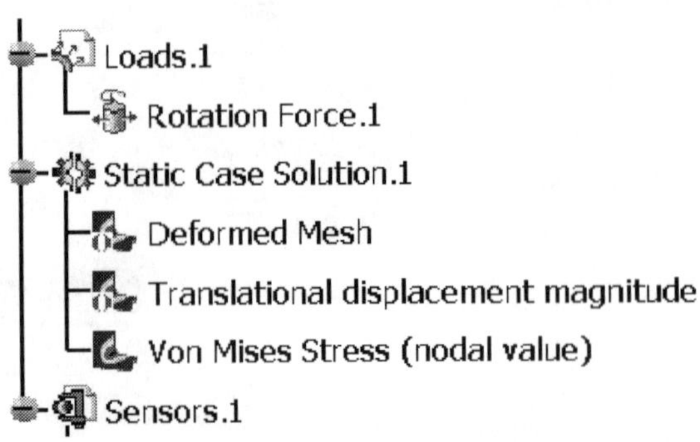

The location and magnitude of the extremum values of a contour (e.g. von Mises stress) can be identified in a plot. This is achieved by using the **Image Extrema** icon in the **Image Analysis** toolbar.

Before the plot is generated, the **Extrema Creation** box pops up as shown to the right. If the default values are maintained, the global maximum and minimum are found and their location pin-pointed in a contour plot as shown below.

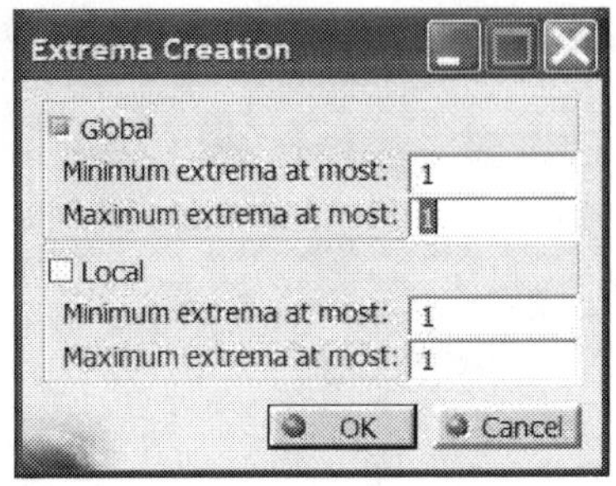


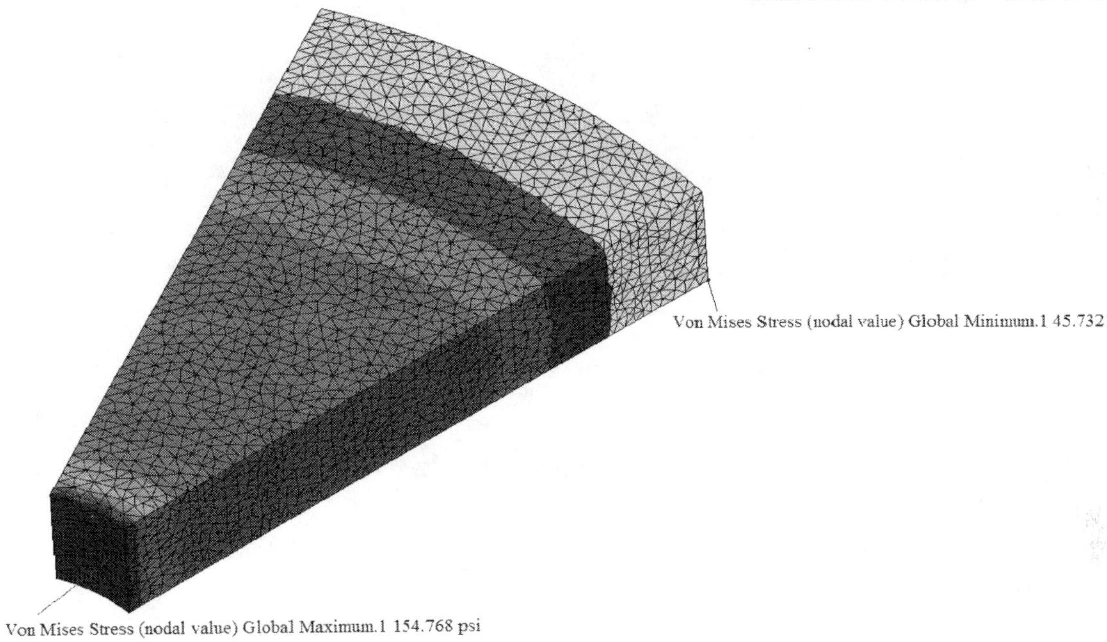


At this point, we have generated two plots. The displacement and the von Mises stress contours which can be displayed individually. However, CATIA also allows you to show both plots side by side.

First make sure that both images to be plotted are active in the tree. If not, point to the graph in the tree, right-click, select **Active**.

Click the **Image Layout** icon from the **Image Analysis** toolbar. The **Images** box, shown to the right, asks you to specify the direction along which the two plots are expected to be aligned. The outcome is side-by-side plots shown next. Here, the **Shading (SHD)** icon from the **View mode** toolbar is selected to create a different style contour.

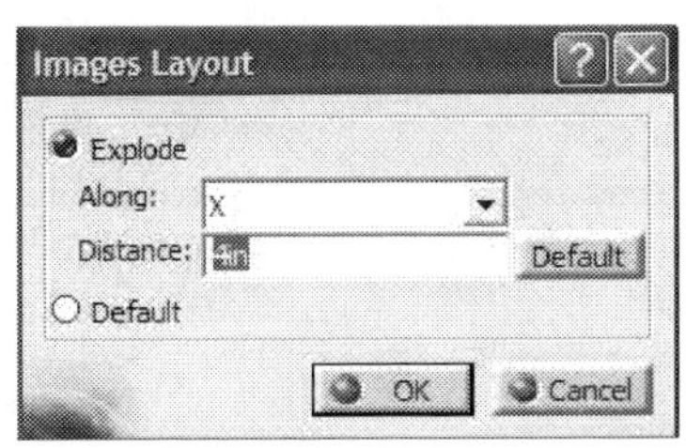

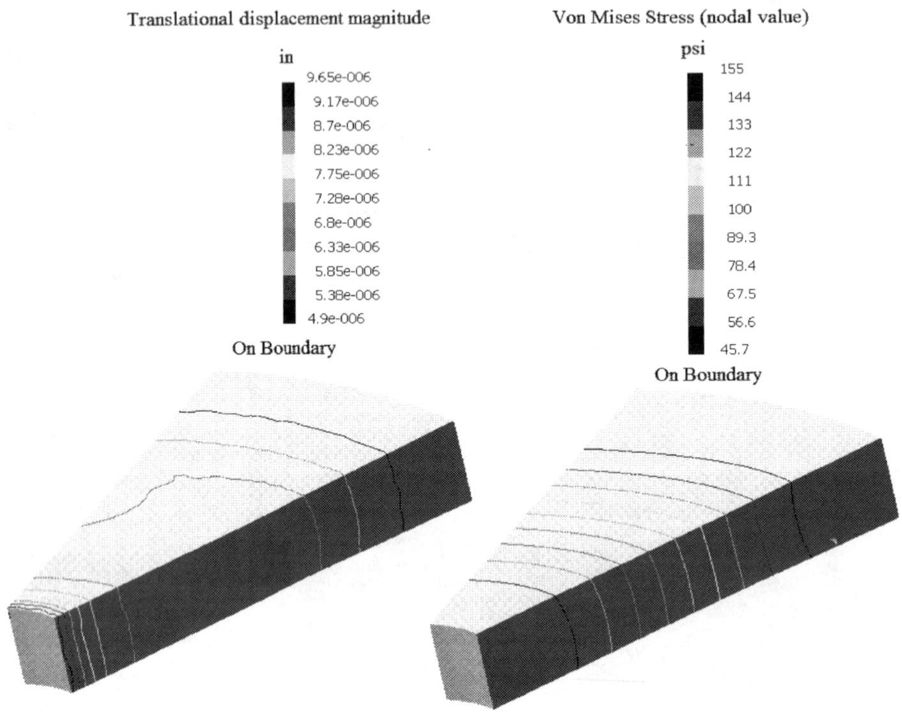


The **Cutting Plane** icon  from the **Analysis tools** toolbar 

can be used to make a cut through the part at a desired location and inspect the stresses inside of the part. The **Cut Plane** box allows you to keep the plane or remove it for display purposes. A typical cutting plane is shown below.

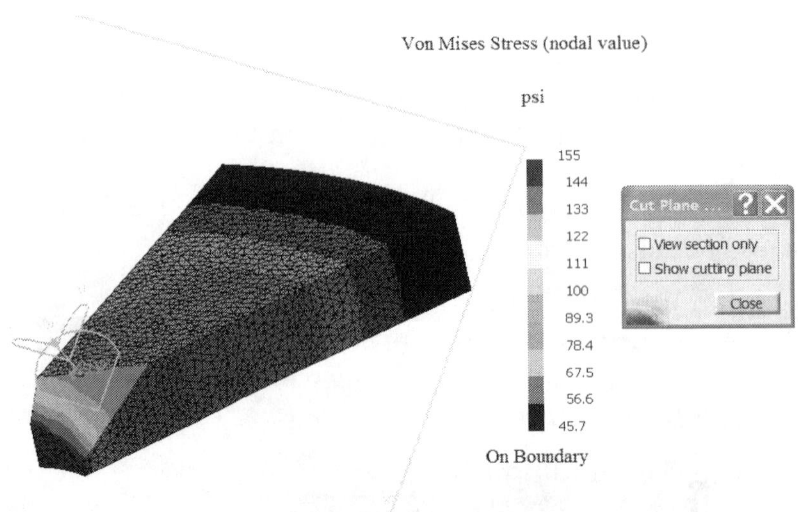


The principal stresses are postprocessed next.

From the **Image** toolbar 

, select the **Principal Stress** icon 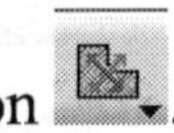.
The result is the principal stress directions in the vector form as displayed on your screen. Due to the large number of arrows, the interpretation of this plot is difficult. You can therefore switch to a different style of plotting. Double-click on the arrows on the screen to open the **Image Edition** box on the right and select **AVERAGE-ISO**.

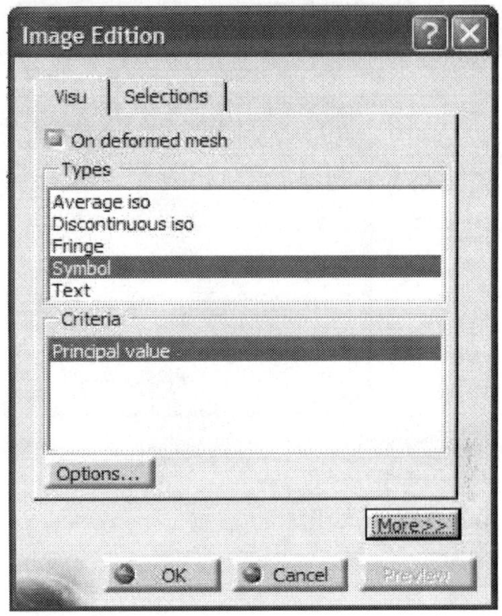


Click on the **More** button to expand the window. Choose the **Component C11**. In CATIA, C11 represents $\sigma_1$, the largest principal stress.

Keep in mind that CATIA uses C11, C22, and C33 to represent the largest, intermediate, and smallest principal stresses.

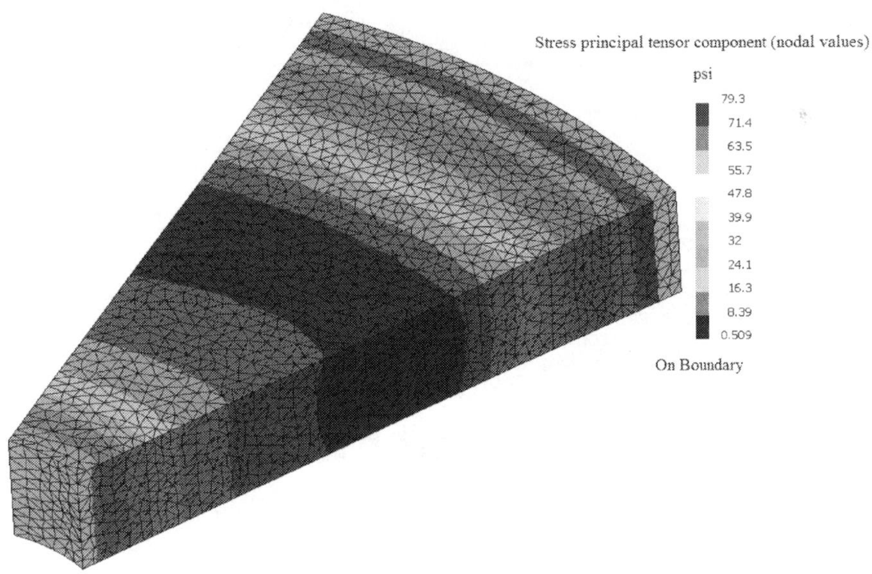

Using the icon **Basic Analysis Results**  in the **Analysis Results** toolbar , an HTML based report can be generated which summarizes the features and results of the FEA model. The first page of this report is displayed below. The location of storage of this report is controlled by the following box.

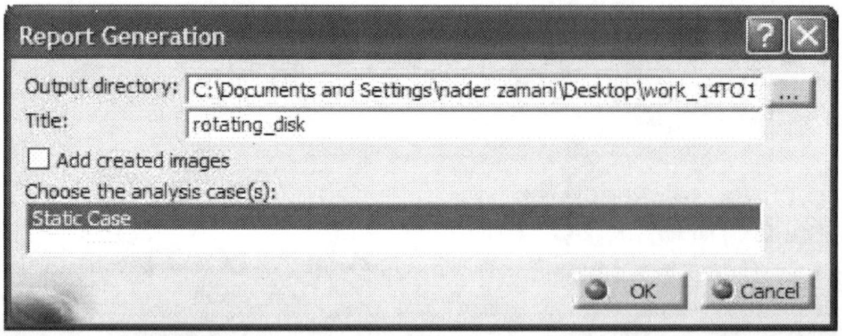


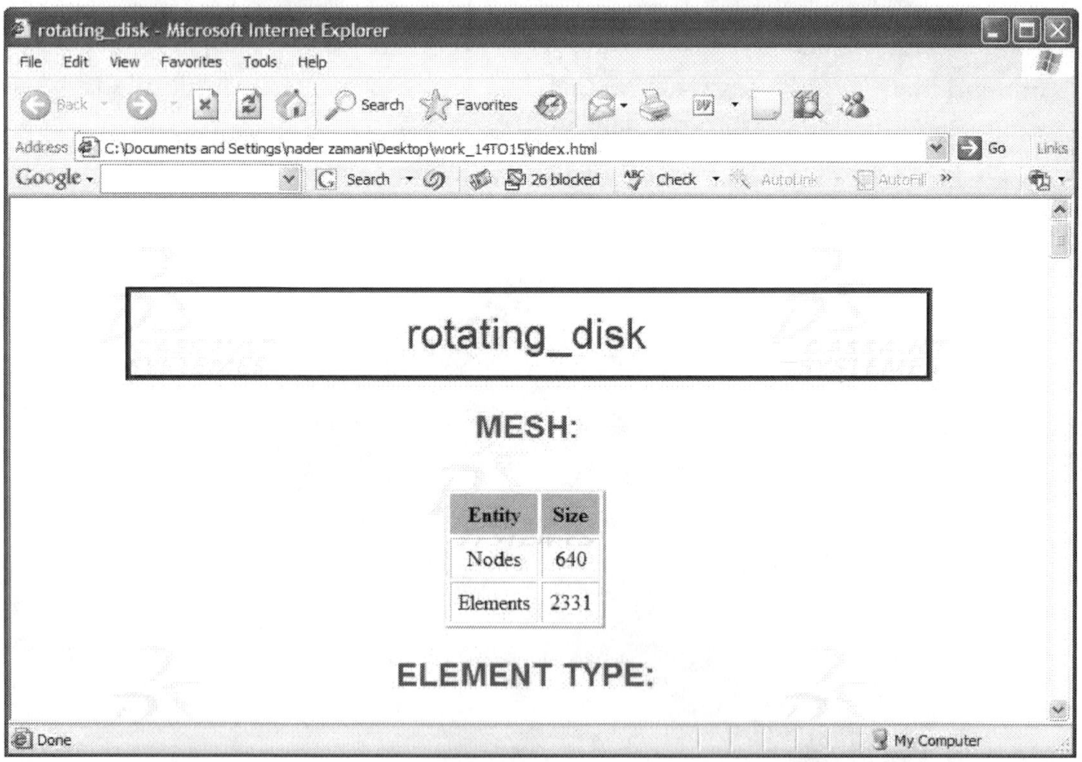


Finally, animation of the model can be achieved through the **Animate** icon  in the **Analysis Tools** toolbar and an AVI file can easily be generated.

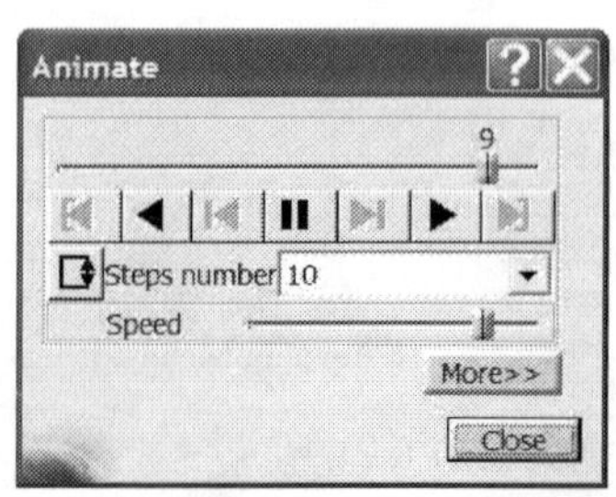

# Exercises for Chapter 4

## Problem 1: Analysis of a Rotating Flywheel

Using reasonable dimensions of your choice create a flywheel that resembles the one shown below. Make the assumption that the flywheel is made of aluminum.
Taking the smallest sector of the geometry, analyze the part when rotating at a constant angular velocity. The two possibilities for the reduction of the model are displayed below.

Contrary to the rotating_disk model in chapter 3, this flywheel has areas of stress concentration which are very much susceptible to static as well as fatigue failure.

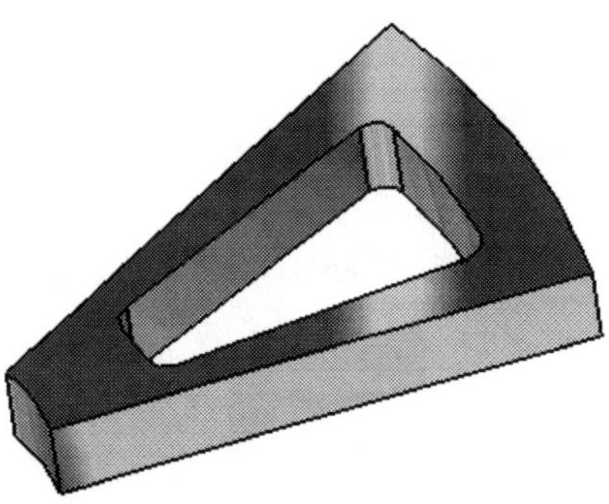

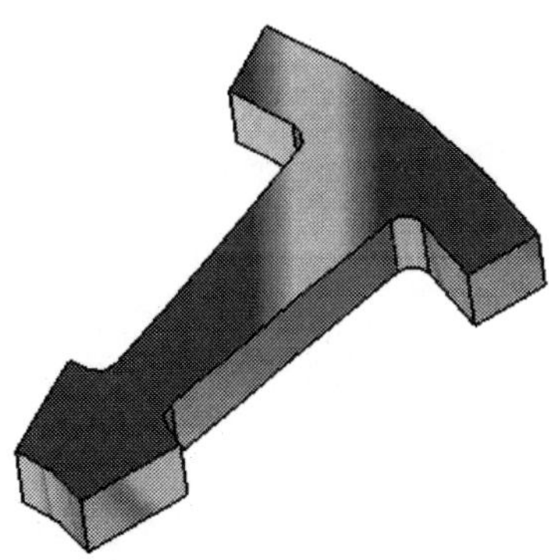

## Problem 2: a Rotating Disk with Angular Acceleration

The disk considered in this chapter was assumed to be spinning at a constant angular velocity. This is reflected in the **Rotation Force** box where the angular acceleration is assumed to be zero.

For the case that the disk is accelerating, or decelerating, the last entry in the box cannot be left as zero. Run the analysis with a reasonable acceleration and observe the displacement pattern which is no longer perfectly circular.

For the value of this angular acceleration, assume that the velocity 113 rad/s was reached in 5 seconds starting from the rest condition. Under this assumption, the acceleration becomes $\frac{113}{5} = 22.6\ \text{rad/s}^2$

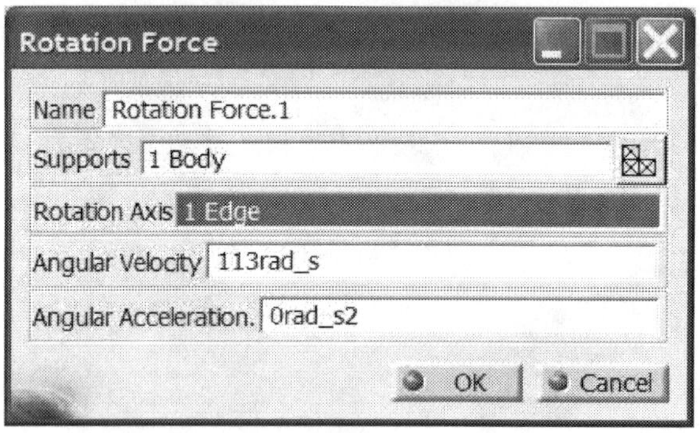


It is also worth investigating the effect of clamping the surface of the interior hole instead of leaving it unrestrained, as done in this chapter.

# Chapter 5

# Deformation of an I-beam under Self-weight

## Introduction

In this tutorial, the solid model of an I-beam is created. The only load present is self-weight which is due to the gravity effect. In CATIA, such an effect is included by providing acceleration in the proper direction.

## 1 Problem Statement

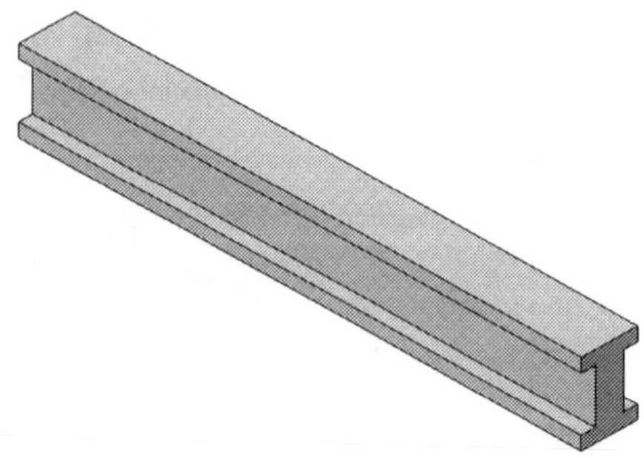

The steel I-beam, shown on the right, is clamped at one end and deflects under its own weight.
The material properties are the default values provided by CATIA. The Young's modulus is $E = 2.901E+7$ psi, Poisson ratio is $\nu = .266$, with the specific weight being $\gamma = .285$ lb/in$^3$. The total length of the beam is $L = 10$ in.

The dimensions of the cross section are such that the resulting area and moment of inertia are $A = 1\text{ in}^2$ and $I = 0.24\text{ in}^4$ respectively.

Elementary strength of materials provides a good estimate of the tip deflection and the maximum stress which exists at the clamp.
The maximum deflection can be estimated from $\delta_{tip} = \dfrac{\gamma A L^4}{8EI}$. With the parameter values supplied, an estimate of $\delta_{tip} = 5.10E-5$ in. is obtained.

The bending stress which is dominant in this problem is calculated from $\sigma = \dfrac{My}{I}$, where y is the distance to the neutral fiber of the beam and M is the moment at a given cross section. If the maximum stress is desired, under the present loading conditions, it is evaluated from $\sigma_{max} = \dfrac{\gamma A L^2 c}{2I}$. For the supplied parameter and cross sectional data, the stress is estimated as $\sigma_{max} = 44.5$ psi.
These values will be used for comparison with the FEA simulation.

In this chapter, the solid tetrahedron element will be used to perform the calculations. A more appropriate family of elements is the so called "Beam" elements which will be discussed in a later chapter. The cost of using beam elements is only a fraction of solids and the accuracy is quite comparable.
Unfortunately, there are several limitations with the beam elements as supplied in CATIA V5.

In the earlier chapters of this tutorial book, the detailed steps were provided at the expense of considerable repetition. Although the remaining tutorials are also self-contained, some of the steps which were already discussed may not be repeated.

## 2 Creation of the Part in Mechanical Design Solutions

Enter the **Part Design** workbench from the standard Windows toolbar, select **File > New**. Rename the part to be **I-beam_Self-weight**.

From the tree, select the **zx** plane and enter the **Sketcher**. In the **Sketcher**, use the icon in the **Profile** toolbar

and dimension as shown below.

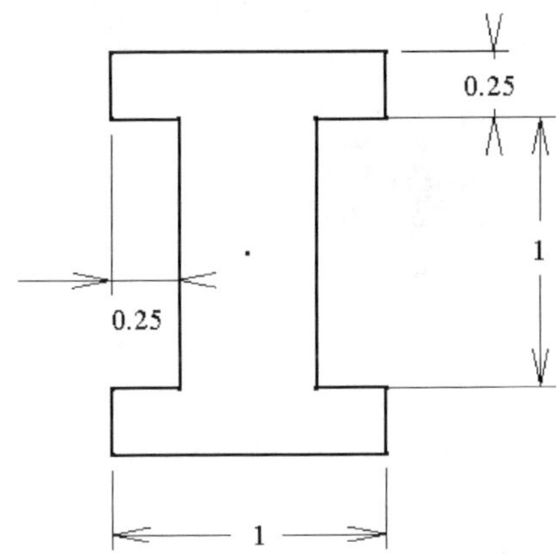


Leave the **Sketcher**.

Using the **Pad** icon, pad the sketch by 10 in. The I-beam is displayed on the screen.

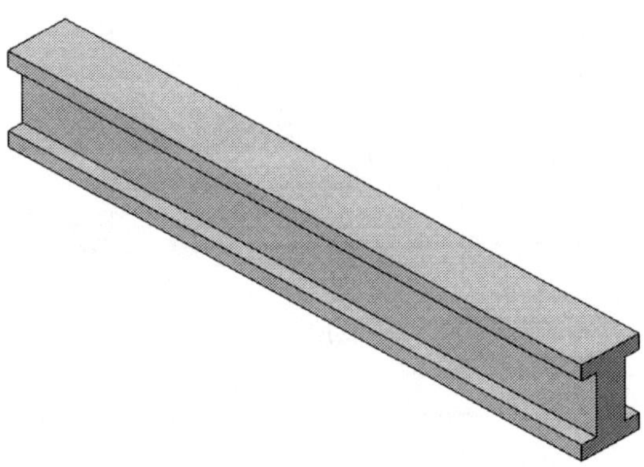

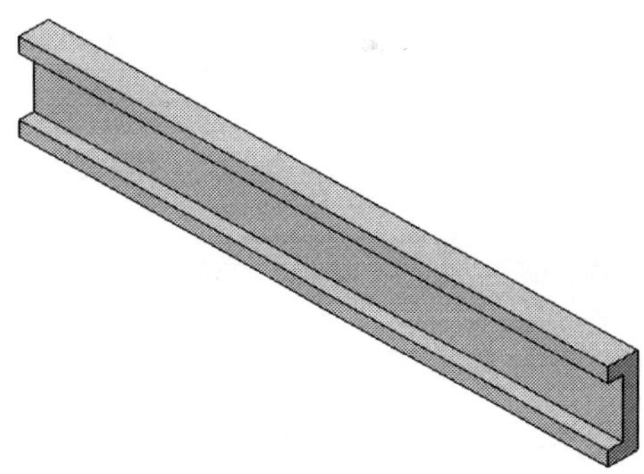

The geometry and the loading (self-weight) is such that the I-beam has a plane of symmetry, however, you will not be exploiting this feature. The entire I-beam will be modeled.

In this chapter, instead of assigning material properties in the **Generative Structural Analysis** workbench, we do it in **Part Design** with the **Apply Material** icon. The use of this icon opens the material database box on the next page.

Use the **Metal** tab on the top; select **Steel**. Use your cursor to pick the part on the screen at which time the **OK** and **Apply Material** buttons can be selected.
Close the box.
The material property is now reflected in the tree.

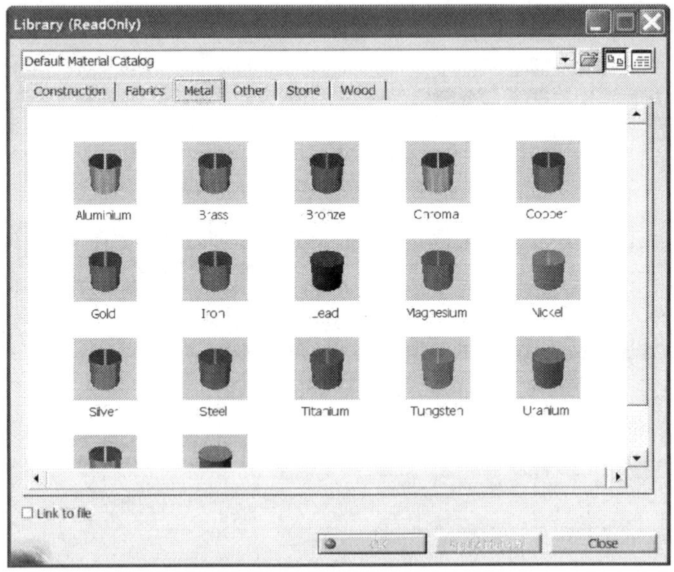


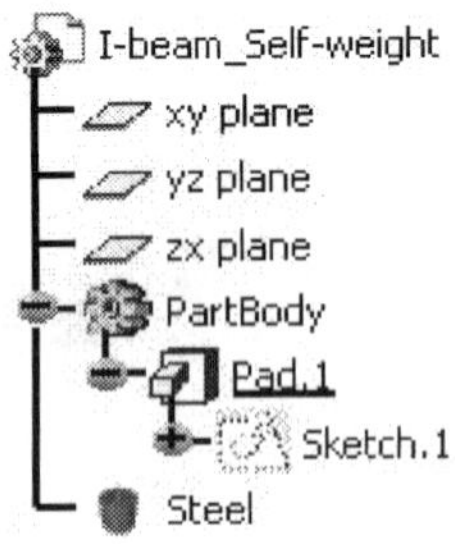


In order to inspect the values of the material properties assigned, double-click on **Steel** in the tree. It may take a few minutes before the database is searched. You will notice that the **Properties** box shown below opens. Choose the **Analysis** tab from this box, and the values will be displayed. Note that these values can be edited.
If the part is still "gray", one can change the rendering style. Select the **Shading with Material** icon  from the **View mode** toolbar 

.

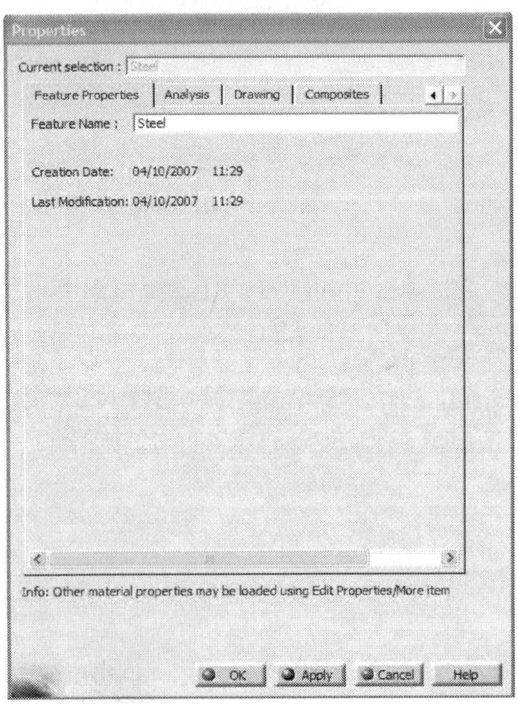


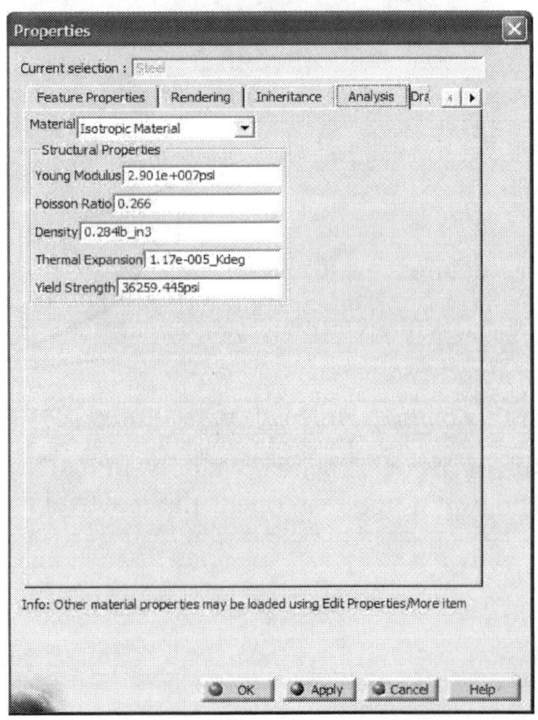

# 3 Entering the Analysis Solutions

From the standard Windows toolbar, select

**Start > Analysis & Simulation > Generative Structural Analysis** 

There is a second workbench known as the **Advanced Meshing Tools** which will be discussed later.

Upon changing workbenches, the box **New Analysis Case** becomes visible. The default choice is **Static Analysis**, which is precisely what we intend to use. Therefore, close the box by clicking on **OK**.

The tree, part, and representative element size and sag (under default values) are displayed below.

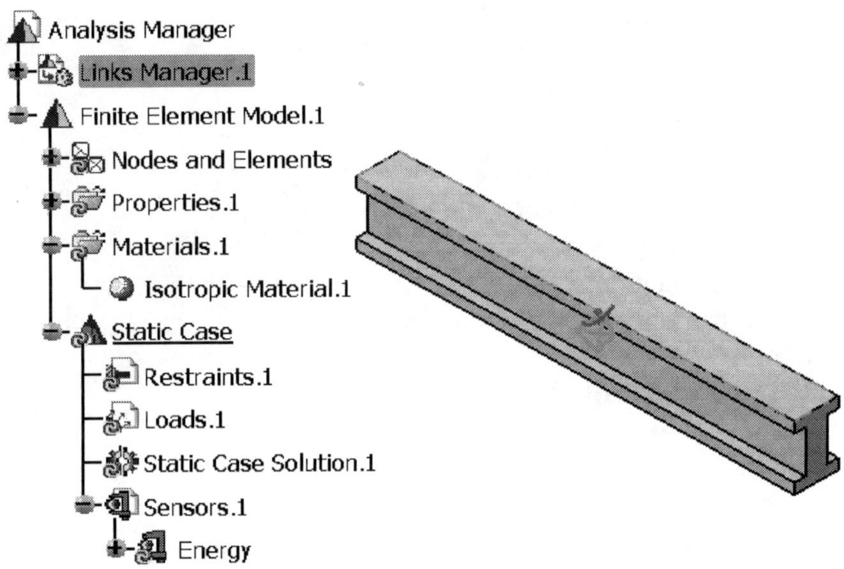


Clearly the representative element is too large and not appropriate for the I-beam. Double-click on the representative icons on the screen and change the default values to match the numbers in the box shown to the right.

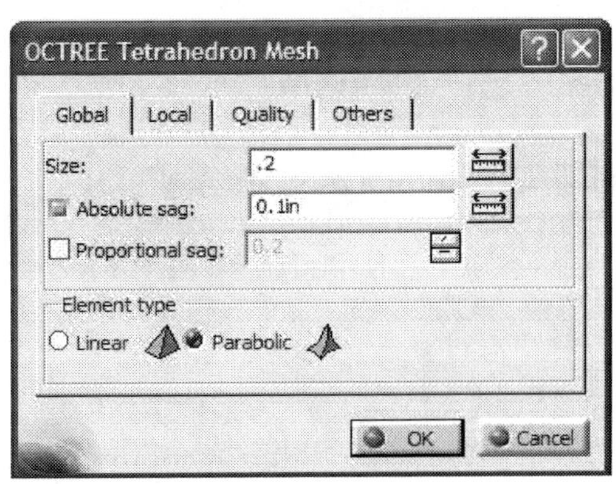


Make sure you select **Parabolic** elements for more accurate results. This is particularly important in the present problem because of thin flanges.

Point the cursor to the branch **Nodes and Elements**, right-click, and select **Mesh Visualization**. See Note #1 in Appendix I. A **Warning** box appears which can be ignored (select **OK**). For the mesh parameters used, the following mesh is displayed on the screen.

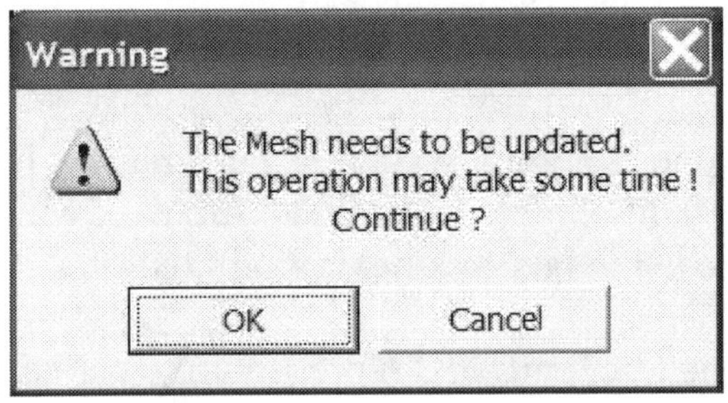


**Applying Restraints:**

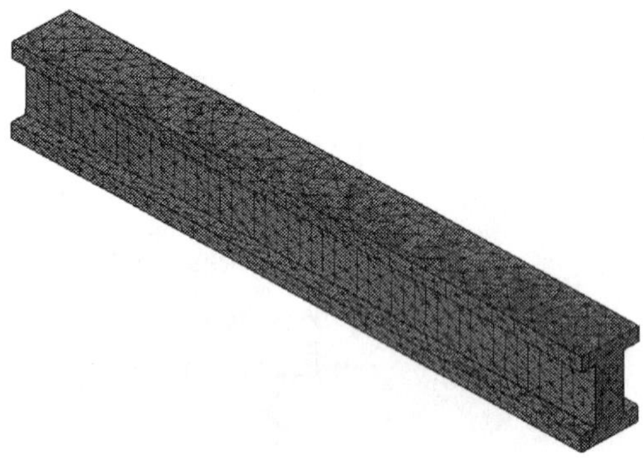

CATIA's FEA module is geometrically based. This means that the boundary conditions cannot be applied to nodes and elements. The boundary conditions can only be applied at the part level. As soon as you enter the **Generative Structural Analysis** workbench, the part is automatically hidden. Therefore, before boundary conditions are applied, the part must be brought to the **Show** mode. This can be carried out by pointing the cursor to the top of the tree, the **Links Manager.1** branch, right-click, select **Show**. At this point, the part and the mesh are superimposed as shown to the right, and you have access to the part.

If, the presence of the mesh is annoying, you can always hide it. Point the cursor to **Nodes and Elements**, right-click, **Hide**.

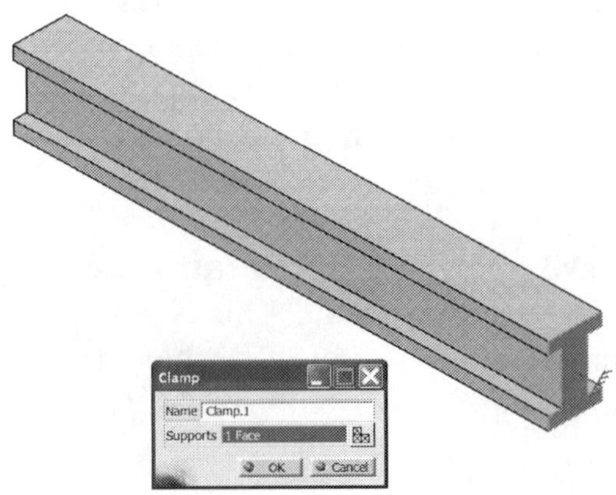


In FEA, restraints refer to applying displacement boundary conditions which is achieved through the **Restraint** toolbar 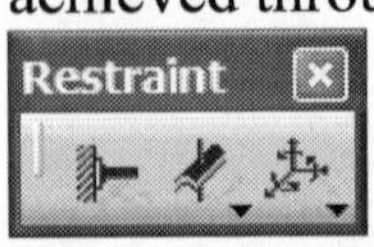

. Select the **Clamp** icon 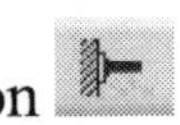 and pick the face of the I-beam that is clamped as shown to the right.

## Applying Loads:

The deflection of the I-beam is due to weight. Self-weight is a particular body force which is due to the interaction of mass and gravity. In a sense, it is the force due to acceleration "g" in the appropriate direction. This is precisely the way it is implemented in CATIA.

From the **Loads** toolbar 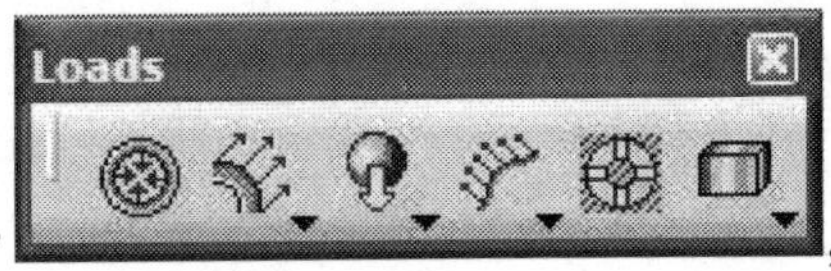

, select the **Acceleration** icon .

The **Acceleration** box shown to the right opens.

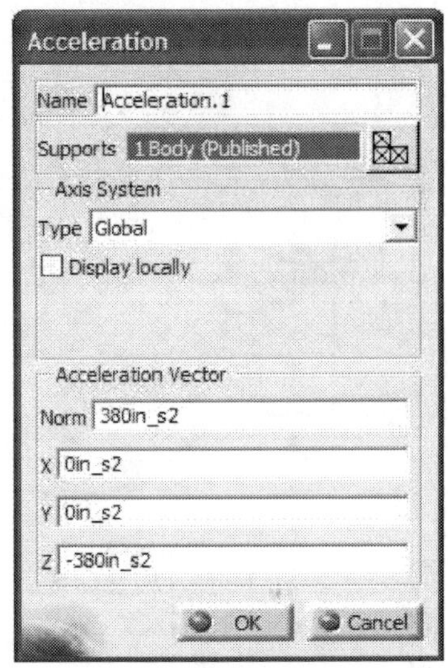


For the **Supports**, select the part from the screen. The z-component of the acceleration is -380 in/s$^2$ which is the standard value of "g" in these units.

The negative sign indicates that this gravity field is pointing in the negative z-direction. Furthermore, these are referred to the global directions.

The acceleration icons appear on the part and reflected in the tree as shown below.

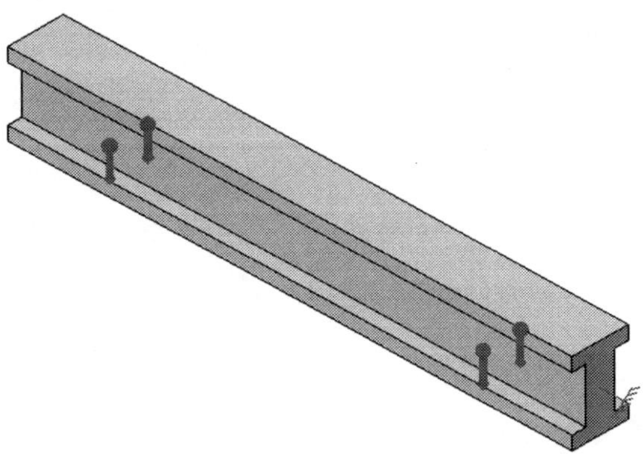

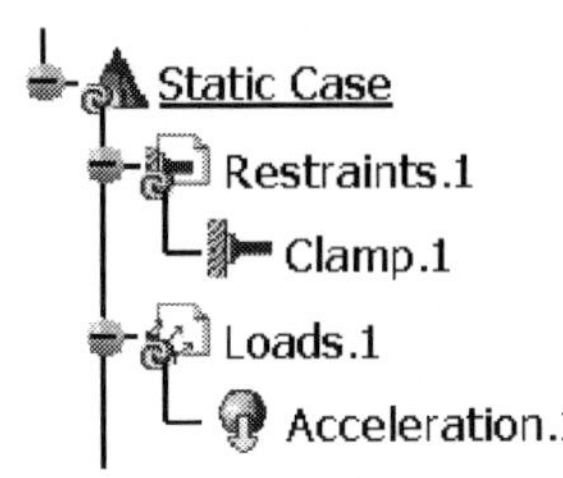


## Launching the Solver:

To run the analysis, you need to use the **Compute** toolbar 

by selecting the **Compute** icon . After a brief pause, a box appears. This box provides information on the resources needed to complete the analysis. If the estimates are all estimates zero in the listing, then there is a problem in the previous step and should be looked into. If all the numbers are zero in the box, the program may run but would not produce any useful results.

The complete tree structure upon a successful run should resemble the one displayed here.

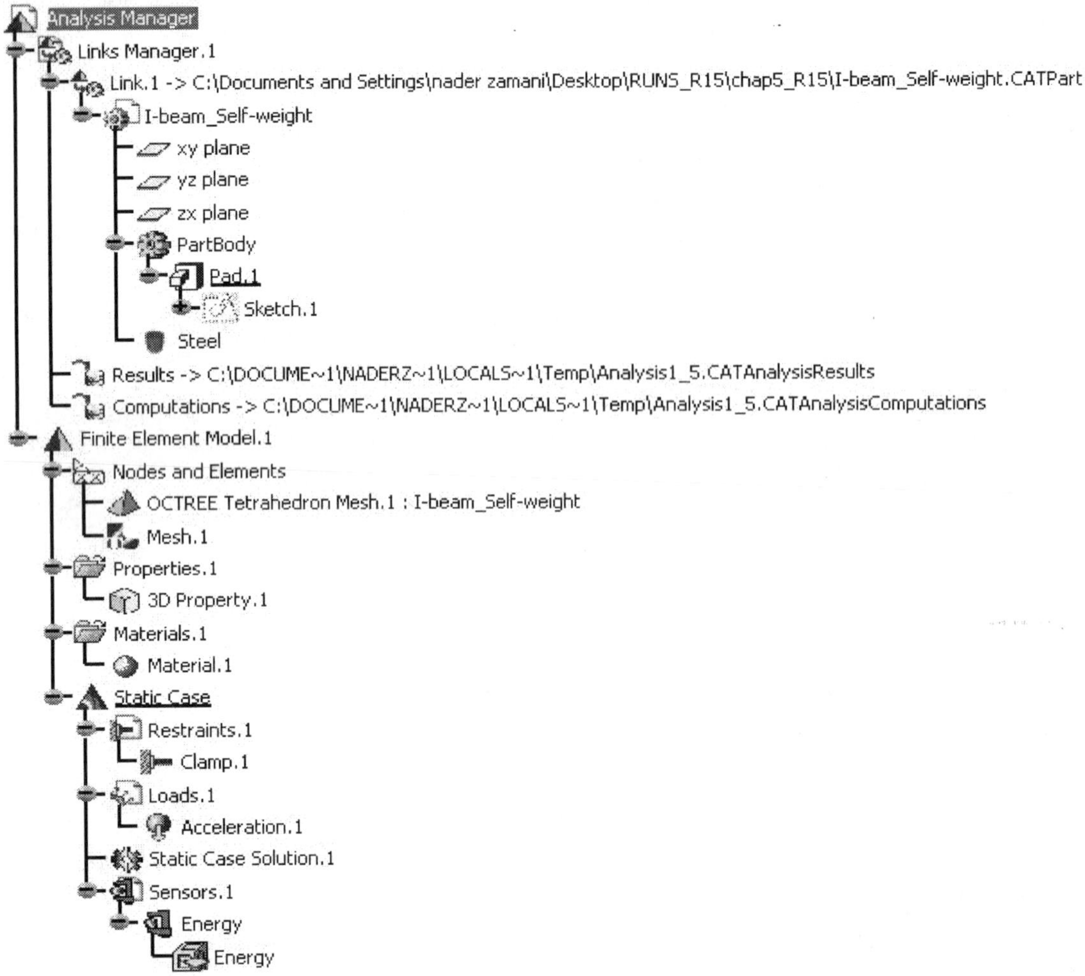


## Postprocessing:

View the deformed shape, using the **Deformation** icon in the **Image** toolbar

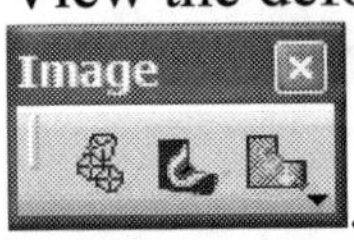


The exaggerated deformed shape is shown to the right. The scale factor can be changed with the **Deformation Scale Factor** icon.

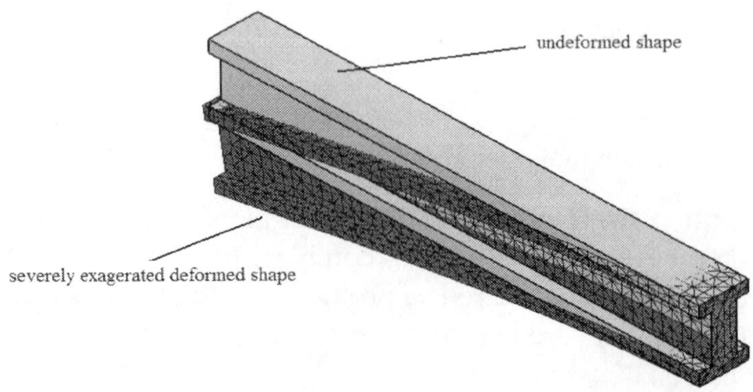

To view the contour of deflection, use the **Displacement** icon . The default plot is in terms of arrows which is not very useful. In order to change this, position the cursor on the arrow field and double-click. In the **Image Edition** box that opens select **AVERAGE-ISO** and press **OK**. The following plot is displayed. To get a shaded contour, you may need to change the render style as described in the previous chapters.

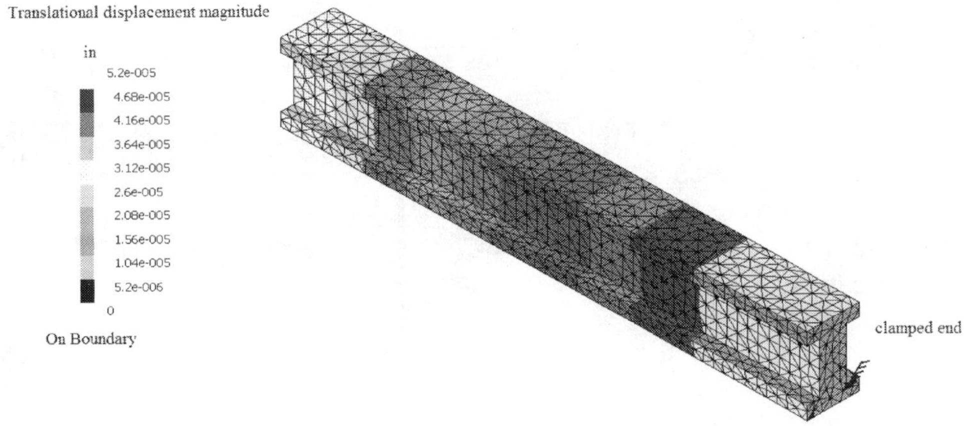


Note that the maximum deflection of 5.2E-5 in. is in excellent agreement with strength of materials value obtained in the beginning of the chapter.
The next step in the postprocessing is to plot the contours of the von Mises stress using the **von Mises Stress** icon  in the **Image** toolbar.
The von Mises stress contour is displayed to the below.

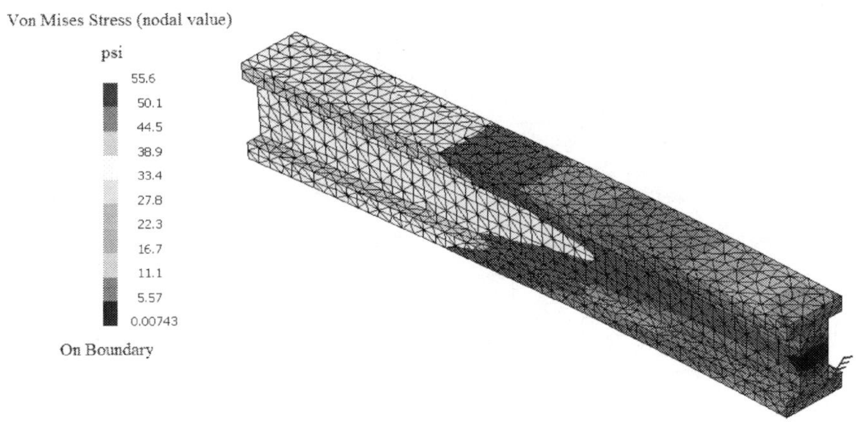

From the toolbar **Groups** 

, select the **Groups by Neighborhood** toolbar 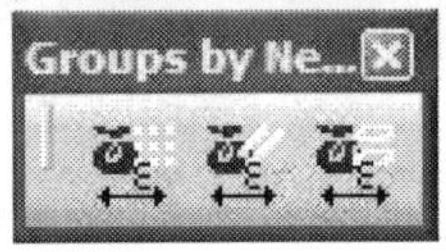

. From this toolbar, select the **Surface Group by Neighborhood** icon . This action leads to the dialogue box shown next.

For the **Supports**, select the face of the I-Beam that was clamped. For the tolerance use 0.3. What this operation does is to create a group of elements which are within 0.3 in of the selected face. The stresses can be plotted for such elements if desired.
In order to achieve this, double-click on the contour levels on the screen to open the image edition box. Next use the **Selections** tab as shown below. Here, you have the choice of selecting different items. Choose **Surface Group by Neighborhood.1**, and use the button . The contour below displays the von Mises stress at the desired section.

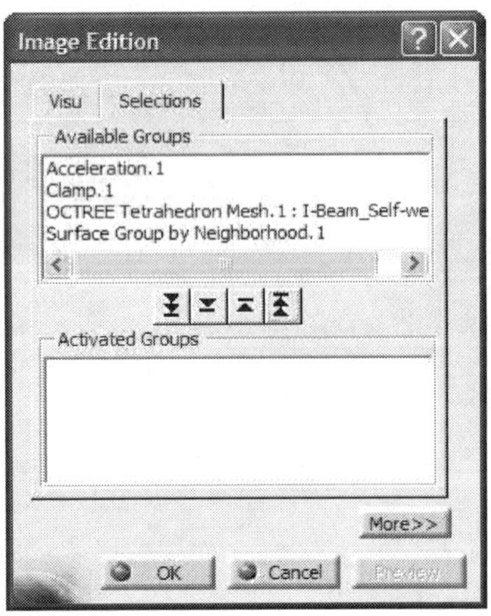

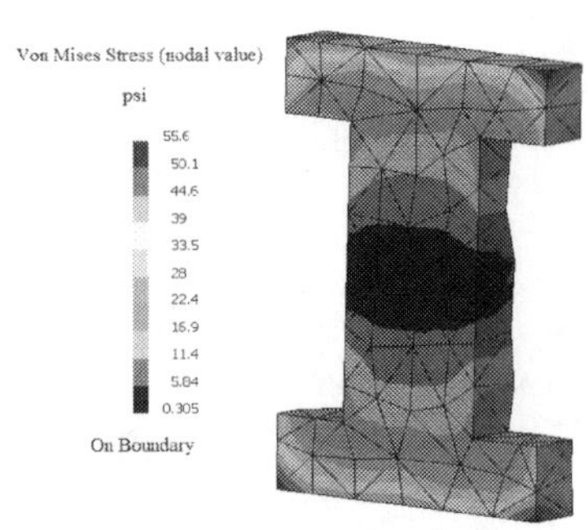

The **Cutting Plane** icon  from the **Analysis tools** toolbar

can be used to make a cut through the part at a desired location and inspect the stresses inside of the part. The **Cut Plane** box allows you to keep the plane or remove it for display purposes. A typical cutting plane is shown next.

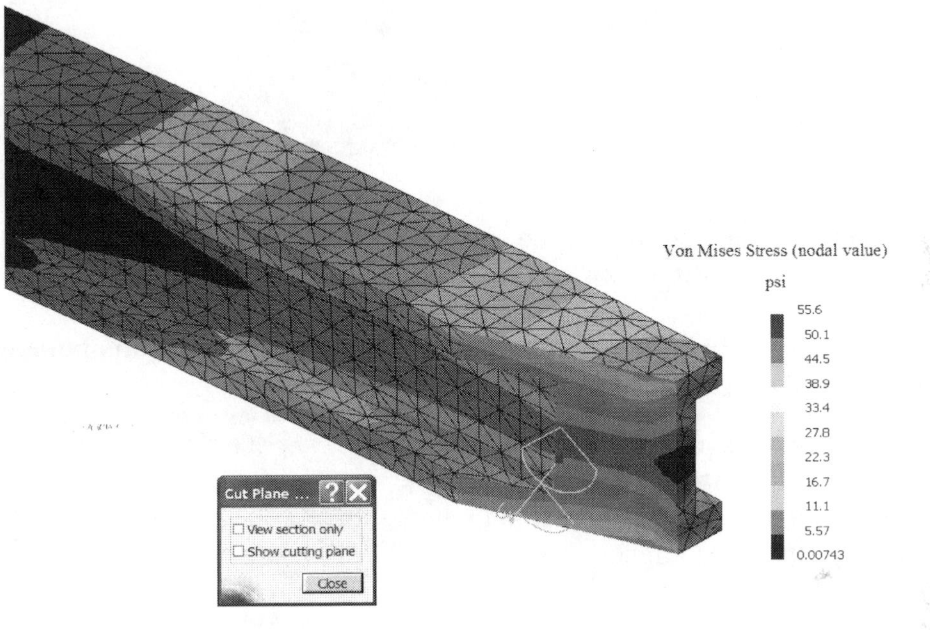


From the **Image** toolbar 

, select the **Principal Stress** icon 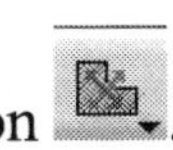. Double-click on the arrows on the screen which causes the **Image Edition**, box to open. Select the **More** button and under **Component** select **C11**. In CATIA, C11 represents the maximum principal stress. Also, from the **Selections** tab choose **Surface Group by Neighborhood.1**.

The result is the contour of maximum principal stress at the wall as displayed below.

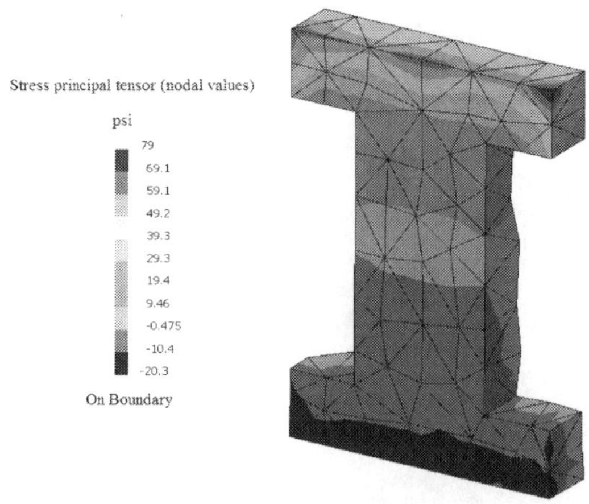


The final task is to tile the contours of the von Mises stress and the maximum principal stress side by side in the x-direction.

First make sure that both images to be plotted are active in the tree, If not, point to the graph in the tree, right-click, select **Active**.

Click the **Image Layout** icon  from the **Image Analysis** toolbar. The **Images** box, shown to the right, asks you to specify the direction along which the two plots are expected to be aligned. The outcome is side-by-side plots shown below.

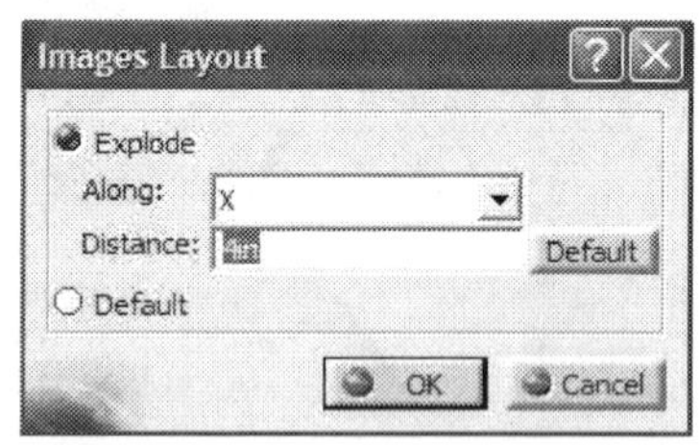


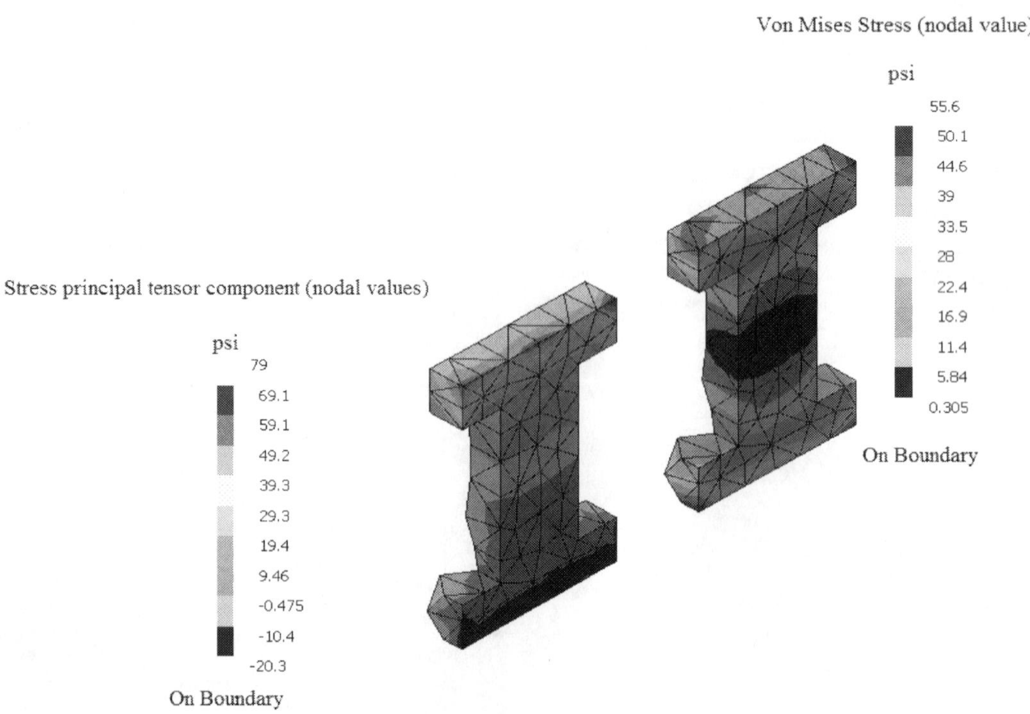

# Exercises for Chapter 5

## Problem 1: Analysis of a Simply Supported I-beam under Self-weight.

The analysis of the I-beam in this chapter is to be repeated with the ends being simply supported. This is achieved by clamping the bottom two edges as shown in the figure below. The deformed shape is also displayed.

Partial Answer:

Elementary strength of materials provides an estimate of the maximum deflection that occurs at the mid-span. This value is computed from $\delta_{max} = \dfrac{5\gamma AL^4}{384EI}$.

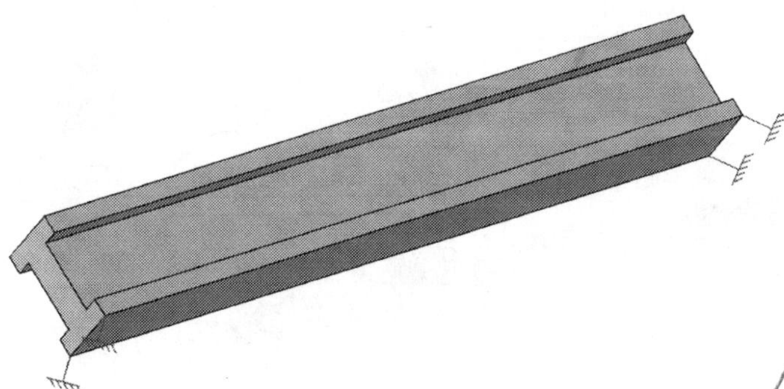

## Problem 2: Modeling "Old Car Radio" Antenna

In the old days, an automobile radio antenna was installed externally in front of the car, on the passenger side. It was a telescopic mechanism made of several hollow tubes as shown below. When the car was accelerating, the cantilever antenna would deflect due to two effects. The wind drag force was the primary culprit with the car acceleration being responsible for the inertial force.

Assuming that the car is driven in vacuum (say on the moon), the drag effect can be ignored. Use reasonable dimensions for the antenna, and a very large acceleration (say a Ferrari), determine the maximum deflection of the antenna and the stresses at the root.

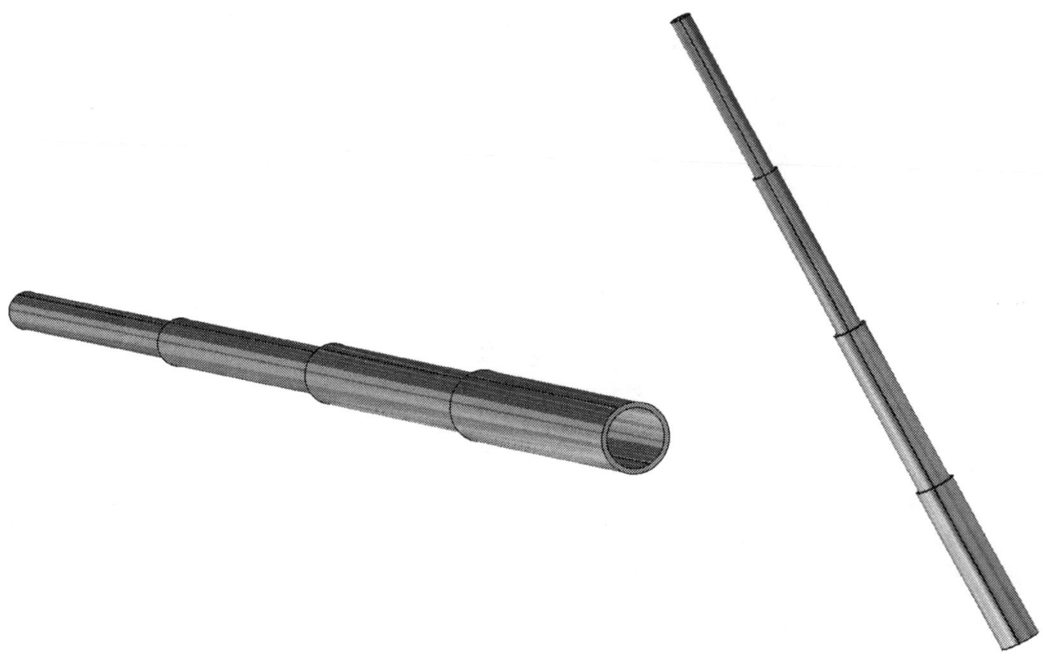

# Chapter 6

# C-clamp Deformed with Enforced Displacement

## Introduction

In this tutorial you will use the “Enforced Displacement” boundary condition in CATIA to analyze the deformation of a C-clamp. Solid elements are employed to mesh the geometry. The sensor icon is used to estimate the force required to cause the deformation.

## 1 Problem Statement

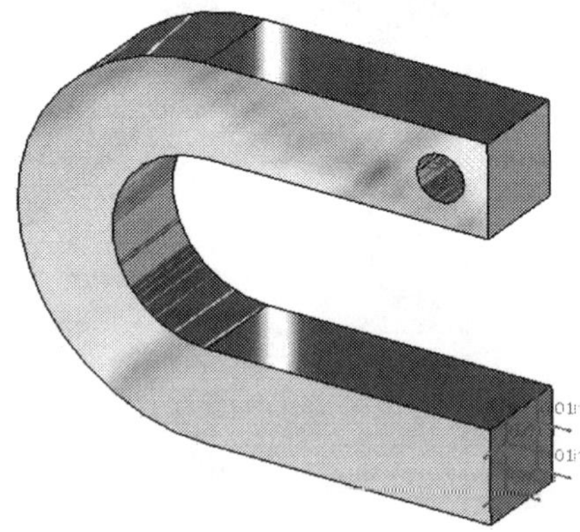

The C-clamp, shown on the right, is made of aluminum with Young’s modulus of 1.015E+7 psi and Poisson ratio 0.346. The interior surface of the top hole is rigidly fixed; whereas a downward displacement of 0.01 in. is applied to the bottom face as displayed.

You will use CATIA to predict the stresses and the deformation in the part. Up until now, the enforced displacements were all zero, but in this example, you will learn how to apply nonzero values.

## 2 Creation of the Part in Mechanical Design Solutions

Enter the **Part Design** workbench from the standard Windows toolbar, select **File > New**. See Note #1 in Appendix I. Rename the part to be **C_Clamp**.

From the tree, select the **zx** plane and enter the **Sketcher**. In the **Sketcher**, use the icon in the **Profile** toolbar

and dimension as shown below.

Leave the **Sketcher**.

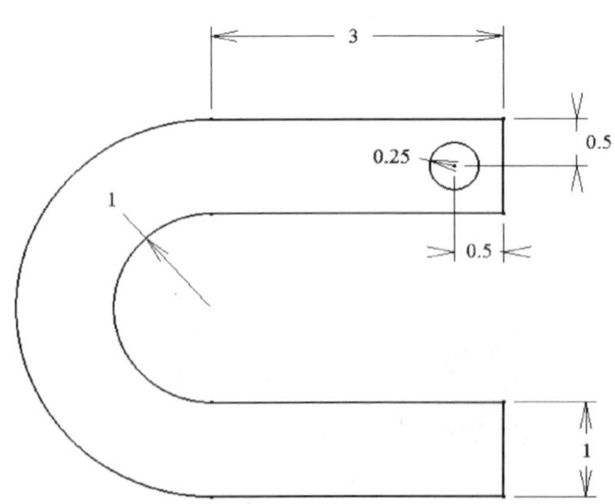


Using the **Pad** icon, pad the sketch by 1 in. The C_Clamp is displayed on the screen.

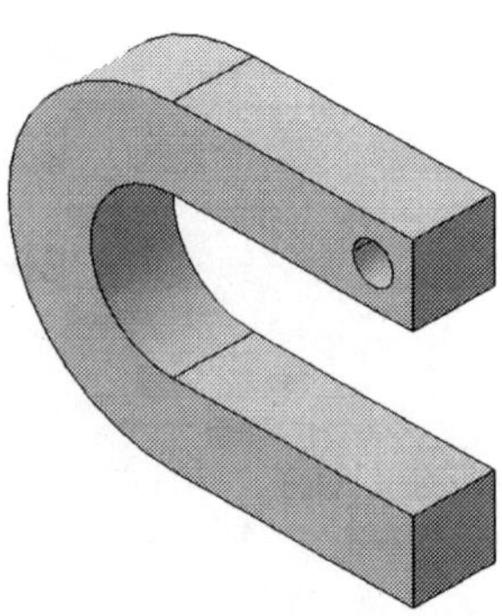

Note that the problem under consideration has a plane of symmetry, but you will not be exploiting that.

Use the **Apply Material** icon  to assign aluminum properties to the C-clamp. Select the **Analysis** tab of the aluminum properties box to confirm the values.

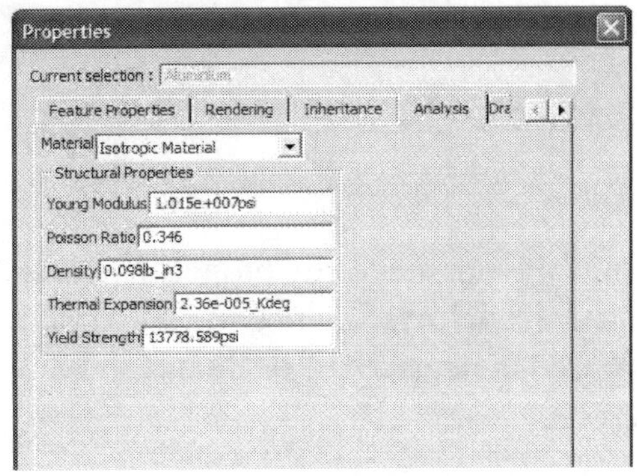


Although an approximate value for the yield strength of a typical aluminum is stated in the box, it is only for information purposes and never used in calculations.

If the part stays "gray", one can change the rendering style from the **View mode** toolbar

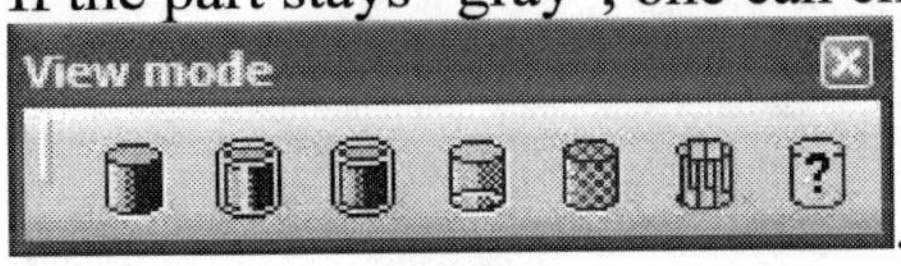


. Select the **Shading with Material** icon .

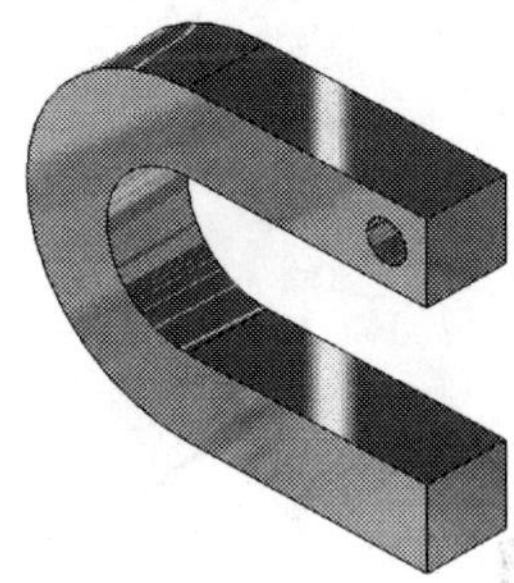

The shiny metal part will be displayed on the screen as shown to the right.

## 3 Entering the Analysis Solutions

From the standard Windows toolbar, select

**Start > Analysis & Simulation > Generative Structural Analysis** 
There is a second workbench known as the **Advanced Meshing Tools** which will be discussed later.

Upon changing workbenches, the box **New Analysis Case** becomes visible. The default choice is **Static Analysis** which is precisely what we intend to use. Therefore, close the box by clicking on **OK**.
The tree, part, and representative element size and sag (under default values) are displayed on the right.

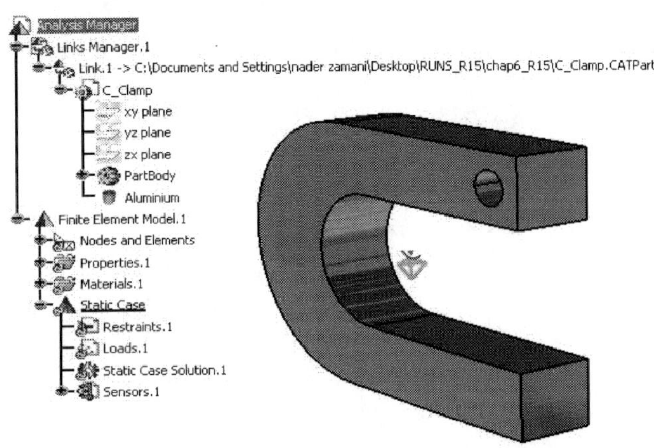

Keep the element size and sag at their default values, however, use parabolic elements instead. Remember, this is done by double-clicking on the representative icons on the screen and selecting **Parabolic** elements.

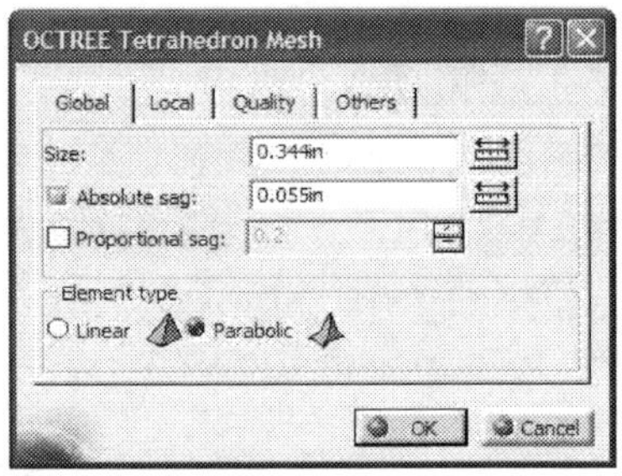


Point the cursor to the branch **Nodes and Elements**, right-click and select **Mesh Visualization**. See note #2 in Appendix I. A **Warning** box appears which can be ignored, select **OK**. For the mesh parameters used, the following mesh is displayed on the screen.

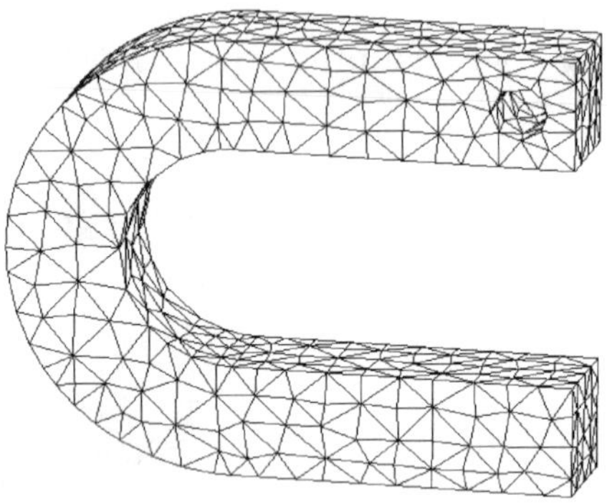

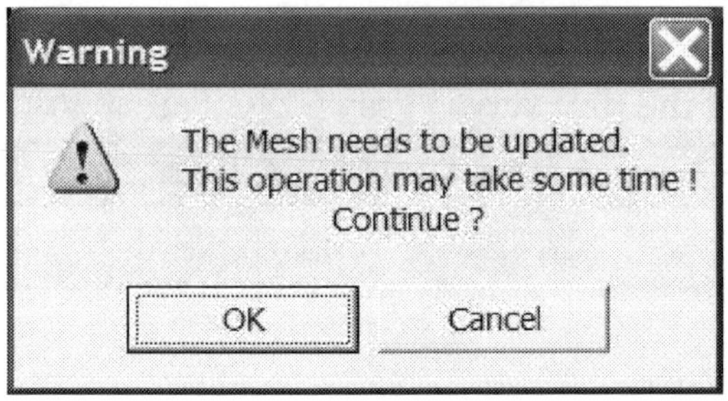


Point the cursor to the mesh, right-click, select **Mesh Object**, followed by **Definition** as shown below on the right.

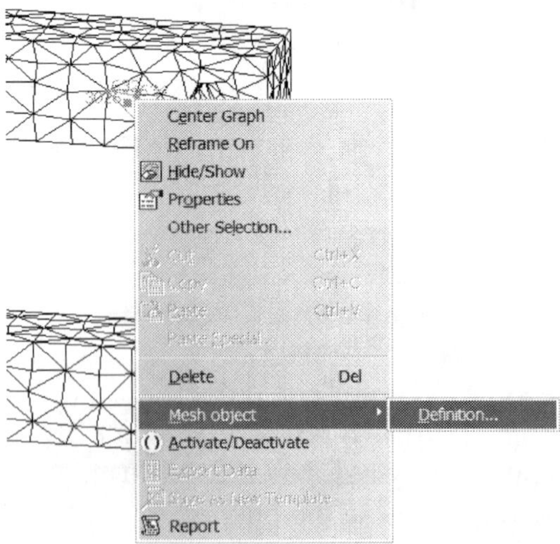


This causes the **Image edition** box to open where you can change the **Shrink Coefficient**. If you use a shrink factor of .80, the mesh will appear as the one shown below.

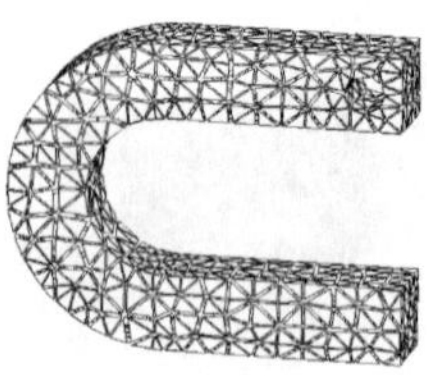

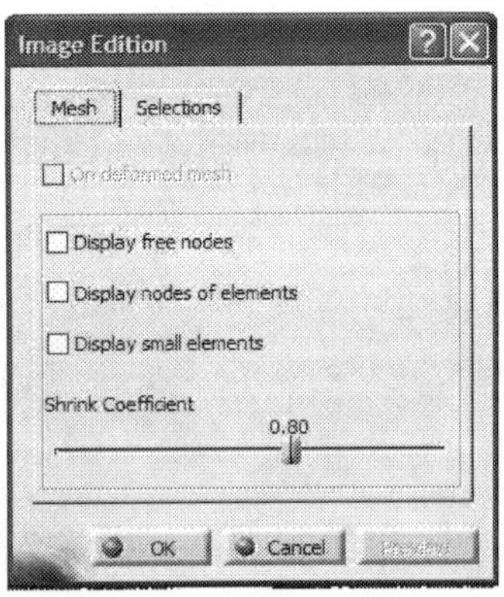

If instead of **Mesh object**, you select **Report**, a summary of your mesh in the HTML format is created as shown below.

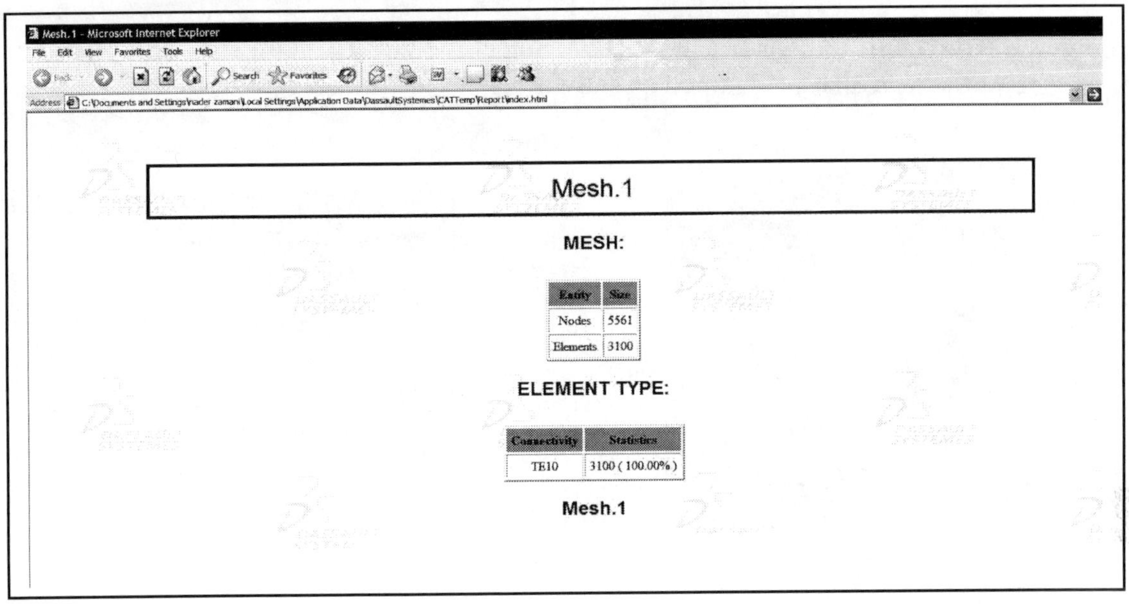


## Applying Restraints:

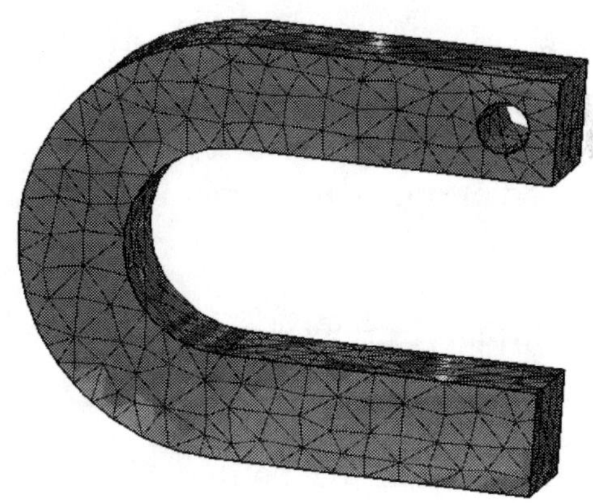

CATIA's FEA module is geometrically based. This means that the boundary conditions cannot be applied to nodes and elements. The boundary conditions can only be applied at the part level. As soon as you enter the **Generative Structural Analysis** workbench, the part is automatically hidden. Therefore, before boundary conditions are applied, the part must be brought to the **Show** mode. This can be carried out by pointing the cursor to the top of the tree, the **Links Manager.1** branch, right-click, select **Show**. At this point, the part and the mesh are superimposed as shown above and you have access to the part.

If, the presence of the mesh is annoying, you can always hide it. Point the cursor to **Nodes and Elements**, right-click, and **Hide**.

Instead of hiding the mesh as indicated above, one can point the cursor to the **Mesh.1** item in the tree, right-click, and select **Activate/Deactivate**. The result is that the mesh is hidden and the part is displayed.

In FEA, restraints refer to applying displacement boundary conditions which is achieved through the **Restraint** toolbar . Select the **Clamp** icon  and pick the inside face of the hole that is clamped as shown below.

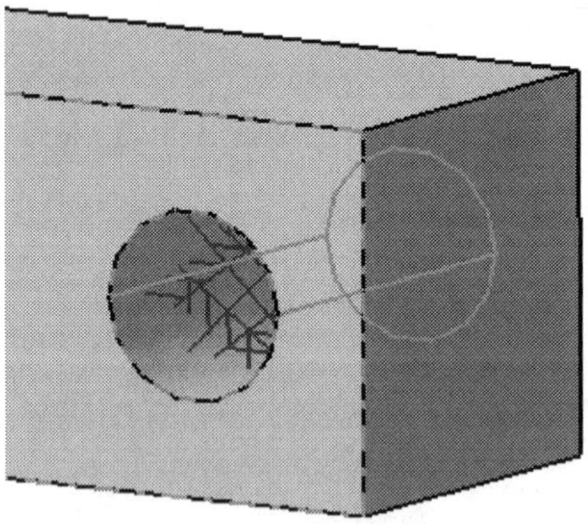

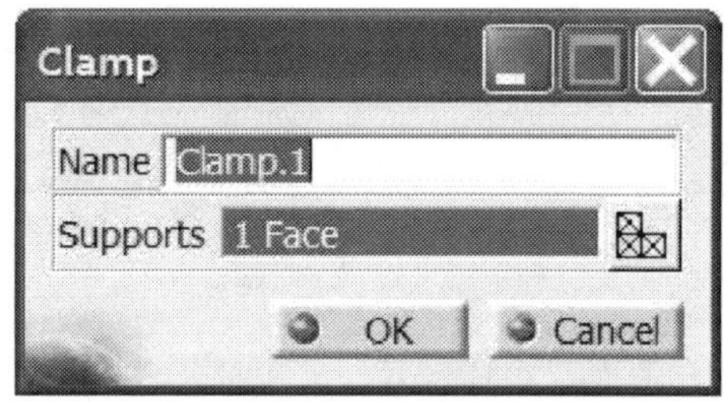


**Applying the Enforced Displacement:**

This involves a two stage process. Use **User-defined Restraint** icon 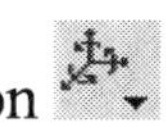 and pick the bottom edge of the C-Clamp as shown.

Make sure that only **Restrain Translation 3** is checked. Whether the last three boxes are checked or not, is irrelevant in this problem.

The current restraints are clearly not what you want. At this point, you have specified zero displacement for the bottom edge whereas it should be -0.01 in.

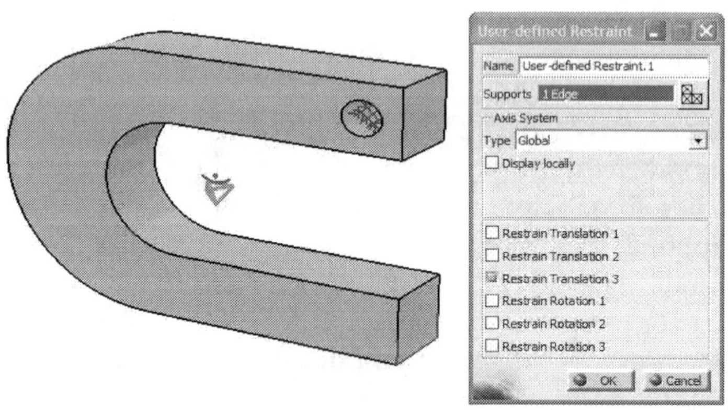


In order to modify this, use the **Enforced Displacement** icon  from the **Loads** toolbar 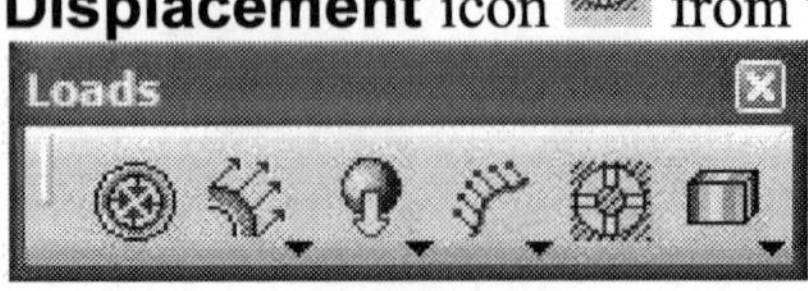.

This opens the box on the right.

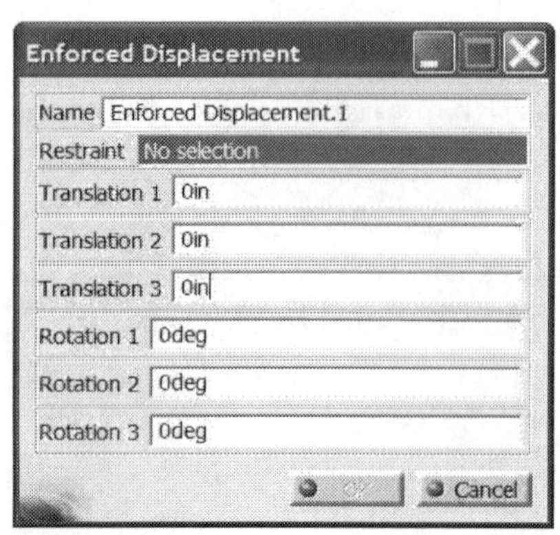

Use the cursor to pick the restraint on the bottom edge. The **Enforced Displacement** box reflects this selection as indicated below. The only restraint that is not "dimmed" and can be changed is **Translation 3**. In this box, type -0.01.
The tree at this point is also shown.

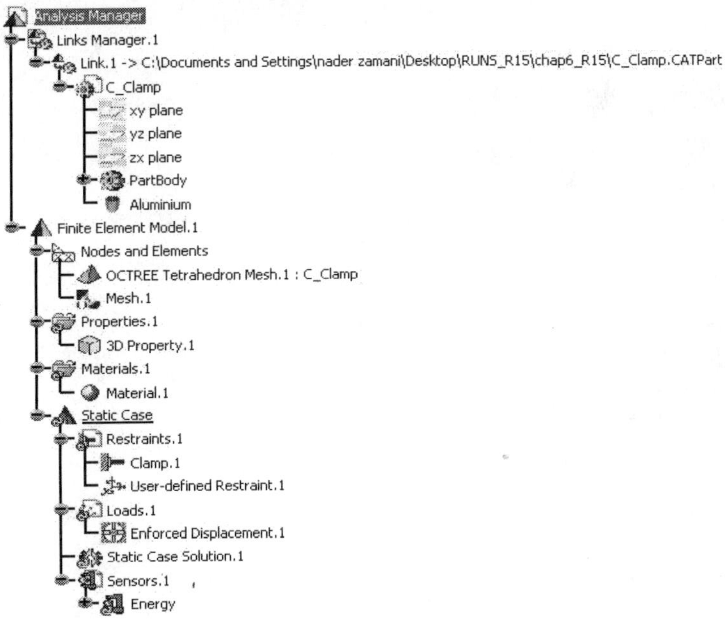

**Launching the Solver:**

To run the analysis, you need to use the **Compute** toolbar  by selecting the **Compute** icon . After a brief pause, a box appears. This box provides information on the resources needed to complete the analysis. If the estimates are all zero in the listing, then there is a problem in the previous step and should be looked into. If all numbers as zero in this box, although the program may run, it will not produce any useful results.

**Postprocessing:**

View the deformed shape, using the **Deformation** icon  in the **Image** toolbar .

The exaggerated deformed shape is shown to the right. The scale factor can be changed with the **Deformation Scale Factor** icon .

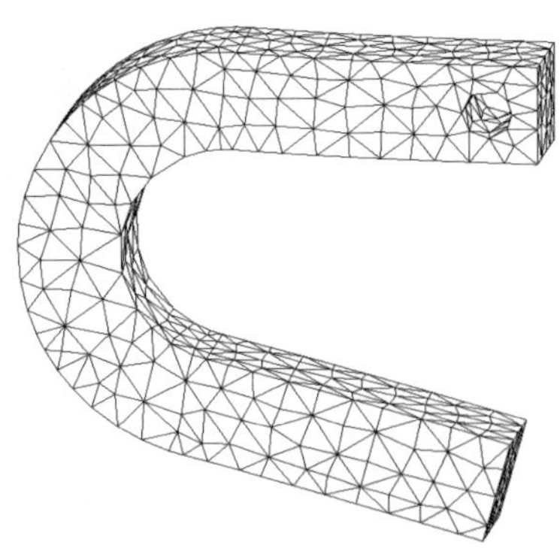

To view the contour of deflection, use the **Displacement** icon. The default plot is in terms of arrows which is not very useful. In order to change this, position the cursor on the arrow field and double-click. In the **Image Edition** box that opens select **AVERAGE-ISO** and press **OK**. You can change the render style by using **Shading with Material** icon in the

**View mode** toolbar 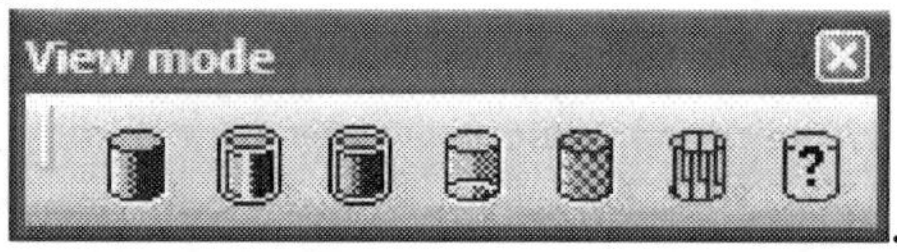.



The following plot is displayed. (Note: The color map has been changed; otherwise everything looks dark.)

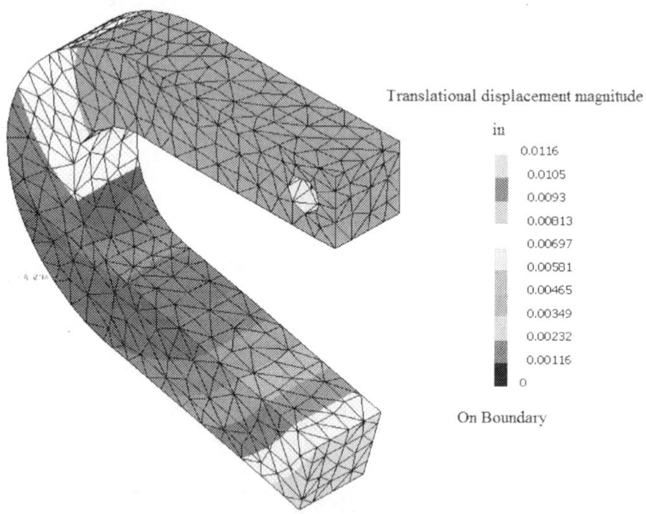


The next step in the postprocessing is to plot the contours of the von Mises stress using the **von Mises Stress** icon in the **Image** toolbar. The von Mises stress is displayed to the below.

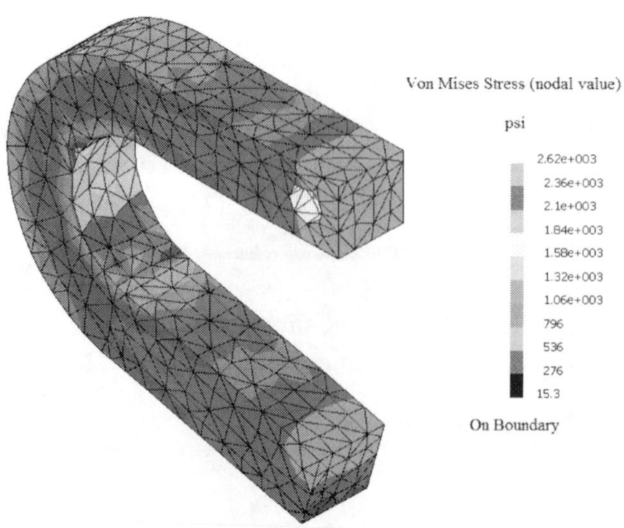

From the toolbar **Groups** 

, select the icon **Surface Group by Neighborhood**. This action leads to the dialogue box shown next.

For the **Supports**, select the curved face of the hole that was clamped. For the tolerance use 0.3. What this process does is to create a group of elements which are within 0.3 in of the selected face. The stresses can be plotted for such elements if desired.
In order to achieve this, double-click on the contour levels on the screen to open the image edition box. Next use the selections tab as shown below. Here, you have the choice of selecting different items. Select **Surface Group by Neighborhood.1**, and use the button. The contour below displays the von Mises stress at the desired section.

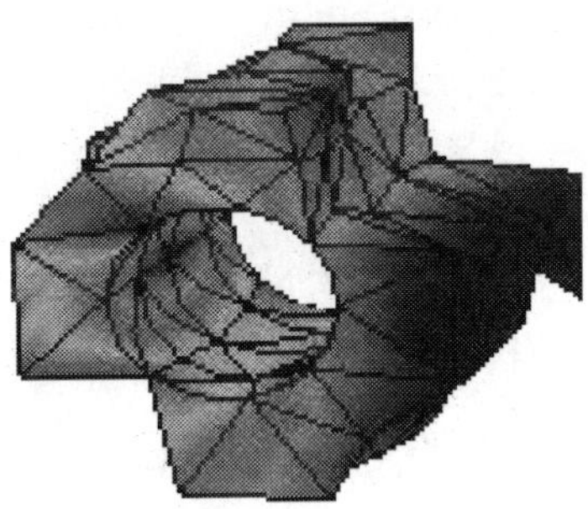

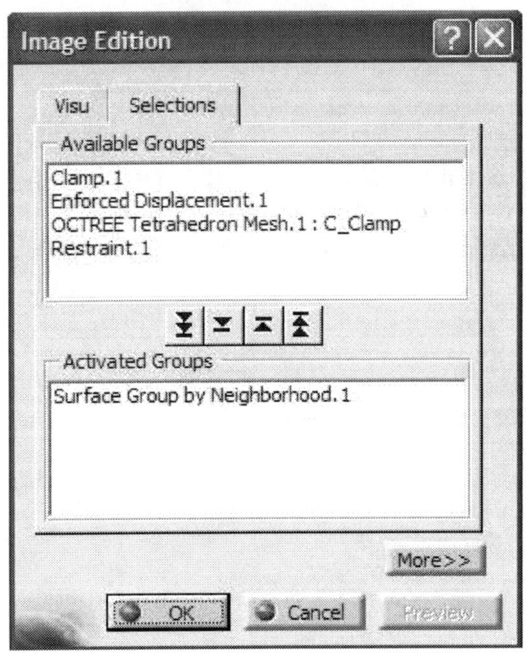


The **Cutting Plane** icon from the **Analysis tools** toolbar

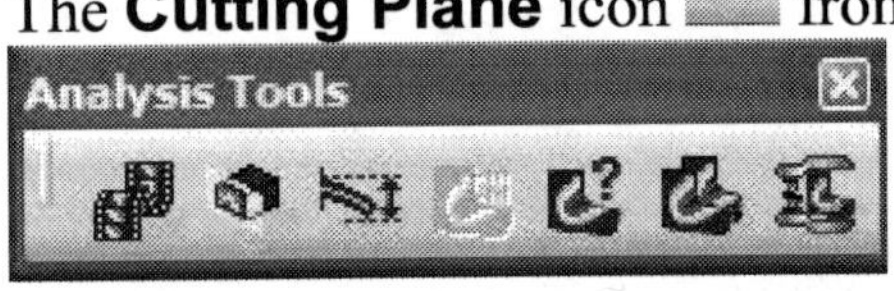


can be used to make a cut through the part at a desired location and inspect the stresses inside of the part. The **Cut Plane** box allows you to keep the plane or remove it for display purposes. A typical cutting plane is shown below.

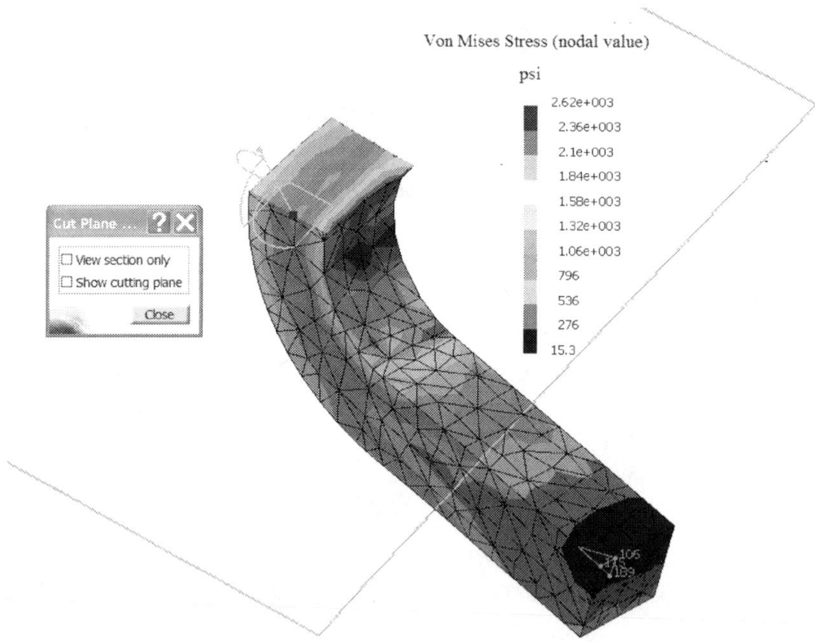


Now we describe the process which allows you to find the force necessary to cause the edge enforced displacement of 0.01 in.

This is achieved by defining a sensor. The sensor definitions are located in the bottom section of the tree as shown on the right.
Point the cursor to the sensor branch in the tree, and right-click.

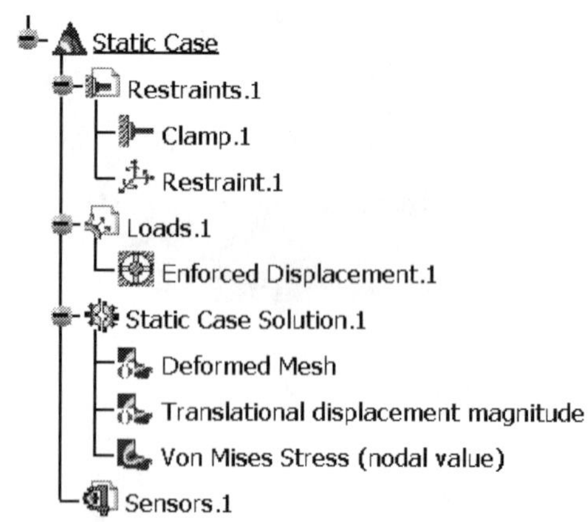


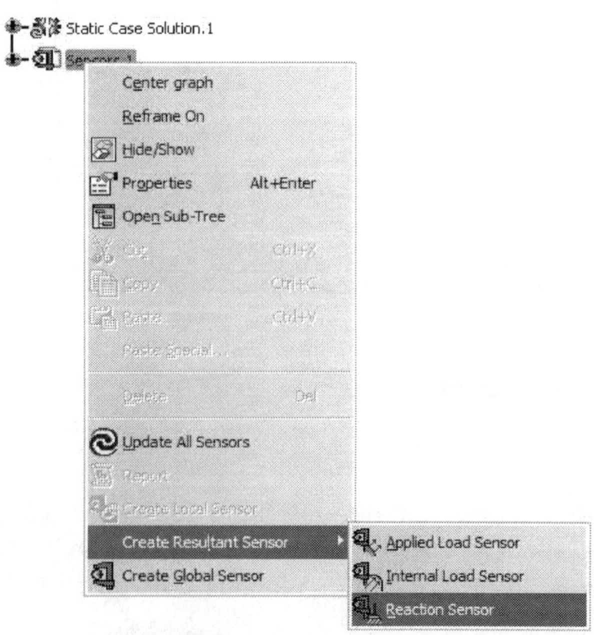

From the contextual menu, select **Create Reaction Sensor**. This forces the following box to open. From this box, select **Clamp.1** and close the box.

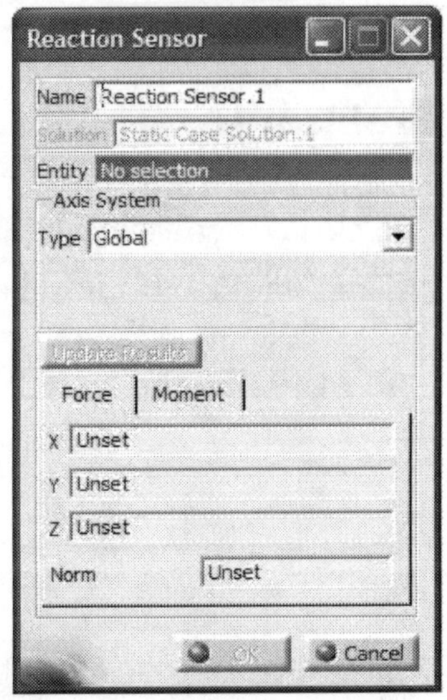


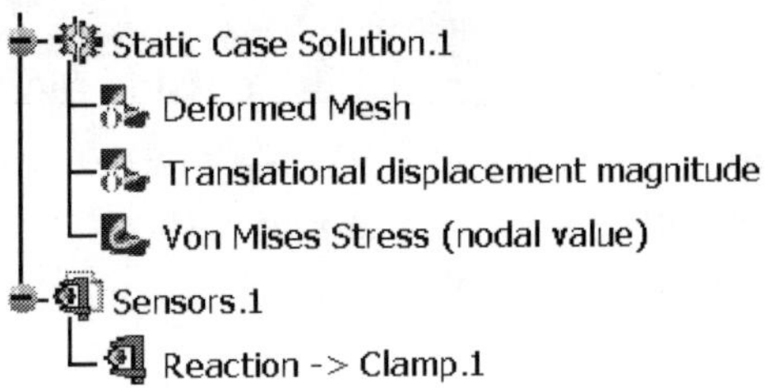


Note that a reaction sensor is created in the tree.

Double-click on the **Reaction Clamp.1** in the tree, the following box opens.
Select the **Update Results** box Update Results. The force necessary to result in the deformation is displayed.
<u>Do not be concerned if your number does not match ours.</u>

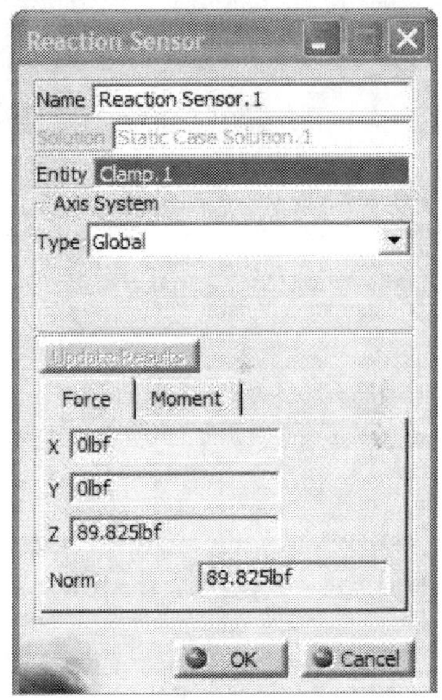


Let us create another sensor which describes the strain energy stored in the C-Clamp due to deformation.

Point the cursor to **Sensor.1** in the tree, right-click and select **Create Global Sensor** from the contextual menu. Upon opening the box below, select **Energy**.

The tree is modified to reflect the **Energy sensor** and indicates a value of 0.046 ft.lbf as displayed below. In order to see the 'Energy" value in the tree, you have to activate certain switches in the CATIA settings. Otherwise, double-click on the "Energy" branch and the value is displayed in a dialogue box as shown below.

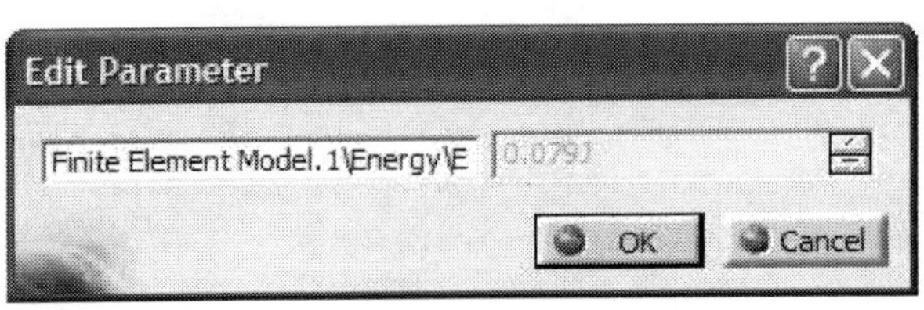


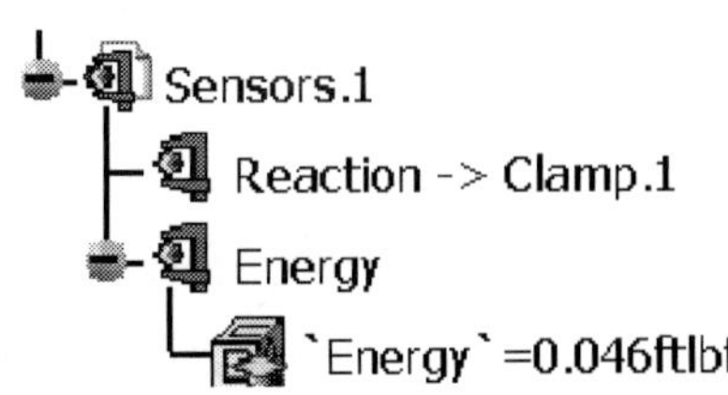

# Exercises for Chapter 6

## Problem 1: a Thick Curved Beam with Enforced Displacement

The curved semi-circular beam shown has inside radius $r_i = 2$ in., outside radius $r_o = 4$ in., and width $b = 1$ in. The beam is clamped at one end and given a displacement of $\delta = .00222$ in. at the other end. Assuming that the beam is made of aluminum, use CATIA to find the force F necessary to create this deformation.

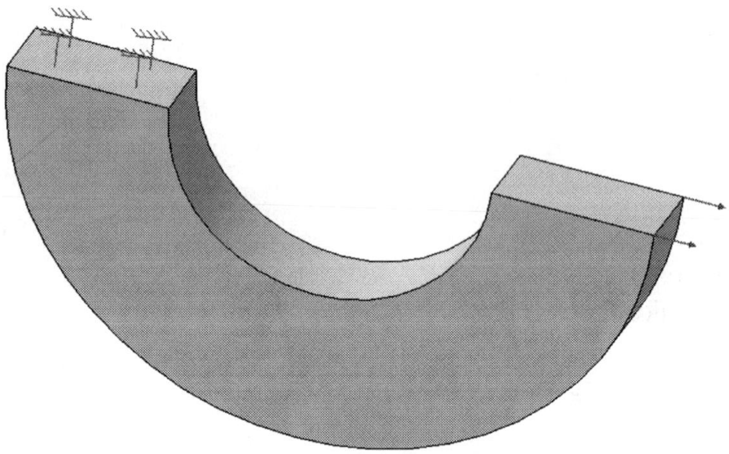

Partial Answer:

Using the Castigliano's theorem, one can find the relationship between the applied force and the resulting displacement. This relationship is expressed by

$$\delta = \frac{\pi}{2}\frac{FR}{EA}\left[\frac{R}{e} - 1 + 2(1+\nu)k\right]$$

where,

| | |
|---|---|
| $R = \dfrac{r_i + r_o}{2}$ | centroidal radius |
| $r_n = \dfrac{A}{b(\ln r_o - \ln r_i)}$ | neutral fiber radius |
| $e = R - r_n$ | eccentricity |
| $k = 1.2$ | for rectangular cross section |
| $A = 2$ | area cross section |

## Problem 2: Finding the Stiffness of a Helical Spring

Design a helical spring with dimensions and material of your choice and use CATIA to estimate its stiffness.

Partial Answer:

Using energy methods, one can derive the expression $k = \dfrac{Gd^4}{8nD^3}$ for the stiffness of the spring. In this expression, "d" is the wire diameter, "D" is the mean coil diameter, "n" is the number of active turns, and "G" is the shear modulus of the material.

# NOTES:

# Chapter 7

# FEA Modeling of the Bent Rod with Beam Elements

## Introduction

In this tutorial, you will be using the one-dimensional beam elements to model a bent rod. The geometry of the model is generated with the **Sketcher** workbench and the results of the beam calculations are compared with the solid elements presented earlier.

## 1 Problem Statement

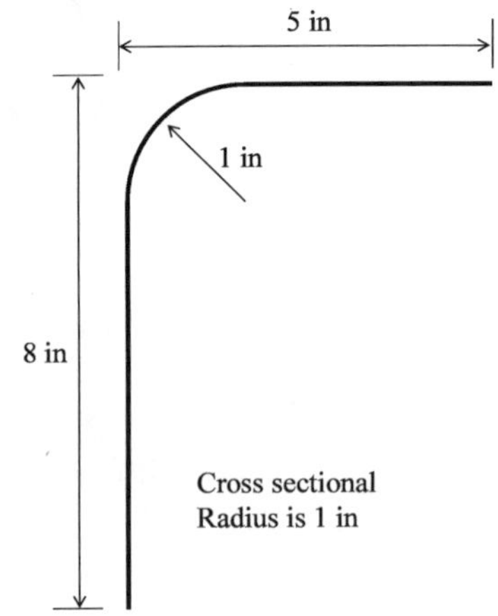


The bent rod, shown to the right, is clamped at bottom end and subjected to a load of 2000 lb perpendicular to the page. The steel rod has a Young's modulus of 30E+6 psi and Poisson ratio 0.3.

This problem was modeled in an earlier chapter using solid elements. It was mentioned that beam elements are more appropriate to model such structures.

Beam elements are extremely versatile and efficient for structures which have unidirectional characteristics. One can site, building skeletons, and automobile frames as typical structures which are routinely modeled with such elements.

A linear beam element has two nodes with six degrees of freedom. The degrees of freedom are three translations and three rotations as shown below. For those who are not familiar with FEA theory, a degree of freedom is an unknown entity that CATIA calculates. Based on the degrees of freedom in a beam element, forces and moments can be directly applied to nodes. As far as the moment is concerned, under ordinary circumstances, it could not have been applied to the nodes of a solid element.

Because of the nature of a beam element, it only requires a wireframe geometry for meshing purposes. However, the section properties have to be defined in order for calculations to proceed. Although for circular cross sections it does not matter, the orientation of the beam in space requires an additional point for proper modeling.

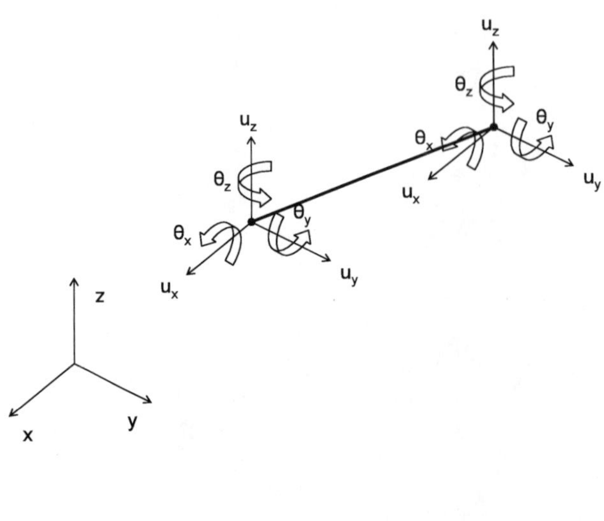

## 2 Creation of the Beam Model in Mechanical Design Solutions

Enter the **Part Design** workbench from the standard Windows toolbar, select **File > New**. Rename the part to be **Beam_Model**.

From the tree, select the **zx** plane and enter the **Sketcher**. In the **Sketcher**, use the icon in the **Profile** toolbar

and dimension as shown below.

Leave the **Sketcher**.

Upon leaving the **Sketcher**, the screen and the tree should be as shown below.

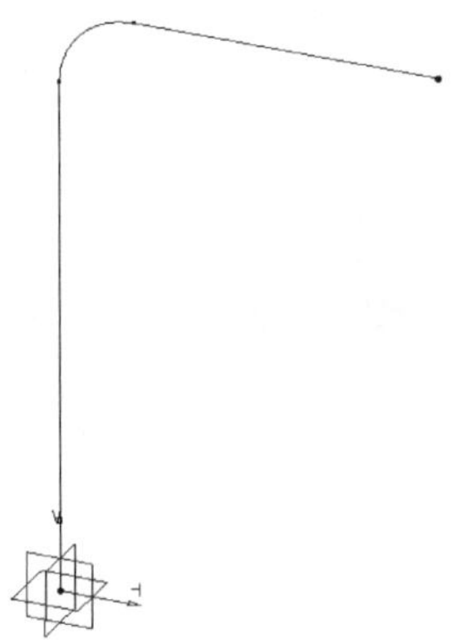

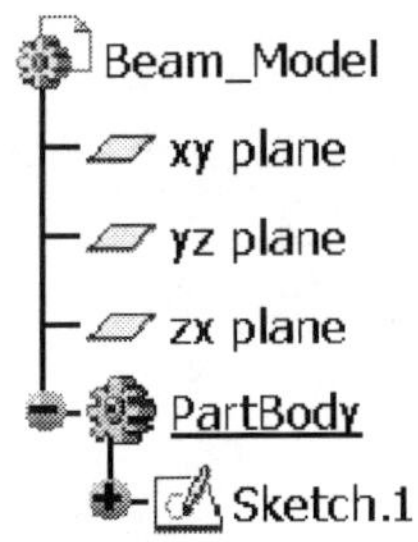


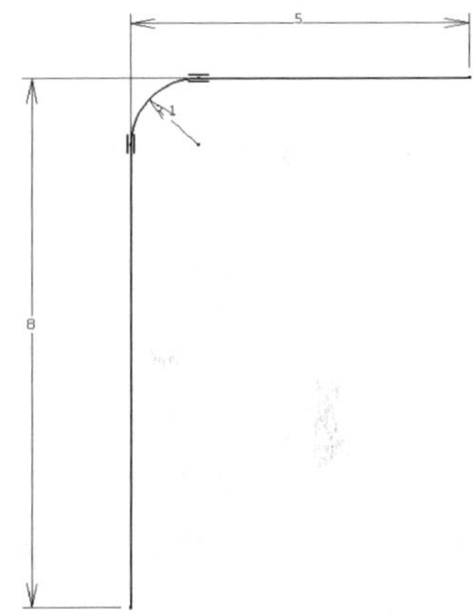

At this point, you need to create a point required to define the cross sectional orientation of the beam. This point must be off the profile that was generated. If the point lies on the profile, you will get an error message.

To create the point, use the **Point** icon in the **Reference Elements** toolbar. If this toolbar is not visible, use **View>Toolbars>Reference Elements (Compact)** to place it on the screen. Clicking on the **Point** icon opens the box shown below.

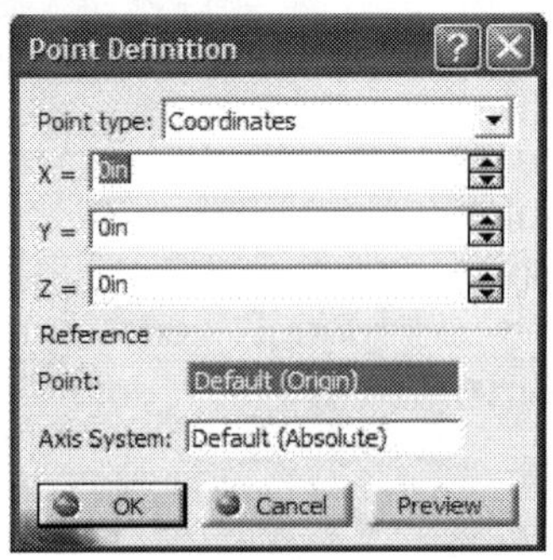


For the "**X**" coordinate, type 2 in. A point with coordinates (2,0,0) is created and shown with an "x" mark on the screen. The actual coordinate is not important as long as the point does not end up on the beam profile. We chose 2 in. to make it better visible on the screen.

<u>The next step which is often forgotten is the **Join** operation</u> for the wireframe.

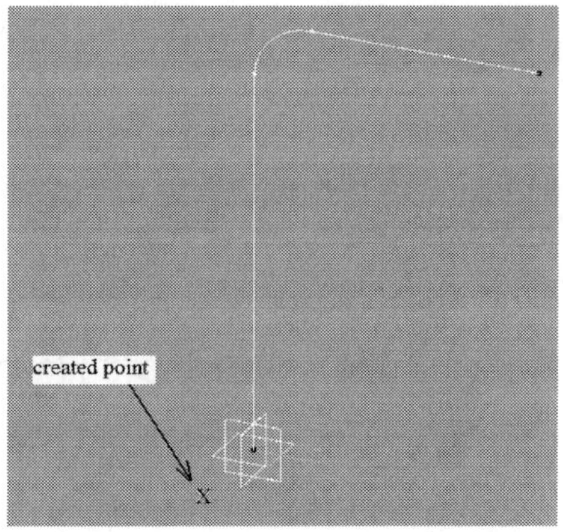


You have to use the **Join** icon 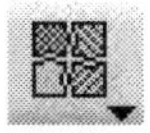 from the **Operations** toolbar 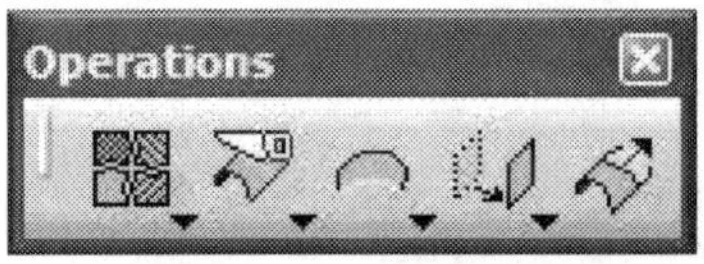

. This toolbar is not ordinarily available in the **Part Design** workbench. In order to access the toolbar, you have to switch to the **Wireframe and Surface Design** workbench from the **Start** menu as shown below (on the right).

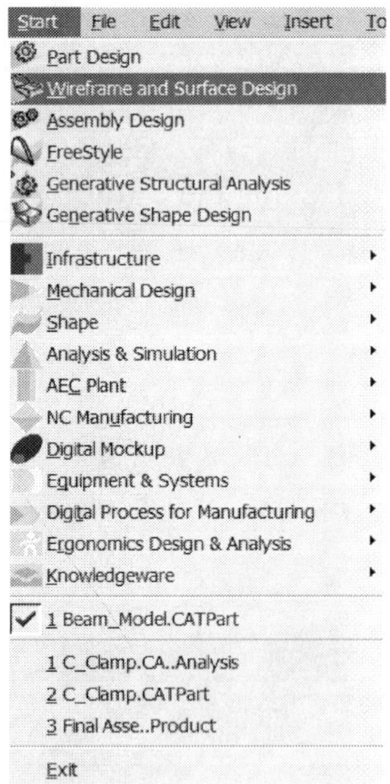


Selecting the **Join** icon, forces the **Join Definition** box to pop up.

For **Elements to Join**, select **Sketch.1** from the tree, or simply pick the beam wireframe from the screen with the cursor. The tree is modified to reflect the join operation process.

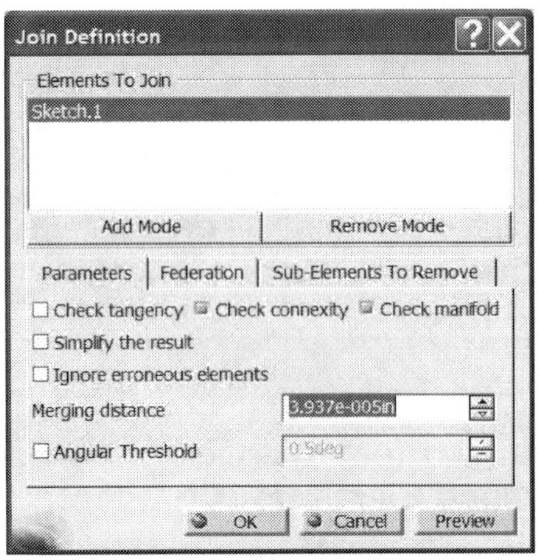


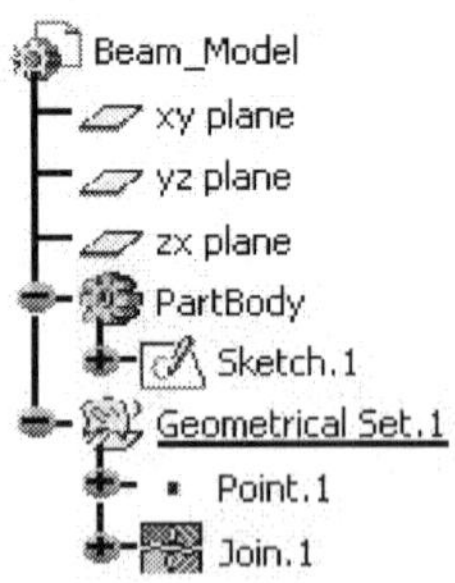


In older releases of CATIA, due to the creation of **Point.1**, an **Open Body.1** would have been created.

The part model is complete and you are ready to move to the **Analysis and Simulation** workbench.

## 3 Entering the Analysis Solutions

From the standard Windows toolbar, select

**Start > Analysis & Simulation > Generative Structural Analysis**

There is a second workbench known as the **Advanced Meshing Tools** which will be discussed later.

The first thing one can note is that although no material properties have been defined, you do not get a warning message as previously. However, the box shown below, **New Analysis Case** is visible on the screen. The default choice is **Static Analysis** which is precisely what we intend to use. Therefore, close the box by clicking on **OK**.

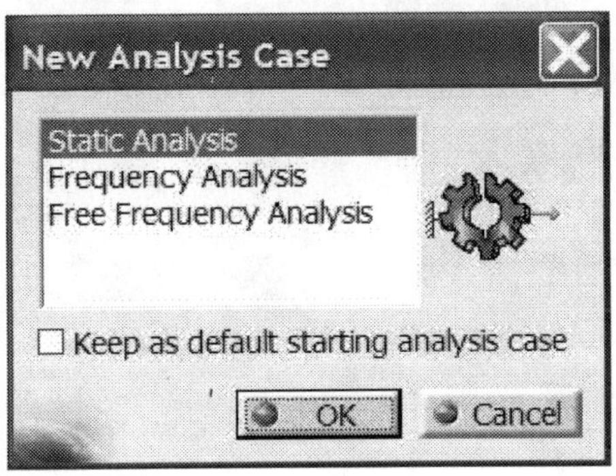


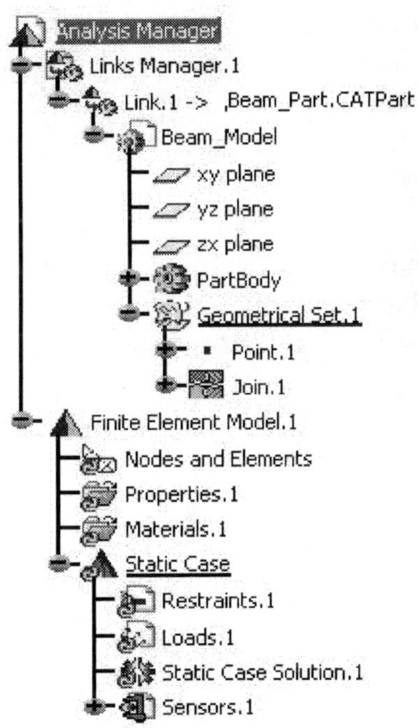


Finally, note that the tree structure gets considerably longer. The bottom branches of the tree are presently "unfilled", and as we proceed in this workbench, assigning loads and restraints, the branches gradually get "filled".

Select the **User Material** icon  in the **Model Manager** toolbar 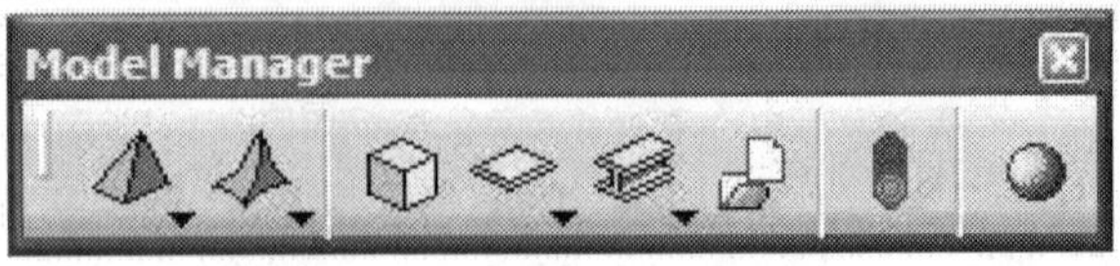

to specify the properties.

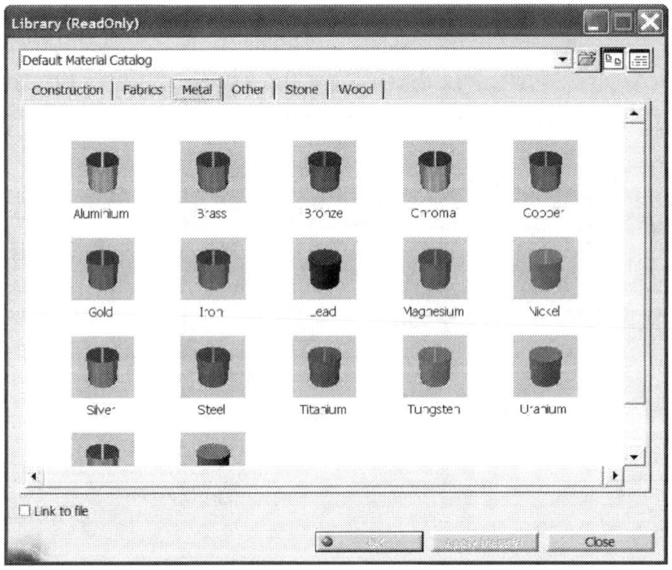


Use the **Metal** tab on the top; select **Steel**. Use your cursor to pick **Join** from the tree at which time the **OK** and **Apply Material** buttons can be selected.
Note that **Join.1** is under the **PartBody** branch.
Close the box.
The material property is now reflected in the tree.

One could have also specified the material at the part level by using the **Apply Material** icon  and selecting **Join** from the tree.

The section of the tree associated with material is shown on the right

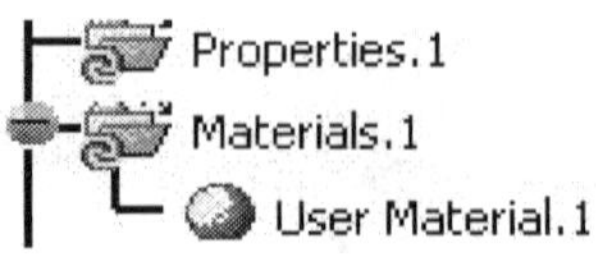


The **Model Manager** toolbar 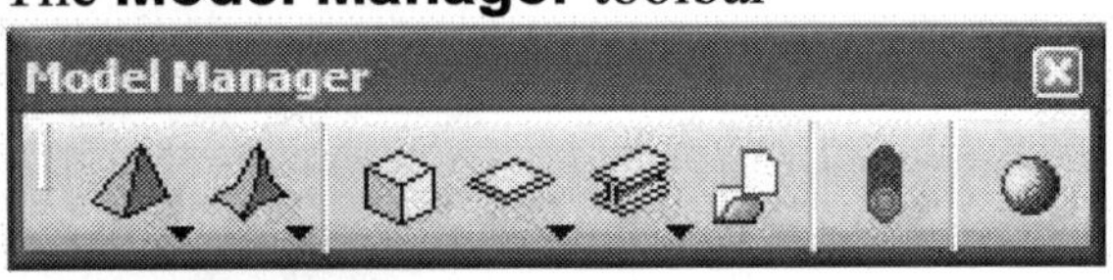

has a sub-toolbar known as **Mesh Parts** 

. Click on the **Beam Mesher** icon 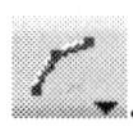.
The **Beam Meshing** box shown below opens.

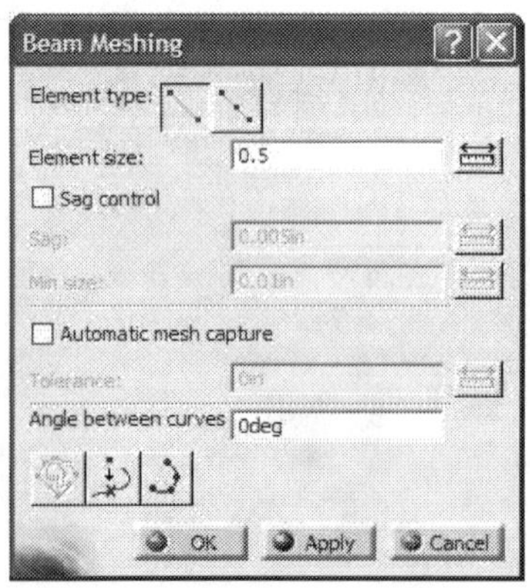


For **Element size** type 0.5 and with the cursor select **Join.1** from the tree or from the screen.

The section of the tree associated with the mesh is shown below.

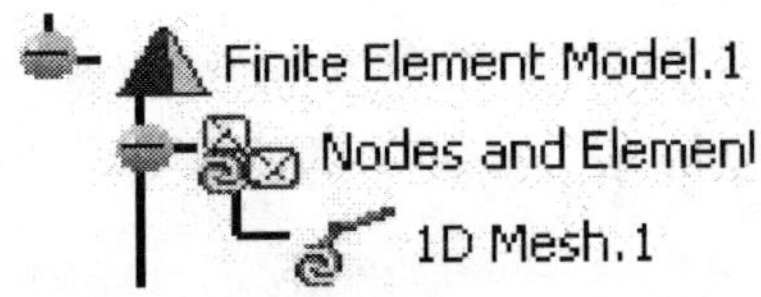


Point the cursor to the branch **Nodes and Elements**, right-click and select **Mesh Visualization** from the contextual menu.

This action opens the standard warning window that you have to close.

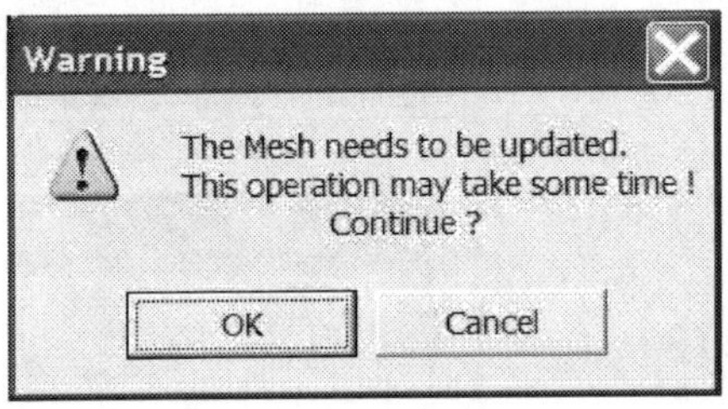


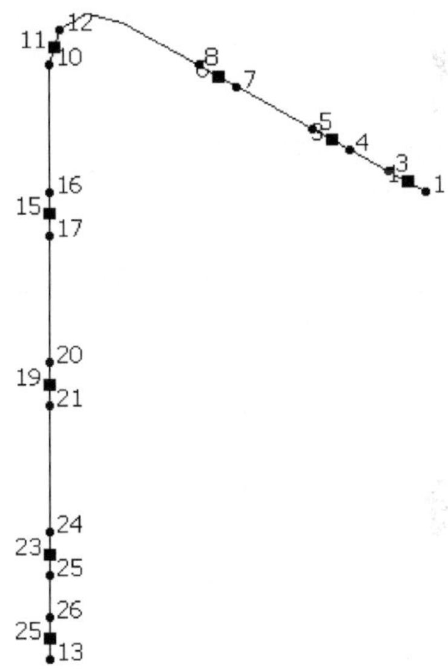


You now have a mesh, but no material properties or section properties are associated with it. In fact, by pointing the cursor to the wireframe on the screen, you can see that the node and element numbers are highlighted.
Some sample elements and nodes are displayed to the right.

Click on the **1D Property** icon  from the **Model Manager** toolbar 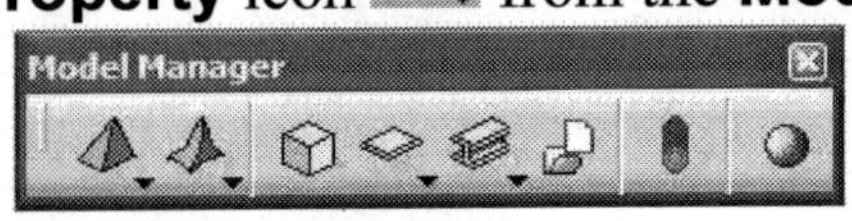

.
The **1D Property** box below opens up.

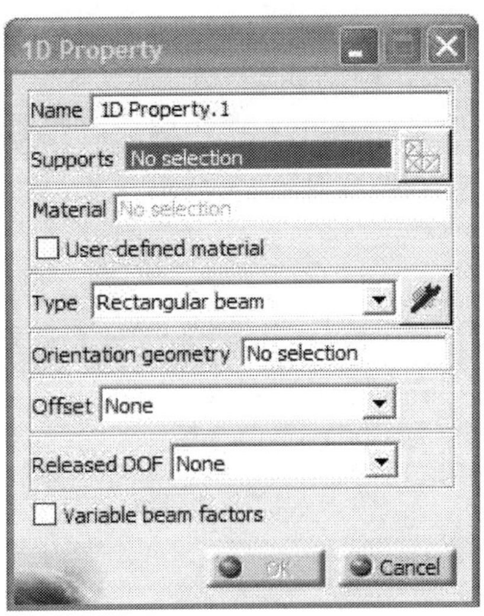


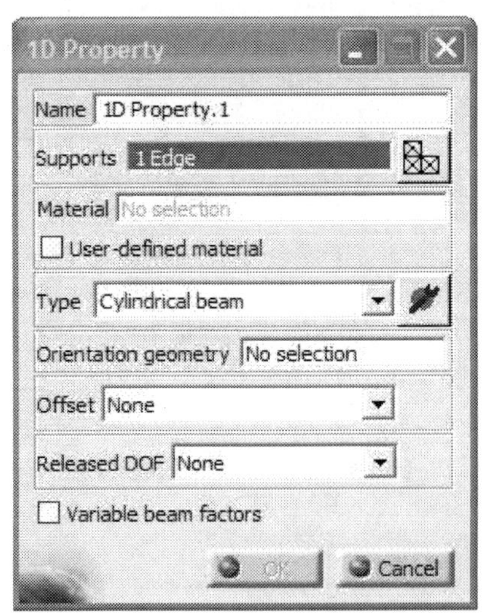

The next several steps are described in detail.

For **Supports** pick **Join.1** <u>in the tree.</u> In fact, this is the only item that can be selected from the tree, or the wireframe.

For **Type** pick **Cylindrical Beam** from the pull down menu.

Using the icon , input the proper cross sectional radius in the pop-up box.
The correct radius is 1 in.

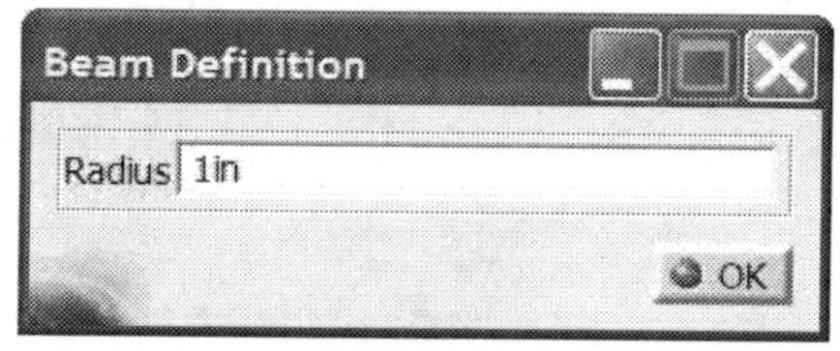


For the **Orientation geometry**, pick **Point.1** from the tree. You may have to expand the tree to reach it. Remember, this is the point with coordinates (2,0,0) which was created earlier. This point can also be picked from the screen provided that your part is in the **Show** mode.

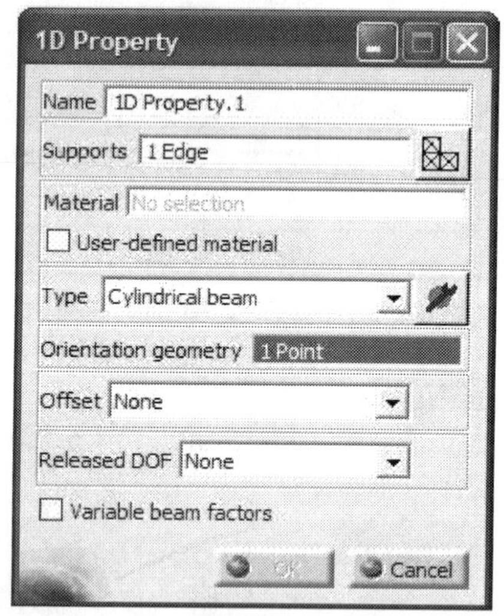


In the box, check the **User-defined Material** and move the cursor to **Material**.

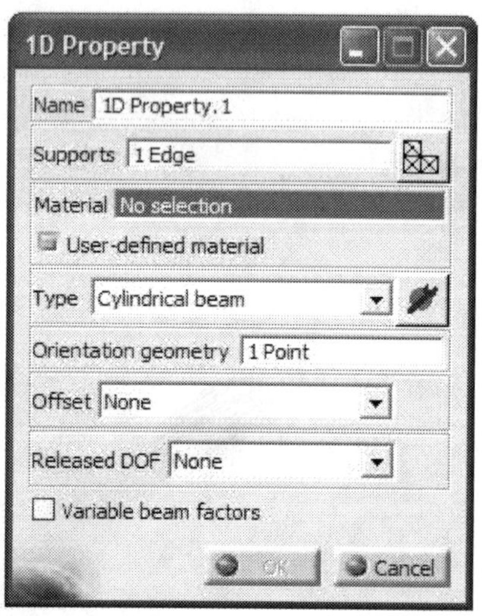


From the tree, select the branch **User Material.1** which was created earlier. The final appearance of the box is shown below and you can close it by pressing **OK**.

The model on the screen, and the portion of the tree reflecting the **1D Properties** are displayed next.

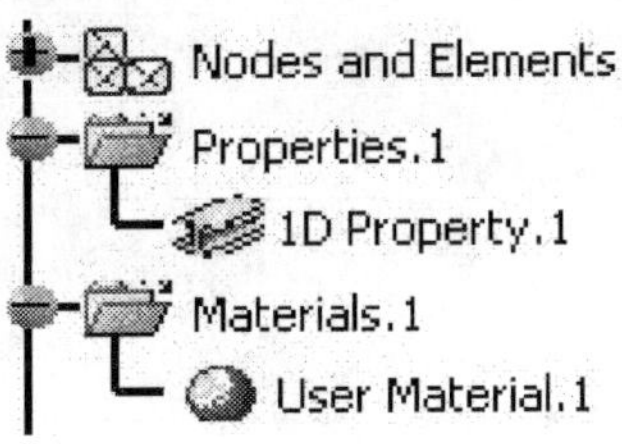


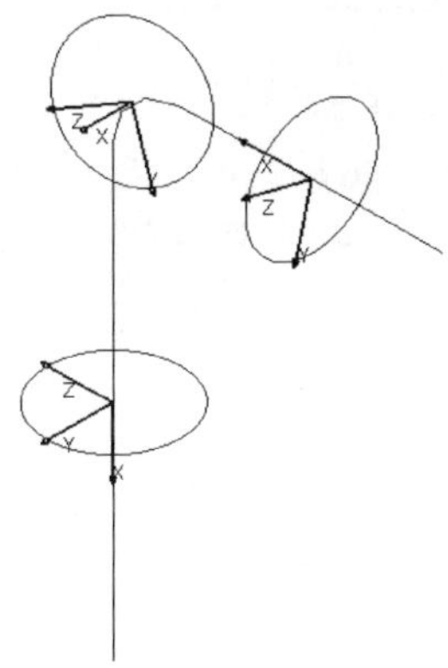

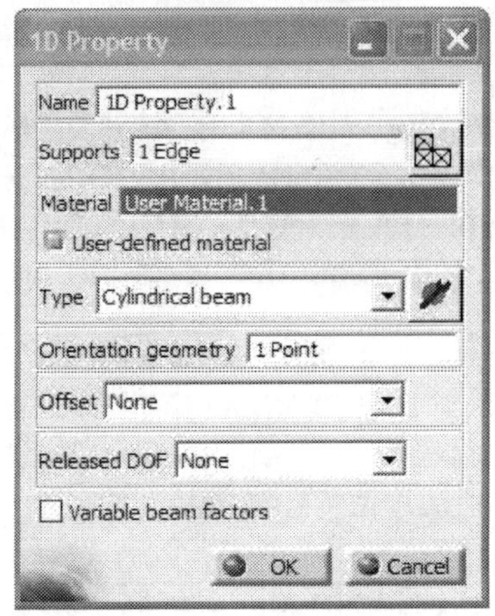


Point the cursor to the branch **Nodes and Elements**, right-click, and select **Mesh Visualization**.

CONGRATULATIONS! You now have a mesh with the correct material properties. **Regularly save your work.**

**Applying Restraints:**

CATIA's FEA module is geometrically based. This means that the boundary conditions cannot be applied to nodes and elements. The boundary conditions can only be applied at the part level. As soon as you enter the **Generative Structural Analysis** workbench, the part is automatically hidden. Therefore, before boundary conditions are applied, the part must be brought to the unhide mode. This can be carried out by pointing the cursor to the top of the tree, the **Links Manager.1** branch, right-click, select **Show**.
**Warning:** Restraints and Loads cannot be applied unless the part is in the show mode. Therefore, if necessary, point the cursor to the **Mesh.1** branch in the tree, right-click, and select **Activate/Deactivate** to remove the mesh and expose the part.

In FEA, restraints refer to applying displacement boundary conditions which is achieved through the **Restraint** toolbar 

. In the present problem, the base of the longer section is clamped. The **Clamp** condition for beams means that, the displacements and rotations in all three directions are zero. Select the **Clamp** icon  and pick the bottom vertex as the pop-up box indicates.

**Applying Loads:**

In FEA, loads refer to forces. The **Loads** toolbar 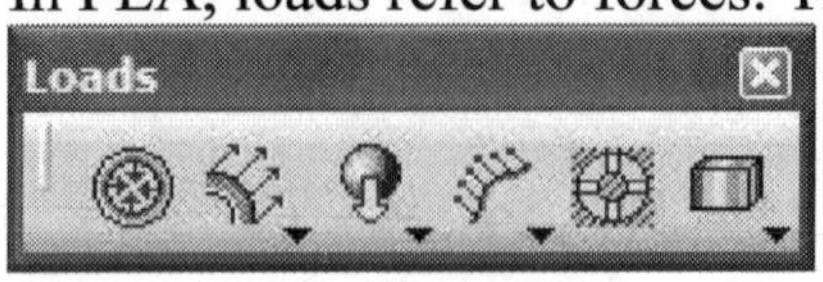

is used for this purpose.

Select the **Distributed Force** icon .
With the cursor, pick the other vertex of the rod which is loaded.

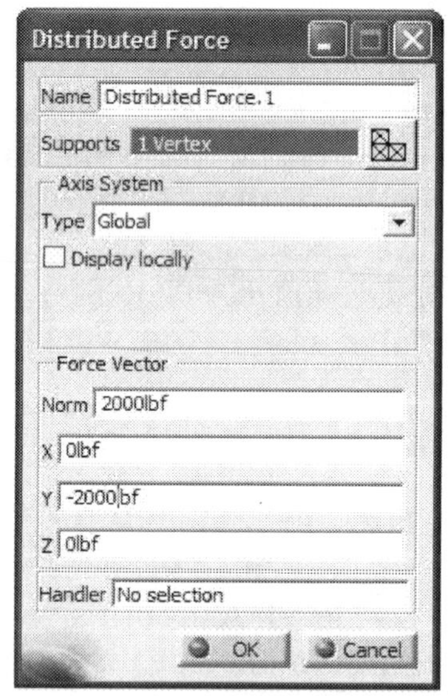


The **Distributed Force** box shown on the right opens. A visual inspection of the global axis in your screen indicates that the force of magnitude 2000 lb (or -2000 lb) should be applied in y-direction

Keep in mind that if your part is in the **Hide** mode, neither of the two vertices can be picked. "Unhide" it first and then proceed.

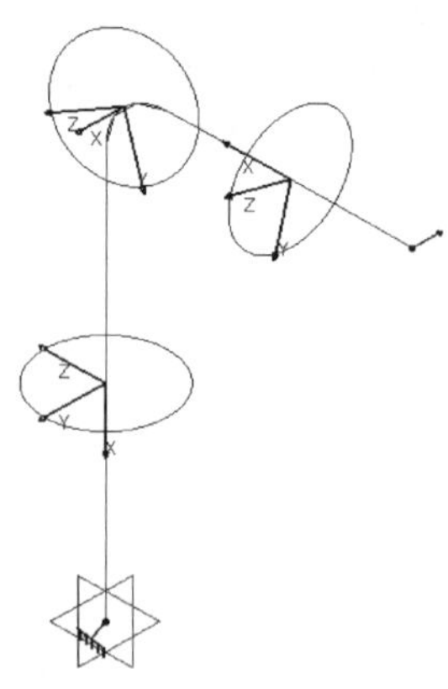

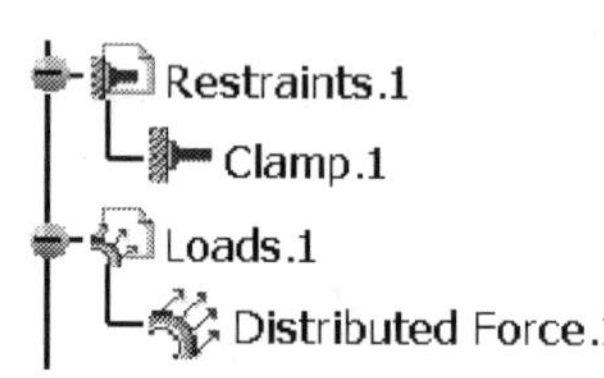


**Launching the Solver:**

To run the analysis, you need to use the **Compute** toolbar 

by selecting the **Compute** icon . This leads to the **Compute** box shown to the right. Leave the defaults as **All** which means everything is computed.

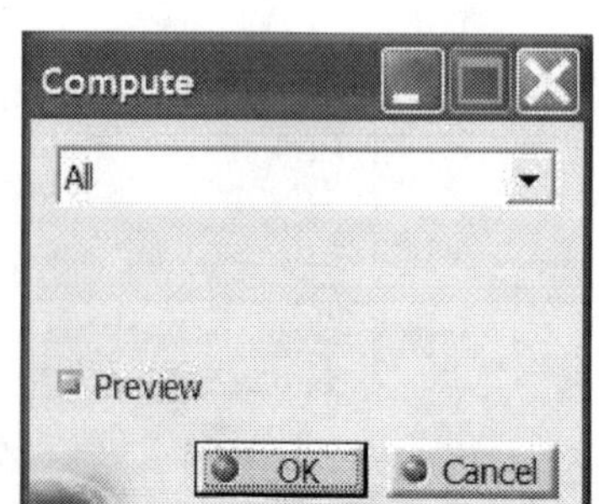

Upon closing this box, after a brief pause the second box shown below appears. This box provides information on the resources needed to complete the analysis. If all estimates are zero in the listing, then there is a problem in the previous step and should be looked into. If all numbers as zero in this box, although the program may run, it will not produce any useful results.

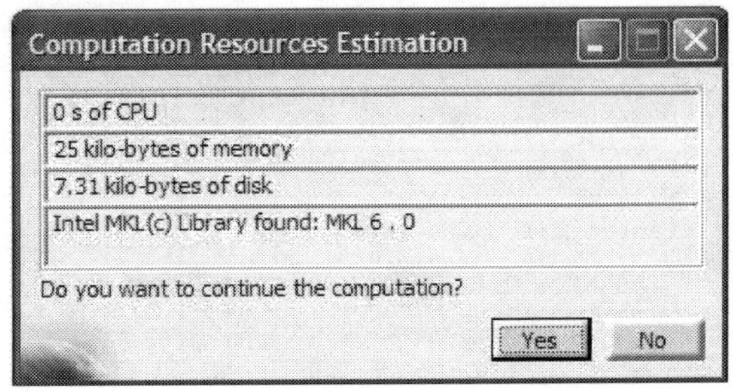


The tree has been changed to reflect the location of the **Results** and **Computations** as shown below.

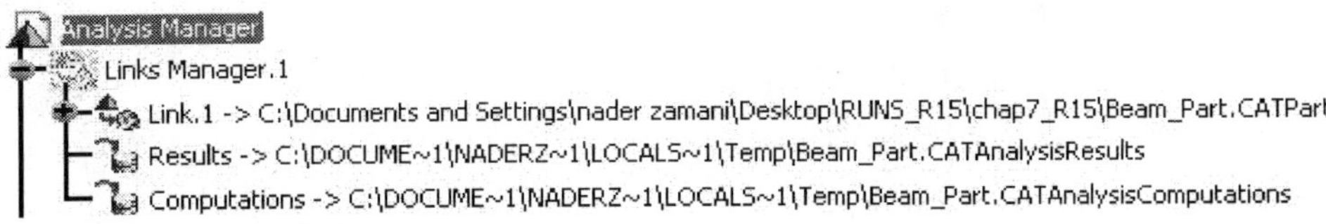


**Postprocessing:**

In the case of beam elements, there is a limited postprocessing available. You can only review the deformed shape and the displacement field. Axial stresses are also available.

The main postprocessing toolbar is called **Image** 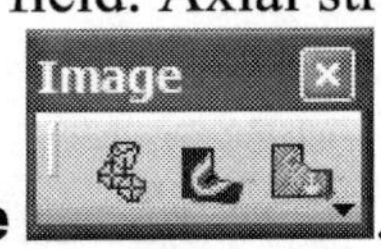

. To view the deformed shape you have use the **Deformation** icon. The deformation image can be very deceiving since one could have the impression that the model actually displaces to that extent. Keep in mind that the displacements are scaled considerably so that one can observe the deformed shape. Although the scale factor is set automatically, one can change this value with the **Deformation Scale Factor** icon in the **Analysis Tools** toolbar 

.

In order to see the displacement field, the **Displacement** icon in the **Image** toolbar should be used. The default display is in terms of displacement arrows as shown on the right. The color and the length of arrows represent the size of the displacement. The contour legend indicates a maximum displacement of .0396 in. This result is in good agreement with the case of the solid elements.

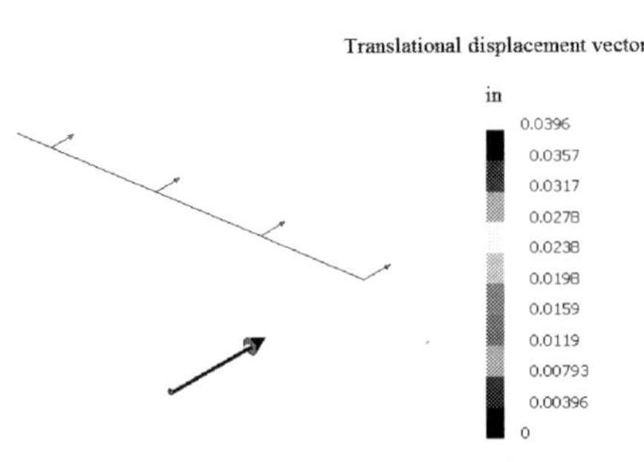


The arrow plot is not particularly useful. In order to view the contour plot of the displacement field, position the cursor on the arrow field and double click. The **Image Edition** box shown below opens.

Note that the default is to draw the contour on the deformed shape. If this is not desired, uncheck the box **On deformed mesh**. Next, select **AVERAGE-ISO** and press **OK**.

The contour of the displacement field is shown below.

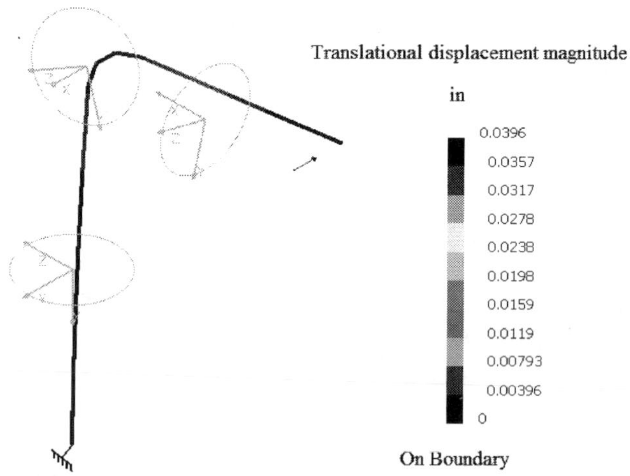


Finally, animation of the model can be achieved through the **Animate** icon 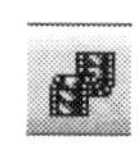 in the **Analysis Tools** toolbar 

. An AVI file can easily be generated.

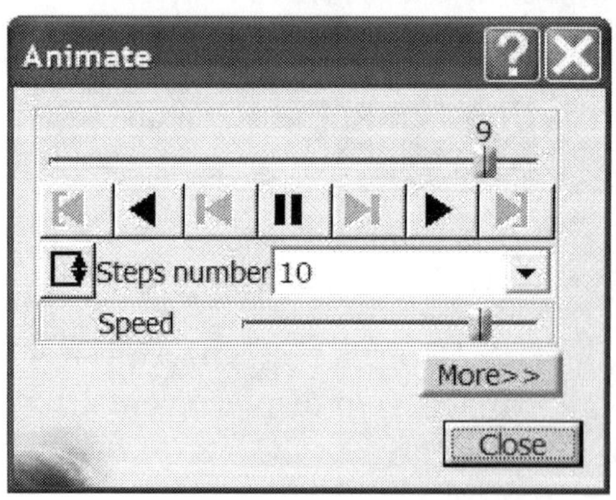

# Exercises for Chapter 7

## Problem 1: Deflection of a Simply Supported Beam under Uniform Load

A Steel beam is 20 inches long having a square cross section 1x1 in This beam is simply supported and carries a uniform load of 30 lb/in as shown. Use the beam elements in CATIA to estimate the maximum deflection occurring at the mid-span of the structure.

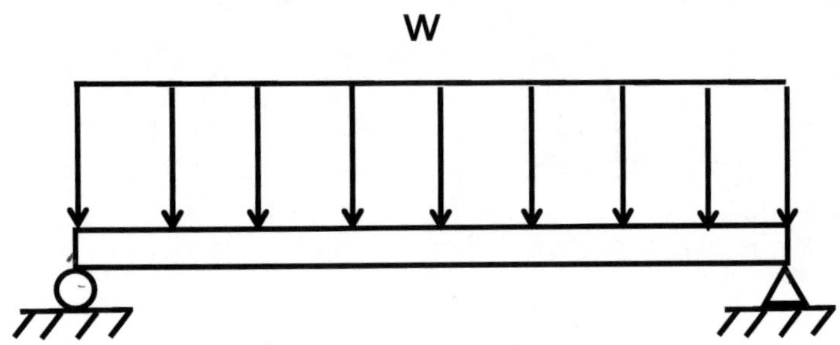


Partial Answer:

Elementary strength of materials estimates this deflection to be $\delta = \dfrac{5wL^4}{384EI}$ where w is the applied load, and I is the cross sectional moment of inertia. For this beam, $I = \dfrac{1}{12}\,in^4$.

Assuming that the Young's modulus is 30E+6 psi, the maximum deflection is approximately $\delta = .025\,in.$

The beam elements are so robust that even very few elements should produce excellent agreement with the above hand calculation.

## Problem 2: Deformation of a Curved Beam under a Concentrated Load

The curved beam shown is made of steel with Young's modulus 30E+6 psi and Poisson ratio 0.29. The cross section of the beam is a square 1x1 in. and the mean radius of the beam is 30 in. A concentrated force $F = 300\,\text{lb}$ is applied to the left end. Use the beam elements in CATIA to estimate the horizontal and vertical deflections of the beam.

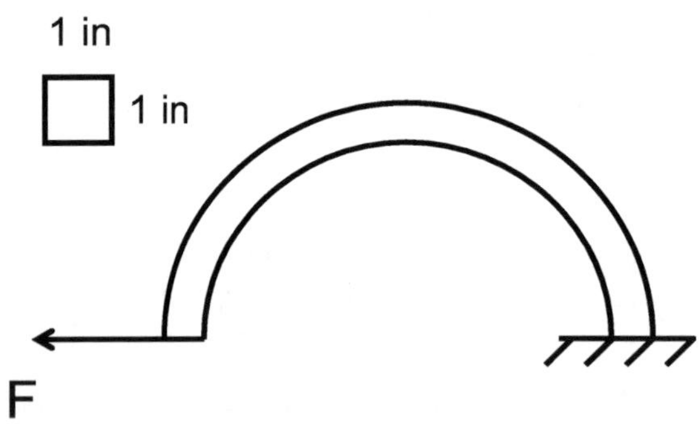


Partial Answer:

Using energy methods such as Castigliano's theorem, the following formulas for the desired entities are obtained.

$$\delta_H = \frac{\pi}{2}\frac{FR^3}{EI} \text{ and } \delta_V = 2\frac{ER^3}{EI}.$$

# Chapter 8

# Beam Elements under Enforced Displacement

## Introduction

In this tutorial, you create a wireframe model of a C-clamp and mesh it with beam elements. An “Enforced Displacement” boundary condition is applied to the beam and using a sensor, the force at the fixed end is computed. The results are compared with the solid model of the same geometry.

## 1 Problem Statement

The C-clamp shown to the right, is made of aluminum with Young’s modulus of 1.015E+7 psi and Poisson ratio 0.346. The “Point.1” is fixed; whereas a downward displacement of 0.01 in. is applied to “Point.5”.

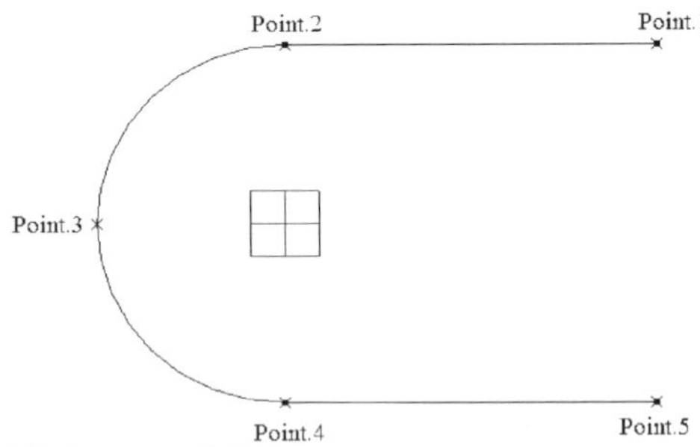


The distance between “Point.1” and “Point.2” is 3 in. with the radius of the arc being 1.5 in. The cross section of the beam elements used is a square, with dimensions 1.x 1. in.

A slight variation of this geometry was modeled earlier with solid tetrahedron elements which will be used for comparison purposes.

## 2 Creation of the Part in Mechanical Design Solutions

Enter the **Part Design** workbench  from the standard Windows toolbar, select **File > New** 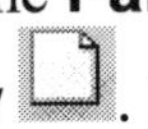. Rename the part to be **Beam_C_Clamp**.

From the standard Windows toolbar select **Start > Wireframe and Surface Design**. This will land you in the **Wireframe and Surface Design** workbench.

Use the **Point** icon  from the **Wireframe** toolbar 

, to create five points with coordinates (3,0,1.5), (0,0,1.5), (-1.5,0,0), (0,0,-1.5), and (3,0,-1.5). These coordinates are associated with **Point.1** through **Point.5**.
A typical box used to create the points is shown below.

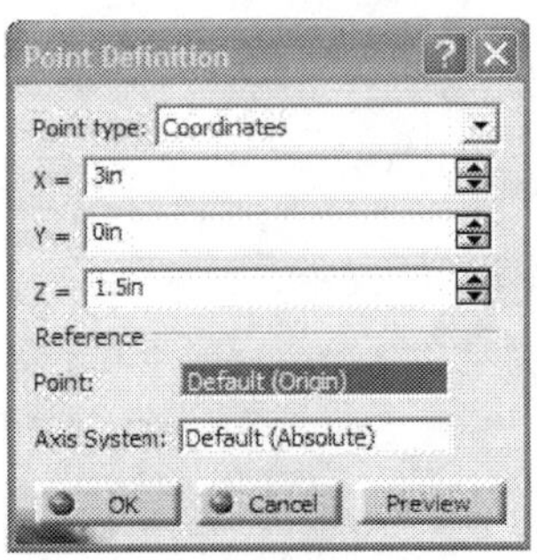

Next, use the **Line** icon , from the **Wireframe** toolbar to create the top and bottom horizontal lines. The **Line Definition** box used to create the first line is shown on the right.

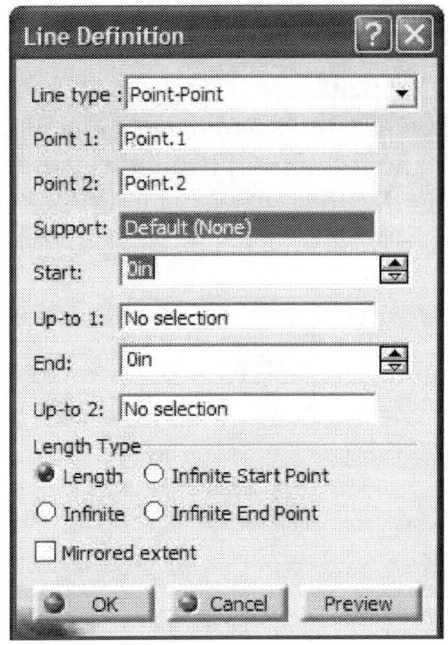


Finally, use the **Circle** icon  from the **Wireframe** toolbar to create an arc between the remaining three points as shown before. The **Circle Definition** box for this operation is shown below. Note that the **Circle type** is **Three points**.

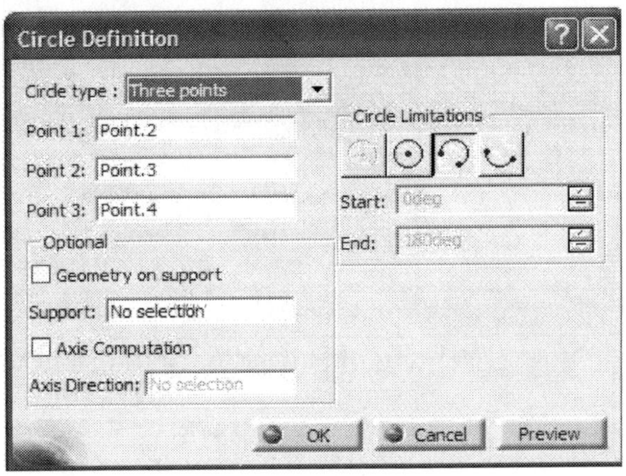


The created geometry in three dimensions and the associated tree structure is displayed below.

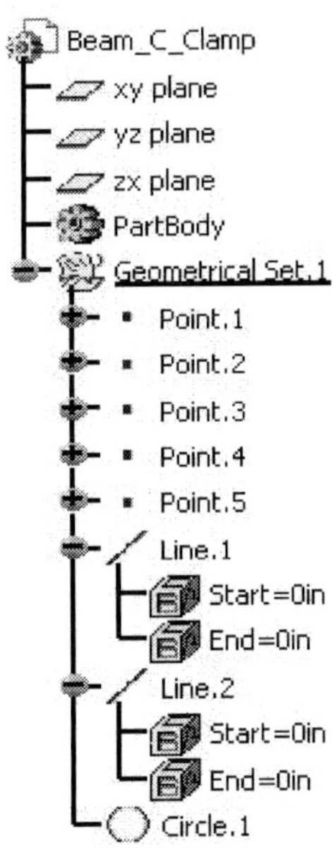


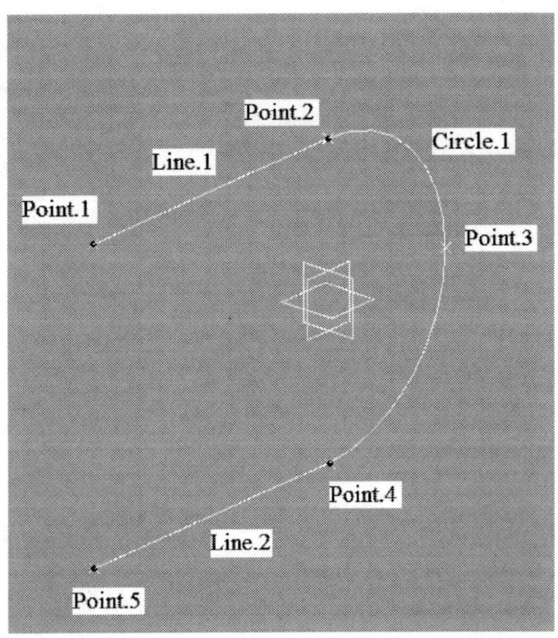

Use the **Join** icon 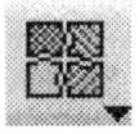 from the **Operations** toolbar 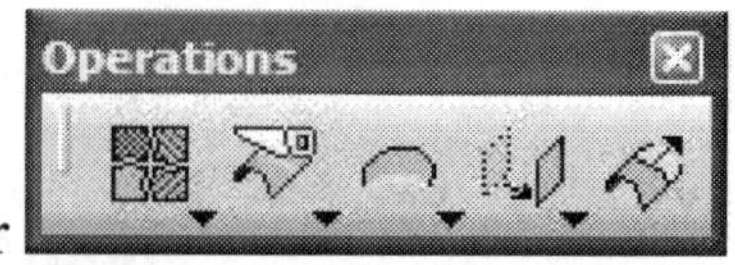

to connect the lines and the arc together. Without this step, which is often forgotten, the lines and the arc although meshed, will not interact with each other in the FEA calculation. The resulting **Join** box is shown where the two lines and the circle have been picked.

The **Join.1** branch is created on the tree as displayed.

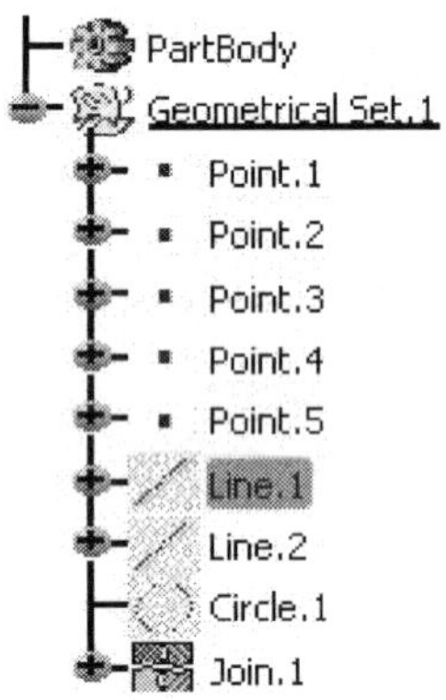


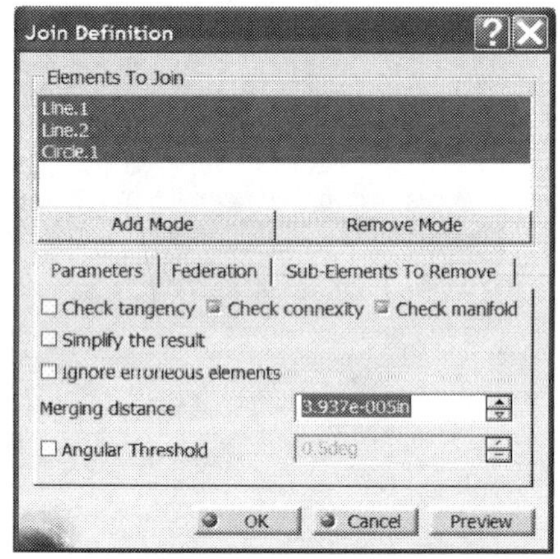


You need to create an additional point (not on the beam) which is used only to orient the cross section. Use the **Point** icon 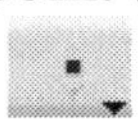 from the **Wireframe** toolbar and give it coordinates (0,0,0).
The geometric model is complete and the all you need to do is to define the material properties.

Use the **Apply Material** icon  to open the **Library** box shown below.

From the **Metal** tab on the top, select **Aluminum**.

Use your cursor to pick the branch **Join.1** from the tree. Finally, select **OK** and **Apply Material**.
Close the box.
The material property is now reflected in the tree.

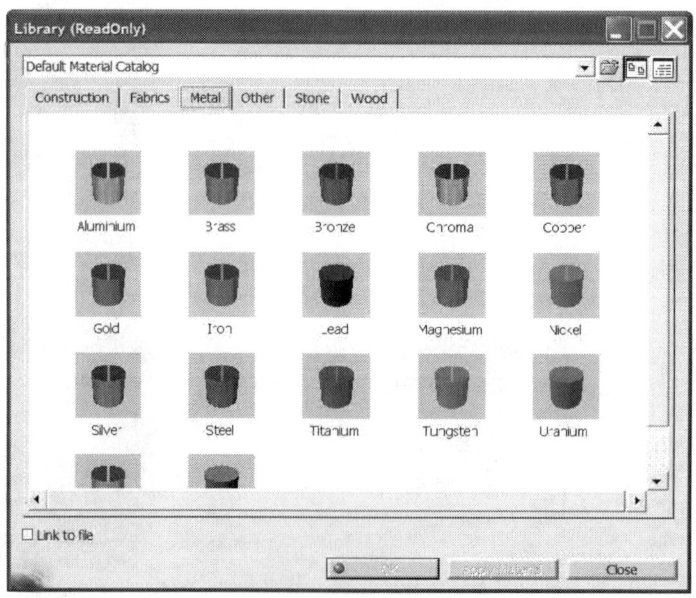


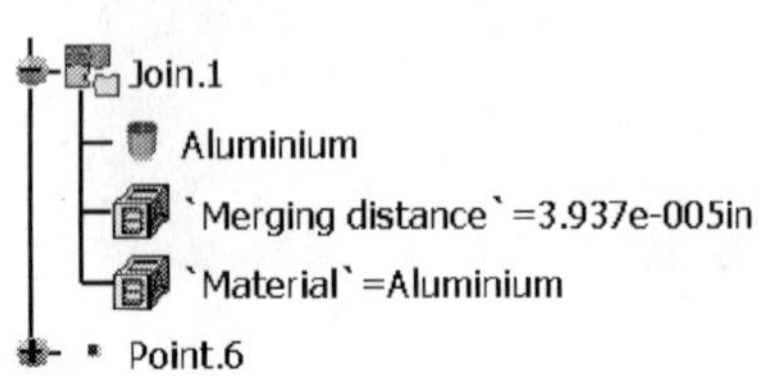

In order to inspect the values of the material properties assigned, double-click on **Aluminum** in the tree. It may take a minute before the database is searched. You will see that the **Properties** box shown below opens. Choose the **Analysis** tab from this box and the values will be displayed. Note that these values can be edited.

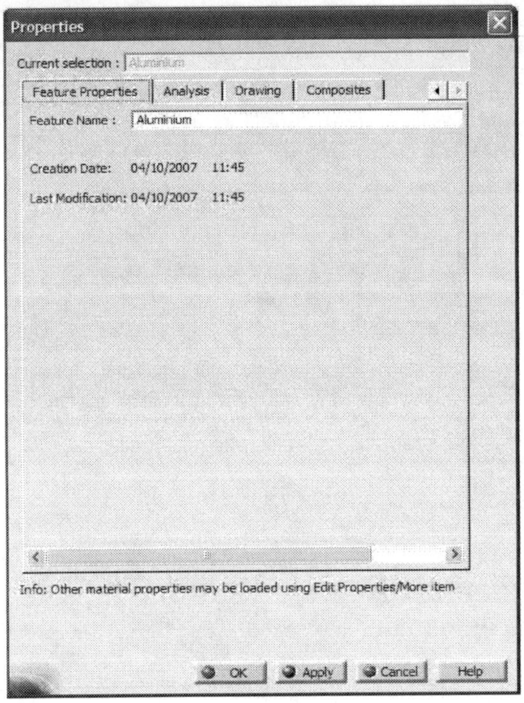


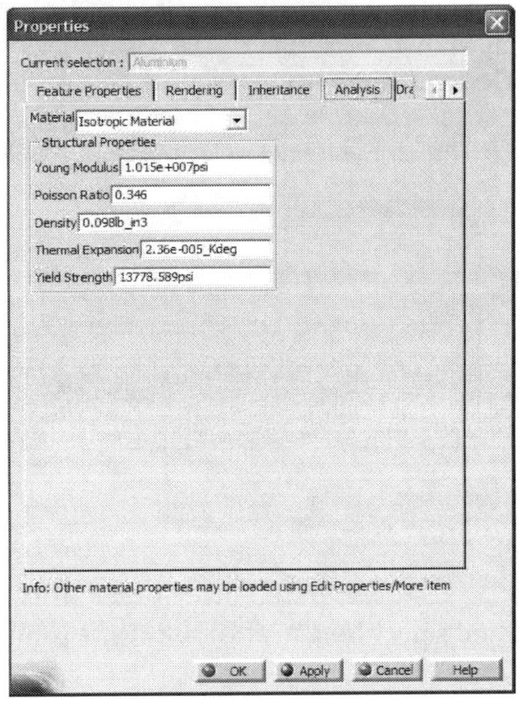


## 3 Entering the Analysis Solutions

From the standard Windows toolbar, select

**Start > Analysis & Simulation > Generative Structural Analysis** 
There is a second workbench known as the **Advanced Meshing Tools** which will be discussed later.

The box shown below, **New Analysis Case** is visible on the screen. The default choice is **Static Analysis** which is precisely what we intend to use. Therefore, close the box by selecting **OK**.

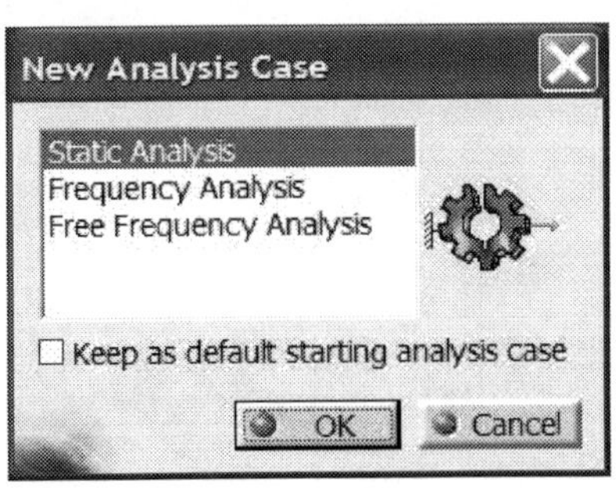

The **Model Manager** toolbar 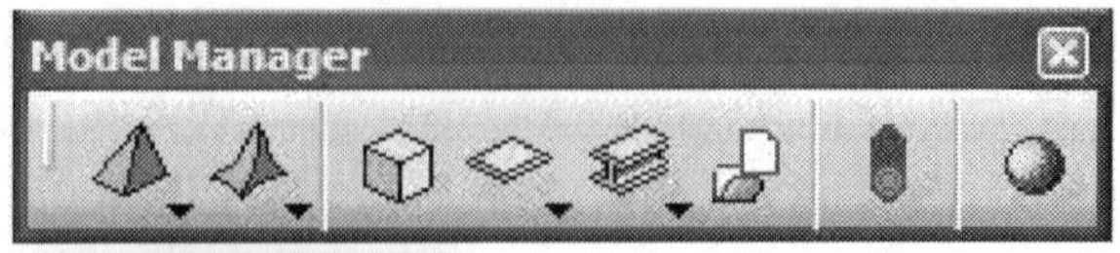

has a sub-toolbar known as **Mesh Parts** 

. Click on the **Beam Mesher** icon . The **Beam Meshing** box shown below opens.

Specify the element size to be 0.1 in and select **Join.1** from the three or the screen.

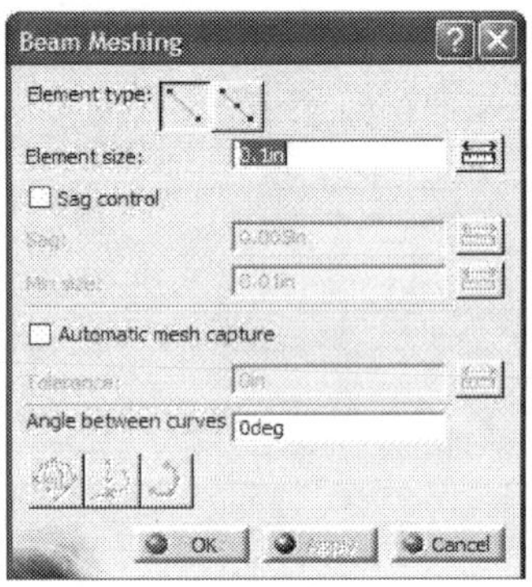


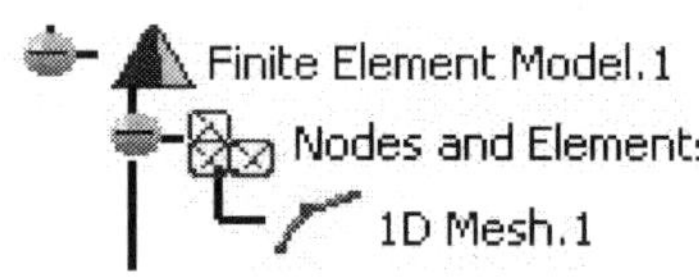


Point the cursor to the branch **Nodes and Elements**, right-click and select **Mesh Visualization** from the contextual menu as shown.

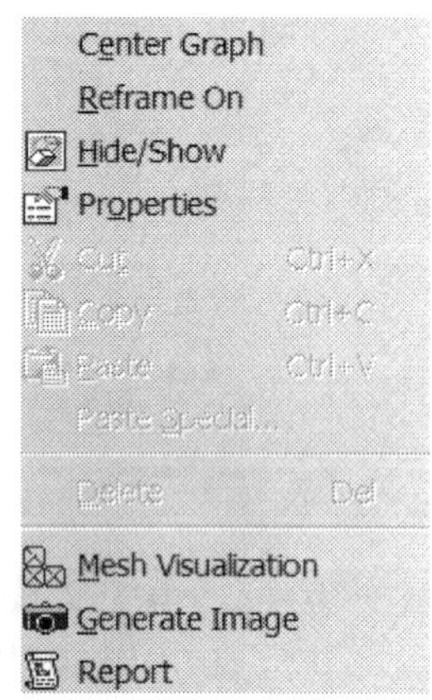


This action opens the standard warning window that you have to close.

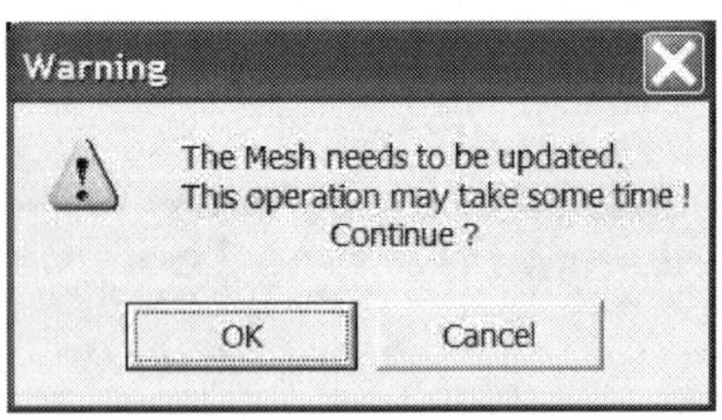


At this point, you have a mesh. In fact, by pointing the cursor to the wireframe on the screen, you can see that the node and element numbers are highlighted. Unless you zoom, it may be difficult to read the numbers. To partially fix this problem, double-click on one of the elements on the screen to open the **Image Edition** box and check the **Display nodes**. The result is the nodes in the model as displayed below giving you a better feeling for the fineness of the mesh.

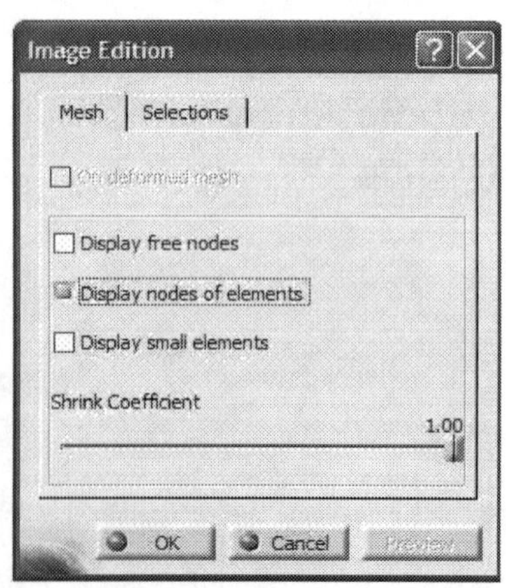

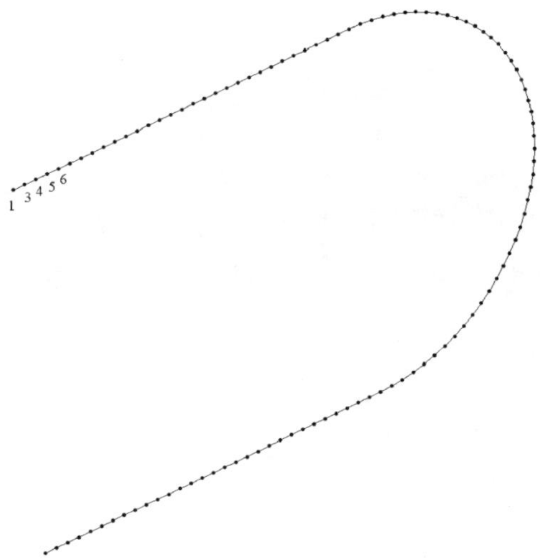


The contextual menu also allows you to generate a report in the HTML format on the nodes and elements. The report indicates that there are 108 nodes and 107 elements.

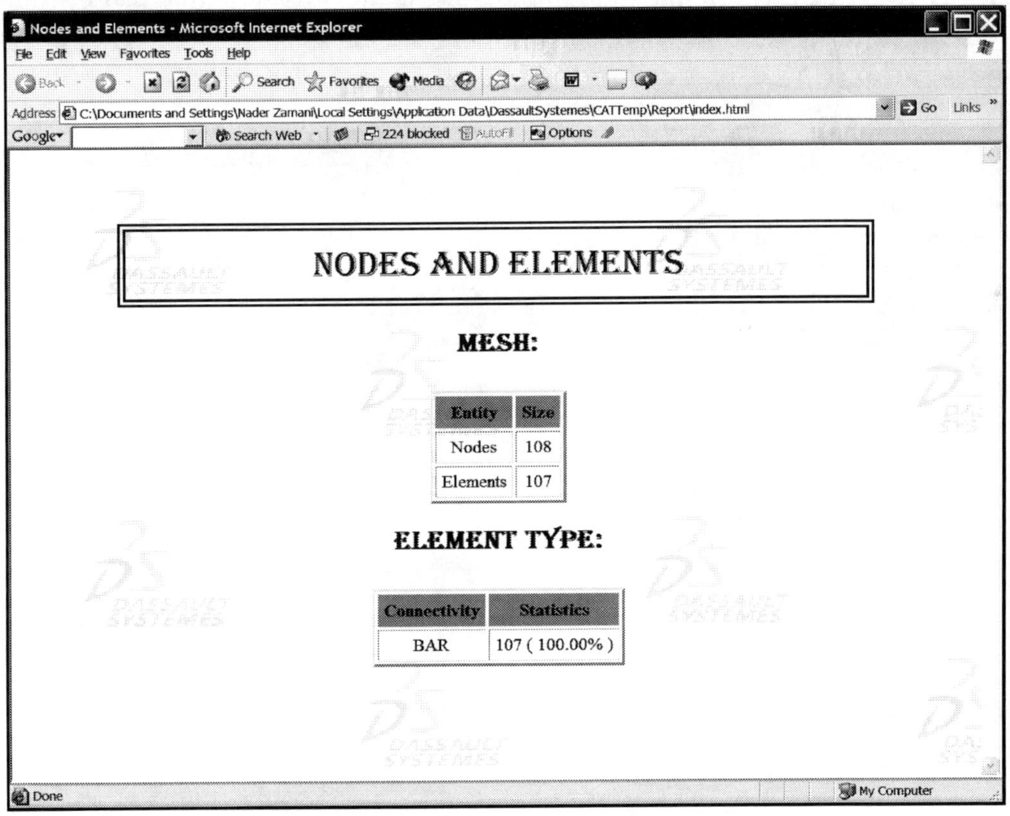


NODES AND ELEMENTS

MESH:

| Entity | Size |
|---|---|
| Nodes | 108 |
| Elements | 107 |

ELEMENT TYPE:

| Connectivity | Statistics |
|---|---|
| BAR | 107 ( 100.00% ) |

You are now in a position to define the cross sectional properties of the C-clamp.

Click on the **1D Property** icon  from the **Model Manager** toolbar

.

The **1D Property** box below opens up.

The next several steps are described in detail.

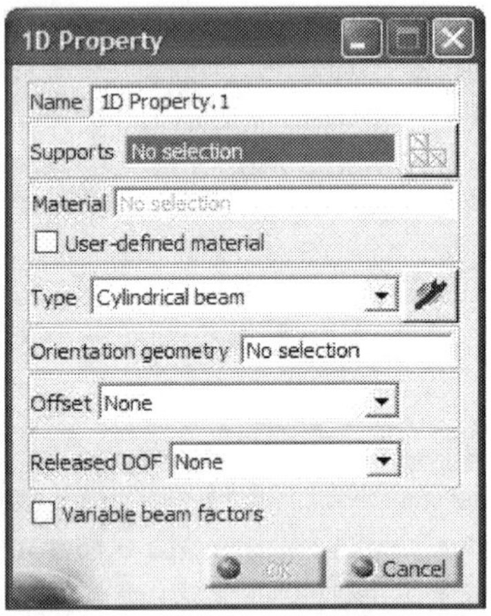


For the **Supports** pick **Join.1** in the tree. In fact, this is the only item that can be selected from the tree, or the wireframe. Choose a **Rectangular beam** from the pull-down menu.

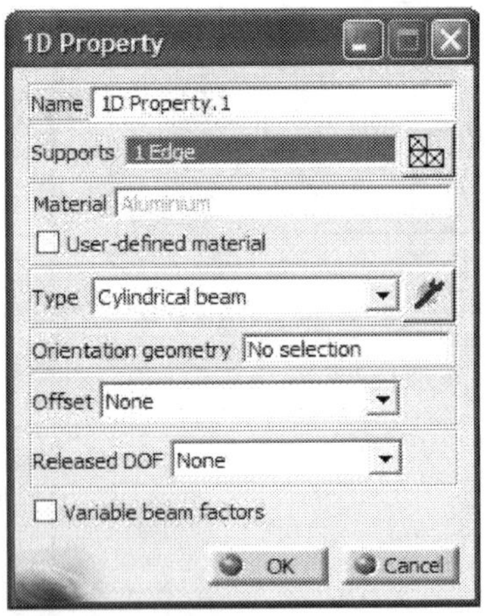


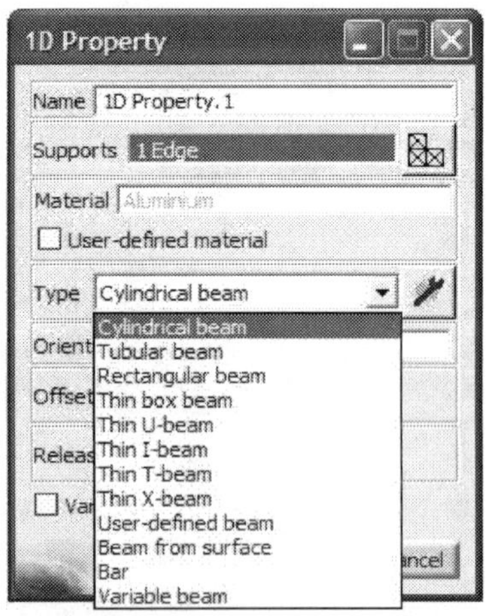


Using the icon , input the proper cross sectional dimensions in the pop-up box. The correct values are shown on the right.

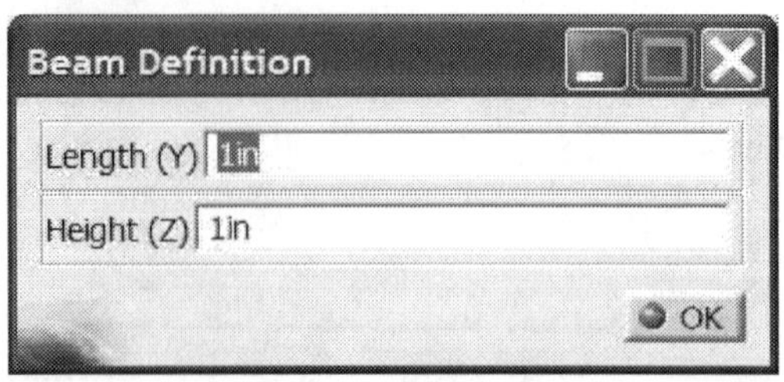


For the **Orientation geometry**, pick **Point.6** from the tree. You may have to expand the tree to reach it. Remember, this is the point with coordinates (0,0,0) which was created earlier. This point can also be picked from the screen provided that your part is in the **Show** mode.

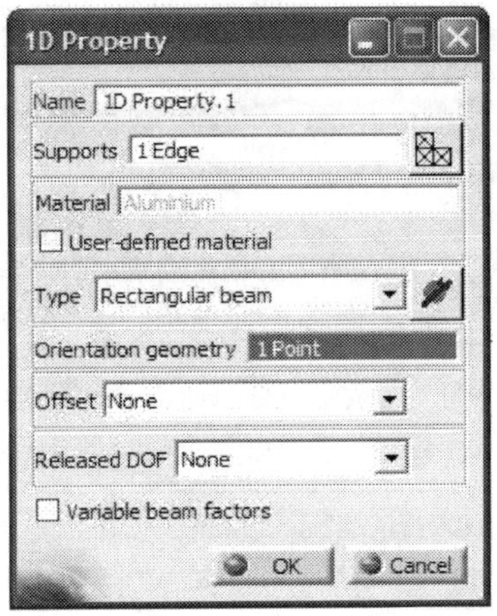


The model on the screen, and the portion of the tree reflecting the beam properties are displayed below.

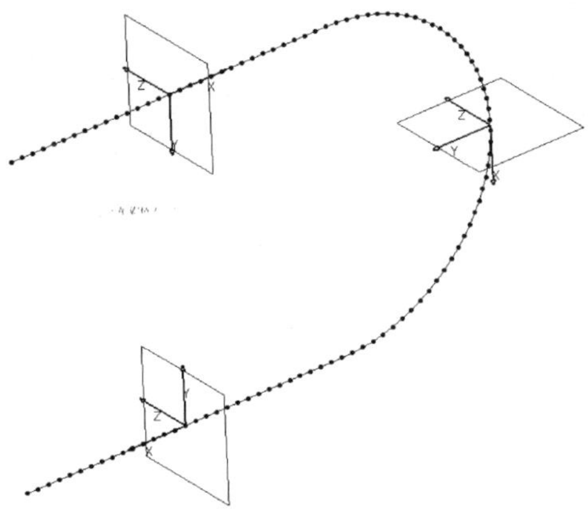

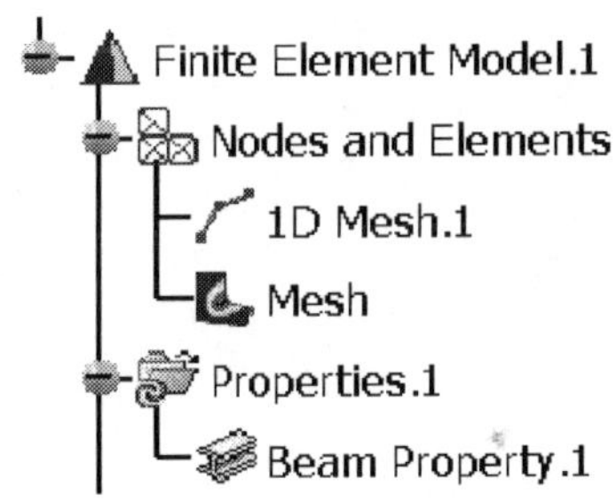


CONGRATULATIONS! You now have a mesh with the correct material properties. Regularly save your work.

**Applying Restraints:**

CATIA's FEA module is geometrically based. This means that the boundary conditions cannot be applied to nodes and elements. The boundary conditions can only be applied at the part level. As soon as you enter the **Generative Structural Analysis** workbench, the part is automatically hidden. Therefore, before boundary conditions are applied, the part must be brought to the show mode. This can be carried out by pointing the cursor to the top of the tree, the **Links Manager.1** branch, right-click, select **Show**.

In FEA, restraints refer to applying displacement boundary conditions which is achieved through the **Restraint** toolbar 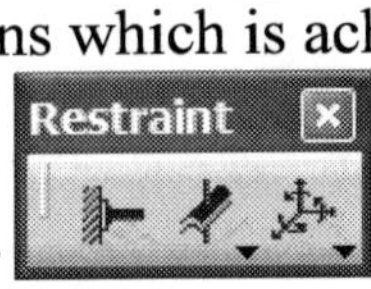

.

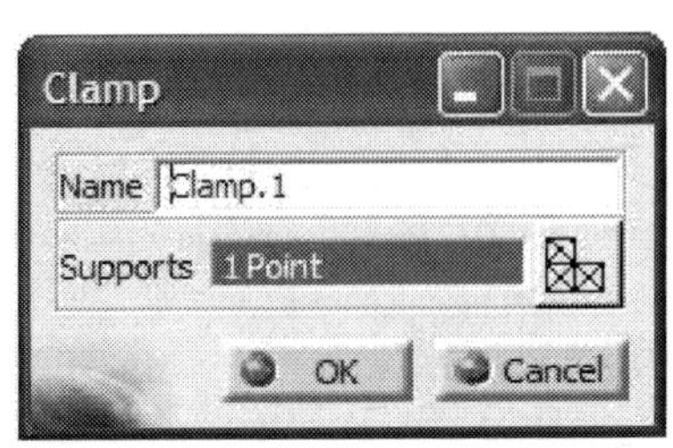

The **Clamp** condition for beams means that the displacements and rotations in all three directions are zero. Select the **Clamp** icon  and pick **Point.1** from the tree (or the screen) as the pop-up box indicates.

The second boundary condition is a downward displacement of 0.01 in. for **Point.5**. Recall that this is a two step process. First, use the icon 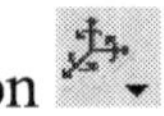 to deal with **Point.5**. The **User-defined Restraint** box should be modified as described below.

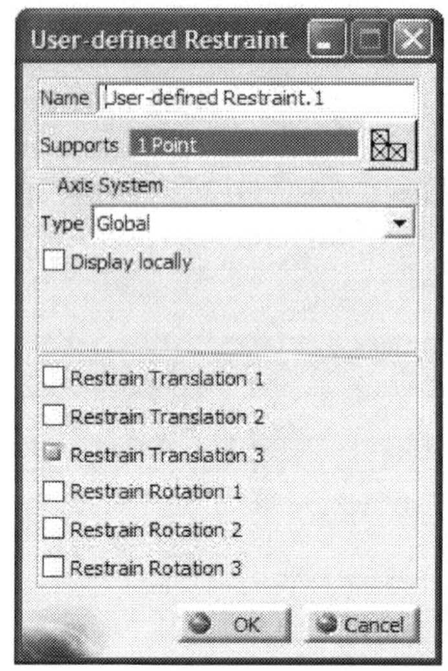


Then, use the **Enforced Displacement** icon 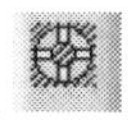 to specify the nonzero values. Clicking on the latter icon opens the box below. For **Restraint** select **Restraint.1** from the tree (or the screen) and use -0.01 for **Translation 3**.

The boundary conditions on your screen should resemble the figure below.

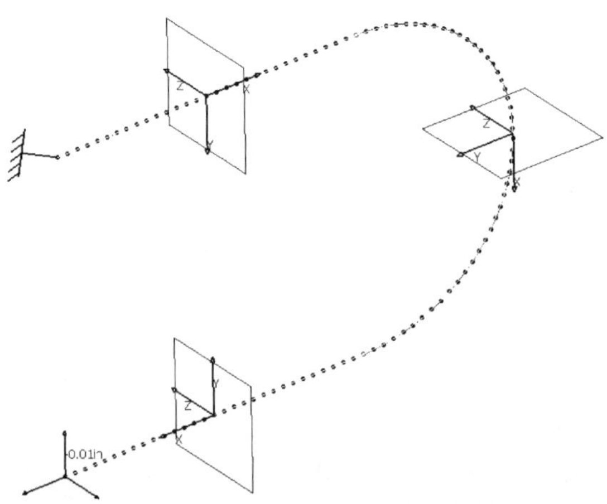

The complete tree structure after the above step is also displayed below.

**Warning:** Restraints and Loads cannot be applied unless the part is in the show mode. Therefore if you were unable to pick Point.1 and Point.5, the part is hiding.

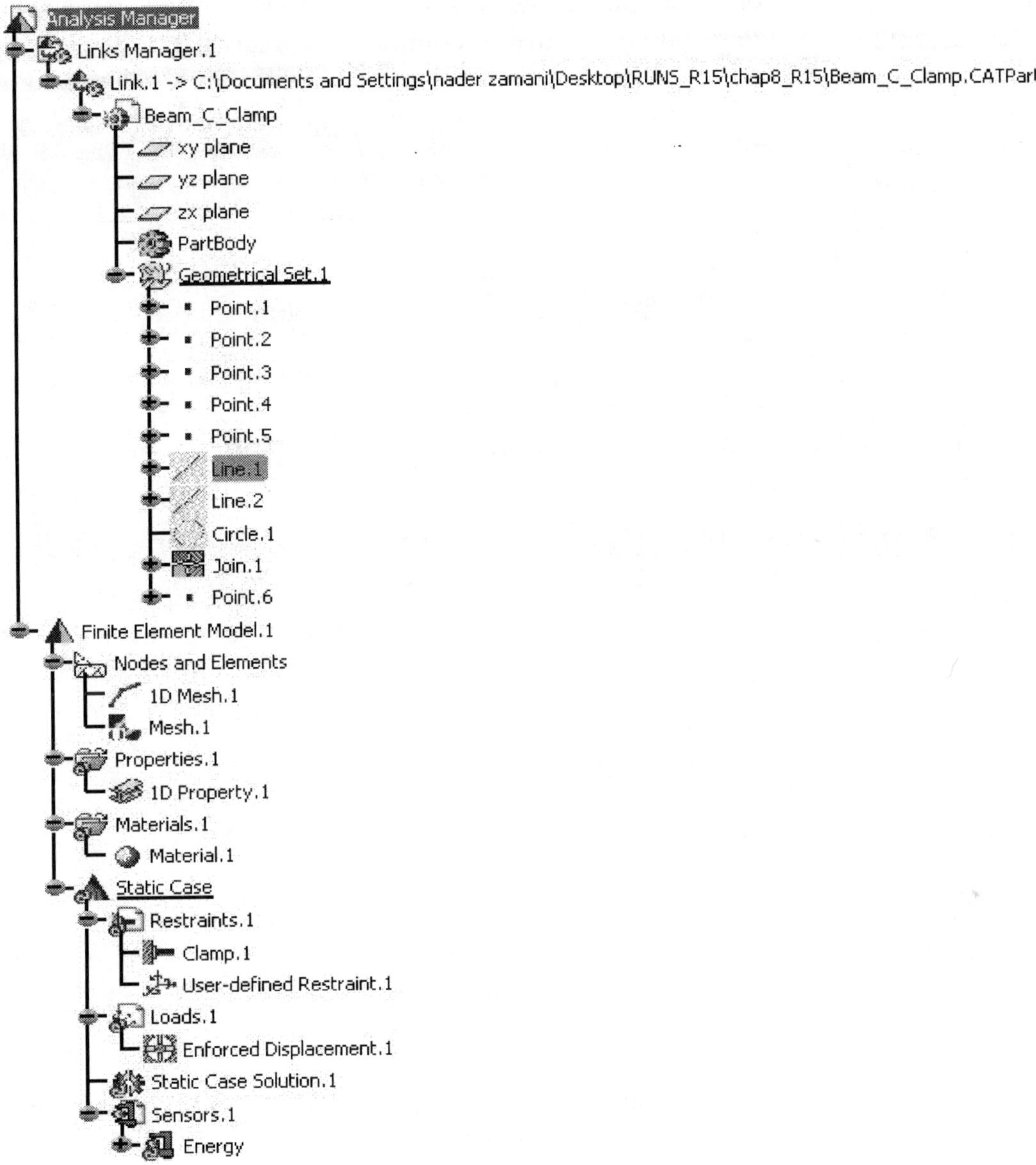


**Launching the Solver:**

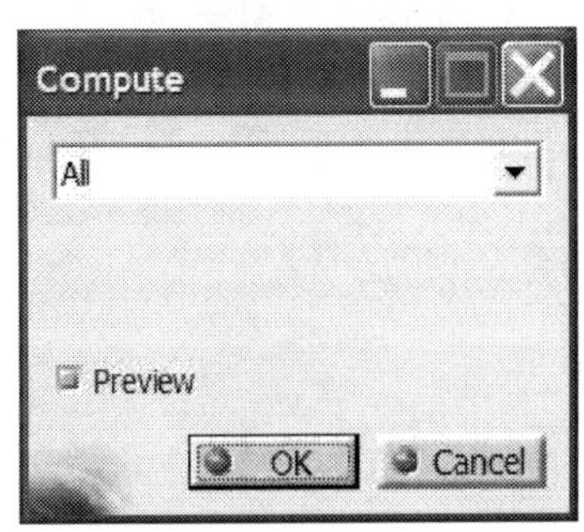


To run the analysis, you need to use the **Compute** toolbar  by selecting the **Compute** icon . This leads to the **Compute** box shown to the right. Leave the defaults as **All** which means everything is computed.

Upon closing this box, after a brief pause, the second box shown below appears. This box provides information on the resources needed to complete the analysis. If the estimates are zero in the listing, there is a problem in the previous step and should be looked into. If all numbers are zero in this box, although the program may run, it will not produce any useful results.

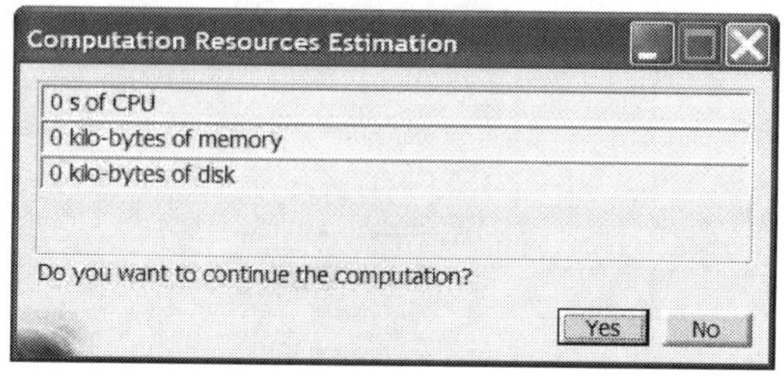


In this problem, in fact all resource estimates will be zero, an indication that there are errors.

In spite of this, ask the computation to proceed. The result is **Error** and **Warning** boxes shown below.

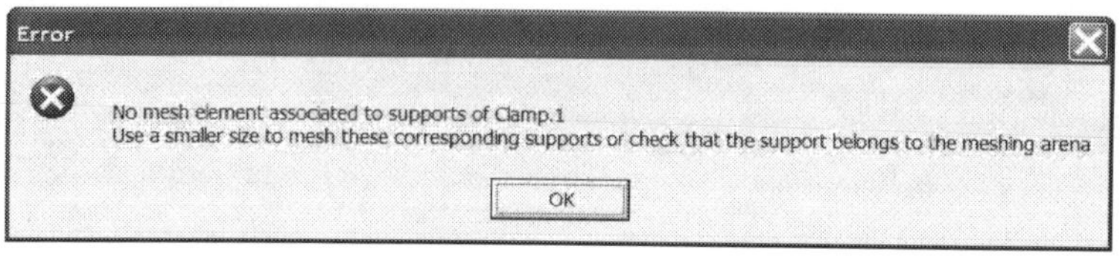


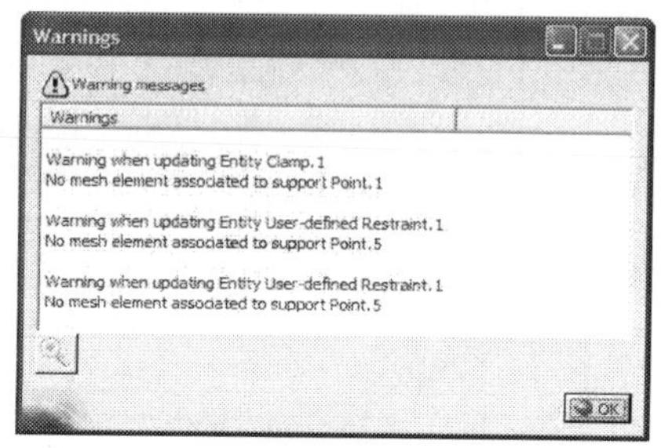


The **Error** message is not very useful. The source of the problem is as follows.

The boundary conditions were applied to **Point.1** and **Point.5** which are not seen by the FEA model. These conditions should have been applied to the same ends but not the above two points. The only way this can be achieved is by hiding **Point.1** and **Point.5**, and then applying the clamps.

First hide **Point.1** and **Point.5**. Next, delete the **Clamp.1**, **Restraint.1**, and **Enforced Displacement.1** from the tree. Repeat the process of applying the boundary conditions as described in the previous page to the ends of the beam.
Make sure that the part is in the **Show** mode. If you cannot pick the ends of the beam, it is an indication that the part is hiding. If so, point the cursor to **Links Manager.1** on the top of the tree, right-click, and select **Hide/Show**.
Upon running the program again, the resource estimates are no longer zero as shown in the new box.

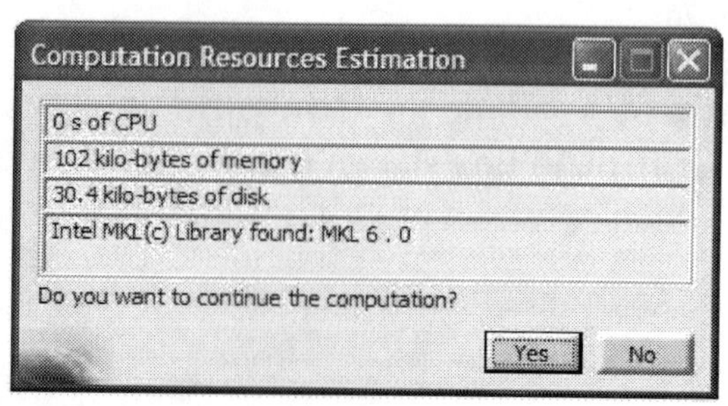

## Postprocessing:

In the case of beam elements, there is a limited postprocessing available. You can only review the deformed shape and the displacement field and the axial stresses.

The main postprocessing toolbar is called **Image** 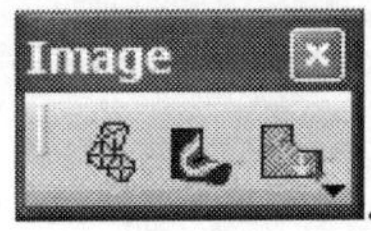

. To view the deformed shape you have use the **Deformation** icon. The deformation image can be very deceiving since one could have the impression that the beam actually displaces to that extent. Keep in mind that the displacements are scaled considerably so that one can observe the deformed shape. Although the scale factor is set automatically, one can change this value with the **Deformation Scale Factor** icon in the **Analysis Tools** toolbar 

.

In order to see the displacement field, the **Displacement** icon in the **Image** toolbar should be used. The default display is in terms of displacement arrows as shown on you screen. The color and the length of arrows represent the size of the displacement.

The arrow plot is not particularly useful. In order to view the contour plot of the displacement field, position the cursor on the arrow field and double-click. The **Image Edition** box opens.

Note that the default is to draw the contour on the deformed shape. If this is not desired, uncheck the box **On deformed mesh**. Next, select **AVERAGE-ISO** and press **OK**.

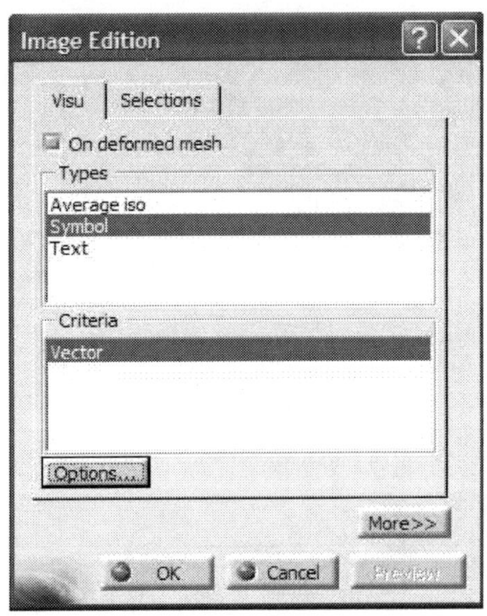

The contour of the displacement field is show below.

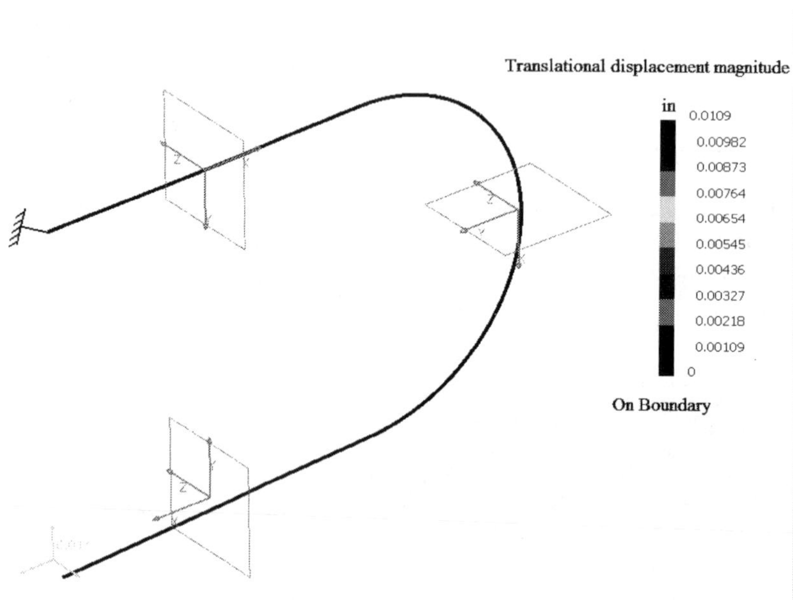


Now, we describe the process which allows you to find, the force necessary to cause the enforced displacement of 0.01 in.

This is achieved by defining a sensor. The sensor definitions are located in the bottom section of the tree as shown on the right.

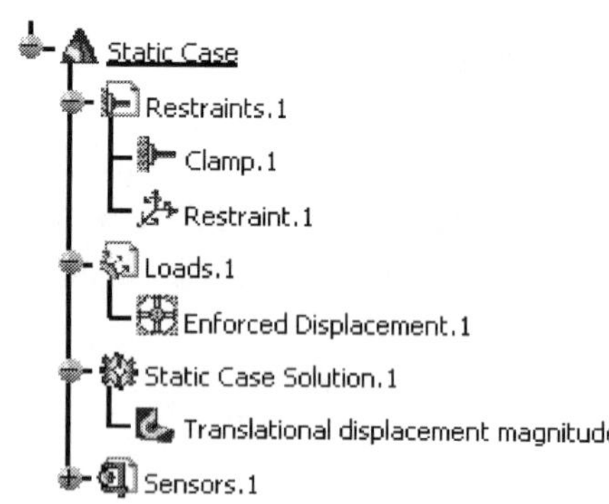


Point the cursor to the sensor branch in the tree, and right-click.

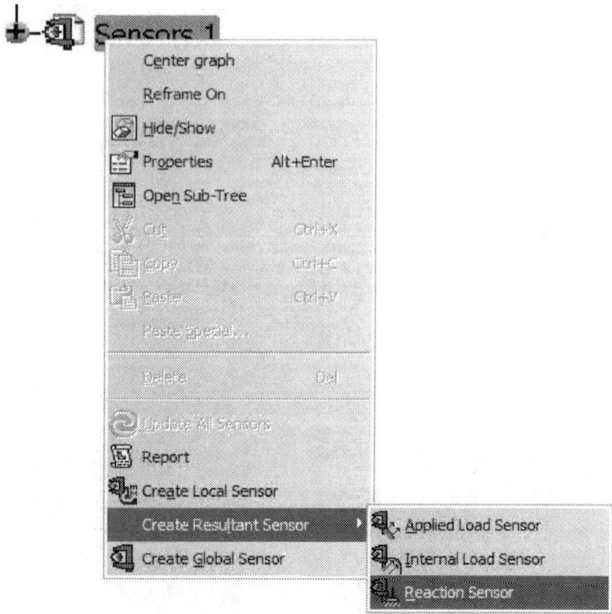

From the contextual menu, select **Create Reaction Sensor**. This forces the following box to open. From this box, select **Clamp.1** and close the window.

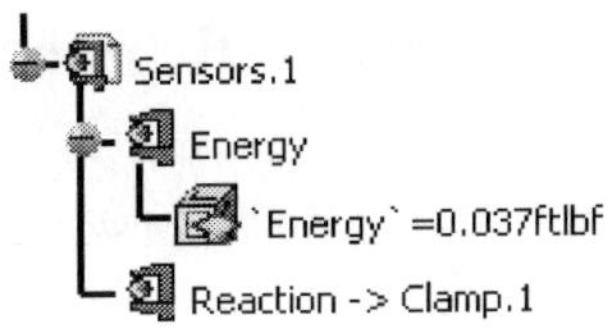


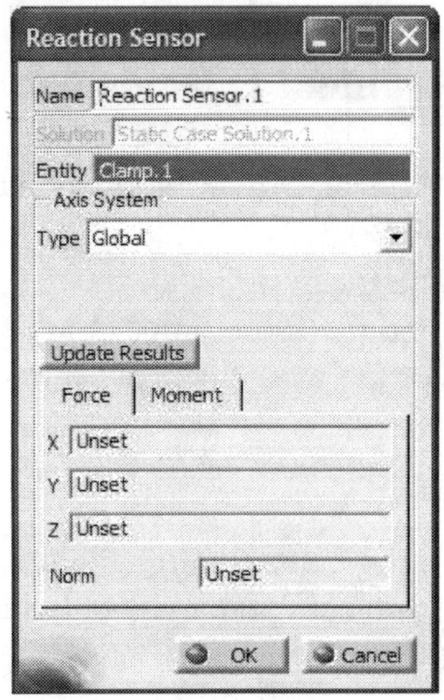


Double-click on the **Reaction Clamp.1** in the tree and the following box on the right opens.
Click on the **Update Results** box. The reaction forces will appear. Do not be concerned with your values not matching our values. Consequently, this is the force required to give the bottom vertex a displacement of 0.01 in. This value is in reasonable agreement with the solid model of the C-clamp previously studied.

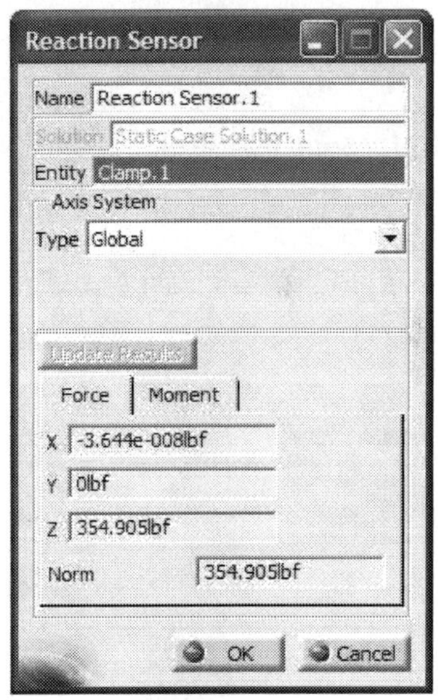


The energy sensor indicates that the stored strain energy due to the deformation is 0.05J . In order to see the 'Energy" value in the tree, you have to activate certain switches in the CATIA settings. Otherwise, double-click on the "Energy" branch and the value is displayed in a dialogue box as shown below.

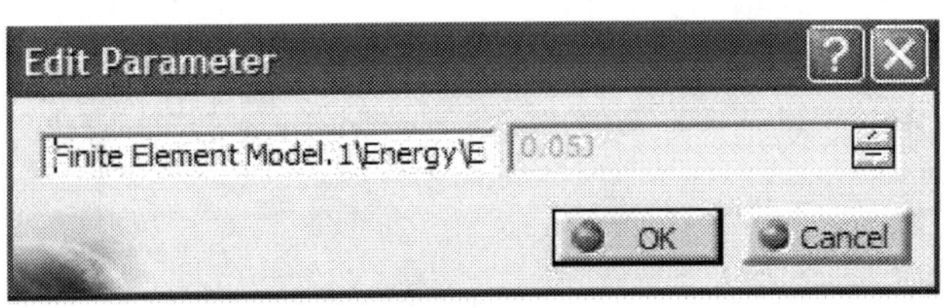

# Exercises for Chapter 8

## Problem 1: Deformation of a Ring due to an Enforced Displacement

The ring shown below is made of steel with Young's modulus .3E+8 psi and Poisson ratio 0.3.
The mean radius of the ring is $R = 10$ in. and the diameter of the cross section is $d = 2$ in.
Find the force F necessary to pull the ring down by 0.01 in.
For the analysis, use beam elements and apply symmetry as deemed necessary.

Partial Answer:

Using Castigliano's theorem, the following relationship between the force and displacement can be obtained;

$$\delta = \left(\frac{\pi}{4} - \frac{2}{\pi}\right)\frac{FR^3}{EI}$$

In this expression, "I" is the cross sectional moment of inertia given by $I = \dfrac{\pi d^4}{64}$.

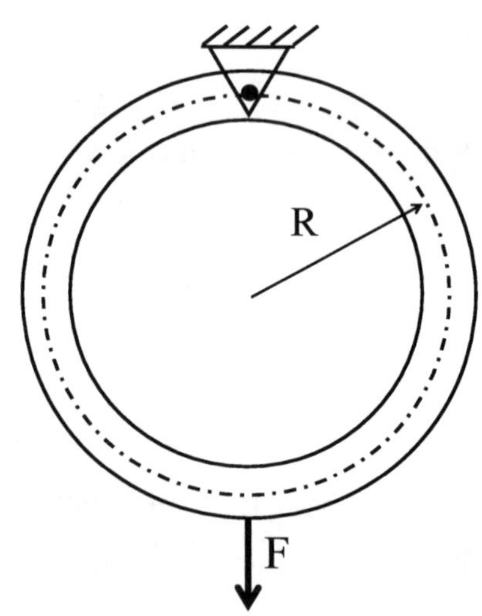

## Problem 2: A Portal Frame with Inclined Columns under an Enforced Displacement.

If the load F is applied horizontally to the top left corner of the portal frame displayed, the translations and rotation of this joint are governed by the following expressions.

$$u = \frac{5L}{24(11+6\sqrt{2})}\frac{FL^3}{EI}$$

$$v = \frac{-5L}{24(11+6\sqrt{2})}\frac{FL^3}{EI}$$

$$\theta = \frac{3(2-\sqrt{2})}{24(11+6\sqrt{2})}\frac{FL^3}{EI}$$

Select your own dimensions and material properties and apply the displacements and rotations according to the above descriptions. Verify the validity of these formulas based on the CATIA output. Use beam element for the FEA model.
The side members are inclined at $45^\circ$.

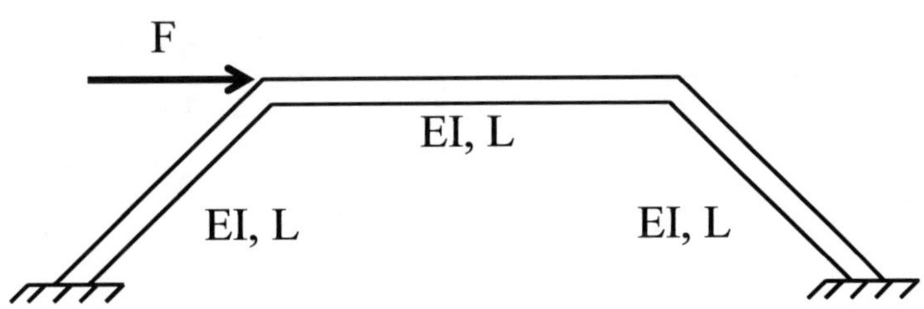

# NOTES:

# Chapter 9

## Bending of a Notched Specimen with Smooth Virtual Part

## Introduction

In this tutorial, a notched specimen consisting of two rectangular sections is modeled with solid elements. The specimen is subjected to bending in its plane. The bending effect is simulated by introducing two "Smooth Virtual Parts" in the model. The concept of "Groups" is used to postprocess the results in the vicinity of the notch.

## 1 Problem Statement

The notched specimen , shown below, is made of aluminum with Young's modulus 10.15E+6 psi and Poisson ratio 0.345. The sample is subjected to a moment of 600 lb.in about the x-axis causing pure bending in the yz plane. The dimensions of the geometry are, $D = 9$ in., $d = 6.923$ in., $R = .9$ in, and $L = 10$ in. The thickness of the plate is $t = 1.5$ in. The problem has "yz" as its plane of symmetry which will be ignored in the model.

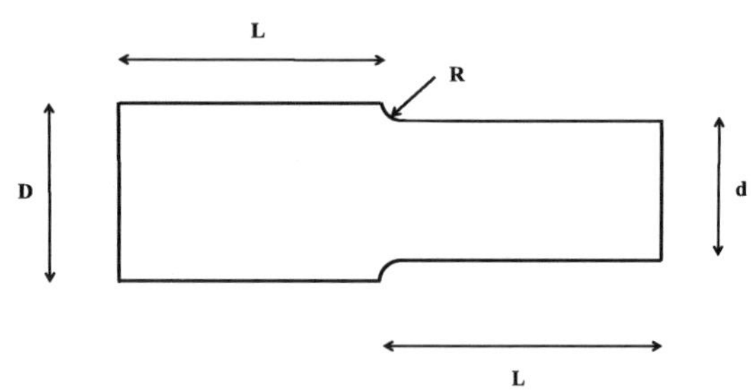


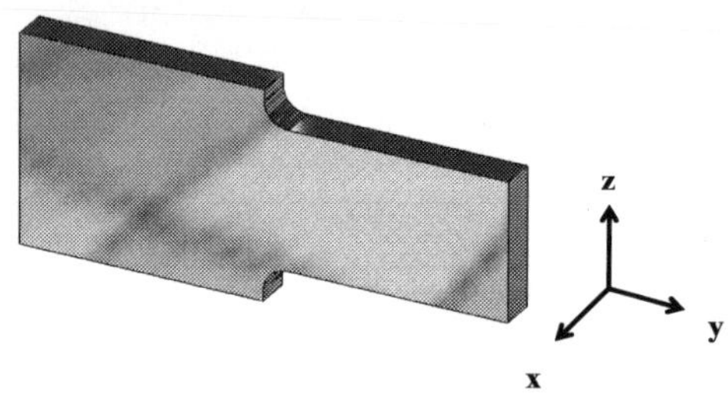


This stress concentration problem has an analytical approximation that can be found in most solid mechanics texts. For the given ratio D/d, the expression for $K_t$, the stress concentration is provided by $K_t(r) = .95880r^{-.27269}$ , where $r = R/d$.
The plot of $K_t$ as a function of r is displayed below. For the particular dimensions provided, $r = .13$ and therefore the analytical estimate of the stress concentration factor is $K_t = 1.67$.

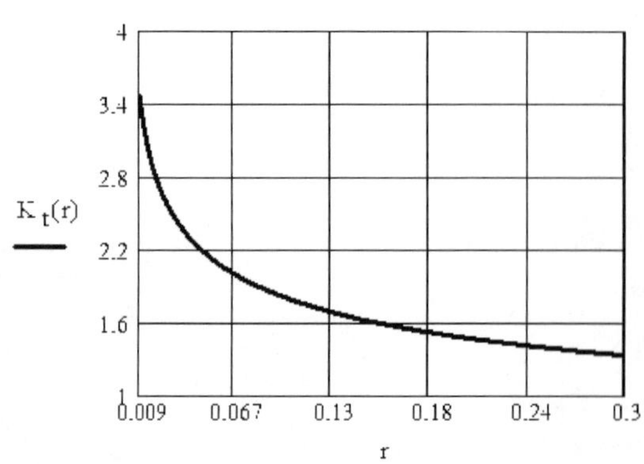

The above stress concentration formula is based on the net section. Let us use the analytical $K_t$ to estimate the maximum stress at the notch.

The cross sectional moment of inertia based on the net section is $I = \frac{1}{12}td^3 = 41.477 \ \text{in}^4$.

The nominal stress is calculated from the flexural formula $\sigma_{nom} = \frac{M(d/2)}{I} = 50 \, \text{psi}$.

Consequently, the maximum stress is $\sigma_{max} = K_t \sigma_{nom} = 83.75 \, \text{psi}$. This is the value that will be used for comparing with CATIA predictions.

Note that although the present problem will be analyzed with solid elements, it is more efficient to carry out the simulation with the shell elements which will be discussed in a later chapter.

## 2 Creation of the Part in Mechanical Design Solutions

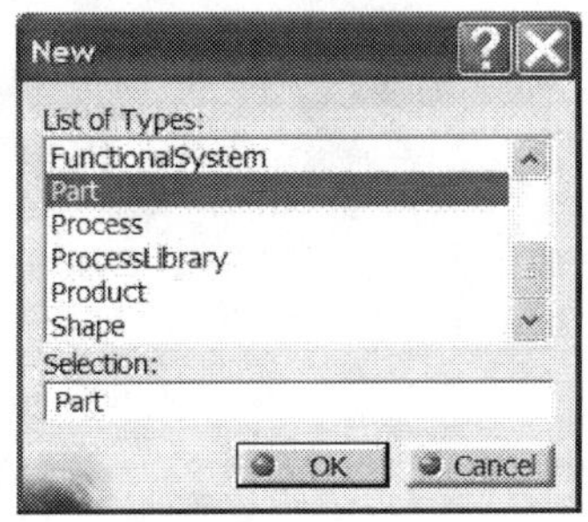


Enter the **Part Design** workbench which can be achieved by different means depending on your CATIA customization. For example, from the standard Windows toolbar, select **File > New** . From the box shown on the right, select **Part**. This moves you to the **Part Design** workbench and creates a part with the default name **Part.1**. In order to change the default name, move the cursor to **Part.1** in the tree, right-click and select **Properties** from the menu list. See Note #1 in Appendix I.

From the **Properties** box, select the **Product** tab and in **Part Number** type **Notched_Sample**. This will be the new part name throughout the chapter. The tree on the top left corner of the screen should look as displayed below.

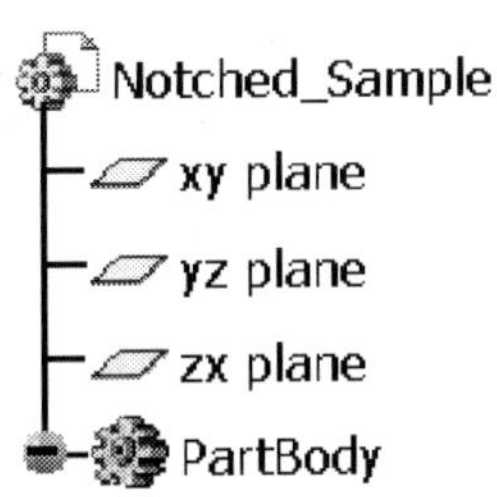


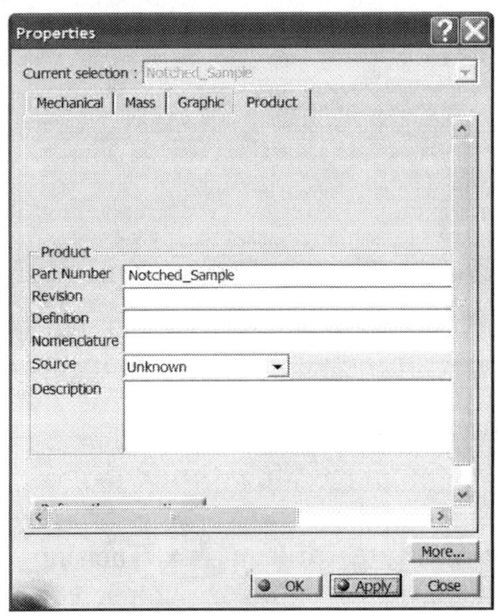

From the tree, select the **yz** plane and enter the **Sketcher**. Draw the sketch shown below and dimension it to match numbers displayed on the sketch.
**STOP**: *Make sure you constrain the geometry so that complete symmetry is maintained about the origin (0,0) of the Sketcher.*

Exit the **Sketcher**, and **Pad** your sketch for 1.5 in. Use a **Length** of 0.75 but check the **Mirrored extent** feature. The **Pad Definition** box is shown below.

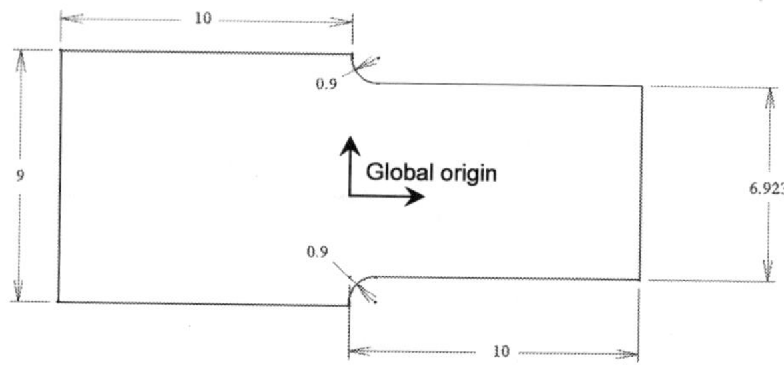


Use the **Apply Material** icon to assign aluminum properties to the notched sample. The **Analysis** tab of the aluminum **Properties** box is selected to confirm the values.

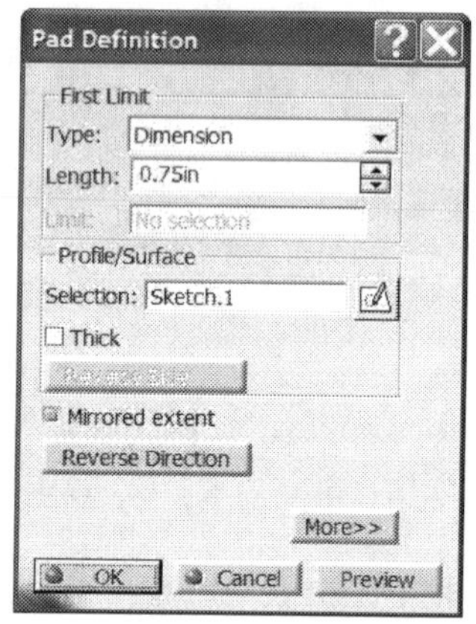


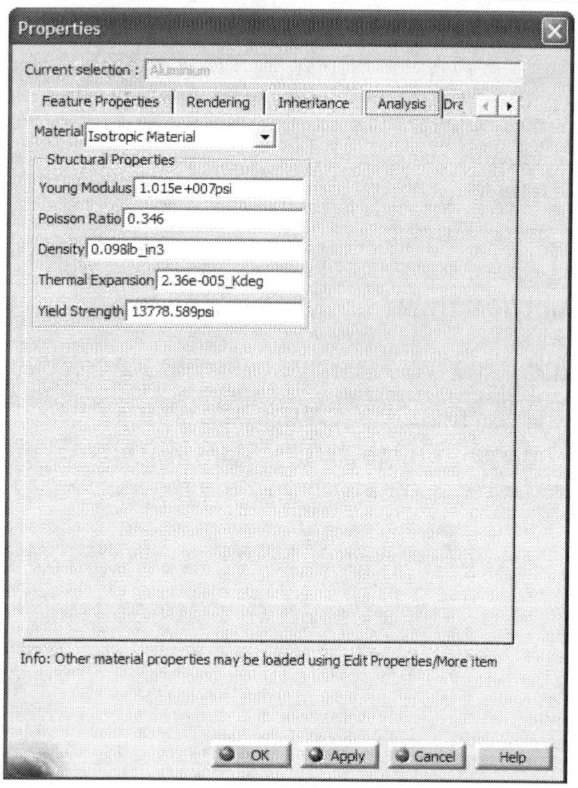


Although a ball park value for the yield strength of a typical aluminum is stated in the box, it is only for information purposes and never used in calculations.

If the part still stays "gray", one can change the rendering style from the **View mode** toolbar. Select the **Shading with Material** icon. The shiny metal part will be displayed on your computer screen as shown on the right.

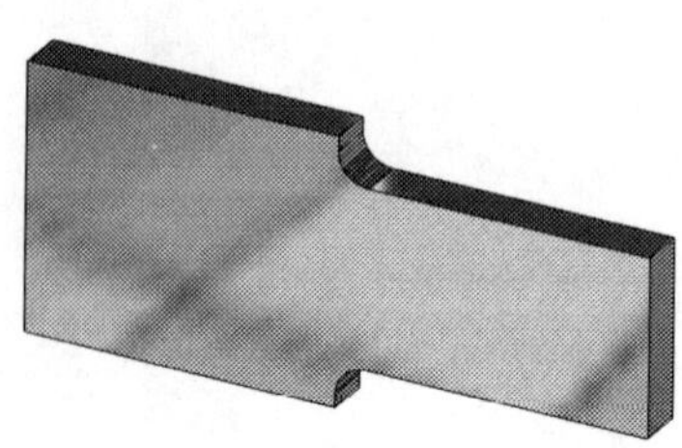

For reasons that may not be obvious at this point, we will create two points with coordinates (0,14,0) and (0,-14,0). *It is assumed that you created the sketch so as to have symmetry about the global origin as shown earlier*.

Select the **Point** icon, from the **Reference Element** toolbar. The box below opens and allows you to input the coordinates. Type the coordinates (0,14,0) in the appropriate locations. Repeat this procedure for creating the point (0,-14,0).

The display on your computer screen and the resulting tree structure are also shown below.

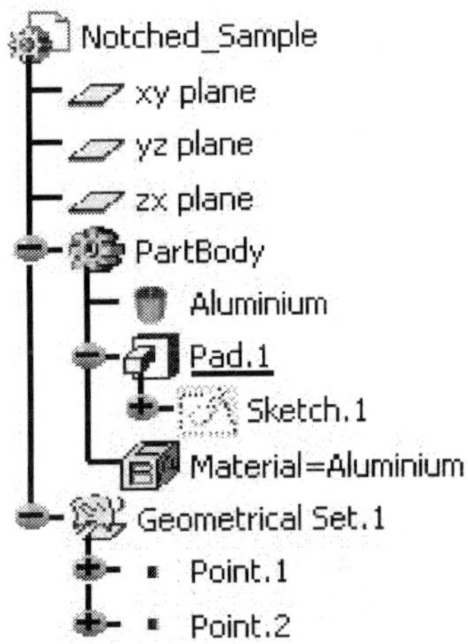


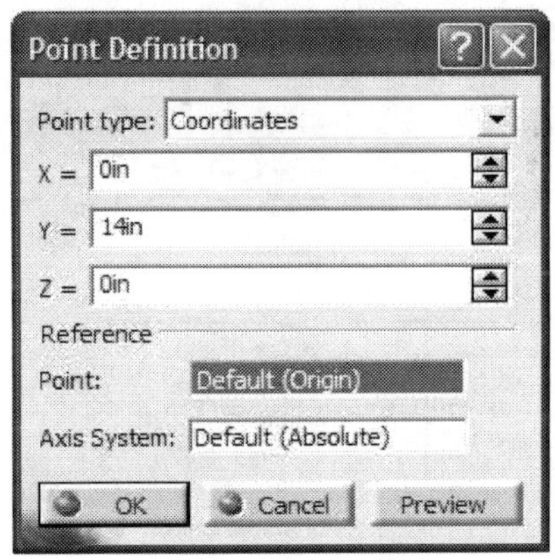


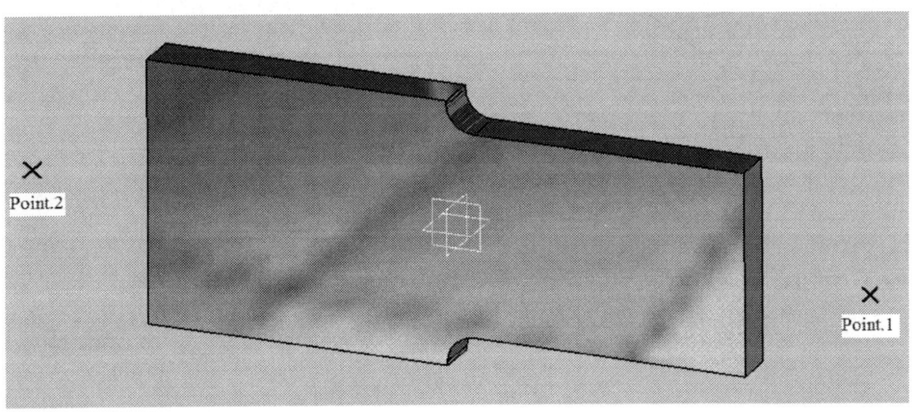


Regularly save your work.

## 3 Entering the Analysis Solutions

From the standard Windows toolbar, select

**Start > Analysis & Simulation > Generative Structural Analysis**
There is a second workbench known as the **Advanced Meshing Tools** which will be discussed later.

Upon changing workbenches, the box **New Analysis Case** becomes visible. The default choice is **Static Analysis** which is precisely what we intend to use. Therefore, close the box by clicking on **OK**.

The tree, the part, and the representative element size and sag (under default values) are displayed below.

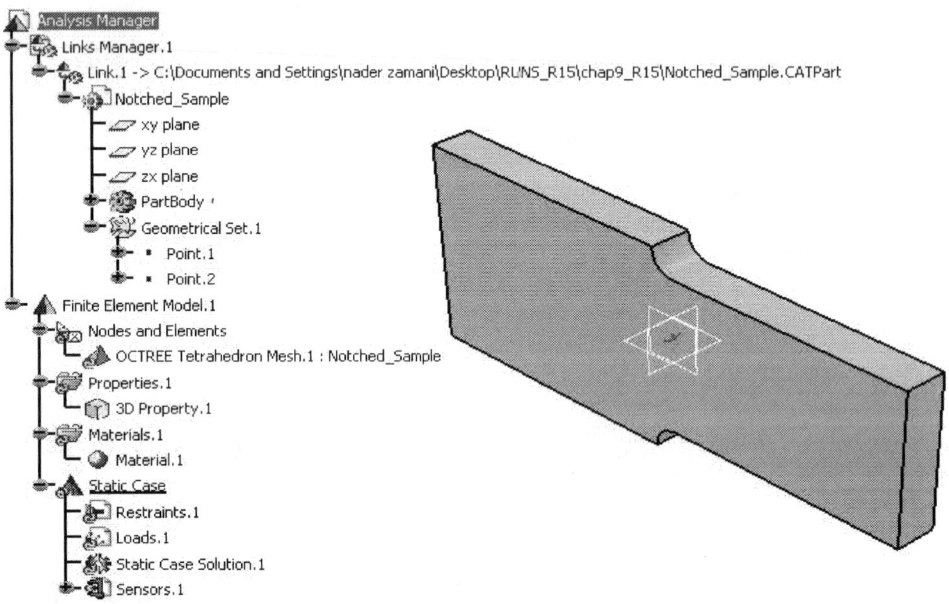


It is obvious that the elements are too big. Double-click on the representative element to open the box below, use the indicated "size" and "sag", and select **Parabolic** elements.

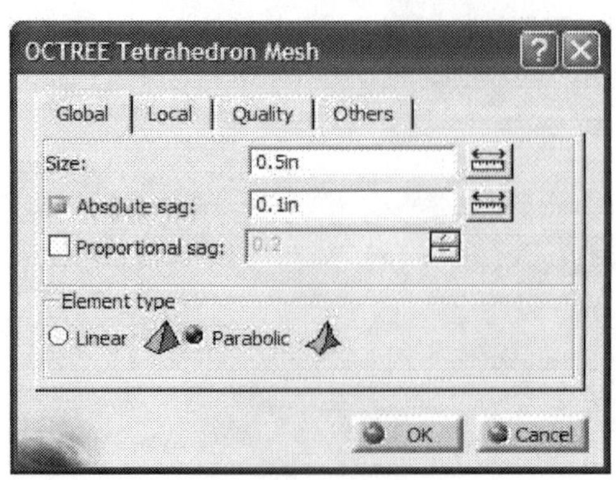

Point the cursor to the branch **Nodes and Elements**, right-click and select **Mesh Visualization**. A **Warning** box appears which can be ignored, select **OK**.
For the mesh parameters used, the following mesh is displayed on the screen. See Note #2 in Appendix I.

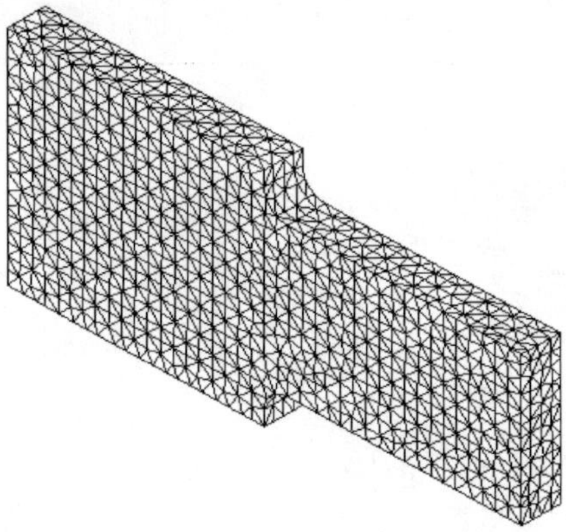

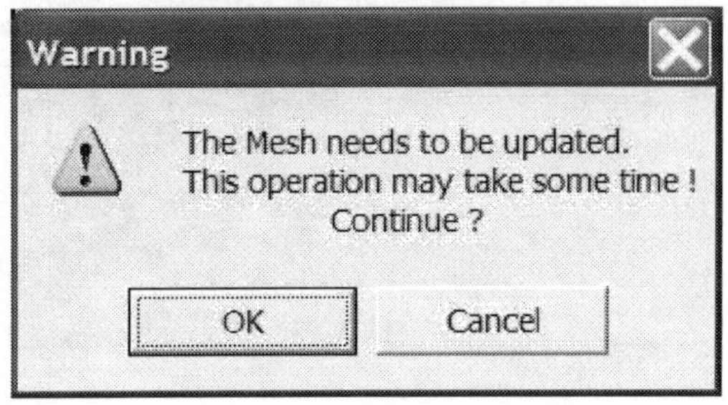


The representative "size" and "sag" icons can be removed from the display by simply pointing to them, right-clicking and selecting **Hide**. This is the standard process for hiding any entity in CATIA V5.

Before proceeding with the rest of the model, a few more points regarding the mesh size are discussed. As indicated earlier, a smaller mesh could result in a more accurate solution; however, this cannot be done indiscriminately. The elements must be small in the regions of high stress gradients such as stress concentrations. These are areas where the geometry changes rapidly such as bends, fillets, and keyways.
Uniformly reducing the element size for the whole part is a poor strategy.

**Creating Smooth Virtual Parts:**

Keep in mind that solid elements do not possess rotational degrees of freedom. The two ends of the notched sample are subjected to a given moment. This boundary condition cannot be directly applied to the present mesh.

One way to achieve this is to create two smooth virtual parts at the constructed end points and apply the boundary condition to them. Select the **Smooth Virtual Part** icon 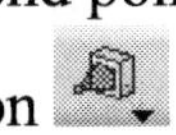 from the **Virtual Part** toolbar 

.

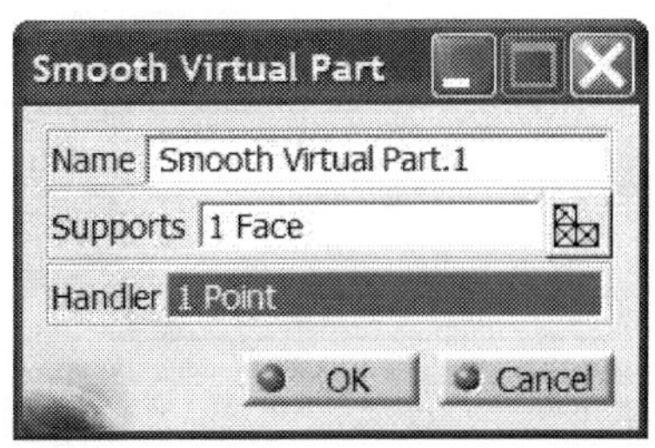


The resulting popup box is shown on the right.
Select the right-end face as the **Supports**, and **Point.1** as the **Handler**.

The **Virtual Part.1** is created as displayed below.

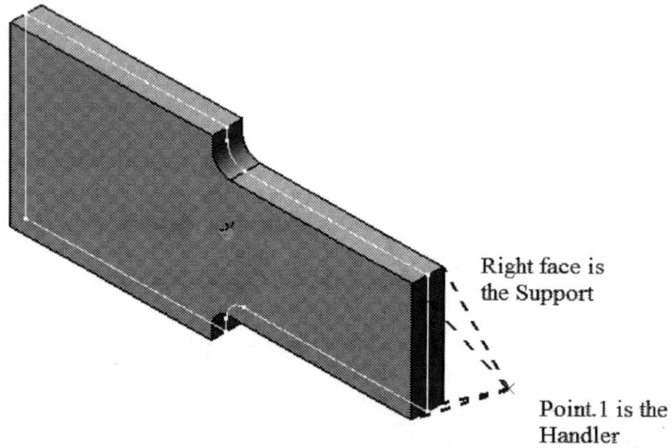


Repeat the same steps with **Point.2** and the left-end face. The two **Smooth Virtual Parts** and their effect on the tree are show next.

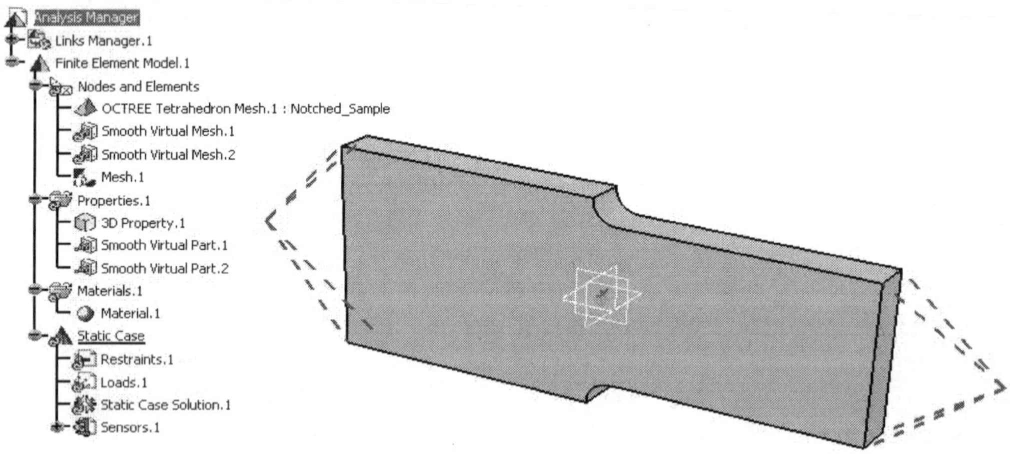


Point the cursor to the **Nodes and Elements** on the tree, right-click, and select **Mesh Visualization**. See Note #2 in Appendix I. This updates the mesh and displays the **Rigid** elements associated with the virtual parts as shown.

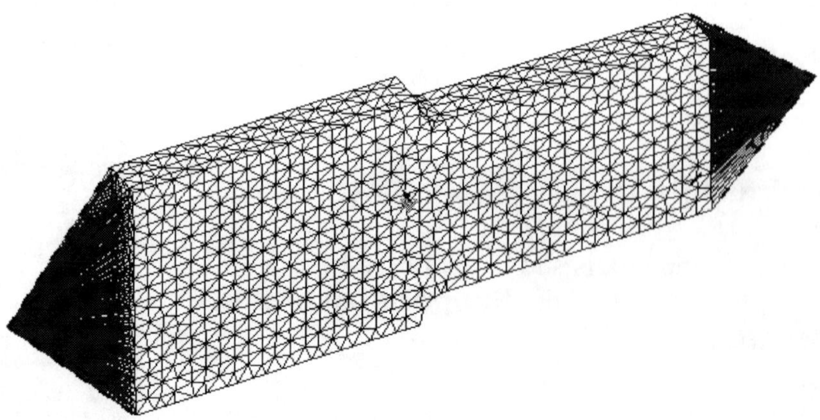

## Applying Restraints:

The restraints are applied to **Point.1** and **Point.2**.

Select the **User-defined Restraint** icon  from the **Restraint** toolbar 

. In the resulting box shown below, pick the virtual part on the right-side from the screen. Restrain all degrees of freedom except **Rotation 1**. The appropriate symbols appear on your computer screen.

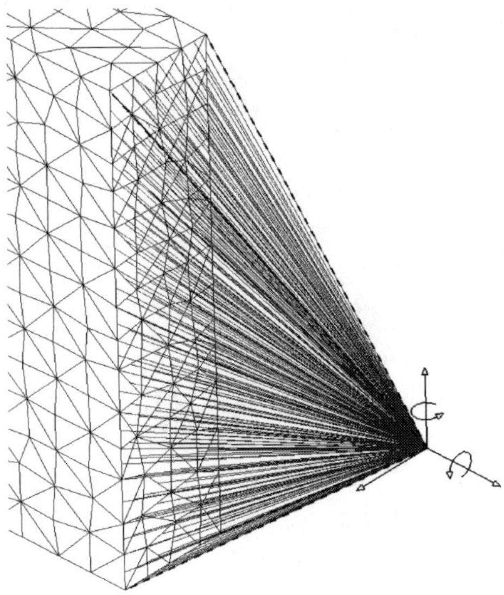

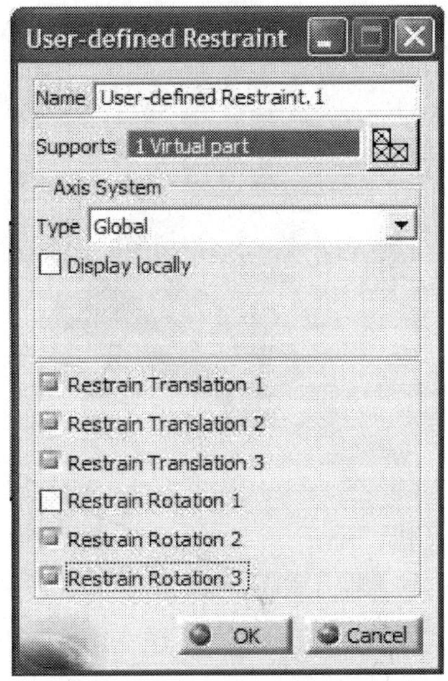


Repeat the above process with the second virtual part but pay attention to the modified restraints as reflected in the box below.

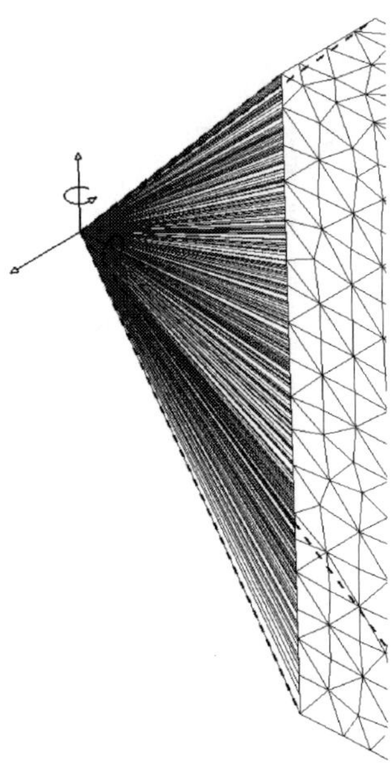

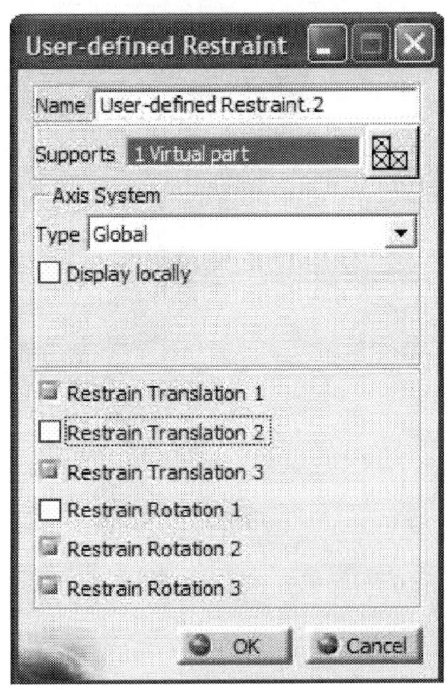

Select the **Moment** icon  from the **Loads** toolbar 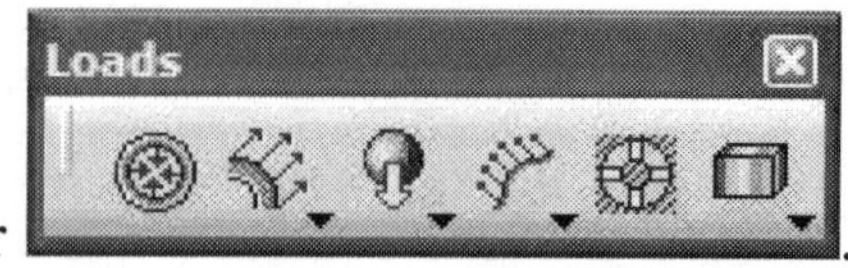

. In the box that opens, for the **Supports** pick the first virtual part and specify a moment of 600 lb.in about the x-axis. The moment symbol appears in your screen as displayed below.

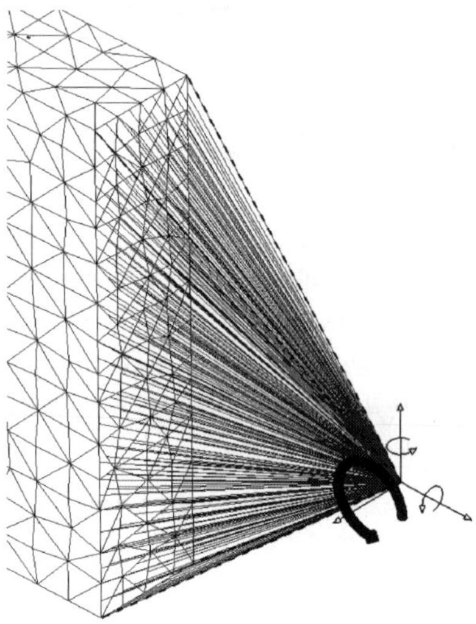

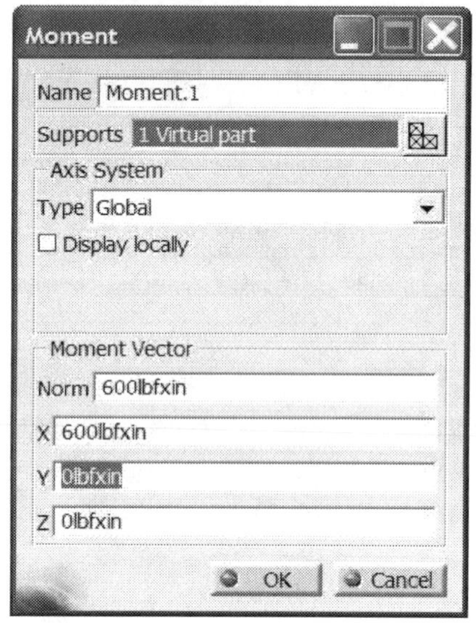


Repeat the process applying a moment of -600 lb.in about the x-axis to the other virtual part. The **Moment** definition box and the resulting symbol are shown below.

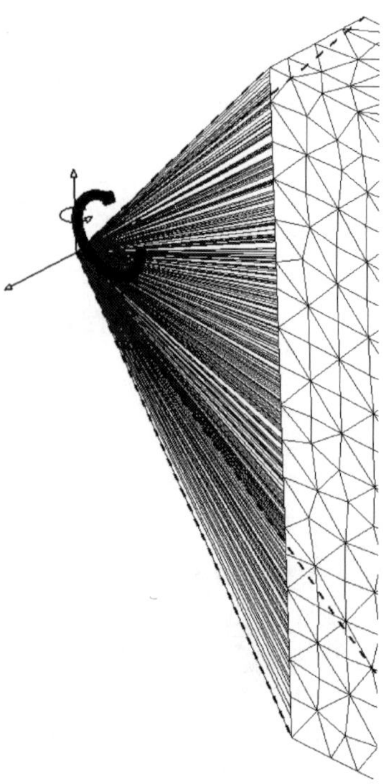

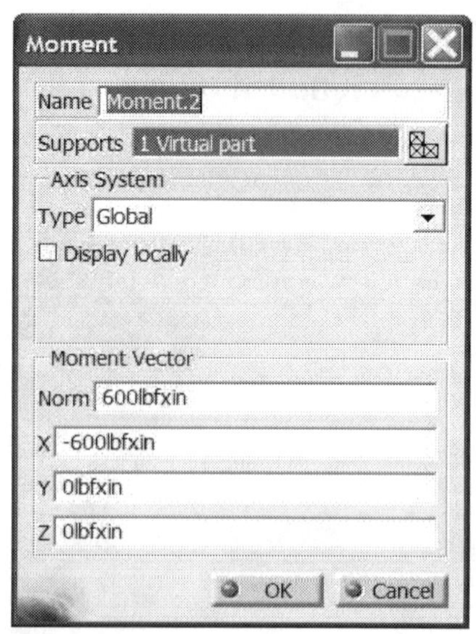

The complete tree after applying the boundary conditions is shown below.

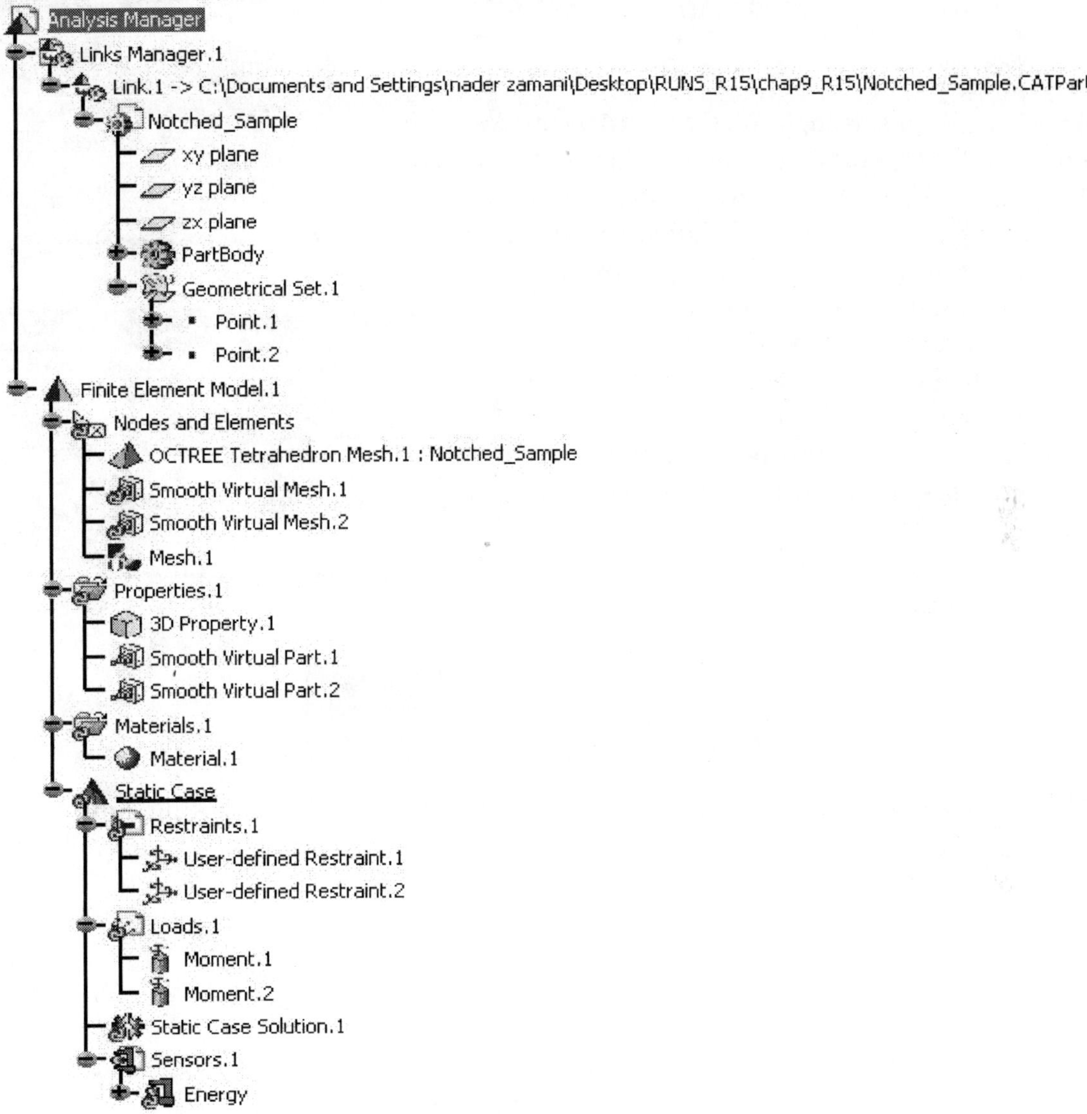

**Launching the Solver:**

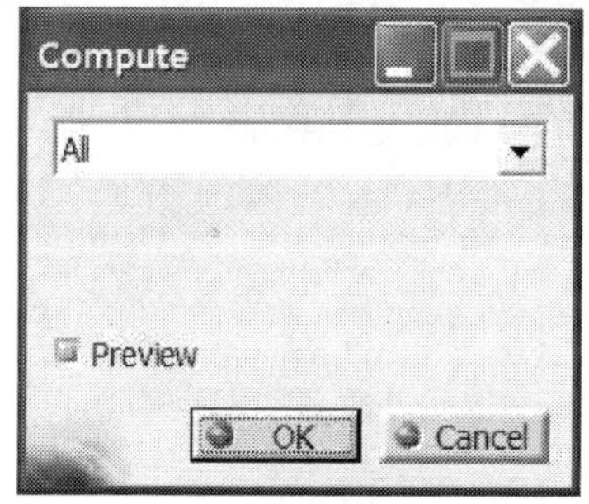


To run the analysis, you need to use the **Compute** toolbar  by selecting the **Compute** icon . This leads to the **Compute** box shown to the right. Leave the defaults as **All** which means everything is computed. Upon closing this box, after a brief pause, the second box shown to the right appears. This box provides information on the resources needed to complete the analysis. If all estimates are zero in the listing, there is a problem in the previous step and should be looked into. If all numbers are zero in this box, although the program may run, it will not produce any useful results.

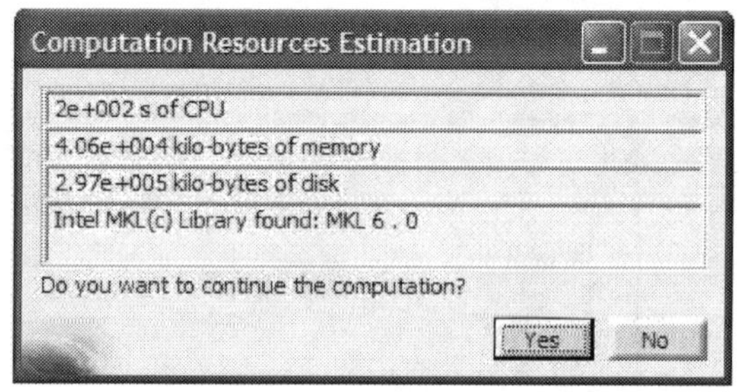


**Postprocessing:**

The main postprocessing toolbar is called **Image** 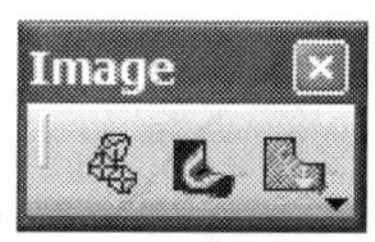

toolbar. To view the deformed shape you have to use the **Deformation** icon . The resulting deformed shape is displayed below.

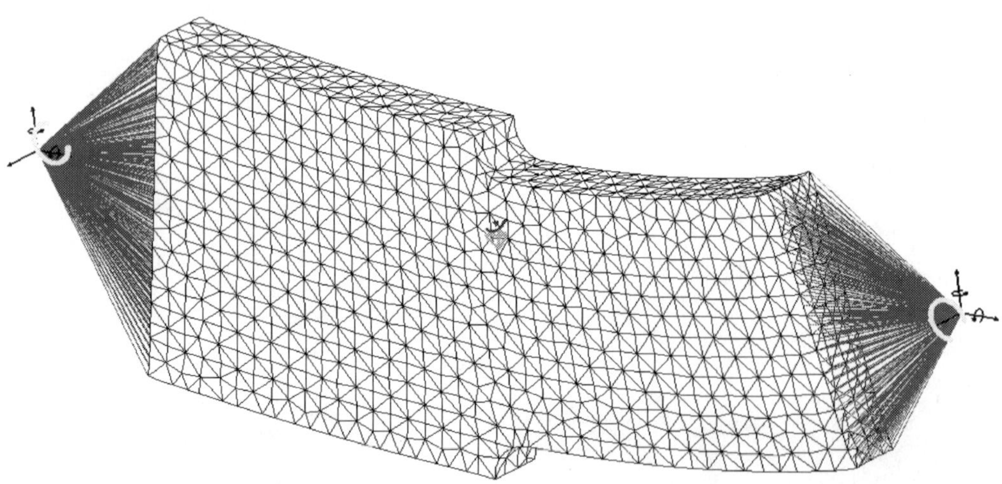

Keep in mind that the displacements are scaled considerably so that one can observe the deformed shape. Although the scale factor is set automatically, one can change this value with the **Deformation Scale Factor** icon  in the **Analysis Tools** toolbar

.

In order to see the displacement field, the **Displacement** icon 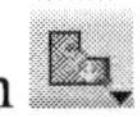 in the **Image** toolbar should be used. The default display is in terms of displacement arrows. The color and the length of arrows represent the size of the displacement.

The arrow plot is not particularly useful. In order to view the contour plot of the displacement field, position the cursor on the arrow field and double-click. The **Image Edition** box shown below opens.

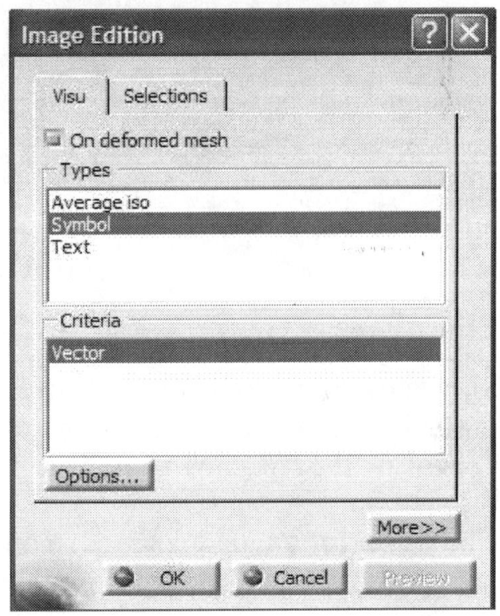


Note that the default is to draw the contour on the deformed shape. If this is not desired, uncheck the box **On deformed mesh**. Next, select **AVERAGE-ISO** and press **OK**.

The contour of the displacement field is shown below.

The maximum deflection is in the middle and happens to be 9.12E-5 in.

Note that the color map has been changed, otherwise, the plot looks all in black.

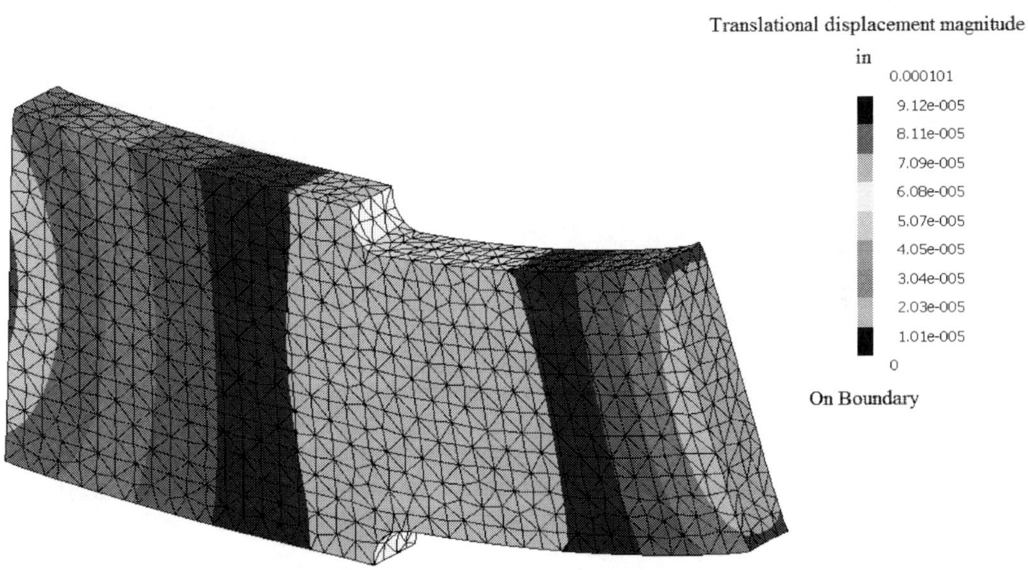

The next step in the postprocessing is to plot the contours of the von Mises stress using the **von Mises Stress** icon  in the **Image** toolbar. The von Mises stress is displayed below. The problem with this contour is that because of the large stresses at the end faces, the stresses at the notched areas are completely masked. Recall that the analytical calculations indicated a maximum stress of 83.5 psi in the notched section.

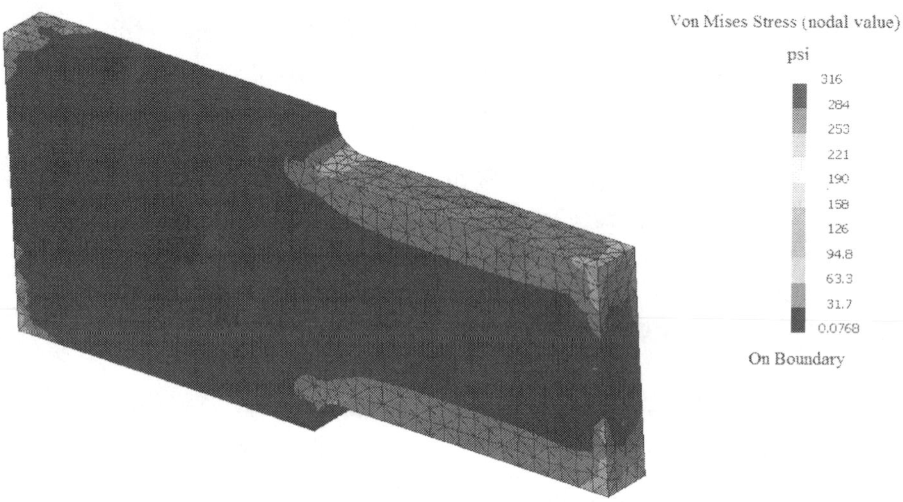


There are two ways this can be corrected. In the first method, you can change the range of stresses that is used for plotting purposes. Double-click on the contour legend which opens up the box shown on the right.

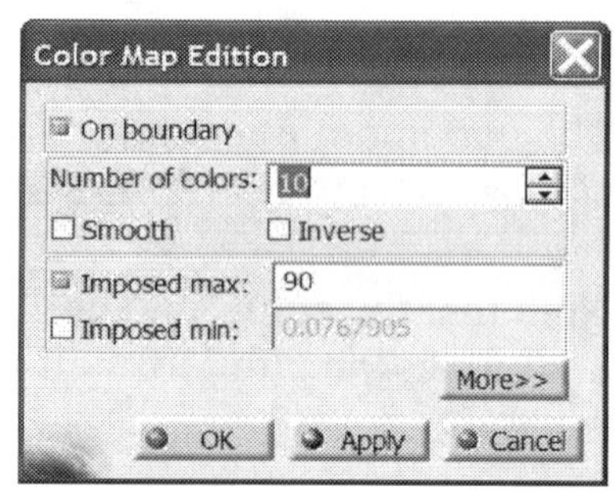


Check **Imposed max**, and enter 90. You are now requesting a contour plot which does not exceed 90 psi. The resulting contour is displayed below.

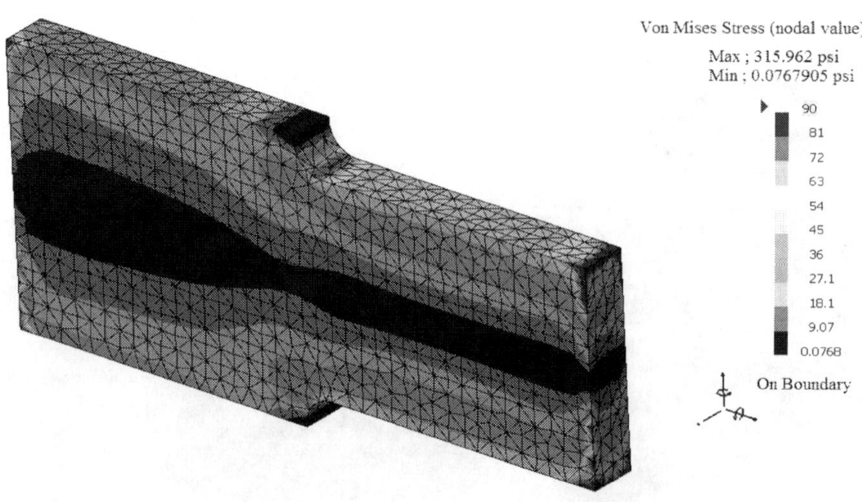

We now propose a second method of capturing the stress in the notched area. Before doing so, make sure that you set the maximum contour value to the original value, i.e., uncheck **Imposed max**.
The second approach uses the **Groups** concept.

The **Groups** toolbar 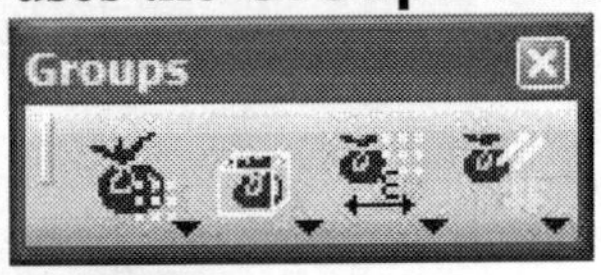

has several sub-toolbars. Select the **Spatial Groups** toolbar 

.

From this toolbar select the **Sphere Group** icon . This allows you to create a sphere of a desired size and location which contains all the elements used for plotting purposes. Clearly, you want to avoid the end faces which have unrealistically large stresses. Upon double-clicking on , the dialogue box shown below opens.
You can change the radius of the sphere and its position.
by clicking on the 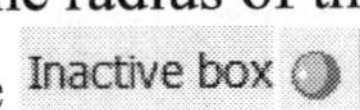

icon. A bigger sphere is depicted below.
If you are having difficulties changing the size of the sphere, read Note #3 in Appendix I. Using the spatial groups takes some practice and exploration.

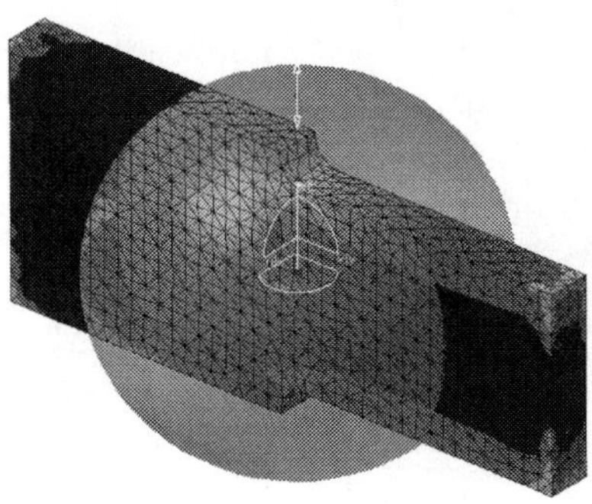

At this point the **Sphere Group.1** is created which encloses the elements trapped by the sphere. This group is listed in the tree as indicated above.

The next step is to plot the von Mises stress for this group. Make sure that the von Mises stress is active.
Double-click on the von Mises stress contour on the screen to open the **Image Edition** box. Next use the selections tab as shown below. Here, you have the choice of selecting different items. Select **Sphere Group.1**, and use the button . The contour below displays the von Mises stress for the desired group.

Notice that the **Sphere Group.1** is in the list. Select it. The screen changes to what is shown below. Notice that the range has a maximum of 84 psi.

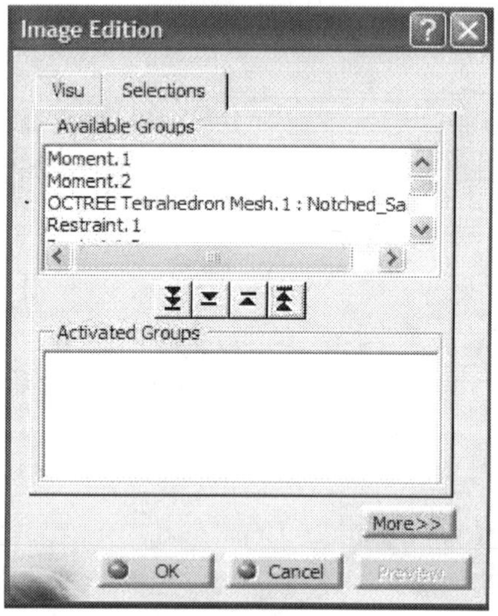


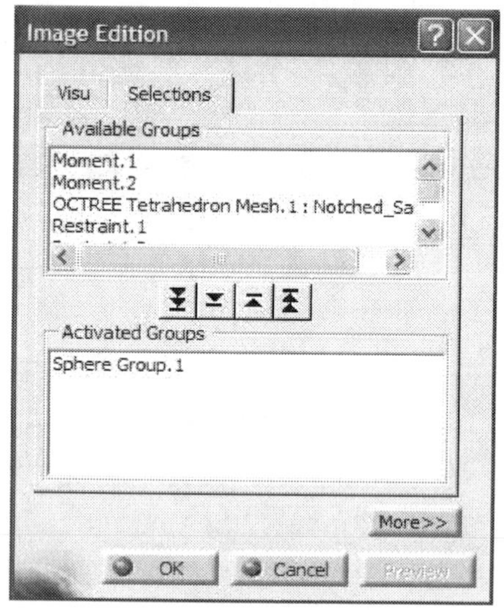


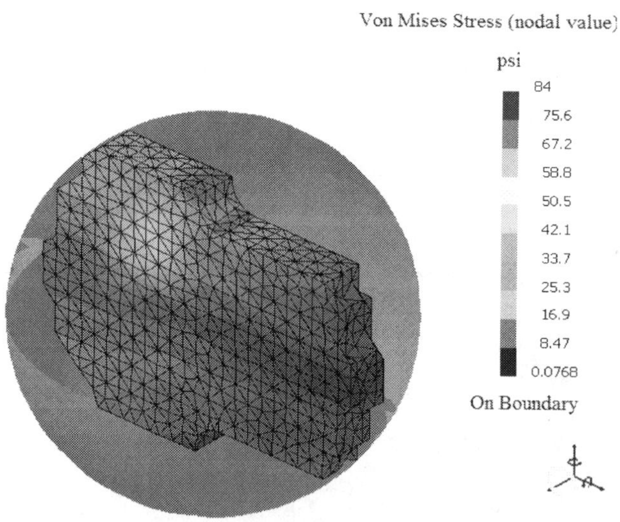


Point the cursor to **Sphere Group.1** in the tree and hide it. The result is a nice contour showing the detailed stress distribution in the notched area as indicated below.

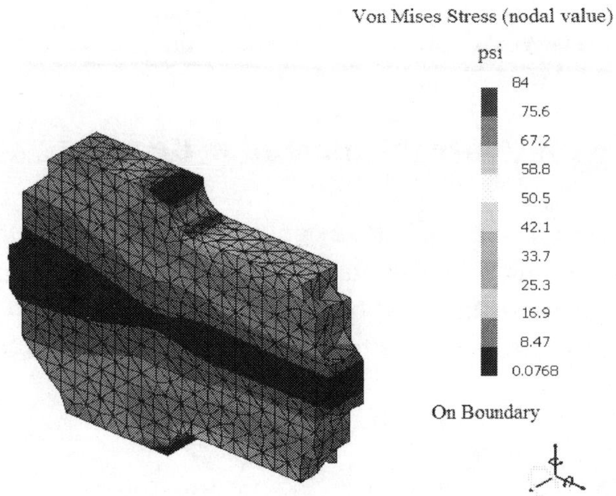
Von Mises Stress (nodal value)
psi
84
75.6
67.2
58.8
50.5
42.1
33.7
25.3
16.9
8.47
0.0768
On Boundary

# Exercises for Chapter 9

## Problem 1: a Plate with Central Hole under Bending

The steel plate shown below has a transverse central hole and subjected to a moment causing an out of plane bending. The dimensions of the plate are $L = 10$ in, $W = 5$ in, $h = 0.5$ in., and $d = 1$ in. Using solid parabolic elements together with the concept of smooth virtual part, find the stress concentration factor due to the presence of the hole.

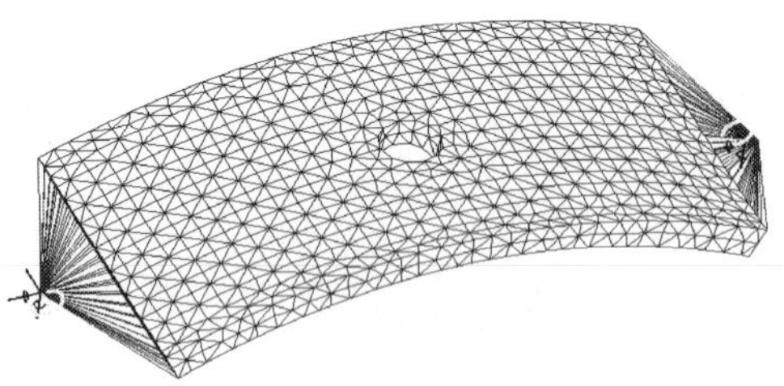

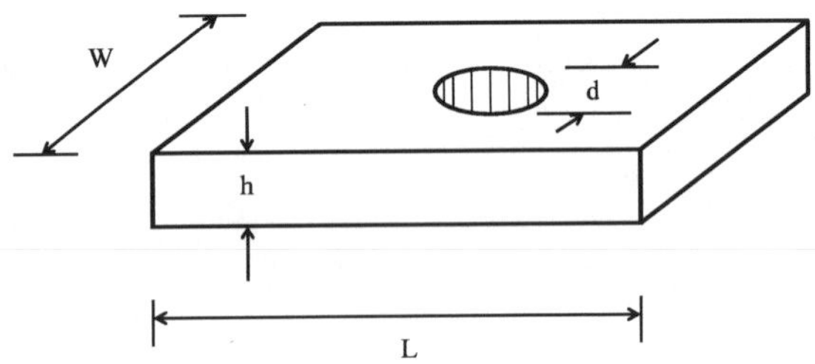


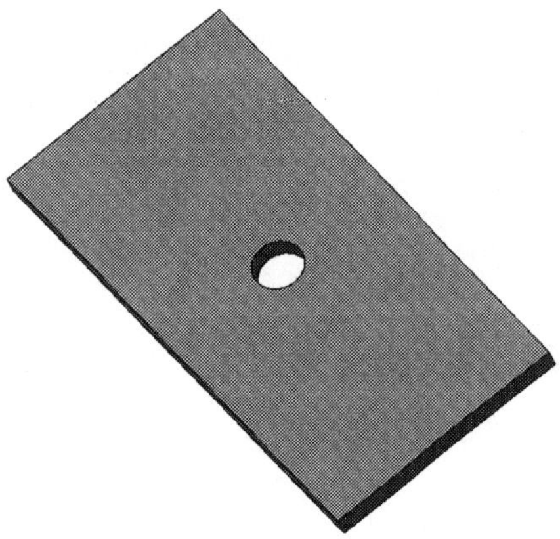

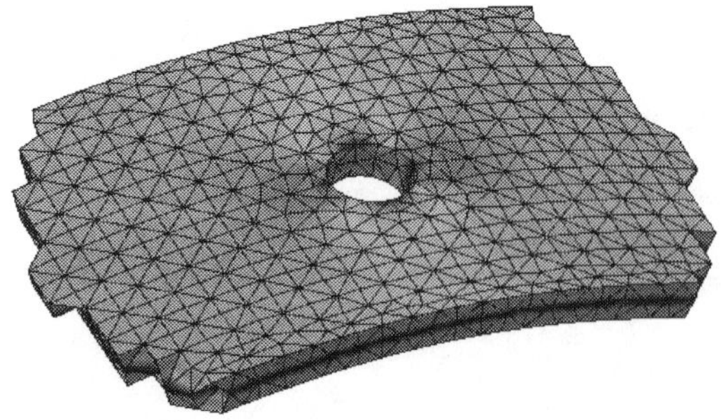

Partial Answer:

It is known that for $\frac{d}{h} \geq .25$, $\frac{d}{W} \leq .65$, and the given dimensions, the stress concentration factor can be estimated from $K_t(r) = 2.02430e^{-.79878r}$. In this formula, $r = \frac{d}{W}$. The plot of this relationship is given below.

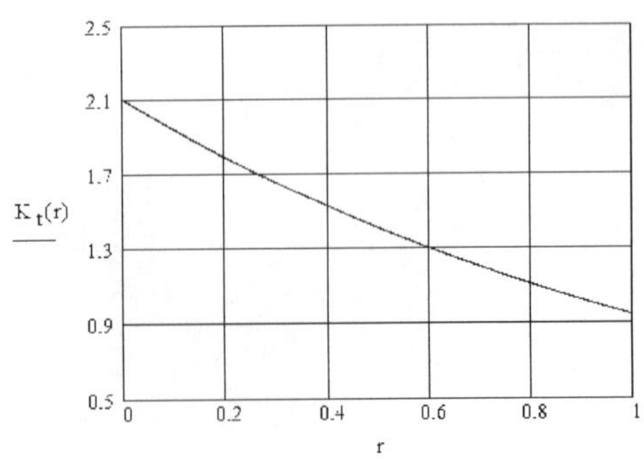

## Problem 2: Twisting of a Grooved Shaft

Using solid elements and the concept of virtual part, find the stress concentration in the grooved shaft subject to torsion. Use, $D = 2$ in., $d = 1$ in., and $r = .1$ in.

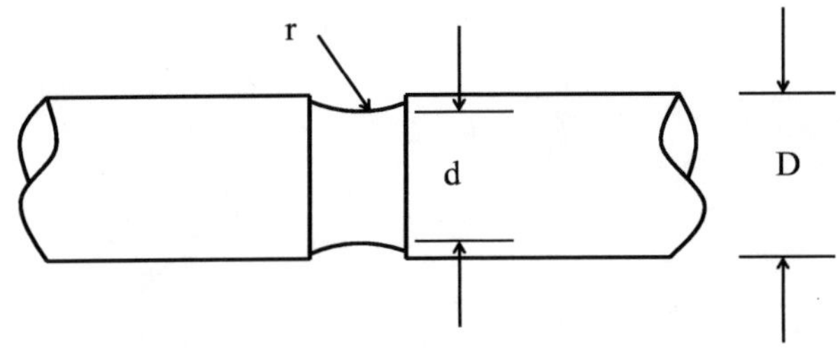


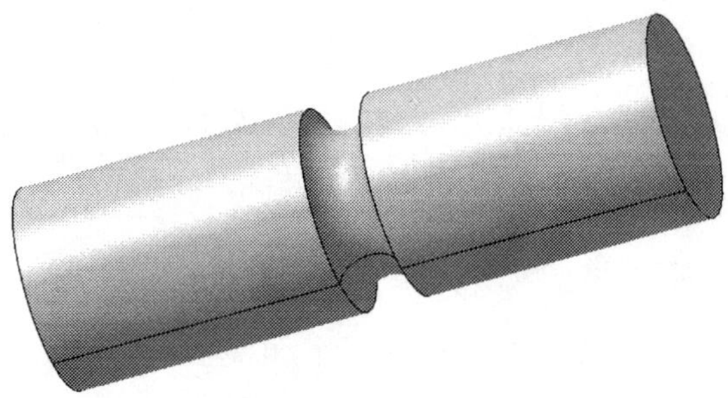

Partial Answer:

For the ratio $\frac{D}{d} = 2$, the stress concentration is estimated from $K_t = .89035\left(\frac{r}{d}\right)^{-.24075}$

# NOTES:

# Chapter 10

## Analyzing a Loaded Bracket with Triangular Shell Elements

## Introduction

In this tutorial, you will model a thin loaded bracket with shell elements. The surface of the bracket is extracted from a solid model and the join operation is used to sew them together. Triangular shell elements which are extremely robust and efficient are used for modeling purposes.

## 1 Problem Statement

The bracket shown below is made of Yellow Brass having a thickness of 0.1 in.
A pressure of 100 psi acts on the top surface. The structure has two planes of symmetry which allows us to model only one quarter of the geometry. The reduced geometry is also displayed.

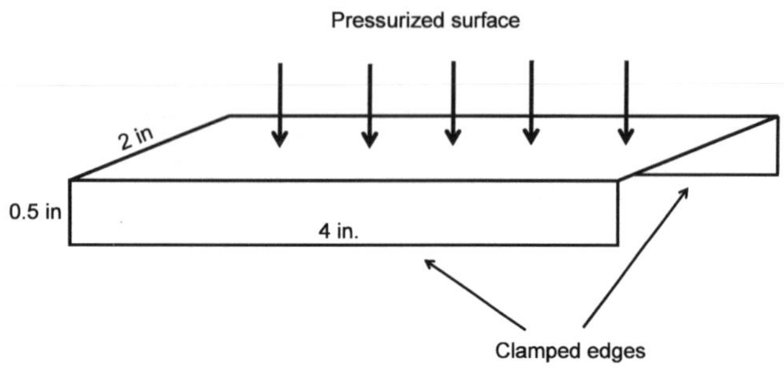


**Full Scale Geometry**

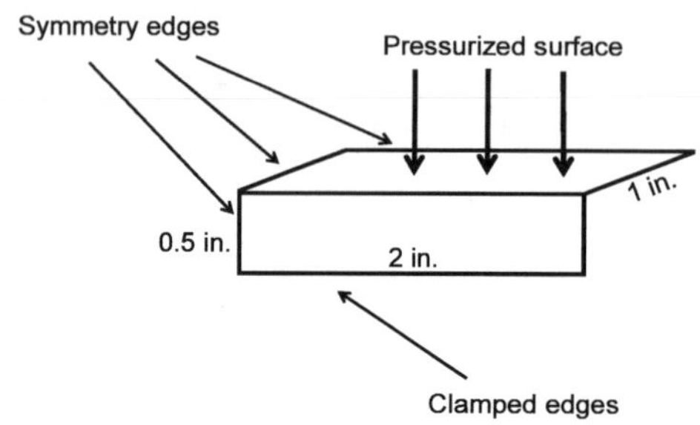


**Reduced Geometry**

Linear triangular shell elements in space have three nodes with each node having six degrees of freedom. Those are, three translations and three rotations. The thickness of the shell has to be provided as an input to CATIA. A typical shell element is displayed below. As in the case of solid elements, CATIA has linear and parabolic shell elements with the latter ones being more accurate. Limited QUAD elements are also available.

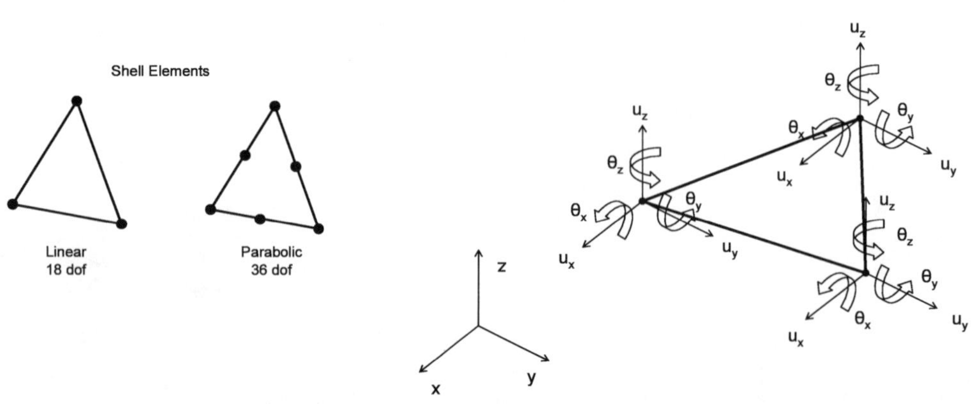


In this tutorial, the surfaces are extracted from a solid part instead of constructing them in the **Wireframe and Surface Design** workbench.

$m_b = 1 \times 10^{-3}$ kg $\quad I_R = 0.06 \quad L_1 = I\omega$

$m_R = 0.5$ kg

$L_R = 0.6$ m $\quad m(r \times \vec{v})$

$L_i = L_f \quad m r . v$

$m_b r . v = I + MR^2 + M_B R^2$

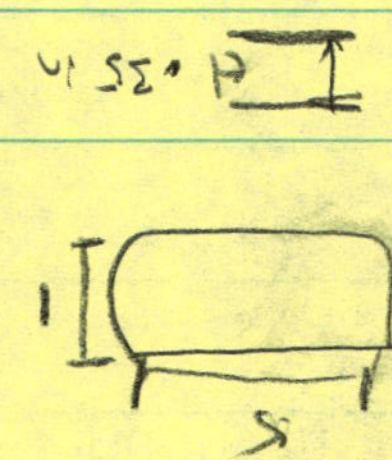

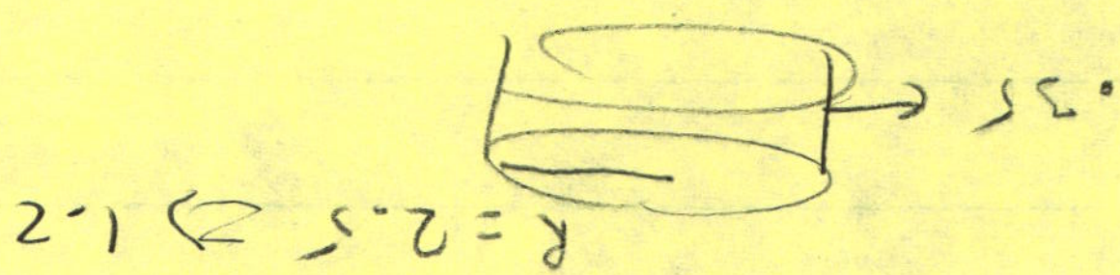

$m_B = 53$ kg $\qquad k = 6000$ N/m

$m_L = 37$ kg

$KE + PE = \frac{1}{2} k x_m^2$

B/ $m_B g(h + x) = \frac{1}{2} k x_m^2$

$519.4 + 519.4x = 3000x^2 \qquad 0.517$

$\omega_1 = \sqrt{\frac{k}{m}} =$

## 2 Creation of the Part in Mechanical Design Solutions

Enter the **Part Design** workbench which can be achieved by different means depending on your CATIA customization. For example, from the standard Windows toolbar, select **File > New**. From the box shown on the right, select **Part**. This moves you to the **Part Design** workbench and creates a part with the default name **Part.1**. See Note #1 in Appendix I.

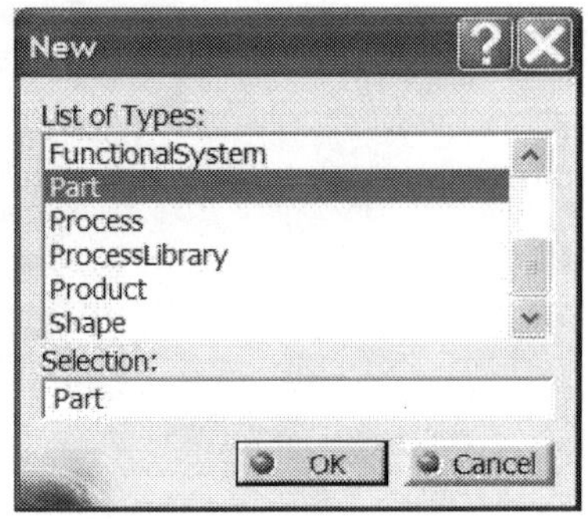


In order to change the default name, move the cursor to **Part.1** in the tree, right-click and select **Properties** from the menu list.
From the **Properties** box, select the **Product** tab and in **Part Number** type **Bracket_Shell**. This will be the new part name throughout the chapter.

From the tree, select the **yz** plane and enter the **Sketcher**. Draw a rectangle of dimensions 0.5x1. in.

Exit the **Sketcher** and **Pad** the sketch by 2 in. The resulting rectangular box represents one quarter of the model.

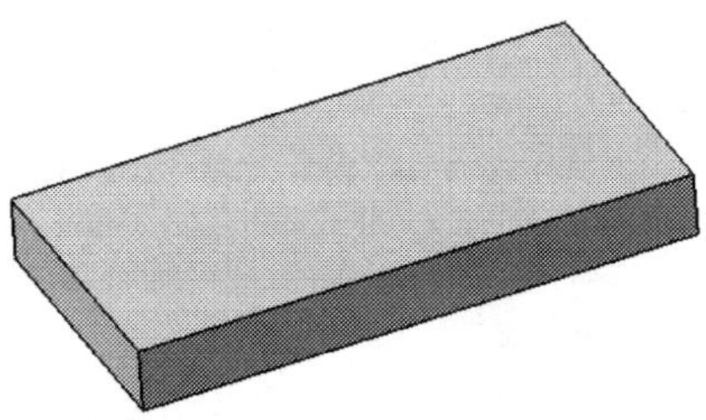

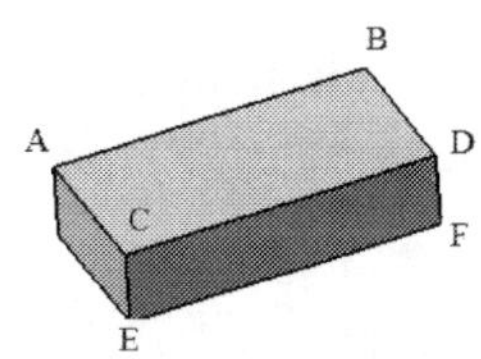


quarter of the box

The next step is to extract the surfaces ABDC and CDFE from the "quarter box" model. To perform this step, you have to change workbenches. From the standard Windows toolbar, select **Start > Wireframe and Surface Design**.

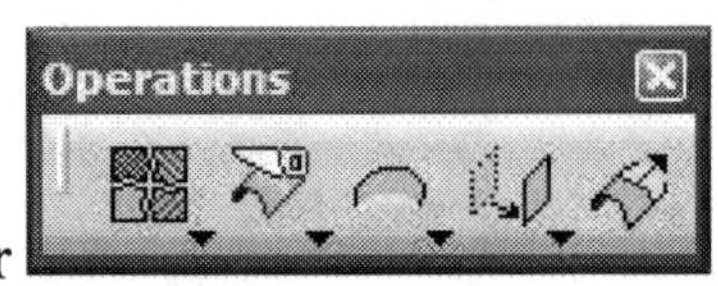


Click on the **Extract** icon in the **Operations** toolbar which leads to the box shown below. For the **Element(s) to extract**, pick the top face.

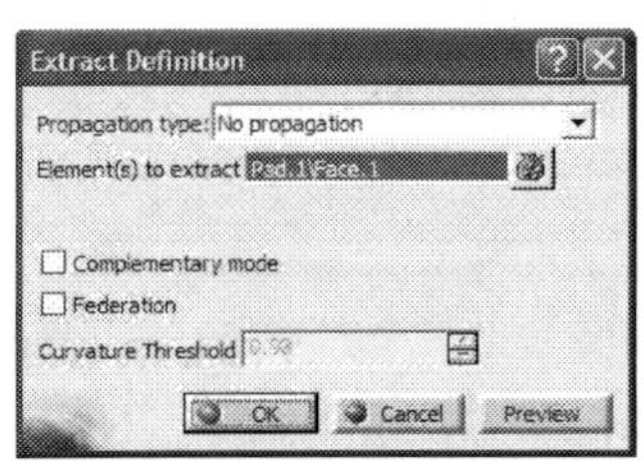

Repeat the extraction process with the side face as displayed.

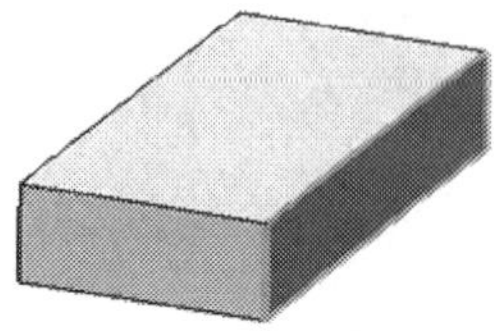

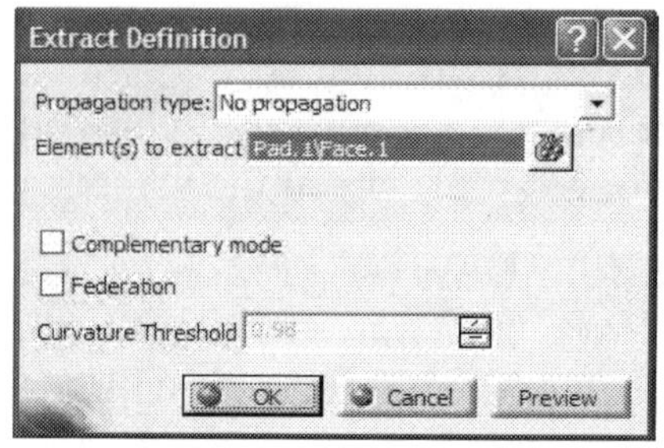


At this point, the two desired surfaces are extracted and the tree has been modified.

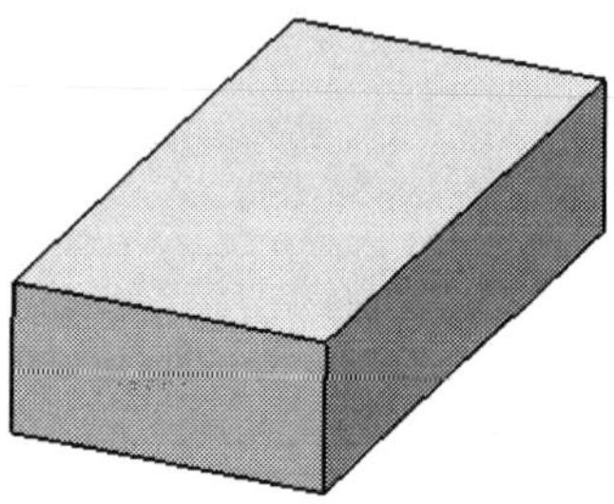

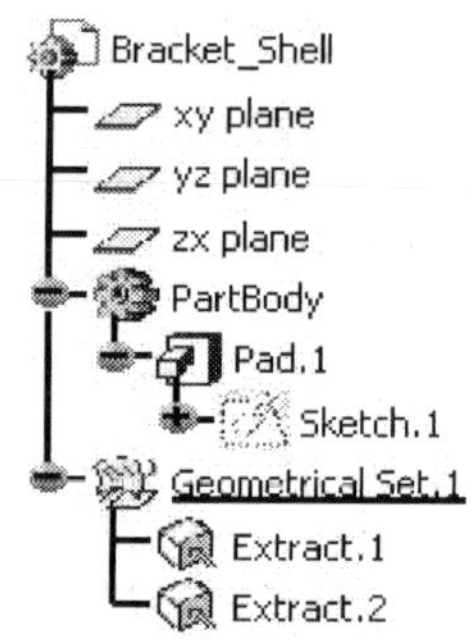


These surfaces have to be joined together; otherwise they will not transfer the load during the finite element analysis.

Use the **Join** icon  from **Operations** toolbar 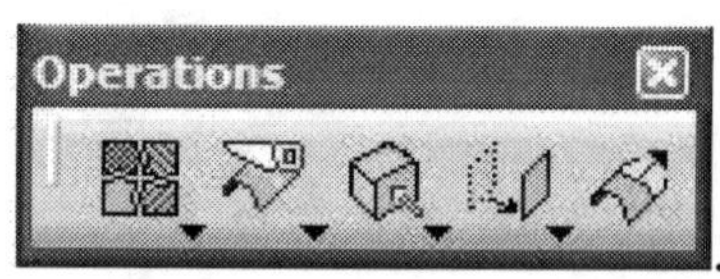.

The following box appears. For **Element To Join**, select the extracted surfaces. The tree is updated reflecting the **Join** operation.

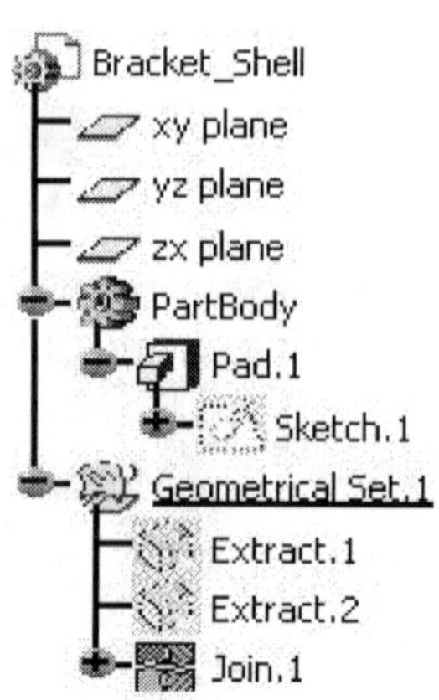


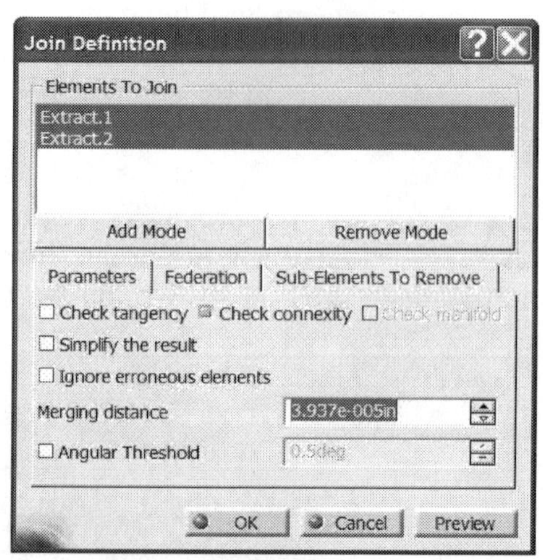

Use the **Apply material** icon to open the database of material properties, selecting **Yellow Brass** from the **Metal** tab. Choose **Join.1** from the tree to complete the process.

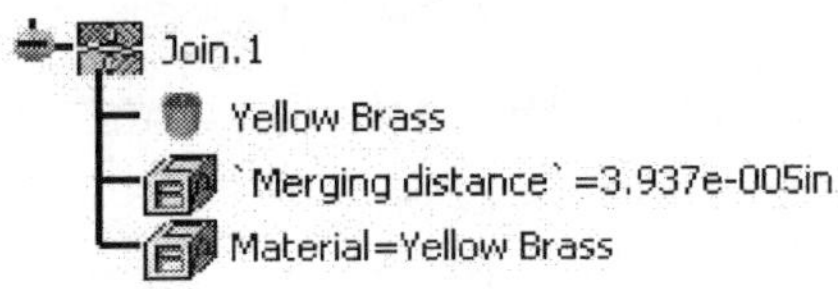


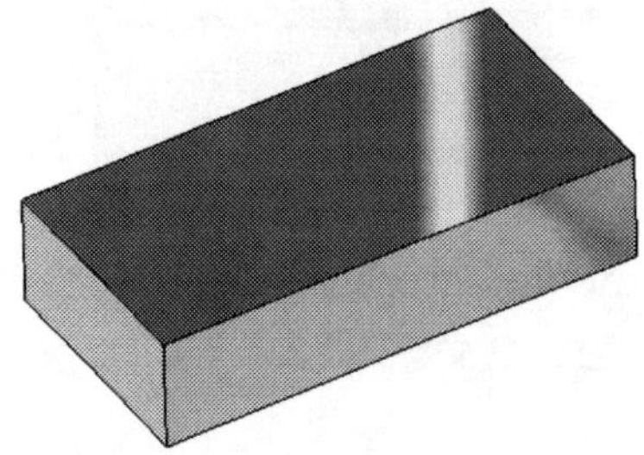

Note that the block is still showing on your computer screen. Right-click on the block, and **Hide** it. At this point, only the joined surface appears on the screen.

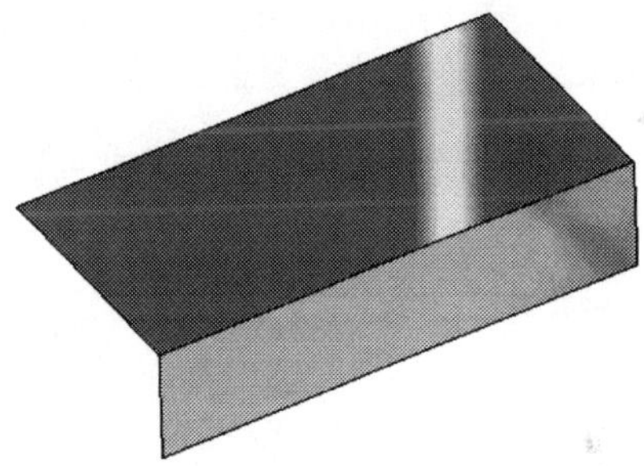

## 3 Entering the Analysis Solutions

From the standard Windows toolbar, select

**Start > Analysis & Simulation > Advanced Meshing Tools** .

**Warning:** If instead of the **Advanced Meshing Tools** workbench, you enter the **Generative Structural Analysis** workbench, immediately a solid mesh on the existing part is generated which is not what is intended. In that case, use the **Cancel** button and exit the **Generative Structural Analysis** workbench.

Upon entering the **Advanced Meshing Tools** workbench, the standard box shown below is displayed. However, you note that the representative element "size" and "sag" is not visible on your display.
This is in contrast to utilizing the **Generative Structural Analysis** workbench for the first time. Therefore, at this point no mesh is present.

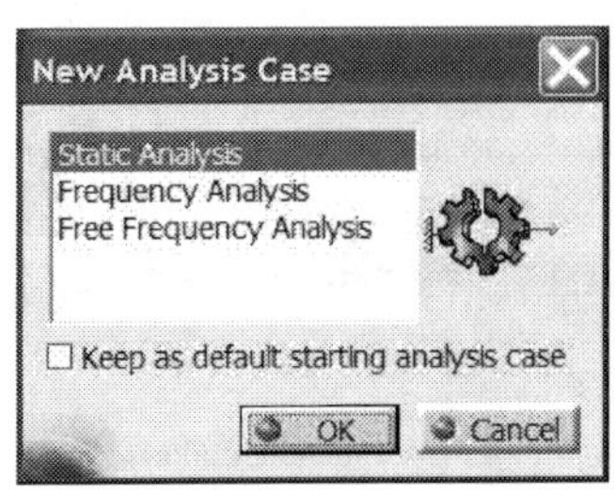

The **Meshing Methods** toolbar 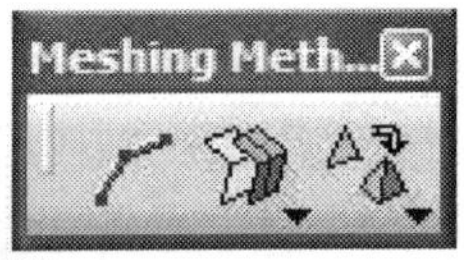 has a sub-toolbar known as the **Surface Mesher** 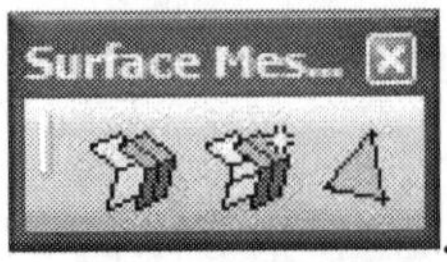. Select **Octree Triangle Mesher** icon 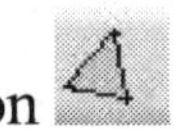 and pick the bracket from the screen. This action leads to the input box shown below. Type the indicated size and sag values and select **Parabolic** elements. Finally, <u>click on the **Apply** button</u>.

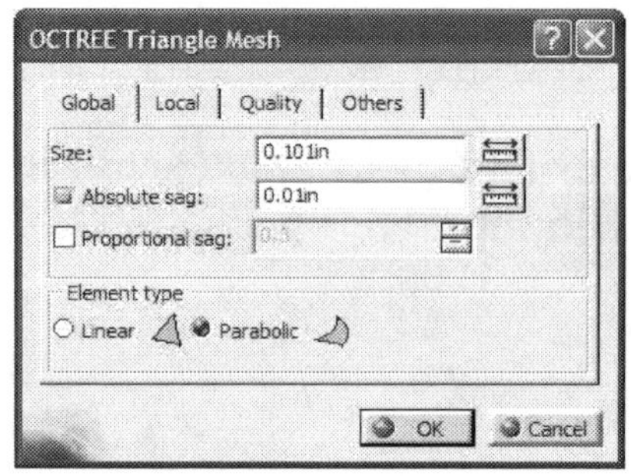


The resulting shell mesh appears on your screen. (Change the render style to **Shading with Edges**  or **Wireframe** .)
The representative "size" and "sag" elements are not tetrahedron anymore but they seem to be planar in shape.

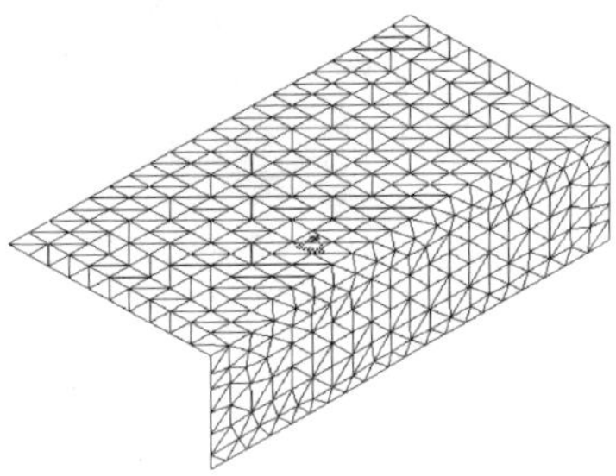

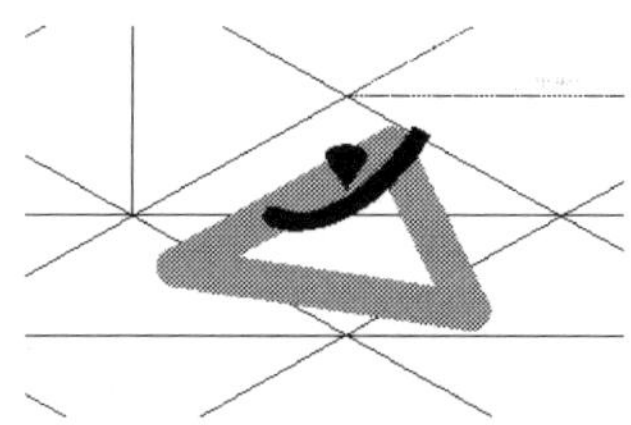

A zoomed view of these entities is displayed on the right.

In the event that you forgot to press the **Apply** button in the **OCTREE Triangle Mesh** box above, no mesh is created. This is in spite of the fact that the mesh "specs" have been set.

In such a situation, point the cursor to the **Nodes and Elements** branch on the tree, right-click, and select **Update All Meshes** as indicated on the right.

Alternatively, double-click on the **OCTREE Triangle Mesh.1** on the tree to open the appropriate box and press on the **Apply** button.

The shell mesh cross sectional properties and the boundary conditions are specified in the **Generative Structural Analysis** workbench. Therefore, switch to this workbench through,

**Start > Analysis & Simulation > Generative Structural Analysis** 

If the mesh disappears from the screen while changing workbenches, point the cursor to the branch **Nodes and Elements**, right-click and select **Mesh Visualization**.

**Assigning Shell Properties:**

The first task is to specify the shell thickness. This can be done two different ways. The properties can be assigned to **Join.1**, or it can be assigned to the **OCTREE Triangle Mesh.1**, selected from the tree. You will follow the latter approach.

Select the **2D Property** icon  from the **Model Manager** toolbar

. The following pop up box appears. For the **Supports**, select the **OCTREE Triangle Mesh.1** from the tree.
The shell **Thickness** is 0.1. Note that the **Material** is automatically picked as **Brass**.

Upon closing the box, the shell thickness is recorded on the mesh as shown below.

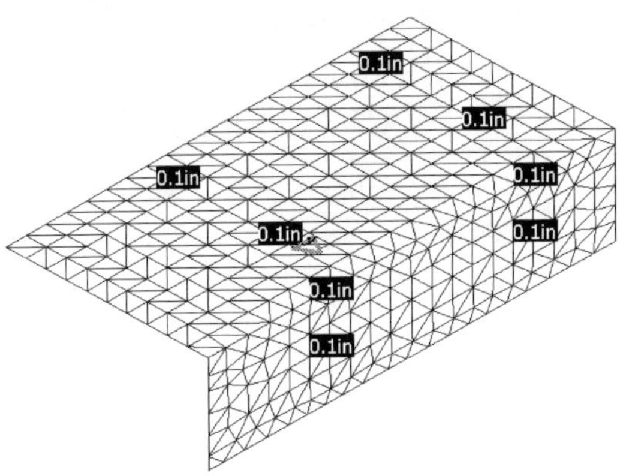


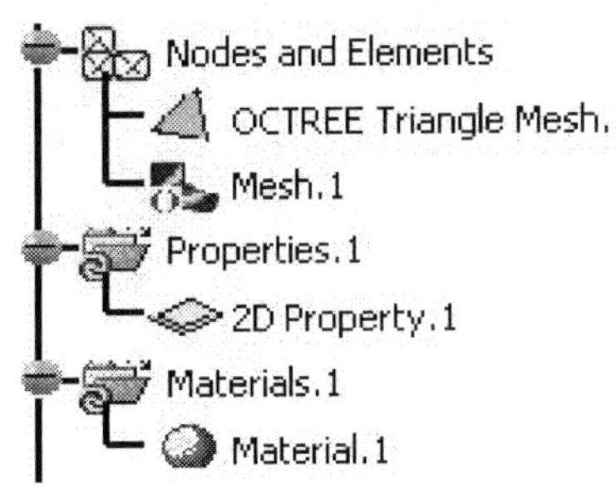


The portion of the tree structure associated with the mesh is also displayed.
CONGRATULATIONS! You now have a mesh with the correct material and shell properties.
Regularly save your work.

**Applying Restraints:**

CATIA's FEA module is geometrically based. This means that the boundary conditions cannot be applied to nodes and elements. The boundary conditions can only be applied at the part level. As soon as you enter the **Generative Structural Analysis** workbench, the part is automatically hidden. Therefore, before boundary conditions are applied, the part must be brought to the **Show** mode. This can be carried out by pointing the cursor to the top of the tree, the **Links Manager.1** branch, right-click, select **Show**. At this point, the part and the mesh are superimposed as shown in the next page and you have access to the part.

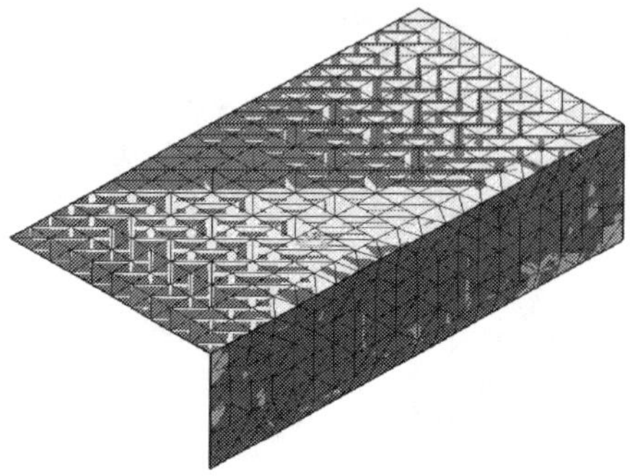

Select the **Clamp** icon  from the **Restraint** toolbar 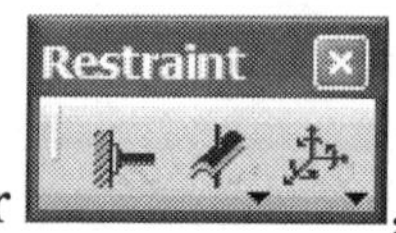

, and pick the bottom edge of the bracket.

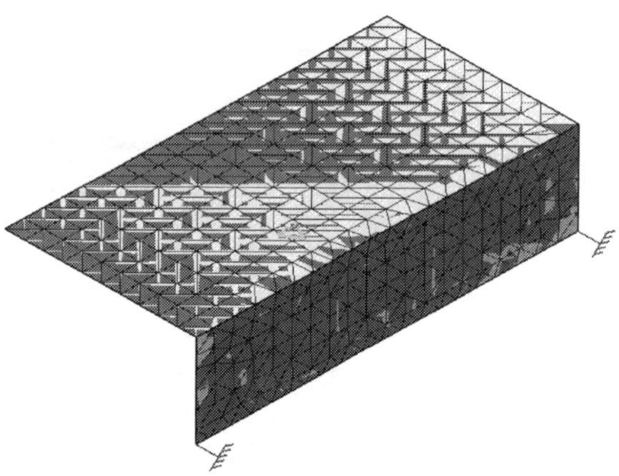

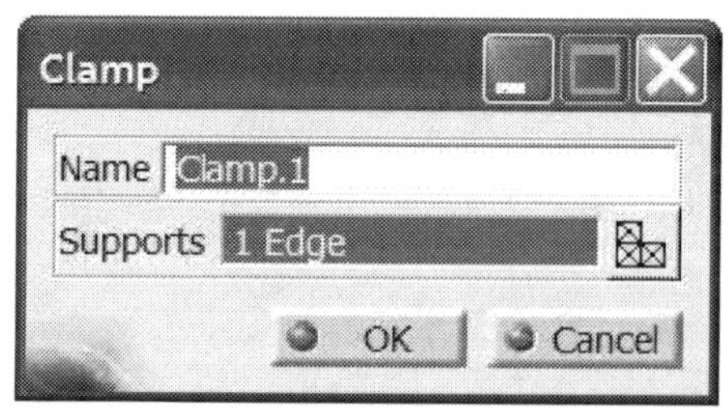


The symmetry edges are restrained with the help of the following table.

| PLANE | $u_x$ | $u_y$ | $u_z$ | $\Theta_x$ | $\Theta_y$ | $\Theta_z$ |
|---|---|---|---|---|---|---|
| yz | zero | free | free | free | zero | zero |
| xz | free | zero | free | zero | free | zero |
| xy | free | free | zero | zero | zero | free |

As an example, the edges AC and CE lie in a plane parallel to the yz plane. Therefore, for these edges, $u_x = \Theta_y = \Theta_z = 0$ .

By the same token, the edge AB lies in a plane parallel to the xz plane. Consequently for this edge, $u_y = \Theta_x = \Theta_z = 0$.

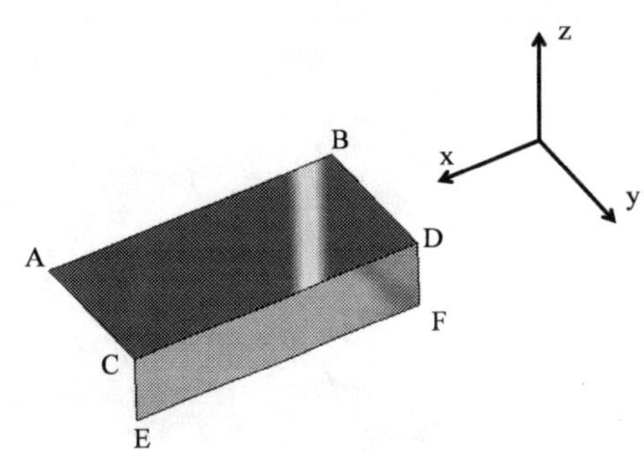


These conditions are enforced with **User-defined Restraint**.

Use **User-defined Restraint** icon 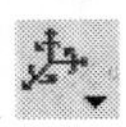 from the **Restraint** toolbar 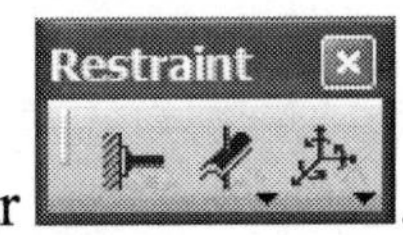

. In the resulting box, pick the AC and CE edges as **Supports**, and check the appropriate restraints as displayed below.

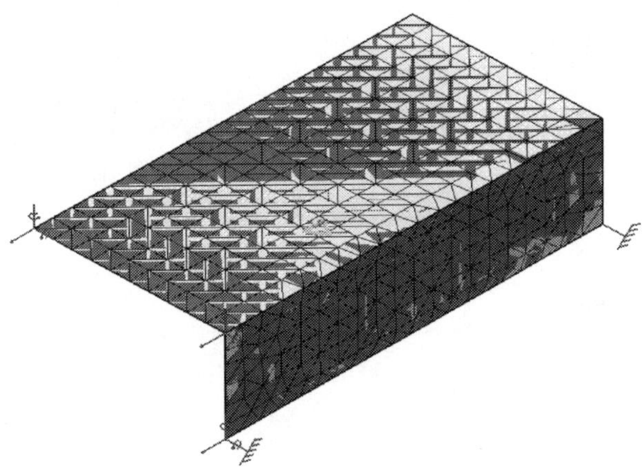

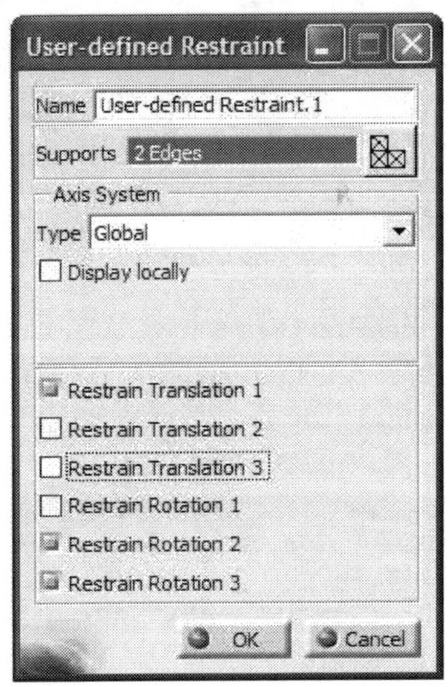

Once again, use the icon 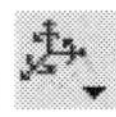 to pick the edge AB and follow the instruction of the box below.

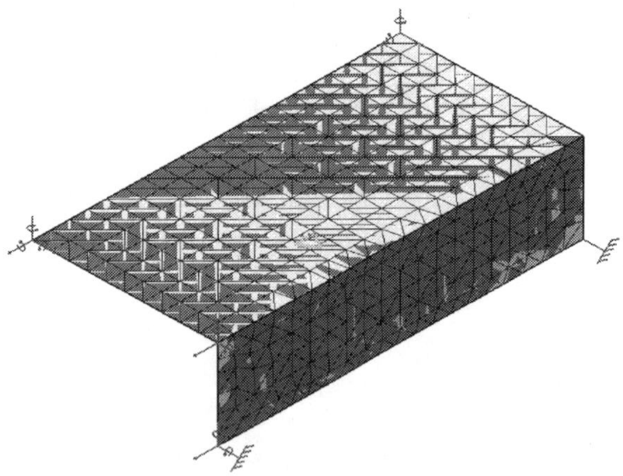

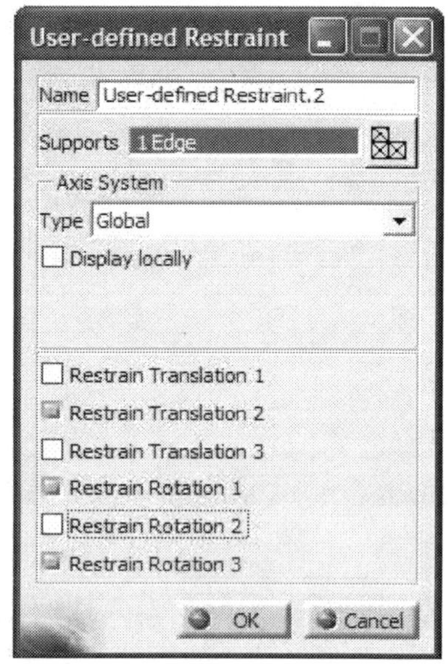


**Applying Loads:**

Use the **Pressure** icon  from the **Loads** toolbar 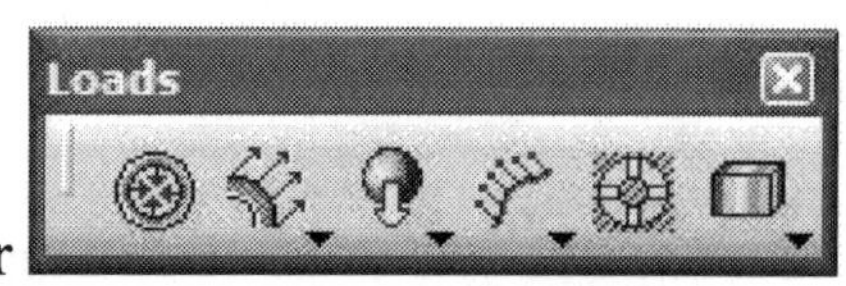

and pick the top face ABCD. Apply a pressure of 100 psi. If the direction is not correct, change the algebraic sign of 100.

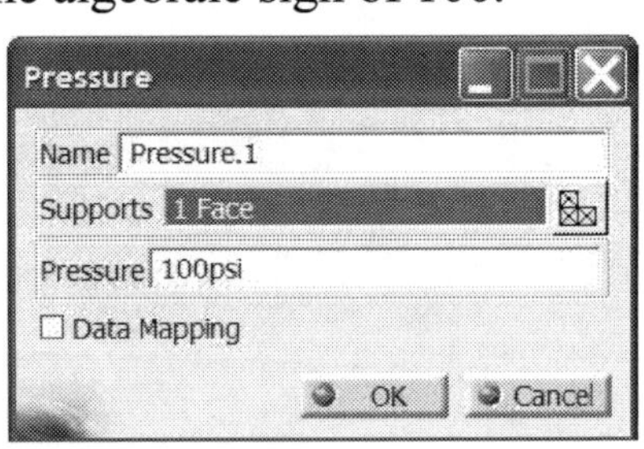


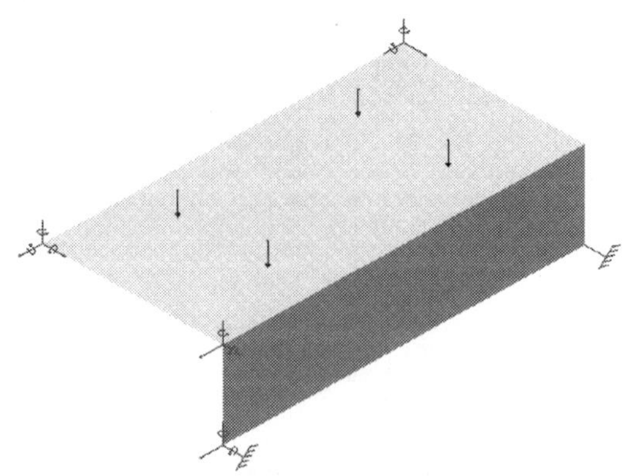

The complete tree at this point is shown below.

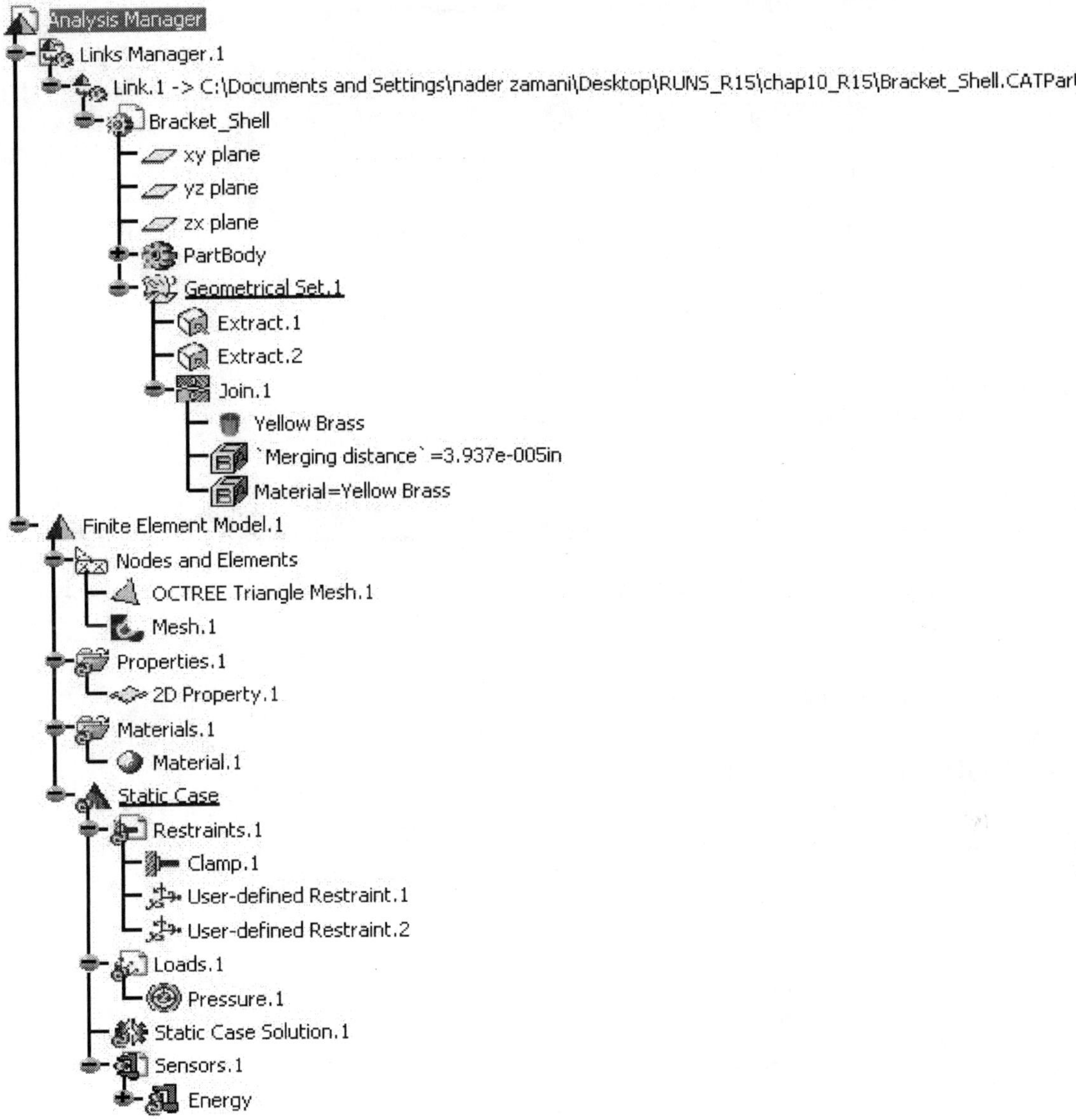


**Launching the Solver:**

To run the analysis, you need to use the **Compute** toolbar by selecting the **Compute** icon. After a brief pause, the box shown below appears. This box provides information on the resources needed to complete the analysis. If the estimates are zero in the listing, there is a problem in the previous step and should be looked into. If the numbers are zero in this box, although the program may run, it will not produce any useful results.

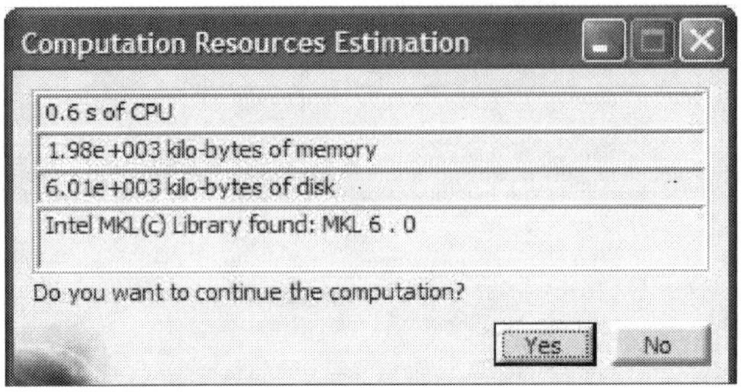


**Postprocessing:**

The main postprocessing toolbar is called **Image** 

toolbar. To view the deformed shape you have use the **Deformation** icon 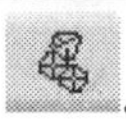. The resulting deformed shape is displayed below.

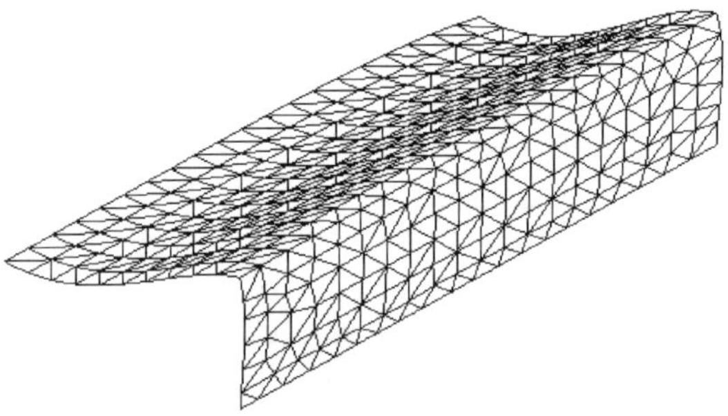

Keep in mind that the displacements are scaled considerably so that one can observe the deformed shape. Although the scale factor is set automatically, one can change this value with the **Deformation Scale Factor** icon  in the **Analysis Tools** toolbar

.

In order to see the displacement field, the **Displacement** icon  in the **Image** toolbar should be used. The default display is in terms of displacement arrows.

The arrow plot is not particularly useful. In order to view the contour plot of the displacement field, position the cursor on the arrow field and double-click. The **Image Edition** box opens.

Note that the default is to draw the contour on the deformed shape. If this is not desired, uncheck the box **On deformed mesh**. Next, select **AVERAGE-ISO** and press **OK**. The contour of the displacement field is shown. (Note: The color map has been changed; otherwise everything looks black.). A maximum displacement of 0.00528 is detected.

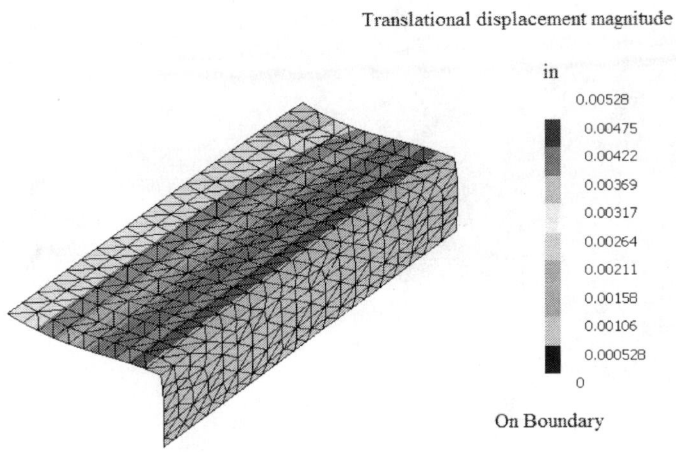


The next step in the postprocessing is to plot the contours of the von Mises stress using the **von Mises Stress** icon in the **Image** toolbar. This is shown below.

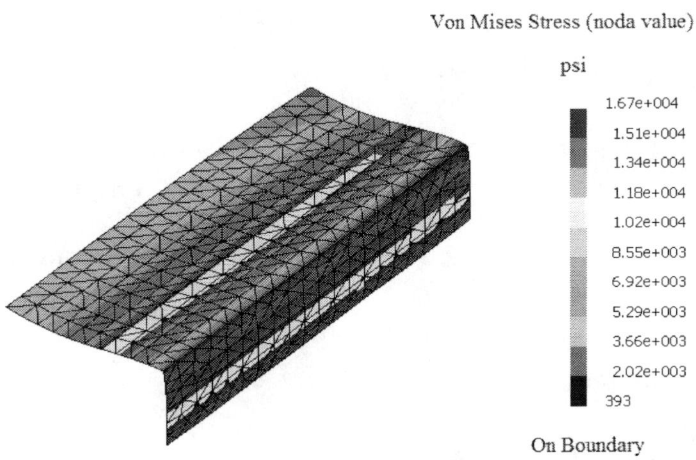

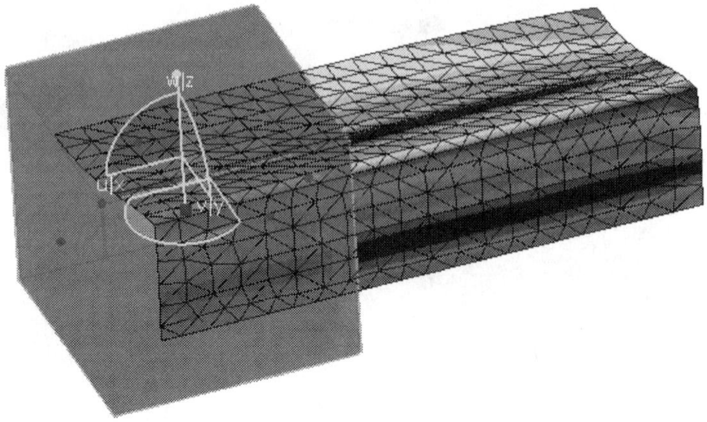

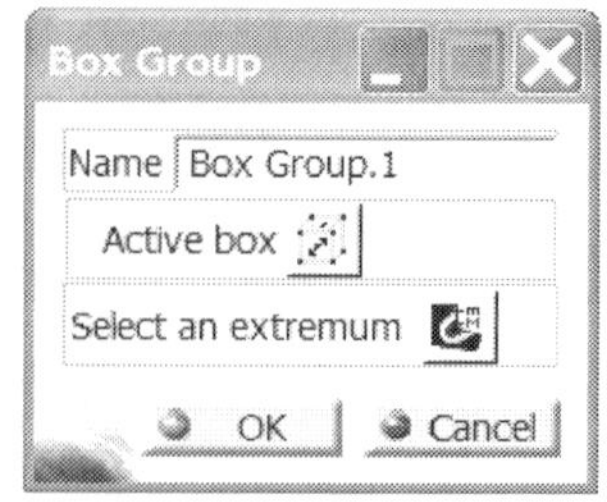


You will now create a group. Read Note #3 in Appendix I.

The **Groups** toolbar 

has several sub-toolbars. Select the **Spatial Groups** toolbar 

.

From this toolbar select the **Box Group** icon . This allows you to create a box of a desired size and location which contains all the elements used for plotting purposes.

Upon double-clicking on , a default box centered at (0,0,0) is constructed.

You can change the size and position of the box by clicking on the 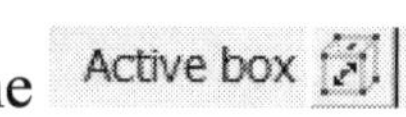

icon and manipulating the compass.

At this point the **Box Group.1** is created which encloses the elements trapped by the sphere. This group is listed in the tree as indicated on the right.

The next step is plotting the von Mises stress for this group. Make sure that the von Mises stress is active. Double-click on the von Mises stress contour on the screen to open the **Image Edition** box. Use the **Selections** tab.

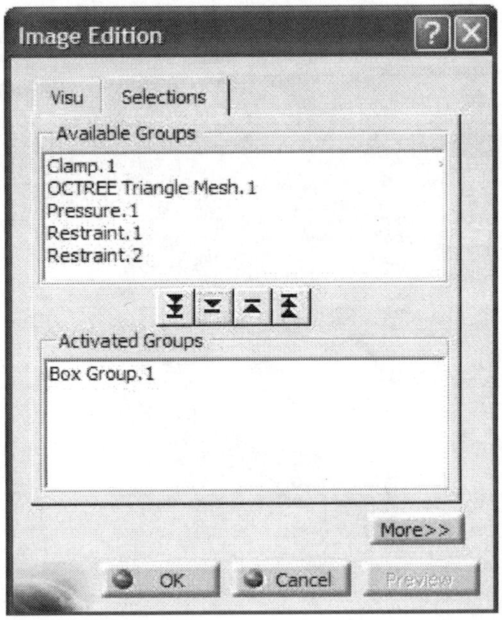


Choose **Box Group.1**. The resulting plot is displayed with the created box also showing.

Point the cursor to **Box Group.1** in the tree and **Hide** it.

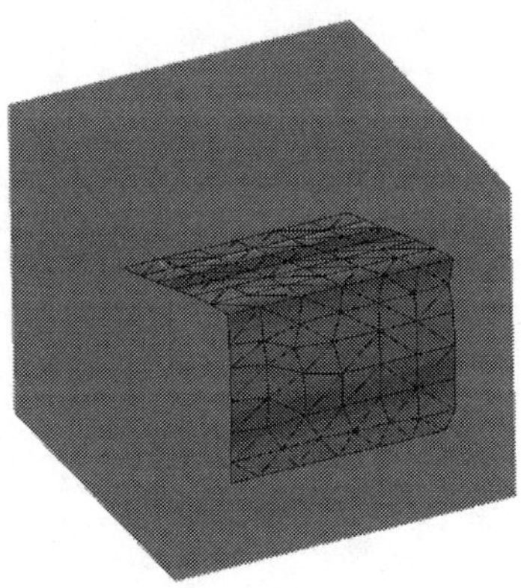

The result is a nice contour showing the detailed stress distribution in the notched area as indicated below. (Note: The color map has been changed; otherwise everything looks black.)

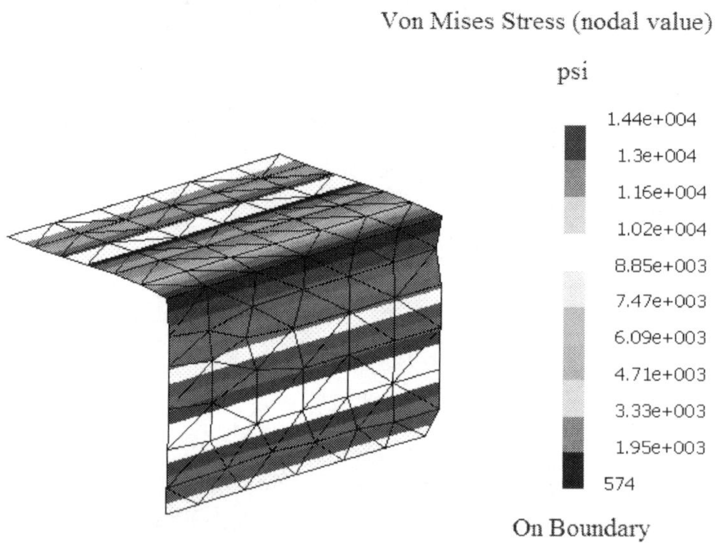


The **Cutting Plane** icon  from the **Analysis tools** toolbar 

can be used to make a cut through the part at a desired location and inspect the stresses, inside of the part. The **Cut Plane** box allows you to keep the plane, or remove it, for display purposes. A typical cutting plane is shown below.

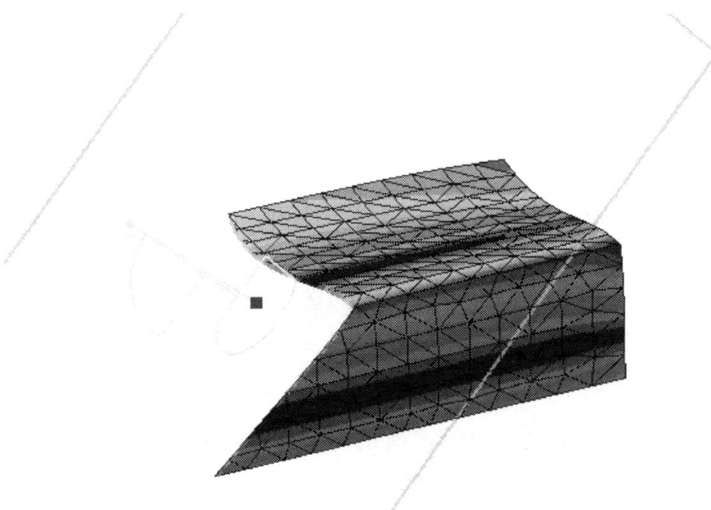

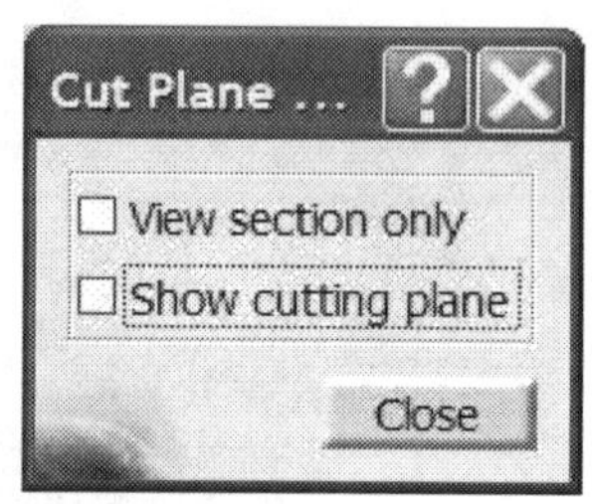


Finally, animation of the model can be achieved through the **Animate** icon  in the **Analysis Tools** toolbar 

. An AVI file can easily be generated.

# Exercises for Chapter 10

## Problem 1: a Plate with Central Hole under Bending, using Shell Elements

The steel plate shown below has a transverse central hole and subjected to a moment, causing an out of plane bending. The dimensions of the plate are $L = 10$ in., $W = 5$ in., $h = 0.5$ in., and $d = 1$ in. Using parabolic shell elements, together with the concept of smooth virtual part, find the stress concentration factor due to the presence of the hole.

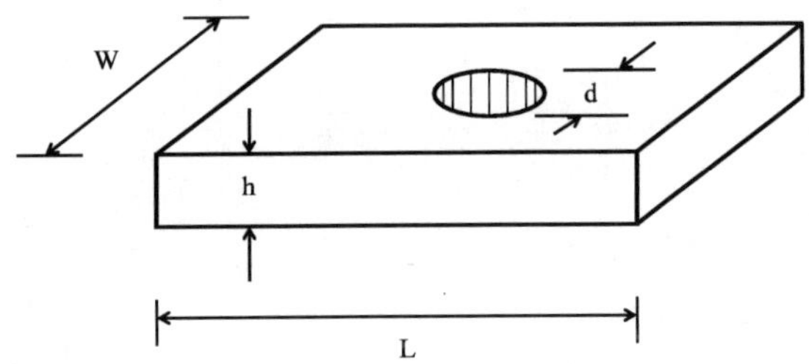


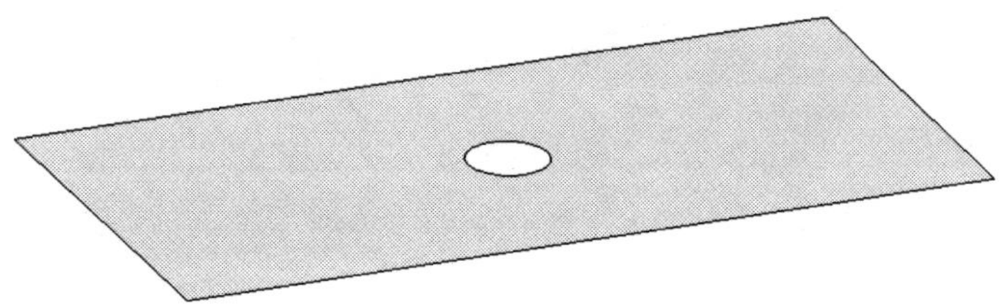

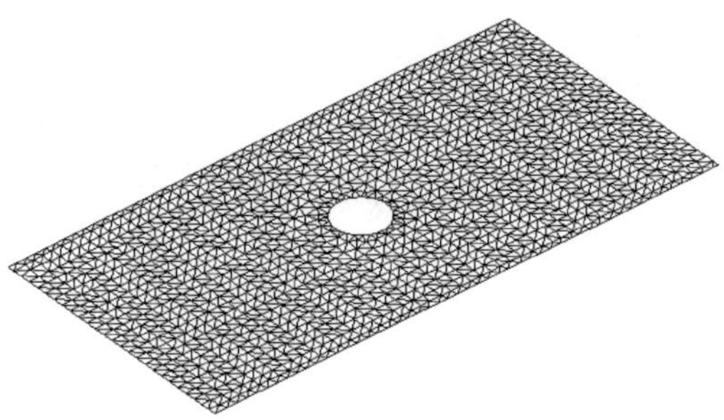

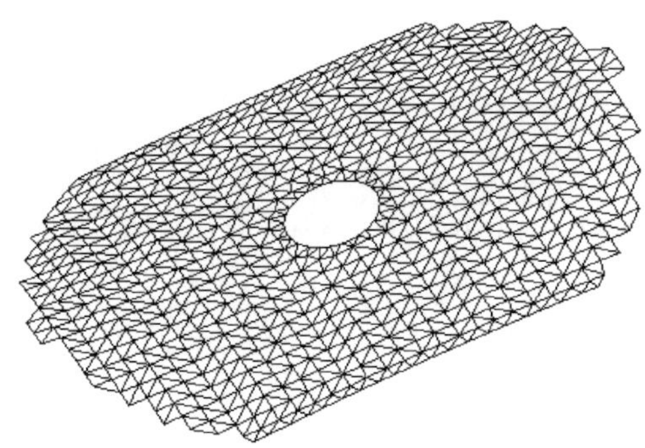

## Problem 2: Deflection of a Clamped Plate under Pressure Loading

A rectangular plate has dimensions $a = 40$ in., $b = 40$ in., and $t = .5$ in. The plate is simply supported at the two edges as shown and is subjected to a pressure of $p = 5$ psi. Calculate the maximum displacement and the maximum stress in the plate. Use shell elements to model the structure.
You can assume that the Young's modulus is .3E8 psi and Poisson ratio is 0.3.

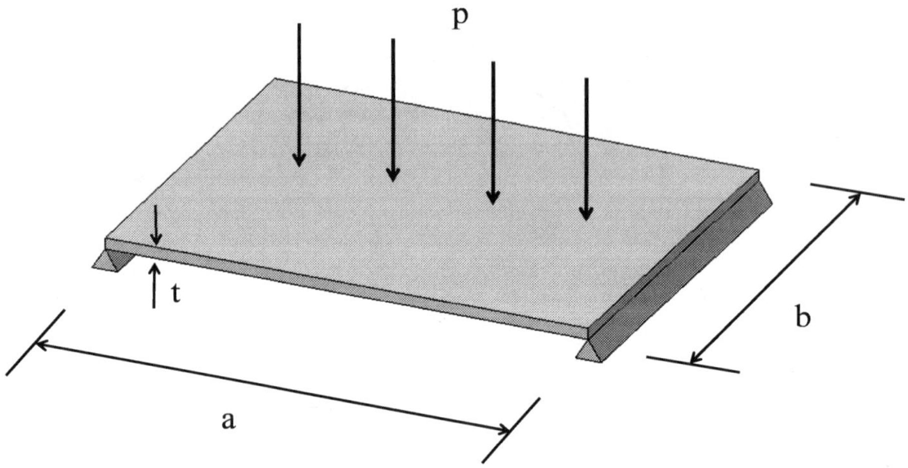


Partial Answer:

Using plate theory one can show that the maximum deflection is at the center of the plate. For a square plate with Poisson ratio 0.3, the deflection is given below.

$$\delta_{max} = 0.00406 \frac{pa^4}{D}$$

The denominator is called the flexural rigidity of the plate and calculated from

$$D = \frac{Et^3}{12(1-\nu^2)}.$$

# Chapter 11

## Modeling Mismatch in Shell Thickness and Surface Mesh

## Introduction

In this tutorial, you will model a thin part consisting of two plates, with different thicknesses, loaded under bending. The two surfaces are meshed with "Surface Mesher" resulting in incompatible nodes at the seam. The two surfaces will be tied together with a rigid connection.

## 1 Problem Statement

The bracket, shown on the right, is made of a horizontal flange and a vertical web. The thicknesses of these plates are 0.05 in. and 0.1 in. respectively. The overall dimensions of the bracket are also shown below.

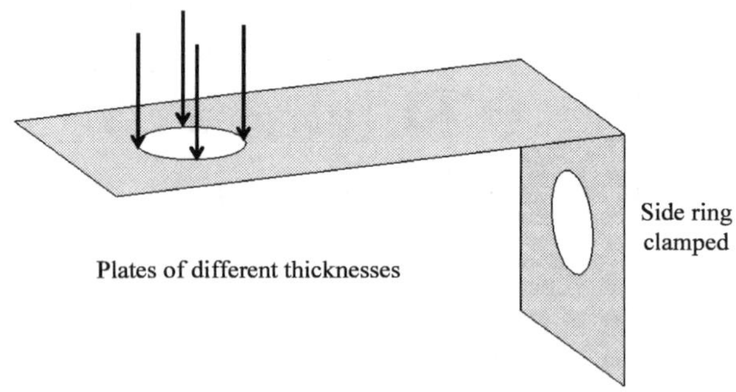


Aluminum is used for fabrication purposes with Young's modulus of 1.015E+7 psi and Poisson ratio 0.346.

The side ring of the web is clamped, whereas the top ring of the flange is loaded with 100 lb force as shown.

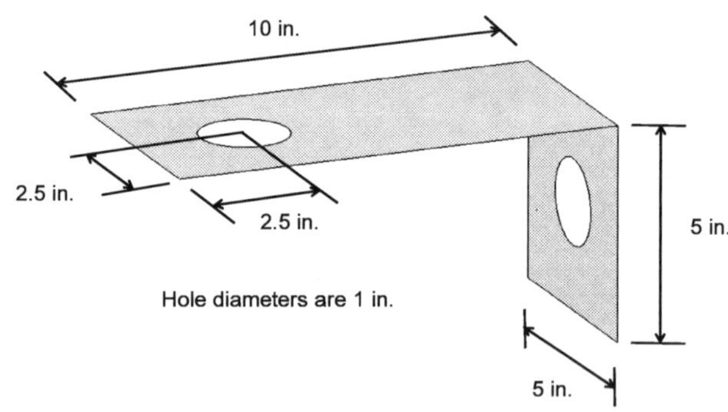


The strategy is to create a solid block of dimensions 10x5x5 in. and drill the holes as pockets in the appropriate locations. Finally, extract the surfaces which represent the flange and the web.

## 2 Creation of the Part in Mechanical Design Solutions

Enter the **Part Design** workbench from the standard Windows toolbar, select **File > New**. Rename the part to be **Mismatch_Thickness**. Read Note #1 in Appendix I.

The first step is straightforward. It involves, drawing a rectangle and padding it. Then, draw two circles on the appropriate faces and create two pockets.
We skip the detailed steps, but provide the reader with the next three figures which can be used as a guide to complete the task.

It is also possible to create the entire bracket directly in the **Wireframe and Surface Design** workbench. This approach will be discussed in a later chapter.

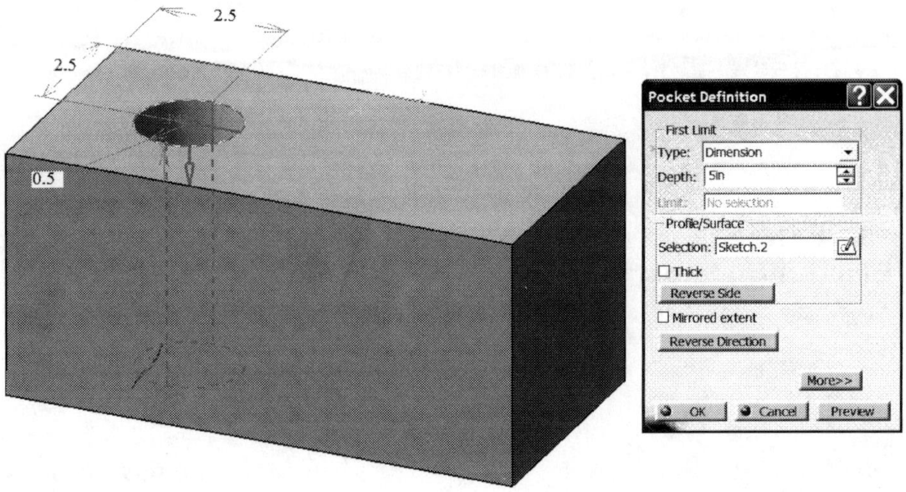


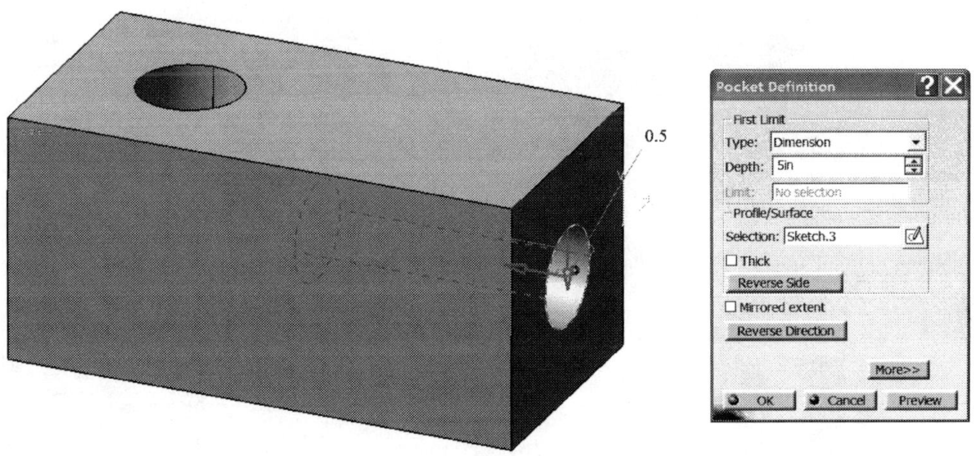


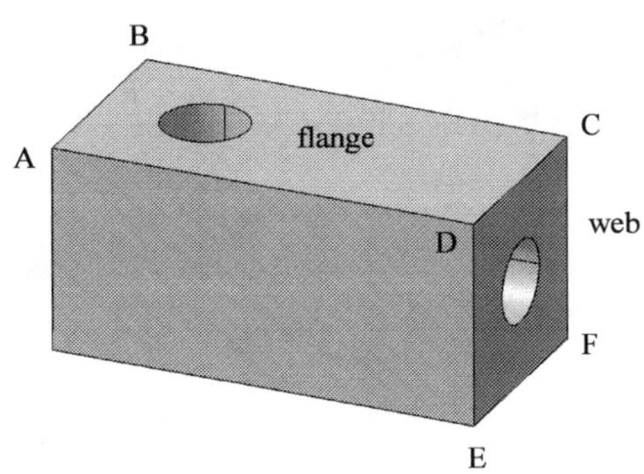


The final three dimensional part is displayed above for your convenience.

The next step is to extract the surfaces ABCD and CDEF from the block. To perform this step, you have to change workbenches. From the standard Windows toolbar, select **Start > Wireframe and Surface Design**.

Click on the **Extract** icon  in the **Operations** toolbar 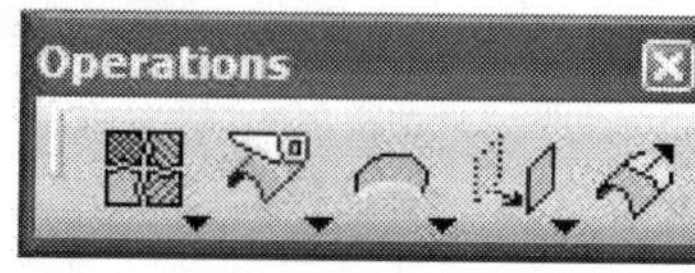

. For the **Element(s) to extract**, pick the ABCD face.

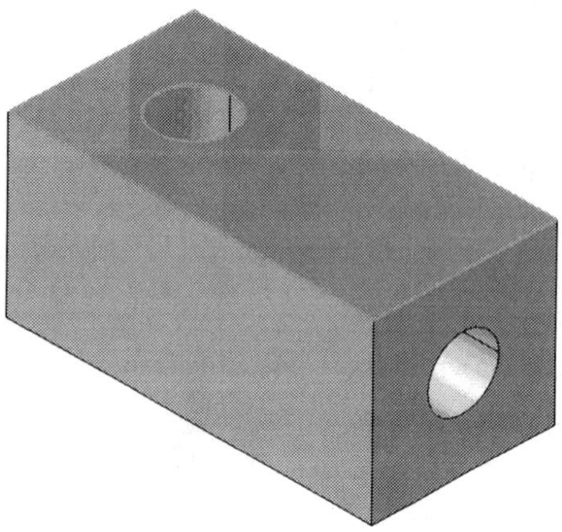

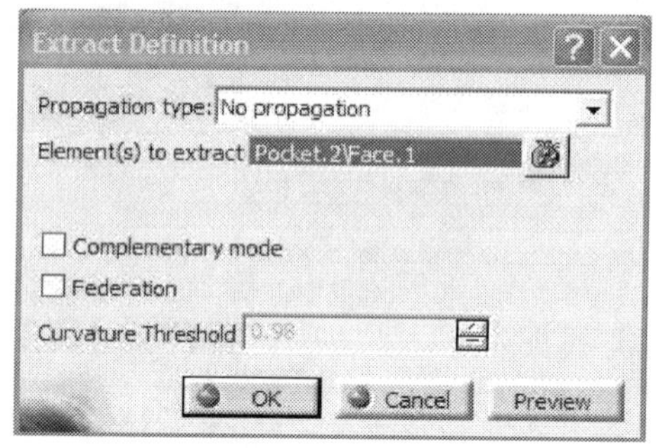


Repeat the steps above, this time extracting the face CDEF.

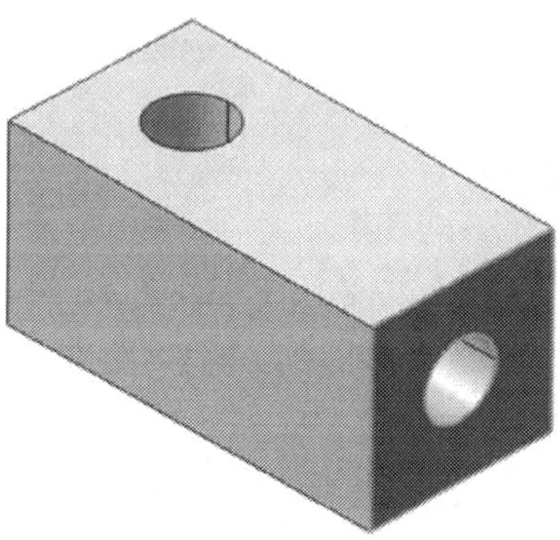

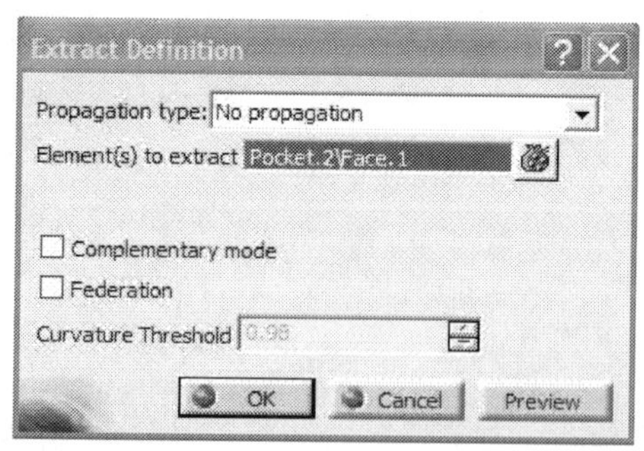


You now have both surfaces extracted and the tree is modified to reflect it.

Note that the block can be hidden by pointing the cursor to it, right-click, and selecting **Hide**.

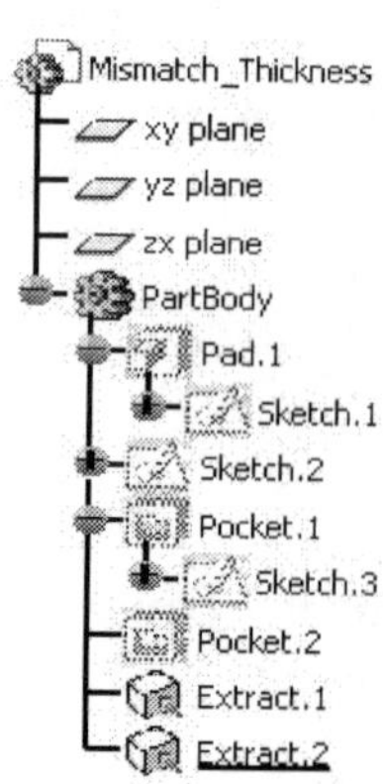

In this tutorial, we purposely <u>will not</u> join the two extracted surfaces. This creates a seam along the CD line which has to be fixed.

Use the **Apply Material** icon  to open the database of material properties, selecting **Aluminum** from the **Metal** tab. Choose **Extract.1** and **Extract.2** from the tree to complete the process.
If the bracket does not look "shiny", you can change the rendering style from the select the **View mode** toolbar 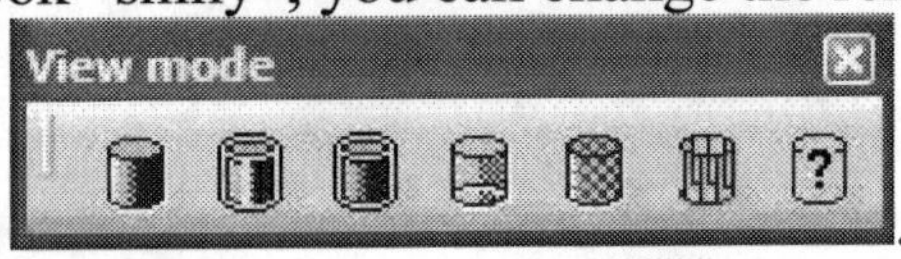

.

Next choose the **Shading with Material** icon .

Select **Applies customized view parameters** icon . This action results in a different rendering displayed below.

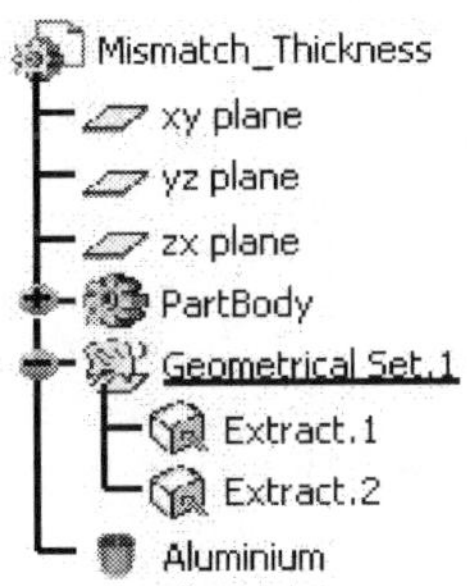


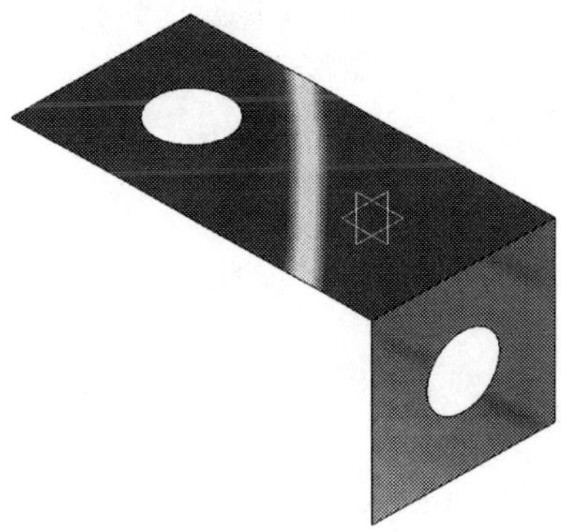

## 3 Entering the Analysis Solutions

From the standard Windows toolbar, select

**Start > Analysis & Simulation > Advanced Meshing Tools** 

<u>**Warning:** If instead of the **Advanced Meshing Tools** workbench, you enter the **Generative Structural Analysis** workbench, immediately a solid mesh on the existing part is generated which is not what is intended. In that case, use the **Cancel** button and exit the **Generative Structural Analysis** workbench</u>.

Upon entering the **Advanced Meshing Tools** workbench, the standard box shown below is displayed. However, you note that the representative element "size" and "sag" is not visible on your display.
This is in contrast to utilizing **Generative Structural Analysis** workbench for the first time.
Therefore, at this point no mesh is present.

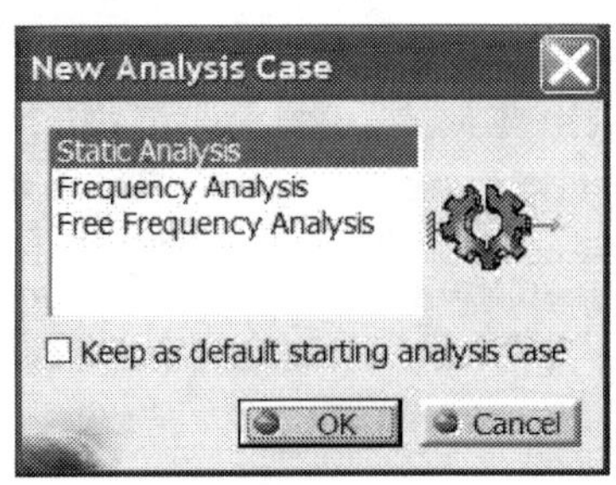

The **Meshing Methods** toolbar 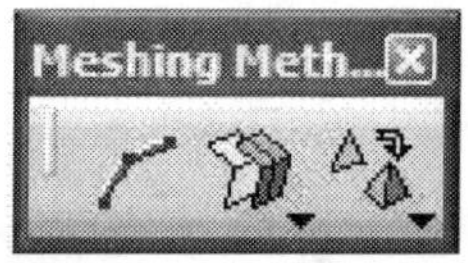

has a sub-toolbar known as the **Surface Mesher** 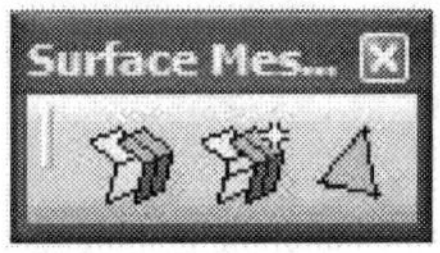

. Select the **Advanced Surface Mesher** icon 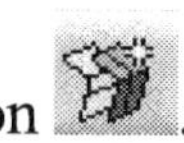.

Pick the top surface to open the **Global Parameters** box shown below.

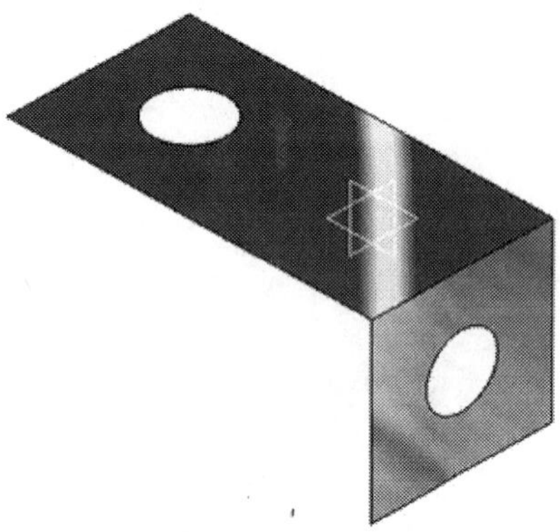

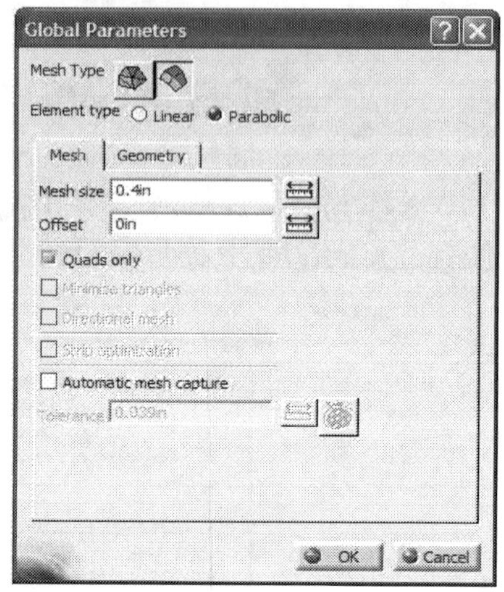


For the element shape select **Set frontal quadrangle method**  and type 0.4 as the **Mesh size**. Once you click on **OK**, the following warning box appears that you can ignore. This warning box may not appear in Release 17.

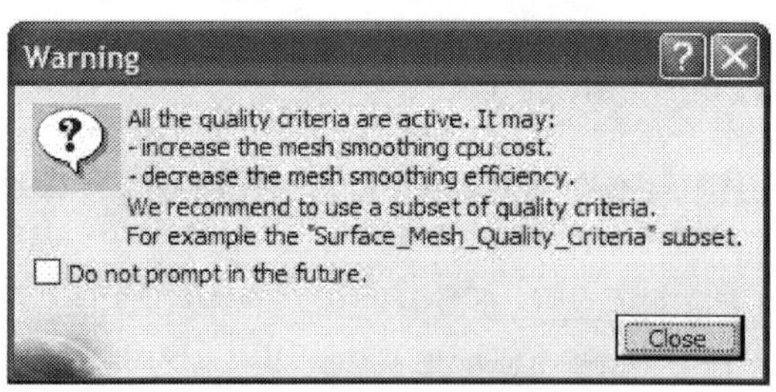


In order to see the mesh while you are in the current workbench, select the **Mesh the Part** icon 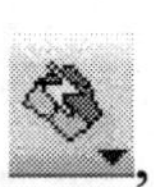, from the **Execution** toolbar 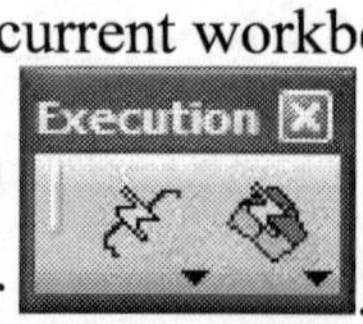

.
The summary box **Mesh the Part** appears which can be ignored.

Use the **Exit** icon  to complete the process.

The meshed part is shown below. Observe that most of the elements are quadrilateral instead of triangular.

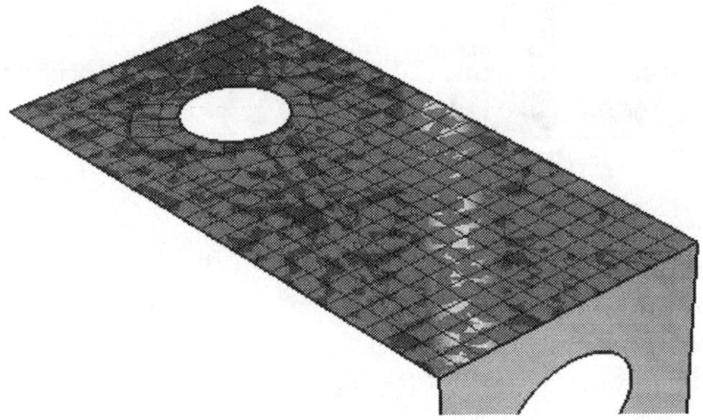

Repeat the exact same process to mesh the CDEF surface.

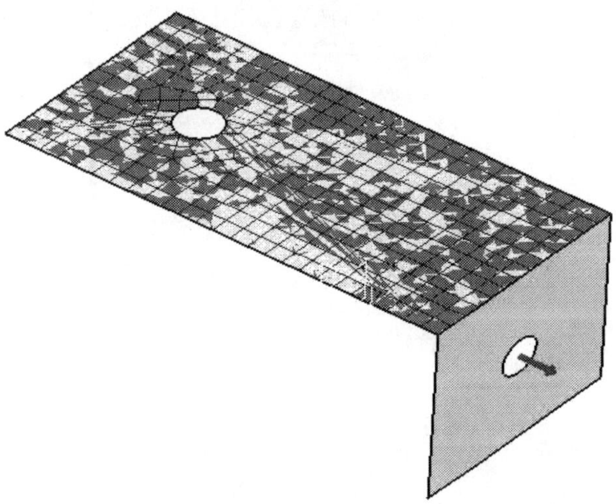

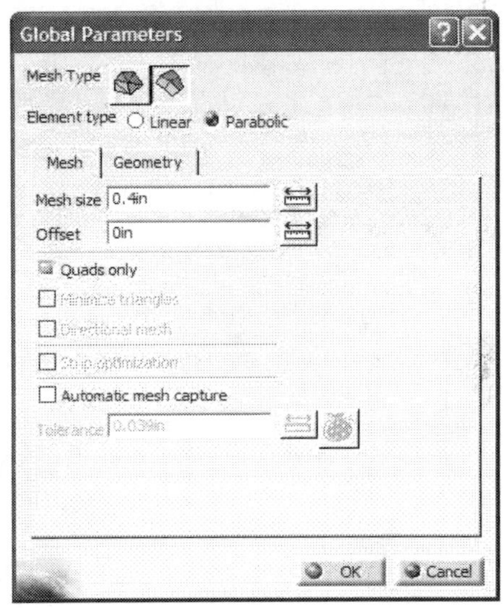


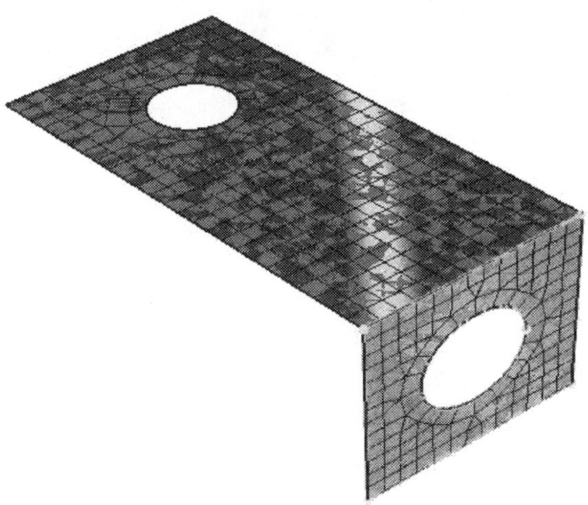

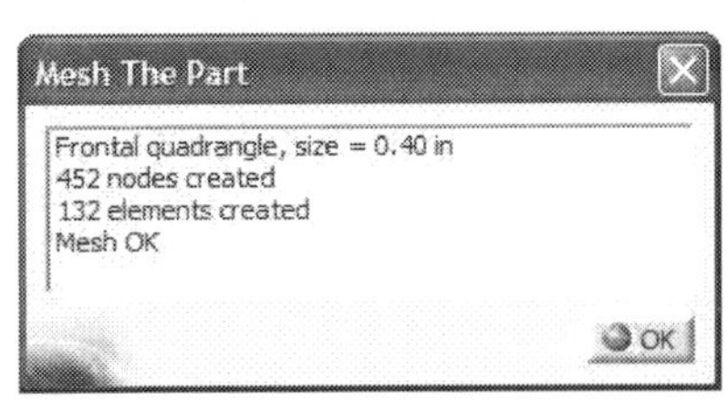

To set the shell thickness, switch workbenches.

**Start > Analysis & Simulation > Generative Structural Analysis**

Select the **2D Property** icon from the **Model Manager** toolbar

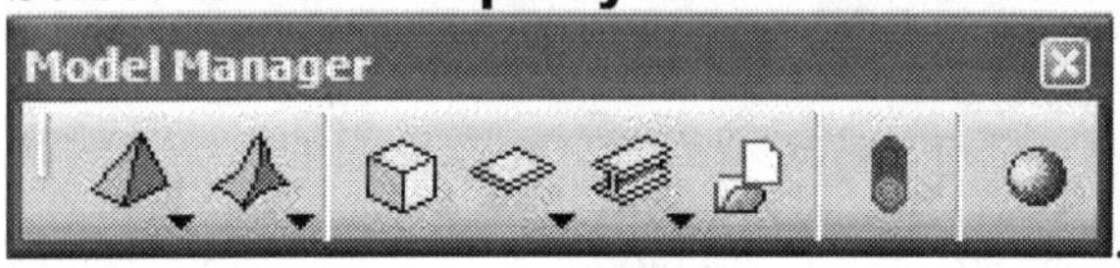


Pick the top surface and type a thickness of 0.05 in. in the appropriate line.
Note that although material may have been defined on the block created earlier, this information is not reflected in the **Materials.1** branch of the tree. For **Supports**, select the top face of the bracket, and type 0.05 for **Thickness**.

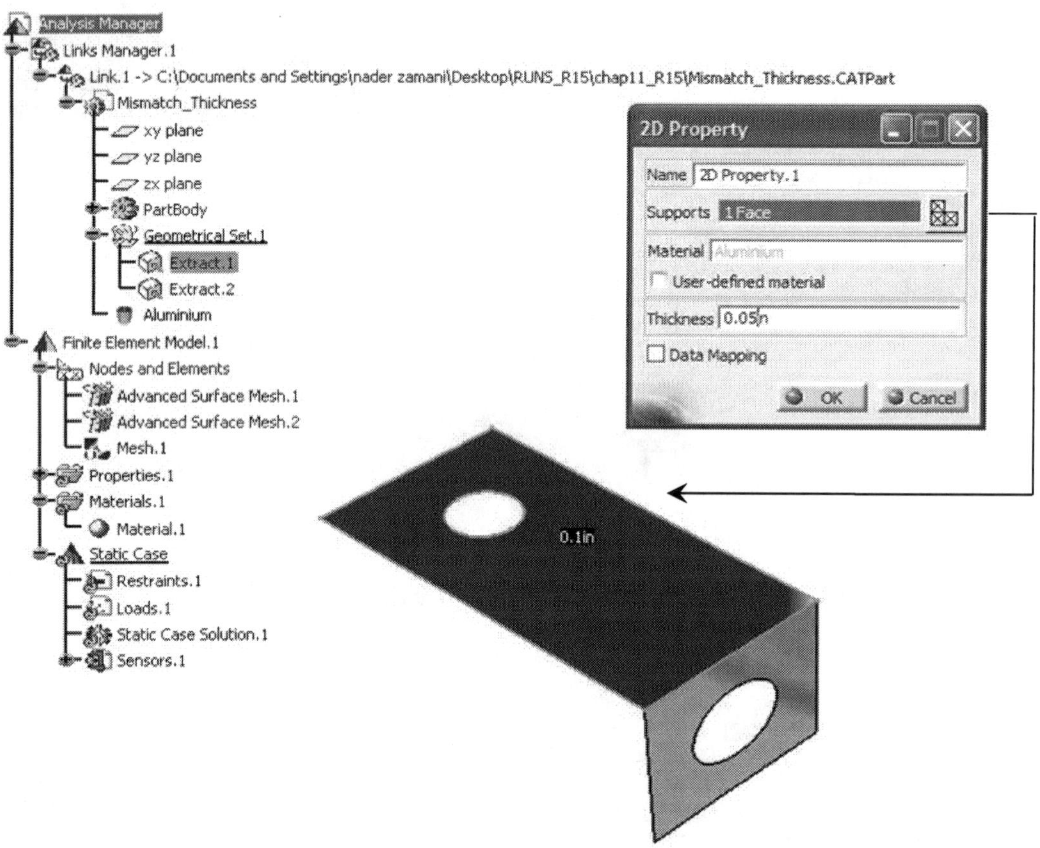


Repeat the process to specify the thickness of the side surface.

Repeat the above step with the side face. Instead of picking the top and side faces, one can also select, **Extract.1** and **Extract.2** from the tree.

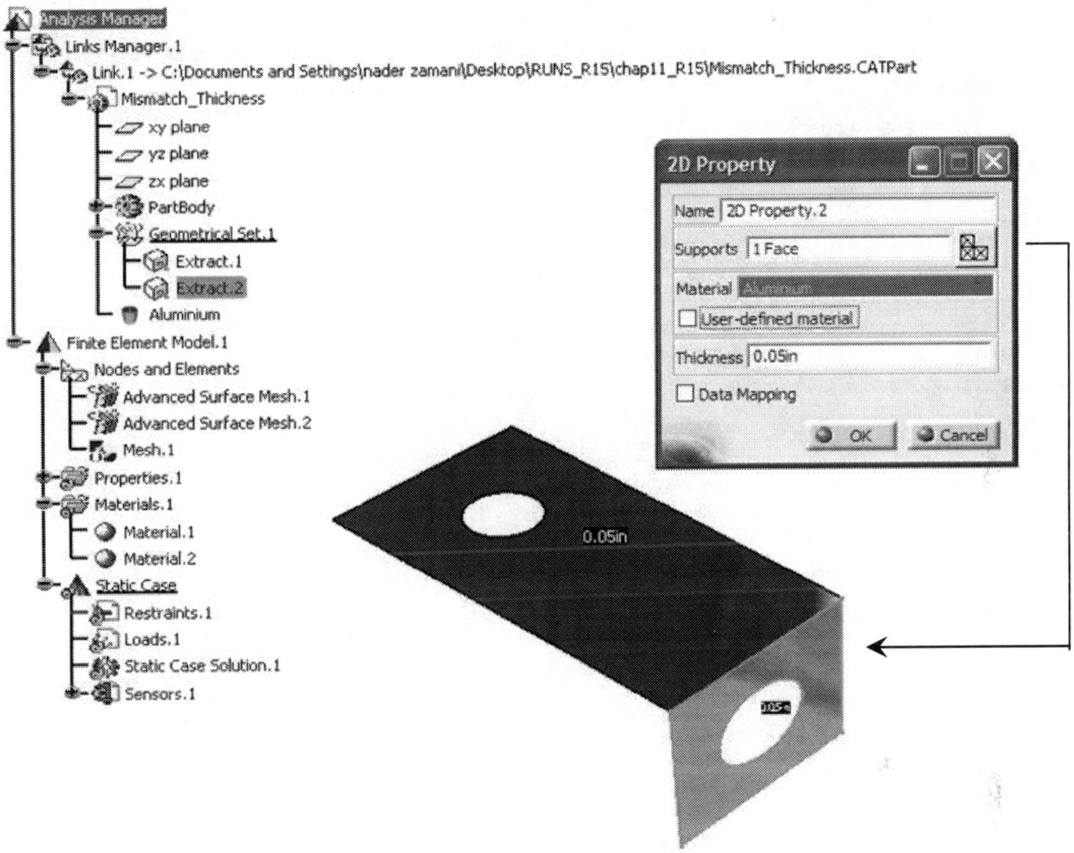


If the mesh disappears from the screen while changing workbenches, point the cursor to the branch **Nodes and Elements**, right-click and select **Mesh Visualization**.

The resulting mesh is displayed below. A zoomed view of the mesh is also shown to emphasize that the two surfaces have a mismatch in the nodes along the line DC. Even if the nodes seem to coincide, using the cursor and picking elements from the top and side surfaces reveal that there are different node numbers along the DC edge.

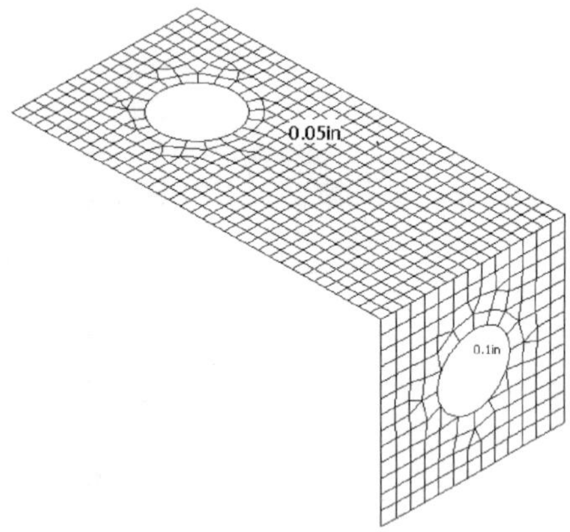


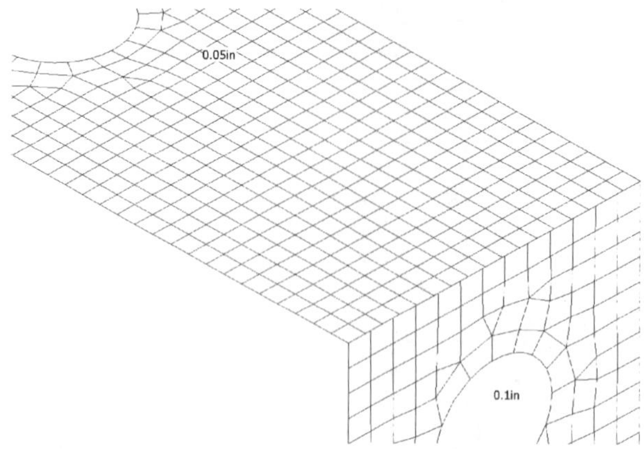


At this point, the branch associated with the **Nodes and Elements** should resemble the one displayed on the right.

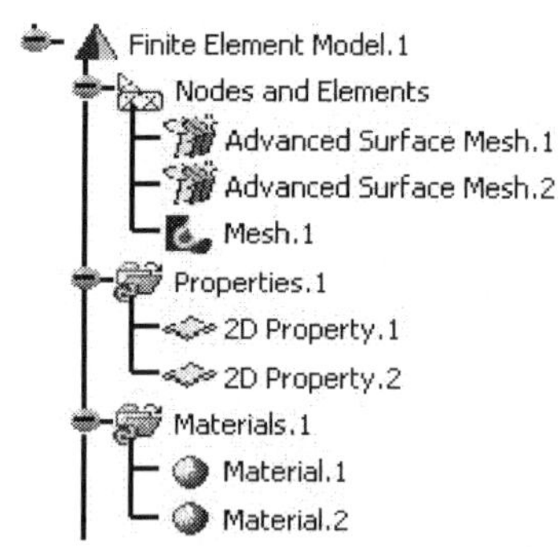


**Creating Analysis Connection:**

The next task is to tie the two meshes along the seam line CD.

Use the **General Analysis Connection** icon  from the **Analysis Supports** toolbar 

.

The result is the input box displayed below. For the **First component**, pick the edge from the web surface. The downward arrow helps to decide whether the correct edge is picked.

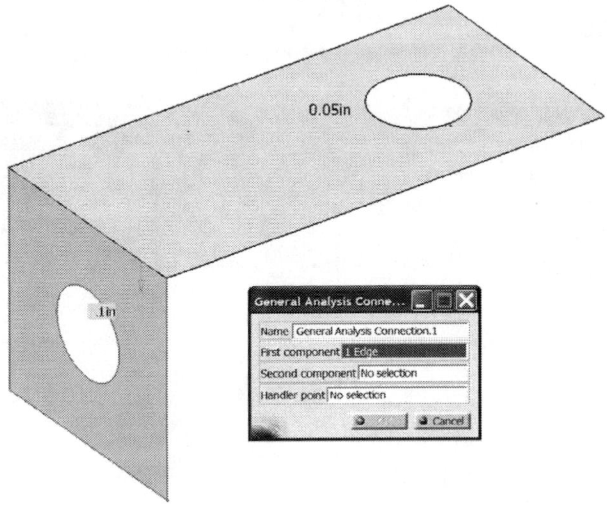


For **Second component** pick the edge from the flange surface. The arrow helps to decide whether the correct edge is picked.

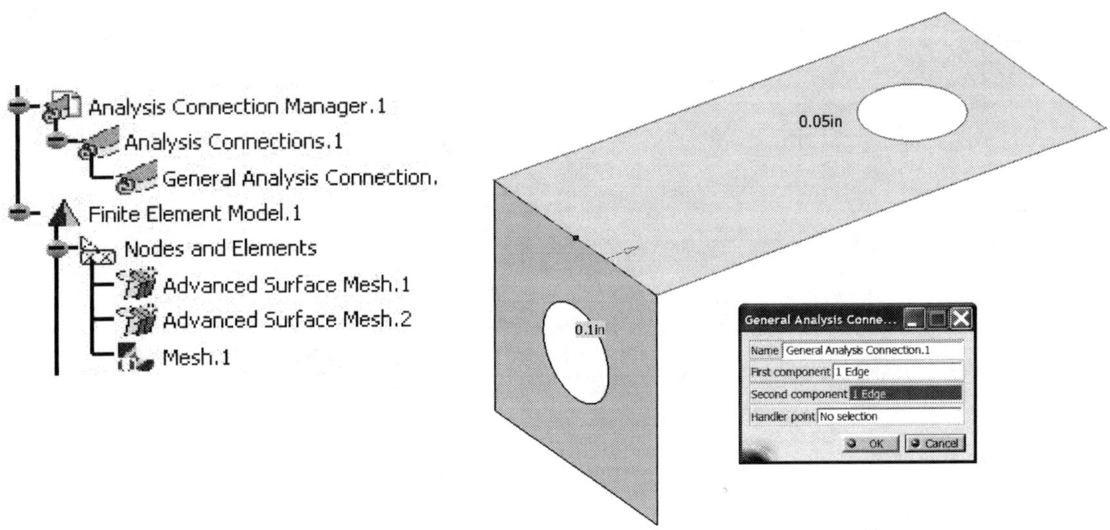


Although the connection between the two edges is established, the nature of this connection is undefined. The **Connection Property** toolbar 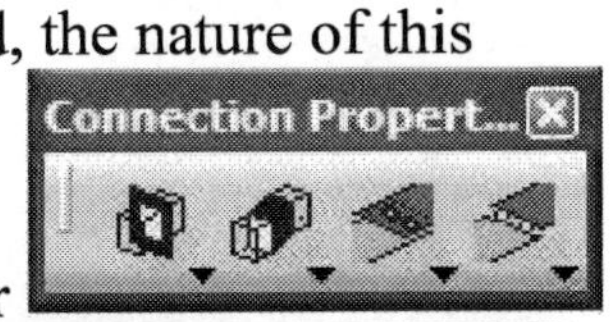

has a sub-toolbar known as **Distant Connection Property** 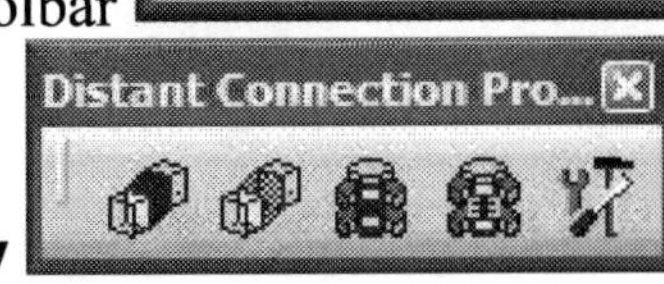

.

Use the **Rigid Connection Property** icon  from this sub-toolbar to open the input box below.

For **Supports** select the **General Analysis Connection**. This can be picked from the tree or from the screen.

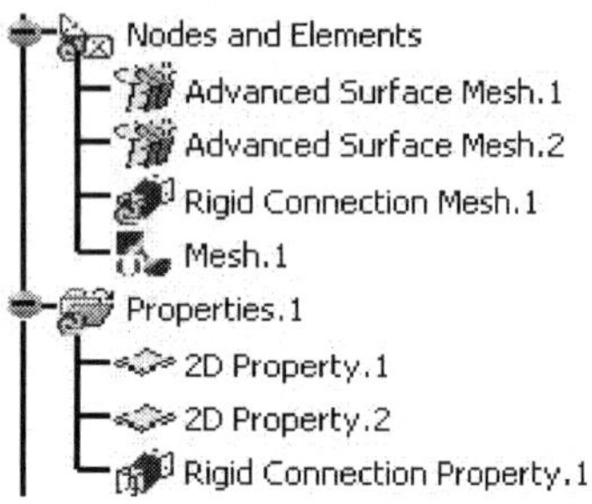

## Applying Restraints:

Select the **Clamp** icon  from the **Restraint** toolbar 

, and pick the ring from the web section.

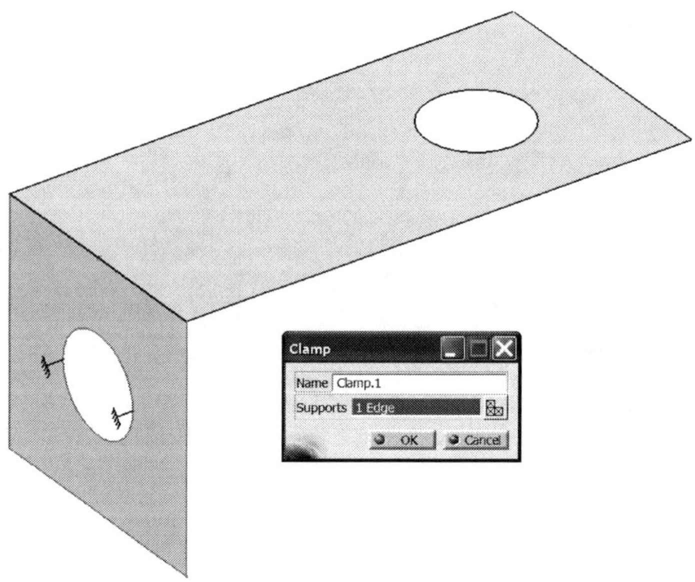

## Applying Loads:

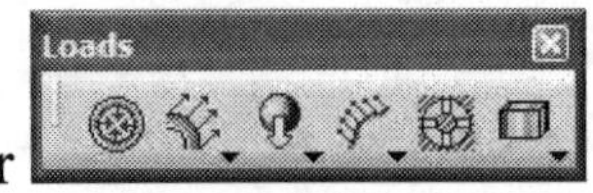


Select the **Distributed Force** icon , from the **Loads** toolbar and pick the ring on the web section. Input a force of -100 lb in the z-direction.

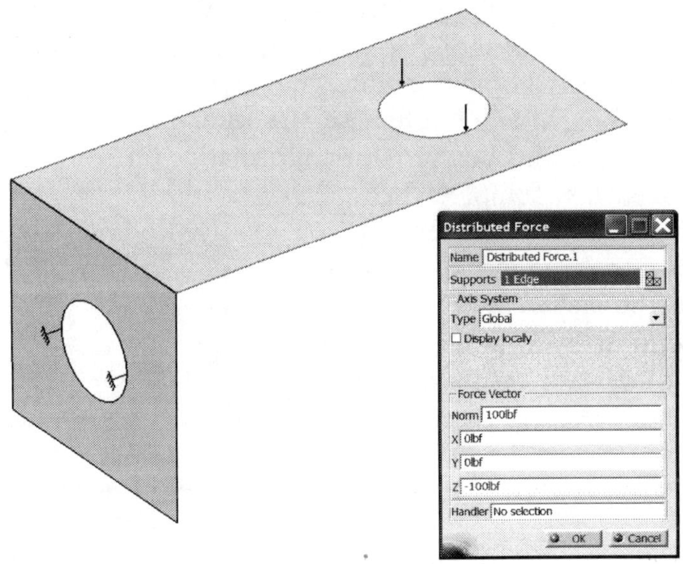


The complete tree before running the analysis is displayed next.

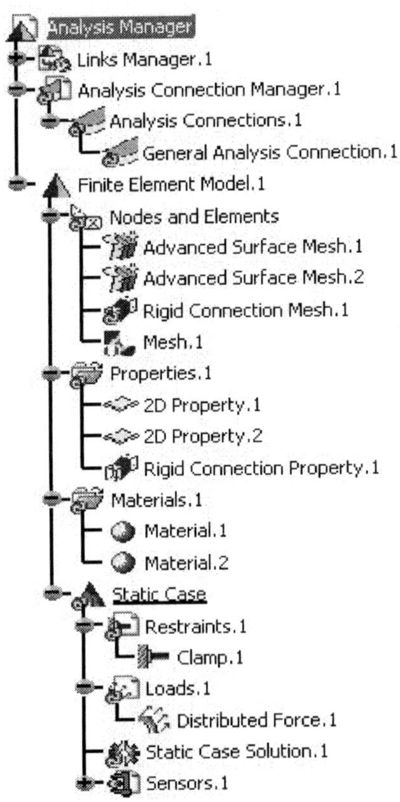

## Launching the Solver:

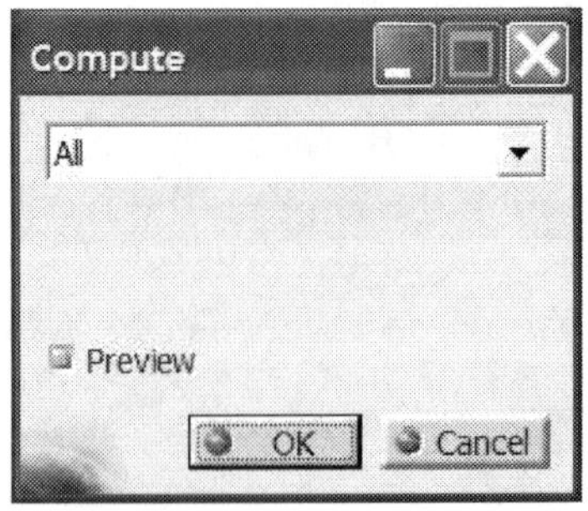


To run the analysis, you need to use the **Compute** toolbar  by selecting the **Compute** icon . This leads to the **Compute** box shown to the right. Leave the defaults as **All** which means everything is computed. Upon closing this box, after a brief pause, the second box shown below appears. This box provides information on the resources needed to complete the analysis. If the estimates are zero in the listing, there is a problem in the previous step and should be looked into. If all numbers are zero in this box, although the program may run, it will not produce any useful results.

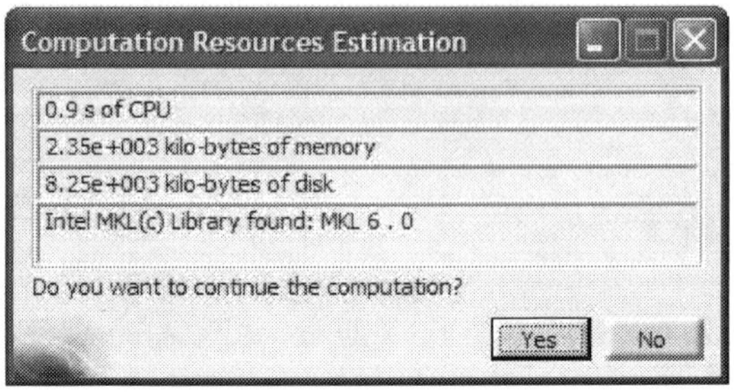


The tree has been changed to reflect the location of the Results and Computations as shown below.

The user can change these locations by double-clicking on the branch after which the box shown on the right opens and can be modified.

**Postprocessing:**

The main postprocessing toolbar is called **Image** 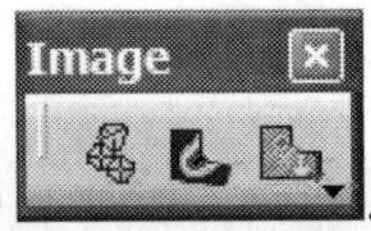

. To view the deformed shape you have to use the **Deformation** icon 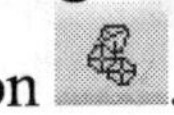. The resulting deformed shape is displayed below.

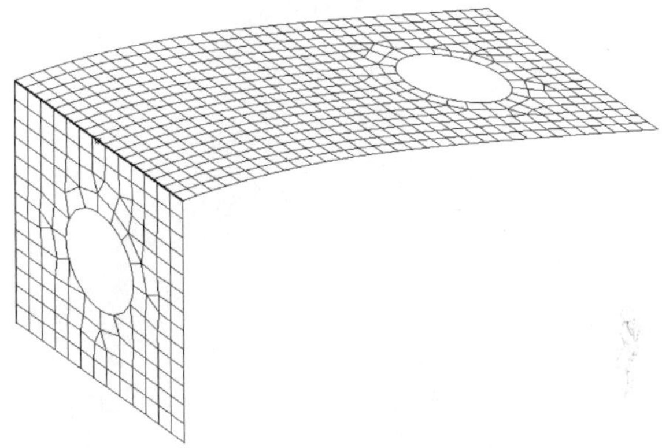

Keep in mind that the displacements are scaled considerably so that one can observe the deformed shape. Although the scale factor is set automatically, one can change this value with the **Deformation Scale Factor** icon  in the **Analysis Tools** toolbar 

.

In order to see the displacement field, the **Displacement** icon 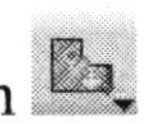 in the **Image** toolbar should be used. The default display is in terms of displacement arrows.

The arrow plot is not particularly useful. In order to view the contour plot of the displacement field, position the cursor on the arrow field and double-click. The **Image Edition** box opens.

Note that the default is to draw the contour on the deformed shape. If this is not desired, uncheck the box **On deformed mesh**. Next, select **AVERAGE-ISO** and press **OK**. The contour of the displacement field is shown. (Note that the color map has been changed; otherwise everything looks black.)

A maximum displacement of 40.9 in. is detected. This value is unrealistic but it is correct.

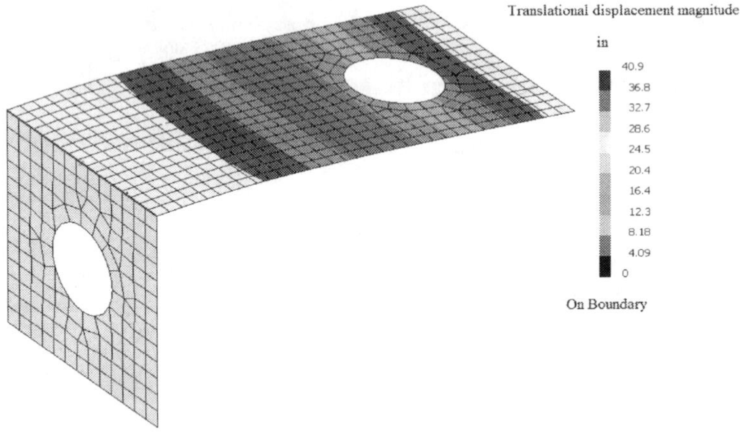


At the first glance, it may appear that the web has not deflected at all. To check the fate of the web, double-click on the contour and in the **Image Edition** box pick the **Selections** tab. From the list, choose **Advanced Surface Mesh.2**.

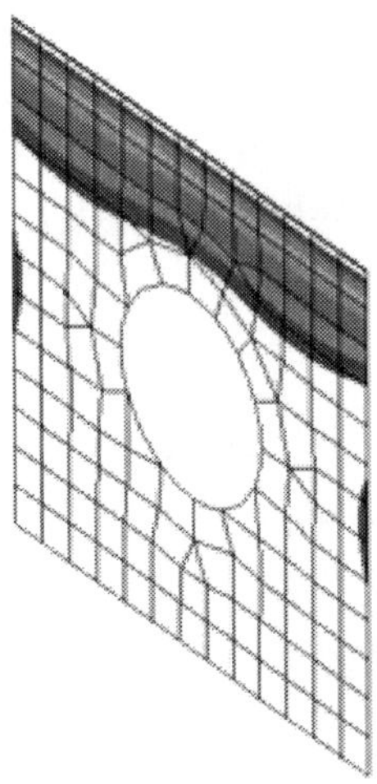

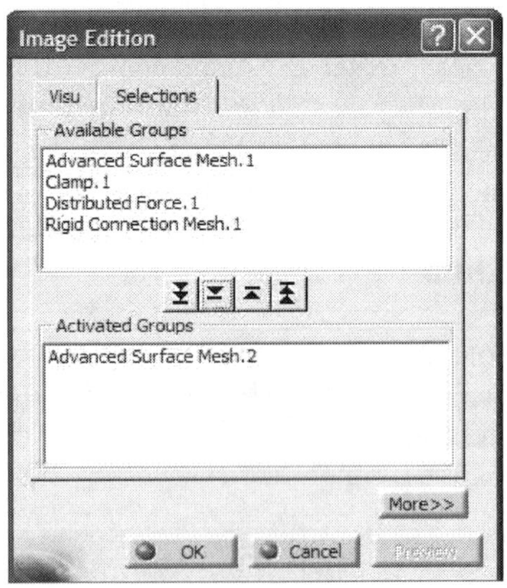


The next step in the postprocessing is to plot the contours of the von Mises stress using the **von Mises Stress** icon  in the **Image** toolbar. This is shown below. Keep in mind that the color map has been changed.

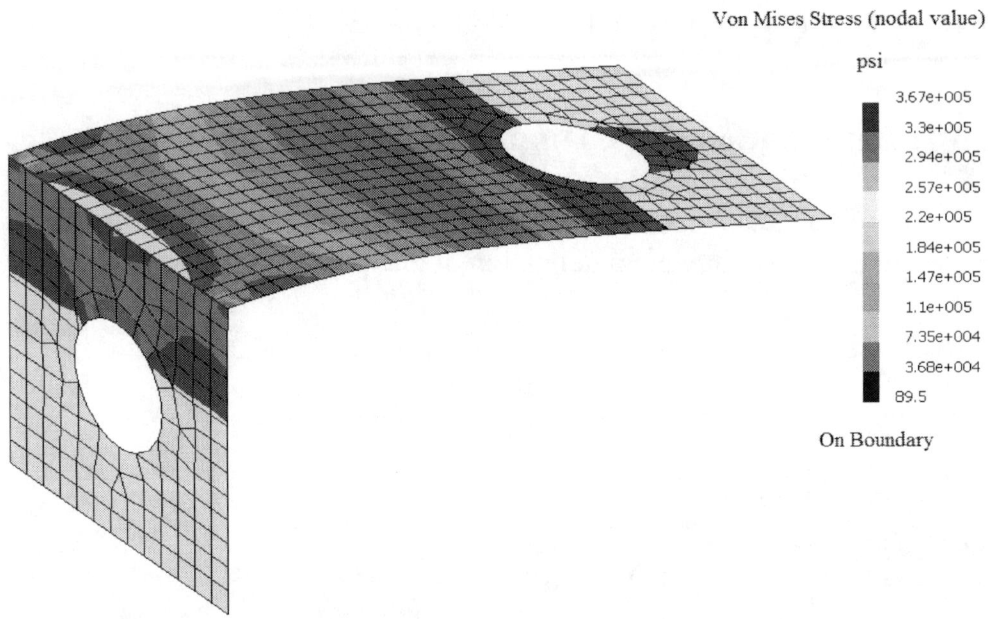
Von Mises Stress (nodal value)
psi
3.67e+005
3.3e+005
2.94e+005
2.57e+005
2.2e+005
1.84e+005
1.47e+005
1.1e+005
7.35e+004
3.68e+004
89.5
On Boundary

# Exercises for Chapter 11

## Problem 1: Deformation of a Clamped Bracket

Use dimensions of your choice to create the clamped bracket shown. Select a material and load level and find the maximum deflection of the part.

Partial Answer:

Use the following sequence of operations for creating the clamp.

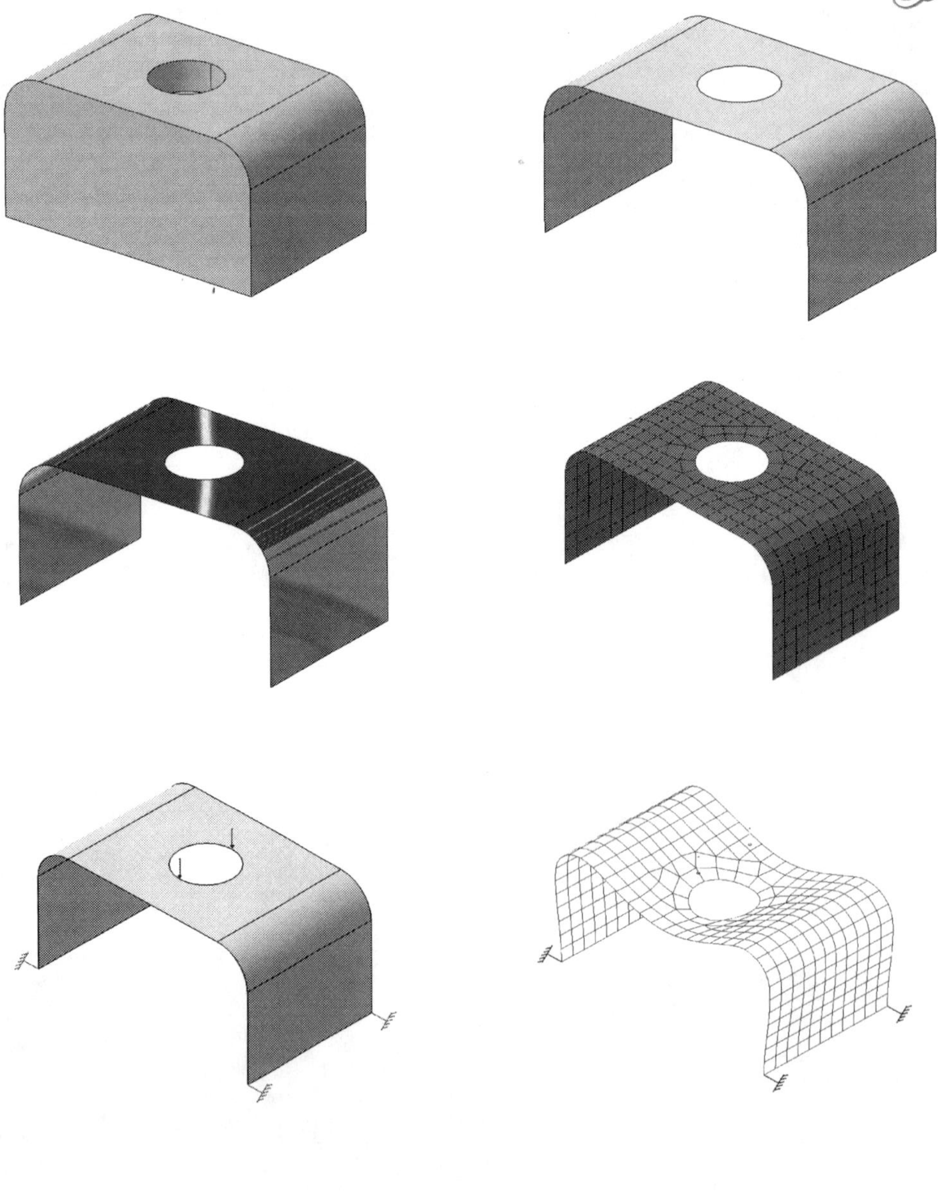

# Chapter 12

# Analysis of Thin Walled Pressure Vessel using Shell Elements

## Introduction

In this tutorial you model a thin walled pressure vessel with shell elements. Symmetry is used to reduce the vessel to a 45 degree sector. The geometry is constructed by taking a broken line segment and revolving it about a suitable axis.

## 1 Problem Statement

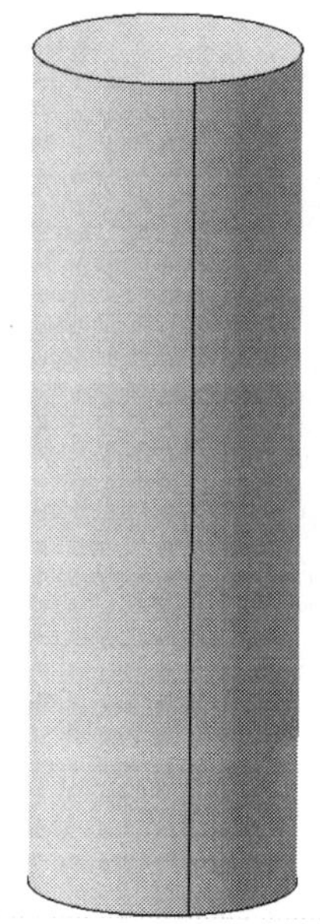

The aluminum thin walled pressure vessel shown has a thickness of $t = 0.1$ in., mean diameter of $r = 6$ in., and a full height of 40 in. The ends are capped and an internal pressure of $p = 100$ psi is present.

Elementary strength of materials provides simple expressions for the principal stresses as provided below.

$$\sigma_{hoop} = \frac{pr}{t}$$

$$\sigma_{axial} = \frac{pr}{2t}$$

$$\sigma_{radial} = 0$$

Because of symmetry, it suffices to model an arbitrary sector of the tank. This need not be at the full length. You will be taking a 45° sector with half height of the tank as displayed below.
Note that one faces is at a 45° orientation with respect to the global coordinate system. Therefore, you will be creating a **User** defined coordinate system for the inclined face and employ it for applying the restraints.

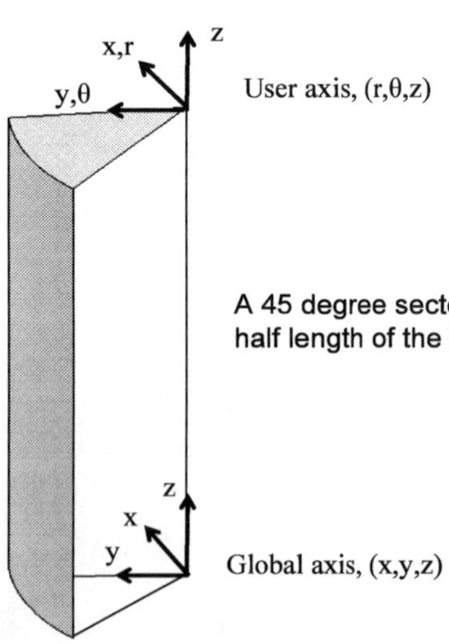

## 2 Creation of the Part in Mechanical Design Solutions

Enter the **Part Design** workbench from the standard Windows toolbar, select **File > New**. Rename the part to be **Pressure_vessel**. See Note #1 in Appendix I.

From the standard Windows toolbar, select **Start > Wireframe and Surface Design**.

Select the **yz** plane and enter the **Sketcher**. Draw the broken line segment shown and dimension it.

Leave the **Sketcher**.

Pick the **Revolve** icon from **Surfaces** toolbar.
In the resulting input box, for **Profile**, select **Sketch.1**.
To select **Revolution axis**, right click, and choose **Z Axis**.
For **Angle 1**, type 45.

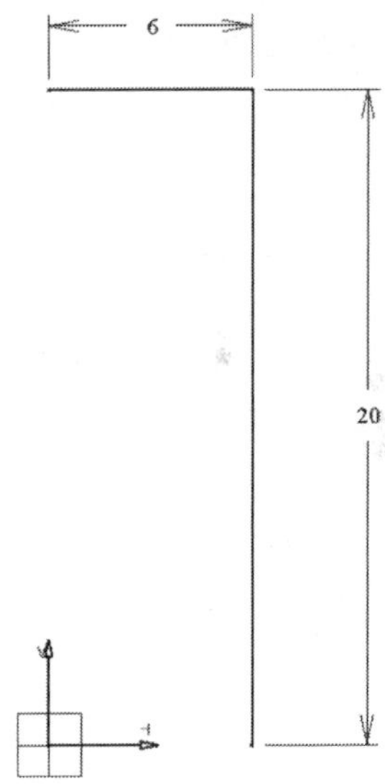


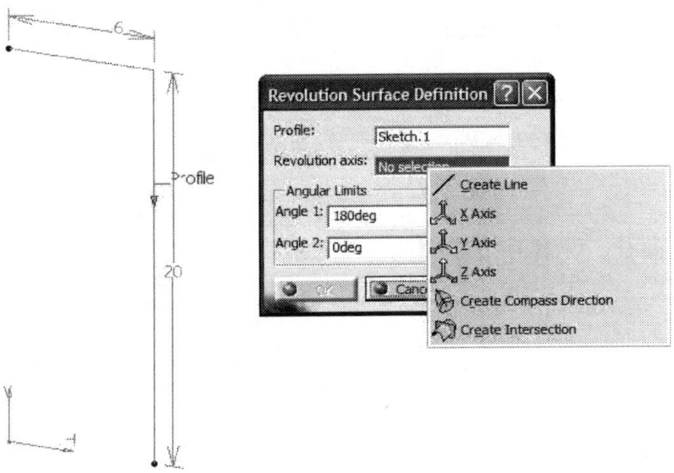


The final appearance of the **Revolution Surface Definition** box and the resulting surface is shown on the right.
Because of the method of construction, a single surface is present, and there is no need for the **Join** operation.

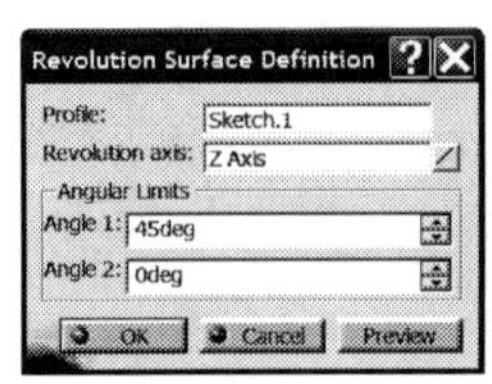

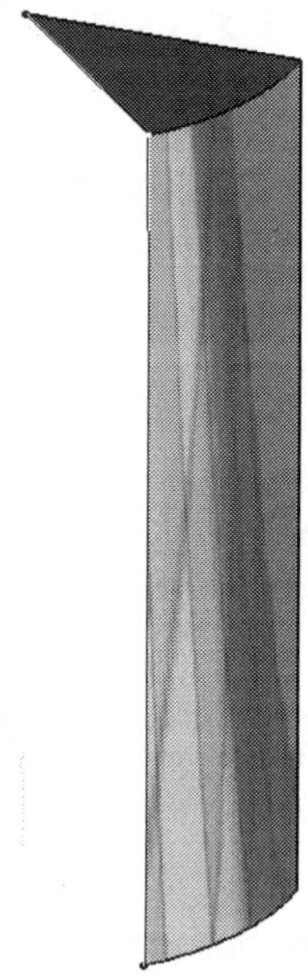

Use the **Apply material** icon to open the database of material properties, selecting **Aluminum** from the **Metal** tab. Choose **Revolve.1** from the tree to complete the process.
If the sector does not look "shiny", you can change the rendering style from the **View mode** toolbar.

Select the **Shading with Material** icon.
This action results in a different rendering displayed on the right.

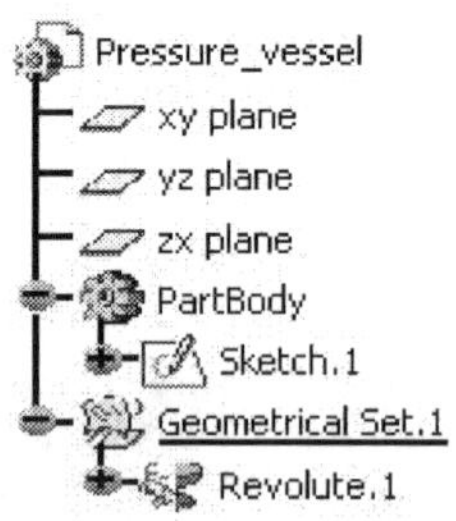


## 3 Entering the Analysis Solutions

From the standard Windows toolbar, select

**Start > Analysis & Simulation > Advanced Meshing Tools**

Upon entering the **Advanced Meshing Tools** workbench, the standard box shown on the right is displayed. However, you note that the representative element "size" and "sag" is not visible on your display.
This is in contrast to the case of entering the **Generative Structural Analysis** workbench for the first time.
Therefore, at this point no mesh is present.

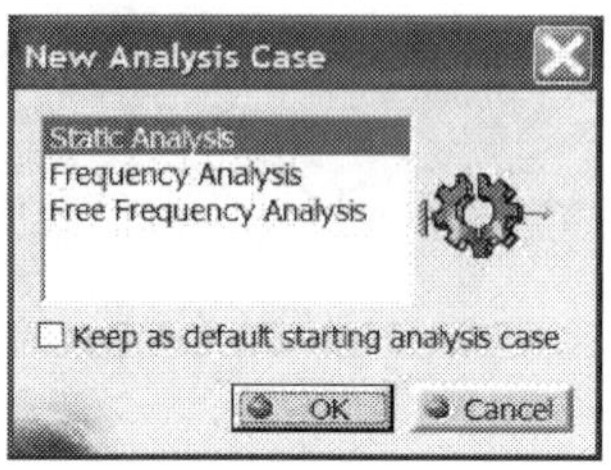


The **Meshing Methods** toolbar 

has a sub-toolbar known as the **Surface Mesher** 

. Select the **Octree Triangle Mesher** icon and pick the surface from the screen and click on the **Apply** button.

The resulting shell mesh appears on your screen.

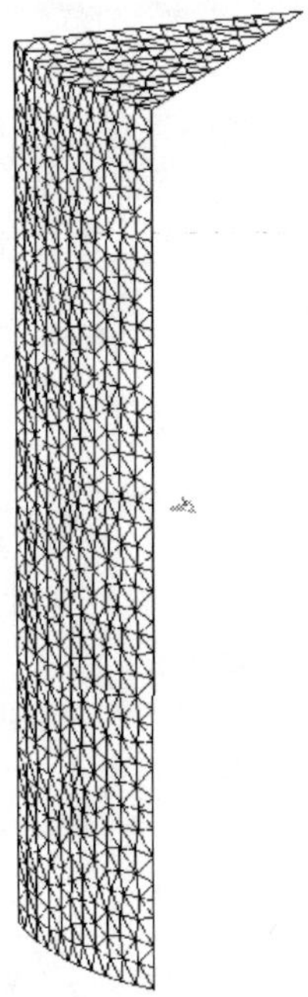

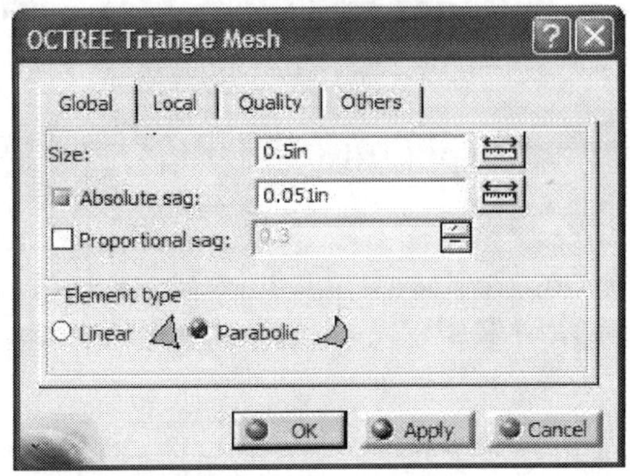


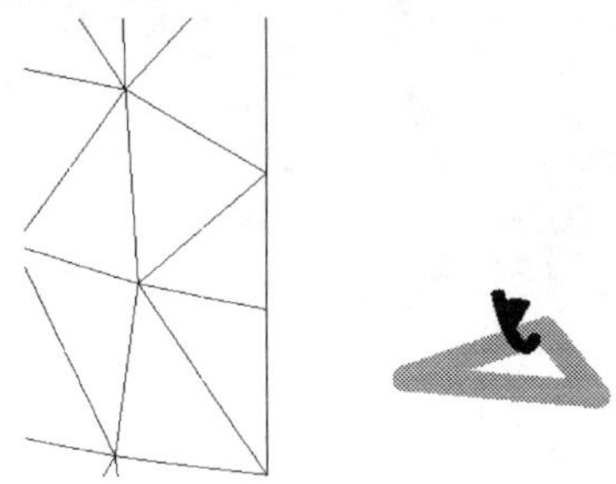

The representative "size" and "sag" elements are not tetrahedron anymore, but they seem to be planar in shape. A zoomed view of these entities is displayed above.

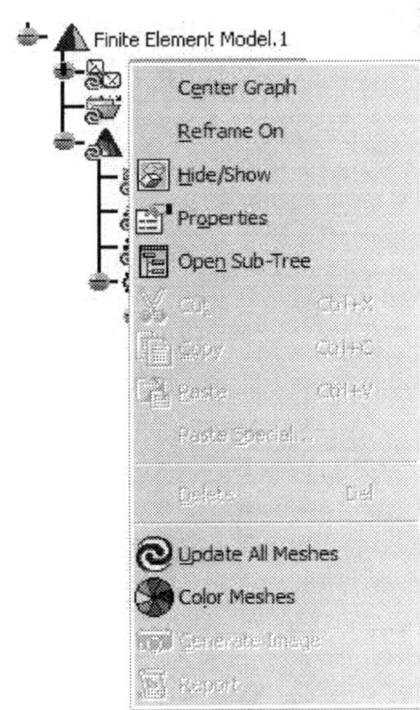


In the event that you forgot to press the **Mesh** button in the **OCTREE Triangle Mesh** box above, no mesh is created. This is in spite of the fact that the mesh "specs" have been set.

In such a situation, point the cursor to the **Nodes and Elements** branch on the tree, right click, and select **Update All Meshes** as indicated on the right.

Alternatively, double click on the **OCTREE Triangle Mesh.1** on the tree to open the appropriate box and press on the **Mesh** button.

The shell mesh cross sectional properties and the boundary conditions are specified in the **Generative Structural Analysis** workbench. Therefore, switch to this workbench through

**Start > Analysis & Simulation > Generative Structural Analysis**

If the mesh disappears from the screen while changing workbenches, point the cursor to the branch **Nodes and Elements**, right click and select **Mesh Visualization**.

### Assigning Shell Properties (2D Properties):

The first task is to specify the shell thickness. This can be done two different ways. The properties can be assigned to **Revolve.1**, or it can be assigned to the **OCTREE Triangle Mesh.1**, selected from the tree. You will follow the latter approach.

Select the **2D Property** icon  from the **Model Manager** toolbar

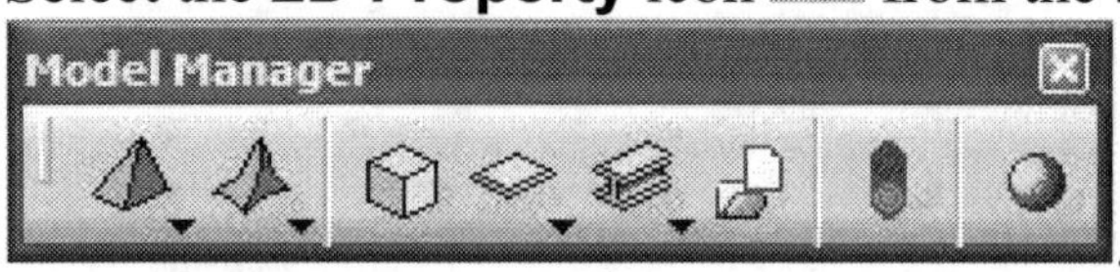


, leading to the following input box. For the **Supports**, select the **OCTREE Triangle Mesh.1** from the tree.
The shell **Thickness** is 0.1. Note that the material is automatically picked as **Aluminum**.

Upon closing the window, the shell thickness is recorded on the mesh as shown below.

The portion of the tree structure associated with the mesh is also displayed.

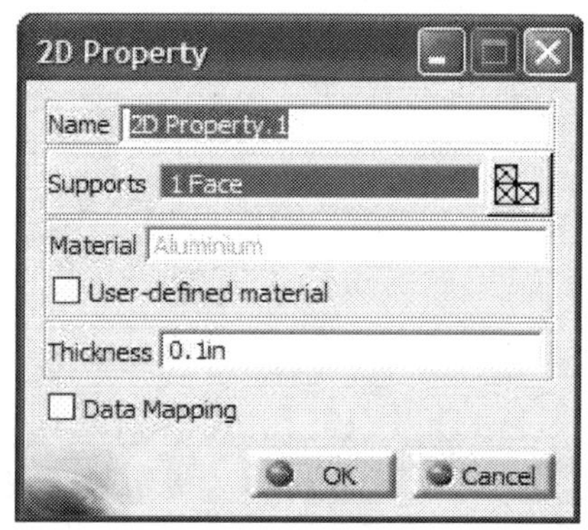


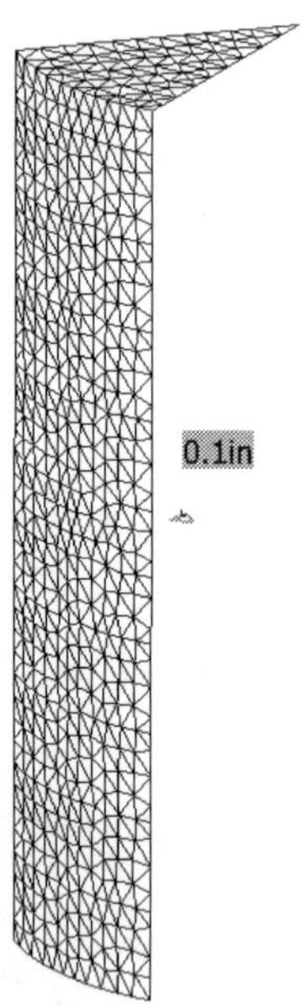


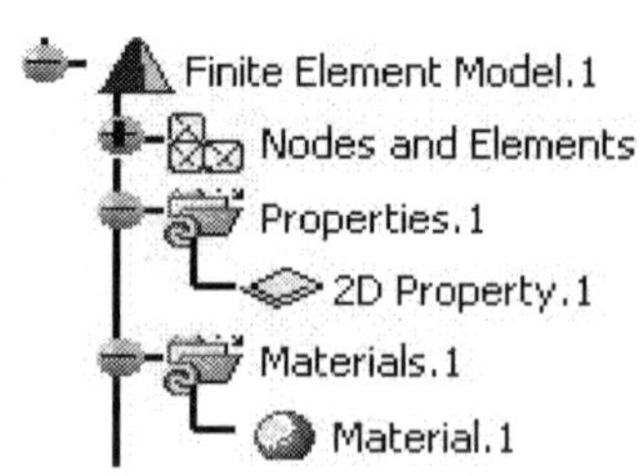


Regularly save your work.

Before applying restraints, switch to the **Wireframe and Surface Design** workbench and create a local coordinate system.

From the **Tools** toolbar 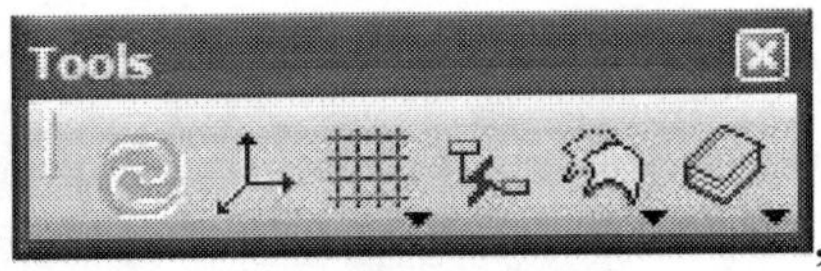

, select the **Axis System** icon 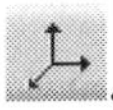. Pick the top vertex as shown below. Select the "**x**", "**y**", and "**z**" axes, so that the coordinate system resembles the figure provided.
Note: Do not pay much attention to the actual picks in the **Axis System Definition** box below. Using trial and error construct the coordinate system so that it resembles what is shown below (exactly).

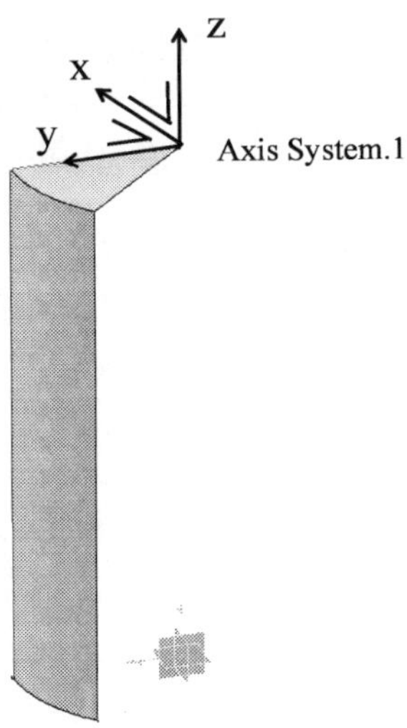


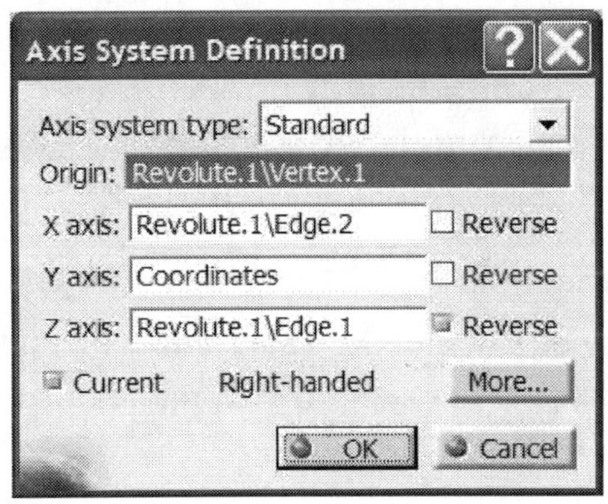


**Applying Restraints:**

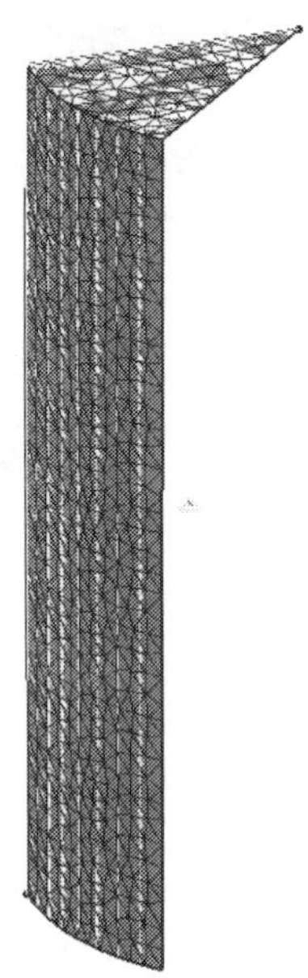

CATIA's FEA module is geometrically based. This means that the boundary conditions cannot be applied to nodes and elements. The boundary conditions can only be applied at the part level. As soon as you enter the **Generative Structural Analysis** workbench, the part is automatically hidden. Therefore, before boundary conditions are applied, the part must be brought to the unhide mode. This can be carried out by pointing the cursor to the top of the tree, the **Links Manager.1** branch, and right click, select **Show**.

At this point, the part and the mesh are superimposed as shown on the right and you have access to the part.

To make your job easier, we have labeled the edges on the right hand side.

The symmetry edges are restrained with the help of the following table.

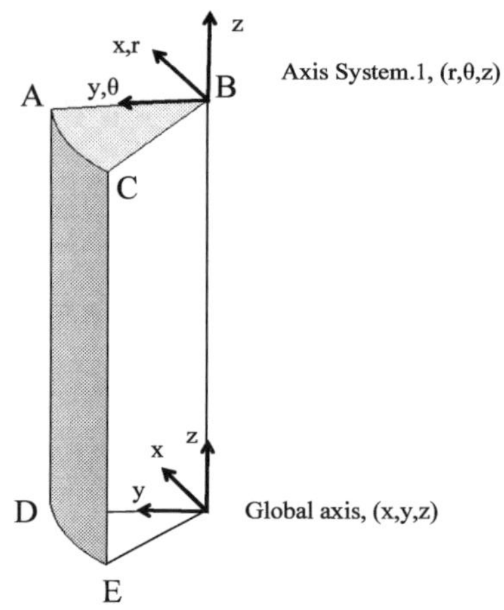


| PLANE | $u_x$ | $u_y$ | $u_z$ | $\Theta_x$ | $\Theta_y$ | $\Theta_z$ |
|---|---|---|---|---|---|---|
| yz | zero | free | free | free | zero | zero |
| xz | free | zero | free | zero | free | zero |
| xy | free | free | zero | zero | zero | free |

If we rely on the local axis for imposing the restraints, the standard directions (1,2,3) in **User-defined Restraints** correspond to (r,Θ,z) directions. Therefore, for imposing restraints, you should be using user **Axis System.1** with the **cylindrical** coordinate system activated.

Consider the edge BCE. When referred to the "Axis System.1", this edge lies in the symmetry plane $\Theta = 135^\circ$. The table indicates that for this edge, $u_y = \Theta_x = \Theta_z = 0$ where (x,y,z) are the (1,2,3) directions.

Select the **User-defined Restraint** icon  from the **Restraint** toolbar .


In the resulting box, pick the BC and CE edges as **Supports**. Most probably you will find out that these edges cannot be picked. The reason being, that the broken line segment used for **Revolving** is in the **Show** mode. Before you can pick these edges, **Hide** the line.

For **Type** select **User** and pick the constructed coordinate system from the screen.
As **Local orientation**, select **Cylindrical**, and check the restraints as shown.

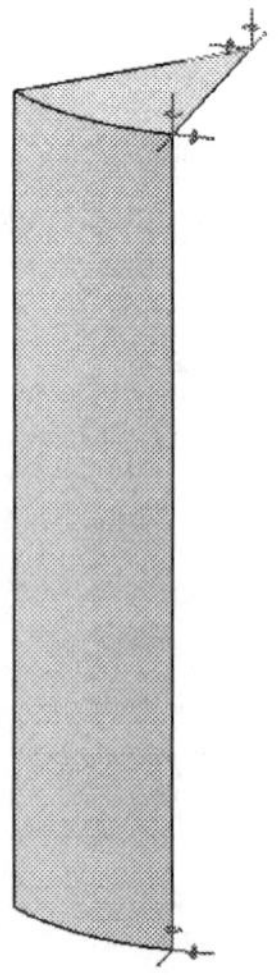

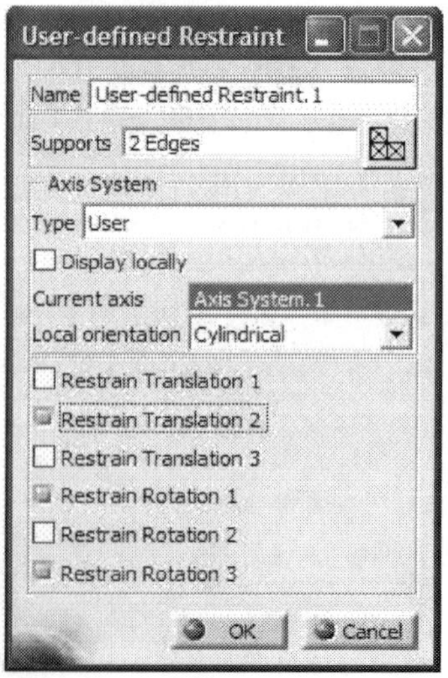

Next, use the **Advanced Restraint** icon to pick the edge BAD. This edge lies in the global yz plane and therefore, $u_x = \Theta_y = \Theta_z = 0$. This information allows us to complete the input box.

For **Type**, select **Global**, and finally restraining the degrees of freedom as indicated.

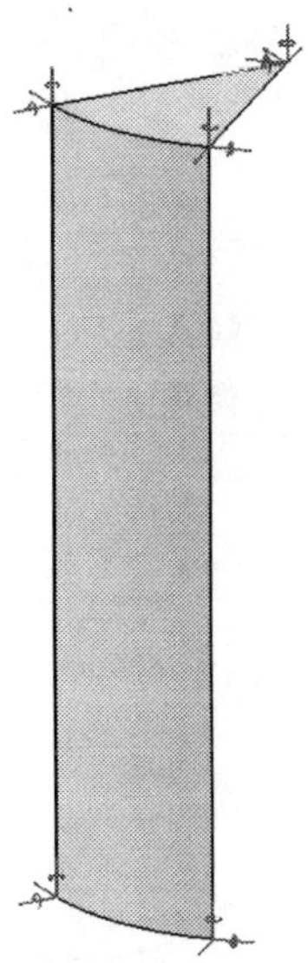

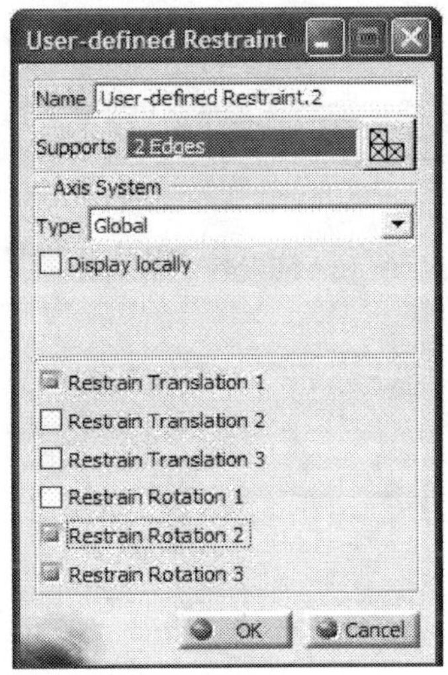


Once again, use the icon to pick the arc DE. This arc lies in the global xy plane. Therefore, the symmetry table indicates that $u_z = \Theta_x = \Theta_y = 0$ where (x,y,z) are the (1,2,3) directions.

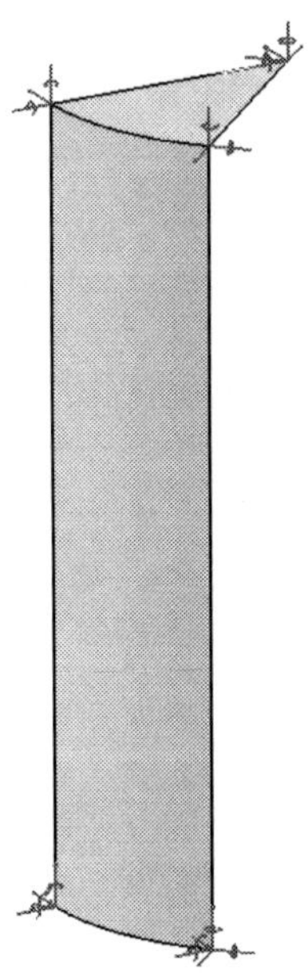

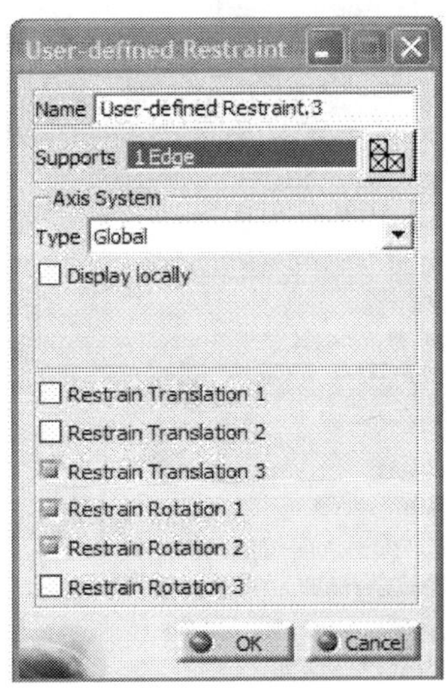

## Applying Loads:

Use the **Pressure** icon  from the **Loads** toolbar 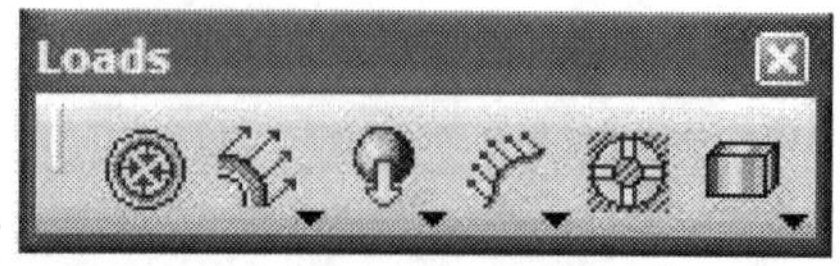

and pick the faces ABC and ACED. Apply a pressure of -100 psi. If the direction is not correct, change the sign of 100.
The complete tree is given below for your information.

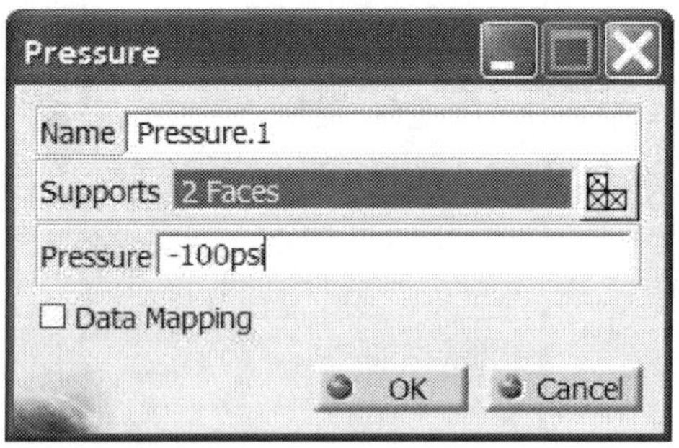


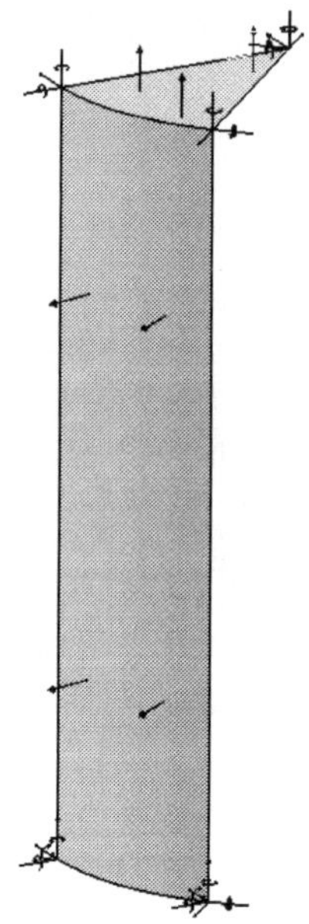

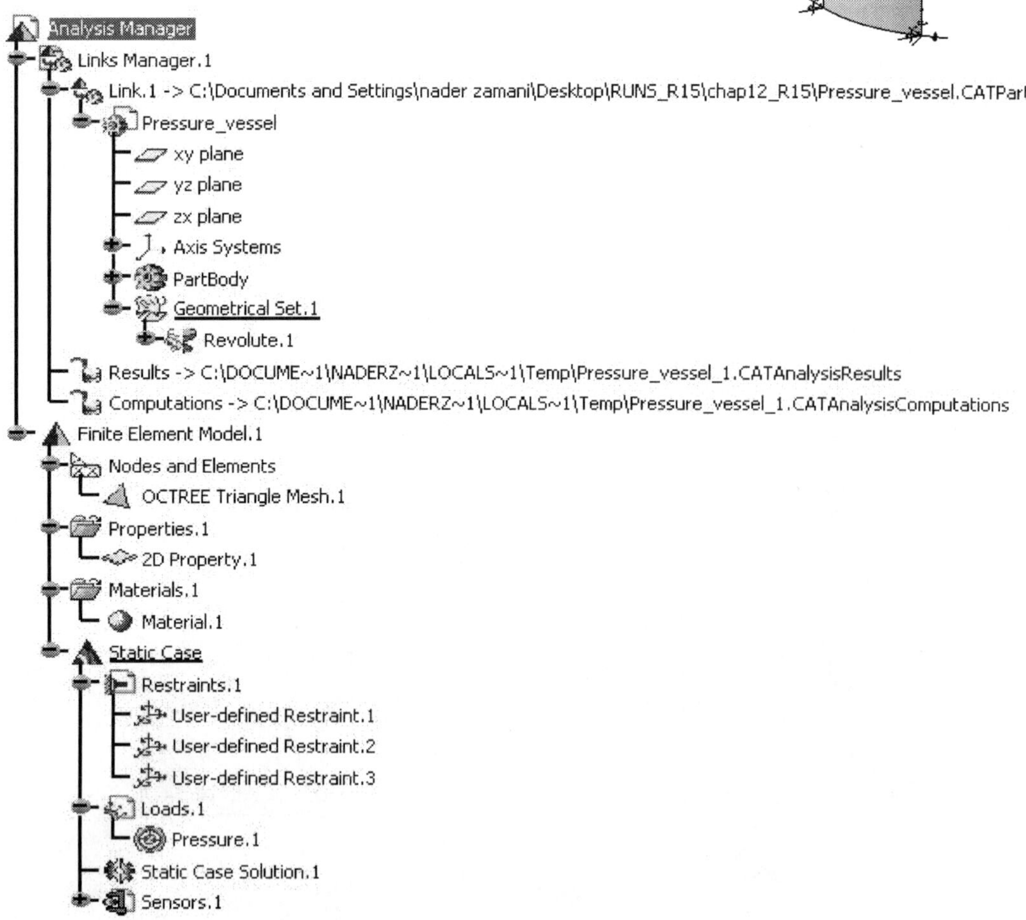

**Launching the Solver:**

To run the analysis, you need to use the **Compute** toolbar 

by selecting the **Compute** icon . After a brief pause, the box shown below appears. This box provides information on the resources needed to complete the analysis. In the event that all estimates are zero in the listing, there is a problem in the previous step and should be looked into. With all numbers as zero in this box, although the program may run, it will not produce any useful results.

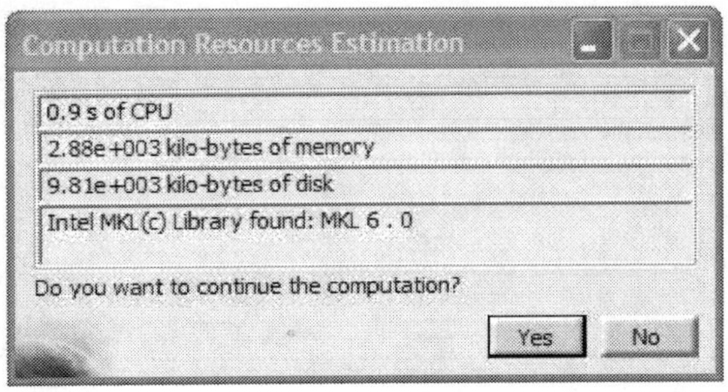


**Postprocessing:**

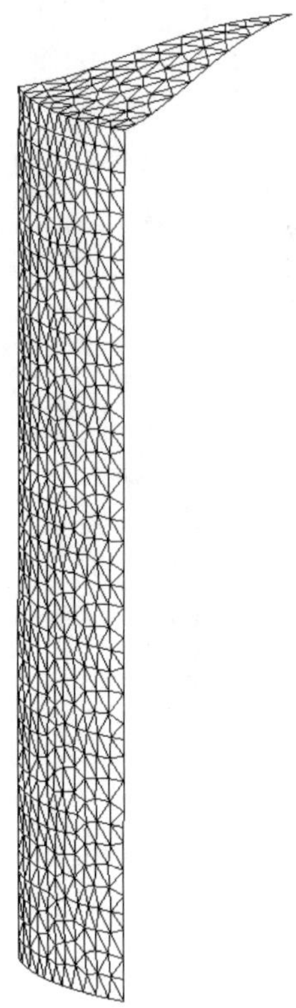

The main postprocessing toolbar is called **Image** 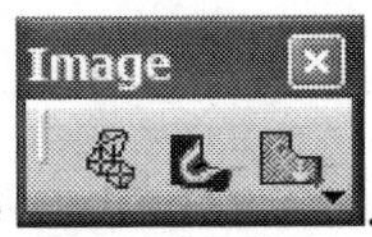

. To view the deformed shape you have use the **Deformation** icon 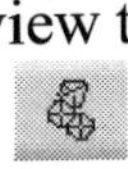. The resulting deformed shape is displayed to the right.

Keep in mind that the displacements are scaled considerably so that one can observe the deformed shape. Although the scale factor is set automatically, one can change this value with the **Deformation Scale Factor** icon  in the **Analysis Tools** toolbar 

.

In order to see the displacement field, the **Displacement** icon  in the **Image** toolbar should be used. The default display is in terms of displacement arrows.

The arrow plot is not particularly useful. In order to view the contour plot of the displacement field, position the cursor on the arrow field and double click. The **Image Edition** box opens.

Note that the default is to draw the contour on the deformed shape. If this is not desired, uncheck the box **On deformed mesh**. Next, select **AVERAGE-ISO** and press **OK**. The contour of the displacement field is shown. The maximum displacement of 2.57 in. is in the capped end.

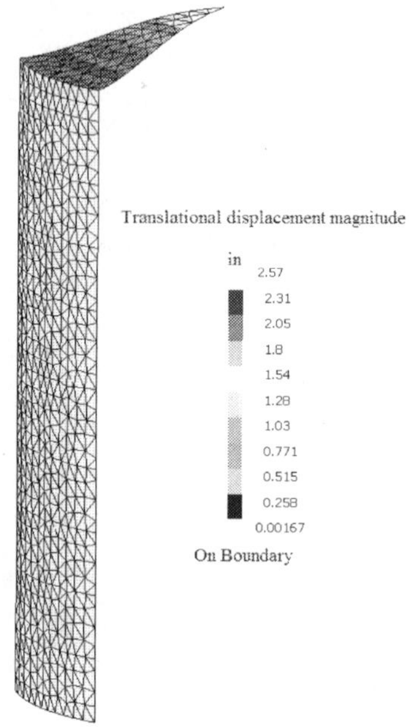


Because of the large displacement of the end cap, it is difficult to read the displacement of the side wall. In order to address that, a **Sphere Group** is created.

Select the **Sphere Group** icon from the **Typed Groups** toolbar

.

This allows you to create a sphere of a desired size and location which contains all the elements used for plotting purposes. Clearly, you want to avoid the capped end which has large displacements. See Note #3 in Appendix I.

Upon double clicking on , a default sphere centered at (0,0,0) is constructed. The box which allows you to resize the sphere is shown below.

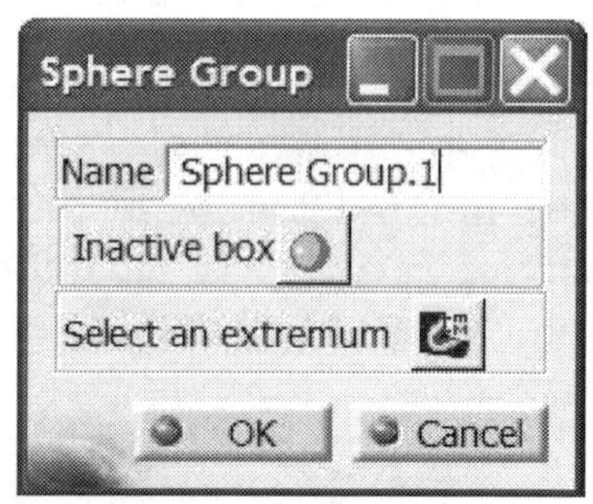


You can change the radius of the box by clicking on the Inactive box icon. A bigger sphere is depicted below.

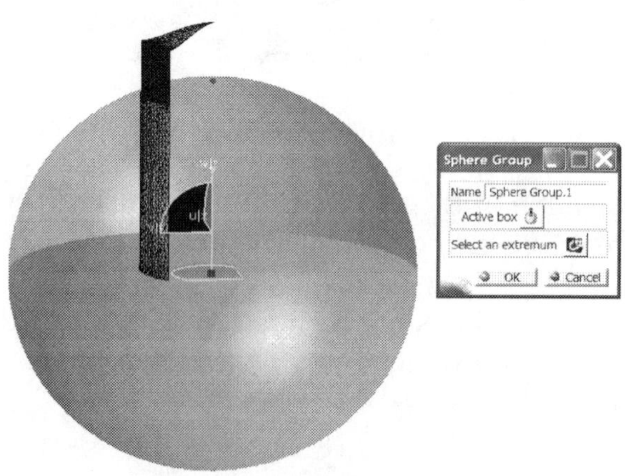

At this point the **Sphere Group.1** is created which encloses the elements trapped by the sphere. This group is listed in the tree as indicated on the right.

The next step is plotting the deflections for this group. Make sure that the plot is active.
Double click on the contour to open the **Image Edition** box and use the **Selections** tab. Select **Sphere Group.1** and use the button . The contour below displays the von Mises stress at **sphere Group.1** section.

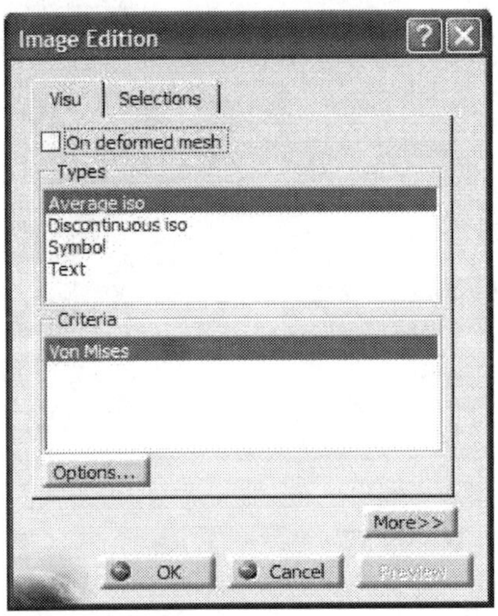


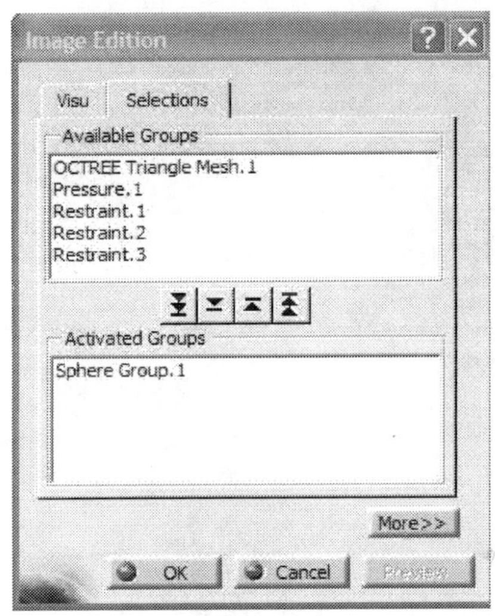


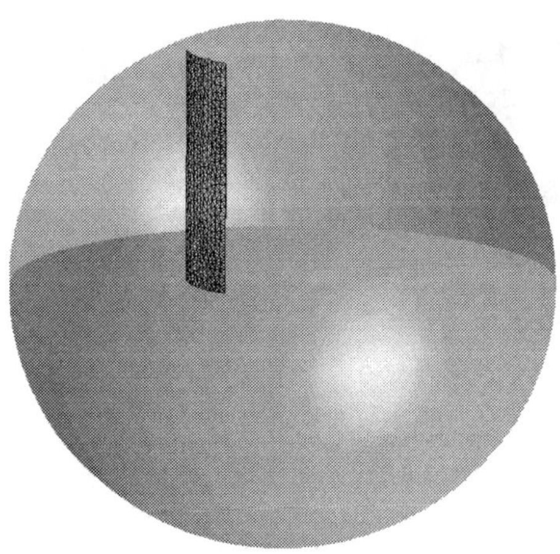

Point the cursor to **Sphere Group.1** in the tree, and **Hide** it. The result is a nice contour showing the detailed displacements in the wall area as indicated below.

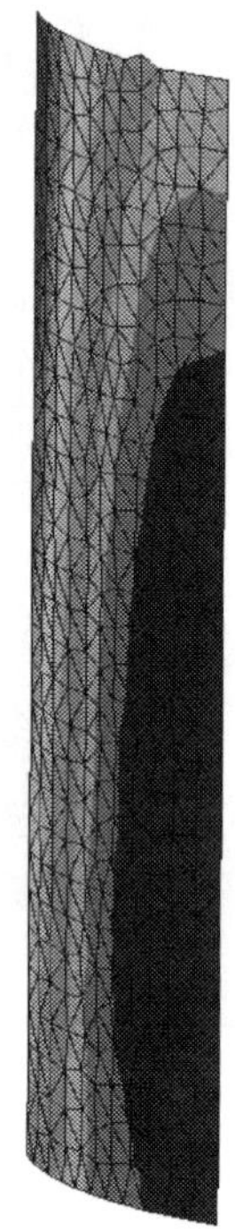

The next step in the postprocessing is to plot the contours of the von Mises stress using the **von Mises Stress** icon  in the **Image** toolbar. The von Mises stress is displayed below. The problem with this contour is that, because of the large stresses at the capped end, the stresses in the wall area are completely masked.
The principal stresses are postprocessed next.

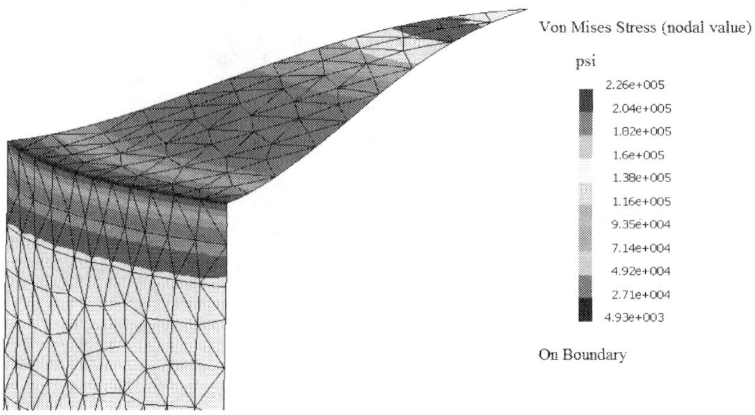


From the **Image** toolbar 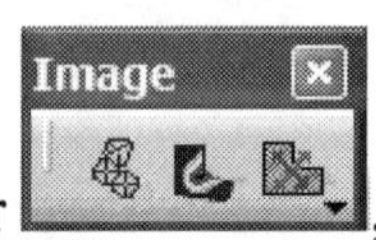

, select the **Principal Stress** icon 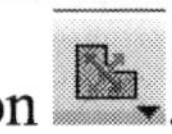. The result is the principal stress directions in the vector form as displayed on your screen. Due to the large number of arrows, the interpretation of this plot is difficult. You can therefore switch to a different style of plotting. Double click on the arrows on the screen to open the **Image Edition** box on the right and select **AVERAGE-ISO**.

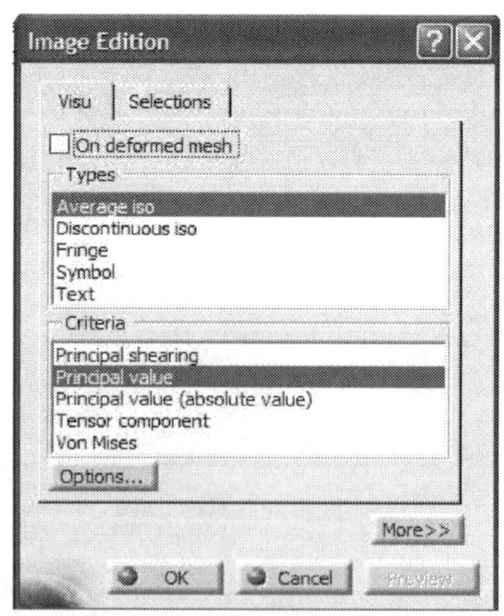

Next, use the **Selections** tab from the top row and choose the **C11** as the component. This results in the contour of the maximum principal stress as displayed below. C11 represents the hoop stress which is uniform away from the capped end.

Keep in mind that CATIA uses C11, C22, and C23 to represent the largest, intermediate, and smallest principal stresses.

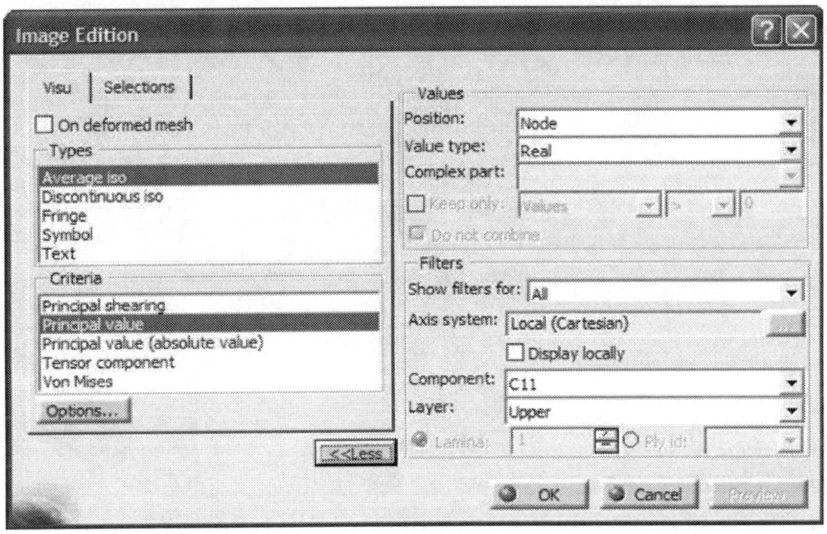


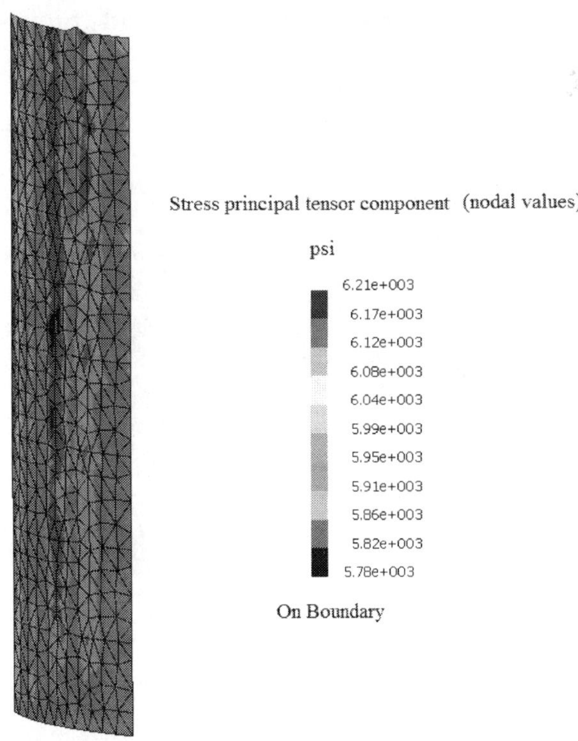


For the supplied parameters, the thin walled pressure vessel formula, $\sigma_{hoop} = \frac{pr}{t}$ predicts a value of 6000 psi which is in good agreement with the FEA contour on the right hand side.

The final task is to tile the contours of hoop stress and displacement field side by side. First make sure that these two plots are active. Point the cursor to the appropriate plot in the tree, right click, and check to see if it is active as displayed below.

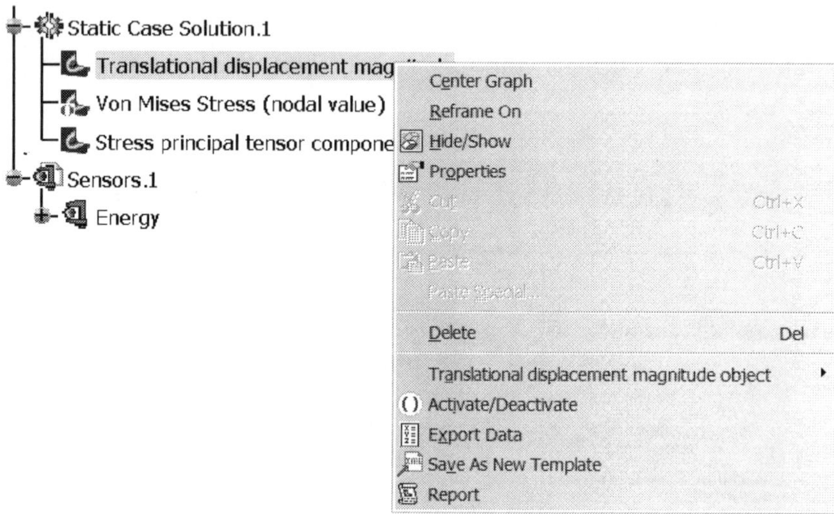


Click the **Image Layout** icon from the **Image Analysis** toolbar. The **Images** box, shown to the right, asks you to specify the direction along which the two plots are expected to be aligned (Make sure that both contours are **Active**). The outcome is side-by-side plots shown below.

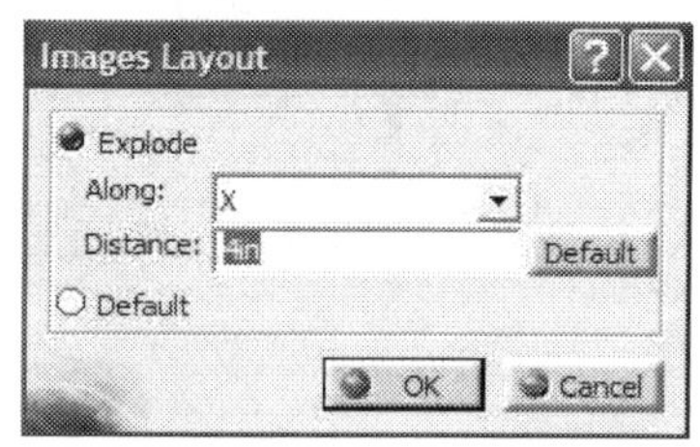


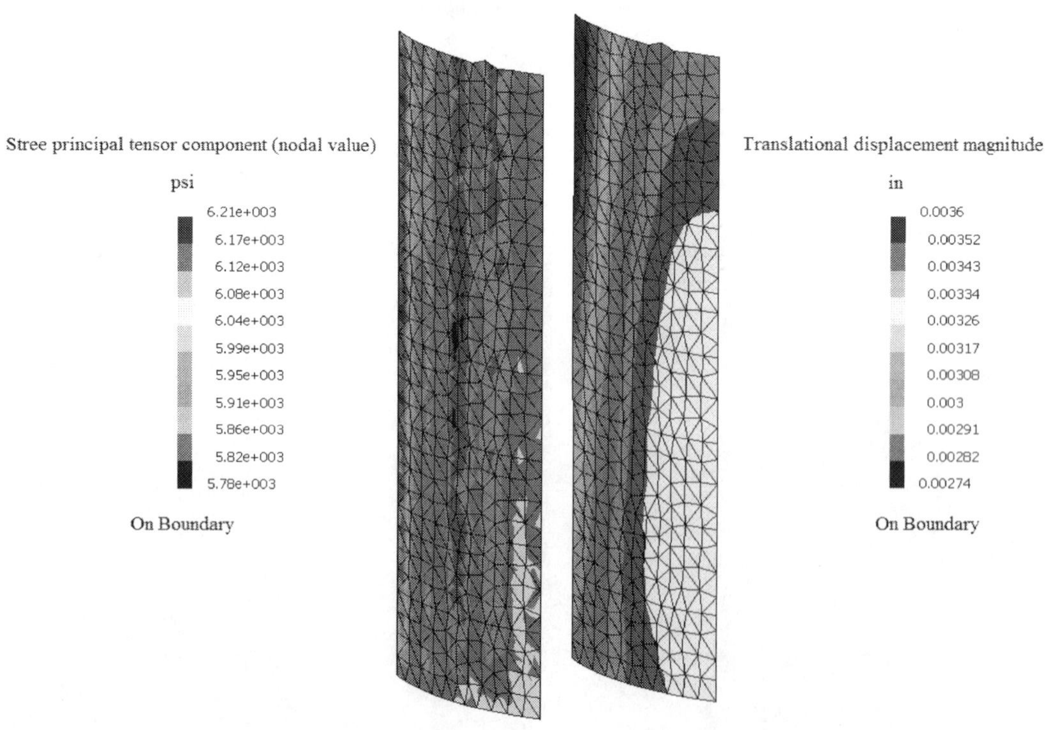

The **Cutting Plane** icon  from the **Analysis Tools** toolbar

can be used to make a cut through the part at a desired location and inspect the stresses inside of the part. The **Cut Plane** box allows you to keep the plane or remove it for display purposes. A typical cutting plane is shown below.

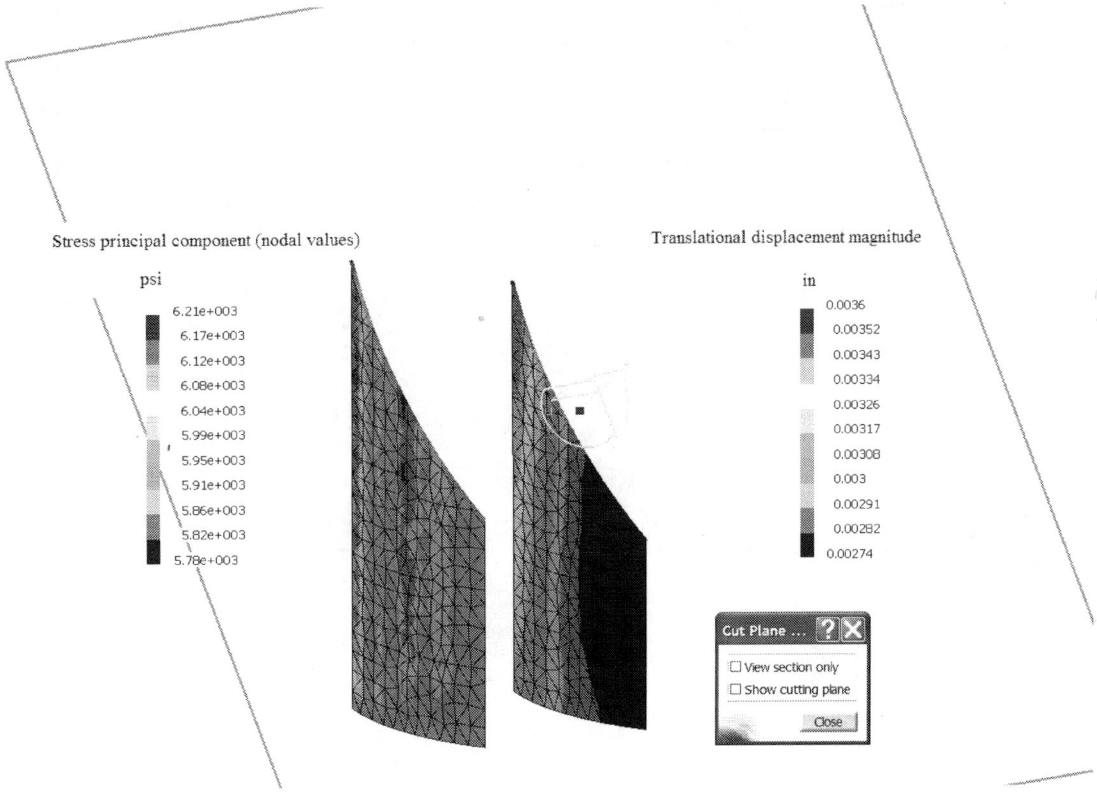


Animation of the model can be achieved through the **Animate** icon  in the **Analysis Tools** toolbar. An AVI file can easily be generated.

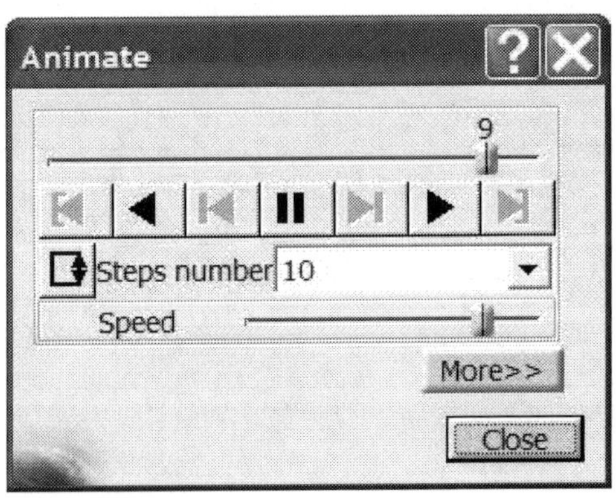

Using the icon **Generate Report**  in the **Analysis Results** toolbar 

, an HTML based report can be generated which summarizes the features and results of the FEA model. The first page of this report is displayed below.

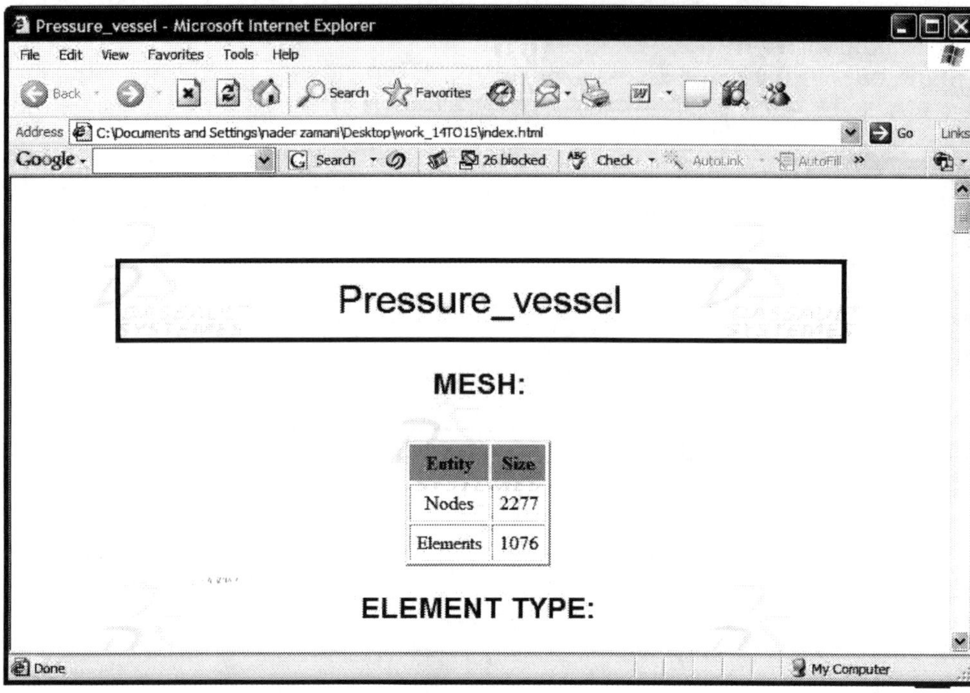

# Exercises for Chapter 12

## Problem 1: Modeling of a Spherical Tank

A steel spherical tank with a mean radius of 40 in. and wall thickness of 0.1 in. is being considered. The tank is subjected to an internal pressure of 100 psi. Use symmetry to reduce the size of the tank by taking a 45 degree slice. Employ shell elements to find the stress distribution in the tank, and the increase in the mean radius of the structure.

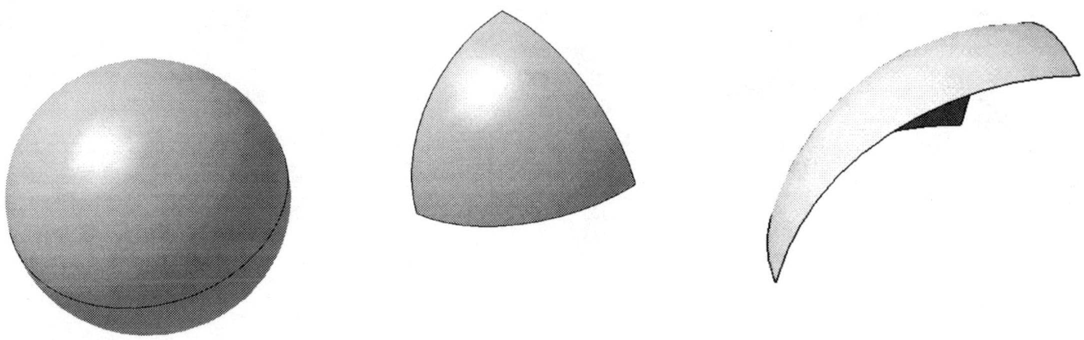

Partial Answer:

Using elementary strength of materials one can show the three principal stresses are given by $\sigma_1 = \sigma_2 = \frac{pr}{2t}$, and $\sigma_3 = 0$.

## Problem 2: Shell Model of a Belleville Spring

A Belleville spring of thickness $t = .1$ in. is depicted below. The geometrical dimensions are $R_1 = .5$ in., $R_2 = .75$ in., and $h = .3$ in. Use shell elements in CATIA, to find the stiffness of this spring. You can assume that the spring is made of steel.

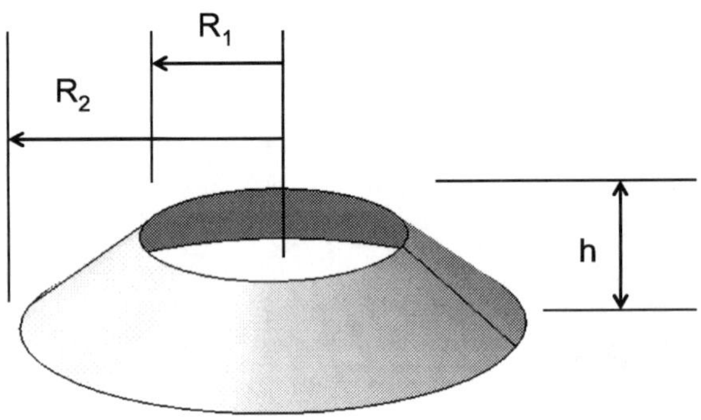


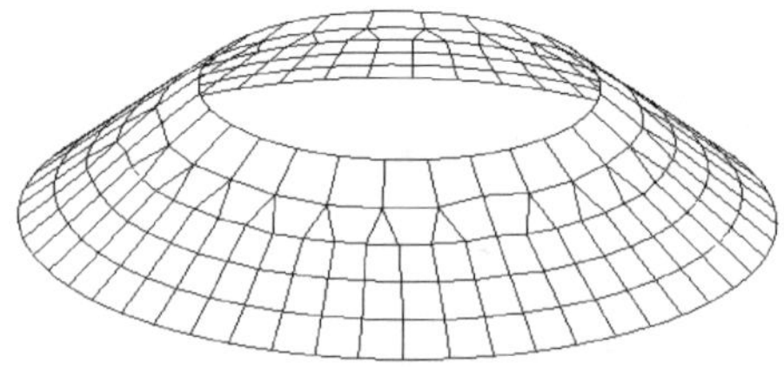

# Chapter 13

## Using the "Surface Mesher" to Simplify Geometry

## Introduction

In this tutorial you will use the Surface Mesher module to simplify the geometry. The mesher is instructed to automatically ignore holes which have a diameter, less than a prescribed value. Furthermore, the surface is constructed directly from points and lines bounding them.

## 1 Problem Statement

The thin surface shown below is made of steel with Young's modulus 10.15E+6 psi and Poisson ratio 0.345. The thickness of the surface is $t = 0.1$ in and the remaining dimensions of the geometry are displayed below.
The surface is subjected to a pressure $p = 5\,\text{psi}$.
For the purpose of analysis, you are expected to ignore the presence of the smaller hole.

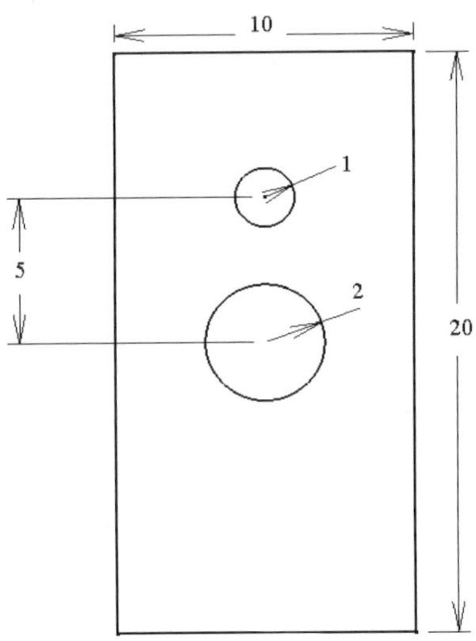


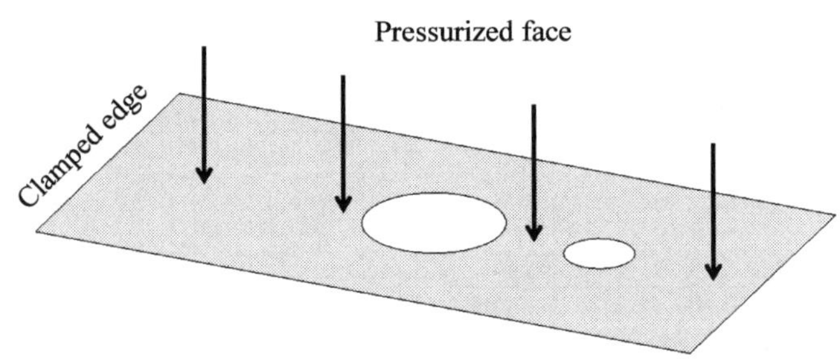


Enter the **Part Design** workbench from the standard Windows toolbar, select **File > New**. Rename the part to be **Plate_with_holes**.

From the standard Windows toolbar, select **Start > Wireframe and Surface Design**.

The strategy for creating the surface is as follows.

Four points will be created, joined together by lines, to define the main plate. Two additional points and circles are constructed on the surface to define the holes.

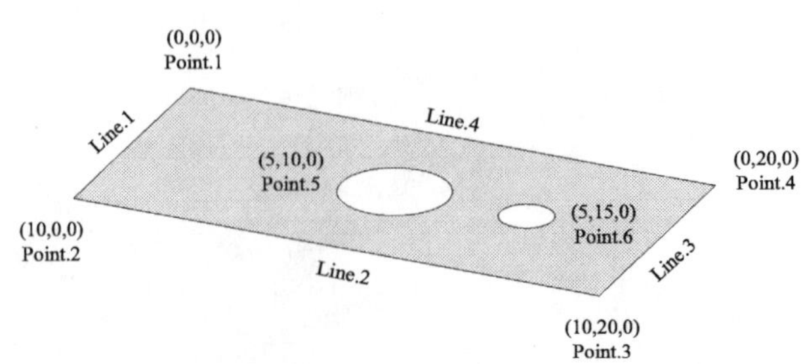

Select the **Point** icon 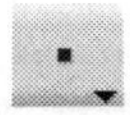 from the **Wireframe** toolbar.
In the resulting input box, type the coordinates of **Point.1** namely (0,0,0).
Repeat this process with the remaining five points, creating them one-by-one.

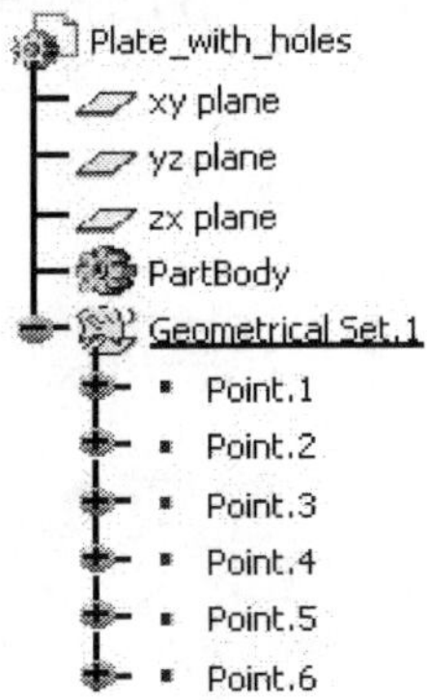


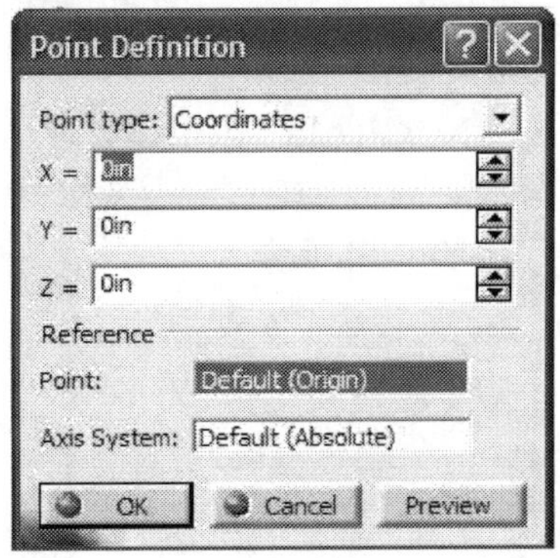


Select the **Line** icon 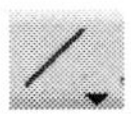 from the **Wireframe** toolbar.
Complete the input box by selecting **Point.1** and **Point.2** as indicated.
Repeat the process to create the remaining three lines.

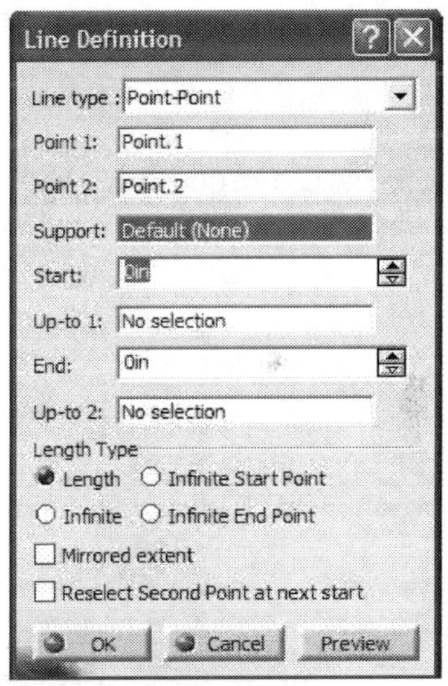


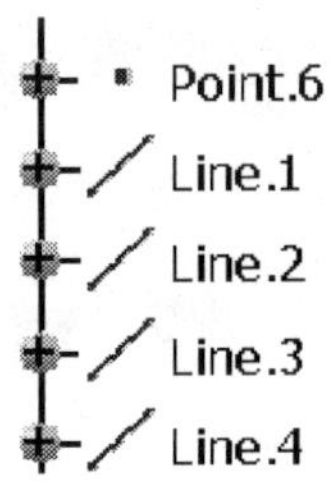


You now have six points and four lines on your computer screen. The next task is to construct the main plate from the four lines.

Select the **Fill** icon  from **Surfaces** toolbar.
Pick the four lines on the screen for the **Boundary** of the plate.

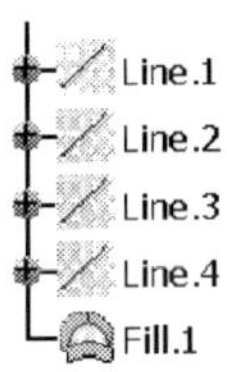


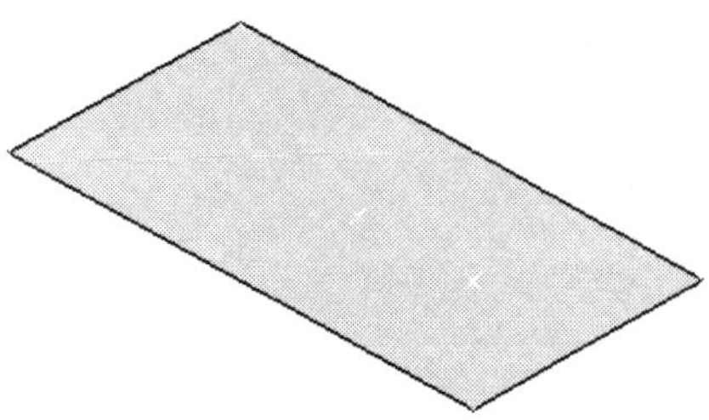

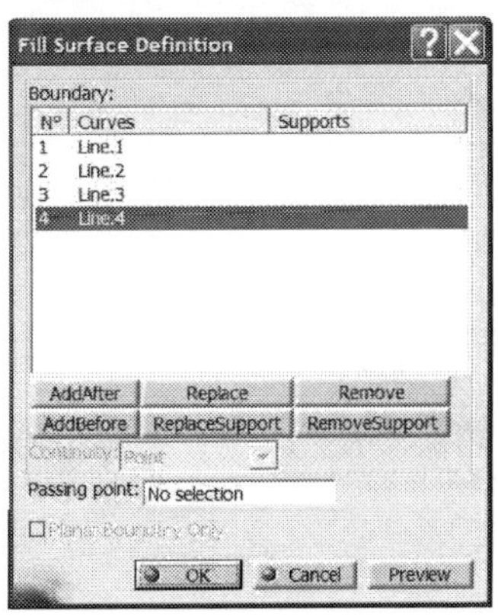

Select the **Circle** icon  from the **Wireframe** toolbar 

.

For the **Center**, select **Point.5**, and for the **Support**, pick **Fill.1** from the tree. Keep in mind that **Fill.1** is the surface constructed. The **Support** could also have been picked from your screen.

Make sure that as the **Circle Limitation** you have selected the icon .

The **Radius** of the circle is 2.

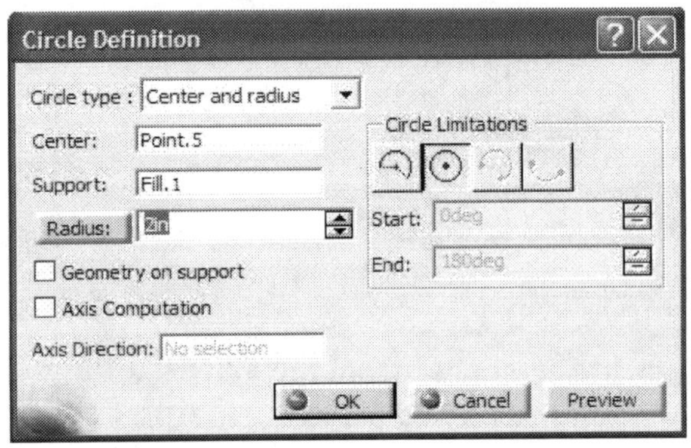


Repeat the process for the smaller circle with **Radius** being 1.

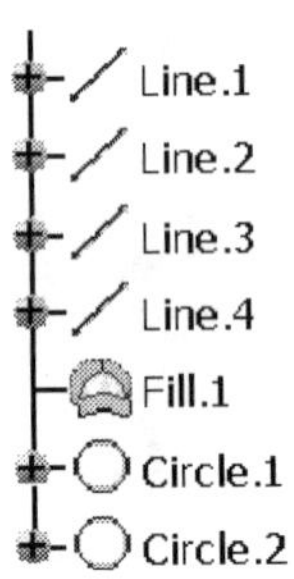


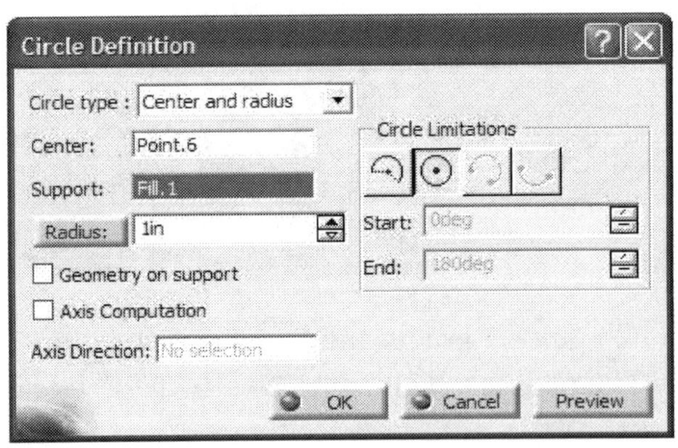


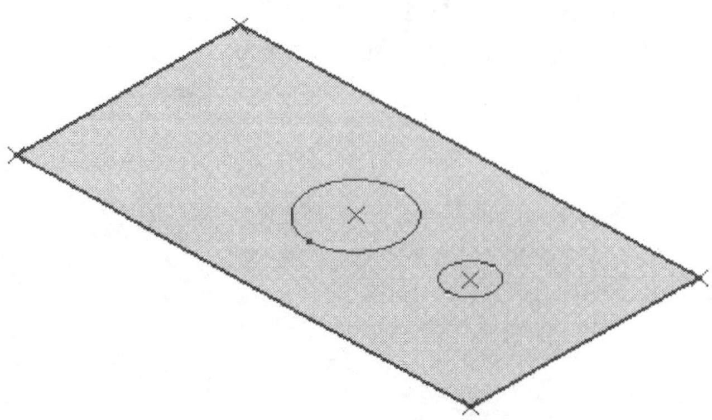

The next task is to use the circles to create holes in the plate.

Use the **Split** icon  from the **Operations** toolbar 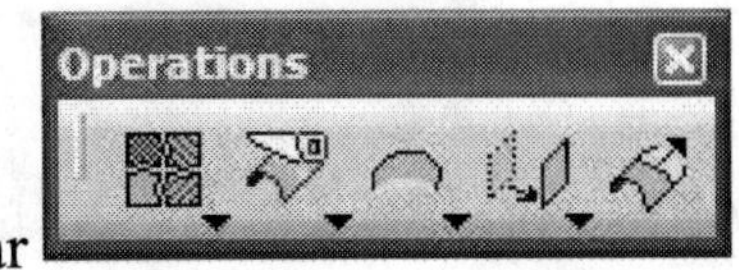

to make the holes.

For **Element to cut** choose **Fill.1**.
For **Cutting elements** select **Circle.1**. If the hole is being kept instead of being removed, use the **Other Side** button.

Repeat the process with **Circle.2**. The result is shown below.

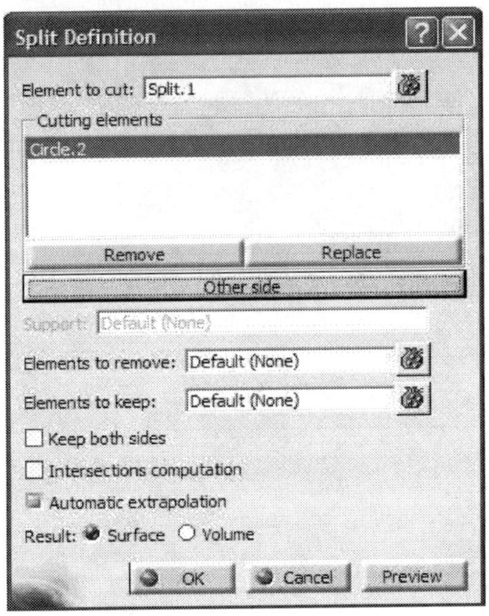


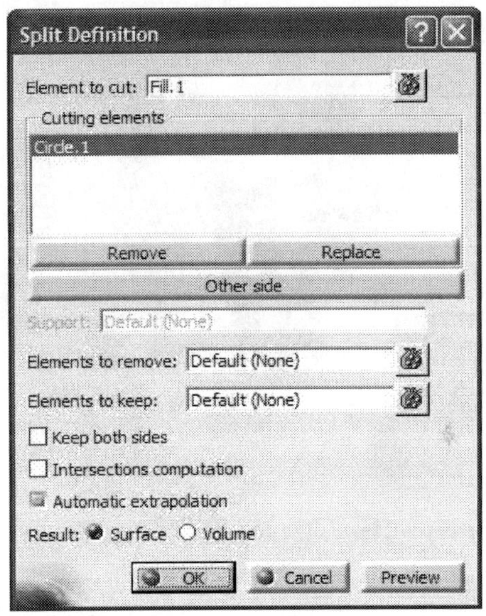


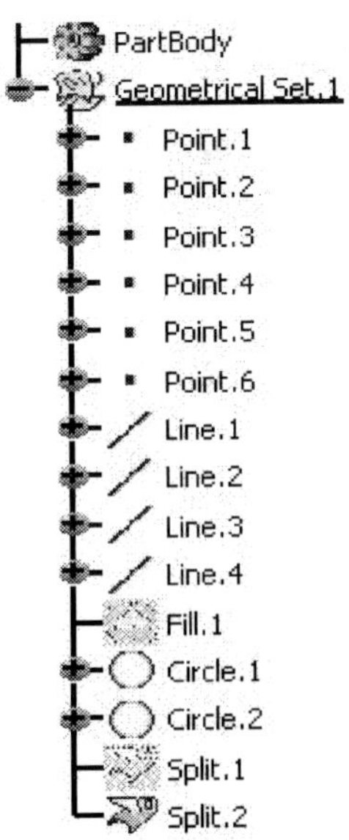


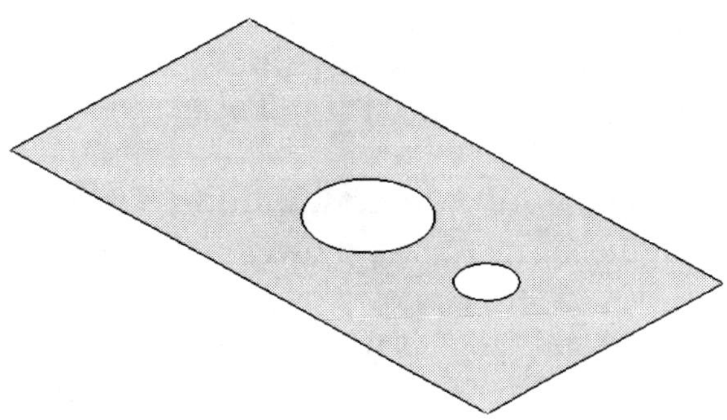

At this point, **Hide** all the points and lines that were created earlier. The reason should be obvious. They will interfere with applying boundary conditions in the finite element model.

Use the **Apply material** icon  to open the database of material properties, selecting **Aluminum** from the **Metal** tab. Choose **Split.2** from the tree to complete the process. If the sector does not look "shiny", you can change the rendering style from the **View mode** toolbar 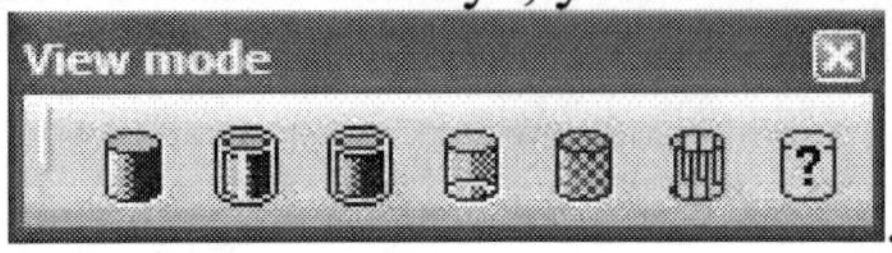

.

Next choose the **Shading with Material** icon 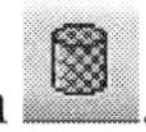.
This action results in a different rendering displayed below.

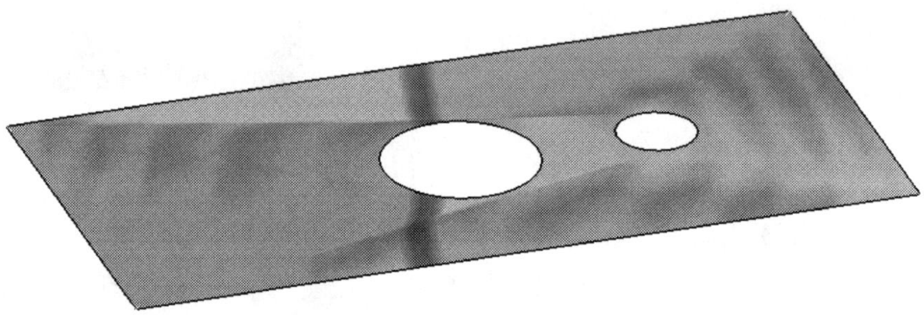

## 3 Entering the Analysis Solutions

From the standard Windows toolbar, select

**Start > Analysis & Simulation > Advanced Meshing Tools** 

**Warning:** If instead of the **Advanced Meshing Tools** workbench, you enter the **Generative Structural Analysis** workbench, use the **Cancel** button to exit and reenter the **Advanced Meshing Tools** workbench.

Upon entering the **Advanced Meshing Tools** workbench, the standard box shown on the right is displayed. However, you note that the representative element "size" and "sag" is not visible on your display. This is in contrast to the case of entering the **Generative Structural Analysis** workbench for the first time. Therefore, at this point no mesh is present.

The **Meshing Methods** toolbar 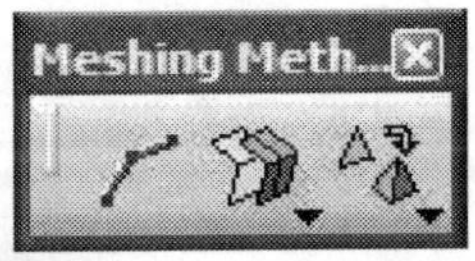

has a sub-toolbar known as the **Surface Mesher** 

. Select the **Advanced Surface Mesher** icon  from this toolbar.

Pick the top surface to open the **Global Parameters** box shown below.

Keep the default **Mesh size**.

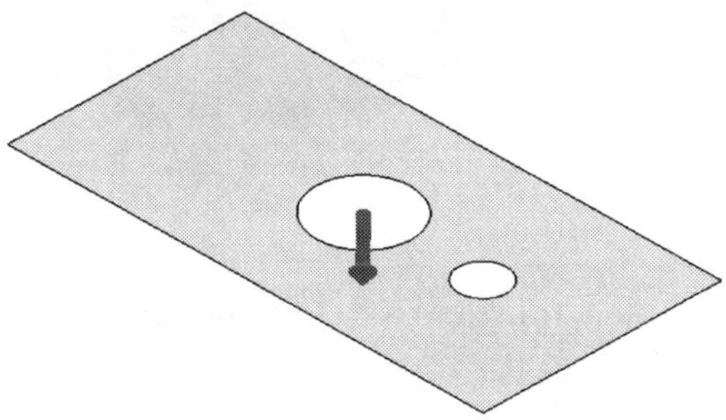

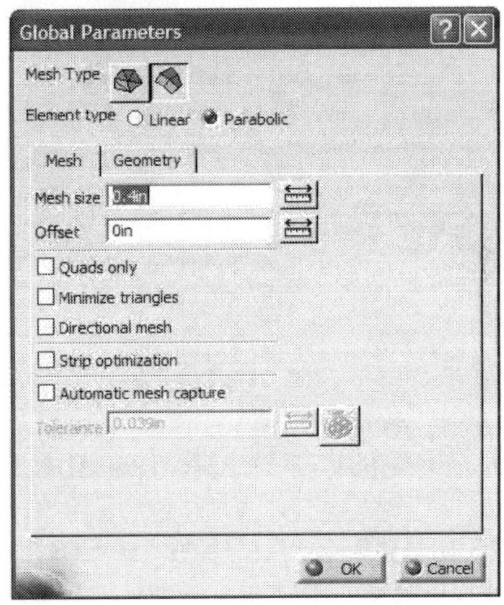


Next, pick the **Geometry** tab which leads to the options displayed below. The input line **Min hole size** is very important. It instructs the software to ignore any holes with diameter less than 0.394 in.

Clearly in the present model none of the holes are affected.

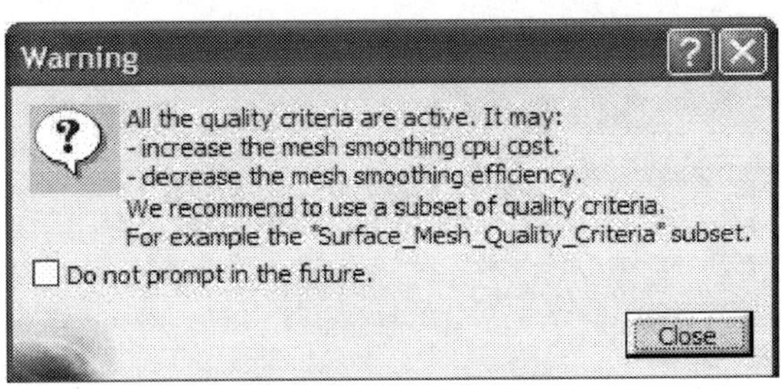


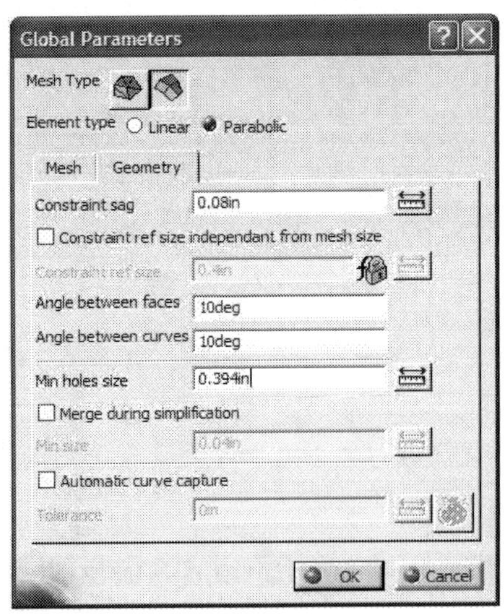


Upon closing the box, nothing happens. However, in order to see the mesh while you are in the current workbench, select the **Mesh the Part** icon 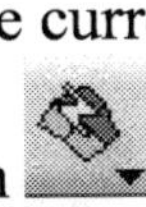 from the **Mesh/Unmesh** toolbar 

.

The summary box **Mesh the Part** appears which can be ignored.

Use the **Exit** icon to complete the process.

In order to see the mesh better, change the render style to **Wireframe (NHR)**. The mesh corresponding to the prescribed parameters is displayed below. Notice that both holes have been taken into consideration.

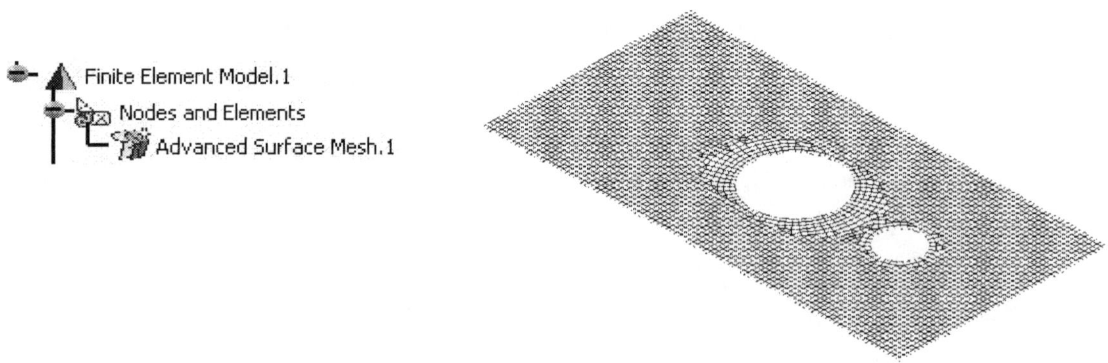


Next, you will remesh by ignoring the smaller hole. In order to delete the above mesh, double-click on the **Nodes and Elements** branch in the tree.

Right-click on **Advanced Surface Mesh.1** in the tree and select **Remove Mesh** as shown.

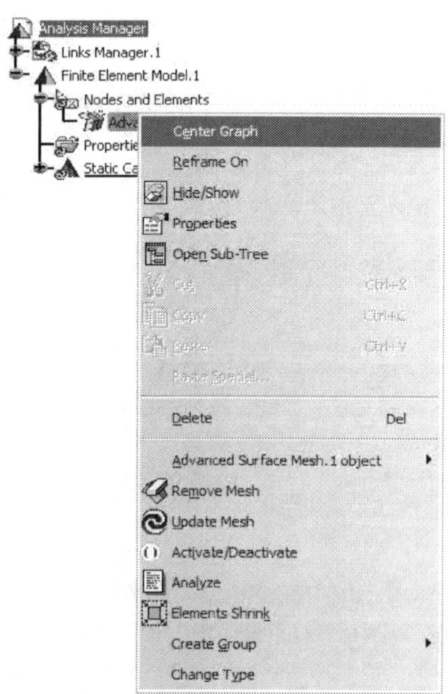


Select the **Advanced Surface Mesher** icon again and pick the surface to be meshed. The resulting pop up window is shown on the next page. For **Mesh size**, type 0.3 in.

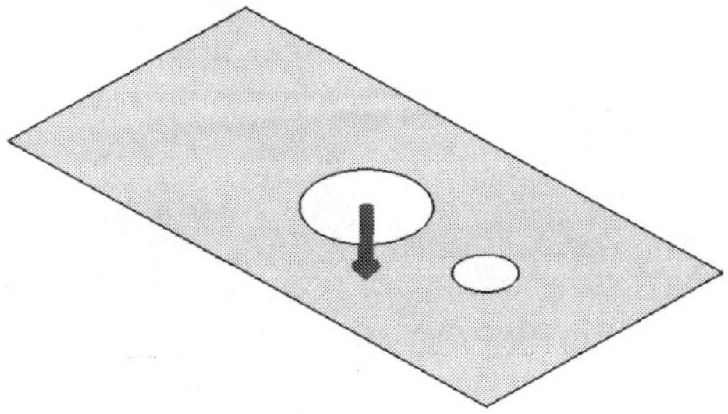

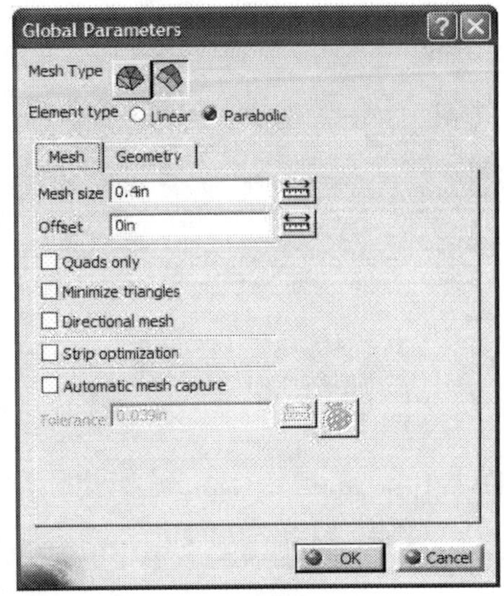


Next, pick the **Geometry** tab and for the **Min hole size**, type 2.2. This tells the software to ignore any holes with diameter less than 2.2 in.

Select the **Mesh the Part** icon 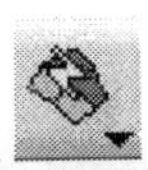 from the **Mesh/Unmesh** toolbar .



The summary box **Mesh The Part** appears which can be ignored.

Use the **Exit** icon 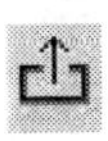 to complete the process.

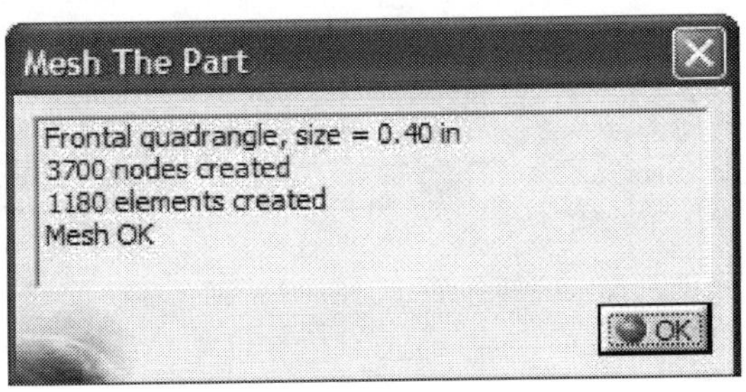


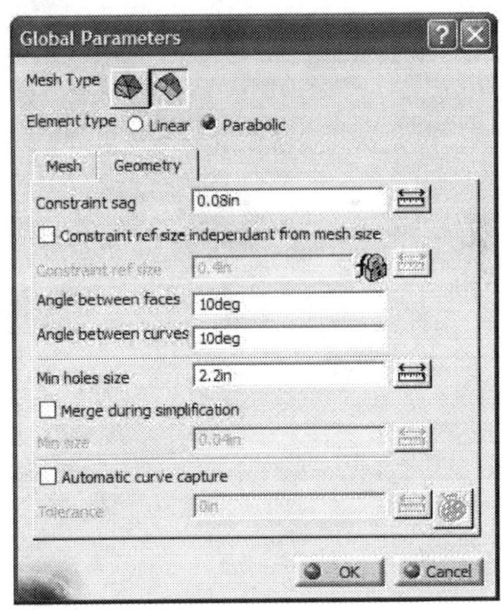


The mesh corresponding to the prescribed parameters is displayed below. Notice that the small hole is eliminated from meshing.

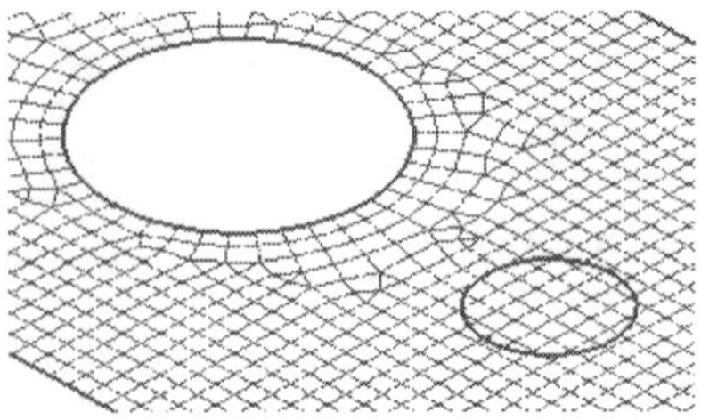

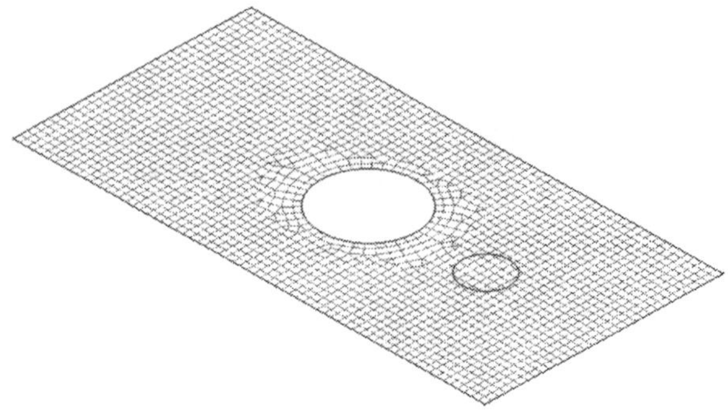

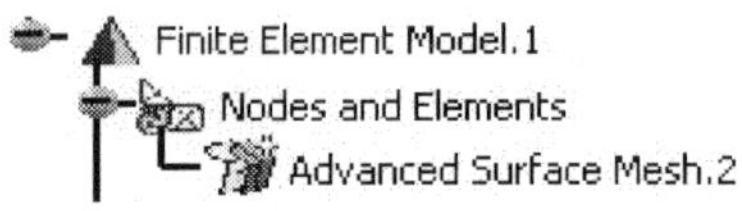


To set the shell thickness, switch workbenches.

**Start > Analysis & Simulation > Generative Structural Analysis**

Select the **2D Property** icon from the **Model Manager** toolbar

, leading to the following input box. Pick the surface and type a thickness of 0.1 in the appropriate line.

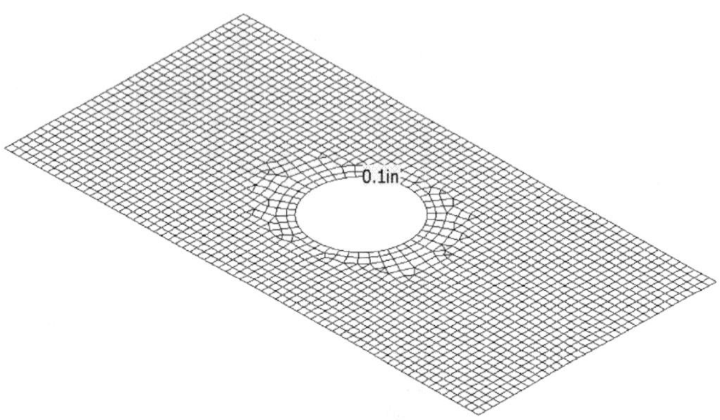


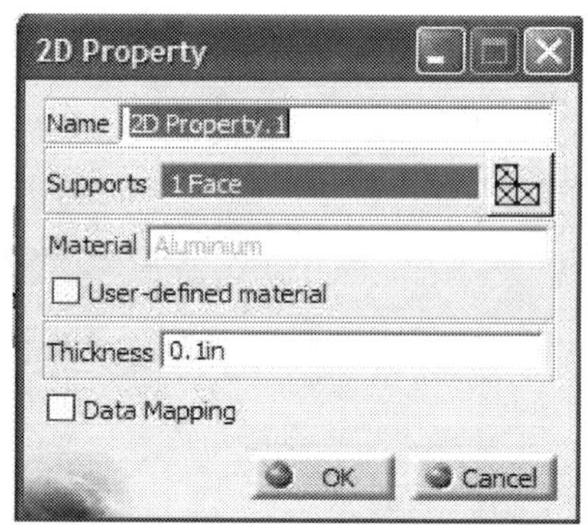

Select the **Clamp** icon from the **Restraint** toolbar and pick the edge.

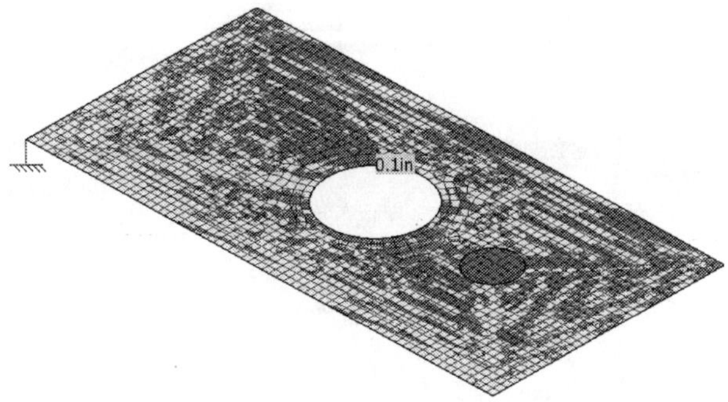


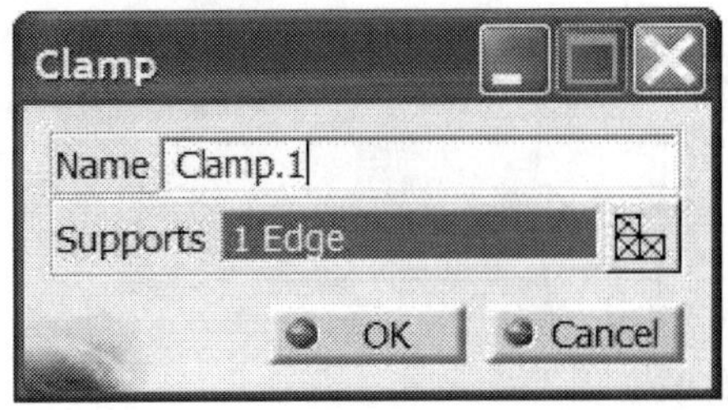


Keep in mind, that part must be in the **Show** mode to apply the boundary conditions. To bring the part in the **Show** mode, point the cursor to the **Links Manager.1**, right-click, and select **Show**. Make sure that the lines 1 through 4 are hidden because you do not want to apply the clamp to these lines. If you do, the **Error** box indicating singularity in the solution will result.

Use the **Pressure** icon  from the **Loads** toolbar 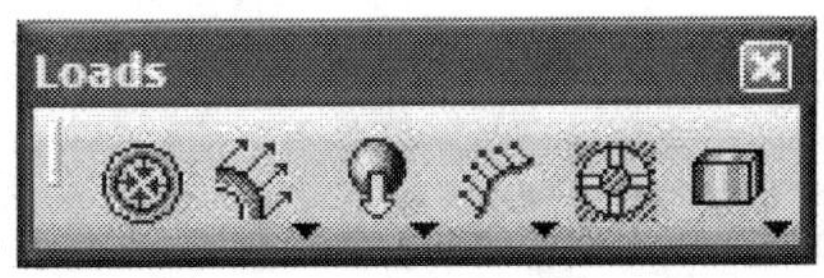

and pick the surface. Apply a pressure of 5 psi.

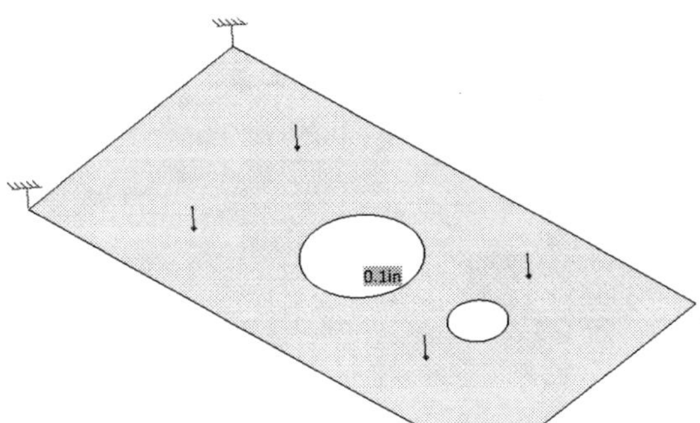


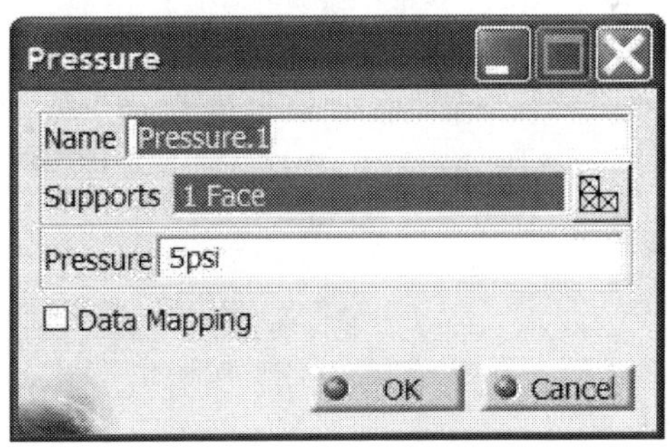

The complete tree structure at this point is shown below.

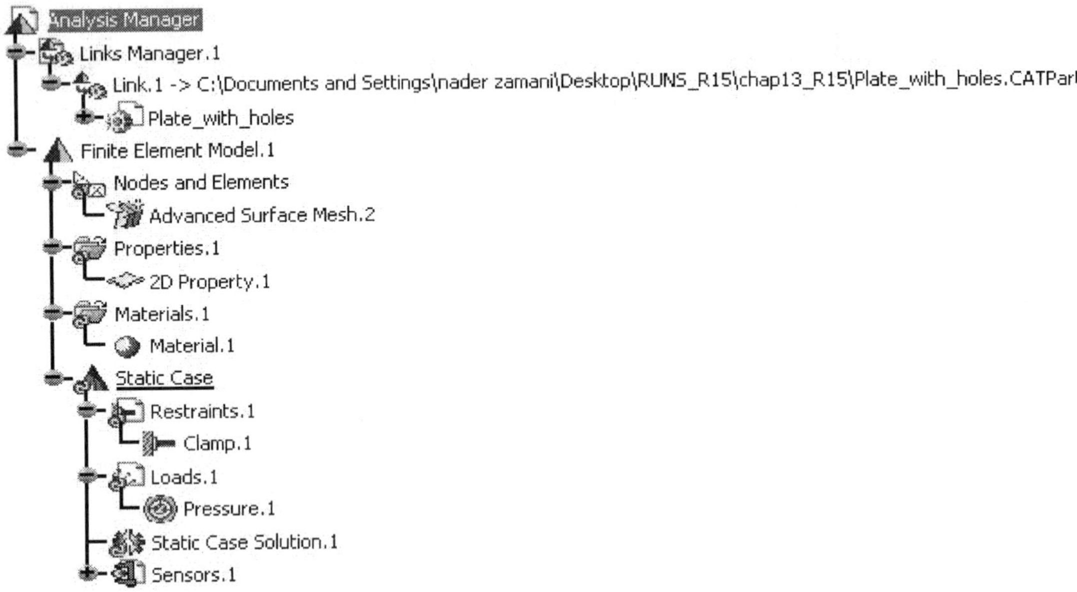


To run the analysis, you need to use the **Compute** toolbar  by selecting the **Compute** icon . This leads to the **Compute** box shown to the right. Leave the defaults as **All** which means everything is computed.
Upon closing this box, after a brief pause the second box shown below appears.
This box provides information on the resources needed to complete the analysis. In the event that all estimates are zero in the listing, there is a problem in the previous step and should be looked into. With all numbers as zero in this box, although the program may run, it will not produce any useful results.

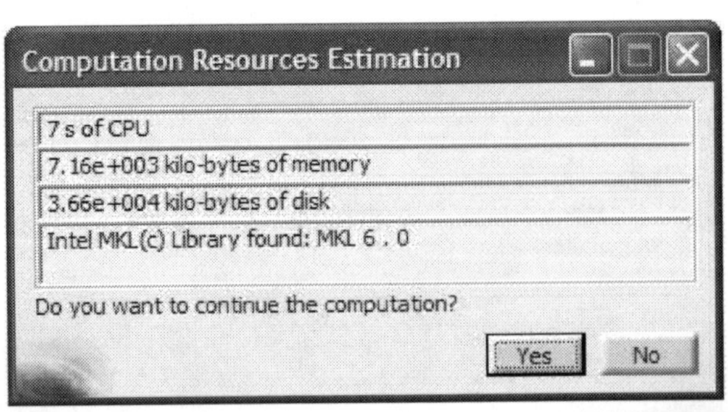


The main postprocessing toolbar is called **Image** 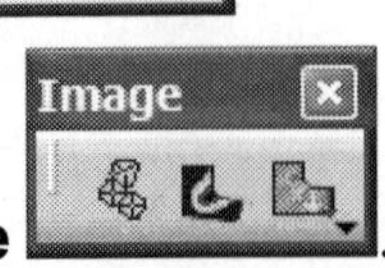. To view the deformed shape you have use the **Deformation** icon . The resulting deformed shape is displayed below.

Keep in mind that the displacements are scaled considerably so that one can observe the deformed shape. Although the scale factor is set automatically, one can change this value with the **Deformation Scale Factor** icon in the **Analysis Tools** toolbar

.

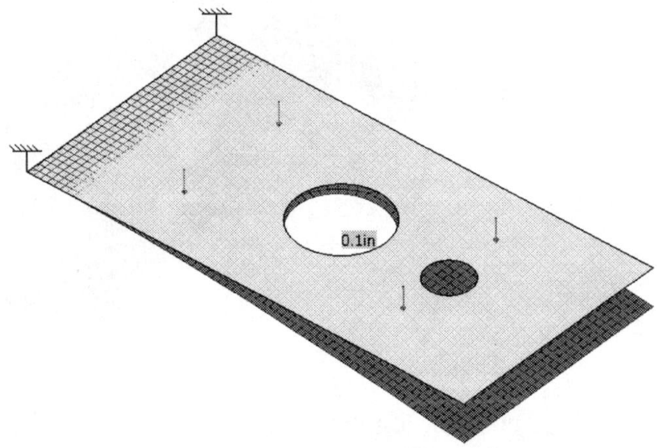


The arrow plot is not particularly useful. In order to view the contour plot of the displacement field, position the cursor on the arrow field and double-click. The **Image Edition** box opens.

Note that the default is to draw the contour on the deformed shape. If this is not desired, uncheck the box **On deformed mesh**. Next, select **AVERAGE-ISO** and press **OK**. The contour of the displacement field is shown.

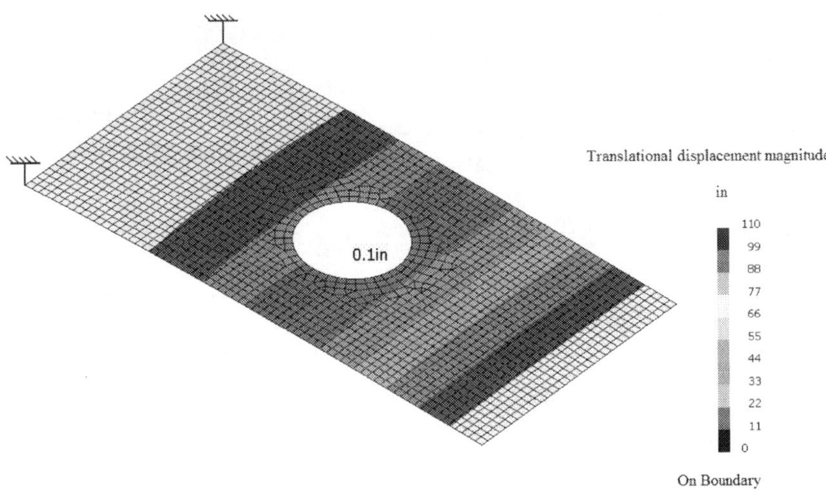

The next step in the postprocessing is to plot the contours of the von Mises stress using the **von Mises Stress** icon in the **Image** toolbar. The von Mises stress is displayed below.

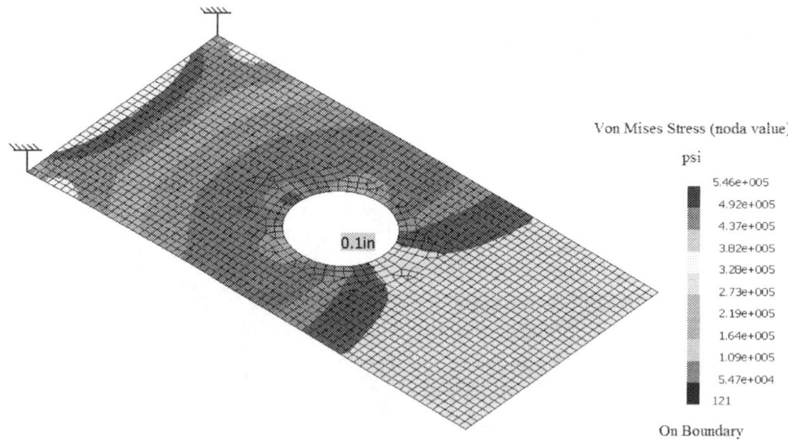


Checking the contour legend it becomes clear that both the displacement and von Mises stress are unrealistically large.

From the toolbar **Groups** 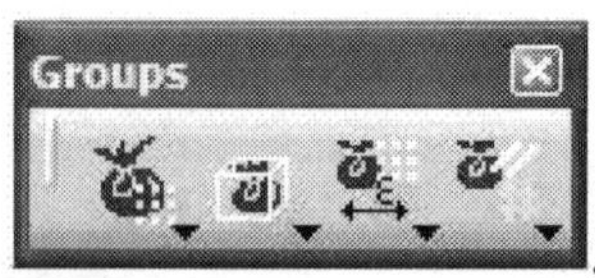

, select the icon **Line Group by Neighborhood**. This action leads to the dialogue box shown next.

For the **Supports**, select the edge of the circle. For the **Tolerance** use 1 in. What this process does is to create a group of elements which are within a neighborhood in of the selected edge. The stresses can be plotted for such elements if desired.
In order to achieve this, double-click on the contour levels on the screen to open the image edition box. Next use the selections tab as shown below. Here, you have the choice of selecting different items. Select **Line Group by Neighborhood.1**, and use the button . The contour below displays the von Mises stress at the desired section.

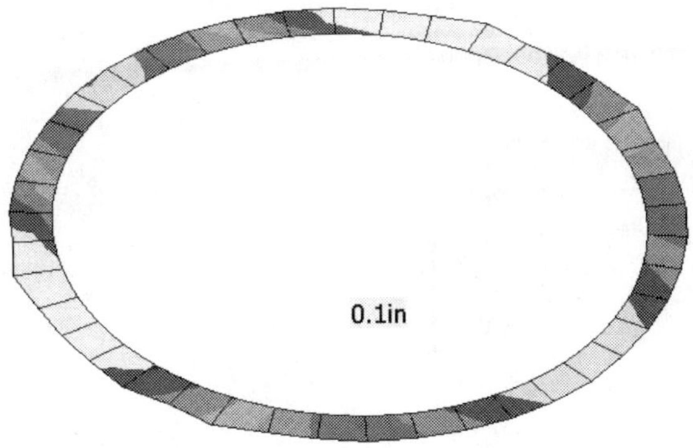


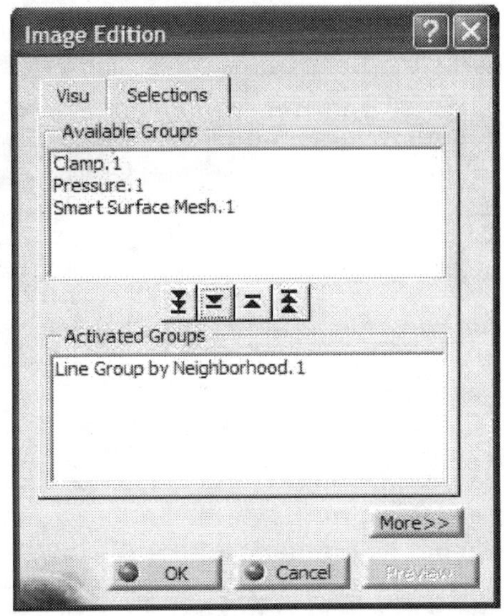


Select the **Image Extrema** icon  from the **Analysis Tools** toolbar

. Double-click on the **von Mises Stress** branch on the tree and pick the **Selections** tab. From the listed items, choose **Line Group by Neighborhood.1**.

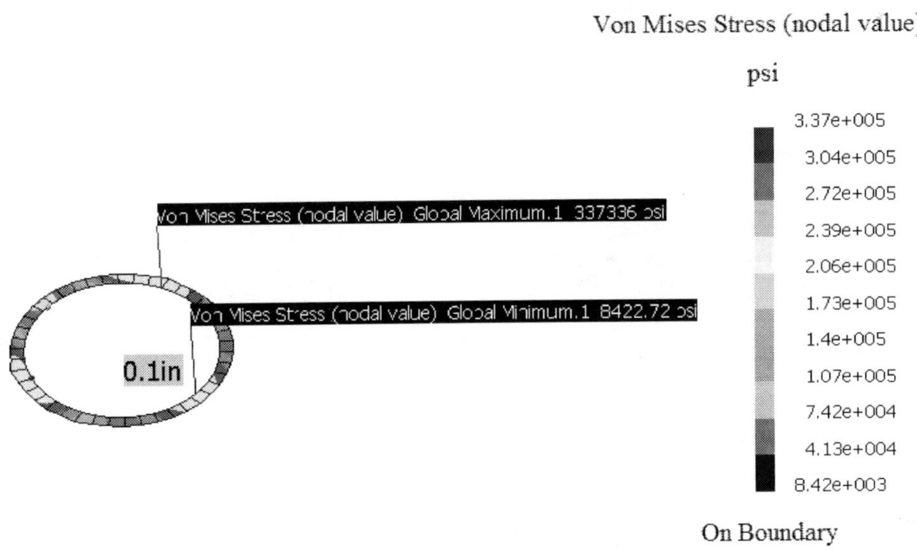

Animation of the model can be achieved through the **Animate** icon in the **Analysis Tools** toolbar. An AVI file can easily be generated.

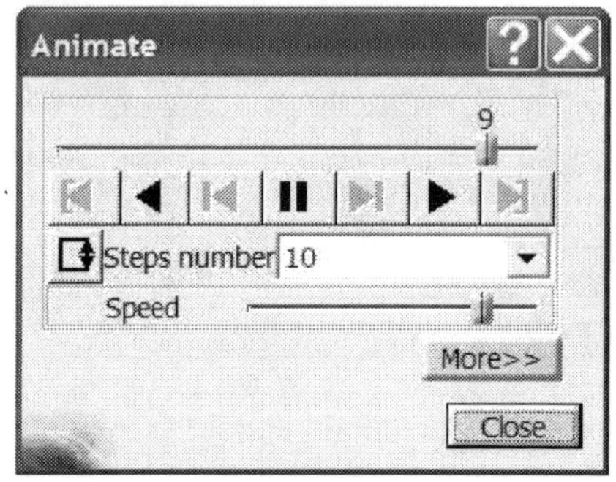


To get a summary listing of the data displayed by the von Mises stress contour, **select it from the tree**, click on the **Information** icon and the following window pops up.

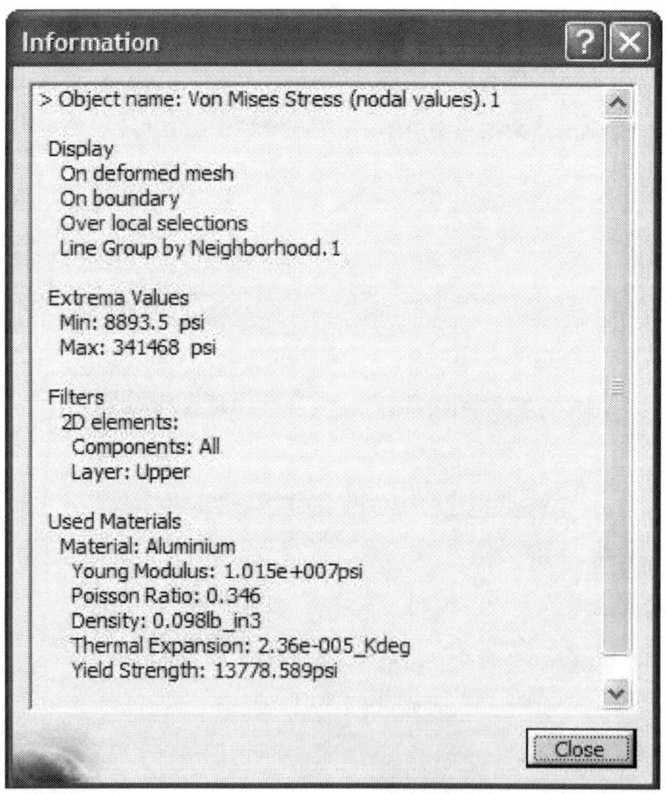

# Exercises for Chapter 13

## Problem 1: Designing a Flywheel with Different Size Holes

Design a flywheel having two different sets of holes as shown. The material should be steel and the dimensions are at your digression. Using CATIA shell elements analyze the behavior of the flywheel under a centrifugal force.

Make sure you instruct the software to ignore the small size holes.

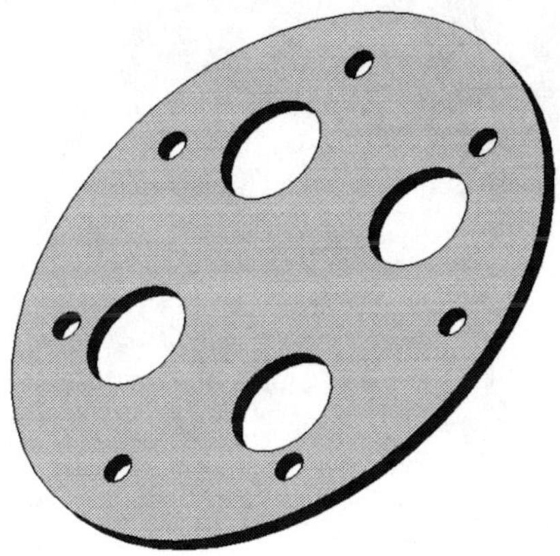

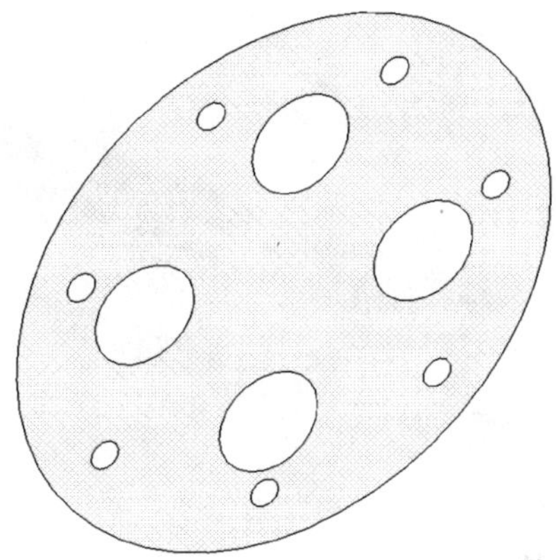

## Problem 2: Analyzing an I-beam with Weight Reduction Holes

The I-beams used in the frame of a trailer truck is often modified to have a large number of wholes in the web sections. These holes are referred as weight reduction holes but are mainly used for attaching other structures to the frame with fasteners.

Your task is to analyze an I-beam as shown, under different restraints with a uniformly distributed load. Leave provisions for the "Surface Mesher" to ignore holes below a prescribed size. Shell elements should be used for analysis purposes.

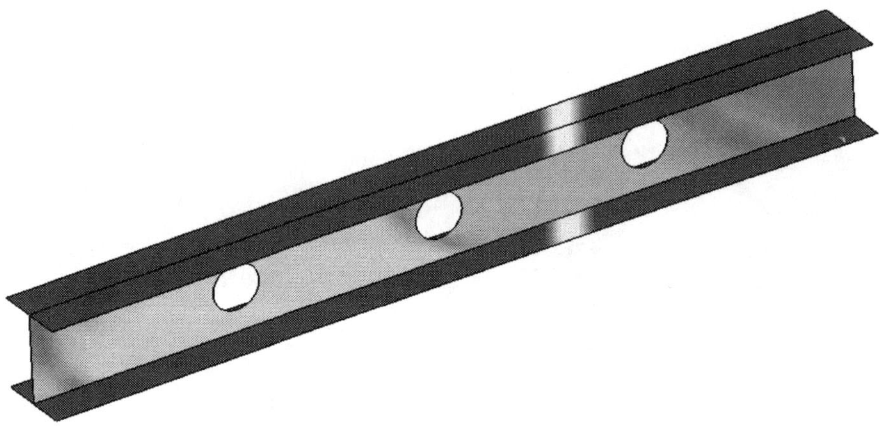

# Chapter 14

# FE Model of a Bearing-Shaft Assembly using Analysis Connection

## Introduction

In this tutorial, you will analyze a shaft-bearing assembly involving contact. The **Analysis Connection** toolbar is used to impose the interaction between the parts. Solid elements will be employed for calculation purposes.

## 1 Problem Statement

The assembly, shown below, consists of a shaft and two bearings with the dimensions as displayed. The thickness of the bearing is 1 in. and the length of the shaft is 6 in. All parts are made of aluminum with $E = 10.15E7$ psi and $\nu = .346$.

The bottom faces of the bearings are clamped and the shaft is subjected to a total downward load of 1000 lb distributed on its surface. The objective is to predict the stresses and deflections of the structure.

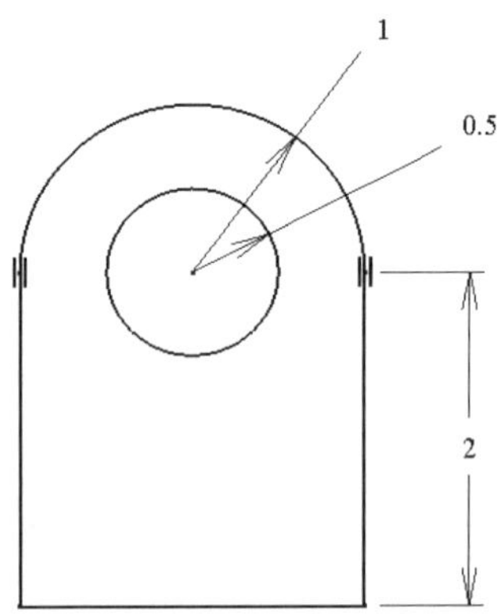


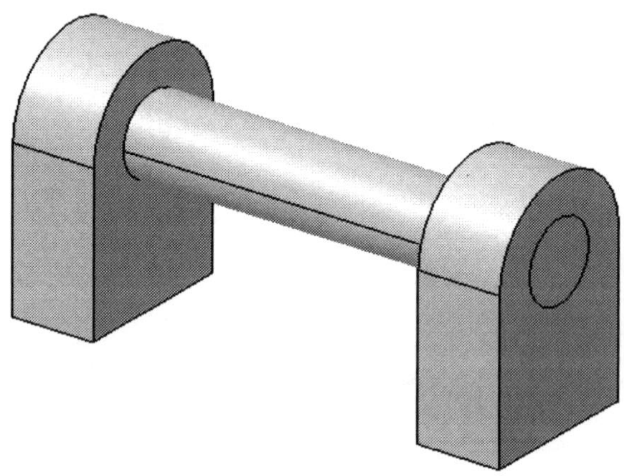

## 2 Creation of the Assembly in the Mechanical Design Solutions

Enter the **Assembly Design** workbench which can be achieved by different means depending on your CATIA customization. For example, from the standard Windows toolbar, select **File > New**. From the box shown on the right, select **Product**. This moves you to the **Assembly Design** workbench and creates an assembly with the default name **Product.1**.

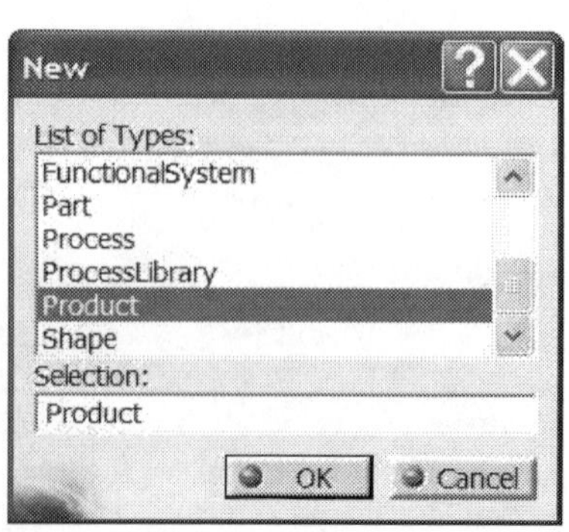


See Note #1 in Appendix I.

In order to change the default name, move the cursor to **Product.1** in the tree, right-click and select **Properties** from the menu list.

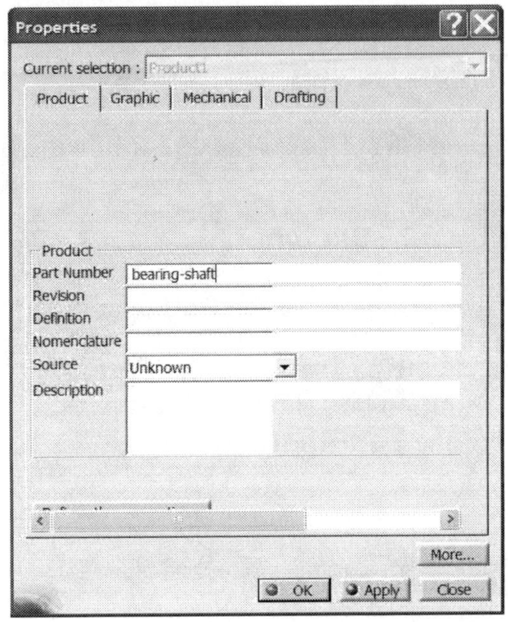


From the **Properties** box, select the **Product** tab and in **Part Number** type **bearing-shaft**.

This will be the new product name throughout the chapter. The tree on the top left corner of your computer screen should look as displayed below.

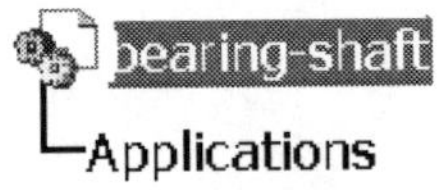


You now create the bearing as a part.
From the standard Windows toolbar, select **Insert > New Part**. The tree is modified to indicate that **Part.1** has been created. Change the default name to **bearing**.
The tree, before and after the name change, is displayed below. Note that the instance name has also been changed to **bearing**.

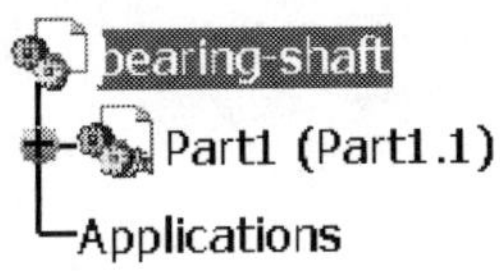


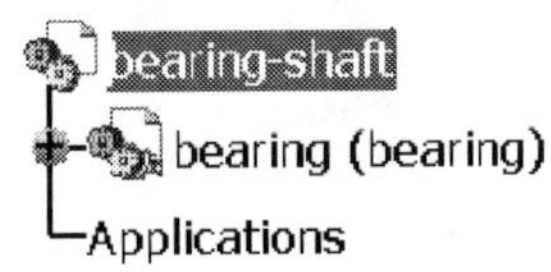


The process of renaming **Part.1** is just like before. Point the cursor to **Part.1** in the tree, right-click, and select **Properties**. The pop up box, after the changes are made is displayed below.

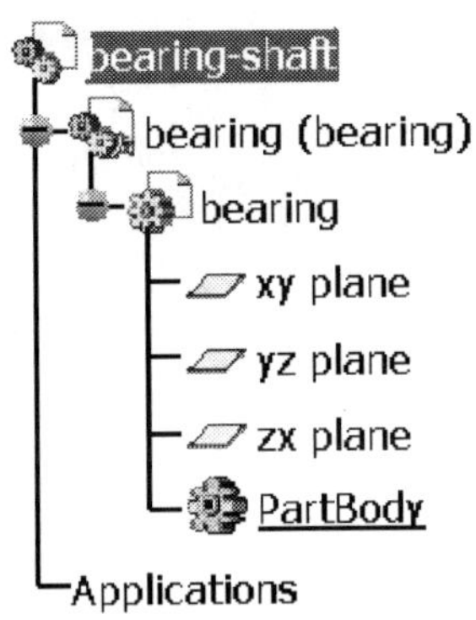


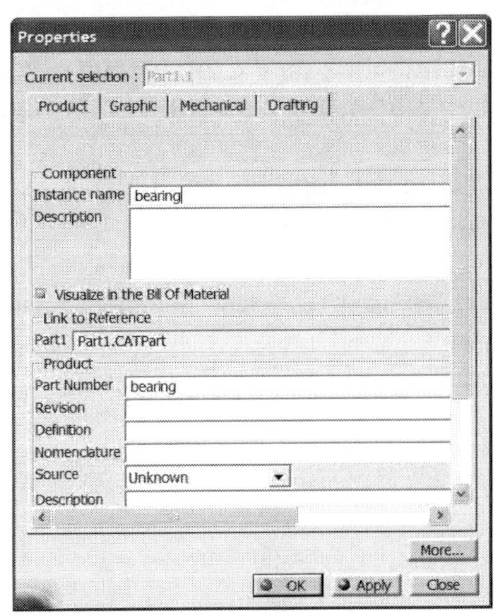

Select the **yz** plane from **bearing** and switch to the **Part Design** workbench.
In **Part Design**, enter the **Sketcher**.

In the **Sketcher**, draw the following profile and dimension as shown.

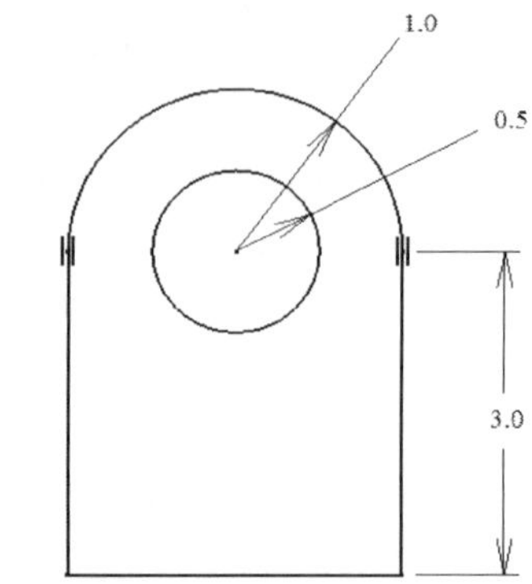


Leave the **Sketcher**.

You will now use the **Pad** operation to extrude the sketch. Upon selecting the **Pad** icon, the pad definition box shown below opens.
For the **Length** use 1.

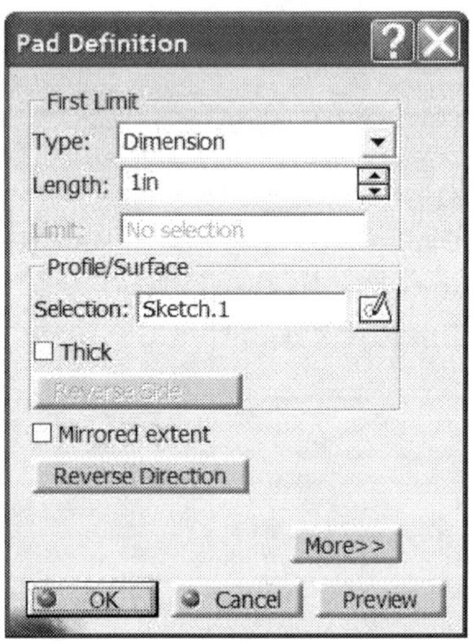


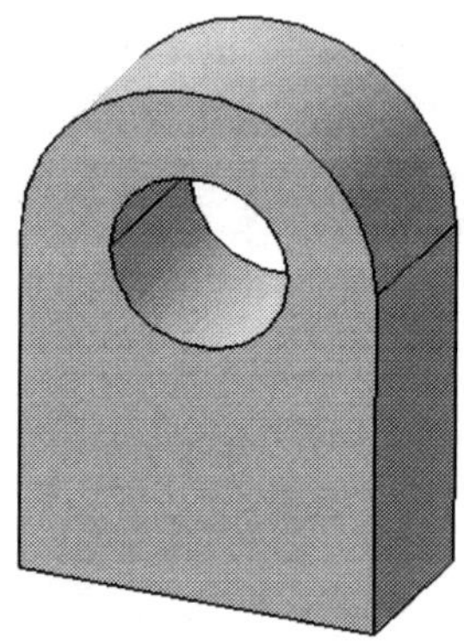

The best way of saving your work is to save the entire assembly. Double-click on the top branch of the tree. This lands you in the **Assembly Design** workbench.

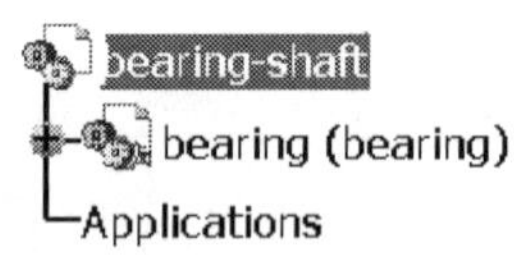


The branch highlights in blue as a confirmation of the new workbench.

Select the **Save** icon. The **Save As** pop up box indicates that saving the assembly activates the saving of the parts. Choose the **Yes** button.

Two bearings are needed in the present problem. One option is to create a second bearing from scratch. The alternative is inserting an instance of the bearing that was just created. We choose to do the latter. This can only be done if the bearing part has been saved.

From the standard Windows toolbar, select **Insert > Existing Component**. The pop up box shown below opens and allows you to select the part to be inserted. Obviously, you have to select the **bearing** and close the window.

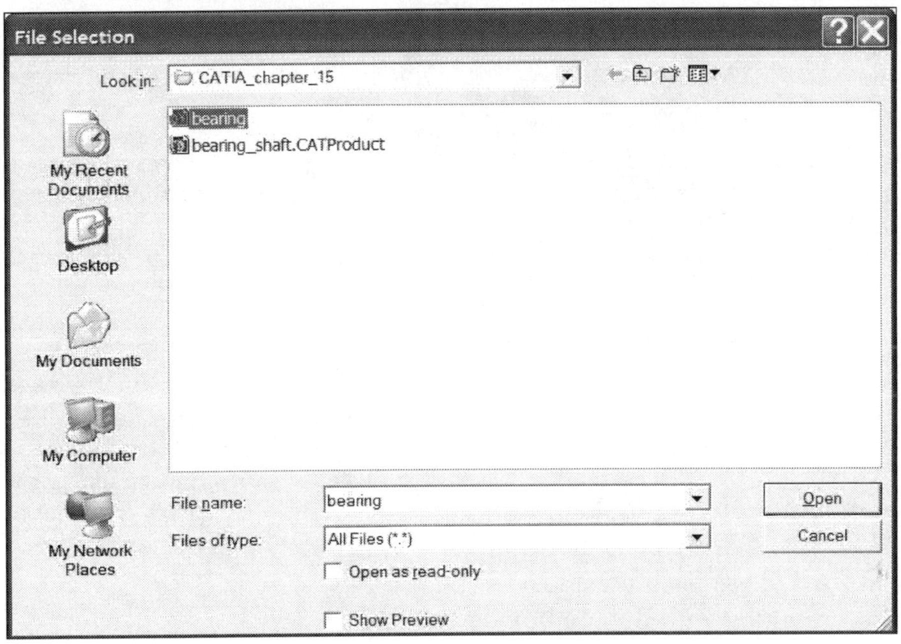


The tree indicates that an instance of the bearing has been created. However, you can see only one bearing on your computer screen.

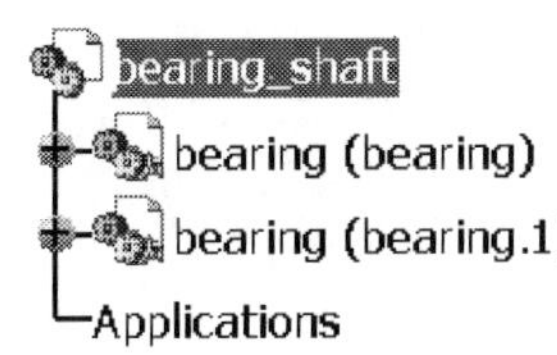


This happens because; the two bearings are coincident at the same location. The procedure for separating the parts is as follows.

Double-click on the top branch of the tree. This lands you in the **Assembly Design** workbench.

The branch highlights in blue as a confirmation of the new workbench.

Select the **Manipulation** icon from the **Move** toolbar .

This leads to the pop up box shown below.

Using the x-direction translation icon, the three parts have been separated as displayed. DO NOT USE ROTATION.

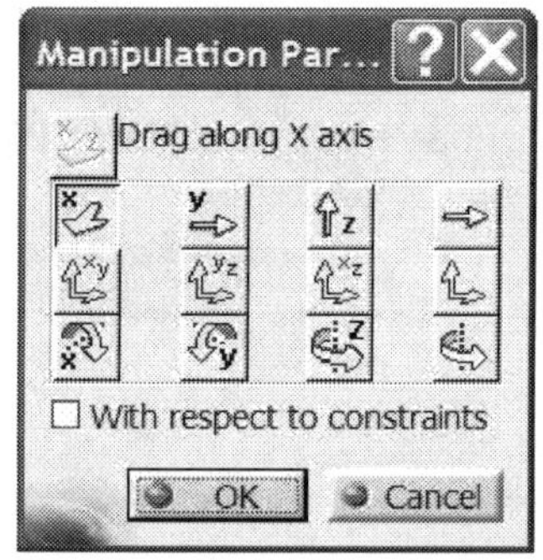


You are now ready to create the shaft.

From the standard Windows toolbar, select **Insert > New Part**. The tree is modified to indicate that **Part.2** has been created.
You are also presented with pop up box on the right. Select **NO** to close the box.

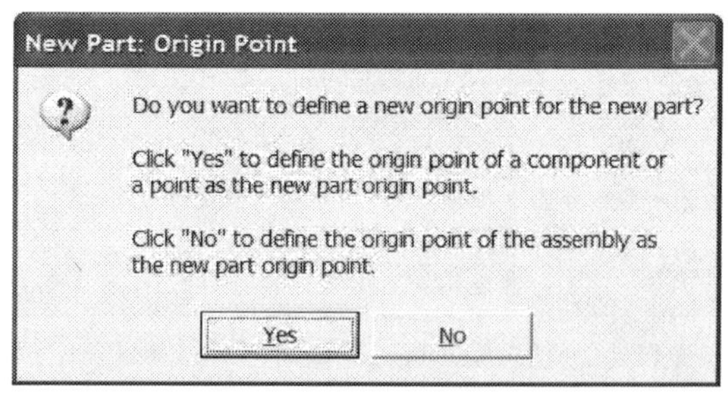


Change the default name to **shaft**.
The tree, after the name change, is displayed on the right. Note that the instance name has also been changed to **shaft**.

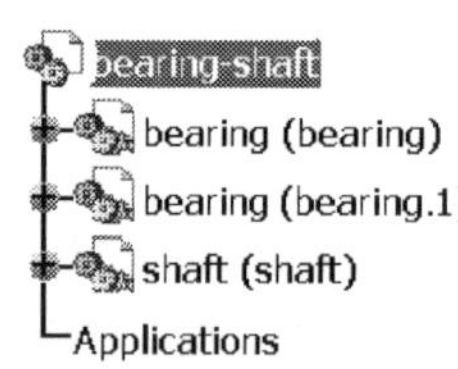


Double-click on the **shaft** branch in the tree so that it is highlighted in blue, as shown on the right.
This lands you in the **Part Design** workbench.

Select the **yz** plane from **shaft** and enter the **Sketcher**.

In the **Sketcher**, draw a circle of radius 0.5 in.

Leave the **Sketcher**.

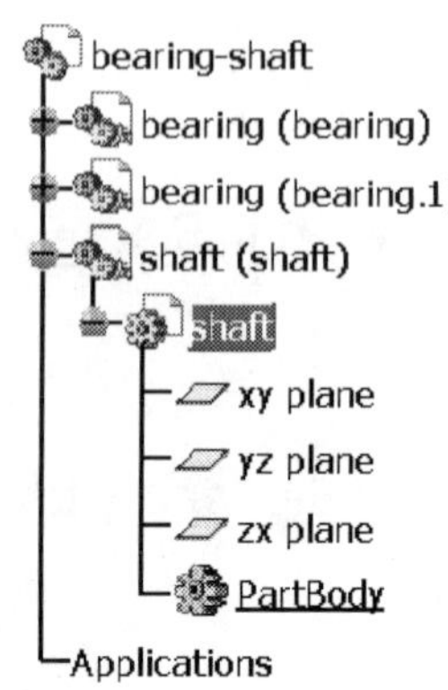

Use the **Pad** icon , to create a shaft of length 6 in.
Save the assembly which automatically saves the two parts.

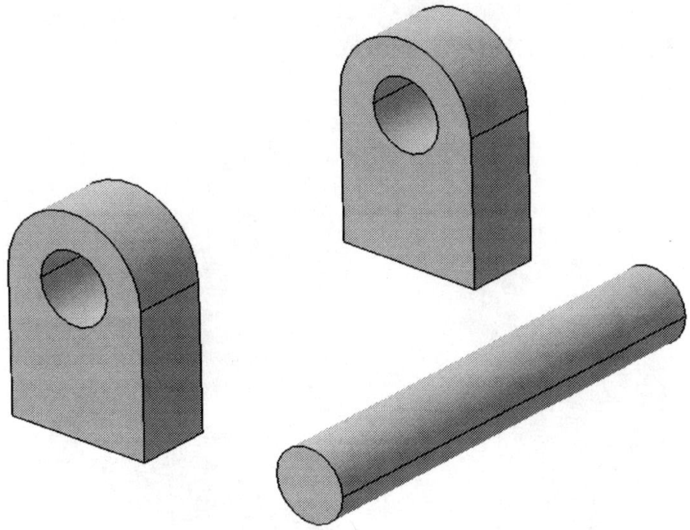

Select the **Apply Material** icon  to activate the material **Library** box below.

Use the **Metal** tab on the top; select **Aluminum**. Use your cursor to pick the top level assembly from the tree at which time the **OK** and **Apply Material** buttons can be selected. Close the box. The material property is now reflected in the tree.

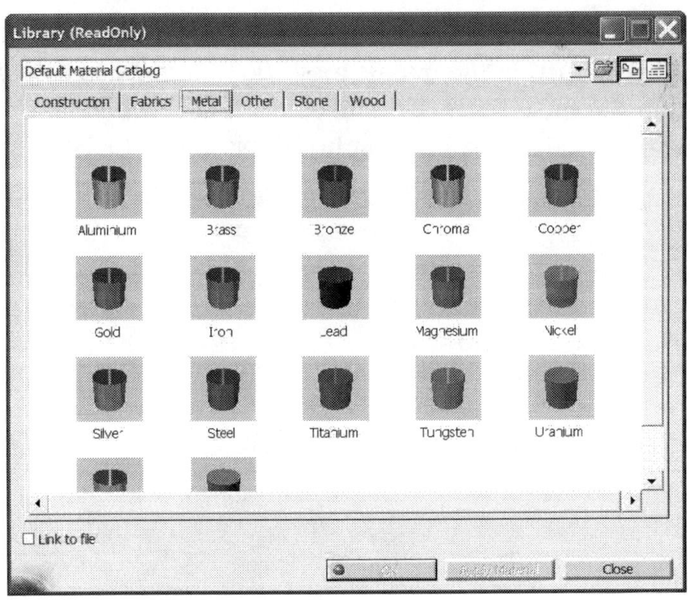


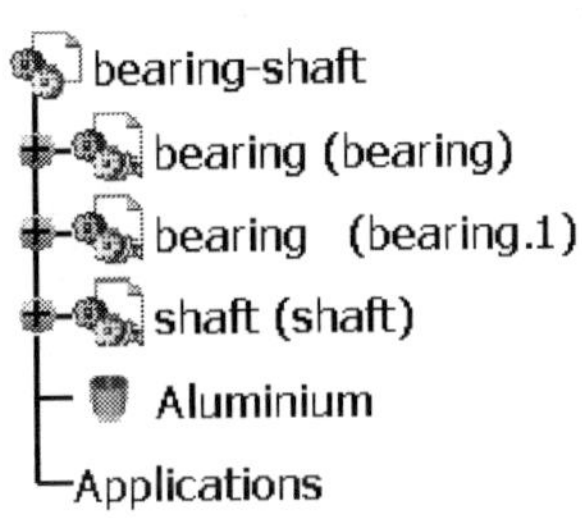

If the assembly does not look "shiny", you can change the rendering style from the **View mode** toolbar 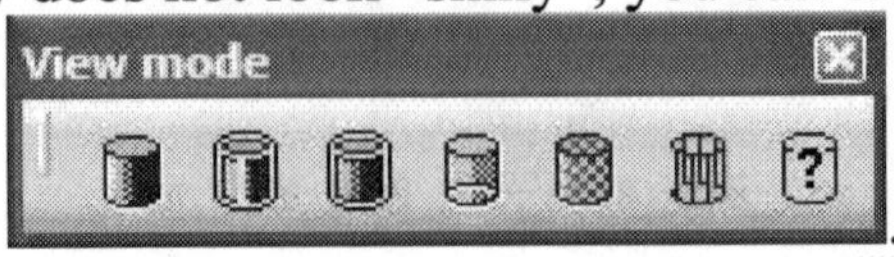
.

Next choose the **Shading with Material** icon . This action results in a different rendering displayed below.

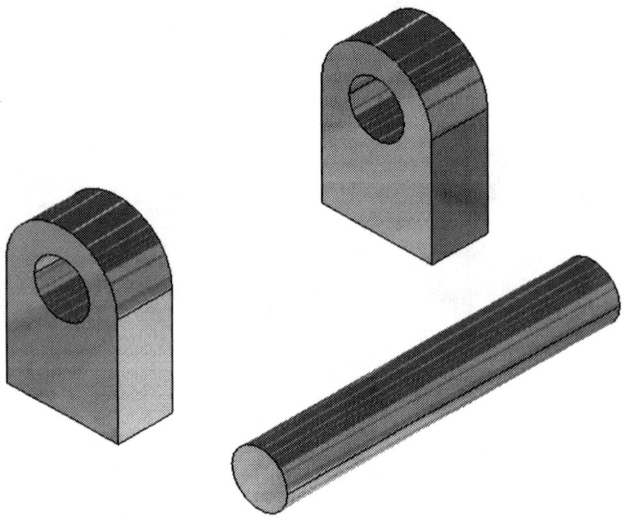

In order to inspect the values of the material properties assigned, double-click on **Aluminum** in the tree. It may take a minute before the database is searched. Next you will see the **Properties** box shown below opens. Chose the **Analysis** tab from this box and the values will be displayed. Note that these values can be edited.

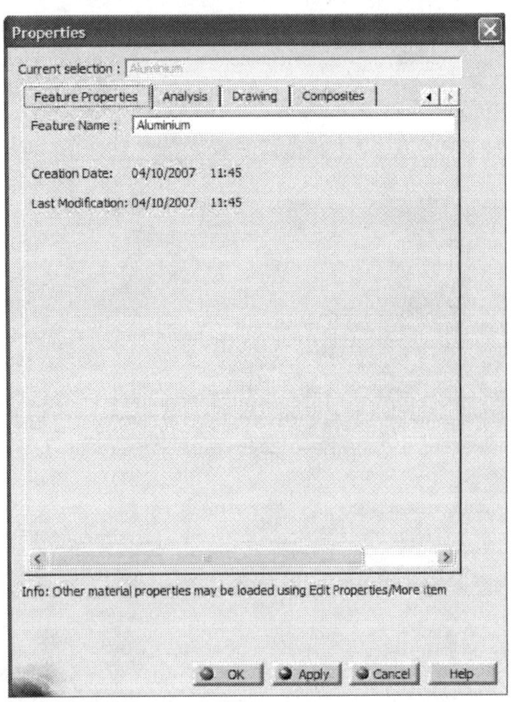


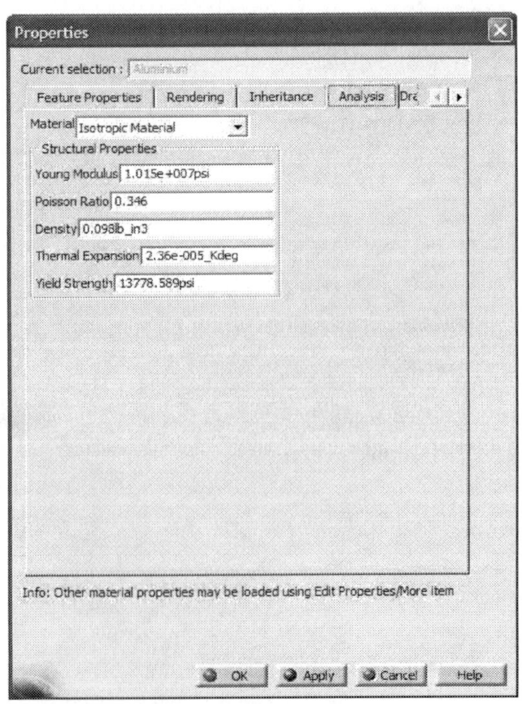

Your next task is to impose assembly constraints.

Pick the **Coincidence** icon  from **Constraints** toolbar .

Select the axis of the shaft and the axis of the hole in the bearing as shown.

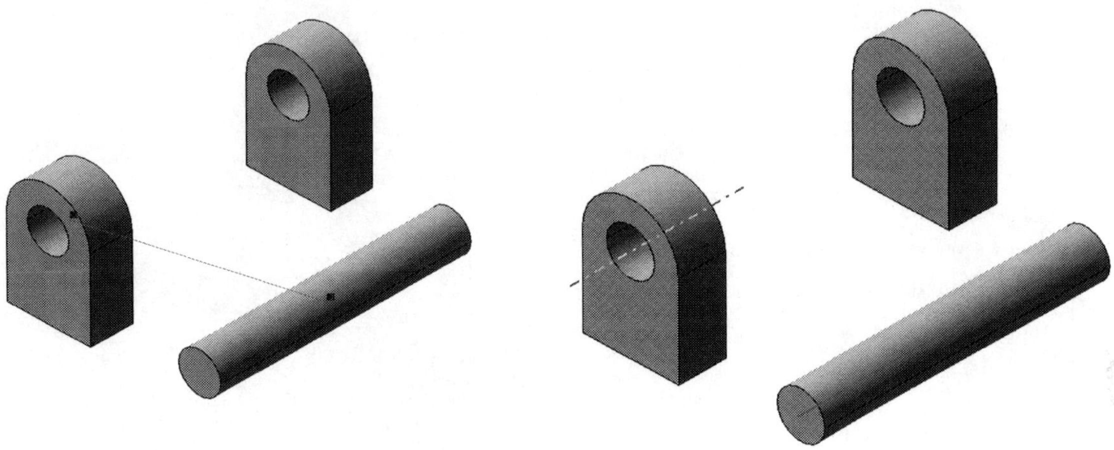

Pick the **Coincidence** icon . Select the end face of the shaft and the face of the bearing as shown.

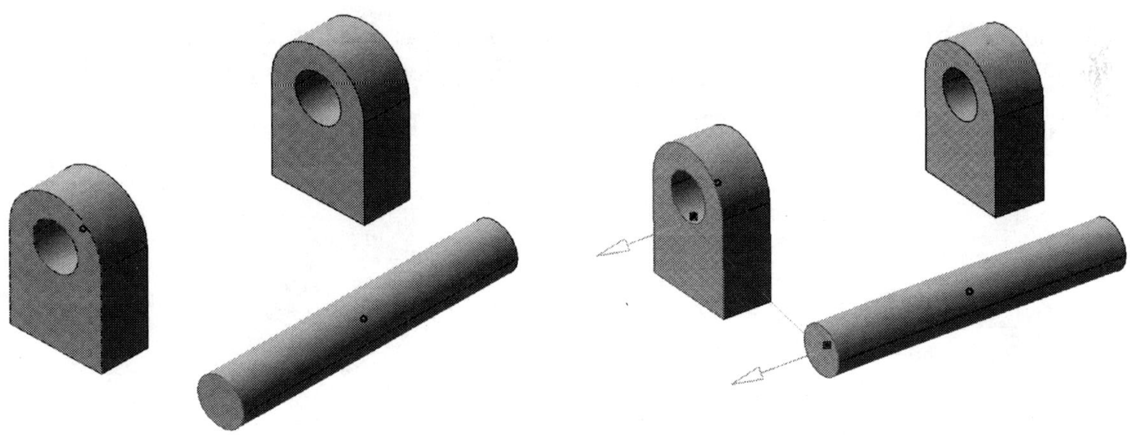

Close the pop up box, shown on the right.

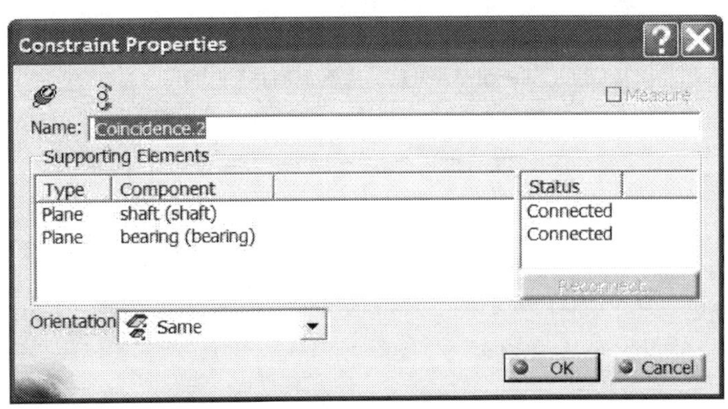

Use the **Update** icon to activate the constraints. This forces the bearing and the shaft to position themselves as displayed below.

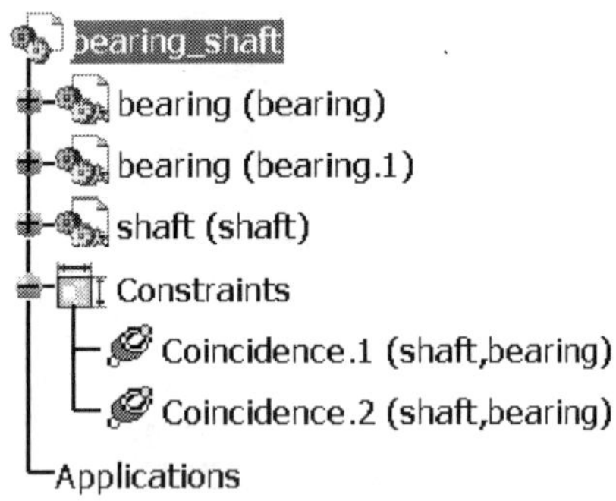

Use the **Anchor** icon from **Constraints** toolbar and select the shaft.
The **Anchor** constraint has no impact on the FEA calculation. Its sole purpose in assembly design is to have a control over the movement of parts.

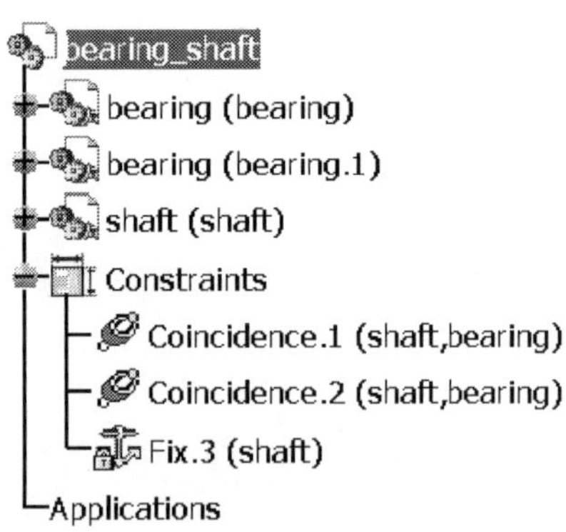


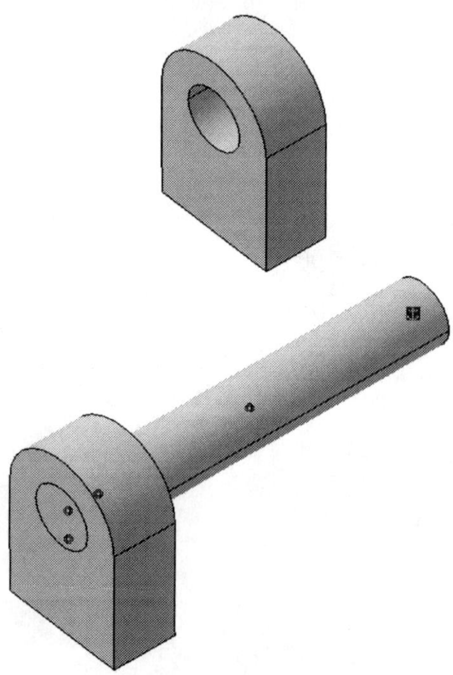

Rotate the assembly to apply the remaining constraints.

Pick the **Coincidence** icon from **Constraints** toolbar .

Select the axis of the shaft and the axis of the hole in the bearing as shown.

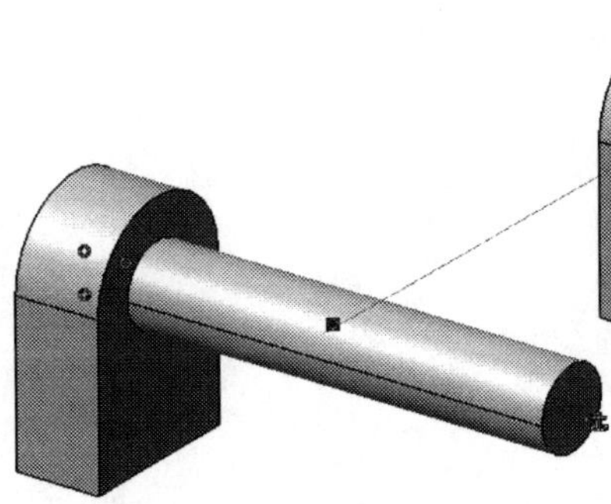

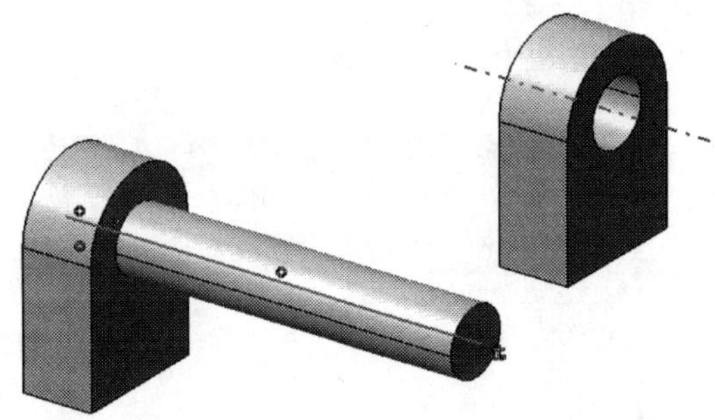

Pick the **Coincidence** icon. Select the end face of the shaft and the face of the bearing as shown and close the pop up box.

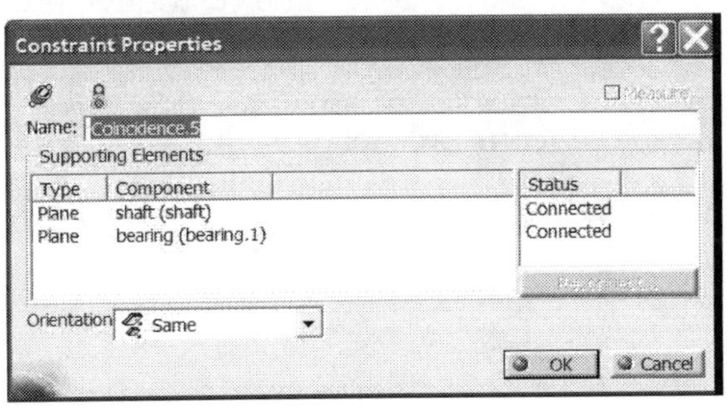


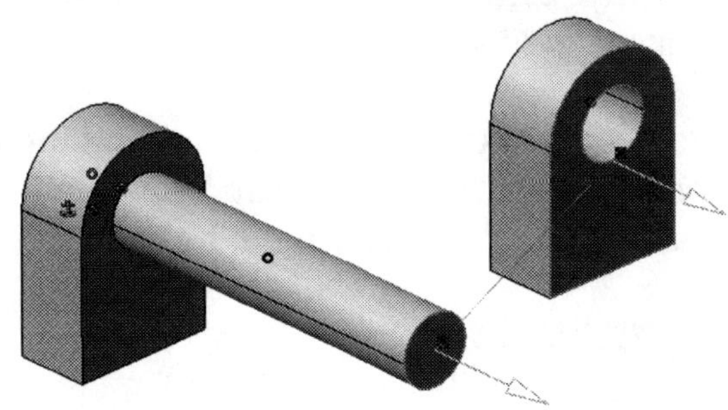

Use the **Update** icon to activate the constraints. This forces the bearing and the shaft to position themselves as displayed below.

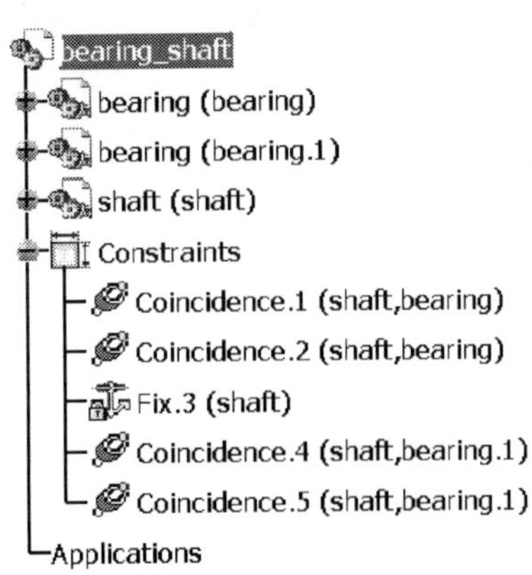

## 3 Entering the Analysis Solutions

From the standard Windows toolbar, select

**Start > Analysis & Simulation > Generative Structural Analysis**

The box shown below, **New Analysis Case**, is visible on the screen. The default choice is **Static Analysis** which is precisely what we intend to use. Therefore, close the box by clicking on **OK**.

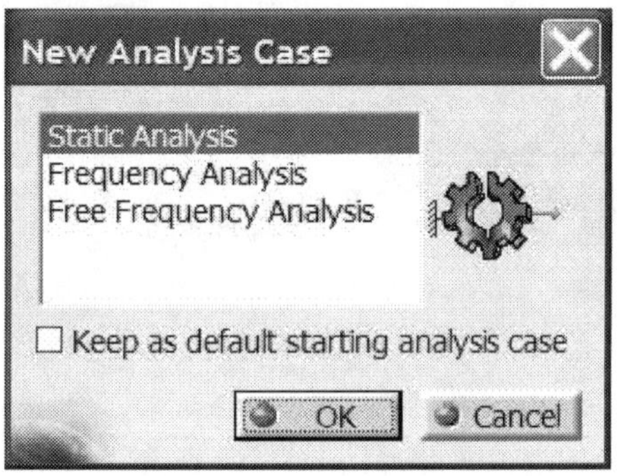


Note that the tree structure gets considerably longer. The bottom branches of the tree are presently "unfilled", and as we proceed in this workbench, assign loads and restraints, the branches gradually get "filled".

Another point that cannot be missed is the appearance of icons on each part that reflect a representative "size" and "sag". It is obvious that each of the three parts has its own mesh. This is displayed in the figure below.

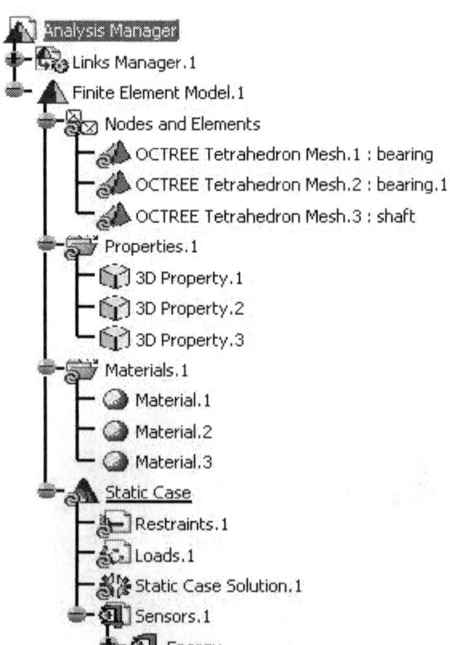

The concept of element size is self-explanatory. A smaller element size leads to more accurate results at the expense of a longer computation time. The "sag" terminology is unique to CATIA. In FEA, the geometry of a part is approximated with the elements. The surface of the part and the FEA approximation of a part do not coincide. The "sag" parameter controls the deviation between the two. Therefore, a smaller "sag" value could lead to better results. There is a relationship between these parameters that one does not have to be concerned with at this point.

The physical sizes of the representative "size" and "sag" on the screen, which also limit the coarseness of the mesh can be changed by the user. There are two ways to change these parameters:
The first method is to double-click on the representative icons on the screen which forces the **OCTREE Tetrahedron Mesh** box to open as shown to the right. This particular box corresponds to the mesh parameters for the **shaft**.

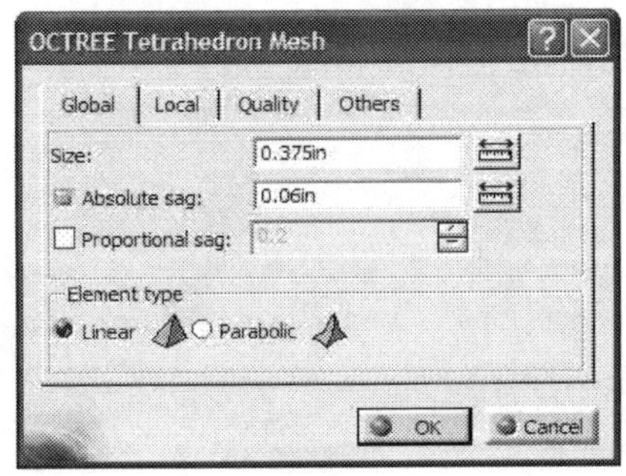


Keep all the default mesh parameters.

Notice that the type of the elements used (linear/parabolic) is also set in this box.
Select **OK**.
The second method of reaching this box is through the tree.
By double-clicking on the branch labeled **OCTREE Tetrahedron Mesh** shown below, the same box opens allowing the user to modify the values.

In order to view the generated mesh, you can point the cursor to the branch **Nodes and Elements**, right-click and select **Mesh Visualization**. This step may be slightly different in some UNIX machines. Upon performing this operation a **Warning** box appears which can be ignored by selecting **OK**. For the mesh parameters used, the mesh shown on the next page is displayed on the screen.
The representative "size" and "sag" icons can be removed from the display by simply pointing to them, right-click and select **Hide**. This is the standard process for hiding any entity in CATIA V5.

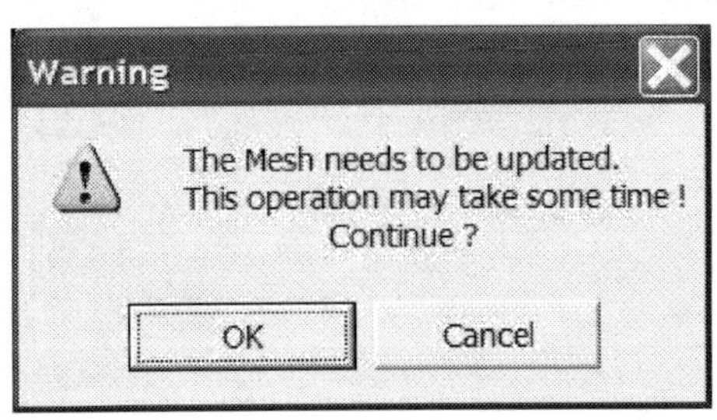

Note that the default mesh size is much smaller for the bearings. The mesh generation algorithm in CATIA takes the size of the part into consideration.

Another important point is the fact that the **shaft** mesh is too coarse. Therefore, the results may be inaccurate.

In general, the elements must be small in the regions of high stress gradient such as stress concentrations.

Uniformly reducing the element size for the whole part is a poor strategy.

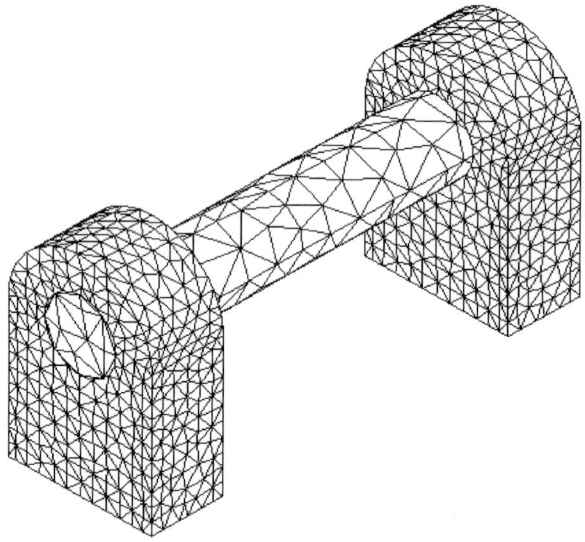

Double-click on **OCTREE Tetrahedron Mesh.3** and change the default values in the pop up box displayed on the right. The mesh corresponding to the revised values is displayed below. This is the mesh that will be used for calculations.

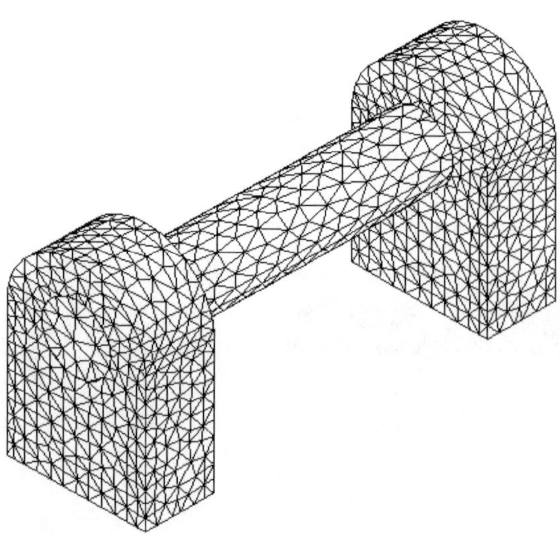

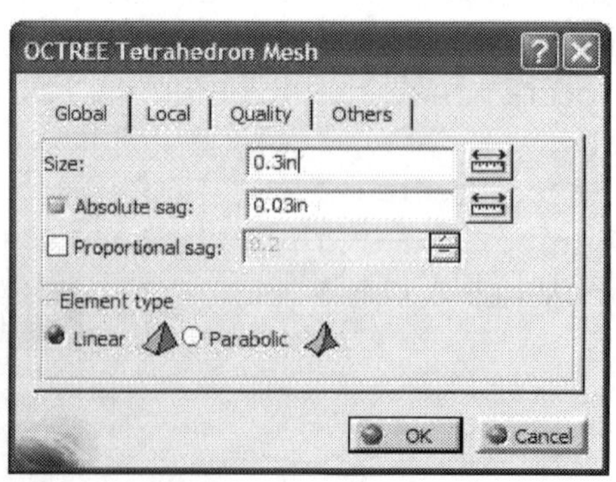

## Applying Restraints:

CATIA's FEA module is geometrically based. This means that the boundary conditions cannot be applied to nodes and elements. The boundary conditions can only be applied at the part level. As soon as you enter the **Generative Structural Analysis** workbench, the parts are automatically hidden. Therefore, before boundary conditions are applied, the part must be brought to the unhide mode. This can be carried out by pointing the cursor to the top of the tree, the **Links Manager.1** branch, right-click, select **Show**. At this point, the parts and the mesh are superimposed as shown below and you have access to the part.

If, the presence of the mesh is annoying, you can always hide it. Point the cursor to **Nodes and Elements**, right-click, **Hide**.

In FEA, restraints refer to applying displacement boundary conditions which is achieved through the **Restraint** toolbar 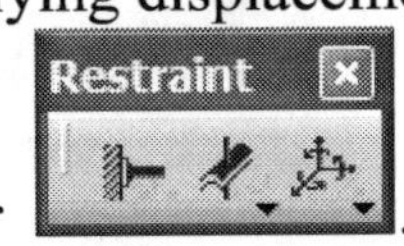.



Select the **Clamp** icon  and pick the bottom faces of the bearings.

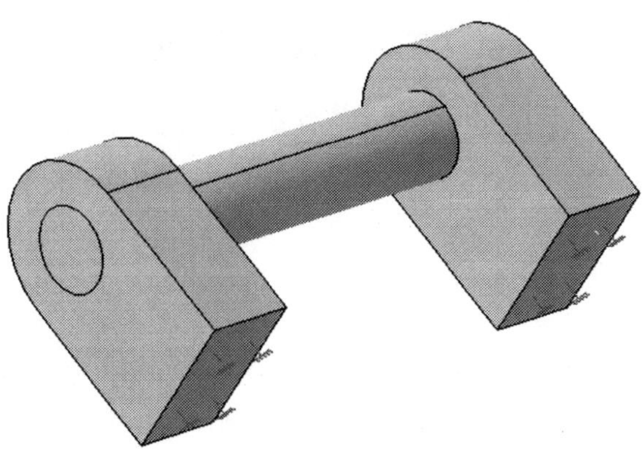

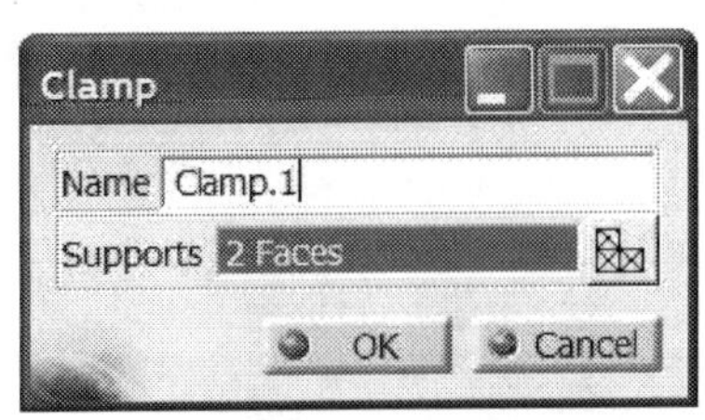

### Applying the Load:

In FEA, loads refer to forces. The **Loads** toolbar 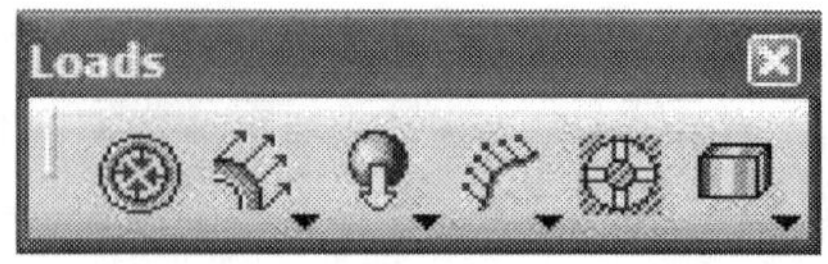

is used for this purpose. Select the **Distributed force** icon 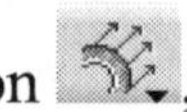, and with the cursor pick the face of the shaft. The **Distributed force** box shown below opens. A visual inspection of the global axis on your screen indicates that the force of magnitude 1000 lb should be applied in the negative z-direction.

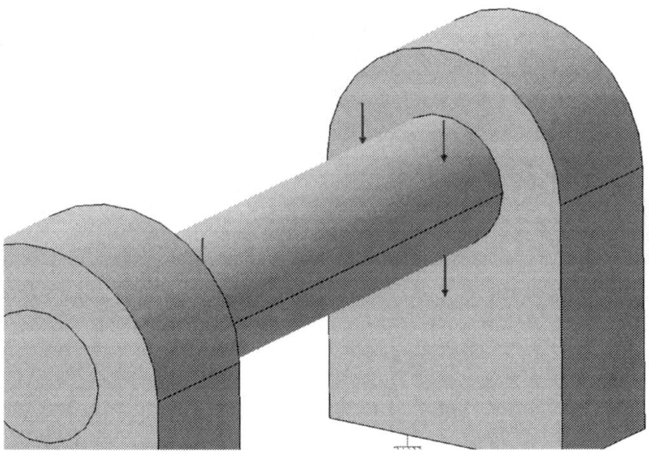

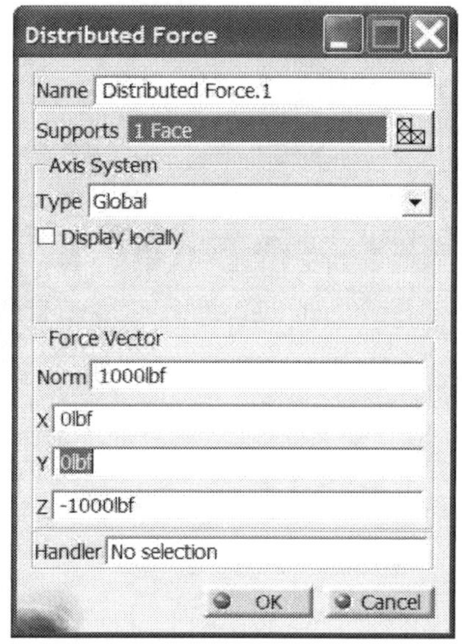


### Creating Analysis Connection:

Use the **General Analysis Connection** icon  from the **Analysis Supports** toolbar 

.
For **First component**, select the face of the shaft.

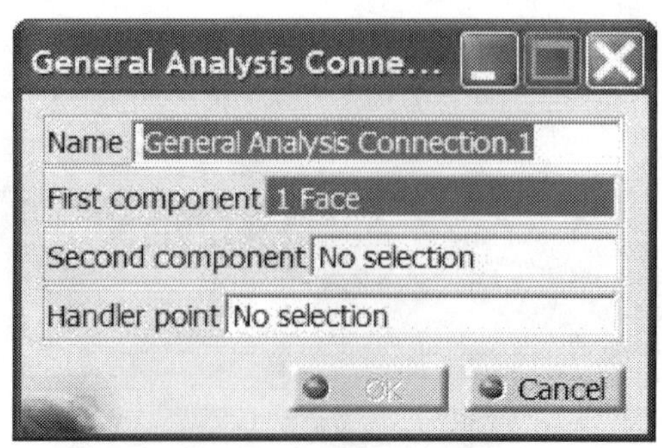

For **Second component**, you need to pick the inside surface of one of the holes. However, this is not easy unless you **Hide** the shaft.

First **Hide** the shaft as shown below, then pick the inside surface of the hole.

Pick inside surface of the hole

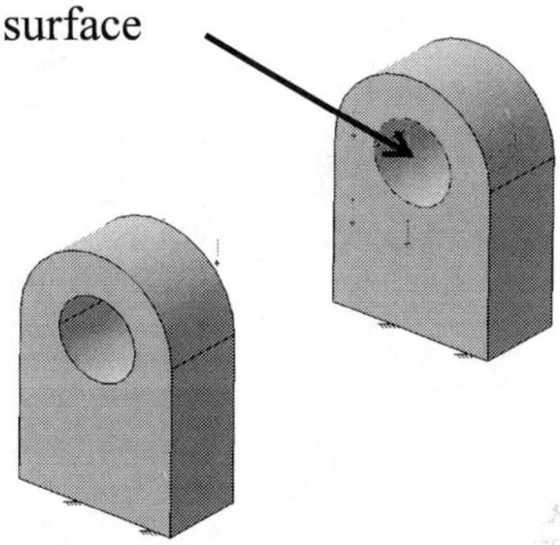

First connection established

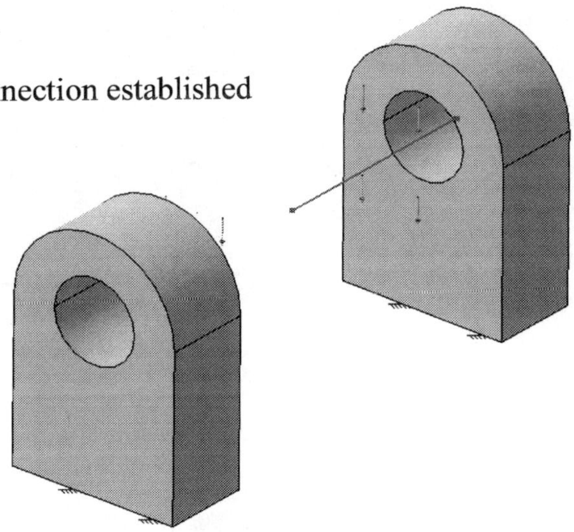

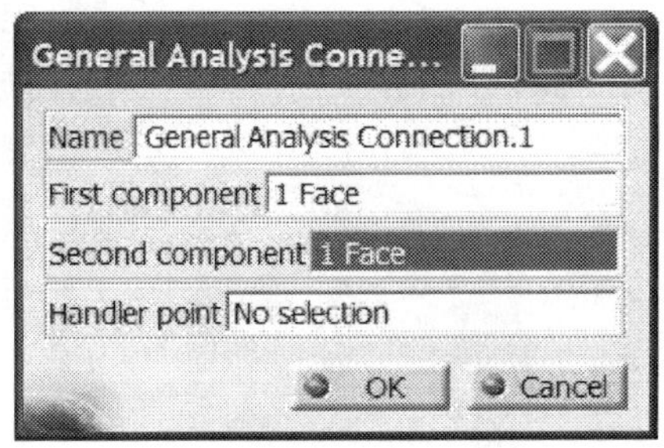


You have to repeat the same process with the shaft and the other bearing.

Use the **General Analysis Connection** icon and select the surface of the shaft as shown below.

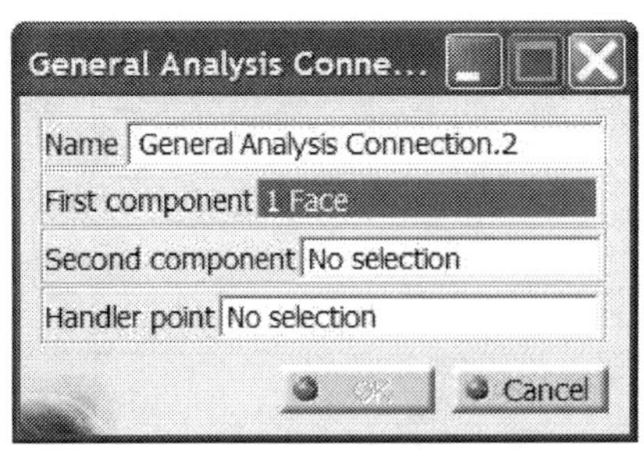

For **Second component**, you need to pick the inside surface of the holes not used before. However, once again, this is not easy unless you **Hide** the shaft.

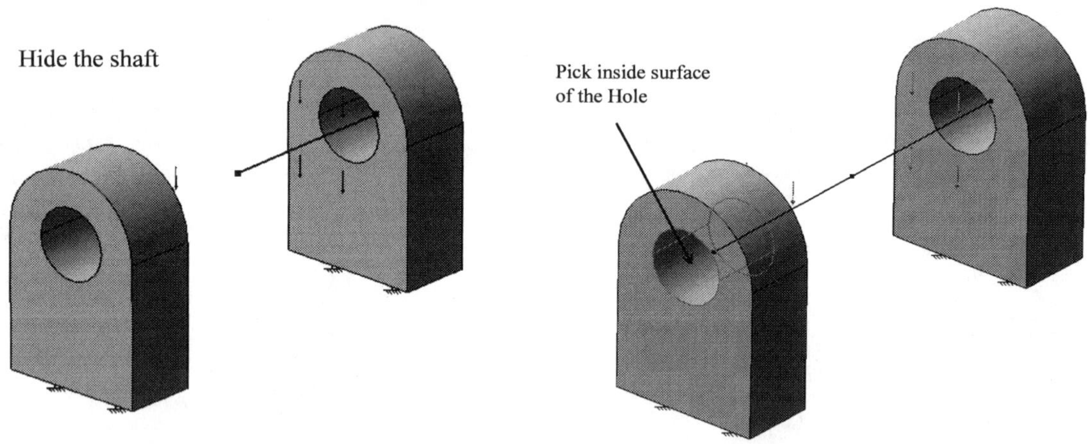


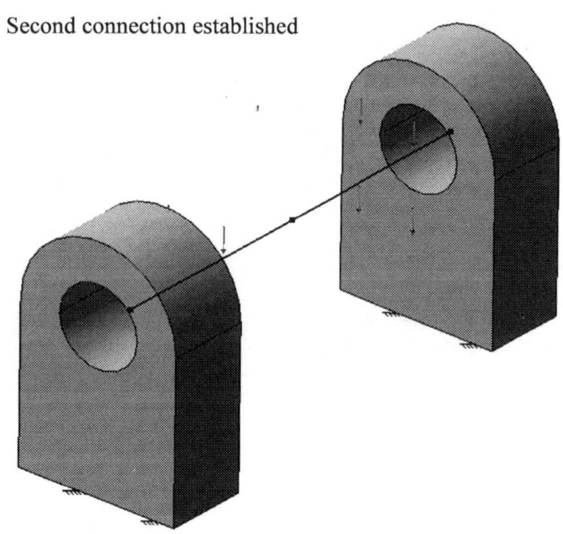


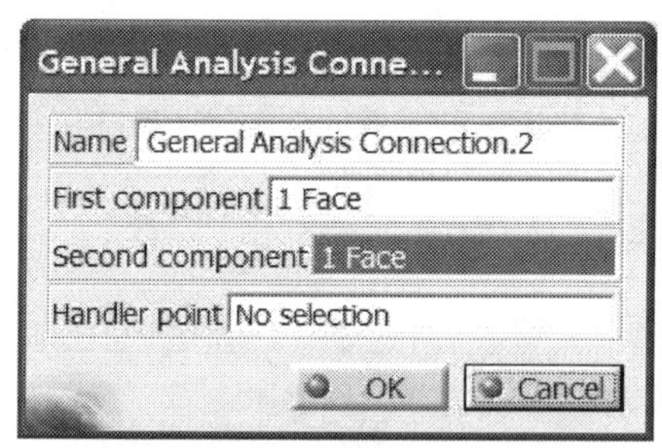


The branch of the tree labeled **Analysis Connection Manager.1** stores the information on the connections being established. The portion of the tree pertaining to this issue is displayed below.

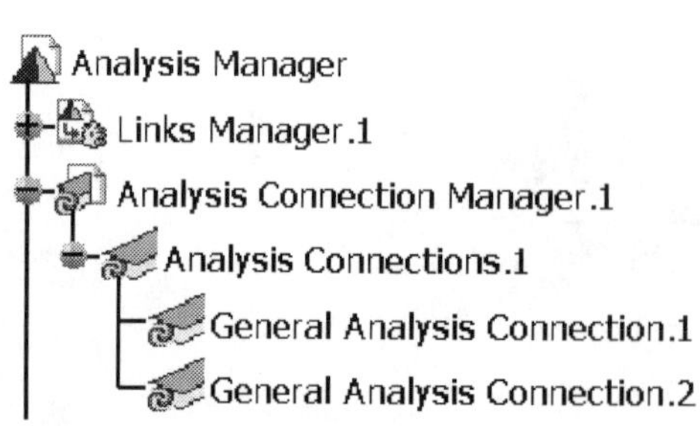

You now define the nature of the connections defined earlier. The **Connection Property** toolbar has a sub-toolbar called **Face Face Connection Property**.

Click on the **Contact Connection Property** icon  from the **Face Face Connection Property** toolbar 

. The following pop up box appears.

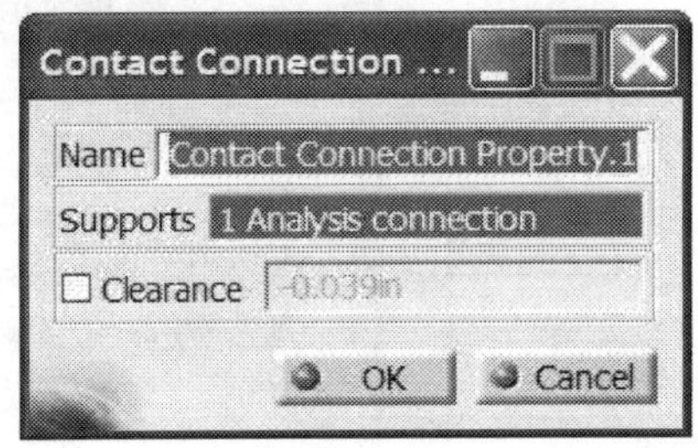


For **Supports**, select **General Analysis Connection.1** from the tree.

On the computer screen, you notice that the standard symbol for contact is created.

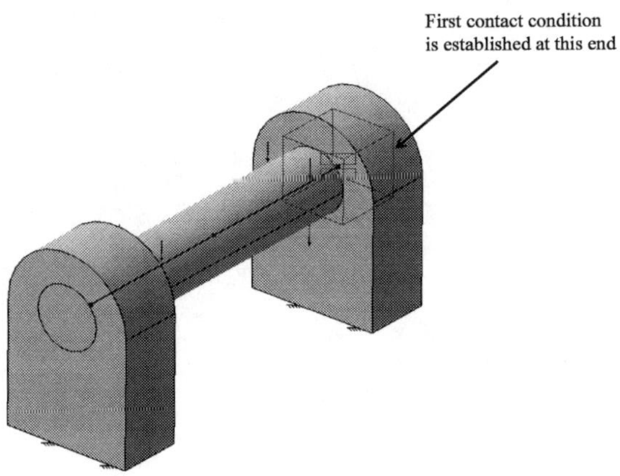


Once again, click on the **Contact Connection property** icon 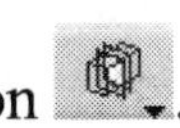.

For **Supports**, select **General Analysis Connection.2** from the tree.

On the computer screen, you notice that the standard symbol for contact is created.

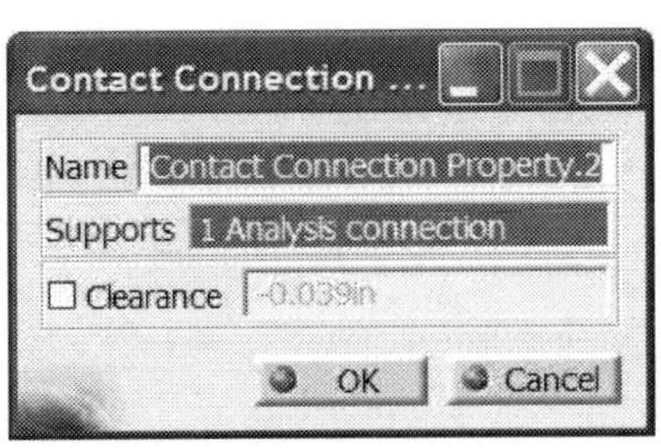


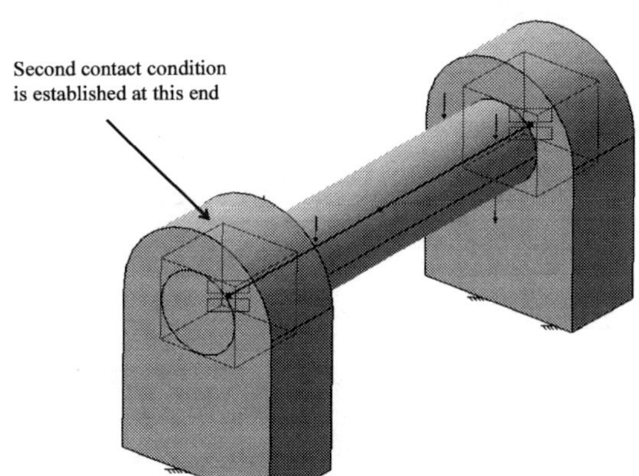

The portion of the tree dealing with the contact branches is shown below.

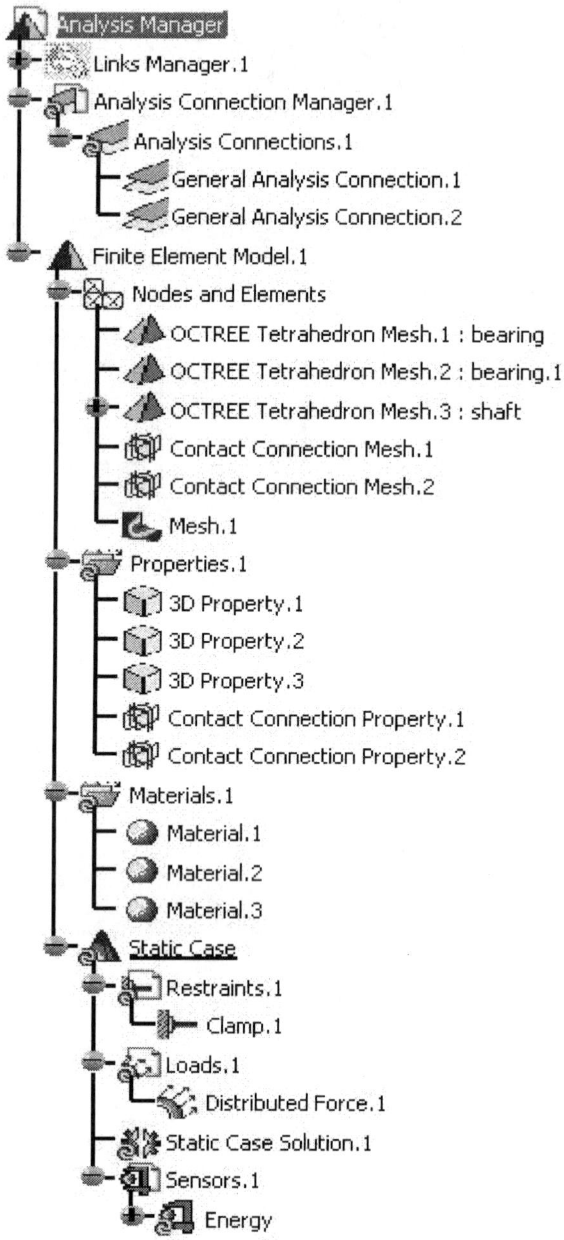


It seems that all restraints have been applied and that the program should run. This is not the case as will be seen shortly. There is one further non-obvious restraint that needs to be applied.

## Launching the Solver:

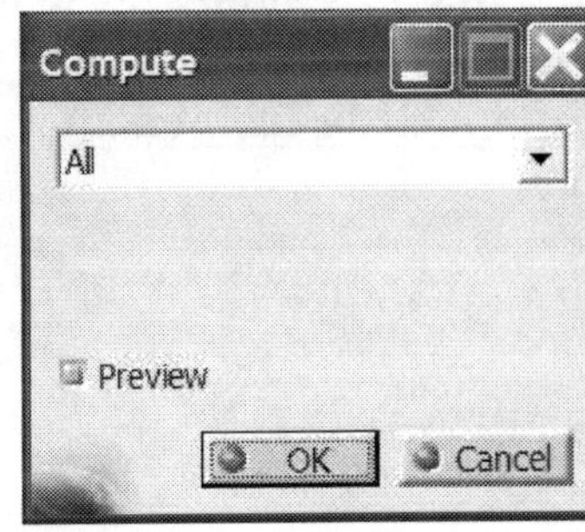


To run the analysis, you need to use the **Compute** toolbar 

by selecting the **Compute** icon . This leads to the **Compute** box shown to the right. Leave the defaults as **All** which means everything is computed.
Upon closing this box, after a brief pause, the second box shown below appears. This box provides information on the resources needed to complete the analysis.
If the estimates are zero in the listing, then there is a problem in the previous step and should be looked into. If all the numbers are zero in the box, the program may run but would not produce any useful results.

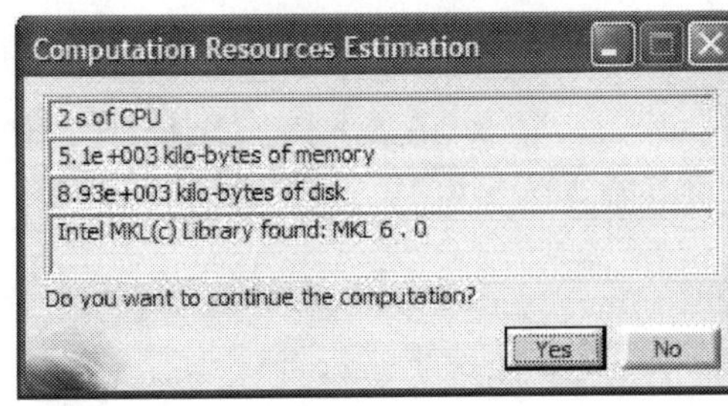


This run terminates with the following **Error** box.

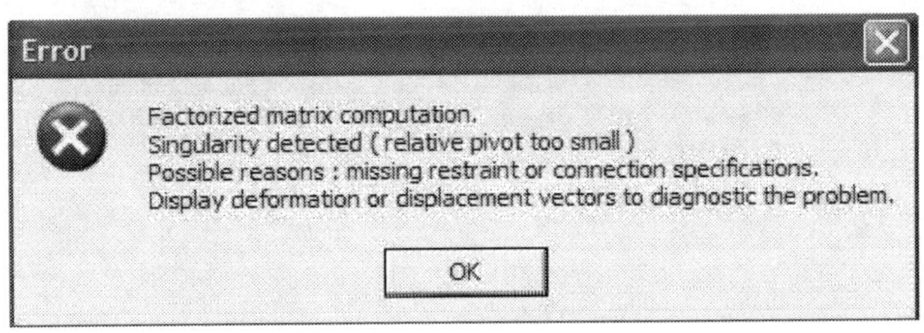


Usually this box implies that the assembly is not fully restrained. In our model, the shaft is free to move along its axis as a rigid body. Some commercial packages rectify the situation by adding a small artificial stiffness in that direction, preventing the rigid body motion. In those packages, effectively they add a "soft" spring in the appropriate direction, resulting in a stiffness.
You prevent this rigid body motion by clamping the circular edge of the shaft.

Select the **Clamp** icon 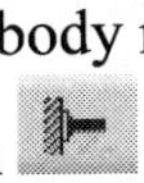 and pick an edge of the shaft.

Pick the circular edge of the shaft

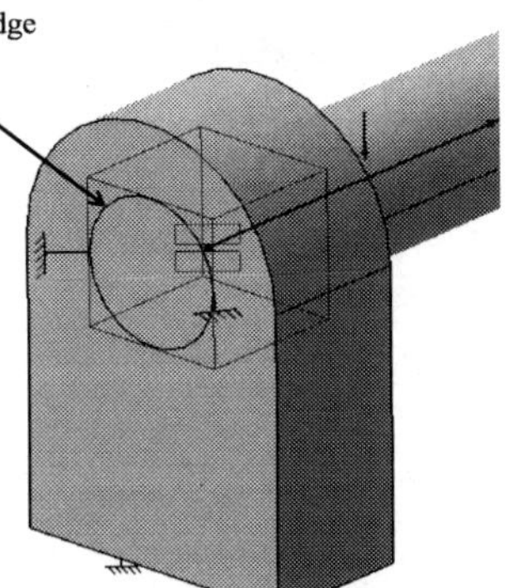

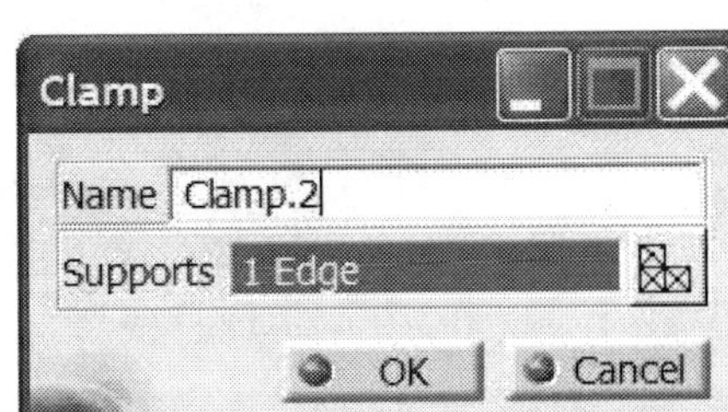

Note that it is very easy to accidentally pick the edge of the hole. Picking the edge of the hole does not stop the shaft from moving as a rigid body. To avoid making this mistake, you can **Hide** the bearing.

Now press on  to run the problem. This time, the run completes without an error.

**Postprocessing:**

The main postprocessing toolbar is called **Image** 

. To view the deformed shape you have to use the **Deformation** icon 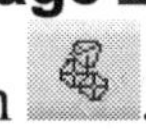. The resulting deformed shape is displayed below.

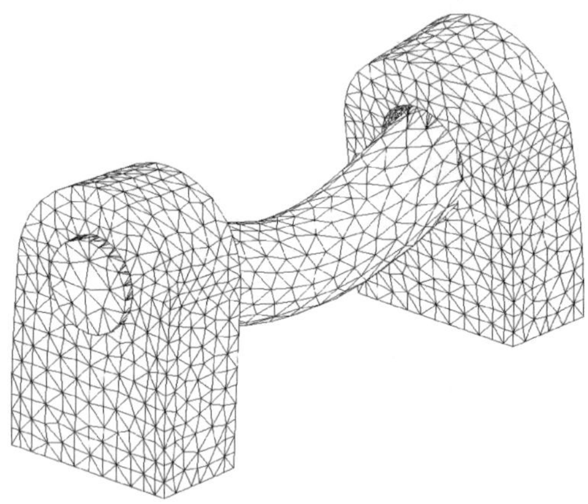

The deformation image can be very deceiving because one could have the impression that the assembly actually displaces to that extent. Keep in mind that the displacements are scaled considerably so that one can observe the deformed shape. Although the scale factor is set automatically, one can change this value with the **Deformation Scale Factor** icon  in the **Analysis Tools** toolbar 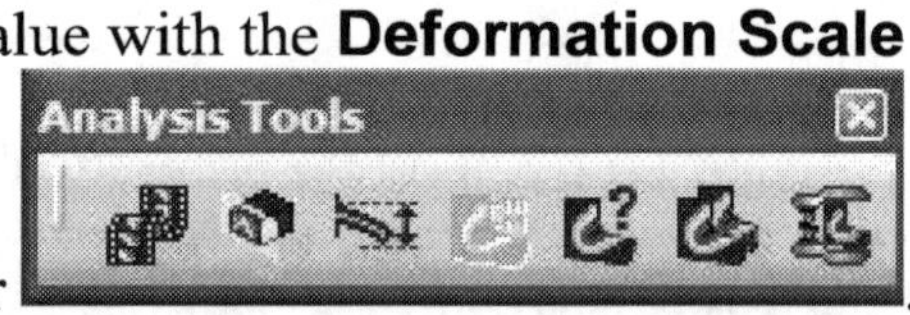

. Clicking on the above icon leads to the box shown below where the desired scale factor can be typed. The deformed shape displayed corresponds to a scale factor of 908.224. The value 0.738665 in. is 908 times the actual maximum displacement.

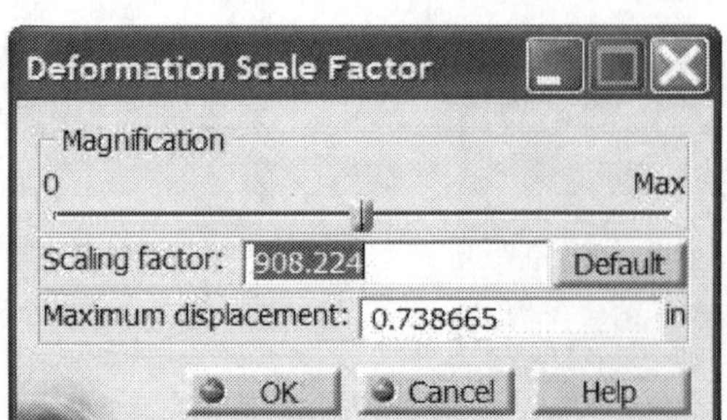

In order to see the displacement field, the **Displacement** icon 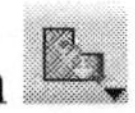 in the **Image** toolbar should be used. The default display is in terms of displacement arrows.

The arrow plot is not particularly useful. In order to view the contour plot of the displacement field, position the cursor on the arrow field and double-click. The **Image Edition** box shown on the right opens.

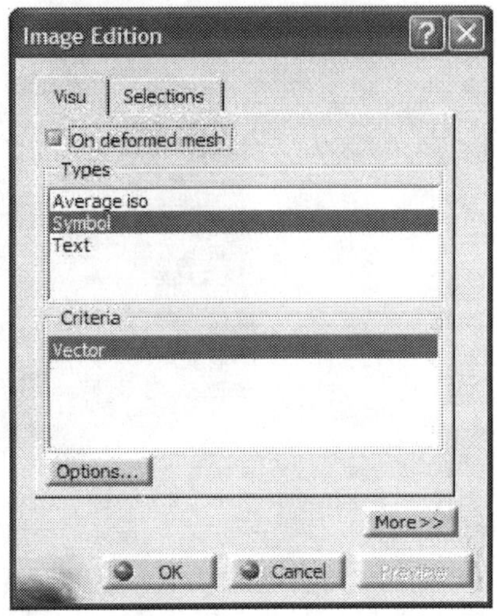


The contour of the displacement field is given below.

Note: The color map has been changed; otherwise everything looks black in the figure.

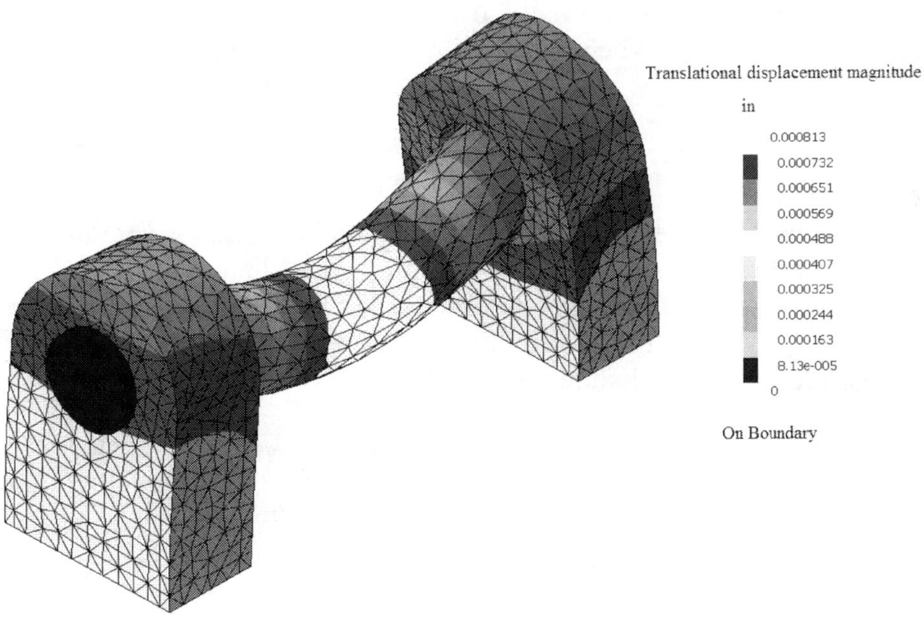


The next step in the postprocessing is to plot the contours of the von Mises stress using the **von Mises Stress** icon  in the **Image** toolbar.
The von Mises stress is displayed on the next page.

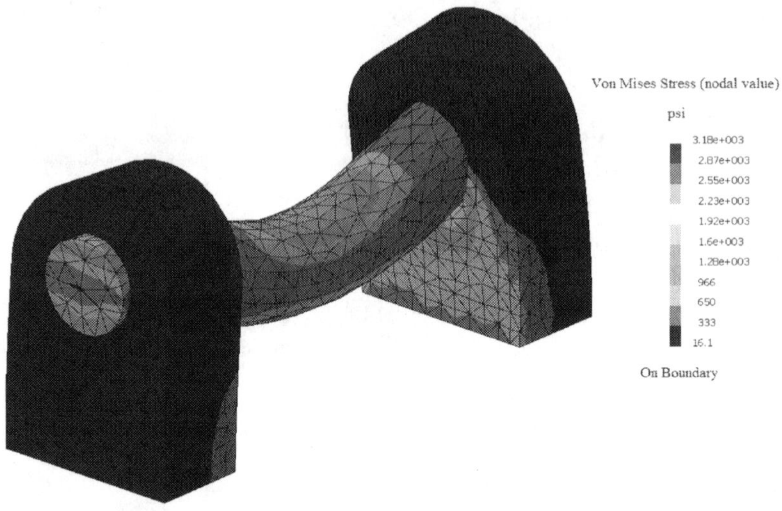


Double-clicking on the contour legend leads to the **Color Map** box displayed on the right. The contour can be plotted as **Smooth** or **Stepped**. The number of color bands is also specified in this box. Finally, the user can describe the range of stresses to be plotted.

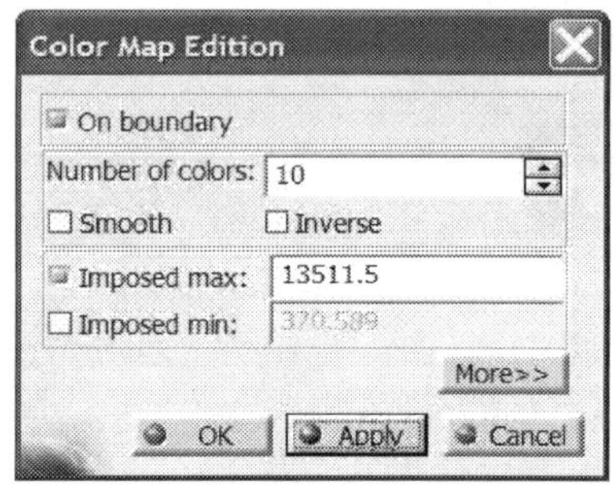


Occasionally, you may be interested in plotting the von Mises stress contour in parts of the assembly or even the supports. In order to achieve this, double-click on the contour levels on the screen to open the image edition box. Next use the **Selections** tab as shown below. Here, you have the choice of selecting different entities. The contour below is the stress distribution in the shaft alone.

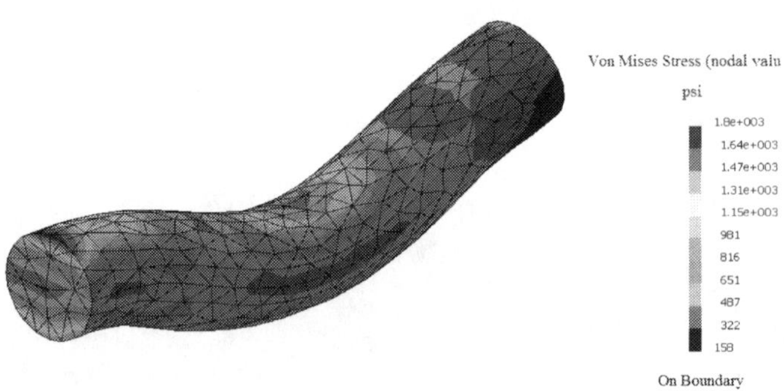


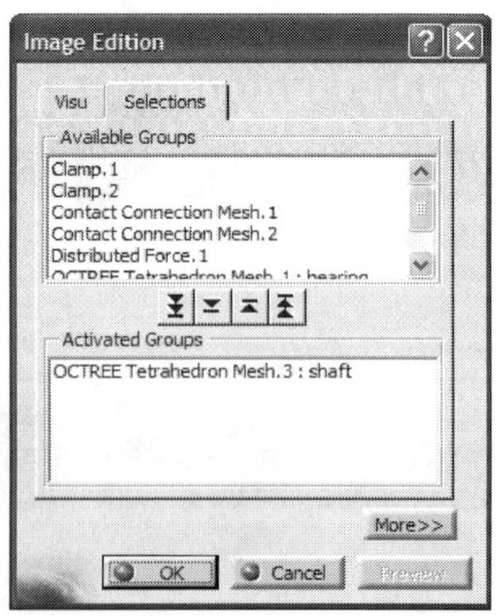


The contour below is the stress distribution in a bearing alone.

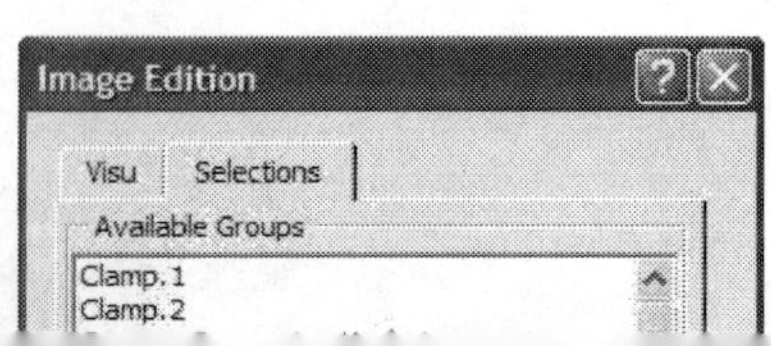

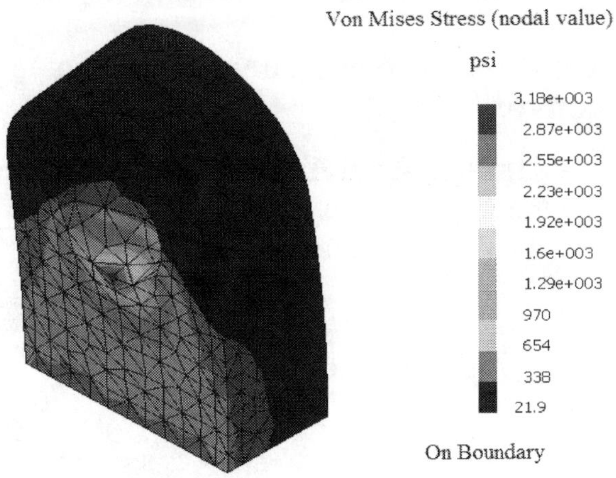


The **Cutting Plane** icon  from the **Analysis Tools** toolbar can be used to make a cut through the part at a desired location and inspect the stresses inside of the part. The **Cut Plane** box allows you to keep the plane or to remove it for display purposes. A typical cutting plane is shown below.

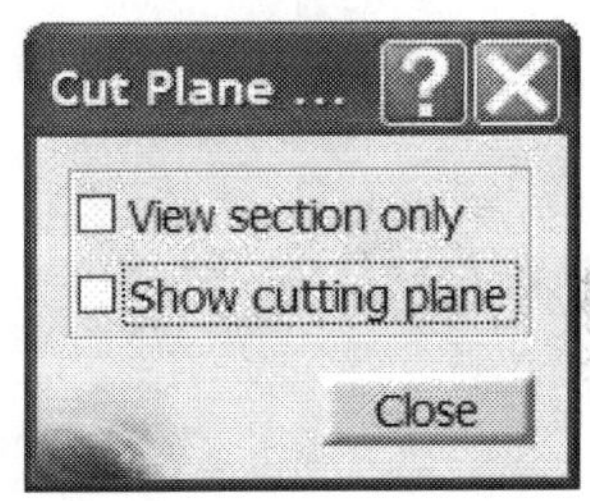


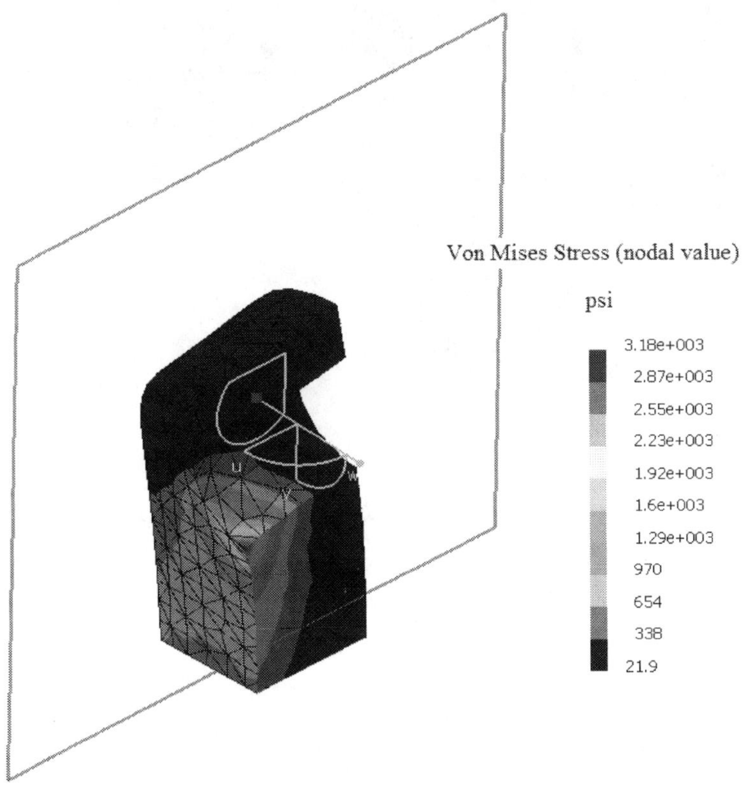

At this point we have generated two plots. The displacement and the von Mises stress contours which can be displayed individually. However, CATIA also allows you to show both plots side by side.

First make sure that both images to be plotted are active in the tree. If not, point to the graph in the tree, right-click, and select **Active**.

Click the **Image Layout** icon from the **Image Analysis** toolbar. The **Images** box, shown to the right, asks you to specify the direction along which the two plots are expected to be aligned. The outcome is side-by-side plots shown below.

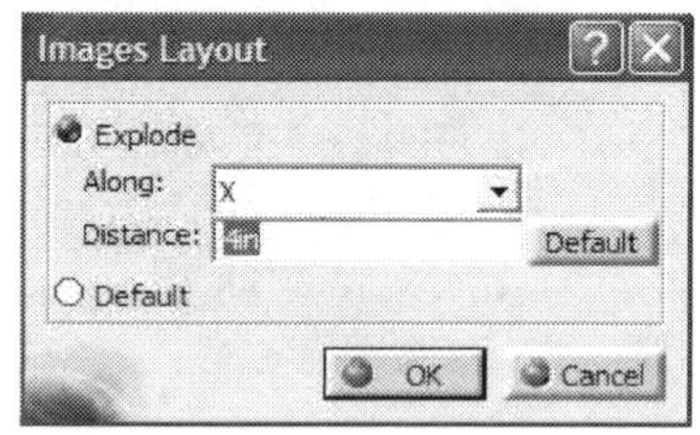

Using the icon **Basic Analysis Results** in the **Analysis Results** toolbar  an HTML based report can be generated which summarizes the features and results of the FEA model.

Animation of the model can be achieved through the **Animate** icon in the **Analysis Tools** toolbar 

and AVI files can easily be generated.

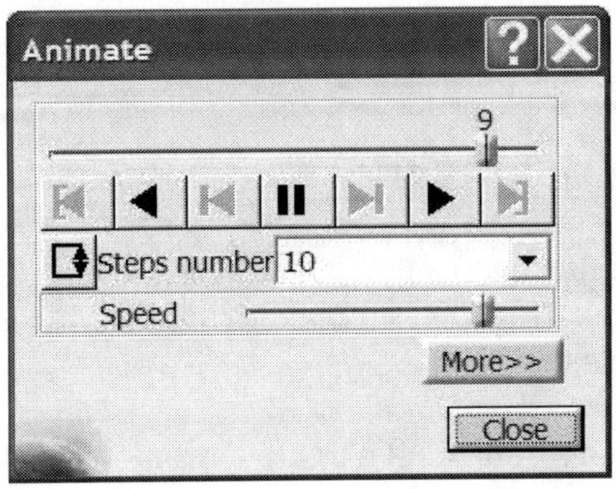


Using the icon **Generate Report** in the **Analysis Results** toolbar, an HTML based report can be generated which summarizes the features and results of the FEA model.

# Exercises for Chapter 14

## Problem 1: Hertz Contact Problem

A famous problem in solid mechanics is the classical Hertz problem. It involves the pressing of two long cylinders together and analyzing the stresses. It is assumed that both materials remain linearly elastic.

In order to be able to compare your CATIA calculations with the exact solution, assume that both materials are identical with Young's modulus E and Poisson ratio $\nu = .3$. Check your results against the analytical solution provided below.

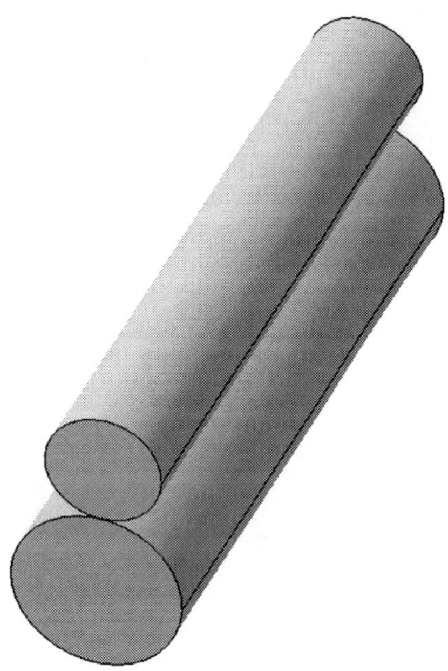

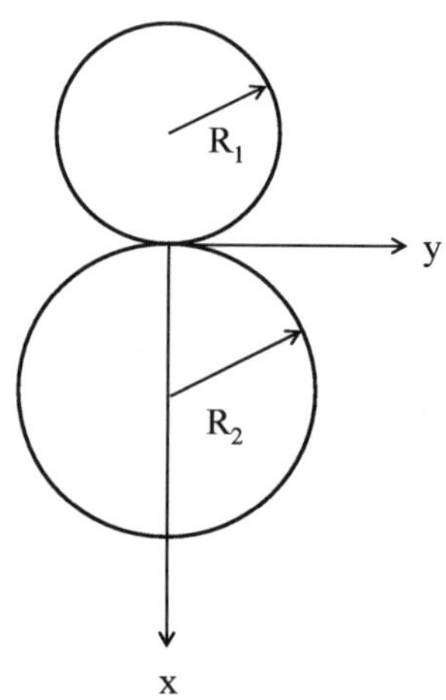


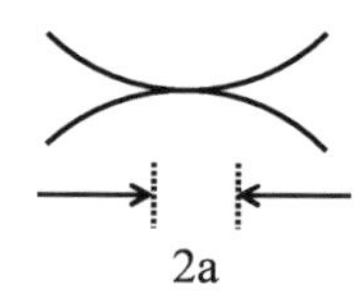


Partial Answer:

Let P be the applied pressure and L the length of the cylinders. Then, using advanced mechanics of materials, one can show the following:

$$a = 1.522\sqrt{\frac{P}{LE}\frac{R_1 R_2}{R_1 + R_2}}$$

$$p_{max} = \frac{2P}{\pi a L}$$

$$\sigma_x = -\frac{p_{max}}{\sqrt{1 + \left(\frac{x}{a}\right)^2}}$$

## Problem 2: Torsion of a Tube

An aluminum tube assembly is supported by two steel pins as shown below. The pins are 6 in. long and subjected to a torque of 1000 lb.in. Use the CATIA solid elements to estimate the stresses developed in the structure.

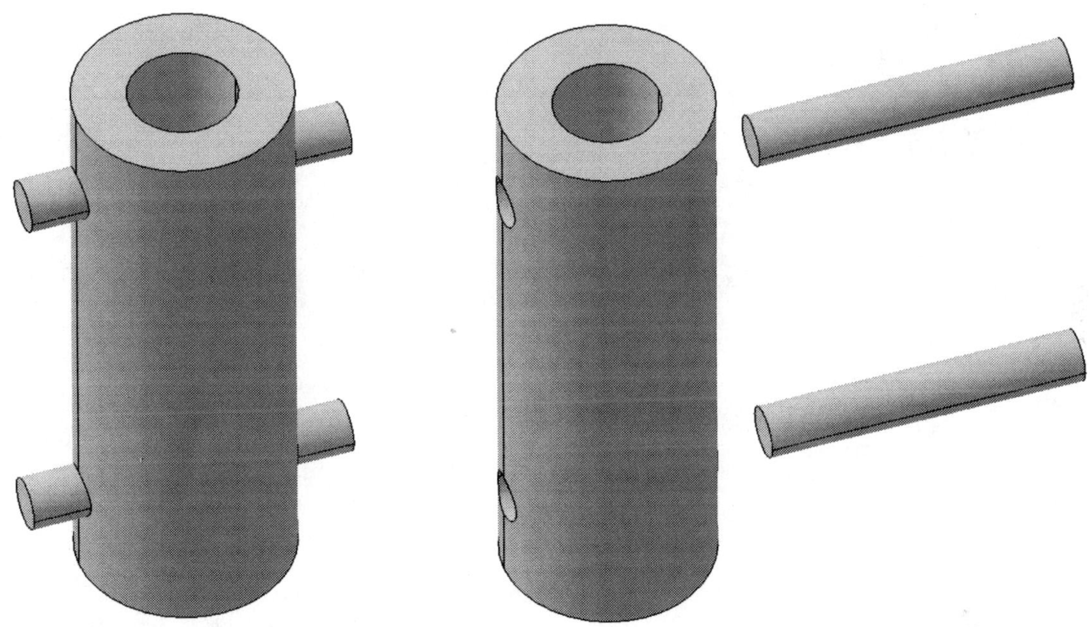

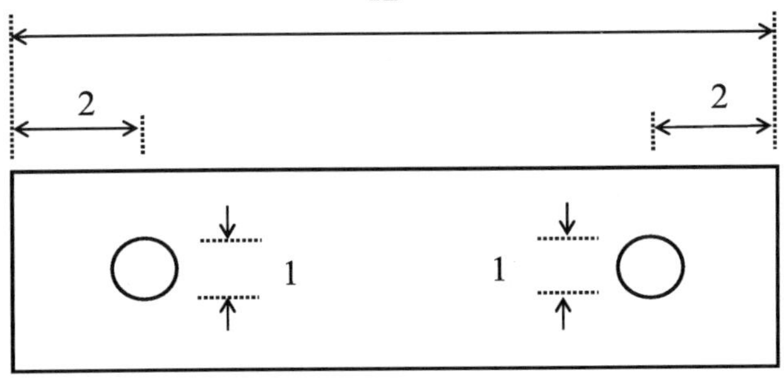


side view

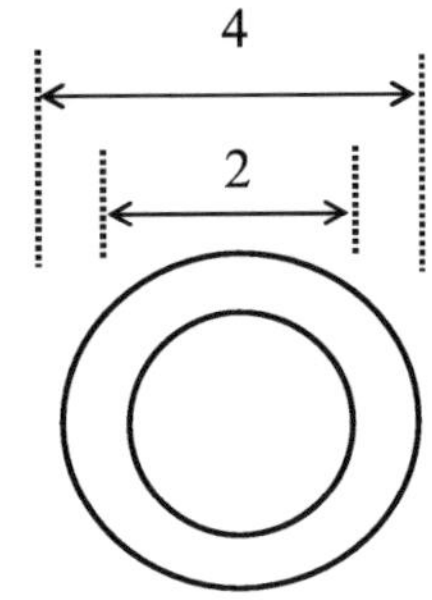


top view

# NOTES:

# Chapter 15

# Shrink Fit Analysis

## Introduction

In this tutorial, you will analyze the assembly of two disks which are shrink fitted within each other. The inside, disk has a diameter which is slightly larger than the outside disk. The **Analysis Connection** toolbar is used for setting up the problem.

## 1 Problem Statement

The two cylinders, shown below, are shrink fitted. The outside cylinder, made of steel, has inside and outside diameters of 4 in. and 5 in. respectively. The inside cylinder, made of brass, has inside and outside diameters of 2 in. and 4.002 in. respectively. This implies that diametral interference is 0.002 in.

The material properties of steel are $E_S = 30E6$ psi and $\nu_S = .29$. The corresponding properties for brass are $E_B = 15E6$ psi and $\nu_B = .32$.

Use CATIA's solid elements to estimate the contact pressure and predict the stress distribution in the assembly.

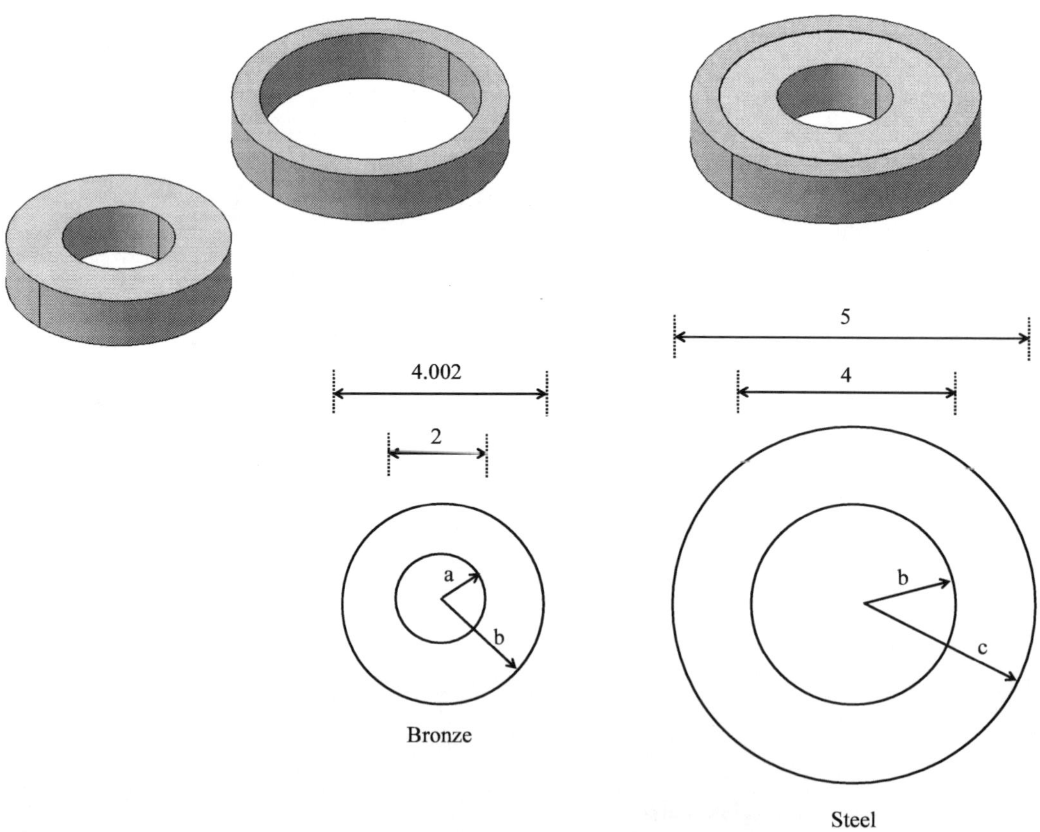


The variables "a", "b" and "c" are called the nominal radii. Here, $a = 1$ in., $b = 2$ in., and $c = 2.5$ in.; furthermore, the radial interference is $\delta = 0.002/2 = .001$ in.

The contact pressure can be calculated from the following expression.

$$p = \frac{\delta}{b\left[\frac{1}{E_S}\left(\frac{c^2+b^2}{c^2-b^2}+\nu_S\right)+\frac{1}{E_B}\left(\frac{b^2+a^2}{b^2-a^2}-\nu_B\right)\right]}$$

Based on the supplied parameters, the contact pressure is estimated as $p = 1990$ psi. The stress distribution can then be evaluated from the following formulas.

For Steel:
$$\begin{cases} \sigma_{hoop} = 3537 + \dfrac{22108}{r^2} \\ \sigma_{radial} = 3537 - \dfrac{22108}{r^2} \end{cases}$$

For Brass:
$$\begin{cases} \sigma_{hoop} = -2653 - \dfrac{2653}{r^2} \\ \sigma_{radial} = -2653 + \dfrac{2653}{r^2} \end{cases}$$

The variable "r" represents the distance of the point under consideration to the origin.

The graphical representation of the hoop and radial stress is provided in the figure below. Note that the radial stress is continuous, whereas there is jump discontinuity in the hoop stress at the interface.

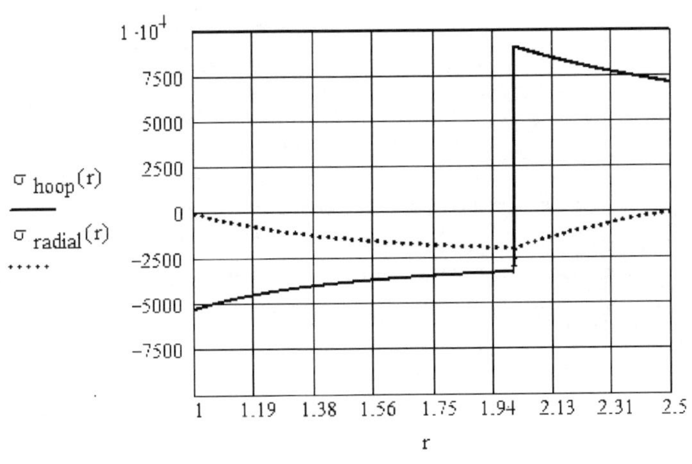


Although for FEA purposes, one needs to take only a sector on the disks, you will ignore symmetry and model the entire geometry.

## 2 Creation of the Assembly in the Mechanical Design Solutions

Enter the **Assembly Design** workbench which can be achieved by different means depending on your CATIA customization. For example, from the standard Windows toolbar, select **File > New** . From the box shown on the right, select **Product**. This moves you to the **Assembly Design** workbench and creates an assembly with the default name **Product.1**. See Note #1 in Appendix I.

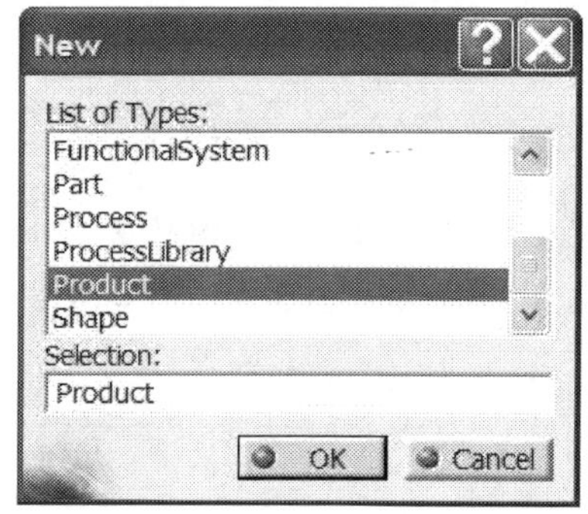


In order to change the default name, move the cursor to **Product.1** in the tree, right-click and select **Properties** from the menu list.

From the **Properties** box, select the **Product** tab and in **Part Number** type **shrink_fit**.

This will be the new product name throughout the chapter. The tree on the top left corner of your computer screen should look as displayed below.

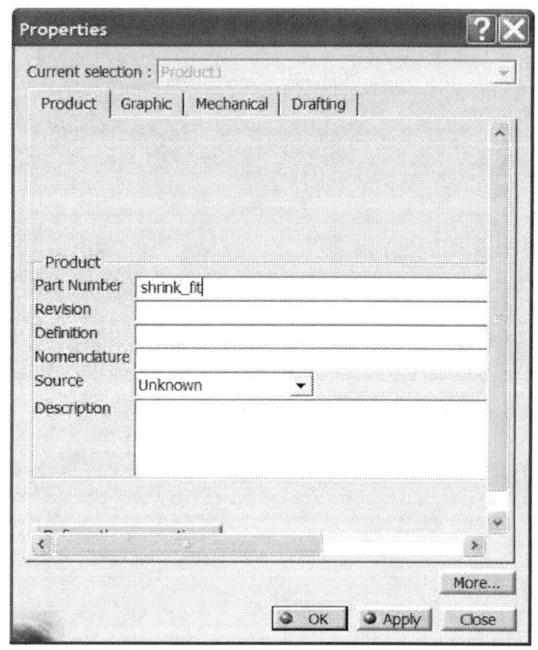

You now create the steel disk as a part.
From the standard Windows toolbar, select **Insert > New Part**. The tree is modified to indicate that **Part.1** has been created. Change the default name to **steel_disk**.
The tree, before and after the name change, is displayed below. Note that the instance name has also been changed to **steel_disk**.

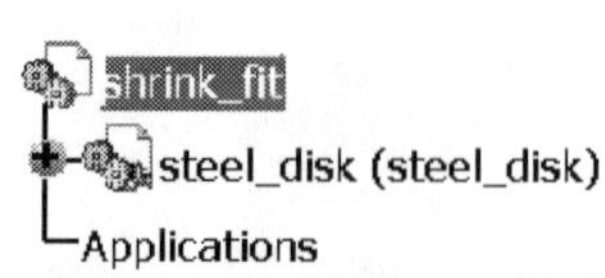


The process of renaming **Part.1** is just like before. Point the cursor to **Part.1** in the tree, right-click, and select **Properties**. The pop box, after the changes are made is displayed below.

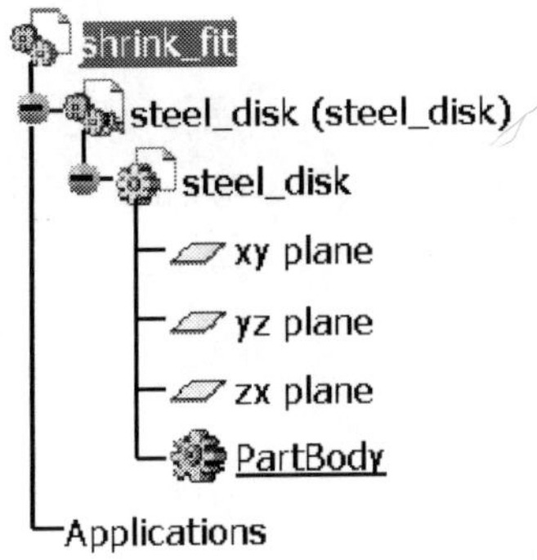


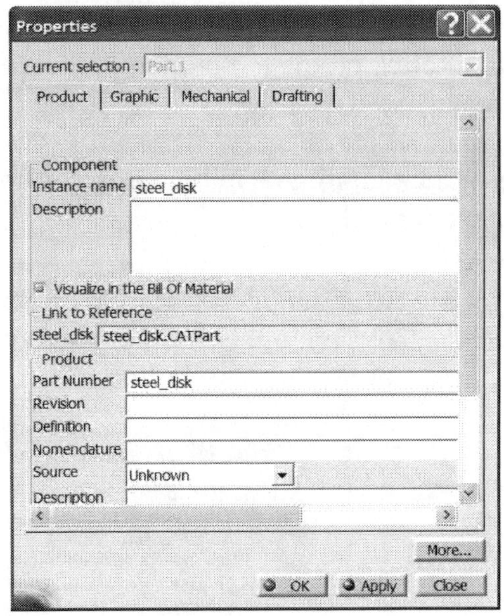


Select the **xy** plane from **steel_disk** and switch to the **Part Design** workbench.

In **Part Design**, enter the **Sketcher** .

In the **Sketcher**, draw two concentric circles ***centered at the origin*** with radii 2 in. and 2.5 in. respectively.

Leave the **Sketcher** .

Use the **Pad** icon to create a hollow disk of height 1 in.

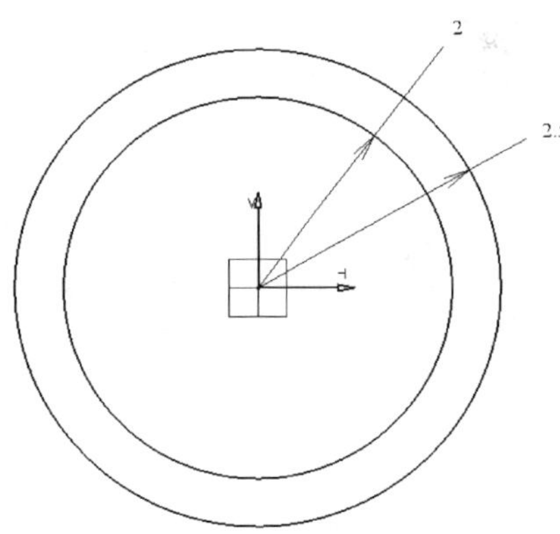


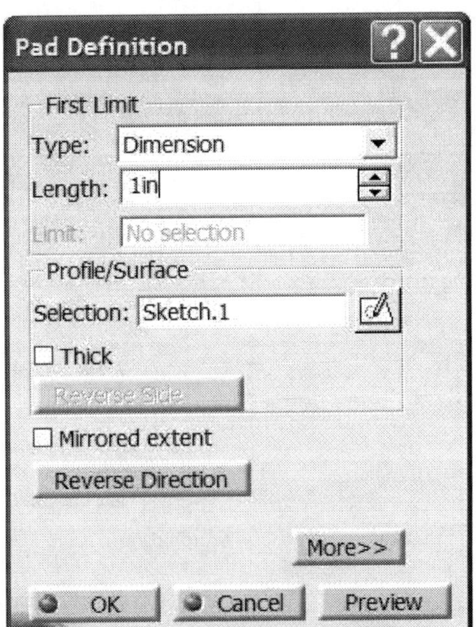


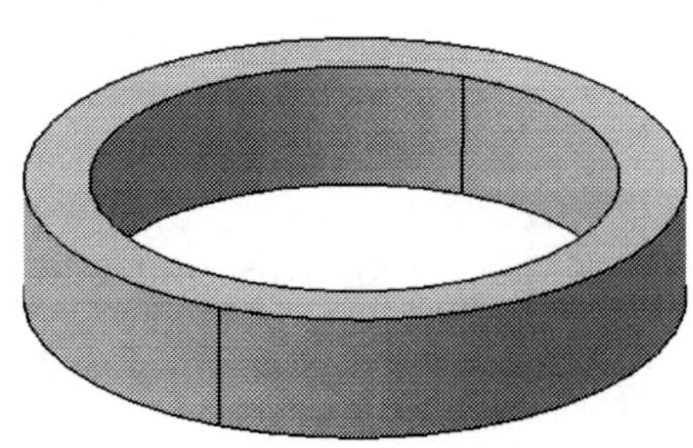

The best way of saving your work is to save the assembly.
Double-click on the top branch of the tree. This lands you in the **Assembly Design** workbench.

The branch highlights in blue as a confirmation of the new workbench.

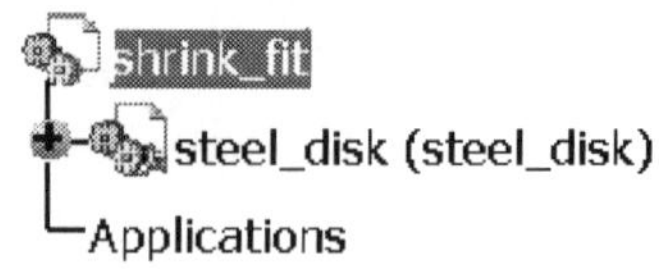


Select the **Save** icon. The **Save As** pop up box indicates that saving the assembly activates the saving of the parts. Choose the **Yes** button.

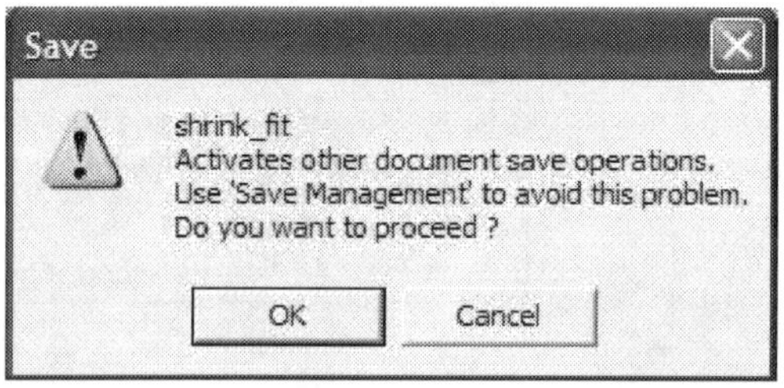


You are now ready to create the brass disk.

From the standard Windows toolbar, select **Insert > New Part**. The tree is modified to indicate that **Part.2** has been created.
You are also presented with pop up box on the right. Select **NO** to close the box.

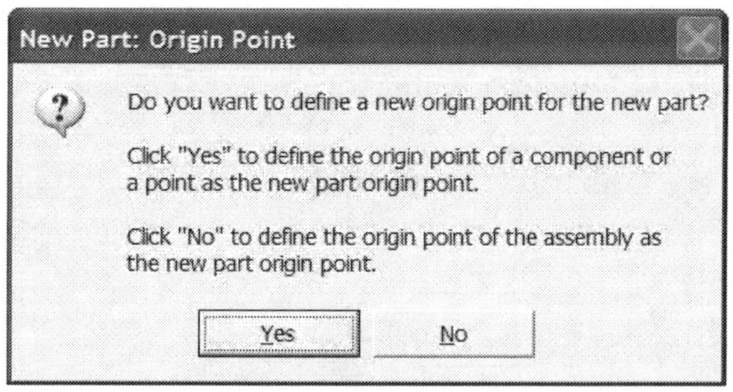


Change the default name to **brass_disk**.
The tree, after the name change, is displayed below. Note that the instance name has also been changed to **brass_disk**.

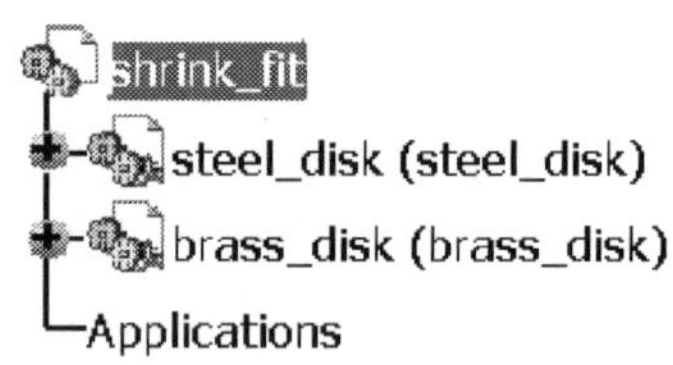


Double-click on the **brass_disk** branch in the tree so that it is highlighted in blue, as shown on the right. This lands you in the **Part Design** workbench.

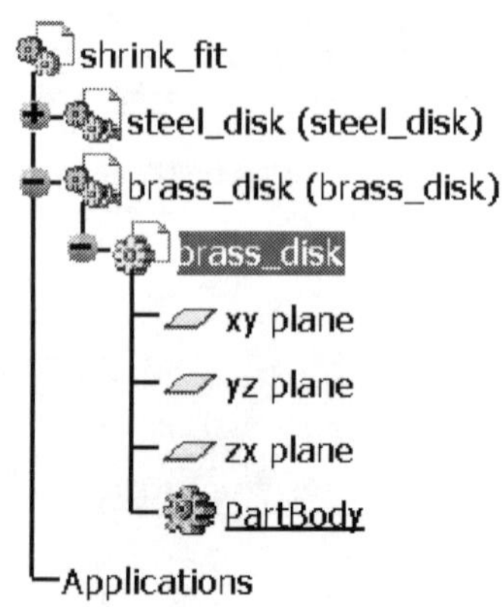


Select the **xy** plane from **brass_disk** and enter the **Sketcher**.

In the **Sketcher**, draw two concentric circles centered at the origin with radii 1 in. and 2 in. respectively.

Leave the **Sketcher**.

Use the **Pad** icon to create a hollow disk of height 1 in.

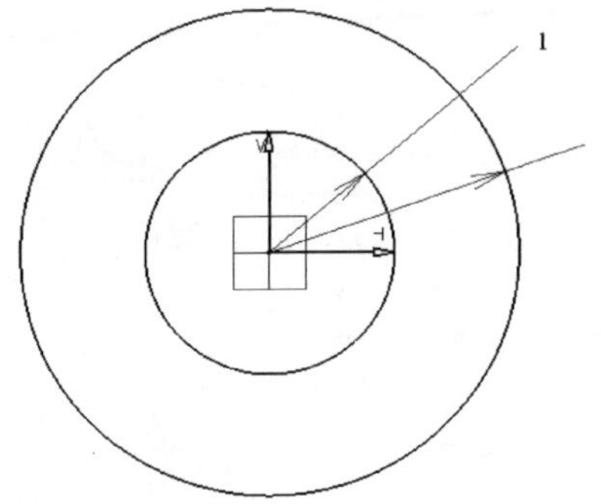


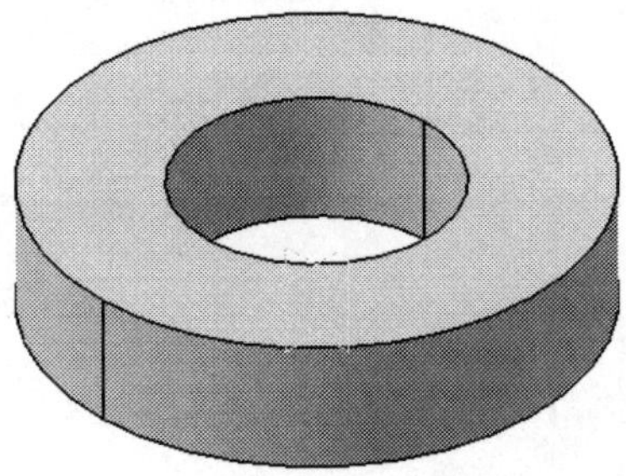

Select the **Apply Material** icon to activate the material **Library** box below.
Use the **Metal** tab on the top; select **Steel**. Use your cursor to pick the **steel_disk** from the tree at which time the **OK** and **Apply Material** buttons can be selected. Close the box.
The material property is now reflected in the tree.

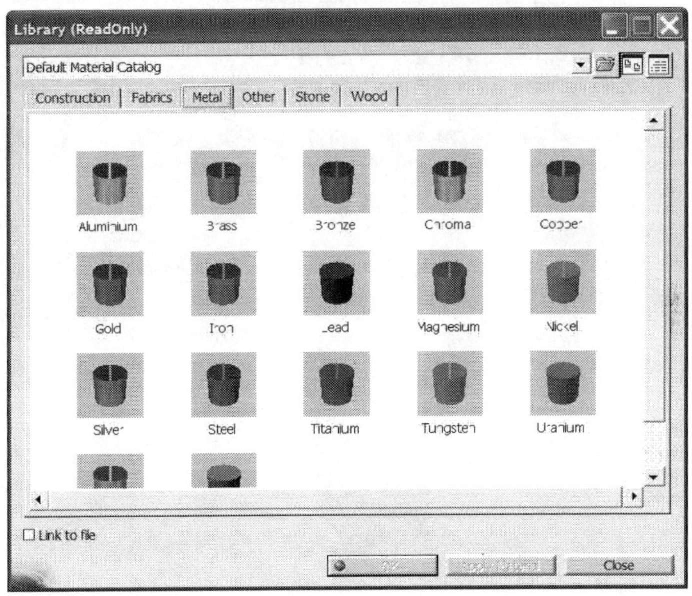


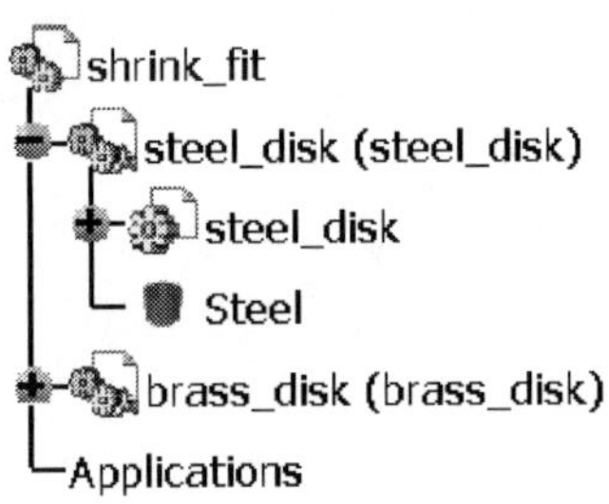


To check the default material properties for steel, double-click on the **Steel** branch in the tree. After a long pause, the pop box for steel properties appears.

Select the analysis tab to read the default values. Since the Young's modulus and the Poisson ratio do not correspond to the data provided, edit them to match the given values. The boxes for default and edited values are shown on the next page.

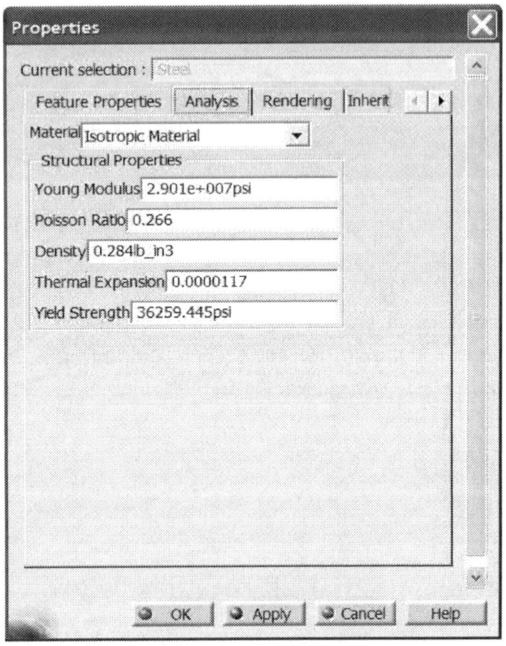


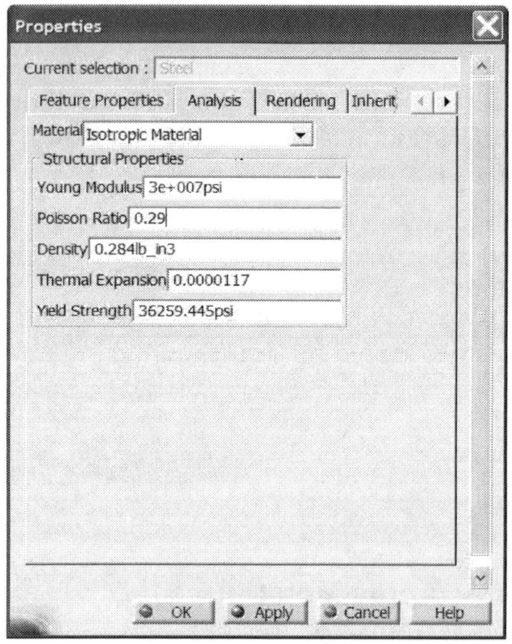


Repeat the same process to apply bras propertied to **brass_disk**.
The boxes for default and edited values are shown below.

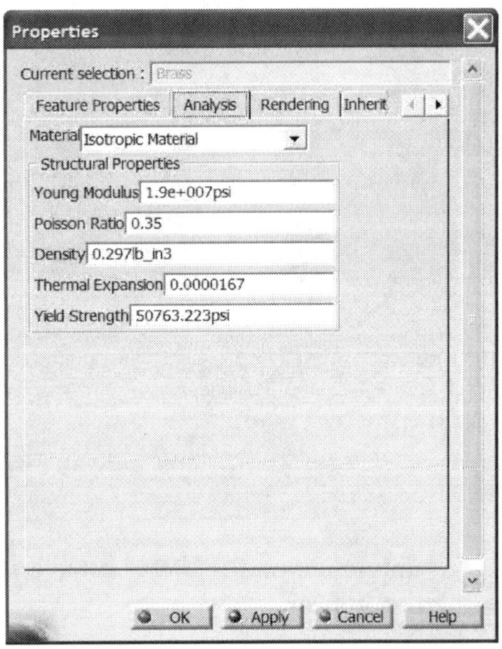


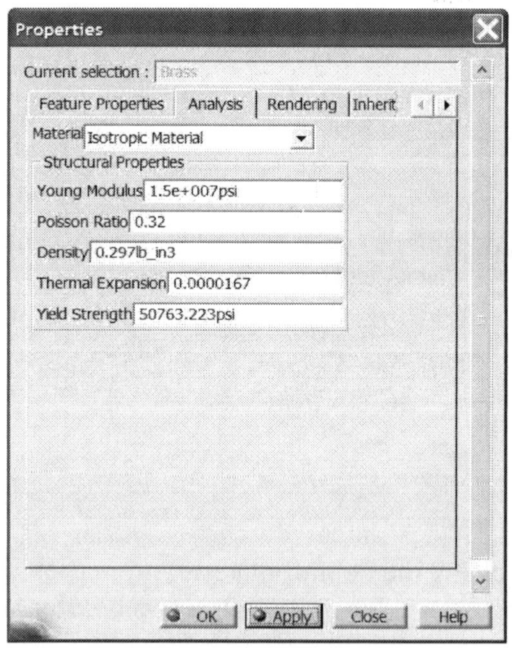


The tree, immediately after material properties have been assigned, is shown on the right.

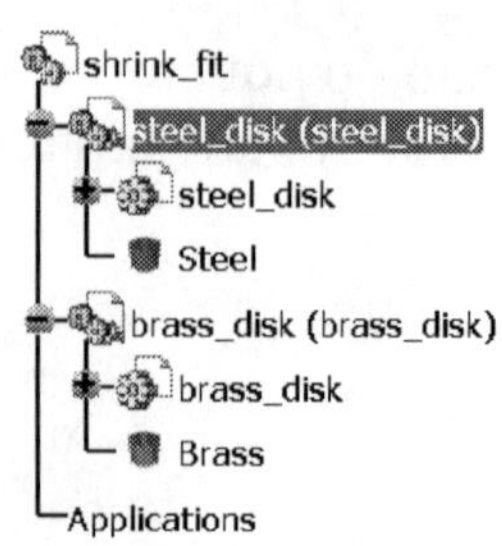

If the assembly does not look "shiny", you can change the rendering style from the **View mode** toolbar 

.

Next choose the **Shading with Material** icon .
This action results in a different rendering displayed below.

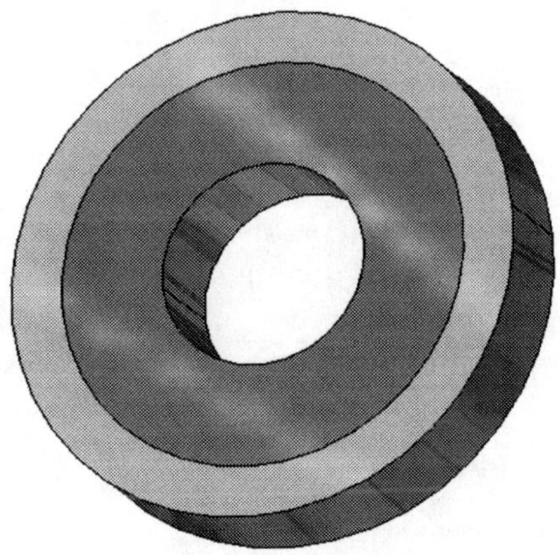

Because of the construction method, the two parts are already positioned correctly and there is no need to apply assembly constraints. The key in this happening was to center all the circles at the origin of the **Sketcher**.

## 3 Entering the Analysis Solutions

From the standard Windows toolbar, select

**Start > Analysis & Simulation > Generative Structural Analysis** 

The box shown below, **New Analysis Case** is visible on the screen. The default choice is **Static Analysis** which is precisely what we intend to use. Therefore, close the box by clicking on **OK**.

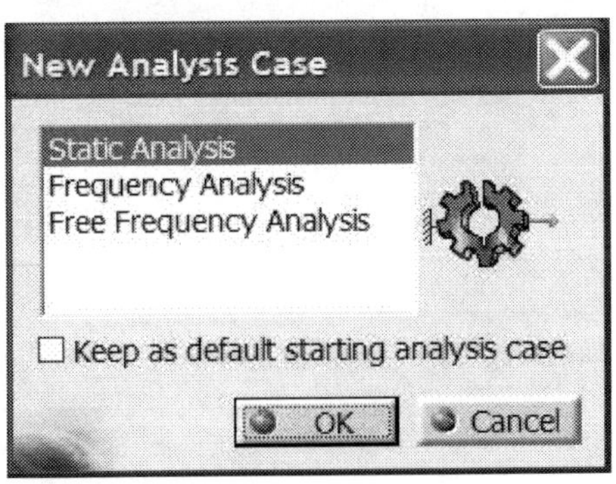

Note that the tree structure gets considerably longer. The bottom branches of the tree are presently "unfilled", and as we proceed in this workbench, assign loads and restraints, the branches gradually get "filled".

Another point that cannot be missed is the appearance of icons on each part that reflect a representative "size" and "sag".
This is displayed in the figure below.

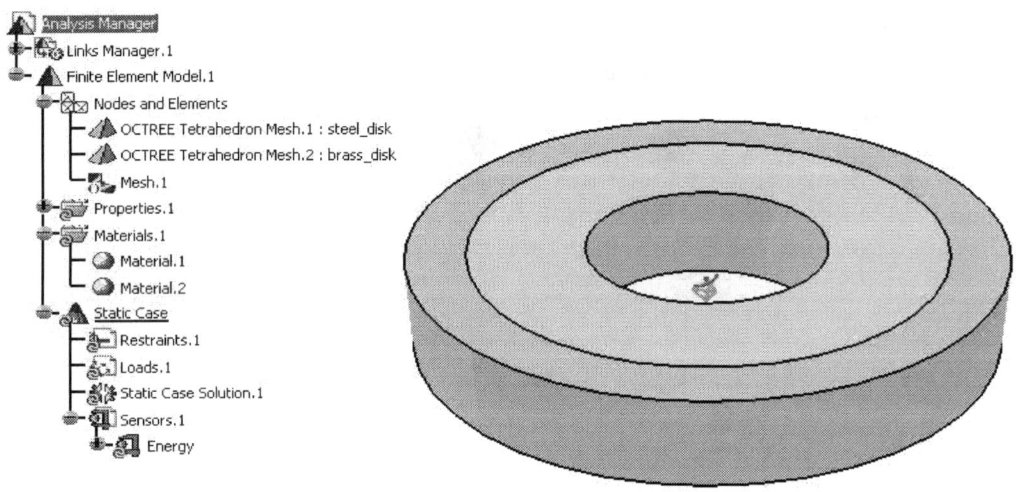


Double-clicking on the branch labeled **OCTREE Tetrahedron Mesh.1** shown below.

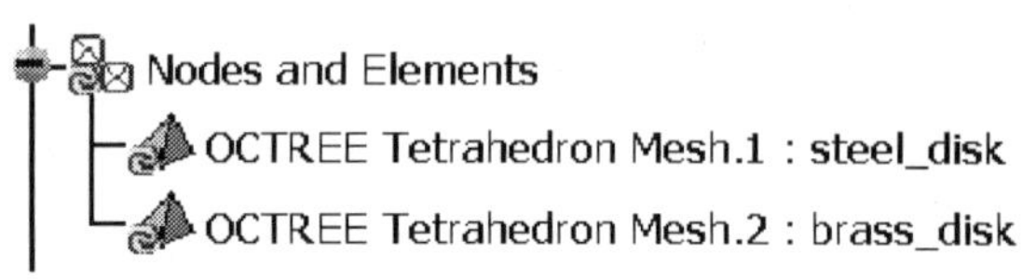


In the pop up box, edit the default "size" and "sag" values to match the numbers shown below.

Repeat the same thing for **OCTREE Tetrahedron Mesh.2** and use same numbers on the right.

Clearly, the default mesh is too coarse.

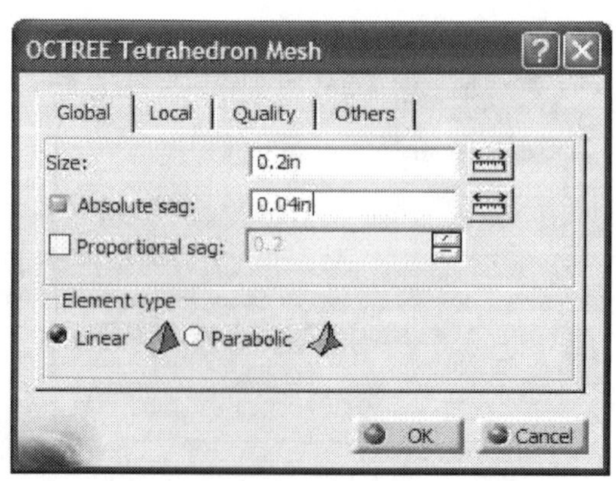

In order to view the generated mesh, you can point the cursor to the branch **Nodes and Elements**, right-click and select **Mesh Visualization**. See Note #2 in Appendix I. This step may be slightly different in some UNIX machines. Upon performing this operation a **Warning** box appears which can be ignored by selecting **OK**. For the mesh parameters used, the mesh shown below is displayed on the screen.

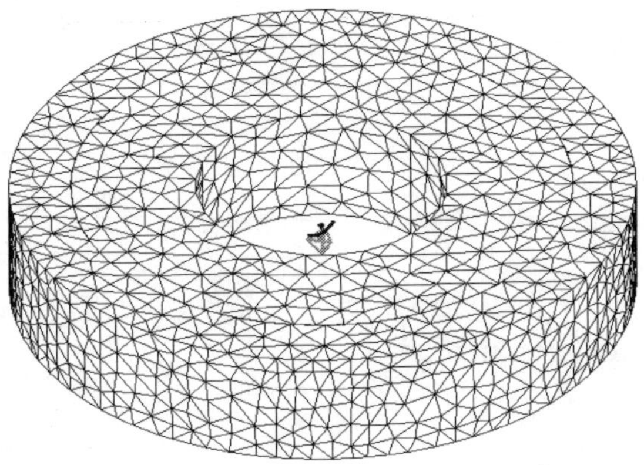

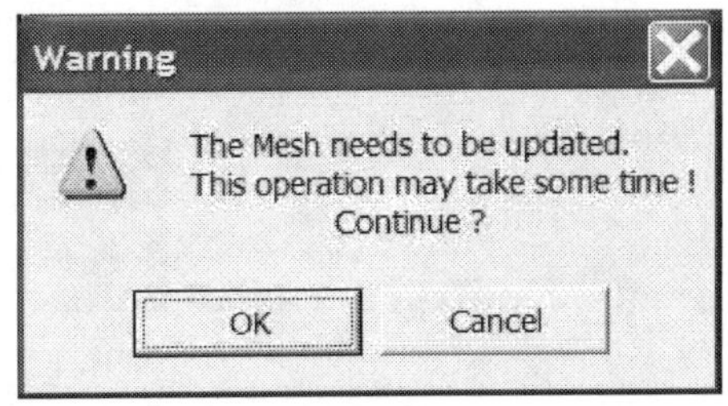


The representative "size" and "sag" icons can be removed from the display by simply pointing to them, right-click and select **Hide**. This is the standard process for hiding any entity in CATIA V5.

**Applying Restraints:**

CATIA's FEA module is geometrically based. This means that the boundary conditions cannot be applied to nodes and elements. The boundary conditions can only be applied at the part level. As soon as you enter the **Generative Structural Analysis** workbench, the parts are automatically hidden. Therefore, before boundary conditions are applied, the part must be brought to the unhide mode. This can be carried out by pointing the cursor to the top of the tree, the **Links Manager.1** branch, right-click, select **Show**. At this point, the parts and the mesh are superimposed as shown below and you have access to the part.

The formulas presented at the beginning of the chapter actually correspond to long cylinders. In order to compare the CATIA results to these formulas, we have to impose the roller boundary conditions to the top and the bottom surfaces of the disks.

If, the presence of the mesh is annoying, you can always hide it. Point the cursor to **Nodes and Elements**, right-click, **Hide**.

In CATIA V5 roller supports are easily modeled by the **Surface Slider** icon .

From the **Restraint** toolbar 

select the **Surface Slider** icon .

The corresponding box shown below opens and for **Supports** you can select the four surfaces of the bottom and the top of the disks as indicated.

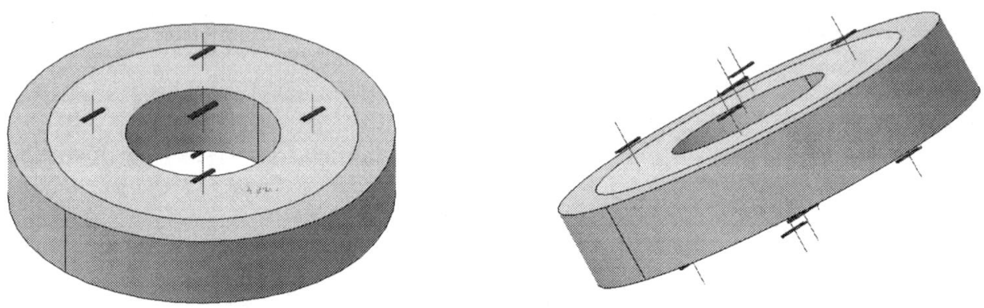

**Creating Analysis Connection:**

Use the **General Analysis Connection** icon 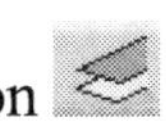 from the **Analysis Supports** toolbar 

.

For **First component**, select the inside face of the steel disk (outer disk). This may be difficult to do because of interference from the inside disk. To fix this problem, you can temporarily hide the inner disk.

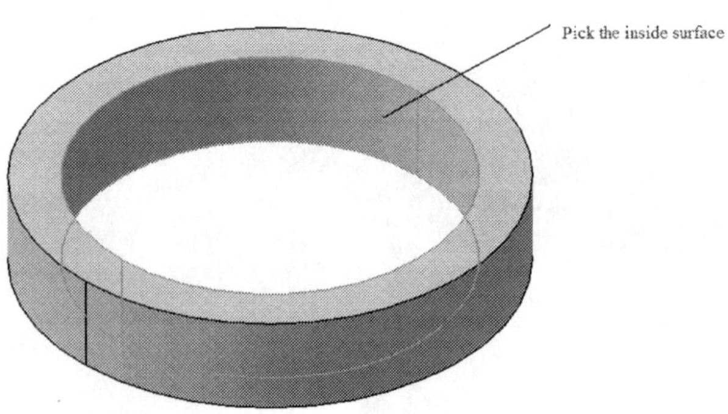


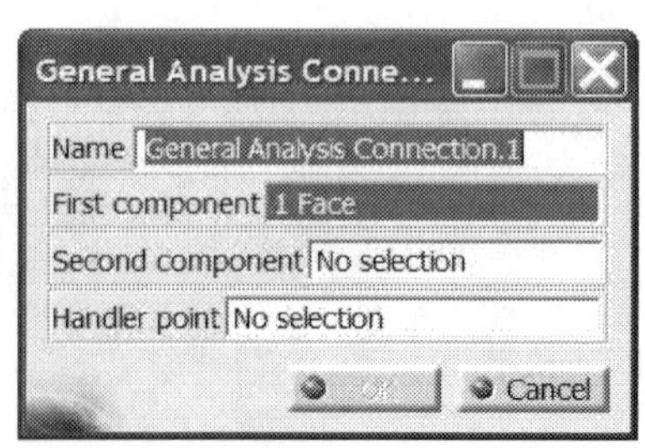

Then **Hide** the outside disk and bring the inside disk into the **Show** mode.
For **Second component**, select the outside surface of the inside disk.

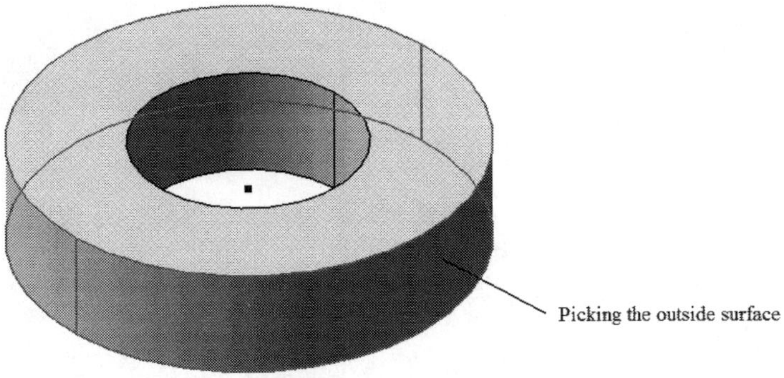


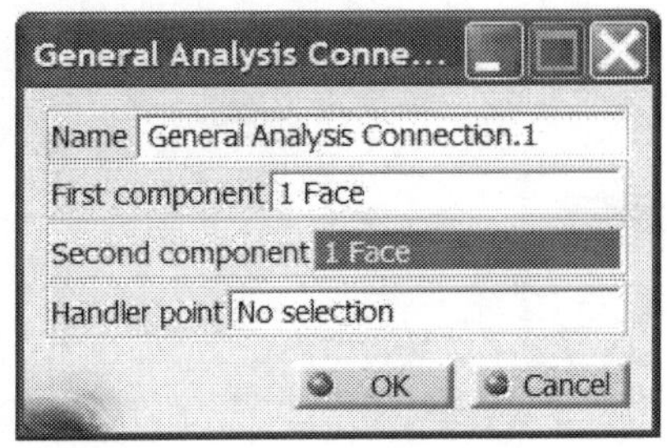


The tree is modified to reflect the creation of the **Analysis Connection**.

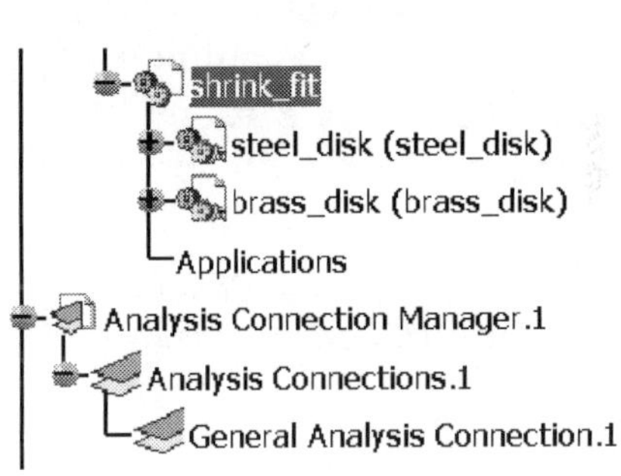


Select the **Pressure Fitting Connection property** icon  from the **Face Face Connections** toolbar 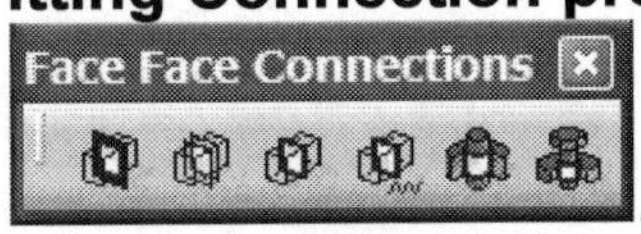

. In the pop up box, for **Supports**, select the **General Analysis Connection.1** created above. This can be selected from the tree or the screen.
For **Overlap** use .001 which is the <u>half</u> of the diametral interference.

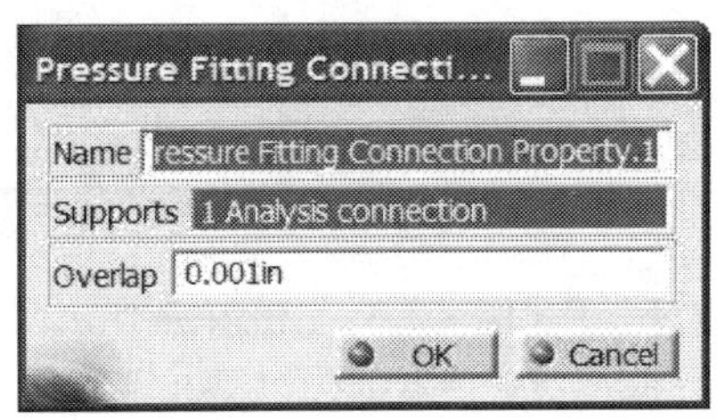


The **Pressure Fit** icon appears on your screen, as displayed below.

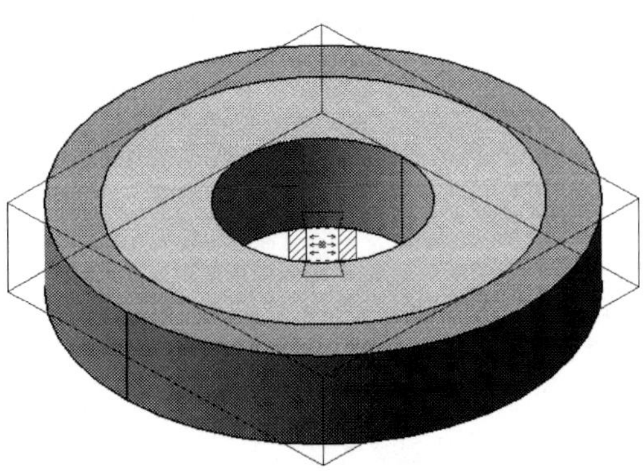

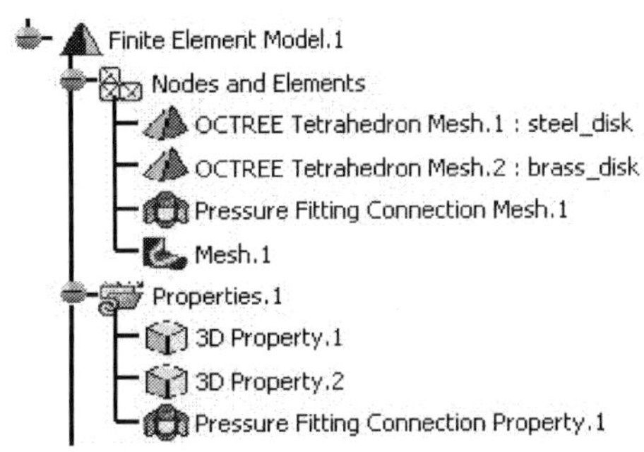

It seems that all restraints have been applied and that the program should run. This is not case as will be seen shortly. There is one further non-obvious restraint that needs to be applied.

**Launching the Solver:**

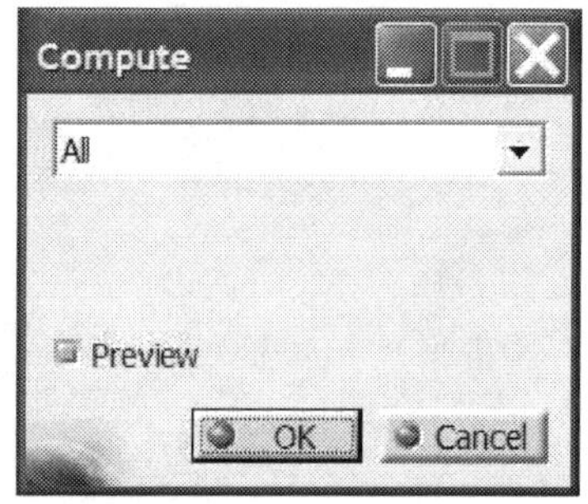


To run the analysis, you need to use the **Compute** toolbar  by selecting the **Compute** icon . This leads to the **Compute** box shown to the right. Leave the defaults as **All** which means everything is computed.
Upon closing this box, after a brief pause, the second box shown below appears. This box provides information on the resources needed to complete the analysis.
If the estimates are zero in the listing, then there is a problem in the previous step and should be looked into. If all the numbers are zero in the box, the program may run but would not produce any useful results.

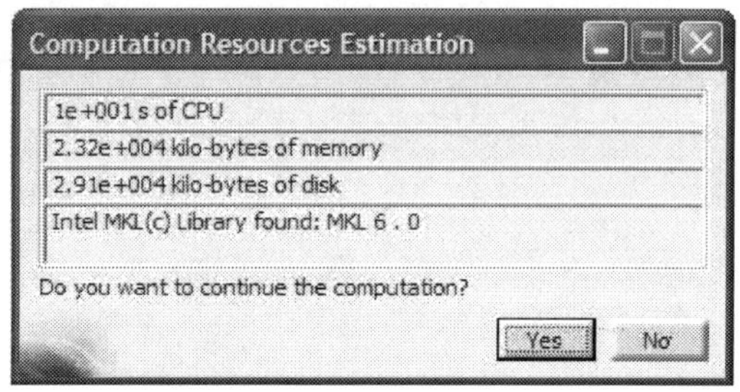


This run terminates with the following **Error** box.

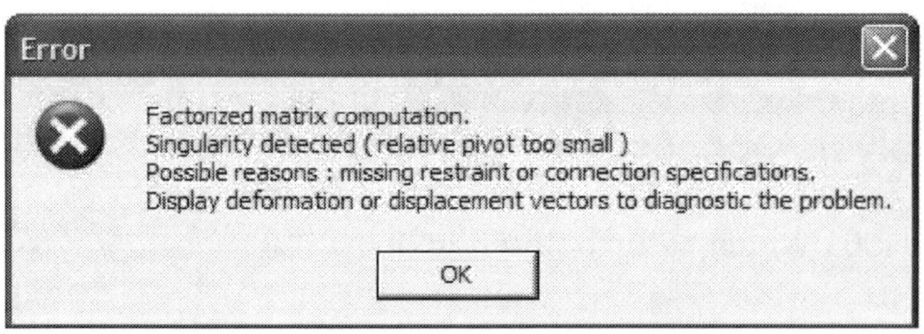


Usually this box implies that the assembly is not fully restrained. In our model, the entire assembly is free to translate in the "xy" plane. Some commercial packages rectify the situation by adding a small artificial stiffness, preventing the rigid body motion. In those packages, effectively they add a "soft" spring in the appropriate direction, resulting in a stiffness.

You will be preventing rigid body motion by clamping one point. The difficulty is that, these disks do not possess vertices that can be picked.

To counteract this problem, you can create a **Smooth Virtual Part** and use its **Handler** to apply the clamp condition.

## Creating a Smooth Virtual Part:

Select the **Smooth Virtual Part** icon 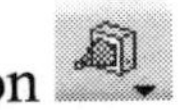 from the **Virtual Part** toolbar .


The resulting popup box is shown on the right. For **Supports**, pick the top surface of the inside (or outside) disk. If the **Handler** is not selected, a default **Handler** is created.

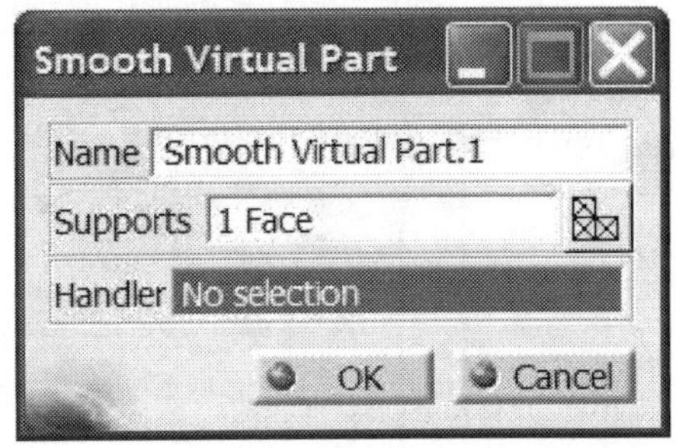


Default "Handler" created at the midpoint of this line

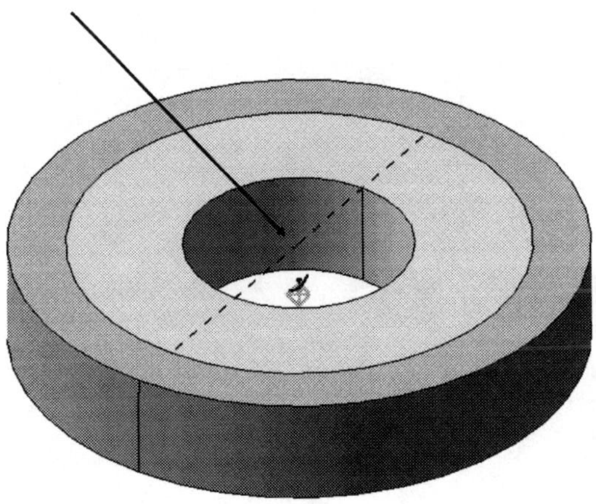

Select the **Clamp** icon  and pick the **Handler** of the **Smooth Virtual Part** created.

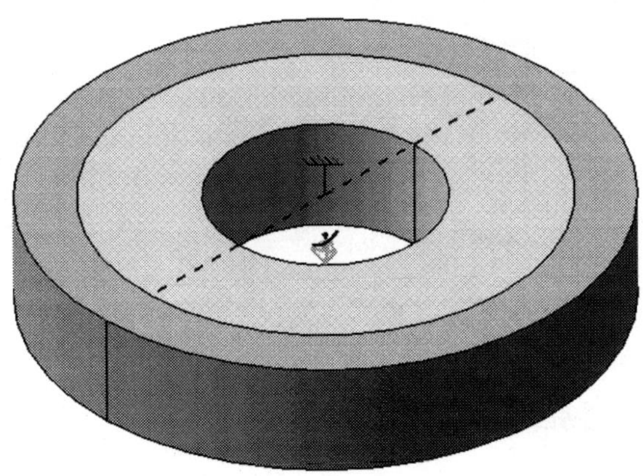

Now press on  to run the problem. This time, the run completes without an error.

The complete tree before running is shown in the next page. It gives you an idea of how the different components are located.

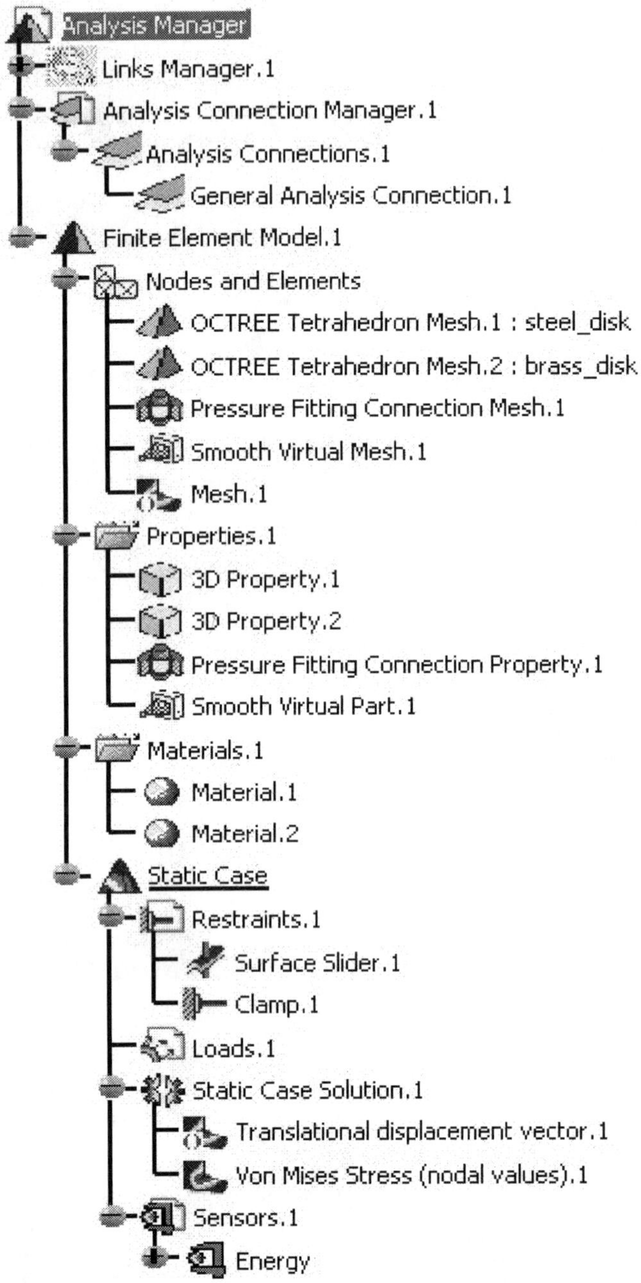
Analysis Manager
Links Manager.1
Analysis Connection Manager.1
Analysis Connections.1
General Analysis Connection.1
Finite Element Model.1
Nodes and Elements
OCTREE Tetrahedron Mesh.1 : steel_disk
OCTREE Tetrahedron Mesh.2 : brass_disk
Pressure Fitting Connection Mesh.1
Smooth Virtual Mesh.1
Mesh.1
Properties.1
3D Property.1
3D Property.2
Pressure Fitting Connection Property.1
Smooth Virtual Part.1
Materials.1
Material.1
Material.2
Static Case
Restraints.1
Surface Slider.1
Clamp.1
Loads.1
Static Case Solution.1
Translational displacement vector.1
Von Mises Stress (nodal values).1
Sensors.1
Energy

## Postprocessing:

The main postprocessing toolbar is called **Image** 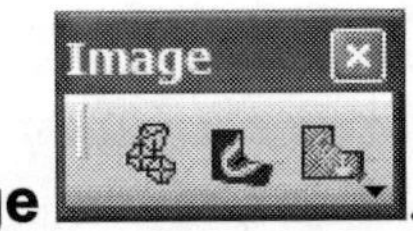

. To view the deformed shape you have to use the **Deformation** icon 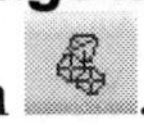. The resulting deformed shape is displayed below.

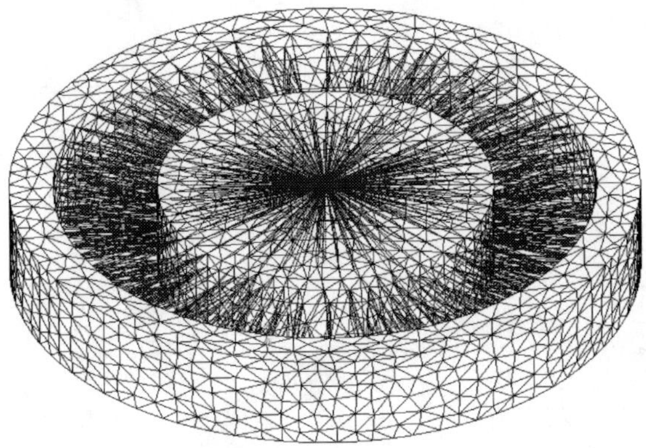

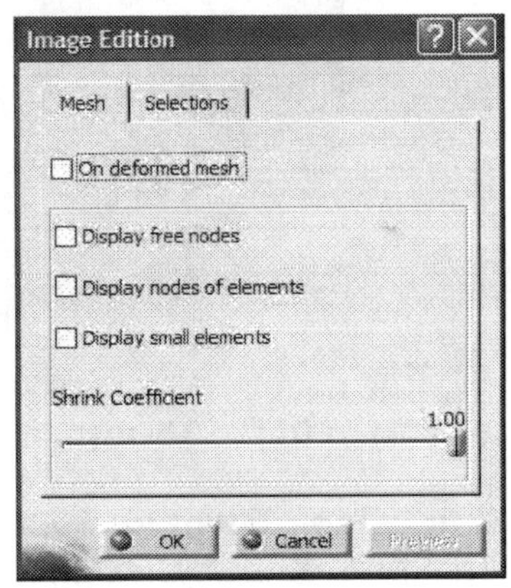


This display is difficult to interpret.
Double-click on the deformation plot. The pop up box shown on the right appears. Uncheck the entry **Display on deformed mesh**.

The plot changes as shown.

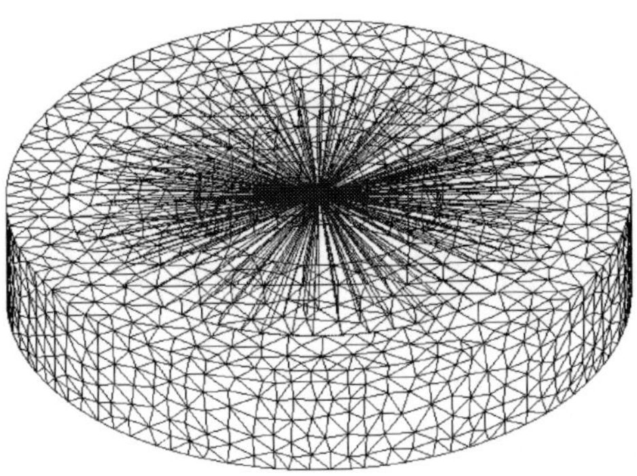

The lines shown in these figures are because of the **Pressure Fitting Connections**. Of course, they can be hidden the usual way.

In order to see the displacement field, the **Displacement** icon  in the **Image** toolbar should be used. The default display is in terms of displacement arrows.

The arrow plot is not particularly useful. In order to view the contour plot of the displacement field, position the cursor on the arrow field and double-click. The **Image Edition** box shown on the right opens.

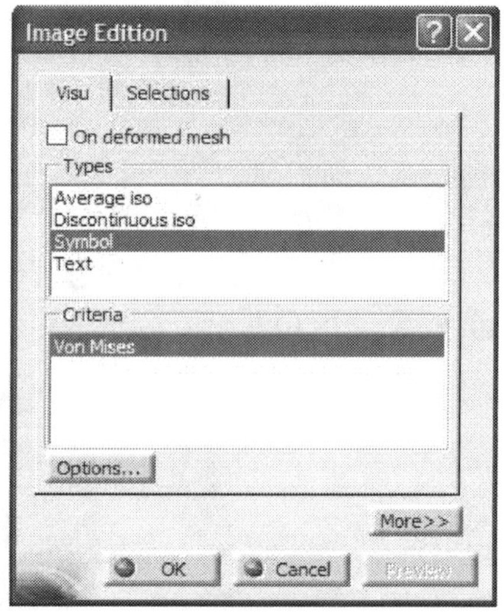


The contour of the displacement field is given below.

Note: The color map has been changed; otherwise everything looks black in the figure.

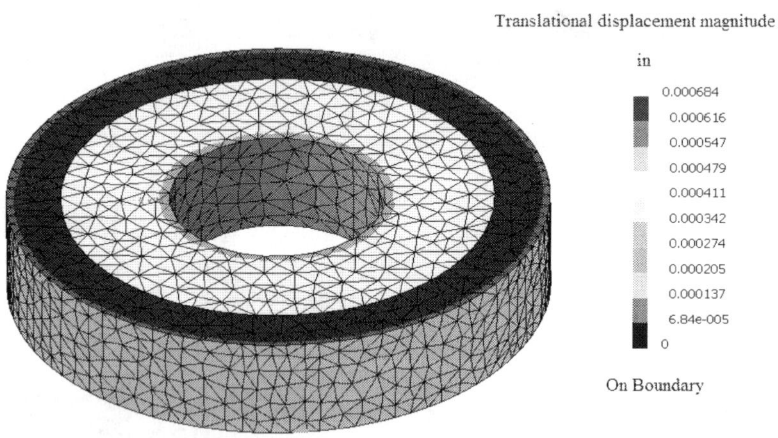


The next step in the postprocessing is to plot the contours of the von Mises stress using the **von Mises Stress** icon in the **Image** toolbar.
The resulting contour of von Mises stress is displayed below.

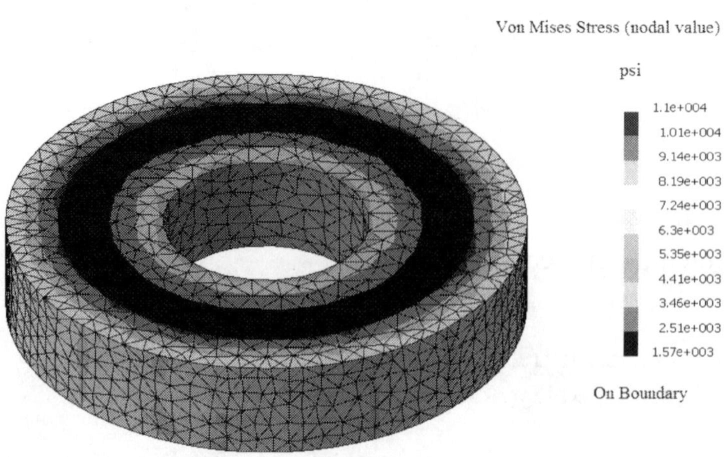

The principal stresses are postprocessed next.

From the **Image** toolbar 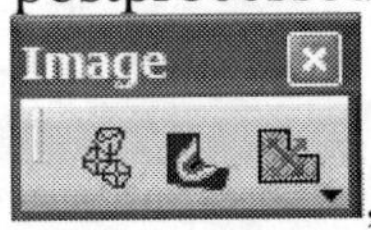

, select the **Principal Stress** icon 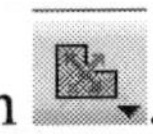. The result is the principal stress directions in the vector form as displayed on your screen. Due to the large number of arrows, the interpretation of this plot is difficult. You can therefore switch to a different style of plotting. Double-click on the arrows on the screen to open the **Image Edition** box on the right and select **AVERAGE-ISO**.

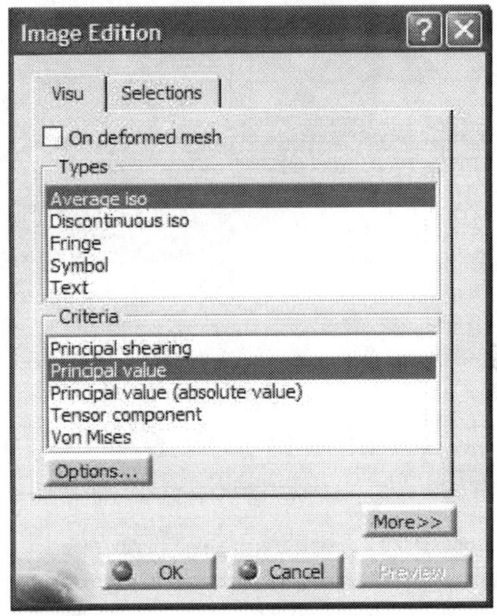


Next, use the **More** button and choose the **C33** as the component. This results in the contour of the smallest principal stress as displayed below.

Keep in mind that CATIA uses C11, C22, and C33 to represent the largest, intermediate, and smallest principal stresses.

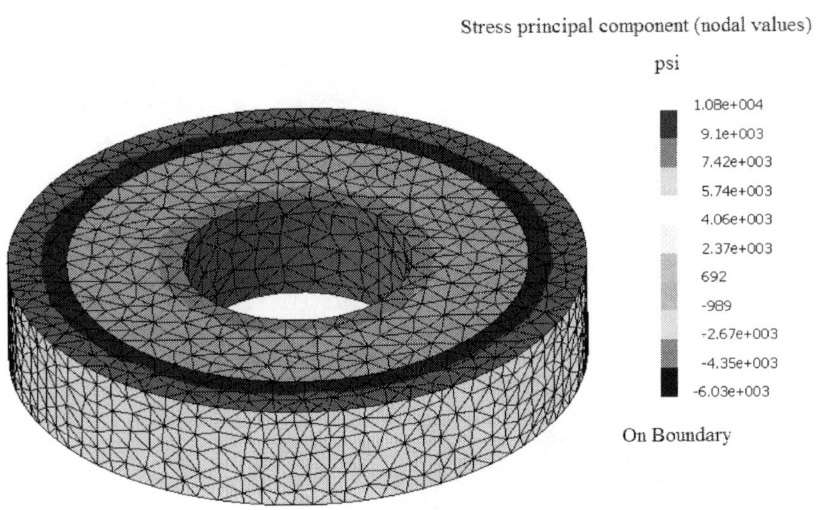


Note that using the **Selections** tab in the **Image Edition** box, the two disks can be handled separately. The stress C22 is plotted on the next page. Both the hoop and radial stress agree well with the formulas presented earlier. CATIA's predicted contact pressure is 1900 psi which is almost identical to the analytical estimate.

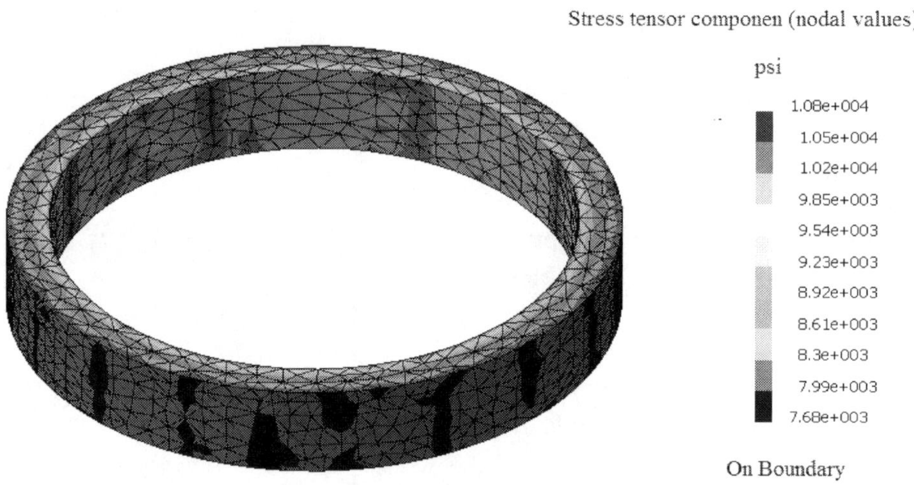


The **Cutting Plane** icon  from the **Analysis Tools** toolbar

can be used to make a cut through the part at a desired location and inspect the stresses inside of the part. The **Cut Plane** box allows you to keep the plane or to remove it for display purposes. A typical cutting plane is shown below.

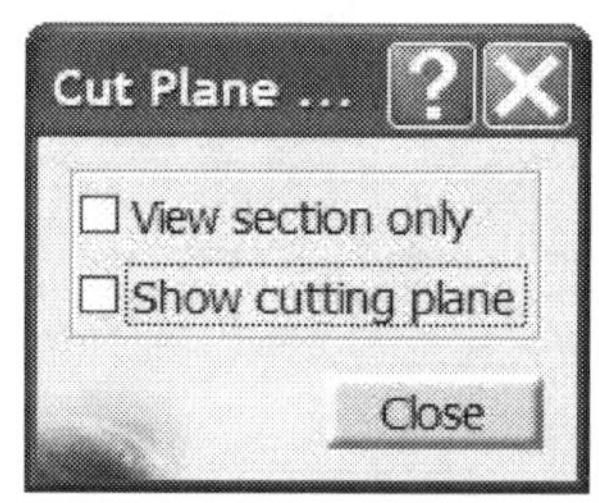


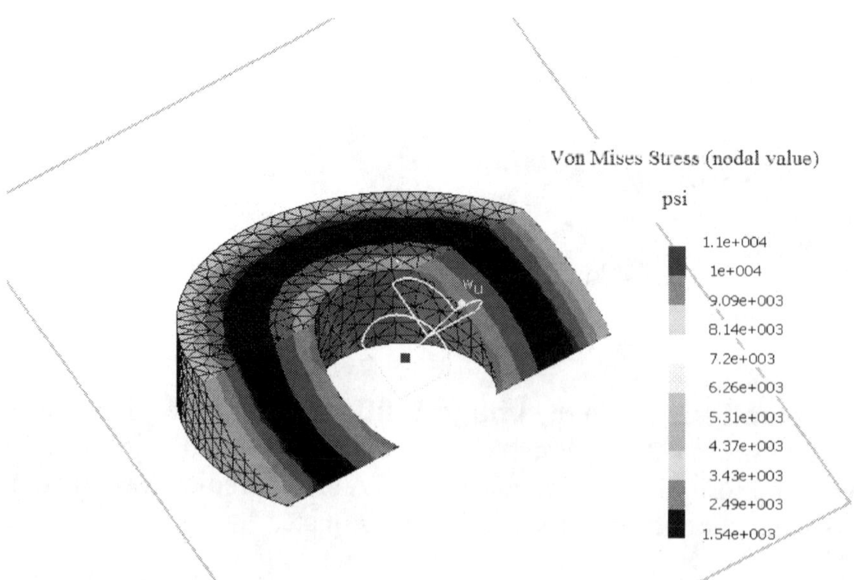

At this point we have generated two plots. The displacement and the von Mises stress contours which can be displayed individually. However, CATIA also allows you to show both plots side by side.

First make sure that both images to be plotted are active in the tree. If not, point to the graph in the tree, right-click, select **Active**.

Click the **Image Layout** icon  from the **Image Analysis** toolbar. The **Images** box, shown to the right, asks you to specify the direction along which the two plots are expected to be aligned. The outcome is side-by-side plots shown below.

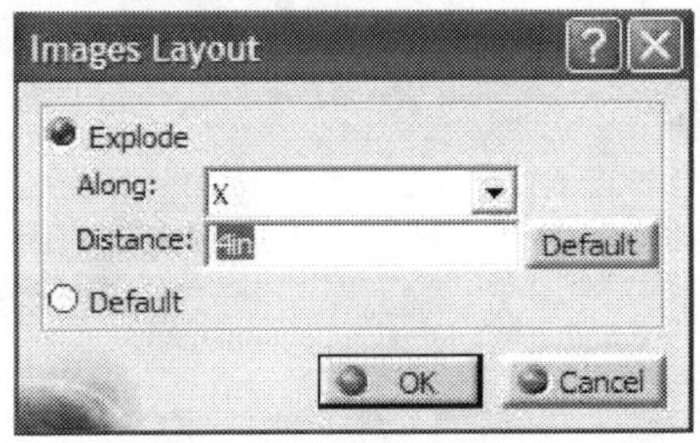


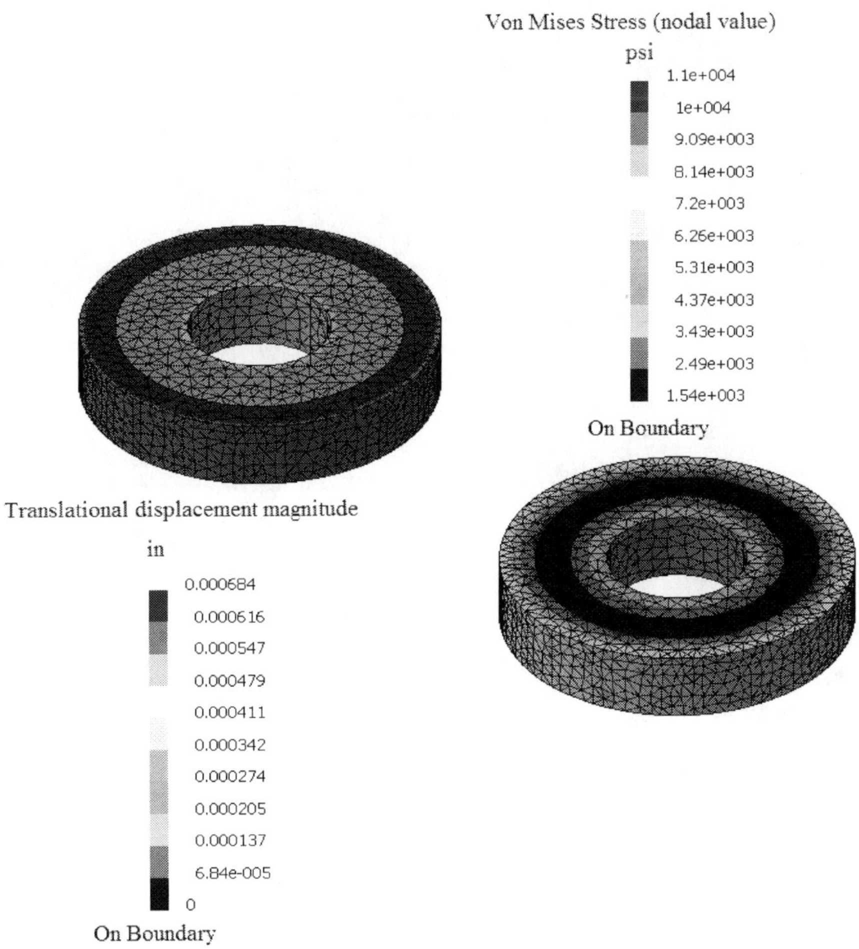

Using the icon **Generate Report**  in the **Analysis Results** toolbar 

an HTML based report can be generated which summarizes the features and results of the FEA model.

Animation of the model can be achieved through the **Animate** icon  in the **Analysis Tools** toolbar 

. An AVI file can easily be generated.

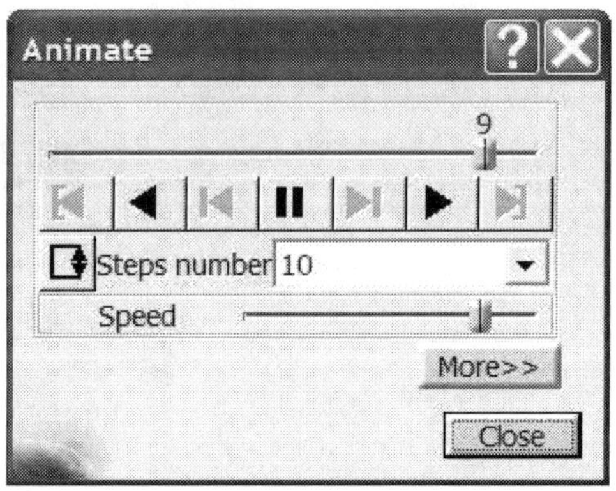

# Exercises for Chapter 15

## Problem 1: Two Rotating Shrink Fitted Disks

The disk with inside radius of 1 in. and outside radius of 6 in. is shrink fitted onto a solid shaft of radius 1.003 in. Both of these components are made of steel with Young's Modulus 30E6 psi and Poisson ratio 0.29. The specific weight of steel is .284 lb/in$^3$. Assuming that the assembly rotates at 5000 rpm, use CATIA to predict the stress distribution in the disk.

Partial Answer:

The contact pressure is 40830 psi and the expressions for the stress distribution in the disk are given by the following formulas.

$$\sigma_{radial} = 4232 - \frac{39017}{r^2} - 82.9r^2$$

$$\sigma_{hoop} = 4232 + \frac{39017}{r^2} - 47.1r^2$$

# NOTES:

# Chapter 16

# Analysis of a Tensile Specimen as an Assembly

## Introduction

In this tutorial, you will analyze a tensile specimen consisting of a block and two pins. The structure is analyzed as an assembly with three interacting parts. Contact conditions are established in the finite element model. A reaction sensor is used to determine the force needed to cause a prescribed deformation.

## 1 Problem Statement

The assembly, shown below, consists of two steel pins and an aluminum block with the dimensions displayed. The end faces of the bottom pin are clamped. However, the end faces of the top pin are given a displacement of 0.01 in causing the block to stretch. The objective is to find the necessary force causing this deformation and predict the stresses in the structure.

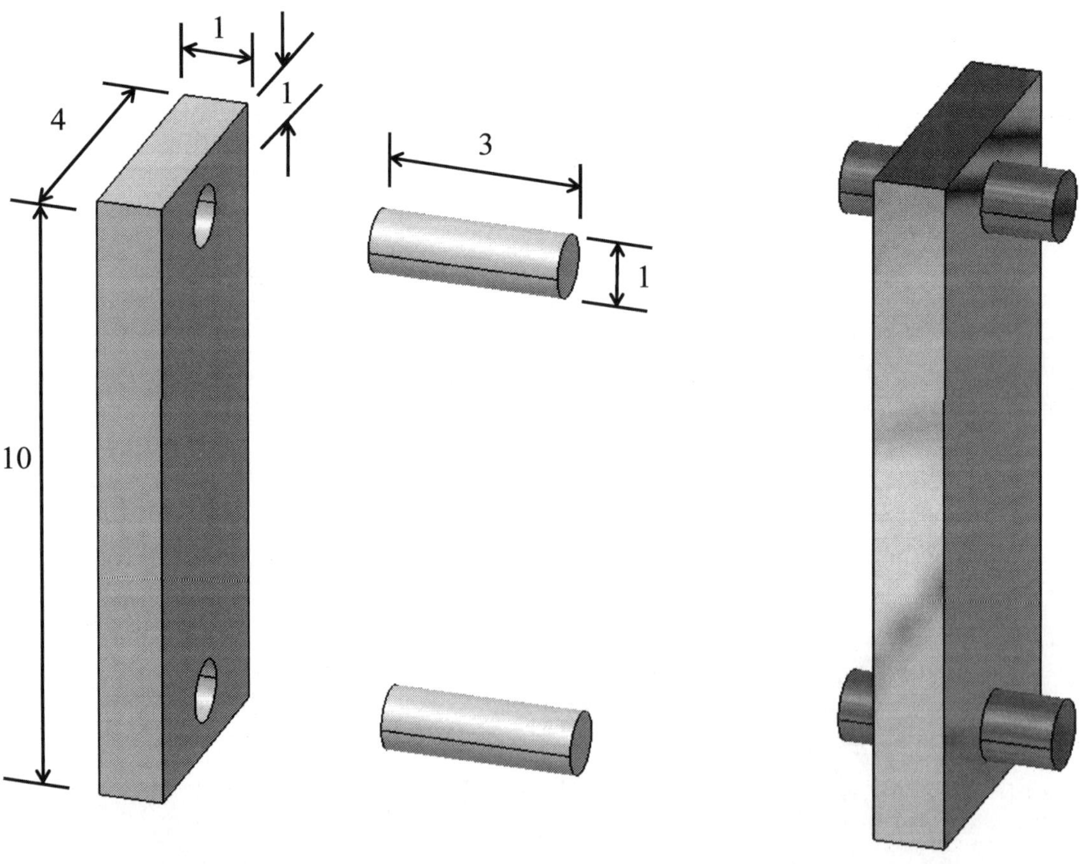

# 2 Creation of the Assembly in the Mechanical Design Solutions

Enter the **Assembly Design** workbench which can be achieved by different means depending on your CATIA customization. For example, from the standard Windows toolbar, select **File > New**.
From the box shown on the right, select **Product**. This moves you to the **Assembly Design** workbench and creates a part with the default name **Product.1**.
See Note #1 in Appendix I.

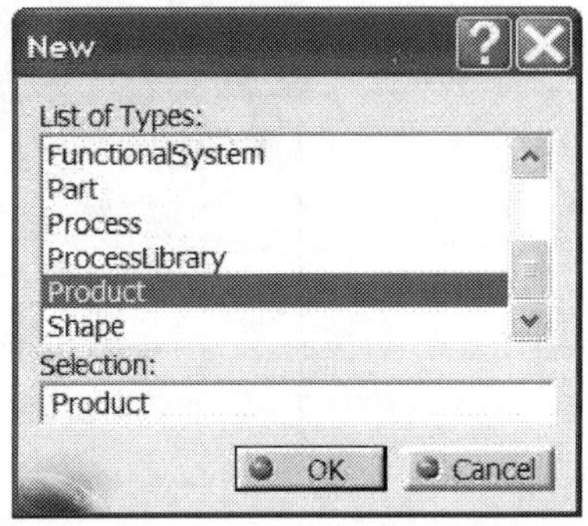


In order to change the default name, move the cursor to **Product.1** in the tree, right-click and select **Properties** from the menu list.

From the **Properties** box, select the **Product** tab and in **Part Number** type **tensile_specimen**.

This will be the new product name throughout the chapter. The tree on the top left corner of your computer screen should look as displayed below.

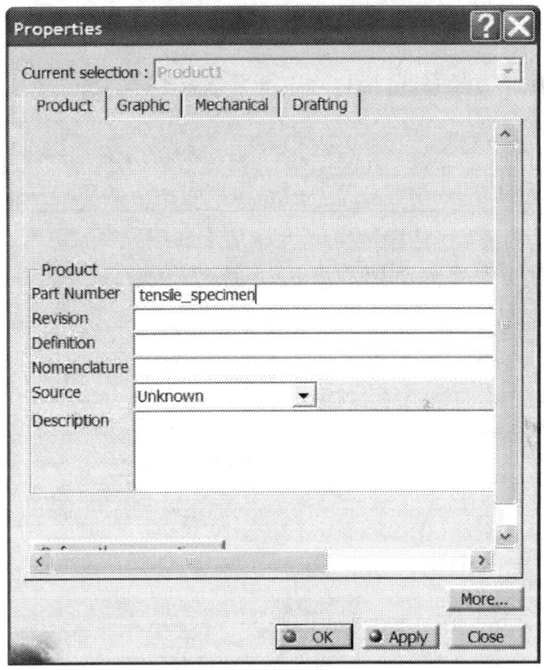


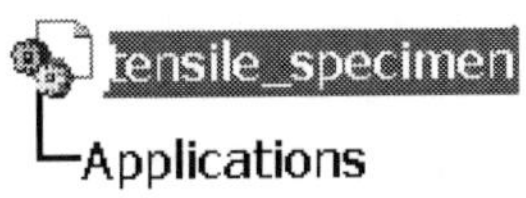


You now create the block as a part.
From the standard Windows toolbar, select **Insert > New Part**. The tree is modified to indicate that **Part.1** has been created. Change the default name to **block**.
The tree, before and after the name change, is displayed below. Note that the instance name has also been changed to **block**.

The process of renaming **Part.1** is just like before. Point the cursor to **Part.1** in the tree, right-click, and select **Properties**. The pop box, after the changes are made is displayed on the next page.

Double-click on the **block** branch in the tree so that it is highlighted in blue.

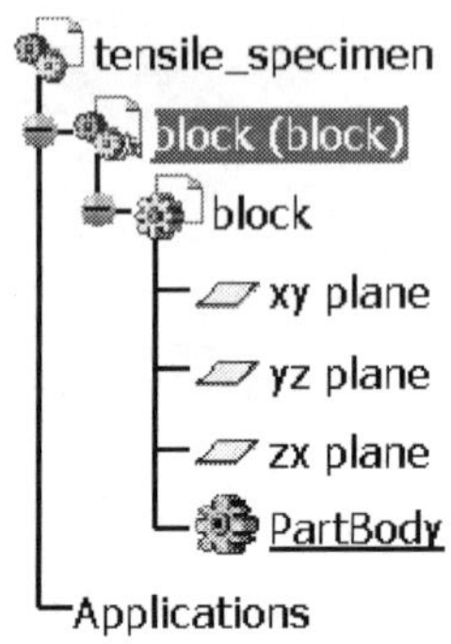


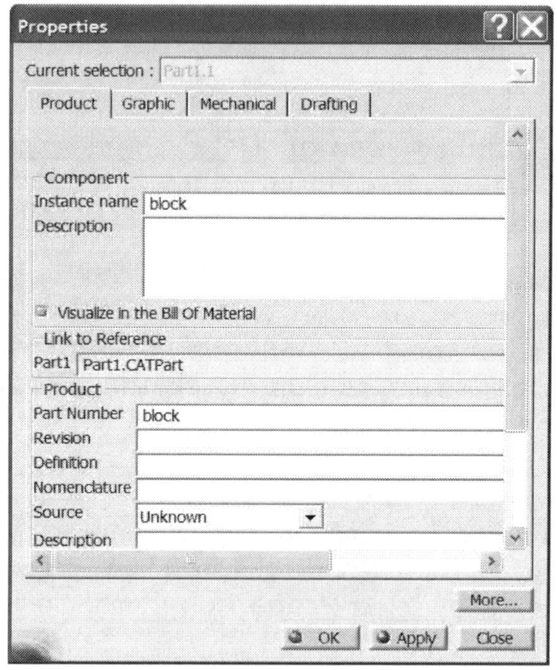


Select the **zx** plane from **block** and switch to the **Part Design** workbench.

In **Part Design**, enter the **Sketcher**.

***In the Sketcher, draw the following profile and dimension as shown. Make sure that the origin is a point of double symmetry, i.e. the rectangle is perfectly symmetric about the point (0,0).***

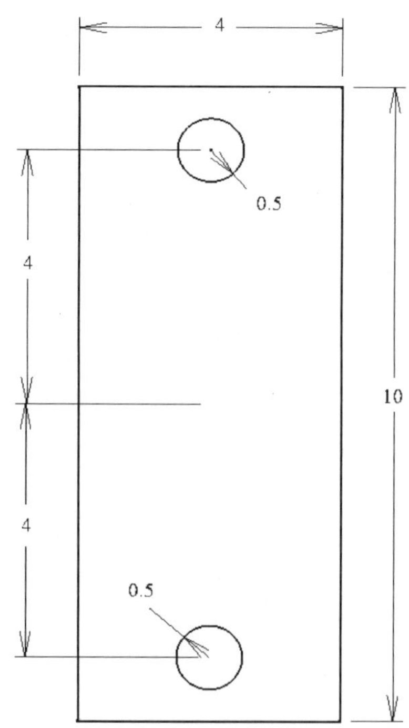


Leave the **Sketcher**.

You will now use the **Pad** operation to extrude the sketch. Upon selecting the **Pad** icon, the **Pad Definition** box shown below opens.

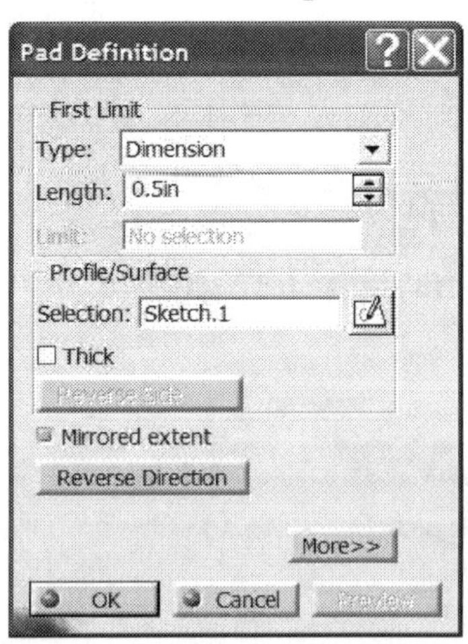


For the **Length** use 0.5, and make sure that the **Mirrored extent** box is selected. The latter feature creates a padded length of 1 in.

Select the **Apply Material** icon  to activate the material **Library** box below.

Use the **Metal** tab on the top; select **Aluminum**. Use your cursor to pick the part on the screen at which time the **OK** and **Apply Material** buttons can be selected. Close the box.
The material property is now reflected in the tree.

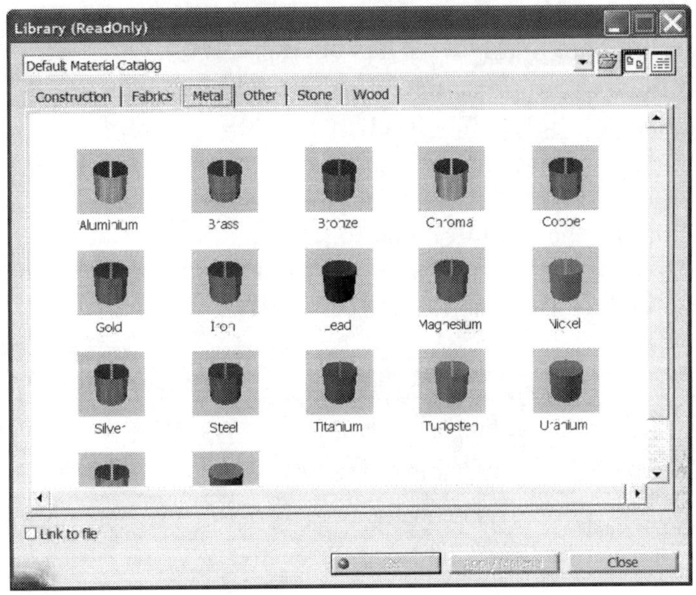


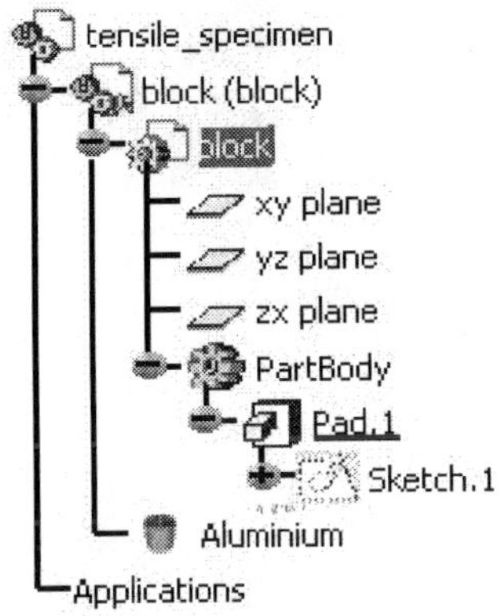


The best way of saving your work is to save the assembly. <u>Double-click on the top branch of the tree</u>. This lands you in the **Assembly Design** workbench.

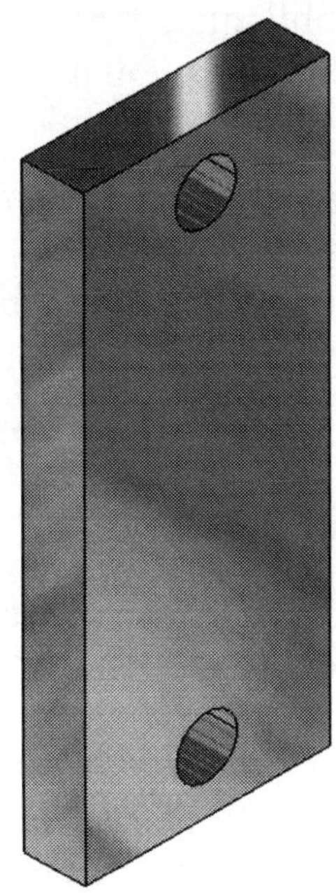

The branch highlights in blue as a confirmation of the new workbench.

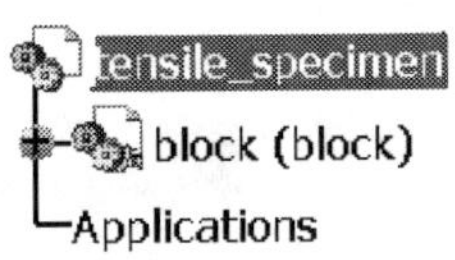


Select the **Save** icon . The **Save As** pop up box indicates that, saving the assembly, activates the saving of the parts. Choose the **Yes** button.

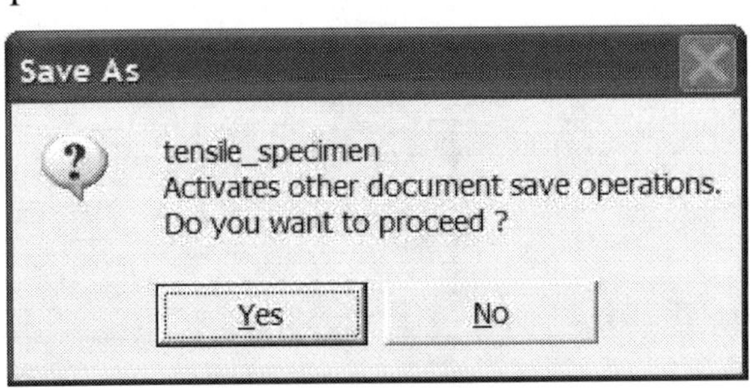

You are now ready to create the pin.

From the standard Windows toolbar, select **Insert > New Part**. The tree is modified to indicate that **Part.2** has been created. You are also presented with pop up box on the right. Select **NO** to close the box.

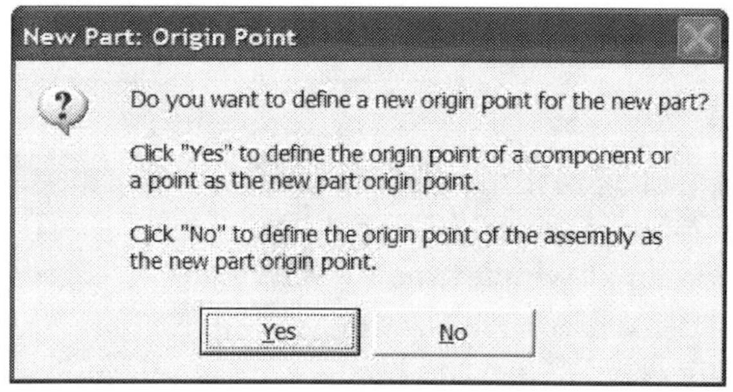


Change the default name to **pin**.
The tree, before and after the name change, is displayed below. Note that the instance name has also been changed to **pin**.

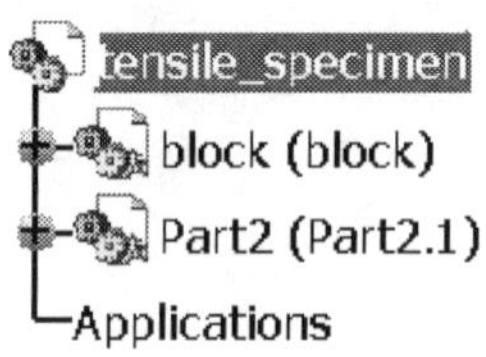


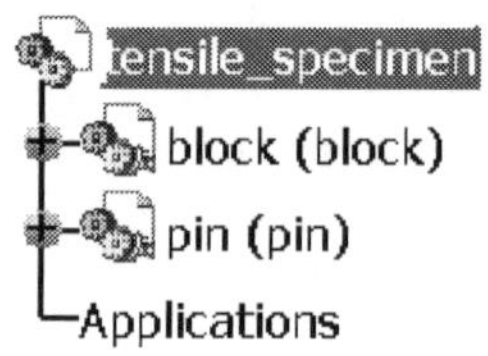


Double-click on the **pin** branch in the tree so that it is highlighted in blue, as shown on the right.
This lands you in the **Part Design** workbench.

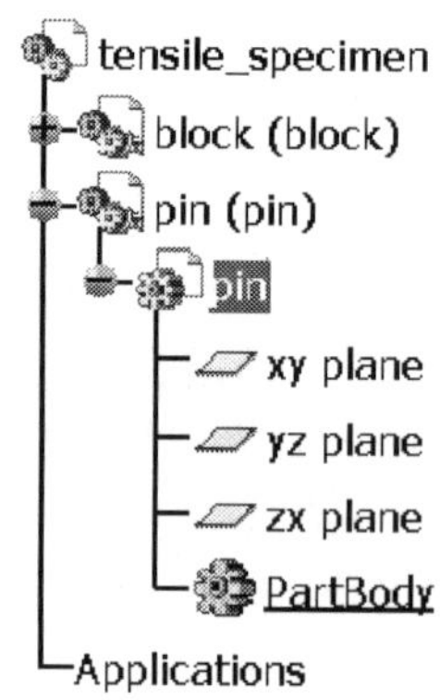


Select the **zx** plane from **pin** and enter the **Sketcher** .

In the **Sketcher**, draw a circle of radius 0.5 ***centered at the origin***.

Leave the **Sketcher** .

You will now use the **Pad** operation to extrude the sketch. Upon selecting the **Pad** icon , the **Pad Definition** box shown below opens.

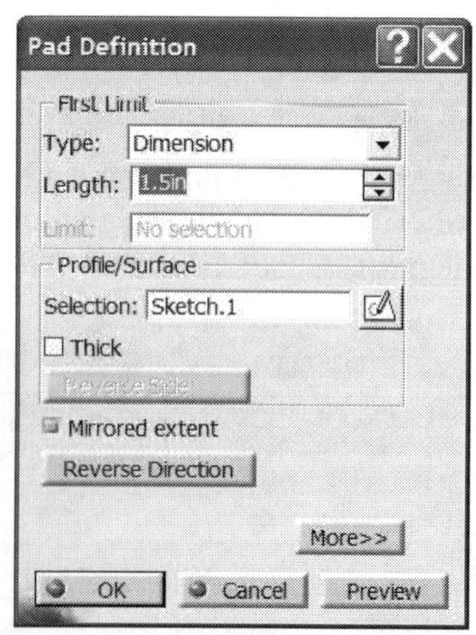


For the **Length** use 1.5, and make sure that the **Mirrored extent** box is selected.
The latter feature creates a padded length of 3 in.

The block and the pin are superimposed but not in the correct position. The assembly constraints will move them into the proper position.

Save the assembly which automatically saves the two parts.

Select the **Apply Material** icon  to assign steel properties to the pin.

At this point, your computer screen resembles the figure shown below.

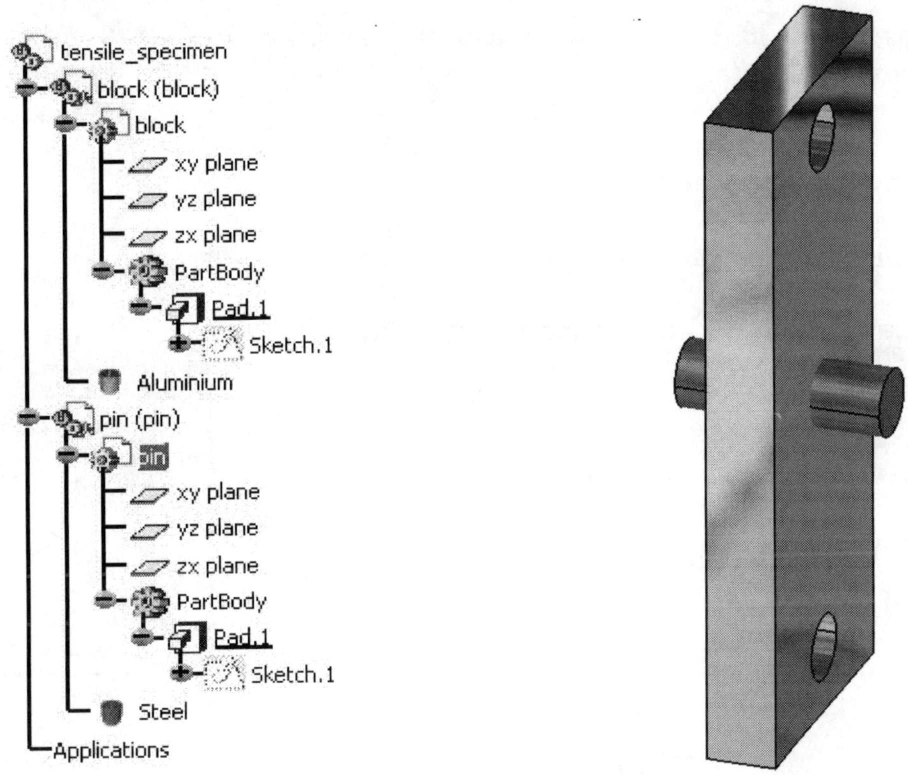


Two pins are needed in the present problem. One option is to create a second pin from scratch. The alternative is, inserting an instance of the pin that was just created. We choose to do the latter.

From the standard Windows toolbar, select **Insert > Existing Component**. The pop up box below opens and allows you to select the part to be inserted. Obviously, you have to select the **pin** and close the window.

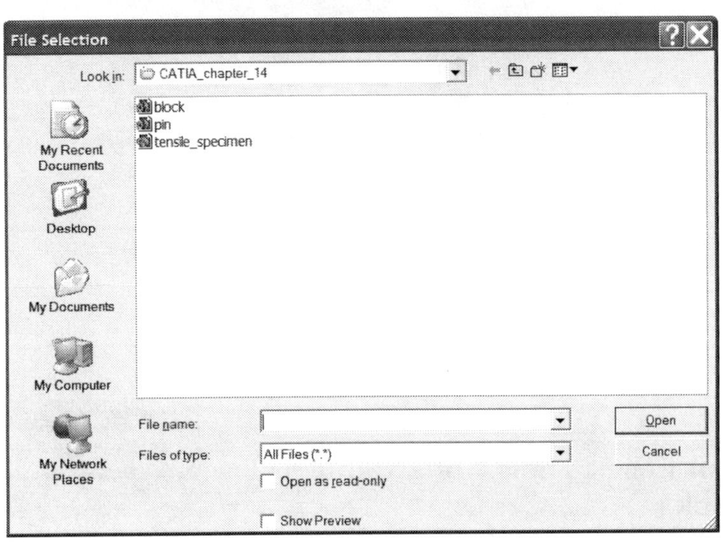

The tree indicates that an instance of the pin has been created. However, you can see only one pin on your computer screen.
***Note: Apply material to the inserted pin if necessary.***

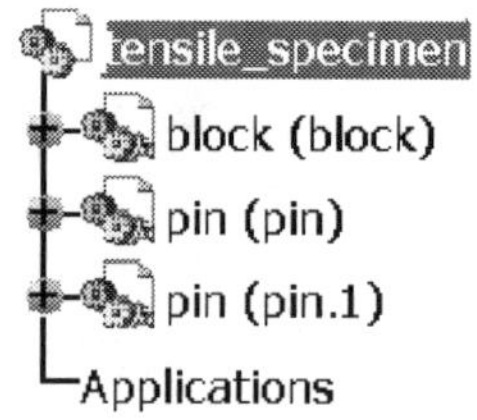


This happens because the two pins are coincident at the same location. The procedure for separating the parts is as follows.

Double-click on the top branch of the tree. This lands you in the **Assembly Design** workbench.

The branch highlights in blue as a confirmation of the new workbench.

Select the **Manipulation** icon from the **Move** toolbar .


This leads to the pop up box shown on the right.

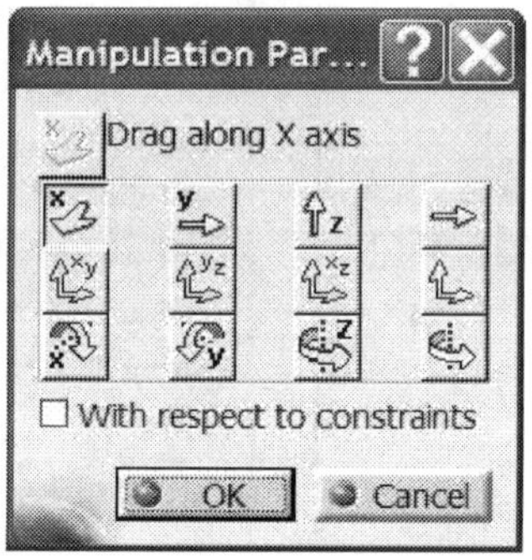


Using the y-direction translation icon , the three parts have been separated as displayed.

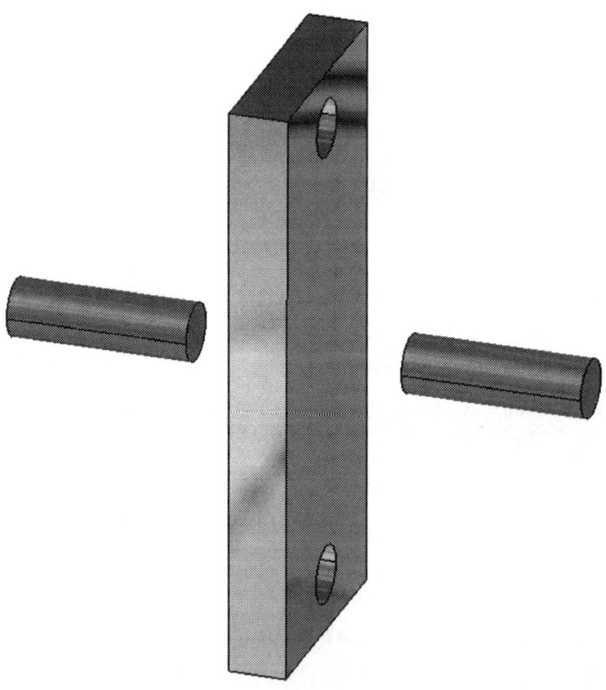

Your next task is to impose assembly constraints.

Use the **Anchor** icon  from **Constraints** toolbar  to anchor the **block**.

Pick the **Coincidence** icon . Select the **zx** planes of the **pin** and the **block**.

The pop up box gives you information regarding the coincidence constraint being established. Select **OK**.

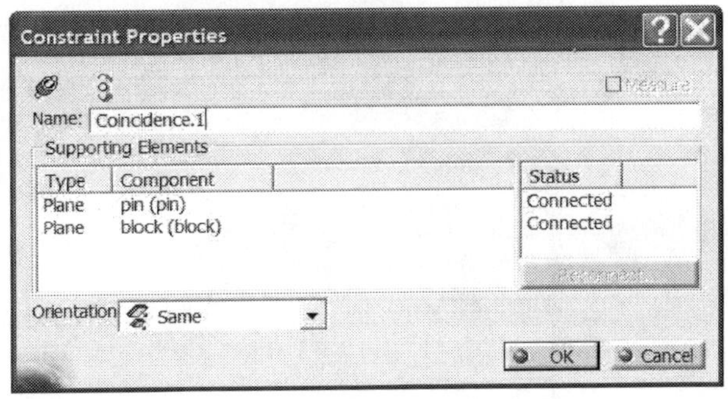


Repeat the last step with the <u>other</u> "**pin**" and the block.

Pick the **Coincidence** icon . Select the axis of the pin and the axis of the <u>top hole</u> as displayed below.

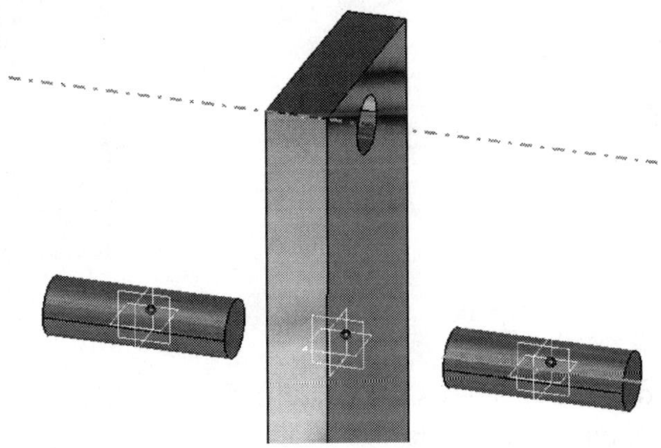

Repeat the last step with the <u>other</u> **pin** and the axis of the <u>bottom hole</u>.

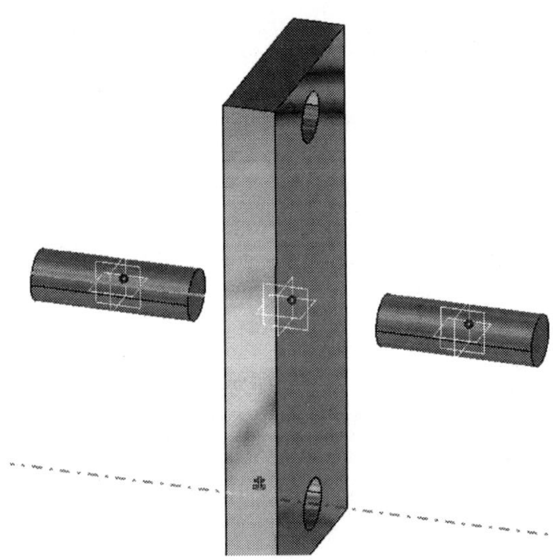

Use the **Update** icon  to activate the constraints. This forces the two pins to position themselves in the holes as displayed below.

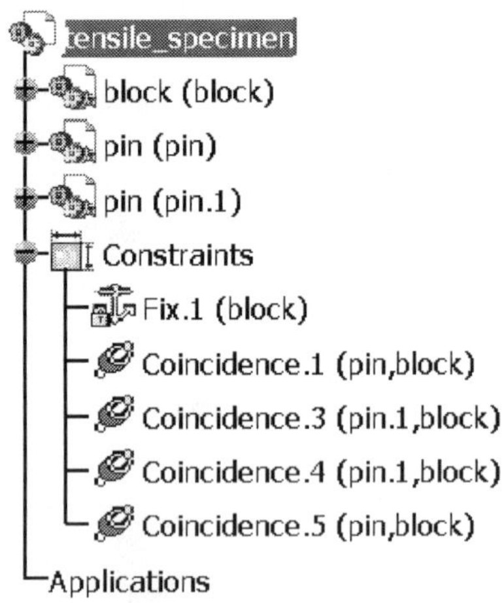


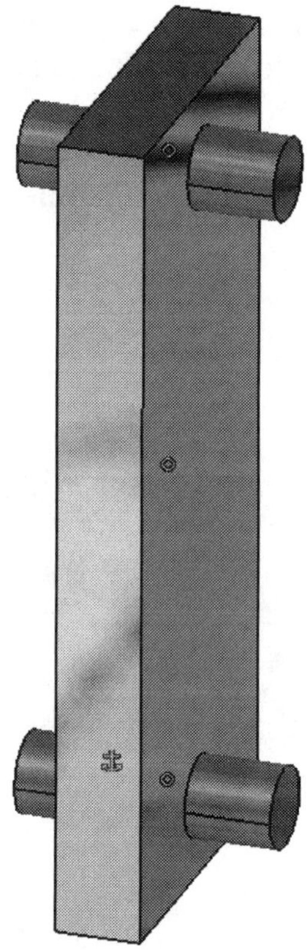

There are two types of solid elements available in CATIA V5: linear and parabolic. Both are referred to as tetrahedron elements and shown below. Limited Hex elements are also available.

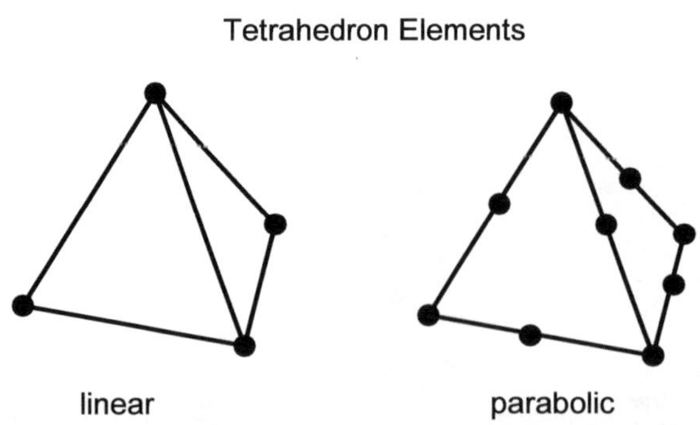


The linear tetrahedron elements are faster computationally but less accurate. On the other hand, the parabolic elements require more computational resources but lead to more accurate results. Another important feature of parabolic elements is that they can fit curved surfaces better. In general, the analysis of bulky objects requires the use of solid elements.

# 3 Entering the Analysis Solutions

From the standard Windows toolbar, select

**Start > Analysis & Simulation > Generative Structural Analysis**

The box shown below, **New Analysis Case** is visible on the screen. The default choice is **Static Analysis** which is precisely what we intend to use. Therefore, close the box by clicking on **OK**.

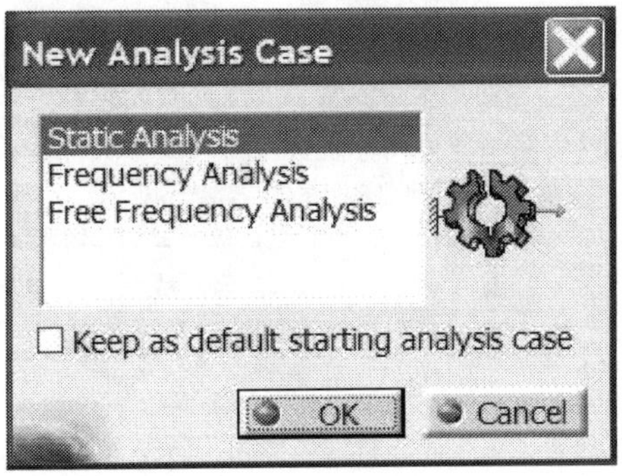


Note that the tree structure gets considerably longer. The bottom branches of the tree are presently "unfilled", and as we proceed in this workbench, assign loads and restraints, the branches gradually get "filled".

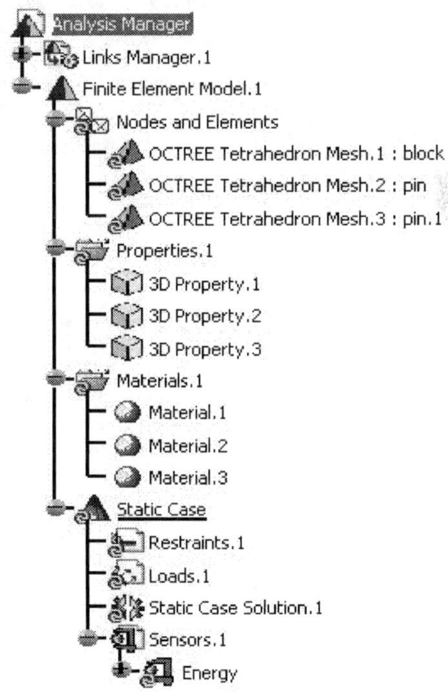


Another point that cannot be missed is the appearance of icons on each part that reflect a representative "size" and "sag". It is obvious that each on the three parts has its own mesh.

This is displayed in the figure below.

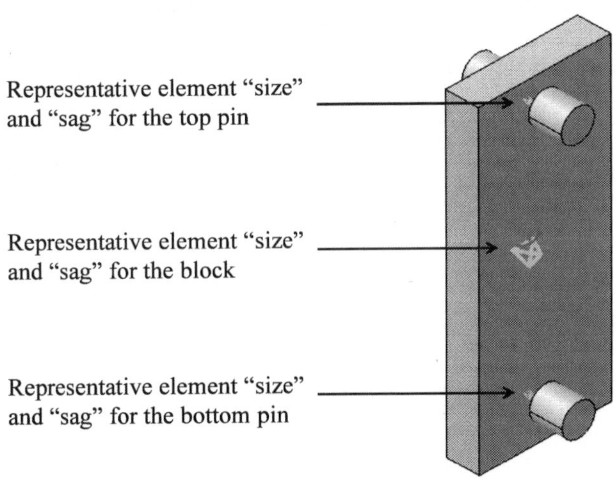

The concept of element size is self-explanatory. A smaller element size leads to more accurate results at the expense of a larger computation time. The "sag" terminology is unique to CATIA. In FEA, the geometry of a part is approximated with the elements. The surface of the part and the FEA approximation of a part do not coincide. The "sag" parameter controls the deviation between the two. Therefore, a smaller "sag" value could lead to better results. There is a relationship between these parameters that one does not have to be concerned with at this point.

The physical sizes of the representative "size" and "sag" on the screen, which also limit the coarseness of the mesh can be changed by the user. There are two ways to change these parameters:
The first method is to double-click on the representative icons on the screen which forces the **OCTREE Tetrahedron Mesh** box to open as shown to the right. This particular box corresponds to the mesh parameters for the **block**.

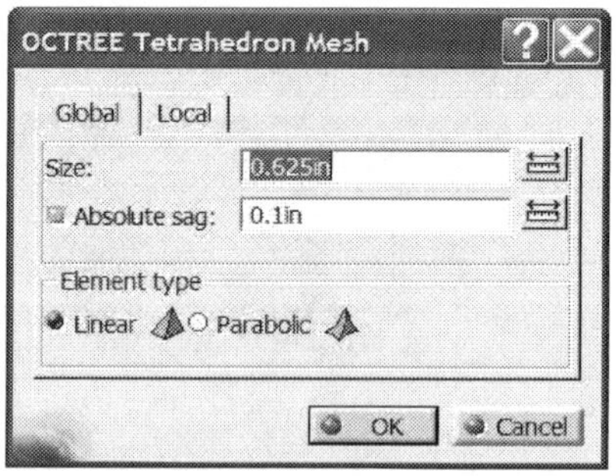


Keep all the default mesh parameters.

Notice that the type of the elements used (linear/parabolic) is also set in this box. Select **OK** to close the box.
The second method of reaching this box is through the tree.
By double-clicking on the branch labeled **OCTREE Tetrahedron Mesh** shown below, the same box opens allowing the user to modify the values.

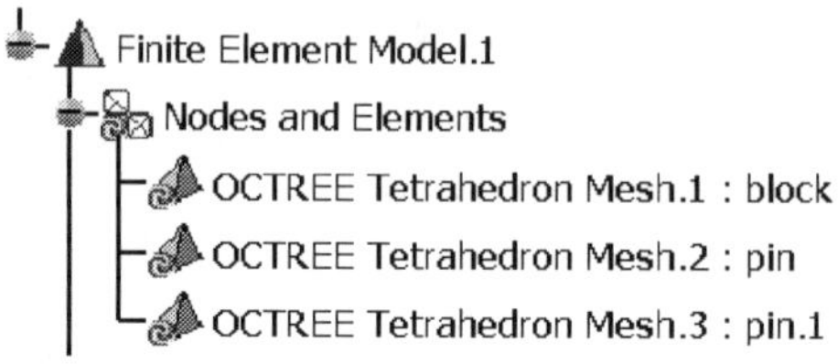


In order to view the generated mesh, you can point the cursor to the branch **Nodes and Elements**, right-click and select **Mesh Visualization**. This step may be slightly different in some UNIX machines. Also read Note #2 in Appendix I. Upon performing this operation a **Warning** box appears which can be ignored by selecting **OK**. For the mesh parameters used, the mesh shown on the next page is displayed on the screen.

The representative "size" and "sag" icons can be removed from the display by simply pointing to them, right-clicking and selecting **Hide**. This is the standard process for hiding any entity in CATIA V5.

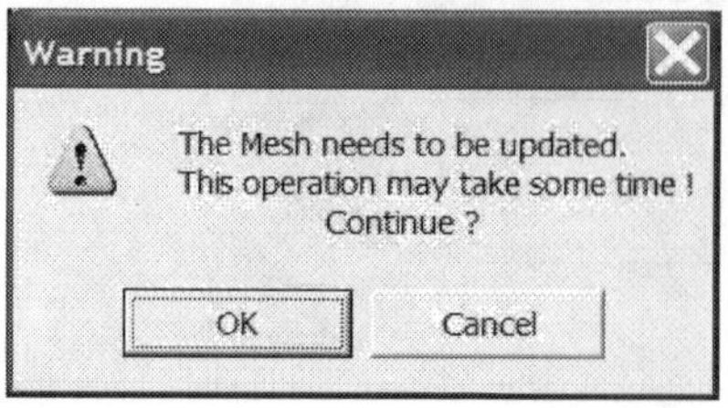

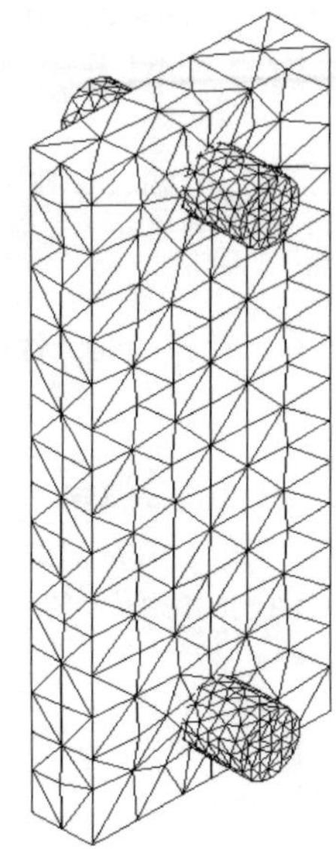

Note that the default mesh size is much smaller for the pins. The mesh generation algorithm in CATIA takes the size of the part into consideration.

Another important point is the fact that the **block** mesh is too coarse. Therefore, the results may be inaccurate.

In general, the elements must be small in the regions of high stress gradient such as stress concentrations.

Uniformly reducing the element size for the whole part is a poor strategy.

**Applying Restraints:**

CATIA's FEA module is geometrically based. This means that the boundary conditions cannot be applied to nodes and elements. The boundary conditions can only be applied at the part level. As soon as you enter the **Generative Structural Analysis** workbench, the parts are automatically hidden. Therefore, before boundary conditions are applied, the part must be brought to the unhide mode. This can be carried out by pointing the cursor to the top of the tree, the **Links Manager.1** branch, right-click, select **Show**. At this point, the parts and the mesh are superimposed as shown below and you have access to the part.

The corresponding tree is also displayed.

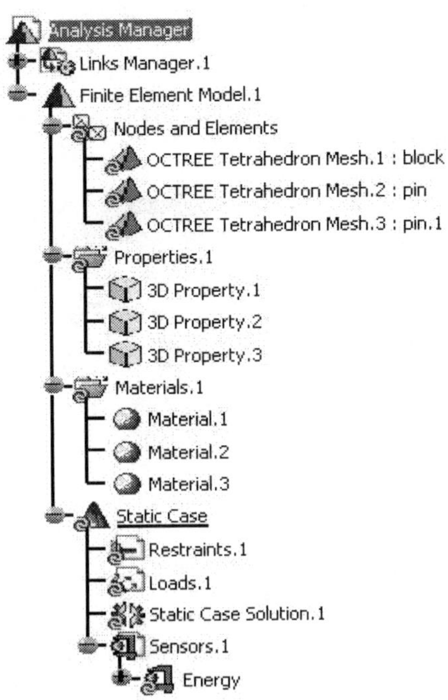


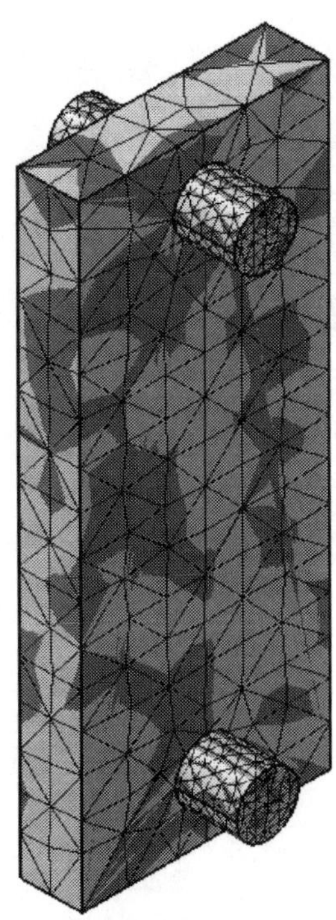

If, the presence of the mesh is annoying, you can always hide it. Point the cursor to **Nodes and Elements**, right-click, **Hide**.

In FEA, restraints refer to applying displacement boundary conditions which is achieved through the **Restraint** toolbar 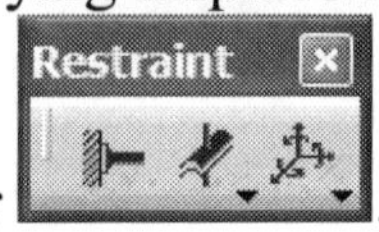

.

Select the **Clamp** icon  and pick the side faces of the bottom pin. Be careful not to pick the circumference (edge) of the circle instead of the face. In this case, only two restraint symbols will be shown attached to the circumference.

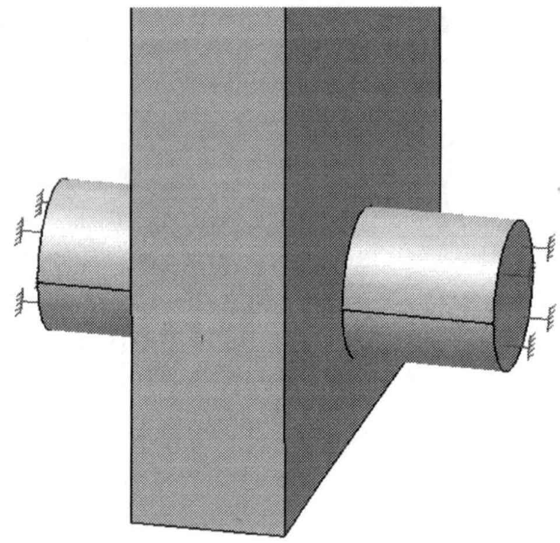

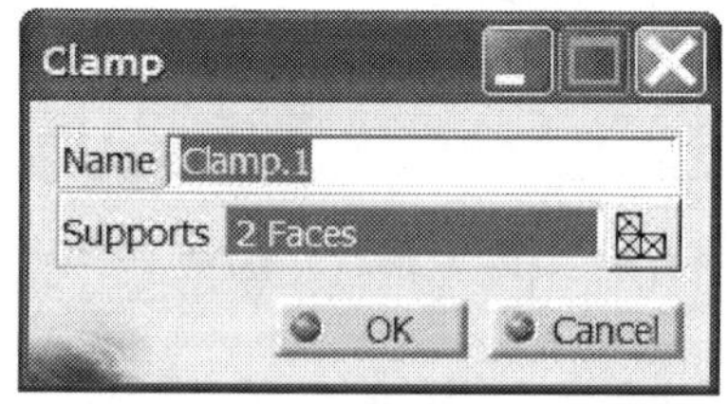


**Applying the Enforced Displacement:**

The next task is to apply a displacement of 0.01 in to the end faces of the top pin. In CATIA this is referred to as **Enforced Displacement**.

This involves a two stage process. Use **User-defined Restraint** icon 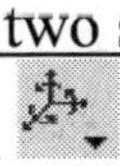 and pick the end faces of the top pin. Make sure that all three translations are checked. Whether the last three boxes are checked or not, is irrelevant in this problem.

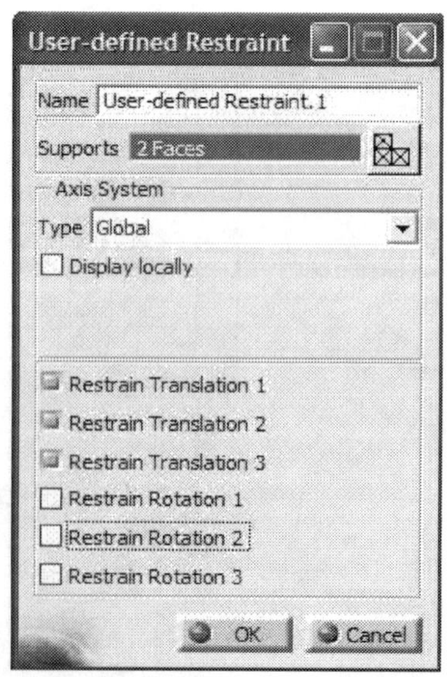


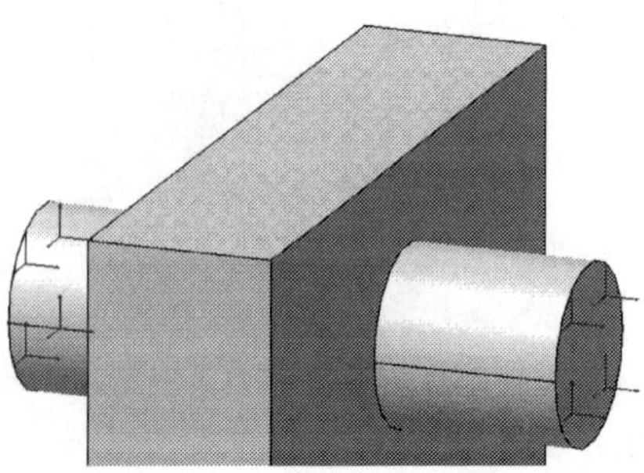

The current restraints are clearly not what you want. At this point, you have specified zero displacement for the end faces of the top pin. This should be 0.01 in.

In order to modify this, use the **Enforced Displacement** icon  from the **Loads** toolbar 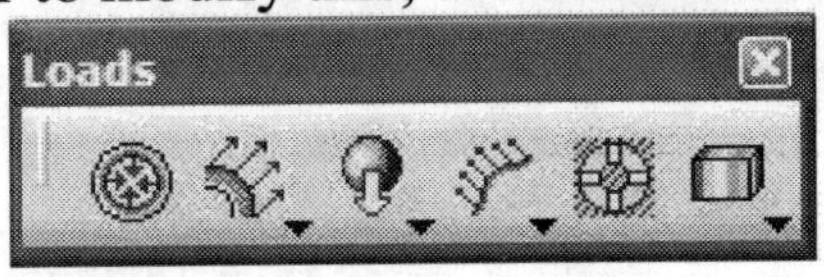

.
This opens the box on the right.

Use the cursor to pick the restraint on the top pin. The **Enforced Displacement** box reflects this selection. Change **Translation 3** to 0.01 and close the box.

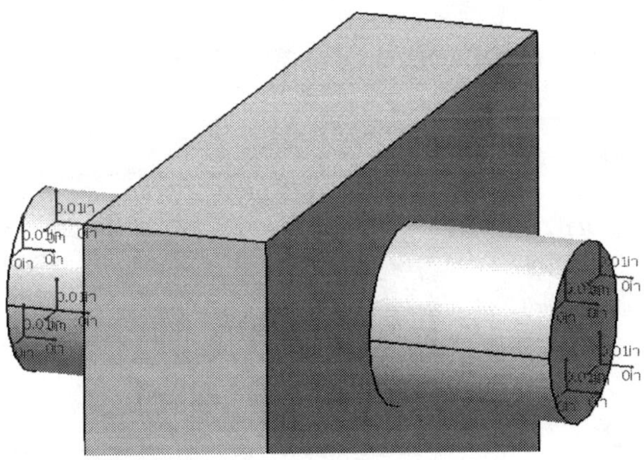

**Creating Analysis Connection:**

Use the **General Analysis Connection** icon 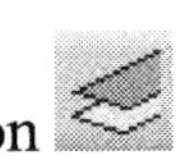 from the **Analysis Supports** toolbar 

. For the **First component**, select the face of the top pin.

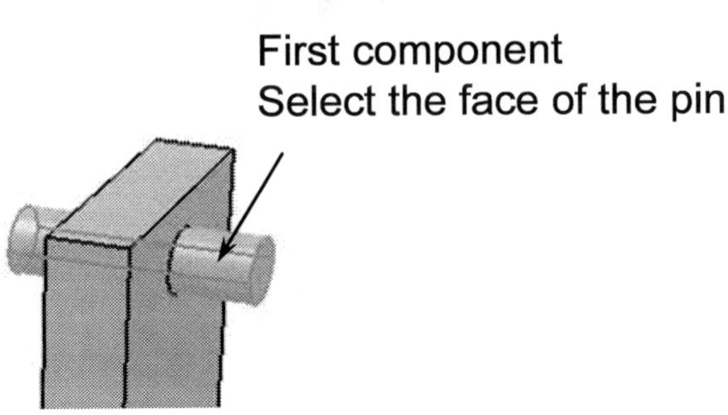


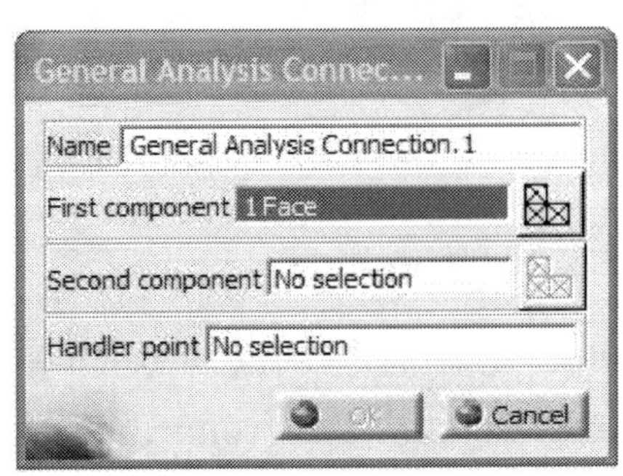

For the **Second component**, you have to select the inside face of the top hole. To do so, hide the top pin. This enables you to select face of the hole.

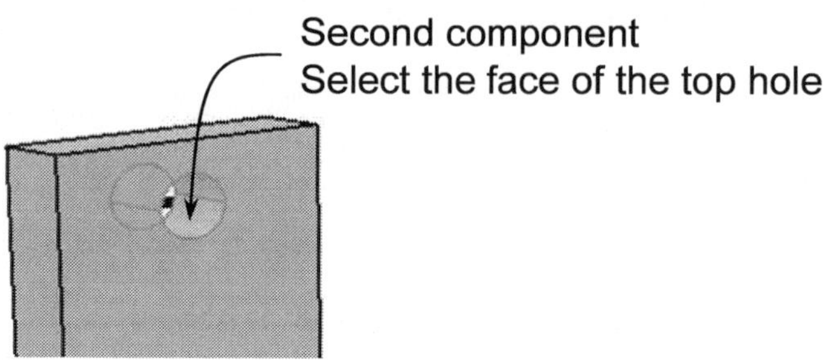


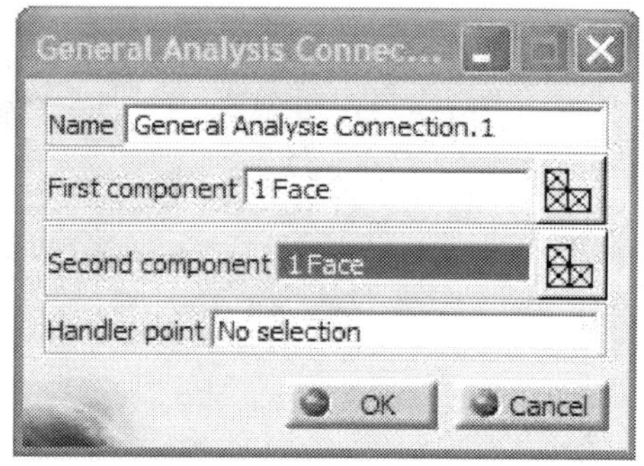


Repeat the process for the bottom pin and the surface of the bottom hole.

Use the **General Analysis Connection** icon  from the **Analysis Supports** toolbar . For the **First component**, select the face of the bottom pin.



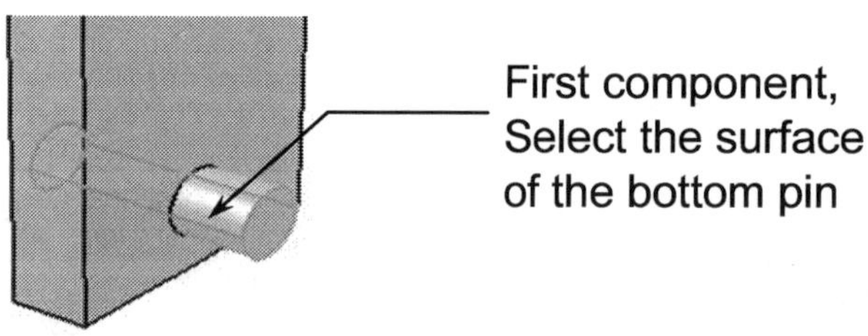


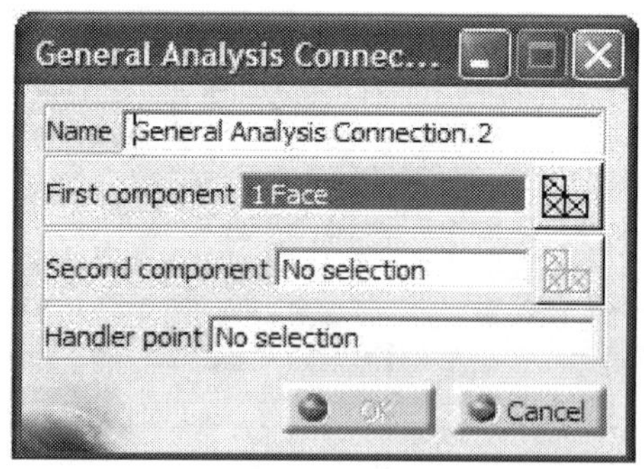


For the **Second component**, you have to select the inside face of the bottom hole. To do so, hide the bottom pin. This enables you to select face of the hole.

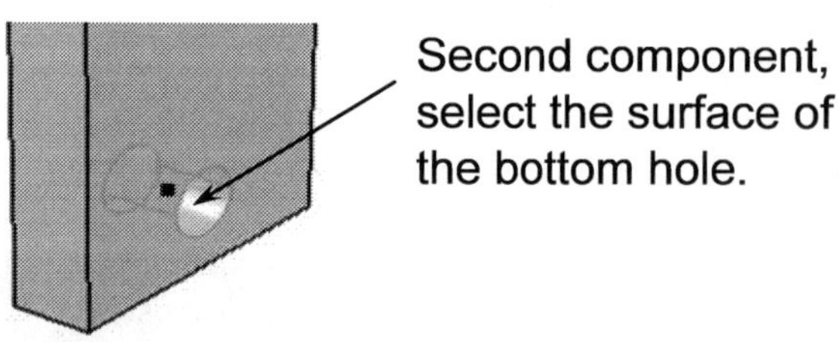


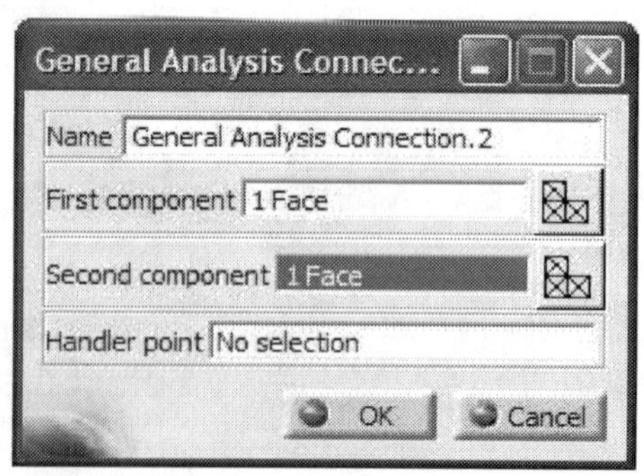


The branch of the tree labeled **Analysis Connection Manager.1** stores the information on the connections just established.

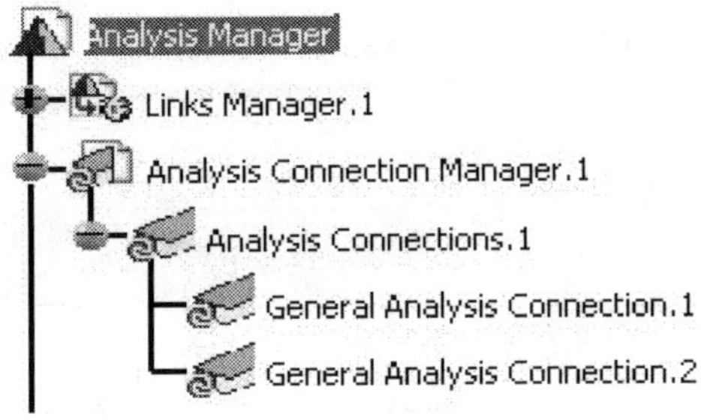


You now define the nature of connection defined earlier. The **Connection Property** toolbar has a sub-toolbar called **Face Face Connection** Property.

Click on the **Contact Connection Property** icon 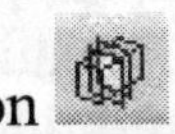 from the **Face Face Connection Property** toolbar 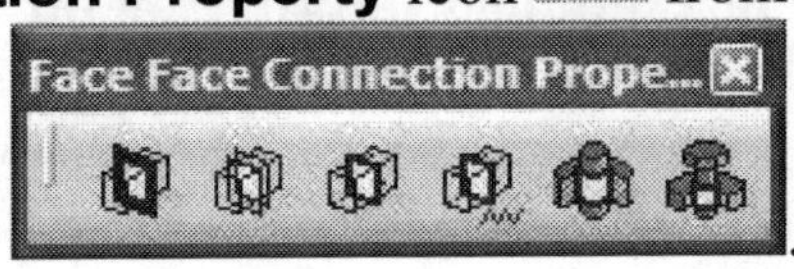

. The following pop up box appears.

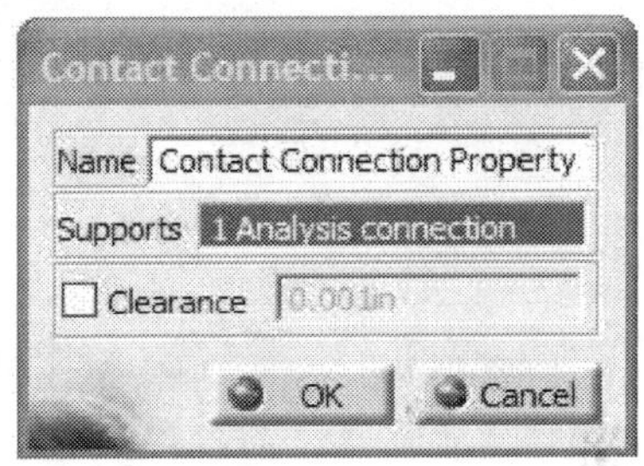


For **Supports**, select **General Analysis Connection.1** from the tree.

On the computer screen, you notice the standard symbol for contact is created (a red box).

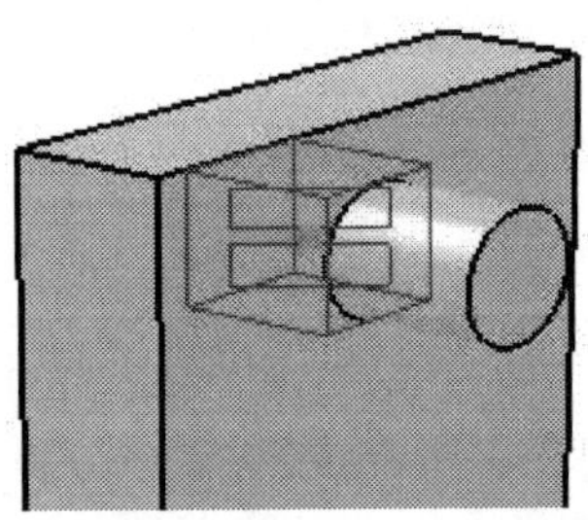

Once again, click on the **Contact Connection Property** icon 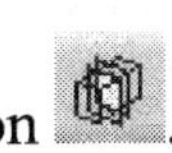.
For **Supports**, select **General Analysis Connection.2** from the tree.
On the computer screen, you notice the standard symbol for contact is created (a red box).

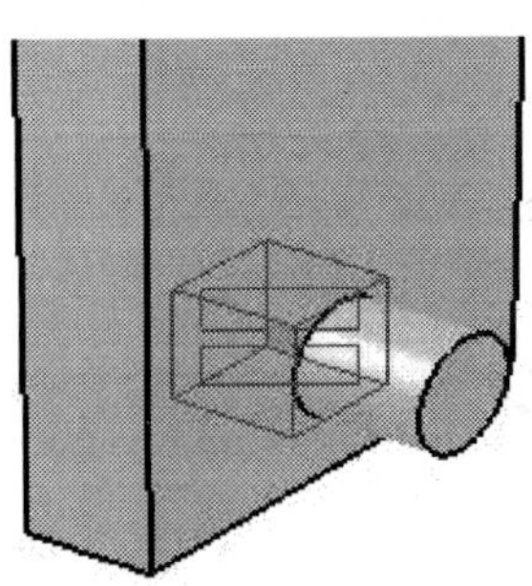

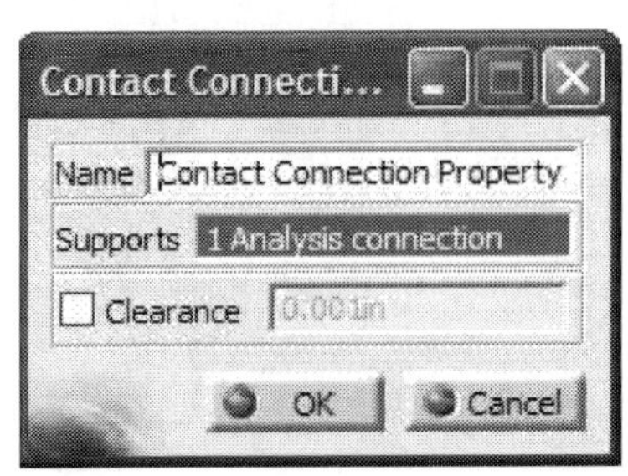

It seems that all restraints have been applied and that the program should run. This is not the case as will be seen shortly. There is one further non-obvious restraint that needs to be applied.

**Launching the Solver:**

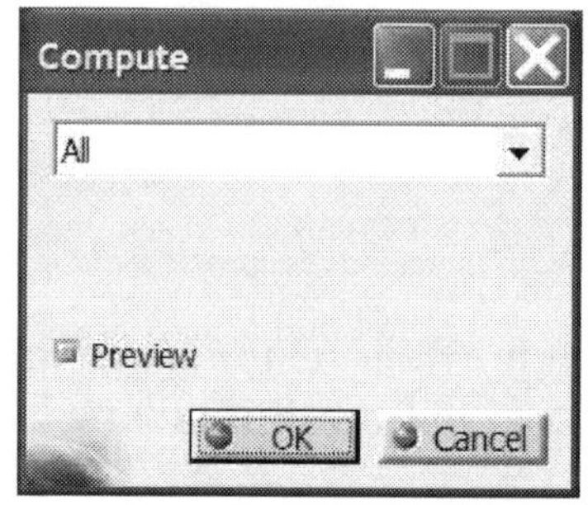


To run the analysis, you need to use the **Compute** toolbar  by selecting the **Compute** icon . This leads to the **Compute** box shown to the right. Leave the defaults as **All** which means everything is computed. Upon closing this box, after a brief pause, the second box shown below appears. This box provides information on the resources needed to complete the analysis. If the estimates are zero in the listing, then there is a problem in the previous step and should be looked into. If all the numbers are zero in the box, the program may run but would not produce any useful results.

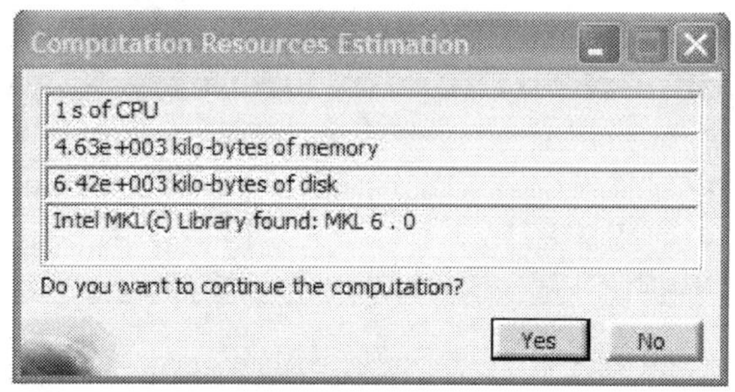


The tree has been changed to reflect the location of the Results and Computations as shown below.

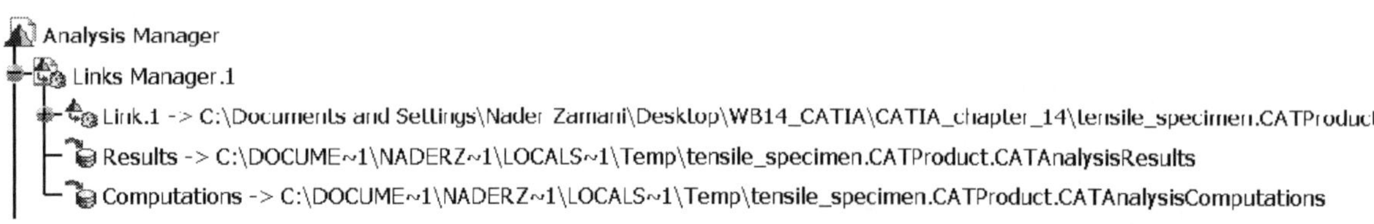


The user can change these locations by double-clicking on the branch. The box, shown on the right, will open and can be modified.

This run terminates with the following **Error** box.

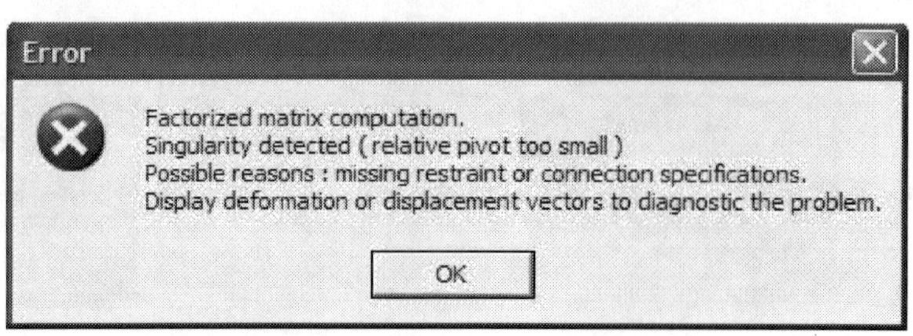

Usually this box implies that the assembly is not fully restrained. In our model, the block is free to move along the pin axis as a rigid body. Some commercial packages rectify the situation by adding a small artificial stiffness in that direction, preventing the rigid body motion. In those packages, effectively they add a “soft” spring in the appropriate direction, resulting in a stiffness.

You achieve the same effect by selecting an arbitrary point (vertex of the block) and prevent it from moving in the y-direction. Use the **Restraint** toolbar 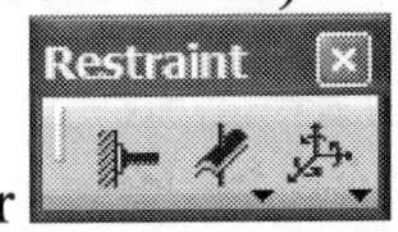

and select the **Advanced Restraint** icon 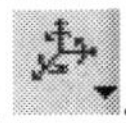.

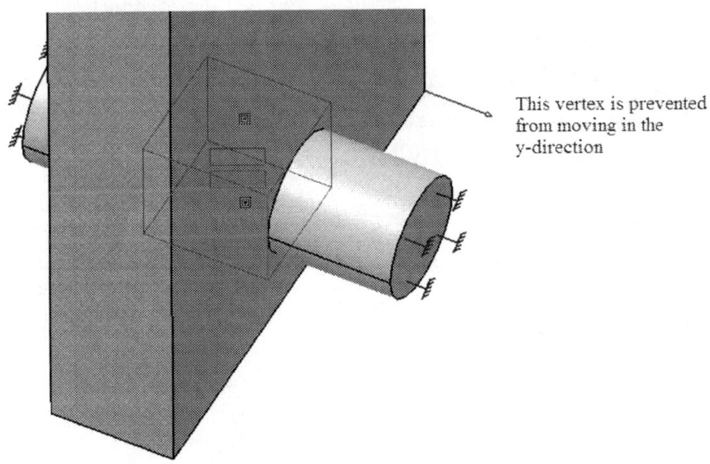


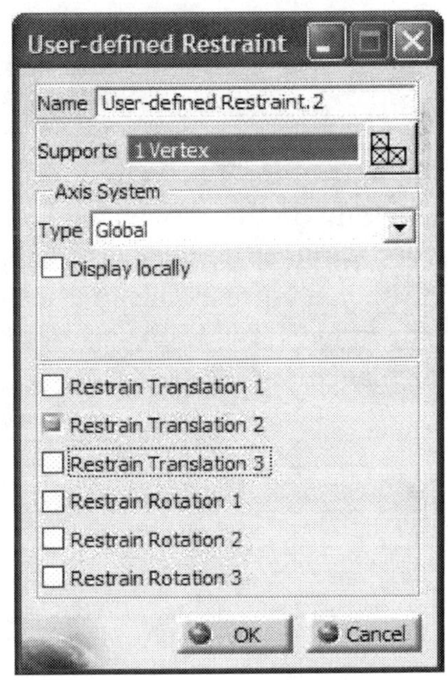


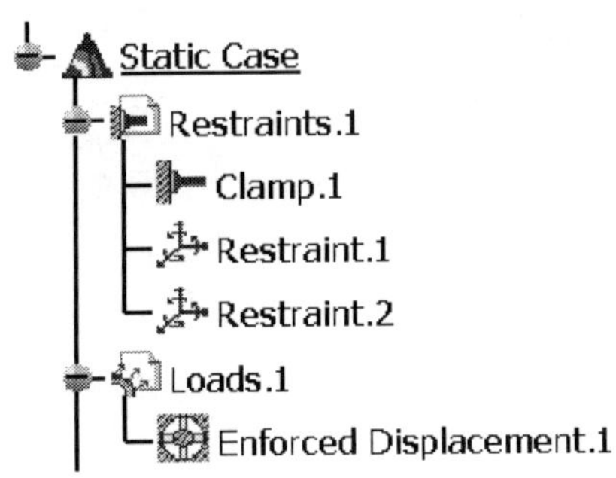


You are reminded that ordinarily the solid tetrahedron elements do not have rotational degrees of freedom; therefore, one cannot directly impose rotation or moment on them. Whether the **Restrain Rotation** boxes are left checked or not, there will be no impact on the results.

Now press on  to run the problem. This time, the run completes without an error.

**Postprocessing:**

The main postprocessing toolbar is called **Image** 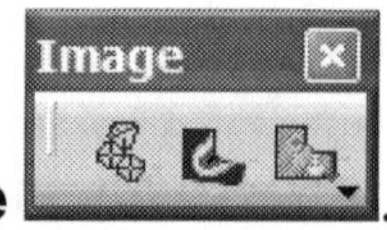

. To view the deformed shape you have to use the **Deformation** icon . The resulting deformed shape is displayed below.

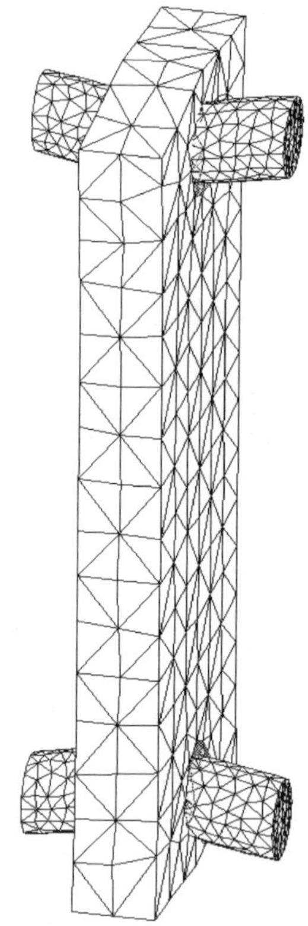

The deformation image can be very deceiving because one could have the impression that the assembly actually displaces to that extent. Keep in mind that the displacements are scaled considerably so that one can observe the deformed shape. Although the scale factor is set automatically, one can change this value with the **Deformation Scale Factor** icon 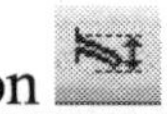 in the **Analysis Tools** toolbar 

.
Clicking on the above icon leads to the box shown below where the desired scale factor can be typed. The deformed shape displayed corresponds to a scale factor of 114.735.
The value 1.14735 in. is 114 times the actual maximum displacement.

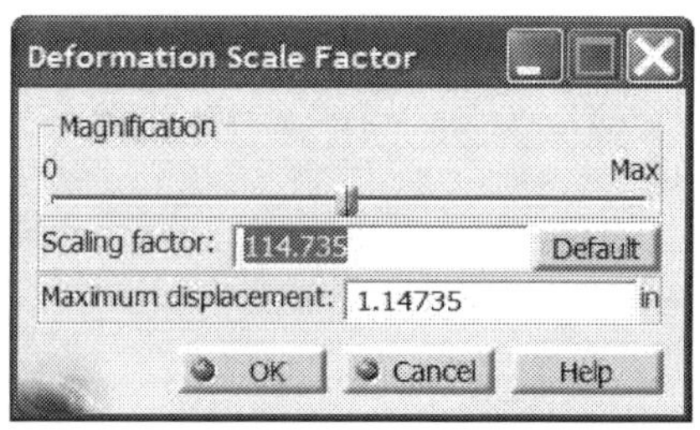


In order to see the displacement field, the **Displacement** icon  in the **Image** toolbar should be used. The default display is in terms of displacement arrows.

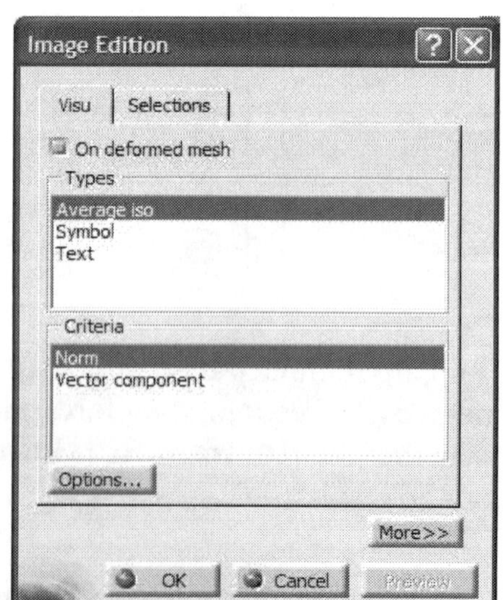


The arrow plot is not particularly useful. In order to view the contour plot of the displacement field, position the cursor on the arrow field and double-click. The **Image Edition** box shown on the right opens.
The contour of the displacement field is given on the next page.
You can change the render style by using **Shading with Material**  icon in the **View mode** toolbar.
Note: The color map has been changed; otherwise everything looks black in the figure.

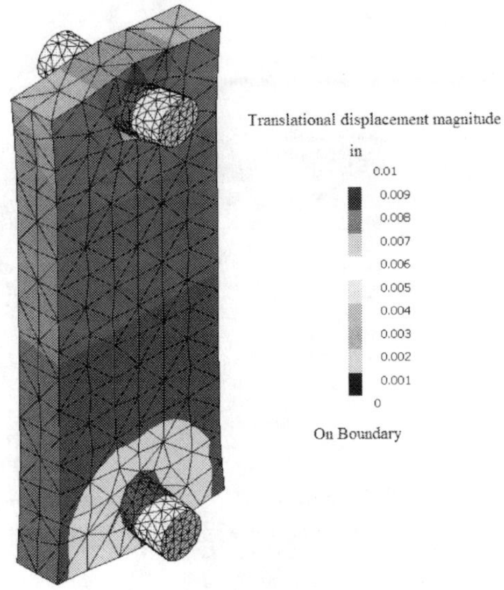


The next step in the postprocessing is to plot the contours of the von Mises stress using the **von Mises Stress** icon  in the **Image** toolbar.
The von Mises stress is displayed below.

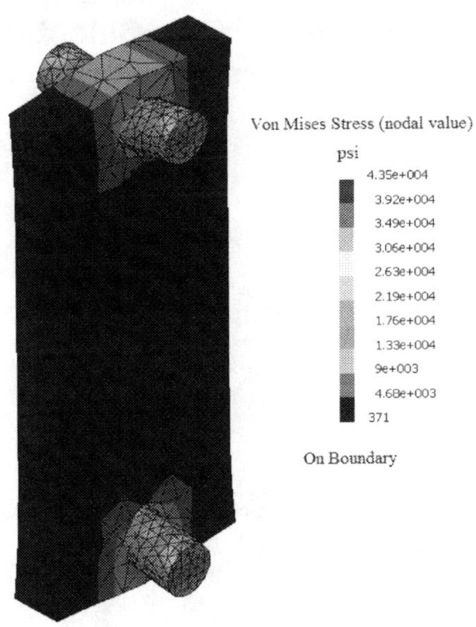


Double-clicking on the contour legend leads to the **Color Map** box displayed on the right. The contour can be plotted as **Smooth** or stepped. The number of color bands is also specified in this box. Finally, the user can describe the range of stresses to be plotted. The contour of von Mises stress corresponding to an **Imposed max** of 15511.5 psi is shown below.

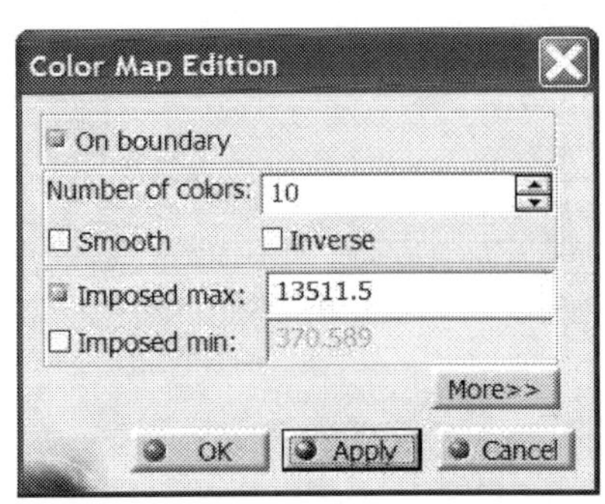

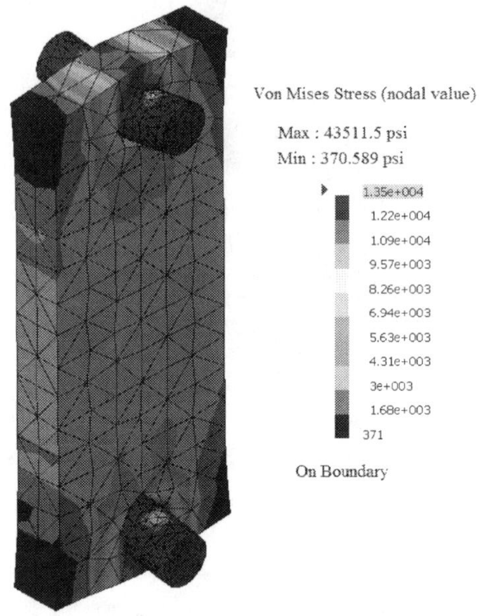


Note that the pins are highly stressed and their large values had masked the stress distribution in the block.

Occasionally, you may be interested in plotting the von Mises stress contour in parts of the assembly or even supports. In order to achieve this, double-click on the contour levels on the screen to open the image edition box. Next use the **Selections** tab as shown below. Here, you have the choice of selecting different entities. The contour below is the stress distribution in the block alone.

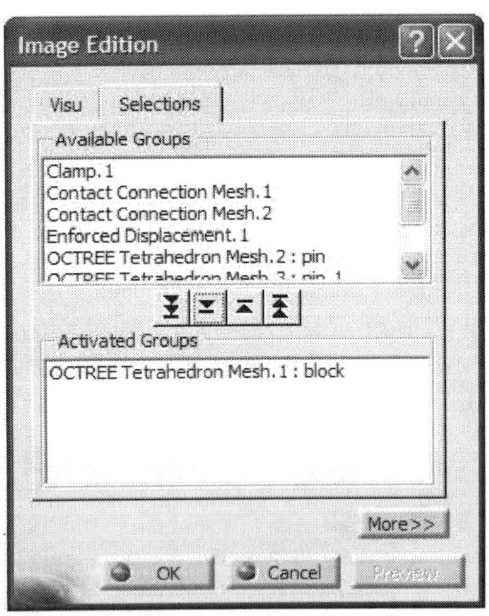


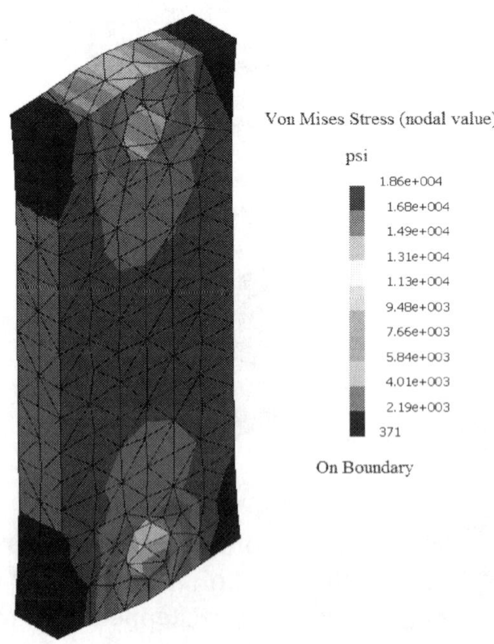

The **Cutting Plane** icon  from the **Analysis Tools** toolbar

can be used to make a cut through the part at a desired location and inspect the stresses inside of the part. The **Cut Plane** box allows you to keep the plane or to remove it for display purposes. A typical cutting plane is shown below.

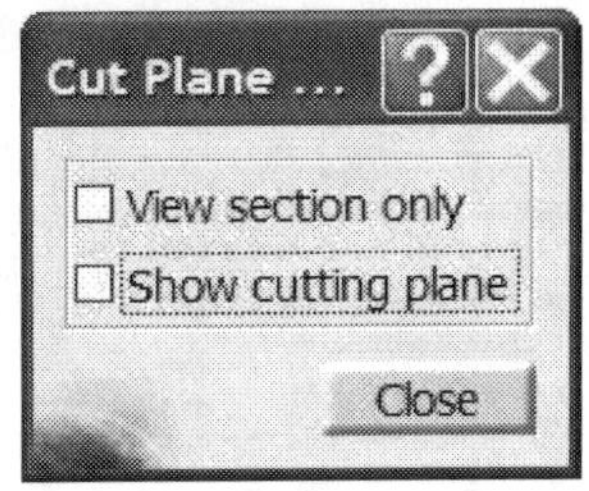


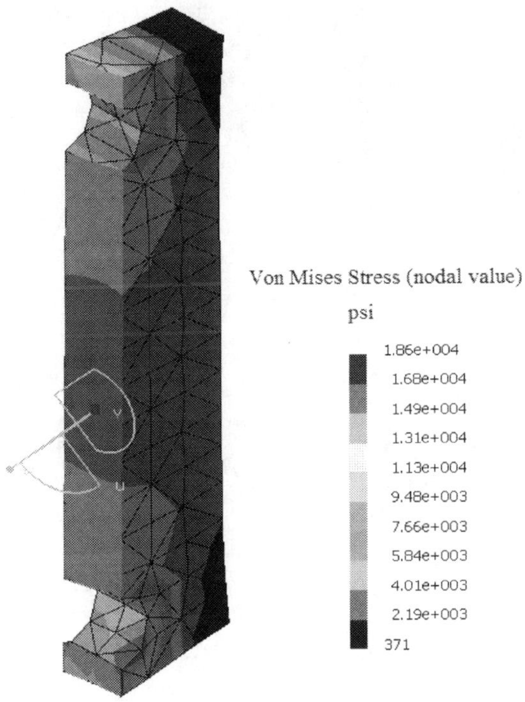


At this point we have generated two plots. The displacement and the von Mises stress contours which can be displayed individually. However, CATIA also allows you to show both plots side by side.

<u>First make sure that both images to be plotted are active in the tree. If not, point to the graph in the tree, right-click, select **Active**.</u>

Click the **Image Layout** icon  from the **Image Analysis** toolbar.

The **Images** box, shown to the right, asks you to specify the direction along which the two plots are expected to be aligned. The outcome is side-by-side plots shown below. (Note: The color map has been changed; otherwise everything looks black.)

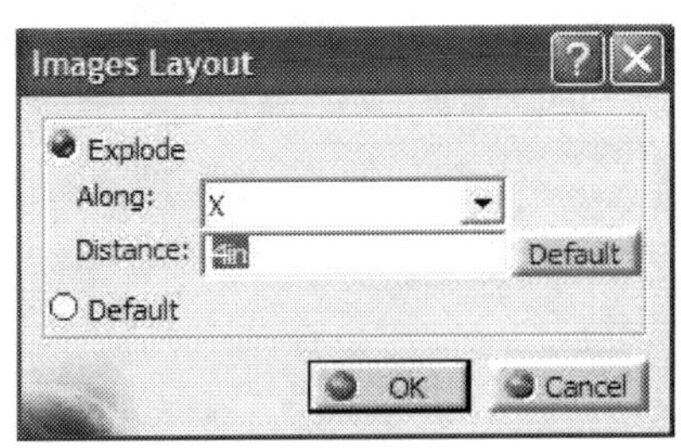

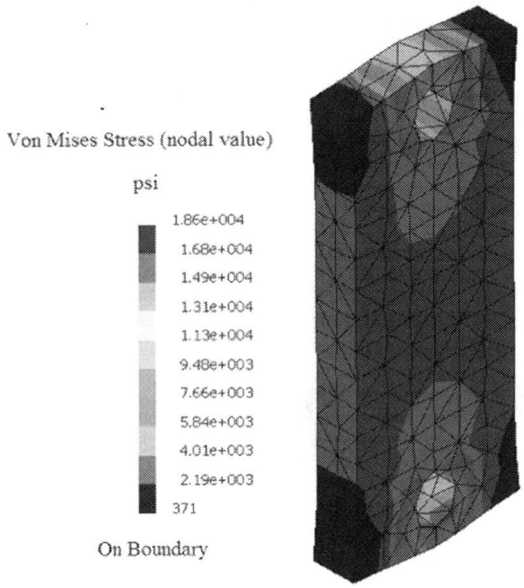


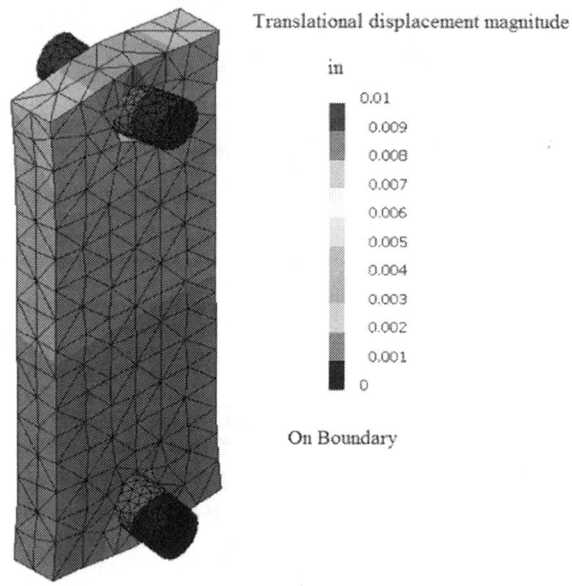


Using the icon **Generate Report** in the **Analysis Results** toolbar an HTML based report can be generated which summarizes the features and results of the FEA model.

Animation of the model can be achieved through the **Animate** icon in the **Analysis Tools** toolbar and AVI files can easily be generated.

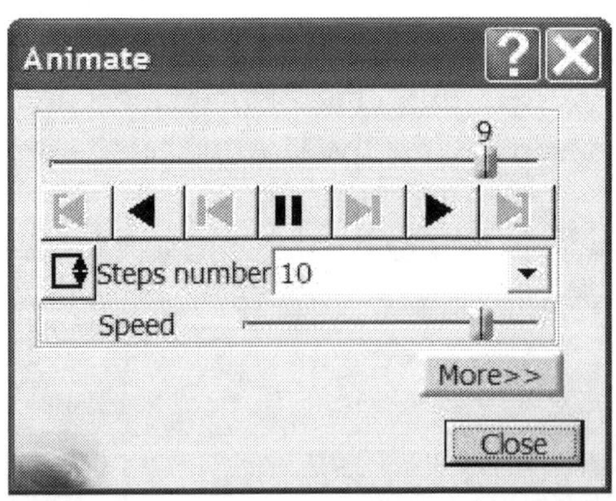

Now we describe the process which allows you to find the force necessary to cause the edge enforced displacement of 0.01 in.

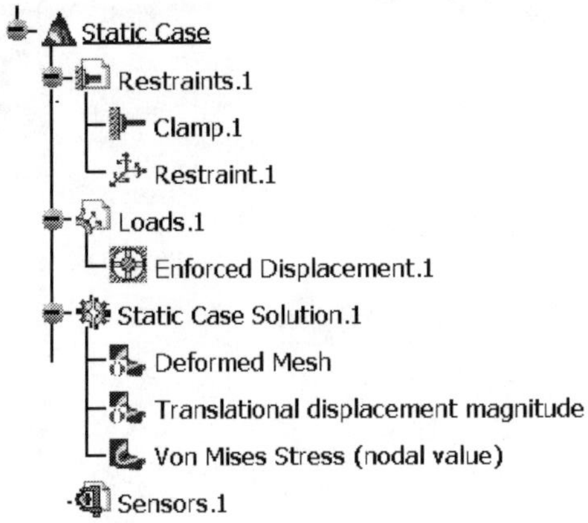


This is achieved by defining a sensor. The sensor definitions are located in the bottom section of the tree as shown on the right.

Point the cursor to the sensor branch in the tree, and right-click.

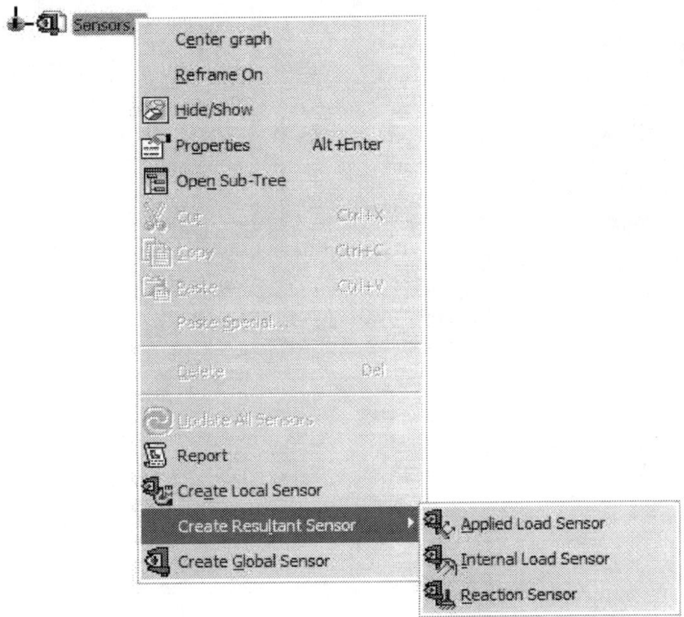


From the contextual menu, select **Create Reaction Sensor**. This forces the following box to open. From this box, select **Clamp.1** and close the window.

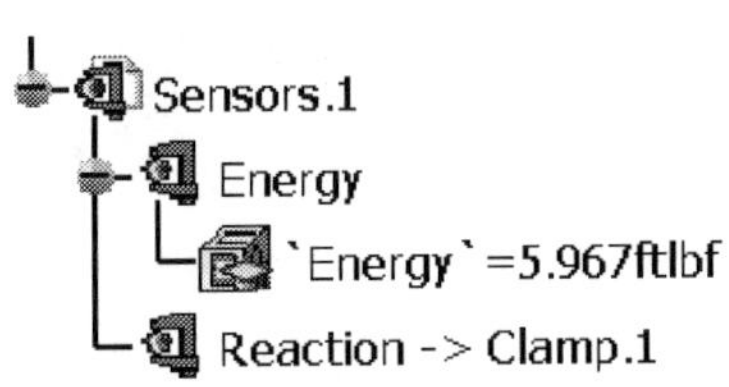


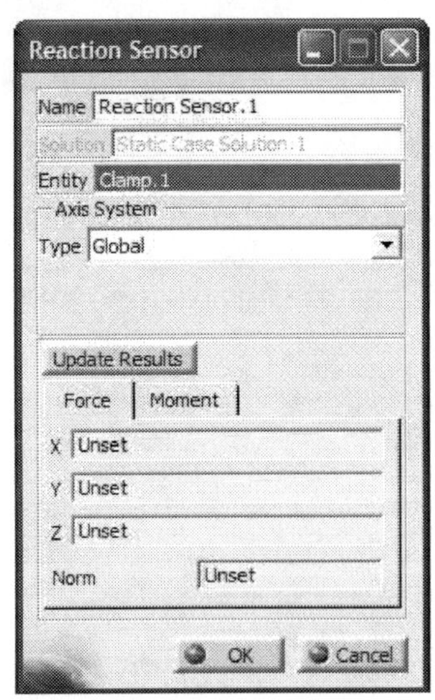


Note that a reaction sensor is created in the tree.

Double-click on the **Reaction Clamp.1** in the tree, the pop up box on the next page opens. Select the **Update Results** box Update Results for the reactions to be recorded.

The data in this box indicates that the reaction at the clamp is 12051.4 lbf. Consequently, this is the force required to give the top pin a displacement of 0.01 in.

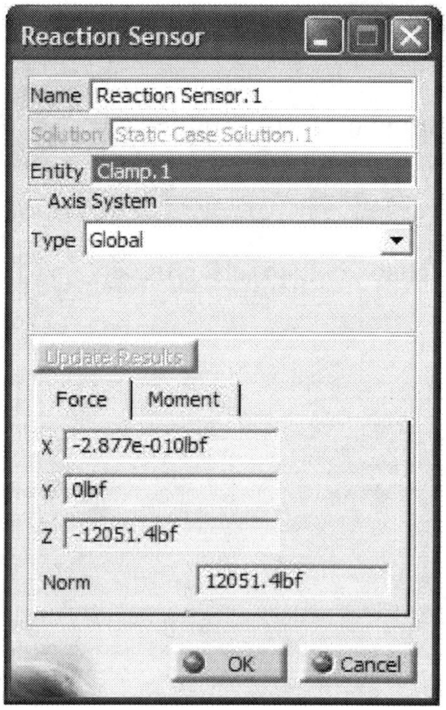
Reaction Sensor
Name
Reaction Sensor.1
Solution
Static Case Solution.1
Entity
Clamp.1
Axis System
Type
Global
Update Results
Force
Moment
X
-2.877e-010lbf
Y
0lbf
Z
-12051.4lbf
Norm
12051.4lbf
OK
Cancel

# Exercises for Chapter 16

## Problem 1: A Tensile Specimen as an Assembly, Symmetry used

Repeat the problem analyzed in this chapter with the one-quarter and the one-eighth model displayed below.

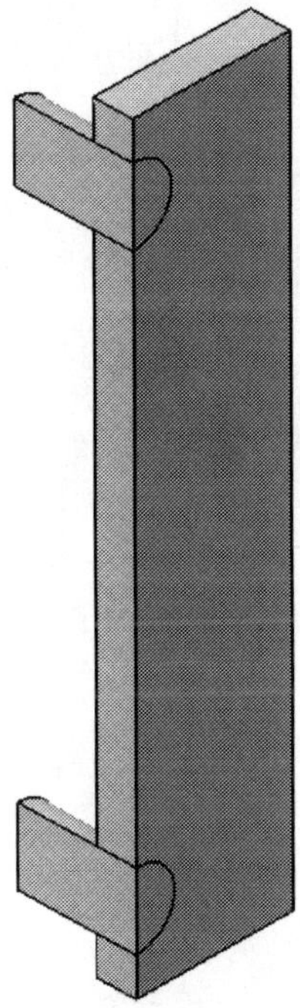

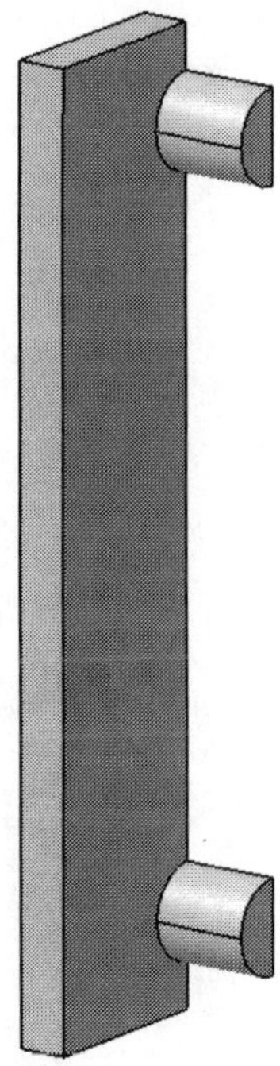

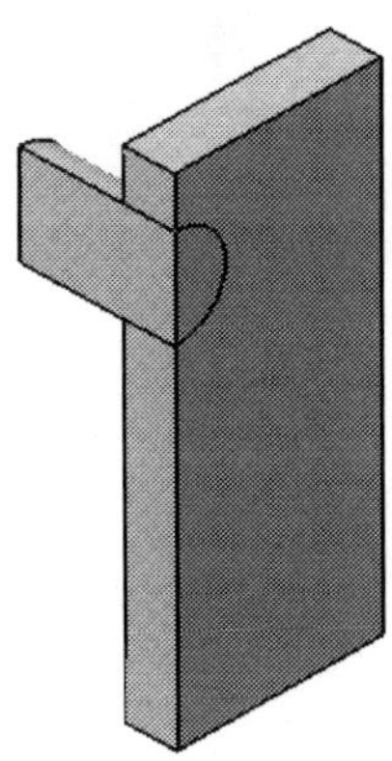

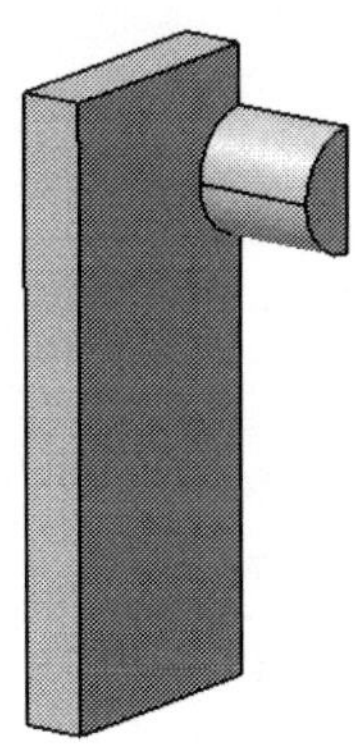

## Problem 2: Bracket Assembly under a Pressure Loading

The bracket assembly, shown below, is supported by two pins. The pin ends are clamped and the bracket of loaded with a pressure of 50 psi. All components are made of steel and the pins are 4 in. long.

The dimensions provided below are all in inches. Use solid elements to find the tip deflection of the bracket.

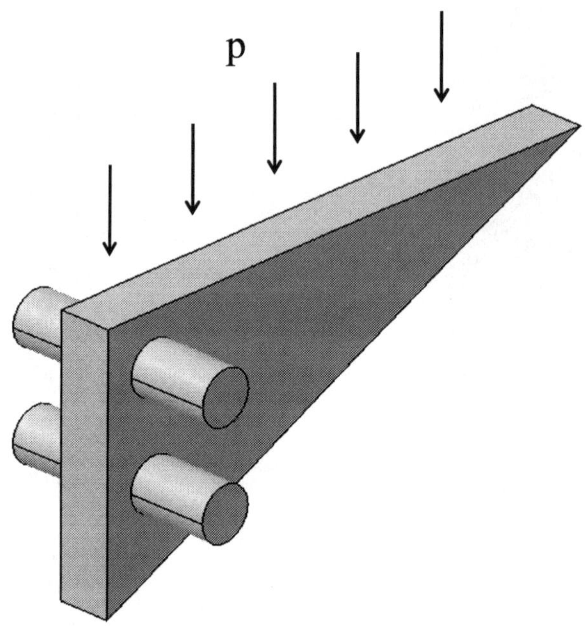


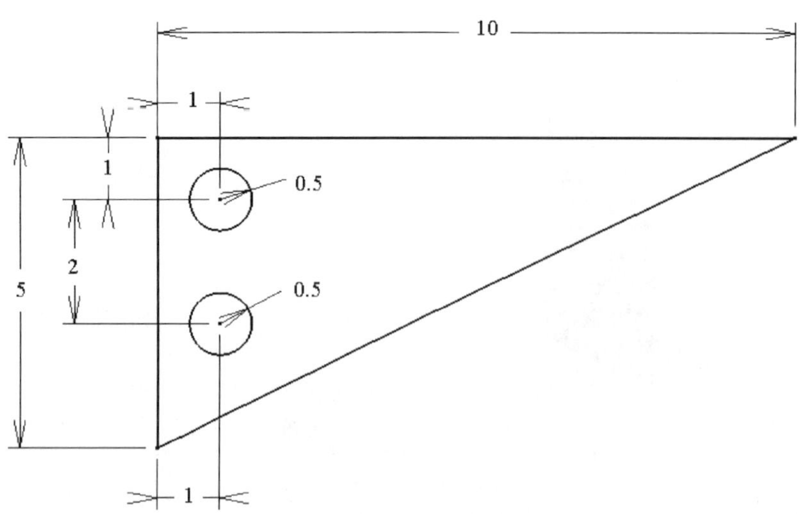

# Chapter 17

# Analysis of a Fastened Assembly

# Introduction

In this tutorial, you model an assembly consisting of two plates, attached together with a preloaded fastener. One plate is loaded, causing the bending of the entire structure. The stresses and deflections are predicted with finite elements.

## 1 Problem Statement

The two steel plates, shown below, are clamped together with a steel bolt.

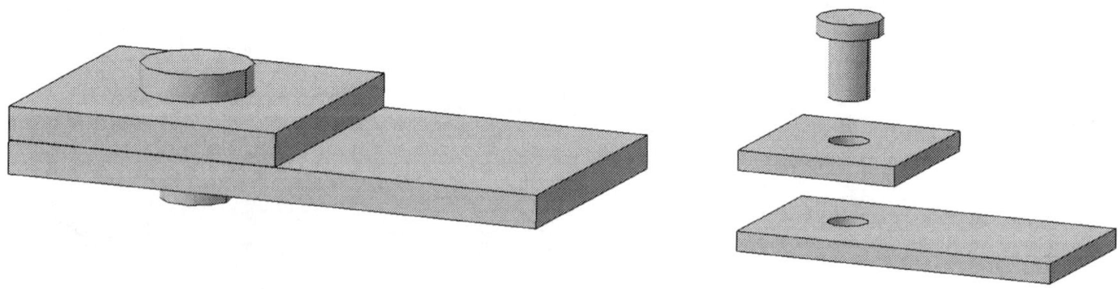

The left ends of both plates are clamped and the bolt has a pretension of 50 lb.
The first step in the analysis is to predict the behavior of the assembly before any other load is applied. In the second step, the longer plate is subjected to a load of 100 lb, causing it to bend. The stress distribution in different parts is to be calculated.

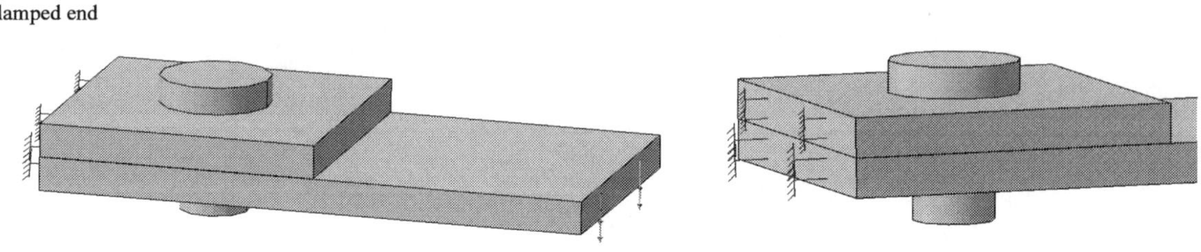


The three parts are created easily and assembled to the correct positions.

## 2 Creation of the Assembly in the Mechanical Design Solutions

Enter the **Assembly Design** workbench which can be achieved by different means depending on your CATIA customization. For example, from the standard Windows toolbar, select **File > New**.
See Note #1 in Appendix I.

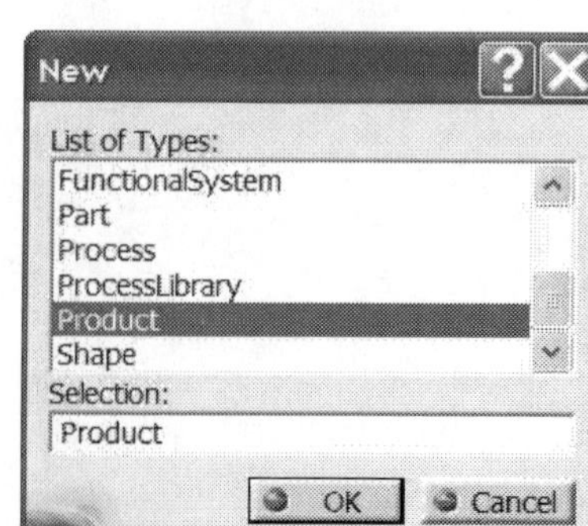

From the box shown on the right, select **Product**. This moves you to the **Assembly Design** workbench and creates a part with the default name **Product.1**.

In order to change the default name, move the cursor to **Product.1** in the tree, right-click and select **Properties** from the menu list.

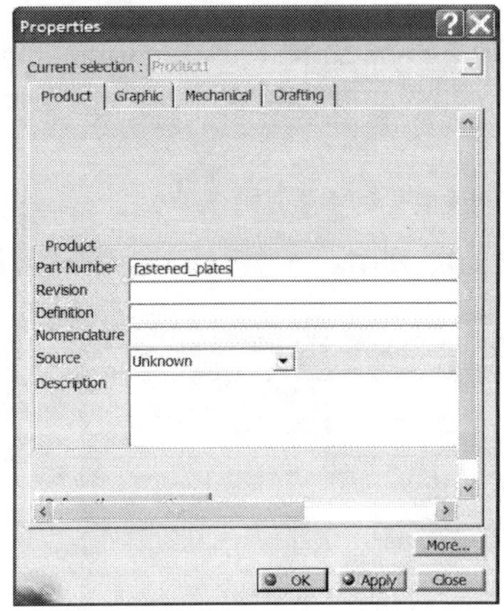


From the **Properties** box, select the **Product** tab and in **Part Number** type **fastened_plates**.

This will be the new product name throughout the chapter. The tree on the top left corner of your computer screen should look as displayed below.

You now create the bolt as a part.
From the standard Windows toolbar, select **Insert > New Part**. The tree is modified to indicate that **Part.1** has been created. Change the default name to **steel_disk**.
The tree, before and after the name change, is displayed below. Note that the instance name has also been changed to **steel_disk**.

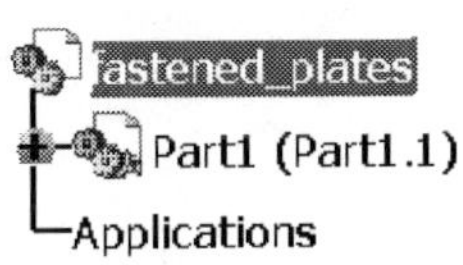


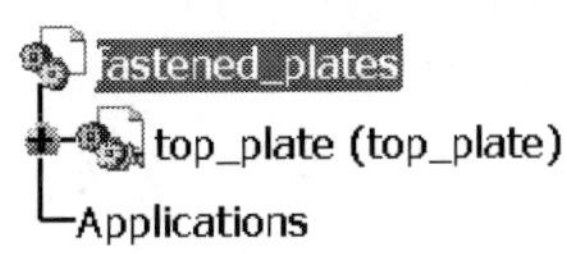


The process of renaming **Part.1** is just like before. Point the cursor to **Part.1** in the tree, right-click, and select **Properties**. The pop up box, after the changes are made is displayed below.

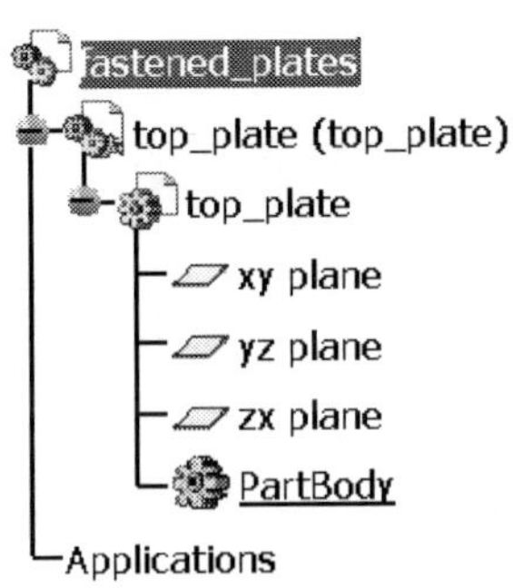


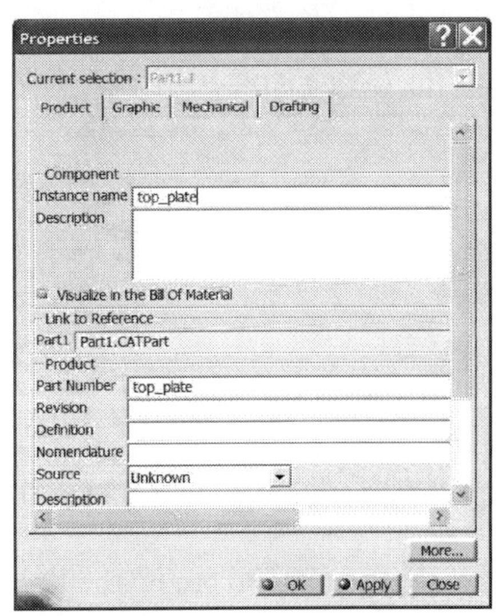

Select the **xy** plane from **top_plate** and switch to the **Part Design** workbench.

In **Part Design**, enter the **Sketcher** .

In the **Sketcher**, draw the following profile with the indicated dimensions.

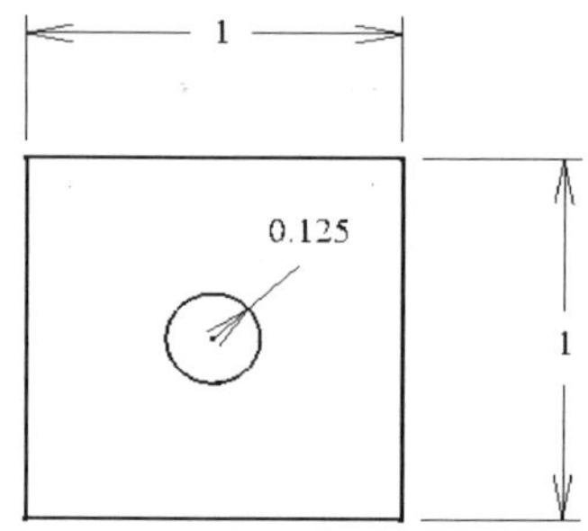


Leave the **Sketcher** .

Use the **Pad** icon , specifying a **Length** of 0.125.

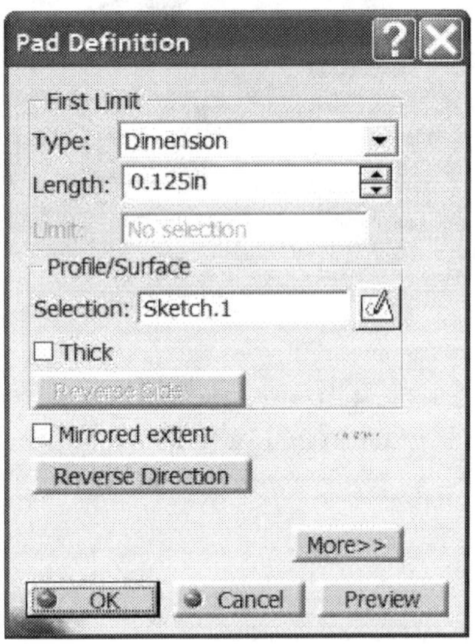


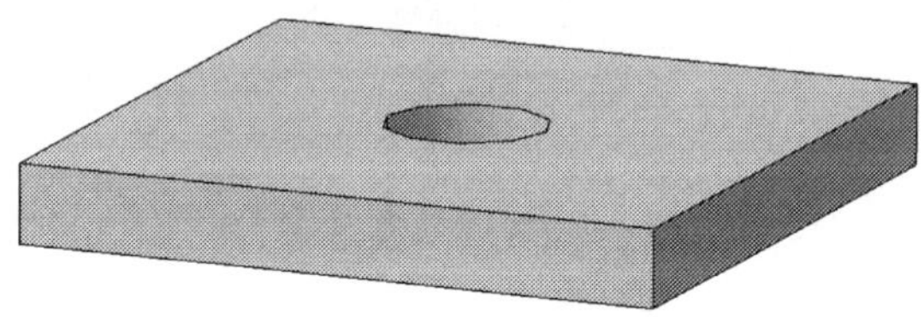

The best way of saving your work is to save the entire assembly. Double-click on the top branch of the tree. This lands you in the **Assembly Design** workbench.

The branch highlights in blue as a confirmation of the new workbench.

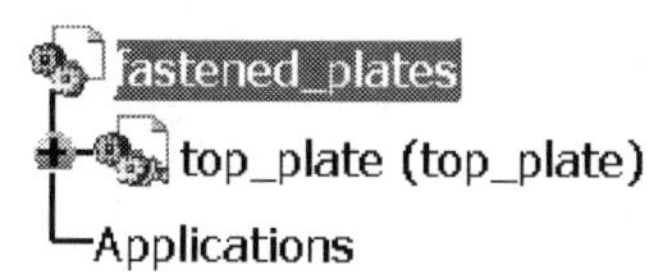


Select the **Save** icon . The **Save As** pop up box indicates that, saving the assembly, activates the saving of the parts. Choose the **Yes** button.

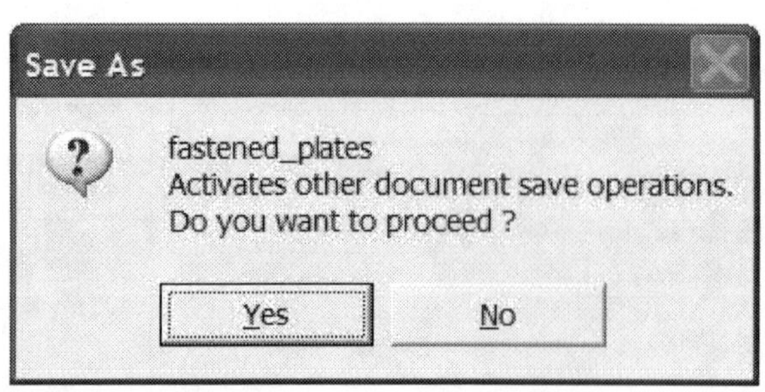


You are now ready to create the bottom_plate.

From the standard Windows toolbar, select **Insert > New Part**. The tree is modified to indicate that **Part.2** has been created.
You are also presented with pop up box on the right. Select **NO** to close the box.

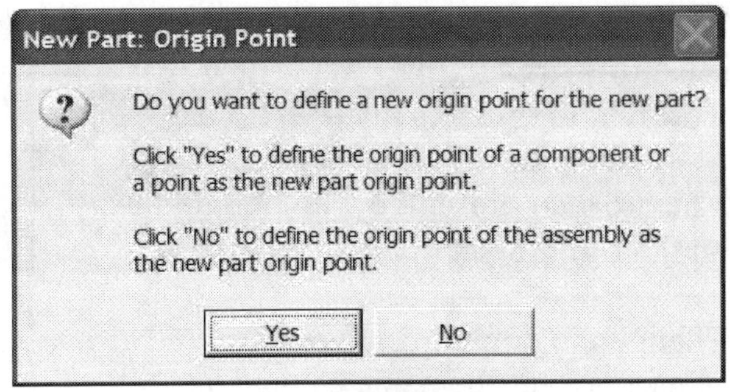


Change the default name to **bottom_plate**.
The tree, after the name change, is displayed on the right. Note that the instance name has also been changed to **bottom_plate**.

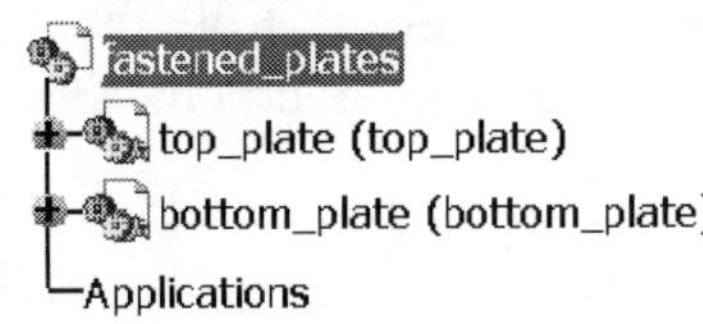


Double-click on the **bottom_plate** branch in the tree so that it is highlighted in blue, as shown on the right. This lands you in the **Part Design** workbench.

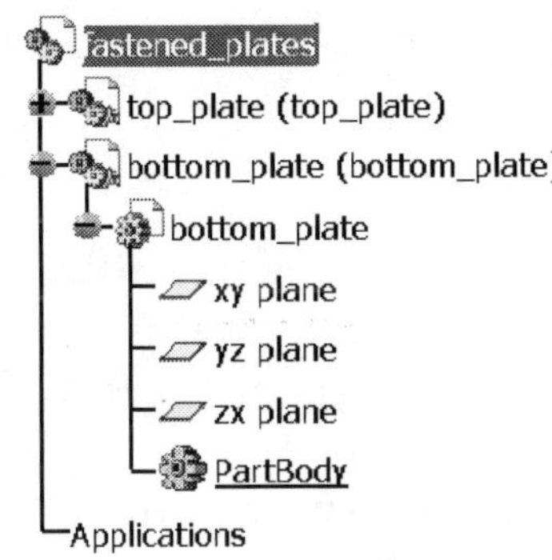


Select the **xy** plane from **bottom_plate** and enter the **Sketcher** .

In the **Sketcher**, draw the following profile with the indicated dimensions.

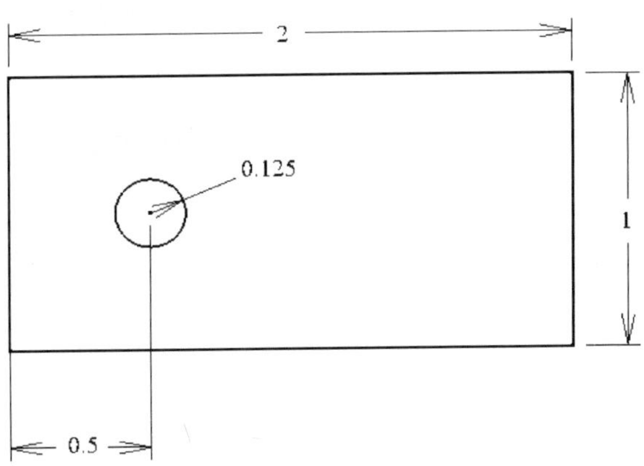


Leave the **Sketcher** .

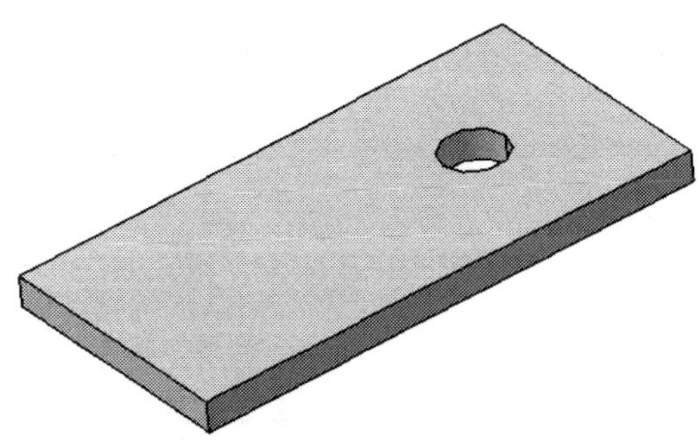

Use the **Pad** icon , specifying a **Length** of 0.125.

Next, you will create the bolt.

From the standard Windows toolbar, select **Insert > New Part**. The tree is modified to indicate that **Part.3** has been created.
You are also presented with pop up box on the right. Select **NO** to close the box.

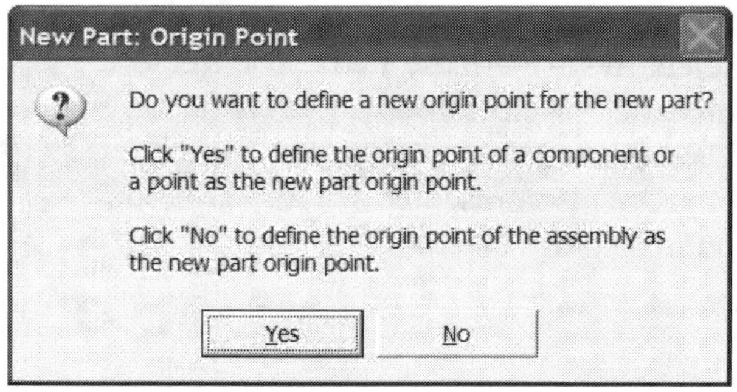


Change the default name to **bolt**.
The tree, after the name change, is displayed below. Note that the instance name has also been changed to **bolt**.

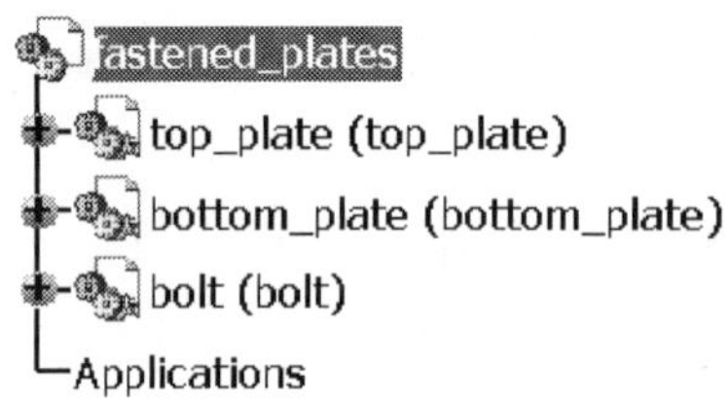


Double-click on the **bolt** branch in the tree so that it is highlighted in blue, as shown on the right.
This lands you in the **Part Design** workbench.

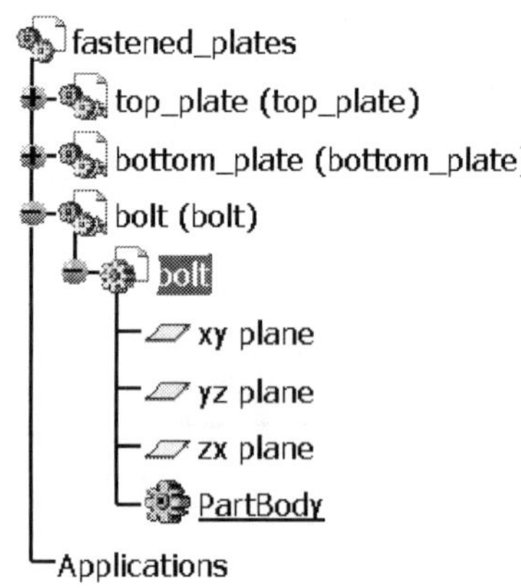


Select the **xy** plane from **bolt** and enter the **Sketcher** .

In the **Sketcher**, draw two concentric circles with the dimensions shown.

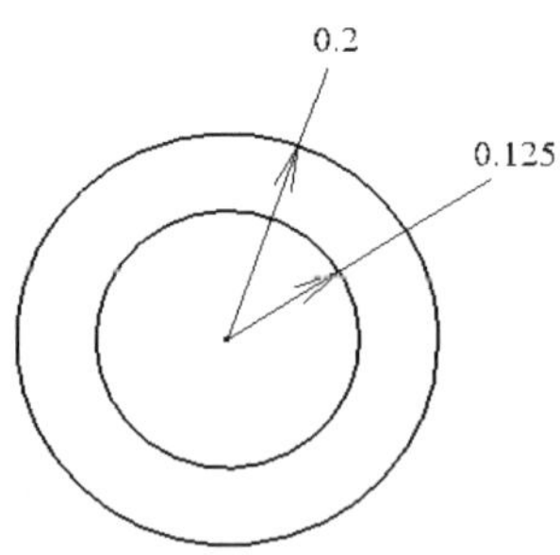


Select the **Multipad** icon , from the **Sketch-Based Features** toolbar

.

The resulting pop up box is shown on the right.
Select **Extrusion domain.1** and use **Length** 0.5 in.

Choose the **Preview** button to see what is done.

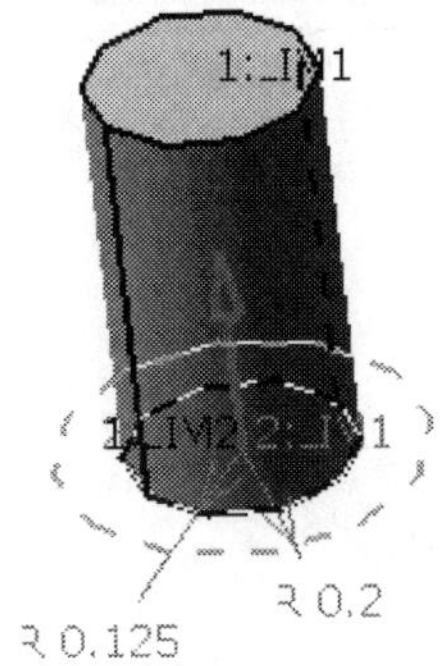


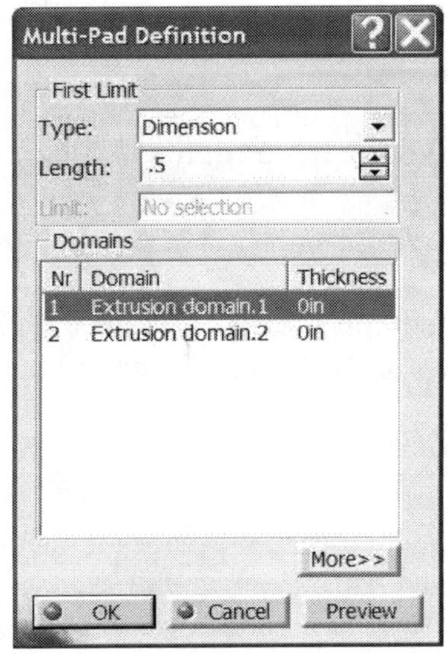


Next, select **Extrusion domain.2** and use **Length** 0.4 in.

Choose the **Preview** button to see what is done.

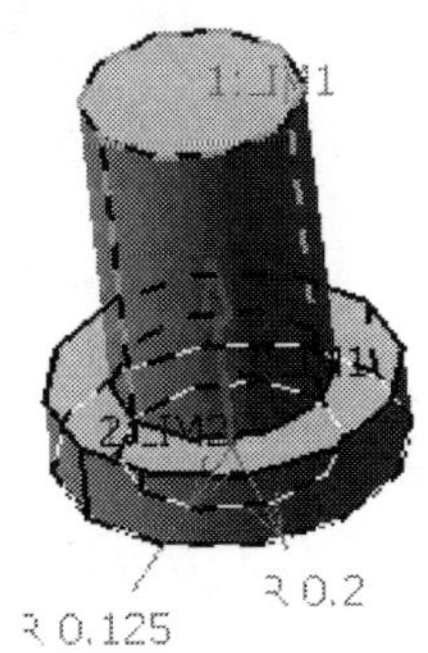


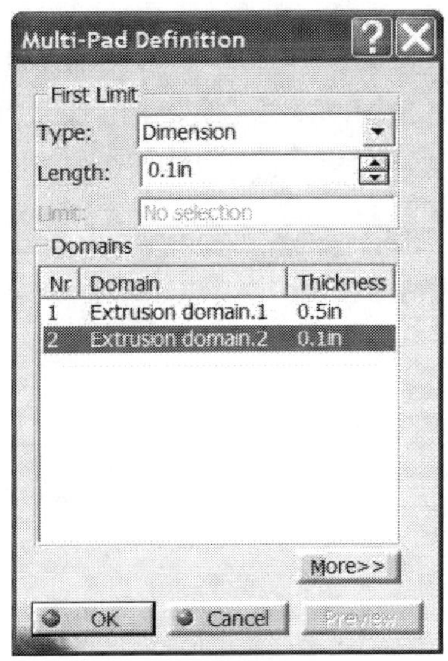


Upon closing the box, the bolt is created. For your convenience, the dimensions of the part are superimposed as displayed below.

The three parts generated, are arbitrarily positioned in space. No attempts were made to create them in their final location.

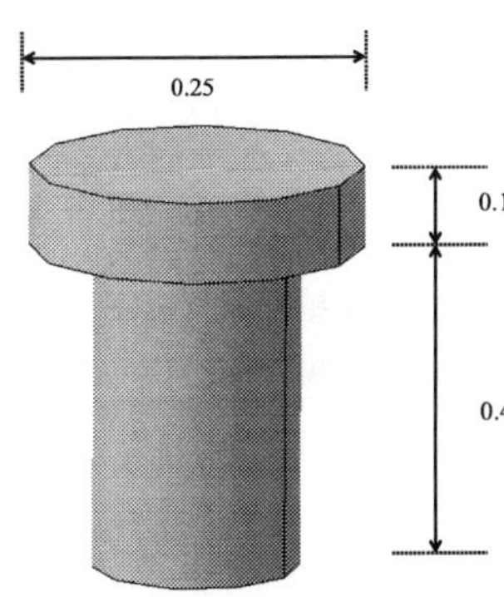


Assembly constraints will be used to move them into the correct position. Keep in mind that these constraints are not used by the **FEA** workbench.

Double-click on the top branch of the tree. This lands you in the **Assembly Design** workbench.

The branch highlights in blue as a confirmation of the new workbench.

Select the **Manipulation** icon from the **Move** toolbar 

. Separate the parts as you find convenient for further manipulation.

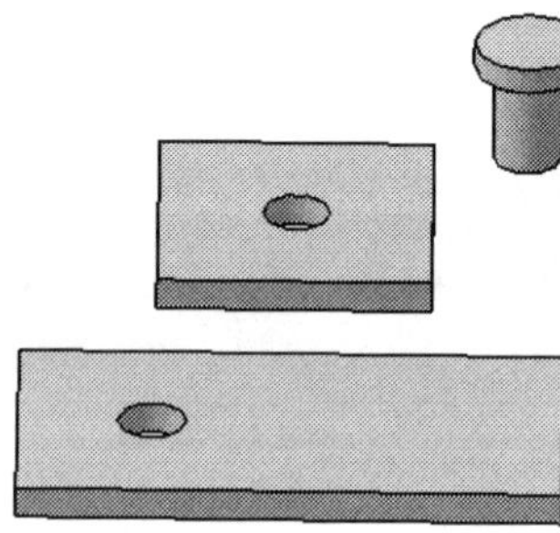

Depending the relative positioning of the parts on your computer screen, your constraints will be different. We will describe the constraints needed to bring the above configuration into the final position.

Pick the **Coincidence** icon  from **Constraints** toolbar 

. Choose the edges shown.

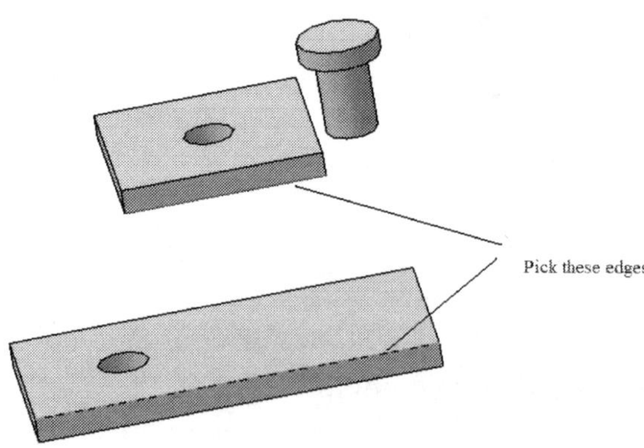


Use the **Update** icon  to activate the constraints. The result is shown on the right.

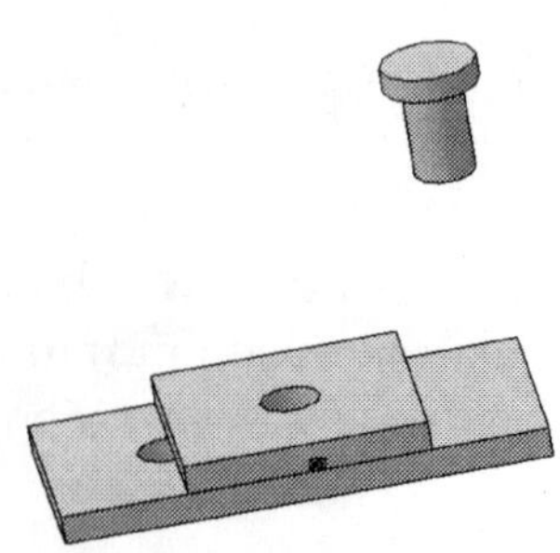

Use the **Coincidence** icon to pick the two vertices shown below.

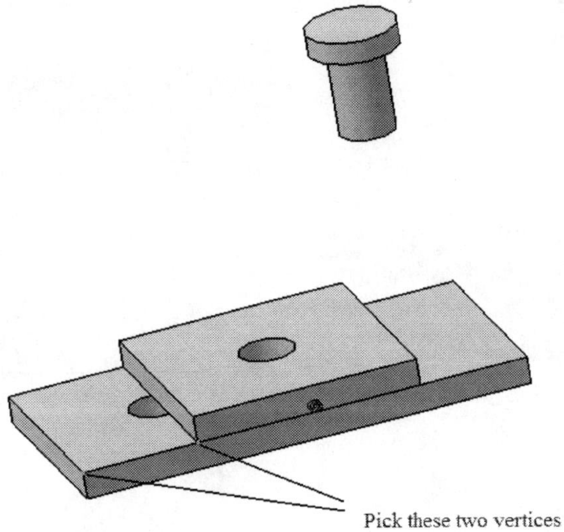


Use the **Update** icon to activate the constraints. The result is shown on the right.

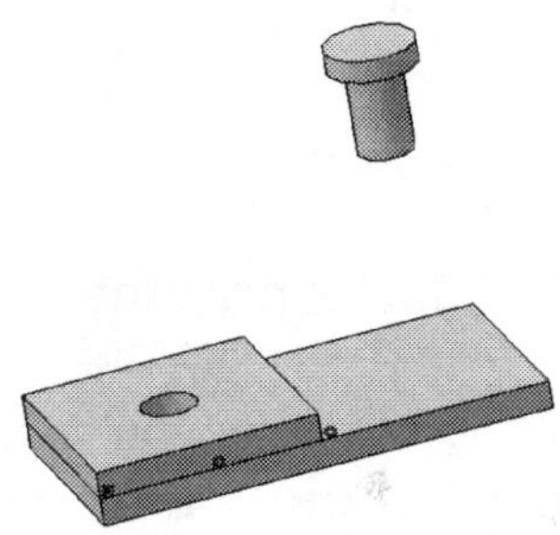

Use the **Coincidence** icon to pick the two axes shown below.

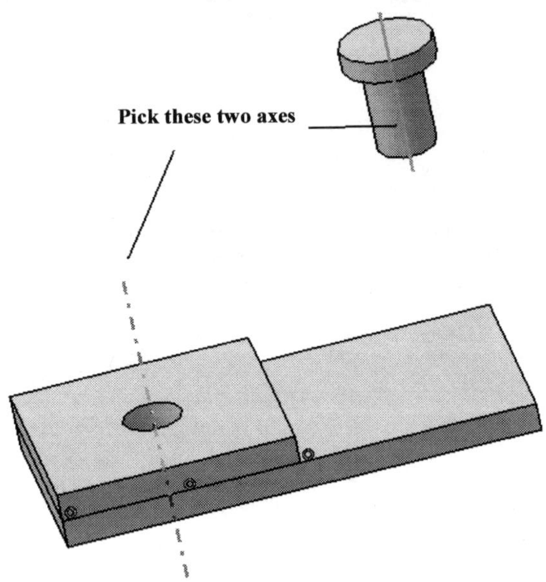


Use the **Update** icon to activate the constraints. The result is shown on the right.

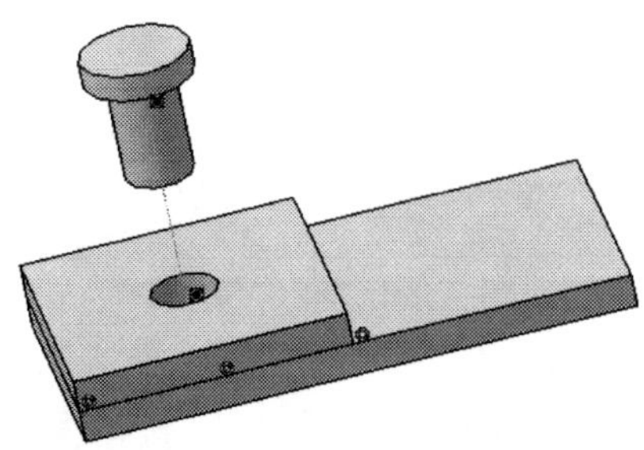

Use the **Coincidence** icon to pick the top face of the small plate and the bottom face of the bolt head. Close the pop up box that appears.

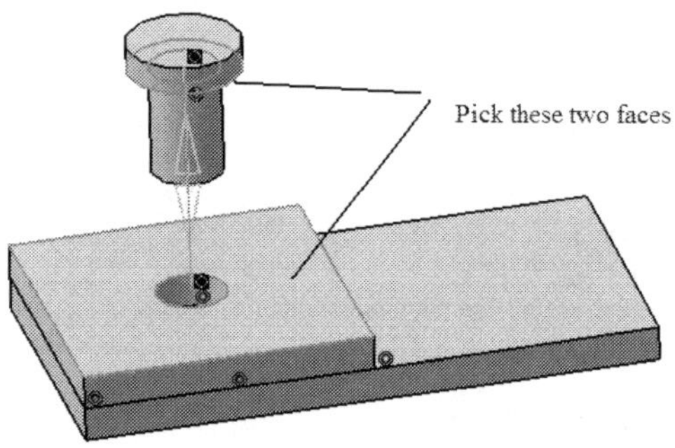


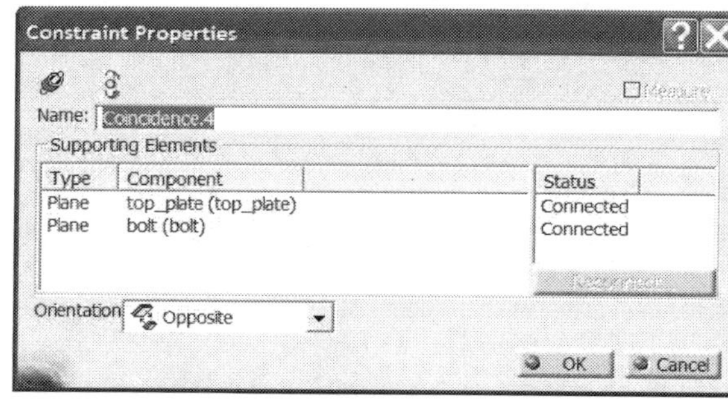


Use the **Update** icon to activate the constraints.
The result is shown on the right.

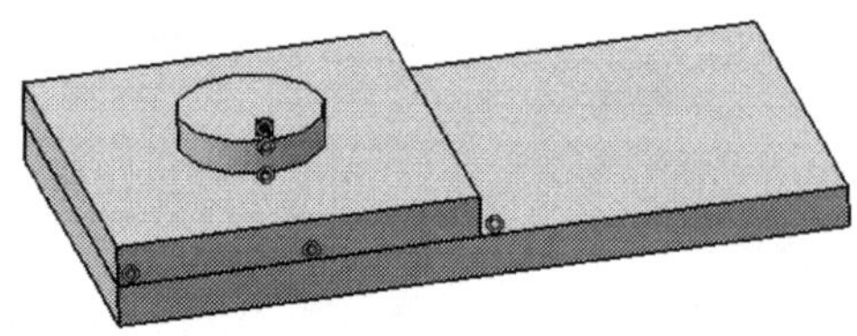

Select the **Apply Material** icon to activate the material **Library** box below.

Use the **Metal** tab on the top; select **Aluminum**. Use your cursor to pick the top level assembly from the tree at which time the **OK** and **Apply Material** buttons can be selected. Close the box.
The material property is now reflected in the tree.

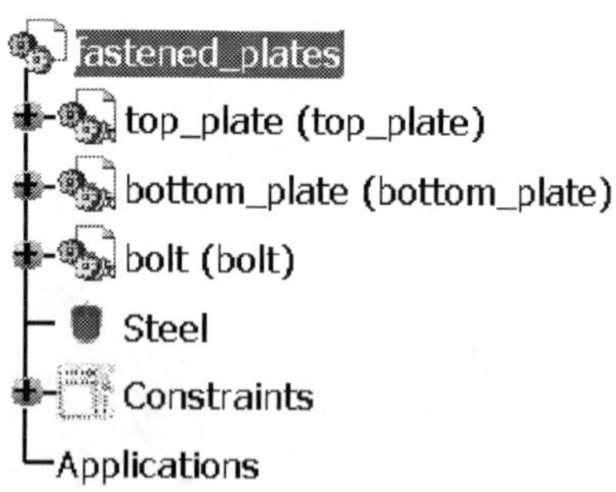


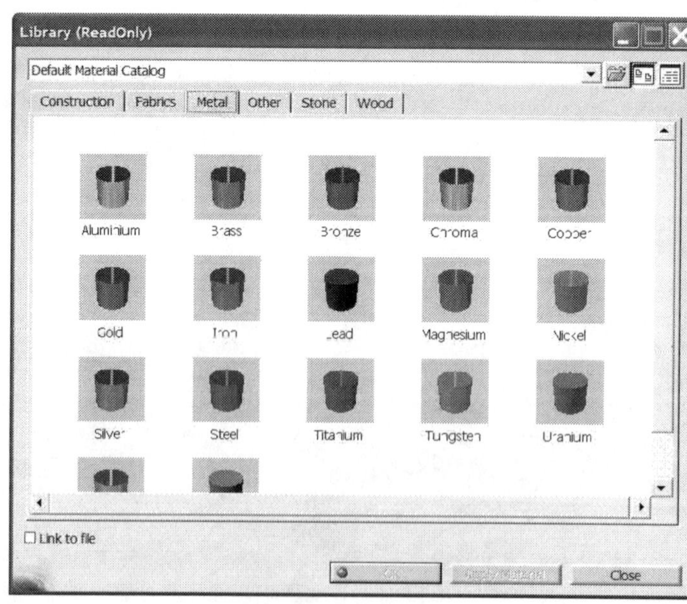

If the assembly does not look "shiny", you can change the rendering style from the **View mode** toolbar 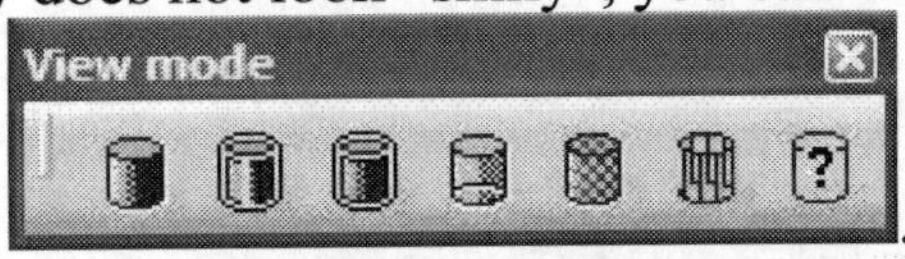

.

Next choose the **Shading with Material** icon 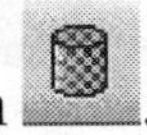.
This action results in a different rendering displayed below.

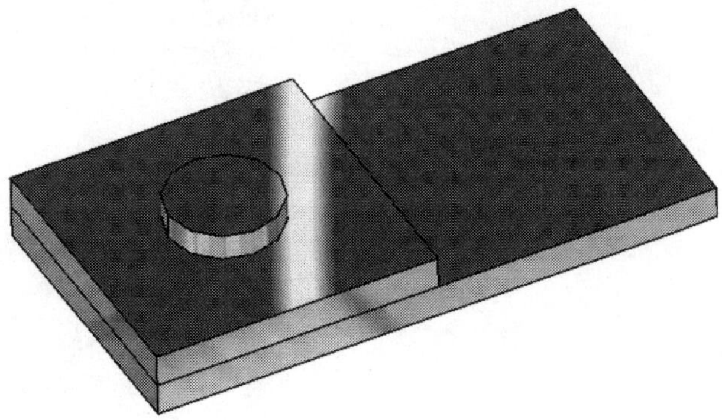

## 3 Entering the Analysis Solutions

From the standard Windows toolbar, select

**Start > Analysis & Simulation > Generative Structural Analysis** 

The box shown below, **New Analysis Case** is visible on the screen. The default choice is **Static Analysis** which is precisely what we intend to use. Therefore, close the box by clicking on **OK**.

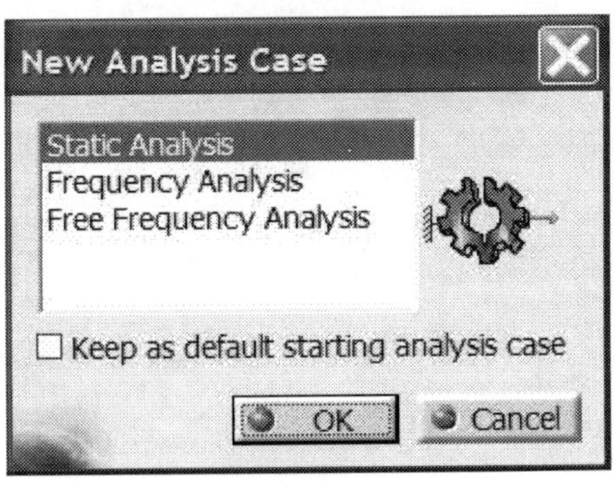


Note that the tree structure gets considerably longer. The bottom branches of the tree are presently "unfilled", and as we proceed in this workbench, assign loads and restraints, the branches gradually get "filled".

Another point that cannot be missed is the appearance of icons on each part that reflect a representative "size" and "sag". It is obvious that each on the three parts has its own mesh.

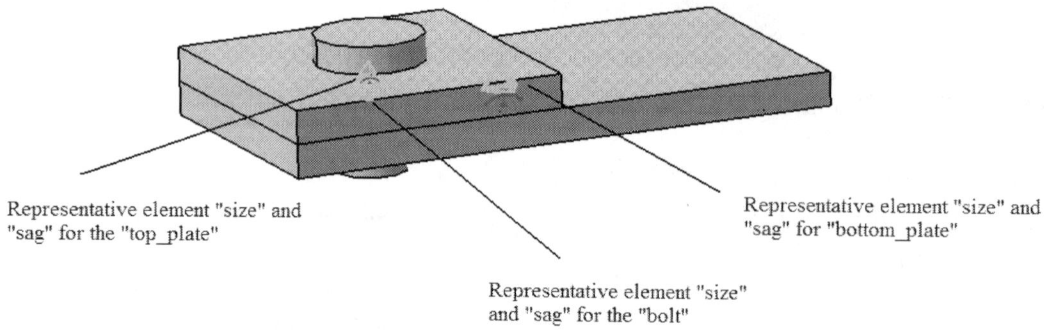


Note that the default “size” and “sag” values have a correlation with the physical size of the part.

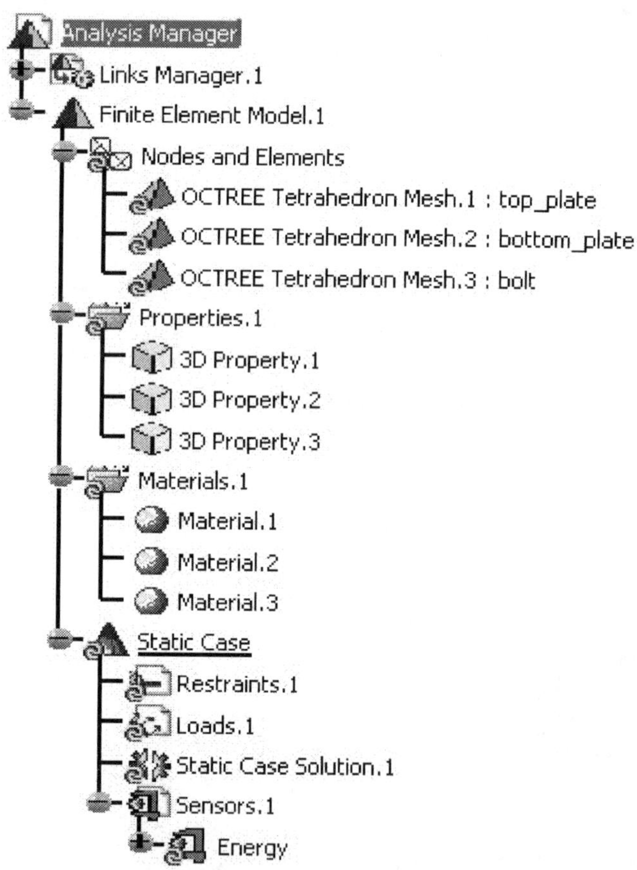

The concept of element size is self-explanatory. A smaller element size leads to more accurate results at the expense of a larger computation time. The "sag" terminology is unique to CATIA. In FEA, the geometry of a part is approximated with the elements. The surface of the part and the FEA approximation of a part do not coincide. The "sag" parameter controls the deviation between the two. Therefore, a smaller "sag" value could lead to better results. There is a relationship between these parameters that one does not have to be concerned with at this point.

The physical sizes of the representative "size" and "sag" on the screen, which also limit the coarseness of the mesh can be changed by the user. There are two ways to change these parameters:
The first method is to double-click on the representative icons on the screen which forces the **OCTREE Tetrahedron Mesh** box to open as shown to the right. This particular box corresponds to the mesh parameters for the **bolt**.

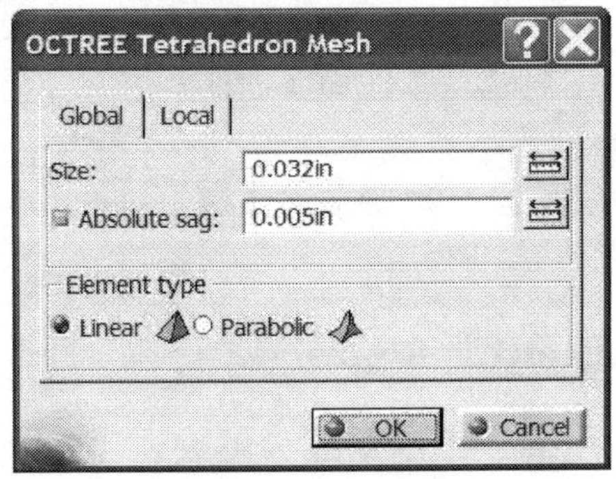


Keep all the default mesh parameters.

Notice that the type of the elements used (linear/parabolic) is also set in this box. Close the box by selecting **OK**.
The second method of reaching this box is through the tree.
By double-clicking on the branch labeled **OCTREE Tetrahedron Mesh** shown below, the same box opens allowing the user to modify the values.

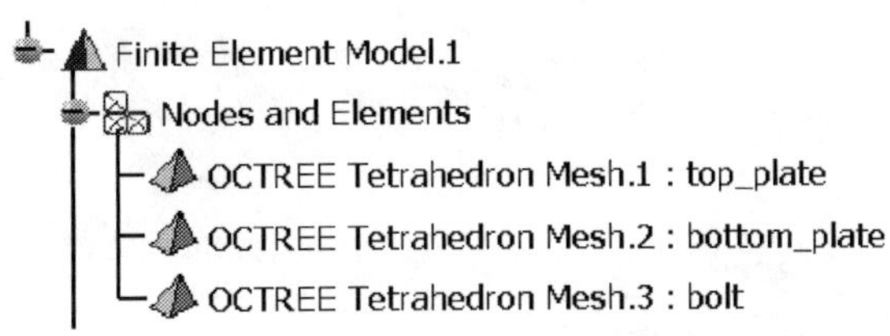


In order to view the generated mesh, you can point the cursor to the branch **Nodes and Elements**, right-click and select **Mesh Visualization**. This step may be slightly different in some UNIX machines. Upon performing this operation a **Warning** box appears which can be ignored by selecting **OK**. For the mesh parameters used, the mesh shown on the next page is displayed on the screen. See Note #2 in Appendix I.

The representative "size" and "sag" icons can be removed from the display by simply pointing to them, right-clicking and selecting **Hide**. This is the standard process for hiding any entity in CATIA V5.

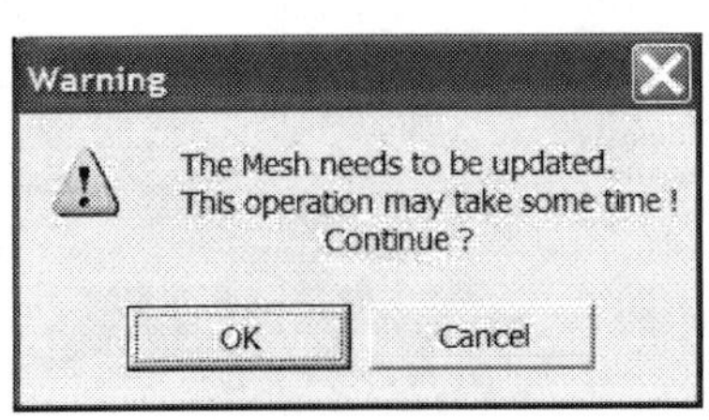

In general, the elements must be small in the regions of high stress gradient such as stress concentrations.

Uniformly reducing the element size for the whole part is a poor strategy.

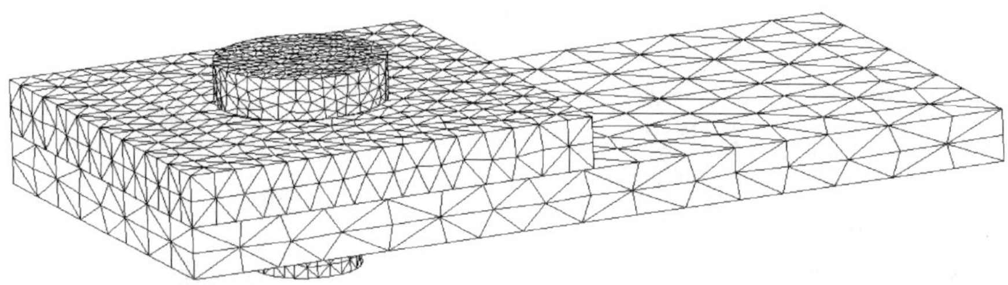

**Applying Restraints:**

CATIA's FEA module is geometrically based. This means that the boundary conditions cannot be applied to nodes and elements. The boundary conditions can only be applied at the part level. As soon as you enter the **Generative Structural Analysis** workbench, the parts are automatically hidden. Therefore, before boundary conditions are applied, the part must be brought to the unhide mode. This can be carried out by pointing the cursor to the top of the tree, the **Links Manager.1** branch, right-click, select **Show**. At this point, the parts and the mesh are superimposed as shown below and you have access to the part.

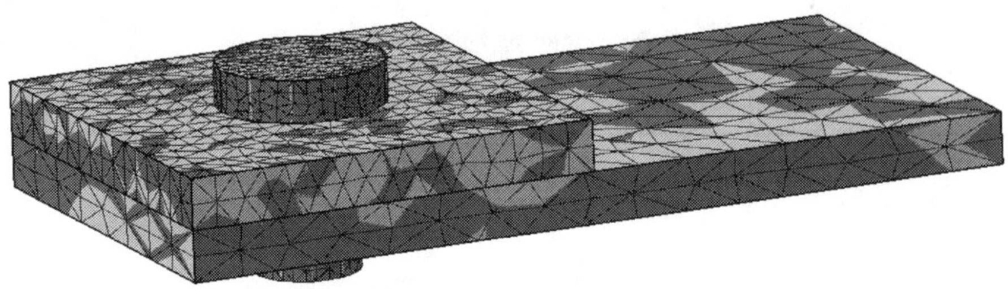

If, the presence of the mesh is annoying, you can always hide it. Point the cursor to **Nodes and Elements**, right-click, **Hide**.
In FEA, restraints refer to applying displacement boundary conditions which is achieved through the **Restraint** toolbar 
.

Select the **Clamp** icon 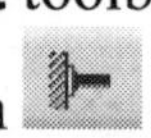 and pick the back faces of the plates.

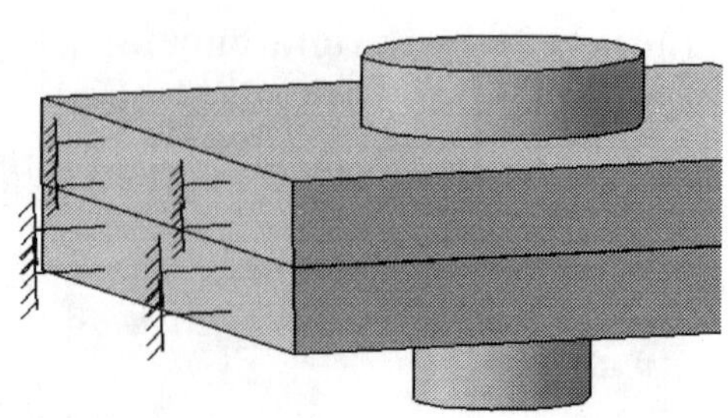

*Note: __The first analysis involves only the preload in the bolt.__*

## Creating Analysis Connection:

In this step, you establish which components interact with each other. The nature of the interaction is to be specified later.

Use the **General Analysis Connection** icon , from the **Analysis Supports** toolbar 

.

### *__Interaction between the "bolt" and the "top_plate":__*

Click on the icon .
For **First component**, select the bottom face of the bolt head.
For the **Second Component,** select the top face of the smaller plate.

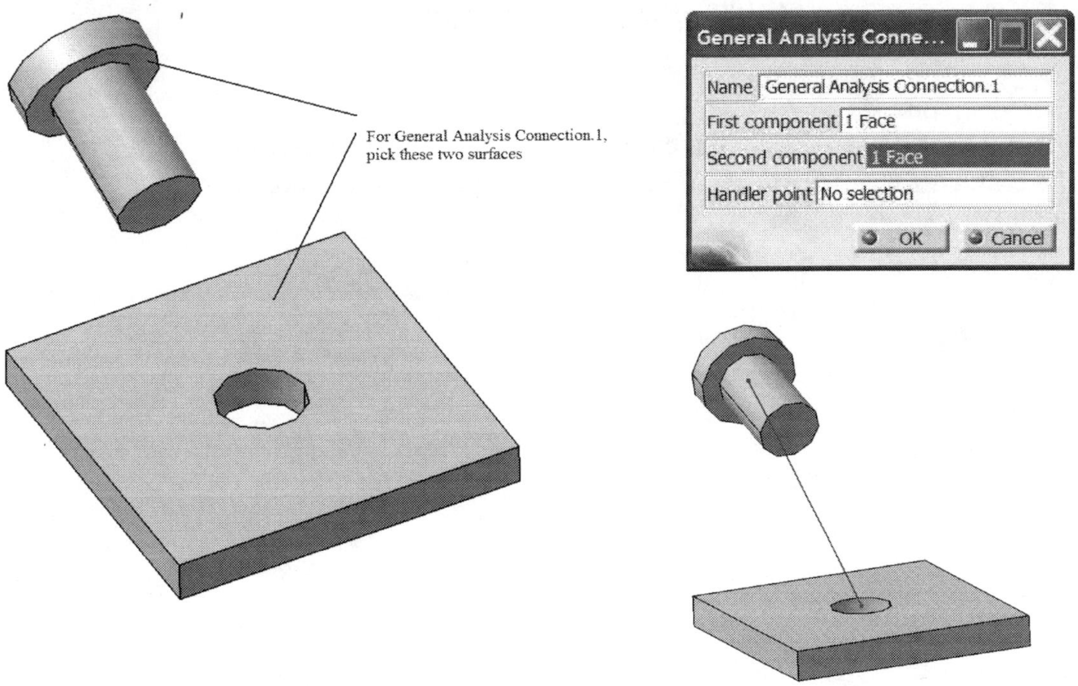


Click on the icon .
For **First component**, select the cylindrical surface of the bolt (threads).
For the **Second Component**, select the inside surface of the hole from top_ plate.
These are displayed in the next page.

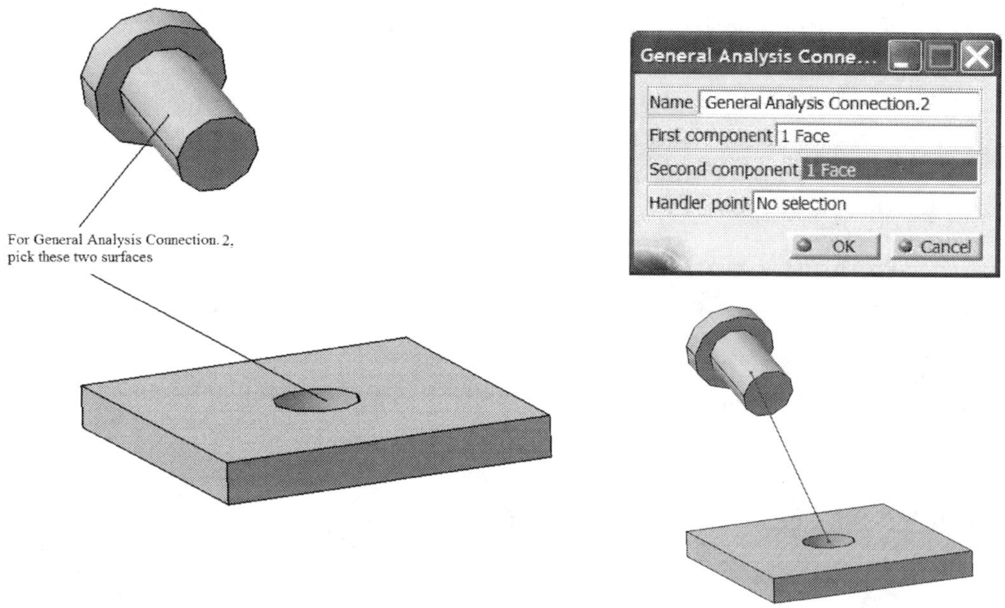


## *Interaction between the "bolt" and the "bottom_plate":*

Click on the icon .
For **First component**, select the cylindrical surface of the bolt (threads).
For the **Second Component**, select the inside surface of the hole from the bottom_plate.

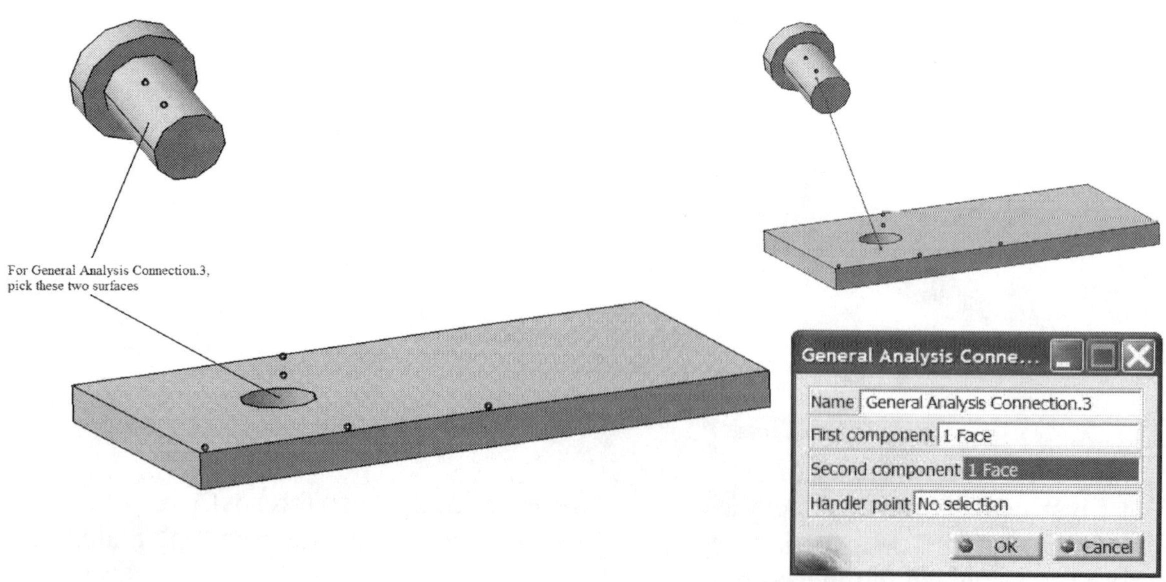

## *Interaction between the "top_plate" and the "bottom_plate":*

Click on the icon .
For **First component**, select the bottom face of the top_plate.
For the **Second Component**, select the top face of the bottom_plate.

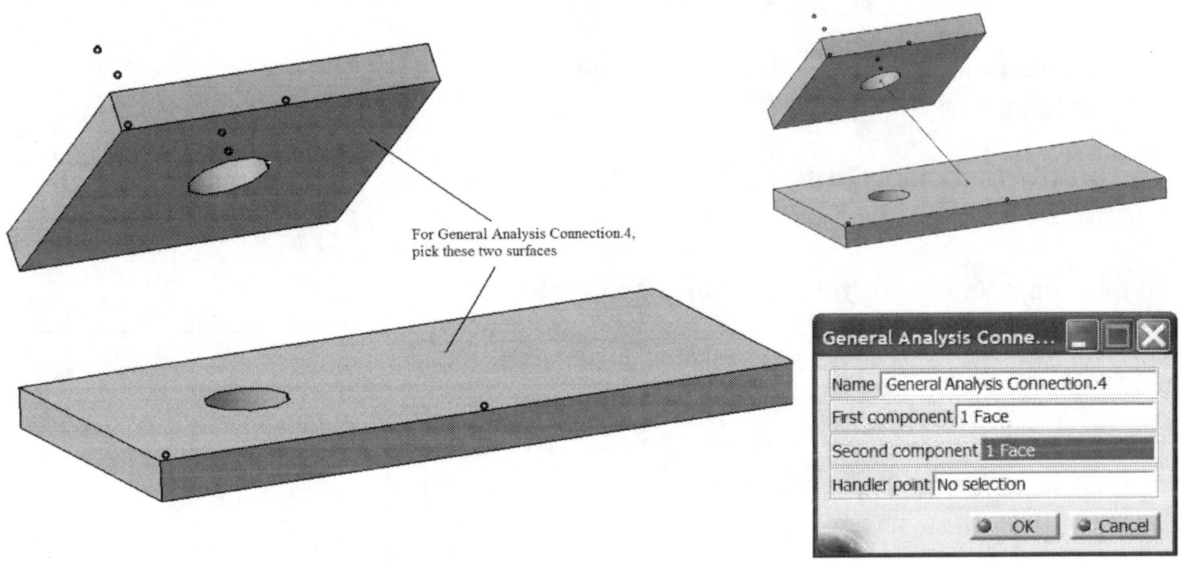


The figure below shows the assembly with all the **General Analysis Connection** icons showing.

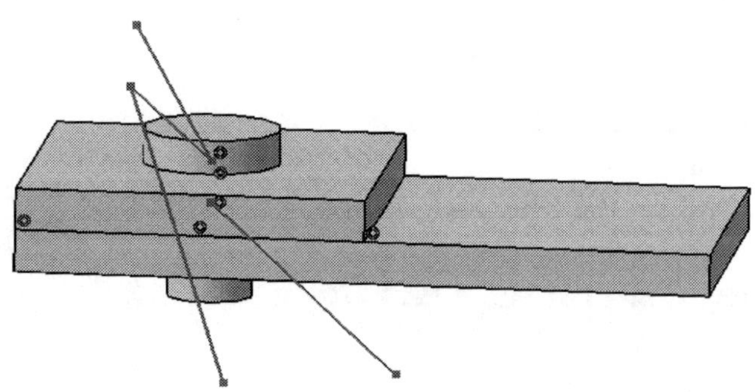

The portion of the tree pertaining to the **Analysis Connections.1** is displayed below.

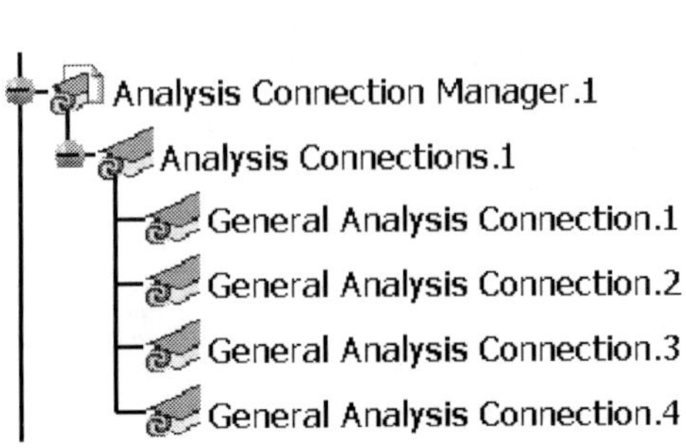

## Defining the Nature of the Analysis Connection:

***Type of Interaction between the "bolt" and the "top plate":***

Click on the **Contact Connection property** icon 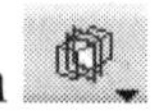 from the **Face Face Connections** toolbar 

.
The pop up box, shown on the right, appears.

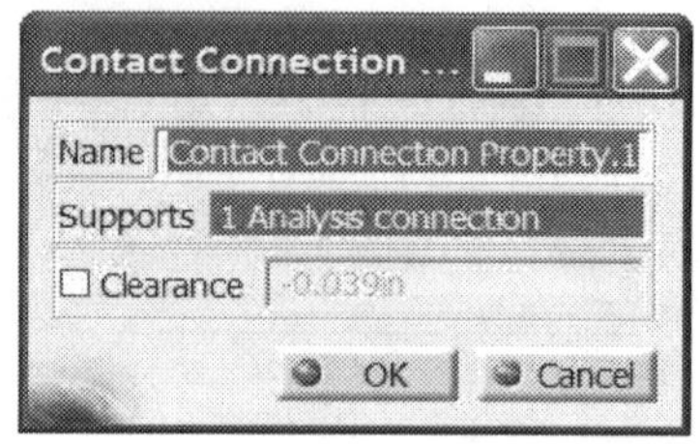


For **Supports**, select **General Analysis Connection.1** from the tree.

On the computer screen, you notice that the standard symbol for contact is created.

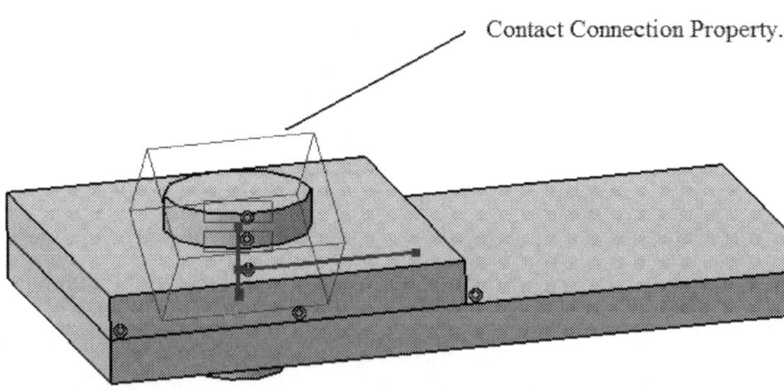

Click on the **Contact Connection property** icon 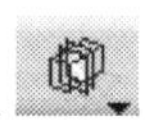 from the **Face Face Connections** toolbar.
The pop up box, shown on the right, appears.

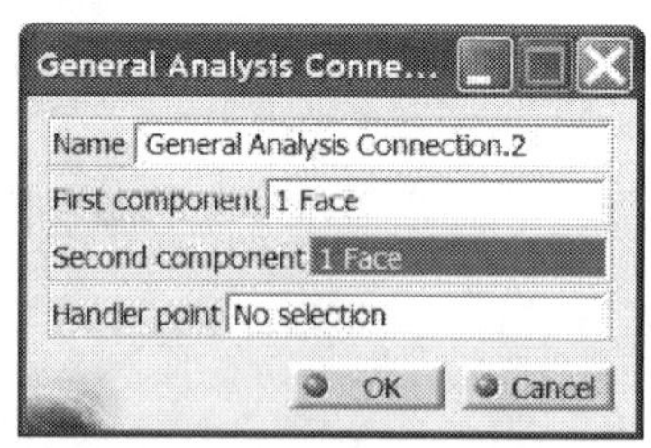


For **Supports**, select **General Analysis Connection.2** from the tree.
On the computer screen, you notice that the standard symbol for contact is created.

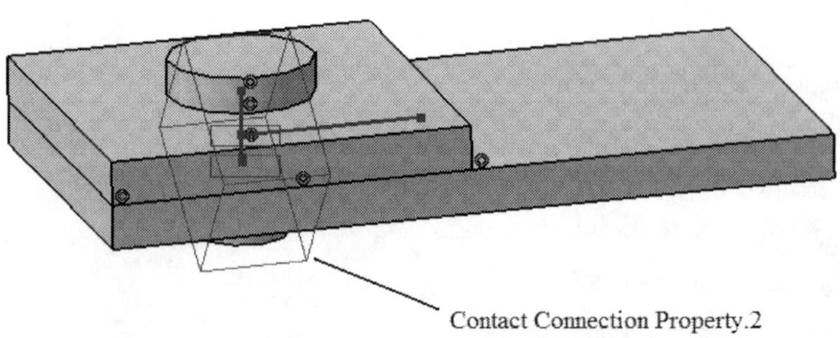

***Type of Interaction between the "bolt" and the "bottom plate":***

Click on the **Contact Connection property** icon from the **Face Face Connections** toolbar.

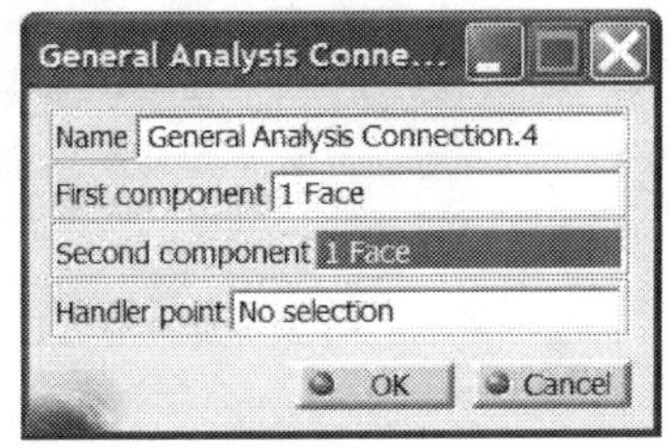


The pop up box, shown on the right, appears.

For **Supports**, select **General Analysis Connection.3** from the tree.

On the computer screen, you notice that the standard symbol for contact is created.

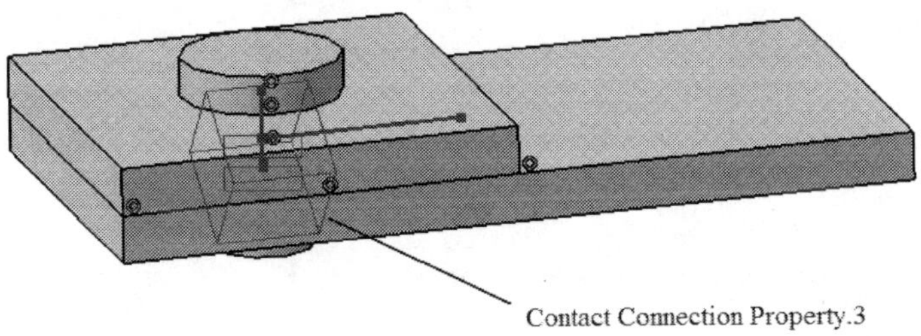


Finally, declare the **General Analysis Connection.4** to be a contact just like above.

Click on the **Bolt Tightening Connection property** icon from the **Face Face Connections** toolbar

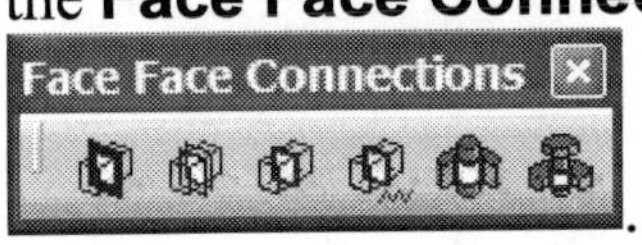


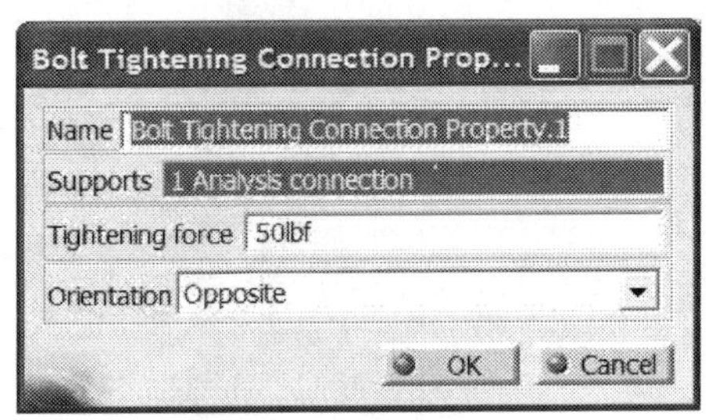


The pop up box, shown on the right, appears.

For **Supports**, select **General Analysis Connection.3** from the tree.

Note: For **Orientation** try **Opposite**; however if the deformation results are unrealistic, change it to **Same**.

Use a **Tightening force** of 50 lb.

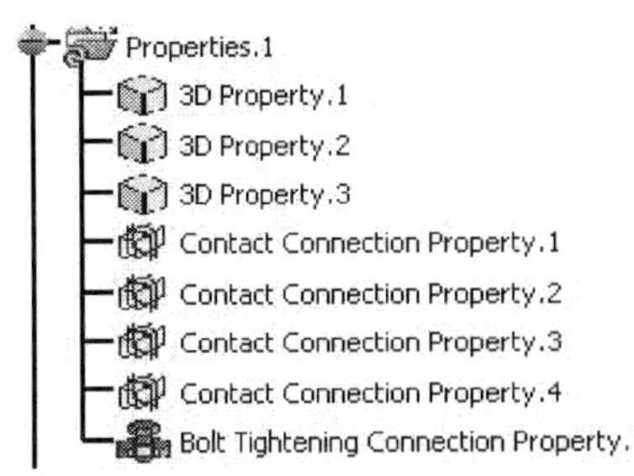


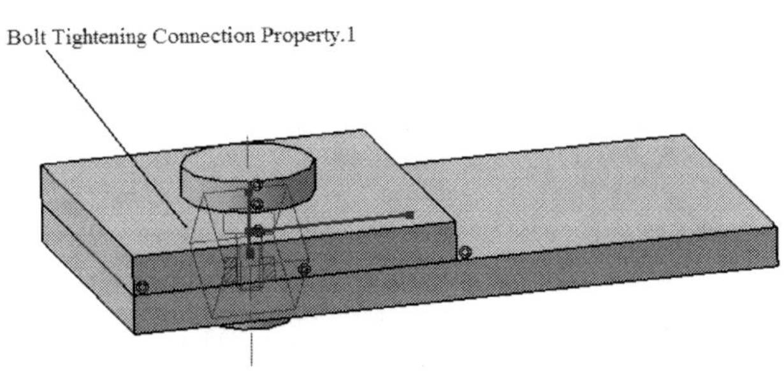

**NOTE:** In your case, you may not see the big red boxes representing contact connection appearing on the screen. This depends on how you had manipulated the parts. It is better to rely on the tree to decide what connections have been established.

On the computer screen, you notice that the standard symbol for contact is created.

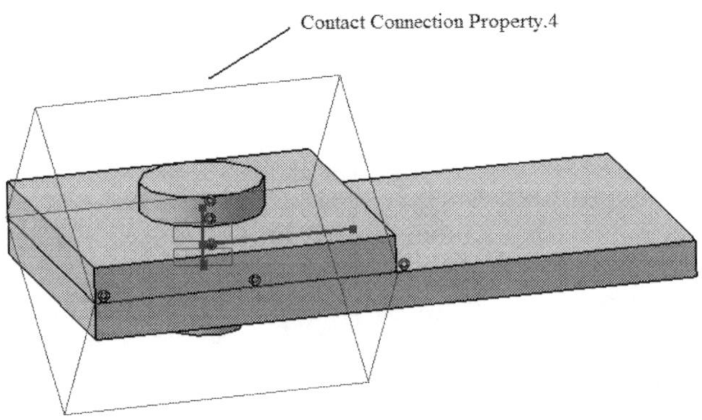


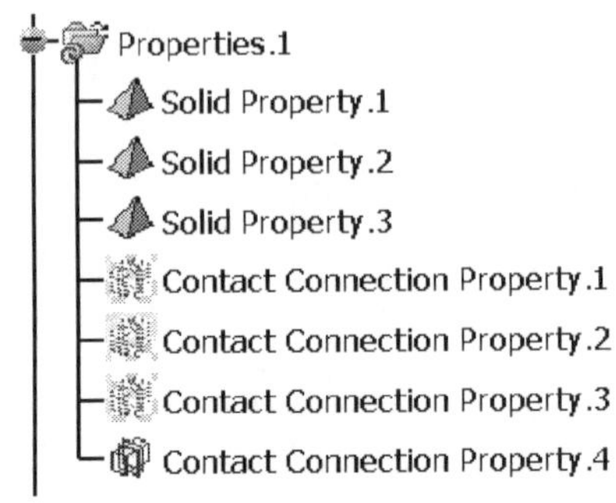


The figure below displays all the connection constraints simultaneously.

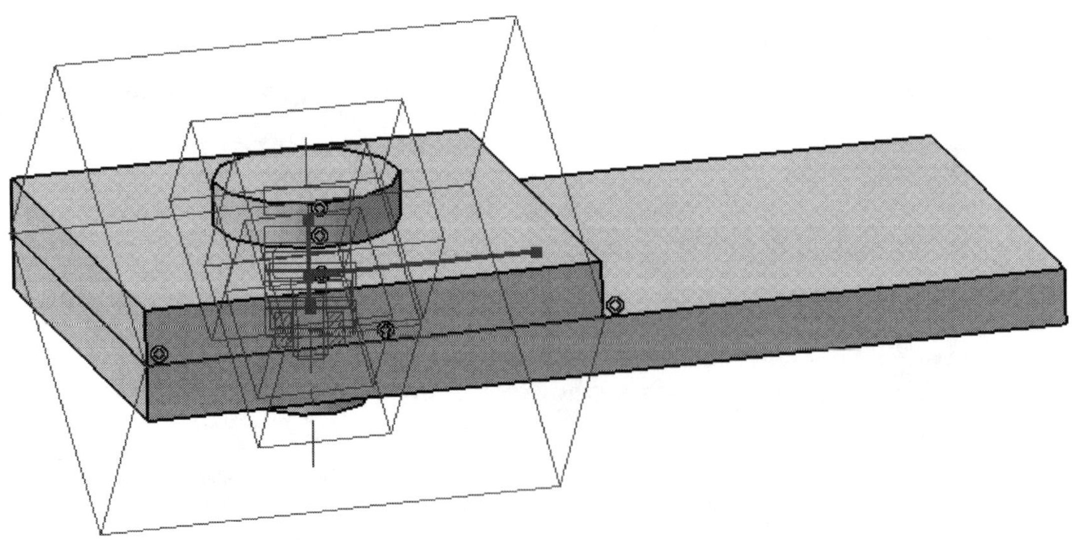

The complete tree is shown for your information.

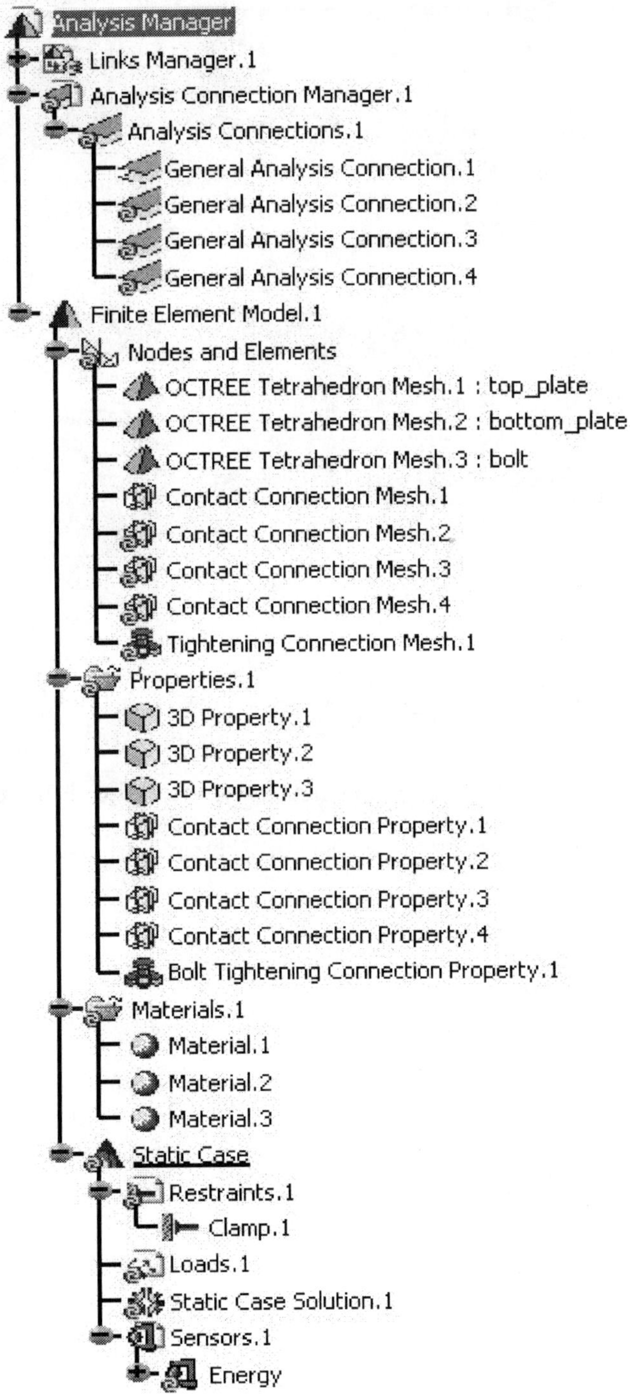

**Launching the Solver:**

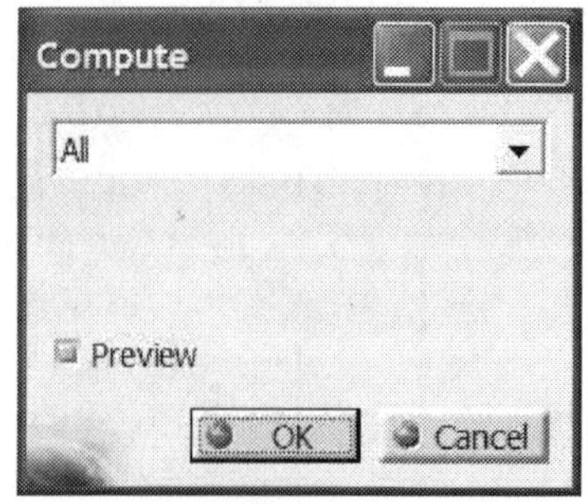


To run the analysis, you need to use the **Compute** toolbar 

by selecting the **Compute** icon . This leads to the **Compute** box shown to the right. Leave the defaults as **All** which means everything is computed.
Upon closing this box, after a brief pause, the second box shown below appears.
This box provides information on the resources needed to complete the analysis. If the estimates are zero in the listing, then there is a problem in the previous step and should be looked into. If all the numbers are zero in the box, the program may run but would not produce any useful results.

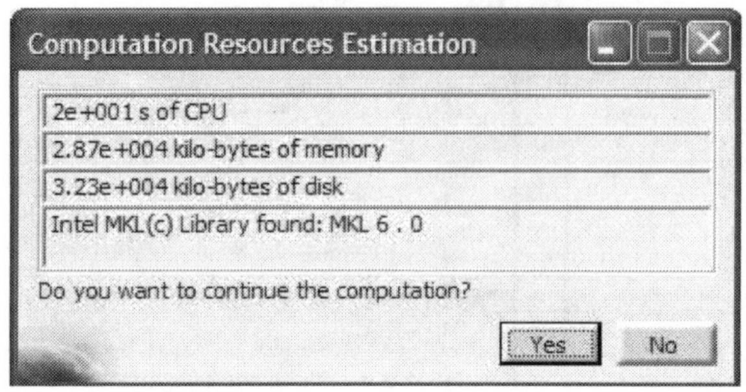


**Postprocessing:**

The main postprocessing toolbar is called **Image** 

. To view the deformed shape you have to use the **Deformation** icon 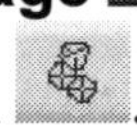. The resulting deformed shape is displayed below.

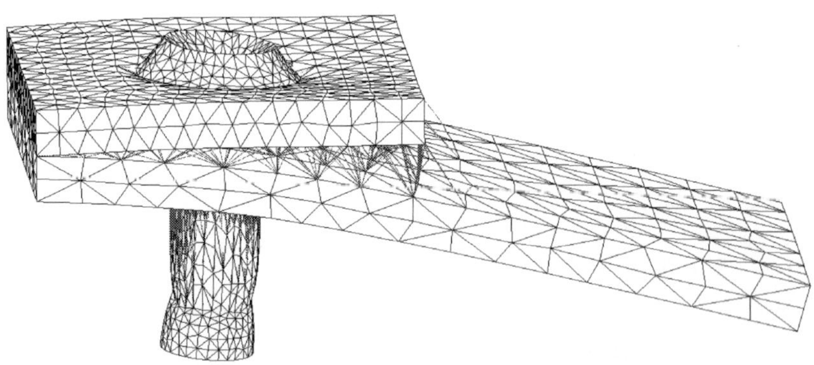

<u>It is important to recall that the only load present is the pre-tension of the bolt</u>.

In order to see the displacement field, the **Displacement** icon  in the **Image** toolbar should be used. The default display is in terms of displacement arrows.

The arrow plot is not particularly useful. In order to view the contour plot of the displacement field, position the cursor on the arrow field and double-click. The **Image Edition** box shown on the right opens.

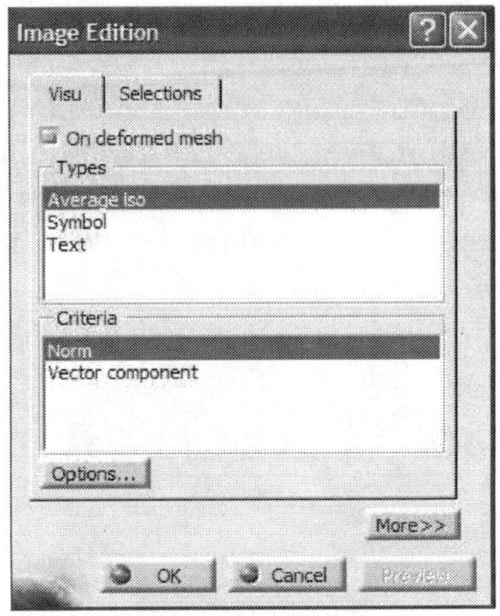


The contour of the displacement field is given below.

Note: The color map has been changed; otherwise everything looks black in the figure.

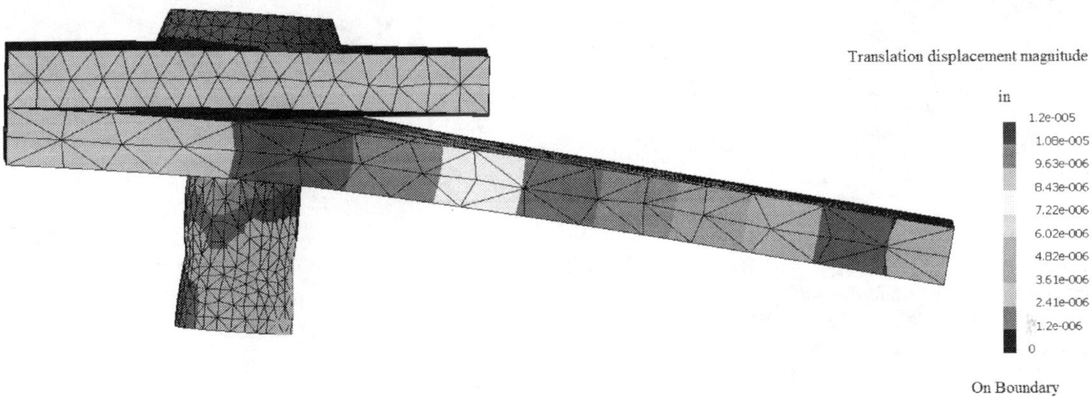


The next step in the postprocessing is to plot the contours of the von Mises stress using the **von Mises Stress** icon  in the **Image** toolbar.
The von Mises stress is displayed below.

Occasionally, you may be interested in plotting the von Mises stress contour in individual parts of the assembly or even the supports. In order to achieve this, double-click on the contour levels on the screen to open the image edition box. Next use the filter tab as shown below. Here, you have the choice of selecting different entities. The contour below is the stress distribution in the bolt alone.

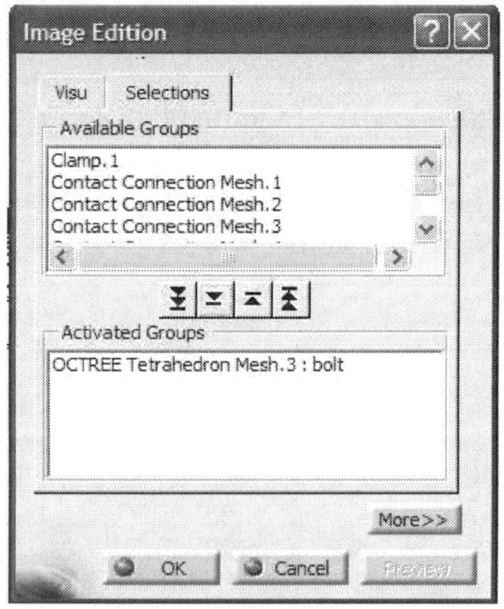


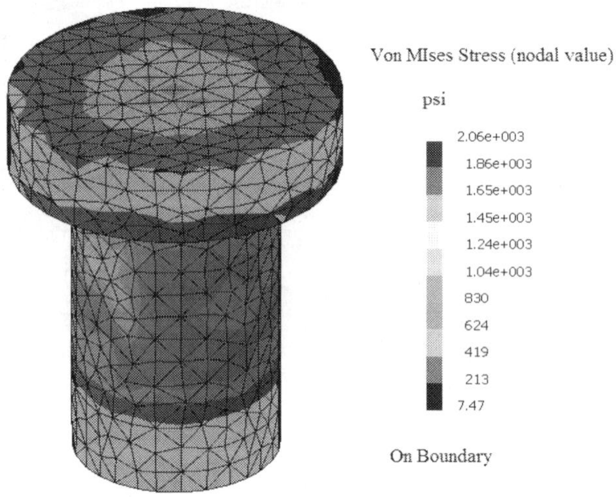


The **Cutting Plane** icon  from the **Analysis Tools** toolbar

can be used to make a cut through the part at a desired location and inspect the stresses inside of the part. The **Cut Plane** box allows you to keep the plane or to remove it for display purposes. A typical cutting plane is shown below.

The frustum associated with pre-loaded bolts is clearly visible with the cutting plane.

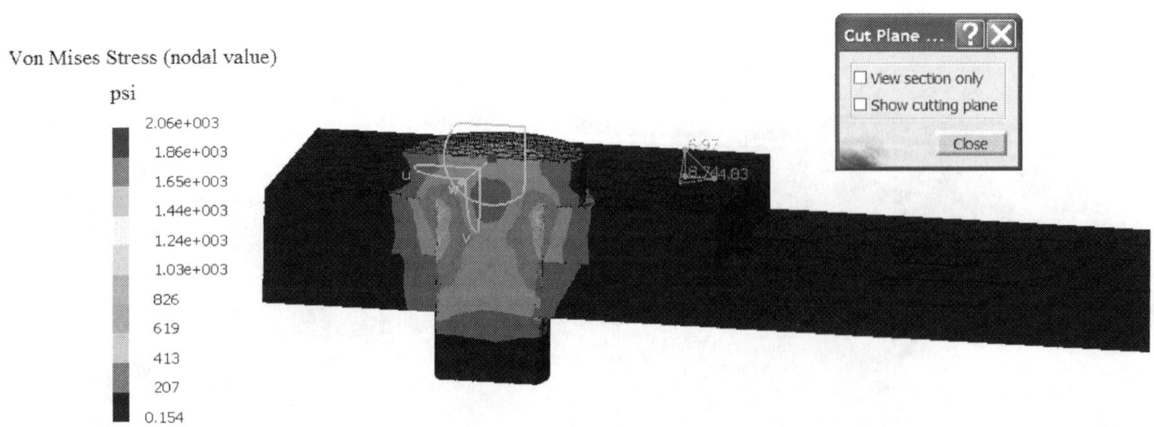

## Applying the Load:

***In view of the fact that during the assembly process, you may have permanently rotated the parts in space, you need to create a User coordinate system. Double-click on the bottom_plate on the screen.*** This lands you in the **Part Design** workbench.

From the **Tools** toolbar 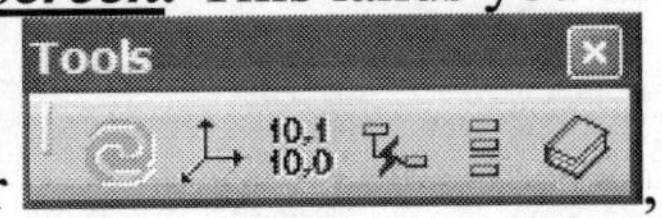



, select the **Axis System** icon 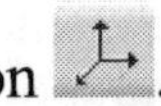. At this point, the **Axis System Definition** box shown on the right opens. Use the cursor to pick the vertex as shown.

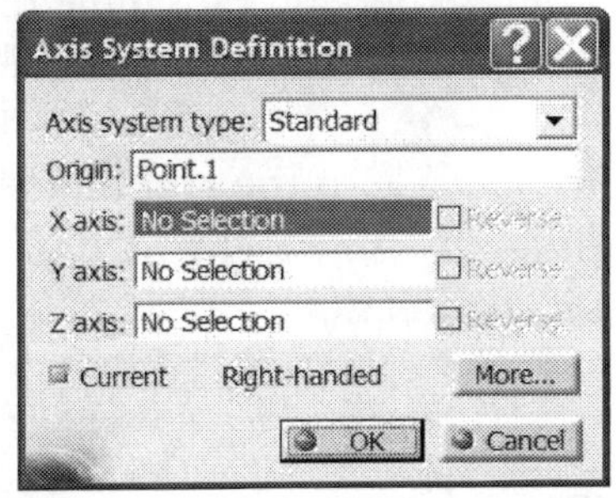



You will see that an axis system is displayed on the screen.

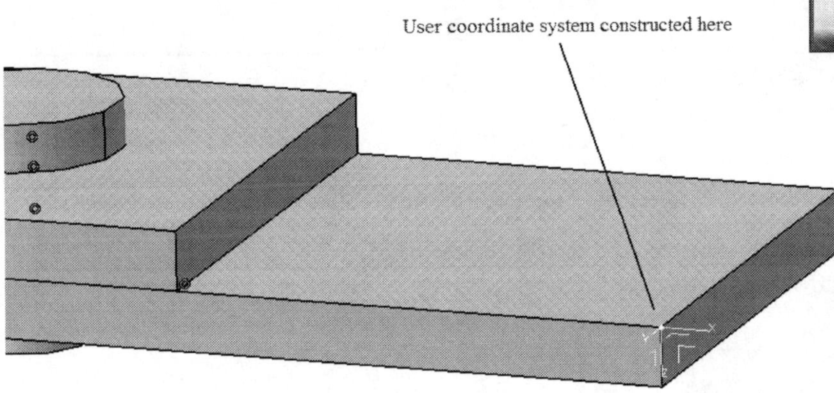



In FEA, loads refer to forces. The **Loads** toolbar 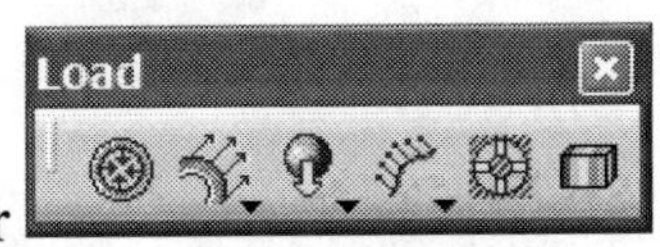



is used for this purpose. Select the **Distributed force** icon , and with the cursor pick the edge of the **bottom_plate** as shown.

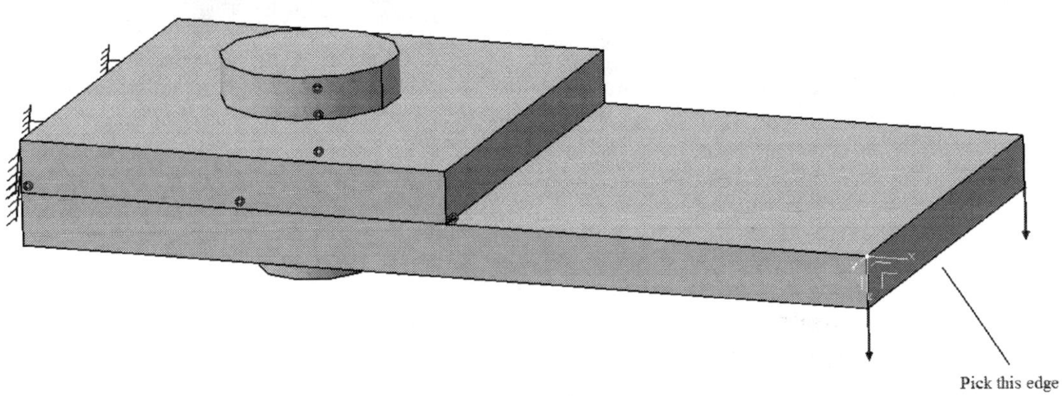

In reference to the **Load** operation above, the following selections in the pop up box have to be made.

For **Supports** select the edge shown.
For **Type** select **User**.
As the **Current Axis**, pick the coordinate system just constructed.
Finally, depending on the orientation of this axis, apply the load in the proper direction.

In the case of the coordinate directions displayed in the previous figure, the load of 100 lb is to be applied in the z-direction.

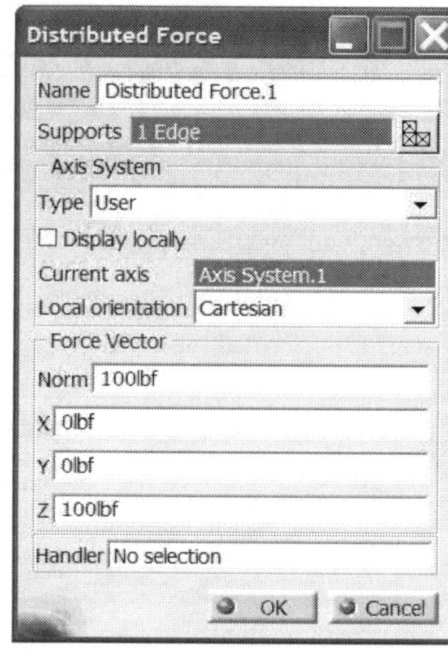


Select the **Compute** icon  to run the analysis.

Pick the **von Mises Stress** icon  in the **Image** toolbar.
The von Mises stress is displayed below. Note that the maximum stress is roughly ten times larger that the unloaded case.

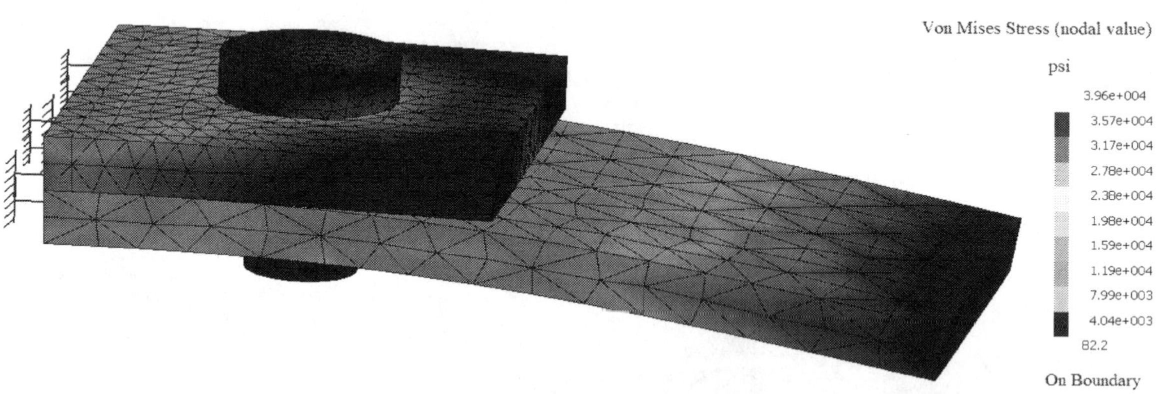

Using the cutting **Cutting Plane** icon, you can see that the von Mises stresss distribution has substantially changed.

Using the icon **Generate Report** in the **Analysis Results** toolbar  an HTML based report can be generated which summarizes the features and results of the FEA model.

Animation of the model can be achieved through the **Animate** icon in the

**Analysis Tools** toolbar  and AVI files can easily be generated.

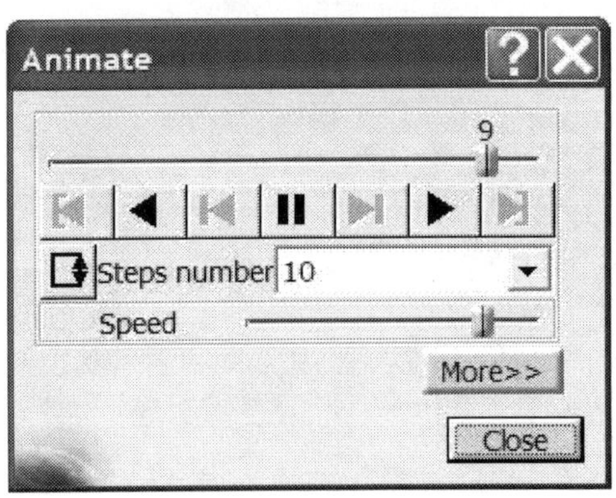

# Exercises for Chapter 17

## Problem 1: Bolt & Nut Assembly

Using dimensions of your choice, model the bolt and nut assembly and give it a specified preload.

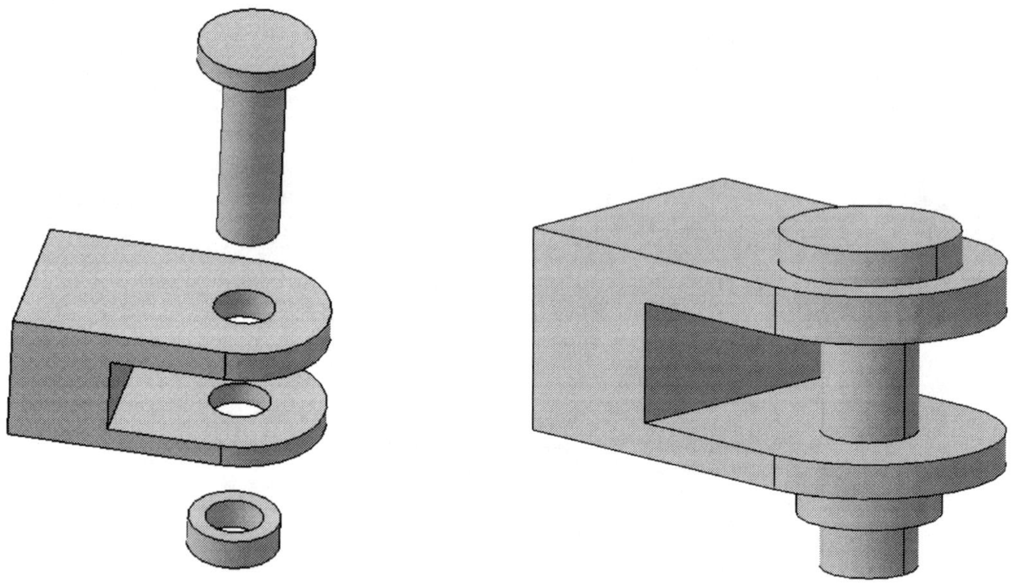

# Chapter 18

# Thermal Stresses in a Bi-metallic Strip

## Introduction

In this tutorial, a bi-metallic strip made of aluminum and steel, bonded together at their interface is analyzed. The strip is subjected to a uniform temperature rise. The difference in the thermal expansion coefficients results in the deflection of the strip.

## 1 Problem Statement

The dimensions in the bi-metallic strip are shown below. This structure is subjected to a uniform temperature rise of $50^{\circ}$ F. Aluminum has a larger coefficient of thermal expansion than steel. Therefore due to the temperature rise, the strip bends down. Use CATIA to find the tip deflection and the von Mises stress distribution in the assembly. In view of the fact that the stresses are developed because of the temperature change, they are referred to as the thermal stresses.

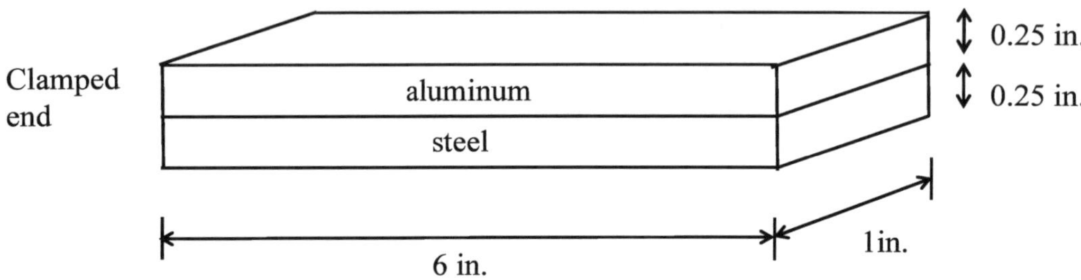


## 2 Creation of the Assembly in the Mechanical Design Solutions

Enter the **Assembly Design** workbench  which can be achieved by different means depending on your CATIA customization. For example, from the standard Windows toolbar, select **File > New** 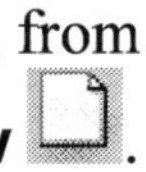.

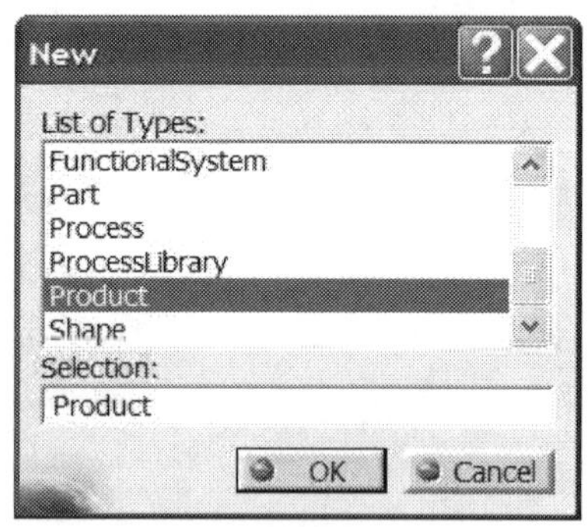


From the box shown on the right, select **Product**. This moves you to the **Assembly Design** workbench and creates a part with the default name **Product.1**.

In order to change the default name, move the cursor to **Product.1** in the tree, right-click and select **Properties** from the menu list.

From the **Properties** box, select the **Product** tab and in **Part Number** type **bi_metallic strip**.

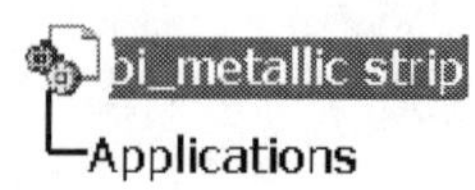


This will be the new product name throughout the chapter.

You now create the aluminum strip as a part.
From the standard Windows toolbar, select **Insert > New Part**. The tree is modified to indicate that **Part.1** has been created. Change the default name to **aluminum_strip**. The tree, before and after the name change, is displayed below. Note that the instance name has also been changed to **aluminum_strip**.

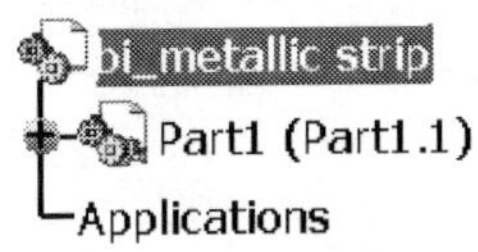


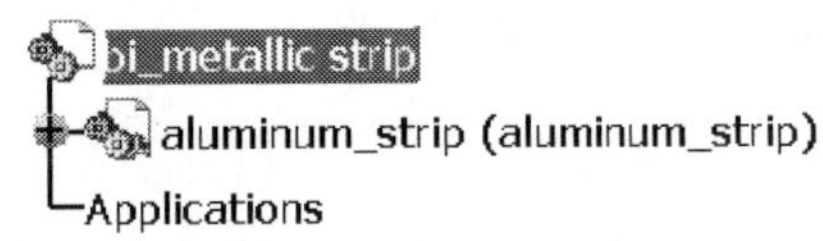


The process of renaming **Part.1** is just like before. Point the cursor to **Part.1** in the tree, right-click, and select **Properties**.

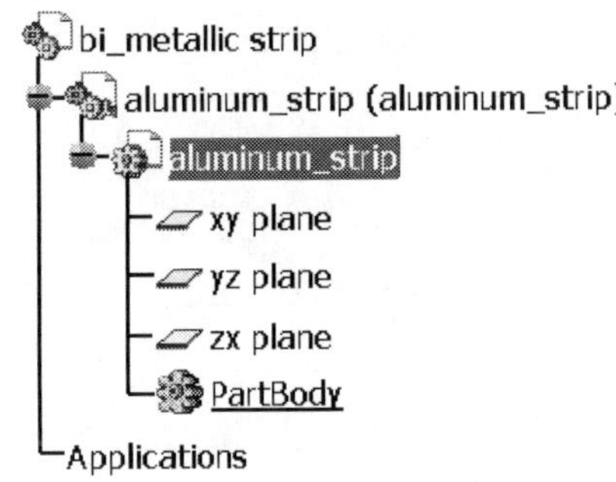


Select the **xy** plane from **aluminum_strip** and switch to the **Part Design** workbench.

In **Part Design**, enter the **Sketcher**.

In the **Sketcher**, use the **Centered Rectangle** icon from the **Profile** toolbar

, draw a rectangle and dimension it, as shown below.

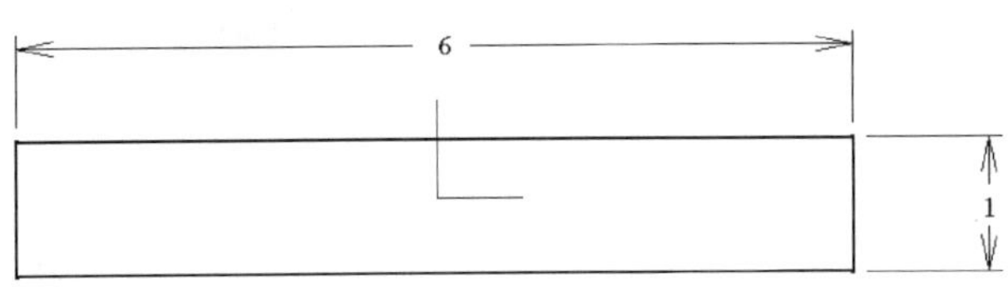


Leave the **Sketcher**.

Use the **Pad** icon, specifying a **Length** of 0.25.

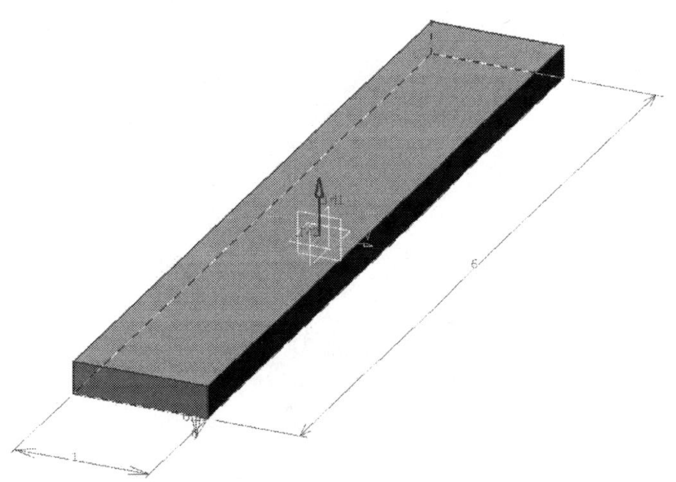

Next, you will create the **steel_strip**.

From the standard Windows toolbar, select **Insert > New Part**. The tree is modified to indicate that **Part.2** has been created. You are also presented with pop up box on the right. Select **NO** to close the box.

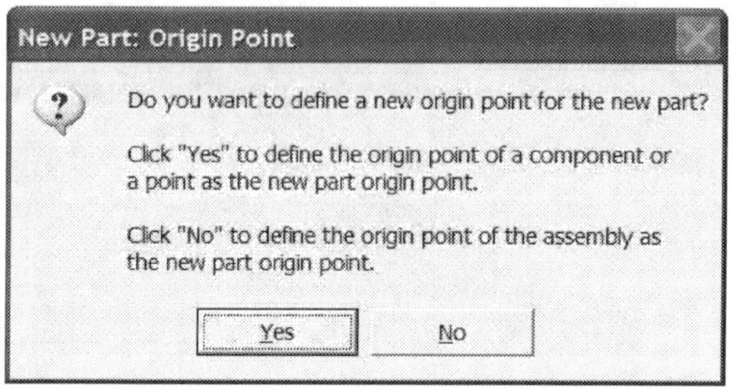


Change the default name to **steel_strip**. The tree, after the name change, is displayed below. Note that the instance name has also been changed to **steel_strip**.

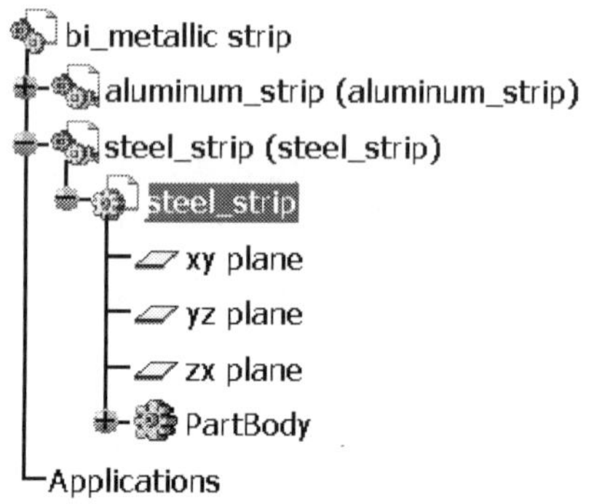


Select the **xy** plane from **steel_strip** and switch to the **Part Design** workbench.

In **Part Design**, enter the **Sketcher**.

Use the **Centered Rectangle** icon to draw another rectangle with the same dimensions as the previous one.

Leave the **Sketcher**.

Use the **Pad** icon, specifying a **Length** of 0.25. Make sure that the **Reverse Direction** button is used to pad in the opposite direction as shown below.

Select the **Apply Material** icon , to activate the material **Library** box below.

Use the **Metal** tab on the top; select **Aluminum**. Use your cursor to pick the **aluminum_strip** from the tree at which time the **OK** and **Apply Material** buttons can be selected. Close the box. The material property is now reflected in the tree.

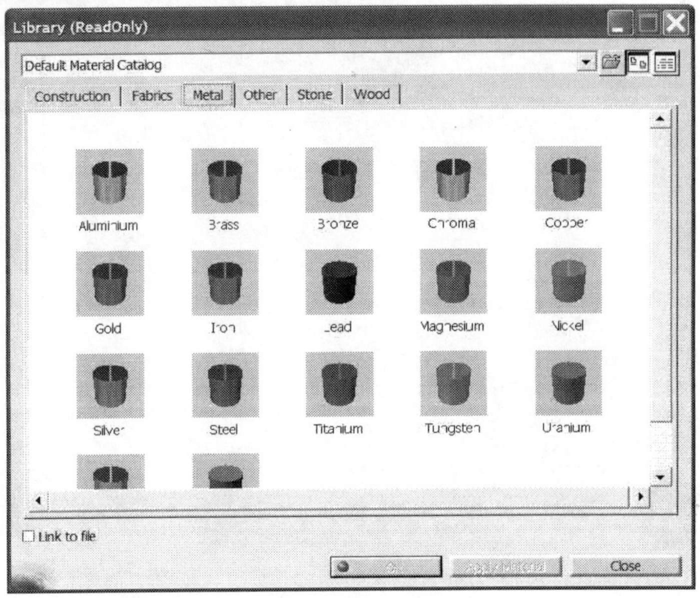


Repeat the process by applying the steel properties to **steel_strip**.

The tree at this point resembles the one shown below.

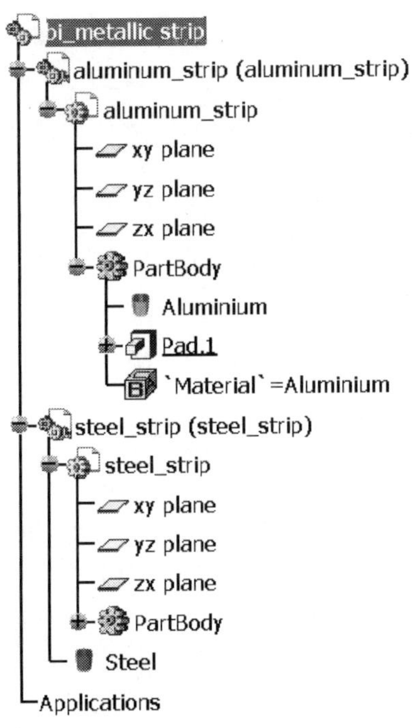

To check the default material properties for steel, double-click on the **Steel** and **Aluminum** branches in the tree. After a long pause, the pop box for steel properties appears.

Select the **Analysis** tab to read the default values. The boxes for default values are shown on the next page. Note that the coefficient of thermal expansion for the aluminum and steel are 0.0000236 and 0.0000117 respectively.

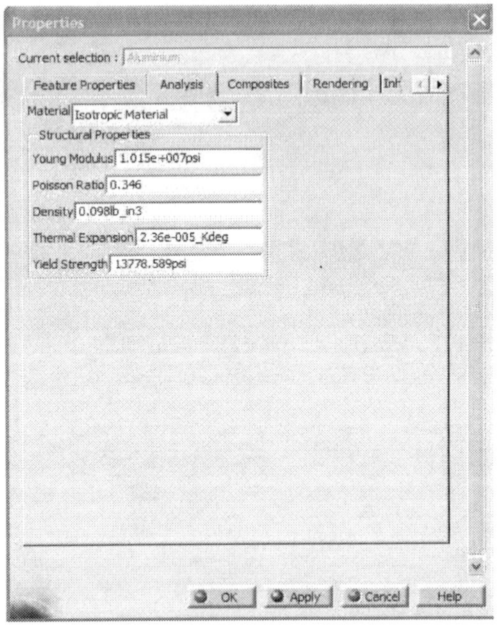


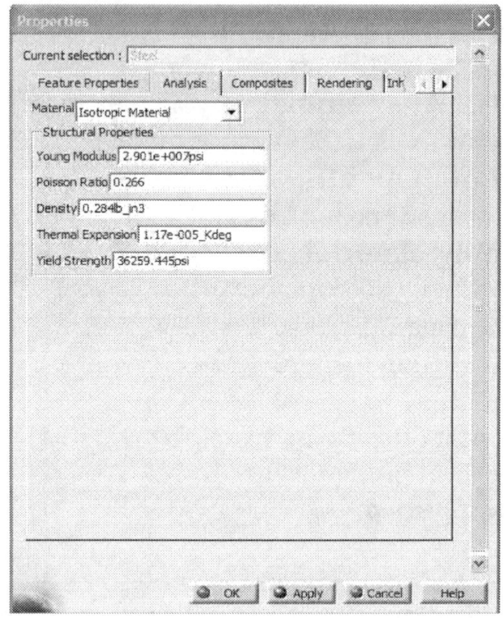


If the assembly does not look "shiny", you can change the rendering style from the **View mode** toolbar 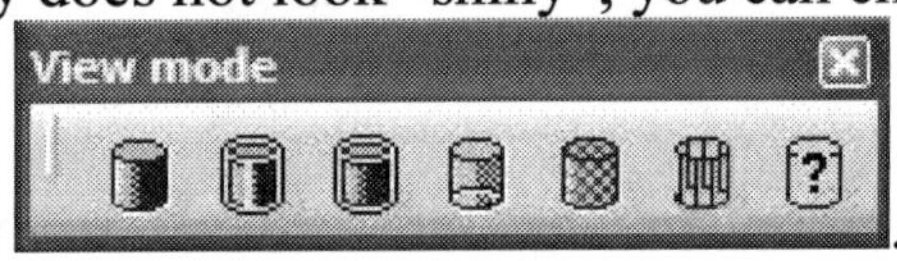
.

Next choose the **Shading with Material** icon .

## 3 Entering the Analysis Solutions

From the standard Windows toolbar, select

**Start > Analysis & Simulation > Generative Structural Analysis** 

The box shown below, **New Analysis Case** is visible on the screen. The default choice is **Static Analysis** which is precisely what we intend to use. Therefore, close the box by clicking on **OK**.

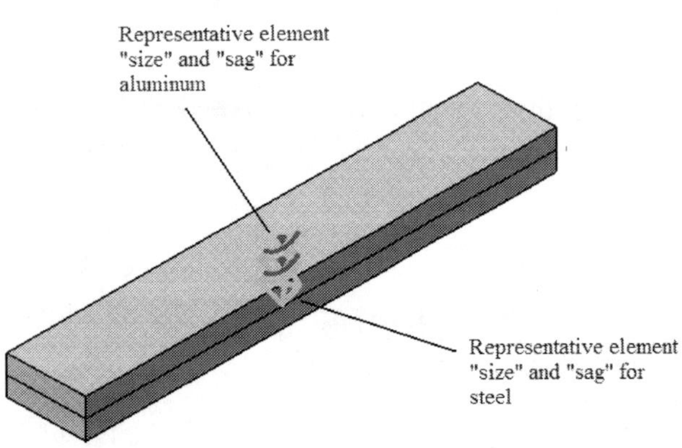

It is clear that the representative element "size" is too large. Double-click on the **OCTREE Tetrahedron Mesh.1** branch in the tree to change the size. In the resulting pop up box, use 0.15 for **Size** and request parabolic type elements.

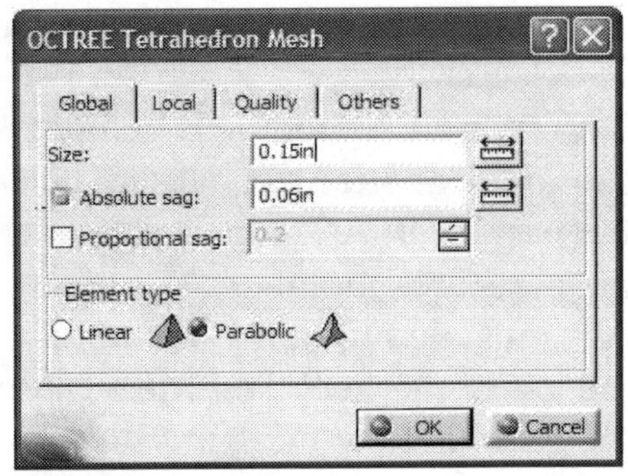


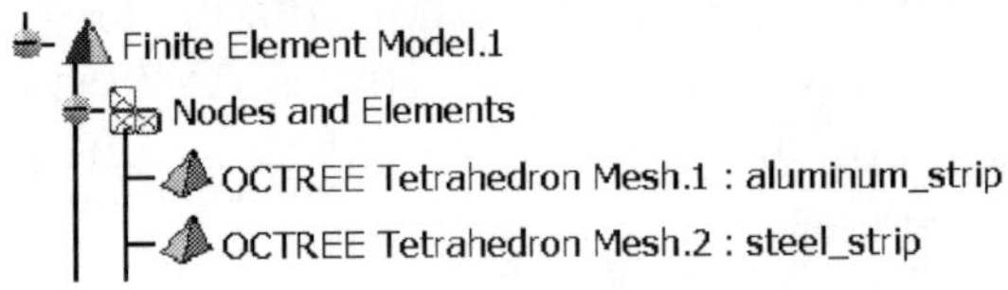


In order to view the generated mesh, you can point the cursor to the branch **Nodes and Elements**, right-click and select **Mesh Visualization**. This step may be slightly different in some UNIX machines. Upon performing this operation a **Warning** box appears which can be ignored by selecting **OK**. For the mesh parameters used, the mesh shown below is displayed on the screen.

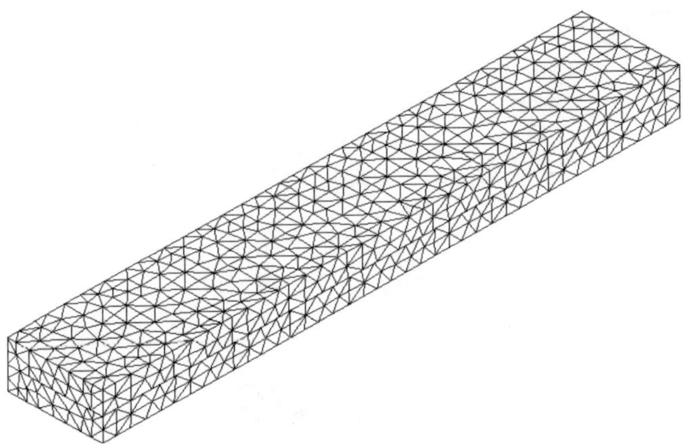

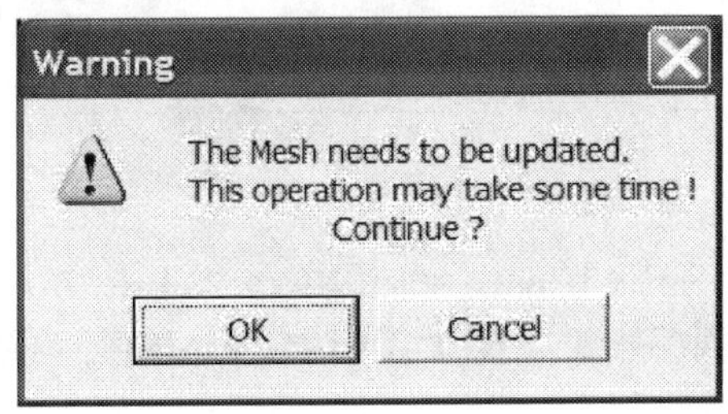


The representative "size" and "sag" icons can be removed from the display by simply pointing to them, right-clicking and selecting **Hide**. This is the standard process for hiding any entity in CATIA V5.

A zoomed view of the mesh at the interface, shown on the right, clearly indicates that the nodes from the top and the bottom strips are not coincident.

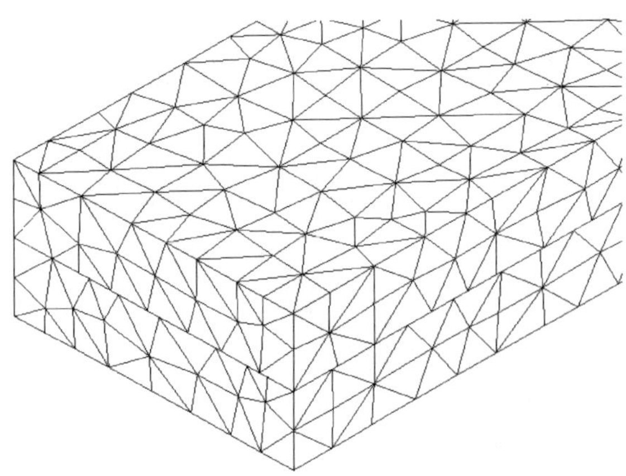

## Applying Restraints:

CATIA's FEA module is geometrically based. This means that the boundary conditions cannot be applied to nodes and elements. The boundary conditions can only be applied at the part level. As soon as you enter the **Generative Structural Analysis** workbench, the parts are automatically hidden. Therefore, before boundary conditions are applied, the part must be brought to the unhide mode. This can be carried out by pointing the cursor to the top of the tree, the **Links Manager.1** branch, right-click, select **Show**. At this point, the parts and the mesh are superimposed as shown below and you have access to the part.

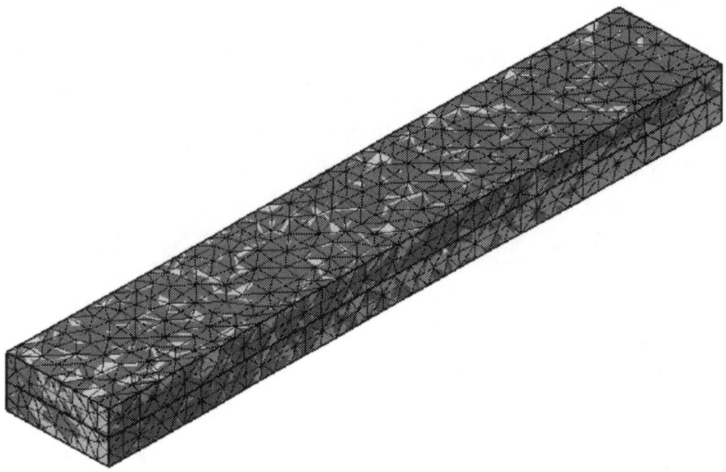

If, the presence of the mesh is annoying, you can always hide it. Point the cursor to **Nodes and Elements**, right-click, **Hide**.

Select the **Clamp** icon  from the **Restraint** toolbar 

and pick the two left faces of the strip as shown.

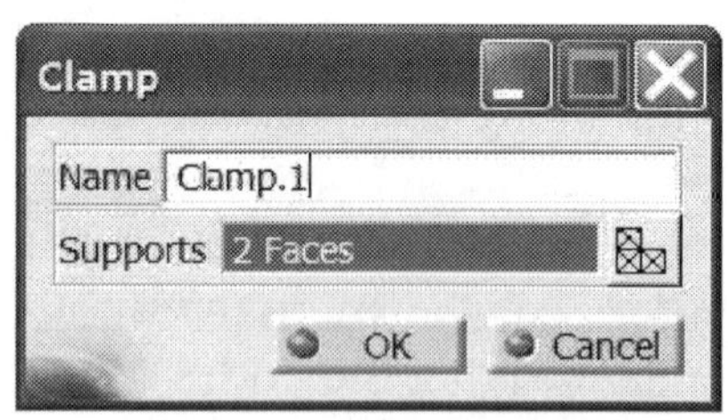


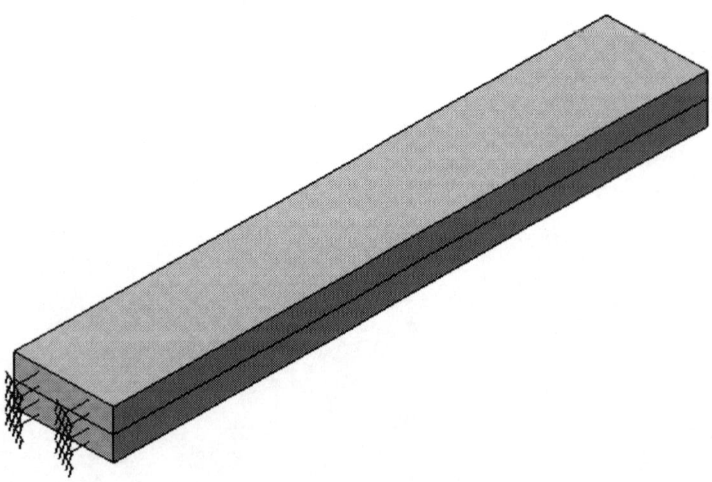

The next step is to apply a uniform temperature rise of 100°F to the assembly. Make sure that the temperature unit in CATIA has been set to Fahrenheit.

Select the **Temperature Field** icon 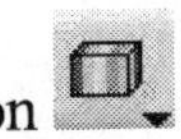 from the **Loads** toolbar

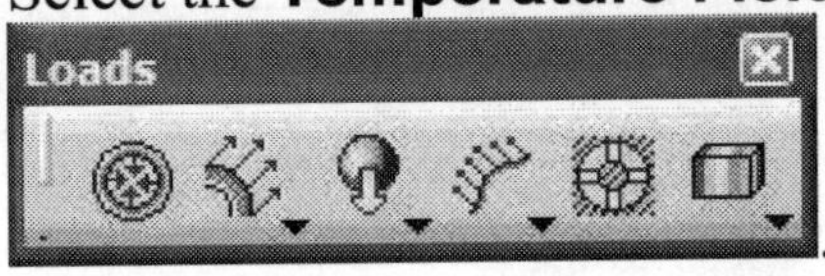

.

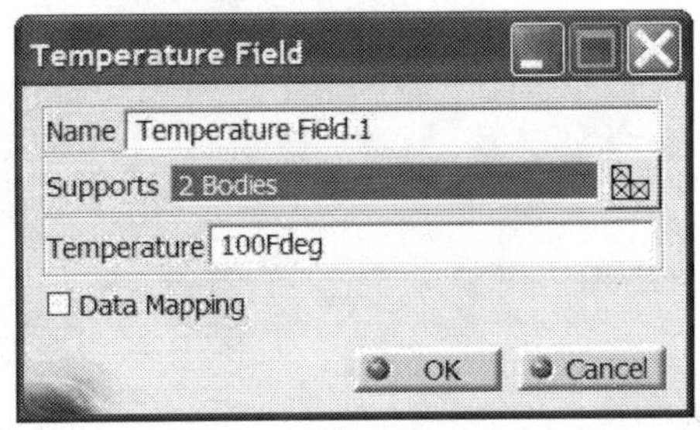


For **Supports**, select the ***top and the bottom strips*** from the screen.

For **Temperature** type 100Fdeg.

The temperature symbol "**T**" appears on both strips as displayed below.

There are no other loads present. Clearly the interfaces of the two strips are bonded and move together. In CATIA, this can be implemented by using the **Fastened Connection** condition.

**Creating Analysis Connection:**

Use the **General Analysis Connection** icon , from the **Analysis Connection** toolbar

.

For **First component**, select the top face of **steel_plate**.
This may be difficult to do because of interference from the **aluminum_plate**. To fix this problem, you can temporarily hide the **aluminum_plate**.

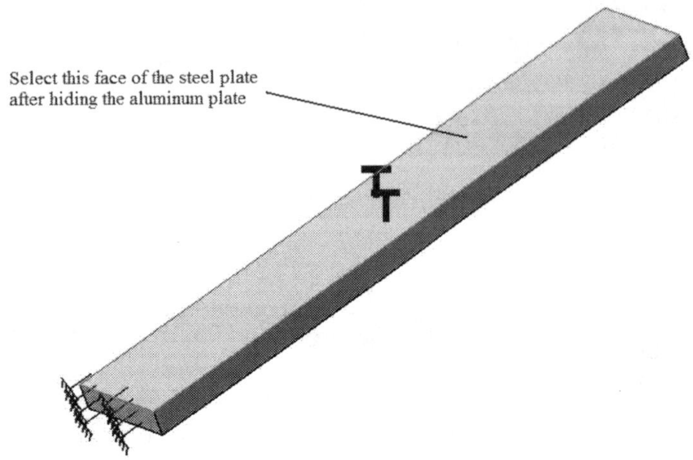


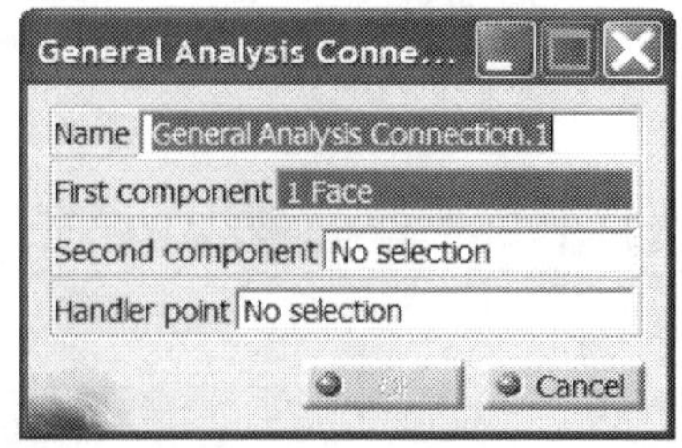


For **Second component**, select the bottom face of the **aluminum_plate**. If you find this difficult, first **Hide** the **steel_plate**.

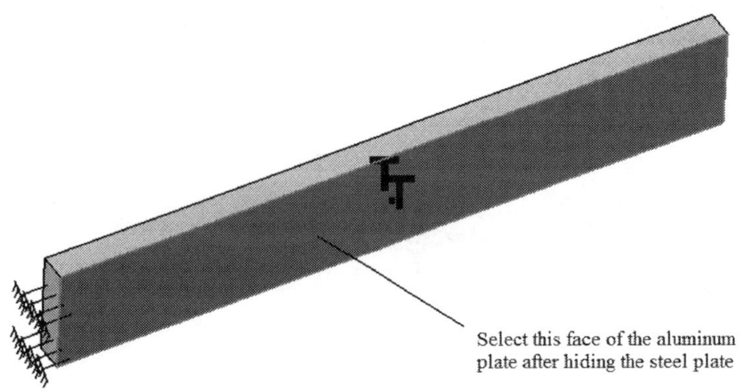


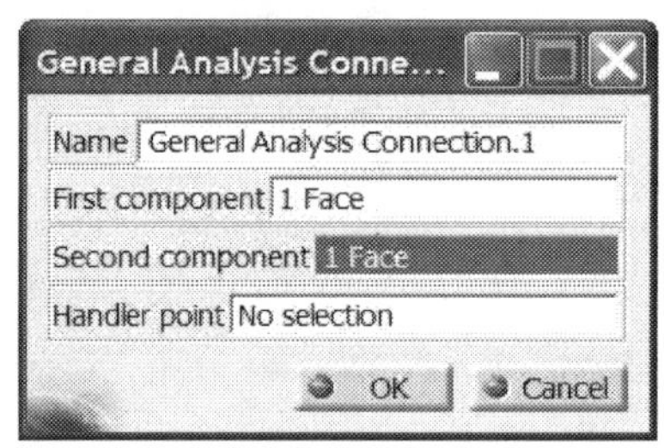


The **General Analysis Connection** just created, modifies the tree as shown on the right.

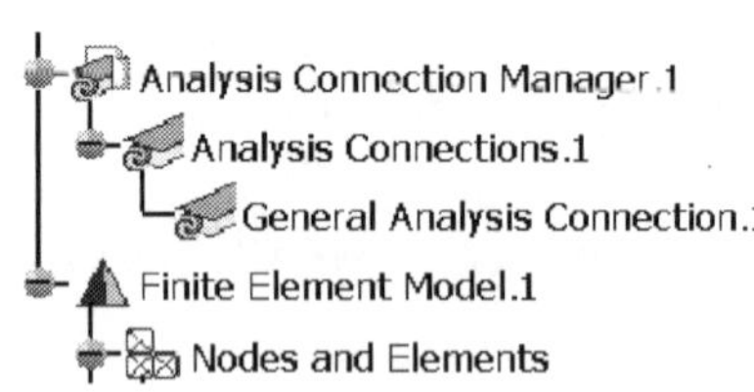


Finally, you have to specify the nature of the above connection.

Select the **Fastened Connection property** icon 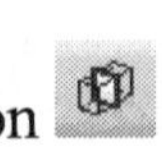 from the **Face Face Connections** toolbar 

. In the pop up box, for **Supports**, select the **General Analysis Connection.1** created above.

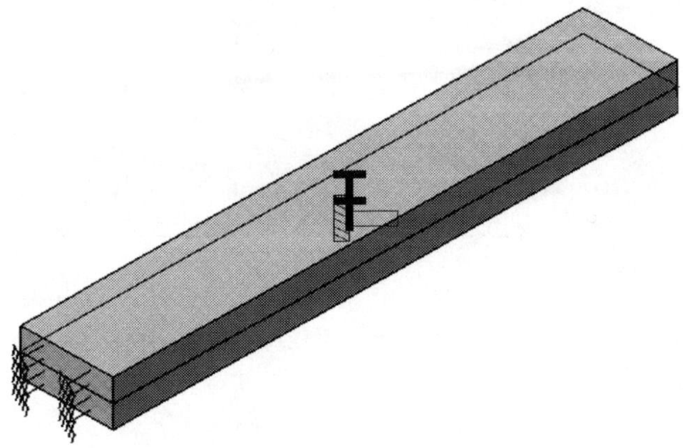

Note that the **Fastened Connection** symbol appears on the assembly.

**Launching the Solver:**

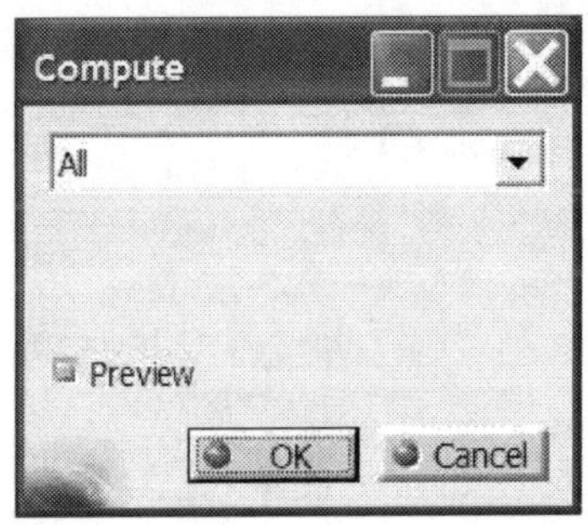


To run the analysis, you need to use the **Compute** toolbar 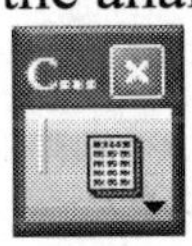 by selecting the **Compute** icon . This leads to the **Compute** box shown to the right. Leave the defaults as **All** which means everything is computed. Upon closing this box, after a brief pause, the second box shown below appears. This box provides information on the resources needed to complete the analysis.
If the estimates are zero in the listing, then there is a problem in the previous step and should be looked into. If all the numbers are zero in the box, the program may run but would not produce any useful results.

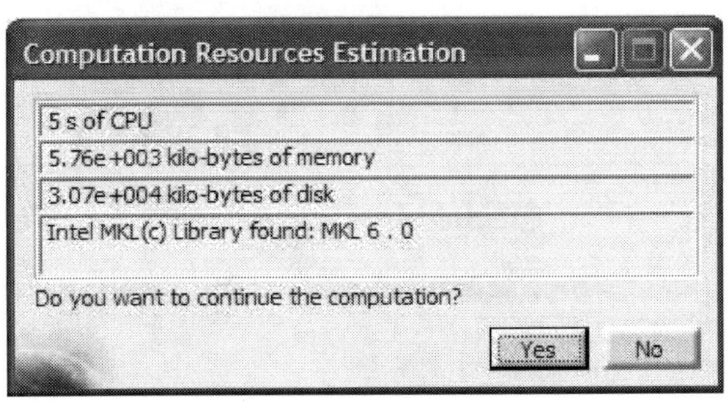

The complete history tree is displayed below for your information.

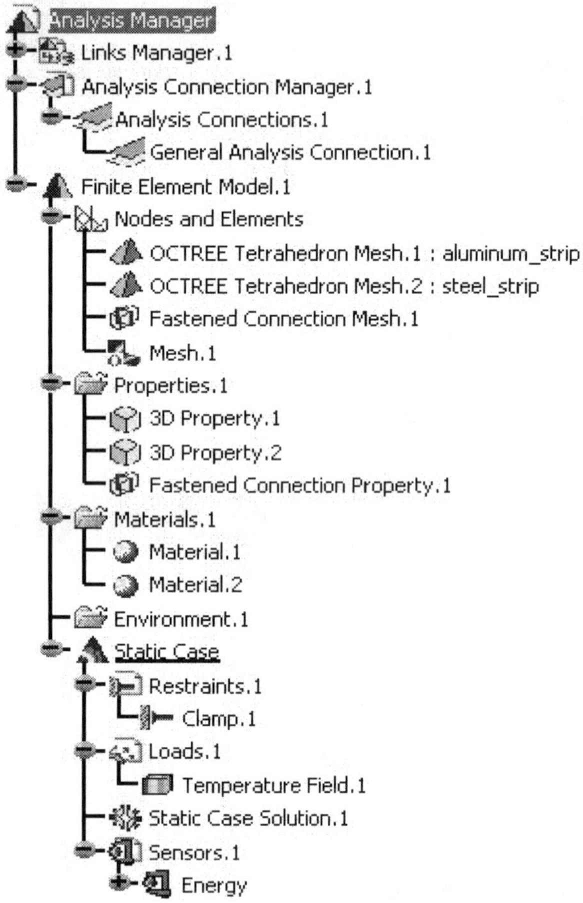


**Postprocessing:**

The main postprocessing toolbar is called **Image** 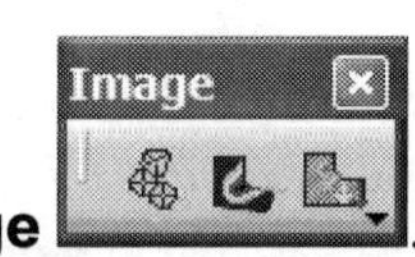

. To view the deformed shape you have to use the **Deformation** icon . The resulting deformed shape is displayed below.

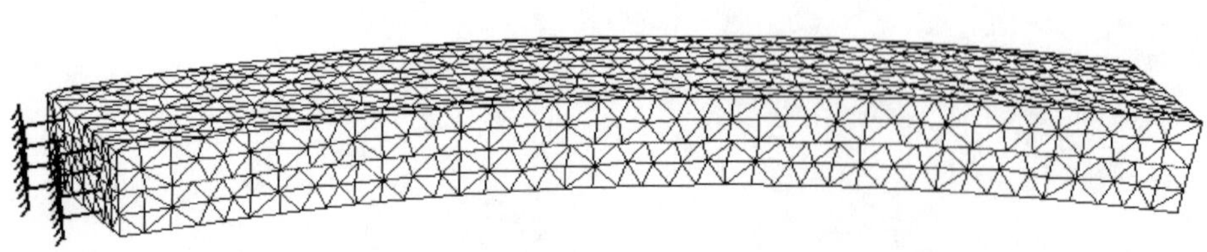

In order to see the displacement field, the **Displacement** icon  in the **Image** toolbar should be used. The default display is in terms of displacement arrows.

The arrow plot is not particularly useful. In order to view the contour plot of the displacement field, position the cursor on the arrow field and double-click. The **Image Edition** box shown on the right opens.

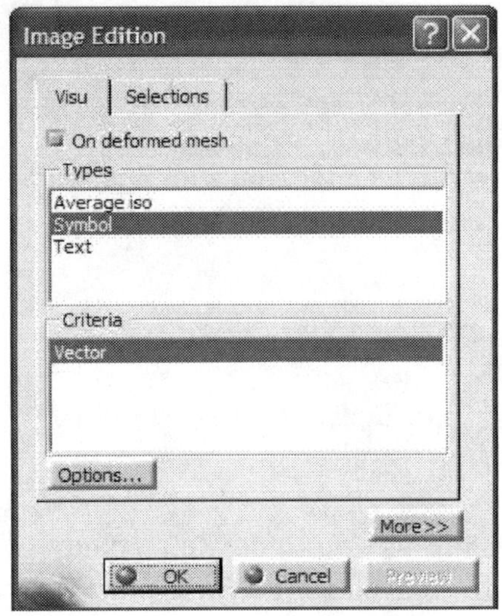


The contour of the displacement field is given below.

Note: The color map has been changed; otherwise everything looks black in the figure.

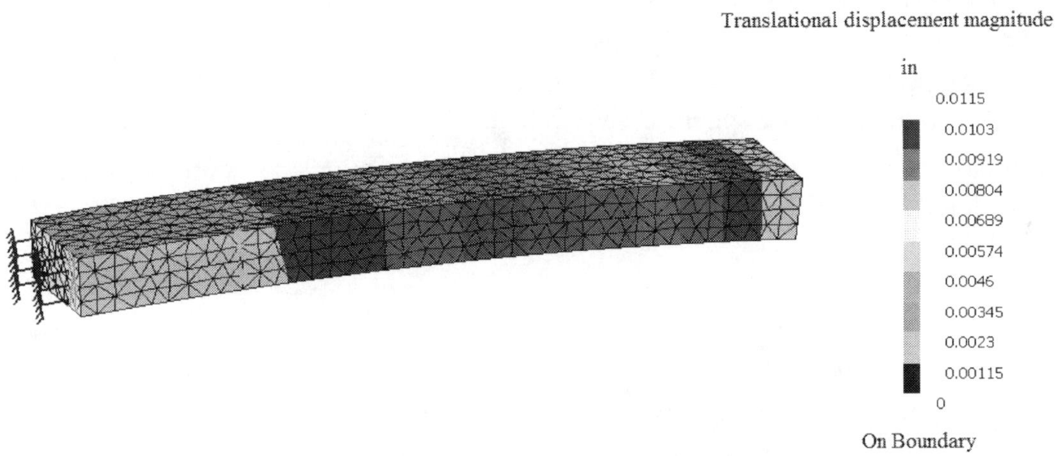


The next step in the postprocessing is to plot the contours of the von Mises stress using the **von Mises Stress** icon  in the **Image** toolbar.
The resulting contour of von Mises stress is displayed below.

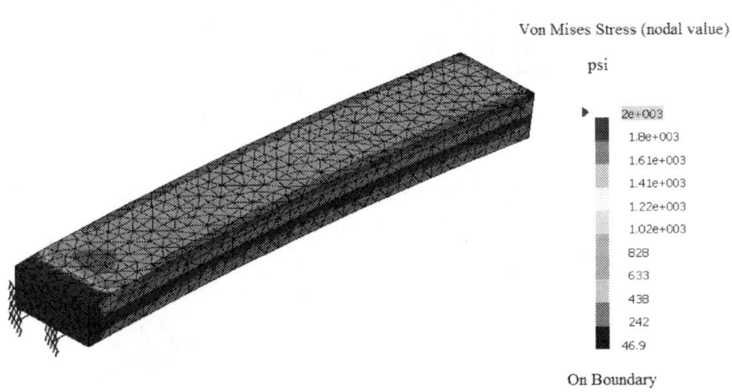

The range for the von Mises stress contour was changed in the previous plot. This was achieved by double-clicking on the contour legend to open the pop up box, shown on the right. The edited range is displayed in the box.

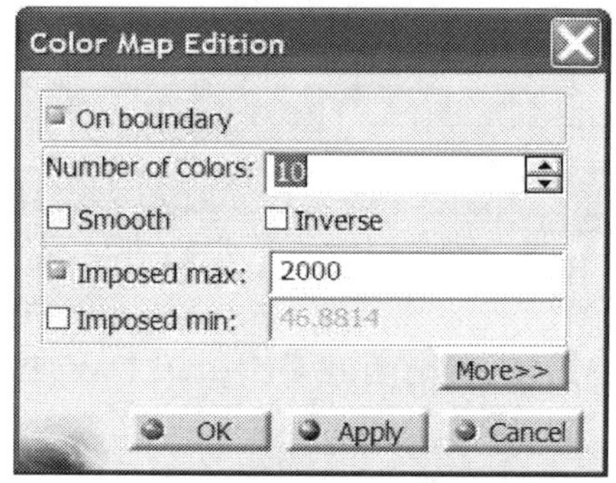


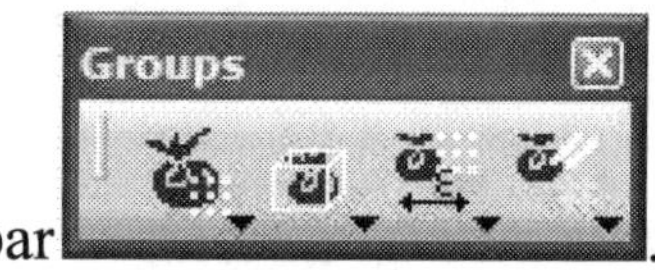


Select the **Sphere Group** icon  from the **Groups** toolbar. See Note #3 in Appendix I.

This allows you to create a sphere of a desired size and location which contains all the elements used for plotting purposes. Clearly, you want to avoid the clamped end which has large stresses.

Upon double-clicking on , a default sphere centered at (0,0,0) is constructed. The box which allows you to resize the sphere is shown below.

You can change the radius of the box by clicking on the 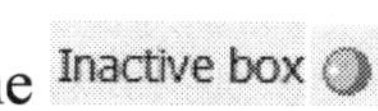

icon. A smaller sphere is depicted below.

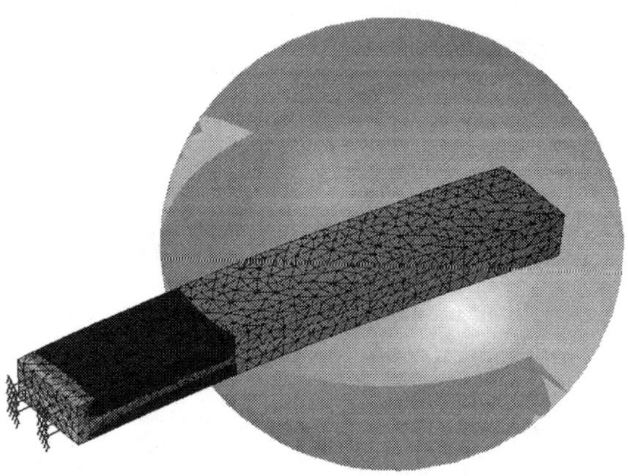

At this point the **Sphere Group.1** is created which encloses the elements trapped by the sphere. This group is listed in the tree as indicated on the right.

The next step is plotting the von Mises stress for this group. Make sure that the plot is active.

Double-click on the contour to open the **Image Edition** box and use the **selections** tab. Select **Sphere Group.1**, and use the button . The contour below displays the von Mises stress at the desired section.

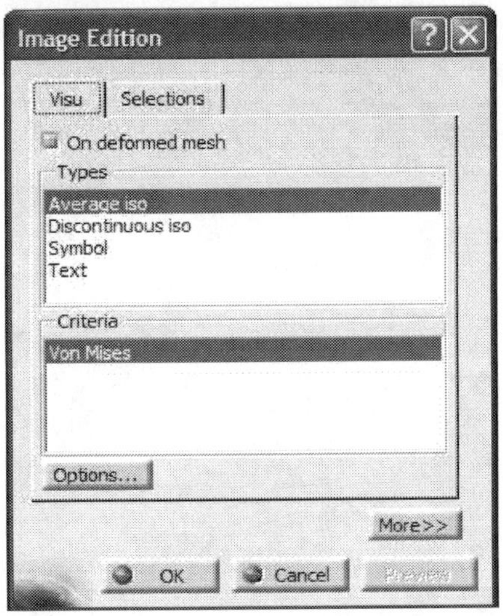


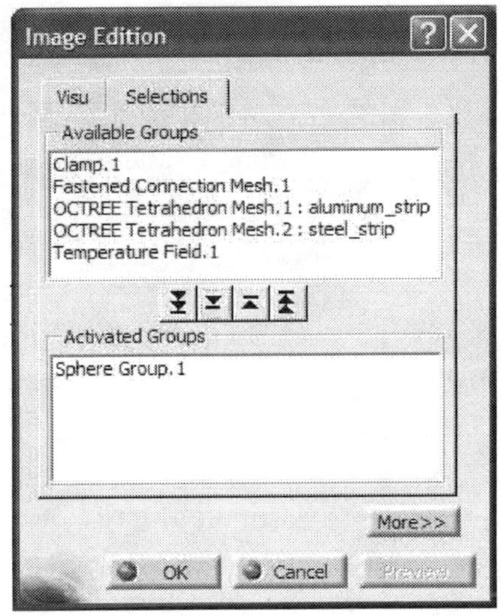


Notice that the **Sphere Group.1** is in the list. Select it. The screen changes to what is shown below. Notice that the range has a maximum of 6.46E+3 psi.

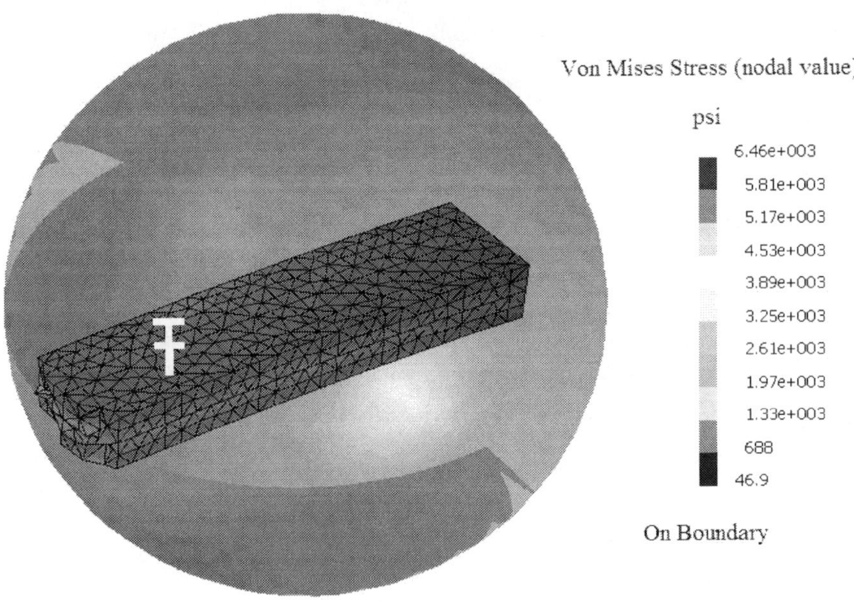


Point the cursor to **Sphere Group.1** in the tree, and **Hide** it. The result is a nice contour showing the detailed displacements in the wall area as indicated in the next page.

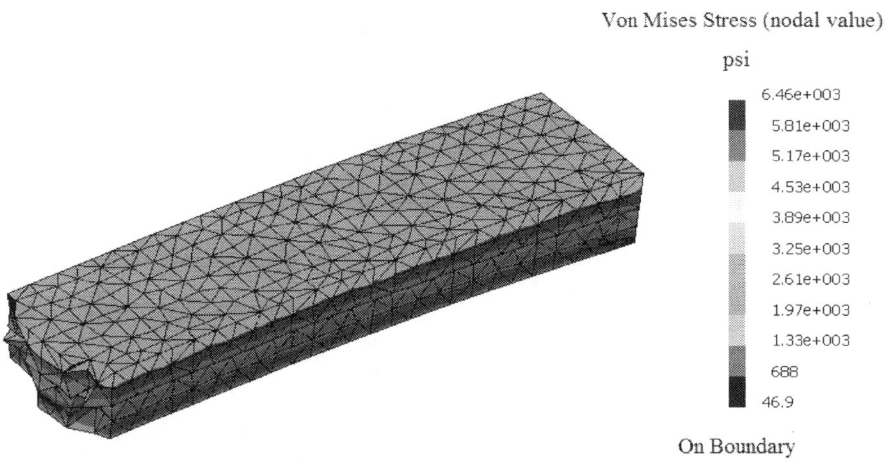


Next we like to estimate the reaction force at the wall.

This is achieved by defining a sensor. The sensor definitions are located in the bottom section of the tree as shown on the right.

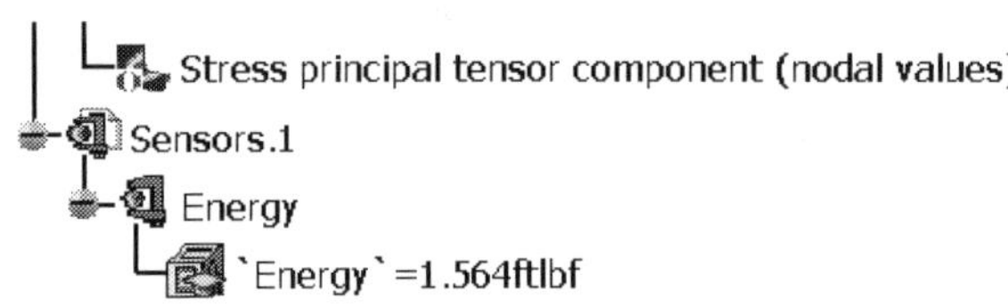


Point the cursor to the sensor branch in the tree, and right-click.

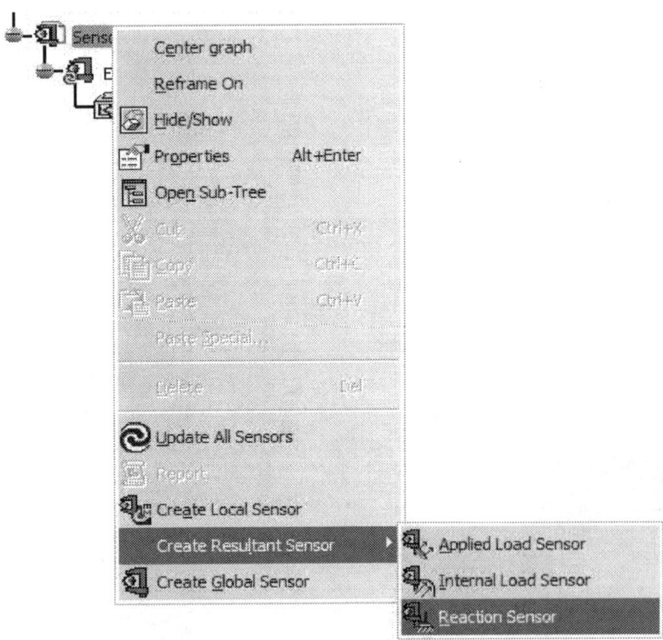


From the contextual menu, select **Create Reaction Sensor**. This forces the following box to open. From this box, select **Clamp.1** and close the box.

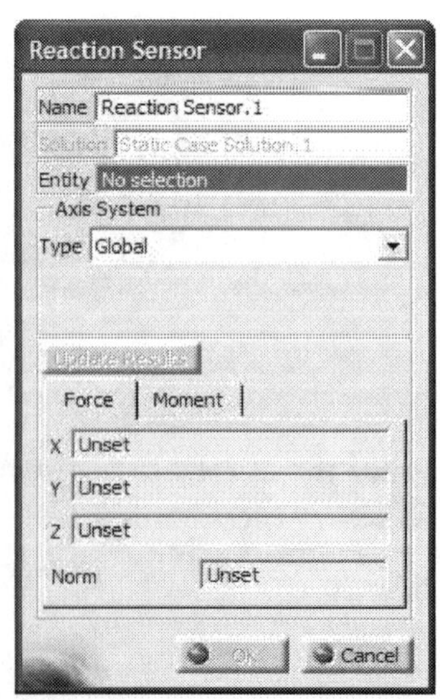

Note that a reaction sensor is created in the tree.

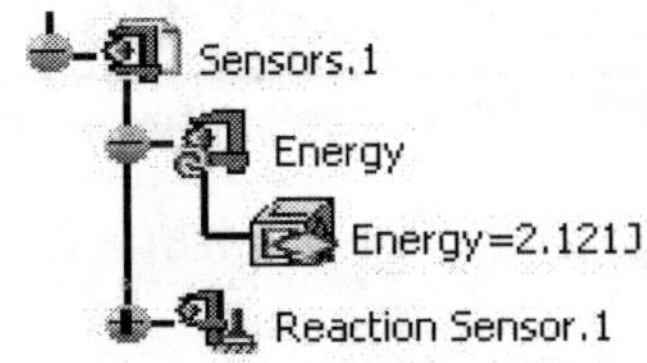


Double-click on the **Reaction Clamp.1** in the tree, the pop up box on the right opens.
Select the **Update Results** box Update Results.

The data in this box indicates that the reaction forces at the clamp are almost zero.
This is not surprising since there are no external forces.

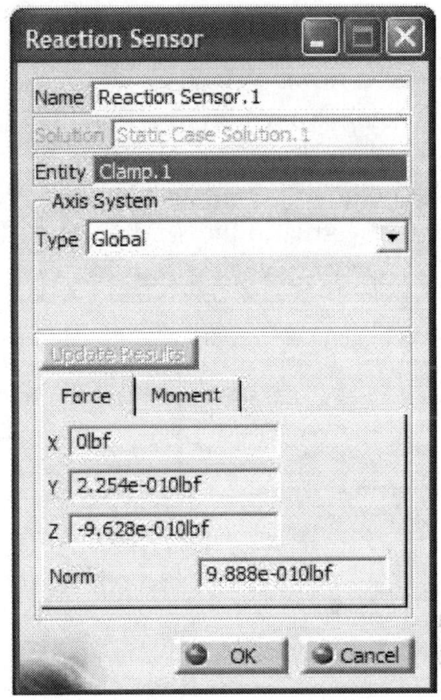

# Exercises for Chapter 18

## Problem 1: The Thermal Expansion of a Clamped beam

The steel beam shown below is clamped at the two ends. The cross section of the beam is a 1x1 in. square with the length of the beam being 6 in. The material properties of the beam are as follows.

Young's modulus, $E = .3E8$ psi
Poisson ratio, $\nu = .29$
Thermal expansion coefficient, $\alpha = .0000117$

The beam experiences a uniform temperature drop of $100^{\circ}$F. Find the stress distribution in the beam and the wall reaction forces.

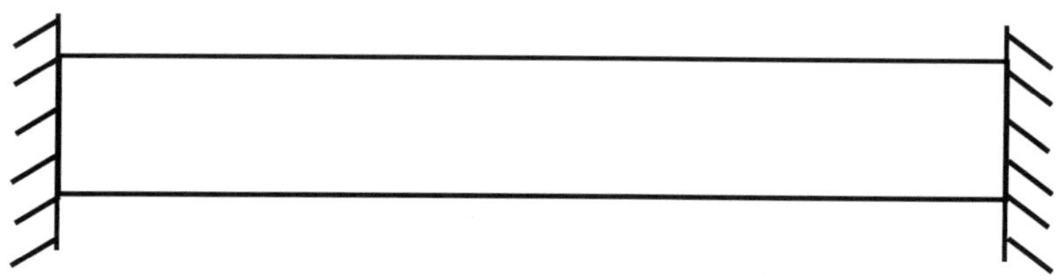

Partial Answer:

As a statically indeterminate problem, there is an exact solution to this model. Removing the wall, the beam freely expands along the axis direction. The developed thermal stress would be $\sigma = \alpha E \Delta T$ and the axial displacement would be zero.

In your FEA model, use the restraints shown below.

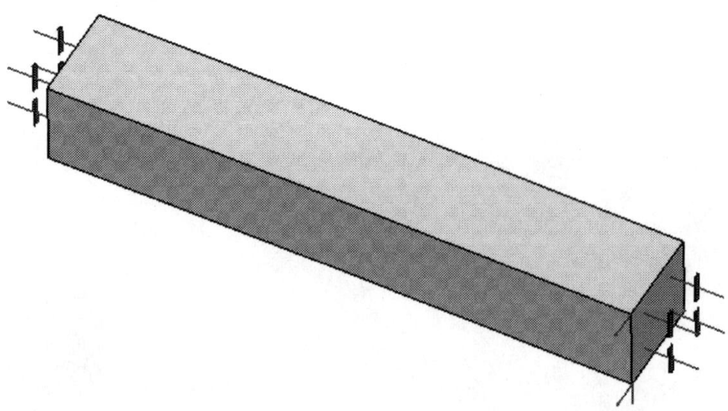

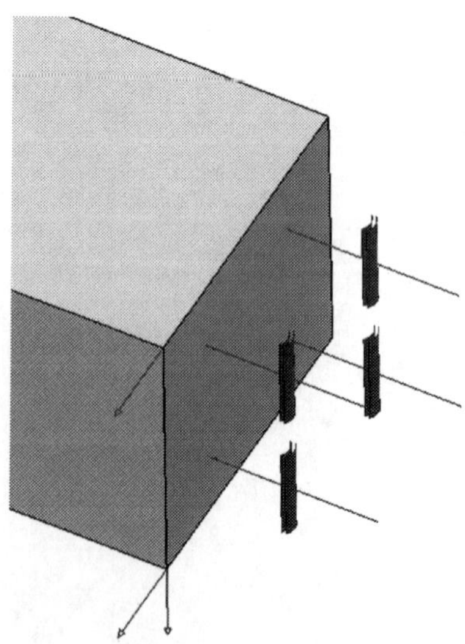

## Problem 2: the Thermal Expansion of a Clamped beam, Revisited

The previous problem can be modeled as an assembly of two parts. A flexible block representing the beam, and another block repressing a rigid wall. Use the same data provided in problem 1 and assume that there is a gap of 0.01 in. between the bar and the wall. Find the stress distribution in the structure.

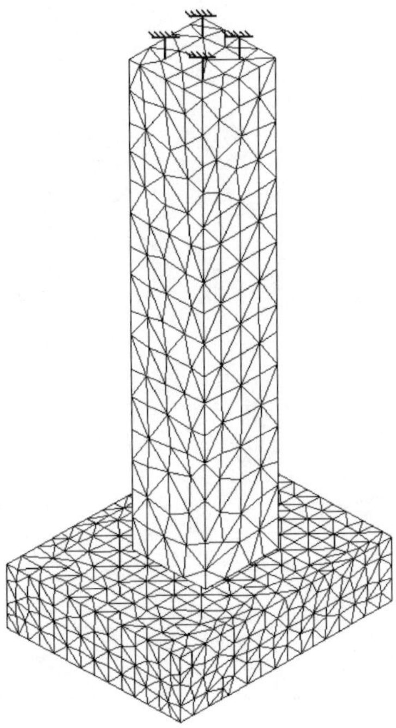

# NOTES:

# Chapter 19

# Hybrid Mesh Analysis

## Introduction

In this tutorial, you will construct an FEA model involving a combination of solid, shell and beam elements. CATIA refers to such models as "Hybrid". The "Analysis Connection Properties" becomes the crucial tool in linking different elements together.

## 1 Problem Statement

The assembly shown on the right is loaded as indicated. Clearly, it is unwise to mesh all the parts with solid elements. Solid elements are suitable for meshing the upright cylinder. The horizontal plate is best represented by shell elements. Finally, the two supporting vertical parts should be meshed with beam elements.

The dimensions are not given explicitly here but described as you progress through the tutorial. The entire structure is modeled as aluminum.

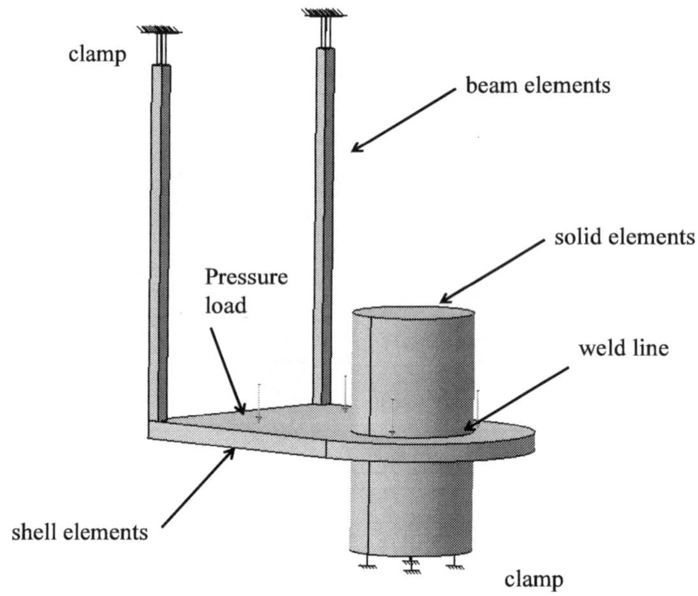


## 2 Creation of the Assembly in the Mechanical Design Solutions

Enter the **Assembly Design** workbench which can be achieved by different means depending on your CATIA customization. For example, from the standard Windows toolbar, select **File > New**.

From the box shown on the right, select **Product**. This moves you to the **Assembly Design** workbench and creates a product with the default name **Product.1**.

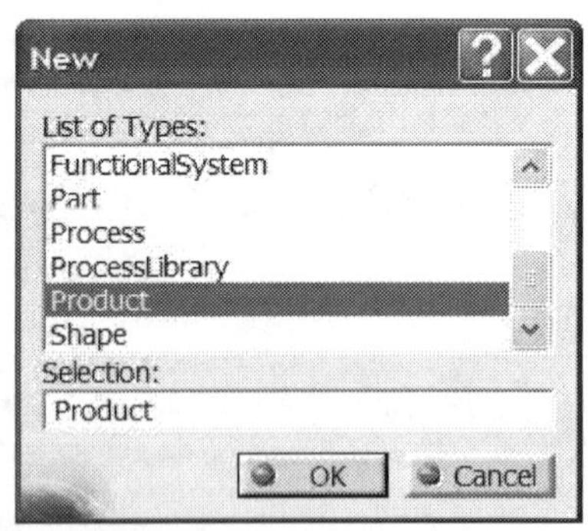


In order to change the default name, move the cursor to **Product.1** in the tree, right-click and select **Properties** from the menu list.

From the **Properties** box, select the **Product** tab and for **Part Number** type **hybrid_mesh**.

This will be the new product name throughout the chapter.

You now create the horizontal_plate as a part. The strategy to do this is to create the solid part as shown, and using only the top surface of it for meshing purposes.
From the standard Windows toolbar, select **Insert > New Part**. The tree is modified to indicate that **Part.1** has been created. Change the default name to **horizontal_plate**. The tree, before and after the name change, is displayed below. Note that the instance name has also been changed to **horizontal_plate**.

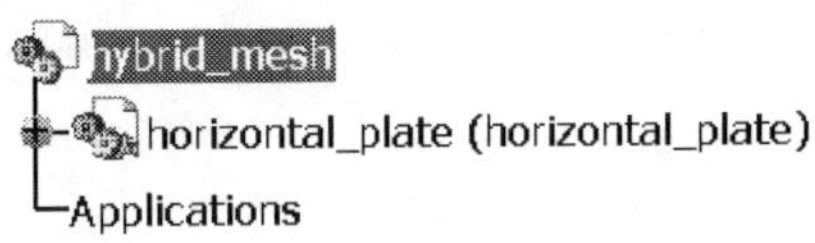


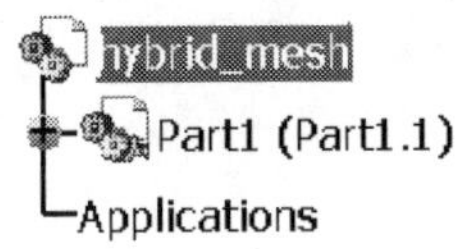


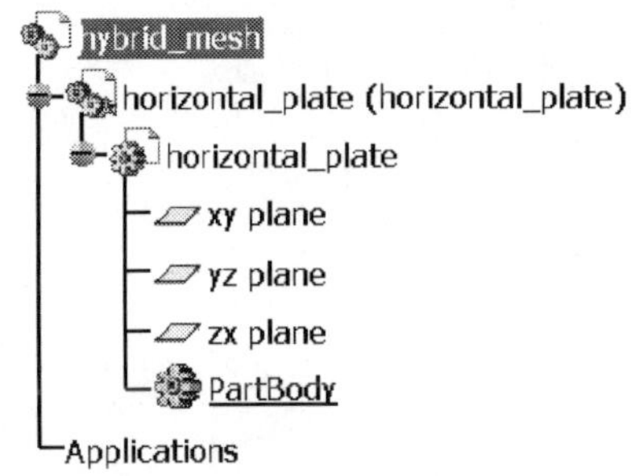


Select the **xy** plane from **horizontal_plate** and switch to the **Part Design** workbench.

In **Part Design**, enter the **Sketcher**.

In the **Sketcher**, use the icons and in the **Profile** toolbar

to draw the cross section of the plate and dimension it as shown below.

Leave the **Sketcher**.

Use the **Pad** icon, specifying a **Length** of 1.

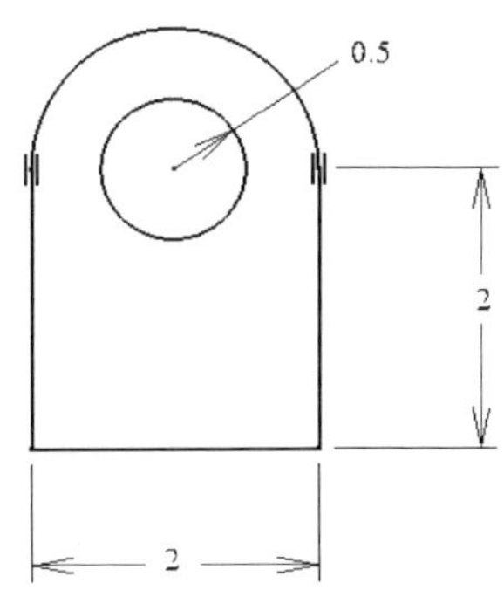


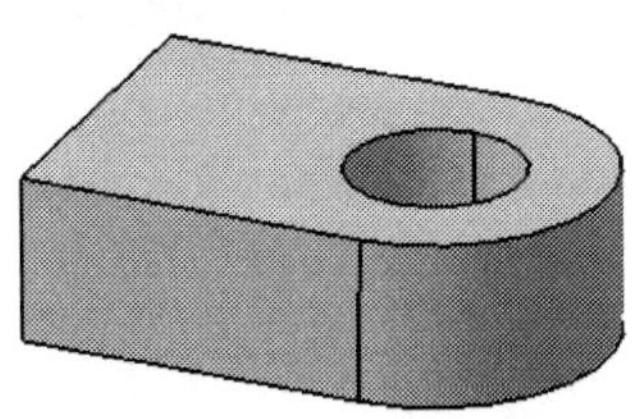

***You next create the two points needed to model the vertical support. This can be done many different ways. You will create two points by selecting the back face and inputting the coordinates in that plane. Pay special attention to the local coordinate system automatically setup in the plane.***

Use the **Reference Element** toolbar , to select the **Point** icon 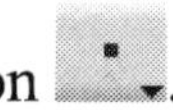. The **Point Definition** box shown below opens.

For **Point type**, choose **On plane**, and for coordinates use the appropriate number. In the figure below, the coordinates are (1,4).

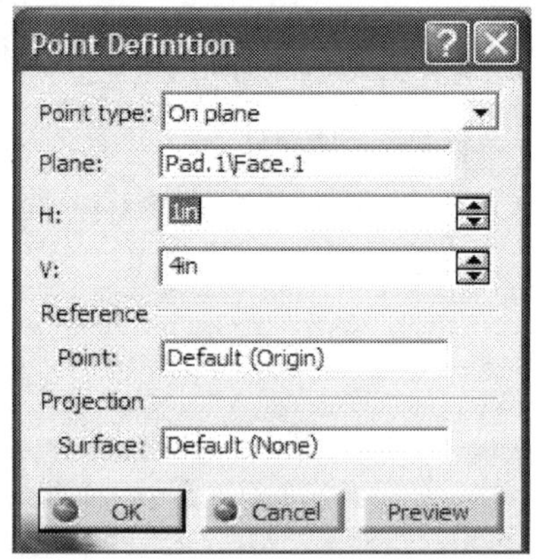


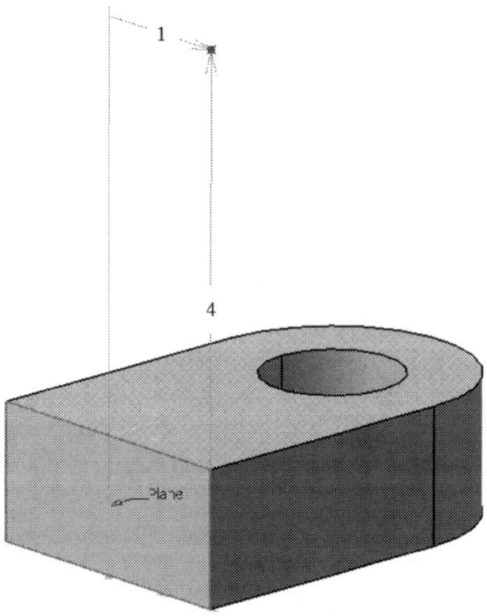


Repeat the same process, creating the second point immediately above the other vertex.

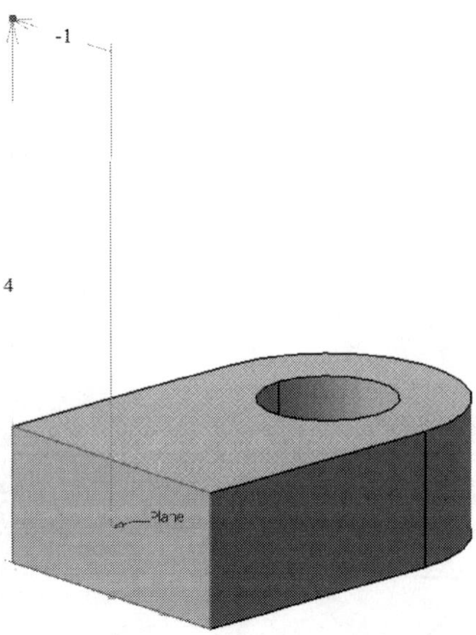


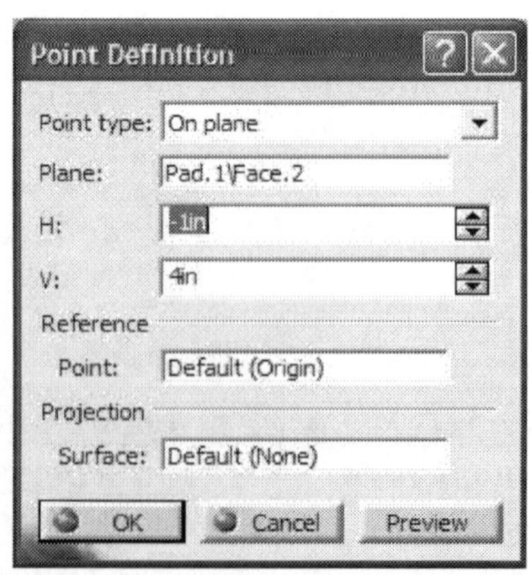

In the next step, you will create the lines representing the vertical supports.

Select the **Line** icon from the **Wireframe** toolbar. Complete the input box by selecting **Point.1** and the vertex immediately below it as shown.

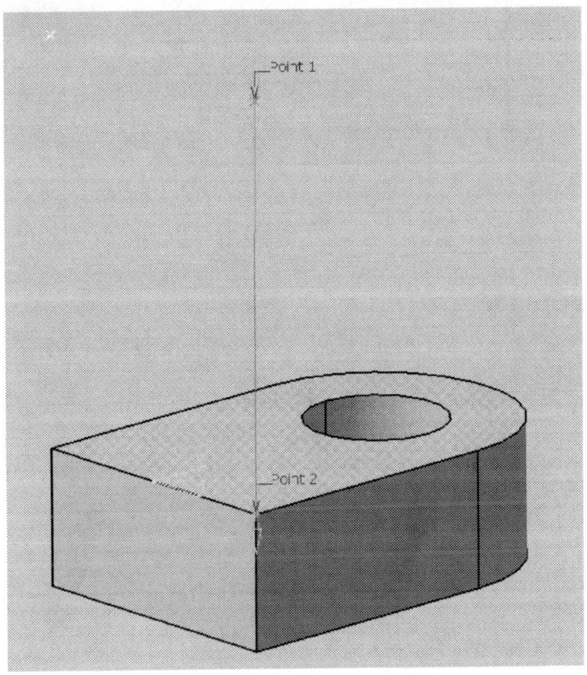


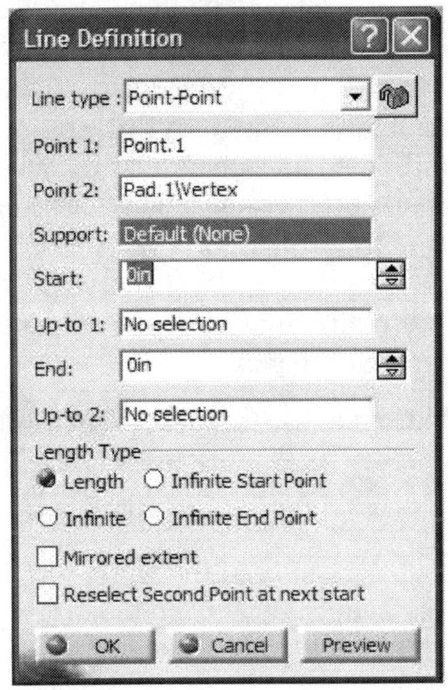


Repeat the same process to construct the second line. This line extends from **Point.2** to the vertex immediately below it.

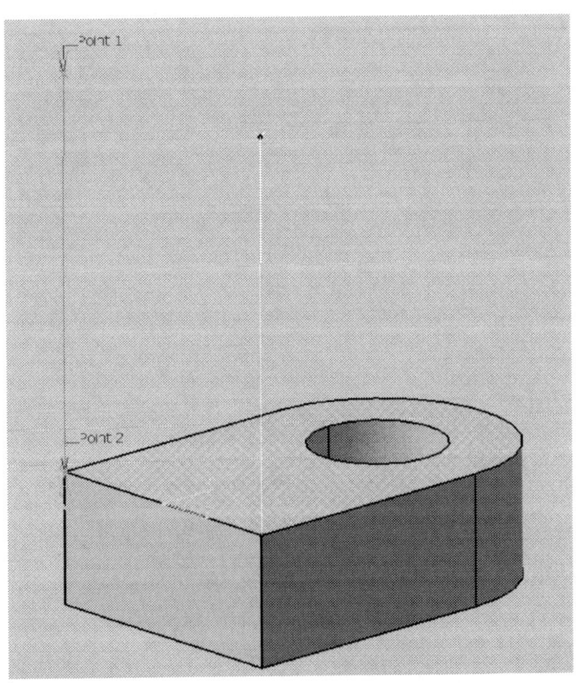


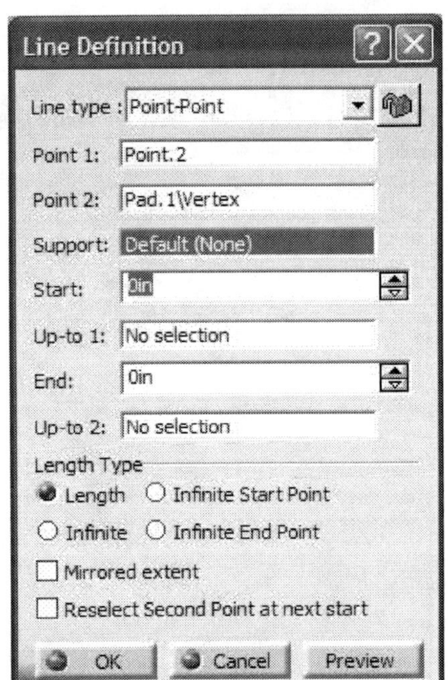

The last step is to create a cylinder of height 3 in. and diameter 1 in.

From the standard Windows toolbar, select **Insert > New Part**. The tree is modified to indicate that **Part.2** has been created. You are also presented with pop up box on the right. Select **NO** to close the box.

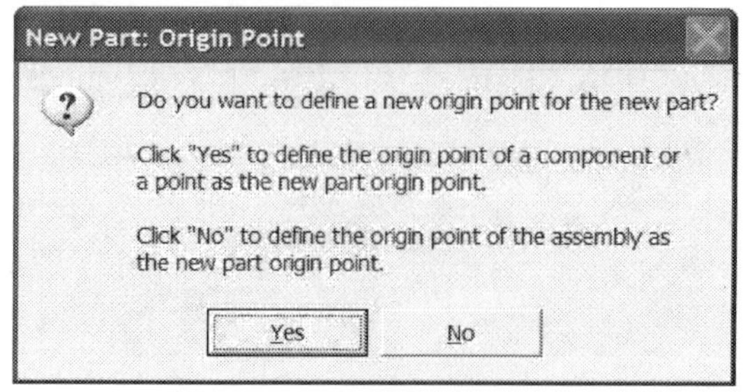


Change the default name to **cylinder**. The tree, after the name change, is displayed below. Note that the instance name has also been changed to **cylinder**.

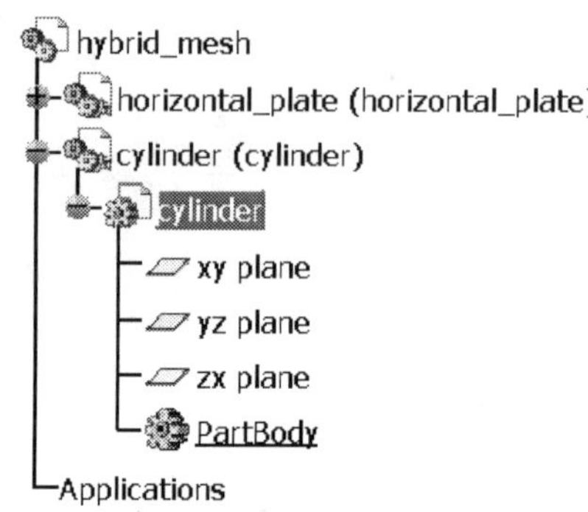


Select the **xy** plane from **cylinder** and switch to the **Part Design** workbench.

In **Part Design**, enter the **Sketcher** .

Draw a circle  of radius 0.5 in. and dimension it  such that the center of the circle lies on the vertical axis, 2 units away from the origin of the **Sketcher**. If the circle is drawn with an arbitrary center, assembly constraints must be used to position the **cylinder** with respect to **horizontal_plate**. Exit the **Sketcher** and **Pad** the circle by 2 inches.

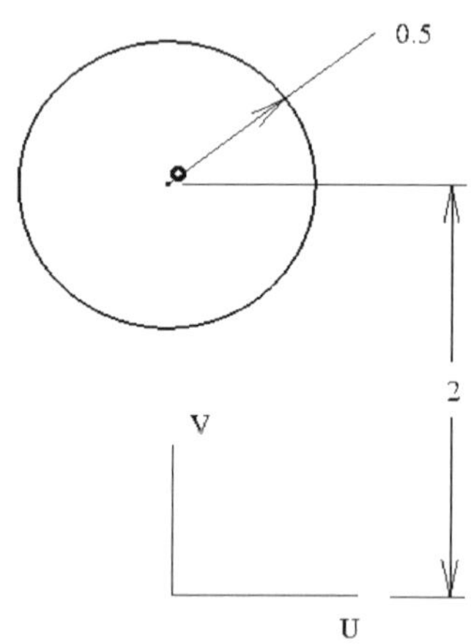


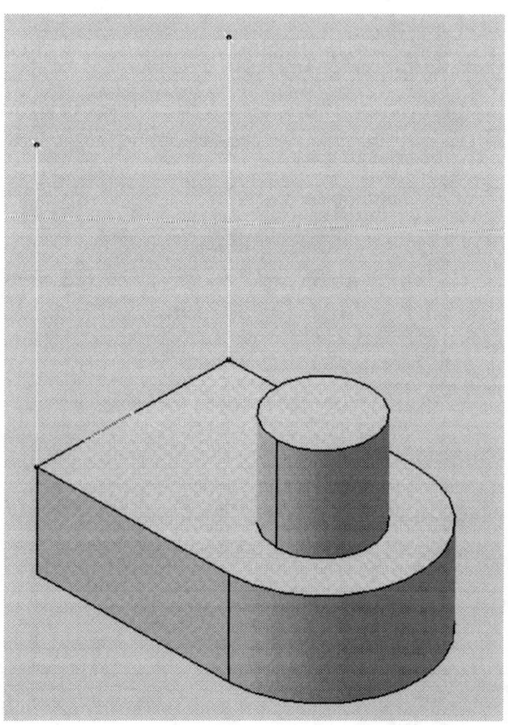

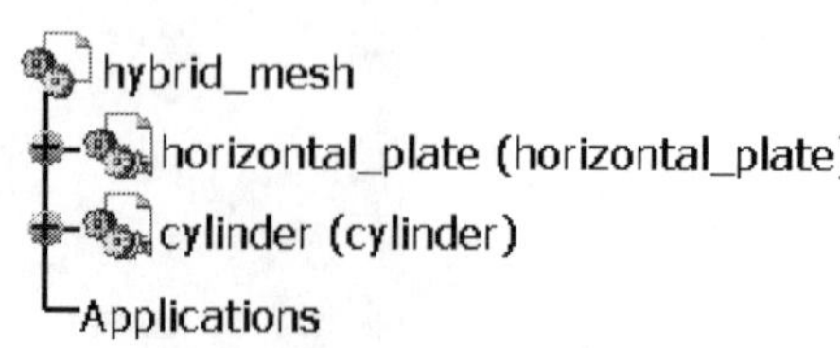

Select the **Apply Material** icon , to activate the material **Library** box below.

Use the **Metal** tab on the top; select **Aluminum**. Use your cursor to pick the top level assembly from the tree at which time the **OK** and **Apply Material** buttons can be selected. Close the box. The material property is now reflected in the tree.

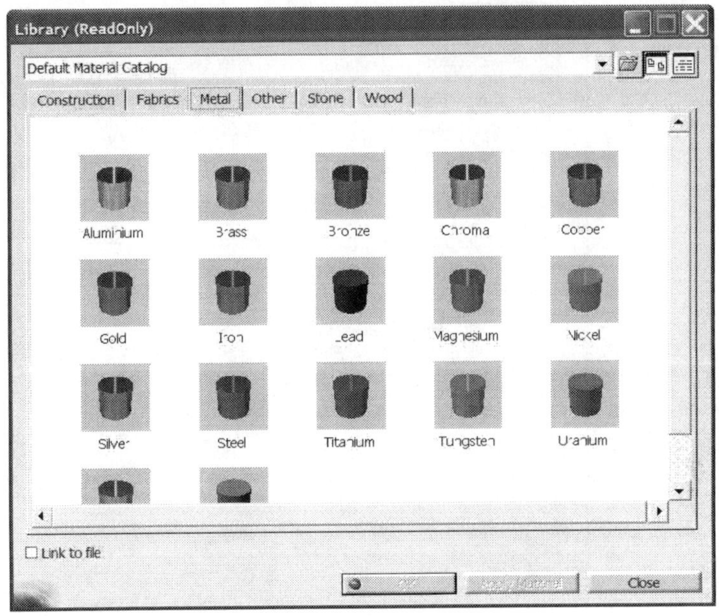


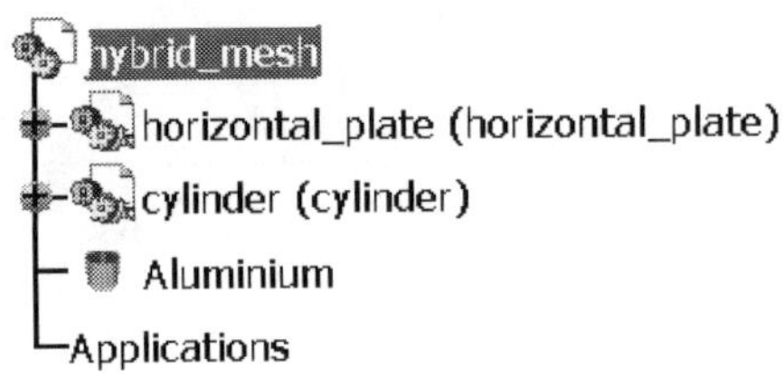


If the assembly does not look "shiny", you can change the rendering style from the **View mode** toolbar

Next choose the **Shading with Material** icon .

The part now appears shaded as shown on the right.

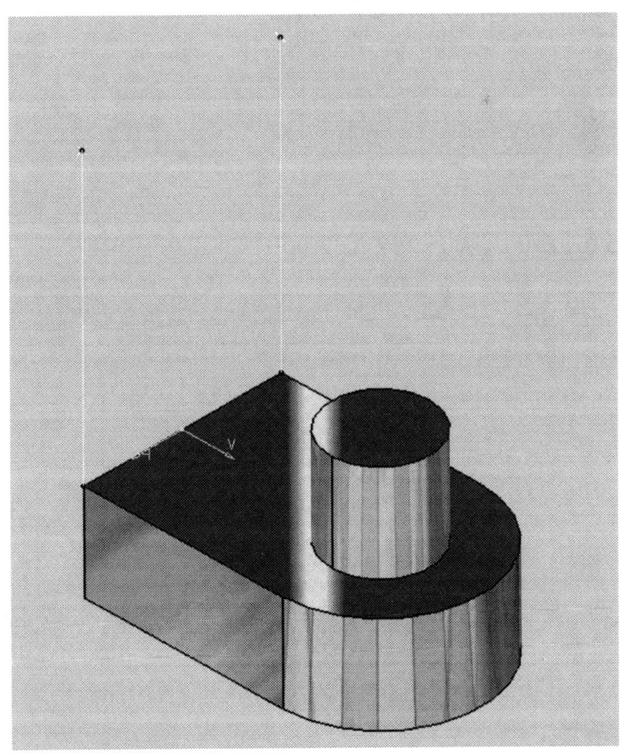

The complete tree structure at this point should resemble the one shown below.

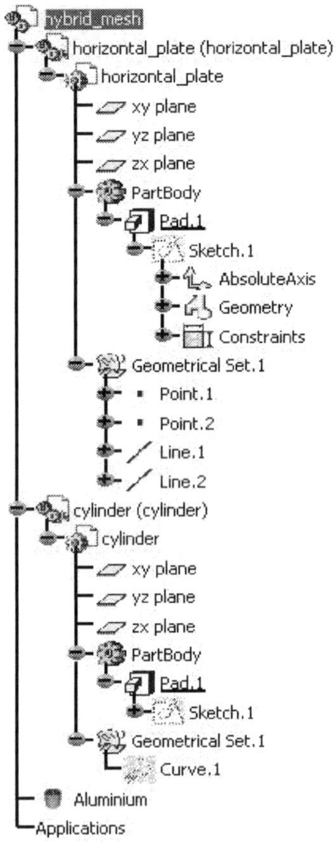


You are now ready to create the FEA model.

Warning: If you enter the **Generative Structural Analysis** workbench, both the **horizontal_plate** and the **cylinder** will be meshed with solid element. This is not desired because the plate is supposed to be meshed with shell elements.

## 3 Entering the Analysis Solutions

From the standard Windows toolbar, select

**Start > Analysis & Simulation > Advanced Meshing Tools** 

Upon entering the **Advanced Meshing Tools** workbench, the standard box shown in the next page is displayed. However, note that the representative element "size" and "sag" is not visible on your display.

This is in contrast to utilizing the **Generative Structural Analysis** workbench for the first time. Therefore, at this point, no mesh is present.

Select the **Advanced Surface Mesher** icon 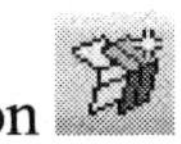 from the **Surface Mesher** toolbar 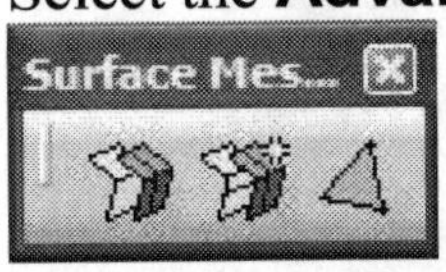

and pick <u>any of the surfaces</u> of the **horizontal_plate** from the screen. This action leads to the input box shown on the right.
For **Mesh size**, type 0.25 and use **Parabolic** elements and close the window.

Select the **Mesh the Part** icon 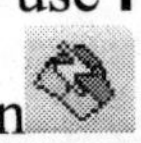 from **Mesh/Unmesh** toolbar 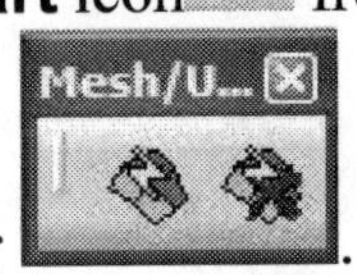.


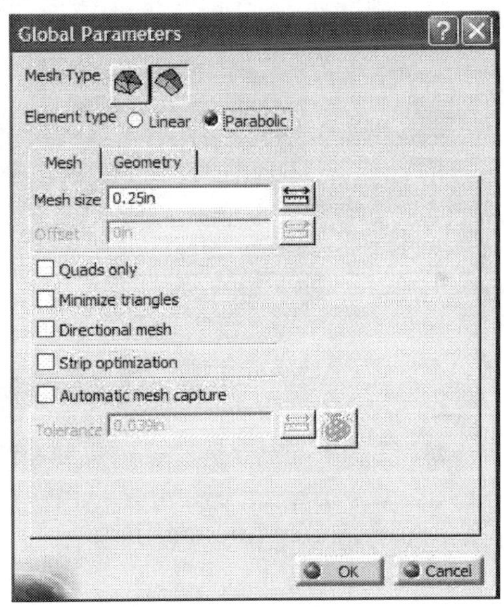


Note that the entire **horizontal_plate** part will be meshed with shell elements. This is not what you want. Only the top face of this part has to be shell meshed.

If you accidentally completed the above step, you have created a hollow volume as shown below.

The easiest way to correct this mistake is as follows. Point the cursor to the **Advanced Surface Mesh.1** branch in the tree, right-click, and select delete. This eliminates the mesh.

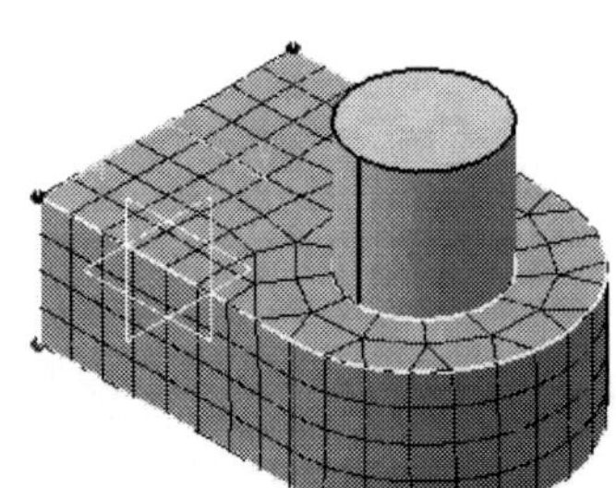

To make the next few steps easier, hide the cylinder.

Select the **Unmesh** icon from **Mesh/Unmesh** toolbar. This deletes the mesh. Exit the workbench by selecting .

Select the **Advanced Surface Mesher** icon once again and pick <u>any of the surfaces</u> of the **horizontal_plate** from the screen. The **Global Parameters** box opens. This action leads to the input box shown below.

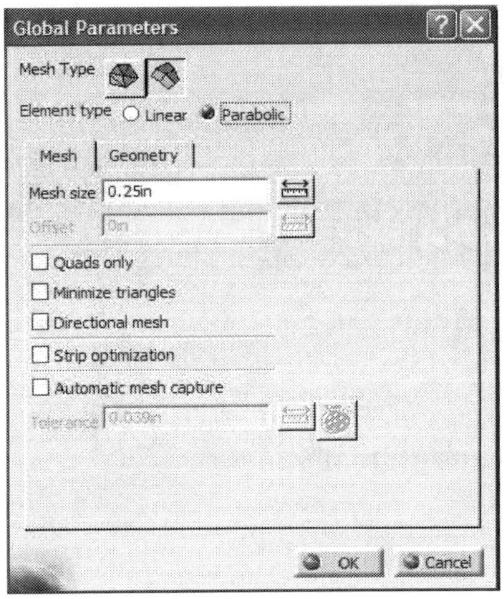


Choose the **Geometry** tab Mesh | Geometry and make sure that **Min hole size** Min holes size 0.1in is smaller that the radius of the hole in the top face. You can use 0.1 in as an example. This makes sure that any hole with radius bigger than 0.1 in is not ignored while meshing.

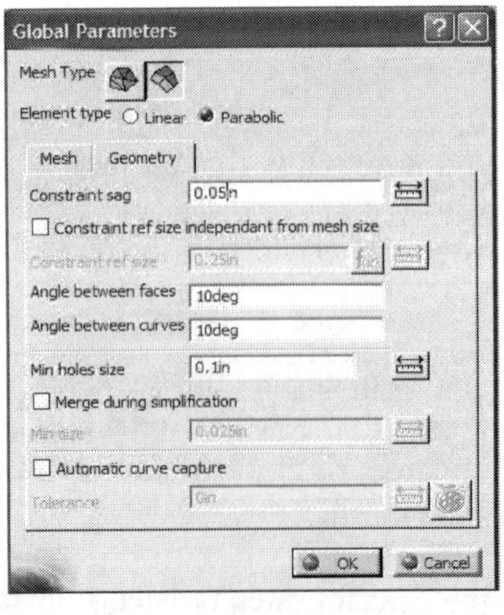


Close the box by pressing **OK**.

Select the **Boundary Simplifications** icon , from the **Local Specifications** toolbar 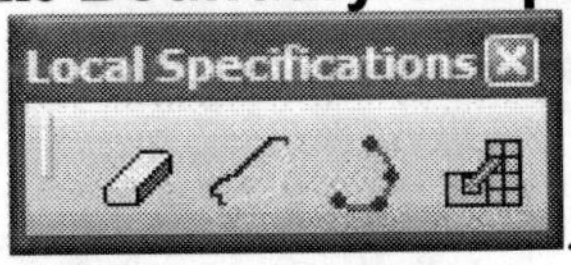

.

The resulting pop up box is shown on the right.

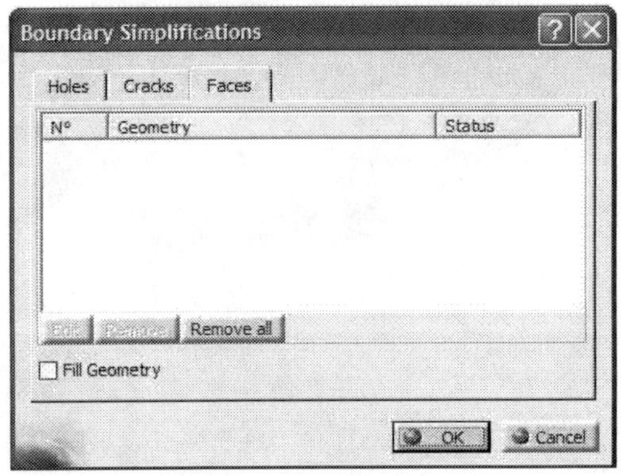


Pick the **Faces** tab from this box.

Select all six faces of **horizontal_plate** except the top face. <u>Do not forget the face of the circular hole</u>.

The purpose of this step is to only leave the surface that has to be meshed, namely, the top face.

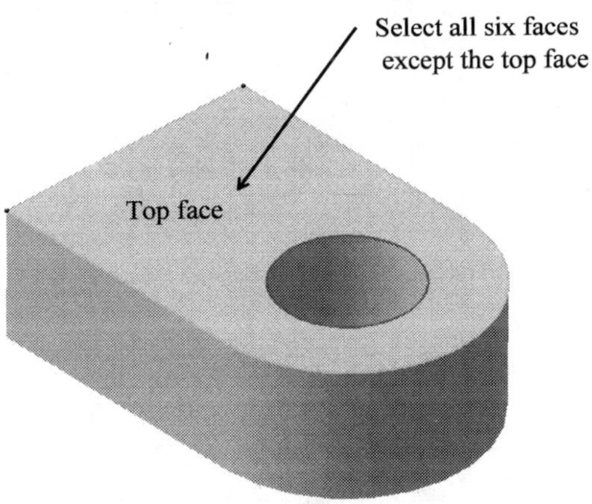


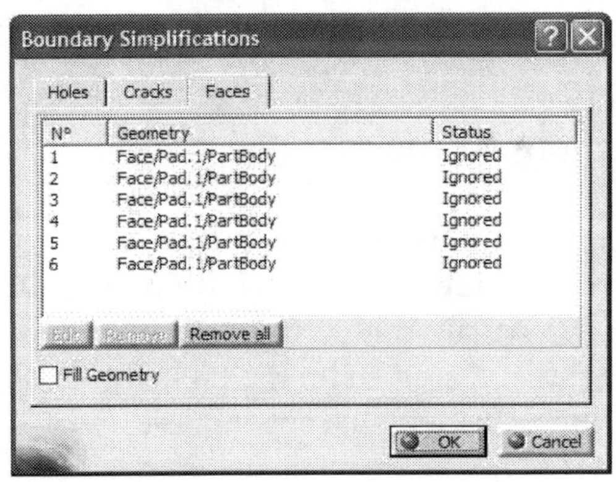


In order to see the mesh while you are in the current workbench, select the **Mesh the Part** icon 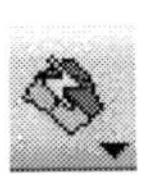 from the **Execution** toolbar 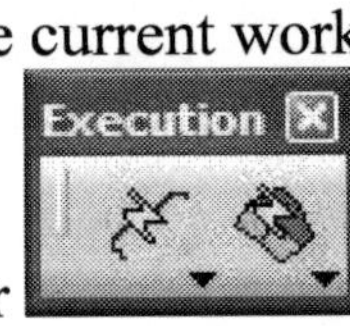

.

The summary box **Mesh the Part** appears which can be ignored.

Use the **Exit** icon  to complete the process.

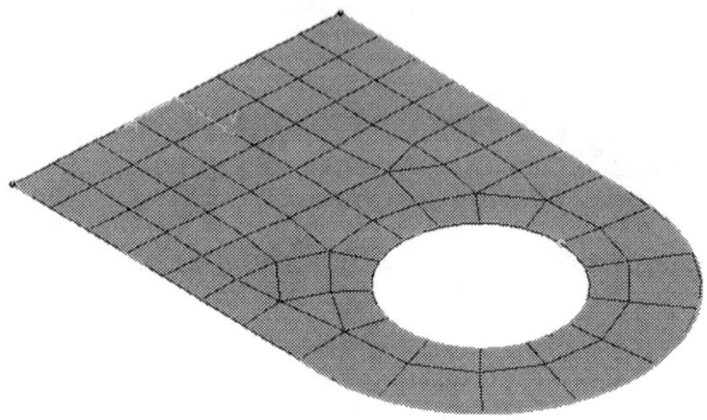

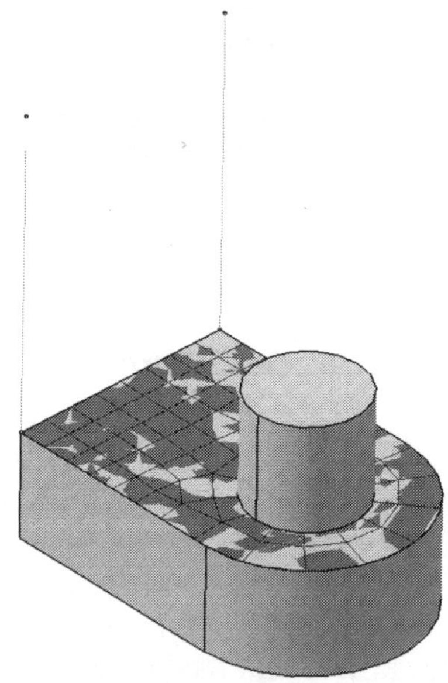

**Exit** the workbench by clicking on 
.

The next step is to mesh the vertical supports with beam elements.

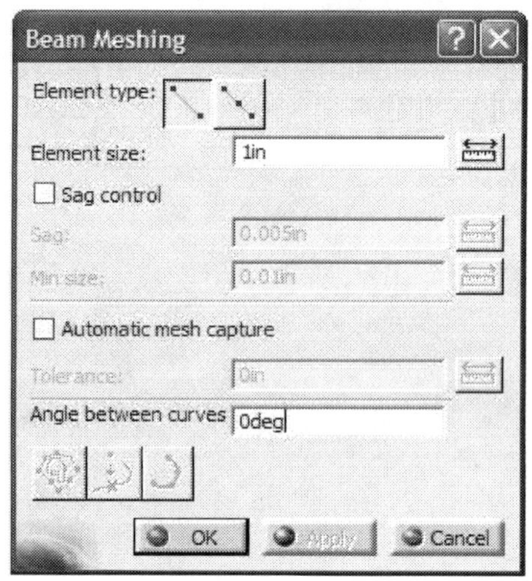


Select the **Beam Mesher** icon 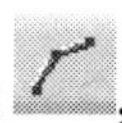, from the **Meshing Methods** toolbar 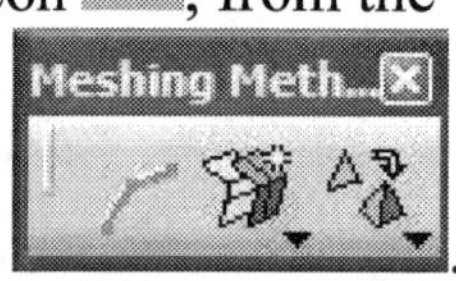
.

In the pop up box shown on the right, type 1 for **Element size**. Select the left line from the screen, then the **Apply** button from the pop up box. Three elements are created on the picked line. Repeat the same process with the second line.
A total of six beam elements are created as indicated below.

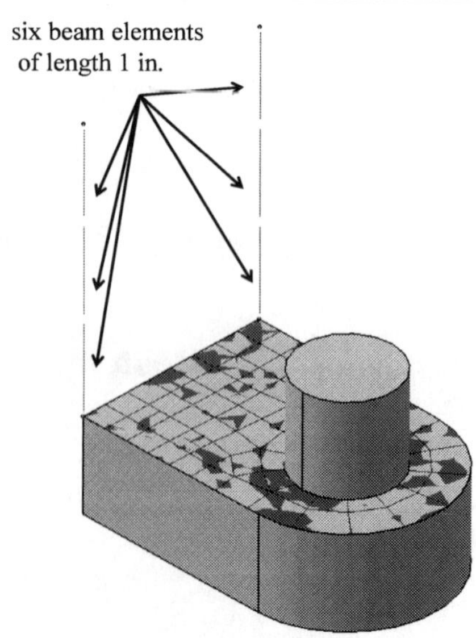


On the surface, it seems that the beam elements are connected to the shell elements at the two vertices. This however is not the case. The connection between the two has to be established later in the **General Connection Property**.

The **cylinder** is to be meshed with the solid tetrahedron elements.

Select the **Octree Tetrahedron Mesher** icon  from the **Solid Meshing** toolbar

and pick the cylinder from the screen.
Use the values indicated below and click on the **Apply** button.

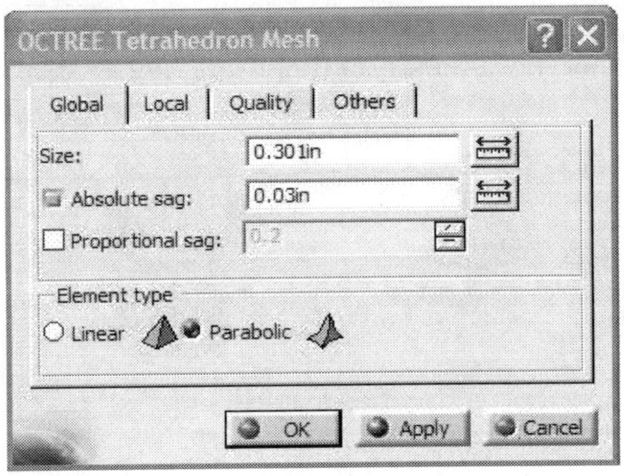


Although the meshing task is complete, the nature of the beam cross section and shell thickness is not defined at this point.

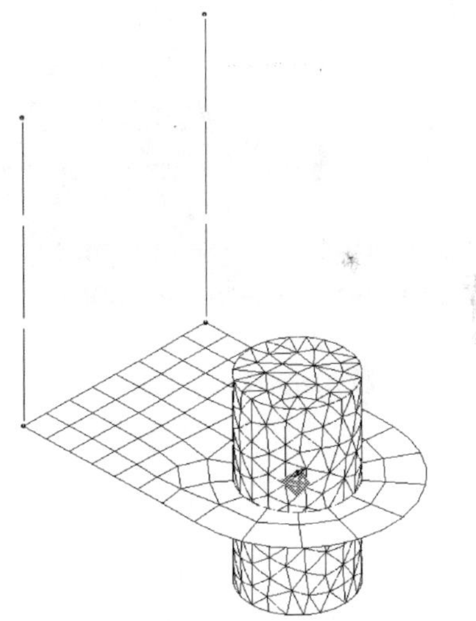

This step has to be done in the **Generative Structural Analysis** workbench.

Make sure that the parts are in the **Show** mode.

Change workbenches by following the usual steps.

**Start > Analysis & Simulation > Generative Structural Analysis** 

If your mesh disappears from the screen, point the cursor to the **Nodes and Elements** branch, right-click, and select **Mesh Visualization**. See Note #2 in Appendix I. Incidentally, the portion of the tree dealing with the mesh is displayed below for your convenience.

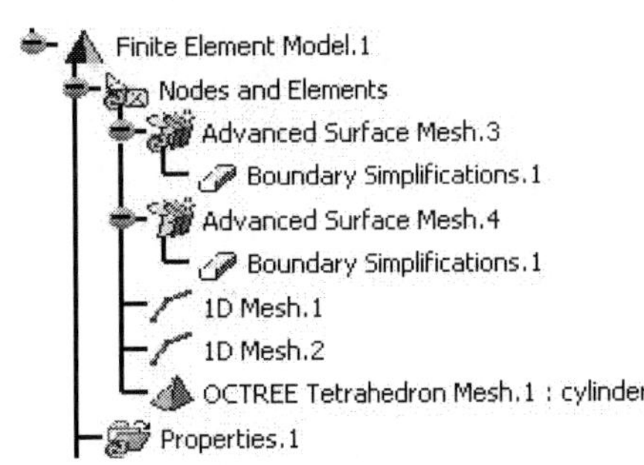


Note that the **Properties.1** and **Materials.1** branches are both unfilled.

If the meshed parts disappear, point the cursor to Nodes and Elements, right-click and select **Mesh Visualization**.

Double-click on the mesh to open the pop up box below. Check **Display nodes**. All the nodes in your model will be shown.

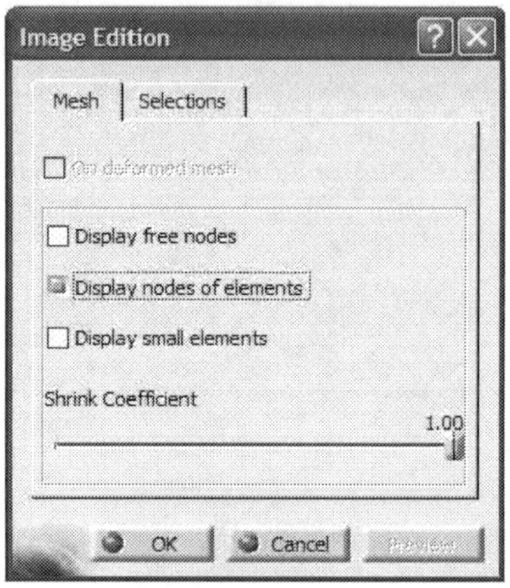


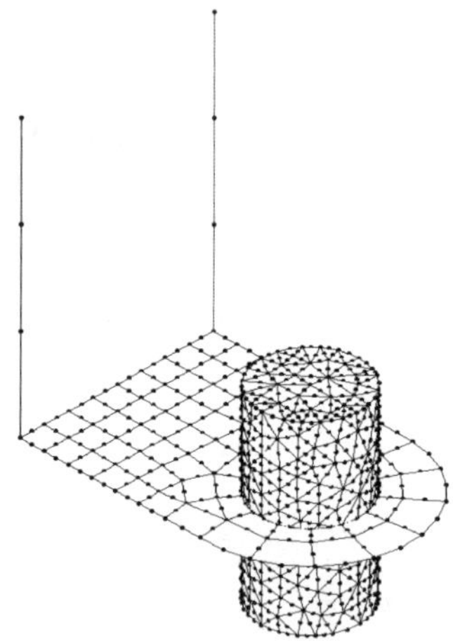

Make sure that the parts are in the **Show** mode.

Select the **3D Property** icon , from the **Model Manager** toolbar

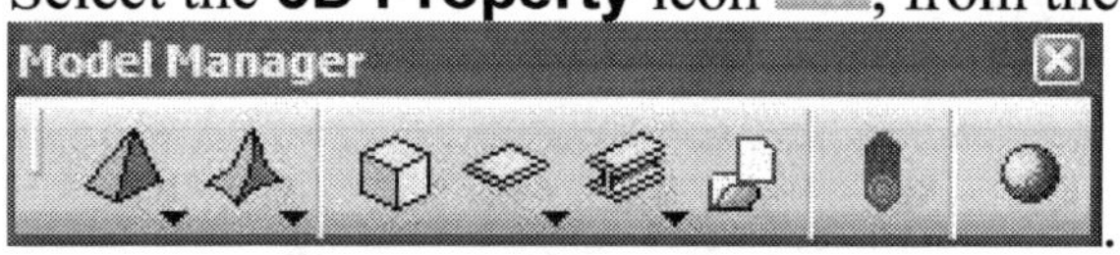


.

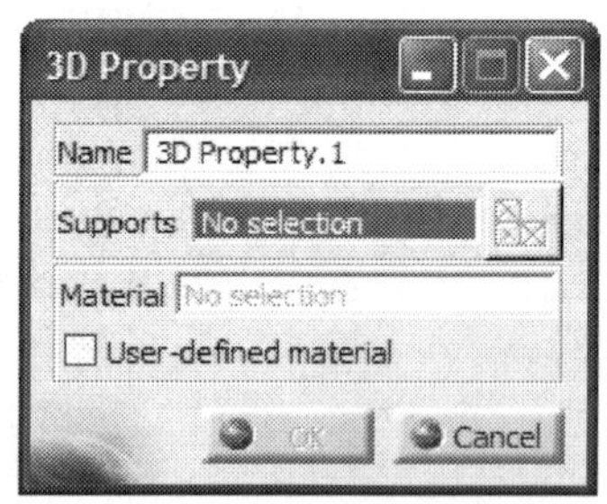


This leads to the pop up box shown on the right. Note that there is no material indicated in this box.

For the **Supports**, select the cylinder from the screen. Immediately, **Aluminum** appears in the material line. The modified pop up box is shown below.

Select the **2D Property** icon  from the **Model Manager** toolbar.
In the resulting pop up box, shown on the right side, no material is specified.
For **Supports**, pick the top surface of the **horizontal_plate**, from the screen.
Note that the box is modified to represent aluminum.

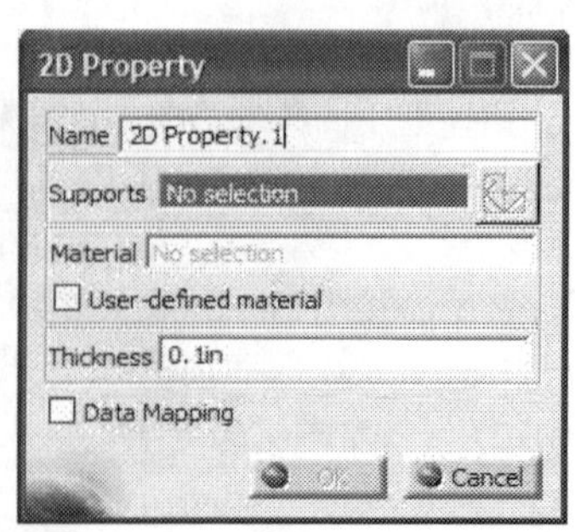


For **Thickness**, use 0.1.

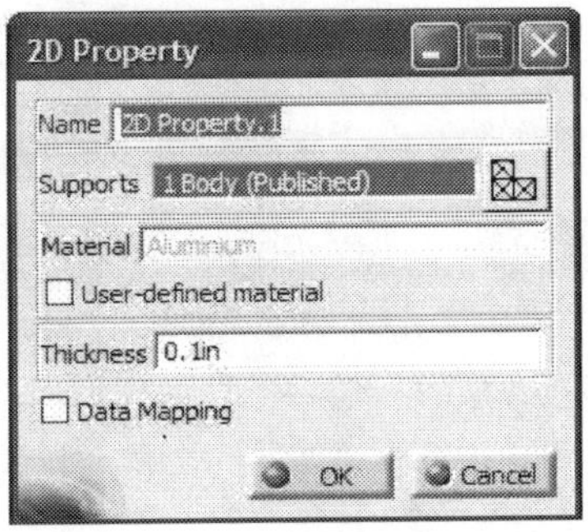


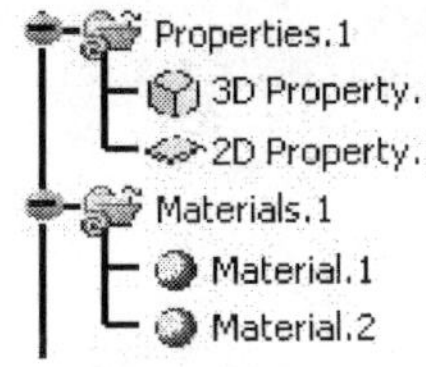


Note that the thickness of the shell elements is displayed on the screen.

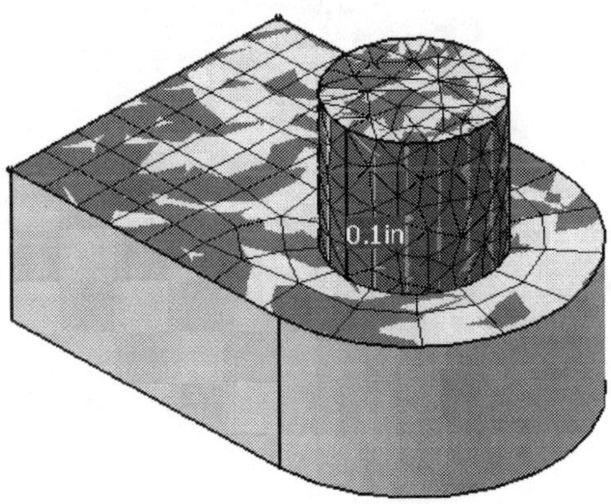


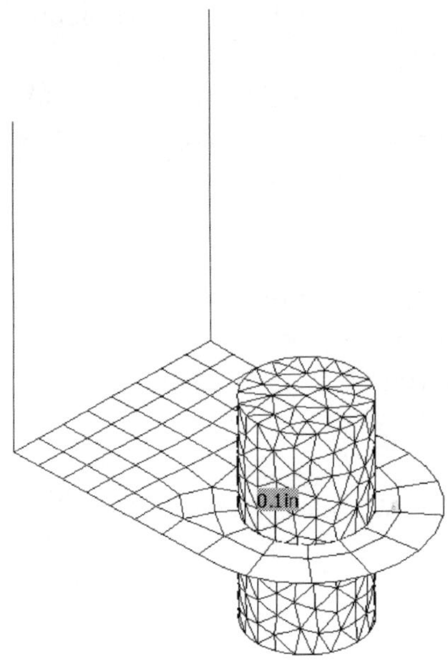


The next step is defining the cross sectional properties of the beam elements.

Select the **1D Property** icon , from the **Model Manager** toolbar

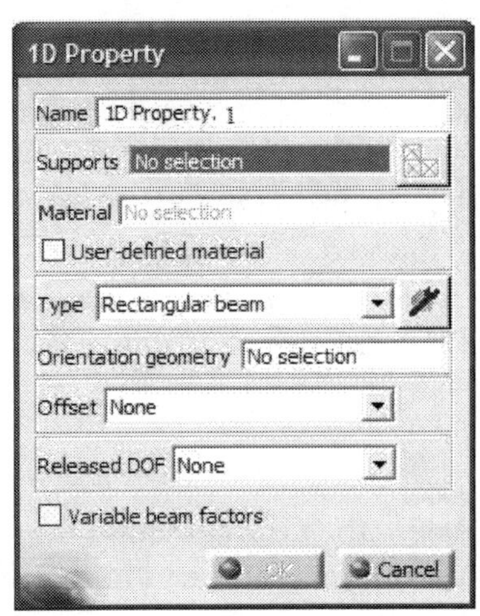


The pop up box shown on the right opens.

For the **Supports**, select the **Line.1**. Keep in mind that **Line.1** is part of the **horizontal_plate** and to be able to pick this line, the part must be in the **Show** mode.

For **Section**, select **Rectangular**, and use 0.1x0.1 as the dimensions. This has to be inputted in a secondary pop up box displayed below.

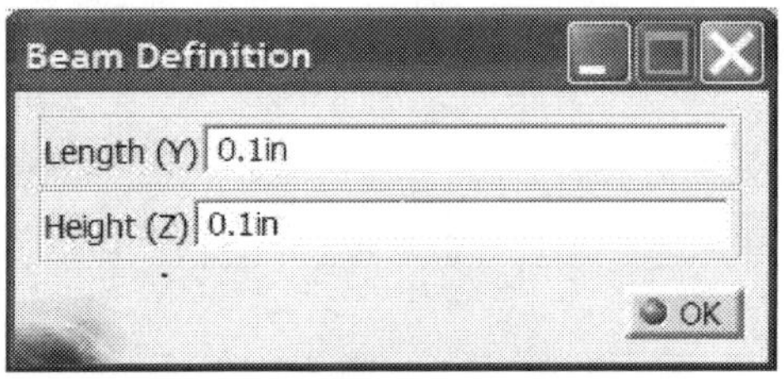


When defining the beam properties for "**line.1**", Use the vertex below as the "**Orientation Point**"

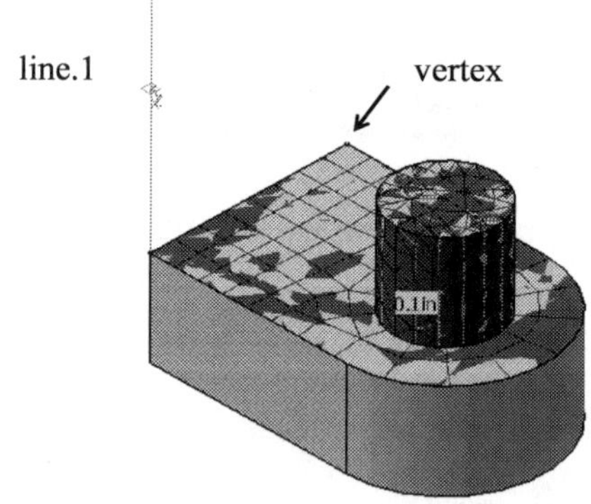


For the **Orientation Geometry** (**Orientation Point**), select the vertex <u>not</u> on the **line.1**, as indicated on the right.
The completed, pop up box for **1D Property** is given below. Note that the material has been correctly assigned.

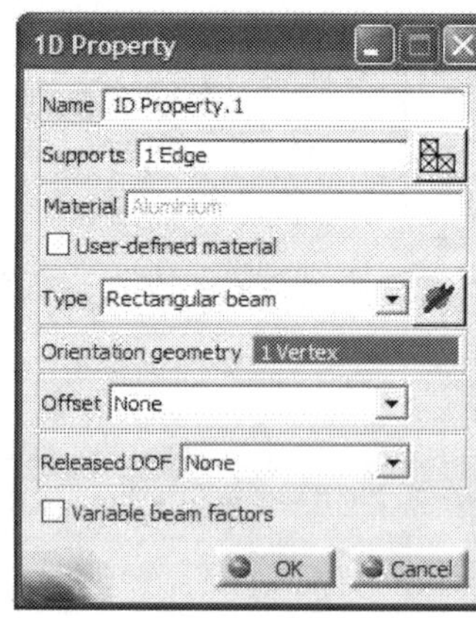


Repeat the same process to define the properties of the beam elements on **line.2**. The only difference being, that the picked vertex has to be switched.

When defining the beam properties for "**line.2**", Use the vertex below as the "**Orientation Point**"

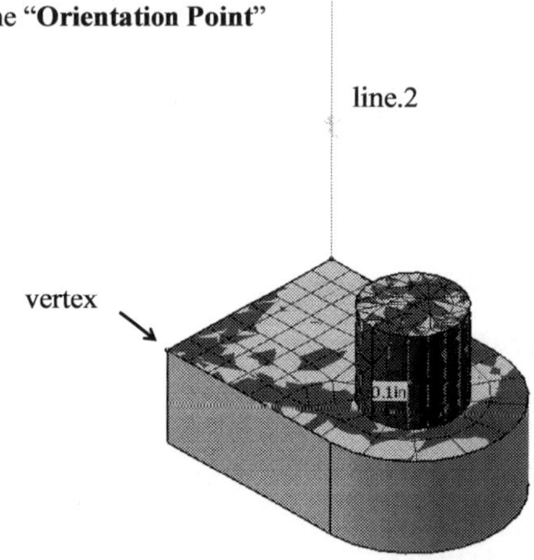


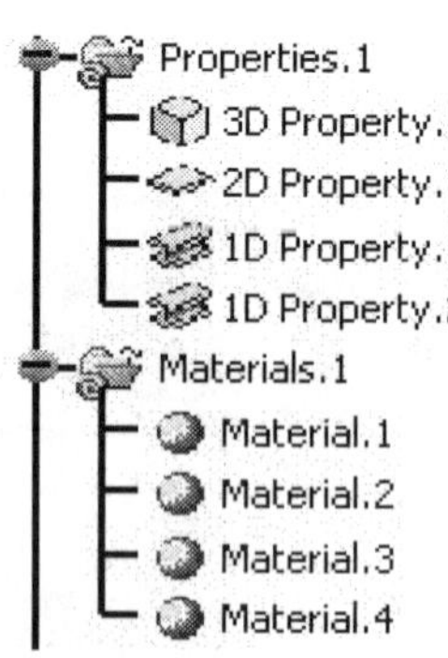


A portion of the tree, after completing the above tasks is displayed on the right.

The next step is to apply the restraints.

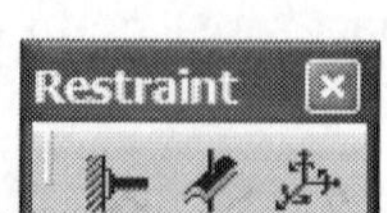


Select the **Clamp** icon  from the **Restraint** toolbar, and pick the bottom face of the cylinder. Keep in mind that the **cylinder** must be in the **Show** mode.

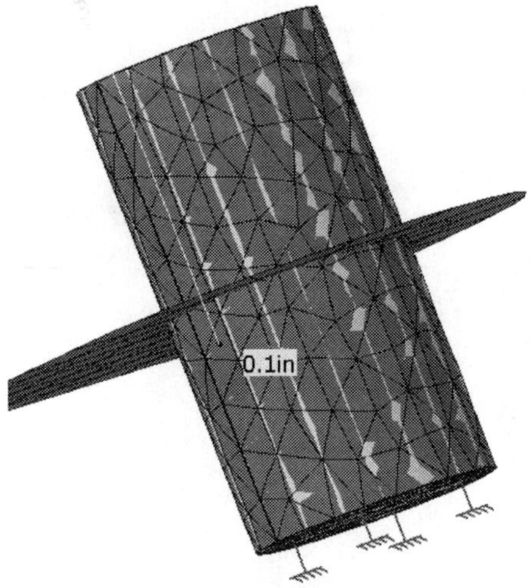


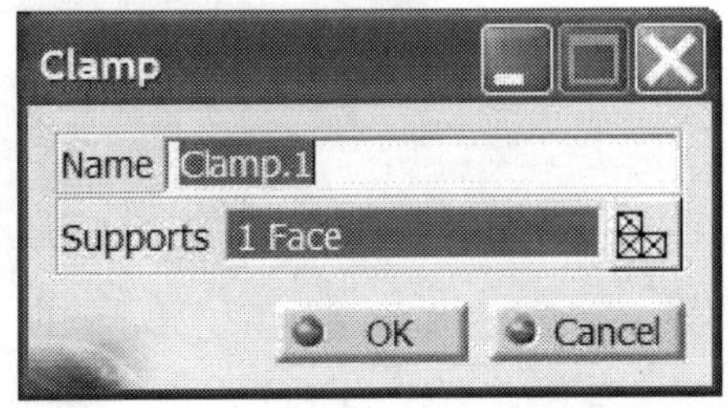


In order to apply the other clamps, make sure that **line.1** and **line.2** are in the **Show** mode. However, **Point.1** and **Point.2** must be in the **Hide** mode.

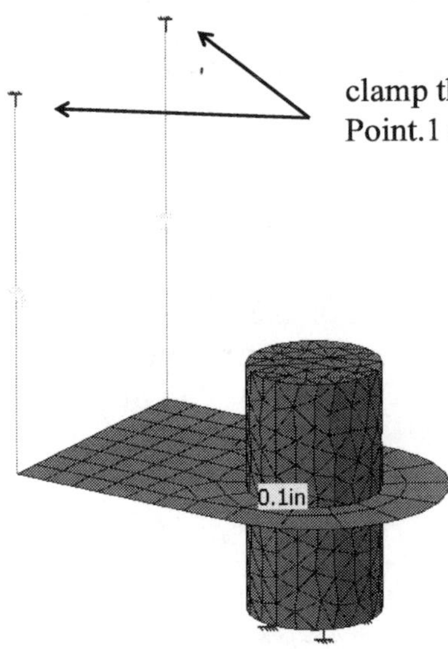


clamp the ends of these two lines while Point.1 and Point.2 are in the "**Hide**" mode

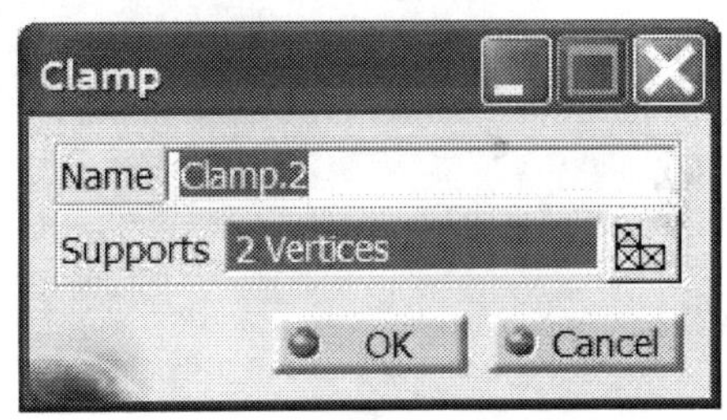


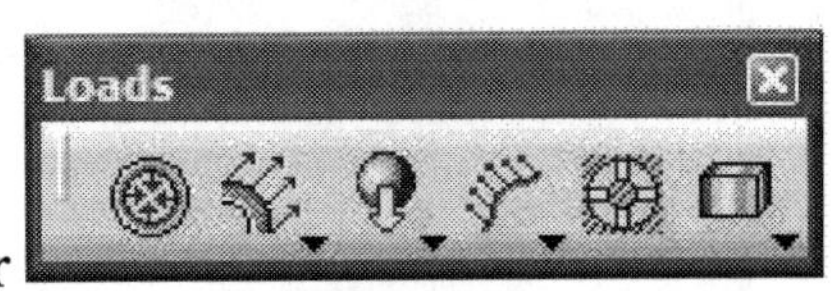


Use the **Pressure** icon from the **Loads** toolbar and pick the surface of the plate. Apply a pressure of 100 psi.

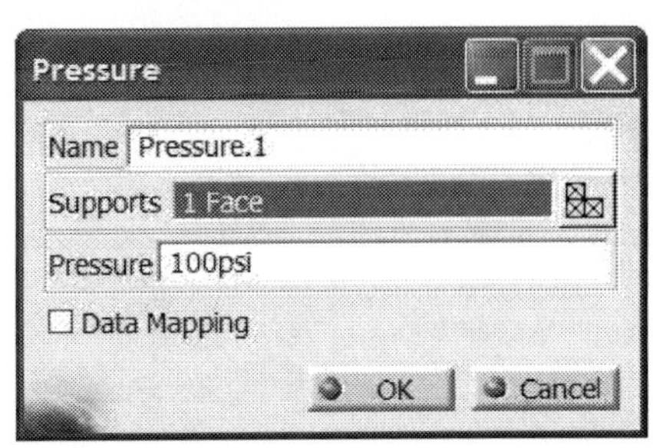

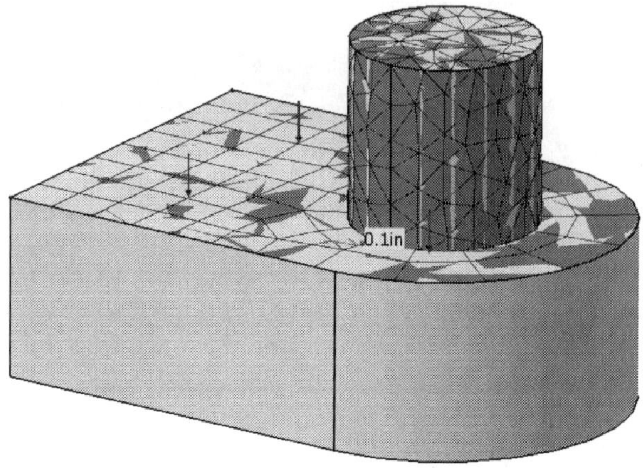


The last step is to apply the connection condition to ensure that the plate does not cut through the cylinder.

Use the **General Analysis Connection** icon , from the **Analysis Connection** toolbar .


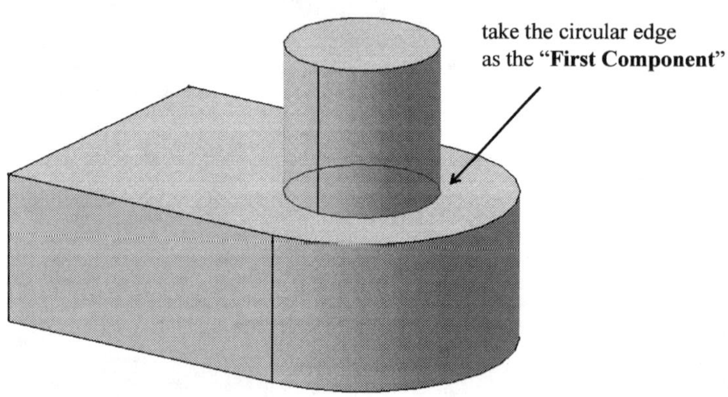


For the **First component**, select the circular edge of the **horizontal_plate**.

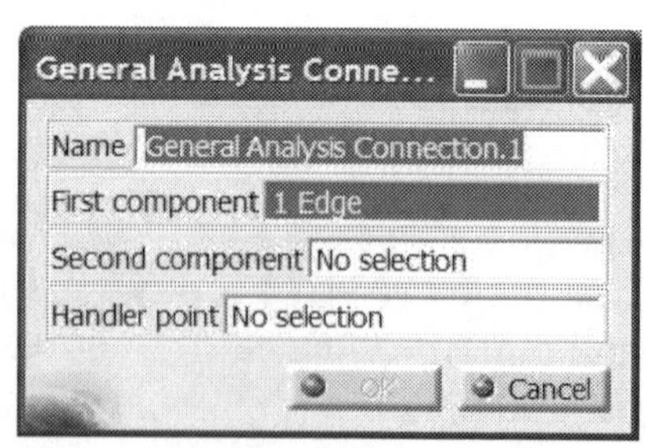


For the **Second Component**, select the outer surface of the cylinder.

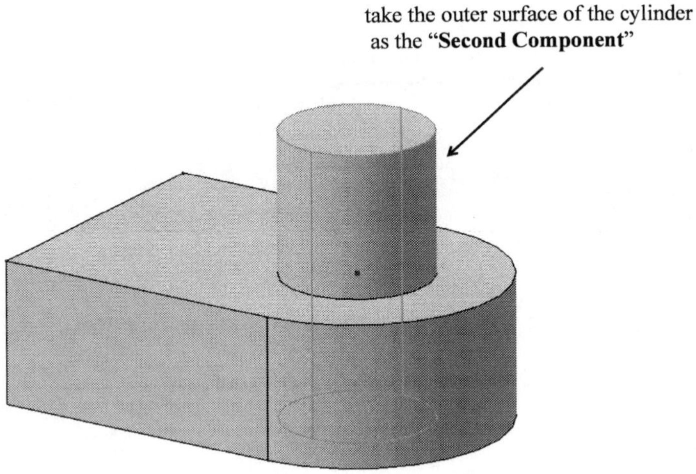


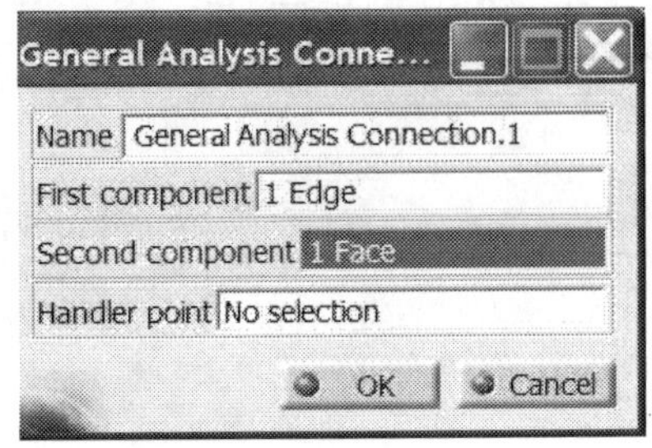


The "little red dot" on the computer screen indicates that a connection between the two picked entities has been established.

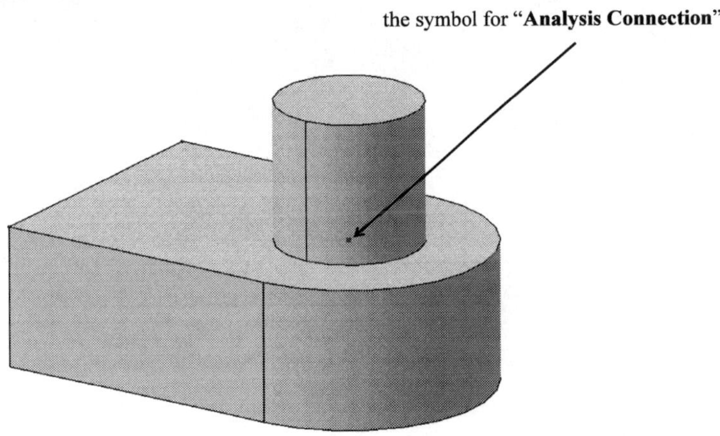


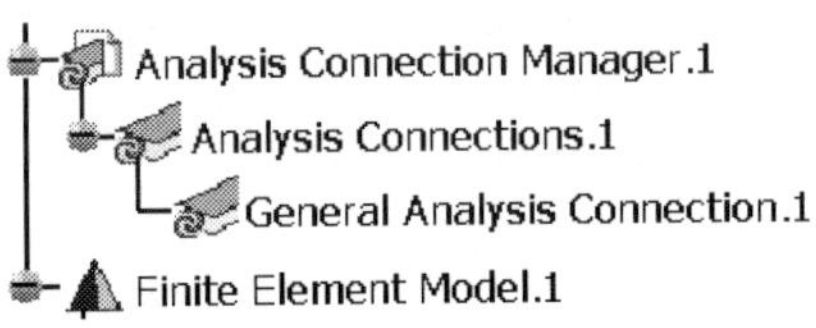


You now define the nature of the connections defined earlier.

Click on the **Smooth Connection property** icon  from the **Distant Connection** toolbar 

. The following pop up box appears.

For **Supports**, select **General Analysis Connection.1** from the tree.

On the computer screen, you notice that the standard symbol for smooth connection is created.

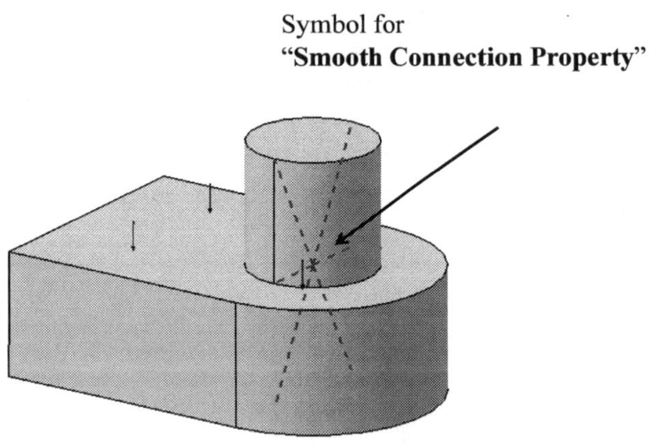


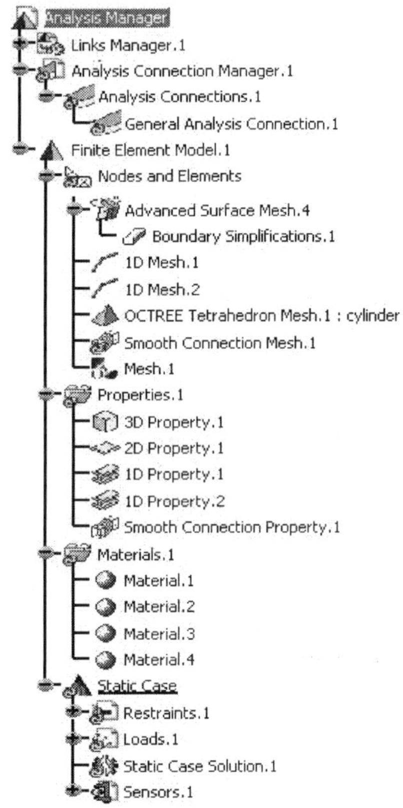


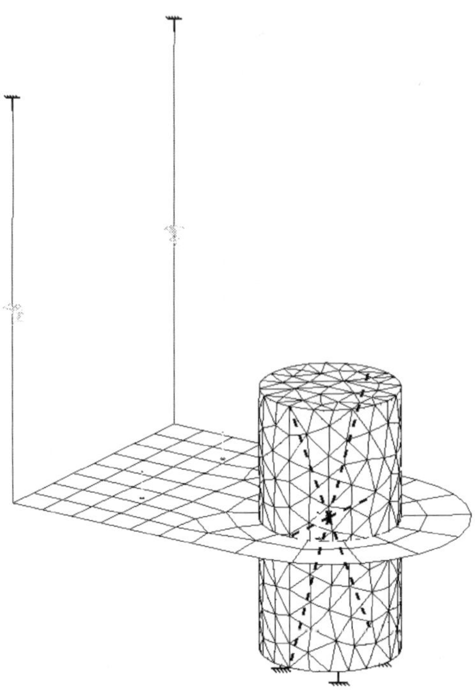

**Launching the Solver:**

To run the analysis, you need to use the **Compute** toolbar  by selecting the **Compute** icon . This leads to the **Compute** box shown to the right. Leave the defaults as **All** which means everything is computed.

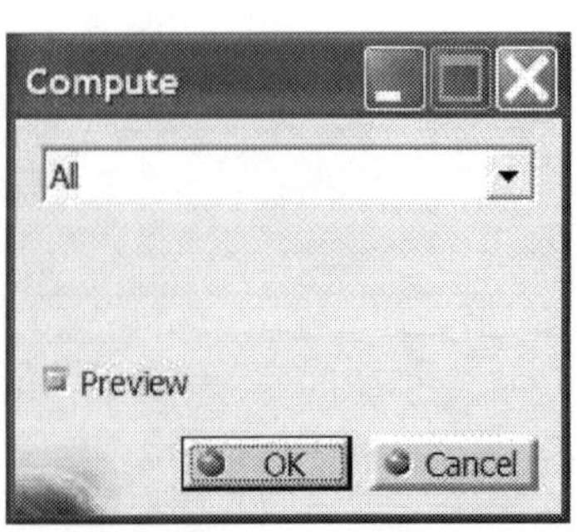

Upon closing this box, after a brief pause, the second box shown below appears. This box provides information on the resources needed to complete the analysis.

If the estimates are zero in the listing, then there is a problem in the previous step and should be looked into. If all the numbers are zero in the box, the program may run but would not produce any useful results.

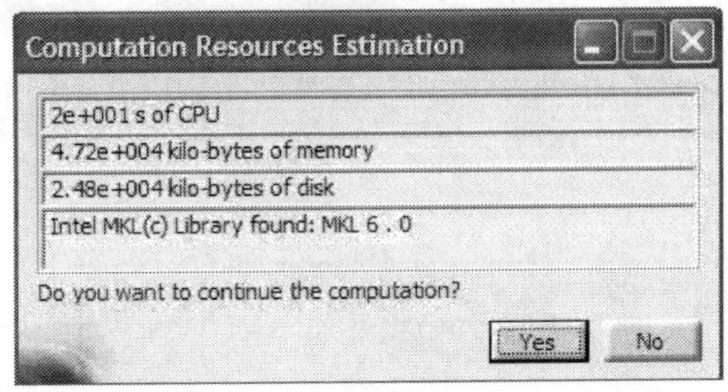


To view the deformed shape you have to use the **Deformation** icon 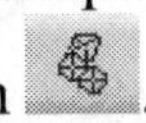. The result is displayed below. It is clear that there is no interaction between the plate and the beam elements. The nodes of the beam and the shell elements have to be tied together.

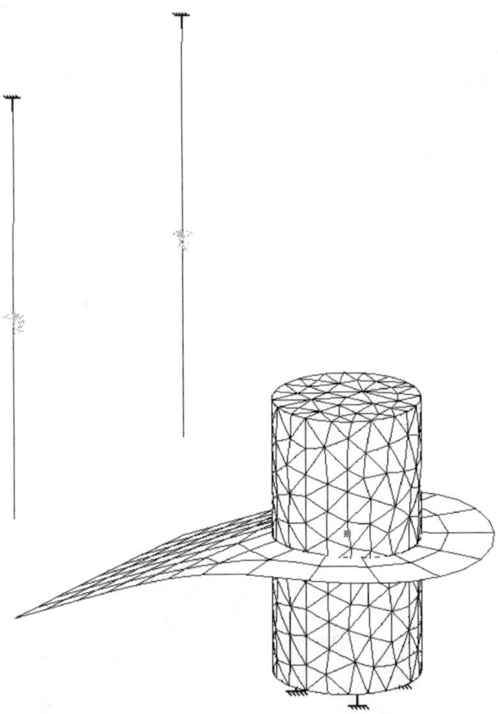

Use the **General Analysis Connection** icon , from the **Analysis Connection** toolbar .


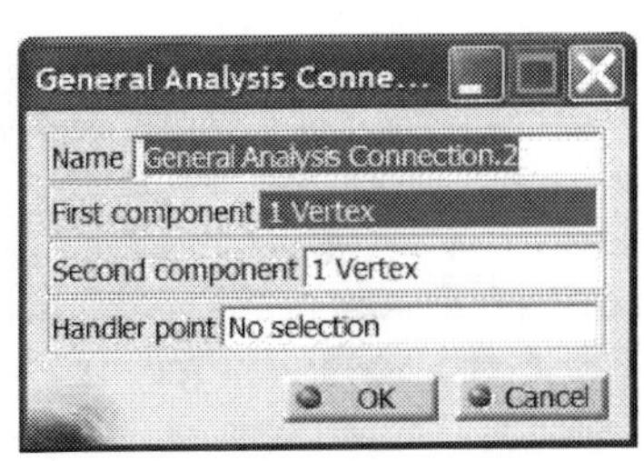


The pop up box, shown on the right opens.
For the **First Component**, select the vertex shown.
You may want to hide **line.1** first.
Bring **line.1** in the **Show** mode. For the **Second Component**, place the cursor close to the end of **line.1** and pick the vertex. If you feel more comfortable, hide the

plate before picking the end point of the line. The important thing to remember is that the two points picked, must be distinct. They should belong to the plate and the line.

Repeat the same process creating another connection between the end of **line.2** and the vertex immediately below it.

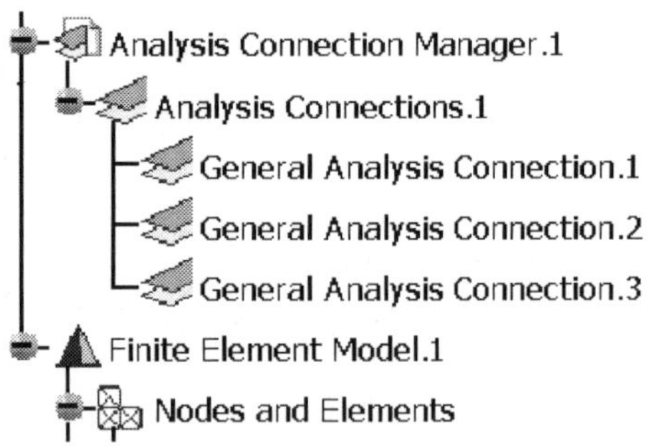


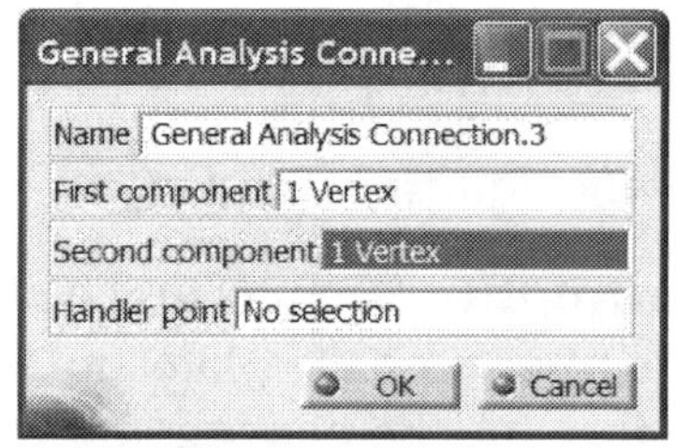


The last step is to describe the nature of the **General Analysis Connection.2** and **General Analysis Connection.3** just created.

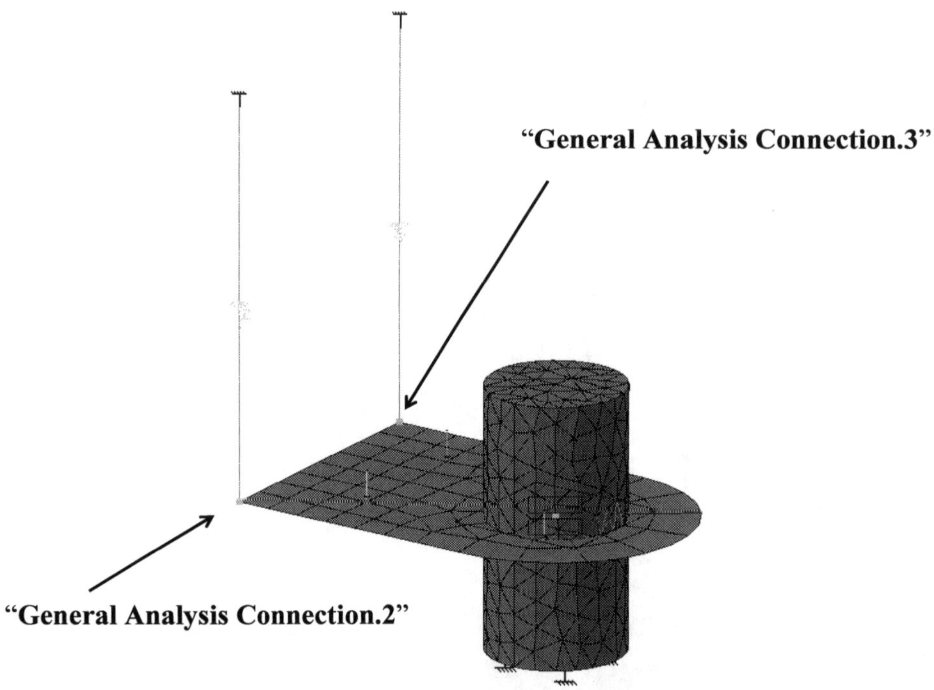


Select the **Rigid Connection property** icon , from the **Distant Connections** toolbar 

. The resulting pop up box is shown below.
For **Supports**, select the **General Analysis Connection.2** from the tree.

Repeat the same process, to create another **Rigid Connection property** for **General Analysis Connection.3** as its **Supports**.

The status of the tree at this point is given below.

Run the problem by the selecting the **Compute** icon.

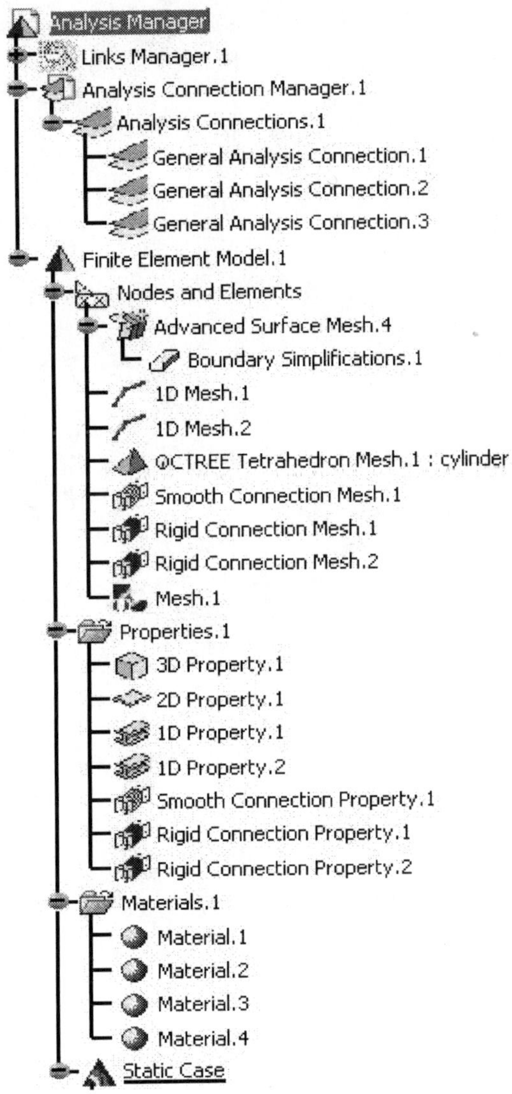

**Postprocessing:**

The main postprocessing toolbar is called **Image** toolbar 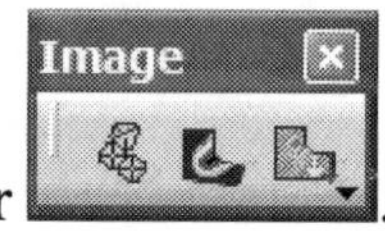. To view the deformed shape, you have use the **Deformation** icon . The resulting deformed shape is displayed below.

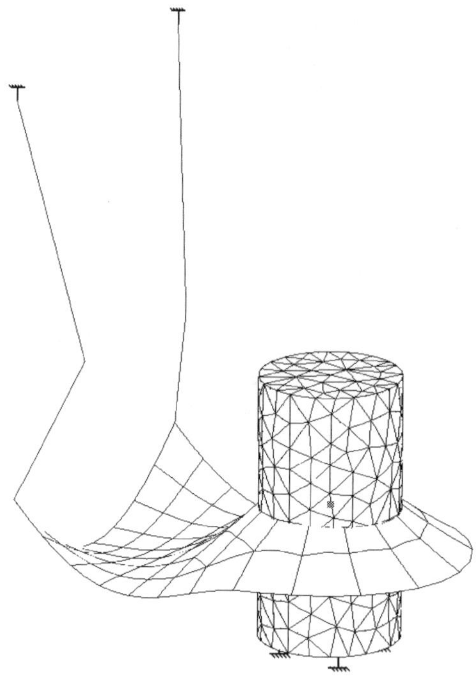

Keep in mind that the displacements are scaled considerably so that one can observe the deformed shape. Although the scale factor is set automatically, one can change this value with the **Deformation Scale Factor** icon  in the **Analysis Tools** toolbar .

In order to see the displacement field, the **Displacement** icon 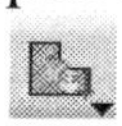 in the **Image** toolbar should be used. The default display is in terms of displacement arrows.

The arrow plot is not particularly useful. In order to view the contour plot of the displacement field, position the cursor on the arrow field and double-click. The **Image Edition** box opens.

Note that the default is to draw the contour on the deformed shape. If this is not desired, uncheck the box **On deformed mesh**. Next, select **AVERAGE-ISO** and press **OK**.

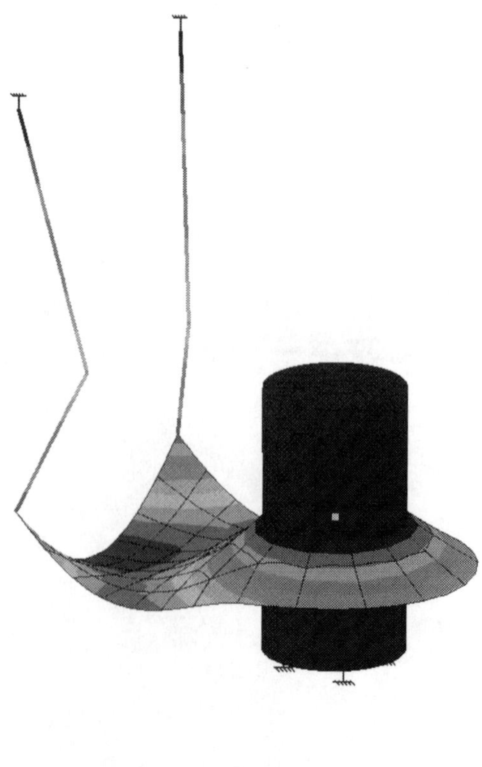

The next step in the postprocessing is to plot the contours of the von Mises stress using the **von Mises Stress** icon  in the **Image** toolbar. The von Mises stress is displayed to the right.

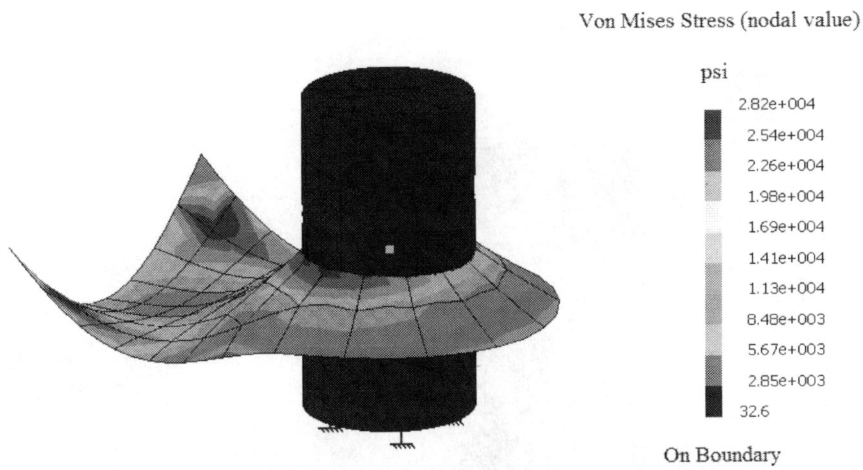


To see the stress distribution in the cylinder, double-click on the contour levels on the screen to open the **Image Edition** box. Next use the **Selections** tab as shown on the right. Here you have the choice of selecting different items.
Select **Octree Tetrahedron Mesh.1** from the list.

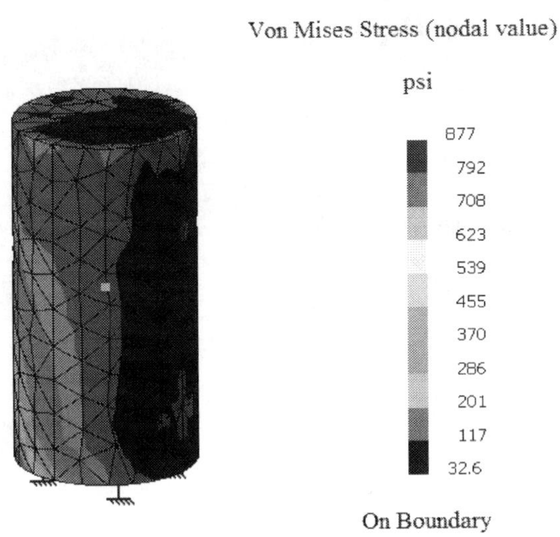


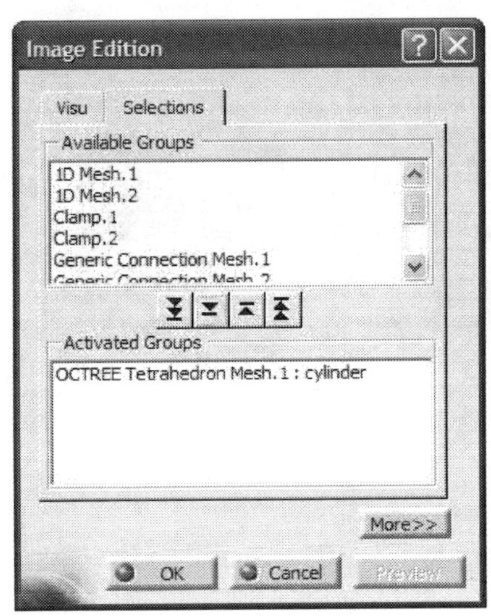

The **Cutting Plane** icon  from the **Analysis Tools** toolbar can be used to make a cut through the part at a desired location and inspect the stresses inside of the part. The **Cut Plane** box allows you to keep the plane or remove it for display purposes. A typical cutting plane is shown below.

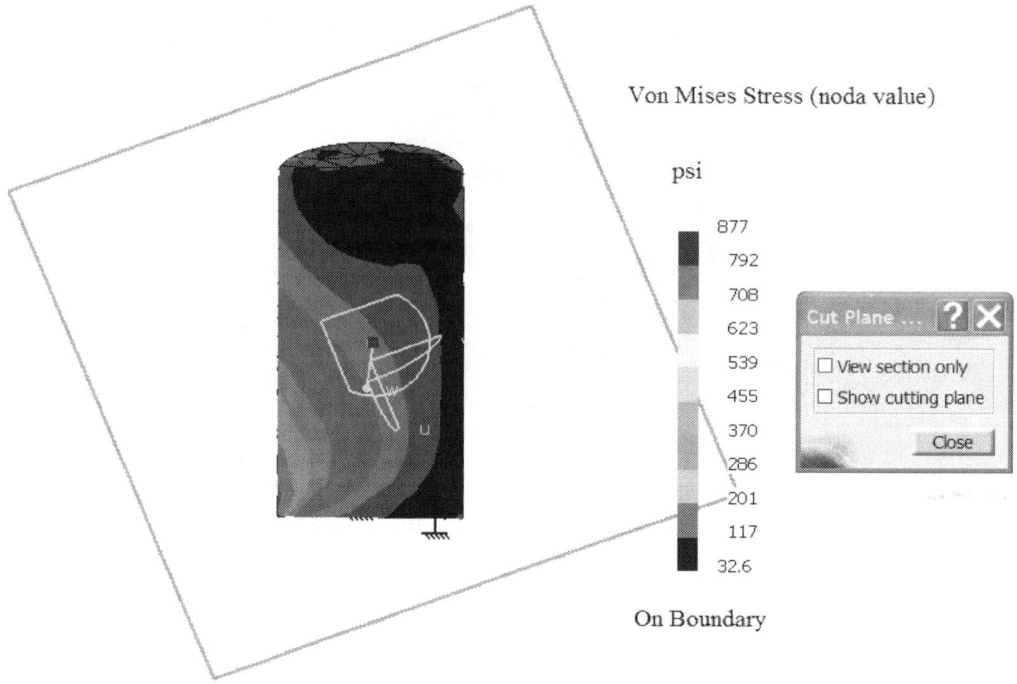


Animation of the model can be achieved through the **Animate** icon  in the **AnalysisTools** toolbar 

. An AVI file can easily be generated.

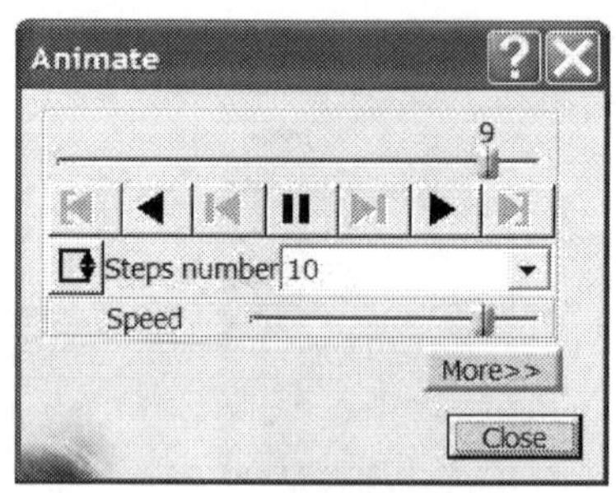

Using the icon **Generate Report** in the **Analysis Results** toolbar, an HTML based report can be generated which summarizes the features and results of the FEA model. The first page of this report is displayed in the next page.

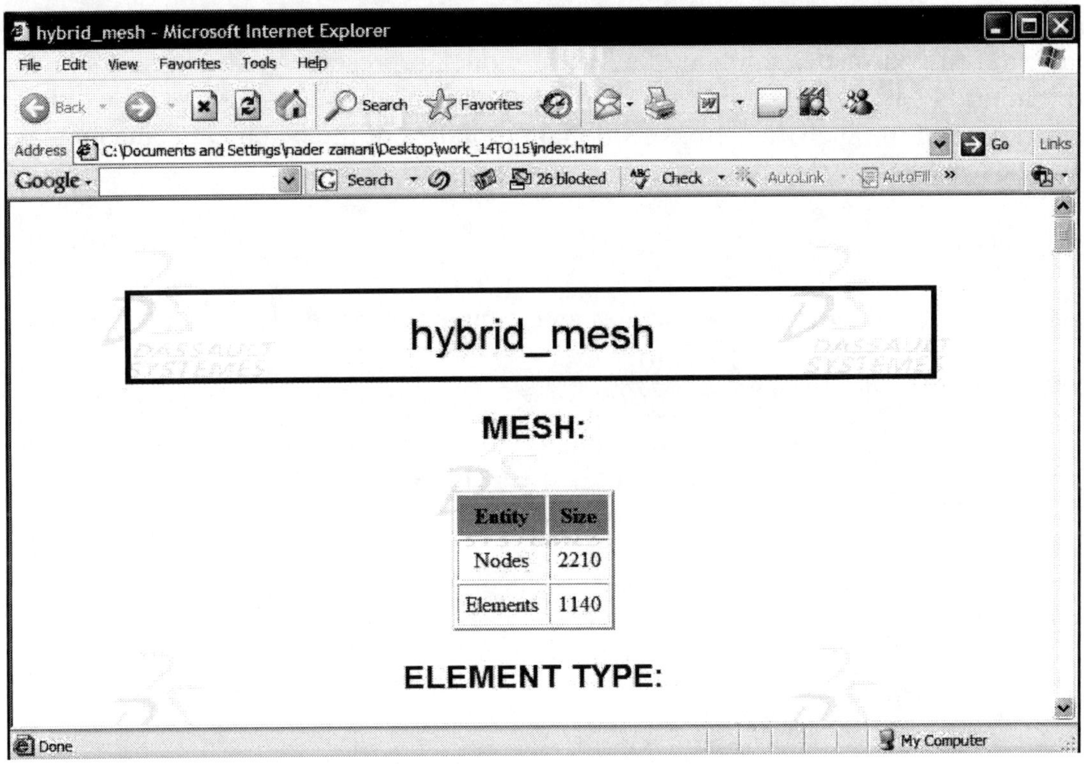


The location of storage of this report is controlled by the pop up box displayed.

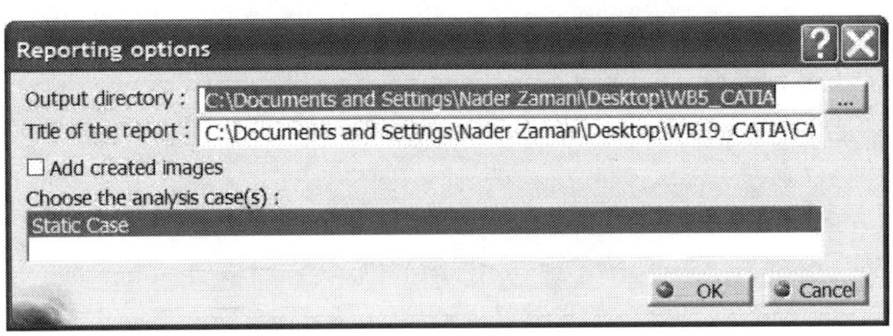

# Exercises for Chapter 19

## Problem 1: Hybrid FEA Model of a Cantilever Beam

The steel cantilever beam of dimensions 1x1x12 in. is deflecting under a load of 500 lb. In order to test your understanding of a hybrid model, represent the structure as a combination of solid, shell, and beam element appropriately tied together at the junctions. The thickness of the shell, and cross sectional properties of the beam elements must be consistent with the existing dimensions.

Partial Answer:

Elementary strength of materials provides an estimate for the tip deflection. This estimate is evaluated from the formula $\delta_{tip} = \frac{FL^3}{3EI}$.

Here, L represents the length of the bar, and I is the cross sectional moment of inertia. In the case of a 1x1 in. square cross section, $I = 1/12 \text{ in}^4$.

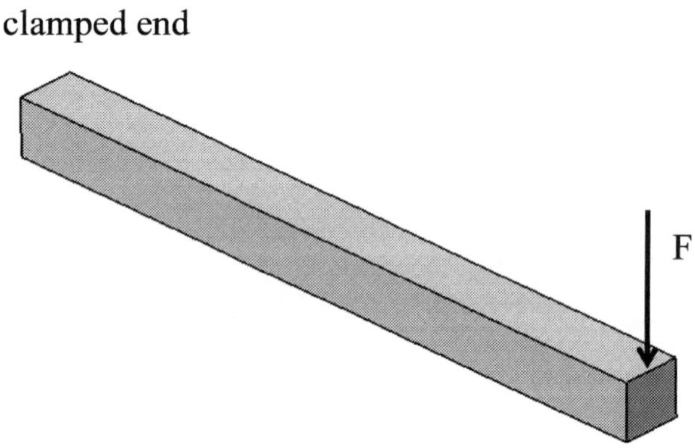


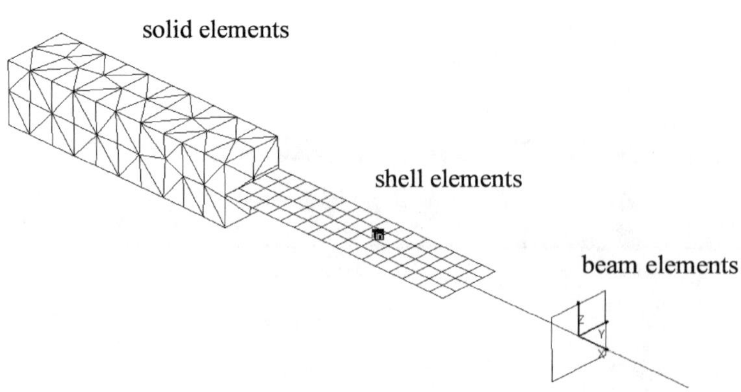

## Problem 2: Hybrid FEA Model of a Tube under Torsion

The purpose of this exercise is to simulate, the torsion of a tube with a hybrid model, consisting of solid and shell elements as displayed below. Assume that the length of the tube is 30 in. with inside and outside radii being 4 in. and 5 in. respectively.

Partial Answer:

The shear stress in the tube is calculated from $\tau = \frac{Tr}{J}$.

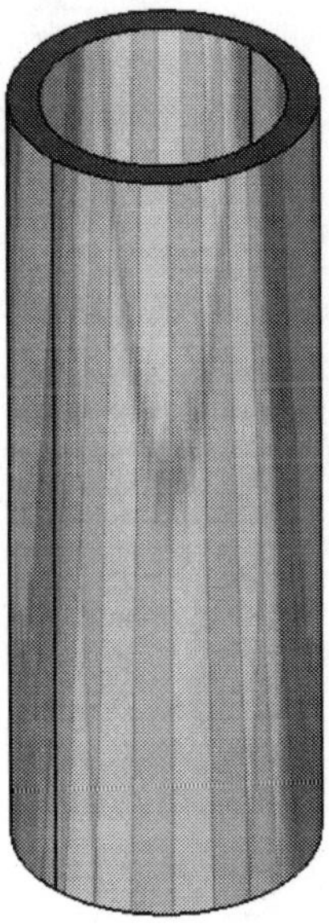

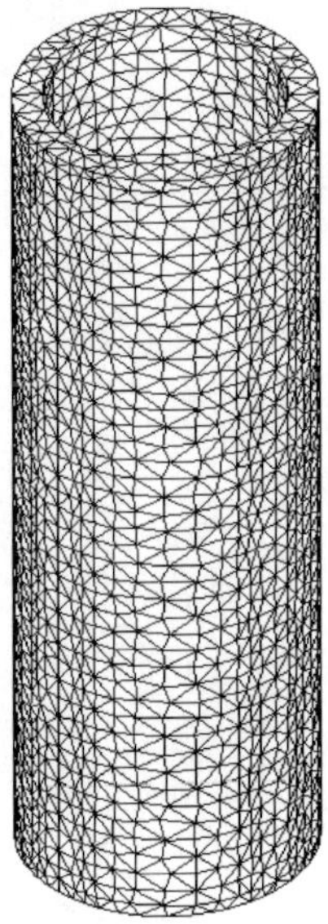

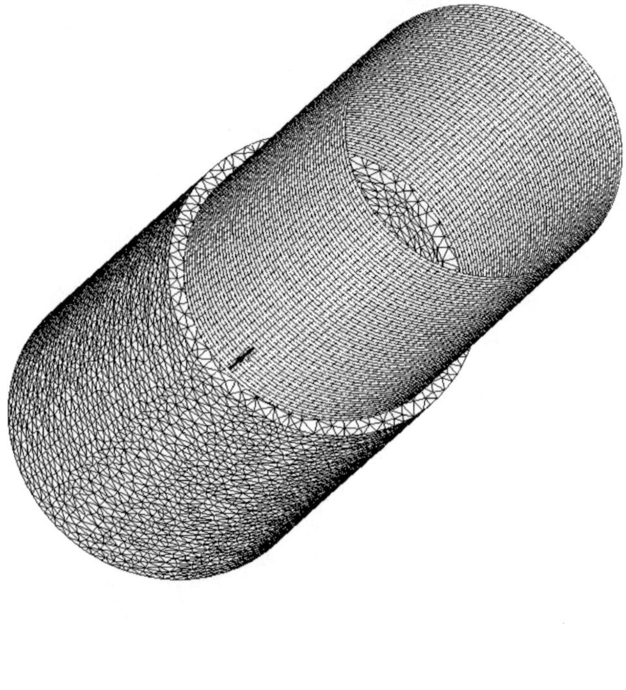

# NOTES:

# Chapter 20

# Spring Elements

# Introduction

In this tutorial, the virtual spring element in CATIA is employed, to predict the deformation of an axially loaded bar. The approximate analytical solution from strength of materials sheds some light on the accuracy of the results.

## 1 Problem Statement

The steel bar shown below is of length $L = 5$ in. and has a $1x1$ in. square cross section.

The structure is clamped at the left end and rests against a spring of stiffness $k = 20E + 6$ lb/in. A force of 1000 lb is applied, causing the bar to elongate. The CATIA solid element, in combination with virtual spring element, is to be used for simulation purposes.

Elementary strength of materials provides an estimate of the tip deflection of the bar according to the following formula.

$$\delta_{tip} = \left[\frac{AE}{L} + k\right]^{-1} F$$

In this expression, "A" and "E" represent the cross sectional area and the Young's modulus of the bar respectively.
Note that the stiffnesses of the bar and the spring are added, because they act in parallel.

Assuming that $E = 2.9E + 7$ psi, a tip deflection of 3.876E-5 in. is predicted.

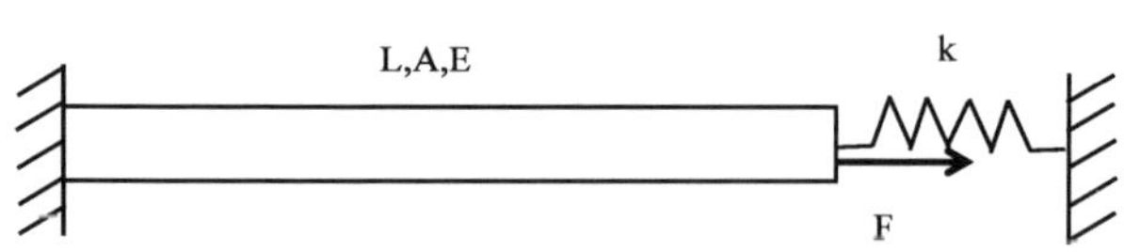


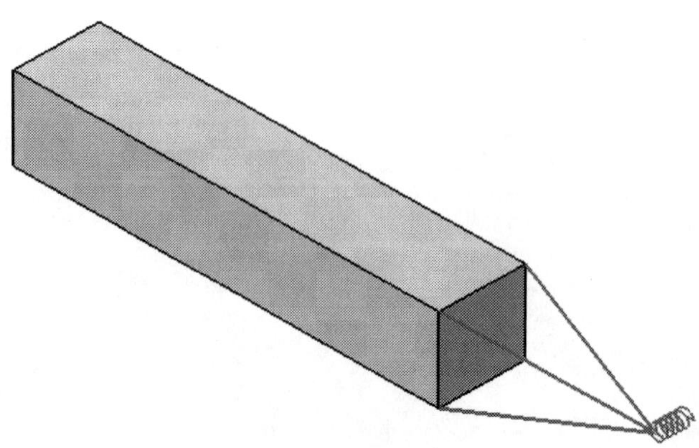

## 2 Creation of the Part in Mechanical Design Solutions

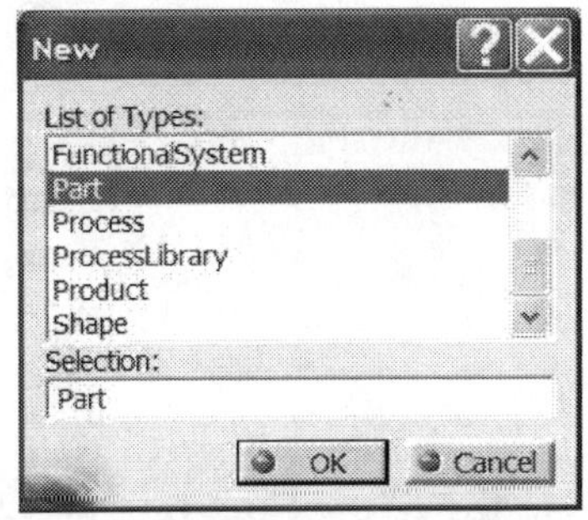


Enter the **Part Design** workbench which can be achieved by different means depending on your CATIA customization. For example, from the standard Windows toolbar, select **File > New**. From the box shown on the right, select **Part**. This moves you to the **Part Design** workbench and creates a part with the default name **Part.1**. Read Note #1 in Appendix I.

In order to change the default name, move the cursor to **Part.1** in the tree, right-click and select **Properties** from the menu list.

From the **Properties** box, select the **Product** tab and in **Part Number** type **spring**. This will be the new part name throughout the chapter. The tree on the top left corner of the screen should look as displayed below.

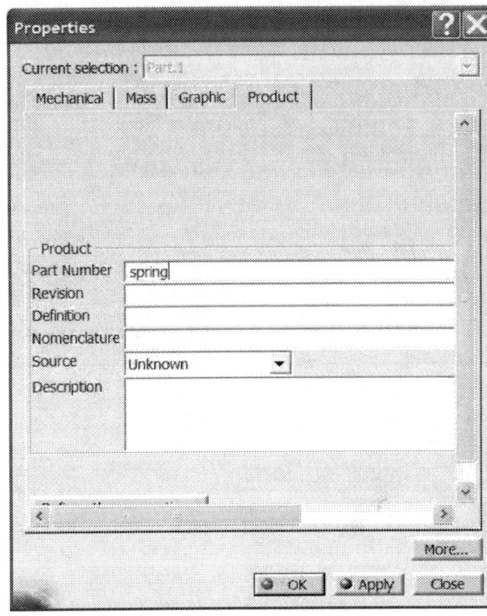


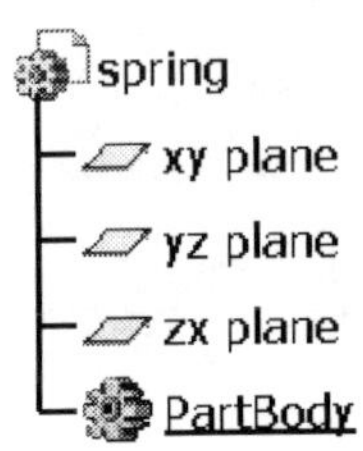


From the tree, select the **zx** plane and enter the **Sketcher**. In the **Sketcher**, use the **Profile** toolbar

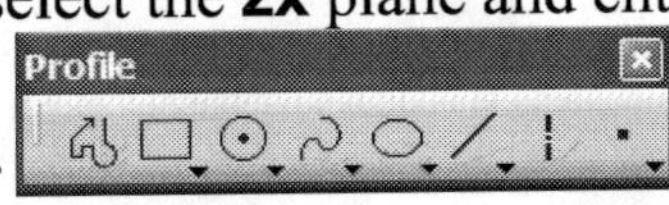


to draw a square, and dimension it.

***Note: The drawn rectangle (square) must be centered at the origin.***

In order to change the dimension, double-click on the dimension on the screen.

Leave the **Sketcher**.

You will now use the **Pad** operation to extrude the sketch.

Upon selecting the **Pad** icon, the **Pad Definition** box shown to the right opens.

In the **Length** box, type 5.

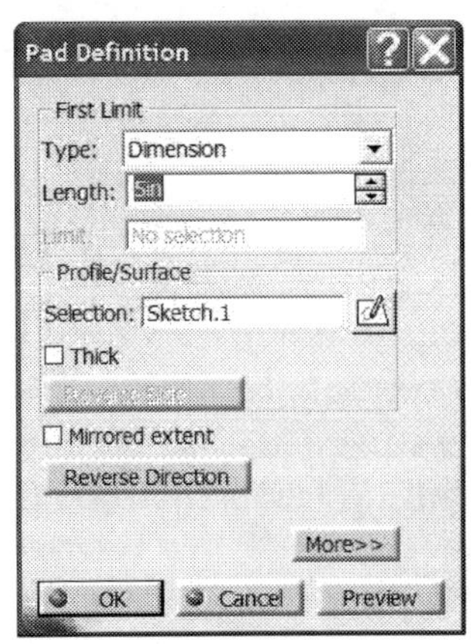


The result is displayed in the next page.

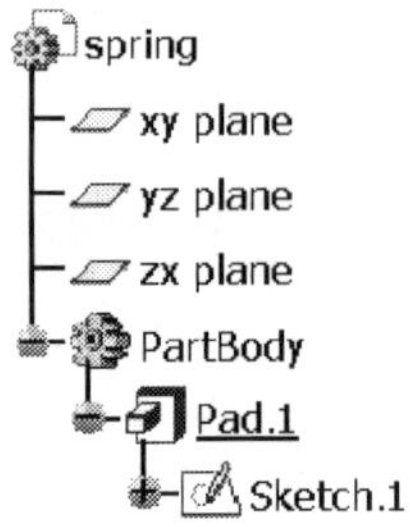


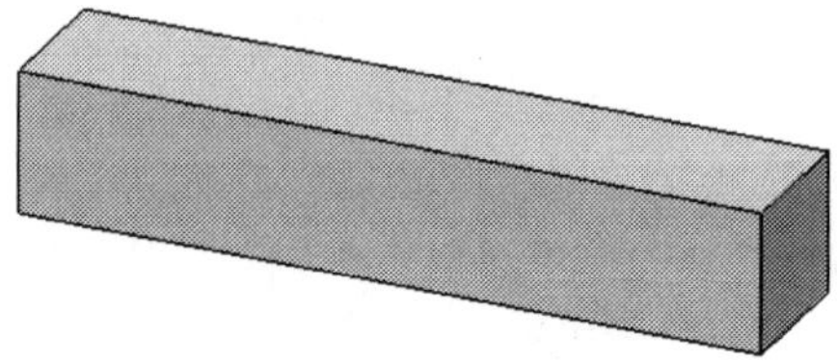

Select the **Apply Material** icon , to activate the material **Library** box below. Use the **Metal** tab on the top; select **Steel**. Use your cursor to pick the **spring** from the tree at which time the **OK** and **Apply Material** buttons can be selected. Close the box. The material property is now reflected in the tree.

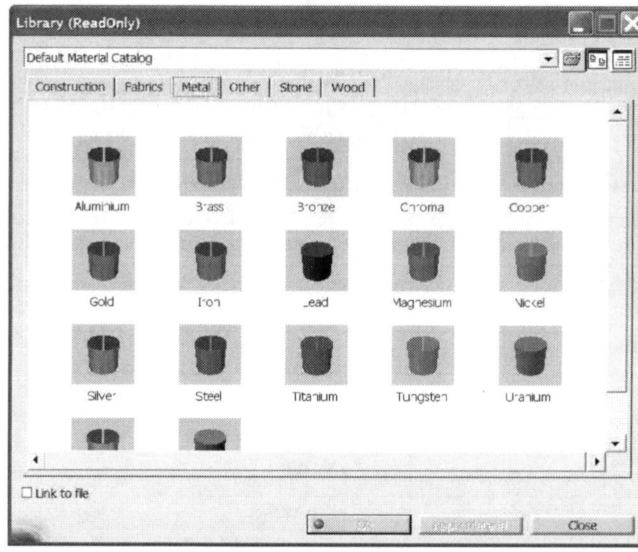


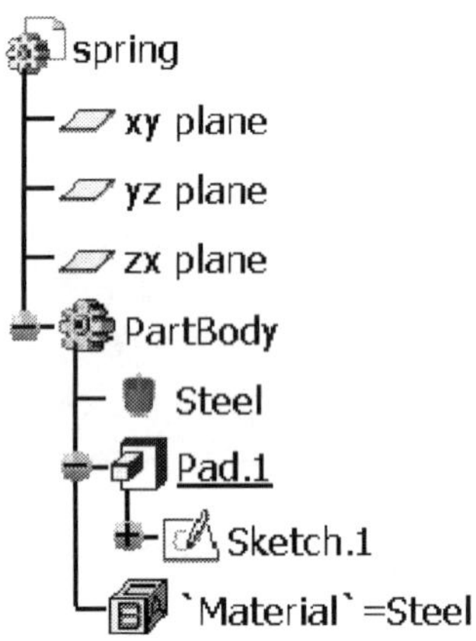


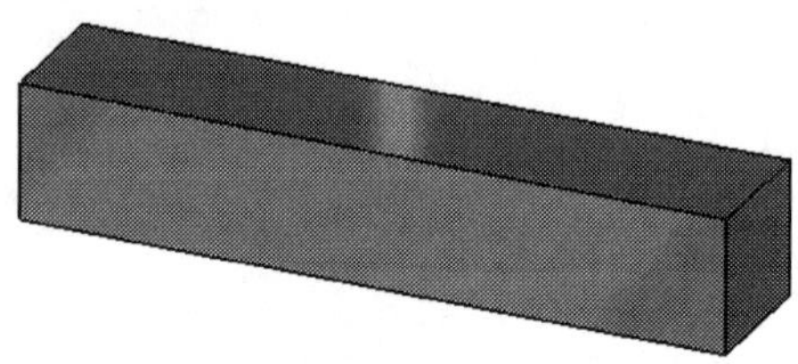

In order to create the **Virtual Spring Element**, you need to create a point which can be used as the **Handler**.

Select the **Point** icon 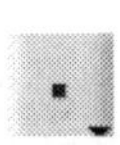 from the **Reference Element** toolbar 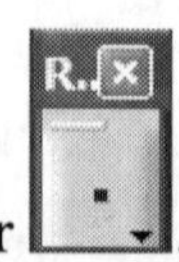. A pop up box opens and allows you to input the coordinates. Type the coordinates (0,7,0) in the appropriate locations. The actual coordinates are irrelevant however with these values you can easily see the point on the screen. The display on your computer screen and the resulting tree structure are also shown below.

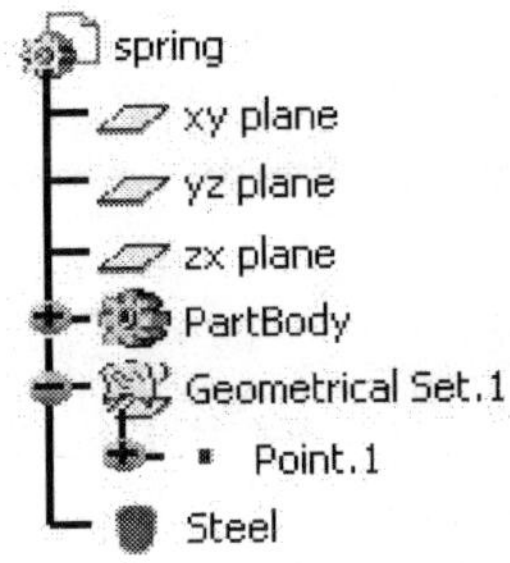


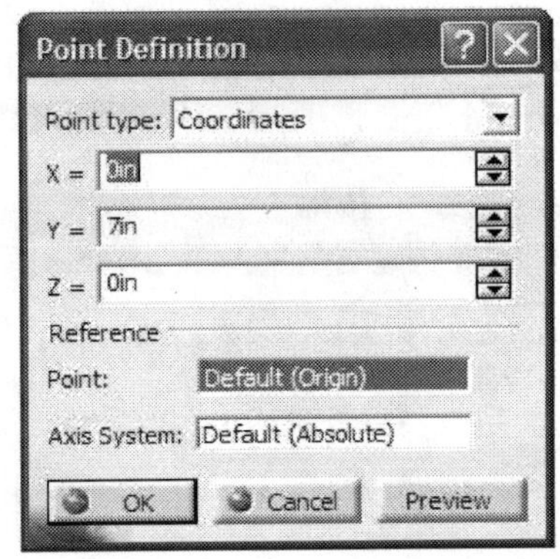


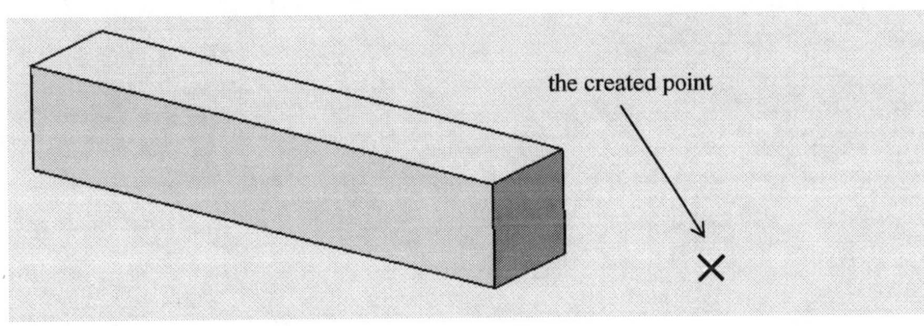


## 3 Entering the Analysis Solutions

From the standard Windows toolbar, select

**Start > Analysis & Simulation > Generative Structural Analysis**

There is a second workbench known as the **Advanced Meshing Tools** which will be discussed later.

Upon changing workbenches, the box **New Analysis Case** becomes visible. The default choice is **Static Analysis** which is precisely what we intend to use. Therefore, close the box by clicking on **OK**.

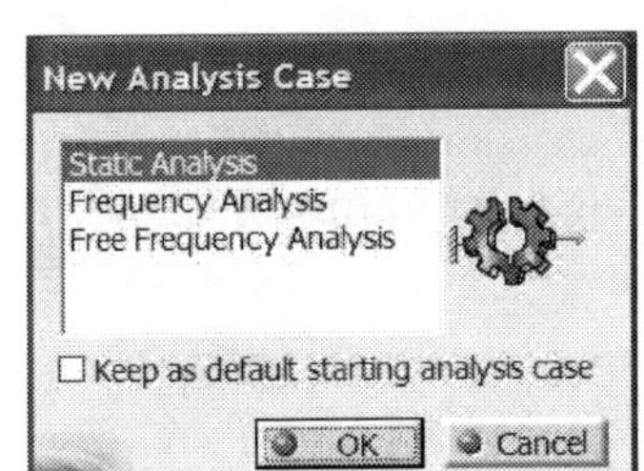


The tree, the part, and the representative element size and sag (under default values) are displayed below.

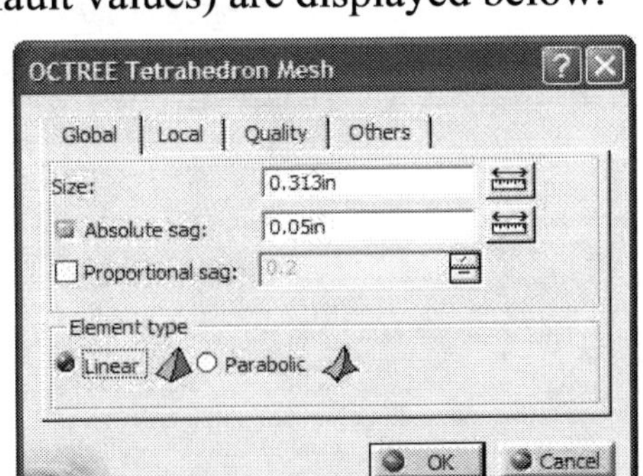

Point the cursor to the branch **Nodes and Elements**, right-click and select **Mesh Visualization**. A **Warning** box appears which can be ignored, select **OK**. For the mesh parameters used, the following mesh is displayed on the screen.

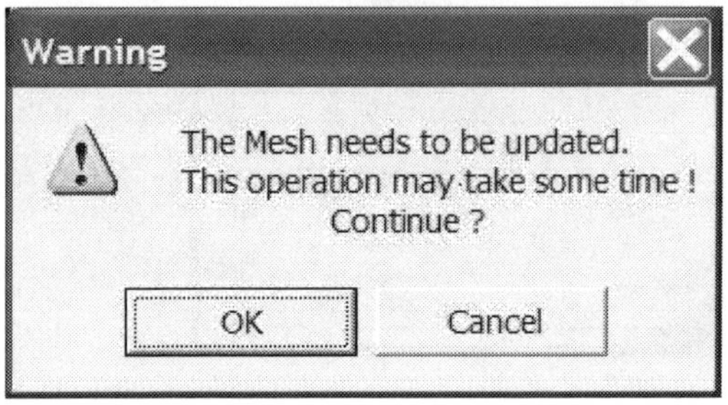


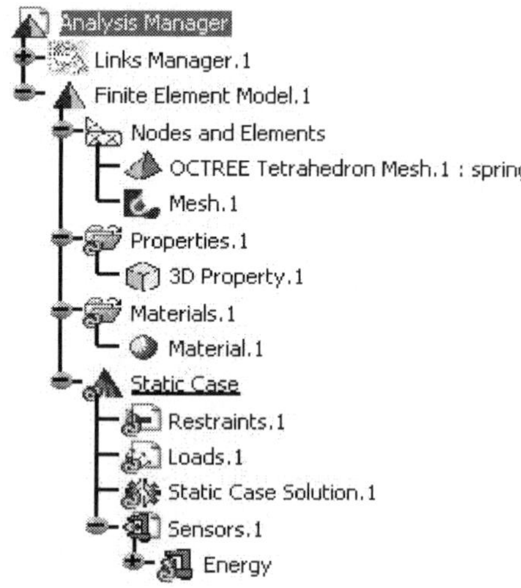


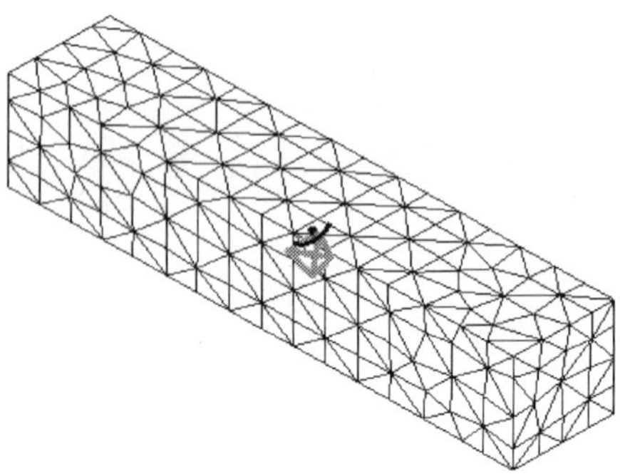

From the **Virtual Part** toolbar 

, select the **Smooth Spring Virtual Part** . The pop up box below opens.

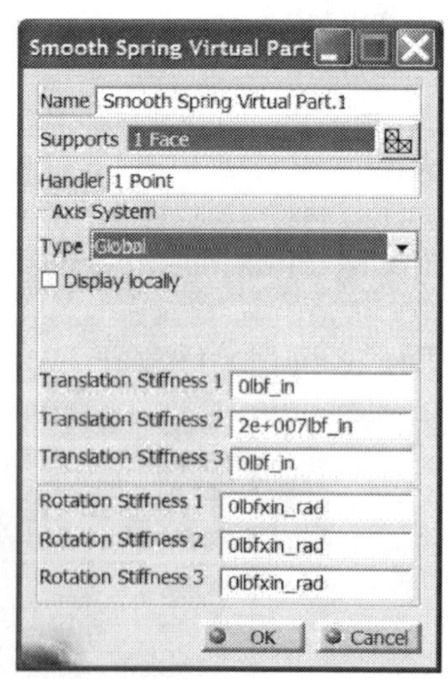


For **Supports**, select the face of the bar which is square.
For the **Handler**, select the point that was created above.
Use the value of 2E+7 lbf/in as **Translational Stiffness 3**.

A spring is created as shown below.

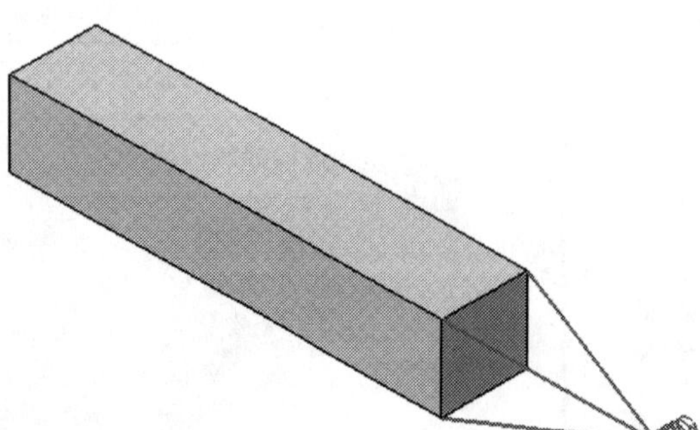

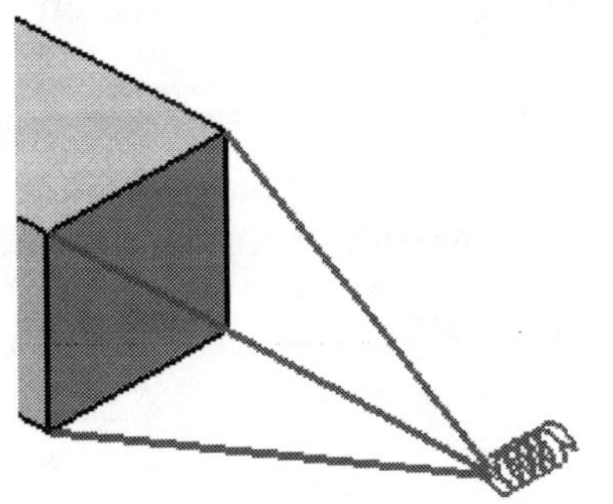

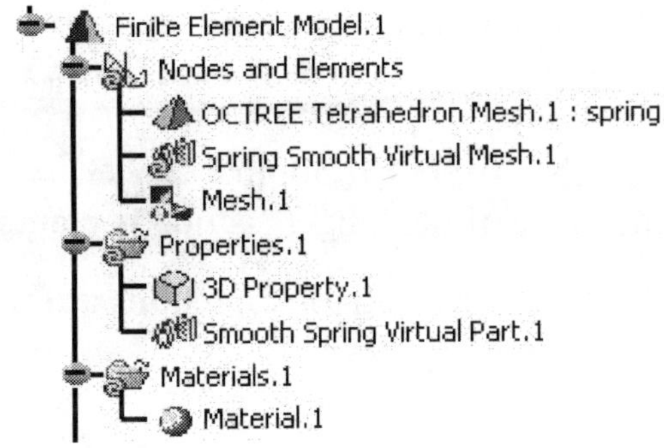


A Spring Smooth Virtual Part is an elastic body connecting a specified point to a specified geometry. This element behaves as a 6-degree of freedom spring in series with a mass-less rigid body which will softly transmit actions (masses, restraints and loads) applied at the handle point, without stiffening the deformable body or bodies to which it is attached. This information is graphically summarized in the figure below.

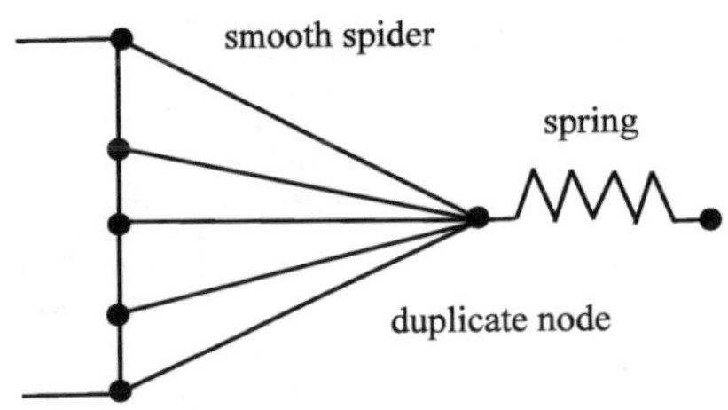


### Applying Restraints:

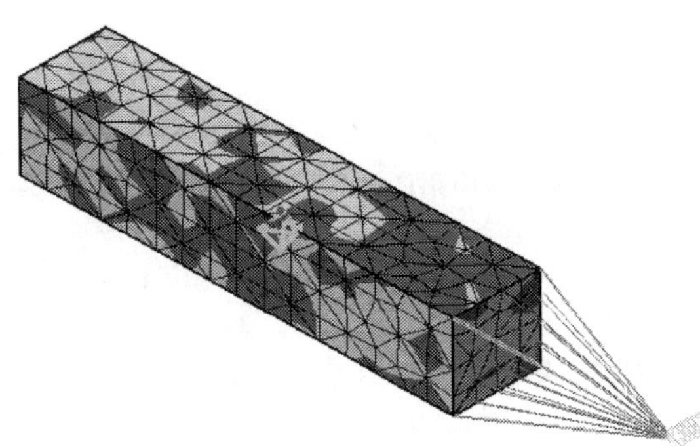

CATIA's FEA module is geometrically based. This means that the boundary conditions cannot be applied to nodes and elements. The boundary conditions can only be applied at the part level. As soon as you enter the **Generative Structural Analysis** workbench, the part is automatically hidden. Therefore, before boundary conditions are applied, the part must be brought to the unhide mode. This can be carried out by pointing the cursor to the top of the tree, the **Links Manager.1** branch, right-click, select **Show**. At this point, the part and the mesh are superimposed as shown above and you have access to the part.

If, the presence of the mesh is annoying, you can always hide it. Point the cursor to **Nodes and Elements**, right-click, **Hide**.

In FEA, restraints refer to applying displacement boundary conditions which is achieved through the **Restraint** toolbar 

. In the present problem, you can assume that the base of the longer section is clamped. The **Clamp** condition means that the displacements in all three directions are zero. Select the **Clamp** icon 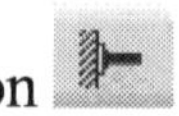 and pick one end of the bar as shown.

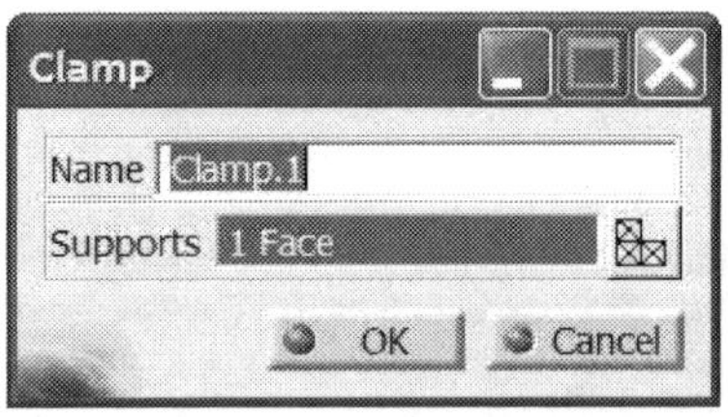


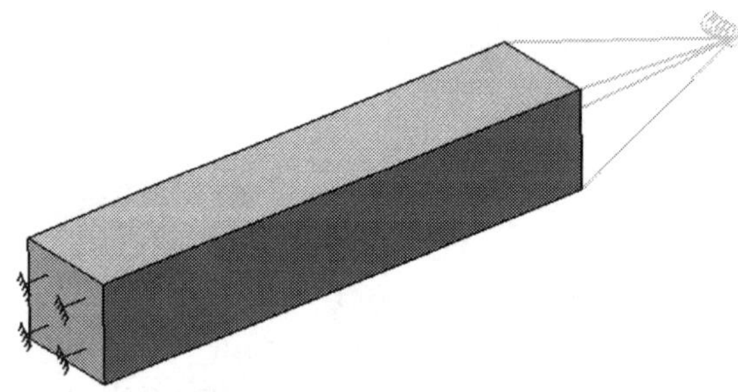

Select the **Clamp** icon  and pick the **Smooth Virtual Spring.1** created above.

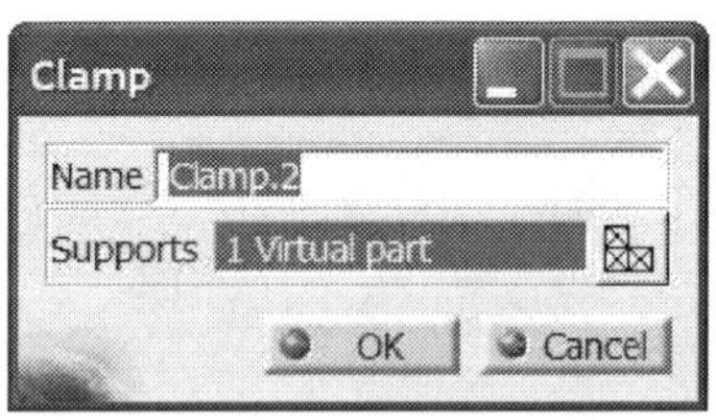


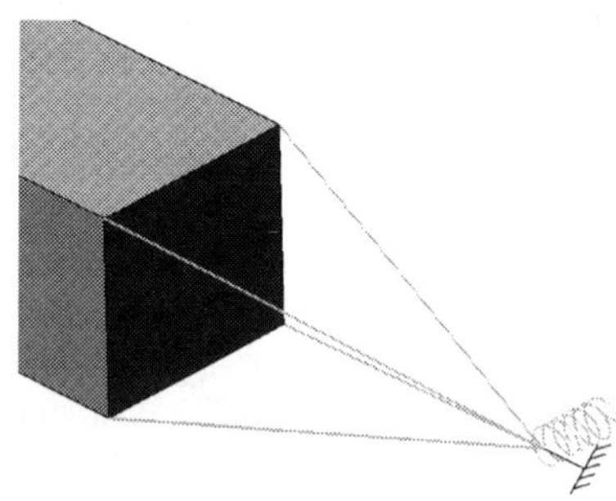

The portion of the tree associated with applying the clamp is displayed on the right.

It is worth mentioning that an alternative to clamping the end of the bar is to use the **Surface Slider** condition. If this approach is used, the rigid body translation should be prevented via the **Advanced Restraint** icon.

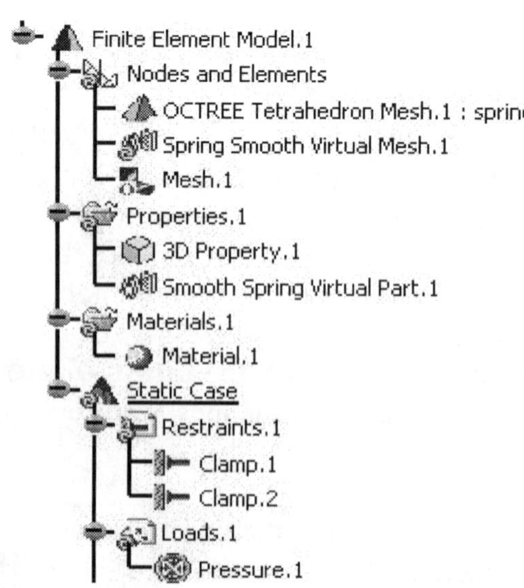

## Applying Loads:

In FEA, loads refer to forces. The **Loads** toolbar 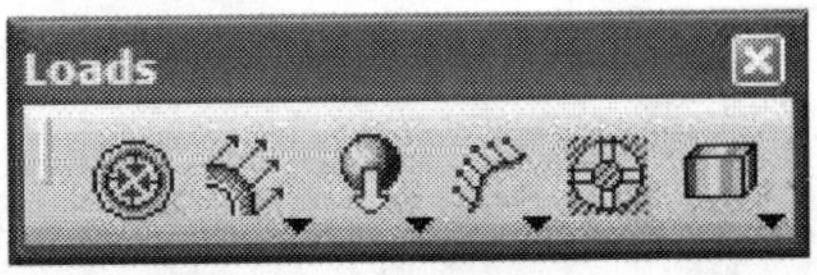 is used for this purpose. We apply the end load as pressure. The force of 1000 lb over the end area is equivalent to a pressure of 1000 psi. Clicking on the **Pressure** icon , opens the **Pressure** box shown below. For the **Support**, select the face where pressure is applied and as value type -1000. All FEA packages have adopted the convention that a positive pressure is compressive while a negative pressure is tensile. The **Pressure** icon will be displayed on the loaded surface of the part as shown.

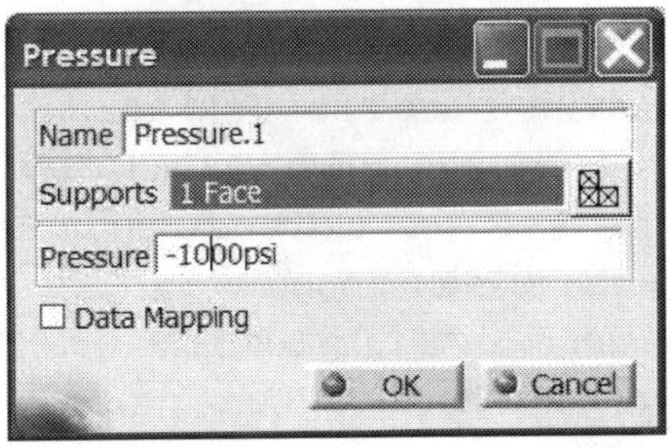


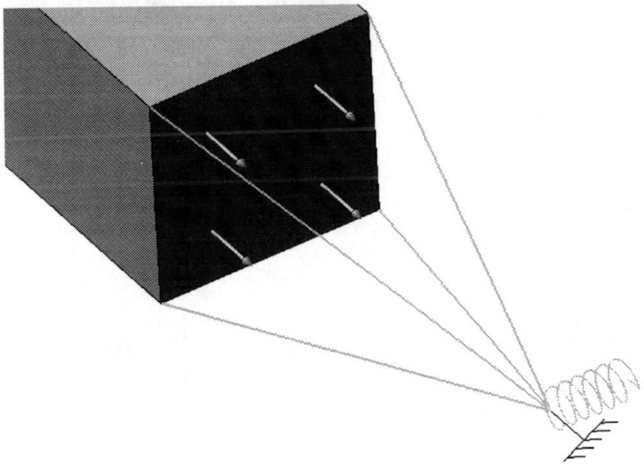

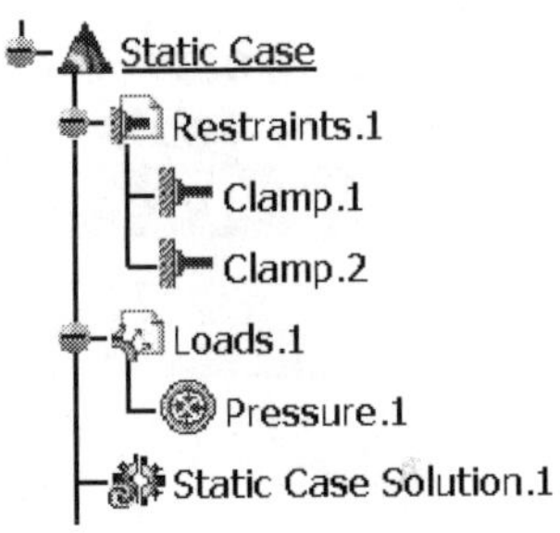


## Launching the Solver:

To run the analysis, you need to use the **Compute** toolbar  by selecting the **Compute** icon . This opens up the **Compute** box. Leave the defaults as **All** which means everything is computed.

Upon closing this box, after a brief pause, the second box shown below appears. This box provides information on the resources needed to complete the analysis.

If the estimates are zero in the listing, then there is a problem in the previous step and should be looked into. If all the numbers are zero in the box, the program may run but would not produce any useful results.

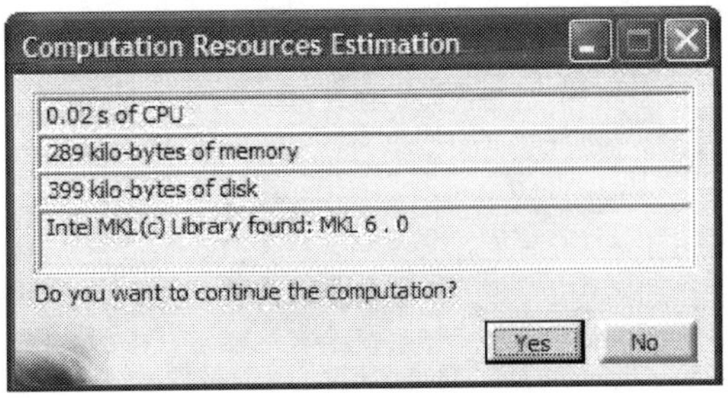

**Postprocessing:**

The main postprocessing toolbar is called **Image** 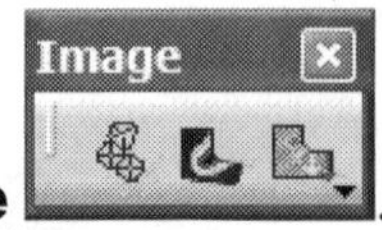

. To view the deformed shape you have to use the **Deformation** icon 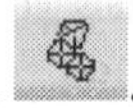. The resulting deformed shape is displayed below.

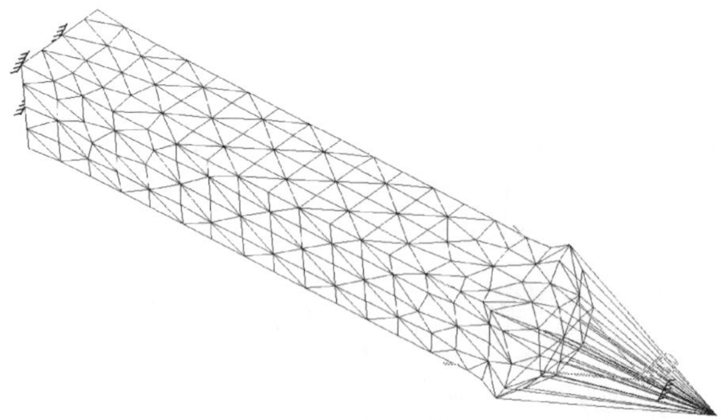

The deformation image can be very deceiving since one could get the impression that the block actually displaces to that extent. Keep in mind that the displacements are scaled considerably so that one can observe the deformed shape. Although the scale factor is set automatically, one can change this value with the

**Deformation Scale Factor** icon 
in the **Analysis Tools** toolbar 

.

In order to see the displacement field, the **Displacement** icon 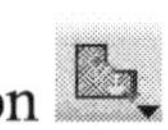 in the **Image** toolbar should be used. The default display is in terms of displacement arrows as shown on your screen. The color and the length of arrows represent the size of the displacement. The contour legend indicates a maximum displacement of 4.66E-5 in.

The arrow plot is not particularly useful. In order to view the contour plot of the displacement field, position the cursor on the arrow field and double-click. The **Image Edition** box shown below opens.

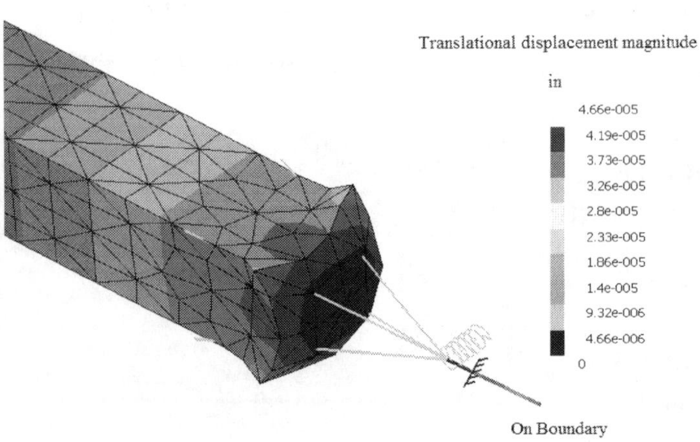


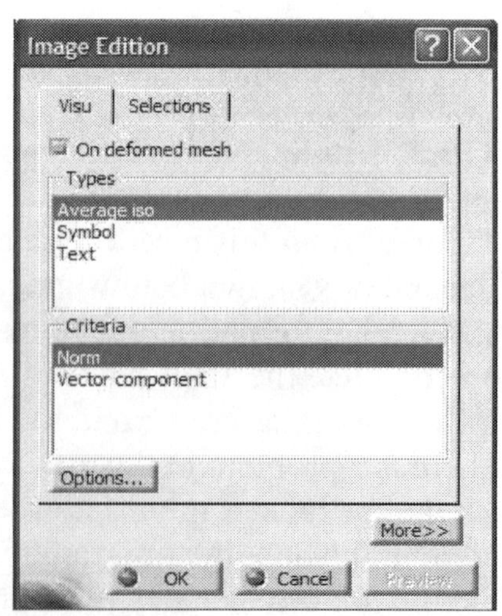

Keep in mind that the above contour represents the resultant displacement of the nodes i.e. $U = \sqrt{u_x^2 + u_y^2 + u_z^2}$ . In order to compare the FEA calculations, with our analytical calculations, zoom in to the tip of the spring element and read the displacement off the screen.

The value 3.81e-005 in. represents the displacement of the duplicate node in the spring. The value agrees quite well with the strength of materials prediction of 3.876E-5 in.

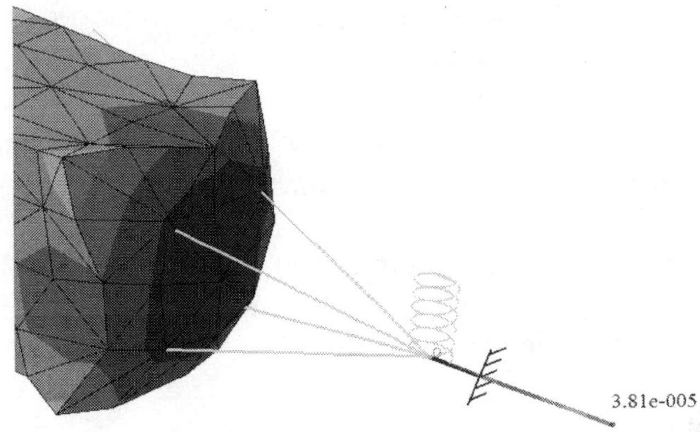


In the event that you had created a **Rigid Spring Virtual Part**, instead of a **Smooth Spring Virtual Part**, the deformation would have been a better representative of the present problems. The results are shown below.

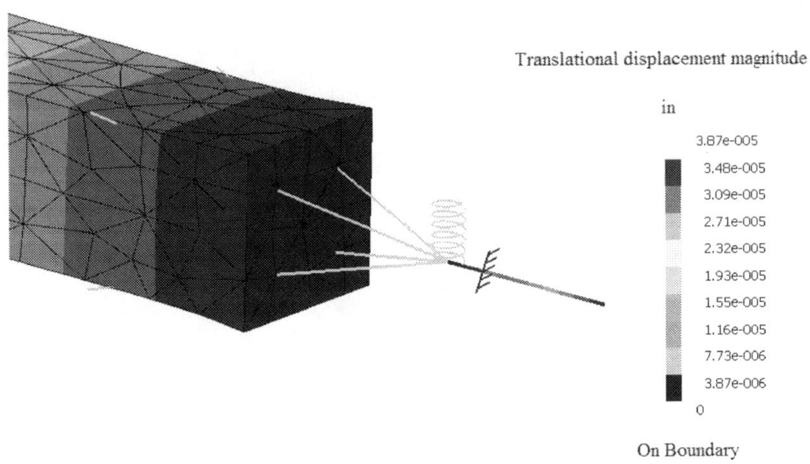


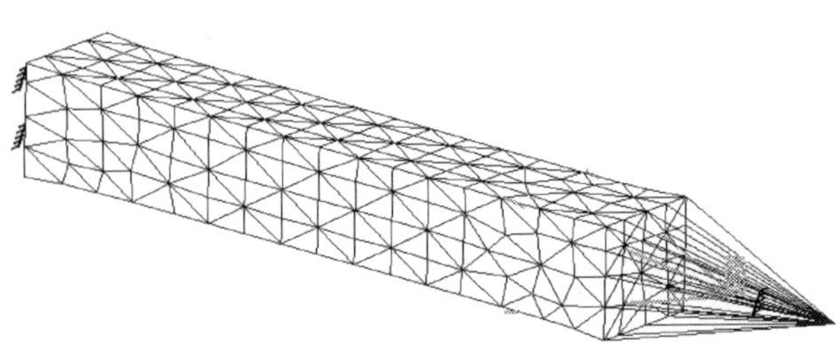

# Exercises for Chapter 20

## Problem 1: Bar Deflection

The steel bar shown below is of length $L = 100$ in. and has a 10x10 in. square cross section.

The structure is clamped at the top end and rests against a spring of stiffness $k = 10E+6$ lb/in.

The structure deflects under its own weight. Use the CATIA solid element, in combination with virtual spring element, to be predict the deflection of tip.

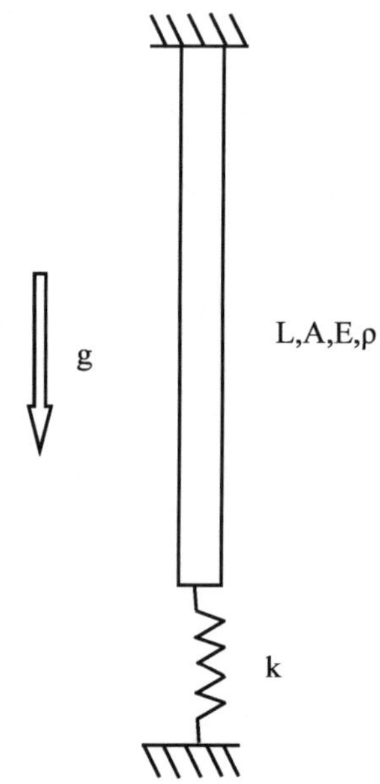


Partial Answer:

Using elementary strength of materials, one can show that the deflection of the bar can be calculated from the following expression.

$$u(x) = -\frac{1}{2E}\rho g x^2 + \frac{1}{E}\frac{2AE\rho gL + k\rho gL^2}{2(AE + kL)}$$

Here, "x" represents the distance to the top support.

Use both the **Smooth Spring Virtual Part**  and the **Rigid Spring Virtual Part** .

## Problem 2: Beam Deflection

The steel bar shown below is of length $2L = 100$ in. and has a 10x10 in. square cross section.

The structure is clamped at the left end and rests against two springs of stiffnesses $k = 5E+6$ lb/in.

The structure deflects under its own weight. Use two beam elements in order to estimate the deflections of the springs.

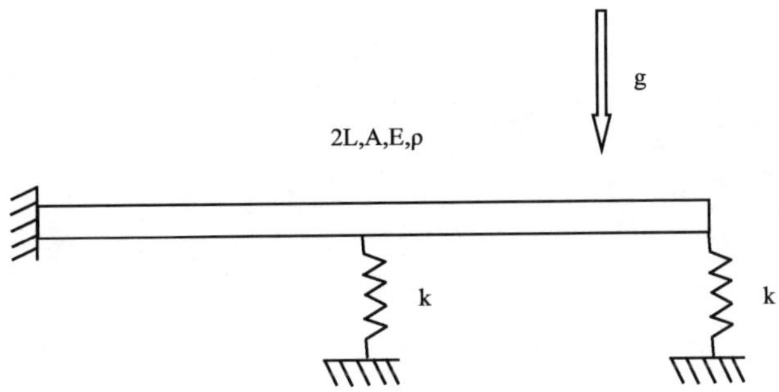


Partial Answer:

Let the finite element model be described by the diagram below.

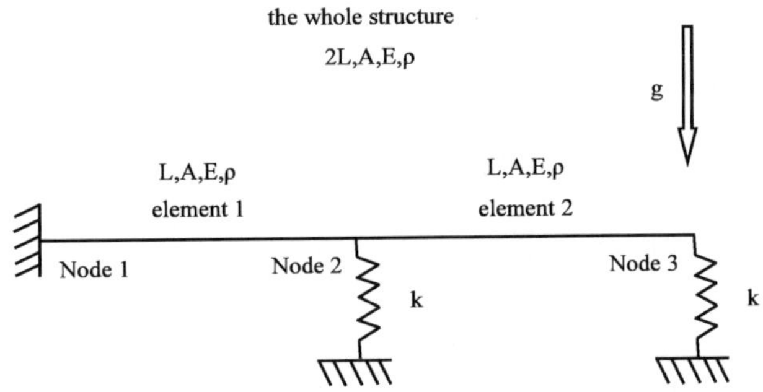


The displacements and rotations of the nodes 2 and 3 are computed from the following system of linear equations.

$$\begin{bmatrix} \frac{24EI}{L^3}+k & 0 & \frac{-12EI}{L^3} & \frac{6EI}{L^2} \\ 0 & \frac{8EI}{L} & -\frac{6EI}{L^2} & \frac{2EI}{L} \\ \frac{-12EI}{L^3} & -\frac{6EI}{L^2} & \frac{12EI}{L^3}+k & -\frac{6EI}{L^2} \\ \frac{6EI}{L^2} & \frac{2EI}{L} & -\frac{6EI}{L^2} & \frac{4EI}{L} \end{bmatrix} \begin{Bmatrix} v_2 \\ \theta_2 \\ v_3 \\ \theta_3 \end{Bmatrix} = \begin{Bmatrix} -\rho AgL \\ 0 \\ -\frac{\rho AgL}{2} \\ \frac{\rho AgL^2}{12} \end{Bmatrix}$$

# NOTES:

# Chapter 21

# Adaptive Refinement

## Introduction

In this tutorial, the concepts of adaptive and local refinement are introduced. These ideas will avoid the need for uniform reduction of the element size through a structure. In the case of adaptive refinement, the CATIA software identifies critical areas and refines the mesh. For local refinement, the user indicates the areas where mesh refinement should take place.

## 1 Problem Statement

The aluminum clamp shown below is fixed at the left end and subjected to a bearing load at the hole. The total bearing load is 1000 lb and tends to stretch the clamp. The dimensions of the part are discussed as the tutorial proceeds.

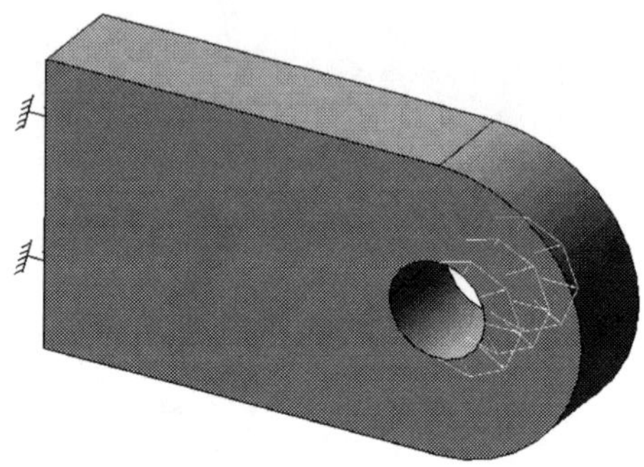

The top and bottom regions around the hole are clearly stress concentration areas. Therefore, one needs a finer mesh in those locations. The clamped area at the wall could also suffer from large stress gradients.

## 2 Creation of the Part in Mechanical Design Solutions

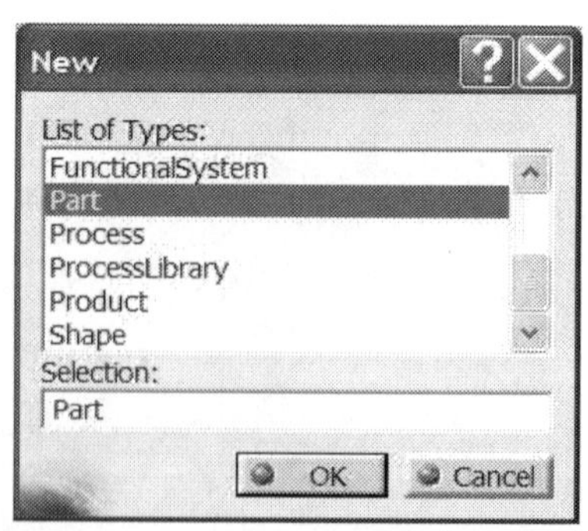


Enter the **Part Design** workbench which can be achieved by different means depending on your CATIA customization. For example, from the standard Windows toolbar, select **File > New**. From the box shown on the right, select **Part**. This moves you to the **Part Design** workbench and creates a part with the default name **Part.1**. Read Note #1 in Appendix I.
In order to change the default name, move the cursor to **Part.1** in the tree, right-click and select **Properties** from the menu list.
From the **Properties** box, select the **Product** tab and in **Part Number** type **refinement**. This will be the new part name throughout the chapter. The tree on the top left corner of the screen should look as displayed in the next page.

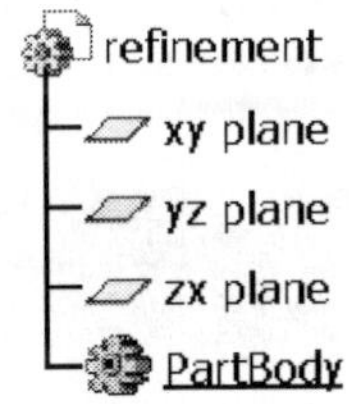


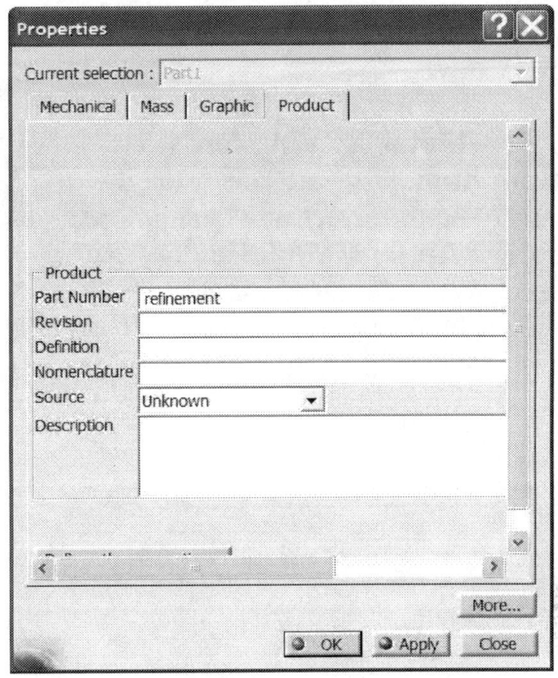


From the tree, select the **xz** plane and enter the **Sketcher**. In the **Sketcher**, use the icon in the **Profile** toolbar

and dimension as shown below. Also, draw a circle of radius 1 as displayed.

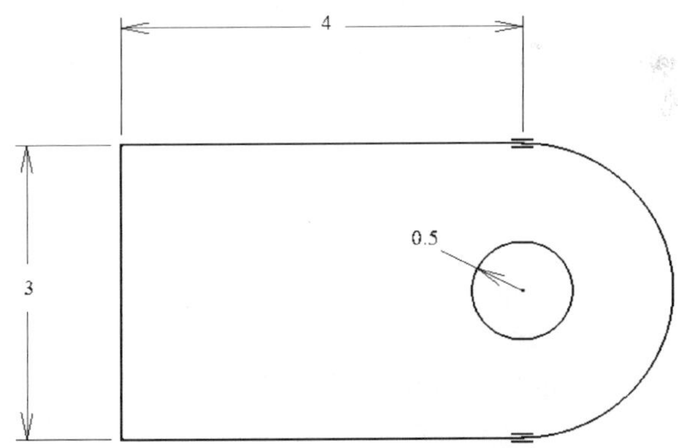


Leave the **Sketcher**.

Using the **Pad** icon, pad the sketch by 1 in.

The clamp is displayed on the screen.

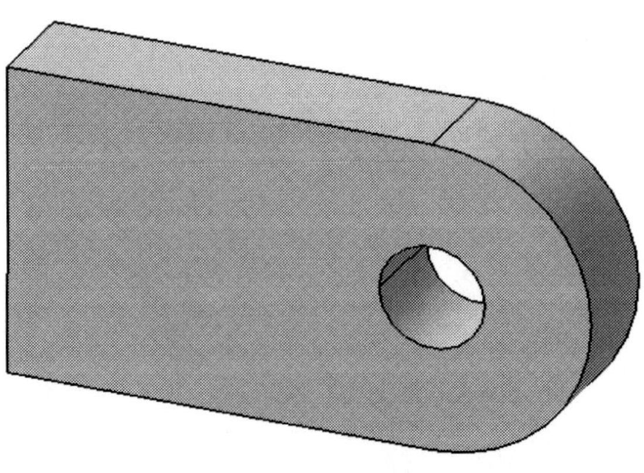

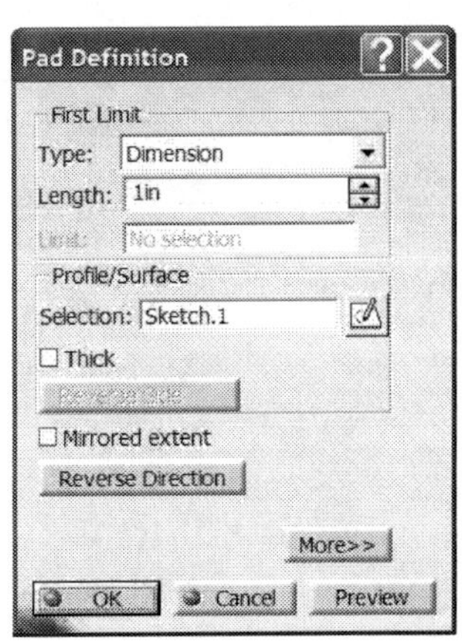

Select the **Apply Material** icon . The use of this icon opens the material database box below.

Use the **Metal** tab on the top; select **Aluminum**. Use your cursor to pick the part on the screen at which time the **OK** and **Apply Material** buttons can be selected. Close the box.
The material property is now reflected in the tree.

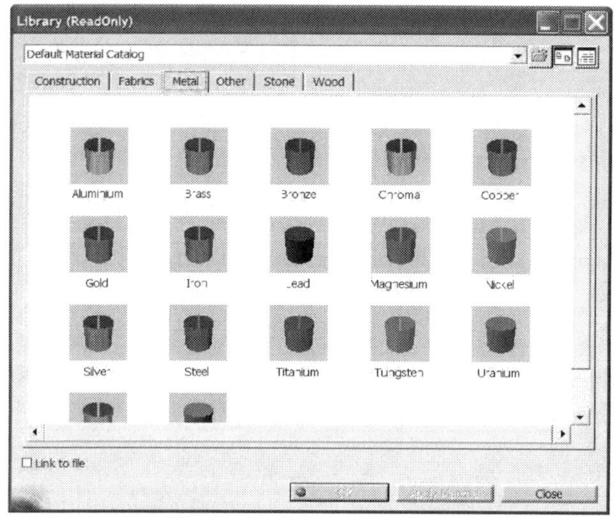


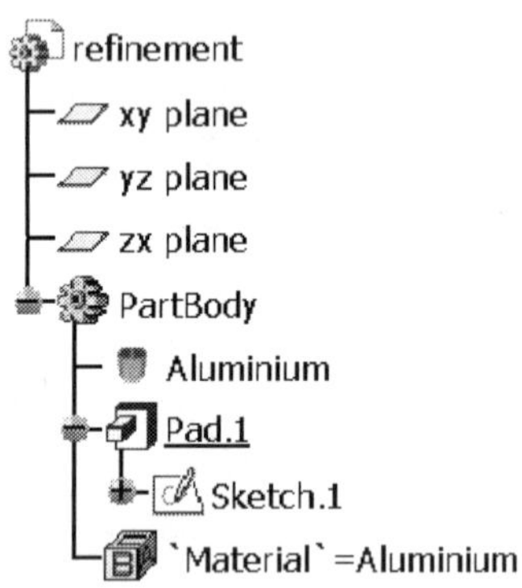


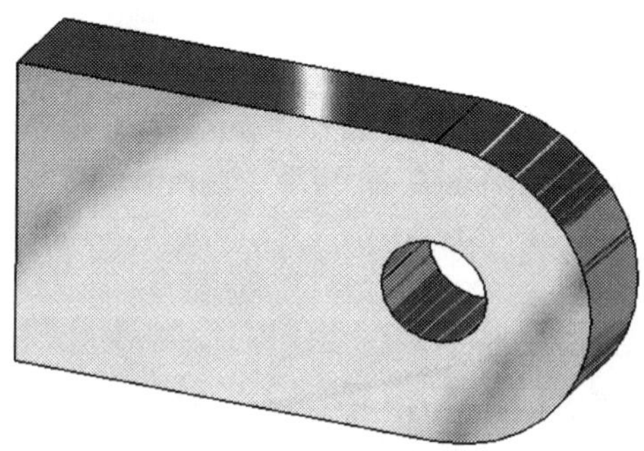

In order to inspect the values of the material properties assigned, double-click on **Aluminum** in the tree. It may take a minute before the database is searched. You will notice that the **Properties** box shown below opens. Choose the **Analysis** tab from this box, and the values will be displayed. Note that these values can be edited.

If the part is still "gray", one can change the rendering style. From the **View** toolbar

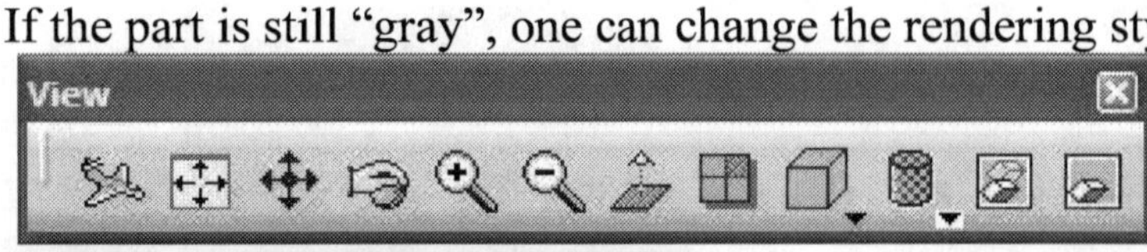


, select the **View mode** toolbar

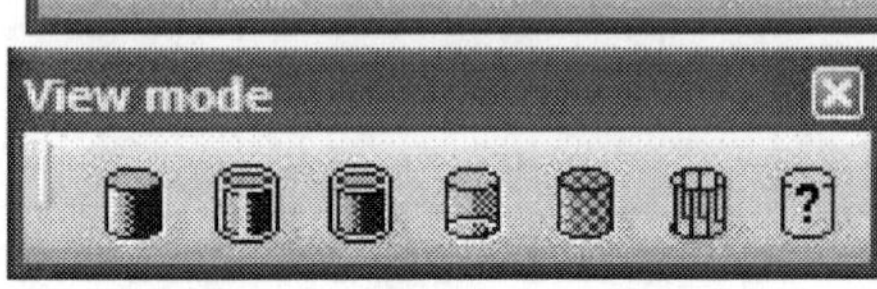


.

Next choose the **Shading with Material** icon .The part now appears shaded as shown above.

## 3 Entering the Analysis Solutions

From the standard Windows toolbar, select

**Start > Analysis & Simulation > Generative Structural Analysis**
There is a second workbench known as the **Advanced Meshing Tools** which will be discussed later.

Upon changing workbenches, the box **New Analysis Case** becomes visible. The default choice is **Static Analysis** which is precisely what we intend to use. Therefore, close the box by clicking on **OK**.

The tree, part, and representative element size and sag (under default values) are displayed below.

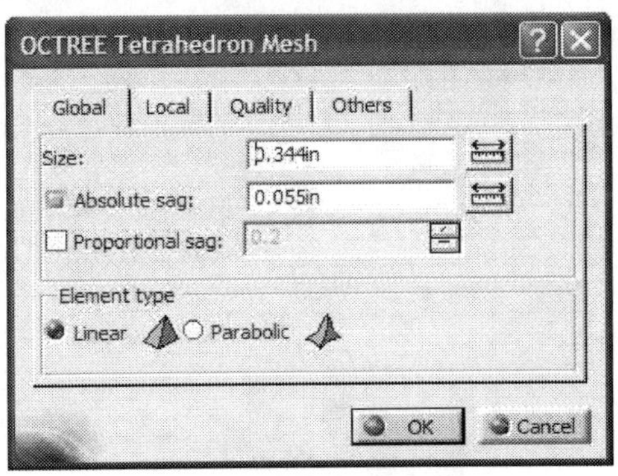


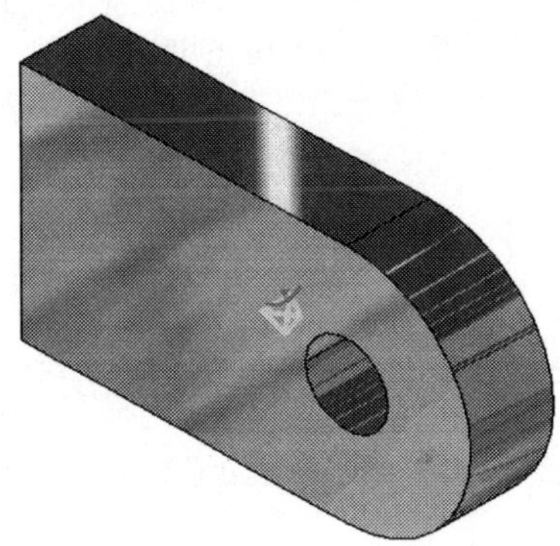

Point the cursor to the branch **Nodes and Elements**, right-click and select **Mesh Visualization**. A **Warning** box appears which can be ignored, select **OK**. For the mesh parameters used, the following mesh is displayed on the screen.
See Note #2 in Appendix I.

Clearly the mesh is very coarse around the hole and will not capture the stress gradient well. You need to refine the mesh in that area. You will perform several refinements in different locations.

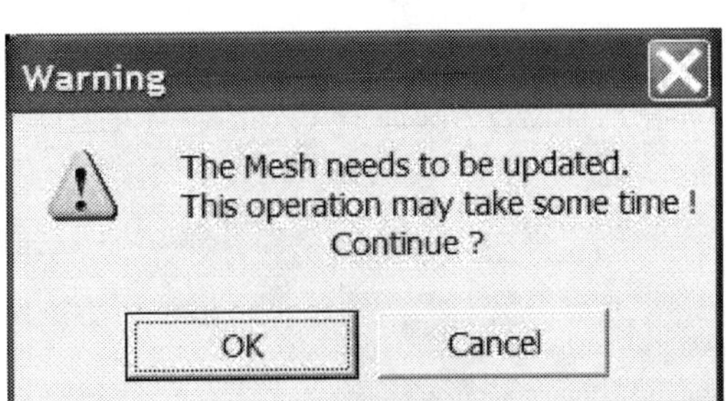


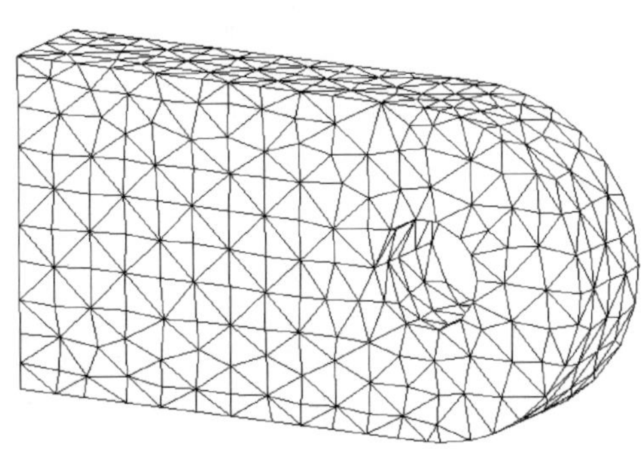

Select the **Local Mesh Size** icon  from the **Mesh Specification** toolbar 

. Note that **Mesh Specification** is a sub-toolbar of the **Model Manager** toolbar 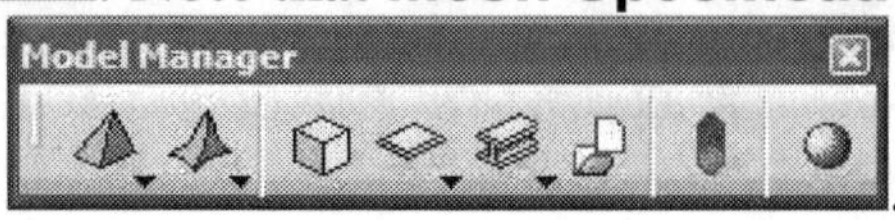

.

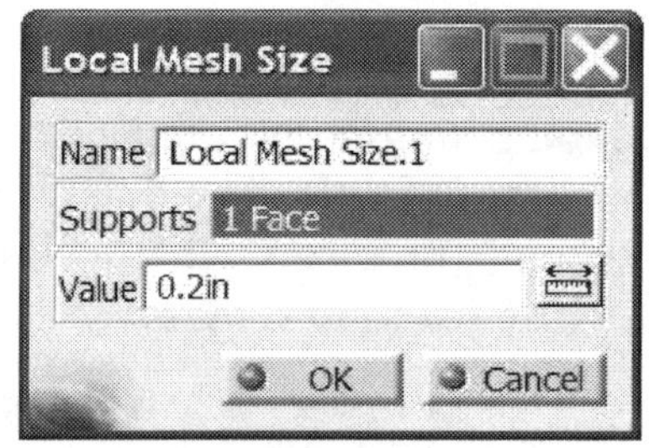


In the pop up box, for **Supports**, select the surface of the hole. For **Value**, type 0.2 in.

Point the cursor to the branch **Nodes and Elements**, right-click and select **Mesh Visualization**.

The refined mesh is displayed on the screen.

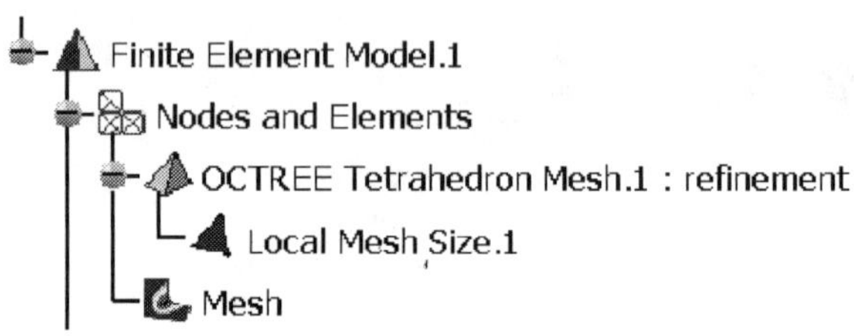


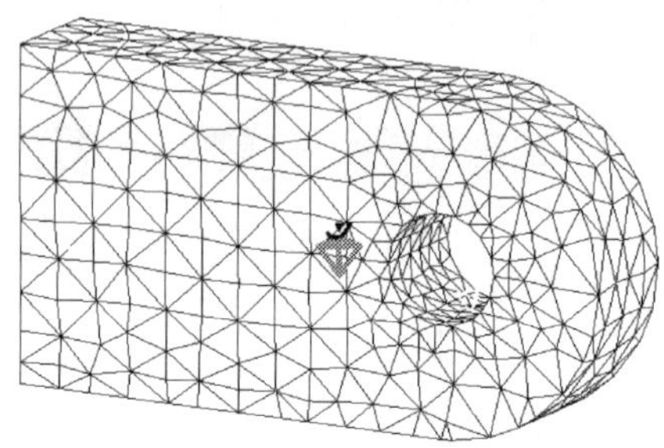

The modification of the tree is also shown below.

Now perform a second refinement.

Select the **Local Mesh Size** icon  again. Pick the surface of the hole for the second time. In the pop up box, change the **Value** to 0.1 in.

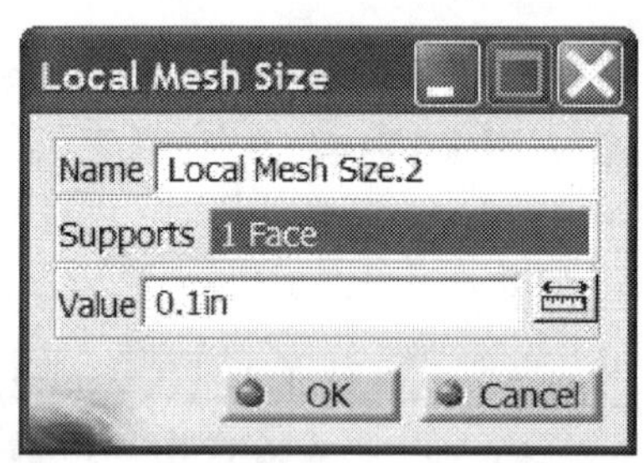


Point the cursor to the branch **Nodes and Elements**, right-click and select **Mesh Visualization**.

The refined mesh is displayed on the screen.
The modification of the tree is also shown below.

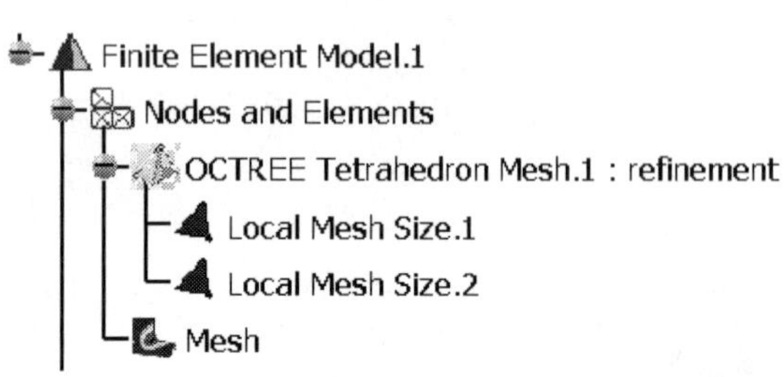


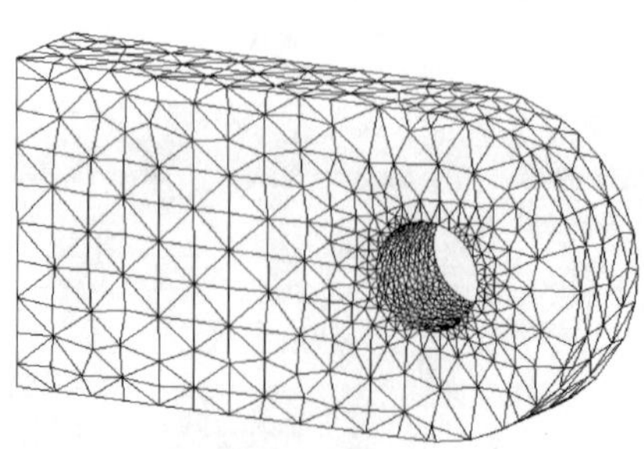

As a third layer of refinement, pick the top flat face of the clamp.

For **Value**, use 0.1 in. and visualize the mesh.

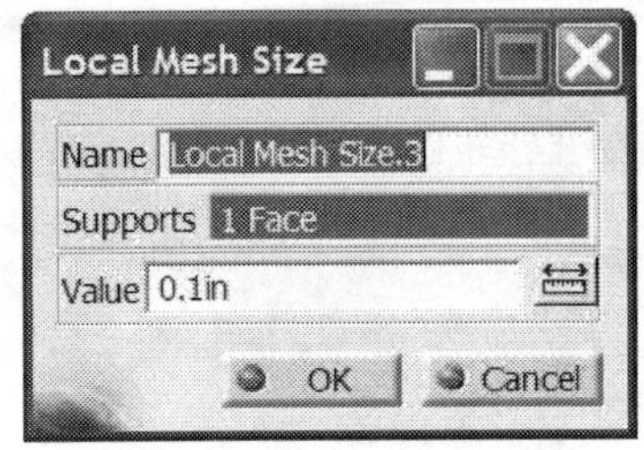


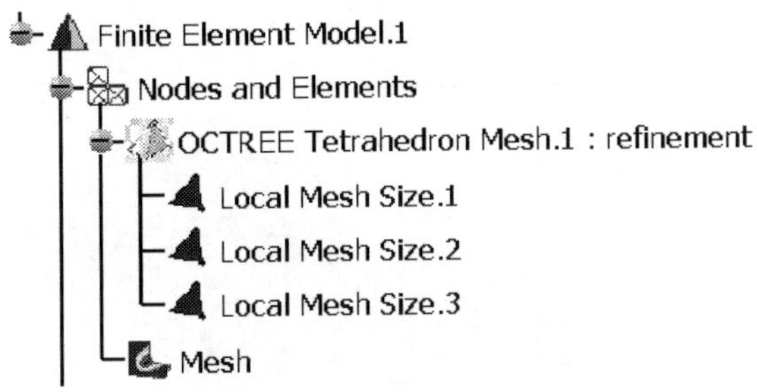


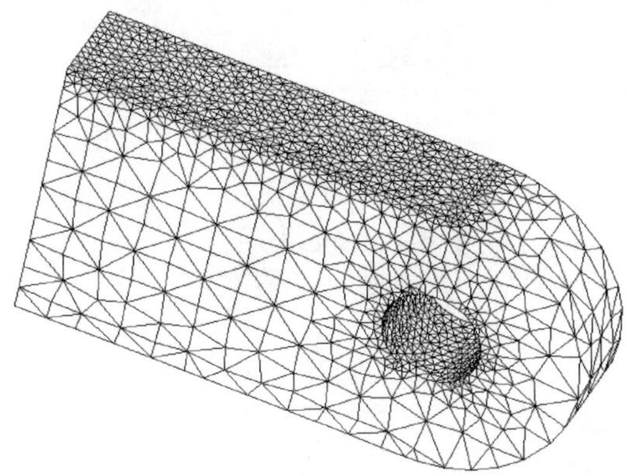

***Now that you have experimented with local mesh refinement, select the three* Local Mesh Size *branches from the tree, right-click, and delete them.***

The next step in the tutorial is to perform an adaptive mesh refinement allowing the software to refine the critical regions. In order to perform such an analysis, you need to make an initial run of your FEA model. This initial run, estimates the possible error in the FEA calculations.

To conduct the initial run, you need to apply the restraints and the loads.

**Applying Restraints:**

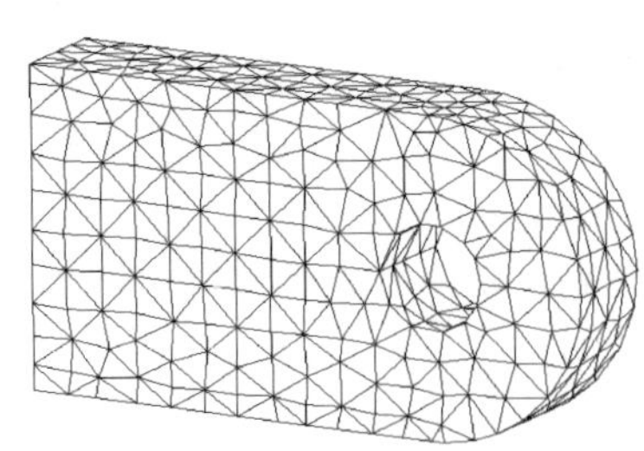

CATIA's FEA module is geometrically based. This means that the boundary conditions cannot be applied to nodes and elements. The boundary conditions can only be applied at the part level. As soon as you enter the **Generative Structural Analysis** workbench, the part is automatically hidden. Therefore, before boundary conditions are applied, the part must be brought to the unhide mode. This can be carried out by pointing the cursor to the top of the tree, the **Links Manager.1** branch, right-click, select **Show**. At this point, the part and the mesh are superimposed as shown above and you have access to the part.

If the presence of the mesh is annoying, you can always hide it. Point the cursor to **Nodes and Elements**, right-click, **Hide**.

Select the **Clamp** icon  and pick the face of the part as shown.

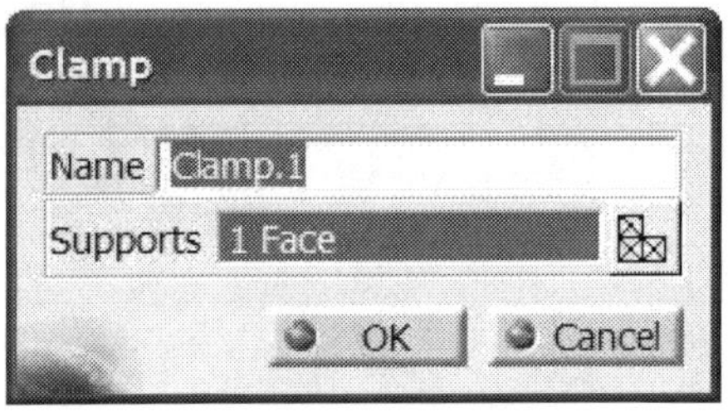


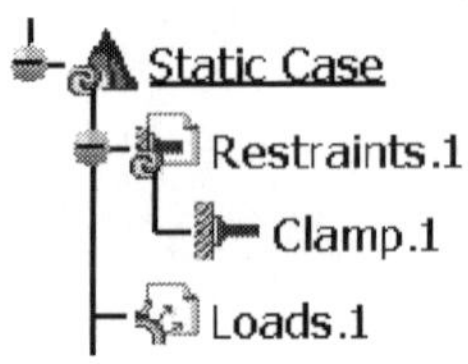


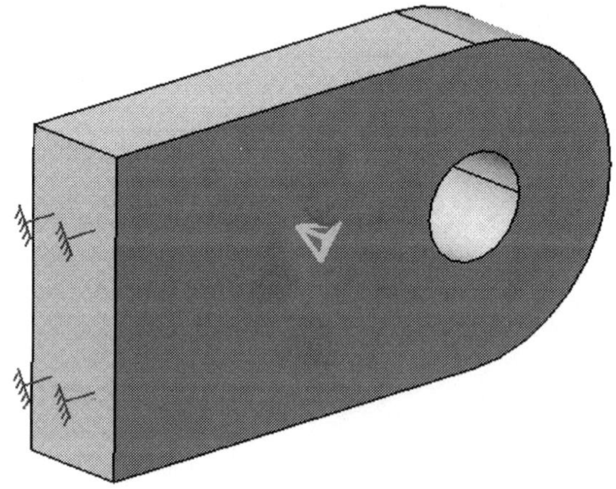

**Applying Loads:**

In FEA, loads refer to forces. The **Loads** toolbar 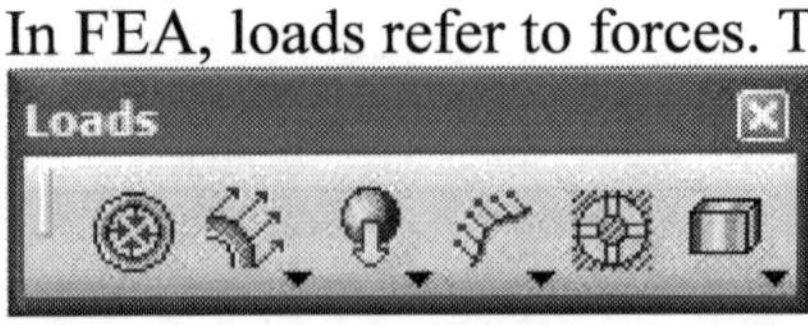

is used for this purpose. Select the **Bearing Load** icon 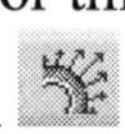 from the **Force** toolbar 

.

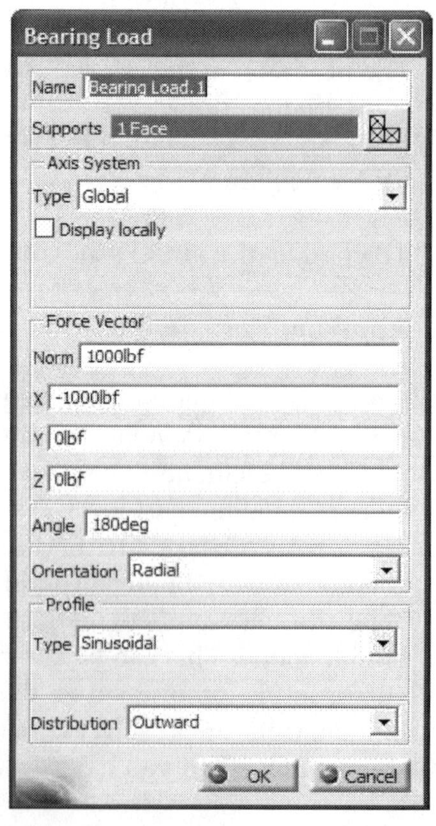


In the pop up box, make the following adjustments.

For **Supports**, select the hole surface.
Use a -1000 lb for **x** direction of the force.

Leave all other options as indicated in the box on the right.

The resulting bearing load is displayed in the next page.

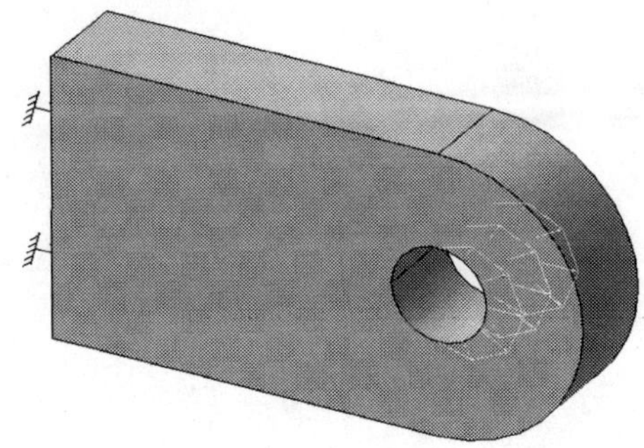

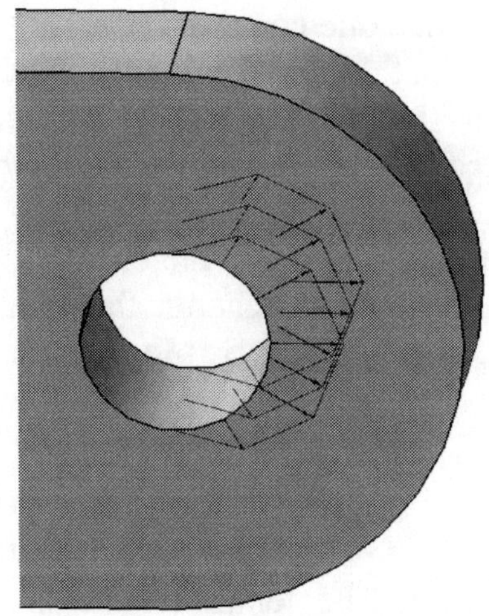

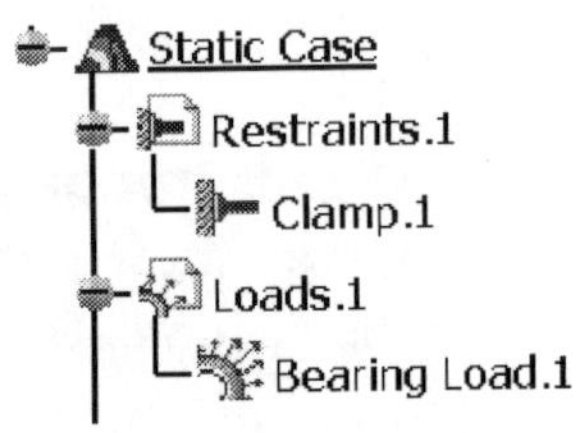


**Launching the Solver:**

To run the analysis, you need to use the **Compute** toolbar by selecting the **Compute** icon. This opens up the **Compute** box. Leave the defaults as **All** which means everything is computed.

Upon closing this box, after a brief pause, the second box shown on the right appears. This box provides information on the resources needed to complete the analysis.

If the estimates are zero in the listing, then there is a problem in the previous step and should be looked into. If all the numbers are zero in the box, the program may run but would not produce any useful results.

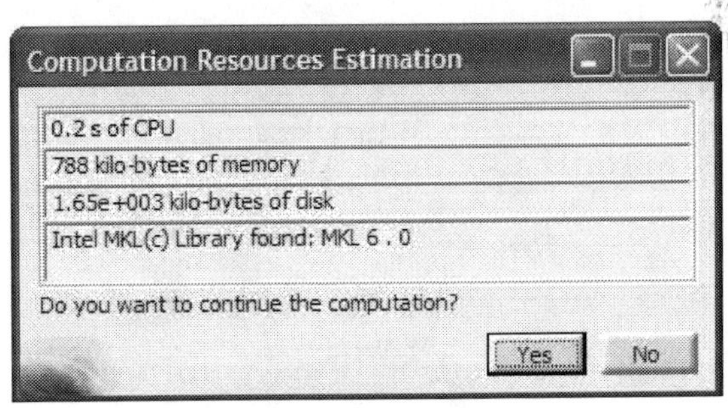


**Postprocessing:**

The main postprocessing toolbar is called **Image**. To view the deformed shape you have to use the **Deformation** icon. The resulting deformed shape is displayed on the next page.

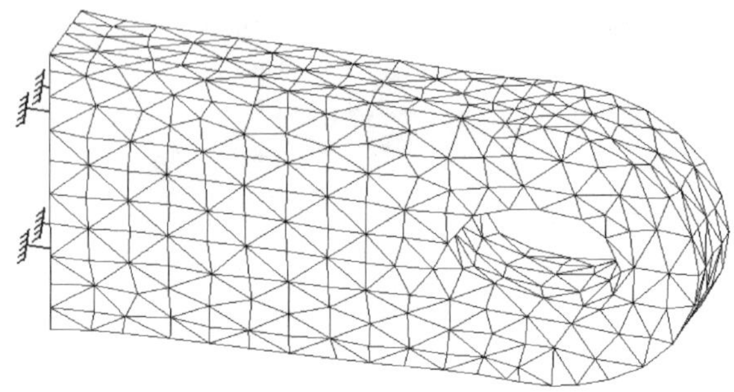

The deformation image can be very deceiving since one could get the impression that the block actually displaces to that extent. Keep in mind that the displacements are scaled considerably so that one can observe the deformed shape. Although the scale factor is set automatically, one can change this value with the **Deformation Scale Factor** icon  in the **Analysis Tools** toolbar.

In order to see the displacement field, the **Displacement** icon  in the **Image** toolbar should be used. The default display is in terms of displacement arrows as shown on your screen. The color and the length of arrows represent the size of the displacement. The contour legend indicates a maximum displacement of 0.00029 in.

The arrow plot is not particularly useful. In order to view the contour plot of the displacement field, position the cursor on the arrow field and double-click. The **Image Edition** box shown below opens.

For the **Type**, select **AVERAGE-ISO**.

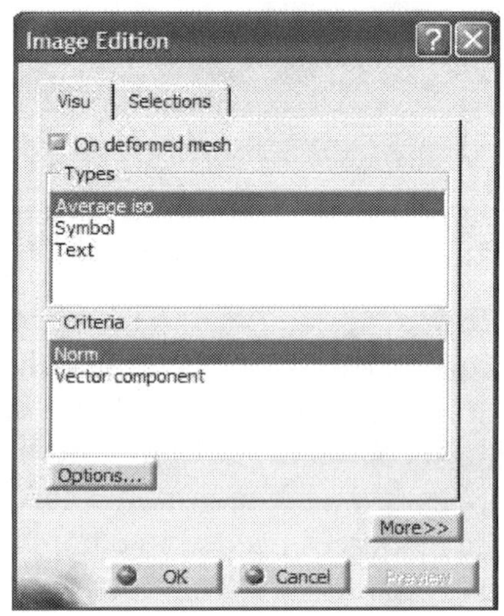


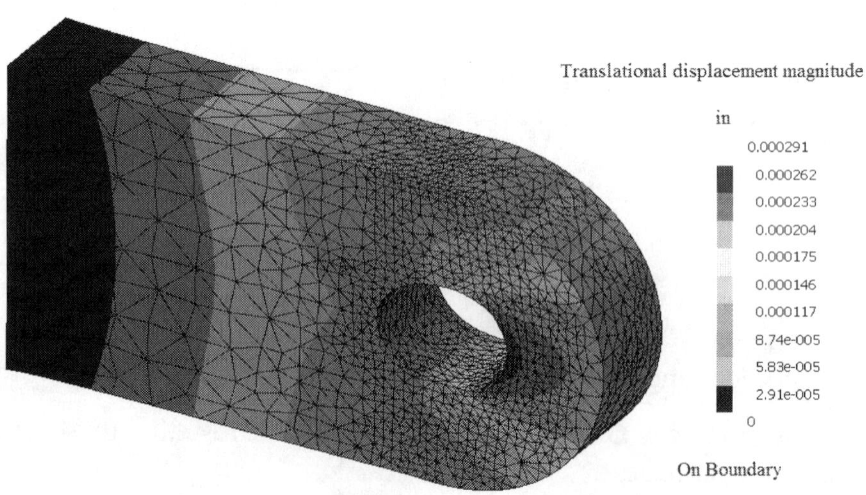

The next step in the postprocessing is to plot the contours of the von Mises stress using the **von Mises Stress** icon in the **Image** toolbar. The von Mises stress is displayed to below. The maximum von Mises stress is 3040 psi.

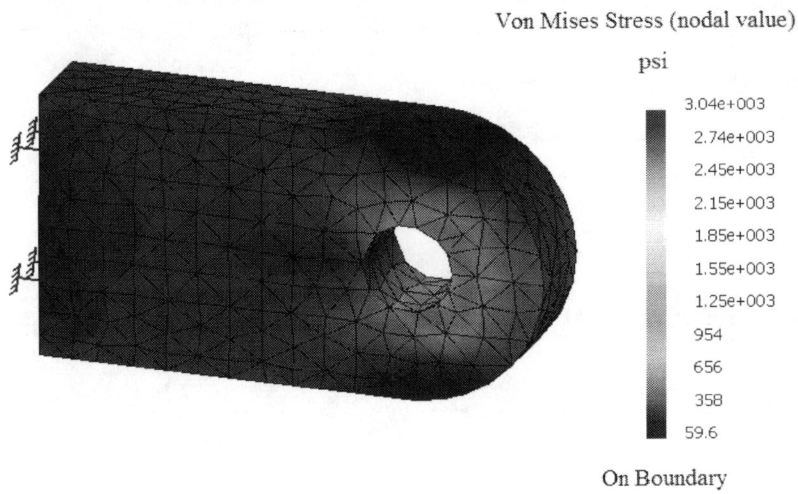


You are now in a position to perform the adaptive refinement.

Select the **New Adaptivity Entity** icon from the **Adaptivity** toolbar. This forces the pop up box, shown on the right, to open.

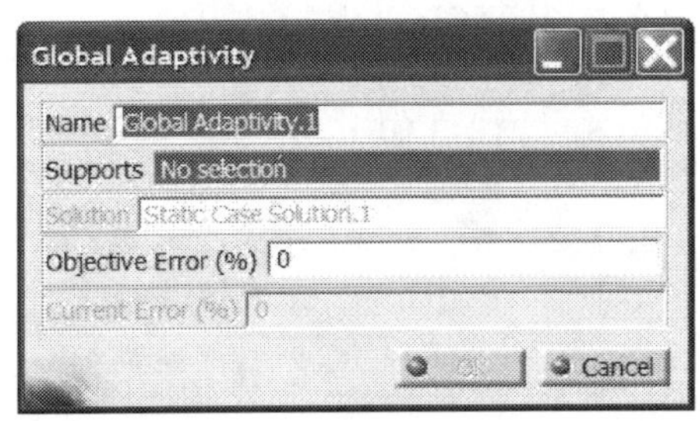


Note that the entry **Current Error(%)**is listed as 0. Point the cursor to the **OCTREE Tetrahedron Mesh.1 : refinement** branch in the tree and select it as the **Supports**.

This selection immediately changes the last line in the box **Current Error(%)**. The new value is displayed in the box below. The pick indicates that the current error is 26.8184%.

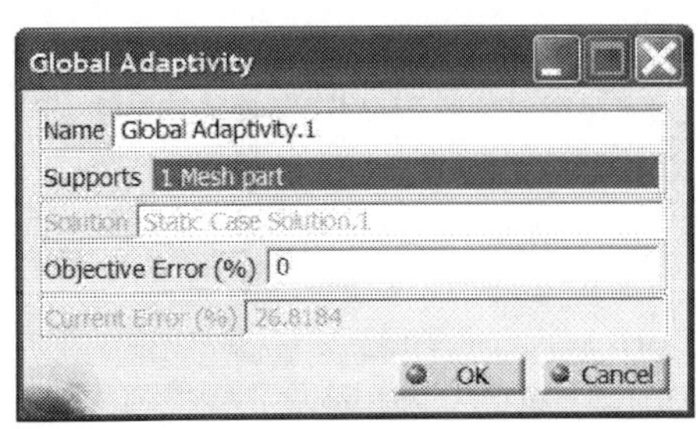


This value is an estimate of the relative error in strain energy.

For **Objective Error(%)**, type 10. The new value is the desired relative error that will be adaptively achieved.

The final content of the **Global Adaptivity** box is shown below.
The portion of the tree pertaining to adaptivity is also displayed.

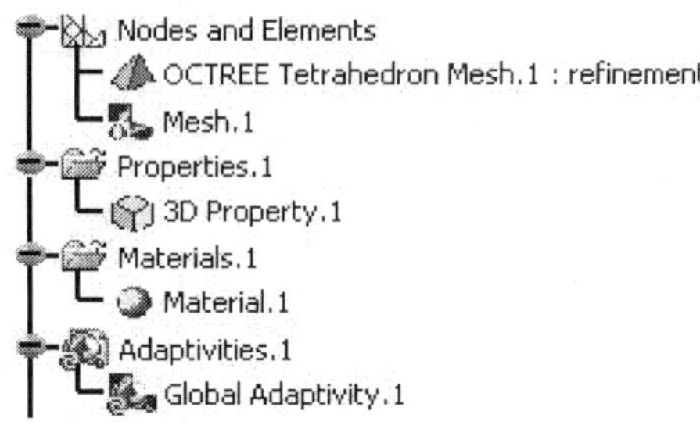


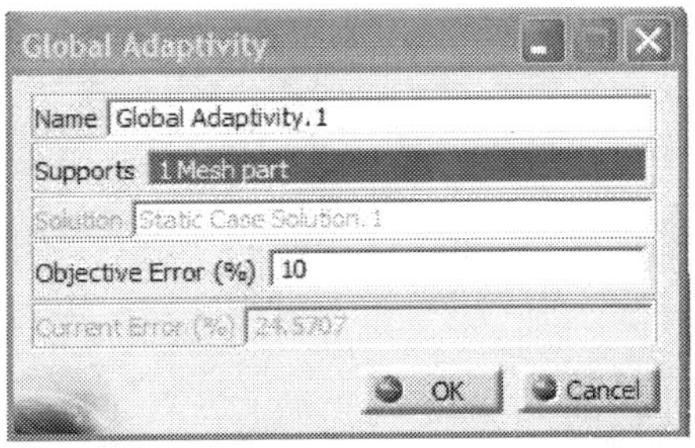


Select the **Compute with Adaptivity** icon  from the **Compute** toolbar

.

The pop up box, shown on the right side, appears.

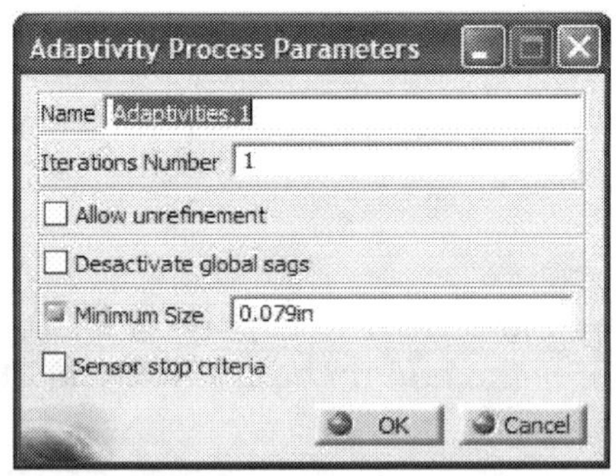


For **Iteration Number**, use 8. (It is suggested that you choose a smaller number, such as 5.)
For **Minimum Size** use 0.1.

The modified **Adaptivity Process Parameters** box is also displayed below.

The selection of these numbers requires some explanation.

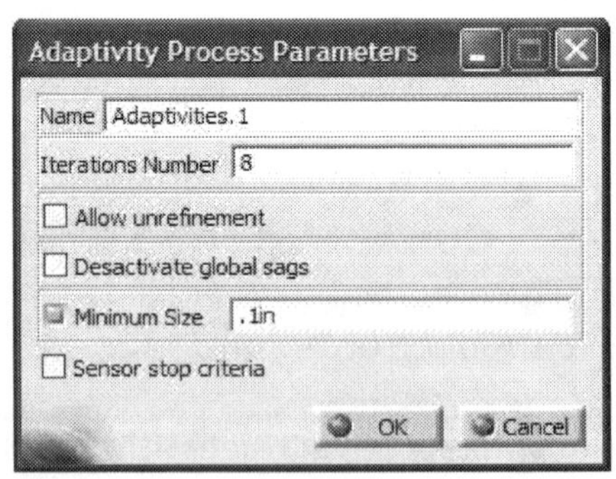


The **Iteration Number** refers to the maximum number of refinements before the error objective is met.

The **Minimum Size** tells the software not to refine an element if the size is less than the specified value.

At this point, select **OK** and start the iteration process. Depending on the speed of your computer, it may take a long time before the run is completed. Basically the problem is run a maximum of 8 times with progressively larger number of elements.

If the error objective is reached, before 8 iterations, the run is terminated. For the present problem, with the parameters specified, the 10% relative error is reached and no **Warning** box appears.

In order to find the estimate of the error, at the end of 8 iterations, double-click on the **Global Adaptivity.1** branch in the tree.
This leads to the pop up box below where the error is estimated as 9.60015%.

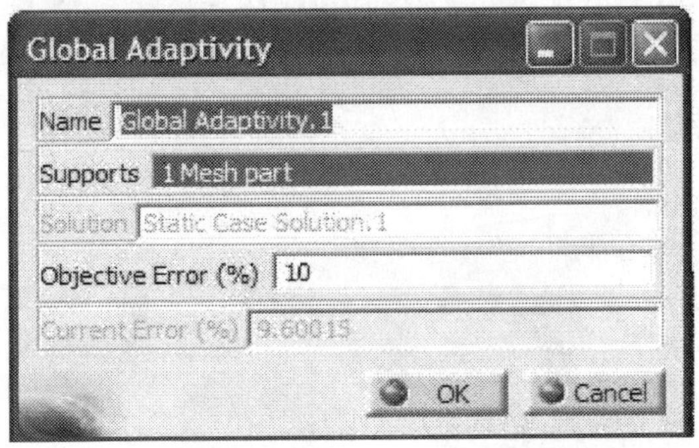


To see the final mesh, point the cursor to the branch **Nodes and Elements**, right-click and select **Mesh Visualization**.

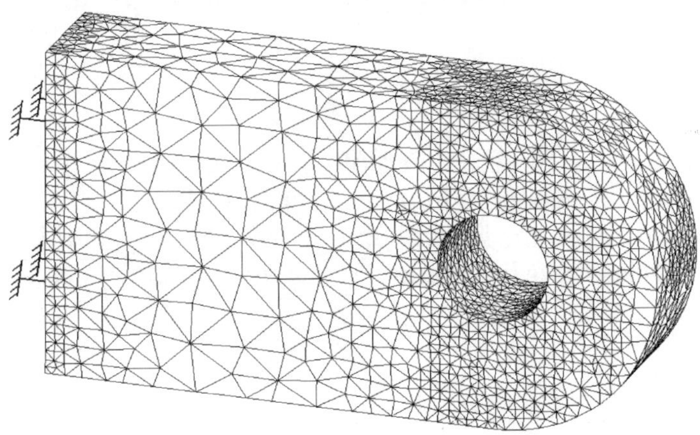

Select the **von Mises Stress** icon  in the **Image** toolbar. The von Mises stress is displayed to below. The maximum von Mises stress is 3470 psi.

The original coarse mesh had a maximum von Mises stress of 3040 psi.

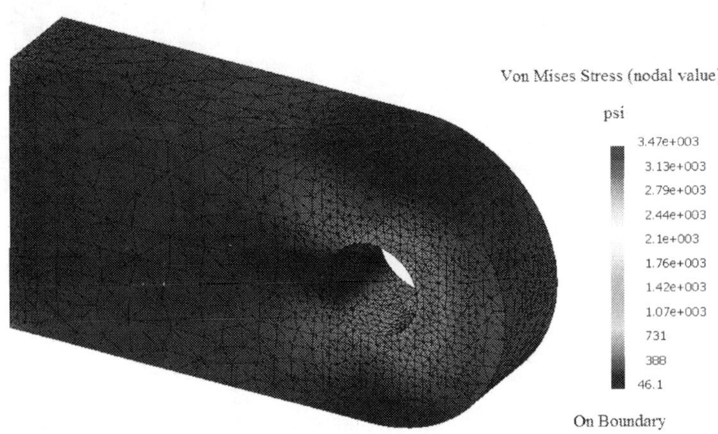

The **Cutting Plane** icon  from the **Analysis Tools** toolbar can be used to make a cut through the part at a desired location and inspect the stresses inside of the part. The **Cut Plane** box allows you to keep the plane or to remove it for display purposes. A typical cutting plane is shown below.

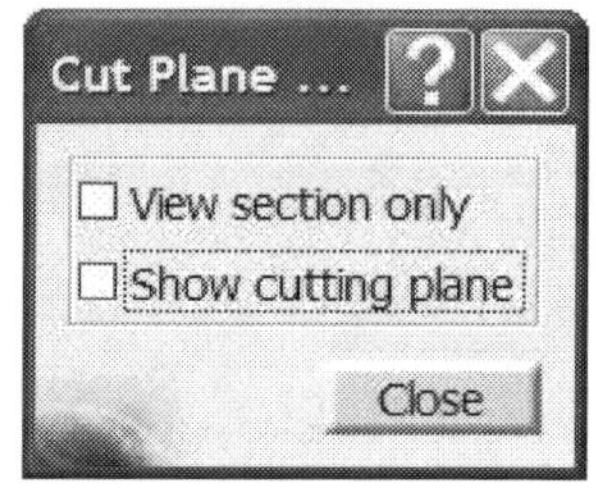


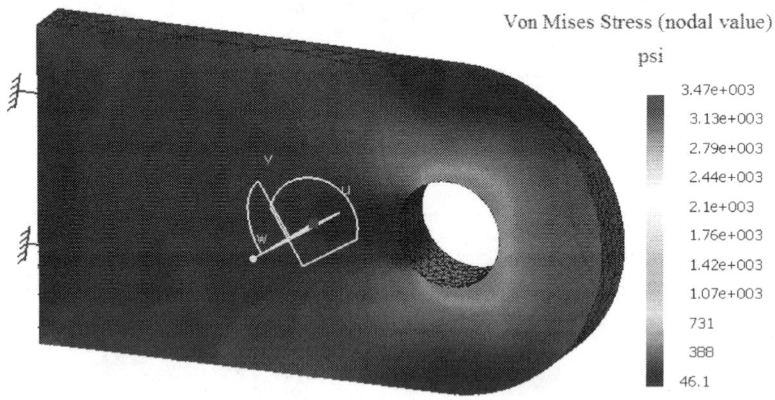


Occasionally, you may be interested in plotting the von Mises stress contour in parts of the assembly or even the supports. In order to achieve this, double-click on the contour levels on the screen to open the image edition box. Use the **Selections** tab and pick **Bearing Load.1**. The stress distribution in the hole region appears on your screen.

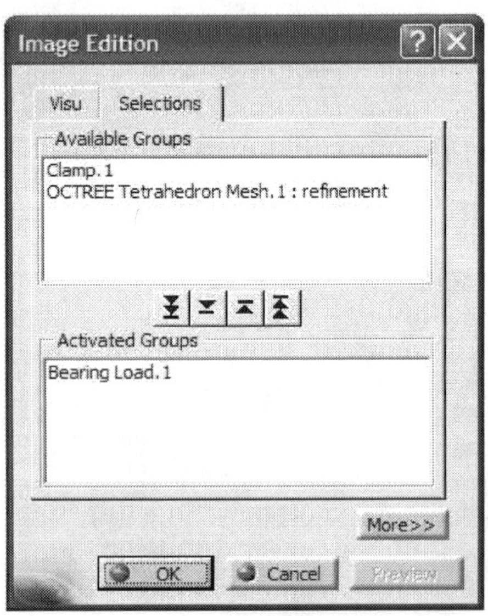

From the toolbar **Groups** 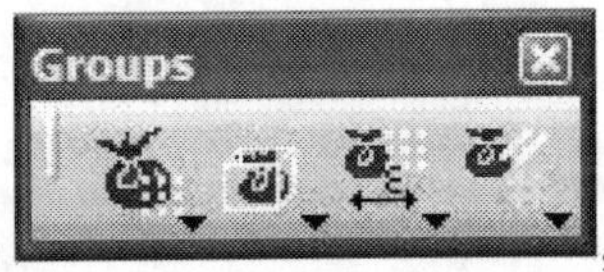, select the icon **Line Group by Neighborhood** . Read Note #3 in Appendix I.
This action leads to the dialogue box shown next.

For the **Supports**, select the edge of the hole. For the **Tolerance** use 1. What this process does is to create a group of elements which are within a neighborhood in of the selected edge. The stresses can be plotted for such elements if desired.
In order to achieve this, double-click on the contour levels on the screen to open the **Image Edition** box. Next use the selections tab as shown below. Here, you have the choice of selecting different items. Select **Line Group by Neighborhood.1**, and use the button . The contour below displays the von Mises stress at the desired section.

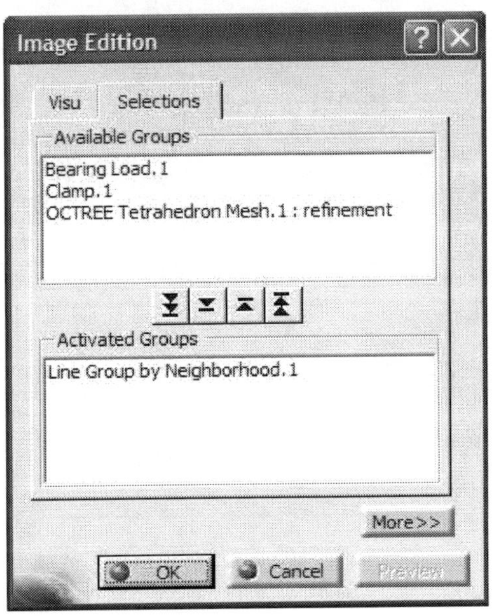

# NOTES:

# Chapter 22

# Free Vibration of a Simply Supported Beam

## Introduction

In this tutorial, a simply supported beam is modeled with solid elements. The first few natural frequencies of the beam are then calculated. The results are compared with the analytical estimates that can be found in most vibration texts.

## 1 Problem Statement

The simply supported beam, shown below, is made of steel. The beam is 10 inches long and has a 1x1 in$^2$ cross section. The objective is to find the natural frequencies and the corresponding vibration modes with solid element. Clearly, the beam elements discussed earlier are more appropriate for this simulation.

The natural frequencies are described by the following expression.

$$\omega_n = \frac{1}{2\pi}\left(\frac{n\pi}{L}\right)^2 \sqrt{\frac{EI}{\rho A}} \qquad n = 1,2,3,\ldots$$

In the above expression, the frequency is in Hertz (Hz).
The beam dimensions under consideration, $L = 10\,\text{in.}$, $A = 1\,\text{in}^2$, $I = 1/12\,\text{in}^4$.
The material properties are, $E = .29E + 8\,\text{psi}$, and $\rho = .72E - 4\,\text{lb.s}^2/\text{in}^4$.
The transverse vibration modes are simple sine curves.

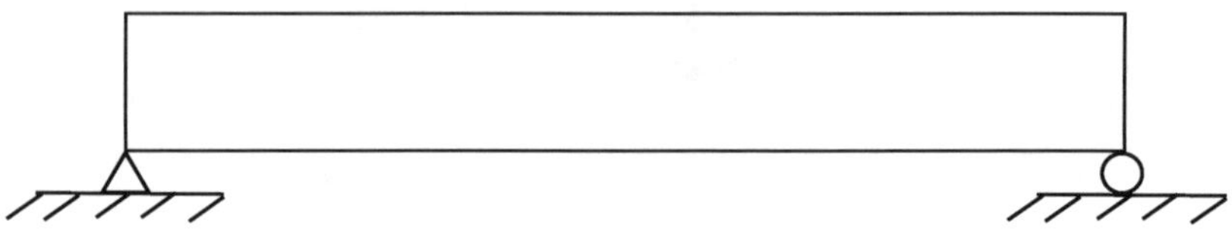

## 2 Creation of the Part in Mechanical Design Solutions

Enter the **Part Design** workbench which can be achieved by different means depending on your CATIA customization. For example, from the standard Windows toolbar, select **File > New**. From the box shown on the right, select **Part**. This moves you to the **Part Design** workbench and creates a part with the default name **Part.1**. Read Note #1 in Appendix I.

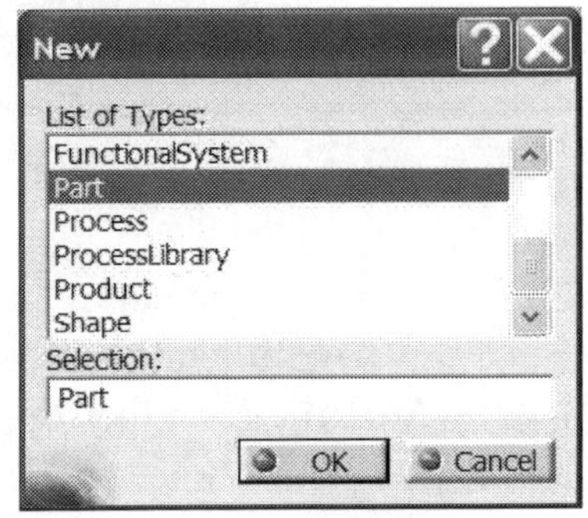


In order to change the default name, move the cursor to **Part.1** in the tree, right-click and select **Properties** from the menu list.

From the **Properties** box, select the **Product** tab and in **Part Number** type **frequencies**. This will be the new part name throughout the chapter. The tree on the top left corner of the screen should look as displayed below.

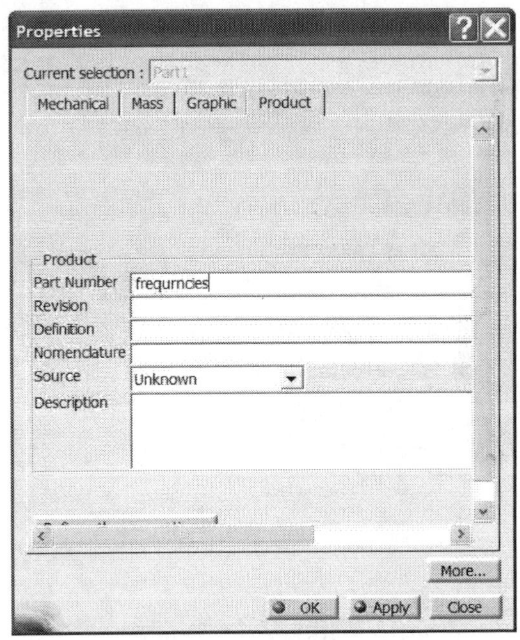


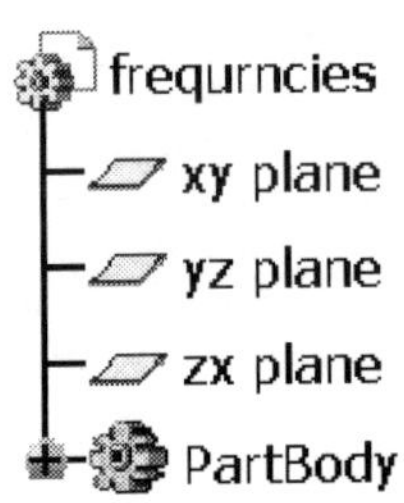


From the tree, select the **yz** plane and enter the **Sketcher**. In the **Sketcher**, use the **Profile** toolbar

to draw a square and dimension it.
In order to change the dimension, double-click on the dimension on the screen.

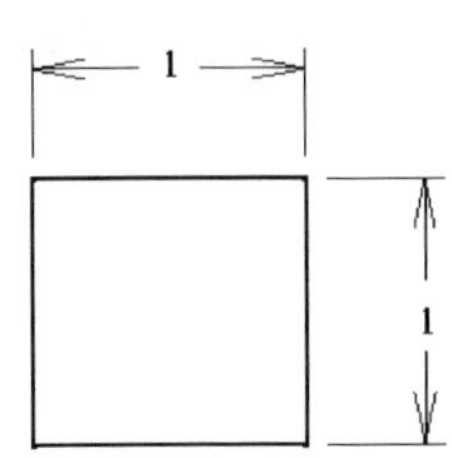


Leave the **Sketcher**.

You will now use the **Pad** operation to extrude the sketch.

Upon selecting the **Pad** icon, the **Pad Definition** box opens.
In the **Length** box, type 10.

The result is displayed on the next page.

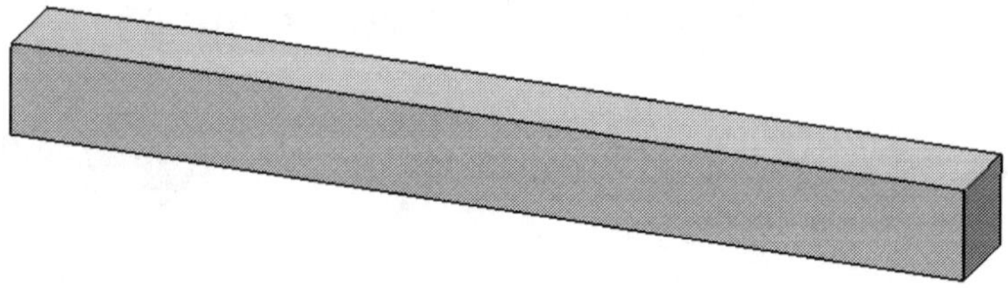

Select the **Apply Material** icon  to activate the material **Library** box below.

Use the **Metal** tab on the top; select **Steel**. Use your cursor to pick the **frequencies** from the tree at which time the **OK** and **Apply Material** buttons can be selected. Close the box.

The material property is now reflected in the tree.

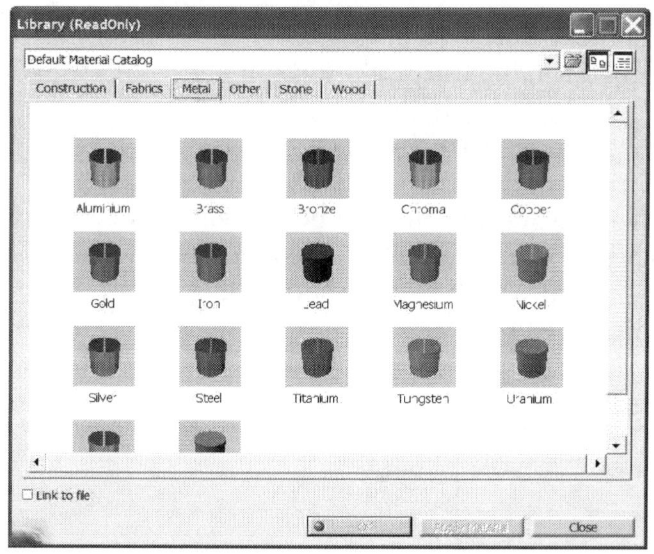


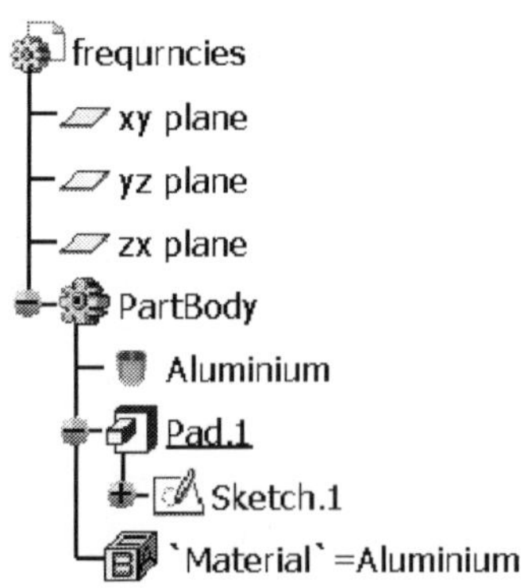


If the part is still "gray", one can change the rendering style. From the **View** toolbar 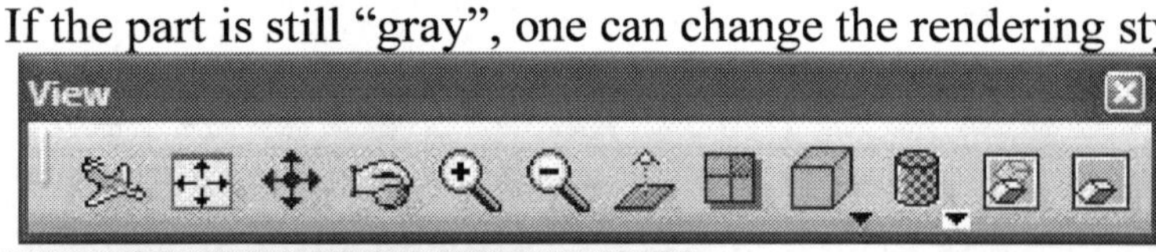

, select the **View mode** toolbar 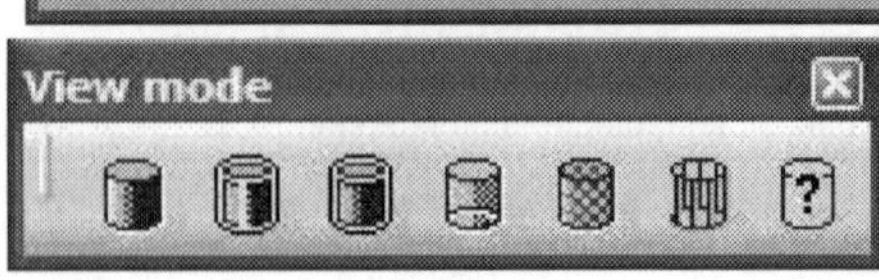

.

Next choose the **Shading with Material** icon .

The part now appears shaded as shown on the right.

## 3 Entering the Analysis Solutions

From the standard Windows toolbar, select

**Start > Analysis & Simulation > Generative Structural Analysis** 

The box shown below, **New Analysis Case** is visible on the screen. The default choice is **Static Analysis**, select the **Frequency Analysis** instead and close the box by clicking on **OK**. The modified portion of the tree reflecting this choice is also displayed.

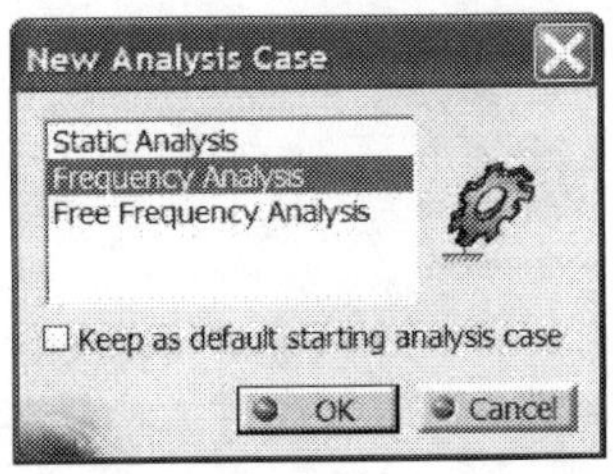


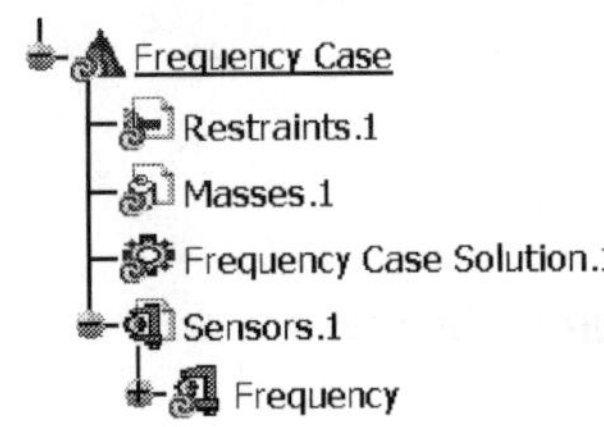


Note that the tree structure gets considerably longer. The bottom branches of the tree are presently "unfilled", and as we proceed in this workbench and assign restraints, the branches gradually get "filled".

Another point that cannot be missed is the appearance of icons on the part that reflect a representative "size" and "sag".

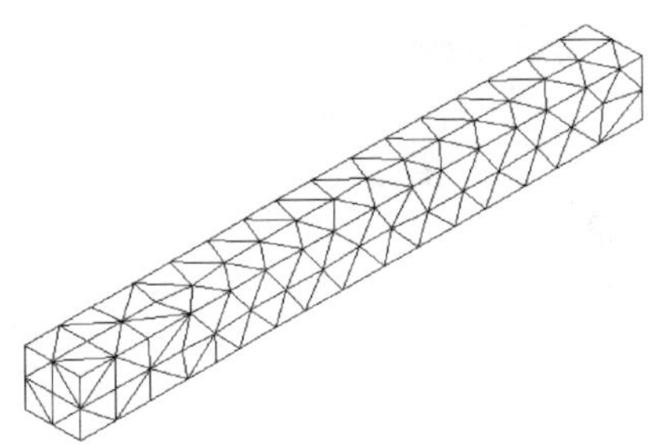

In order to view the generated mesh, you can point the cursor to the branch **Nodes and Elements**, right-click and select **Mesh Visualization**.

In a frequency analysis, the loads play no role.

In fact, the **Loads** toolbar 

is dimmed. In such a case only restraints can be applied. In order to impose the simple support condition in a straight forward way, you will create two smooth virtual parts first.

**Creating Virtual Parts:**

First make sure that the part is in the **Show** mode.

Select the **Smooth Virtual Part** icon  from the **Virtual Part** toolbar 

.
The resulting pop up box is shown below.
Select the right-end face as the **Supports** and leave **Handler** as blank. Since no handler is defined, the centroid of the face will be the default **Handler**.

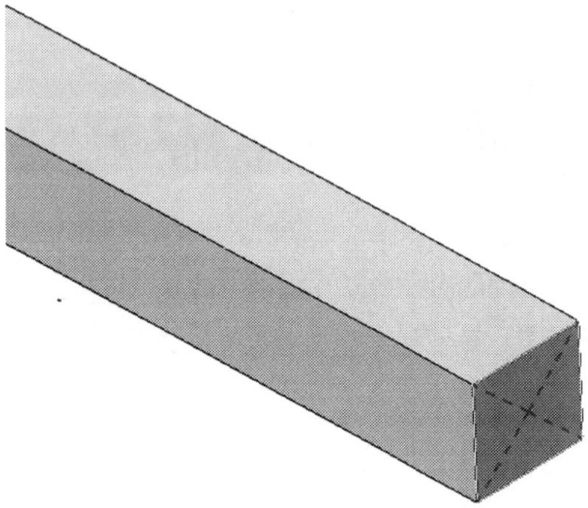

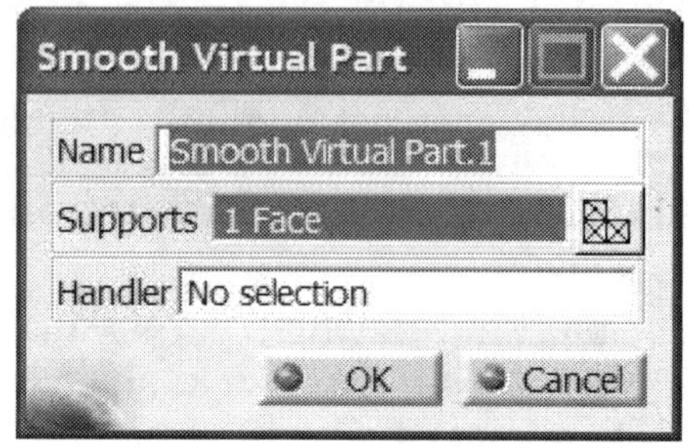


Repeat the same process with the other end.

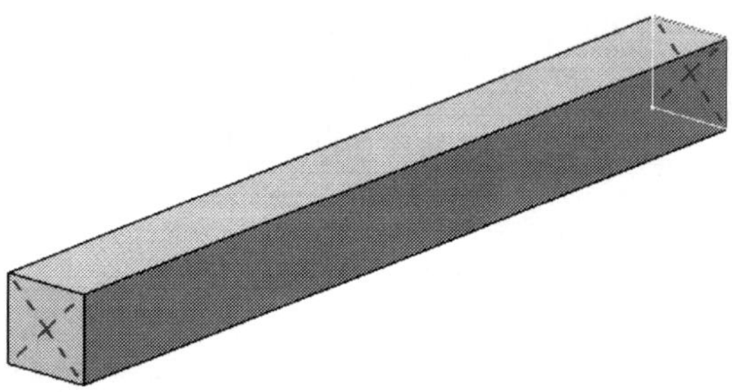

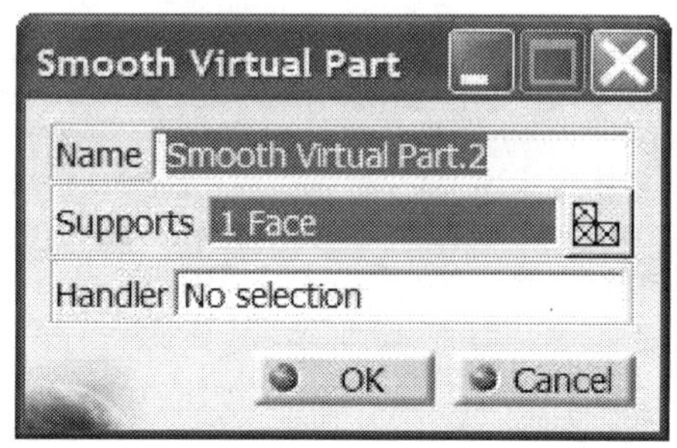


The portion of the tree associated with the virtual parts created is shown below.

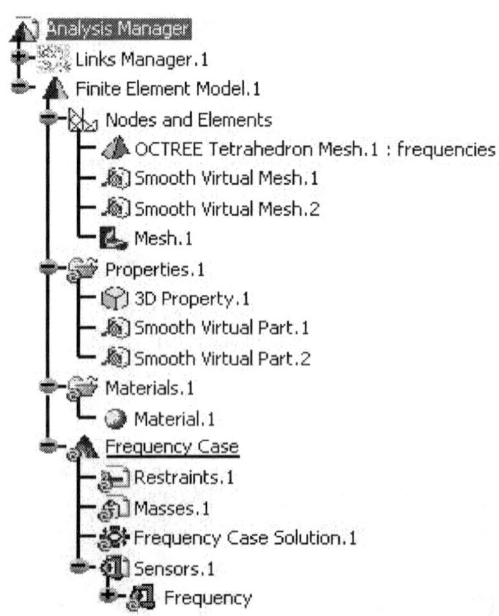

## Applying Restraints:

CATIA's FEA module is geometrically based. This means that the boundary conditions cannot be applied to nodes and elements. The boundary conditions can only be applied at the part level. As soon as you enter the **Generative Structural Analysis** workbench, the parts are automatically hidden. Therefore, before boundary conditions are applied, the part must be brought to the unhide mode. This can be carried out by pointing the cursor to the top of the tree, the **Links Manager.1** branch, right-click, select **Show**. At this point, the part and the mesh are superimposed as shown below and you have access to the part.

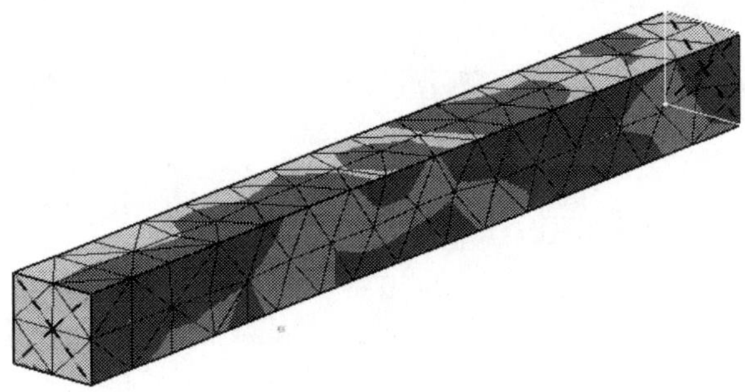

If, the presence of the mesh is annoying, you can always hide it. Point the cursor to **Nodes and Elements**, right-click, **Hide**.
In FEA, restraints refer to applying displacement boundary conditions which is achieved through the **Restraint** toolbar 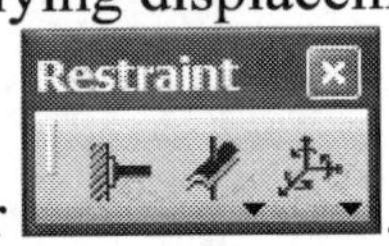

.

Using the downward black arrow, shown in the toolbar above, extract the **Mechanical Restraints** toolbar 

.

Select the **Pivot** icon . The pop up box shown to the right allows you to pick the pivot axis. In the present model, it is the y- axis. Type "**1**" for **Y**.

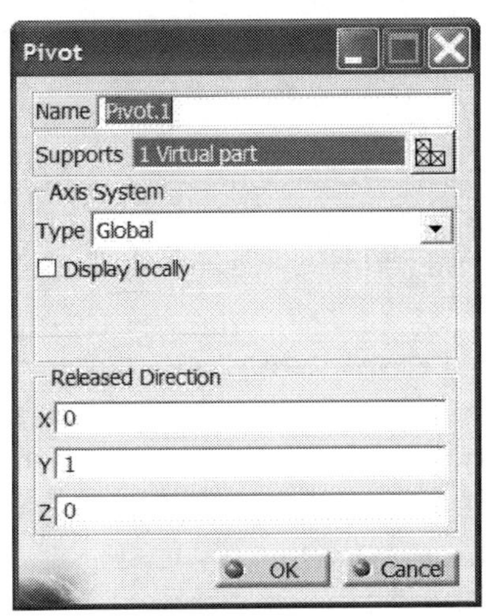


For the **Supports**, select **Smooth Virtual Part.1**. This can be done through the tree or a screen pick.

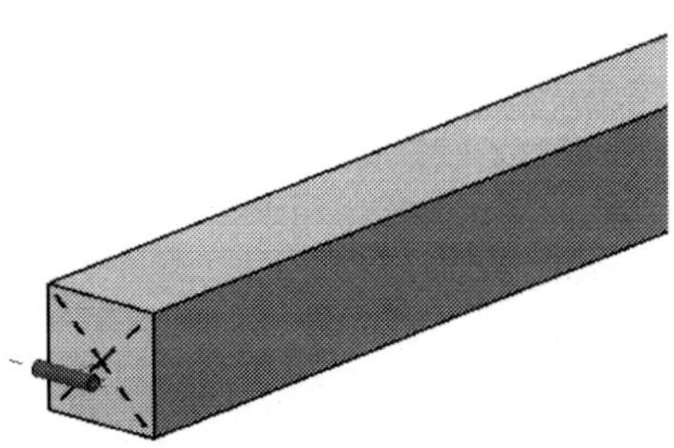

Repeat the same process to create **Pivot.2**, at the other end.

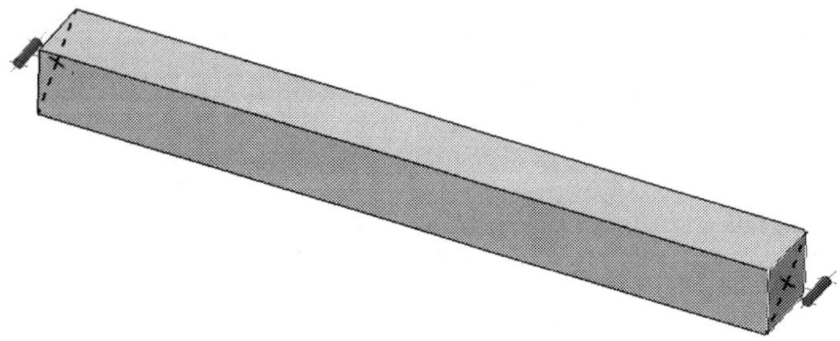

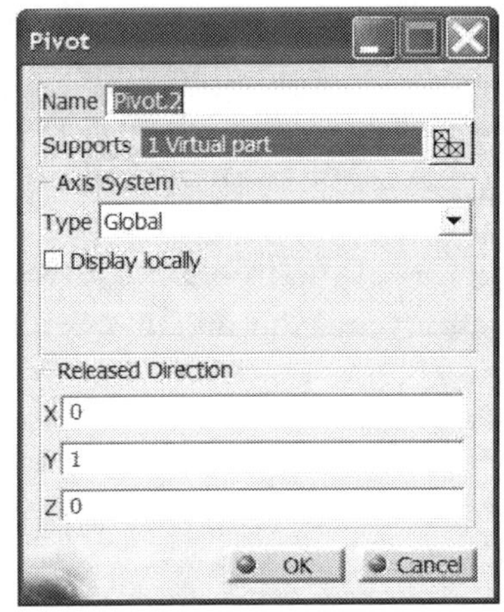


The portion of the tree reflecting the pivoted restraints is displayed below.

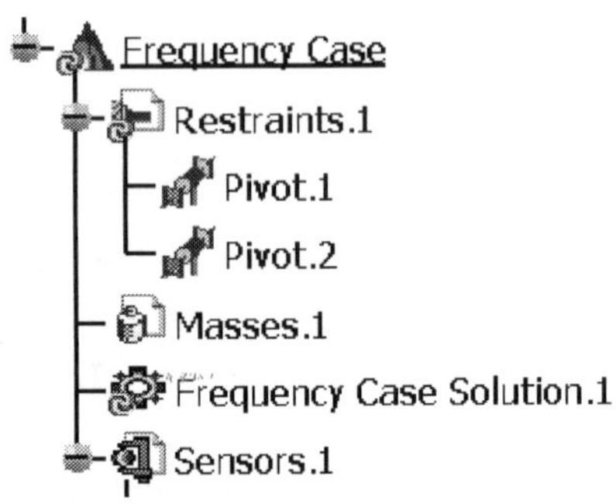


Double-click on the **Frequency Case Solution.1** branch of the tree. In the resulting pop up box you can specify the number of frequencies to be extracted and the algorithm to be used. Keep all the defaults.

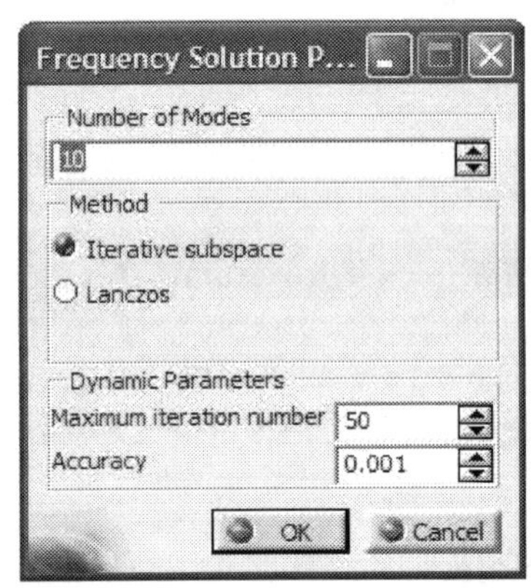


**Launching the Solver:**

To run the analysis, you need to use the **Compute** toolbar  by selecting the **Compute** icon . This leads to the **Compute** box shown to the right. Leave the defaults as **All** which means everything is computed.
Upon closing this box, after a brief pause, the second box shown on the next page appears. This box provides information on the resources needed to complete the analysis.

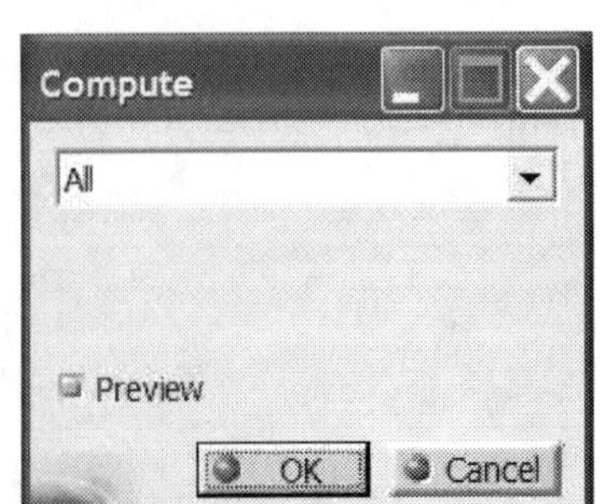

If the estimates are zero in the listing, then there is a problem in the previous step and should be looked into. If all the numbers are zero in the box, the program may run but would not produce any useful results.

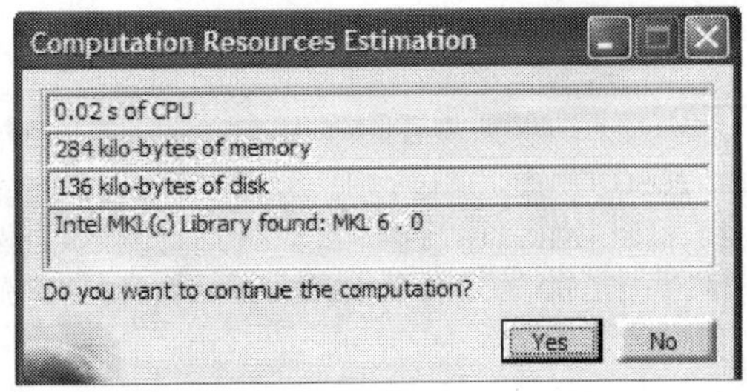


## Postprocessing:

The main postprocessing toolbar is called **Image** 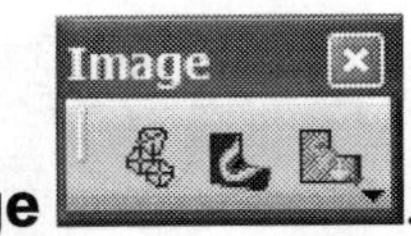

. To view the deformed shape you have to use the **Deformation** icon 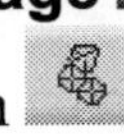. The resulting deformed shape is displayed below. This deformed shape corresponds to the smallest natural frequency. The side view is also displayed. It clearly represents half a sine wave.

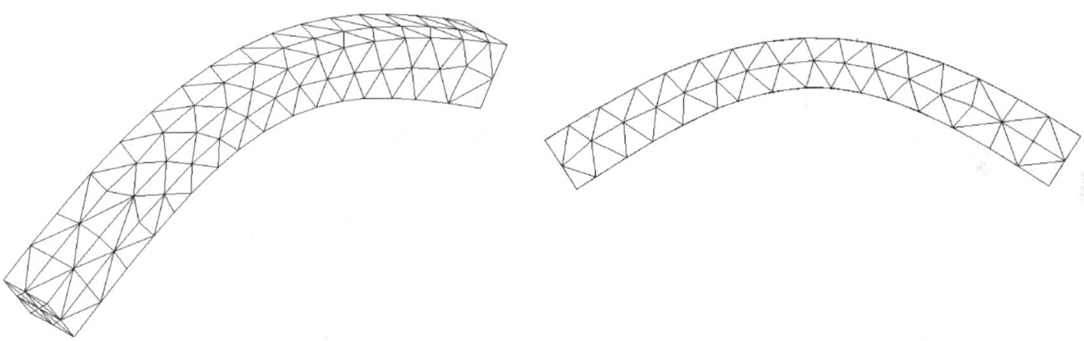

Double-click on the deformed shape on the screen and pick the **Selections** tab. The pop up box, shown on the right, list all ten extracted frequencies. Select the fourth mode from the list and the corresponding mode shape appears on the screen. This is shown below.

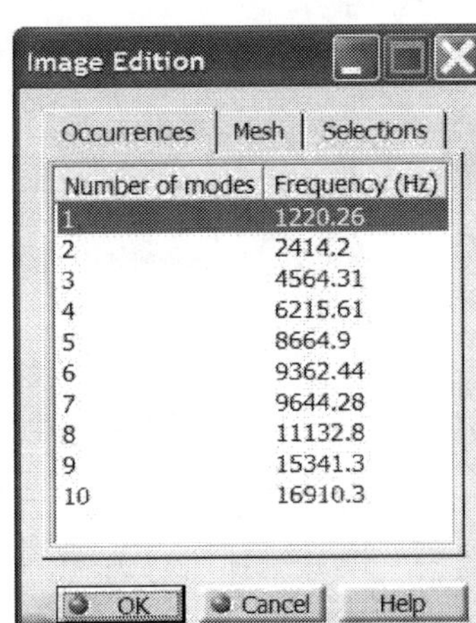


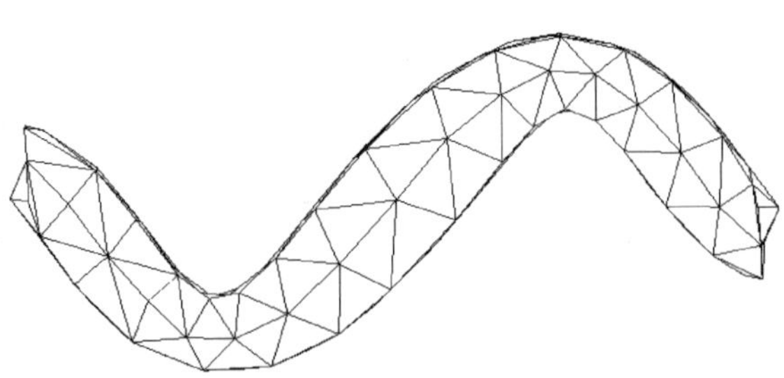

The next step in the postprocessing is to plot the contours of the von Mises stress using the **von Mises Stress** icon  in the **Image** toolbar.
The resulting contour of von Mises stress is displayed below.
Although the von Mises can be plotted for vibration mode, the magnitude of such a stress is meaningless. It gives the user only an idea of the relative stress distribution in the part.

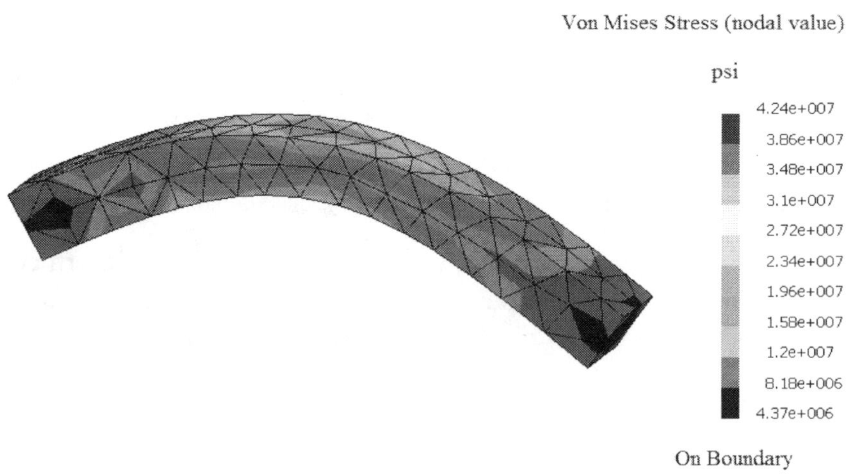


Suppose you are interested in extracting two natural frequencies in the range 2000Hz to 18000 Hz. Double-click on the **Frequency** branch of the tree in the **Sensors** section. The pop up box shown below opens.

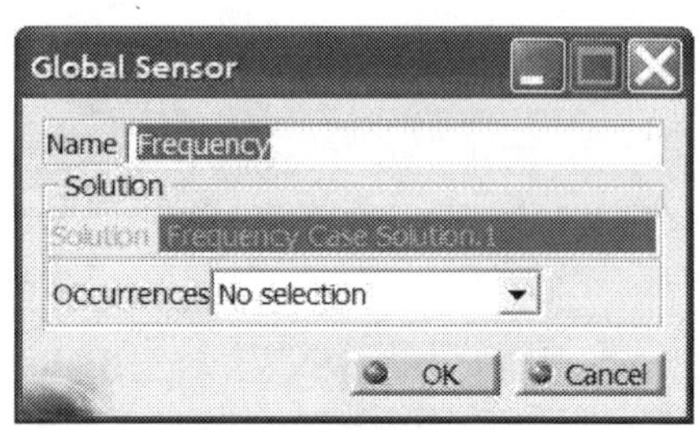


For **Occurrences**, select **Intervals** and use the  icon from the pop up box.

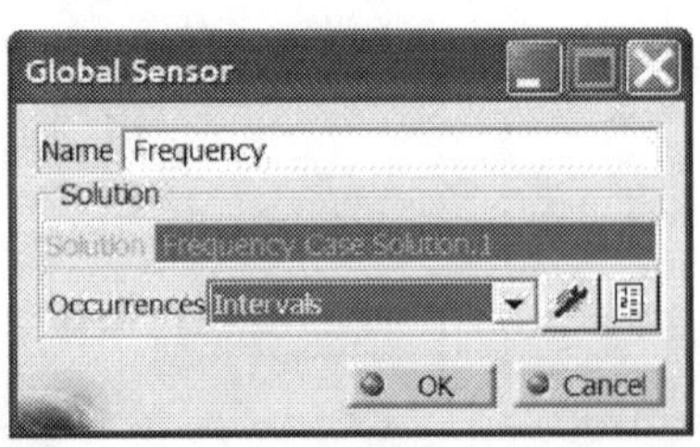


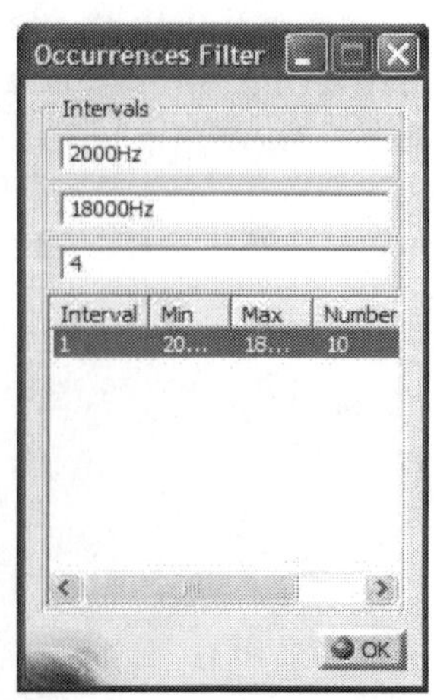


This leads to a second pop up box displayed to the right where the range and the number of frequencies can be specified.

Select the **Compute** icon  to run the problem once again.

Once the run is complete, double-click on **Frequency List** branch in the tree. The list extracted frequencies in the specified range will appear on the screen. This is shown below. In this case, there are only four frequencies in the requested range.

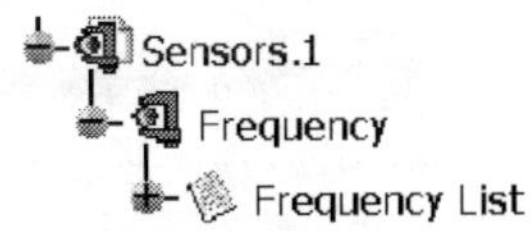


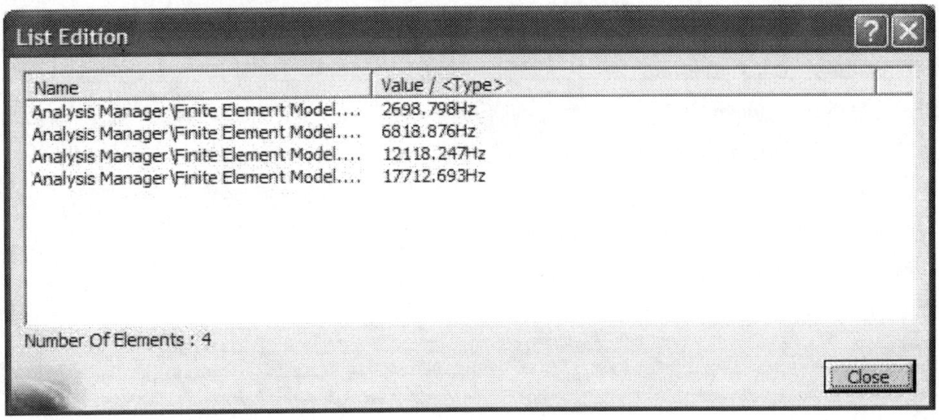


Suppose you want to make another run with the beam being cantilevered instead. Use the standard Windows toolbar and the following sequence.

**Insert > Frequency Case**

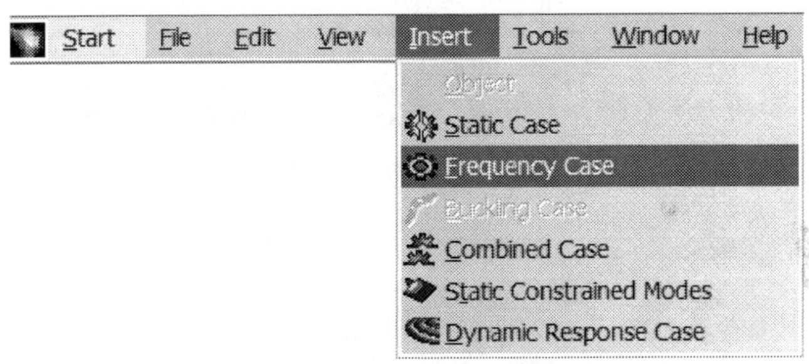


In the pop up box, shown below, keep all the default entities.

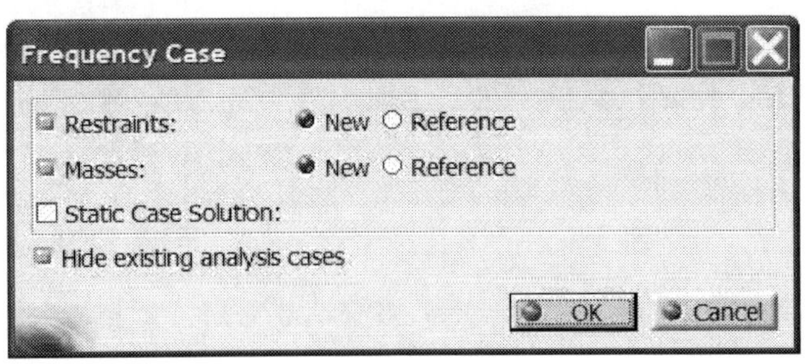

Note the tree is modified to reflect the new frequency analysis to be performed.

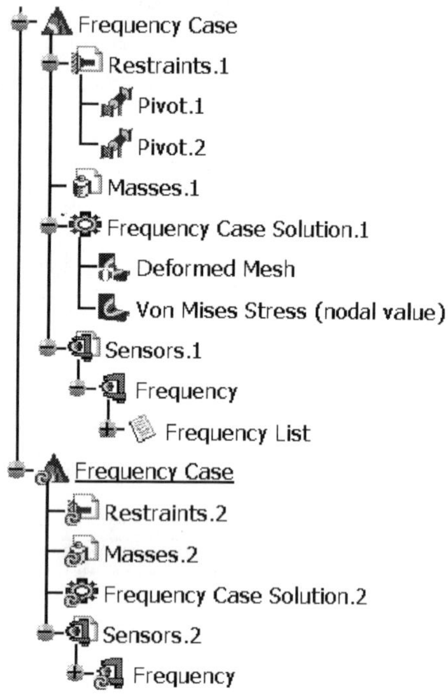


Select the **Clamp** icon  and pick the face of the part as shown.

This clamp restraint appears in the new **Frequency Case** indicated to the right.

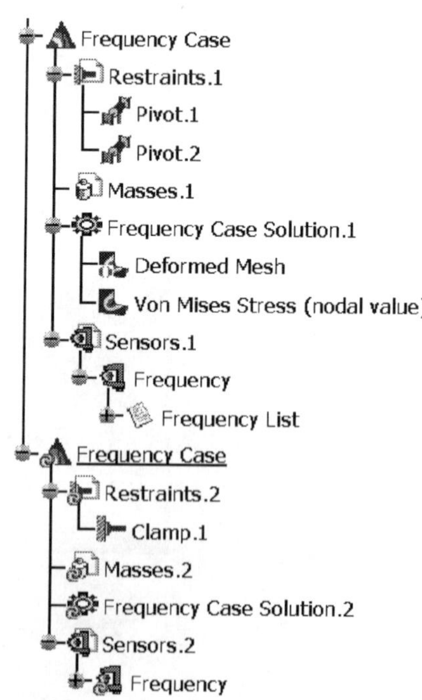


Select the **Compute** icon  to run the problem once again.

To view the deformed shape you have to use the **Deformation** icon 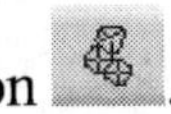. The resulting deformed shape is displayed below.

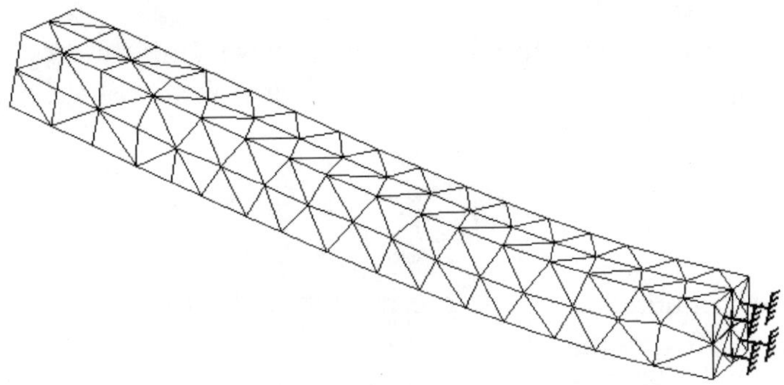

Double-click on the deformed shape. The pop up box, shown below, lists all ten extracted frequencies.

Finally, animation of the model can be achieved through the **Animate** icon 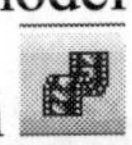 in the **Analysis Tools** toolbar 

.
An AVI file can easily be generated.

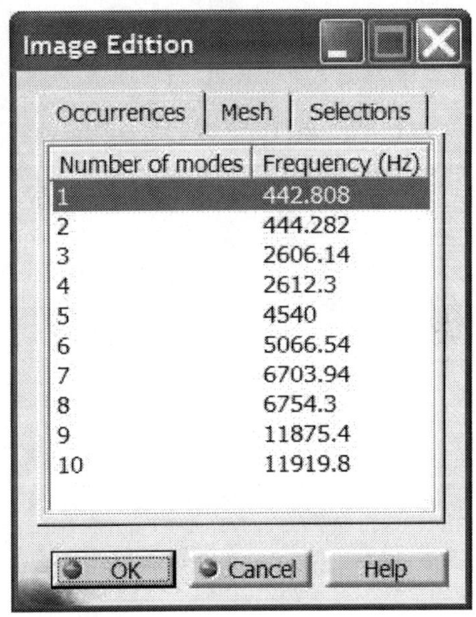


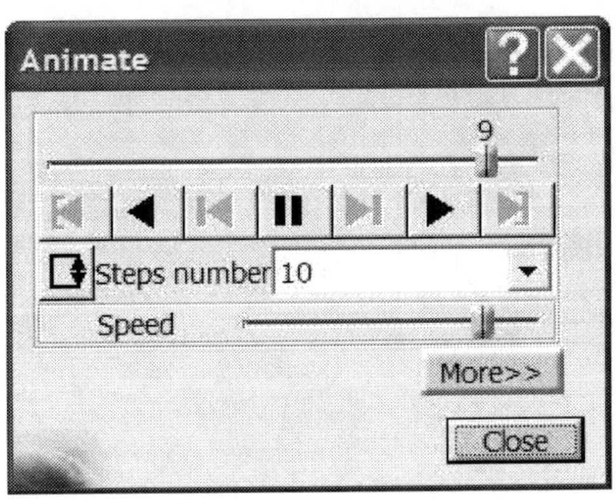

# Exercises for Chapter 22

## Problem 1: Natural Frequencies of a Two Member Frame

Using dimensions of your choice, and properties of steel, find the first two natural frequencies of the frame shown below. The finite element model should include only beam elements.

Partial Answer:

The first two natural frequencies, due to the in-plane vibration of the frame, can be approximated from the following formulas.

$$\omega_1 = 1.172\sqrt{\frac{EI}{mL^4}}$$

$$\omega_2 = 3.198\sqrt{\frac{EI}{mL^4}}$$

These frequencies are in radians per second. Furthermore, "m" represents the mass of each member.

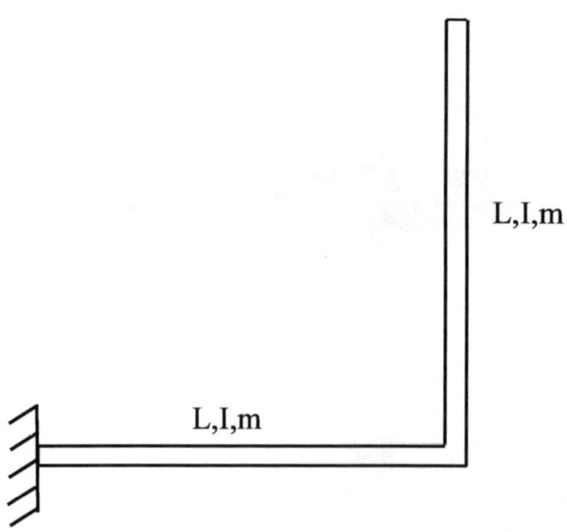

# Chapter 23

# Buckling Analysis

## Introduction

In this tutorial, the buckling analysis of a plane frame is performed. An approximate analytical solution is available which is used to asses the quality of the FEA predictions.

## 1 Problem Statement

The frame structure shown on the right hand side is made of aluminum with Young's modulus $E = 1.015E + 7$ psi. The two members have a 1x1 $in^2$ cross section and a nominal length of $L = 10$ in. The axial loads P could lead to the buckling of the structure. The solid elements in CATIA will be used to predict the buckling load. The solid and FEA model are displayed below.

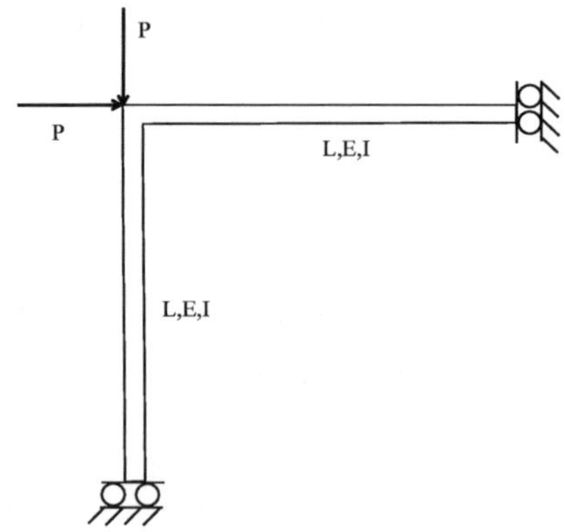


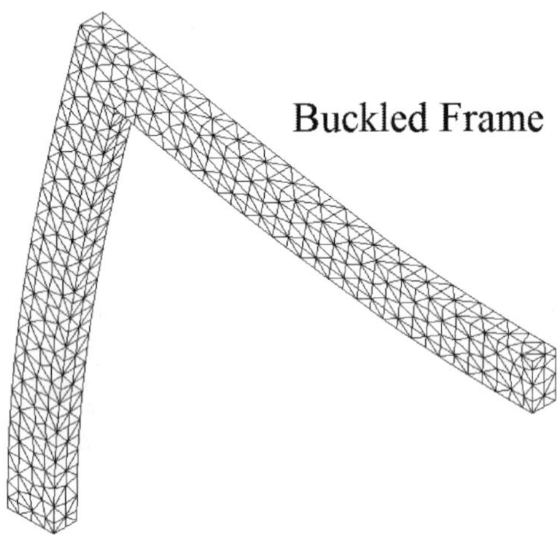

Note that, to best represent the problem, only half of the cross section is used. However, this requires imposing a symmetry condition as a restraint.

Elementary theory of strength of materials provides an estimate of the smallest buckling load from the formula $P_{cr} = \dfrac{\pi^2 EI}{4L^2}$. In this expression, $I = \dfrac{1}{12}\,in^4$ and $L = 9.5$ in. The length L has been adjusted to take into account the thickness.

The critical load, based on these values and Young's modulus, is 23125 lb.

The first step of performing a buckling calculation is to carry out a static analysis with a unit dummy load.

## 2 Creation of the Part in Mechanical Design Solutions

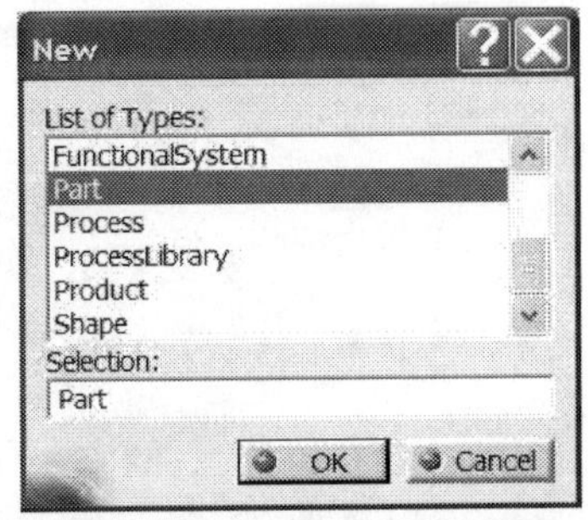


Enter the **Part Design** workbench which can be achieved by different means depending on your CATIA customization. For example, from the standard Windows toolbar, select **File > New**. From the box shown on the right, select **Part**. This moves you to the **Part Design** workbench and creates a part with the default name **Part.1**. Read Note#1 in Appendix I.

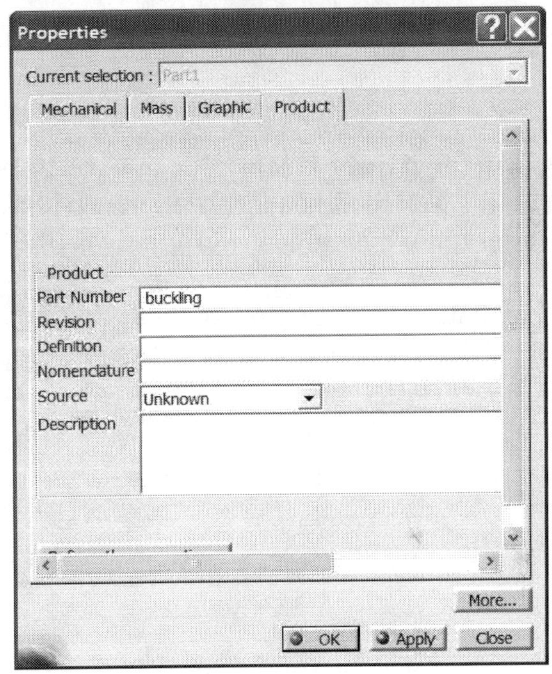


In order to change the default name, move the cursor to **Part.1** in the tree, right-click and select **Properties** from the menu list. From the **Properties** box, select the **Product** tab and in **Part Number** type **buckling**. This will be the new part name throughout the chapter. The tree on the top left corner of the screen should look as displayed below.

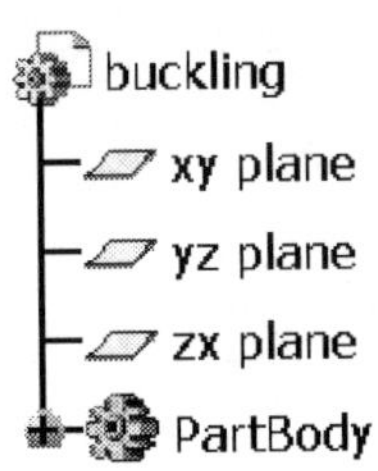


From the tree, select the **yz** plane and enter the **Sketcher**. In the **Sketcher**, use the **Profile** toolbar

to draw the wireframe shown below, and dimension it. In order to change the dimension, double-click on the dimension on the screen.

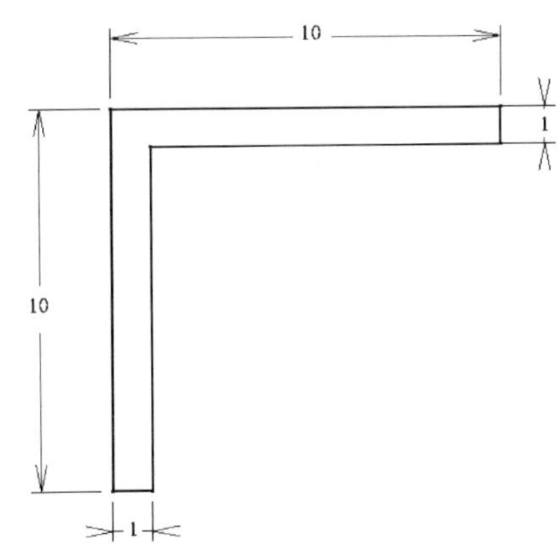


Leave the **Sketcher**.

You will now use the **Pad** operation to extrude the sketch.

Upon selecting the **Pad** icon, the **Pad Definition** box opens.
In the **Length** box, type 0.5 in.

The result is displayed below.

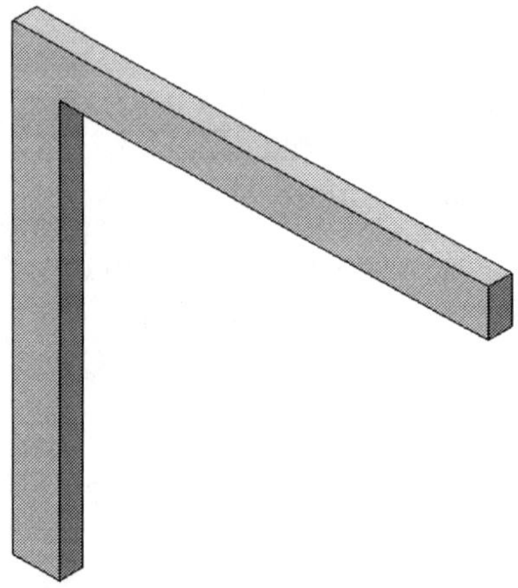

Select the **Apply Material** icon  to activate the material **Library** box below. Use the **Metal** tab on the top; select **Steel**. Use your cursor to pick the **buckling** from the tree at which time the **OK** and **Apply Material** buttons can be selected. Close the box.

The material property is now reflected in the tree.

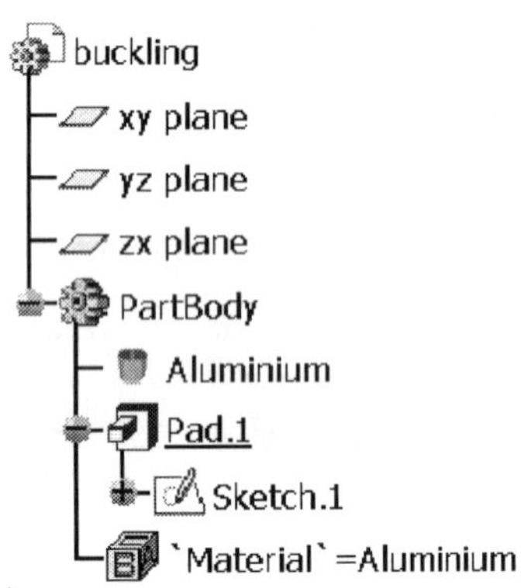


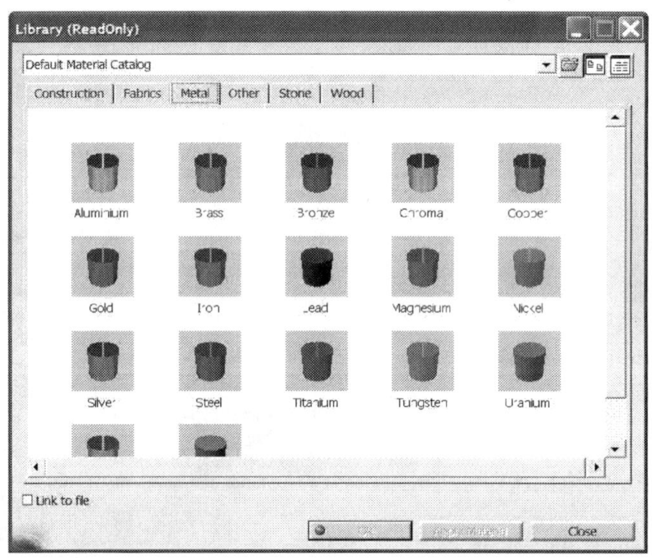


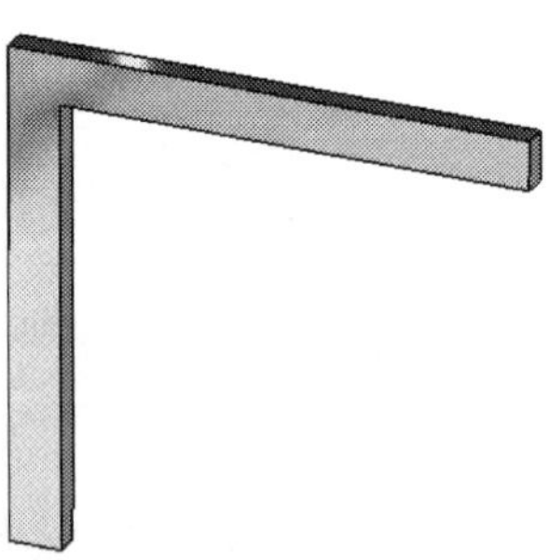

From the **View mode** toolbar 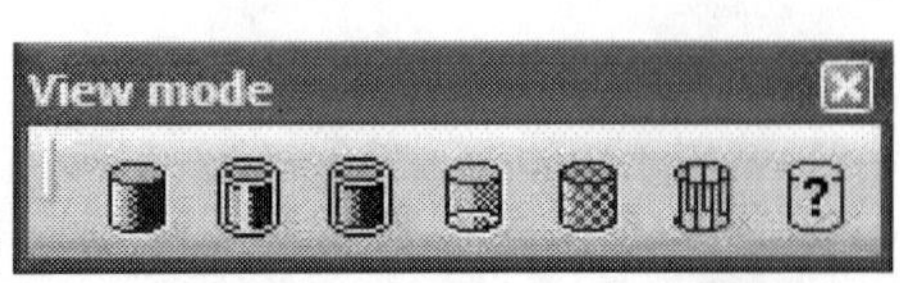 select the **Shading with Material** icon .


The part now appears shaded as shown above.

## 3 Entering the Analysis Solutions

From the standard Windows toolbar, select

**Start > Analysis & Simulation > Generative Structural Analysis** 

The box shown below, **New Analysis Case** is visible on the screen. The default choice is **Static Analysis**, click on **OK** to close the box. The modified portion of the tree reflecting this choice is also shown.

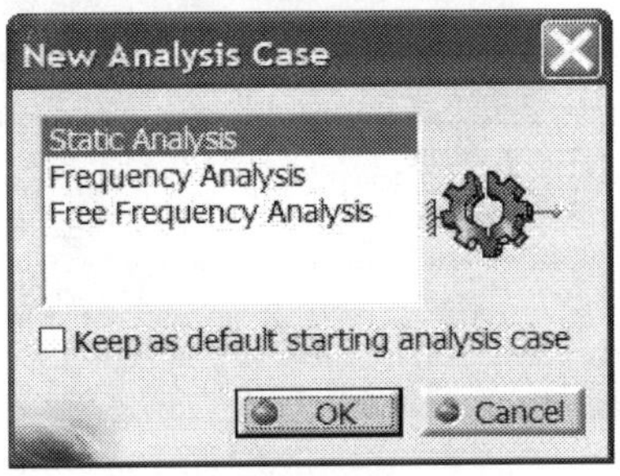


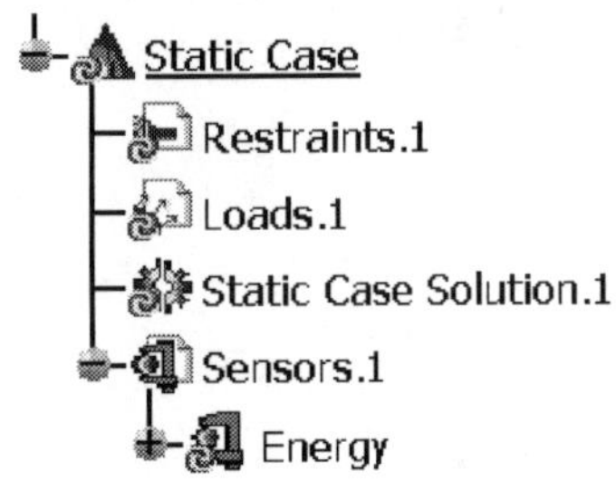


Note that the tree structure gets considerably longer. The bottom branches of the tree are presently "unfilled", and as we proceed in this workbench, assign loads and restraints, the branches gradually get "filled".

Another point that cannot be missed is the appearance of icons on each part that reflect a representative "size" and "sag".

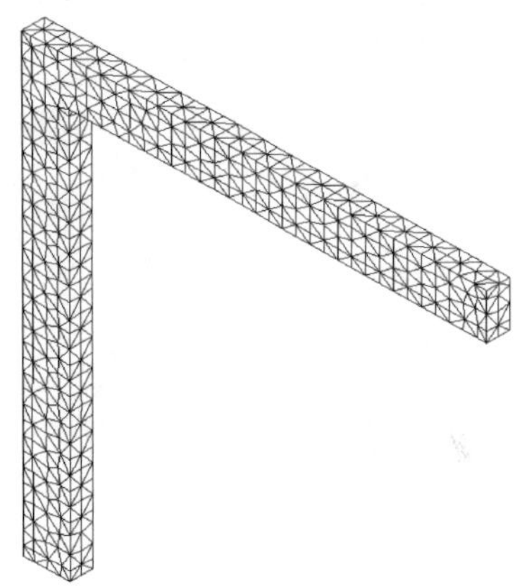

In order to view the generated mesh, you can point the cursor to the branch **Nodes and Elements**, right-click and select **Mesh Visualization**.

**Applying Restraints:**

CATIA's FEA module is geometrically based. This means that the boundary conditions cannot be applied to nodes and elements. The boundary conditions can only be applied at the part level. As soon as you enter the **Generative Structural Analysis** workbench, the parts are automatically hidden. Therefore, before boundary conditions are applied, the part must be brought to the unhide mode. This can be carried out by pointing the cursor to the top of the tree, the **Links Manager.1** branch, right-click, select **Show**. At this point, the parts and the mesh are superimposed as shown on the right and you have access to the part.

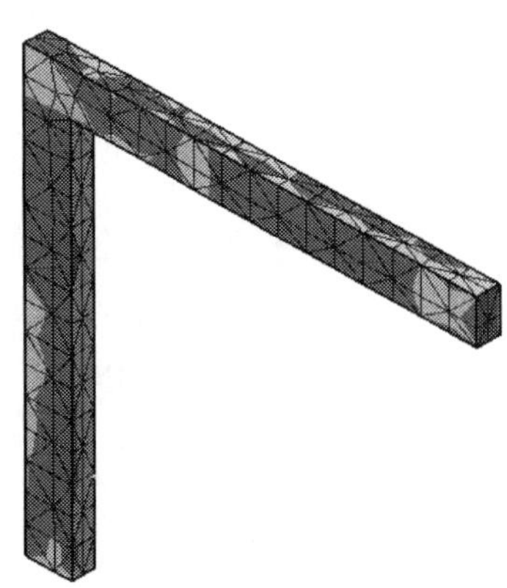

If the presence of the mesh is annoying, you can always hide it. Point the cursor to **Nodes and Elements**, right-click, **Hide**.

From the **Restraint** toolbar 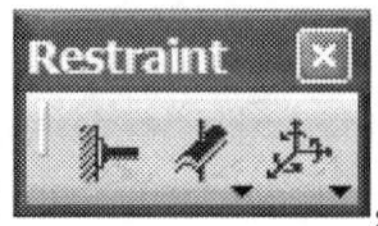

, select the **Surface Slider** icon 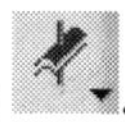. Once the box shown on the right opens, using the cursor, pick the three faces of the part as indicated below.

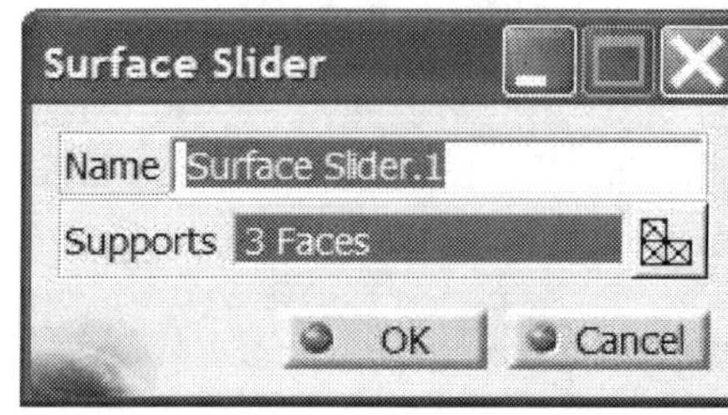


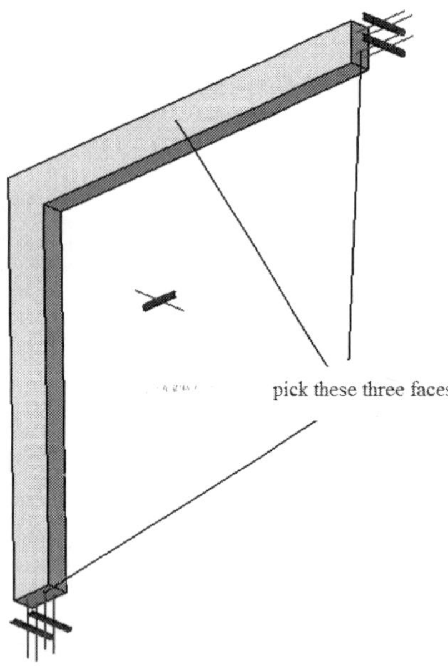


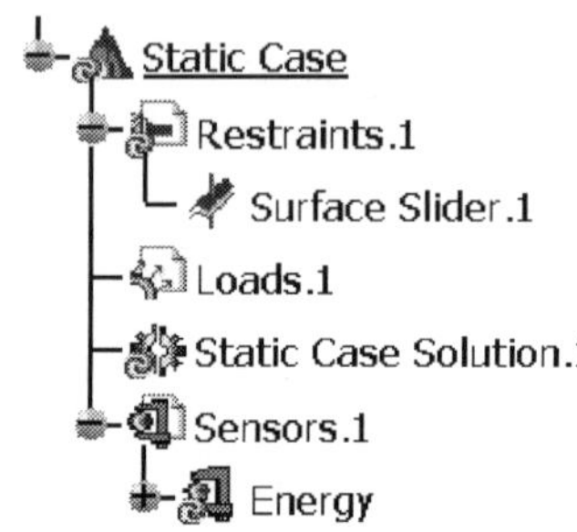


**Applying Loads:**

In FEA, loads refer to forces. The **Loads** toolbar 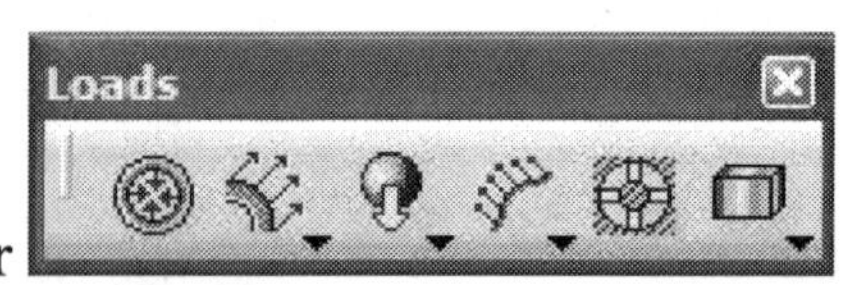

is used for this purpose. Select the **Distributed force** icon , and with the cursor pick the edge shown.

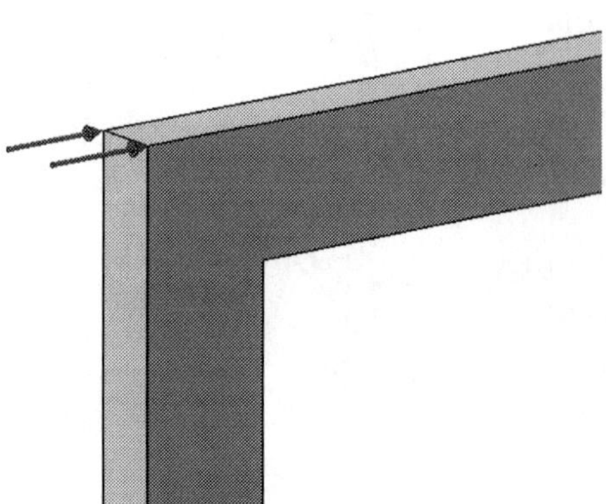

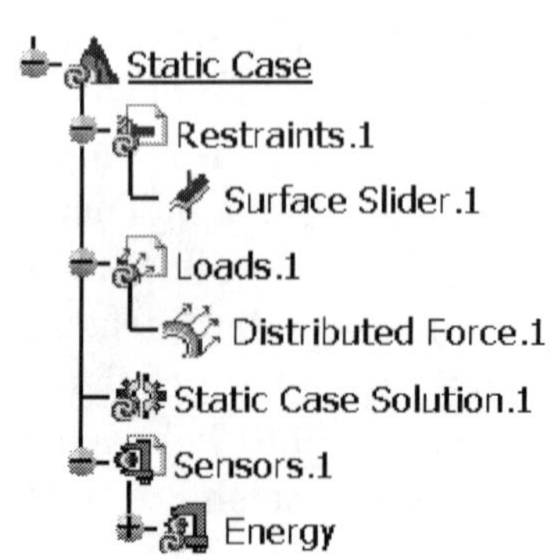

The **Distributed force** box shown below opens. Repeat the same process, however, this time apply a unit dummy load of "-1" in the z-direction. This is shown the pop up box below.

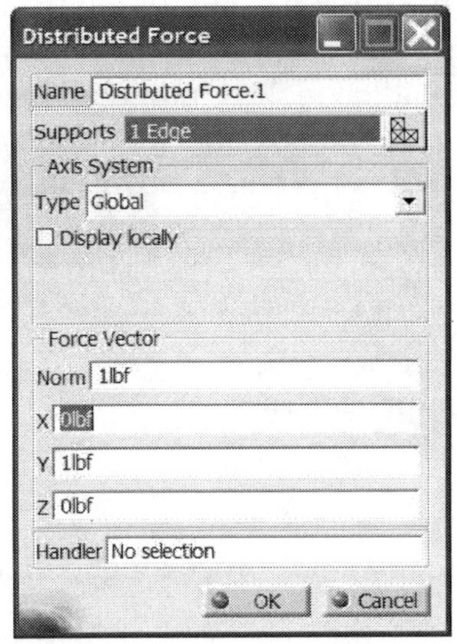


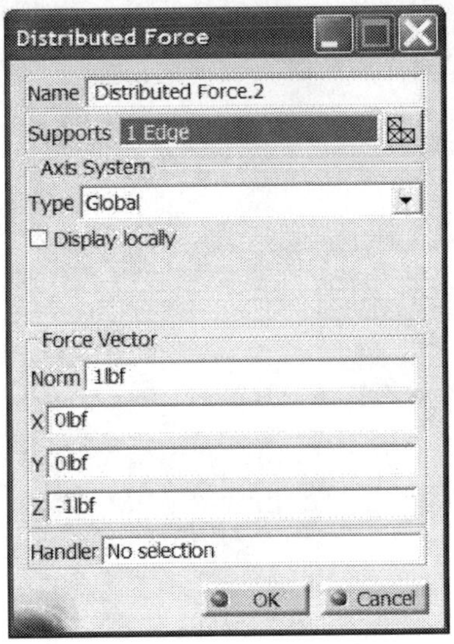


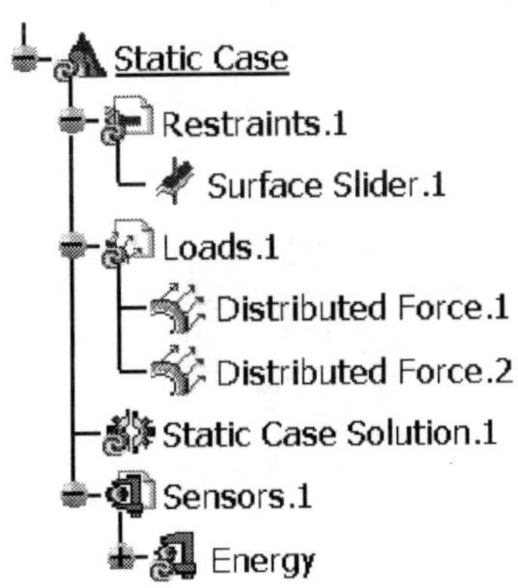


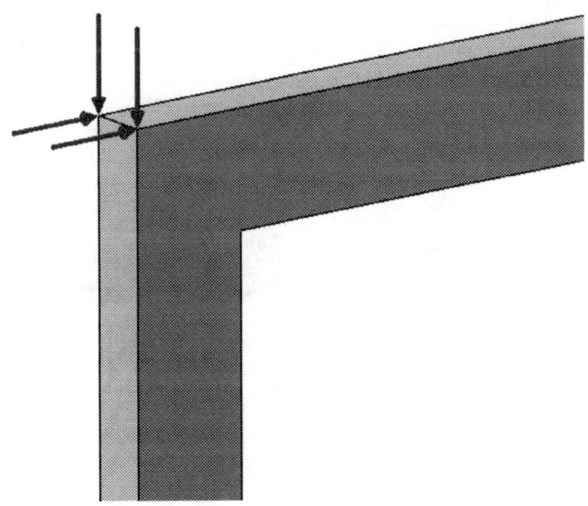

**Launching the Solver:**

To run the analysis, you need to use the **Compute** toolbar  by selecting the **Compute** icon . This leads to the **Compute** box shown to the right. Leave the defaults as **All** which means everything is computed.
Upon closing this box, after a brief pause, the second box shown on the next page appears. This box provides information on the resources needed to complete the analysis.

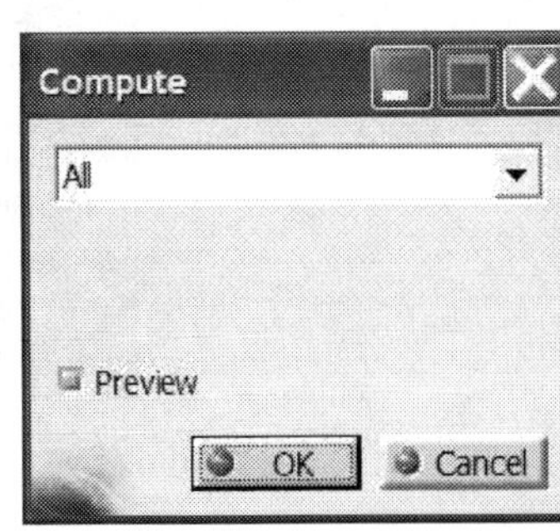

If the estimates are zero in the listing, then there is a problem in the previous step and should be looked into. If all the numbers are zero in the box, the program may run but would not produce any useful results.

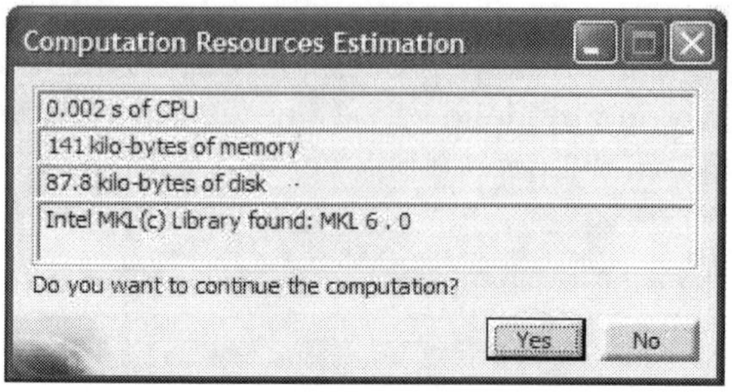


**Postprocessing:**

The main postprocessing toolbar is called **Image** 

. To view the deformed shape you have to use the **Deformation** icon . The figure below indicates the deformed shape under a dummy unit load. Note that no buckling analysis has been performed yet.

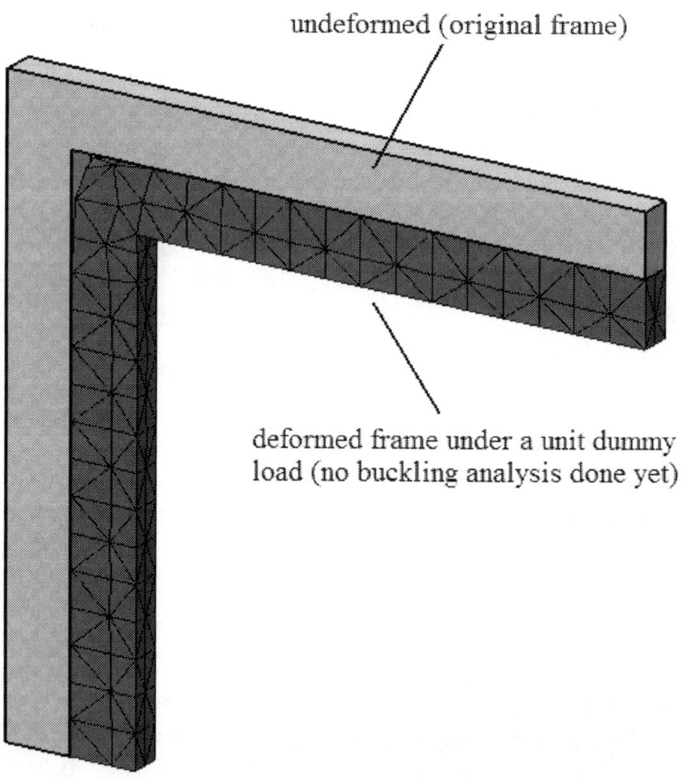

## Proceeding with the Buckling Analysis:

Once an initial static analysis is performed, the buckling analysis can follow. Use the standard Windows toolbar and pick

**Insert > Buckling Case**

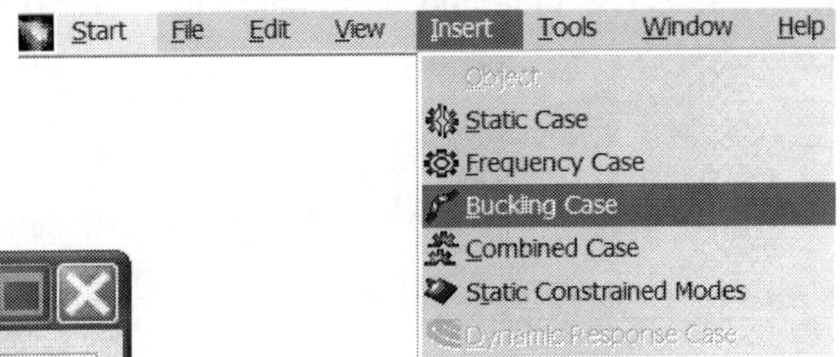


The pop up box shown below appears on your screen.

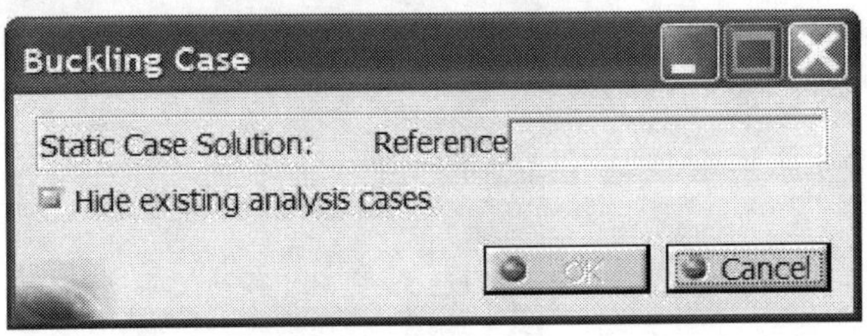


For **Reference**, select the **Static Case Solution.1** branch of the tree as indicated below.

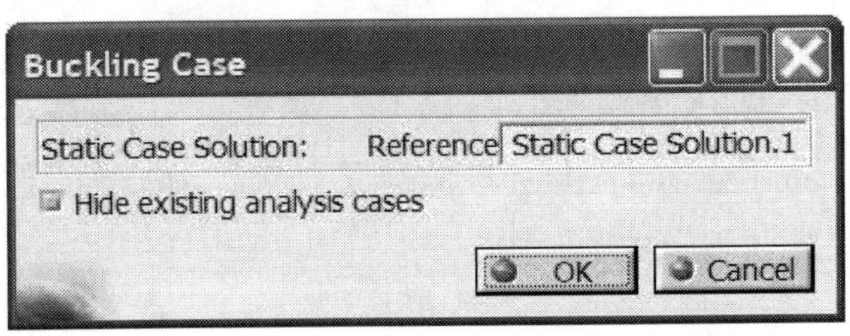


This procedure leads to the insertion of a buckling case as reflected in the modified tree.

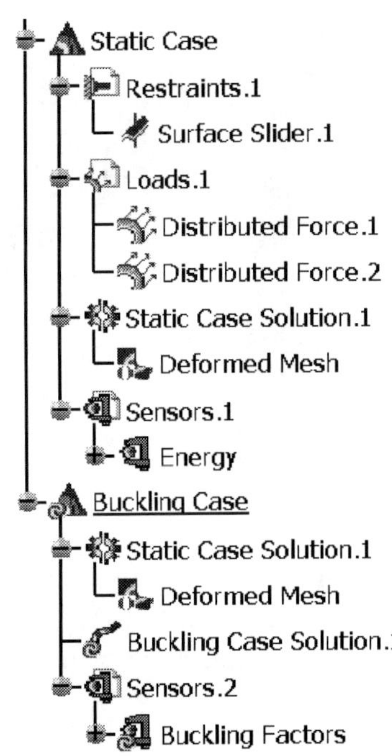

Select the **Compute** icon to run the problem once again.

To view the deformed shape (first buckling mode) you have to use the **Deformation** icon. The side and isometric views are displayed below.

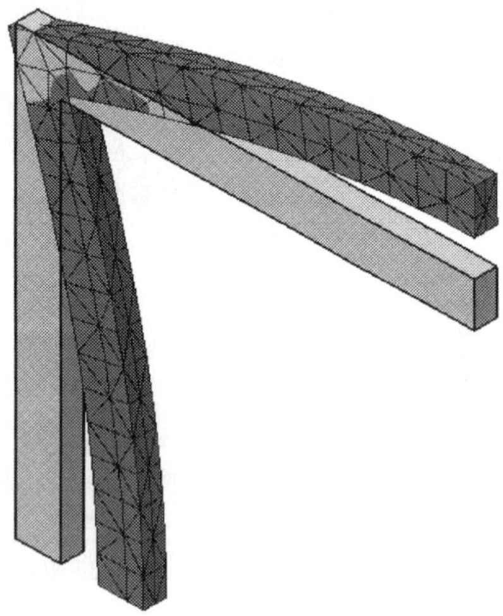

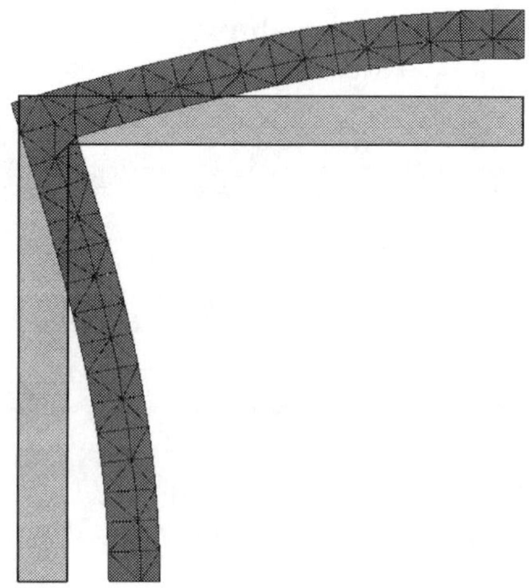

Double-click on the deformed shape. The pop up box, shown on the right, lists ten extracted buckling modes. Select the second mode from the list and the corresponding mode shape appears on the screen. This is shown below.

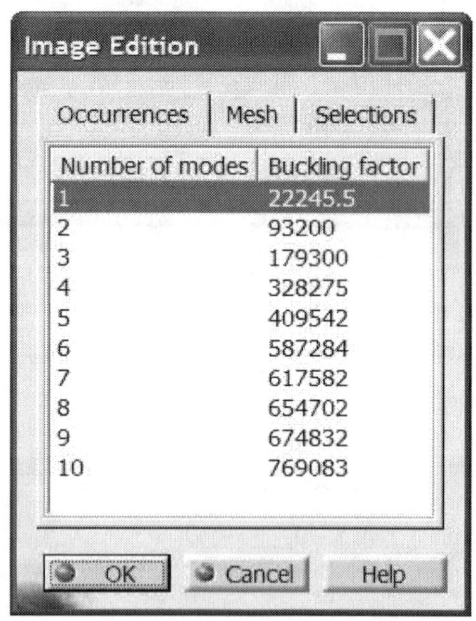


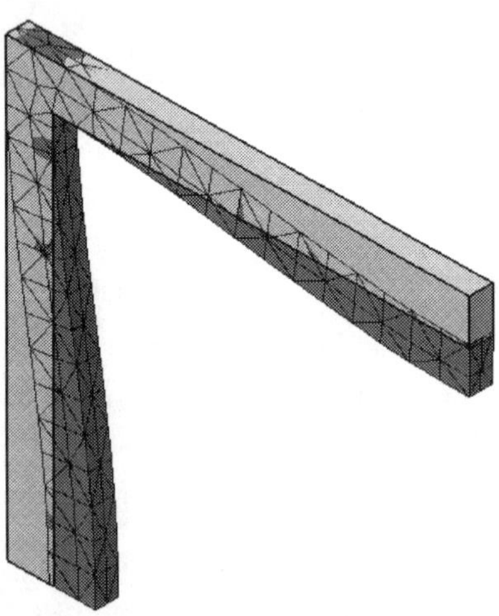

Since symmetry was used to reduce the thickness of the frame, the predicted smallest buckling load is 2(22245.5), namely 44491 lb. This value is considerably different from the hand calculations earlier. The agreement will be much better if beam elements are used.

# Exercises for Chapter 23

## Problem 1: Buckling Analysis of a Cylindrical Tube

An aluminum tube has a wall thickness of 0.1 in, nominal radius of 12 in., and length of 48 in. The bottom edge of the tube is clamped (no translation or rotation). Using shell elements, estimate the smallest buckling load applied in the axial direction.

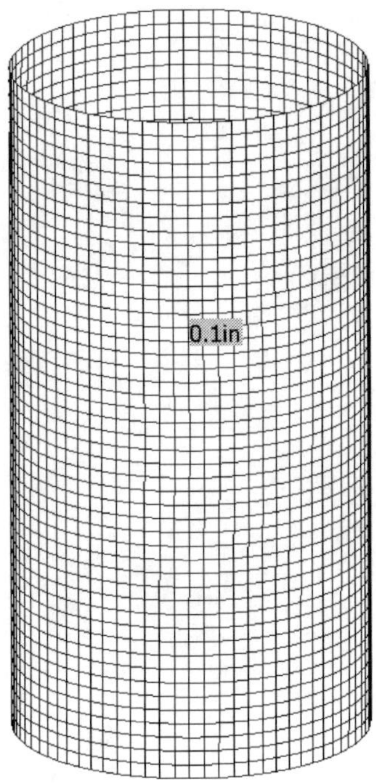


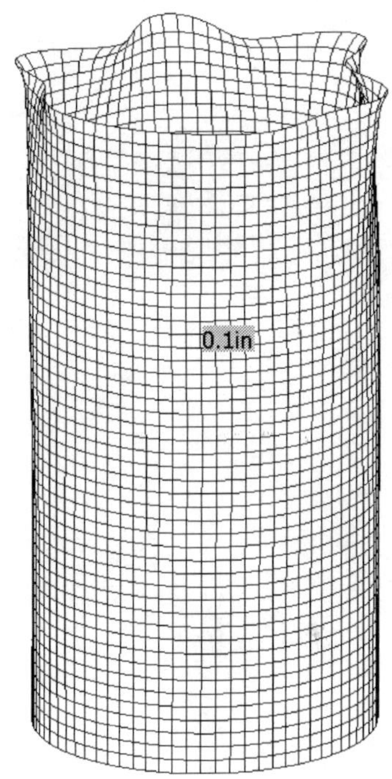


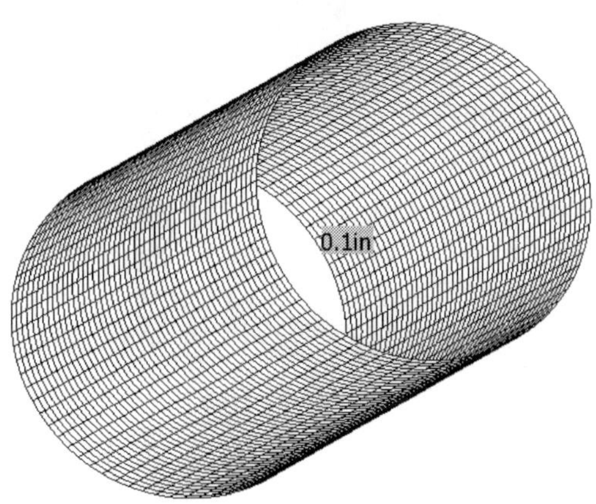


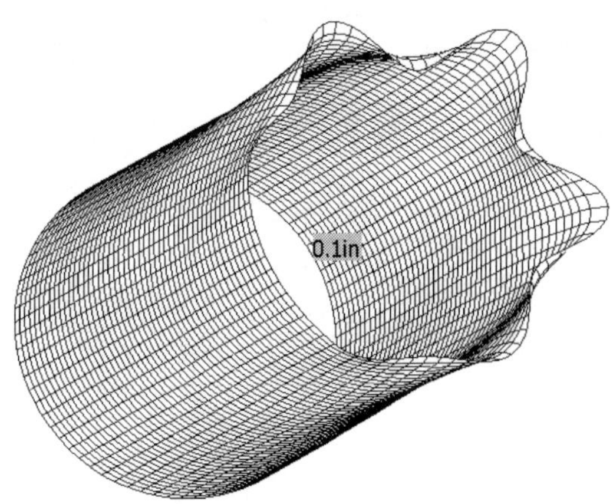

# NOTES:

# Chapter 24

# A Simple Spot Weld Model

# Introduction

In this tutorial, two thin steel sheets are spot welded together. The sheet metals are modeled with shell elements. The spot welds are introduced using the analysis connection feature in CATIA.

# 1 Problem Statement

The two sheet metals shown are made of steel having a thickness of 0.03 in. and spot welded together at the four dotted points. The edge AB of the bottom plate is clamped and the edge CD of the top L-sheet is loaded with a 10 lb force.
All the dimensions shown are in inches. The objective is to use CATIA to predict the stresses in these parts.

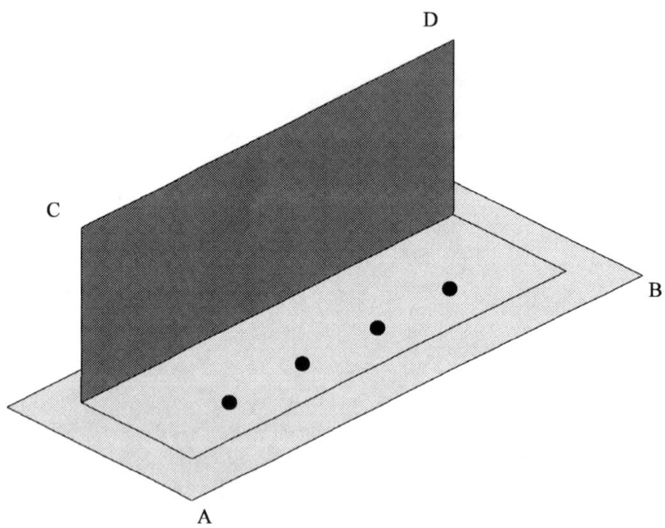


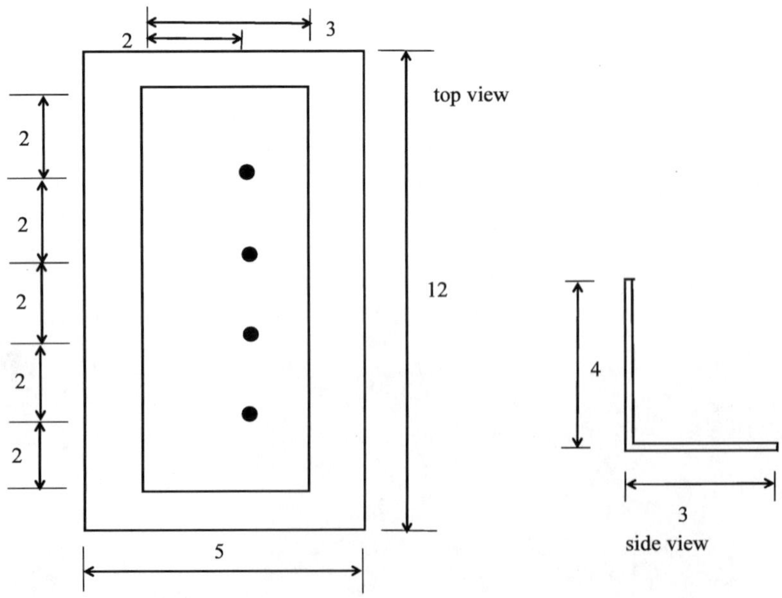

## 2 Creation of the Assembly in the Mechanical Design Solutions

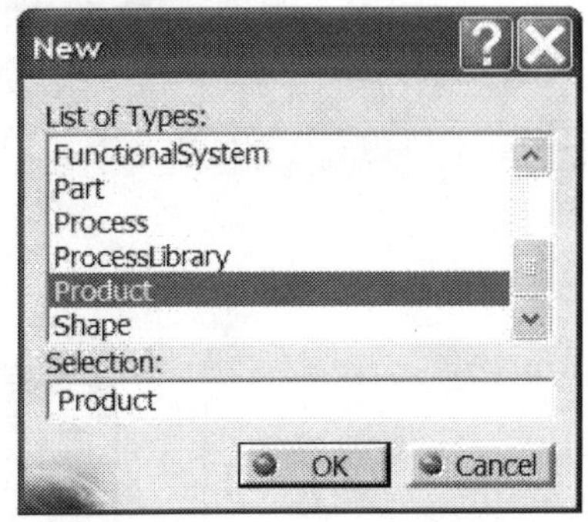



Enter the **Assembly Design** workbench 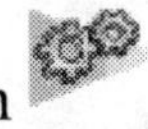 which can be achieved by different means depending on your CATIA customization. For example, from the standard Windows toolbar, select **File > New** 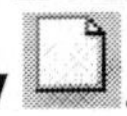. See Note #1 in Appendix I.

From the box shown on the right, select **Product**. This moves you to the **Assembly Design** workbench and creates a product with the default name **Product.1**.

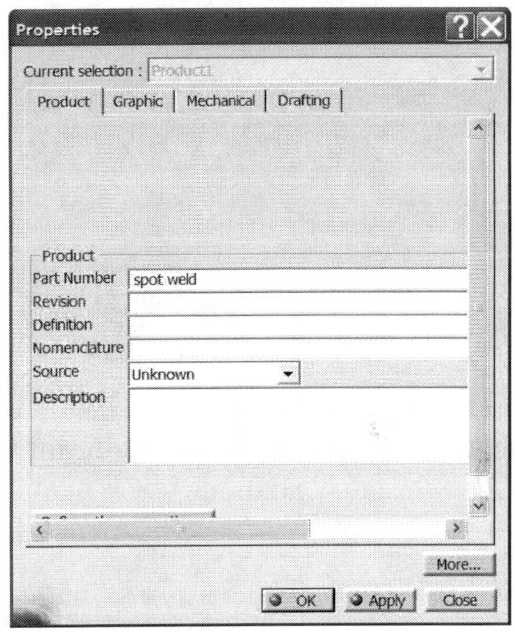



In order to change the default name, move the cursor to **Product.1** in the tree, right-click and select **Properties** from the menu list.

From the **Properties** box, select the **Product** tab and in **Part Number** type **spot weld.**

This will be the new product name throughout the chapter. The tree on the top left corner of your computer screen should look as displayed below.

You now create the bottom plate as a part.
From the standard Windows toolbar, select **Insert > New Part**. The tree is modified to indicate that **Part.1** has been created. Change the default name to **bottom**.
The tree, before and after the name change, is displayed below. Note that the instance name has also been changed to **bottom**.

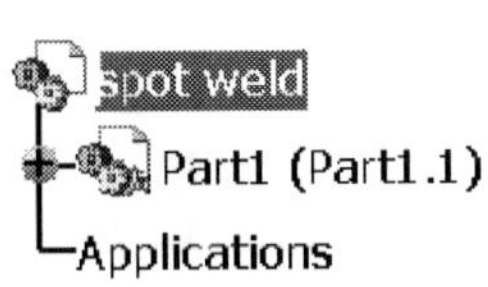



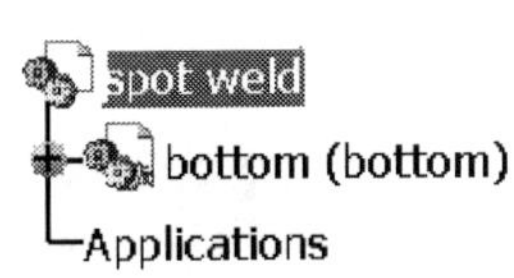



From the standard Windows toolbar, select **Start > Wireframe and Surface Design**. This lands you in the **Wireframe and Surface Design** workbench. The concept of **Geometrical Sets** defined in the next page is new. So the detailed steps are discussed and displayed.

From the standard Windows toolbar, select **Insert > Geometrical Set …** as shown.

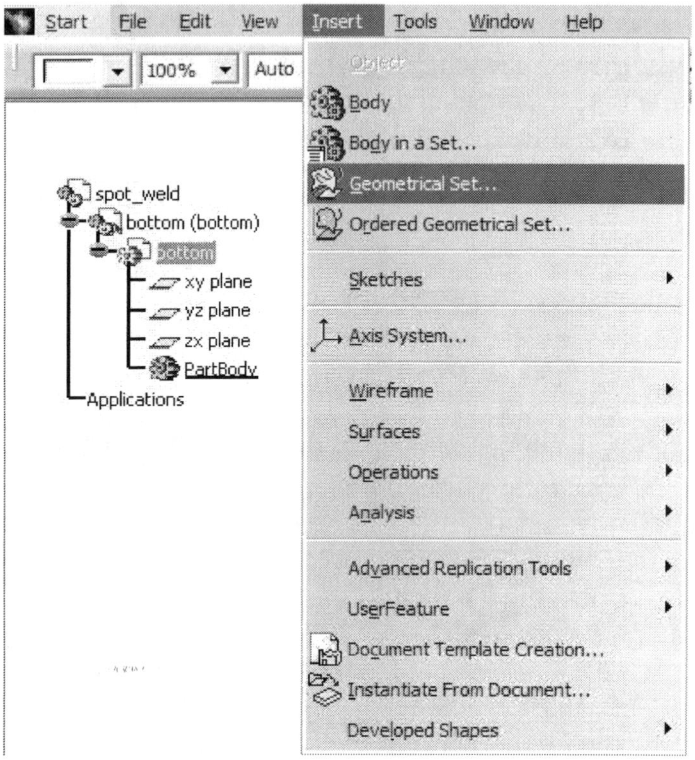


The pop up box shown on the right is appearing on the screen.
For **Name**, type **My_First_Geometrical_Set**.
Upon closing the box, the tree is modified to reflect the set created.

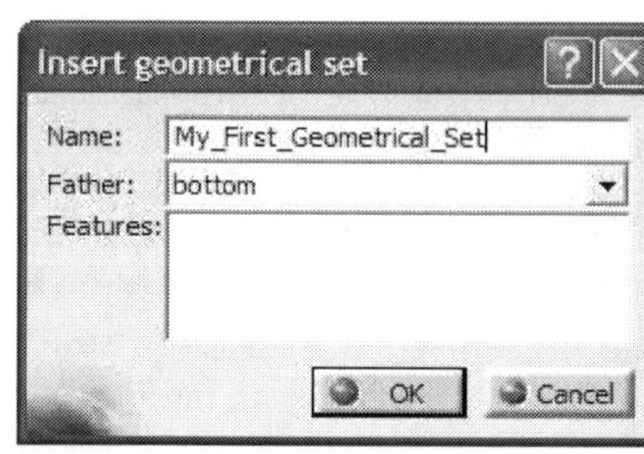


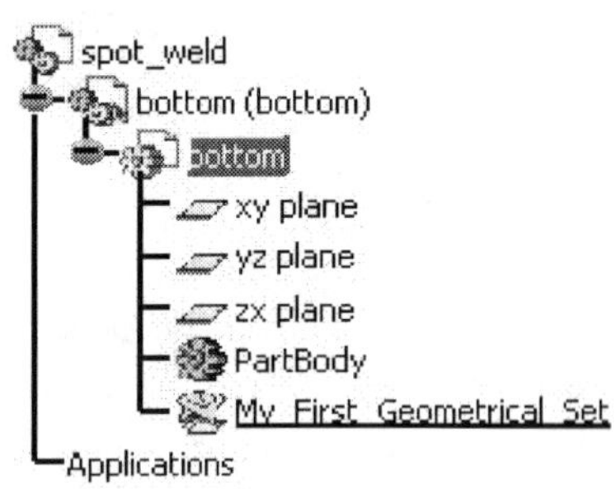


Select the **yz** plane and enter the **Sketcher** . Draw a horizontal line, and dimension it as indicated on the next page. ***Make sure that the line starts on the vertical axis exactly one unit above the origin.***

Leave the **Sketcher** .

Your computer screen immediately after exiting the **Sketcher** resembles the figure below.

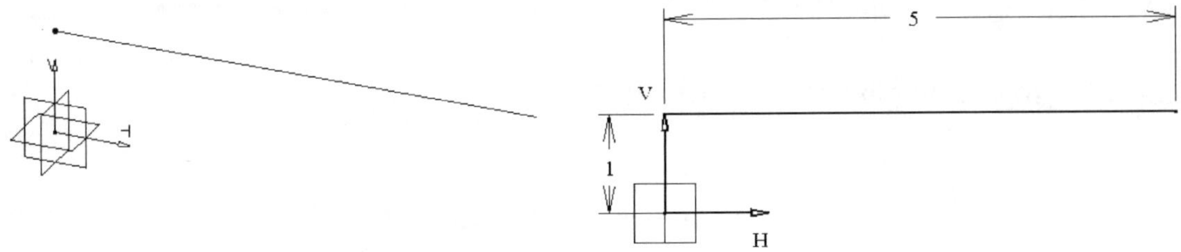


The tree is modified as shown.

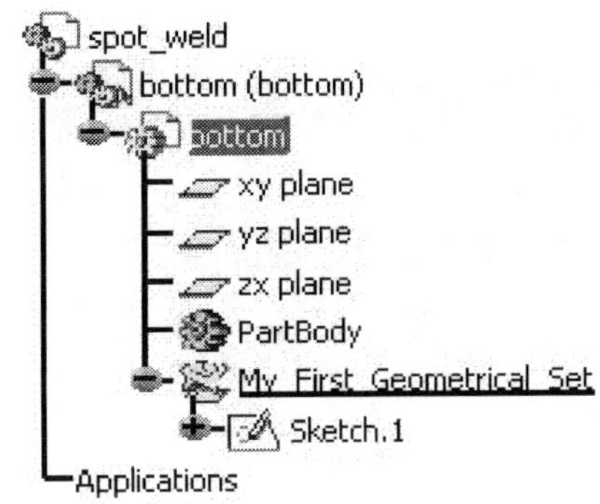


Select the **Extrude** icon  from the **Surfaces** toolbar

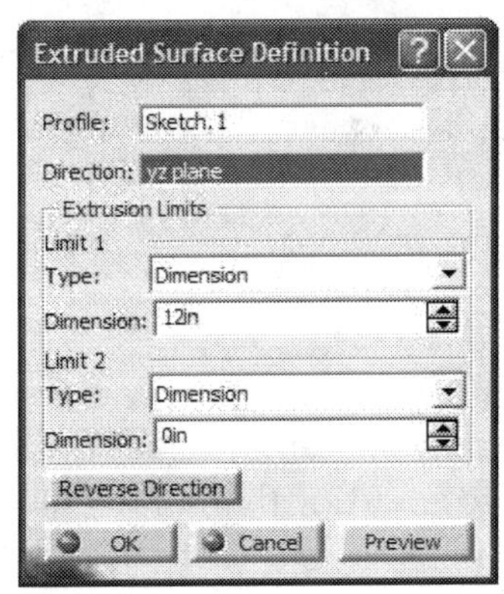


In the pop up box, shown on the right side, make the following selections. For **Profile** choose **Sketch.1**. The **Direction** will automatically be set as **yz**. For **Limit 1**, type 12. The result is a 5x12 in. plate as displayed below.

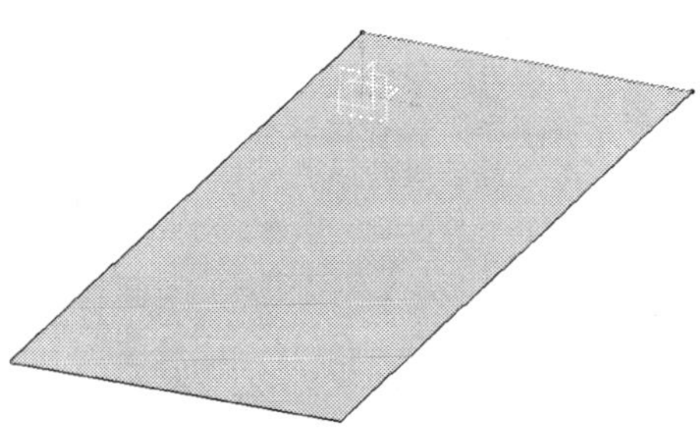

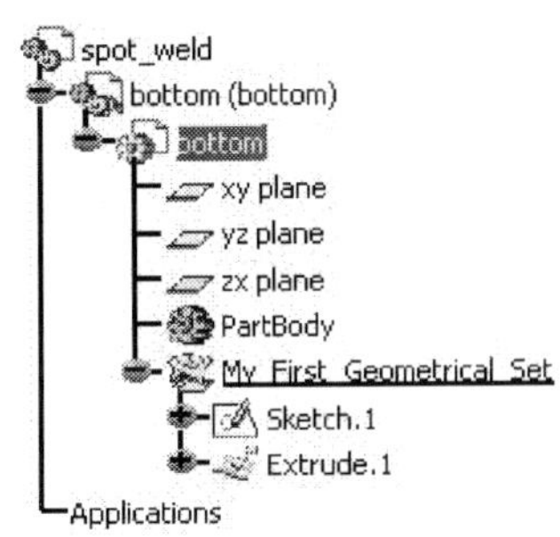

The best way of saving your work is to save the entire assembly. Double-click on the top branch of the tree. This lands you in the **Assembly Design** workbench.

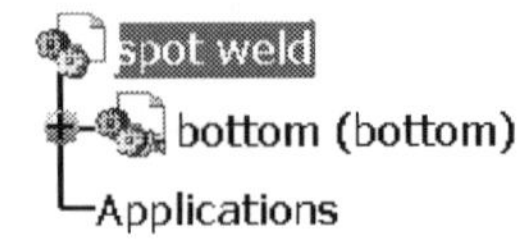


The branch highlights in blue as a confirmation of the new workbench.

Select the **Save** icon. The **Save As** pop up box indicates that saving the assembly activates the saving of the parts. Choose the **Yes** button.

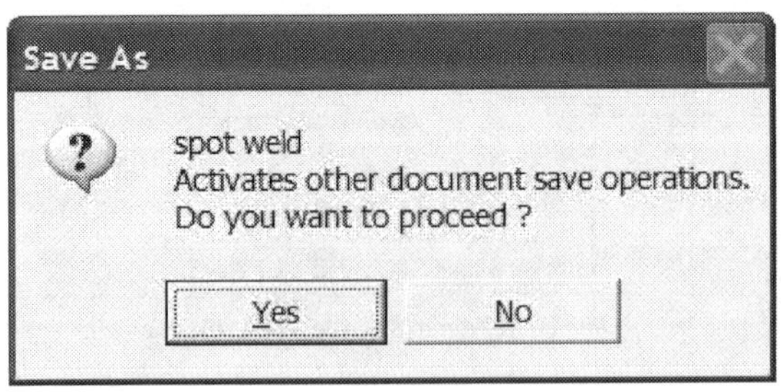


You are now ready to create the top plate.

From the standard Windows toolbar, select **Insert > New Part**. The tree is modified to indicate that **Part.2** has been created.
You are also presented with pop up box on the right. Select **NO** to close the box.

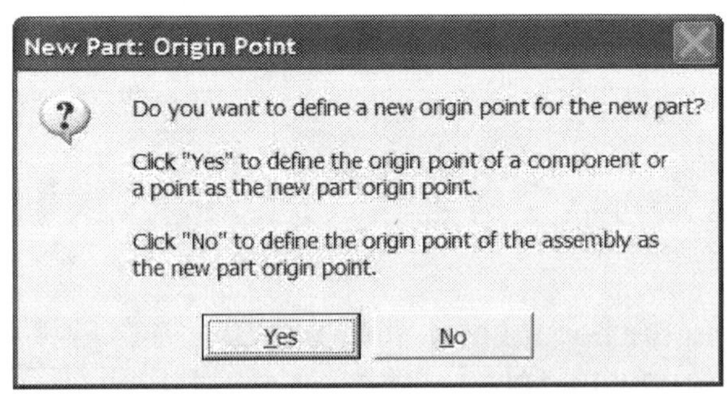


Change the default name to **top**.
The tree, after the name change, is displayed below. Note that the instance name has also been changed to **top**.

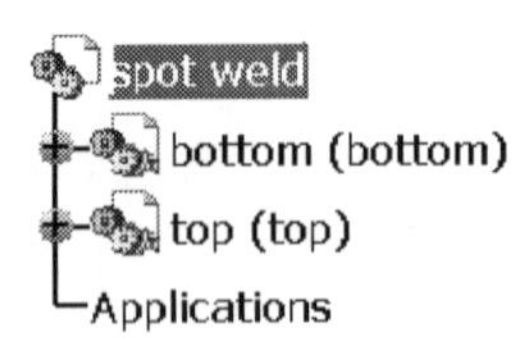


Double-click on the **top** branch in the tree so that it is highlighted in blue, as shown on the right.
This lands you in the **Wireframe and Surface Design** workbench.

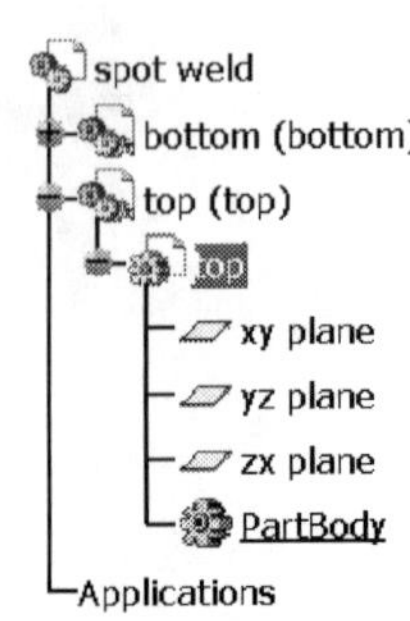

From the standard Windows toolbar, select **Insert > Geometrical Set ...** as shown.

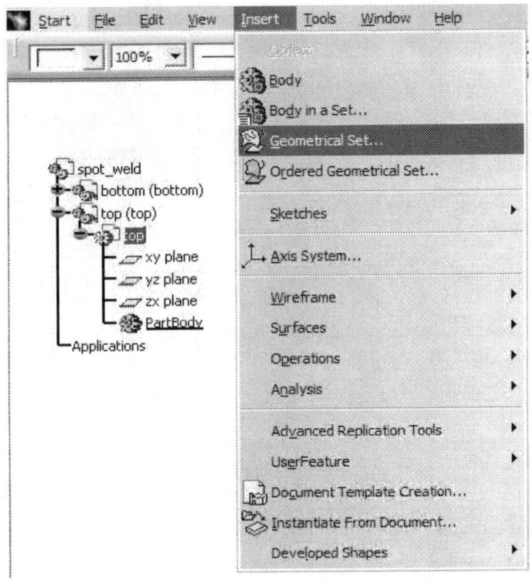


The pop up box shown below appears on the screen.
For **Name**, type **My_Second_Geometrical_Set**.
Upon closing the box, the tree is modified to reflect the set created.

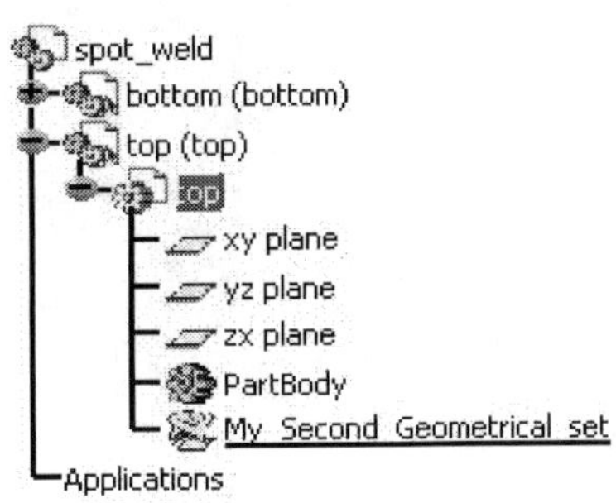


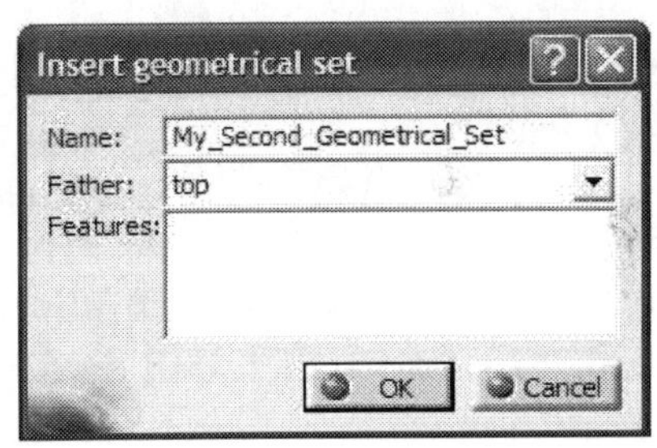


Select the **yz** plane from **top** and enter the **Sketcher**.

In the **sketcher**, draw the L-shaped line and dimension as shown in the next page.

Leave the **Sketcher**.

Note that there is 0.1 in. gap between the top and bottom plates.

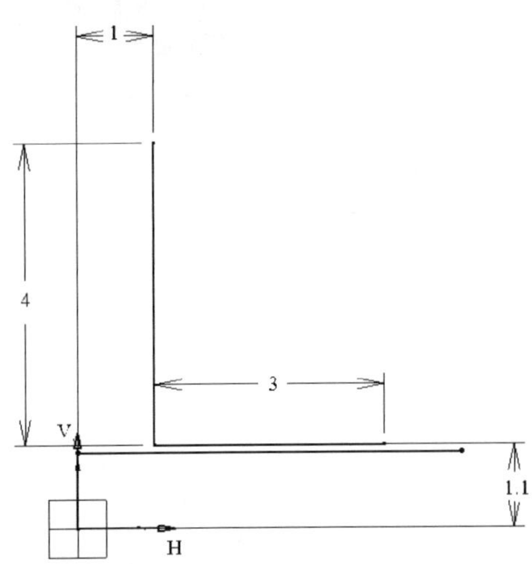

After exiting the **Sketcher**, your screen should resemble below.

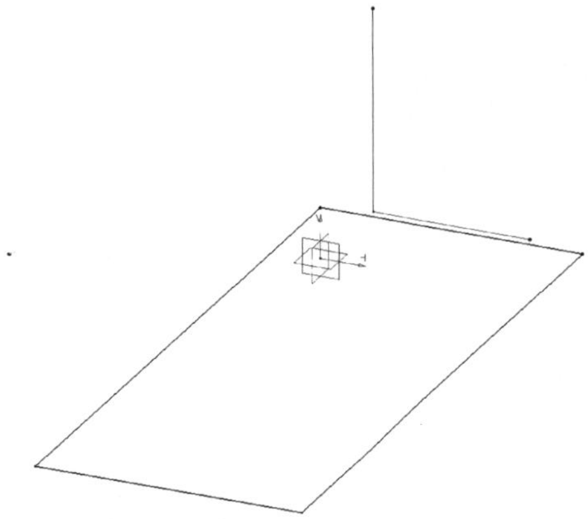

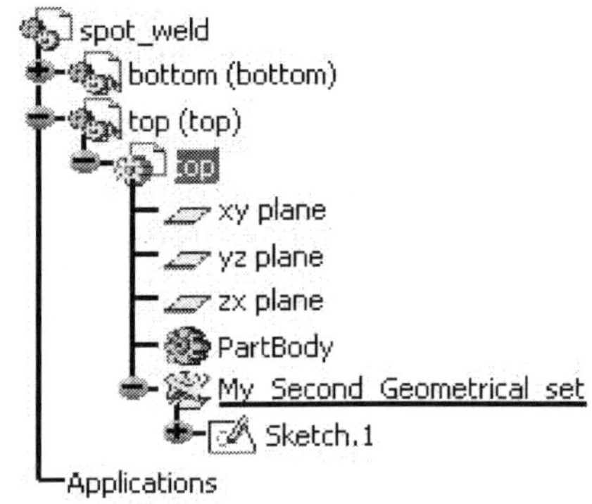


Select the **Extrude** icon 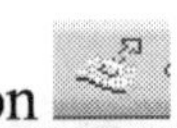 from the **Surfaces** toolbar

.

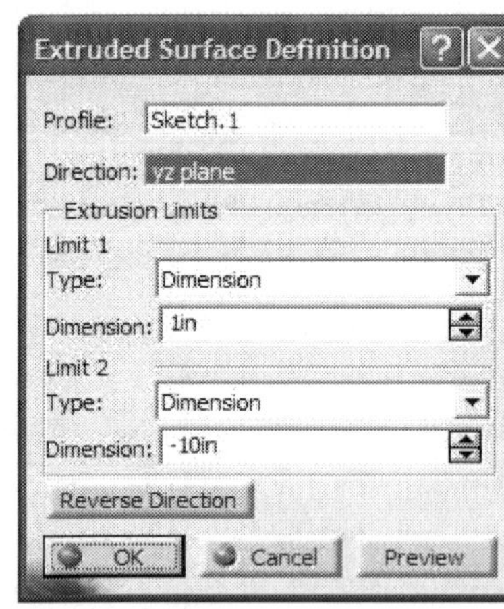


In the pop up box, shown on the right side, make the following selections.
For **Profile** choose **Sketch.1**.
The **Direction** will automatically be set as **yz**.
For **Limit 1**, type 11, and for **Limit 2**, type -10.
The result is a 3x10 in. L-plate as displayed below.

The next step is to create 4 points at the correct locations on the **top** part which will be designated as the spot welds.

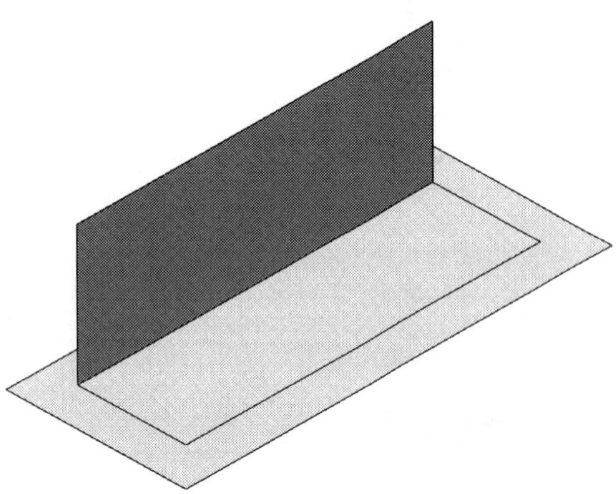

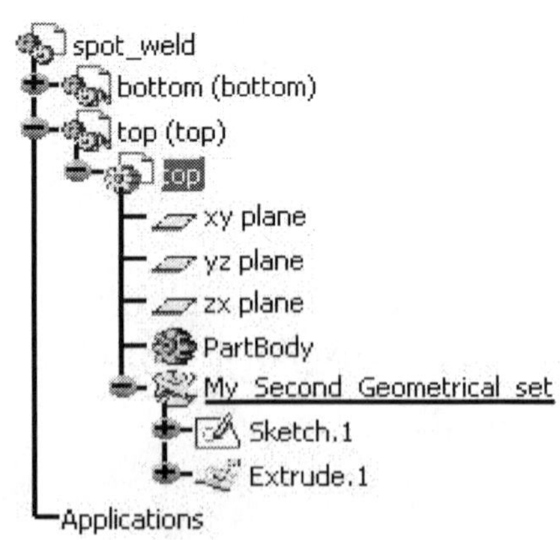


Make sure you are in the **top** part.

From the standard Windows toolbar, select **Insert > Geometrical Set ...** as shown.

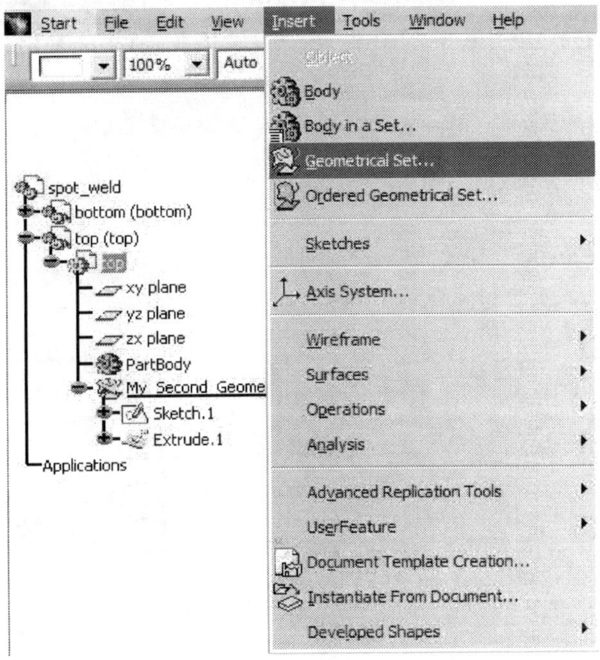

The pop up box shown on the right is appearing on the screen.
For **Name**, type **My_Third_Geometrical_Set**.
Upon closing the box, the tree is modified to reflect the set created.

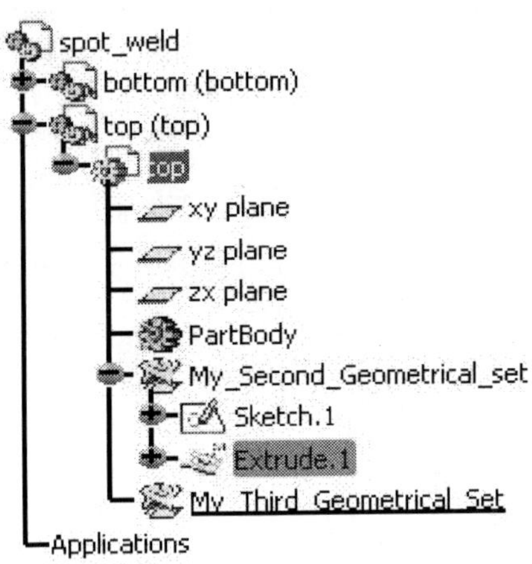

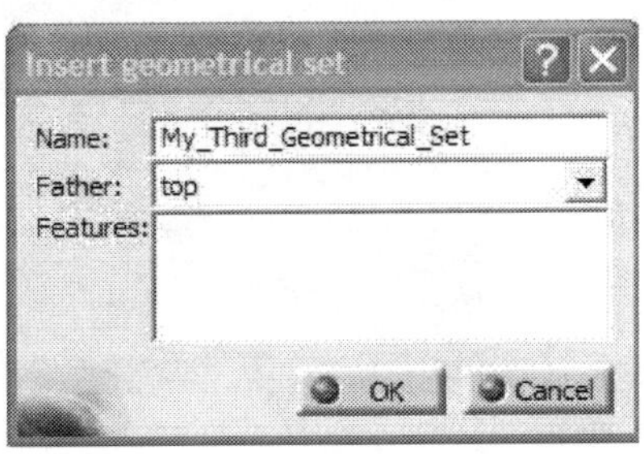

Select the **Point** icon  from the **Wireframe** toolbar 

.
In the resulting input box, type the coordinates of **Point.1** namely (3,3,1.1).

Repeat the same process three more times creating **Point.2**, **Point.3**, and **Point.4**.

The coordinates are described below.
**Point.2** has coordinates (5,3,1.1).
**Point.3** has coordinates (7,3,1.1).
**Point.4** has coordinates (9,3,1.1).

The four points and the modified tree are displayed below.

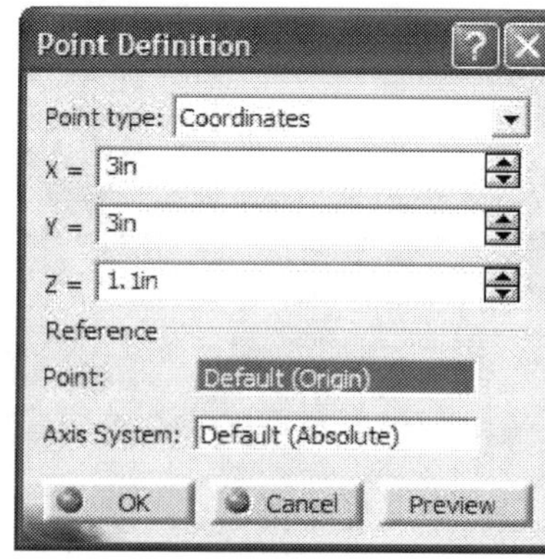


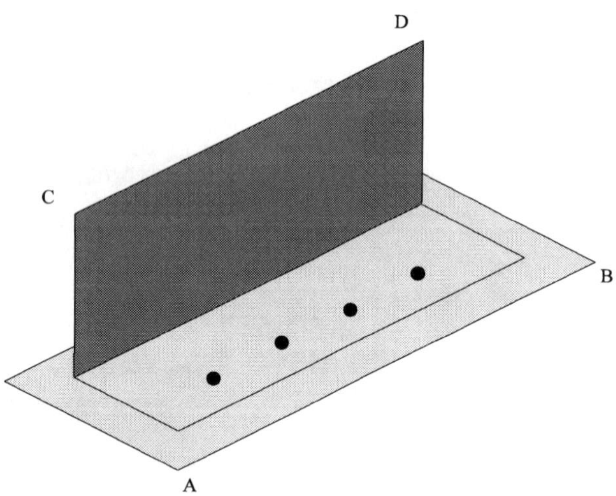


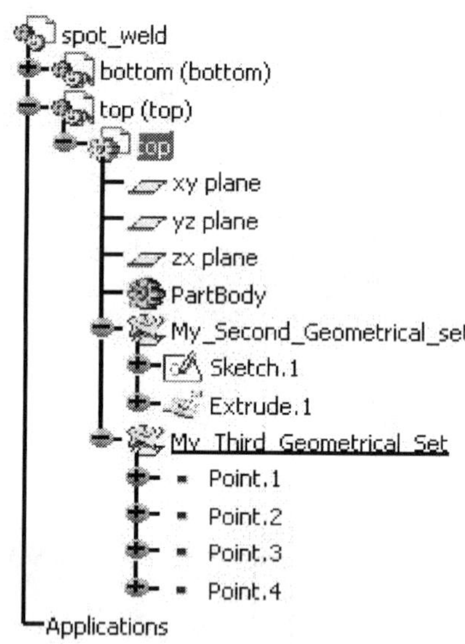


Note that, on your computer screen, you do not see "black" dots. Instead, the points are represented by "white" x-marks which may be hardly visible.

Note that the four points generated in the My_Third_Geometric_Set will be used to define the spot weld locations.

Select the **Apply Material** icon , to activate the material **Library** box below.

Use the **Metal** tab on the top; select **Steel**. Use your cursor to pick the top level <u>assembly</u> from the tree at which time the **OK** and **Apply Material** buttons can be selected. Close the box. The material property is now reflected in the tree.

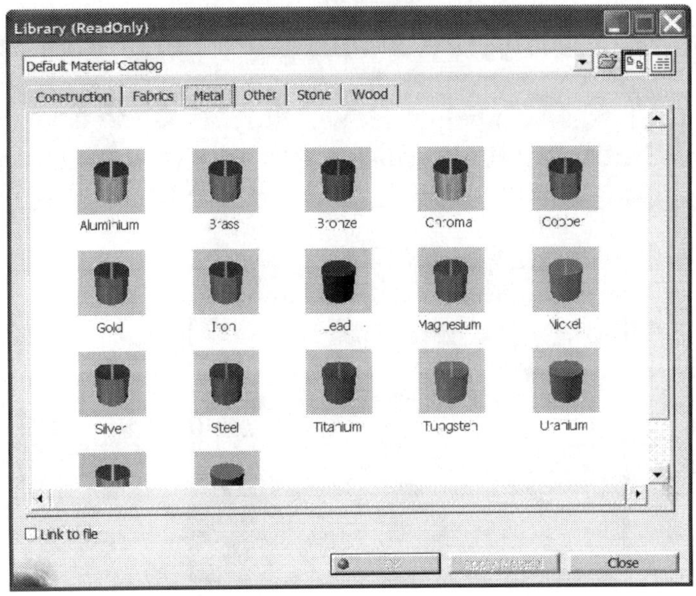


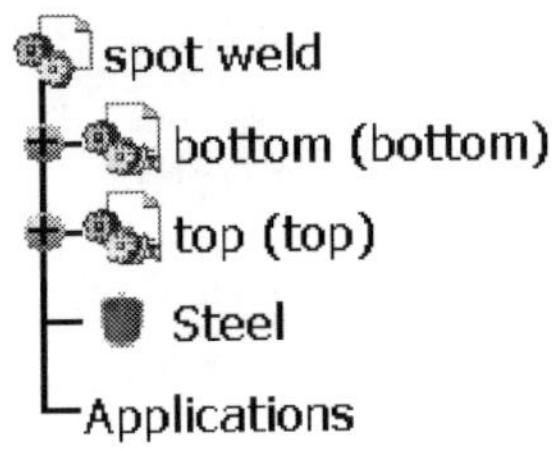


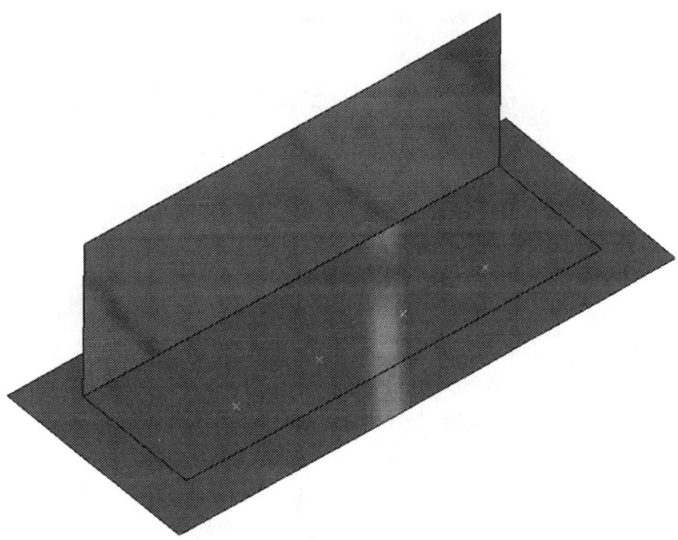

From the **View mode** toolbar 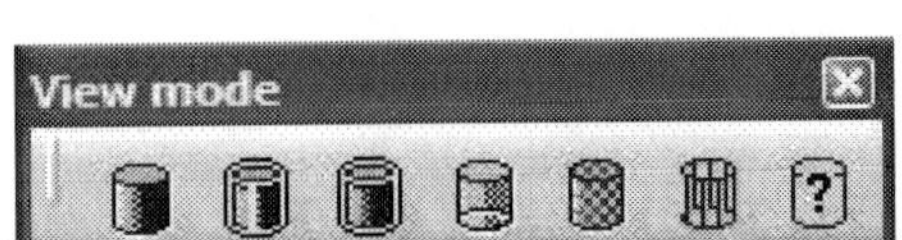

select the **Shading with Material** icon . The part now appears shaded as shown above.

## 3 Entering the Analysis Solutions

From the standard Windows toolbar, select

**Start > Analysis & Simulation > Generative Structural Analysis**

The box shown below, **New Analysis Case** is visible on the screen. The default choice is **Static Analysis** which is precisely what we intend to use. Therefore, close the box by clicking on **OK**. IGNORE THE WARNING BOX.

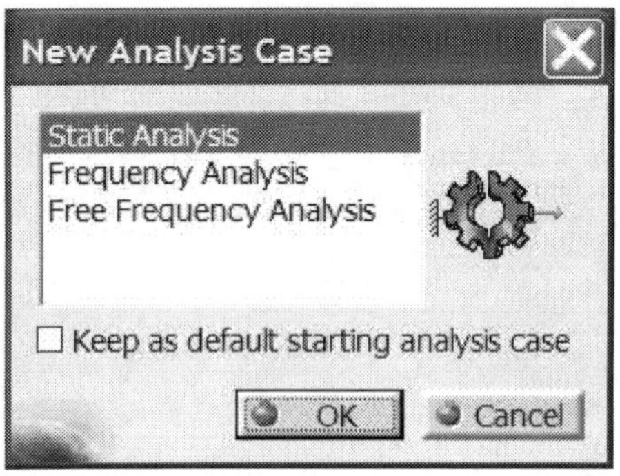


Note that the tree structure gets considerably longer. The bottom branches of the tree are presently "unfilled", and as we proceed in this workbench, assign loads and restraints, the branches gradually get "filled".

Select the **OCTREE Triangle Mesher** icon from the **Meshing Method** toolbar

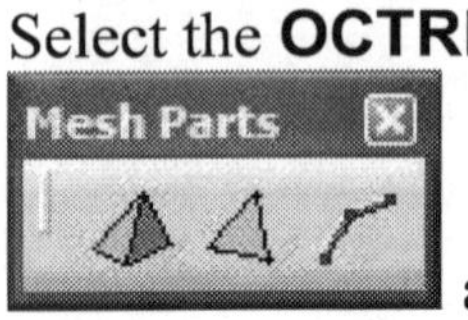


and pick the **top** surface from the screen. If tree is being used for this selection, pick the **Extrude.1** from this part.

In the pop up box, type 0.3 for **Size**.
In order to view the generated mesh, you can point the cursor to the branch **Nodes and Elements**, right-click and select **Mesh Visualization**.

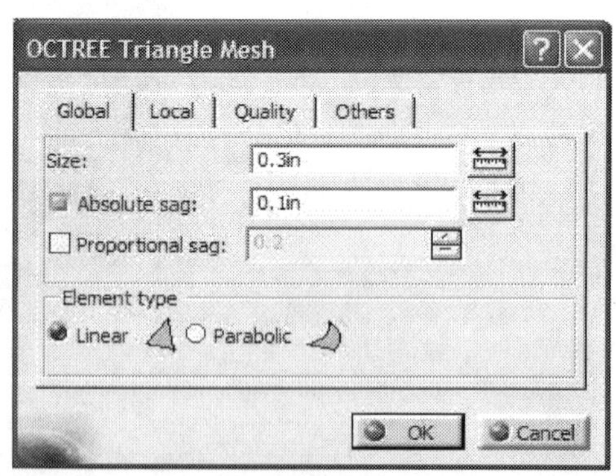


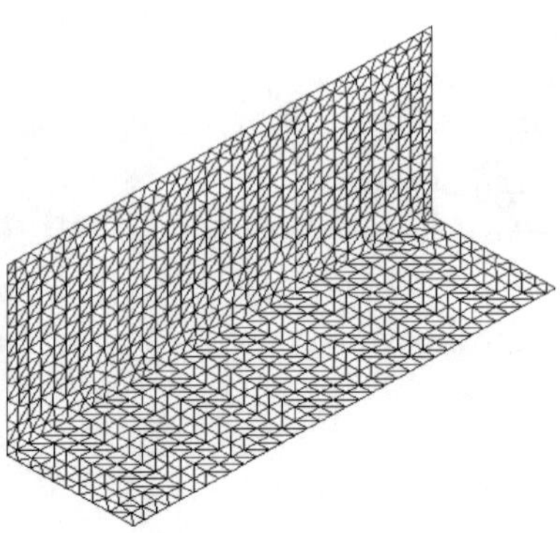

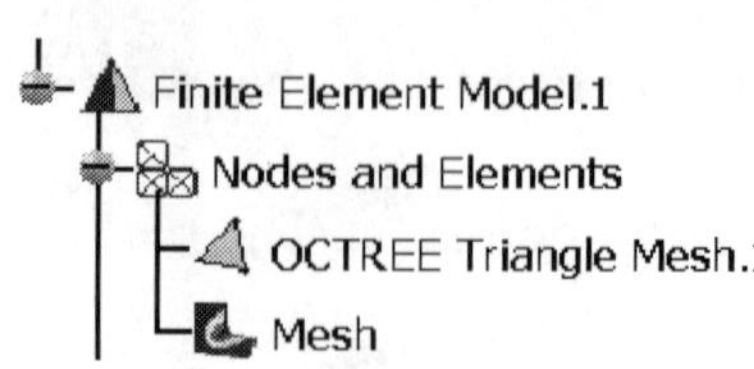

Repeat the same process as above to mesh the bottom plate where **Extrude.1** from the bottom part is selected.

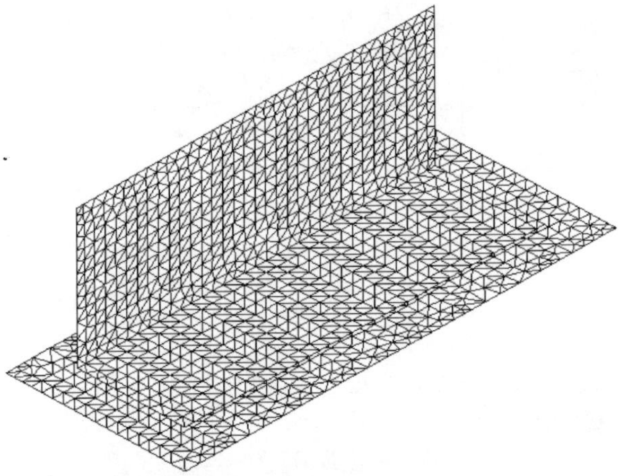

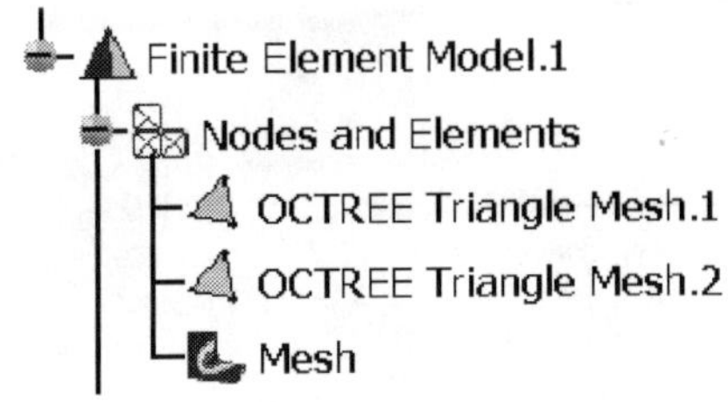


The next step is to assign the shell thicknesses. Make sure that **top** and **bottom** are in the **Show** mode; otherwise you will have to make selections from the tree.

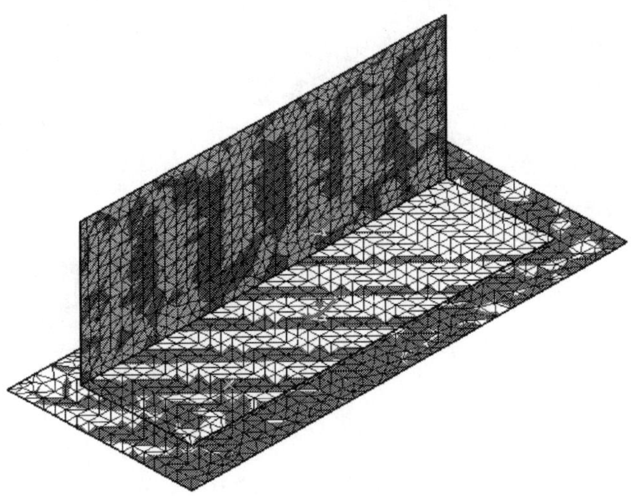

Select the **2D Property** icon  from the **Model Manager** toolbar

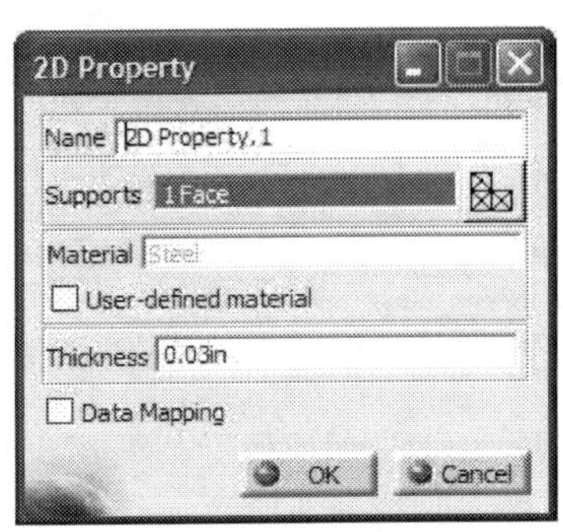


The pop up box ,shown on the right, appears. For the **Supports**, select the **Extrude.1** from the tree belonging to the **bottom** part.
The shell **Thickness** is 0.03. Note that the material is automatically picked as **Steel**.

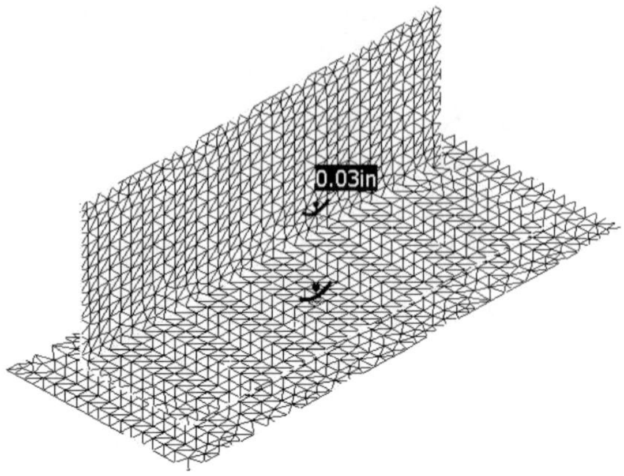

Repeat the same process with the **bottom** plate. For the **Supports**, select the **Extrude.2** from the tree belonging to the **bottom**.

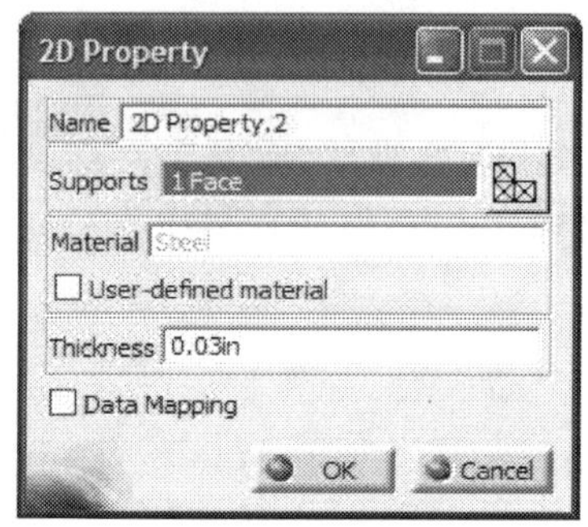


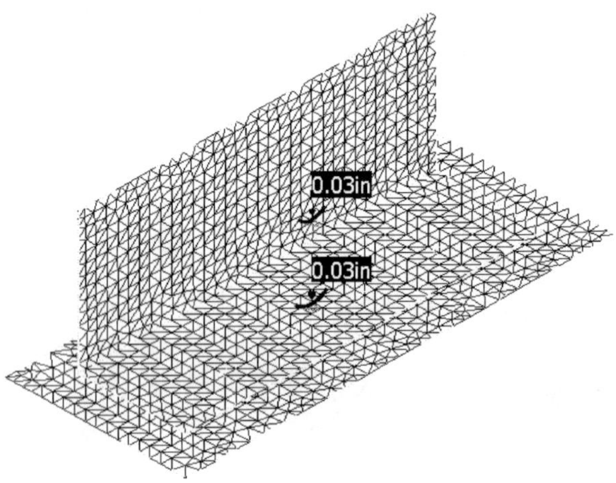


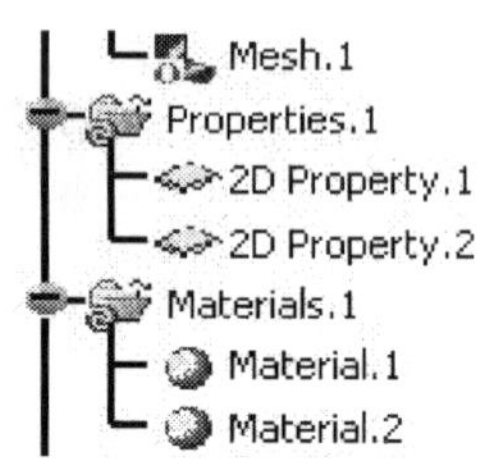


The next step is establishing a connection between the top plate, the bottom plate and the four points created earlier.

Select the **Point Analysis Connection** icon , from the **Analysis Connections** toolbar

.

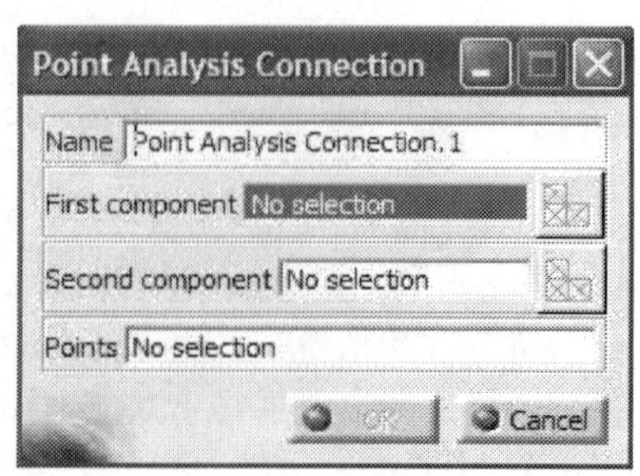

The pop up box, shown below, opens.
For **First component**, select the top plate (or **Extrude.1** from the **top** part).
For **Second component**, select the bottom plate (or **Extrude.1** from the **bottom** part).

For **Points**, select **My_Third_Geometrical_Set** from the tree or the screen. The modified pop up box is shown below.

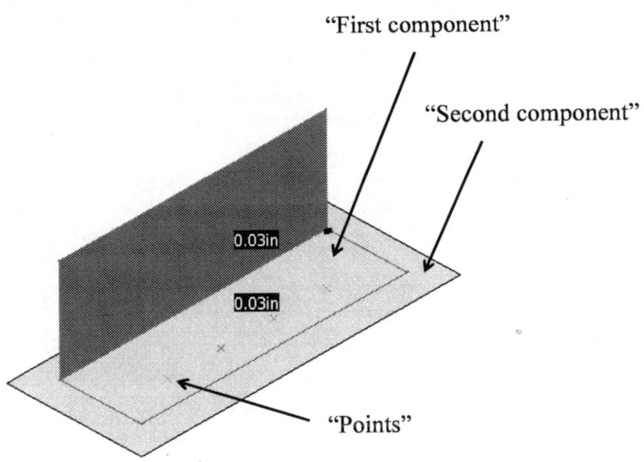


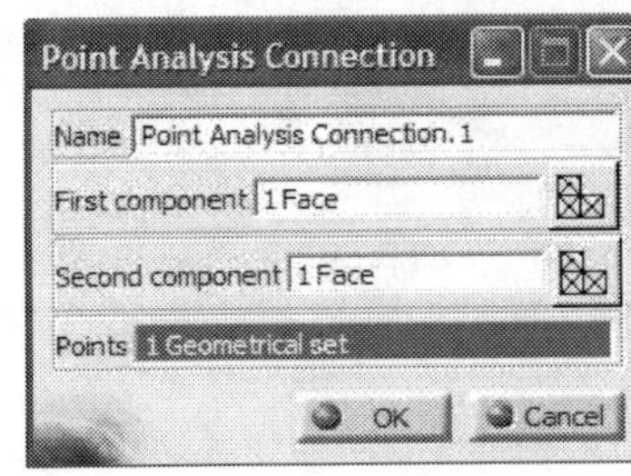


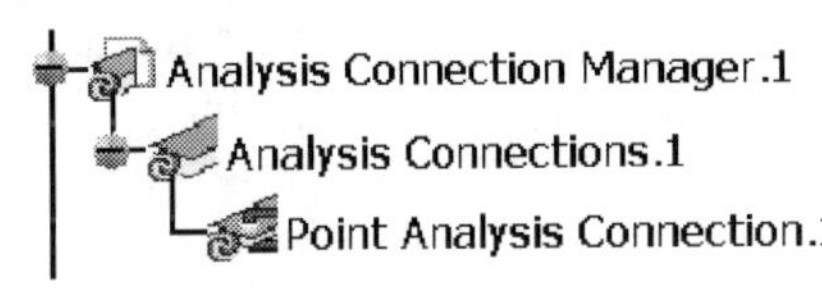


The nature of this connections is now established as a spot weld.

Select the **Spot Welding Connection property** icon  from the **Welding Connection** toolbar 

. In the pop up box, shown below, for **Supports** select the **Point Analysis connection.1** created earlier from the tree. Leave the type as **Rigid**.

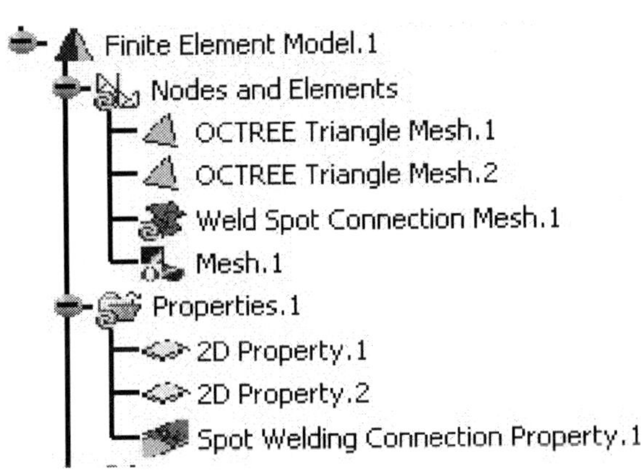


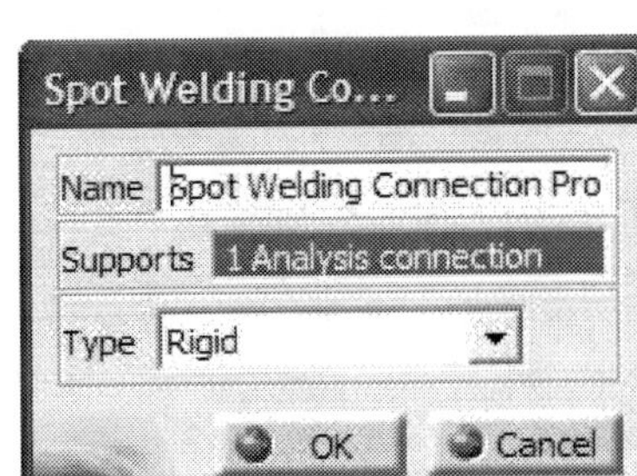

Select the **Clamp** icon from the **Restraint** toolbar, and pick the edge of the bottom plate as indicated.

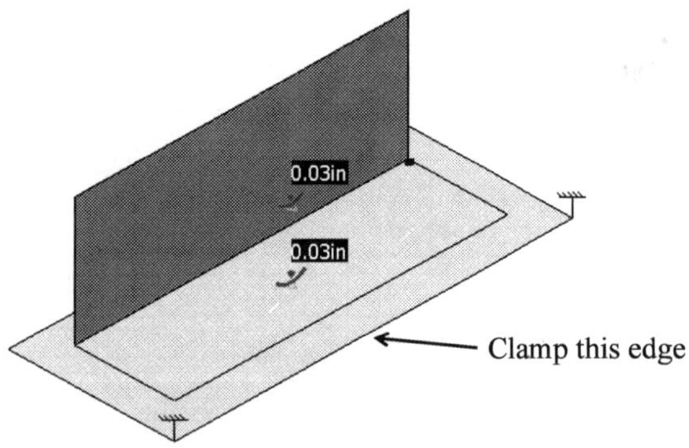


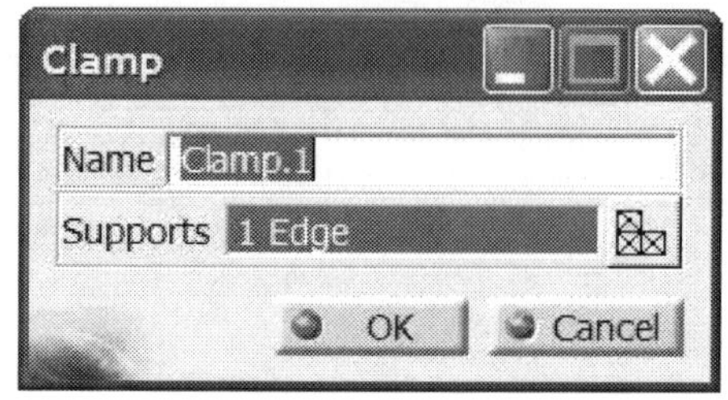


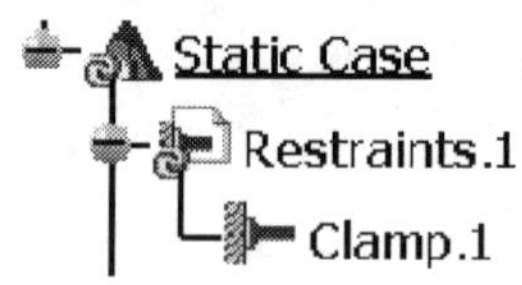


Select the **Distributed force** icon, and with the top edge shown, applying a load of 10 lb perpendicular to the face.

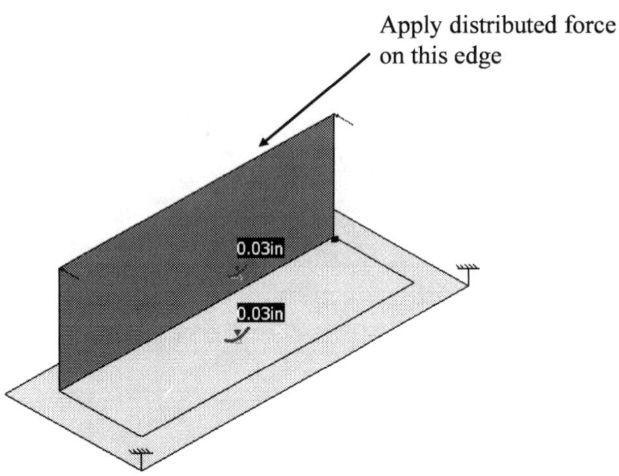


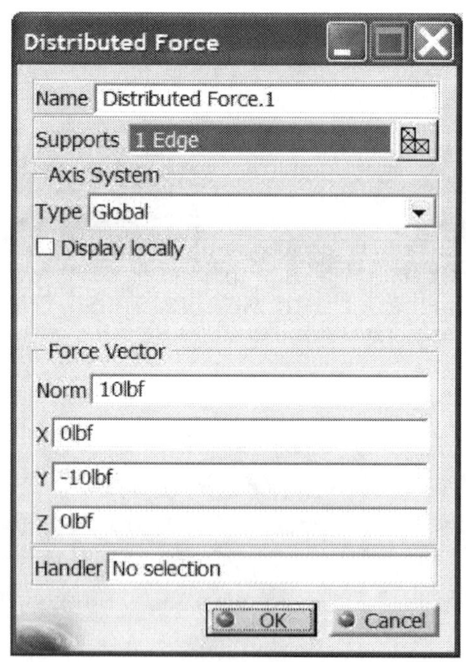


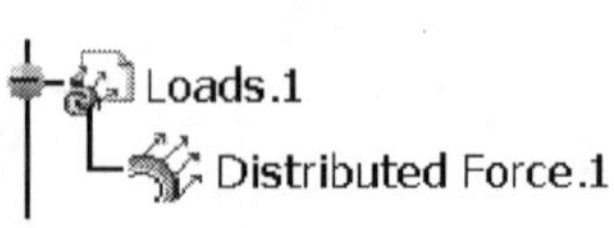

## Launching the Solver:

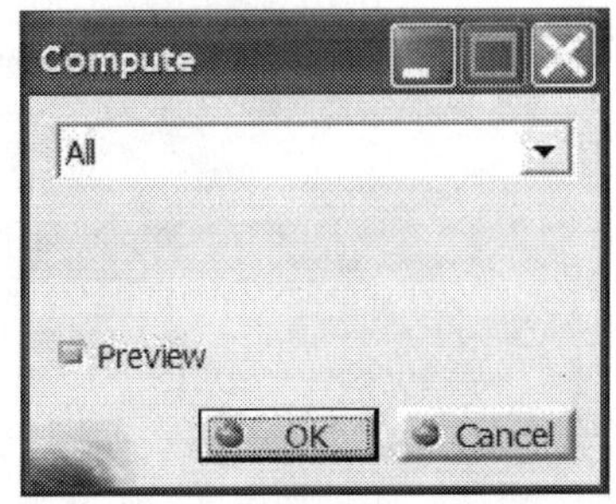


To run the analysis, you need to use the **Compute** toolbar 

by selecting the **Compute** icon . This leads to the **Compute** box shown to the right. Leave the defaults as **All** which means everything is computed.

Upon closing this box, after a brief pause, the second box shown below appears. This box provides information on the resources needed to complete the analysis.

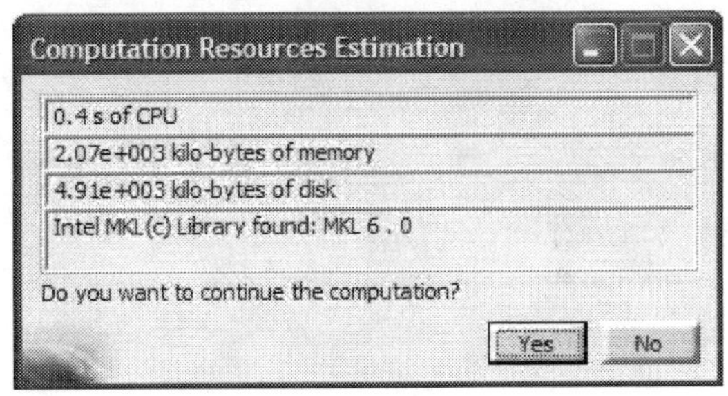


If the estimates are zero in the listing, then there is a problem in the previous step and should be looked into. If all the numbers are zero in the box, the program may run but would not produce any useful results.

## Postprocessing:

Select the **von Mises Stress** icon  in the **Image** toolbar 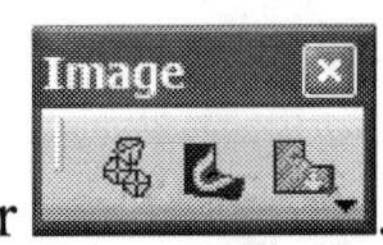
.
The stress distribution in both parts is displayed. Note that the color map has been changes; otherwise everything looks dark.

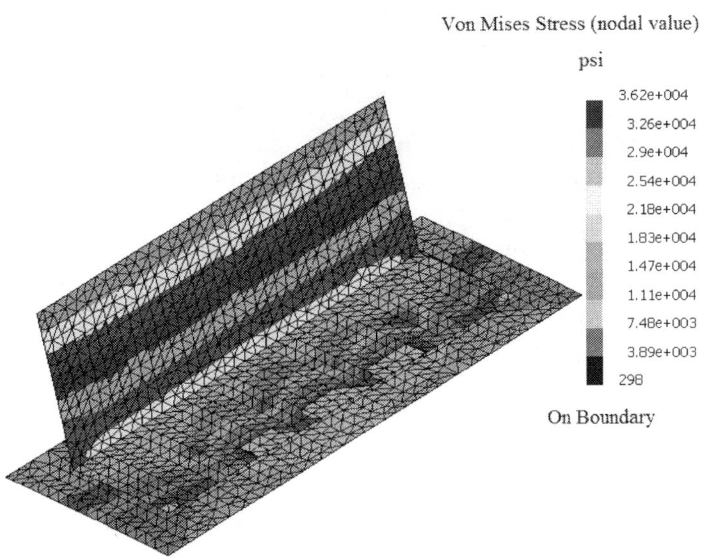

In order to see the stress distribution in the top and bottom plates separately, double-click on the contour displayed on the screen. In the pop up box shown below, pick the **Selections** tab. You can now choose the different components to be displayed.

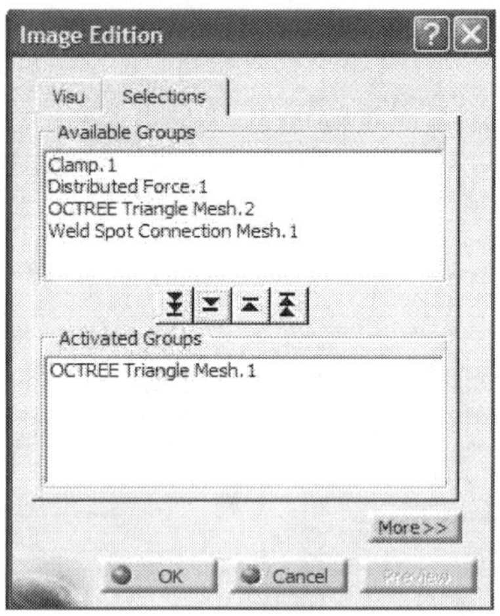


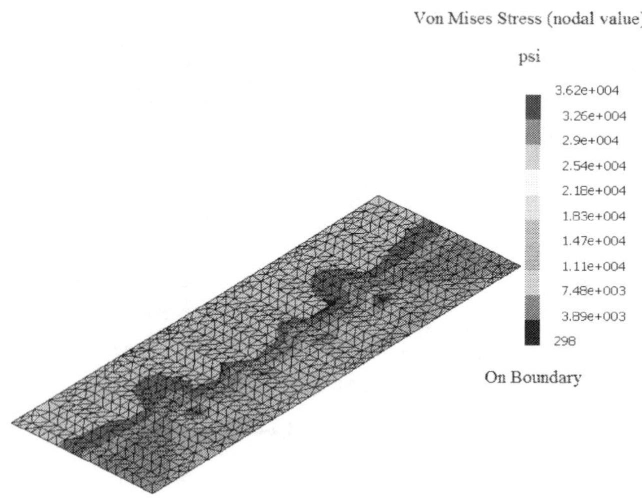


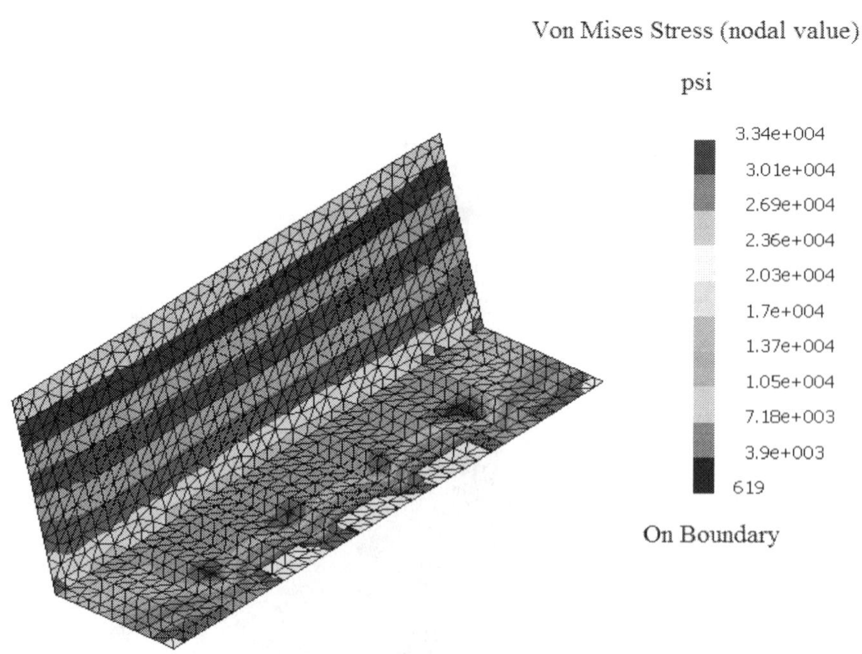

# Chapter 25

# Defining Restraints or Loads on Patches

## Introduction

In this tutorial, you will learn how to define loads on parts which have no geometric support associated with them.

## 1 Problem Statement

The aluminum plate shown below is clamped at one end and subjected to pressure load of 1000 psi on a circular patch of radius 0.25 in. The problem would have been straight forward if instead of the patch, the entire rectangular face was loaded.

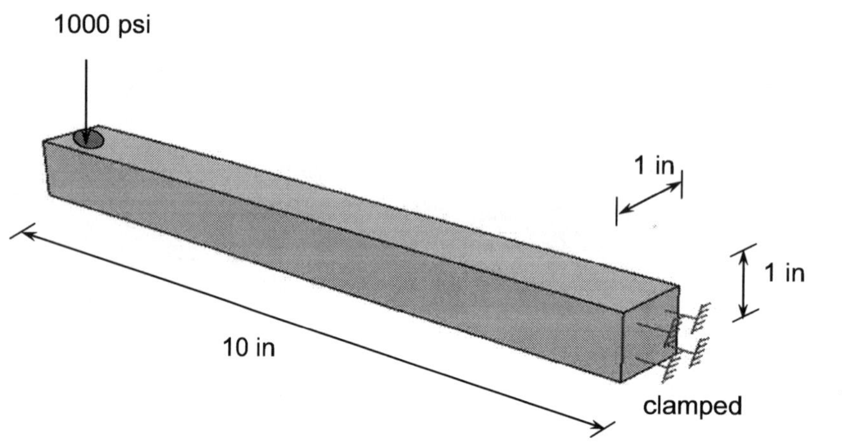


Top view, not drawn top scale

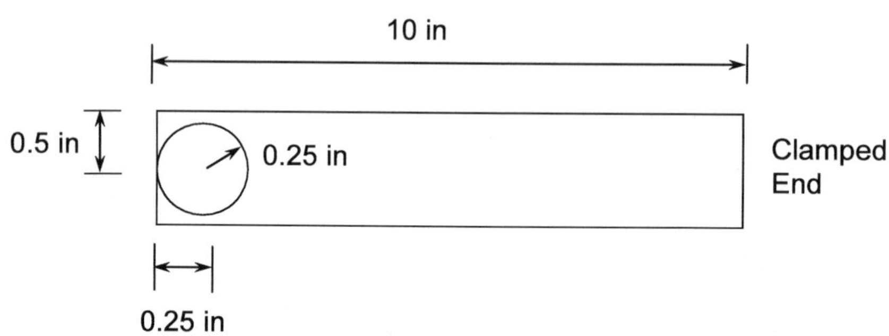


## 2 Creation of the Assembly in the Mechanical Design Solutions

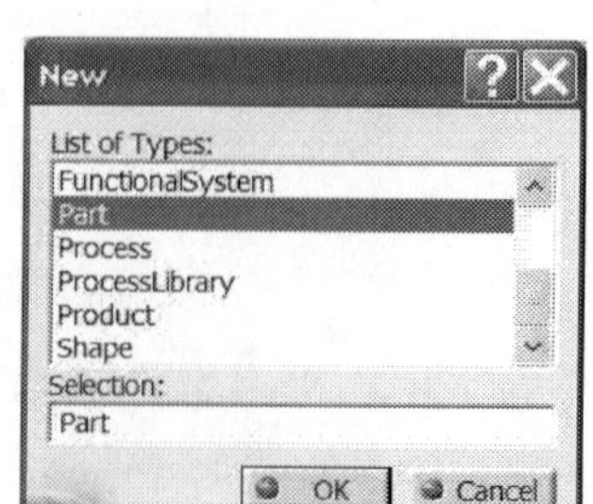


Enter the **Part Design** workbench  which can be achieved by different means depending on your CATIA customization. For example, from the standard Windows toolbar, select **File > New** 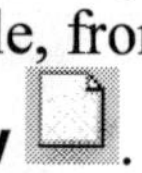.

From the box shown on the right, select **Part**. This moves you to the Part Design workbench and creates a part with the default name **Part.1**.

In order to change the default name, move the cursor to **Part.1** in the tree, right-click and select **Properties** from the menu list.

From the **Properties** box, select the **Product** tab and in **Part Number** type **patch_load**.

This will be the new part name throughout the chapter.

From the tree, select the **yz** plane and enter the **Sketcher**. In the Sketcher, draw a **centered rectangle** and dimension it as shown. Leave the **Sketcher**.

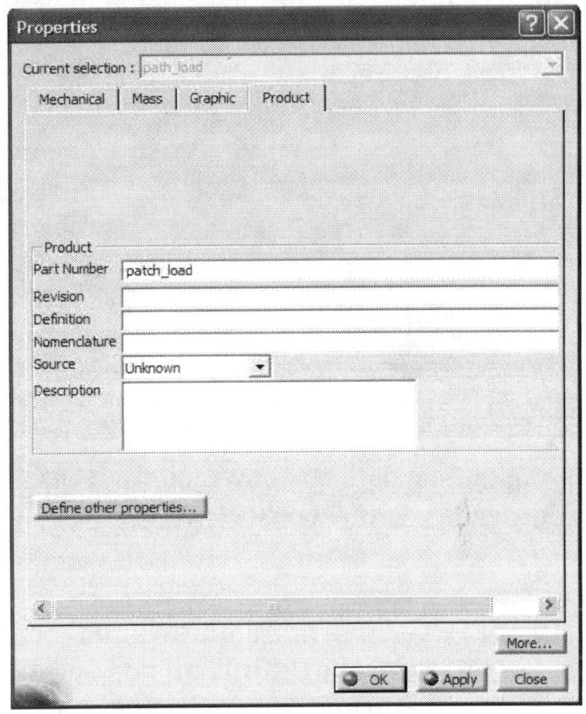


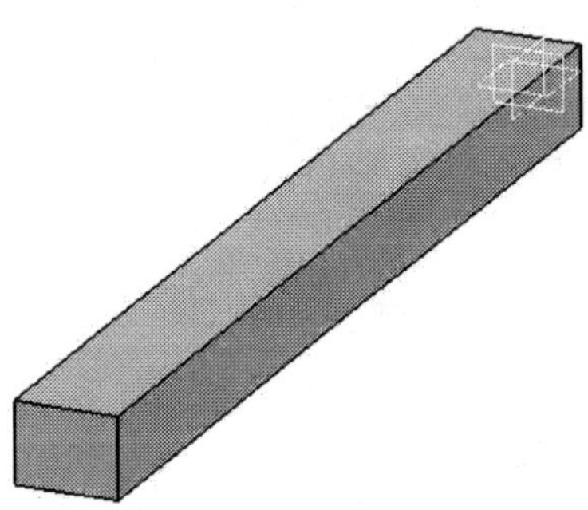

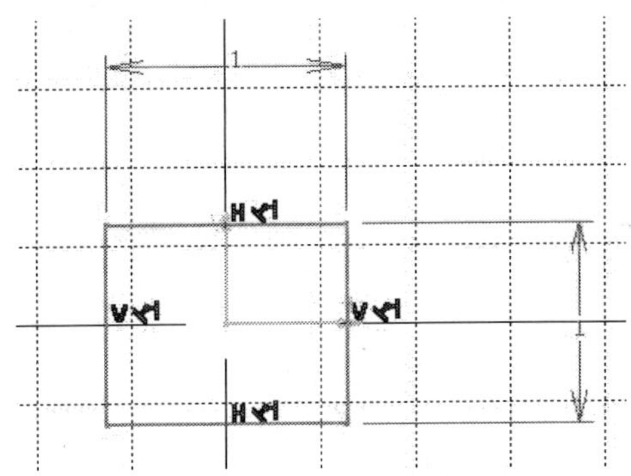

You will now use the **Pad** operation to extrude the sketch. Upon selecting the **Pad** icon, the pad definition box shown to the right opens. For **Length** use 10.in.

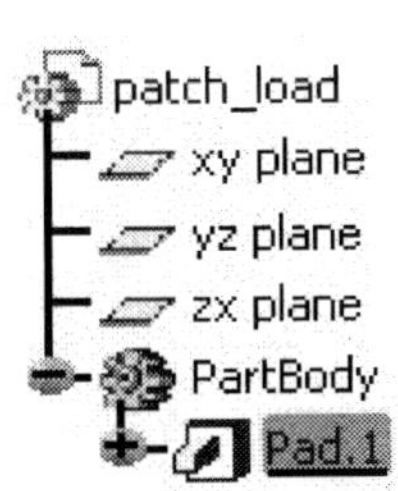


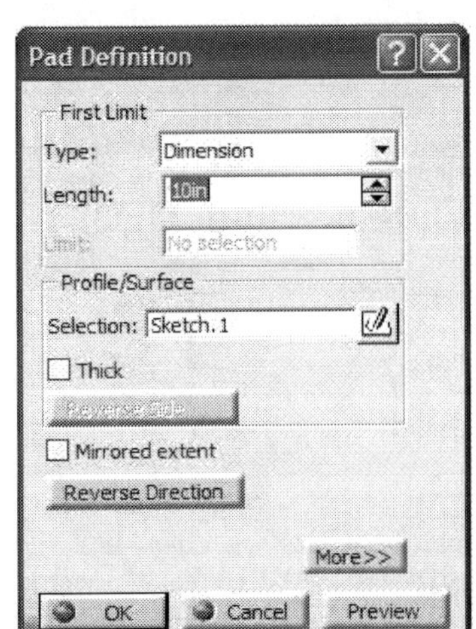

Select the top surface of the block just created and enter the **Sketcher**. Use the **Circle** icon to draw a circle of radius 1 as shown. Leave the **Sketcher**.

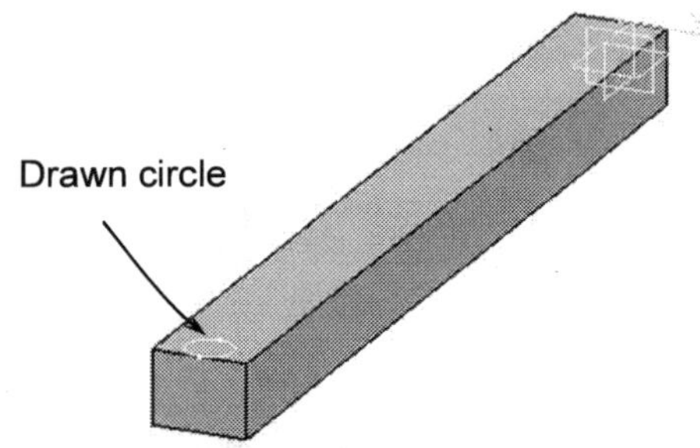


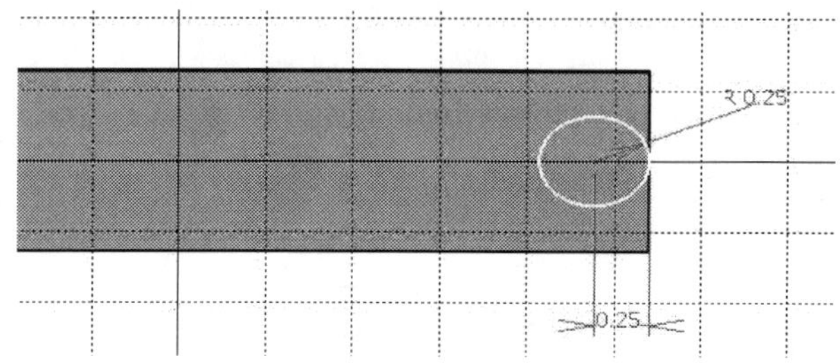


From the standard Windows toolbar, select **Start > Wireframe and Surface Design**. This lands you in the **Wireframe and Surface Design** workbench.

Use the **Fill** icon from **Surfaces** toolbar

.

In the **Fill Surface Definition** pop up box, for **Boundary Curves**, select **Sketch.2**. Close the box.

The outcome is a surface patch with **Sketch.2** as its boundary.

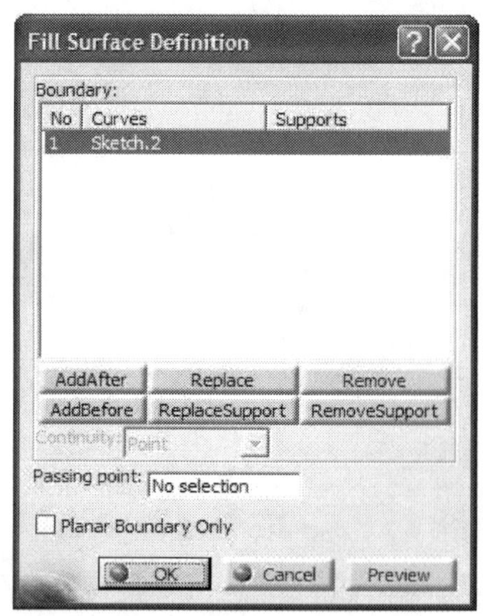


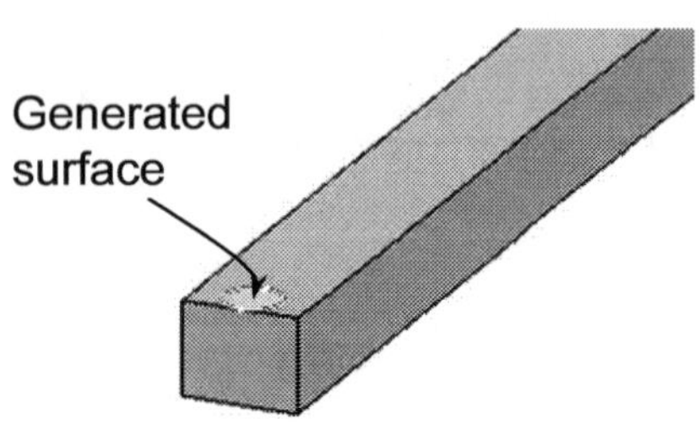


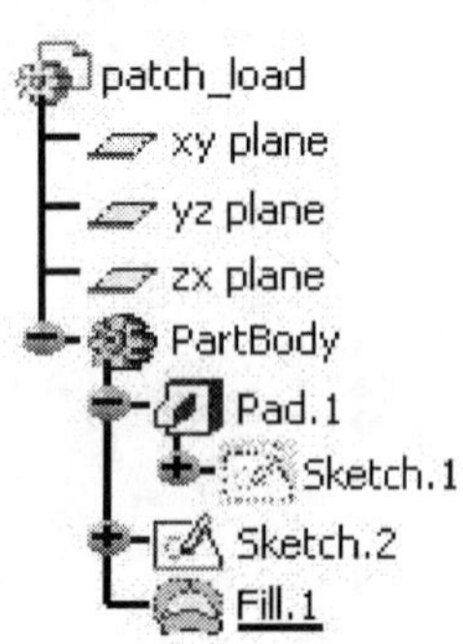


The specification tree at this point is displayed for your reference.
Switch to the **Part Design** workbench.

At this point we apply the default aluminum material properties to the part. Select the **Apply Material** icon . The use of this icon opens the material database box below.

Use the **Metal** tab on the top; select **Aluminum**. Use your cursor to pick the part on the screen at which time the **OK** and **Apply Material** buttons can be selected.
Close the box.
The material property is now reflected in the tree.

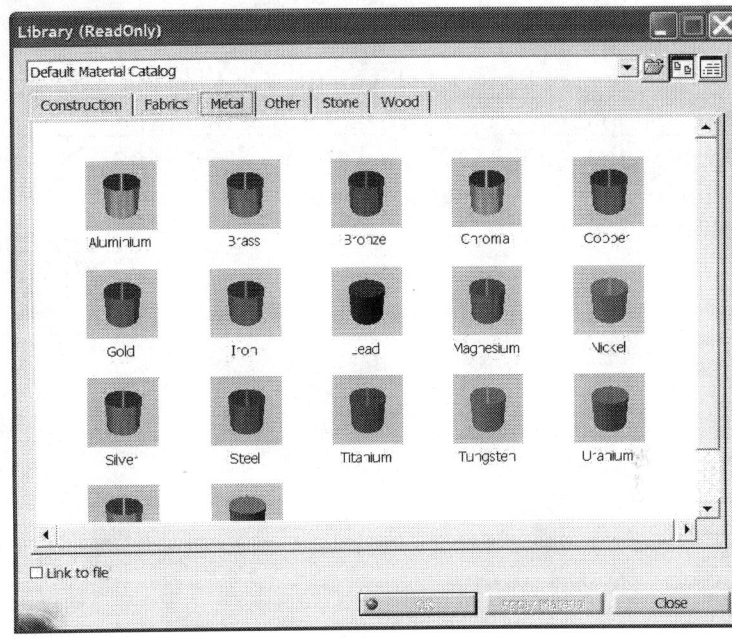


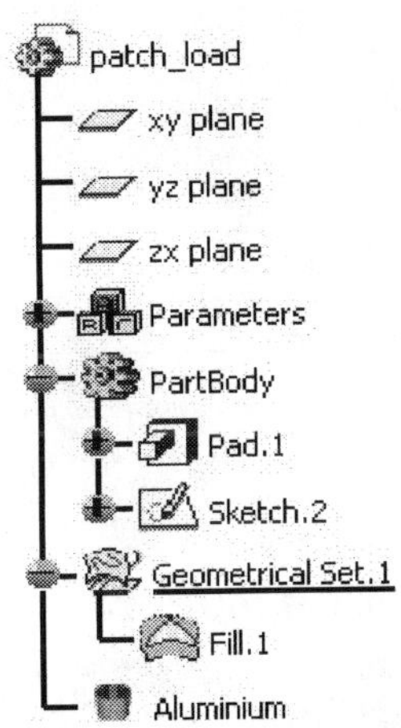


## 3 Entering the Analysis Solutions

From the standard Windows tool bar, select

**Start > Analysis & Simulation > Generative Structural Analysis** 

The box shown below, **New Analysis Case** is visible on the screen. The default choice is **Static Analysis** which is precisely what we intend to use. Therefore, close the box by clicking on **OK**.

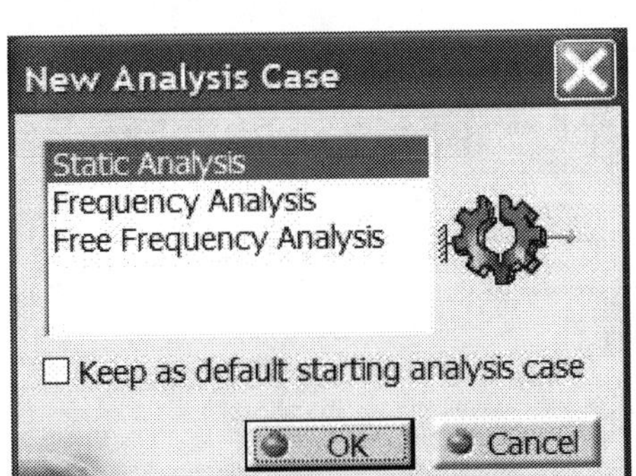

**Important Note:**
The block has been automatically meshed with solid tetrahedron elements. The created patch however has no mesh associated with it. The patch is not a finite element entity at this point.

**Refining the mesh on the top surface:**
The reader may be puzzled with the need for the next step. However, to have a better idea of the adopted approach, we will refine the mesh on the top face of the block.
Double-click on the **Octree Tetrahedron Mesh** branch of the tree.
In the resulting dialogue box make sure that **Linear** is selected. This is to avoid excessive computation time.

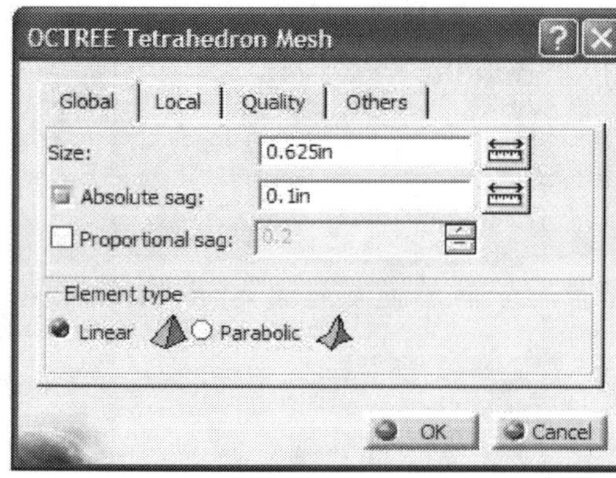


Select the **Local Mesh Size** icon  from the **Mesh Specification** toolbar 

. In the pop up box, for the **Supports** select the top face of the block, and for **Value** type 0.1.

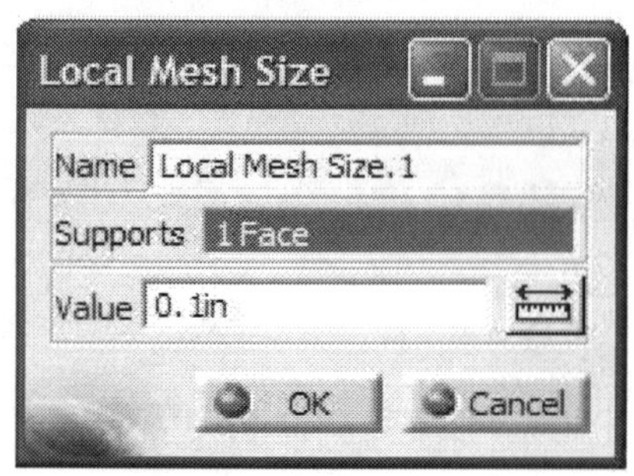


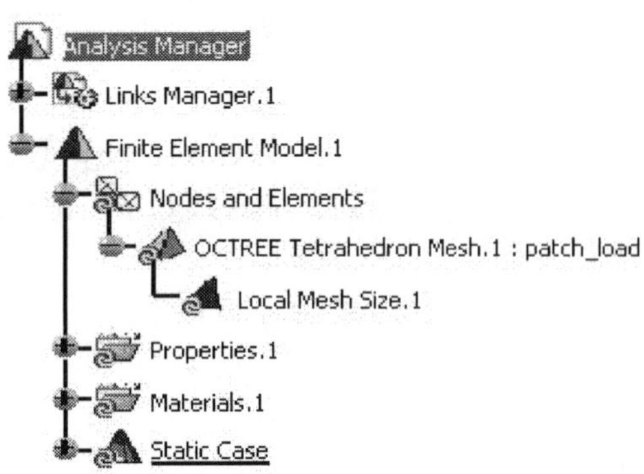


To see the locally refined mesh, point the cursor to the branch **Nodes and Elements** in the tree, right-click and select **Mesh Visualization**.

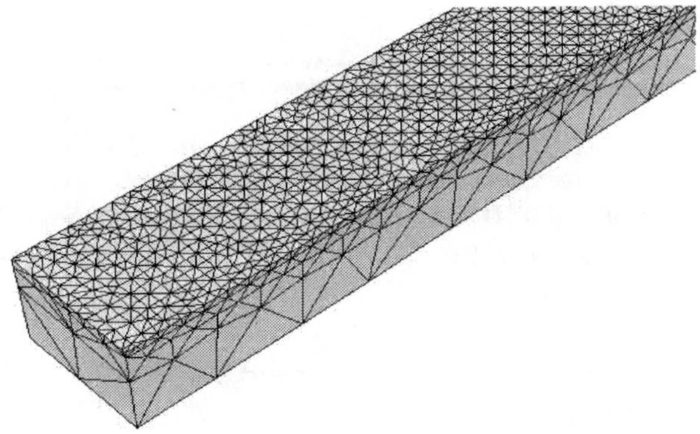

To proceed with the rest of the problem, point the cursor to the branch of the tree, containing the mesh plot, right-click and select **Activate/Deactivate**.

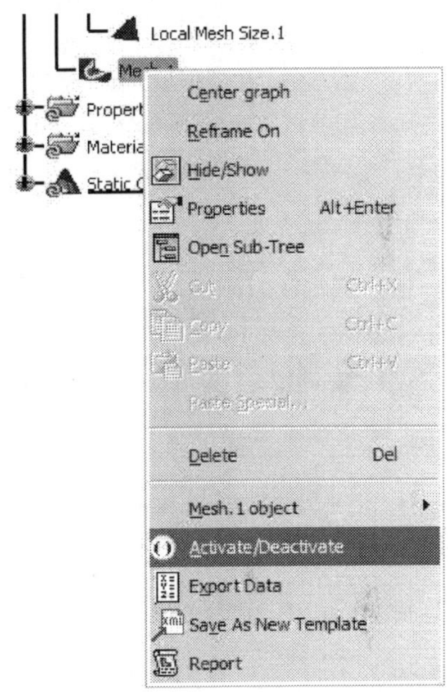


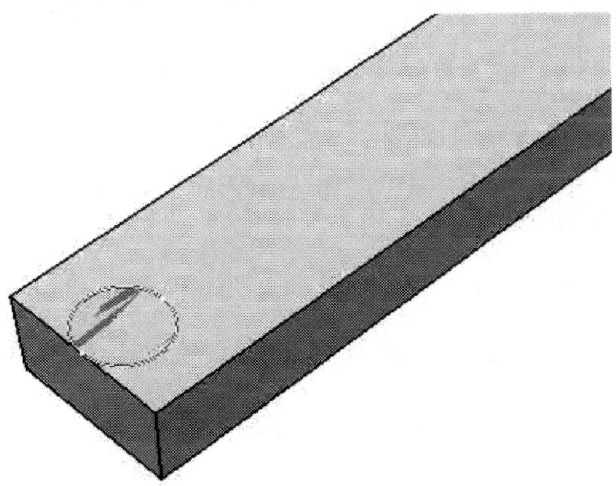

## Creating a Surface Group by Neighborhood:

Select the **Surface Group by Neighborhood** icon  from the **Groups by Neighborhood** toolbar 

.

In the resulting pop up box, for **Supports** select the circular patch created earlier, and for **Tolerance** use 0.000001 in. Close the box by choosing **OK**.

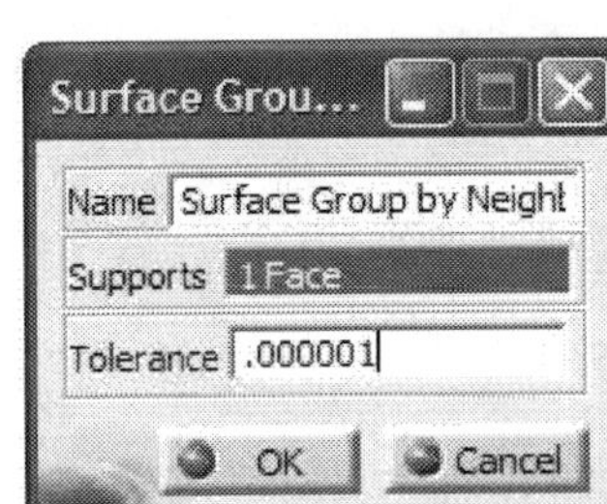


The group is recorded in the tree.

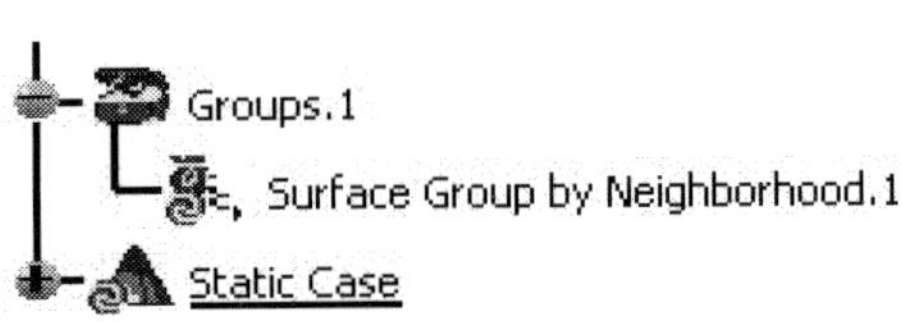

## Applying Loads:

In FEA, loads refer to forces. The **Load** toolbar 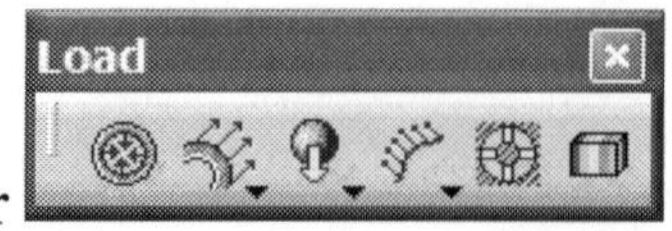

is used for this purpose. Click on the **Pressure** icon 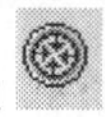; for **Supports** select **Surface Group by Neighborhood.1** from the tree. For **Pressure**, input **1000** psi.

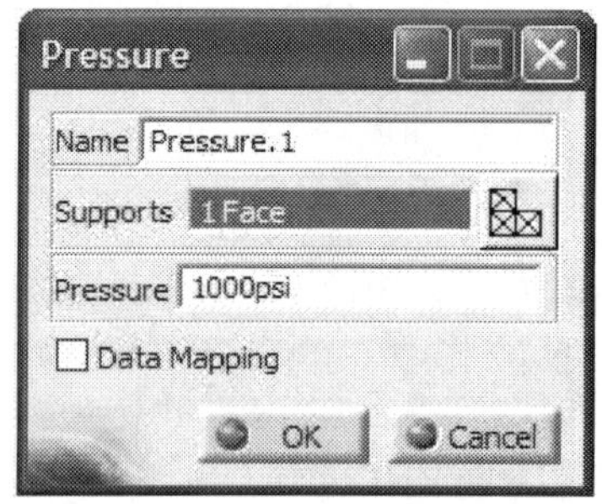


## Applying Restraints:

In FEA, restraints refer to applying displacement boundary conditions which is achieved through the **Restraint** toolbar 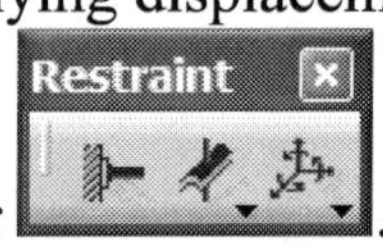

.
The **Clamp** condition means that the displacements in all three directions are zero. Select the **Clamp** icon  and pick the side face for the block as shown below.

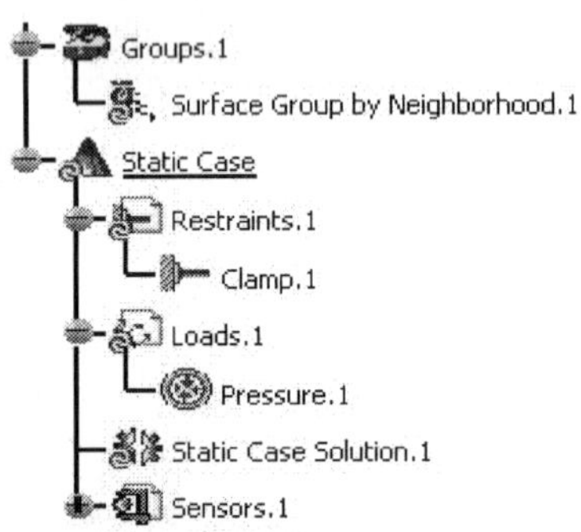


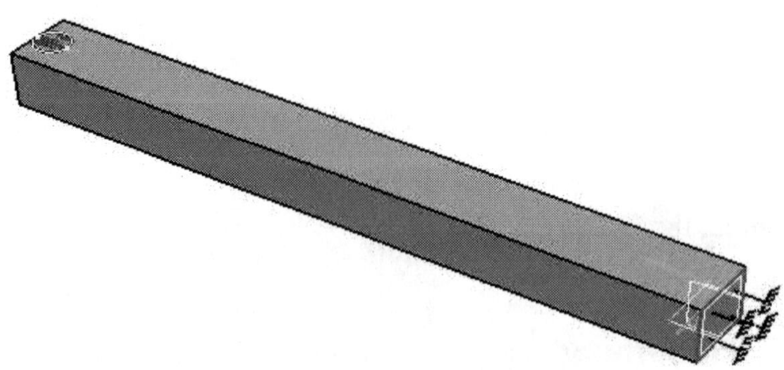

### Launching the Solver:

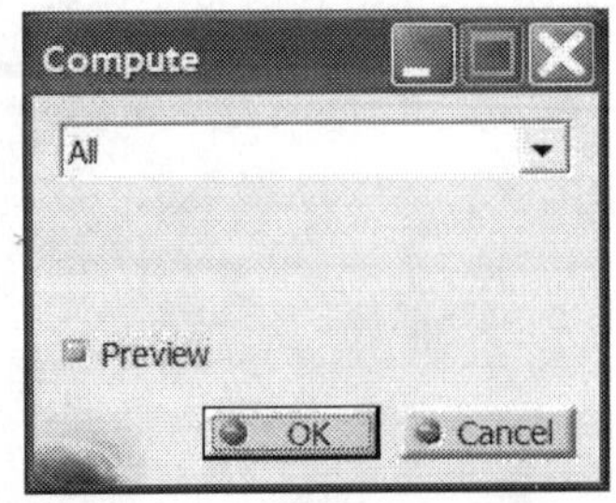


To run the analysis, you need to use the **Compute** toolbar 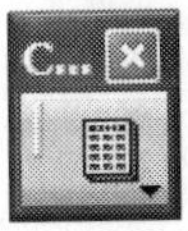

by selecting the **Compute** icon . This leads to the **Compute** box shown to the right. Leave the defaults as **All** which means everything is computed.

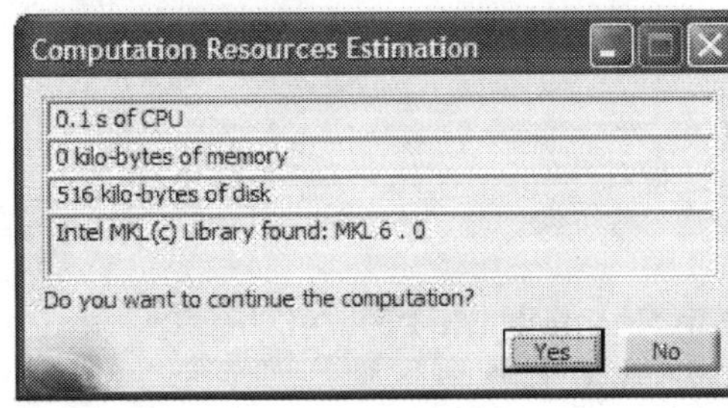


Upon closing this box, after a brief pause, the second box shown below appears. This box provides information on the resources needed to complete the analysis.
If the estimates are zero in the listing, then there is a problem in the previous step and should be looked into. If all the numbers are zero in the box, the program may run but would not produce any useful results.

### Postprocessing:

The main postprocessing toolbar is called **Image** 

. To view the deformed shape you have to use the **Deformation** icon 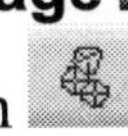. The resulting deformed shape is displayed below.

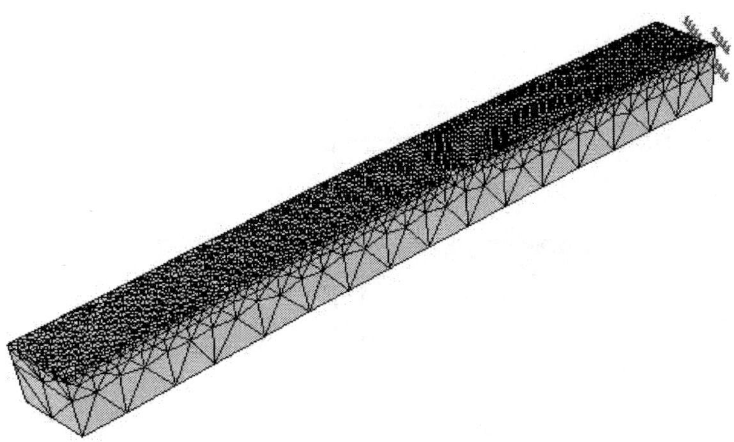

This plot does not reveal much information. In particular it is not clear whether the load has been applied on the desired location. To see this, plot the C33 components of the principal stress. Select the **Principal Stress** icon 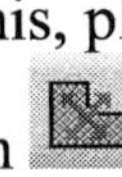 from the **Other Image** toolbar 

.

The principal stresses are plotted in the vector form as shown below.

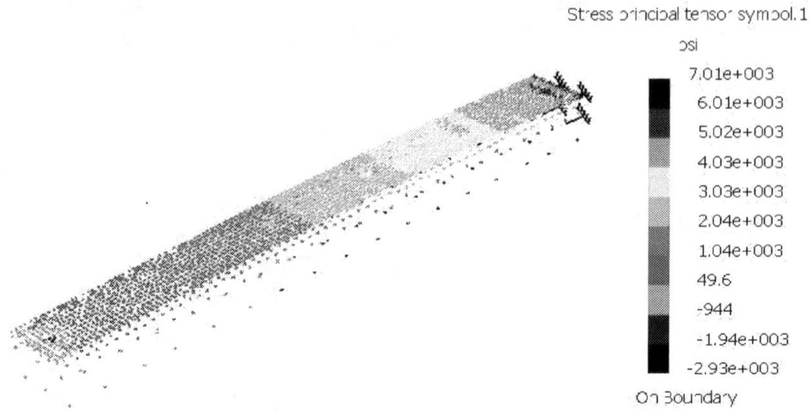


Double-click the plot on the screen. From the **Image Edition** pop up box, select **Average iso**.

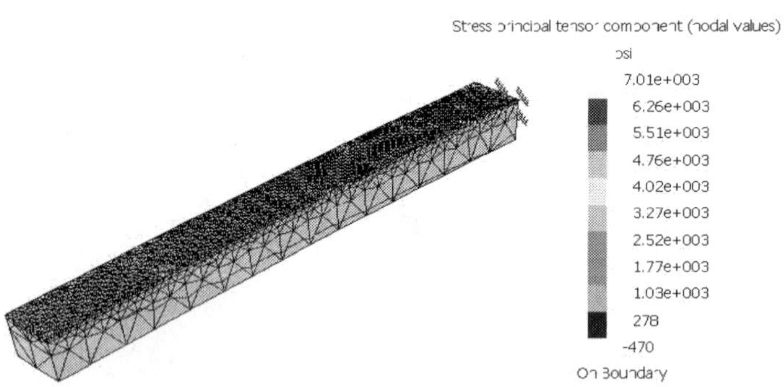


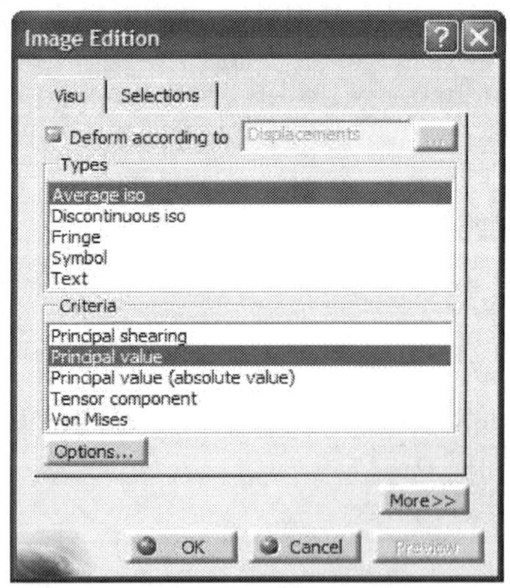


Use the **Selections** tab; from the list, choose **Surface Group by Neighborhoods.1** and click on ⩡.

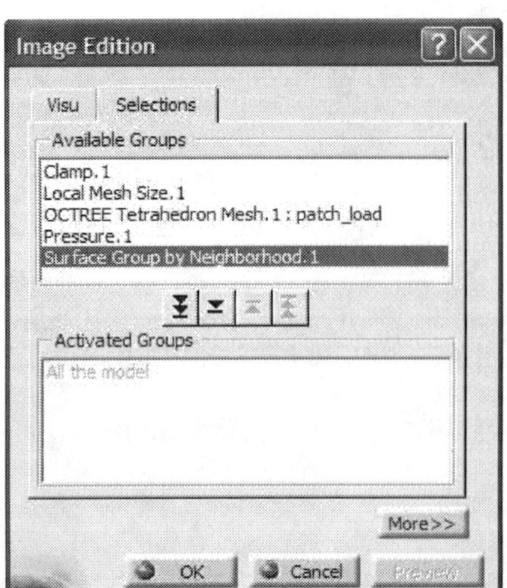


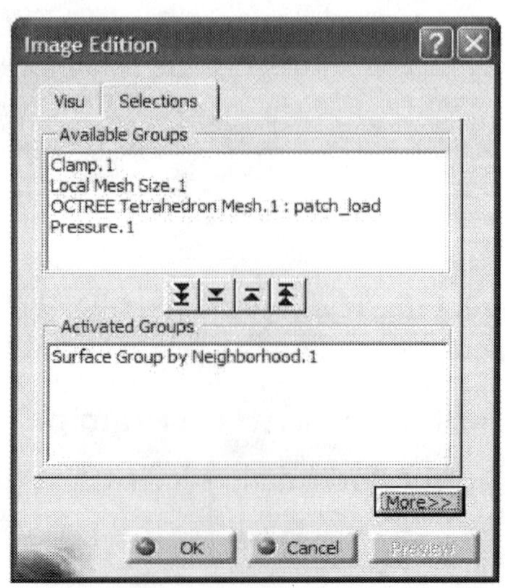

Select the more button to expand the dialogue box More>>.

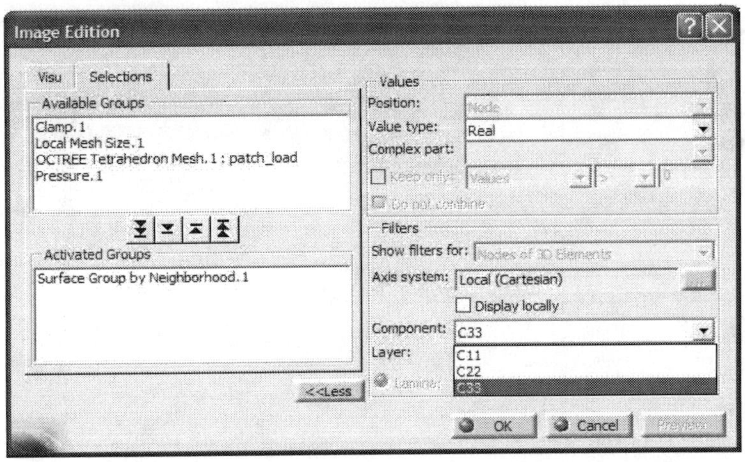


For **Components** select **C33**. This is the smallest component of principal stress. The circular pattern clearly indicates that the pressure of 1000 psi was applied in the desired location.

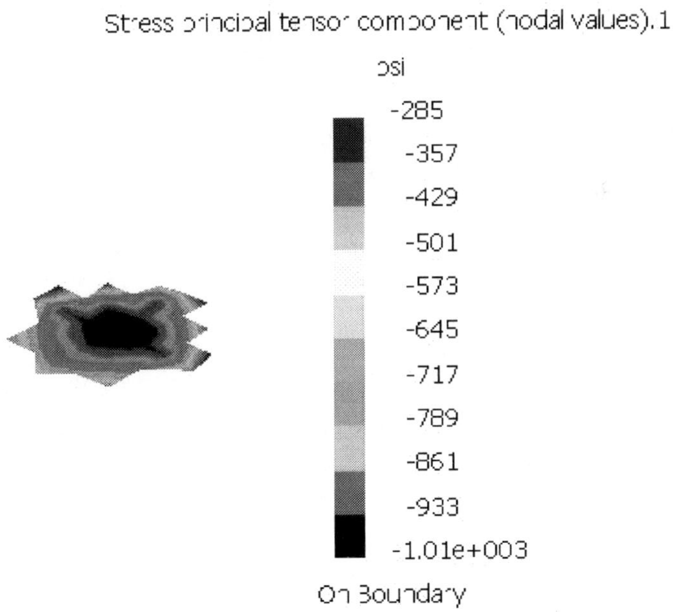

# NOTES:

# Chapter 26

# Limited Hexahedral Element Capabilities

## Introduction

In this tutorial, you will experiment with the hexahedral elements in CATIA V5. These elements are obtained by dragging shell elements in a prescribed direction. The Hex capabilities are very limited and do not enjoy all the functionalities of the tetrahedral elements in CATIA.

## 1 Problem Statement

A steel rectangular block having a central hole is being pulled from both ends as shown. The dimensions of the block are described below and the resulting stress at the end faces is 100 psi. The block is to be modeled without taking symmetry into consideration and hexahedral elements are to be used. The block's thickness is assumed to be 2 inches.

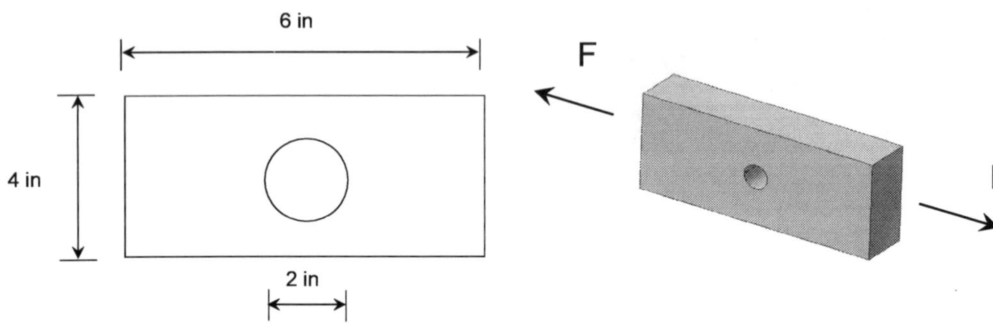


## 2 Creation of the Assembly in the Mechanical Design Solutions

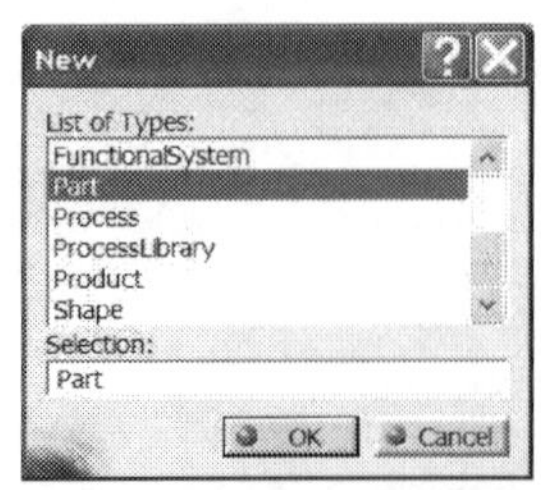


Enter the **Part Design** workbench which can be achieved by different means depending on your CATIA customization. For example, from the standard Windows toolbar, select **File > New**. Read Note #1 in Appendix I.

From the box shown on the right, select **Part**. This moves you to the **Part Design** workbench and creates a part with the default name **Part.1**.

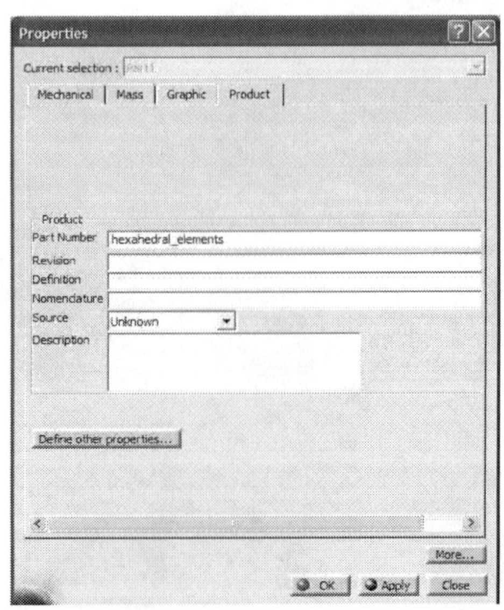


In order to change the default name, move the cursor to **Part.1** in the tree, right-click and select **Properties** from the menu list.

From the **Properties** box, select the **Product** tab and in **Part Number** type **hexahedral_elements**.

This will be the new part name throughout the chapter.

From the tree, select the **yz** plane and enter the **Sketcher**. In the **Sketcher**, draw a rectangle and dimension it.

Use the **Circle** icon to draw a circle of radius 1 centered in the rectangle. Leave the **Sketcher**.

You will now use the **Pad** operation to extrude the sketch. Upon selecting the **Pad** icon, the **Pad Definition** box shown to the right opens.

For **Length** use 2 in.

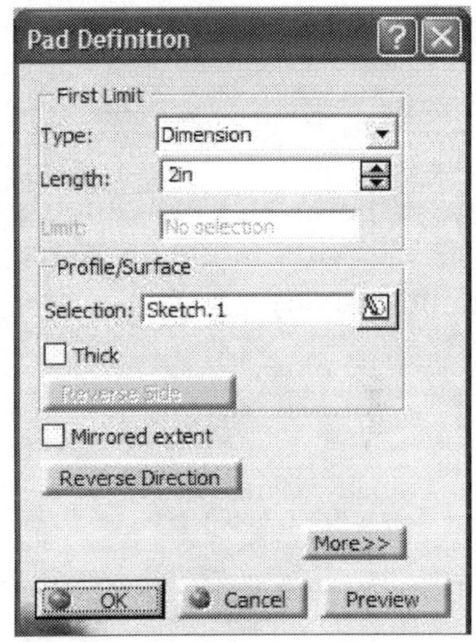


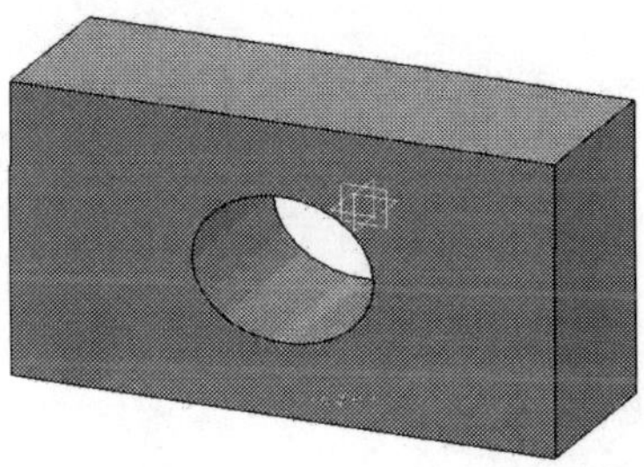

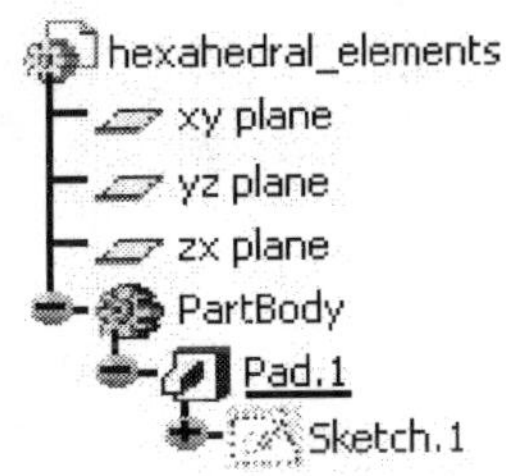


From the standard Windows toolbar, select **Start > Wireframe and Surface Design**. This lands you in the **Wireframe and Surface Design** workbench.

Select the **Extract** icon from **Extracts** toolbar

.

In the resulting pop up box, for **Element(s) to extract**, select the face of the block as shown.

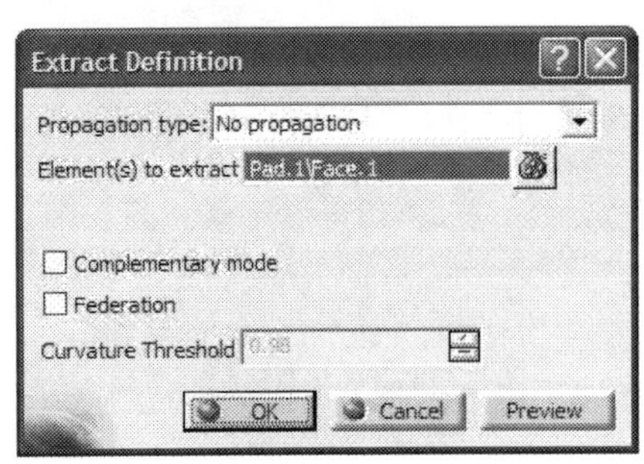


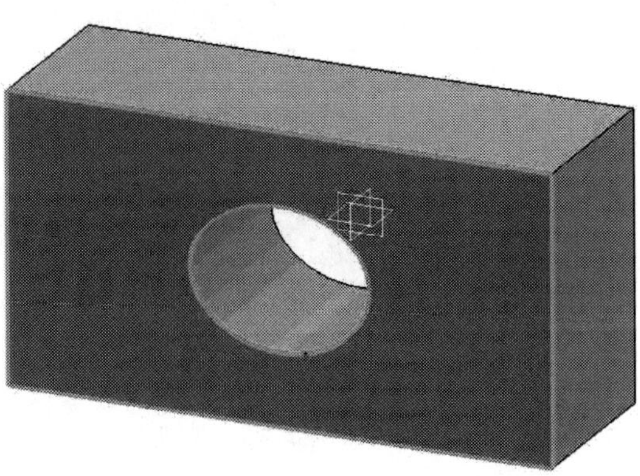

The first extracted surface is shown below.

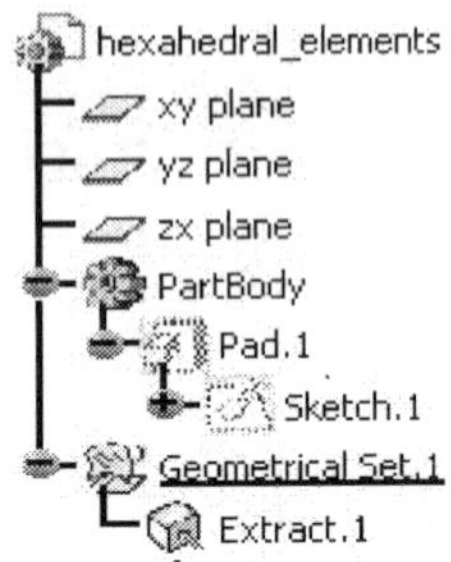


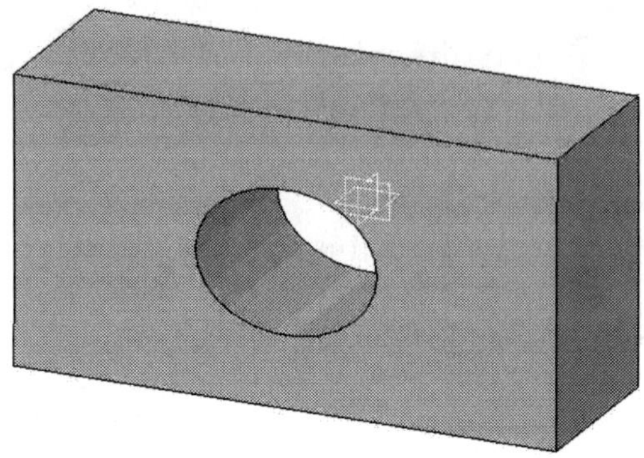

Repeat the surface extraction process to obtain the opposite surface and the other two side surfaces. After hiding the three dimensional block, the surfaces are displayed simultaneously.

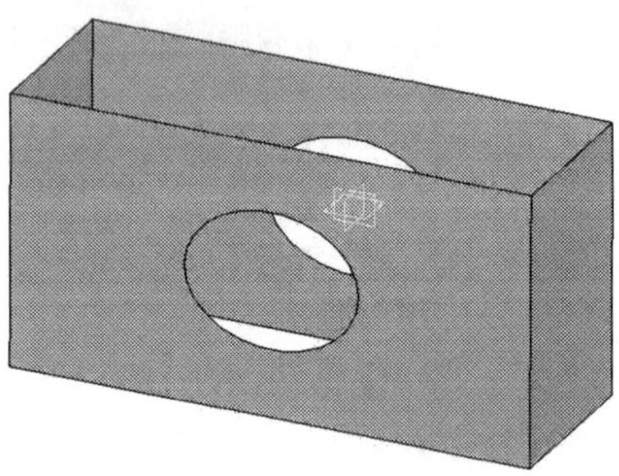

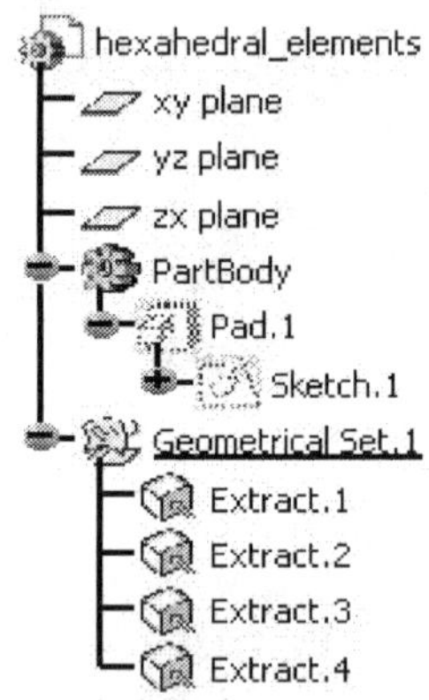


Using the **Line** icon  in the **LineAxisPoly** toolbar 

, create the line AB. This line will define the direction of the mesh extrusion. ***You may find it easier if the side planes are hiding.***

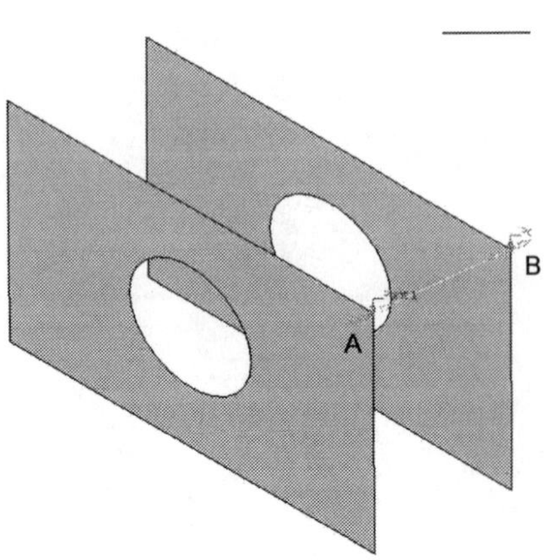


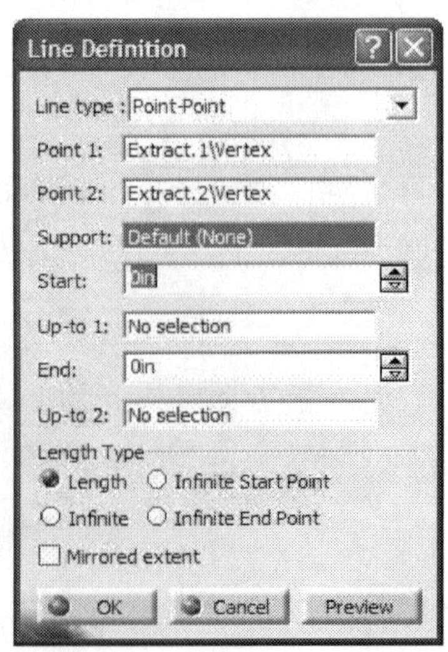

Select the **Apply Material** icon  to activate the material **Library** box below. Use the **Metal** tab on the top; select **Steel**. Use your cursor to pick the **hexahedral_elements** from the tree at which time the **OK** and **Apply Material** buttons can be selected. Close the box.
The material property is now reflected in the tree.

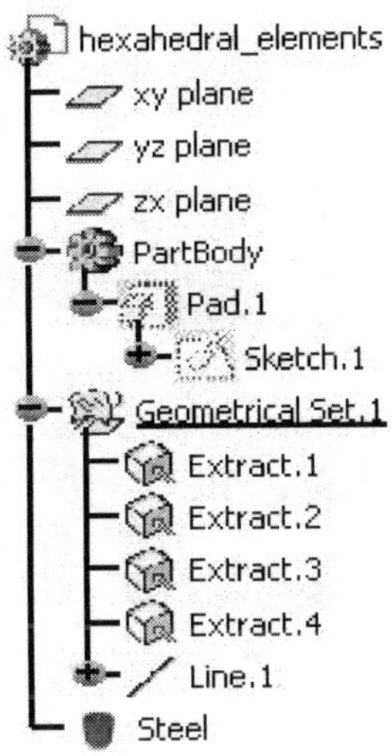


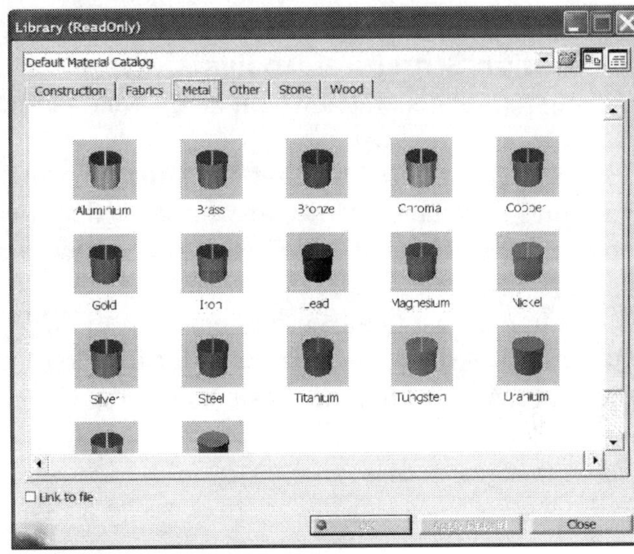


From the **View mode** toolbar 

select the **Shading with Material** icon .
The part now appears shaded as steel.

## 3 Entering the Analysis Solutions

From the standard Windows toolbar, select

**Start > Analysis & Simulation > Advanced Meshing Tools** 

**Warning:** If instead of the **Advanced Meshing Tools** workbench, you enter the **Generative Structural Analysis** workbench, immediately a solid mesh on the existing part is generated which is not what is intended.

Upon entering the **Advanced Meshing Tools** workbench, the standard box shown on the right is displayed. However, you note that the representative element "size" and "sag" is not visible on your display.
This is in contrast to the case of entering the **Generative Structural Analysis** workbench for the first time. Therefore, at this point no mesh is present.

The **Meshing Methods** toolbar 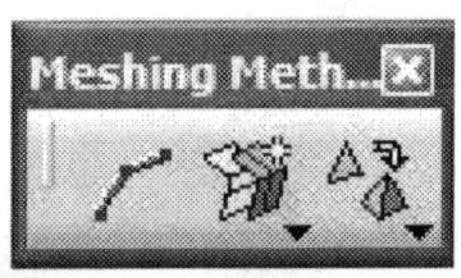

has a sub-toolbar known as the **Surface Mesher** 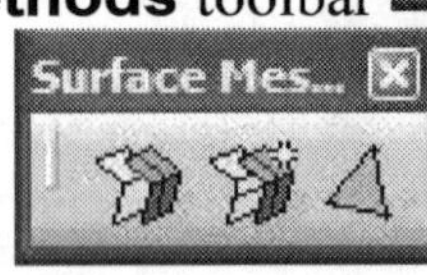

. Select the **Advanced Surface Mesher** icon .

Pick the ***surface*** with the point "A" on it. This leads to the **Global Parameters** box shown below. Keep the default **Mesh size**. In the event that you get an error message regarding the **Sag size**, select the **Geometry** tab and modify the **Sag** value to comply with the error message. Also, make sure that the minimum hole size is zero. A nonzero value may have been used in one of your previous runs.

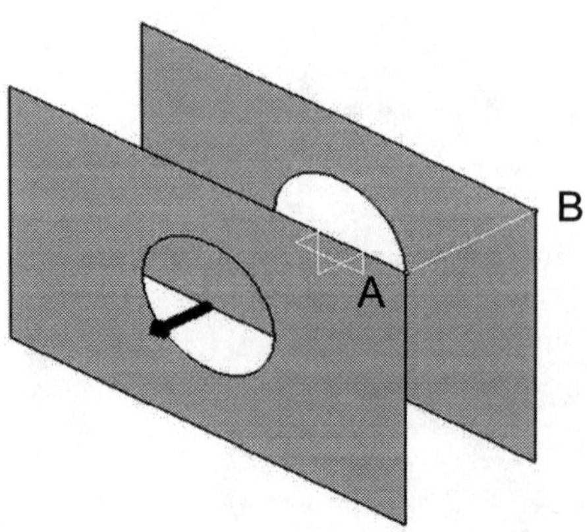


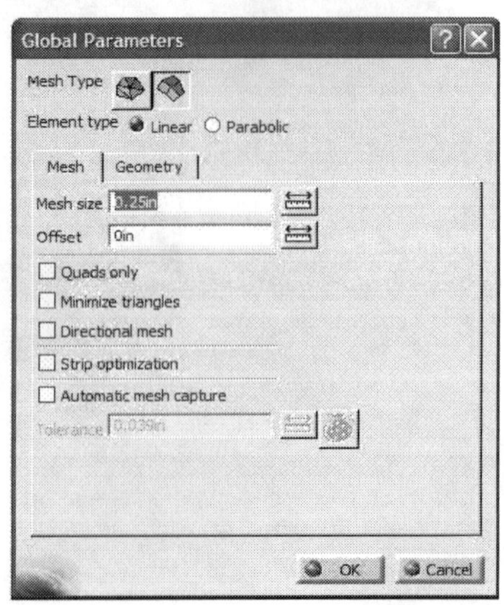

Close the resulting **Warning** pop up box.

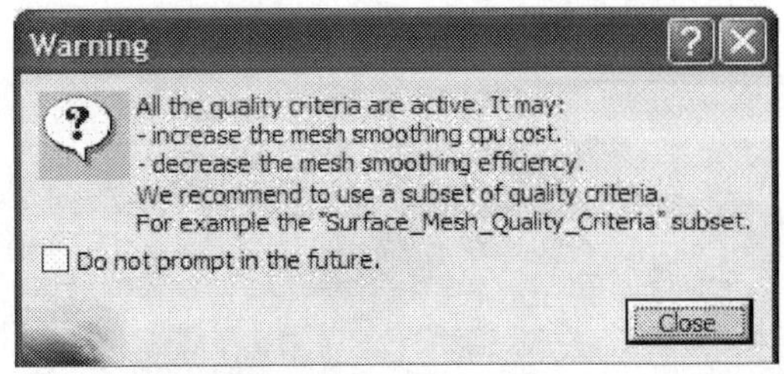


In order to see the mesh while you are in the current workbench, select the **Mesh the Part** icon, from the **Mesh/Unmesh** toolbar 

. This is a sub-toolbar of the **Execution** toolbar 

.
The summary box **Mesh the Part** appears which can be ignored.

Use the **Exit** icon to complete the process.

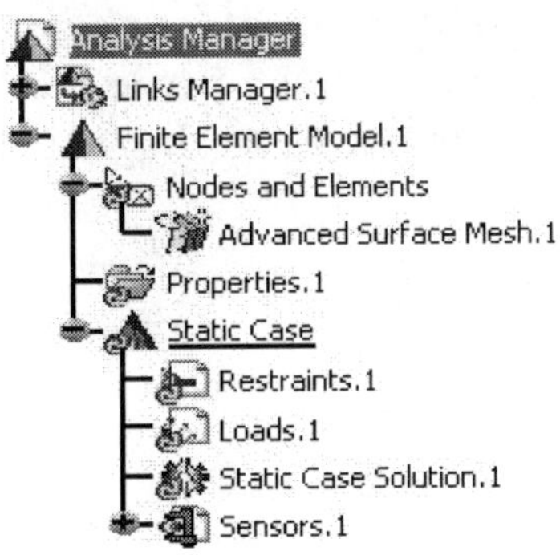


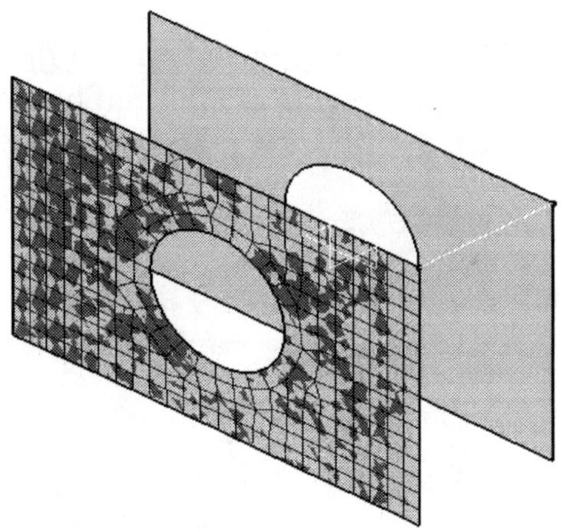

Select the **Extrude Mesher with Translation** icon in the **Extrude Transformation** toolbar 

.

In the resulting pop up box, the following selections have to be made.
For **MeshPart**, select the **Advanced Surface Mesh.1** from the tree, simply the meshed surface from the screen.
For **Axis**, pick the line AB constructed earlier.
For **Start**, type 0
For **End**, type 2, which is the thickness of the block.
For the number of layers, type 8.
Finally select the **Apply** button.

The completed pop up box and the resulting hexahedral mesh is shown below.

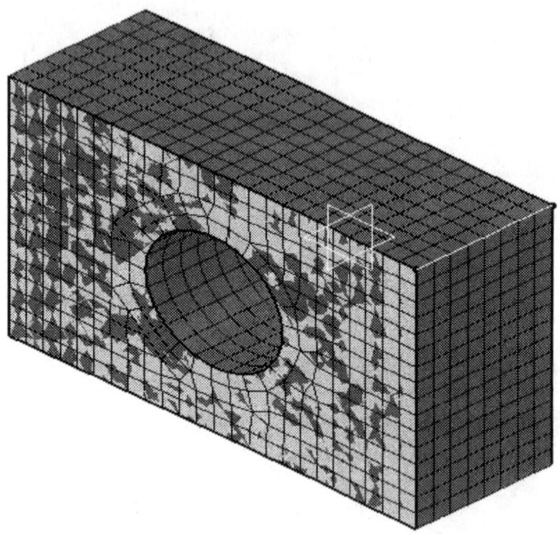

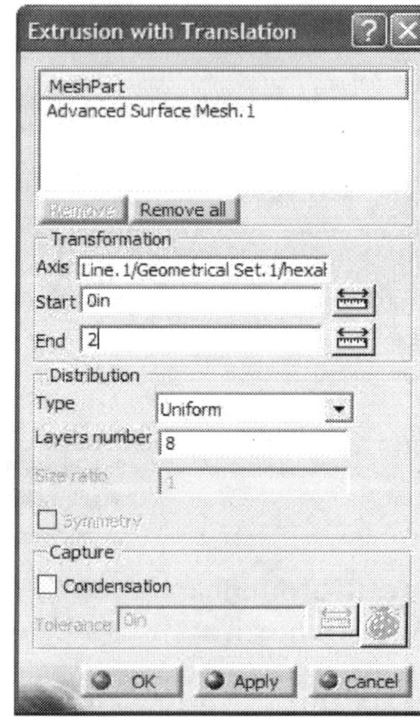


***The shell mesh initially constructed has no further purpose and therefore should be removed from the model.*** This is achieved by pointing the cursor to the **Smart Surface Mesh.1** in the tree, right-clicking, and selecting **Active/Deactivate** as shown below.

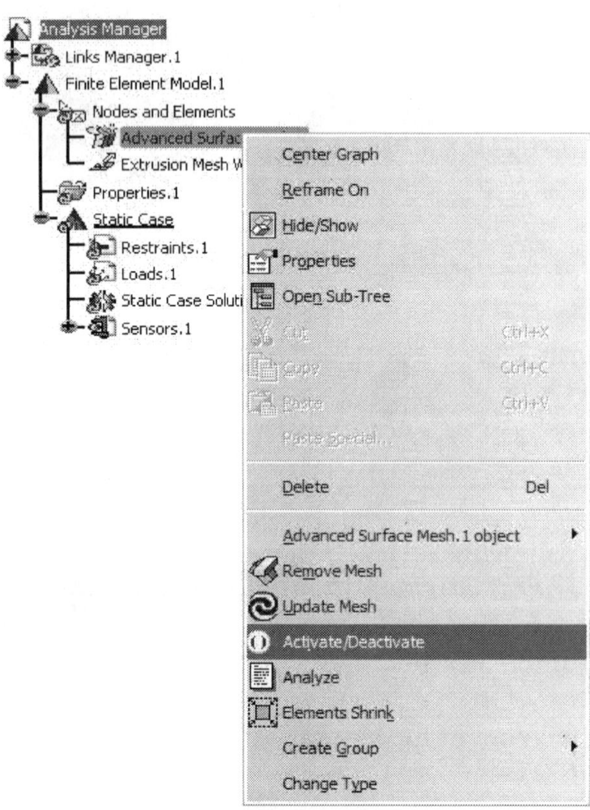

You are done with the **Advanced Meshing Tools**.
From the standard Windows tool bar, select

**Start > Analysis & Simulation > Generative Structural Analysis**

In order to view the generated mesh, you can point the cursor to the branch **Nodes and Elements**, right-click and select **Mesh Visualization**.

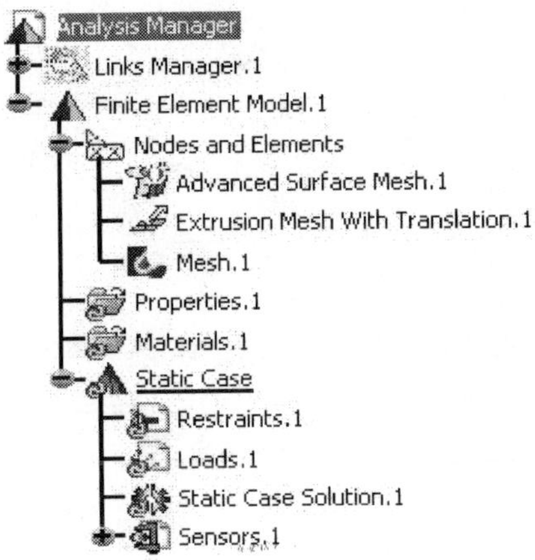


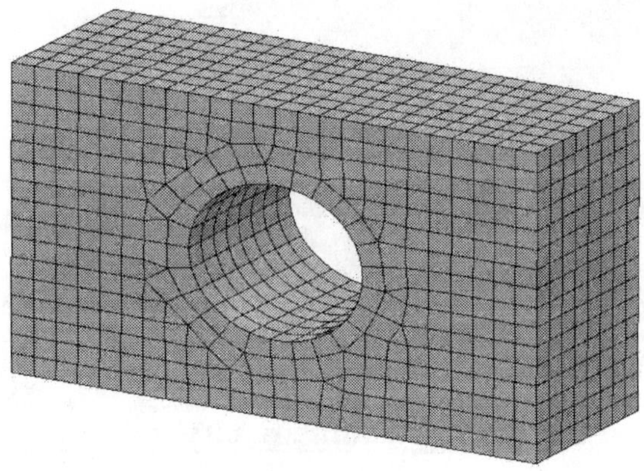

Point the cursor to **Mesh.1** in the tree, right-click and select **Activate/Deactivate**.

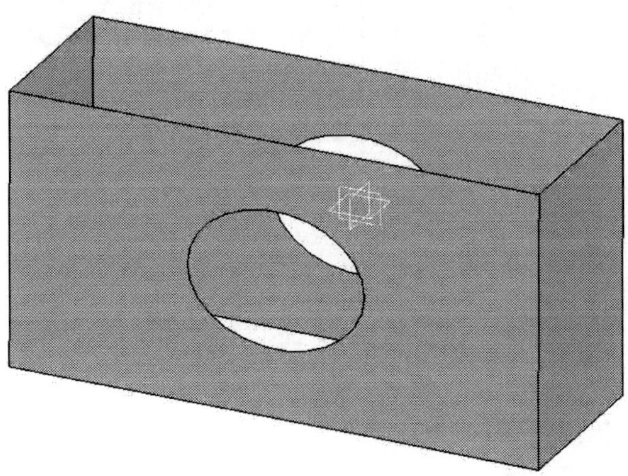

The key in dealing the hexahedral mesh is the concept of **Surface Group by Neighborhood**. You will define two such groups.

Select the **Surface Group by Neighborhood** icon 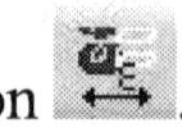. In the pop up box, for the **Supports** pick the extracted shown below. For **Tolerance** choose a small number such as 0.001.

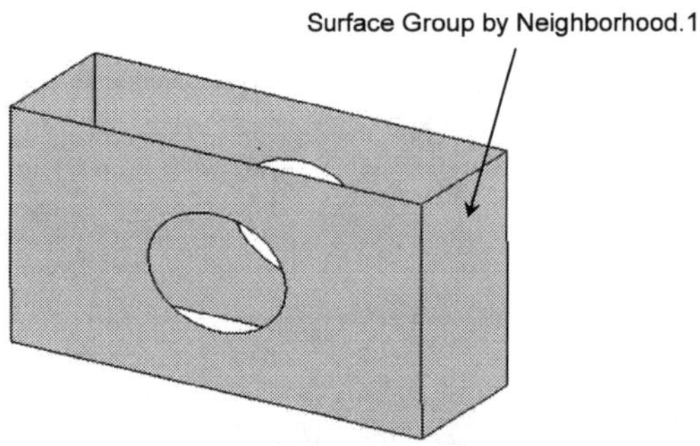

Once again, select the **Surface Group by Neighborhood** icon 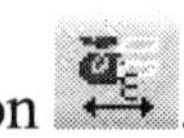. In the pop up box, for the **Supports** pick the extracted surface as shown. <u>For **Tolerance** choose a small number such as 0.001.</u> **<u>It is extremely important to use a small value for tolerance. In the present problem .001 is sufficient.</u>**

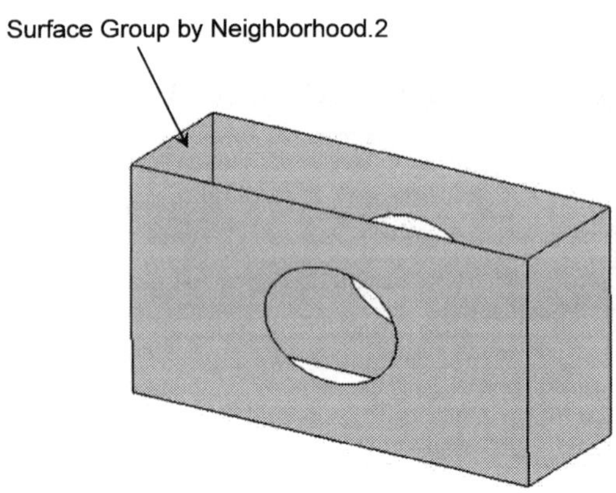


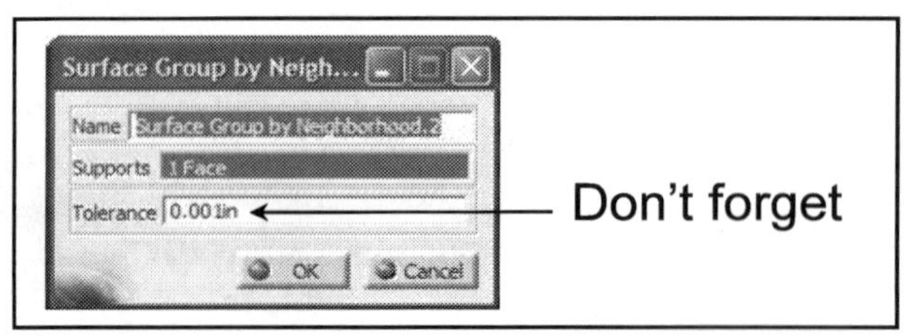


The tree is modified to reflect these groups.

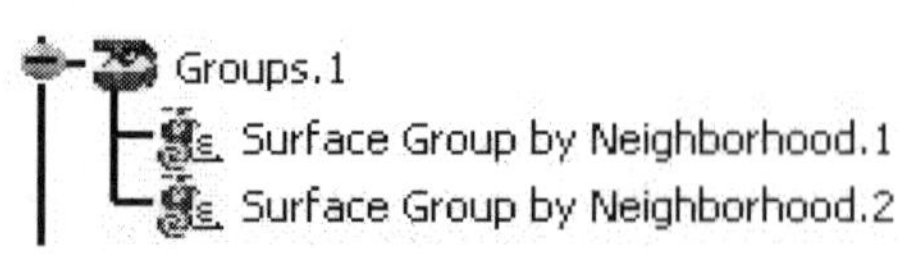


***<u>You now have to define the 3D property associated with the hexahedral mesh.</u>***

Select the **3D Property** icon  from the **Model Manager** toolbar

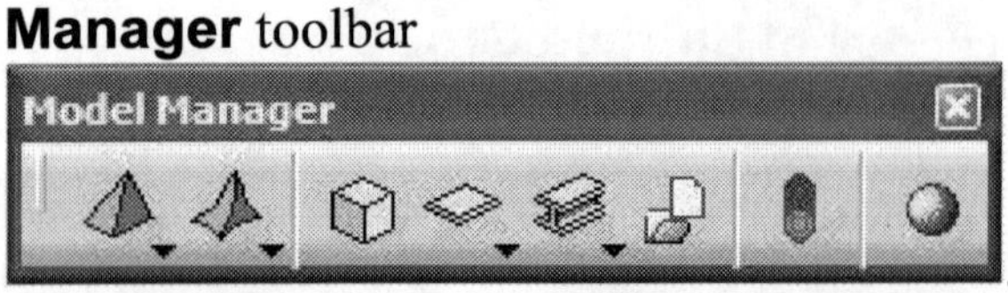


For Supports, pick the **Extrusion Mesh with Translation.1** in the tree.

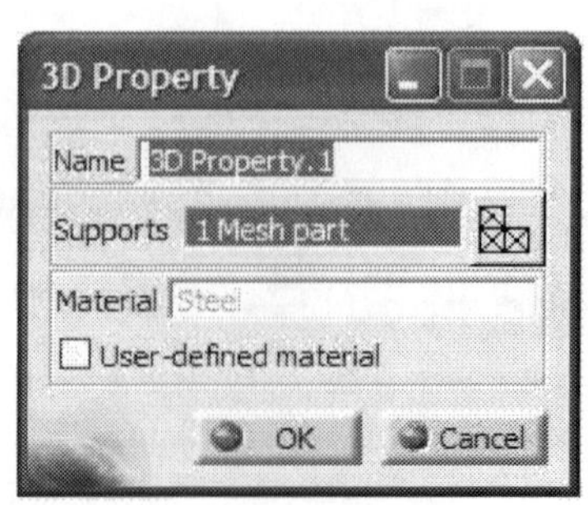

## Applying Restraints:

Use the **Isostatic** icon  from the **Advanced Restraint** toolbar 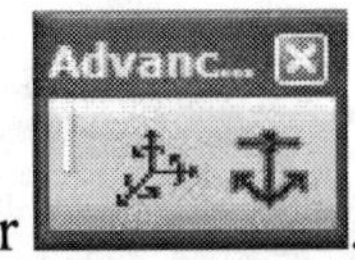

. You need not worry about picking an entity. The isostatic restraint is automatically applied.

## Applying Loads:

Click on the **Pressure** icon , for **Supports**, select **Surface Group by Neighborhood.1**. For **Pressure**, input **-100** psi.

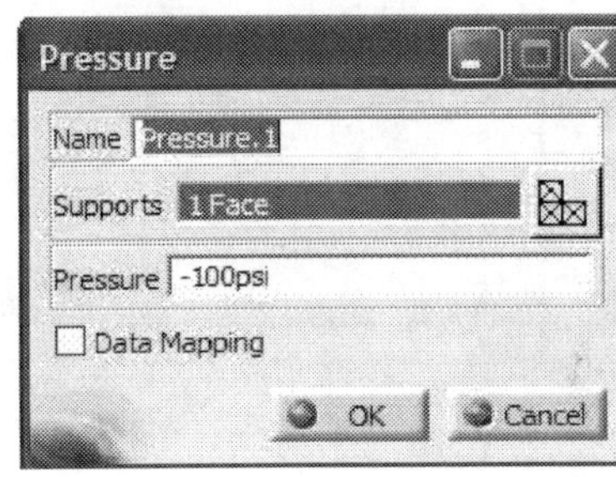


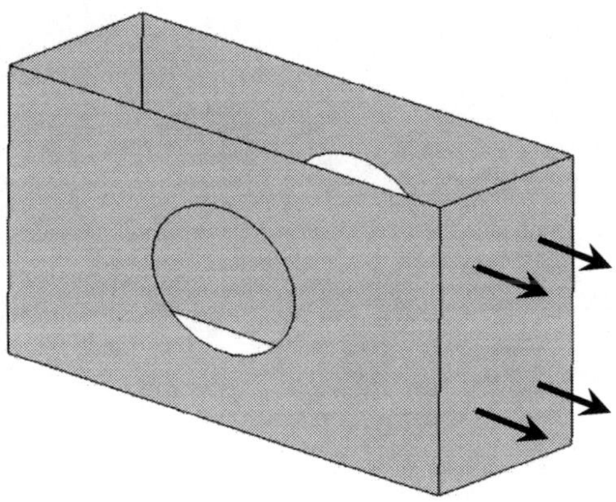

Click on the **Pressure** icon  again. For **Supports**, select **Surface Group by Neighborhood.2**. For **Pressure**, input **-100** psi.

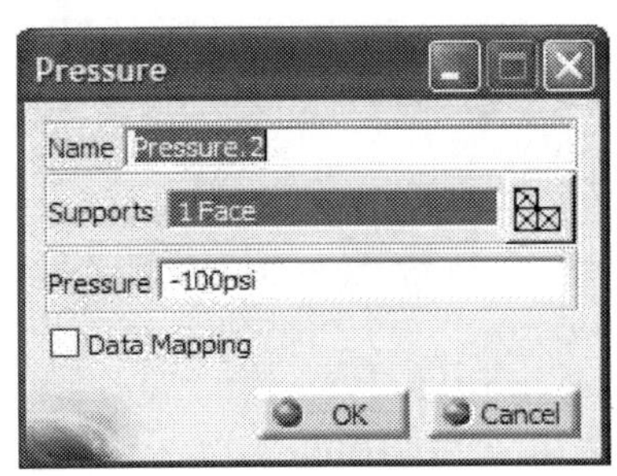


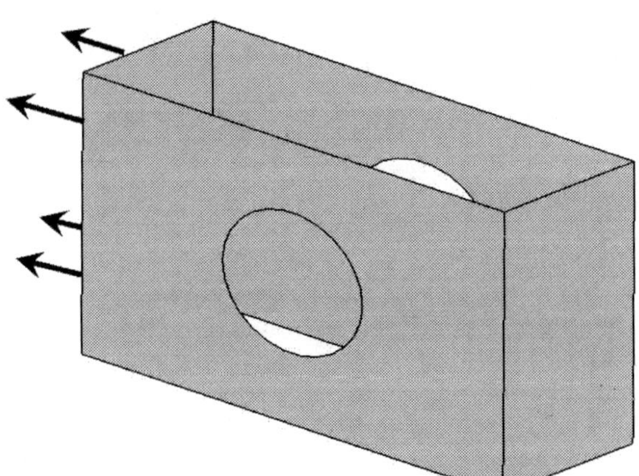

The complete tree is given below for your reference.

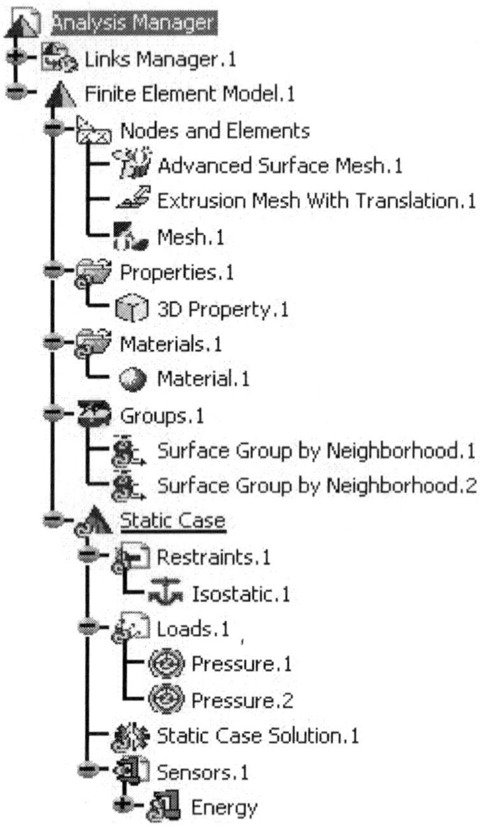


**Launching the Solver:**

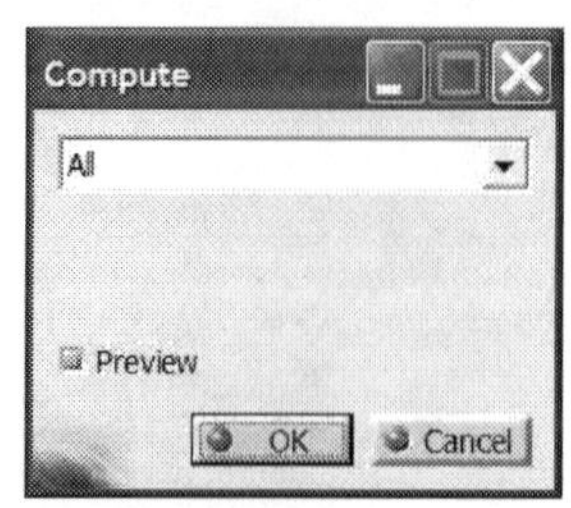


To run the analysis, you need to use the **Compute** toolbar 

by selecting the **Compute** icon . This leads to the **Compute** box shown to the right. Leave the defaults as **All** which means everything is computed.

Upon closing this box, after a brief pause, the second box shown below appears. This box provides information on the resources needed to complete the analysis.

If the estimates are zero in the listing, then there is a problem in the previous step and should be looked into. If all the numbers are zero in the box, the program may run but would not produce any useful results.

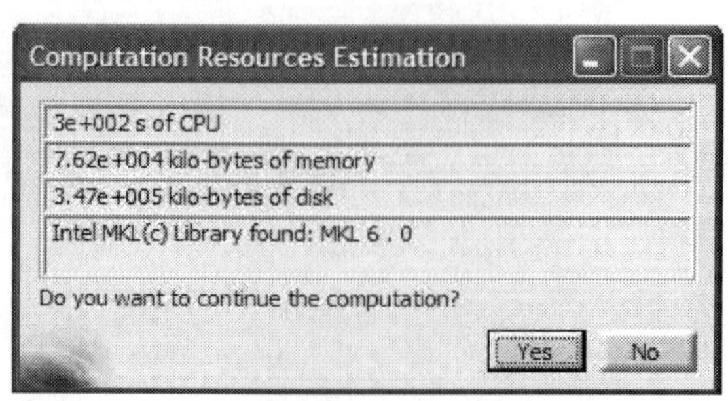

## Postprocessing:

The main postprocessing toolbar is called **Image** 

. To view the deformed shape you have to use the **Deformation** icon 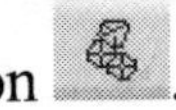. The resulting deformed shape is displayed below.

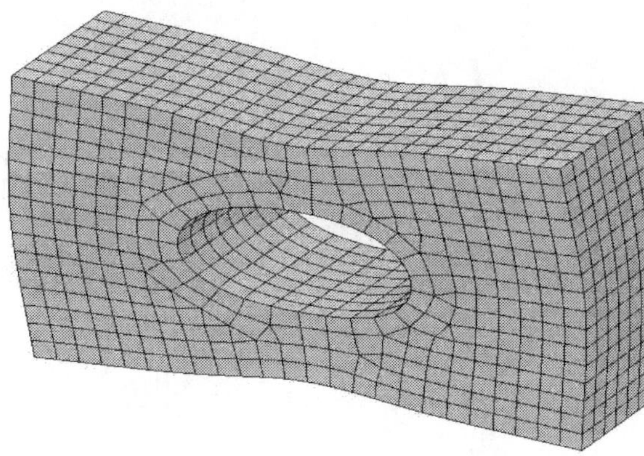

The next step in the postprocessing is to plot the contours of the von Mises stress using the **von Mises Stress** icon  in the **Image** toolbar.
The von Mises stress is displayed below.

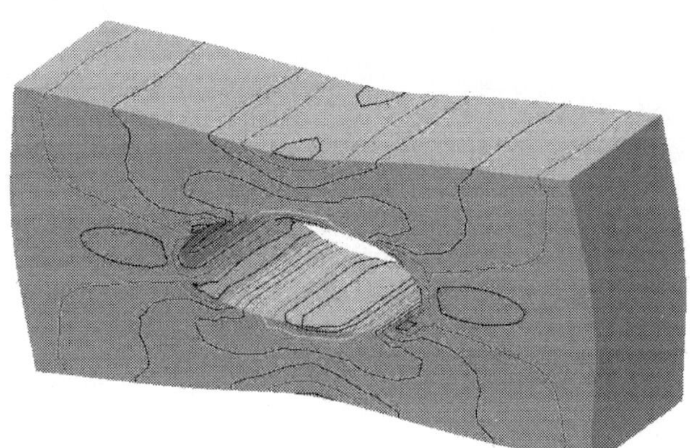

# NOTES:

# Chapter 27

# Frequency Response Analysis of a Simply Supported Beam

## Introduction

In this tutorial, the midspan of a simply supported beam is subject to sinusoidal (harmonic) load causing it to vibrate in the transverse direction. The objective is to find the amplitude of the vibration of a node as a function of the applied frequency.

## 1 Problem Statement

The simply supported beam shown below is subjected to the harmonic load $F(t) = 4000\sin(\omega t)$ lb at its midspan.

The beam is assumed to be made of steel (with properties specified by CATIA) , L =20 inches, and a square 1x1 cross section. The deflection of the beam at the midpoint is described by the expression $w(t) = \dfrac{2*(4000)}{\rho AL}\sum_{n=1}^{\infty}\dfrac{1}{\omega_{2n-1}^2 - \omega^2}\sin\omega t$ where $\omega_n$ represents the natural frequency of a simply supported beam given by $\omega_n = (n\pi)^2\sqrt{\dfrac{EI}{\rho AL^4}}$ rad/s.

Instead of using infinite modes in the above expansion, we employ only three modes and compare it with the results generated by CATIA's **Harmonic Dynamic Response Solution**. In the CATIA model, to ensure that the three dimensional model closely approximates the beam bending solution, the side faces of the beam are prevented from out of plane motion by using Surface Sliders. Only half of the beam is modeled and therefore Surface Slider is used at the plane of symmetry.

Note that CATIA generates the amplitude of the response which needs to be compared with $A(\omega) = \left|\dfrac{2*(4000)}{\rho AL}\sum_{n=1}^{3}\dfrac{1}{\omega_{2n-1}^2 - \omega^2}\right|$. CATIA results are plotted in terms of frequencies in Hz and consequently the above expression needs to be scaled as $\dfrac{A(\omega)}{4\pi^2}$. The final comment is that, 1% damping is used for the three modes in CATIA calculations.

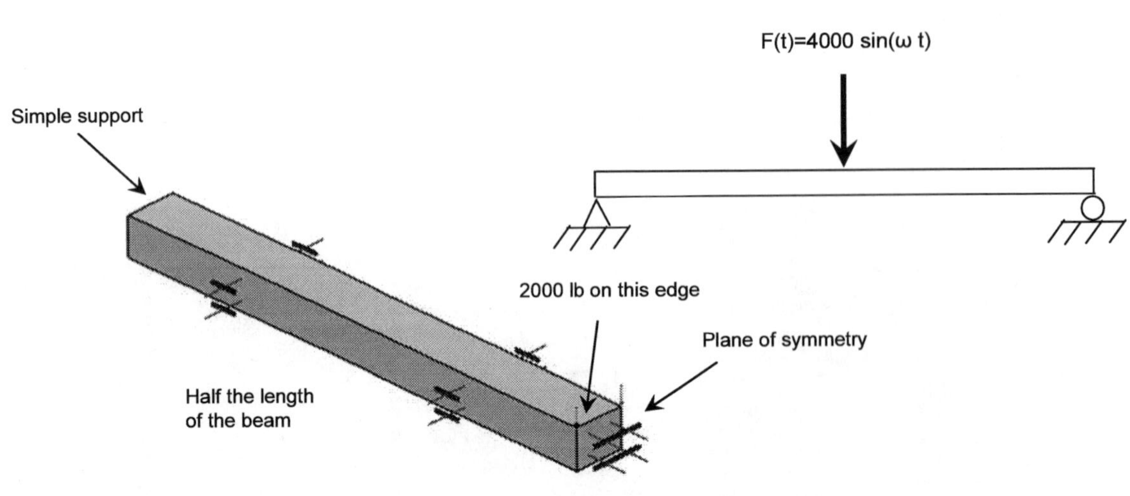

## 2 Creation of the Part in Mechanical Design Solutions

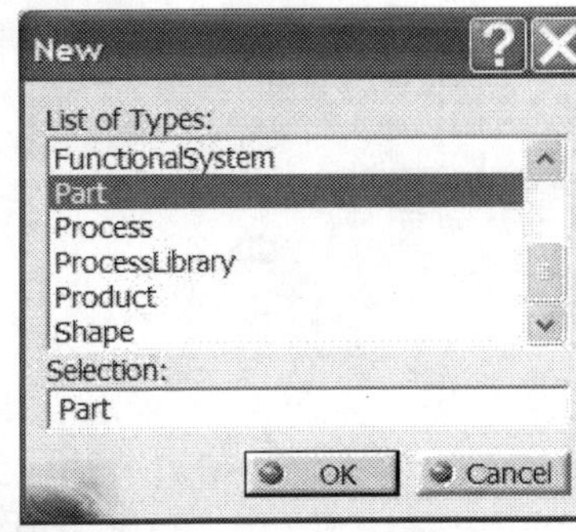


Enter the **Part Design** workbench which can be achieved by different means depending on your CATIA customization. For example, from the standard Windows toolbar, select **File > New**. From the box shown on the right, select **Part**. This moves you to the **Part Design** workbench and creates a part with the default name **Part.1**. Read Note #1 in Appendix I.

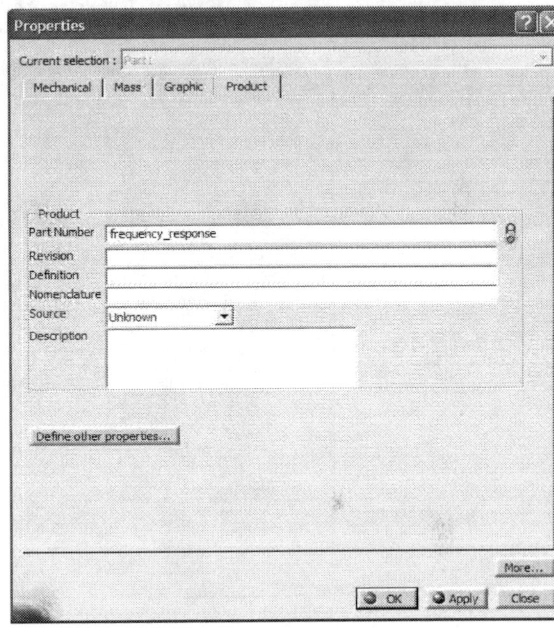


In order to change the default name, move the cursor to **Part.1** in the tree, right-click and select **Properties** from the menu list. From the **Properties** box, select the **Product** tab and in **Part Number** type **frequency_response**.

This will be the new part name throughout the chapter. The tree on the top left corner of the screen should look as displayed below.

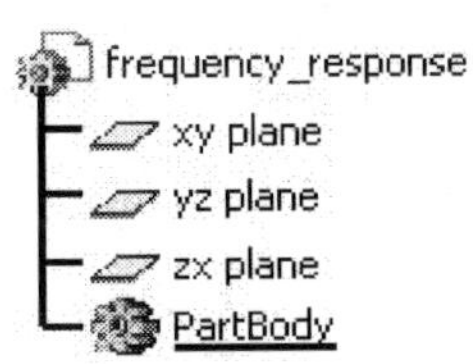


From the tree, select the **zx** plane and enter the **Sketcher**. In the **Sketcher**, use the **Profile** toolbar

to draw a 1x1 square, and dimension it.

In order to change the dimension, double-click on the dimension on the screen.

Leave the **Sketcher**.

You will now use the **Pad** operation to extrude the sketch.

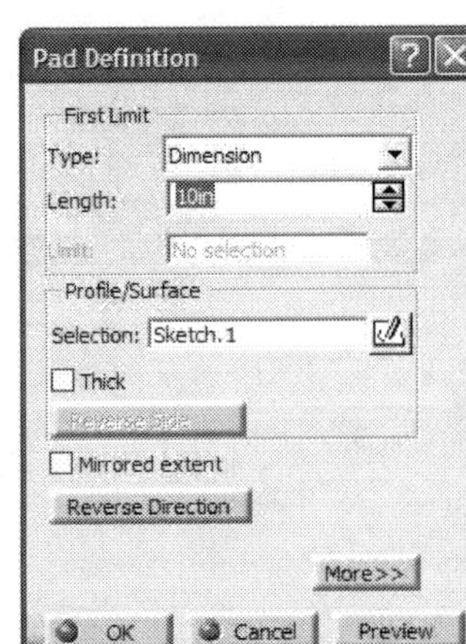


Upon selecting the **Pad** icon, the **Pad Definition** box shown to the right opens.
In the **Length** box, type 10.

The result is displayed on the next page.

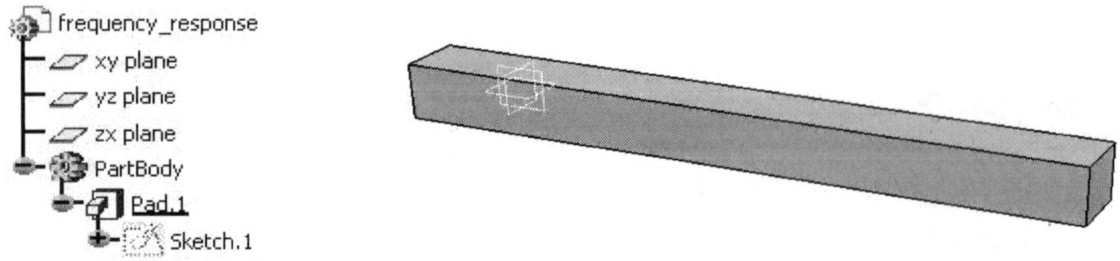


Select the **Apply Material** icon  to activate the material **Library** box below. Use the **Metal** tab on the top; select **Steel**. Use your cursor to pick the part from the screen at which time the **OK** and **Apply Material** buttons can be selected. Close the box.

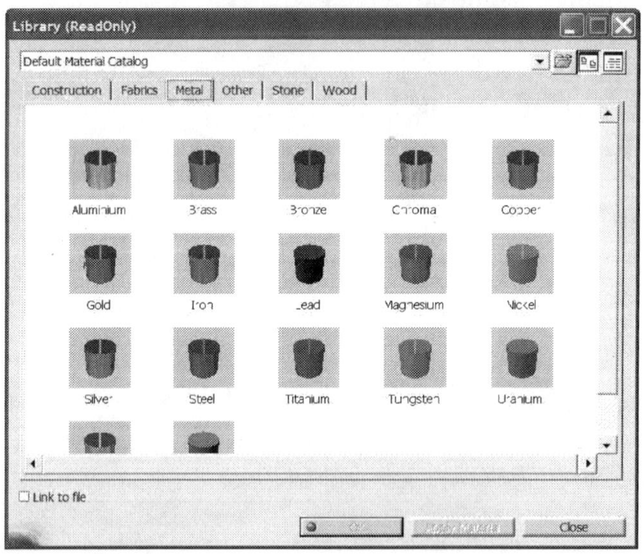


The material property is now reflected in the tree.

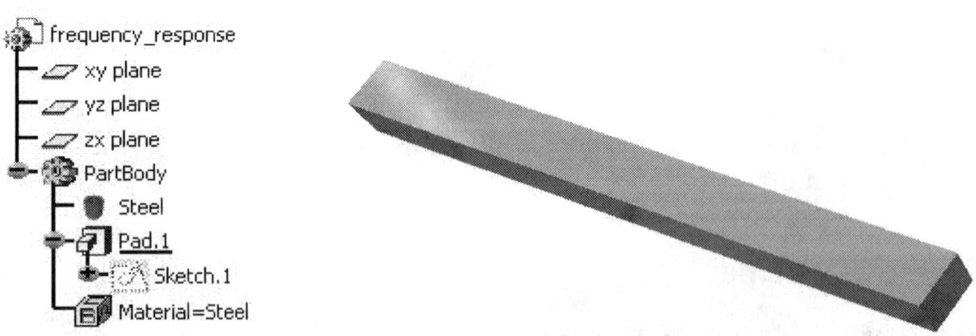

## 3 Entering the Analysis Solutions

From the standard Windows toolbar, select

**Start > Analysis & Simulation > Generative Structural Analysis** 
There is a second workbench known as the **Advanced Meshing Tools** which is used for other purposes.

Upon changing workbenches, the box **New Analysis Case** becomes visible. The default choice is **Static Analysis** which is precisely what we intend to use. Therefore, close the box by clicking on **OK**.

The tree, part, and representative element size and sag (under default values) are displayed below.

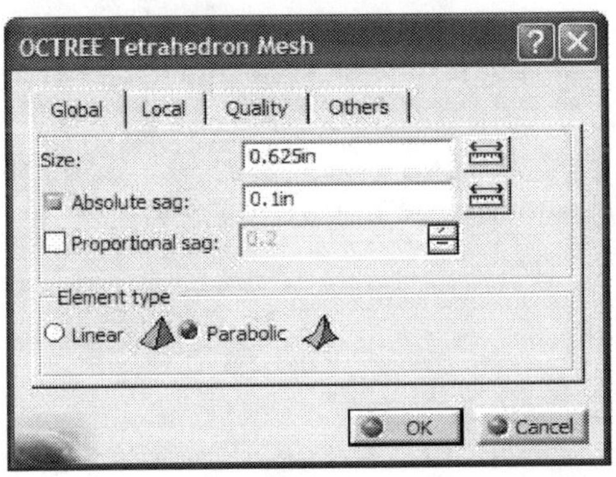


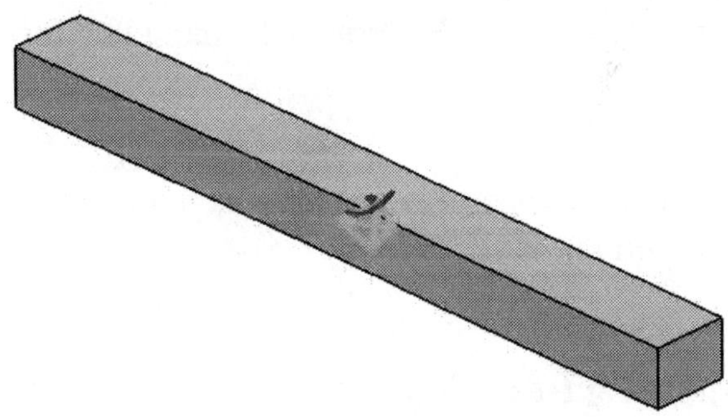

Point the cursor to the branch **Nodes and Elements**, right-click and select **Mesh Visualization**. A **Warning** box appears which can be ignored, select **OK**. For the mesh parameters used, the following mesh is displayed on the screen.

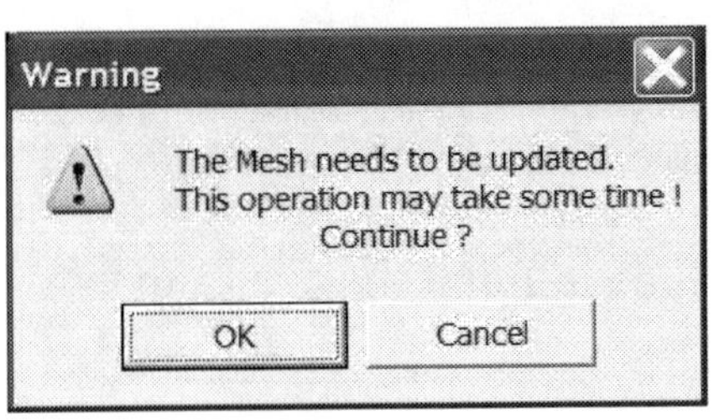


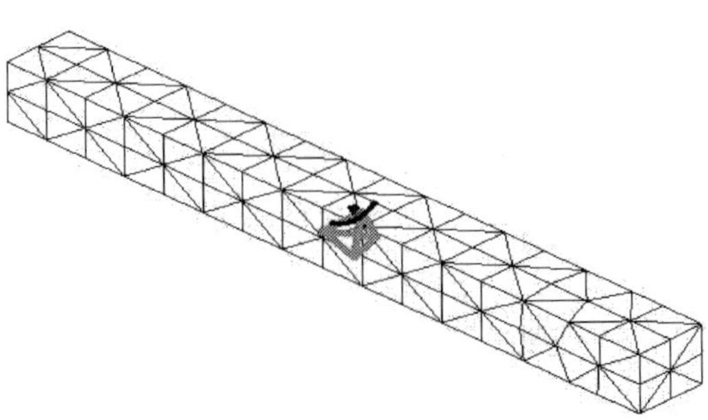

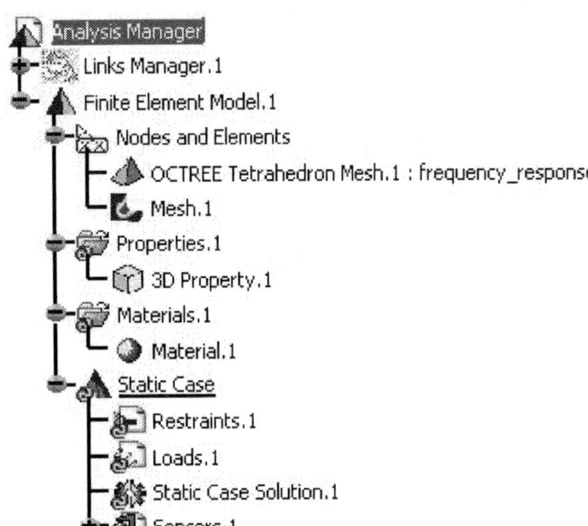

From the **Virtual Part** toolbar 

, select the **Smooth Virtual Part** . From the pop up box below select the face shown as the **Support**.

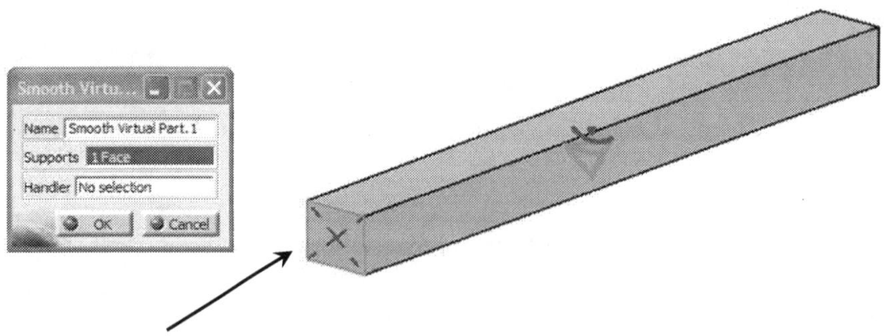


For support, select this face

For the **Handler**, no selection is made. This implies that the handler is the centroid of the selected the face.

**Applying Restraints:**

CATIA's FEA module is geometrically based. This means that the boundary conditions cannot be applied to nodes and elements. The boundary conditions can only be applied at the part level. As soon as you enter the **Generative Structural Analysis** workbench, the part is automatically hidden. Therefore, before boundary conditions are applied, the part must be brought to the unhide mode. This can be carried out by pointing the cursor to the top of the tree, the **Links Manager.1** branch, right-click, and select **Show**. At this point, the part and the mesh are superimposed and you have access to the part.

If the presence of the mesh is annoying, you can always hide it. Point the cursor to **Nodes and Elements**, right-click, **Hide**.

In FEA, restraints refer to applying displacement boundary conditions which is achieved through the **Restraint** toolbar 

. Use the **Mechanical Restraints** sub-toolbar 

. From this sub-toolbar, select the **Pivot** icon .

In the resulting pop up box, make the selections as described below. Note that the selection of "1" for "**X**" in this box is to align the pivoting in the correct orientation. If your coordinate system is oriented differently, you may have to pick "**Y**" or "**Z**" and specify "1" for it.

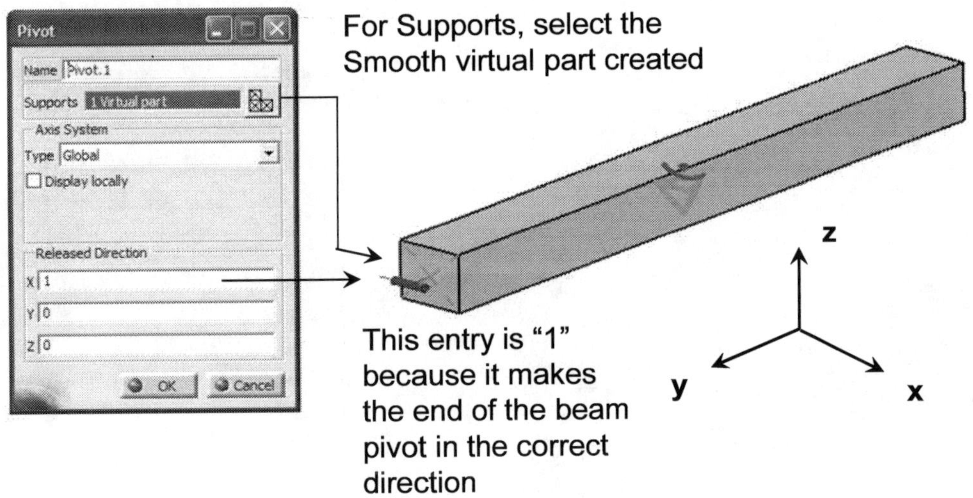


Apply the **Surface Slider** icon to the three faces shown below. The reason behind picking the two side faces is to be able to create a three dimensional solution which can be compared to the beam bending derivations described in the chapter introduction.

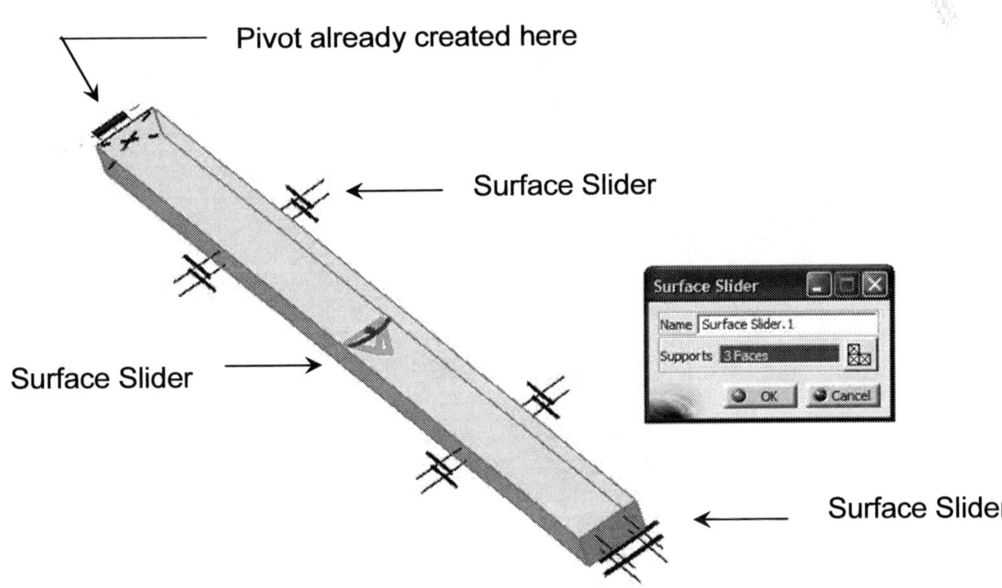

## Applying Loads:

Select the **Distributed Force** icon 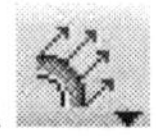 from the **Loads** toolbar 

.
Make the edge selection as shown below and apply 2000 lb in the downward direction.

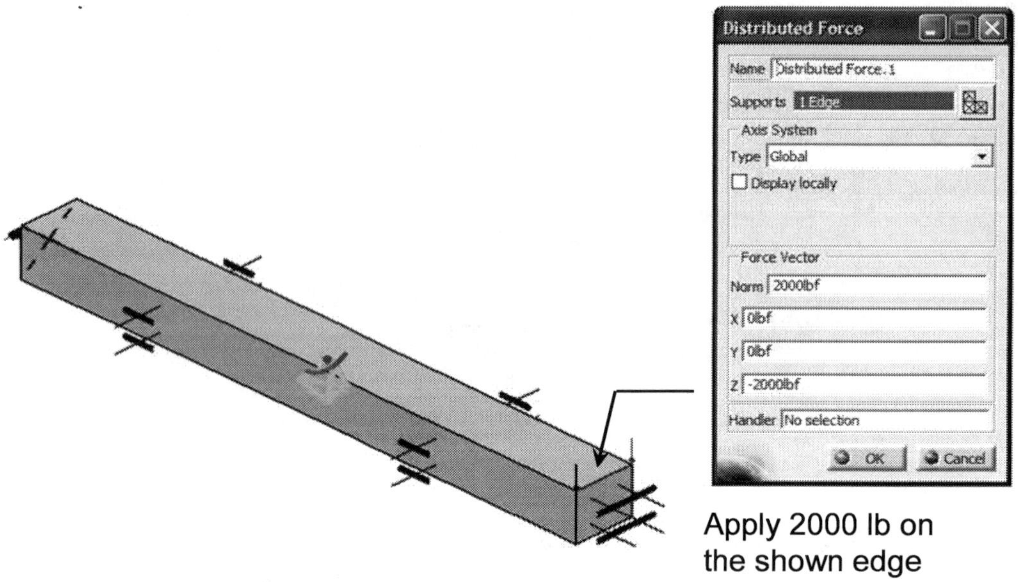


The tree structure is also shown below for your reference.

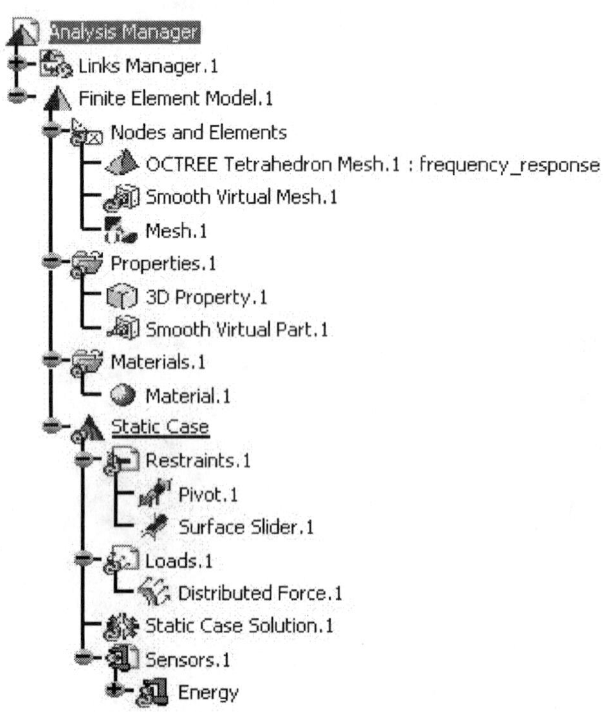

## Launching the Solver:

To run the analysis, you need to use the **Compute** toolbar  by selecting the **Compute** icon . This opens up the **Compute** box. Leave the defaults as **All** which means everything is computed.

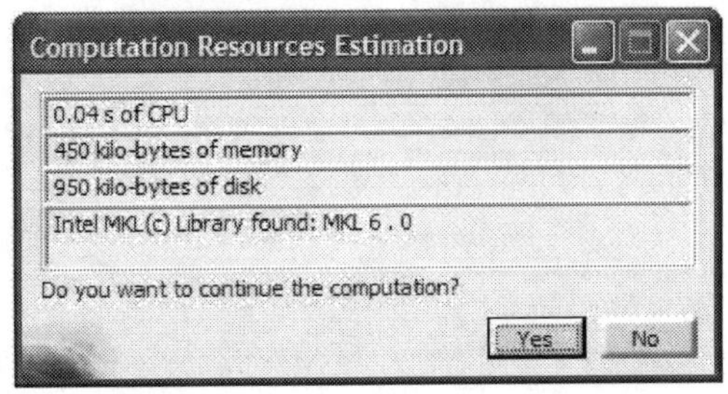


Upon closing this box, after a brief pause, the second box shown below appears. This box provides information on the resources needed to complete the analysis.
If the estimates are zero in the listing, then there is a problem in the previous step and should be looked into. If all the numbers are zero in the box, the program may run but would not produce any useful results.

## Postprocessing (Static Results):

The main postprocessing toolbar is called **Image** 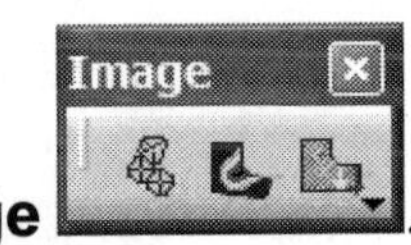. To view the deformed shape you have to use the **Deformation** icon 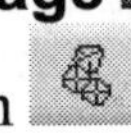. The resulting deformed shape is displayed below.

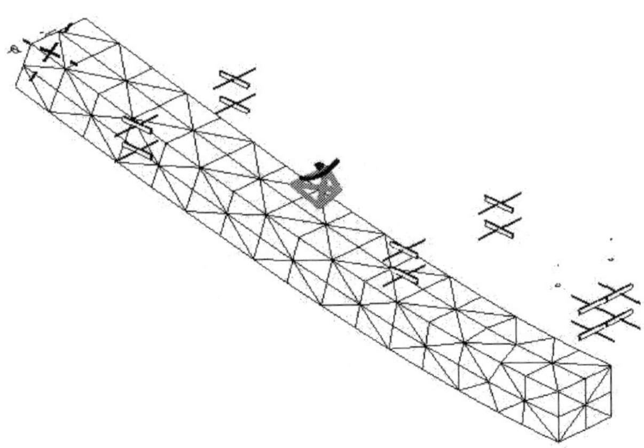

## Inserting a Frequency Case:

In order to carry out a frequency-response analysis (or **Harmonic Dynamic Response Case** as known in CATIA V5), first the natural frequencies of the structure have to be calculated. This is why we you have to insert a Frequency Case.
Point the cursor to the top menu bar (standard Windows toolbar), and follow **Insert>Frequency Case** as displayed in the next page.

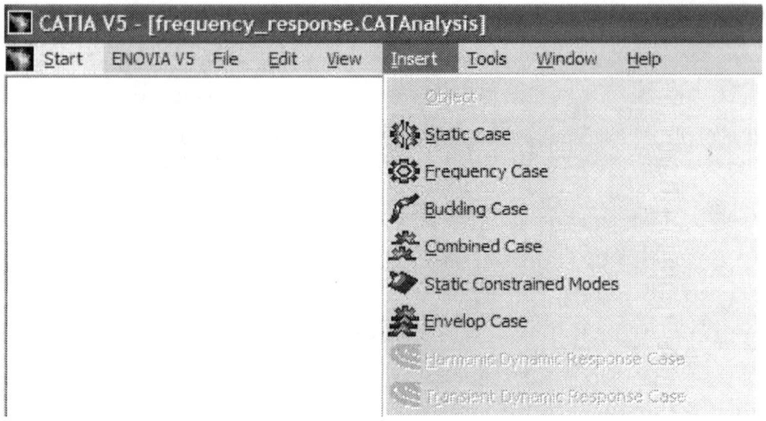


At this point, the pop up box below opens.

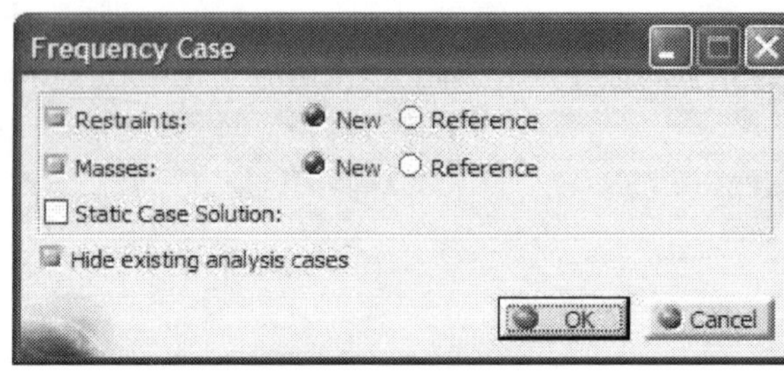


Since we intend to use the same restraints as in the static case, Select the **Reference** radio button, and with the cursor pick **Restraint.1** from the tree.

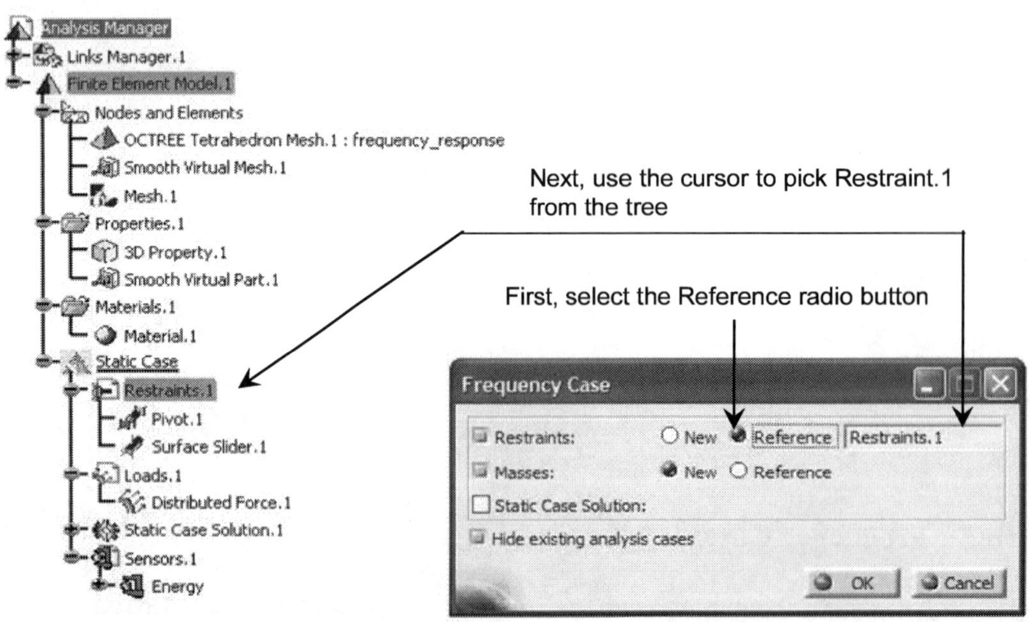


Otherwise, you need to specify the same restraints (Surface Slider and Pivot once again on the desired Supports.)

Note that a **Frequency Case** has been added to the tree.

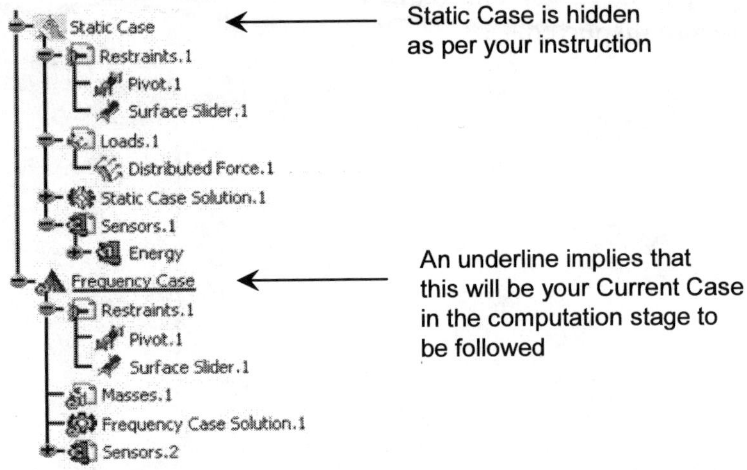


Double-click on **Frequency Case Solution.1** from the tree and request "3" modes to be computed.

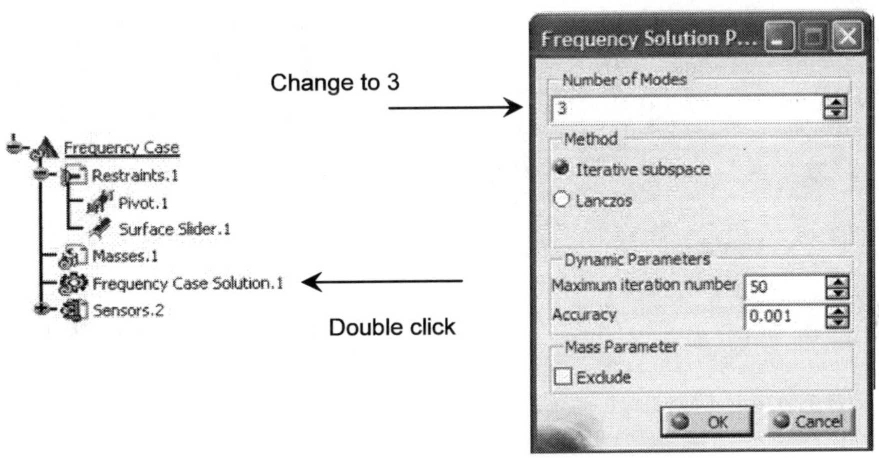


To run the analysis, you need to use the **Compute** toolbar  by selecting the **Compute** icon . This opens up the **Compute** box. Leave the defaults as **All** which means everything is computed. Keep in mind that your **Current Case** is the **Frequency Case** which is underlined in the tree. Since you requested only three modes, the results are returned very quickly.

**Postprocessing (Frequency Results):**

The main postprocessing toolbar is called **Image** 

. To view the deformed shape you have to use the **Deformation** icon . The resulting deformed shape is displayed on the next page.

By double-clicking on the deformed shape and choosing the **Occurences** tab from the **Image Edition** box, the calculated frequencies are listed. By selecting any one of them, the modes shapes are displayed.

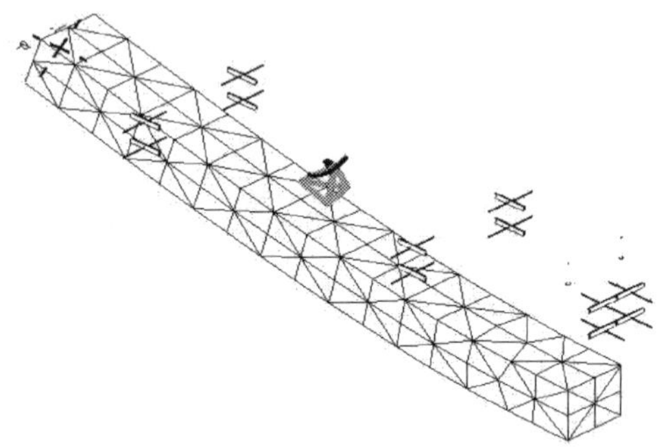

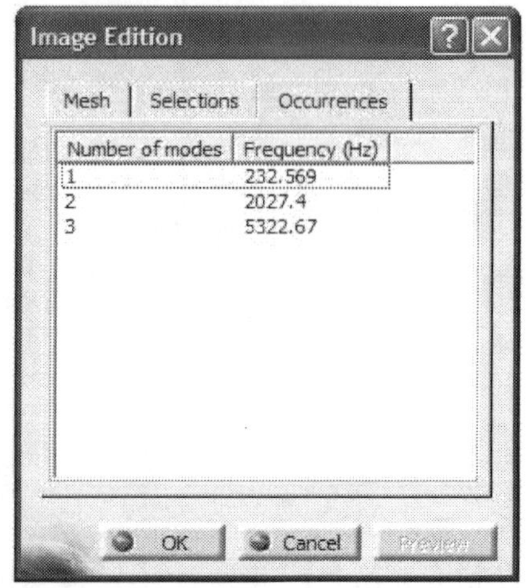


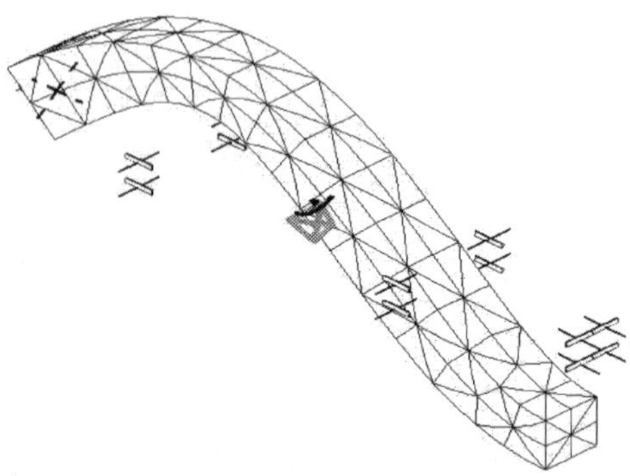

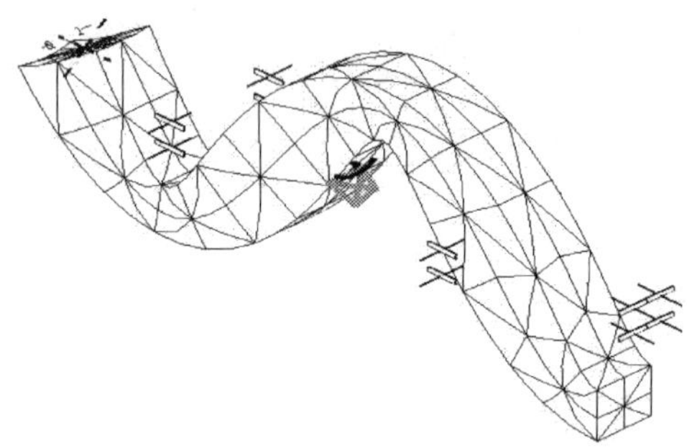

At this point you are ready to insert a **Harmonic Dynamic Response Case**.

**Inserting a Harmonic Dynamic Response Case:**

Point the cursor to the top menu bar (standard Windows toolbar), and follow **Insert > Harmonic Dynamic Response Case** as displayed below.

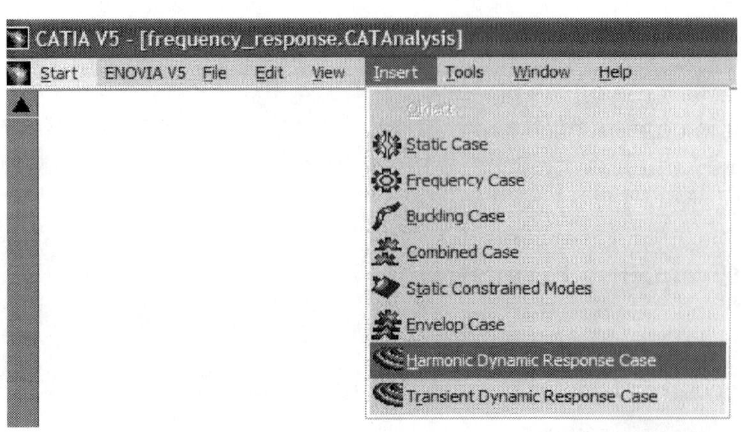

The pop up box shown below appears on the screen.

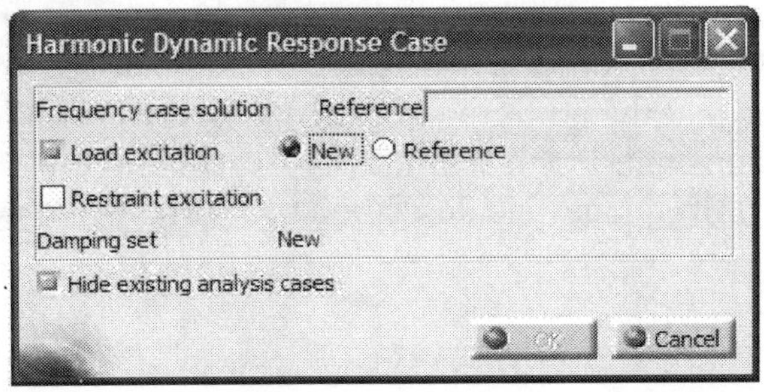


Note that we can use the **Frequency Case Solution.1** just completed as the **Reference**.

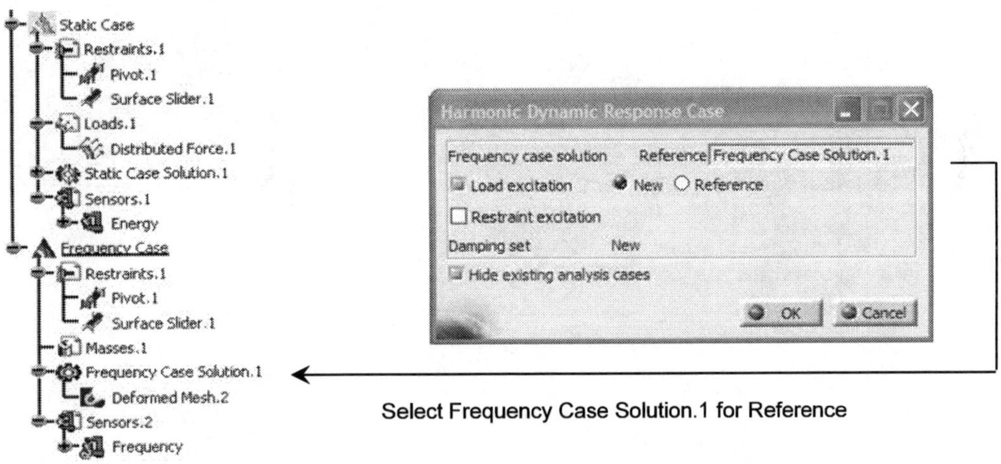


Note that a **Harmonic Dynamic Response Case** has been added to the tree.

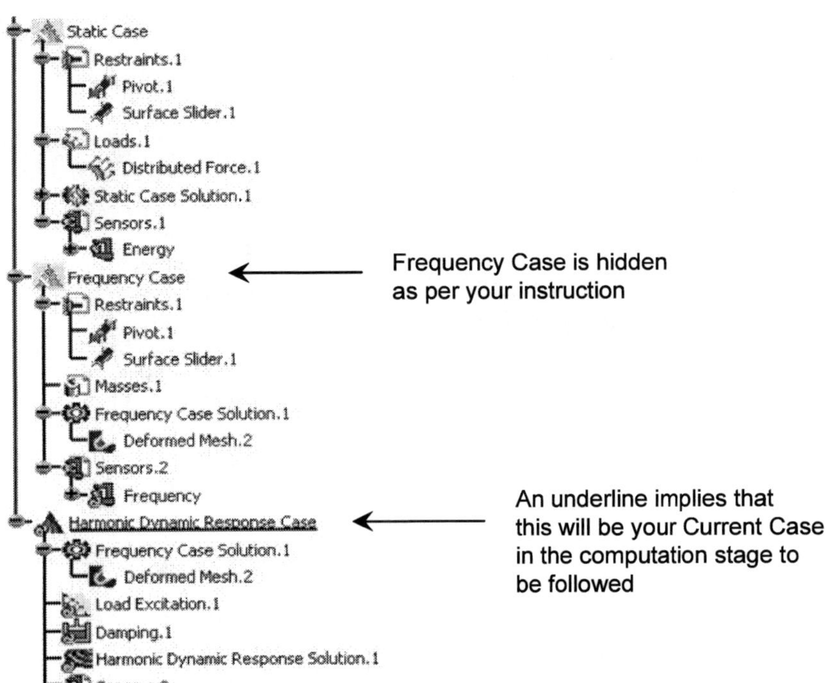

Select the **White Noise** icon 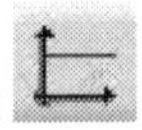 from the **Modulation** toolbar 

. In CATIA, white noise indicates that the amplitude of the applied sinusoidal load as a function of the frequency is constant. If this is not the case, the functional dependence of the amplitude (as a function of frequency) is described by **Frequency Modulation**.

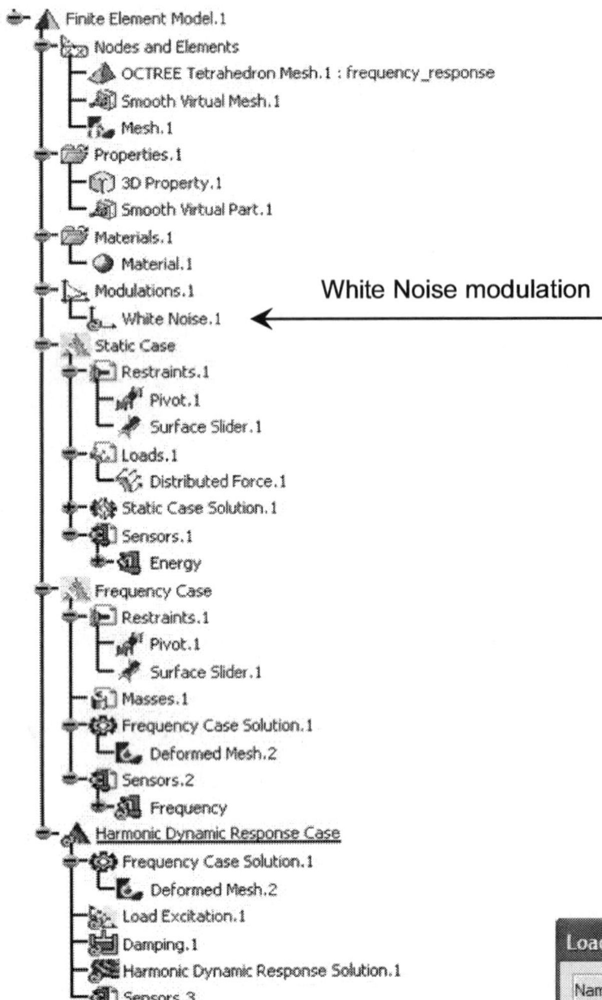


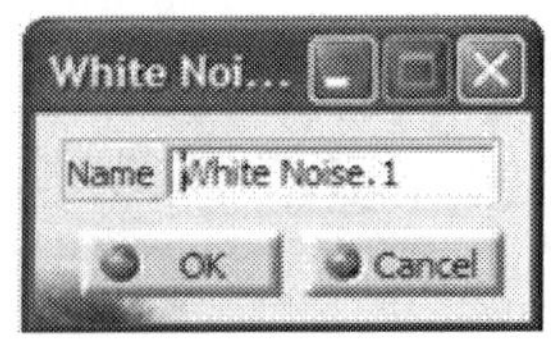


Double-click on the **Load Excitation.1** from the tree which appears under the **Harmonic Dynamic Response Case** in the tree. This opens the pop up box shown on the right.

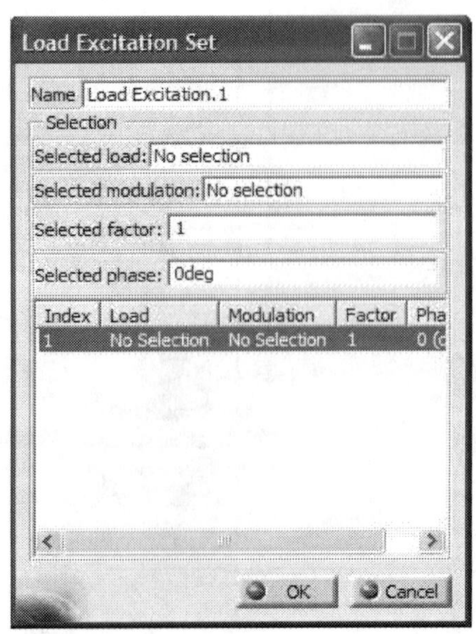

For **Selected load**, pick **Loads.1** which was created in the **Static Case**.
For **Selected modulation**, pick **White Noise.1** from the tree.

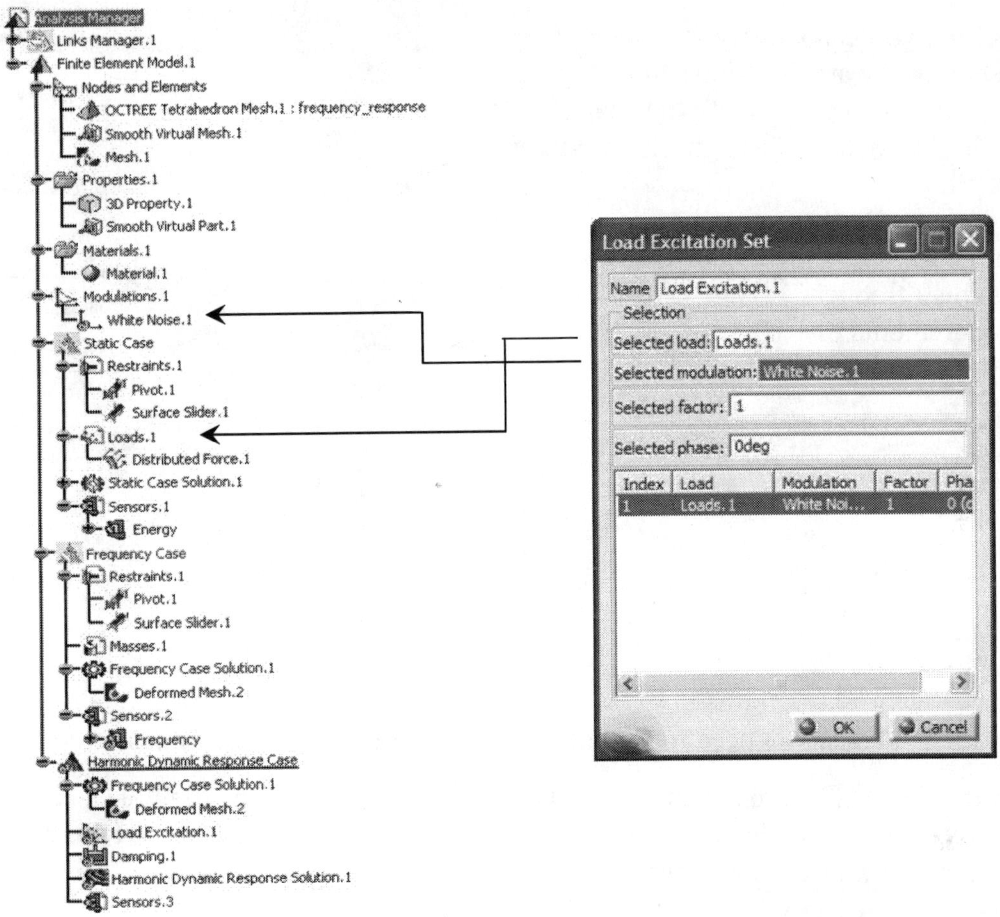


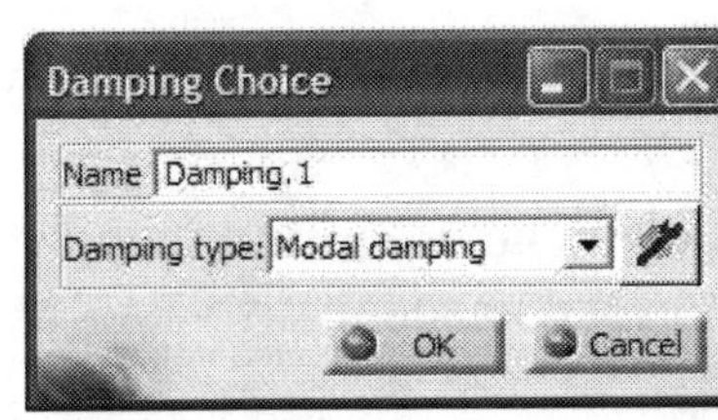


Double-click on the **Damping.1** branch in the tree which leads to the **Damping Choice** shown on the right.

Under the **Damping type**, keep **Modal damping** and select the icon  to specify individual values. Keep the default values of 1% for all three modes. Note that the damping ratio can be specified mode by mode. Close the box by pressing **OK**.

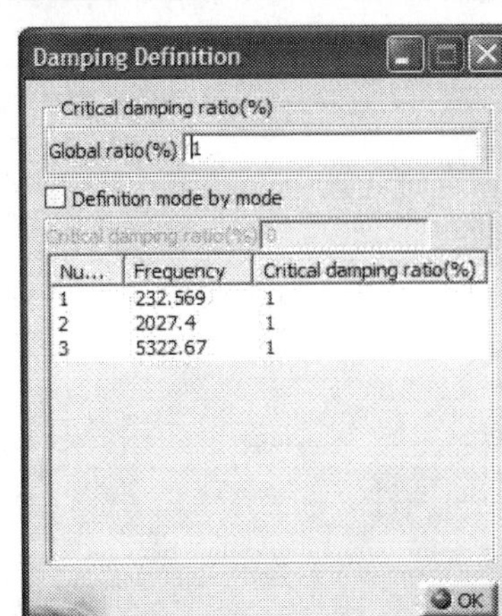

Double-click on the **Harmonic Dynamic Response Solution.1** branch from the tree leading to the box shown on the right.

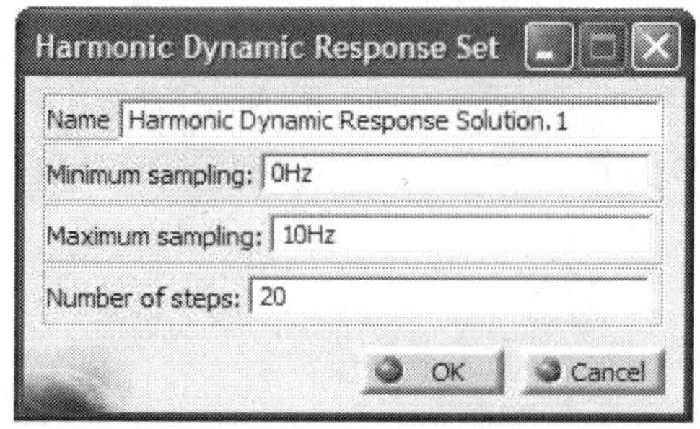


In this box, you can specify the range of frequency of the applied sinusoidal load. Furthermore, you can specify the spacing of the desired frequency through The **Number of steps**.

Fill in the lines as shown below. We are requesting a frequency range of $0 \leq \omega \leq 6000$ Hz in increments of 1 HZ.

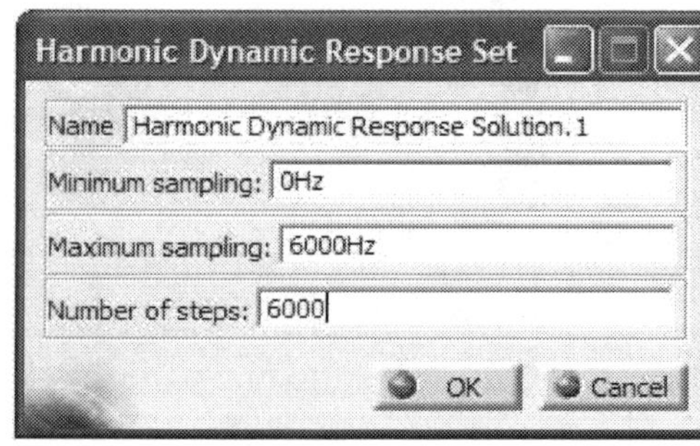


To run the analysis, you need to use the **Compute** toolbar  by selecting the **Compute** icon. This opens up the **Compute** box. Leave the defaults as **All** which means everything is computed. Keep in mind your **Current Case** is the **Harmonic Dynamic Response Case** which is underlined in the tree.

**Postprocessing (Harmonic Dynamic Results):**

To view the deformed shape you have to use the **Deformation** icon. The resulting deformed shape is displayed below.

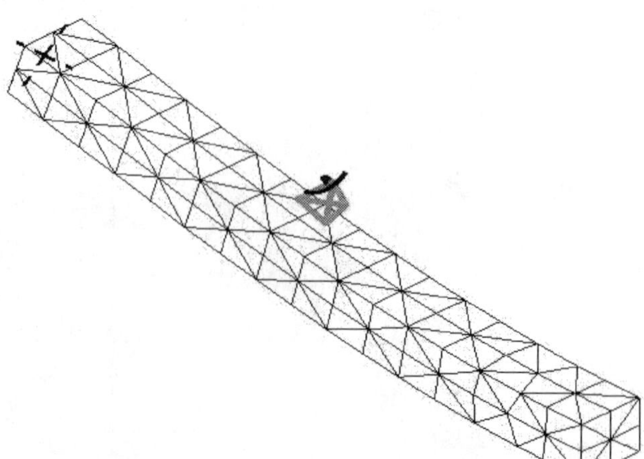

Double-click on the deformed shape on the screen, to open the **Image Edition** box shown below. Select the **Occurrences** tab to get the list of all available frequencies and their deformed shapes.

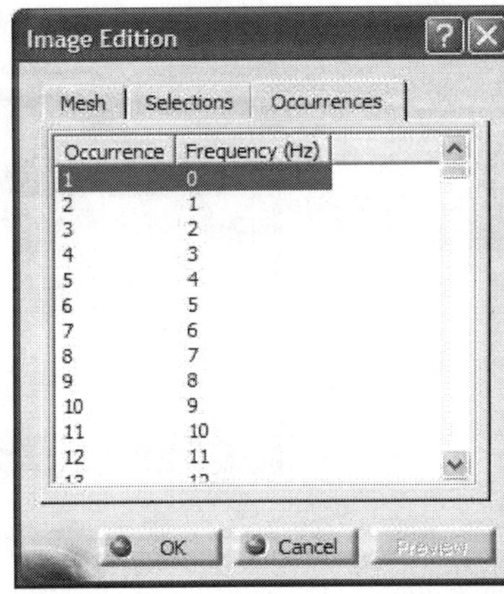


Note that if you select a deformed shape in the vicinity of 230 Hz, the deformed shaped indicates that you are close to the resonant frequency. This is displayed below.

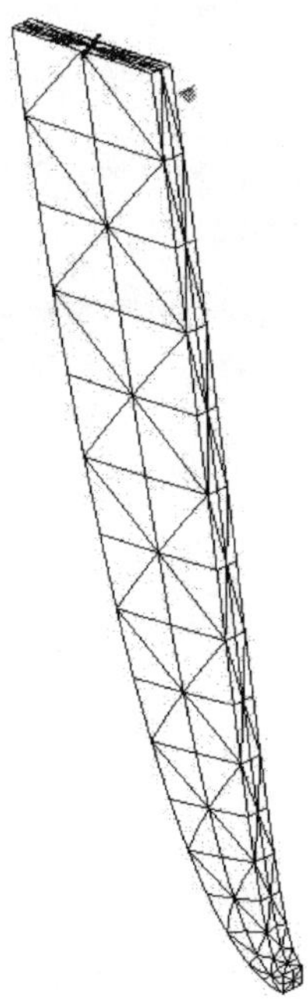

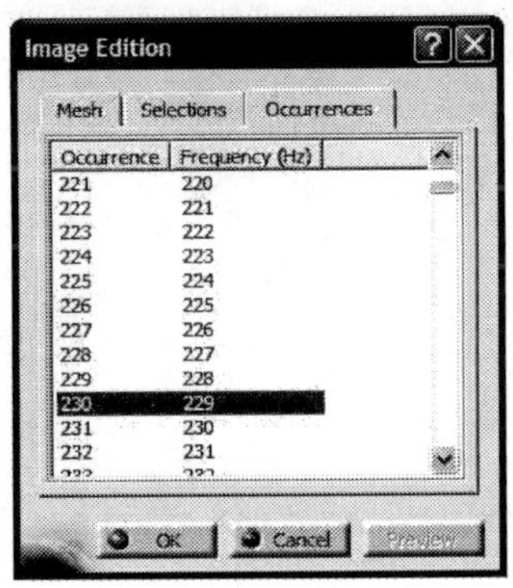


Your next task is to generate a two dimensional graph which displays the variation of the amplitude of any desired node as a function of the applied load frequency.

Point the cursor to the branch **Harmonic Dynamic Response Solution.1** in the tree, right-click, and select **Generate 2D Display** 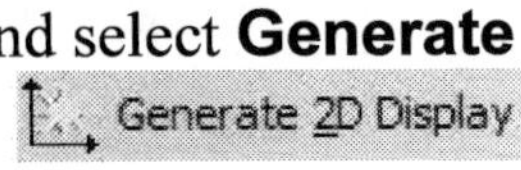
.

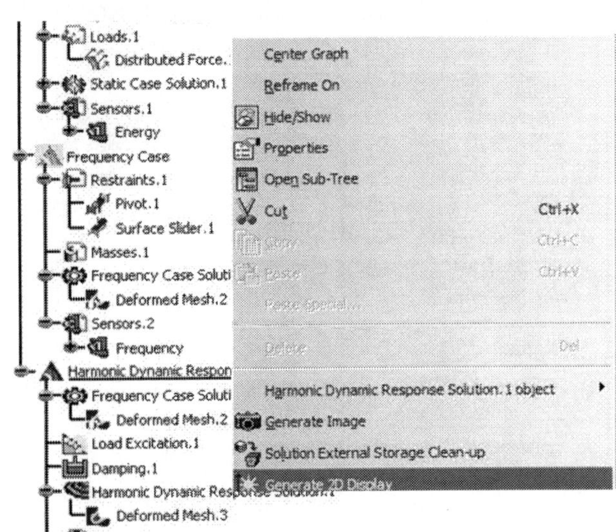

In the resulting pop up box, select **Next**. Keep the default **1 graph** and select **Finish**.

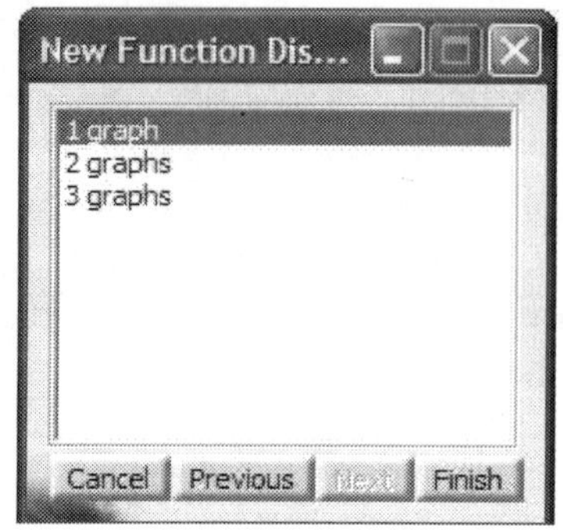


At this point, two windows open which are shown below. The large window is labeled **Results in relative axis graph.1** and eventually will display your desired graph.

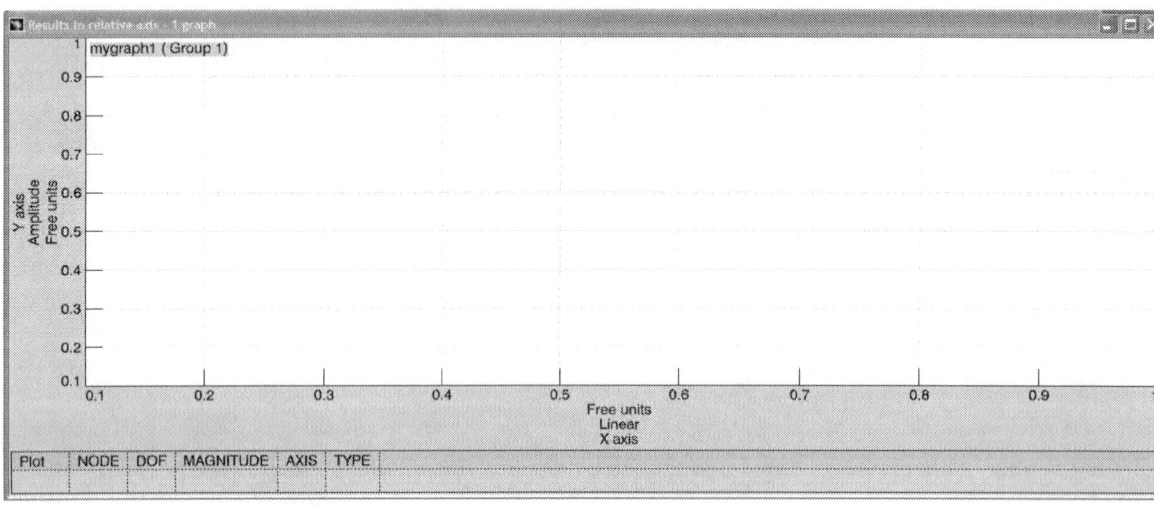


The second window is labeled Select Data and will enable you to pick the desired node and that data to be displayed. This window is shown below.

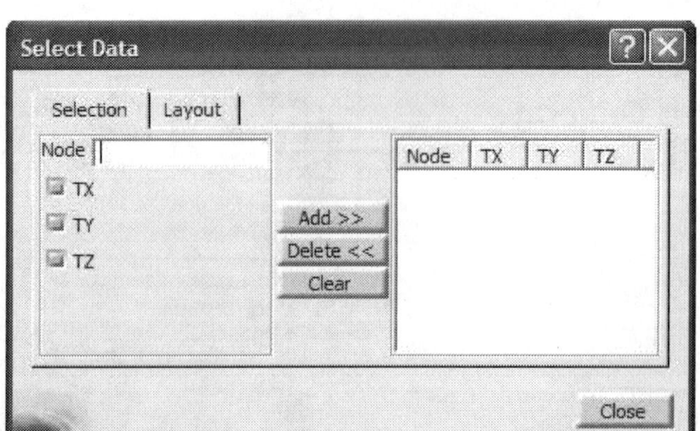

The desired node has to be picked from the screen. In order to do so, bring the window labeled **frequency-response.CATAnalysis** in the front and place the cursor at the desired node (the node will be highlighted) and click.

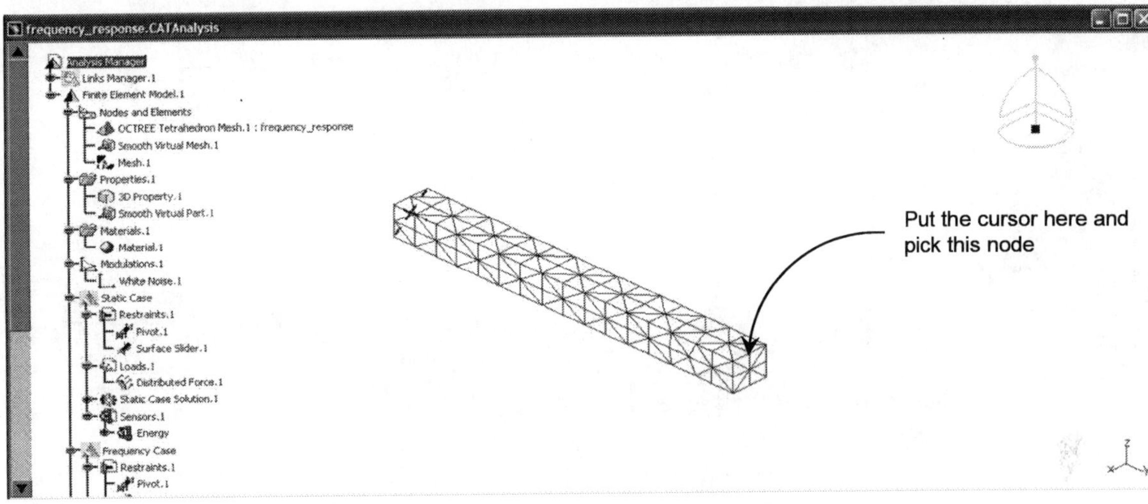


Since we are primarily interested in the display of the amplitude in the "**Z**" direction, uncheck the options **Tx** and **Ty**.

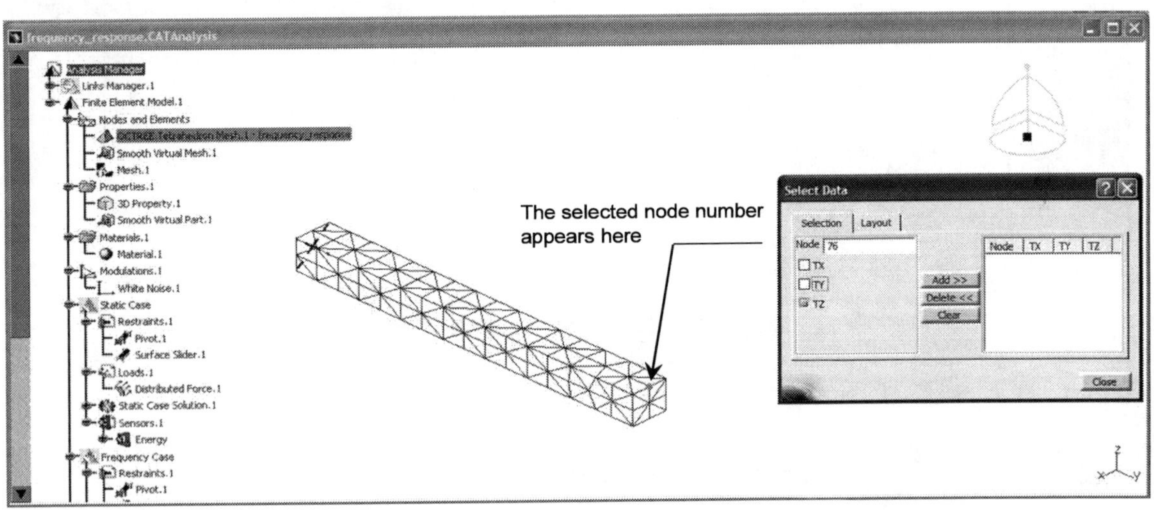


Click on the **Add>>** button Add >>.

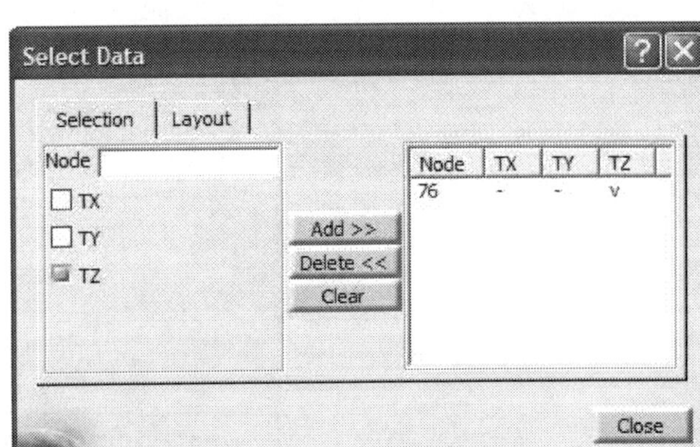

At this point the desired graph appears in the **Results in relative axis graph.1** which can be brought in the front if it is hiding behind the **frequency-response.CATAnalysis** window.

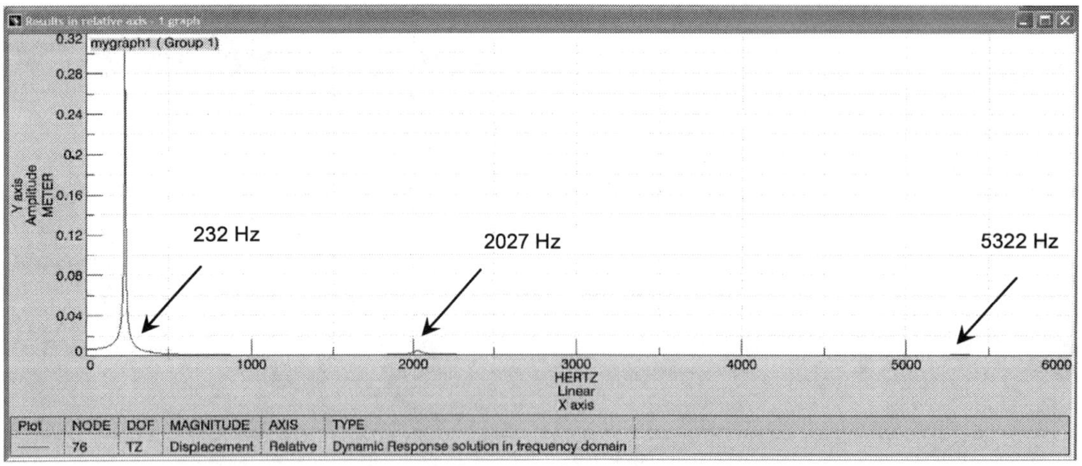


If you wish to see the above plotted restricted to the range $1500 \leq \omega \leq 2500$ Hz, point the cursor to the horizontal axis, right-click and select **Limits>Fixed** as displayed below.

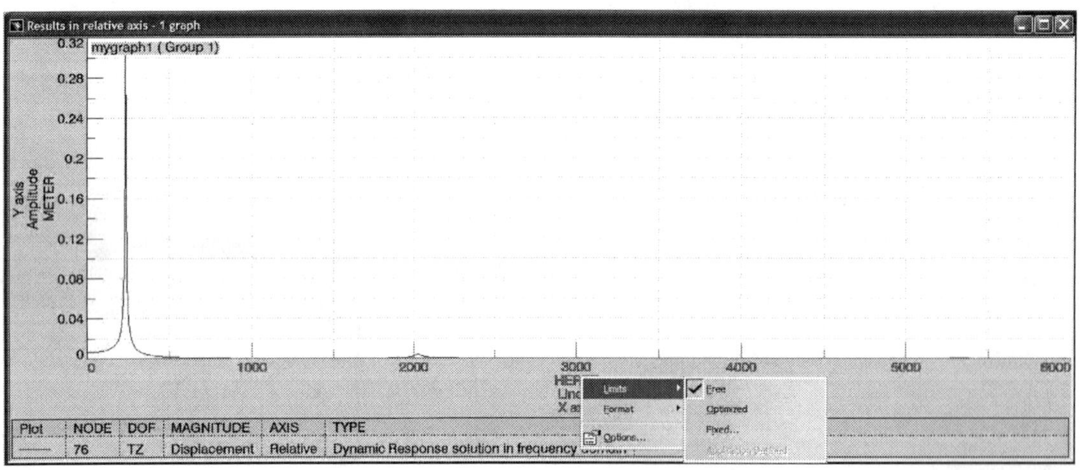


This enables you to input the desired range in the place holders shown.

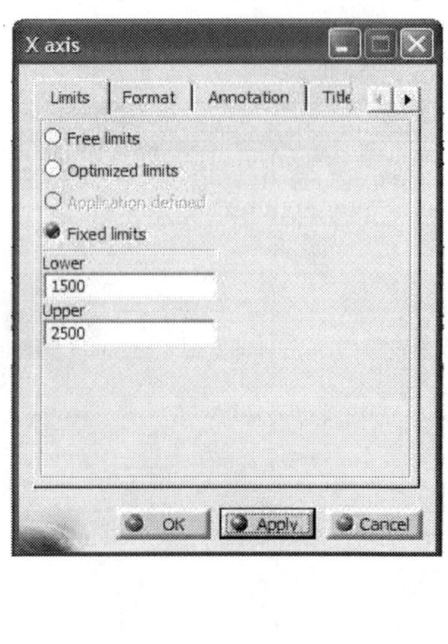


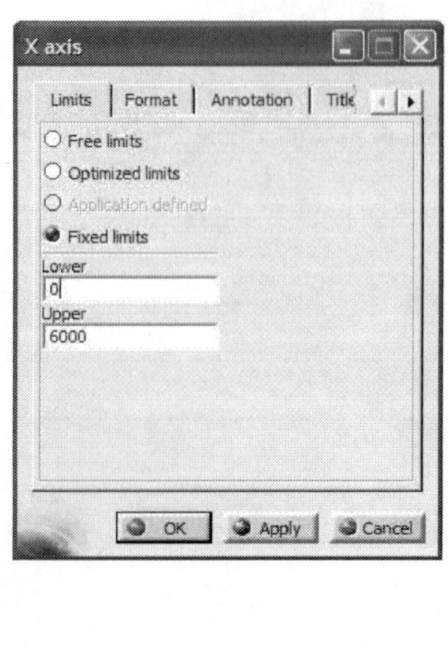

The amplitude curved is then displayed in the new range.

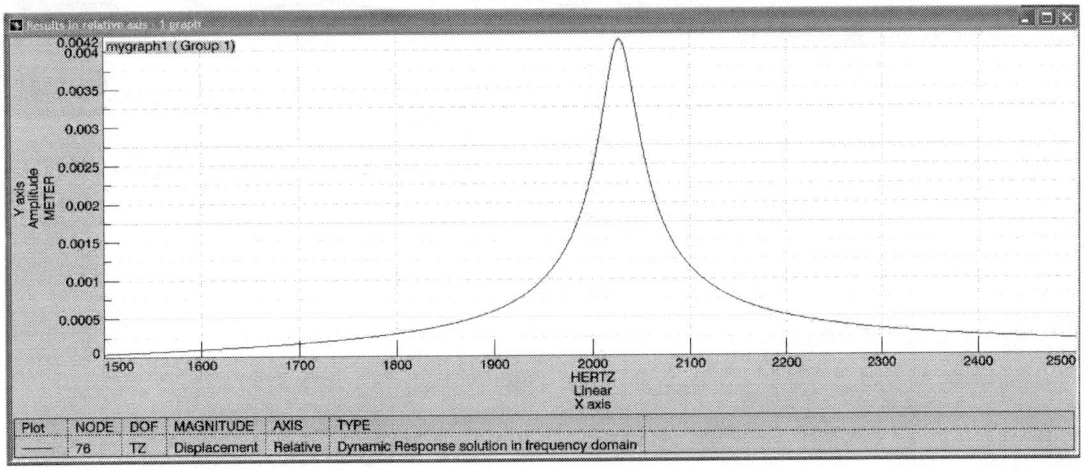


The amplitudes on other ranges are also shown below.

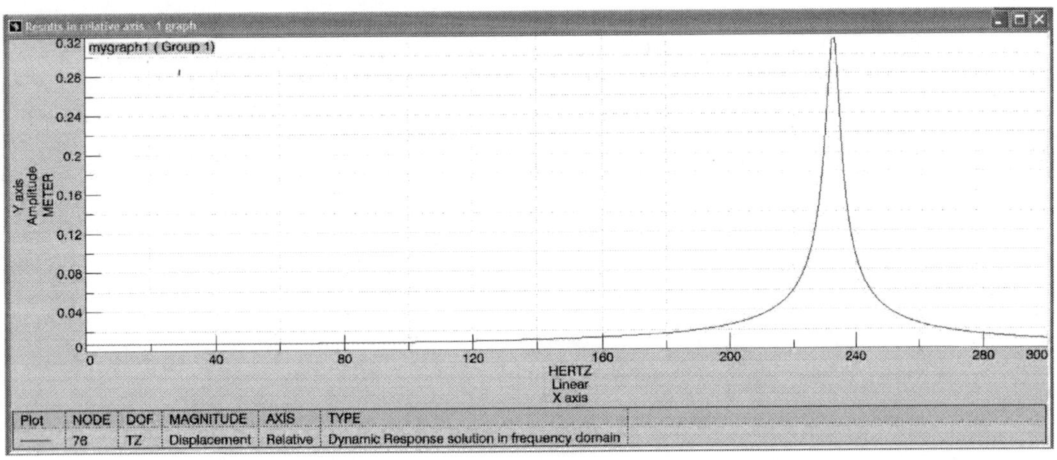


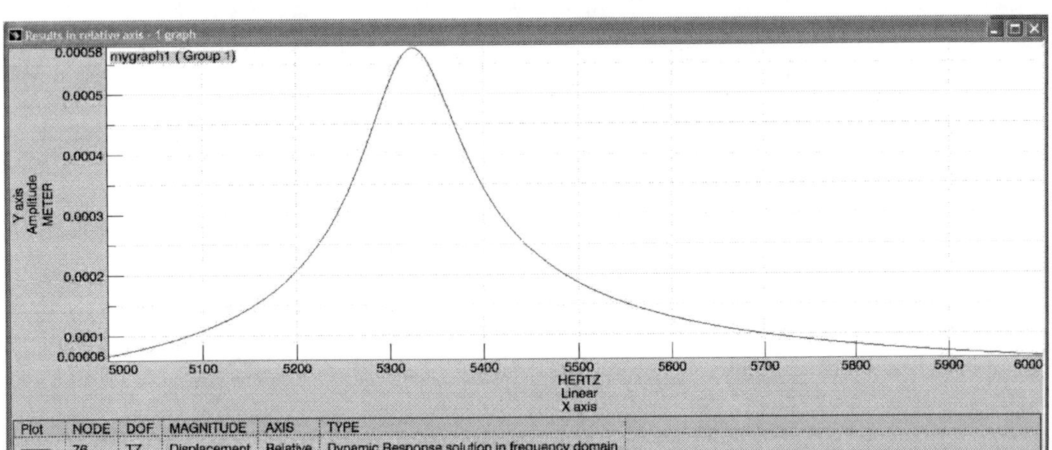

# NOTES:

# Appendix I

# Miscellaneous Comments

**Note #1**:

In recent releases of CATIA V5, once a **Part** (or **Product** file) is being created, a **New Part** dialogue box shown below is activated. Here, you have a choice of selecting different options. Throughout this book it is assumed that none of the top three options are selected. It is also possible to rename the part through this dialogue box.

In the event that the second box is checked, a geometrical set is automatically created and your tree structure may have an additional branch as shown.

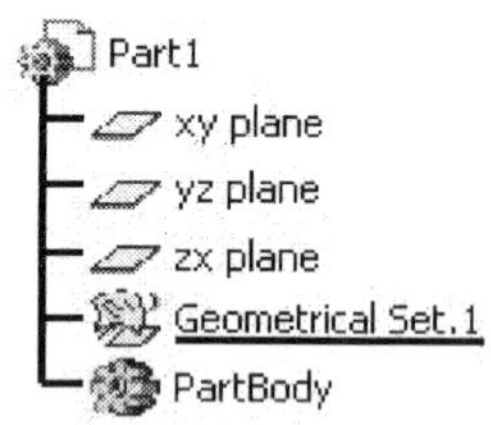


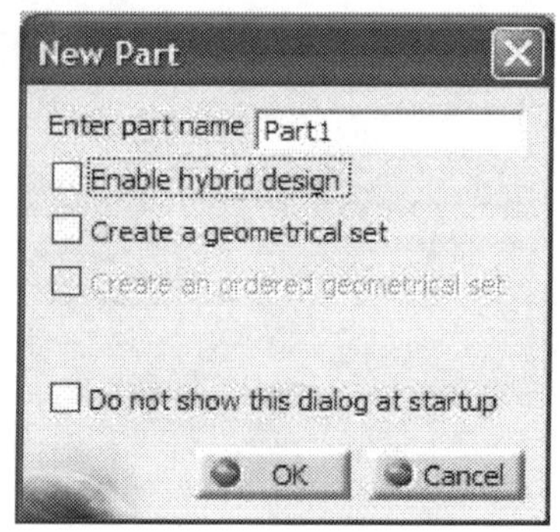


**Note #2**:

In order to view the generated mesh, you can point the cursor to the branch **Nodes and Elements**, right-click and select **Mesh Visualization**. However, the render style may be such that the resulting elements do not have their edges displayed as shown below.

Use the render type **Shading with Edges** from the **View mode** toolbar

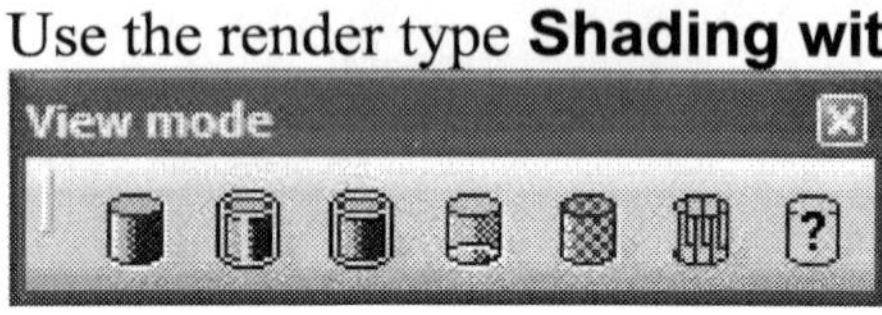


to see the element edges.

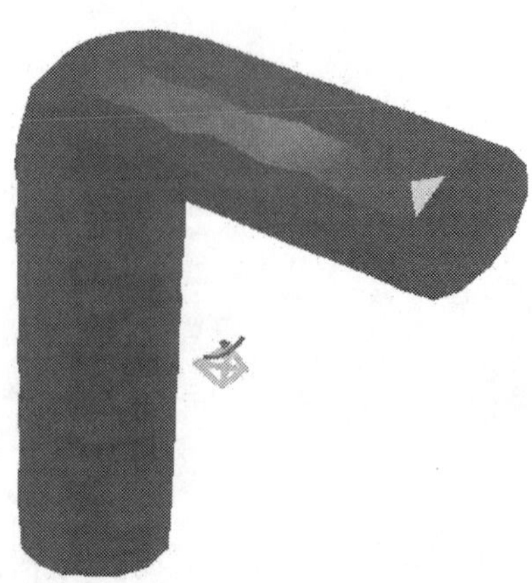

**<u>Note #3</u>:**

The use of the **Spatial Groups** 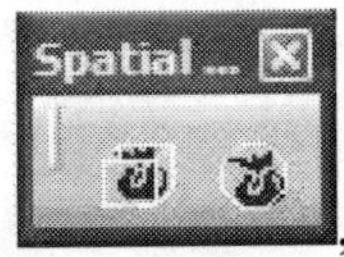, such as **Box Group**  and **Sphere Group** , takes some practice and exploring. If you are having difficulties changing the size of the box or the sphere, point the cursor to the compass, right-click, and select one of the options. In order to change the size of such entities, you have to drag the little red dots shown on the box or sphere.

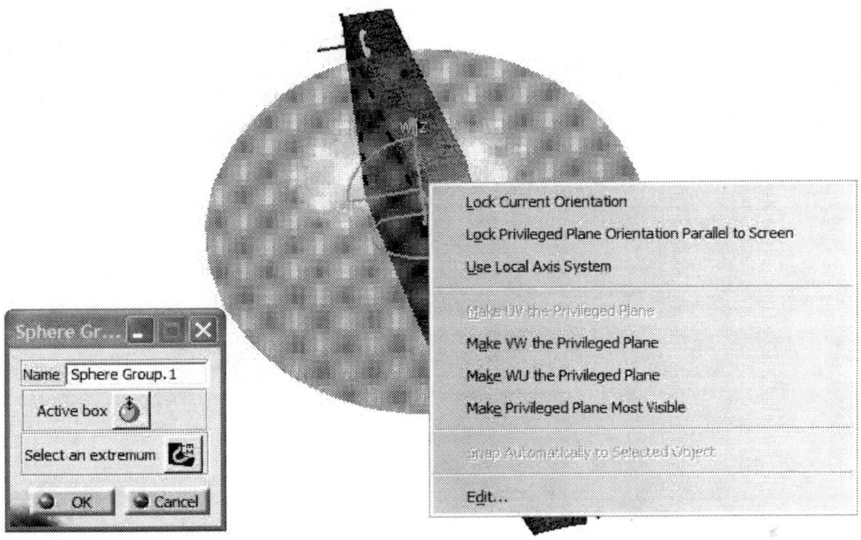